Neuropsychology of Memory

Neuropsychology of Memory

Edited by
LARRY R. SQUIRE *and* **NELSON BUTTERS**

University of California at San Diego School of Medicine
Veterans Administration Medical Center, San Diego

THE GUILFORD PRESS
New York   London

© 1984 The Guilford Press
A Division of Guilford Publications, Inc.
200 Park Avenue South, New York, N.Y. 10003

Printed in the United States of America

LIBRARY OF CONGRESS CATALOGING IN PUBLICATION DATA
Main entry under title:

Neuropsychology of memory.

 Bibliography: p.
 Includes index.
 1. Amnesia. 2. Memory—Physiological aspects.
3. Memory—Effect of drugs on. 4. Neuropsychology.
I. Squire, Larry R. II. Butters, Nelson.
RC394.A5N48 1984   616.85′232   84-4642
ISBN 0-89862-638-2

To my teachers, the late Hans-Lukas Teuber and Samuel H. Barondes.—L.R.S.

To all my teachers: Morton Wiener, H. Enger Rosvold, Mortimer Mishkin, Harold Goodglass, and Edith Kaplan; and to my wife, Arlene, for her love, warmth, and friendship for the past 27 years.—N. B.

Contributors

Marilyn Albert, PhD, Departments of Psychiatry and Neurology, Massachusetts General Hospital, Division on Aging, Harvard Medical School, Boston, Massachusetts

Mark Baker, BSc, Psychological Laboratory, University of St. Andrews, St. Andrews, Fife, Scotland

Michel Baudry, PhD, Center for the Neurobiology of Learning and Memory, University of California, Irvine, California

Edward L. Bennett, PhD, Melvin Calvin Laboratory, Lawrence Berkeley Laboratory, Berkeley, California

Theodore W. Berger, PhD, Departments of Psychology and Psychiatry, University of Pittsburgh, Pittsburgh, Pennsylvania

Neil E. Berthier, PhD, Brain Research Institute, Mental Retardation Research Center, Departments of Anatomy and Psychiatry, University of California at Los Angeles Medical Center, Los Angeles, California

Michael A. Bixler, Department of Psychology, University of Vermont, Burlington, Vermont

Herman Buschke, MD, Department of Neurology, Albert Einstein College of Medicine, Bronx, New York

Nelson Butters, PhD, Psychology Service, Veterans Administration Medical Center, San Diego, California; Department of Psychiatry, University of California at San Diego School of Medicine, La Jolla, California

Laird S. Cermak, PhD, Psychology Research, Boston Veterans Administration Medical Center, Boston, Massachusetts; Neurology Department, Boston University School of Medicine, Boston, Massachusetts

Gregory A. Clark, PhD, Center for Neurobiology and Behavior, Columbia University, New York, New York

Neal J. Cohen, PhD, Department of Psychology and Clinical Research Center, Massachusetts Institute of Technology, Cambridge, Massachusetts

Fergus I. M. Craik, PhD, Department of Psychology, Erindale College, University of Toronto, Mississauga, Ontario, Canada

Terry Crow, PhD, Department of Physiology, School of Medicine, University of Pittsburgh, Pittsburgh, Pennsylvania

Hasker P. Davis, PhD, Department of Psychology, St. John's University, Jamaica, New York

Diana Deutsch, PhD, Department of Psychology, University of California at San Diego, La Jolla, California

J. A. Deutsch, DPhil, Department of Psychology, University of California at San Diego, La Jolla, California

Bruce V. DiMattia, MS, Department of Psychology, University of Utah, Salt Lake City, Utah

Nelson H. Donegan, PhD, Department of Psychology, Stanford University, Stanford, California

Robert W. Doty, PhD, Center for Brain Research, University of Rochester Medical Center, Rochester, New York

Howard M. Eisenberg, MD, Division of Neurosurgery, The University of Texas Medical Branch, Galveston, Texas

Joaquin M. Fuster, MD, Department of Psychiatry and Brain Research Institute, School of Medicine, University of California at Los Angeles, Los Angeles, California

Michela Gallagher, PhD, Department of Psychology, University of North Carolina, Chapel Hill, North Carolina

Arnold L. Glass, PhD, Department of Psychology, Rutgers University, New Brunswick, New Jersey

Paul E. Gold, PhD, Department of Psychology, University of Virginia, Charlottesville, Virginia

Elkhonon Goldberg, PhD, Division of Neuropsychology, Department of Psychiatry, Albert Einstein College of Medicine and Montefiore Medical Center, Bronx, New York

Eric Halgren, PhD, Veterans Administration Southwest Regional Epilepsy Center, Los Angeles, California; Department of Psychiatry and Biobehavioral Sciences, and Brain Research Institute, University of California at Los Angeles School of Medicine, Los Angeles, California

David F. Hall, PhD, Department of Psychology, Thiel College, Greenville, Pennsylvania; Department of Psychology, University of Washington, Seattle, Washington

Larry L. Jacoby, PhD, Department of Psychology, McMaster University, Hamilton, Ontario, Canada

Terry L. Jernigan, PhD, Psychology Service, Veterans Administration Medical Center, Palo Alto, California

Bruce S. Kapp, PhD, Department of Psychology, University of Vermont, Burlington, Vermont

Raymond P. Kesner, PhD, Department of Psychology, University of Utah, Salt Lake City, Utah

Richard Kovner, PhD, Department of Neurology, Montefiore Medical Center and Albert Einstein College of Medicine, Bronx, New York

John L. Kubie, PhD, Department of Physiology, Downstate Medical Center, Brooklyn, New York

David G. Lavond, PhD, Department of Psychology, Stanford University, Stanford, California

Harvey S. Levin, PhD, Division of Neurosurgery, The University of Texas Medical Branch, Galveston, Texas

Elizabeth F. Loftus, PhD, Department of Psychology, University of Washington, Seattle, Washington

Gary Lynch, PhD, Center for the Neurobiology of Learning and Memory, University of California, Irvine, California

John Madden IV, PhD, Departments of Physiology and of Psychiatry and the Behavioral Sciences, Stanford University Medical School, Stanford, California

Helen Mahut, PhD, Department of Psychology, Northeastern University, Boston, Massachusetts

Robert G. Mair, PhD, Neurology Service, Veterans Administration Medical Center, Providence, Rhode Island; Division of Neurology, Section of Psychiatry and Human Behavior, Brown University, Providence, Rhode Island

Laura A. Mamounas, Department of Psychology, Stanford University, Stanford, California

Steven Mattis, PhD, Department of Psychiatry, New York Hospital–Cornell Medical Center, Westchester Division, White Plains, New York

Michael D. Mauk, Department of Psychology, Stanford University, Stanford, California

Andrew R. Mayes, DPhil, Department of Psychology, University of Manchester, Manchester, England, United Kingdom

David A. McCormick, PhD, Department of Neurology, Stanford University Medical School, Stanford, California

John McDowall, PhD, Department of Psychology, Porirua Hospital, Porirua, New Zealand

William J. McEntee, MD, Neurology Service, Veterans Administration Medical Center, Providence, Rhode Island; Division of Neurology, Section of Psychiatry and Human Behavior, Brown University, Providence, Rhode Island

Peter R. Meudell, PhD, Department of Psychology, University of Manchester, Manchester, England, United Kingdom

Donald R. Meyer, PhD, Department of Psychology, Ohio State University, Columbus, Ohio

Patricia Morgan Meyer, PhD, Department of Psychology, Ohio State University, Columbus, Ohio

Mortimer Mishkin, PhD, Laboratory of Neuropsychology, National Institute of Mental Health, Bethesda, Maryland

John W. Moore, PhD, Department of Psychology, University of Massachusetts, Amherst, Massachusetts

Richard Morris, DPhil, Psychological Laboratory, University of St. Andrews, St. Andrews, Fife, Scotland

Morris Moscovitch, PhD, Psychology Department, Centre for Studies in Human Development and Unit for Memory Disorders, Erindale College, University of Toronto, Mississauga, Ontario, Canada

Mark Moss, PhD, Department of Anatomy, Boston University School of Medicine, Boston, Massachusetts; Department of Psychiatry, Massachusetts General Hospital, Harvard Medical School, Boston, Massachusetts

David S. Olton, PhD, Department of Psychology, Johns Hopkins University, Baltimore, Maryland

Marlene Oscar-Berman, PhD, Department of Biobehavioral Sciences, Division of Psychiatry, and Aphasia Research Center, Department of Neurology, Boston University School of Medicine, Boston, Massachusetts; Aphasia Research Center, Boston Veterans Administration Medical Center, Boston, Massachusetts

Andrew Papanicolaou, PhD, Division of Neurosurgery, The University of Texas Medical Branch, Galveston, Texas

Jeffrey P. Pascoe, PhD, Department of Psychology, University of Vermont, Burlington, Vermont

Herbert L. Petri, PhD, Department of Psychology, Towson State University, Baltimore, Maryland

Constantine X. Poulos, PhD, Addiction Research Foundation, Toronto, Ontario, Canada

Karl H. Pribram, MD, Neuropsychology Laboratories, Departments of Psychology and of Psychiatry and the Behavioral Sciences, Stanford University, Stanford, California

James B. Ranck, Jr., MD, Department of Physiology, Downstate Medical Center, Brooklyn, New York

H. L. Roitblat, PhD, Department of Psychology, Columbia University, New York, New York

Edmund T. Rolls, DPhil, Department of Experimental Psychology, University of Oxford, Oxford, England, United Kingdom

Steven Rose, PhD, Brain Research Group, Department of Biology, The Open University, Milton Keynes, MK76AA, United Kingdom

Mark R. Rosenzweig, PhD, Department of Psychology, University of California, Berkeley, California

Aryeh Routtenberg, PhD, Departments of Psychology and Neurobiology/Physiology, Northwestern University, Evanston, Illinois

Daniel L. Schacter, PhD, Department of Psychology, University of Toronto, Toronto, Ontario, Canada

Paul R. Solomon, PhD, Department of Psychology, Williams College, Williamstown, Massachusetts

Larry R. Squire, PhD, Department of Psychiatry, Veterans Administration Medical Center, San Diego, California; Department of Psychiatry, University of California at San Diego School of Medicine, La Jolla, California

Joy L. Taylor, PhD, Laboratory of Clinical Psychopharmacology and Psychophysiology, Veterans Administration Medical Center, Palo Alto, California; Department of Psychiatry and Behavioral Sciences, Stanford University School of Medicine, Stanford, California

Garth J. Thomas, PhD, Center for Brain Research,

University of Rochester Medical Center, Rochester, New York

Richard F. Thompson, PhD, Department of Psychology, Stanford University, Stanford, California

Robert Thompson, PhD, Fairview State Hospital, Costa Mesa, California; Department of Physical Medicine and Rehabilitation, University of California at Irvine Medical Center, Orange, California

Jared R. Tinklenberg, MD, Laboratory of Clinical Psychopharmacology and Psychophysiology, Veterans Administration Medical Center, Palo Alto, California; Department of Psychiatry and Behavioral Sciences, Stanford University School of Medicine, Stanford, California

Norman M. Weinberger, PhD, Department of Psychobiology and Center for the Neurobiology of Learning and Memory, University of California at Irvine, Irvine, California

Herbert Weingartner, PhD, Laboratory of Psychology and Psychopathology, National Institute of Mental Health, Bethesda, Maryland

D. Adrian Wilkinson, DPhil, Addiction Research Foundation, Toronto, Ontario, Canada

Gordon Winocur, PhD, Department of Psychology, Trent University, Peterborough, Ontario, Canada

Charles D. Woody, MD, Brain Research Institute, Mental Retardation Research Center, Departments of Anatomy and Psychiatry, University of California at Los Angeles Medical Center, Los Angeles, California

Stuart Zola-Morgan, PhD, Veterans Administration Medical Center, San Diego, California; Department of Psychiatry, University of California at San Diego School of Medicine, La Jolla, California

Steven F. Zornetzer, PhD, Office of Naval Research, Arlington, Virginia

Preface

The past 20 years have witnessed an exponential growth in studies of the neuropsychology of memory. Even for the avid student of this area, it has been impossible to keep abreast of the entire field and to integrate the findings of human and animal studies. While this difficulty with integration is due partially to the vast volume of investigations published each year, some of the problems appear to us to be related to a lack of understanding of investigators' implicit underlying assumptions about memory. For this reason, we have assembled in this volume contributions from a group of scientists who have assessed the neuropsychology of memory from the molecular as well as the molar perspective; have employed physiological, anatomical, pharmacological, and behavioral techniques; and have dealt with the complexities of memory in animals and humans. The contributors were assigned the task of reaching beyond their empirical data and currently favored theories and of making explicit their long-term programmatic goals. To facilitate the reader's appreciation of the various chapters, we have organized this volume into three sections: "Studies of Normal and Abnormal Memory in Humans"; "Studies of Memory in Nonhuman Primates"; and "Studies of Memory in Nonprimates: Physiology, Pharmacology, and Behavior." Within each of these three sections, the chapters have been further ordered to provide additional continuity and cohesion of the subject matter.

L. R. S.
N. B.

Contents

Studies of Normal and Abnormal Memory in Humans

No phenomenon in the neuropsychology of human memory has generated greater interest than the amnesic syndrome. Following the classical demonstration by Scoville and Milner in the late 1950s that severe and lasting amnesia follows bilateral ablation of the mesial temporal lobe region of the brain, numerous investigators have turned their attention to the neurological and psychological bases of this disorder. What has been confusing to the reader of this literature is that although all of the investigators have focused upon the deficits and preserved capacities of amnesic patients, the various definitions of "amnesia," the criteria for selection of patients, and the ultimate purposes of the rash of studies published in the 1960s and 1970s often appeared contradictory. For example, while some investigators combined patients with medial temporal or diencephalic lesions into a single "amnesic" group, others segregated and compared their amnesic populations according to lesion site (e.g., hippocampal or diencephalic lesions) or etiology of the disorder (e.g., virus, anoxia, trauma, vascular disorder, long-term alcoholism). In fact, this conflict has been more apparent than real and reflects the disparate goals of the investigators. In studies in which a single "amnesic" group was used, the aim was often to identify a single cognitive deficit (e.g., storage, retrieval, encoding) that might account for all amnesic conditions, whereas in the studies in which different amnesic populations were defined, the goal was often to uncover differences in the memory disorders of etiologically distinct clinical populations.

Our own review of the human literature has led to the identification of four types of amnesic research, two of which are theoretically oriented and two of which are primarily concerned with clinical issues. Readers should be aware that our divisions are arbitrary and perhaps too finely drawn, but they will, we believe, find these divisions to have some validity and didactic value.

The most common type of human study attempts to develop or substantiate a particular model or set of concepts about memory. For example, attempts to demonstrate that amnesia may be reduced to a retrieval or an encoding deficit fall into this category of research. Similarly, attempts to show that amnesia represents a loss of episodic (rather than semantic) memory or a deficiency in acquiring declarative knowledge are interested in more than just understanding the neurological syndrome. In these cases, the investigators often commence their investigations of abnormal memory with definite preconceptions about normal human memory; consequently, the amnesic patient then becomes the tool through which the normal model is tested. Among investigators interested in the construction of such memory models, the etiology or the locus of their amnesic patients' lesions are sometimes ignored or treated in a casual manner.

Other investigators of the neuropsychology of memory have focused primarily on the functions of particular brain regions (e.g., the hippocampus, the midline diencephalic region). These experimenters attempt to locate patients with lesions limited to a particular structure; to stimulate specific anatomical sites, via implanted electrodes; or to correlate memory deficits with changes in the CT or PET scans, via neuroradiological techniques. The major goal in these studies is always a *neural model* rather than a psychological theory of memory. To be sure, the scientist interested in neural models of memory will frequently borrow concepts from the theorist studying normal learning, but the concepts are treated as heuristic implements, to be discarded quickly when better ones are available.

A third group of human investigations is primarily interested in particular disease states (e.g., alcoholic Korsakoff syndrome, Alzheimer disease); such studies attempt to explain the specific memory deficits associated with these diseases. Investigators engaged in such clinical research tend to cluster their groups on the basis of etiology, under the assumption that similar etiologies result in similar constellations or clusters of brain lesions and memory deficits. In some cases, these investigators may also borrow concepts from normal human memory for heuristic purposes, while others are less theoretically oriented and rely more heavily upon specific techniques or test paradigms used in human and animal research. Some of the resulting studies assume a comparative flavor; that is, the investigator compares two or more patient populations (e.g., alcoholic Korsakoff patients, patients with Alzheimer disease, patients with transient amnesia following bilateral ECT) with the hope of finding double dissociations between tasks and patient populations. Such double dissociations would then provide valuable clues as to the differential processes underlying the patients' anterograde and retrograde memory disorders.

A fourth type of neuropsychological study of human memory disorders focuses upon the role of neurotransmitters (e.g., acetylcholine, dopamine). Typically, a particular patient group with an assumed common etiology (e.g., Alzheimer disease) and neurochemical abnormality (e.g., cholinergic deficiency) is tested before and after the administration of a pharmacological agonist or antagonist. The critical question is whether the patient improves or not with such drug trials. The investigator pursuing the pharmacological basis of memory disorders may or may not borrow concepts from theories of normal human memory. As in other clinically oriented studies, the use of such terms as "episodic" and "semantic" memory is purely heuristic and secondary to the major neurochemical goals of the study. The investigator who eschews all theoretical concepts usually selects a battery of validated memory tasks (e.g., the Wechsler Memory Scale) with little reference to or concern with the processes underlying normal performance on such tests. If a particular pattern of improvement occurs among the individual tests, the atheoretical investigator may then become interested in whether his or her particular drug treatment is affecting "storage," "retrieval," "encoding," or "attention."

The chapters following this brief introduction exemplify all four types of neuropsychological studies of human memory. In addition, several of the initial chapters dicuss in detail some of the current concepts and theories of normal human memory. These chapters are included for two reasons: (1) to supply readers with a theoretical background that will aid their appreciation of other contributions in this volume; and (2) to underscore the interdependence between basic knowledge in normal human memory and attempts to understand the cognitive processes that underlie the severe memory disorders of various amnesic and demented patient populations. In human neuropsychology, the schism between basic cognitive research and the understanding of abnormal behavior is small, if it exists at all!

Age Differences in Remembering

1

Fergus I. M. Craik

In this chapter I outline my current views on the human memory system, and illustrate a number of points by drawing on work concerning age differences in remembering. In this way I can put forward some ideas on how the normal system breaks down in one set of circumstances; furthermore, there is evidence to suggest that the effects of aging are quite similar (in some respects at least) to the effects of other conditions affecting memory performance.

A View of the Memory System

The last 20 years of memory research have seen a progressive trend away from theories concerned with structure and mechanism toward theories dealing with processes and operations. Thus early models in the information-processing tradition (see Murdock, 1967, for a review) focused on various memory "stores" (e.g., sensory memory, short-term store or STS, and long-term store or LTS) containing memory traces whose information content varied as a function of the store they occupied. Research questions were primarily concerned with the capacity of each store, the rate and mechanism of forgetting, and the coding characteristics of the traces within the various stores. Some processes were also necessary to transfer information from one store to another; thus the processes (and possibly mechanisms) of attention served to transfer information from sensory storage to the STS, and the processes of rehearsal served to transfer information from the STS to the LTS (Murdock, 1967). Memory failures within this scheme were attributed to such factors as reduced capacity of the stores (particularly the STS), faster forgetting of information from one or more stores, and a failure of the transfer mechanisms to shift information from one store to the next.

These structural models are attractive in many respects. They led to a clearly defined program of behavioral research in which the capacity, forgetting functions, and coding characteristics of the various stores were explored and measured; also, the structural models held out the hope of identifying neurological mechanisms underlying parts of the behavioral model. But there are drawbacks, too; for example, Lockhart and I (Craik & Lockhart, 1972) pointed to findings showing that the characteristics of the memory stores varied markedly with changes in materials, subjects, tasks, and strategies. Whereas it is plausible that mental *processes* might be context-dependent, it is surely less reasonable for mechanisms to vary in this respect.

Fergus I. M. Craik. Department of Psychology, Erindale College, University of Toronto, Mississauga, Ontario, Canada.

3

Later models have continued this shift of emphasis from mechanism to process. One solution (which might be characterized as the adoption of a "mixed" model) was to suggest an interactive mixture of structures and processes; a more radical solution was essentially to abandon structure altogether, and to describe the activities of learning and remembering entirely in terms of mental processes. Atkinson and Shiffrin's (1968) buffer model is in the first category. Their model is basically structural, but with a major and more explicit role for processes, especially the "rehearsal buffer" in the STS, and its associated transfer function from STS to LTS. One source of memory disorders within the Atkinson and Shiffrin model is obviously the process of rehearsal or transfer, since permanent registration suffers if these processes are impaired. The other major source of disorders is presumably the retrieval process as described, for example, by Shiffrin (1970). One serious objection to the notion of transfer put forward by Atkinson and Shiffrin is that subsequent experimental work (e.g., Craik & Watkins, 1973; Woodward, Bjork, & Jongeward, 1973) has shown that the adequacy of registration in LTS is not simply a function of rehearsal time, but depends critically on the qualitative nature of the operations performed during rehearsal.

The "levels-of-processing" view (Craik & Lockhart, 1972) suggested that memory was the record of operations carried out primarily for the purposes of perception and comprehension. Since "deeper" semantic traces were associated with higher levels of memory performance, a central notion of the levels-of-processing position was that "rehearsal" comprised qualitatively different types, and that different types of rehearsal had different effects on subsequent memory. The set of ideas was still fairly structural, however, in that analysis of incoming information took place within a hierarchically organized system largely constructed from past experience. Short-term or primary memory was seen as continued processing (or activation) of some part of the system; thus residence "in primary memory" was synonymous with "continued attention paid to" an event. That is, primary memory was seen as a process rather than a store. Memory failures by this point of view might again arise from inefficient encoding (e.g., failure to process information deeply) or from ineffective retrieval (e.g., failure to reinstate the same processing operations at retrieval that had been operative at encoding). The levels-of-processing position also came in for its share of criticism (e.g., Baddeley, 1978) on various grounds, including the circularity of the notion of "depth," the lack of an independent measure of depth, the suggestion of a fixed series of analyzers, and the fact that retrieval processes were left unspecified.

The levels-of-processing viewpoint was clearly more process-oriented than most previous information-processing models, but it may still have been too structural. Both the hierarchical analyzing system (past knowledge in some sense) and the resulting "records" of the analyses performed are structural concepts. If remembering is really like perceiving, then it is perhaps no more likely that records or memory traces exist in the absence of remembering than it is that percepts exist in the absence of perceiving. There are perhaps no such things as "engrams" to be found by even the most advanced neuroanatomical techniques. That is, if remembering is best viewed as an activity (rather than as a thing loosely termed "memory"), it can only be studied while the activity is occurring. Clearly *something* must change as the result of experience—some change in the system must underlie the phenomena of learning and remembering—but it may be a change in the "interpretative machinery" of the cognitive system so that the machinery now interacts differently with recurring stimulus events, rather than the initial experience being recorded in a series of copies, records, or traces. This general view of remembering as an activity was suggested by Bartlett (1932), and has been developed more recently by Kolers (1973) and by Bransford and his colleagues (e.g., Bransford, McCarrell, Franks, & Nitsch, 1977).

In two recent reviews (Craik, 1979, 1981), I have put forward a "general-processing" view of memory, which stems partly from the levels-of-processing position but also draws on the work of colleagues in the Toronto region (principally Larry Jacoby, Marcel Kinsbourne, Paul Kolers, Morris Moscovitch, and Endel Tulving). In outline, the view is that memory can be understood in terms of encoding processes, retrieval processes, and their interactions. Encoding processes are seen as interpretations of the stimulus pattern in terms of qualitatively different types of past experience (or in terms of innate analyzing procedures, in the case of basic pattern-recognition operations). Thus an event can be analyzed in terms of its sensory qualities, or (in addition) in terms of its meaning and significance in various different dimensions. Later memory of the event will reflect those analyses that have been emphasized at the time of encoding; thus we may remember only the gist of a conversation if that was particularly important during the initial exchange, or we may remember "surface" aspects of the stimulus in cases where such information was important (or received extensive analysis) during initial perception and comprehension. By "surface information" I mean sensory qualities, such as color, loudness, taste, and smell; sensory combinations, such as voice quality and visual patterns; and physical details of patterns, such as typescript, specific words used, and specific details of pictures. These aspects stand in contrast to "deeper," "semantic" interpretations of the stimulus pattern, although I would emphasize that "sensory" and "semantic" lie on a continuum in many cases (e.g., bringing past knowledge and expertise to bear on appreciating a painting or a glass of wine, or in recognizing a friend's voice).

Whereas Lockhart and I (Craik & Lockhart, 1972) argued that memory was a function of depth of processing, with sensory aspects of the stimulus being forgotten rapidly, more recent work has shown that conclusion to be only partially correct. Specific "surface" aspects of unfamiliar typescripts are well remembered (Kolers, 1973), as are unusual and unexpected objects in a picture (Friedman, 1979) and the specific words used in a conversation, especially if the words were emotional or personally relevant (Keenan, MacWhinney, & Mayhew, 1977; Rogers, Kuiper, & Kirker, 1977). Perhaps a more adequate statement of the relation between memory performance and the qualitative type of initial analysis would be that an event will be well remembered, provided, first, that some well-organized body of past experience (schema or expertise) is brought to bear on the event, and, second, that the resulting analysis is somewhat different from highly practiced routine procedures performed by the schemas in question. That is, for an event to be well remembered, it must be "meaningful" in terms of past experience, yet also distinctive from the many routine past applications of the relevant analytic procedures. Such distinctive encodings naturally require more attention and processing resources (and often involve deliberate, conscious decisions). Correspondingly, if sufficient processing resources are not available for whatever reason, the processing system must fall back on relatively effortless, automatic procedures; this falling back leads to an analysis that is very similar to many previous analyses, and thus to a nondistinctive encoding and poor subsequent recollection of the event.

In this general-processing view of memory, retrieval processes are regarded as being very similar (perhaps identical) to encoding processes. That is, retrieval processes also vary qualitatively, reflecting different mixtures of surface and semantic processing; and, like encoding processes, they require greater or lesser amounts of processing resources, depending on the degree of prior practice. Thus, retrieval processes are not seen as a "search" for the wanted trace, but rather as a reinstatement of the initial encoding operations (cf. Kolers, 1973). The system literally "re-cognizes" the original event.

If this account is accurate in general terms, how does a person know that he or she is "remembering" rather than simply perceiving and comprehending? That is, what is the correlate of *pastness* in this system? One answer (suggested to me by Marcel Kinsbourne) is that the current context is "appropriate" for perceiving (in that our mental processes reflect what is currently present in our surroundings), whereas this is not true of remembering: There is invariably some mismatch between the processes associated with remembering an event and those processes that are driven by the current context. However, remembering will be easier, and more likely to be successful, to the extent that aspects of the present environment induce the appropriate processing operations. Thus recognition is a particularly effective retrieval method (especially if the initial context is also present during remembering); cued recall is reasonably effective, especially if the cues were salient aspects of the original event and are processed in the same way as they were initially; but free recall is relatively difficult and often unsuccessful, since in this case the system must somehow reinstate the appropriate operations with minimal help from the environment. In this last case, the subject attempts to "reconstruct" the initial context by relying partly on general knowledge ("semantic memory" in Tulving's [1972] terms) and partly, perhaps, on bootstrapping feedback from the relevant operations constructed thus far—that is, the subject experiences feelings of partial recognition as parts of the original episode are reconstructed. As a final point, accurate recollection also seems to depend on the distinctiveness of the mental operations in question. Thus, if the original event was familiar, expected, or treated cursorily with relatively routine automatic operations, then even a very complete reinstatement of these operations at retrieval may not yield strong feelings of recollection, since the operations necessarily refer to many other occasions also (i.e., highly practiced "automatic" operations must necessarily have been run off on many previous occasions). To repeat, good recollection of an event necessitates the involvement of distinctive combinations of processes at encoding (thereby necessitating the expenditure of conscious effort to integrate these novel components of the encoded event). Correspondingly, the same processing operations must be reinstated at retrieval, and this will again require deliberate effortful processing, unless the initial event is itself re-presented very completely; in this case, the event will drive the system into very much the same configuration as before.

Clearly these notions are imprecise and incomplete. In the remainder of the chapter, I briefly discuss some empirical findings from the literature on age difference and memory and use these concrete instances as illustrations of the points made above.

Age Differences in Remembering

In this very brief treatment of adult age differences in memory, the terms "old" and "older" usually refer to people over 60 years of age. In the experiments cited, the older subjects are typically aged 60–80, and are in good health; they are usually matched for verbal intelligence or educational level with a young control group whose members are in their late teens or early 20s. Fuller details of the arguments, and studies on which they are based, are provided in previous reviews (Craik, 1977; Craik & Rabinowitz, 1984).

In overview, my position is that there *are* age-related decrements in memory functioning, but that these decrements are much more apparent in some tasks than in others; this observation has led many workers to adopt the view that aging affects only certain stores, systems, or functions. A second general observation is that the decrements often appear to reflect *inefficient* functioning, rather than true "breakage" or "loss" of component structures. I say this, since (as illustrated later) changes in the task, in the instructions, or in the environment can restore an older person's functioning to the level of young adults.

In general, age differences appear to be slightest when the relevant mental processes are "driven" rather directly by the stimulus or are strongly determined or supported by the environment. Thus age differences are minimal in situations characterized by strong stimulus–response connections—either where the processes concerned are relatively peripheral and "wired in" (e.g., those that are involved in simple sensory–motor functions; see Cerella, Poon, & Williams, 1980), or where the processes are highly practiced and over-learned (as with older active chess and bridge players; see Charness, 1982). Age differences are greatest, on the other hand, when the task requires going "beyond the information given"—where processes must be self-initiated (as opposed to driven by the stimulus), where new connections or patterns must be formed (as opposed to reliance on existing schemas), and/or where a different "set" must be established from the person's habitual set or the set induced by the environment. Thus large age differences are found in free-learning situations (especially using novel or unfamiliar material), as well as in unstructured free-recall situations (Craik, 1977), in situations demanding the use of inference (Cohen, 1979), and in situations requiring novel approaches to problem-solving tasks (Rabbitt, 1977).

The older cognitive system appears to *reflect* the environment in a somewhat passive manner, rather than to *modify* the environment actively. Active modification requires more effort and more cognitive resources, and it appears to be these effortful mental operations that older people are unable, or unwilling, to perform (Hasher & Zacks, 1979).

Short-Term and Long-Term Memory

Previous research workers into age differences in memory have attempted to systematize the area by suggesting that aging effects only some parts of the total system. Thus, Welford (1958) made a persuasive case for the existence of age differences in short-term memory, but not in long-term memory. My position is that age differences may or may not appear in short-term retention—equally, they may or may not appear in long-term retention—as a function of *the type of task* being performed, not the "memory store" in question.

Within the domain of short-term retention, it may be useful to distinguish between "primary-memory" and "working-memory" tasks (Craik & Rabinowitz, 1984). In our review, Rabinowitz and I used "primary memory" to refer to situations in which small amounts of material are held briefly in memory and are then retrieved in a relatively untransformed fashion. Examples of primary-memory tasks are digit span, recalling the last few words from a free-recall list (the recency effect), and the Brown–Peterson paradigm. Age differences are negligible in these three tasks (Craik, 1977), although all three involve short-term memory. By way of illustration, Figure 1-1 (Craik, 1977) shows two studies using the Brown–Peterson paradigm. In contrast, working-memory tasks show large age differences (Craik & Rabinowitz, 1984). I use "working memory" to refer to situations in which the subject must hold, manipulate, and transform the material before responding. Thus backward digit span, the transformed word span tasks devised by Talland (1965), and various dual-task paradigms (e.g., Kirchner, 1958; Wright, 1981) require active manipulation of the material—and all show large age decrements.

The conclusion drawn in our review (Craik & Rabinowitz, 1984) was therefore that age decrements appear in short-term memory tasks as a function of the degree of active manipulation involved, not merely as a result of involving the short-term memory system. Within long-term memory situations, the same case can be made; in line with recent terminology, the work on long-term retention is discussed under the heading of semantic and episodic memory.

Semantic and Episodic Memory

Following Tulving's (1972) distinction, "semantic memory" refers to a person's store of general knowledge, whereas "episodic memory" refers to contextually bound events whose time and place of occurrence form part of the remembered information. It has been

FIGURE 1-1. Short-term forgetting rate as a function of age. (A) Data from a study by D. Schonfield. (B) Data from a study by F.I.M. Craik. (From F.I.M. Craik, Age differences in human memory. In J. E. Birren & K. W. Schaie [Eds.], *Handbook of the psychology of aging*. New York: Van Nostrand Reinhold, 1977. Reprinted by permission.)

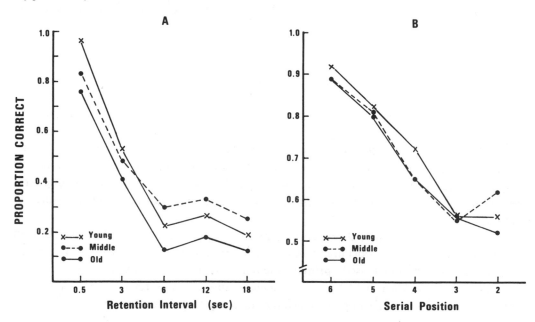

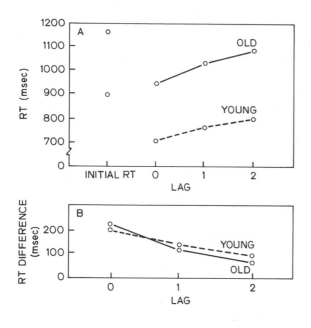

FIGURE 1-2. Reaction times in a category-decision task as a function of age and lag. Data from a study by Mark Byrd. (From F.I.M. Craik & M. Byrd, Aging and cognitive deficits: The role of attentional resources. In F.I.M. Craik & S.E. Trehub [Eds.], *Aging and cognitive processes*. New York: Plenum, 1982. Reprinted by permission.)

suggested that age decrements occur in episodic but not in semantic memory (Perlmutter, 1978); however, I wish to argue again that age differences may or may not appear in either memory system as a function of the degree of active, novel manipulation required by the task, not simply as a function of the "system" involved.

Within semantic memory, two very different situations showing negligible age differences are, first, cases of semantic activation or "priming" (Byrd, reported by Craik & Byrd, 1982; Howard, Lasaga, & McAndrews, 1980; Howard, McAndrews, & Lasaga, 1981); and, second, cases in which well-practiced (and well-maintained) complex cognitive skills are tapped. As an example of the first type of case, Mark Byrd (reported by Craik & Byrd, 1982) conducted a study in which subjects were shown a series of category-exemplar pairs (e.g., "fruit–cherry" or "furniture–tiger"). The subject's task was to decide as rapidly as possible whether the exemplar belonged to the category. In a long series of such pairs, the same category was sometimes repeated (but with a different exemplar) at lags of 0, 1, or 2 intervening items. On such repeated trials, decision times were shorter, but the facilitation effect was just as large for older as for younger subjects (see Figure 1-2); that is, these relatively automatic priming effects appear to be independent of age.

When more complex semantic-memory tasks are considered, age decrements sometimes do and sometimes do not occur. For example, Schaie (1980) presented data showing that whereas performance on a multiple-choice vocabulary test of verbal ability showed an *improvement* with age, at least until the 60s, a test of word fluency (generating as many words as possible beginning with a given letter) declined markedly from the mid-20s on. Both of these tests appear to tap "semantic memory," but whereas the former relies on well-practiced routines and is "guided" by the test situation, the latter is not. That is, performance appears to be determined by the nature of the task, not by the memory system involved.

When episodic-memory tasks are considered, it is again apparent that age decrements may be large or small, depending on the support provided by the task. In cases where little "guidance" is provided, either at encoding or at retrieval, age differences are large. Thus, if a list of words is presented with instructions simply to learn the list for a later test, and the subsequent test is one of free recall, large age decrements are typically observed. This extreme case may be contrasted with one in which effective encoding operations are induced by means of a semantic orienting task (e.g., subjects may be asked to fit each word into a sentence frame, or decide whether the word belongs to a specified category, or to image the word in interaction with other words), and this encoding task is coupled with a retrieval test in which processes are again guided—for example, cued recall or recognition. In this second case, age differences are slight or nonexistent (Craik, 1977; Craik & Rabinowitz, 1984; Rabinowitz, Craik, & Ackerman, 1982). These findings are not consonant with the idea that aging is associated with a decrement in the functioning of some unitary "system" (such as episodic memory), but they are consistent with the idea that older subjects perform certain types of mental operations inefficiently, unless the operations are induced and guided by the task, by specific instructions, or by other supportive aspects of the current environment. Rabbitt (1982) provides a nice example: Older people are quite poor at describing a route through city streets, although the same people can find their own way perfectly well—in the latter situation, the context provides "support and guidance" with respect to each successive turn and decision.

If older people are capable of carrying out effective processing operations, why do they often fail to produce them spontaneously? My colleagues and I (e.g., Craik & Byrd, 1982; Craik & Rabinowitz, 1984) have suggested that older people may have fewer "processing resources" to drive mental operations. If this is so, it would be reasonable to expect that difficult and novel operations would suffer first, whereas highly practiced stereotyped operations would continue to be performed. But novel combinations are essential in order to encode events distinctively from many previous similar events; thus if the older person fails to modify the event in light of the specific current context, it will be encoded in a stereotyped fashion and thus will not be easily retrieved. The idea of reduced processing resources suggests that if such resources could be reduced artificially in young subjects, their memory performance should resemble that of their older counterparts. We have carried out a series of experiments on young subjects using a second concurrent task (i.e., divided attention) to reduce resources, and these studies have indeed yielded results similar to the pattern seen in normal aging (Rabinowitz et al., 1982). Although the speculation of reduced processing resources appears plausible, it may not be the only factor underlying age decrements in episodic memory. For example, lack of recent practice—especially with the rather artificial tasks given in laboratory experiments—may well be a factor. It is also possible that older subjects are less likely to realize that elaborate semantic operations are associated with good retention, and thus they may fail to carry them out unless explicitly instructed to do so (e.g., Hulicka & Grossman, 1967).

Conclusions

In the present chapter, I have suggested first that memory (or, more properly, *remembering*) may be best understood in terms of encoding processes, retrieval processes, and their interactions. This approach stands in contrast to approaches whose goal is to describe specific memory stores or systems. Good memory for an event is associated with situations in which the event is related to the subject's past knowledge in a meaningful way, yet is also treated in a way that is distinctive from this past knowledge. In many cases, this distinctiveness will be conferred by integrating the event with its specific context. At retrieval, the same mental operations that took place at encoding must be reinstated either by the event itself, by similarities in the retrieval environment, or by the subject's own reconstructive operations. It is apparently somewhat difficult and effortful for the subject to treat each event in a distinctive fashion, and the present suggestion is that, because of reduced processing resources, older people often fail to carry out effective encoding and retrieval operations. These deficiencies can be overcome, however, if the task and the environment are structured to induce effective operations in older subjects. A similar pattern of memory deficiency has been found in young subjects working under conditions of divided attention, and it is an interesting question for further research to explore how far the current ideas might be extended to describe memory failures in other conditions (e.g., fatigue, alcoholic intoxication, and at least some amnesias). As a final word on theory, the present approach, with its emphasis on mental processes in dynamic interaction with aspects of the environment, suggests that students of memory should not be striving to model the system "at rest" or in isolation—that is, as some entity with an existence separate from its activities. Rather, our goal should be to model the interactions themselves—the interactions among tasks, environmental events, and mental representations of prior knowledge.

REFERENCES

Atkinson, R. C., & Shiffrin, R. M. Human memory: A proposed system and its control processes. In K. W. Spence & J. T. Spence (Eds.), *The psychology of learning and motivation* (Vol. 2). New York: Academic Press, 1968.

Baddeley, A. D. The trouble with levels: A re-examination of Craik and Lockhart's framework for memory research. *Psychological Review*, 1978, *85*, 139–152.

Bartlett, F. C. *Remembering.* Cambridge, England: Cambridge University Press, 1932.

Bransford, J. D., McCarrell, N. S., Franks, J. J., & Nitsch, K. E. Toward unexplaining memory. In R. Shaw & J. Bransford (Eds.), *Perceiving, acting, and knowing.* Hillsdale, N.J.: Erlbaum, 1977.

Cerella, J., Poon, L. W., & Williams, D. M. Aging and the complexity hypothesis. In L. W. Poon (Ed.), *Aging in the 1980's.* Washington, D.C.: American Psychological Association, 1980.

Charness, N. Problem solving and aging: Evidence from semantically rich domains. *Canadian Journal of Aging*, 1982, *1*, 21–28.

Cohen, G. Language comprehension in old age. *Cognitive Psychology*, 1979, *11*, 412–429.

Craik, F. I. M. Age differences in human memory. In J. E. Birren & K. W. Schaie (Eds.), *Handbook of the psychology of aging.* New York: Van Nostrand Reinhold, 1977.

Craik, F. I. M. Human memory. *Annual Review of Psychology*, 1979, *30*, 63–102.

Craik, F. I. M. Encoding and retrieval effects in human memory: A partial review. In J. Long & A. D. Baddeley (Eds.), *Attention and performance IX.* Hillsdale, N.J.: Erlbaum, 1981.

Craik, F. I. M., & Byrd, M. Aging and cognitive deficits: The role of attentional resources. In F. I. M. Craik & S. E. Trehub (Eds.), *Aging and cognitive processes.* New York: Plenum, 1982.

Craik, F. I. M., & Lockhart, R. S. Levels of processing: A framework for memory research. *Journal of Verbal Learning and Verbal Behavior*, 1972, *11*, 671–684.

Craik, F. I. M., & Rabinowitz, J. C. Age differences in the acquisition and use of verbal information. In H. Bouma & D. G. Bouwhuis (Eds.), *Attention and performance X.* Hillsdale, N.J.: Erlbaum, 1984.

Craik, F. I. M., & Watkins, M. J. The role of rehearsal in short-term memory. *Journal of Verbal Learning and Verbal Behavior*, 1973, *12*, 599–607.

Friedman, A. Framing pictures: The role of knowledge in automatized encoding and memory for gist. *Journal of Experimental Psychology: General*, 1979, *108*, 316–355.

Hasher, L., & Zacks, R. T. Automatic and effortful processing in memory. *Journal of Experimental Psychology: General*, 1979, *108*, 356–388.

Howard, D. V., Lasaga, M. I., & McAndrews, M. P. Semantic activation during memory encoding across the adult life span. *Journal of Gerontology*, 1980, *35*, 884–890.

Howard, D. V., McAndrews, M. P., & Lasaga, M. I. Semantic priming of lexical decisions in young and old adults. *Journal of Gerontology*, 1981, *36*, 707–714.

Hulicka, I. M., & Grossman, J. L. Age group comparisons for the use of mediators in paired-associate learning. *Journal of Gerontology*, 1967, *22*, 46–51.

Keenan, J. M., MacWhinney, B., & Mayhew, D. Pragmatics in memory: A study of natural conversation. *Journal of Verbal Learning and Verbal Behavior*, 1977, *16*, 549–560.

Kirchner, W. K. Age differences in short-term retention of rapidly changing information. *Journal of Experimental Psychology*, 1958, *55*, 352–358.

Kolers, P. A. Remembering operations. *Memory and Cognition*, 1973, *1*, 347–355.

Murdock, B. B., Jr. Recent developments in short-term memory. *British Journal of Psychology*, 1967, *58*, 421–433.

Perlmutter, M. What is memory aging the aging of? *Developmental Psychology*, 1978, *14*, 330–345.

Rabbitt, P. M. A. Changes in problem solving in old age. In J. E. Birren & K. W. Schaie (Eds.), *Handbook of the psychology of aging*. New York: Van Nostrand Reinhold, 1977.

Rabbitt, P. Breakdown of control processes in old age. In T. M. Field, A. Huston, H. C. Quay, L. Troll, & G. E. Finley (Eds.), *Review of human development*. New York: Wiley, 1982.

Rabinowitz, J. C., Craik, F. I. M., & Ackerman, B. P. A processing resource account of age differences in recall. *Canadian Journal of Psychology*, 1982, *36*, 325–344.

Rogers, T. B., Kuiper, N. A., & Kirker, W. S. Self-reference and the encoding of personal information. *Journal of Personality and Social Psychology*, 1977, *35*, 677–688.

Schaie, K. W. Cognitive development in aging. In L. K. Obler & M. L. Albert (Eds.), *Language and communication in the elderly: Clinical, therapeutic and experimental issues*. Lexington, Mass.: Lexington Books, 1980.

Shiffrin, R. M. Memory search. In D. A. Norman (Ed.), *Models of human memory*. New York: Academic Press, 1970.

Talland, G. A. Three estimates of the word span and their stability over the adult years. *Quarterly Journal of Experimental Psychology*, 1965, *17*, 301–307.

Tulving, E. Episodic and semantic memory. In E. Tulving & W. Donaldson (Eds.), *Organization of memory*. New York: Academic Press, 1972.

Welford, A. T. *Aging and human skill*. London: Oxford University Press, 1958.

Woodward, A. E., Jr., Bjork, R. A., & Jongeward, R. H., Jr. Recall and recognition as a function of primary rehearsal. *Journal of Verbal Learning and Verbal Behavior*, 1973, *12*, 608–617.

Wright, R. E. Aging, divided attention, and processing capacity. *Journal of Gerontology*, 1981, *36*, 605–614.

Toward the Multidisciplinary Study of Memory: Ontogeny, Phylogeny, and Pathology of Memory Systems

2

Daniel L. Schacter

The observation that the study of memory proceeds on many different levels can be safely regarded as a contemporary truism. Even a casual survey of recent literature reveals a multitude of approaches to the problem, each characterized by different experimental methods, empirical phenomena, and theoretical issues. The contributors to the present volume themselves represent a significant proportion of the various sectors of memory research, including psychology, biochemistry, neuroanatomy, phylogeny, and pharmacology of memory, as well as the experimental and clinical neuropsychology of memory disorders. There are other areas, too, that should be included in a census of research enterprises concerned with memory, such as artificial intelligence, human and animal development, psychophysiology, hypnosis, and functional psychopathology.

The number of studies of memory produced by any one of the foregoing disciplines ranges from modest to huge; the total volume of published research is staggering. Yet in spite of the impressive amount of data and theory generated by individual areas of memory research, the level of cross-disciplinary communication has been relatively limited, and a systematic multidisciplinary attack on problems of memory has not yet emerged. Such a situation may not be entirely surprising, because the task of staying abreast of unfolding developments in one's own research area—or in just a segment of it—can sometimes leave even the most dedicated scholar gasping for breath. If we must constantly monitor the activity in our own backyard, then it is difficult to invest too much attention in our neighbor's business.

It is unlikely, however, that the relative lack of multidisciplinary approaches to memory can be wholly attributed to the mind-numbing powers of the seemingly endless flow of articles that emanate from contemporary journals. One other factor contributing to the present situation concerns the diversity of theoretical issues that occupy the attention of scientists in the various sectors of memory research. It would be difficult to identify any one theme or issue that is common to the study of memory in all, or even most, of its numerous manifestations. In fact, issues that are crucial theoretically in one area of study may be little understood by, or totally unfamiliar to, practitioners in another. Such a state of affairs may not be terribly troubling to many researchers, for at least two reasons. First, individual areas of memory research operate at different levels of analysis and derive from conceptual contexts that are characterized by distinct theoretical goals and different methods of achieving them. Second, there is often lack of agreement about what issues are

Daniel L. Schacter. Department of Psychology, University of Toronto, Toronto, Ontario, Canada.

important theoretically *within* a given discipline (Tulving, 1979). Hence there would be little reason to expect any degree of cohesion across conceptual and methodological boundaries, and a survey of the contemporary scene reveals that there is indeed little consensus about what issues might be pursued from a multidisciplinary perspective (for some recent attempts to bridge cross-disciplinary gaps, see Cermak, 1982, Moscovitch, 1984, and Rosenzweig & Bennett, 1976).

The purposes of the present chapter are (1) to delineate some reasons why a multidisciplinary approach to memory is desirable at the present time; (2) to suggest issues that can be fruitfully examined from a multidisciplinary perspective; and (3) to present some data concerning a particular problem whose investigation requires multidisciplinary integration.

Reasons for a Multidisciplinary Approach

A case for a multidisciplinary approach to the study of memory can be made on the grounds that it may provide some research opportunities that would not be otherwise available, and that it may help us to avoid some pitfalls all too frequently encountered within some specific subareas of memory research. One benefit that might be reaped by a multidisciplinary approach is that it can take advantage of the fact that different areas of memory research are characterized by different strengths. For example, the neuro-psychology of memory disorders provides useful tools for fractionating memory into component processes or subsystems by observing patterns of dissociation in neuropathological cases of amnesia; the cognitive psychology of adult memory possesses many research paradigms that permit a relatively sophisticated analysis of people's performance on both simple and complex tasks; animal lesion research is capable of a level of precision in determining the relation between brain structure and mnemonic function that is not possible in work with humans; and developmental as well as comparative studies have a unique opportunity to shed light on the relation between memory and language. Ongoing work in these and other areas of memory research reflects the particular strengths associated with each discipline. It is easy to become enthusiastic when one imagines the analytic power that might be achieved by bringing to bear a number of different perspectives on an issue of cross-disciplinary concern. A similar sentiment has been expressed by Shallice (1979), who speculated that a multidisciplinary attack on problems of memory might yield a broad understanding in which "the strength of the whole would be much greater than that of the sum of its parts" (p. 274).

A multidisciplinary focus might also help to guard against a danger that has been discussed by several students of memory: the tendency of research to be driven by specific paradigms and experimental phenomena, rather than by general theoretical goals. Newell (1973), for instance, pointed out that cognitive psychologists are all too often concerned solely with the discovery of isolated experimental phenomena. Research then focuses on explaining an individual phenomenon—in the manner of the "20 Questions" game described by Newell—rather than on attempting to elucidate the relation of the phenomenon to other sets of phenomena, or to place it in a more general theoretical framework. Neisser (1978/1982) has lamented the fact that psychological students of memory are so easily beguiled by an experimental paradigm that yields orderly data; he noted that the Sternberg paradigm "has been so thoroughly investigated and described that everything is known except what it means" (p. 7). In a critique of the literature on infant memory, Sophian (1980) argued that the almost exclusive use of the habituation paradigm has yielded a narrow view of infants' mnemonic capabilities, and implored researchers to become less "paradigm bound" in future work. Other students of memory have articulated similar concerns (e.g., Allport, 1975; Tulving, 1979).

I am not naive enough to believe that a multidisciplinary research focus would eliminate the problems noted by these authors. But it does seem probable that such difficulties would be less likely to emerge in a multidisciplinary context that is focused specifically on theoretical issues that are sufficiently broad to interest researchers from different areas. To the extent that a multidisciplinary perspective encourages us to keep the "big picture" in mind, it may reduce the chances of researchers' becoming entangled in the intricacies of isolated experimental paradigms and phenomena.

Areas of Multidisciplinary Concern: Four Candidate Issues

How might we develop a fruitful multidisciplinary perspective on the understanding of memory? Such an accomplishment would not be a simple one. As Rosenzweig (1976) pointed out in his summary of a multidisciplinary conference on learning and memory, it is not a trivial task for researchers to overcome the conceptual constraints imposed by training and experience in a particular discipline, although this is a necessary condition for the development of cross-disciplinary interaction. And it is unlikely that the goal of multidisciplinary understanding could be attained by simply urging researchers to incorporate data and theories from other areas of memory research into their own work; the vastness of the literature, alluded to earlier, could leave even the most enthusiastic multidisciplinarians frozen in their tracks at the beginning of the attempted journey across disciplinary boundaries. Clearly, some sort of focus is required before the journey begins. It is probably not enough to say that we want a multidisciplinary understanding of "memory": We may have to specify particular issues and problems that seem amenable to cross-disciplinary research if we are going to have a reasonable chance for success.

Not all issues, of course, are best pursued from a multidisciplinary perspective; interest in many is restricted—and appropriately so—to practitioners within a specific discipline. We do not expect students of memory development to be concerned with the mechanisms underlying free recall in hypnotized subjects, nor do we expect researchers who study single-cell preparations to participate in a debate over the role of frontal lobes in memory processes. Many other examples could be cited: A substantial proportion of memory research focuses on problems that are of largely local concern. What are the issues that are of interest to, and can be usefully studied by, participants in different sectors of memory research?

Let me mention briefly several problems that seem ripe for multidisciplinary study, and then discuss in somewhat more detail one issue that seems particularly well suited for such analysis. First, consider the problem of the relationship between affect and memory. This issue has long been of interest to investigators concerned with psychoanalytic phenomena (e.g., Erdelyi & Goldberg, 1979; Rapaport, 1950), and has also been pursued in studies of the neural and biochemical substrates of memory (Kety, 1976). More recently, there has been an upsurge of interest in the affect–memory interaction among cognitive psychologists (Bower, 1981), social psychologists (Isen, Shalker, Clark, & Karp, 1978), and researchers concerned with clinical depression (Clark & Teasdale, 1982). There has not yet been, however, a systematic attempt to integrate data and theory from all of the foregoing approaches, although the results of some recent work indicate that such cross-fertilization can yield useful insights (Derry & Kuiper, 1981). A multidisciplinary focus at this juncture might well lead to a more general understanding of the relationship between affect and memory than has so far been accomplished.

Similar comments could be made about the problem of infantile amnesia. Once solely the province of psychoanalysts, this problem has recently garnered attention from students of animal memory (Spear, 1979), social development (White & Pillemer, 1979), and adult cognition (Rubin, 1982). Each of these disciplines brings a unique perspective to this difficult issue. How are their respective insights related to one another? We do not yet know.

Another issue that might be clarified by multidisciplinary integration concerns the effects of context on memory. "Context" is a term that few researchers seem to like, yet many use it for lack of a better alternative. "Context effects"—defined roughly as the influence of learning and retrieval environments on mnemonic processes—have been observed and discussed by researchers concerned with intact human memory (Smith, Glenberg, & Bjork, 1978), animal memory (Spear, 1978; Winocur, 1982), memory disorders (Winocur, 1982), drug effects (Eich, 1980), infant (Ruff, 1981) and child memory (Perlmutter, Sophian, Mitchell, & Cavanaugh, 1981), and neuroanatomy (O'Keefe & Nadel, 1978). What are the implications of the many manifestations of context effects? Could the construct itself be better understood by increased cross-disciplinary communication? The possibility may be worth pursuing.

Memory consolidation is another problem that has been studied by researchers in many different disciplines. The issue remains a controversial one. Investigators who work at a purely psychological level tend to reject the usefulness of the concept altogether (e.g., Crowder, 1982), whereas researchers with biological and neurochemical inclinations look upon it much more favorably (e.g., McGaugh & Hertz, 1972). While refraining from discussing the utility of the concept in the present chapter, I should note that ideas put forward recently by Wickelgren (1979) and by Squire, Cohen, and Nadel (1983)—which draw upon and integrate data from various sectors of memory research—go a long way toward settling problems that had arisen within different disciplines that did not formerly enjoy active communication with one another. Perhaps further cross-disciplinary efforts will yield an even clearer understanding of this basic issue.

Dissociable Memory Systems and the Multidisciplinary Approach

The issues mentioned above are all particularly promising areas for multidisciplinary integration, because (1) they are problems of fundamental importance that have attracted the attention of investigators within a number of disciplines; (2) cross-disciplinary interaction concerning each issue has been rather limited; and (3) the current level of understanding in each case is somewhat modest. The same comments apply to an issue that I would like to discuss in somewhat more detail: the nature and number of memory systems.

The notion that what we call "memory" is not a monolithic entity, but can be better described as a number of separate but interacting systems, is not a new one. Many students of the subject, dating back at least to the early 19th century, have put forward various hypotheses that entail distinctions among fundamentally different kinds of memory. One reason why this issue now seems especially suitable for multidisciplinary study is that investigators in different sectors of memory research are demonstrating a great deal of interest in it. Concern with this issue was originally sparked by the debate concerning short-term memory and long-term memory, about which I have more to say shortly; however, it has recently focused on what we might call "varieties of long-term memory." Without attempting to construct an exhaustive list, one can point to distinctions among different kinds of memory that have been made in experimental psychology (Herrmann, 1982; Johnson, 1983; Schacter & Tulving, 1982b; Tulving, 1972, 1983), neuropsychology of amnesia (Cohen & Squire, 1980; Kinsbourne & Wood, 1975, 1982; Moscovitch, 1982; Warrington & Weiskrantz, 1982), animal memory (Olton, Becker, & Handelmann, 1979), artificial intelligence (Winograd, 1975), hypnosis research (Kihlstrom, 1980), and developmental studies of both humans (Nelson & Brown, 1978; Schacter & Moscovitch, 1984) and animals (Nadel & Zola-Morgan, 1984). Moreover, in spite of existing disagreements concerning the precise nature of the distinctions to be made, the ideas put forward by many of these researchers share much in common. In most cases, a memory system that makes possible the acquisition and utilization of knowledge of specific facts or events, and whose products may be accessible to conscious awareness, is contrasted with a system that underlies the acquisition of skills or general knowledge of rules and strategies, and that may not be accessible to conscious awareness. In view of this wide-ranging interest in a common problem, there are both methodological and theoretical reasons why increased multidisciplinary convergence on the issue of multiple memory systems may be particularly useful at the present time.

A multidisciplinary focus may help to define exactly what we mean when we speak of "different memory systems," and may also help to elucidate the operational criteria that are needed to distinguish among them. It would be all too easy for researchers in different disciplines who are concerned with this problem to define it in terms of experimental paradigms and theoretical constructs that are unique to their own disciplines. The danger here is that research concerning the nature and number of memory systems could become paradigm-bound. It seems clear that a satisfying understanding of this rather broad issue will not be attained by endless studies of one paradigm—be it the fragment-completion task of cognitive psychology, the radial maze used in animal research, or the mirror-reading task given to amnesics. Rather, we want to interrelate data from different paradigms both within and across disciplines, and, if possible, to extend laboratory observations of mnemonic dissociations to natural environments (Schacter, 1983). In order to accomplish this objective, it is important that researchers in different disciplines reach some sort of understanding concerning the kind of memory that their different paradigms measure. It is instructive to consider the fate of an issue that has been noted earlier: the relationship between short-term and long-term memory. This problem has probably sparked enough research and theory in different disciplines—including experimental psychology, neuropsychology, and neurochemistry—to provide sufficient material for a revealing monograph by an enterprising historian of science. However, as recent discussions indicate clearly, there is not only lack of consensus about the theoretical status of the issue, there is even lack of agreement about how to define "short-term memory" and "long-term memory" operationally. I would suggest that the current confusion may be partly attributable to the fact that investigators in different disciplines have used a variety of paradigms to assess short-term memory, that their respective ideas about what constitutes "short-term memory" became closely tied to their paradigms, and that there has been relatively little cross-disciplinary communication about the issue at the level of defining and delineating the constructs of interest. This sequence of events could well serve as a model of exactly what we do not want to happen in the "new wave" of research on multiple memory systems.

The history of the short-term memory–long-term memory issue also highlights a problem that may require a multidisciplinary perspective in order to be addressed satisfactorily: the specification of criteria for determining the kind of evidence that permits one to argue for separate memory systems. It is difficult to find any discussion in the short-term–long-term memory literature about the kinds of evidence that do and do not support distinctions between different memory systems (for an exception, see Wickelgren, 1973). Similarly, there has been little analysis of this problem in the recent research discussed above. How can we say that a particular set of data provides evidence in favor of different memory *systems*, rather than different *processes* operating within a unitary system? Or how can we know when the results of an experiment are telling about different attributes of a memory trace, rather than about different memory systems? There are as yet no good answers to these questions, and I suspect that a failure to grapple with them directly will lead to a state of conceptual confusion in the literature. It does seem clear, however, that we need criteria that would be applicable to the interpretation of data in different sectors of memory research; to this end, it would be useful for investigators in different disciplines to propose and debate criteria that could guide interpretation of experiments concerned with the nature and number of memory systems.

A multidisciplinary focus may also help to deal with a problem that could become acute, and is already evident in the literature: an undesirable proliferation of postulated memory systems (for discussion, see Jacoby, 1983; Schacter & Tulving, 1982b). Imagine that we treated each of the proposed binary distinctions between memory systems (e.g., short-term–long-term, episodic–semantic, declarative–procedural, working–reference) as orthogonal to one another. The astronomical number of systems that would be postulated by enumerating all possible combinations and permutations of existing distinctions might lead one to beg earnestly for forgiveness from the Lord of Parsimony. Of course, many researchers would argue that current distinctions overlap substantially with one another, and I would tend to agree. But the basic problem that we are left with is similar in either case: How can we choose among the many proposed distinctions and keep the number of theoretical possibilities to a manageable level? There is a way in which a multidisciplinary perspective could help to resolve this question. If researchers could agree among themselves that empirical support for a given distinction needs to be obtained from different sectors of memory research in order to establish its theoretical utility, then we may be able to avoid a situation in which a multitude of distinctions abound, each deriving its support from a relatively narrow data base. Such a proposal entails difficulties of its own (e.g., how many different disciplines must provide evidence supporting a given distinction before its theoretical usefulness can be ascertained?), but it provides an alternative to the state of theoretical anarchy that we might encounter otherwise.

Ontogeny, Phylogeny, and Pathology of Memory Systems

In the foregoing paragraphs I have pointed to methodological and strategic issues pertaining to the problem of the nature and number of memory systems that might be clarified by multidisciplinary integration. What about theoretical ideas? Are there any theoretical issues related to the basic problem of multiple memory systems that could be viewed more clearly, or tackled more readily, in a multidisciplinary context than in a unidisciplinary setting? I would like to suggest as a candidate a problem that was of considerable interest to some late 19th-century students of psychology and neurology, and has reemerged in recent discussions of memory and memory pathology (e.g., Nadel & Zola-Morgan, 1984; Rozin, 1976b; Schacter & Tulving, 1982a; Squire, in press). This is the idea that there is an important relationship among the ontogeny, phylogeny, and pathology of memory systems. The general form of the relationship, which derives from Jacksonian notions about the evolution and dissolution of the nervous system, is captured in which might be called the "last in, first out" hypothesis: Memory systems that develop late in evolution also appear relatively late in ontogeny, and are the first to be affected in cases of generalized brain disease. This idea may seem uncomfortably familiar to some researchers, because it is related to the controversial notion, championed by Ernst Haeckel and other 19th-century biologists, that ontogeny recapitulates phylogeny. There is indeed a flavor of recapitulationism to the "last in, first out" hypothesis, but this need not be a barrier to its investigation. Although the radical and overly simplistic form of recapitulationism entailed in proposals such as Haeckel's "biogenetic law" is no longer tenable, there is a good deal of biological evidence that points to significant relationships between ontogeny and phylogeny (Gould, 1977). In fact, such relationships have played a major role in recent discussions of the evolution of intelligence (Parker & Gibson, 1979; Rozin, 1976a).

Is there any evidence that supports the "last in, first out" hypothesis with respect to memory? Not surprisingly, there have been relatively few direct experimental investigations of this problem. However, consideration of studies of both animal and human memory indicates that there are many reasons to believe that the mnemonic capacities of infants and adult amnesics are similar (Nadel & Zola-Morgan, 1984; Schacter & Moscovitch, 1984). More specifically, the evidence suggests that a memory system that entails retention of modifications of procedures or processing operations (Cohen & Squire, 1980; Moscovitch, 1982) is preserved in amnesics and appears early in ontogeny, whereas a system that depends upon establishment of propositional representations is impaired in amnesics and develops later in ontogeny—in human infants, at the age of about 8–10 months (Schacter & Moscovitch, 1984).

We examined the possible relationship between amnesic and infant memory in a study of amnesic patients' ability to remember the location of hidden and visible objects (Schacter & Moscovitch, 1984). Our study was patterned after object-search tasks that have been used in research concerning infant cognition (cf. Gratch, 1976). Such studies have revealed that 9- to 10-month-old infants are capable of remembering the location of an object over a brief delay if the object is hidden at just one location (Location A). However, if after several successful searches at Location A, the object is hidden at a different location (Location B), many infants continue to search at A, even though the displacement is visible and the infant attends to it. This pattern of preservative search, first reported by Piaget (1954), is known as the "A$\overline{\text{B}}$

error." Piaget believed that the $A\overline{B}$ error constitutes evidence of an incompletely developed object concept, and numerous other interpretations have been offered. There is, however, a good deal of evidence to indicate that forgetting associated with proactive interference is a major source of the $A\overline{B}$ error (Schacter & Moscovitch, 1984). If, as suggested above, mnemonic abilities of infants and amnesics are similar, then we might expect that amnesic patients —who can be highly sensitive to proactive interference (e.g., Kinsbourne & Winocur, 1980; Warrington & Weiskrantz, 1974; Winocur & Weiskrantz, 1976)—would perform in a manner similar to infants on object-search tasks.

Our study included six severely amnesic patients of mixed etiologies (four in the early stages of Alzheimer disease, one with an anterior communicating artery aneurysm, and one without a firm diagnosis) and six control patients who were characterized by mild cognitive impairments, but no significant memory loss (two cerebrovascular accidents, one early Alzheimer, one anterior communicating artery aneurysm, and two without a firm diagnosis). The performance of the amnesics on the Wechsler Memory Scale was significantly impaired in comparison with that of the controls, but the two groups did not differ on age, education, or IQ. Because our amnesic patients demonstrated signs of frontal lobe pathology, performance of amnesics and controls was matched on the Wisconsin Card Sort, a task that is sensitive to perseverative tendencies associated with dorso-lateral frontal lobe damage.

Patients were instructed to remember that a common object had been hidden behind a stack of books on a desk (Location A); the actual hiding of the object was done in full view of the patients. Each of the three trials at Location A included an immediate test, as well as a delayed test that followed a 2.5-minute filled retention interval. On both tests, patients attempted to find the object that was hidden on that particular trial; a different object was used on each trial (e.g., a stapler, a pencil, etc.). On delayed tests, patients' memory for the identity of the hidden object was probed. Both amnesics and controls searched successfully for the object on the delayed tests of the first three A trials (see Figure 2-1, panel A); performance on immediate tests was also perfect. When an object was then hidden at Location B (behind a book or a plant on a filing cabinet), all of the amnesics and controls found it when tested immediately. After the delay, however, four of the six amnesics searched incorrectly at A. The second phase of the experiment began with two more A trials (A_4 and A_5 in Figure 2-1). An object was then placed on a desk at Location C, about halfway between the patient and Location A, and in his or her *direct view*. Developmental studies have found that some infants commit the $A\overline{B}$ error on a delayed test even if the object is visible at B (see Schacter & Moscovitch, 1984). We observed a similar phenomenon. Although the amnesics performed well on the A_4 and A_5 trials, and all patients "found" the object on the immediate test at Location C, only one amnesic could "find" it on the delayed test at C (see Figure 2-1, panel A). The five patients who erred searched for the object at A, and failed to pick out the correct object when asked to choose among the several visible objects on the desk. In contrast, all but one of the controls performed flawlessly on the C trial. This patient searched initially at A, but unlike the amnesics, corrected himself spontaneously and then selected the object at Location C.

Amnesics' recall of the *identity* of the object (see Figure 2-1, panel B) was perfect on the first delayed trial, but declined sharply on the next trial and remained low; control patients' object recall was high on all delayed tests. Because it looks as though the first trial exerted a powerful interfering effect on amnesics' ability to remember new objects and

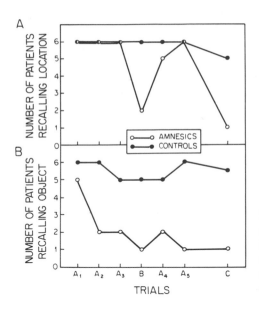

FIGURE 2-1. Delayed recall of location (panel A) and object (panel B) by amnesic and control patients on consecutive trials of an object-search task. Objects were hidden at an initial location (A) and a second location (B), and were visible at a third location (C). A different object was used on each trial.

locations on subsequent trials, we have called this phenomenon "mnemonic precedence." We have observed mnemonic precedence in a different object-search task, and have also found that patients with bilateral damage to the frontal lobes, who are characterized by marked perseverative tendencies but not by severe memory loss, easily recall both object location and identity on our tasks. These observations suggest that a memory deficit attributable to proactive interference may be a major (if not the only) source of mnemonic precedence, and encourage the idea that the occurrence of mnemonic precedence in amnesics and the $A\overline{B}$ error in infants reflects a point of genuine correspondence between their mnemonic abilities. The parallel performance of the two groups may reflect the operation of a memory system that is degraded in amnesics, and is not yet fully developed in 8- to 10-month-old infants. Although this hypothesis is clearly somewhat tentative and requires further empirical corroboration, it does provide a first step in the direction of thinking seriously about the relation between the ontogeny and pathology of memory systems, and suggests that the "last in, first out" hypothesis may merit consideration. The more general point to note is that investigation of this issue requires some degree of multidisciplinary integration.

Some students of memory may hesitate at the prospect of approaching such a wide-ranging issue at a time when understanding of much simpler problems is difficult to come by. Such caution is well founded; the history of psychology and biology is dotted by unifying schemes that have proven to be no more than temporary distractions that did not lead to any real advances in understanding (cf. Schacter, 1982, Chapter 7). In spite of such a risk, it seems likely that exploration of such a multifaceted issue as the ontogeny, phylogeny, and pathology of memory systems would facilitate multidisciplinary interaction, would encourage us to view familiar ideas in new theoretical contexts, and would provide a reminder that the study of memory is intimately connected with the investigation of basic issues in development and evolution. And that might move us closer to the kind of broad understanding of memory that investigators in all disciplines would like to achieve.

ACKNOWLEDGMENTS

Preparation of this chapter was supported by a Special Research Program Grant from the Connaught Fund, University of Toronto. Neal Cohen, Morris Moscovitch, Larry Squire, and Endel Tulving have provided useful discussion of relevant issues. Carol A. Macdonald provided help in preparation of the manuscript. Morris Freedman and Marlene Oscar-Berman provided access to the frontal patients for the object-search task.

REFERENCES

Allport, D. A. The state of cognitive psychology. *Quarterly Journal of Experimental Psychology*, 1975, *27*, 147–152.

Bower, G. H. Mood and memory. *American Psychologist*, 1981, *36*, 129–148.

Cermak, L. S. (Ed.). *Human memory and amnesia*. Hillsdale, N.J.: Erlbaum, 1982.

Clark, D. M., & Teasdale, J. D. Diurnal variation in clinical depression and accessibility of memories of positive and negative experiences. *Journal of Abnormal Psychology*, 1982, *91*, 87–95.

Cohen, N. J., & Squire, L. R. Preserved learning and retention of pattern-analyzing skill in amnesia: Dissociation of knowing how and knowing that. *Science*, 1980, *210*, 207–210.

Crowder, R. G. General forgetting theory and the locus of amnesia. In L. S. Cermak (Ed.), *Human memory and amnesia*. Hillsdale, N.J.: Erlbaum, 1982.

Derry, P. A., & Kuiper, N. A. Schematic processing and self-reference in clinical depression. *Journal of Abnormal Psychology*, 1981, *90*, 286–297.

Eich, J. M. The cue-dependent nature of state-dependent retrieval. *Memory and Cognition*, 1980, *8*, 157–173.

Erdelyi, M. H., & Goldberg, B. Let's not sweep repression under the rug: Toward a cognitive psychology of repression. In J. F. Kihlstrom & F. J. Evans (Eds.), *Functional disorders of memory*. Hillsdale, N.J.: Erlbaum, 1979.

Gould, S. J. *Ontogeny and phylogeny*. Cambridge, Mass.: Harvard University Press, 1977.

Gratch, G. On levels of awareness of objects in infants and students thereof. *Merrill–Palmer Quarterly*, 1976, *22*, 157–176.

Herrmann, D. J. The semantic–episodic distinction and the history of long-term memory typologies. *Bulletin of the Psychonomic Society*, 1982, *20*, 207–210.

Isen, A. M., Shalker, T. E., Clark, M., & Karp, L. Affect, accessibility of material in memory, and behavior: A cognitive loop? *Journal of Personality and Social Psychology*, 1978, *36*, 1–12.

Jacoby, L. L. Perceptual enhancement: Persistent effects of an experience. *Journal of Experimental Psychology: Learning, Memory, and Cognition*, 1983, *9*, 21–38.

Johnson, M. A multiple-entry, modular memory system. In G. H. Bower (Ed.), *The psychology of learning and motivation* (Vol. 17). New York: Academic Press, 1983.

Kety, S. S. Biological concomitants of affective states and their possible role in memory processes. In M. R. Rosenzweig & E. L. Bennett (Eds.), *Neural mechanisms of learning and memory*. Cambridge, Mass.: MIT Press, 1976.

Kihlstrom, J. F. Posthypnotic amnesia for recently learned materials: Interactions with "episodic" and "semantic" memory. *Cognitive Psychology*, 1980, *12*, 227–251.

Kinsbourne, M., & Winocur, G. Response competition and interference effects in paired-associate learning by Korsakoff amnesics. *Neuropsychologia*, 1980, *18*, 541–548.

Kinsbourne, M., & Wood, F. Short-term memory and the amnesic syndrome. In D. D. Deutsch & J. A. Deutsch (Eds.), *Short-term memory*. New York: Academic Press, 1975.

Kinsbourne, M., & Wood, F. Theoretical considerations regarding the episodic–semantic memory distinction. In L. S. Cermak (Ed.), *Human memory and amnesia*. Hillsdale, N.J.: Erlbaum, 1982.

McGaugh, J. L., & Herz, M. J. *Memory consolidation*. San Francisco: Albion, 1972.

Moscovitch, M. Multiple dissociations of function in amnesia. In L. S. Cermak (Ed.), *Human memory and amnesia*. Hillsdale, N.J.: Erlbaum, 1982.

Moscovitch, M. (Ed.). *Infant memory*. New York: Plenum Press, 1984.

Nadel, L., & Zola-Morgan, S. Infantile amnesia: A neurobiological perspective. In M. Moscovitch (Ed.), *Infant memory*. New York: Plenum Press, 1984.

Neisser, U. Memory: What are the important questions? In U. Neisser (Ed.), *Memory observed*. San Francisco: W. H. Freeman, 1982. (Originally published in M. M. Bruneberg, P. E. Morris, & R. N. Sykes [Eds.], *Practical aspects of memory*. London: Academic Press, 1978.)

Nelson, K., & Brown, A. L. The semantic–episodic distinction in memory development. In P. A. Ornstein (Ed.), *Memory development in children*. Hillsdale, N.J.: Erlbaum, 1978.

Newell, A. You can't play 20 Questions with nature and win. In W. G. Chase (Ed.), *Visual information processing*. New York: Academic Press, 1973.

O'Keefe, J., & Nadel, L. *The hippocampus as a cognitive map*. London: Oxford University Press, 1978.

Olton, D. S., Becker, J. T., & Handelmann, G. E. Hippocampus, space, and memory. *Behavioral and Brain Sciences*, 1979, *2*, 313–365.

Parker, S. T., & Gibson, K. R. A developmental model for the evolution of language and intelligence in early hominids. *Behavioral and Brain Sciences*, 1979, *2*, 367–408.

Perlmutter, M., Sophian, C., Mitchell, D. B., & Cavanaugh, J. C. Semantic and contextual cuing of preschool children's recall. *Child Development*, 1981, *52*, 873–881.

Piaget, J. *The construction of reality in the child*. New York: Basic Books, 1954.

Rapaport, D. *Emotions and memory*. New York: International Universities Press, 1950.

Rosenzweig, M. R. Conference summary. In M. R. Rosenzweig & E. L. Bennett (Eds.), *Neural mechanisms of learning and memory*. Cambridge, Mass.: MIT Press, 1976.

Rosenzweig, M. R., & Bennett, E. L. (Eds.). *Neural mechanisms of learning and memory*. Cambridge, Mass.: MIT Press, 1976.

Rozin, P. The evolution of intelligence and access to the cognitive unconscious. In J. M. Sprague & A. N. Epstein (Eds.), *Progress in physiological psychology* (Vol. 6). New York: Academic Press, 1976. (a)

Rozin, P. The psychobiological approach to human memory. In M. R. Rosenzweig & E. L. Bennett (Eds.), *Neural mechanisms of learning and memory*. Cambridge, Mass.: MIT Press, 1976. (b)

Rubin, D. C. On the retention function for autobiographical memory. *Journal of Verbal Learning and Verbal Behavior*, 1982, *21*, 21–38.

Ruff, H. A. Effects of context on infants' responses to novel objects. *Developmental Psychology*, 1981, *17*, 87–89.

Schacter, D. L. *Stranger behind the engram: Theories of memory and the psychology of science*. Hillsdale, N.J.: Erlbaum, 1982.

Schacter, D. L. Amnesia observed: Remembering and forgetting in a natural environment. *Journal of Abnormal Psychology*, 1983, *92*, 236–242.

Schacter, D. L., & Moscovitch, M. Infants, amnesics, and dissociable memory systems. In M. Moscovitch (Ed.), *Infant memory*. New York: Plenum Press, 1984.

Schacter, D. L., & Tulving, E. Amnesia and memory research. In L. S. Cermak (Ed.), *Human memory and amnesia*. Hillsdale, N.J.: Erlbaum, 1982. (a)

Schacter, D. L., & Tulving, E. Memory, amnesia, and the episodic/semantic distinction. In R. L. Isaacson & N. E. Spear (Eds.), *The expression of knowledge*. New York: Plenum Press, 1982. (b)

Shallice, T. Neuropsychological research and the fractionation of memory systems. In L.-G. Nilsson (Ed.), *Perspectives on memory research*. Hillsdale, N.J.: Erlbaum, 1979.

Smith, S. M., Glenberg, A. M., & Bjork, R. A. Environmental context and human memory. *Memory and Cognition*, 1978, *6*, 342–353.

Sophian, C. Habituation is not enough: Novelty preferences, search, and memory in infancy. *Merrill–Palmer Quarterly*, 1980, *26*, 239–257.

Spear, N. E. *The processing of memories: Forgetting and retention*. Hillsdale, N.J.: Erlbaum, 1978.

Spear, N. E. Experimental analysis of infantile amnesia. In J. F. Kihlstrom & F. J. Evans (Eds.), *Functional disorders of memory*. Hillsdale, N.J.: Erlbaum, 1979.

Squire, L. R. Memory and the brain. In S. Friedman, K. A. Klivington, & R. W. Peterson (Eds.), *Brain, cognition, and education*. New York: Academic Press, in press.

Squire, L. R., Cohen, N. J., & Nadel, L. The medial temporal region and memory consolidation: A new hypothesis. In H. Weingartner & E. Parker (Eds.), *Memory consolidation*. Hillsdale, N.J.: Erlbaum, 1983.

Tulving, E. Episodic and semantic memory. In E. Tulving & W. Donaldson (Eds.), *Organization of memory*. New York: Academic Press, 1972.

Tulving, E. Memory research: What kind of progress? In L.-G. Nilsson (Ed.), *Perspectives on memory research.* Hillsdale, N.J.: Erlbaum, 1979.

Tulving, E. *Elements of episodic memory.* London: Oxford University Press, 1983.

Warrington, E. K., & Weiskrantz, L. The effect of prior learning on subsequent retention in amnesic patients. *Neuropsychologia,* 1974, *12,* 419–428.

Warrington, E. K., & Weiskrantz, L. Amnesia: A disconnection syndrome? *Neuropsychologia,* 1982, *20,* 233–248.

White, S. H., & Pillemer, D. B. Childhood amnesia and the development of a socially accessible memory system. In J. F. Kihlstrom & F. J. Evans (Eds.), *Functional disorders of memory.* Hillsdale, N.J.: Erlbaum, 1979.

Wickelgren, W. A. The long and the short of memory. *Psychological Bulletin,* 1973, *80,* 425–438.

Wickelgren, W. A. Chunking and consolidation: A theoretical synthesis of semantic networks, configuring in conditioning, S-R versus cognitive learning, normal forgetting, the amnesic syndrome, and the hippocampal arousal system. *Psychological Review,* 1979, *86,* 44–60.

Winocur, G. The amnesic syndrome: A deficit in cue utilization. In L. S. Cermak (Ed.), *Human memory and amnesia.* Hillsdale, N.J.: Erlbaum, 1982.

Winocur, G., & Weiskrantz, L. An investigation of paired-associate learning in amnesic patients. *Neuropsychologia,* 1976, *14,* 97–110.

Winograd, T. Understanding natural language. In D. Bobrow & A. Collins (Eds.), *Representation and understanding.* New York: Academic Press, 1975.

The Fate of Memory: Discoverable or Doomed?

3

David F. Hall and Elizabeth F. Loftus

Over the past several years, we have been investigating the circumstances under which information received subsequent to a complex natural event, such as an accident or a crime, causes a systematic and predictable change in recollection of the event (see Loftus, 1979, for a review of this work). Such research was intended, in part, to disclose factors that can affect the reliability of eyewitness reports in civil and criminal cases. While the eyewitness research program has retained its practical orientation, a consistent finding of largely irreversible alterations in subjects' recollections soon began to suggest basic, general questions about the nature of human memory. In particular, it gradually became apparent that one of the most commonly held assumptions about memory—the assumption that there exist permanent, unalterable traces of information about past experience—must be carefully reexamined (Loftus & Loftus, 1980).

It must be acknowledged from the beginning that the terms "memory" and "recollection" have distinct meanings; at least in scientific writing, the distinction should be made clear. "Memory" refers to a store of information, as well as to the processes involved in accessing that store. "Recollection" refers to recall or recognition, or to other actions dependent on memory. Cognitive psychology tries, in part, to make inferences about memory—inferences that are necessarily based on observations of human recollection. In the present chapter, we review a smoldering controversy that has developed within cognitive psychology over the permanence and the unalterability of underlying human memory. To lay the groundwork, we first review recent findings about the alteration of recollection. Next, we consider the implications of these recent findings for the assumption of memory permanence. Finally, we briefly present the outline of an emerging theoretical framework for understanding change in human recollection.

Alteration of Recollection

A large number of experiments have shown that recollection of details of complex events can under some circumstances be affected by postevent experiences. The experimental paradigm employed in such studies can be briefly described in terms of three essential stages.

David F. Hall. Department of Psychology, Thiel College, Greenville, Pennsylvania; Department of Psychology, University of Washington, Seattle, Washington.

Elizabeth F. Loftus. Department of Psychology, University of Washington, Seattle, Washington.

1. Acquisition: A subject views a film or a slide sequence depicting a complex event, such as a simulated crime or an automobile accident.
2. Retention and change: A subject encounters new information subsequent to the initial event. The source of new information might include biasing suggestions or questions, photographs, or even rehearsal of the original event. Whatever the source, postevent information is added to original memory for the event, and creates the potential for altered recollection.
3. Retrieval: Subsequent recollection tests reveal that postevent experiences appear to have altered the content of what is recalled or recognized.

A study by Loftus, Miller, and Burns (1978) typifies the usual procedure. In that study, subjects viewed a series of slides depicting an automobile accident. The slides included a view of a red Datsun stopped at a yield sign, or, for some subjects, a view of the same red Datsun stopped at a stop sign. Either immediately or following a period of delay, subjects were given a set of questions that for some subjects included a potentially misleading item of information. In particular, the item "Did another car pass the red Datsun while it was stopped at the stop sign?" contained misinformation when asked of subjects who had actually viewed a yield sign. Finally, subjects were tested for recollection of the sign. Depending on the time intervals that occurred between the slides and the intervening questions, and between the slides and the final recollection, up to 80% of the subjects indicated that their recollections had been affected by the misinformation. That is, they remembered a stop sign when a yield sign and actually been seen, or a yield sign when a stop sign had been seen. Thus, under some circumstances, postevent information not only is added to original memory, but appears actually to replace original memory in subjects' recollections. What follows is a summary of some of the major experimental variables that have been found to affect alterations in recollection.

Critical Factors in Recollection Change: Retention Intervals, Warnings, and Syntax

A number of variables have been shown to moderate the effectiveness of postevent information in altering subsequent recollections. While it is not feasible in this chapter to offer a comprehensive review of the growing body of literature on recollection change, some factors that are already fairly well understood can be described. These include (1) the intervals between an event, a subsequent misleading message, and a final test of recollection; (2) the presence of warnings; and (3) the syntactic form of questions and messages.

INTERVALS BETWEEN AN EVENT, A SUBSEQUENT MISLEADING MESSAGE, AND A FINAL TEST OF RECOLLECTION

The intervals between viewing an initial event, reading a subsequent misleading message, and engaging in a final test of recollection have been found to be critical determinants of changes in subjects' recollections (Loftus *et al.*, 1978). Results of the Loftus *et al.* study indicate that the number of subjects for whom recollection alterations occurred increased with longer as opposed to shorter intervals before encountering the postevent message. As a corollary finding, the number of subjects for whom recollection change occurred was greatest when the final test of recollection occurred immediately after reading the postevent misinformation. Thus, recollection change appears to be facilitated by the weakening of original memory with the passing of time, and the change is most successfully secured if tested while the misinformation is still relatively current.

WARNINGS

Research by Greene, Flynn, and Loftus (1982) indicates that alteration of recollection can be effectively prevented if subjects are warned in advance that a postevent message might contain misinformation. However, the precise timing of the warning appears to be critical.

In a series of experiments, subjects first viewed slides that depicted the snatching of a wallet. Five minutes after this viewing, subjects read a brief message recapitulating details of the event. For some subjects, the brief message included incorrect, potentially misleading information. Some of those subjects were warned that the message might contradict some of the actual details of the original event. For different groups of subjects, the warning was received either immediately before viewing the slides, immediately after viewing, immediately before reading the misleading message, or immediately before engaging in the final recollection test. The final test presented 20 items, including the four critical items about which subjects had received misinformation.

Results indicated that warnings received immediately prior to reading the misinformation facilitated subjects' resistance to the misinformation, and effectively averted changes in recollection. However, warnings received at other times, earlier or later, were of little or no avail to subjects. A covariate in the study—the amount of time taken by subjects to read misinformation—proved to be helpful in explaining these results. In short, subjects who had been given warnings immediately prior to reading the misinformation read more slowly, and presumably more carefully, than did subjects given warnings at other points in the procedure.

Thus, there appears to be only one brief, opportune moment when warnings influence the otherwise gullible and incautious subjects. That crucial moment comes immediately before subjects begin to read and to assimilate the potentially misleading message.

THE SYNTACTIC FORM OF MISLEADING QUESTIONS

We have seen that properly timed warnings can help subjects to detect discrepancies in a postevent message. In a strikingly similar manner, the syntax of a postevent message can also serve to conceal, or to reveal, misinformation.

In one experiment (Loftus, 1981; Loftus & Greene, 1980), students attending a lecture watched as an intruder unexpectedly entered the lecture hall, aggressively insulted the professor, and then quickly departed. Following the unexpected melodrama, students read and answered 15 questions about details of the event. For some subjects, one of the questions contained a false and potentially misleading reference to a nonexistent mustache. In fact, two versions of the misleading question were read by different groups of subjects. In one version, the mustache appeared as the subject of a simple interrogative sentence:

"Was the mustache worn by the tall intruder light or dark brown?" In the second version, the mustache appeared as the object of an auxiliary clause: "Did the intruder who was tall and had a mustache say anything to the professor?"

A day later, subjects were tested again for recollection of details of incident, including recollection of the nonexistent mustache. On this final occasion, subjects were asked whether they had previously encountered any reference to the intruder's mustache.

Results indicated that misinformation presented as the object of an auxiliary clause was more likely to alter subjects' recollections than was the same misinformation presented as the subject of a simple sentence. A clue to explaining the first result lies in the complementary result that subjects were less likely to remember a reference to a mustache when that reference had appeared obscurely as the object of an auxiliary clause than when it had been boldly presented as the subject of a sentence.

It seems reasonable to expect that a greater amount of attention would be directed to the main subject of a simple sentence than to the relatively obscure object of a minor clause. This line of inference suggests that subjects' recollections are more readily altered when misinformation has been casually assimilated than when it has been given full and careful attention. The results also suggest that misinformation that has been carefully scrutinized is likely to be rejected, whereas misinformation that is assimilated with minimal attention can be added indiscriminately to existing memory.

In summary, we have reviewed a sample of studies demonstrating several variables that affect the alteration of recollection. In many of these studies, the subject's capacity to detect discrepancies while initially reading a postevent message appears to have been a critical factor. Indeed, retention intervals, warnings, and syntax are all variables that appear likely to affect a subject's capacity to detect points of discrepancy in a postevent message. Thus, the detection of discrepancy appears to be a common, mediating factor underlying the operation of a number of circumstantial variables.

Recollections are, we must presume, based on memory. Memory for any mundane natural event must often withstand an influx of new information about the same, or similar, events. The experimental evidence indicates that in some circumstances original memory is, in some manner that is not yet well understood, buried, or obscured, or replaced, or recombined with new information. Indeed, the possible interactions of old and new information have not yet been adequately described, let alone categorized. One question that is engendered by the phenomenon of recollection change is this: What happens to the original memory for a natural event? Is it erased, changed, or merely filed in some obscure storehouse of outdated information, like a scarce, out-of-print book?

Does Memory Really Change?

Although an impressive amount of research shows that a subject's recollections are readily altered by exposure to postevent information, debate continues to be waged over what happens to the original information in memory. Has the original information actually been altered or lost, beyond all possibility of recovery? Or has such information merely been rendered relatively inaccessible, but still potentially retrievable under optimal conditions? Loftus and Loftus (1980) have taken the position that some memories may undergo irreversible transformations, but other researchers continue to look for evidence supporting the permanence of information in memory (Mand & Shaughnessy, 1981; Morton, Hammersley, & Bekerian, 1981).

Morton *et al.*'s (1981) theory of "headed records" proposes that for each distinct experiential episode, a person creates a permanent record or file in memory. The notion that a new file is created for each and every mundane experience implies that human memory must operate as a liberally rendundant and continuously expanding store of information—a store in which nothing is ever really lost, but in which some things may nevertheless be difficult to find. Redundancy is further ensured by the fact that whenever a recollection requires the retrieval of an existing memory file, the file is recopied. However, the new, recopied file typically differs from the original file. In particular, new details have typically been added and original details deleted in the recopying process. Thereafter, the recopied file may be retrieved from memory, rather than the original file. Presumably, each incident of retrieval results in yet another file, each progressively more distant in content from the original. The accumulation of recopied files makes recovery of the original increasingly difficult. Yet, recovery of the original is never, according to Morton *et al.*, totally impossible. Given some set of optimal cues, the original file should be recoverable. One is reminded of some college libraries in which books have been carelessly reshelved and apparently lost, yet in which there is often some amazing librarian with an uncanny sense for the whereabouts of lost books. Given the right librarian, and enough time, anything can be found.

Indeed, proponents of the headed-records theory have offered recent experimental evidence indicating that in some circumstances a judicious selection of test cues can facilitate retrieval of the original memory for an event, rather than retrieval of more recently acquired postevent information (Bekerian & Bowers, 1983). In short, the headed-records theory offers an explanation for alterations in recollection, while at the same time suggesting a system whereby original memory would still be locked away in the dusty, but still sometimes accessible, recesses of memory.

In a similar vein, Mand and Shaughnessy (1981) have interpreted changes in recollection for natural events in terms of Underwood's (1971) frequency theory of recognition memory. According to the frequency theory, a subject's ability to recognize a target stimulus is a function of the number of presentations of the target relative to the number of presentations of distractor items, with allowance made for other factors, such as the order and recency of presentation of each item. Presumably, recognition of the target stimulus is facilitated by each successive presentation. Thus, an experiment could be designed to demonstrate that a lingering remnant of original memory enhances subsequent acquisition of compatible information, even after misleading postevent information had at some point gained temporary ascendancy. Regrettably, no such experiment has been reported to date.

In brief, both the headed-records theory and the frequency theory suggest the continued existence of original memory for a natural event. Both of these theories offer the hypothesis that memory is neither changed nor lost, but rather that original memory coexists with, and competes for retrieval with, more recent information.

One difficulty with both coexistence theories, however, is the fact that a crucial hypothesis—that of coexistence—cannot be scientifically disproven. Even if a particular item in memory, item *x*, cannot be retrieved from memory in spite of exhaustive efforts to retrieve it, one might nevertheless argue that item *x* still exists, but is merely temporarily irretrievable. Now, prove that x does not exist! Indeed, techniques have been devised to induce the retrieval of stubbornly intractable memories (Loftus & Loftus, 1980). Such efforts have included multiple probes using a variety of question forms and using recognition as well as recall; the use of the postexperimental debriefing period as an occasion for a final, introspective memory probe (Loftus et al., 1978, Experiment 2); monetary incentives for correct responding (Loftus, 1979); the "second-guess" technique (Loftus, 1979); and, finally, hypnosis (Putman, 1979; Sanders & Simmons, 1983; Zelig & Beidleman, 1981).

It is sufficient for present purposes to note that sometimes, in some circumstances, these techniques have been used successfully to uncover the existence of otherwise surprisingly intractable memories. However, within the context of naturalistic studies of alteration in memory for complex events by misleading postevent information, these techniques have usually failed to resurrect lost memories, in spite of every reasonable effort to make them do so. In many experiments, memory that would have been demonstrably present had subjects not encountered a misleading postevent experience seems to have vanished as if it had never existed. At some point, depending on one's personal criterion, one might begin to suspect that something that cannot be found does not exist.

In summary, the jury is still out on the question of memory permanence. Indeed, there does not appear to be any clear scientific route to a resolution of the question. Still, the question beckons like a theoretical siren, and enchanted investigators will no doubt continue to bolster one side or the other of the issue.

An Emerging Framework for Reconstructive Memory

An emerging framework for the study of alterations in recollection (Hall, Loftus, & Tousignant, 1983) suggests that the coexistence of original memory with postevent information is only one of a number of possible outcomes in a process of memory reconstruction. This emerging framework assumes that novel memories are frequently being constructed from fragments of existing memories and elements of current experience. The construction of novel memories, which are the basis of novel recollections, is assumed to occur regardless of whether any lingering trace of original memory persists. The questionable permanence of memory is perhaps of less theoretical and practical significance than is the increasingly apparent capability of human subjects to treat new information as if it had always been a part of existing memory.

Our emerging theoretical framework includes a paradigm for demonstrating the alteration of recollection; a set of principles summarizing the circumstances that have been found to affect recollection change; and, finally, a preliminary categorization of different phyla and species of memory construction, including a set of hypotheses about the circumstances in which each species of alteration is likely to be encountered. In this chapter, the paradigm has been discussed, and one of the principles—that of the importance of the subject's detection of discrepancies—has been presented. Some of the other principles can only be mentioned briefly here. To begin with, we believe that memory must be activated (e.g., employed in current, ongoing problem solving) in order to undergo alteration. Furthermore, we regard the form of recollection (i.e., recall, recognition, color matching, estimation of probabilities, or other responses) as important in consolidating the alteration of memory. Finally, we consider "memory alteration" to be a fairly broad concept that includes the simple addition of new details to the total store of information about a complex event; the simple deletion of information from memory for an event; and more complex processes requiring the integration of diverse information to produce novel, reconstructed memories.

The body of experimental findings on recollection change is already sufficiently large to demand a theoretical framework. The question of sustaining interest at this point is not "Is memory permanent?", but rather, "Under what circumstances, and by what processes, is information integrated to yield novel recollections?" The fascinating phenomenon of compromise memories can serve as one concluding example of a species of recollection change that seems to require a new theoretical perspective. Compromise memories are perhaps best demonstrated in studies of change in recollection for colors (Bornstein, 1976; Loftus, 1977; Thomas, Caronite, LaMonica, & Hoving, 1968). In Loftus's (1977) study, subjects viewed an automobile accident involving a green car. Afterwards, subjects were asked a question that referred misleadingly to "the blue car." Finally, a color-recognition test was given. Results indicated that subjects who had been exposed to the misleading question tended to shift their color selection in the direction of the misleading information. However, the color most frequently selected appeared to have been influenced not only by the postevent misinformation (blue), but also by the original color (green). Indeed, many subjects selected a blue–green hue that apparently represented a compromise between the two sources of information. Thomas et al. (1968), Bornstein (1976), and others have reported similar results, indicating a compromise, or blending, in memory between information derived from verbal cues (labels) and visual cues (colors). The existence of compromise memories creates a paradox for theories that do not allow for changes in underlying memory traces. However, from the emerging perspective of memory integration, compromise memories are viewed as an example of a novel recollection, derived not as a static trace of a single experience, but rather as a function of information obtained at different times and from different sources.

ACKNOWLEDGMENTS

The writing of this chapter was supported by a grant from the National Science Foundation, and a supplement to that grant enabled David F. Hall to spend a sabbatical year at the University of Washington. We are grateful for support provided for David F. Hall by Thiel College.

REFERENCES

Bekerian, D. A., & Bower, J. M. Eyewitness testimony: Were we misled? *Journal of Experimental Psychology: Learning, Memory, and Cognition*, 1983, 9(1), 139–145.
Bornstein, M. H. Name codes and color memory. *American Journal of Psychology*, 1976, 89, 269–279.
Greene, E., Flynn, M. S., & Loftus, E. F. Inducing resistance to misleading information. *Journal of Verbal Learning and Verbal Behavior*, 1982, 21, 207–219.
Hall, D. F., Lotfus, E. F., & Tousignant, J. P. Post-event information and changes in recollection for a natural event. In G. L. Wells & E. F. Loftus (Eds.), *Eyewitness testimony: Psychological perspectives*. London: Cambridge University Press, 1983.

Loftus, E. F. Shifting human color memory. *Memory and Cognition*, 1977, *5*, 696–699.

Loftus, E. F. *Eyewitness testimony*. Cambridge, Mass.: Harvard University Press, 1979.

Loftus, E. F. Mentalmorphosis: Alterations in memory produced by bonding of new information to old. In J. B. Long & A. D. Baddeley (Eds.), *Attention and performance IX*. Hillsdale, N.J.: Erlbaum, 1981.

Loftus, E. F., & Greene, E. Warning: Even memory for faces may be contagious. *Law and Human Behavior*, 1980, *4*, 323–334.

Loftus, E. F., & Loftus, G. R. On the permanence of stored information in the human brain. *American Psychologist*, 1980, *35*, 409–420.

Loftus, E. F., Miller, D. G., & Burns, H. J. Semantic integration of verbal information into visual memory. *Journal of Experimental Psychology: Human Learning and Memory*, 1978, *4*, 19–31.

Mand, J. L., & Shaughnessy, J. J. *How permanent are memories for real life events?* Unpublished manuscript, Hope College, 1981.

Morton, J., Hammersley, R., & Bekerian, D. A. *Headed records: A framework for remembering and its failures.* Unpublished manuscript, MRC Applied Psychology Unit, Cambridge, England, 1981.

Putman, W. H. Hypnosis and distortions in eyewitness memory. *International Journal of Clinical and Experimental Hypnosis*, 1979, *27*, 437–448.

Sanders, G. S., & Simmons, W. L. The use of hypnosis to enhance eyewitness accuracy: Does it work? *Journal of Applied Psychology*, 1983, *68*, 70–77.

Thomas, D. R., Caronite, A. D., LaMonica, G. L., & Hoving, K. L. Mediated generalization via stimulus labelling: A replication and extension. *Journal of Experimental Psychology*, 1968, *78*, 531–533.

Underwood, B. J. Recognition memory. In H. H. Kendler & J. T. Spence (Eds.), *Essays in neobehaviorism*. New York: Appleton-Century-Crofts, 1971.

Zelig, M., & Beidleman, W. B. The investigative use of hypnosis: A word of caution. *International Journal of Clinical and Experimental Hypnosis*, 1981, *29*, 401–412.

Control of Cognitive Processing

4

Herman Buschke

It is generally agreed that learning and remembering depend on attention, use of an effective strategy, and the cognitive abilities needed to carry out that strategy. The identification and interpretation of memory deficits depend on assurance that effective cognitive processing has been carried out in learning and recall, since apparent memory deficits can be due to inattention, failure to use effective kinds of processing despite the ability to do so, or inability to carry out appropriate processing because of cognitive impairment. Control of cognitive processing will therefore be needed to induce effective processing. Processing can be controlled either by appropriate training, based on a task analysis as described by Belmont and Butterfield (1977), or by structuring the task in a way that induces the appropriate processing. Since such training of neurological patients is difficult (see Kovner, Mattis, & Goldmeier, 1983), the present discussion is limited to processing control achieved by appropriate task structuring. In either case, it must be shown that the intended kind of processing was actually carried out, since without such assurance "impaired recall" may mean only that training or task design did not succeed. Decreased recall can be attributed to memory impairment only when it can be shown independently that appropriate cognitive processing has been carried out successfully— that is, that recall is limited, despite cognitive processing sufficient for better recall by appropriate control subjects.

This chapter considers some of the reasons why cognitive processing should be controlled during learning and recall. While this discussion is limited to verbal learning, many of these considerations also apply to other kinds of memory. The discussion focuses on the problem of production deficiencies, the effects of cognitive processing on the number and kind of memory units, and the use of cued or conceptually guided recall to evaluate storage and retrieval.

Overcoming Production Deficiencies

It is well established that apparent limitations of memory may result from failure to use effective kinds of cognitive processing, despite the ability to do so. Such limitation of memory is due to "production deficiency" (Flavell, 1970), rather than to memory deficiency. Production deficiency is shown by inducing the appropriate kind of processing by training or task structuring, leading to reduction or elimination of the apparent memory deficit. Persistent memory deficit despite training or task structuring may be due either to

Herman Buschke. Department of Neurology, Albert Einstein College of Medicine, Bronx, New York.

memory deficit or to the failure of training or task structuring to overcome production deficiencies.

It has been shown that apparent memory deficits in normal aging can be ameliorated by control of cognitive processing in learning and recall. Improvement of apparent memory deficits was found by Hulicka and Grossman (1967) when normal aged and young adults were helped to use the same kinds of mediational strategies in paired-associate learning, and by Hultsch (1971) when aged and young adults were required to sort items for organized free recall. Smith (1977) and Perlmutter (1979) required normal aged and young adults to study unrelated words under conditions designed to induce controlled processing of the items, as well as under conditions where encoding was left uncontrolled. Both studies tested memory either by controlled free recall or by cues to control processing during recall and found that age-related memory deficits were greater when processing was not controlled. Such deficits were reduced (Perlmutter, 1979), or eliminated (Smith, 1977) by controlled processing during learning and by cuing during recall. Similar results were obtained by Till and Walsh (1980), who investigated the effects of various kinds of encoding tasks on memory for implicational sentences by normal aged and young adults. Their subjects performed a word-estimation task, a "pleasantness"-rating task, or a comprehension task on sentences presented for subsequent recall. Memory for sentences learned under different processing conditions was tested either by uncontrolled free recall or by conceptually controlled cued recall (using implicational cues that could be inferred from the sentences). Even though their aged subjects did not appreciate the implication of all sentences, Till and Walsh (1980) found that age-related differences were reduced or eliminated by such controlled processing. Their aged adults were able to recall as many sentences as the young adults when provided with cues for controlled recall. Other studies of conceptual memory by myself and Michael Macht, which also show such amelioration of apparent memory deficits in normal aged adults, are discussed later.

Such findings make it clear that learning and memory of normal aged adults may be limited by production deficiencies, which must be overcome for accurate assessment of memory and learning. Since the memory of aged adults with neurological impairment also will be limited by such production deficiencies, neuropsychological evaluation of their memory also will require control of processing to overcome the effects of production deficiencies. Studies showing that production deficiencies can be corrected by controlled processing also indicate the value of comparing memory of aged and young adults or of patients and control subjects under conditions in which all are carrying out the same kind of cognitive processing. Because different kinds of strategies and cognitive processing may be used for what is supposed to be the same memory task, such as imagery, organizing, or generating a story in learning for free recall, it seems desirable to control processing so that comparisons can be made under conditions in which all are using the same specific kind of processing. Furthermore, different strategies may not be equally effective, so that control of processing will be needed to show that apparent memory deficits are not due to use of less effective strategies. The best possible recall should be obtained in order to evaluate the memory abilities of patients and control subjects accurately. This will require control of processing to induce the most effective kind of processing. Comparison of memory using different strategies for processing will be needed to investigate the relationship between cognitive processing and memory and to evaluate cognitive processing in patients. These considerations also apply to serial neuropsychological evaluations of memory in an individual patient, since cognitive processing abilities, as well as memory, may change with recovery or progression.

Cognitive Processing, Memory Units, and Conceptual Memory

The units that are learned and recalled by a subject need not, and often do not, correspond to the units presented for learning (Tulving, 1968). Cognitive processing will affect the number and nature of the memory units learned and remembered by individual subjects (Miller, 1956). In free-recall learning of unrelated items, organization results in the recall of multi-item chunks, so that the number of *items* recalled may not accurately reflect the number of *units* learned and remembered (Bower, 1970; Buschke, 1976, 1977; Liebster, Macht, & Buschke, 1981; Tulving, 1962). Unless cognitive processing is controlled, some subjects may have fewer units to learn and recall, because they can group or organize the individual items into a smaller number of larger units, while patients with impaired cognitive processing may have to learn and remember a larger number of smaller units. In learning and recall of organized coherent text, the conceptual units of recall need not correspond to sentences or propositions, and special procedures may be needed to identify the conceptual units (Buschke & Schaier, 1979). Since evaluation of memory depends on an accurate measure of the amount remembered, control of cognitive processing is needed to specify the number of memory units to be learned and remembered.

The number of memory units should be controlled in order to evaluate memory of patients and control subjects when all are attempting to learn and recall the same number and kind of units, so that decreased recall will indicate memory deficits, rather than effects of production deficiencies or cognitive impairment on the number of units to be learned and remembered. Furthermore, when cognitive processing is not controlled, different subjects may learn and remember different kinds of memory units, because uncontrolled grouping may result in units composed of differing numbers of different items related to each other in different ways. Therefore, grouping should be controlled either by training or by structuring the task so that all subjects learn either the same multi-item units or the same ungrouped single-item units.

Since evaluation of verbal memory is usually intended to evaluate semantic memory for meaningful items, controlled processing will also be needed to ensure that it is the concept represented by each item and not just the name that is learned and remembered. Saying or writing an item will not be sufficient. Some kind of response indicating conceptual processing is needed. One method to induce such processing in free recall of unrelated items is described later.

One way to investigate conceptual memory while minimizing grouping of items and inducing the same kind of processing by all subject is to present unrelated but clear ideas in the form of sentences for learning and recall. Unrelated ideas such as "The quiet librarian was about to shriek," "The hungry couple went ice-skating," and "The nervous governor spilled his soup" are likely to be learned and remembered as separate memory units because they are difficult to organize or group into larger memory units. They are likely to be processed in the same way by all who know and can use the language. Additional explanations ("The quiet librarian shrieked/because she saw a mouse run under the table") or qualifications that also induce additional processing but do not increase understanding ("The quiet librarian was about to shriek/even though the students were busy working") can be used to constrain processing further by making all subjects think about each base idea in the same specific way. Such explanations or qualifications can be used to provide contextual elaboration during encoding and to obtain conceptually guided cued recall by reinstating the context at recall.

Conceptual memory of normal aged and young adults for such unrelated ideas has been investigated in several experiments by myself and Macht (Buschke & Macht, 1983). In each experiment, there were 16 aged and 16 young adults who learned sets of 16 unrelated ideas, either with or without additional explanations or qualifications, in a counterbalanced order. A within-subject design was used to minimize effects of individual differences in cognitive processing. There was only one presentation of each idea, one at a time, followed by free recall in any order. The subjects were allowed to use their own words for recall if necessary, since these experiments were concerned with memory for ideas rather than sentences. Recall was scored as "complete" or "incomplete" by consensus of three raters, using a liberal criterion to score "incomplete" only if recall was clearly incomplete, in order to determine whether the aged might recall less complete ideas. "Total recall" was the sum of complete and incomplete ideas, since even incomplete recall indicates recall of a distinct memory unit. Incomplete recall may be due to ineffective cognitive processing during learning or to ineffective retrieval during recall.

In the first experiment, aged and young adults were asked to learn and remember either the ideas alone or the ideas and their explanations when the explanations were also presented. While the aged recalled fewer ideas than the young and recalled ideas less completely, both aged and young were able to recall as many ideas with explanations as ideas alone. This indicates that such explanations can be integrated with the ideas they explain as part of larger conceptual memory units. Such integration reflects the effectiveness of cognitive processing, while the total number of ideas recalled indicates the number of units stored and retrieved.

In the second experiment, aged and young adults were asked to learn and remember only the base ideas, whether presented alone or together with explanations. The aged recalled fewer ideas and recalled ideas less completely than the young, but free recall by aged as well as by young was greater when ideas were processed with explanations than when ideas were presented alone. This indicates that such contextual elaboration can induce additional, more specific processing by constraining subjects to think about each idea in a specific way, thus enhancing the meaning of each base idea. Subsequent presentation of the subject of each idea (e.g., "the librarian") for cued recall of the rest of that idea increased recall by both aged and young, although the aged still recalled fewer ideas and recalled them less completely than the young. Cued recall by aged as well as by young was greater when the base ideas were processed together with the explanations than when the base ideas were processed alone; this indicates that additional processing of the base ideas in the context of their explanations can increase storage. This effect may be due to better encoding of the relationship between the subject and predicate of each idea, since these explanations were designed to explain the relationship between the subjects and their predicates, which should have led to more effective cued recall of the predicates when recall was cued by the subjects. Although the use of subjects as cues for recall may underestimate storage, such cued recall was very good (14 out of 16) when ideas were processed with explanations by the young.

In the third experiment, aged and young adults were asked to learn and remember only the base ideas, which were always presented together with either an explanation or a qualification. They were told to remember only the base ideas, but were asked to rate the relationship between base ideas and explanations or qualifications in order to induce processing. In this experiment, the explanations and qualifications themselves were used to cue recall by reinstating the context of learning. Cued recall of both sets of ideas was tested together after free recall of both sets was completed, so that the subjects would not try to learn the explanations or qualifications. This experiment was intended to overcome the limitations of subject cues, to test the generality of such contextual elaboration during learning, and to determine whether the increased recall found in the second experiment was due to better comprehension of the base ideas because of explanation or might be due to additional processing and contextual elaboration provided by both qualifications and explanations.

Comparison of the low levels of free recall (when only the base ideas alone were processed) with the high level of cued recall (when the ideas were processed with their explanations or qualifications) illustrates the need to control cognitive processing for accurate evaluation of memory. When ideas alone were learned, the aged seemed to show substantial memory deficits. However, when cognitive processing was controlled by contextual elaboration in learning and recall, the aged were able to learn and recall nearly as many memory units as the young. Although the aged recalled less than the young, the differences between recall by aged and young was reduced markedly by control of cognitive processing in both learning and recall; this indicates that most of the apparent memory deficits in aging reflect ineffective cognitive processing rather than impaired memory. The aged responded to the manipulations of cognitive processing used in these experiments in the same way as the young, which indicates that they can still use the same recall processes. These experiments do not reveal any specific memory deficits in normal aged adults and show the value of testing memory under conditions of optimal processing for accurate evaluation of memory abilities.

Use of Cued Recall

Cued recall is needed to show the full extent of storage and recall, since free recall alone will not recover all of the recallable memory units available in storage. Tulving and Pearlstone (1966) found that "availability" normally exceeds "accessibility." Without recovery of all memory units available in storage, neither storage nor retrieval can be evaluated accurately. Just as evaluation of recall depends on effective learning, evaluation of learning depends on effective recall (Kobasigawa, 1977). Cued recall will provide maximal estimates of storage and will identify those recall failures due to retrieval failures, so that both storage and retrieval can be evaluated accurately (Burke & Light, 1981; Buschke, 1974). Without cued recall, neither storage nor retrieval can be evaluated fully, and it will not be possible to determine whether recall failure is due to impairment of storage or retrieval. However, if cues are to be effective, they must be processed together with their targets during learning (Fisher & Craik, 1977; Thompson & Tulving, 1970;

Tulving & Osler, 1968; Tulving & Thompson, 1973). Since maximally effective cuing is needed to evaluate memory, this means that controlled processing is needed during learning to obtain effective cued recall, as well as to ensure effective storage. Therefore, control of cognitive processing in both learning and recall is needed in order to evaluate either.

One way to control cognitive processing, even in brief clinical evaluation of patients, is illustrated by the following simple method (Buschke, in press): A set of target items is placed in front of the patient so that all are visible during learning. The items can be words, pictures, or objects; they are selected so that each belongs to a different category. The patient is asked to search for and name each item when given the appropriate category label (such as "clothing") or description (such as "something to wear"). Naming all of the items in this way shows that this kind of processing has been carried out successfully, shows that the patient can name all of the items, and provides a basis for effective cued recall using the same category labels (Wood, 1967). After interference, the patient attempts free recall of the items in any order. Then the category labels for any items not recovered by free recall are presented to test for storage of those items by cued recall. Successful cued recall shows that the item is available in storage and that failure of free recall is due to retrieval failure. Adding cued recall to free recall provides an estimate of storage. The difference between cued recall and free recall provides a measure of retrieval ability.

If desired, recognition can also be tested by presenting any target items not retrieved by cued recall together with a new distractor item from the same category, and asking the patient to choose the target item. Such recognition is difficult to interpret, because it may only indicate some degree of familiarity, which must be distinguished from guessing (Craik, 1977). When recognition is restricted in this way to only those items not recovered either by free recall or by cued recall (which probably would have been recognized), recognition has been close to chance. Since cued recall convincingly shows storage of items that have been sufficiently well learned for recall, it is not clear that the use of recognition will improve the evaluation of memory when cued recall can be used effectively.

Although the initial search and naming may be slow, it can be done by patients as well as by normal control subjects when a set of 10 outline pictures (Snodgrass & Vanderwart, 1980) is presented for learning. Normal subjects can retrieve at least six out of ten items by free recall and can recover all of the rest by cued recall. Patients retrieve fewer items by free recall, indicating retrieval deficits, and may not recover all of the rest by cued recall, indicating storage deficits. Patients can recover at least some items by cued recall even when they do not retrieve any by free recall; this provides evidence of learning and recall that would not have been obtained without the use of cued recall.

The usefulness of such controlled processing for evaluation of memory is illustrated by the following case. A 66-year-old woman with moderately severe dementia of the Alzheimer type, who is a patient of Leon Thal, had a Blessed score of 23 errors out of a possible 33. She was able to name all of the items in a linear array of 10 pictures when asked to tell what "animal," what "tool," what "clothing," and so on was included among the pictures. After interference by counting and conversation, she retrieved two items by free recall. Then she recovered five additional items when cued by the category labels. The addition of cued recall to free recall shows storage of seven recallable items. In forced-choice recognition she chose two out of the remaining three items, but it is not clear whether this represents true recognition or guessing. Her performance differs from that of normal subjects of similar age, who were able to retrieve at least six items by free recall and all of the rest by cued recall; their performance highlights the patient's decreased storage and impaired retrieval under conditions in which both the patient and the normal control subjects used the same specific kinds of cognitive processing in learning and free recall (Frase & Kamman, 1974).

Conclusions

This chapter has considered some of the reasons why control of cognitive processing is needed for accurate evaluation of memory. Control of processing is needed mainly to overcome production deficiencies and to make effective cued recall possible, so that memory deficits can be identified and analyzed when maximum learning and recall have been elicited. In addition, control of cognitive processing is needed to compare memory of patients and control subjects when they are using the same specific kinds of effective cognitive processing, and to compare memory in the same patient at different times. Controlled memory testing should improve correlation of memory deficits with neuro-pathological and neurochemical changes by providing more complete evaluation of memory. It should also be useful in research on the pharmacological treatment of impaired memory, by inducing the same processing in experimental and placebo conditions and by making it possible to evaluate pharmacological effects under conditions in which appropriate and effective kind of cognitive processing are carried out.

It is worth noting that the strategies for control of cognitive processing, as well as the reasons why such control is needed to identify and interpret memory deficits, are applications of the concepts of production deficiency (Flavell, 1970), depth of processing (Cermak & Craik, 1979; Craik & Lockhart, 1972), encoding specificity (Tulving & Thompson, 1973), cued recall (Fisher & Craik, 1977; Tulving & Osler, 1966; Tulving & Pearlstone, 1966), organization and memory units (Bower, 1970; Miller, 1956; Tulving, 1962, 1968), and information processing (Cermak, 1980; Miller, 1956). These concepts, and their beneficial contributions to evaluations of clinical memory impairment, are the result of several decades of research by experimental cognitive and developmental psychologists concerned with normal human memory.

ACKNOWLEDGMENTS

The research described in this chapter was supported by USPHS Grants NS-03356 and HD-01799 from the National Institutes of Health, and AGO-2478 from the National Institute on Aging.

REFERENCES

Belmont, J. M., & Butterfield, E. C. The instructional approach to developmental cognitive research. In R. V. Kail, Jr., & J. W. Hagen (Eds.), *Perspectives on the development of memory and cognition*. Hillsdale, N.J.: Erlbaum, 1977.
Bower, G. H. Organizational factors in memory. *Cognitive Psychology*, 1970, *1*, 18–46.
Burke, D. M., & Light, L. L. Memory and aging: The role of retrieval processes. *Psychological Bulletin*, 1981, *90*, 513–546.
Buschke, H. Spontaneous remembering after recall failure. *Science*, 1974, *184*, 579–581.

Buschke, H. Learning is organized by chunking. *Journal of Verbal Learning and Verbal Behavior*, 1976, *15*, 313–324.

Buschke, H. Two-dimensional recall: Immediate identification of clusters in episodic and semantic memory. *Journal of Verbal Learning and Verbal Behavior*, 1977, *16*, 201–215.

Buschke, H. Cued recall in amnesia. *Journal of Clinical Neuropsychology*, in press.

Buschke, H., & Macht, M. L. Explanation and conceptual memory. *Bulletin of the Psychonomic Society*, 1983, *21*, 397–399.

Buschke, H., & Schaier, A. H. Memory units, ideas and propositions in semantic remembering. *Journal of Verbal Learning and Verbal Behavior*, 1979, *18*, 549–563.

Cermak, L. S. Memory as a processing continuum. In L. W. Poon, J. L. Fozard, L. S. Cermak, D. Arenberg, & L. Thompson (Eds.), *New directions in memory and aging*. Hillsdale, N.J.: Erlbaum, 1980.

Cermak, L. S., & Craik, F. I. M. (Eds.). *Levels of processing in human memory*. Hillsdale, N.J.: Erlbaum, 1979.

Craik, F. I. M. Age differences in human memory. In J. E. Birren & K. W. Schaie (Eds.), *Handbook of the psychology of aging*. New York: Van Nostrand Reinhold, 1977.

Craik, F. I. M., & Lockhart, R. S. Levels of processing: A framework for memory research. *Journal of Verbal Learning and Verbal Behavior*, 1972, *11*, 671–684.

Fisher, R. P., & Craik, F. I. M. The interaction between encoding and retrieval operations in cued recall. *Journal of Experimental Psychology: Human Memory and Learning*, 1977, *3*, 701–711.

Flavell, J. H. Developmental studies of mediated memory. In H. Reese & L. Lipsett (Eds.), *Advances in child development and behavior* (Vol. 5). New York: Academic Press, 1970.

Frase, L. T., & Kamman, R. Effects of search criteria on unanticipated free recall of categorically related words. *Memory and Cognition*, 1974, *2*, 181–184.

Hulicka, I. M., & Grossman, J. L. Age-group comparisons for the use of mediators in paired-associate learning. *Journal of Gerontology*, 1967, *22*, 46–51.

Hultsch, D. F. Adult age differences in free classification and recall. *Developmental Psychology*, 1971, *4*, 338–342.

Kobasigawa, A. Retrieval strategies in the development of memory. In R. V. Kail, Jr., & J. W. Hagen (Eds.), *Perspectives on the development of memory and cognition*. Hillsdale, N.J.: Erlbaum, 1977.

Kovner, R., Mattis, S., & Goldmeier, E. A technique for promoting robust free recall in chronic organic amnesia. *Journal of Clinical Neuropsychology*, 1983, *5*, 65–71.

Liebster, N., Macht, M. L., & Buschke, H. Memory units and the composition of recall. *Bulletin of the Psychonomic Society*, 1981, *18*, 179–182.

Miller, G. A. The magical number seven plus or minus two: Some limits on our capacity for processing information. *Psychological Review*, 1956, *63*, 81–97.

Perlmutter, M. Age differences in adults' free recall, cued recall and recognition. *Journal of Gerontology*, 1979, *34*, 533–539.

Smith, A. D. Adult age differences in cued recall. *Developmental Psychology*, 1977, *13*, 326–331.

Snodgrass, J. G., & Vanderwart, M. A standardized set of 260 pictures: Norms for name agreement, image agreement, familiarity, and visual complexity. *Journal of Experimental Psychology: Human Learning and Memory*, 1980, *6*, 174–215.

Thompson, D. M., & Tulving, E. Associative encoding and retrieval: Weak and strong cues. *Journal of Experimental Psychology*, 1970, *86*, 255–262.

Till, R. E., & Walsh, D. A. Encoding and retrieval factors in adult memory for implicational sentences. *Journal of Verbal Learning and Verbal Behavior*, 1980, *19*, 1–16.

Tulving, E. Subjective organization in free recall of "unrelated" words. *Psychological Review*, 1962, *69*, 344–354.

Tulving, E. Theoretical issues in free recall. In T. R. Dixon & D. L. Horton (Eds.), *Verbal behavior and general behavior theory*. Englewood Cliffs, N.J.: Prentice-Hall, 1968.

Tulving, E., & Osler, S. Effectiveness of retrieval cues in memory for words. *Journal of Experimental Psychology*, 1968, *77*, 593–601.

Tulving, E., & Pearlstone, Z. Availability versus accessibility of information in memory for words. *Journal of Verbal Learning and Verbal Behavior*, 1966, *5*, 381–391.

Tulving, E., & Thompson, D. M. Encoding specificity and retrieval processes in episodic memory. *Psychological Review*, 1973, *80*, 352–373.

Wood, G. Category names as cues for the recall of category instances. *Psychonomic Science*, 1967, *9*, 323–324.

The Computer as a Model of Mind

Arnold L. Glass

In the last two decades, a full-fledged scientific paradigm (Kuhn, 1962) has emerged in part of the area that was once occupied by what was called "experimental psychology." Cognitive psychology is based on an analogy between the computer and human beings. The analogy implies certain assumptions about what the brain is, about what the mind is, and about the relationship between the two.

To begin with, a distinction must be drawn between the hardware of a computer and the programs that run on it. The computer hardware is the "medium," while the program is the "code." Both the hardware and the program are essential aspects of the computer. A program must be expressed in some physical medium, whether this medium consists of ink and paper or the magnetic dipoles within a computer. Conversely, a computer that has not been programmed is functionally inert. However, many different kinds of hardware (e.g., 8-bit machines, 16-bit machines) may run the same program, and many different programs may be run on the same machine. So programs and hardware are distinct entities. When this distinction is applied to humans, the brain is classified as the medium, and the mind as the code. Hence, the description of the medium is the subject matter of neuroanatomy and neurophysiology; the description of the code is the subject matter of cognitive psychology.

A code consists of two parts: a set of "data" and a "procedure" that operates on it. A procedure is a sequence of actions that do something to the data. For example, consider the following computer program:

1. Read number from keyboard into memory position 1 (MP1).
2. Read number from keyboard into memory position 2 (MP2).
3. Add MP1 and MP2 to memory position 3 (MP3).
4. Write the content of MP3 to the video monitor.

The program is a procedure for adding two numbers together. The data that the program operates on are typed in from a keyboard. So if someone typed in the numbers 2 and 3, these would be the data. By analogy, the data of the human mind are a person's sensory impressions, perceptions, and memories.

When a computer is examined further, one finds that it consists of several different media, each with its own characteristic code. The central processor interacts with the environment through two or more peripheral devices. In the example given above, the peripheral devices are a keyboard and a visual display. The code of the central processor is a pattern of 0's and 1's, which are represented in the medium by magnetic dipoles. The code of the keyboard is a position in an array (i.e., the position of the number key on the

Arnold L. Glass. Department of Psychology, Rutgers University, New Brunswick, New Jersey.

keyboard), and the code of the display is the shape of the visual character. A procedure such as the one shown above performs two kinds of actions. A "transduction" transforms information from one code to another; statements 1, 2, and 4 in the example perform transductions. An "operation" changes the data within a code in some way: For example, statement 3 performs the operation of addition.

The human brain involves many different codes, and many different transductions are performed on inputs as they pass from the sensory receptors (which are peripheral devices) to the cortex. Mental procedures also perform operations on the data within a code. When you decide whether "sun" and "done" rhyme, you are performing a comparison operation within an auditory code, and when you decide whether the letter "M" is a rotation of the letter "W," you are performing a comparison operation within the visual code.

We have access to three kinds of information about the mind. We have incomplete but still considerable anatomical and physiological information about its medium, the brain. We have phenomenological knowledge through introspection about what we can perceive and what kinds of mental operations we can perform. Finally, we have behavioral information—data about how much we know and how quickly we can respond. This last category also includes the results of experiments that indicate our limits, such as experiments that vary auditory or visual inputs along various physical dimensions (e.g., frequency) to determine what inputs can and cannot be perceived. It also includes experiments in which auditory and visual inputs are varied in more complicated ways, such as experiments involving visual and auditory illusions, which determine the regularities in the environment that influence perception. The task of cognitive psychology is to combine the information from the various sources in order to infer the structure of the underlying mental code. The following is an example of how this is done.

Speech would not be a practical means of communication if it took 5 minutes to understand each sentence. You would not spend your time reading this book if it took 5 or 6 hours to read each page. In general, the brain must be able to process information rapidly, so that it can deal with the huge amount of information that is transmitted whenever people communicate. Suppose that you read this book in the following manner: You have in your brain a list consisting of all the words you know and their meanings; each list item is something like a dictionary entry. A college graduate knows about 25,000 words, so assume this is how many words the list contains. Let us further suppose that when you see a word on this page, in order to find its meaning you compare it to each word on the list in your memory, one at a time, until you find the one each matches exactly. Since it takes about 1 millisecond for a neuron to transmit information, the shortest time that a comparison could take is 1 millisecond. On the average, you can expect to get about halfway through the list before you find a match, so you can expect to make an average of about 12,500 comparisons for each word. If you make 12,500 comparisons, one at a time, for each word, and each comparison takes about 1 millisecond, then on the average it should take 12.5 seconds to find the meaning of each word as you read. Clearly, there is something wrong with this estimate; reading does not take so long. If we assume that the most frequently used words are at the top of the list, we can reduce the estimated reading speed somewhat. But even rare words to not take 25 seconds to recognize.

Suppose we also assume that the word list in memory is organized alphabetically, just like a dictionary. The main word list is divided into 26 sublists, each containing words beginning with a different letter of the alphabet. These lists, in turn, are each organized into 26 sub-sublists by their second letter, and so on. Then, when an input word is compared to the word list in memory, it is compared a letter at a time. First, the first letter of the word is compared to the main list to find which sublist contains words that begin with the same letter. By the same logic used above, since there are 26 letters on the list, the comparison process should take about 13 milliseconds before a match is found. Then the second letter of the word is compared to the appropriate sublist, the third letter to the appropriate sub-sublist, and so forth, until all the letters of the input word are matched and its meaning in memory is found. On the average, if a word has n letters, it would take n times 13 milliseconds to find its meaning by this process, so it would take about 65 milliseconds on the average to identify the meaning of a five-letter word. Since people read at a rate of about 250–350 milliseconds per word, this estimate of the time it takes to retrieve each word's meaning is now fast enough to be compatible with how fast people can actually process sentences.

The point of this example is not that people read letter by letter, or that the human memory is organized like a dictionary. Both of these hypotheses are in fact false. Rather, the point of the example is to show how consideration of behavioral and physiological facts can rule out specific hypotheses about mental procedures. These considerations rule out a procedure that recognizes words by comparing them holisticly and serially. The domain of possible comparison procedures is narrowed to those procedures that segment the input into a set of features such as the letters of the alphabet, and/or that compare it to many memory traces at the same time. In fact, we know from the research in this area that groups of letters that form spelling units form features used by the recognition procedure, and that the visual input may undergo transduction to an auditory code that provides a second set of features for recognition (Conrad, 1964). Furthermore, each feature is compared in parallel to the descriptions of more than one word at a time (Morton, 1969). Hence, in this case, experimental results have confirmed the general explanation suggested by the underlying assumptions of the model.

The analogy between a computer and a human provides a well-defined starting point for the investigation of cognition, since it provides a set of initial assumptions and a set of problems to work on. Also, it provides a way of combining three different kinds of information within a descriptive framework. As in the example above, physiological, phenomenological, and behavioral evidence can frequently be combined to converge on a single hypothesis. However, the analogy can only be carried so far, because there are also major differences between computers and people. First, people are many orders of magnitude more complex than computers. Computers are essentially simple systems involving two levels of code, one for a peripheral device and the other for the central processor. In contrast, human information processing involves many kinds of codes, and an auditory or visual input is recoded many times as it passes through layers of the brain. Second, the architecture of the neural medium is fundamentally different from the medium of a computer. In particular, the computer provides no analogue for neural plasticity, and it is not a model of how learning occurs at the neural level.

Third, if we make a distinction between analysis and storage, the computer provides a model for how an input might be initially analyzed, but the resulting memory trace is very different for a computer from what it is for a human. In a computer, a datum, whether it is a letter, a word, or the meaning of a sentence, is stored at a specific location. So if the information in a particular location is erased, that word or letter is gone forever, while other data are unaltered. In contrast, Lashley (1950) showed that a rat retained a learned visual discrimination after as much as 90% of the visual cortex was removed. However, the errors on the task increased with the size of the lesion. The implication is that information is stored over a wide area in the mammalian brain. Destroying any single cell does not remove a particular datum, but rather adds noise to the system, so that all data become a little more difficult to recover. So a model that is fundamentally different from a computer is needed for how information is stored in human memory. One kind of structure that might provide a better analogue of human memory has been described by Hinton and Anderson (1981). This model treats memory as a large matrix and treats inputs as vectors. Each vector alters the entire matrix in some way; however, if a vector is repeated, the matrix undergoes a predictable alteration. Hence, a vector can be "recognized" by the matrix as old. Unfortunately, this model is very abstract, and it is not clear how to apply it to human memory. The only physical instantiations of the model are holograms, and they are not very useful as models of human memory.

Finally, a computer model of memory does not provide a good explanation of forgetting due to associative interference. A computer memory is neutral with respect to its contents. Similar data are not automatically stored adjacently, as they appear to be in human memory. So similar data do not affect each other's encoding and retrieval any more than unrelated data do. Associative computer models of memory (e.g., Anderson & Bower, 1973) are no more than traditional associative theories couched in computer terminology. It may be that an implementation of an associative theory on a computer makes the theory more explicit. However, it has not solved the problems of associative theory in accounting for experimental results. For example, there is still no good account of the buildup of proactive interference in the distractor task (Keppel & Underwood, 1962).

To summarize, the computer seems to be a useful analogue for the encoding process, but also appears to say nothing at all about storage. It remains to be seen whether the correspondences of the computer to the brain prove useful, despite the divergences. Ultimately, the fruitfulness of the computer analogy to the study of psychology will be determined by the efforts of the psychologists who use it. If the analogy is a false one, then a vigorous effort to apply it will only lead to results of limited generalizability, which in turn will lead to frustration and eventual abandonment of the model. On the other hand, if there are some true correspondences between mechanical and human information processing, then an effort to apply the model should lead to the discovery of broad generalizations about the human information-processing system.

REFERENCES

Anderson, J. A., & Bower, G. H. *Human associative memory*. Washington, D.C.: Winston, 1973.
Conrad, R. Acoustic confusion in immediate memory. *British Journal of Psychology*, 1964, *55*, 75–84.
Hinton, G. E., & Anderson, J. A. *Parallel models of associative memory*. Hillsdale, N.J.: Erlbaum, 1981.
Keppel, G., & Underwood, B. J. Proactive inhibition in short-term retention of single items. *Journal of Verbal Learning and Verbal Behavior*, 1962, *1*, 153–161.
Kuhn, T. S. *The structure of scientific revolutions*. Chicago: University of Chicago Press, 1962.
Lashley, K. S. In search of the engram. *Symposium of the Society for Experimental Biology*, 1950, *4*, 454–482.
Morton, J. Interaction of information in word recognition. *Psychological Review*, 1969, *76*, 165–178.

6

Memory for Nonverbal Auditory Information:
A Link between Behavioral and Physiological Studies

Diana Deutsch

Introduction

When objects and events are represented in memory, much of this representation must be in terms of dimensions of variation. Thus, the representation of visually perceived objects must include colors, brightnesses, locations, and so on. The representation of sounds must analogously include pitches, durations, loudnesses, and locations. Such representational dimensions need not be confined to first-order attributes. Lines are perceived as having length, curvature and orientation; at a higher level, objects are perceived as having such characteristics as volume and distance. Pitch sequences may be described at one level as a succession of melodic and harmonic intervals, and at a higher level in terms of steps along scalar alphabets (Deutsch & Feroe, 1981). Certain complex attributes appear to be internally represented in terms of several dimensions. For example, the perceptual space for musical timbre appears to be bi- or tridimensional (Grey, 1975; Risset & Wessel, 1982).

Let us assume that an incoming stimulus gives rise to a memory representation in terms of values along several different dimensions. A number of general questions may then be posed: How do such memory dimensions relate to physical dimensions? How do the different elements of a given memory dimension interact with one another? How do the outputs of different memory dimensions interact in retrieval? And so on. To examine these questions, the system underlying memory for pitch and pitch relationships was investigated. The findings reveal the existence of a finely tuned multidimensional memory system, which displays characteristics that are formally analogous to those found in systems handling sensory information at the incoming level, and whose physiological substrates are well understood.

Memory for Pitch: General Considerations

A number of hypotheses may be advanced concerning the characteristics of pitch memory. One is that pitch memory is the function of an unstructured buffer store, in which information deteriorates simply through a process of temporal decay. A second hypothesis

Diana Deutsch. Department of Psychology, University of California at San Diego, La Jolla, California.

is that pitch information is retained in a general store of limited capacity, and that memory loss occurs as a result of such capacity limitation. A third hypothesis is that pitch memory is the function of a specialized system, whose elements interact in a systematic fashion.

In order to decide between these various hypotheses, we may begin with the following set of observations. Suppose that a tone is presented, and this is followed shortly by another tone that is either identical in pitch or that is a semitone removed. Most listeners have no difficulty in determining whether these two tones are the same or different. When a pause of 6 seconds' duration is interpolated between the tones to be compared, the judgment is still a very easy one. Various investigators have shown that memory for pitch is subject to a process of temporal decay (Bachem, 1954; Harris, 1952; Koester, 1945; Wickelgren, 1966, 1969); however, in the present situation, the difference in pitch to be discriminated is so large that the decay is not subjectively apparent. Suppose now that eight extra tones are interpolated between the two to be compared, and the listener is asked to ignore them. The task now becomes strikingly more difficult. In fact, if listeners are selected for errorless performance in comparing such tone pairs when these are separated by a silent retention interval of 6 seconds, they will typically make over 40% errors when eight extra tones are interpolated during the retention interval.

We can conclude that the system underlying memory for pitch is one in which information is subject to a slow rate of temporal decay, but is also subject to a sizable interference effect produced by interpolated tones. This leads us to inquire as to the cause of this interference effect, and again various hypotheses may be considered. The first is that attention to the tone to be remembered is necessary to prevent memory decay, and that the interpolated tones produce attention distraction. If this were the case, then other interpolated materials that distract attention should also produce memory loss. A second hypothesis is that pitch information is retained in a general memory store together with other types of material, and that this store is of limited capacity. We should then expect that other interpolated materials would produce memory impairment, provided that they entered memory. A third hypothesis is that pitch information is retained in a specialized system, and that memory impairment results from interactions within this system.

An experiment was performed to decide between these various hypotheses (Deutsch, 1970). In one condition, subjects compared the pitches of two tones, which were separated by a retention interval during which six extra tones were interpolated. The test tones either were identical in pitch or differed by a semitone. The second condition was the same as the first, except that six spoken digits were interpolated instead of tones. In both these conditions, subjects were asked to judge whether the test tones were the same or different in pitch, and to ignore that interpolated materials. The third condition was identical to the second, except that the subjects were asked to recall the digits in addition to comparing the pitches of the test tones. This ensured that the digits were attended to and were committed to memory. In the fourth condition, digit recall was required alone.

The interpolated tones were found to produce a substantial increase in errors of pitch recognition. However, the interpolated digits produced only a minimal decrement, even when their recall was required. Further, the requirement to perform the pitch-recognition task did not produce an increase in errors of digit recall. We can conclude from this experiment that the impairment of memory for pitch that occurs when other tones are interpolated is the result of interactions within a specialized system.

Lateral Inhibition in the Pitch-Memory System

We now inquire more specifically into the nature of the interactions that result in loss of memory for pitch. One possibility is that tones are retained in a store that is limited in terms of the number of tones that it can hold at any one time. When new tones enter this store, old ones are bumped out. On this hypothesis, the amount of memory impairment produced by an interpolated tone would be the same, regardless of its pitch relationship to the tone to be remembered. However, if the effect of one tone on memory for another were found to vary as a function of their pitch relationship, then this would indicate instead a system in which memory elements interact in a specific fashion.

In one experiment to evaluate these two hypotheses (Deutsch, 1972b), subjects were presented with a test tone, which was followed by six interpolated tones, and then by a second test tone. The pitches of the test tones either were identical or differed by a semitone. The experiment investigated the effects of placing in the second serial position of the interpolated sequence a tone whose pitch bore a critical relationship to that of the first test tone. This relationship varied in steps of 1/6 tone between identity and a whole-tone separation.

The results of the experiment are displayed in Figure 6-1. It can be seen that the error rate varied systematically, depending on the degree of similarity between the first test tone and the critical interpolated tone. When these two tones were identical in pitch, memory was facilitated. Errors increased gradually as the pitch difference between the first test tone and the critical interpolated tone increased. Errors peaked at a difference of 2/3 tone, and then decreased, reaching baseline at around a whole-tone separation.

The plot displayed in Figure 6-1 was obtained by superimposing plots from sequences in which the test tones were positioned at different points along the pitch continuum, spanning a range of an octave. Since the musical scale is a logarithmic function of waveform frequency, an identical difference along this scale is based on an increasing

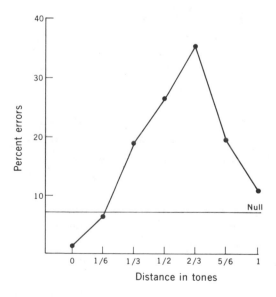

FIGURE 6-1. Percentage of errors in pitch-comparison judgment as a function of the distance in pitch between the first test tone and a critical interpolated tone. The line labeled *Null* indicates the percentage of errors in a control condition, in which all interpolated tones were at least 1½ tones removed in pitch from the first test tone. (From D. Deutsch, Mapping of interactions in the pitch memory store. *Science*, 1972, *175*, 1020–1022. Copyright 1972 by the American Association for the Advancement of Science. Reprinted by permission.)

frequency difference as the scale is ascended; this difference doubles over an octave. In the present experiment, the error rate varied systematically as a function of the log frequency difference between the interacting tones, and this was independent of their absolute position along the scale. Given this finding, it was proposed that pitch information is retained along an array whose elements are activated by tones of specific pitch. Elements that are activated by tones whose fundamental frequencies are separated by the same distance in log frequency units are spaced the same distance apart on this array. It was further hypothesized that interactions occur along this array which are a function of the distance between the interacting elements.

But what might be the physiological basis of these interactions? An interesting analogy here presents itself with lateral inhibitory interactions found in systems that handle sensory information at the incoming level (Alpern & David, 1959; Carterette, Friedman, & Lovell, 1970; Hartline, Ratliff, & Miller, 1961; Klinke, Boerger, & Gruber, 1970; Ratliff, 1965; Sachs & Kiang, 1968; Von Békésy, 1960). Indeed, the relative frequency range over which the present interference effect was found to occur corresponds well with the relative frequency range over which centrally acting lateral inhibition has been found in physiological studies of the auditory system (Klinke et al., 1970). As further evidence, the present effect was found to cumulate when two interpolated tones were presented in this disruptive range, placed one on either side of the test tone along the pitch continuum (Deutsch, 1973). Analogously, in lateral inhibitory networks, a cumulation of inhibition occurs from stimuli that are placed one on either side of a test stimulus (Ratliff, 1965).

If a lateral inhibitory network were indeed involved, an effect might be expected that would be most unlikely to occur on other grounds. It has been found in some physiological studies that when a neural unit that is inhibiting another unit is itself inhibited by a third unit, there is a release of the originally inhibited unit from inhibition. This phenomenon is known as disinhibition, and is a property of recurrent but not nonrecurrent lateral inhibitory networks. The demonstration of disinhibition should thus provide convincing evidence that a lateral inhibitory network underlies the present memory effects.

More specifically, one might expect that if a tone that was inhibiting memory for another tone were itself inhibited by a third tone, memory for the first tone would return. That is, in sequences where the test tones are identical in pitch, if two critical tones were interpolated—one always 2/3 tone removed from the first test tone, and the other further removed along the pitch continuum—then the error rate should vary systematically as a function of the pitch relationship between these two interpolated tones. As indicated by the open circles in Figure 6-2, the error rate should be greatest when these two tones are identical in pitch, should decline as the second test tone moves away from the first, should dip maximally at a separation of 2/3 tone, and then should return to baseline. The plot produced should thus be roughly the inverse of the plot produced by the original disruptive effect.

This experiment was performed, and the results are displayed by the closed circles in Figure 6-2 (Deutsch & Feroe, 1975). The open circles display the function that was obtained theoretically from the baseline function shown by the open triangles, assuming a lateral inhibitory network. It can be seen that there is a very good correspondence between the experimentally and theoretically obtained functions. This provides strong evidence that elements of the pitch-memory system are arranged as a recurrent lateral inhibitory network.

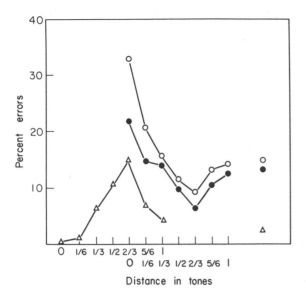

FIGURE 6-2. Percentages of errors in pitch recognition obtained experimentally and predicted theoretically from the model of lateral inhibition. See text for details. (From D. Deutsch & J. Feroe, Disinhibition in pitch memory. *Perception and Psychophysics*, 1975, *17*, 320–324. Copyright 1975 by The Psychonomic Society, Inc. Reprinted by permission.)

We may then ask why such a system should have evolved; that is, in what ways it might be useful to the organism. In the case of systems that handle sensory information at the incoming level, two main functions for lateral inhibition have been postulated. The first is a sharpening of the sensory image (Cornsweet, 1970; Ratliff, 1965). Such a sharpening effect would clearly be valuable in preserving the fineness of a memory image as well. The second function concerns that abstraction of higher-order information. For example, Barlow and Levick (1965) have proposed that the responses of directionally sensitive ganglion cells in the rabbit retina are very likely to be influenced by lateral inhibition. If this type of information abstraction is performed in the case of stimuli that are presented simultaneously or near-simultaneously, than it is also likely to be performed in the case of stimuli that are presented in temporal succession. Thus it would appear that lateral inhibition is a useful feature to have built into a memory system.

A more general point should also be made in this context. From the evidence described, the system that retains pitch information appears to be organized in certain important respects along the same lines as the system that handles such information at the incoming level. We can therefore envisage the former system in terms of a direct projection from the latter. This view contrasts with the concept of a rapidly deteriorating "preperceptual" buffer store, in which auditory information is retained in uncategorized from (Massaro, 1972). Indeed, it is difficult to see how a store with such properties could be useful. We would have to suppose that information is initially categorized at the incoming level, then translated into uncategorized form for retention in the "preperceptual" store, and finally translated back into the form in which it had first been categorized. No mechanism has been suggested whereby the information that has been lost can be retrieved for recategorization. The concept of a memory array that results as a direct projection from the sensory array, preserving the original form of stimulus categorization, does not run into such difficulties.

Retention of Temporal or Order Information

A memory system must be capable of retaining information concerning not only *what* event had occurred, but also *when* the event had occurred. I conjectured (Deutsch, 1972a) that pitch information is retained both along a pitch continuum and also along a temporal or order continuum, resulting in a distribution such as the one shown in Figure 6-3. It was further conjectured that as time proceeds, this memory distribution spreads in both directions, but particularly along the temporal continuum. Depending on the stimulus conditions, and the task required of the subject, such a spread can lead either to increased errors or to enhanced performance in pitch-recognition judgment.

First, suppose that subjects are required to determine whether two test tones are the same or different in pitch, when these are separated by a sequence of interpolated tones. Then, in conditions where the test tones differ, the interpolation of a tone that is of the same pitch as the second test tone should lead to errors of misrecognition. In other words, due to the spread of the memory distribution along the temporal continuum, the subject should recognize correctly that a tone of the same pitch as the second test tone had occurred, but should be uncertain *when* it had occurred, and so should sometimes conclude erroneously that it had been the first test tone. This effect should be greater when the critical interpolated tone is placed early in the interpolated sequence rather than late. Such findings have indeed been obtained (Deutsch, 1975b).

A second prediction arises from the hypothesized loss of temporal or order information. Suppose that errors were plotted as a function of the pitch relationship between the first test tone and the critical interpolated tone, and that the pitch difference between the two test tones was also varied. Then in sequences where the critical interpolated tone and the second test tone are placed on the same side of the pitch continuum relative to the first test tone, the peak of errors should occur where the critical interpolated tone and the second tone are identical in pitch. In other words, a shift in the pitch of the second test tone, when the pitch of the first test tone is held constant, should result in a parallel shift in the peak of errors produced by the critical interpolated tone. This result has also been obtained (Deutsch, 1975b).

The spread of a memory distribution along a temporal or order continuum may also be expected to give rise to memory enhancement, or consolidation. Suppose that a test tone is presented, followed later by a tone of identical pitch, such that the distributions

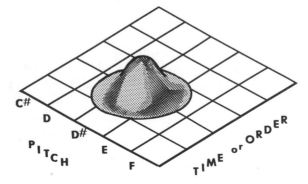

FIGURE 6-3. Hypothesized distribution underlying memory for the pitch of a tone. (From D. Deutsch, Effect of repetition of standard and comparison tones on recognition memory for pitch. *Journal of Experimental Psychology*, 1972, *93*, 156–162. Copyright 1972 by the American Psychological Association. Adapted by permission.)

underlying memory for these two tones overlap along the temporal continuum. The overlapping portions of these distributions should then sum, resulting in a stronger memory trace for the pitch of the test tone. This should, in turn, lead to enhanced recognition performance (Deutsch, 1972a).

An experiment was performed to test this prediction (Deutsch, 1975a). Subjects made pitch-comparison judgments when the tones to be compared were separated by a retention interval during which a sequence of six extra tones was interpolated. In one condition, a tone of the same pitch as the first test tone was included in the second serial position of the interpolated sequence. In another condition, such a tone was included in the fifth serial position. In a third condition, no such tone was included. The repeated tone was found to give rise to enhanced recognition performance at both serial positions. However, this effect was substantially and significantly greater when the repeated tone was placed early in the interpolated sequence rather than late. This is as expected from the hypothesis of a spread of the memory distributions along a temporal or order continuum, since the closer the repeated tone is to the test tone, the greater should be the overlap of their memory distributions.

Organization of Memory for Pitch Relationships

We may conjecture that the form of organization that exists in the case of memory for first-order attributes exists in the case of memory for higher-order attributes also. As an example, let us consider memory for pitch relationships. When two tones are presented simultaneously or in temporal succession, there results the perception of a musical interval. Further, when the fundamental frequencies of two tone pairs are related by the same ratio, these intervals are of the same apparent size (Deutsch, 1969). We may then hypothesize that there exists a memory continuum whose elements are activated by the presentation of pairs of tones. Tone pairs that stand in the same ratio project onto the same point along this continuum; tone pairs standing in adjacent ratios project onto adjacent points; and so on. A monotonic continuum of interval size is thus formed. We may further conjecture that interactions occur along this continuum that are analogous to those found in the system underlying memory for absolute pitch values.

An experiment was performed to test this hypothesis (Deutsch, 1978). Subjects compared the pitches of two test tones when these were both accompanied by tones of lower pitch. The test tones either were identical in pitch or differed by a semitone. However, the tone accompanying the first test tone was always identical in pitch to the tone accompanying the second test tone. So when the test tones were identical, the intervals formed by the test tone combinations were also identical. Further, when the test tones differed, the intervals formed by the test tone combinations also differed.

The test tone combinations were separated by a retention interval during which six extra tones were interpolated. The tones in the second and fourth serial positions of the interpolated sequence were also accompanied by tones of lower pitch. When the intervals formed by the interpolated combinations were identical in size to the interval formed by the first test tone combination, errors were fewer than when the sizes of the intervals formed by the interpolated combinations were chosen at random. Further, when the intervals formed by the interpolated combinations differed in size by one semitone from the interval formed by the first test tone combination, errors were more numerous than when the sizes of the intervals formed by the interpolated combinations were chosen at random.

This experiment demonstrates that effects which are analogous to those found in the system that retains absolute pitch values exist in the system retaining pitch abstractions also. These effects are memory enhancement through repetition, and similarity-based interference in the same relative frequency range.

Interactions between Outputs of Two Memory Systems

Finally, we may inquire how the outputs of two memory systems interact in producing recognition judgments. When comparisons are made between stimuli that vary along one (relevant) dimension, how are these affected by simultaneously varying the stimuli along a different (irrelevant) dimension?

This question was addressed by considering the influence of relational context on judgments concerning the absolute pitches of two test tones. In one experiment (Deutsch & Roll, 1974), subjects compared the pitches of two tones when these were both accompanied by tones of lower pitch. The test tone combinations were separated by a retention interval during which a sequence of extra tones was interpolated. In some conditions, the harmonic intervals formed by the test tone combinations were identical, and in others they differed; these patterns of relationship were present both when the test tones were identical and also when these differed. A strong effect of harmonic context was found. When the pitches of the test tones were identical, but when these were placed in different harmonic contexts, there resulted an increased tendency to judge them as different. Also, when the pitches of the test tones differed, but when these were placed in the identical harmonic context, there was an increased tendency to judge them as identical. In further study (Deutsch, 1982), the effect of melodic context was examined. Here, subjects compared the pitches of two test tones when these were each preceded by tones of lower pitch. Again, the test tone combinations were separated by a retention interval during which a sequence of extra tones was interpolated. A strong effect of melodic context was demonstrated, which was analogous to that found for harmonic context.

Conclusion

An important goal of neuropsychology is to explain behavior in terms of its neurophysiological and neuroanatomical substrates. In attempting to reach this goal, it is useful to seek out paradigms in which patterns of behavior are produced that can be most directly explained in terms of known physiological mechanisms. In the case of memory, one approach is dissect out specific dimensions of representation by behavioral means. Interactions between elements along such dimensions can then be studied, together with interactions between outputs of different dimensions.

This chapter has presented findings which indicate that the above approach is a particularly useful one. Where single dimensions are concerned, findings indicate that memory elements interact in ways analogous to lateral inhibitory interactions that have been studied at the physiological level in sensory systems. This leads us to conjecture that other effects described here—such as memory enhancement through repetition, and loss of temporal or order information—can also be explained relatively directly in terms of hypothesized neural mechanisms. At the same time, such findings appear as examples of memory phenomena that are commonly obtained in a wide variety of situations. These are, for instance, similarity-based interference, consolidation through repetition, and loss of memory for when events had occurred. Such phenomena have generally been studied in situations where multiple memory representations must have been involved, and so where the physiological correlates must have been highly complex. The present findings therefore provide a link between cognitive studies of human memory on the one hand, and studies of relatively simple physiological mechanisms on the other.

ACKNOWLEDGMENT

This work was supported by U.S. Public Health Service Grant MH-21001.

REFERENCES

Alpern, M., & David, H. The additivity of contrast in the human eye. *Journal of General Physiology*, 1959, *43*, 109–126.

Bachem, A. Time factors in relative and absolute pitch determination. *Journal of the Acoustical Society of America*, 1954, *26*, 751–753.

Barlow, H. B., & Levick, W. R. The mechanism of directionally selective units in the rabbit's retina. *Journal of Physiology*, 1965, *178*, 477–504.

Carterette, E. C., Friedman, M. P., & Lovell, J. D. Mach bands in auditory perception. In R. Plomp & G. F. Smoorenburg (Eds.), *Frequency analysis and periodicity detection in hearing*. Sijthoff: Leiden, 1970.

Cornsweet, T. N. *Visual perception*. New York: Academic Press, 1970.

Deutsch, D. Music recognition. *Psychological Review*, 1969, *76*, 300–307.

Deutsch, D. Tones and numbers: Specificity of interference in short-term memory. *Science*, 1970, *168*, 1604–1605.

Deutsch, D. Effect of repetition of standard and comparison tones on recognition memory for pitch. *Journal of Experimental Psychology*, 1972, *93*, 156–162. (a)

Deutsch, D. Mapping of interactions in the pitch memory store. *Science*, 1972, *175*, 1020–1022. (b)

Deutsch, D. Interference in memory between tones adjacent in the musical scale. *Journal of Experimental Psychology*, 1973, *100*, 228–231.

Deutsch, D. Facilitation by repetition in recognition memory for tonal pitch. *Memory and Cognition*, 1975, *3*, 263–266. (a)

Deutsch, D. The organization of short-term memory for a single acoustic attribute. In D. Deutsch & J. A. Deutsch (Eds.), *Short-term memory*. New York: Academic Press, 1975. (b)

Deutsch, D. Interactive effects in memory for harmonic intervals. *Perception and Psychophysics*, 1978, *24*, 7–10.

Deutsch, D. The influence of melodic context on pitch recognition judgment. *Perception and Psychophysics*, 1982, *31*, 407–410.

Deutsch, D., & Feroe, J. Disinhibition in pitch memory. *Perception and Psychophysics*, 1975, *17*, 320–324.

Deutsch, D., & Feroe, J. The internal representation of pitch sequences in tonal music. *Psychological Review*, 1981, *88*, 503–522.

Deutsch, D., & Roll, P. L. Error patterns in delayed pitch comparison as a function of relational context. *Journal of Experimental Psychology*, 1974, *103*, 1027–1034.

Grey, J. M. *An exploration of musical timbre*. Unpublished doctoral dissertation, Stanford University, 1975.

Harris, J. D. The decline of pitch discrimination with time. *Journal of Experimental Psychology*, 1952, *43*, 96–99.

Hartline, H. K., Ratliff, F., & Miller, W. H. Inhibitory interaction in the retina and its significance in vision. In E. Florey (Ed.), *Nervous inhibition.* New York: Pergamon Press, 1961.

Klinke, R., Boerger, G., & Gruber, J. The influence of the frequency relation in dichotic stimulation upon the cochlear nucleus activity. In R. Plomp & G. F. Smoorenburg (Eds.), *Frequency analysis and periodicity detection in hearing.* Sijthoff: Leiden, 1970.

Koester, T. The time error in pitch and loudness discrimination as a function of time interval and stimulus level. *Archives of Psychology*, 1945, *297*(whole issue).

Massaro, D. W. Preperceptual images, processing time and perceptual units in auditory perception. *Psychological Review,* 1972, *79*, 124–145.

Ratliff, F. *Mach bands: Quantitative studies of neural networks in the retina.* San Francisco: Holden-Day, 1965.

Risset, J.-C., & Wessel, D. L. Exploration of timbre by analysis and synthesis. In D. Deutsch (Ed.), *The psychology of music.* New York: Academic Press, 1982.

Sachs, M. B., & Kiang, N. Y.-S. Two-tone inhibition in auditory nerve fibers. *Journal of the Acoustical Society of America,* 1968, *43*, 1120–1128.

Von Békésy, G. *Experiments in hearing.* New York: McGraw-Hill, 1960.

Wickelgren, W. A. Consolidation and retroactive interference in short-term recognition memory for pitch. *Journal of Experimental Psychology*, 1966, *72*, 250–259.

Wickelgren, W. A. Associative strength theory of recognition memory for pitch. *Journal of Mathematical Psychology*, 1969, *6*, 13–61.

7

The Episodic–Semantic Distinction in Amnesia

Laird S. Cermak

The study of amnesia has become increasingly interesting to theorists of cognition, memory, and information processing because of the possibility of demonstrating dissociable sets of memory systems within this population. The amnesic syndrome was long viewed as the last bastion of support for a short-term memory–long-term memory dichotomy (Wickelgren, 1975), and then later seen as a means to dissociate encoding from retrieval. Now, the study of amnesia represents the area with the greatest potential of demonstrating a distinction between semantic memory and episodic memory. Any one of these three issues could be highlighted to make the point that amnesia can represent a testing ground for memory theorists, and, indeed, documentation of the first two topics has been numerous. Consequently, a good deal of this chapter is devoted to exploring the dissociation of semantic and episodic memory in the amnesic patient.

Prior to this discussion, an observation concerning the use of the amnesic patient as a testing ground for one's theories ought to be mentioned. Unlike the study of college sophomores, the plight of the individual patient and his or her overwhelming difficulties often becomes as important to the investigator as the pursuit of data to prove or disprove a hypothesis. Furthermore, the so-called "testing ground" often tends to take on a fertility of its own, becoming the source for formulations about the nature and consequences of the syndrome itself. Thus, the study of amnesia often tends to lead, rather than follow, the thinking about normal memory in the investigator's research program. This reversal of priorities in the present investigator's research program is probably most obvious in later sections of this chapter.

The Episodic–Semantic Distinction

Contemporary memory theorists have found it theoretically profitable to divide long-term verbal memory into two components, namely, "episodic" and "semantic" memory (Tulving, 1972). "Episodic" memory has been defined as memory for specific, personally experienced events, while memory for general principles, associations, rules, and the like has been defined as "semantic" memory. Because episodic memory includes information learned in laboratory situations, it has traditionally received more attention than semantic memory from experimental psychologists. Also, it has been the arena for most of the controversies existing in the amnesia literature.

Laird S. Cermak. Psychology Research, Boston Veterans Administration Medical Center, Boston, Massachusetts; Neurology Department, Boston University School of Medicine, Boston, Massachusetts.

Attempts to differentiate episodic from semantic memory have only recently been initiated by investigators of the amnesic syndrome. Kinsbourne and Wood (1975) were among the first to suggest that perhaps amnesics have an intact semantic memory in the presence of their highly dramatic impairments in episodic memory. If this were true, it would provide exceptionally good evidence for the independence of the two systems. But Kinsbourne and Wood's evidence was based solely on clinical observation coupled with a rather informal experiment. Patients were asked first to describe what an object such as a railroad ticket was (Kinsbourne and Wood felt that this tapped semantic memory); then they were asked to describe an instance in which they had used that particular object (an index of episodic memory). Since the amnesic patients could do the former but not the latter, these authors felt that their thesis had been proven.

At approximately this same time, Collins and Loftus (1975) were in the process of demonstrating two components of semantic memory, which they labeled "lexical" and "conceptual." My colleagues and I (Cermak, Reale, & Baker, 1978) used these authors' technique of assessing semantic memory, using response time as a measure; we found that, while amnesic patients had little to no impairment in lexical-search rate, they did show an impaired rate of search through conceptual memory. From this it was concluded that amnesic patients' search rate through semantic memory is not necessarily normal and seems to depend upon the sophistication of the search, in that the more cognitively complex the search, the less normal the rate of search. However, it has to be noted quite strongly that the patients were always able to come up with acceptable answers to even the most complex semantic questions; this confirms the notion that semantic memory is intact for these individuals. The slower search rate meant either that the semantic organization is a little less stable for these patients or that amnesics simply proceed with greater caution.

This impaired search speed through conceptual semantic memory might actually help to explain the often-reported notion that analysis of incoming episodic information is deficient for amnesic Korsakoff patients (see Butters & Cermak, 1980, for a review of this "encoding-deficits theory"). Since semantic memory must be searched in order to compare and contrast each new episode with what is already known, when such comparison is slow, analysis may be delayed and search terminated prematurely. Thus, impaired search rate of semantic memory might underlie some of the encoding deficits seen in amnesic patients.

On the other hand, when retrieval from semantic memory is relatively easy and automatic, as when primary associations or initial letters are used as cues, the intactness of semantic memory may actually appear to facilitate episodic retention, as in the case of cuing following a learning task (Warrington & Weiskrantz, 1978, 1982), or in the case of encoding specificity tasks (Cermak & Stiassny, 1982). In other words, semantic memory may facilitate episodic recall in instances when its organization conforms to expectations of a task, and may interfere with episodic recall when its organization does not conform to these expectations.

This interdependence of the two memory systems is also seen in research with normals whenever it is demonstrated that a previous episode can have a stimulating effect on semantic-memory search rate. For instance, Loftus and Cole (1974) demonstrated that when two consecutive semantic-memory searches of the same category (e.g., animals) are made, the second search proceeds more rapidly than expected, even when searching for different exemplars. Loftus and Cole explain this by proposing that the subjects (here, college students) "remember" the category searched on the first trial and do not need to search all exemplars from that category again. Unfortunately, amnesics' retention of their search once it is completed is poor because of their impaired episodic memory. Consequently, facilitation of subsequent same-category searches does not occur (Cermak *et al.*, 1978). Thus, instances where semantic-memory search is impaired might sometimes represent an inability to utilize an impoverished episodic-memory system. This, coupled with the results described previously, suggests a dependence of one memory system upon the other, yet an independence of the two systems in terms of mode of access and method of retrieval. Retrieval from semantic memory may be available to the patient, since its structure was established prior to brain injury, while retrieval from episodic memory may demand creativity at the time of input and thus is not available for the brain-injured patient to use. This thesis is more fully developed in the next section of this chapter.

On a more general level, Schacter (1982) and Zola-Morgan, Cohen, and Squire (1983) do report that amnesic patients have some ability to remember episodes from their "distant" past, even though such retrieval is not evident for present events. If this is true, then it provides retrograde evidence (memory for events occurring prior to brain injury) against Kinsbourne and Wood's (1975) theory of the dissociation of the two systems in amnesia. In other words, it suggests that retrieval from both semantic and episodic memory may exist for very long-term memories retained by amnesics. However, the issue takes on added complexity because of a recent report (Cermak & O'Connor, 1983) testing the long-term episodic recall of a postencephalitic amnesic patient. This patient, who has been described elsewhere (Cermak, 1976), is an extremely intelligent but highly amnesic patient; all attempts to encourage episodic retrieval from his retrograde memory have failed. The initial attempt employed a procedure originally developed by Robinson (1976) and used successfully by both Schacter and Cohen. Essentially, all that was done was to give the patient a word such as "boat" and then ask him to describe any incident from his past that involved a boat. Our postencephalitic patient was able to deduce some probable situations involving the items given him, such as "I imagine I sailed as a youngster because we lived near the harbor," but, as he himself said it, he "could not remember a specific instance concerning a boat." Subsequent testing of Korsakoff patients has also revealed equally empty phrases in response to each item, and of course this was the outcome originally reported by Kinsbourne and Wood (1975). Some patients were able to remember that they often went sailing, but could not describe the boat or remember any specific instance surrounding boating.

Our postencephalitic patient did, however, often regale us with specific stories about his youth that seemed episodic. These tales were quite consistent (read: repetitious) and were usually given verbatim from instance to instance. We discovered, however, that he could not embellish these stories and, even when queried extensively, never seemed to know any of the circumstances surrounding the saga. To confirm his stories and to gather more folklore, we questioned the patient's mother. She could confirm his tales to some extent, but she found it difficult to provide us with very many other stories. However, even those few she could provide were not remembered by our patient when we asked him about these other events.

It seemed that our patient's "apparent" retrograde episodic retrieval really represented nothing more than retrieval from a very personal base of semantic knowledge, which concerned what he knew to be true about himself. He could make logical deductions in response to queries, much as he would concerning questions about the rest of the real world. However, this "personal folklore" ought not to be construed as being episodic memory. Furthermore, it is not clear that any amnesic's memory of events—past or present, personal or otherwise—is anything other than this type of semantic-memory retrieval. More is said on this in the next section on retrograde amnesia, but for now it seems fair to conclude that amnesics' long-term recall ability provides a good argument for differentiating episodic from semantic memory.

Retrograde Amnesia

The question has been raised earlier as to whether retrograde amnesia (i.e., the inability to retrieve information learned prior to onset of brain injury) is largely the result of loss of episodic memories or of some change in semantic organization. The normal pattern of forgetting remote events has been documented by Bahrick, Bahrick, and Whittlinger (1975), who tested 392 high-school graduates for retention of their classmates' names. They found that free recall of names declined with negative acceleration by 60% over an interval ranging from 2 weeks to 57 years. Bahrick (1981) has now also found comparable results for retention of street and building names as well as for events. Thus, normal "remote" forgetting is quite extensive itself and is, as one might expect, a gradually declining function of the age of the event. Quite possibly, this melting of memories represents a shift in time from specific retention involving episodes to a more general retention of "knowledge about" names and events.

Sanders and Warrington (1971) found a similar decline in retention when they tested normals on a questionnaire of public events that had occurred over the past 40 years. However, on this same test for amnesics, they found profound impairments; these extended equally for recall of quite recent as well as of distant events. In other words, amnesics' ability to retrieve information across the decades remained fairly constant, and quite poor, across the board. Their performance might best be described as being fairly flat across the retention intervals tested.

Not only was this result different from that expected from the normal aging process, but it turned out to be quite at odds with findings of Seltzer and Benson (1974) and Marslen-Wilson and Teuber (1975) with other amnesic populations. These authors found that retrieval of remote memories by amnesics is actually much better than their retrieval of more recent memories; that is, retrieval is precisely the opposite of the normal aging process. This "shrinking" retrograde amnesia has also been documented by Albert, Butters, and Levin (1979), who tested recognition of famous faces and famous events from the 1920s through the 1970s. They found that normals were more accurate at identifying famous people and/or events from recent decades than from earlier decades, while amnesics performed in exactly the opposite direction.

Thus, it can be seen that at least three patterns of remote-memory abilities have emerged. Perhaps each represents the same underlying function, with different amnesic overlays superimposed. It could be that the brain degeneration of Korsakoff patients (used in the Seltzer & Benson, Marslen-Wilson & Teuber, and Albert *et al.* studies) is gradual, and so they simply "store" less and less each year. Or, it may be that Sanders and Warrington's patients demonstrated only straight "retrieval" deficits. Cohen and Squire

(Cohen & Squire, 1981; Squire & Cohen, 1982) have suggested that these differences may be a result of the etiology of the disorder, in that temporal lobe damage (or disruption, as with ECT patients), inhibits consolidation (or storage) of recent memory, while diencephalic lesions disrupt retrieval from an already existent storage.

Recently, I have proposed (Cermak, 1982) that the retrieval-deficit theory of retrograde amnesia may actually be stronger than initial data have suggested, because, if the test is repeated with the same patients, what is recalled one day varies considerably from what is recalled the next day. In fact, we (Cermak & O'Connor, 1983) found that our postencephalitic patient's day-to-day retrieval varied as much as 50%. In other words, the patient recalled many items on a second testing that he had failed to retrieve on initial testing, and seemingly "forgot" others. His overall retrieval probability remained the same, even across decades, but the specific items that he recalled varied considerably. It seemed as if the limitation was more on the number recallable than on the number still in memory. If this is so, then it argues that the patient, if tested often enough, might be able to demonstrate knowledge of as many facts as normals, but cannot demonstrate such at any one sitting. Recently, a comparable result has been reported (Cermak, 1982) for Korsakoff patients as well.

The existence of a retrograde retrieval deficit, and the various "slopes" seen in different patient populations, just might be explained by the very same episodic–semantic distinction described in the preceding section. Although most investigators of the amnesic process have tended to view retrograde amnesia as removed from the episodic–semantic distinction, such may not be the case. It is quite likely that normal individuals remember fewer episodes from their youth and childhood than they do from more recent years. Even those distant episodes that do appear vivid may actually be more familial folklore than truly retained episodes (see Loftus, 1980, for more on this possibility). As a consequence, normals may tend to answer more of the queries about distant decades on a retrograde-memory test from their semantic memory and more of the recent items from their episodic memory. An event from the 1950s might be remembered more as a matter of general knowledge, while an event from the 1970s might still retain a personal episodic component. An individual might recall where he or she was when Nixon resigned, but not know where he or she was when Eisenhower had a heart attack.

As a consequence, "normal" retrograde retrieval may change from being primarily retrieval from semantic memory to being primarily retrieval from episodic memory (with a great deal of midterm overlap possible). Tests based on normal remote recall may thus be biased first toward semantic memory (for distant decades) and then toward episodic memory (for recent decades). Even attempting to make all test items equally retrievable by a group of normal individuals does not change or reduce this bias. Given that Korsakoffs do have better semantic than episodic memory (as argued in the preceding section), then this shifting bias alone can explain their apparent "shrinking" retrograde amnesia. The more the question depends on semantic knowledge (as queries about earlier decades do), the better these patients perform. The more the question depends on retention of an episode (as queries about recent events do), the less well they perform. Their highly variable recall can also be explained, since retrieval from semantic memory probably involves some form of organized search process, and this process has been shown to be slow and probably quite random in these patients. The postencephalitic patient (Cermak &

O'Connor, 1983), who shows a flatter gradient of remote recall than do the Korsakoff patients, may reflect the possibility that his semantic memory is not as normal as that of Korsakoffs. He not only seems to have more of a search problem than Korsakoffs do, but he may truly have lost more information, due to the cortical nature of his disorder. While the validity of this assumption awaits verification, for now it is evident that the post-encephalitic patient's search of semantic memory is more impoverished than that of Korsakoffs. In addition, he, even more than the Korsakoffs, has trouble rejecting the incorrect items encountered during a semantic-memory search.

Further Implications

As the reader can undoubtedly appreciate, the distinction between episodic and semantic memory can resolve a good number of the issues and conflicts that remain in the field of amnesia. If it can be demonstrated that amnesics have good semantic memory and poor episodic memory, then not only can the nature of retrograde amnesia be brought into perspective, but so also can the roles of encoding, associative interference, and context in determining rate of loss from anterograde memory.

   The conflict between encoding versus associative interference in the retrieval deficits of amnesics would boil down to a conclusion that under those conditions where cuing appears to facilitate episodic retrieval, either a patient's strongest associate in semantic memory is being cued, or else some item in semantic memory has been so well primed that it appears most appropriate to the patient. In other words, it can be proposed that the episode is not retained (i.e., the patient does not actually remember the most recent presentation), but his or her "guess" based on a momentary associative strengthening of semantic memory happens to be correct in this situation. The encoding-deficits theory is still correct, in that the "episode" is not analyzed in a manner that permits its recon-struction. The associative retrieval-deficits theory is also correct in that the subject will always face interference from his or her highest semantic associate to any cue and can only be cued "correctly" under those conditions that manipulate his or her semantic hierarchy in such a way that a new response appears appropriate to the patient.

   Context can be viewed as having a part in the amnesic's retrieval deficit if it is proposed that the patient is truly unable to analyze and reconstruct the context of "episodes." Since context plays no role in semantic retrieval, its special status in amnesia becomes reasonable, since the amnesic's disorder is almost entirely episodic. Both Hirst's (1982) and Stern's (1981) emphasis on context is well taken, but they overlook a great deal of other encoding data, because they do not seem to realize that the amnesic's deficit is in all of episodic memory, not just in one obvious episodic feature (namely, context).

   "Semantic" and "episodic" may not be the best terms to define these two in-dependent systems—particularly since "semantic" seems to imply retention of only "ver-balizable" material, and much more than this is implicated in the amnesic syndrome. Terms suggested by others seem equally specific to types of learning and recall situations (e.g., "pro-cedural" and "declarative," "knowing how" and "knowing that," "vertical" and "hori-zontal" associations, etc.). Probably one ought to stick with "retrieval from generalized knowledge" versus "retrieval of specific events." Nevertheless, and regardless of the ulti-mate titles chosen, the incorporation of the semantic–episodic distinction into our understanding of amnesia seems to be absolutely necessary, and the amount gained by awareness of this distinction in amnesia might be important to theorists of the normal memory process.

ACKNOWLEDGMENT

My research reported in this chapter is supported by NIAAA Grant AA-00187 to Boston University School of Medicine, and by the Medical Research Service of the Veterans Administration.

REFERENCES

Albert, M. S., Butters, N., & Levin, J. Temporal gradients in the retrograde amnesia of patients with alcoholic Korsakoff's disease. *Archives of Neurology*, 1979, *36*, 211–216.

Bahrick, H. P. *Long-term ecological memory.* Paper presented at the Sixth Annual Interdisciplinary Conference, Park City, Utah, 1981.

Bahrick, H. P., Bahrick, P. S., & Wittlinger, R. P. Fifty years of memory for names and faces: A cross-sectional approach. *Journal of Experimental Psychology: General*, 1975, *104*, 54–75.

Butters, N., & Cermak, L. S. *Alcoholic Korsakoff's syndrome: An information processing approach to amnesia.* New York: Academic Press, 1980.

Cermak, L. S. The encoding capacity of a patient with amnesia due to encephalitis. *Neuropsychologia*, 1976, *14*, 311–326.

Cermak, L. S. *The effects of alcohol on the aging brain.* Paper presented at the Sixth Annual Conference on Addiction Research and Treatment: Drugs, Alcohol and Aging, Coatesville, Pennsylvania, August 1982.

Cermak, L. S., & O'Connor, M. The retrieval capacity of a patient with amnesia due to encephalitis. *Neuropsychologia*, 1983, *21*, 213–234.

Cermak, L. S., Reale, L., & Baker, E. Alcoholic Korsakoff patients' retrieval from semantic memory. *Brain and Language*, 1978, *5*, 215–226.

Cermak, L. S., & Stiassny, D. Recall failure following successful generation and recognition of responses by alcoholic Korsakoff patients. *Brain and Cognition*, 1982, *1*, 165–176.

Cohen, N. J., & Squire, L. R. Retrograde amnesia and remote memory impairment. *Neuropsychologia*, 1981, *19*, 337–356.

Collins, A. M., & Loftus, E. F. A spreading activation theory of semantic processing. *Psychological Review*, 1975, *82*, 407–428.

Hirst, W. The amnesic syndrome: Descriptions and explanations. *Psychological Bulletin*, 1982, *91*, 435–460.

Kinsbourne, M., & Wood, F. Short-term memory processes and the amnesic syndrome. In D. Deutsch & J. A. Deutsch (Eds.), *Short-term memory.* New York: Academic Press, 1975.

Loftus, E. F. *Memory: Surprising new insights into how we remember and why we forget.* Reading, Mass.: Addison-Wesley, 1980.

Loftus, E. F., & Cole, W. Retrieving attribute and name information from semantic memory. *Journal of Experimental Psychology*, 1974, *102*, 1116–1122.

Marslen-Wilson, W. D., & Teuber, H.-L. Memory for remote events in anterograde amnesia: Recognition of public figures from new photographs. *Neuropsychologia*, 1975, *13*, 347–352.

Robinson, J. A. Sampling autobiographical memory. *Cognitive Psychology*, 1976, *8*, 578–595.

Sanders, H. I., & Warrington, E. K. Memory for remote events in amnesic patients. *Brain*, 1971, *94*, 661–668.

Schacter, D. L. *Approaches to the study of memory pathology: Issues and data.* Paper presented at the meeting of the Lake Ontario Neuroscience Society, Syracuse, New York, 1982.

Seltzer, B., & Benson, D. F. The temporal pattern of retrograde amnesia in Korsakoff's disease. *Neurology*, 1974, *24*, 527–530.

Squire, L. R., & Cohen, N. J. Remote memory, retrograde amnesia, and the neuropsychology of memory. In L. S. Cermak (Ed.), *Human memory and amnesia.* Hillsdale, N.J.: Erlbaum, 1982.

Stern, L. D. A review of the theories of human amnesia. *Memory and Cognition*, 1981, *9*, 247–262.

Tulving, E. Episodic and semantic memory. In E. Tulving & W. Donaldson (Eds.), *Organization of memory*. New York: Academic Press, 1972.

Warrington, E. K., & Weiskrantz, L. Further analysis of the prior learning effect in amnesic patients. *Neuropsychologia*, 1978, *16*, 169–177.

Warrington, E. K., & Weiskrantz, L. Amnesia: A disconnection syndrome? *Neuropsychologia*, 1982, *20*, 233–248.

Wickelgren, W. A. The long and the short of memory. In D. Deutsch & J. A. Deutsch (Eds.), *Short-term memory*. New York: Academic Press, 1975.

Zola-Morgan, S., Cohen, N. J., & Squire, L. R. Recall of remote episodic memory in amnesia. *Neuropsychologia*, 1983, *21*, 487–500.

8

Processing Capacity and Recall in Amnesic and Control Subjects

John McDowall

In current memory research, much attention has been focused on the nature of processing operations that occur at both the encoding and retrieval stages of a memory task. The theoretical impetus for this focus largely developed from the levels-of-processing approach (Craik & Lockhart, 1972), and the concepts developed from it have influenced the experimental investigation of amnesia. Thus, the literature on amnesia is largely concerned with investigating the role of encoding and retrieval operations in subjects in an attempt to assess the relative contributions of these to the amnesic state (see Knight & Wooles, 1980, for a recent review).

Recently, the view that an individual has a limited amount of attentional resource or processing capacity with which to carry out cognitive demands has been investigated. Shiffrin and Schneider (1977) and Hasher and Zacks (1979) have argued that cognitive operations vary along an active–passive continuum, with "passive" (automatic) operations defined as those that can be carried out at little or no cost to the individual's overall processing capacity and that can be carried out simultaneously with other cognitive demands. "Active" (controlled) operations, on the other hand, are assumed to require considerable processing capacity and are impaired when this resource becomes overloaded, as, for example, by the requirements of other cognitive operations. Examples of passive operations include the encoding of temporal and spatial information, while active processes include rehearsal, cognitive decisions and strategies, and search from long-term memory.

In a recent paper investigating recall deficits in aged subjects, Rabinowitz, Craik, and Ackerman (1982) showed that the experimental reduction of processing capacity using a divided-attention procedure resulted in younger subjects' mimicking the recall deficits typically found in older subjects. Specifically, these authors argued that a substantial amount of processing capacity is required in order to encode a stimulus in such a way as to differentiate it from other stimuli held within the semantic store. When processing capacity is reduced, active processing is impaired, and stimuli are encoded in a passive manner— that is, in a manner that does not provide the stimulus with sufficient distinctiveness to facilitate recall.

The concept of a reduced processing capacity, and its consequences for encoding and retrieval operations, have possible implications for the study of amnesia. Specifically, to what extent are the known encoding and retrieval deficits typically found in amnesic subjects the result of, or influenced by, a limited processing capacity? Are amnesic subjects capable of encoding stimuli above a passive level? The aim of this chapter is to use the

John McDowall. Department of Psychology, Porirua Hospital, Porirua, New Zealand.

concept of processing capacity to investigate the failure of amnesic subjects to demonstrate "list learning," defined as the ability to recall an increasing number of words over trials. Fuld (1976) has argued that the inability to retrieve increasing numbers of words over trials reflects a failure to organize words according to some higher-order structure. In this chapter, it is hypothesized that such higher-order organization requires active processing, and therefore will be impaired if overall processing capacity is reduced.

The experiment briefly described below compares the recall of Korsakoff subjects in a multitrial free-recall procedure with those of two groups of nonamnesic subjects, one group memorizing stimulus words, the other group memorizing stimulus words while also engaged in a letter-monitoring task. If a failure to recall an increasing number of words over trials is due to a reduced opportunity to engage in active processing of stimuli, the nonamnesic subjects engaged in the divided-attention task should demonstrate a recall pattern similar to that of the amnesic subjects.

Method

A total of 30 subjects served in this experiment. One group was comprised of 10 subjects diagnosed as Korsakoff patients with alcoholic histories. All of these subjects had severe anterograde and retrograde amnesia, but were free from any major global confusional state. Subjects in this group were required to have an IQ (Wechsler Adult Intelligence Scale, verbal) of 80 points or more (mean = 96.60, range = 83–105). The other groups were chosen from hospital staff members matched for education and socioeconomic status with the Korsakoff group; one group of 10 subjects was assigned to a learning task, and another group of 10 subjects was assigned to a divided-attention task. All subjects were matched for age (mean = 53 years, range = 41–66). Twenty high-frequency nouns chosen from separate taxonomic categories were selected from the Battig and Montague (1969) norms. These words were displayed on a video monitor one at a time to subjects, who were informed that they would be given a memory test at the end of the presentation. Each word was presented for 1.5 seconds, and at the end of the trial subjects were given a recall test. This procedure was repeated until four trials had been completed. After the recall test on the last trial, subjects were given a cued-recall test: The taxonomic category label for each stimulus word was read to the subjects, who were asked to name the appropriate exemplar.

In the divided-attention group, subjects had to view the stimulus words while performing a letter-monitoring task. In this task, subjects listened through headphones to a series of letters presented to either the right or the left ear. Subjects were instructed to push a trigger held in the left hand whenever the letter "B" was heard in the left ear, and to push the trigger held in the right hand whenever the letter "J" was heard in the right ear. A target letter occurred, on the average, every 2.5 seconds. Subjects in this group were told that the letter-monitoring task was important and that they should try hard to avoid mistakes.

Results and Discussion

A 3 (groups) $\times$ 4 (trials) analysis of variance with repeated measures on the last factor revealed a significant main effect for type of group, $F(2, 27) = 169.60, p < .001$. The main effect of trials was also significant, $F(3, 81) = 117.27, p < .001$, as was the group $\times$ trials interaction, $F(6, 81) = 23.89, p < .001$. An inspection of Figure 8-1 shows a similar pattern of recall over trials for both the amnesic group and the divided-attention group. These two groups did not differ in the total amount of words recalled, and both showed a small increase in words over the four trials.

Both the divided-attention group and the amnesic group recalled significantly more words when recall was cued. For the divided-attention group, the mean number of words recalled under the cued condition was 12.2, compared with a mean of 4.3 words averaged over the four free-recall trials. For the amnesic group, the difference was 10.9 words for the cured condition and 4.2 for the free-recall condition. The full-attention control group did not recall more words under the cued condition.

These results show that nonamnesic subjects engaged in a divided-attention task display a word recall that is identical to that obtained by amnesic subjects. This is true for (1) total number of words recalled per trial, (2) numbers of words recalled over trials, and (3) the ability of both and the amnesic group and the divided-attention group to benefit by the provision of semantic cues. This last finding is an important one and suggests that despite a dramatically impaired free recall, subjects in the divided-attention group were able to encode stimuli to a semantic level and thus were able to take advantage of the general category cues provided. The study by Rabinowitz *et al.* (1982) on aged subjects suggested that general semantic features of stimuli appear to be encoded automatically (i.e., in a way requiring little processing capacity), and that a general category cue, such as a category-superordinate label, would be effective in improving recall.

Despite the ability to encode stimuli to a semantic level, subjects in the divided-attention group were unable to freely recall more words than amnesic subjects. The same discrepancy between free recall and cued recall has been demonstrated in amnesic subjects (McDowall, 1979, 1981) and implies that effective free recall requires more than encoding stimuli to a semantic level. Additional processes might include encoding the higher-order relational properties of stimuli and encoding contextual information. A working hypothesis

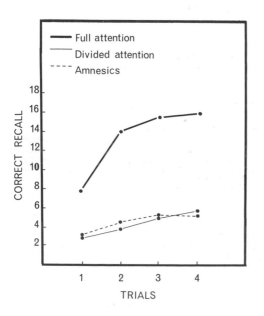

FIGURE 8-1. Number of words recalled over trials for three experimental groups.

is that these types of cognitive processes are necessary for effective free recall, but require active processing and therefore considerable processing capacity. Without this active processing, stimuli are encoded to a semantic level, but in a way that does not facilitate retrieval or distinguish them from words held in semantic memory. This view would also account for the high rate of intrusion found in the recall of amnesic subjects, since correct rejection of intrusions would require that subjects discriminate between episodic information (information presented during acquisition) and semantic information (information existing in some permanent store).

The question remains as to the role played by a limited processing capacity on the nature and extent of amnesic memory. It is one thing to demonstrate that by the experimental reduction of processing capacity, normal control subjects can mimic the results found in amnesic subjects; however, this does not necessarily warrant the conclusion that processing capacity *per se* is the fundamental impairment in amnesia. Relevant to this issue is the question of whether amnesic forgetting is qualitatively similar to normal forgetting. If recall deficits in amnesic subjects can be explained largely on the basis of a severely impaired processing capacity, then normal subjects should show identical patterns of deficits under divided-attention conditions. Similarly, subjects under experimentally reduced processing capacity should also benefit from those procedures that have been shown to aid amnesic recall (e.g., cuing, recognition, list blocking, etc.).

Using a divided-attention procedure could also prove valuable in clarifying specific memory deficits in amnesic subjects. In particular, the extent to which divided-attention subjects produce results that are different from those of amnesic subjects might clarify areas in which amnesic subjects are impaired, over and above a limited processing capacity.

REFERENCES

Battig, W. F., & Montague, W. E. Category norms for verbal items in 56 categories: A replication and extention of the Connecticut category norms. *Journal of Experimental Psychology Monograph*, 1969, *80*(3, Part 2).

Craik, F. I. M., & Lockhart, R. S. Levels of processing: A framework for memory research. *Journal of Verbal Learning and Verbal Behavior*, 1972, *11*, 671–684.

Fuld, P. A. Storage, retention, and retrieval in Korsakoff's syndrome. *Neuropsychologia*, 1976, *14*, 225–236.

Hasher, L., & Zacks, R. T. Automatic and effortful processes in memory. *Journal of Experimental Psychology: General*, 1979, *108*, 356–388.

Knight, R. G., & Wooles, I. M. Experimental investigation of chronic organic amnesia: A review. *Psychological Bulletin*, 1980, *88*, 753–771.

McDowall, J. Effects of encoding instructions and retrieval cuing on recall in Korsakoff patients. *Memory and Cognition*, 1979, *7*(3), 232–239.

McDowall, J. Effects of encoding instructions on recall and recognition in Korsakoff patients. *Neuropsychologia*, 1981, *19*, 43–48.

Rabinowitz, J. C., Craik, F. I. M., & Ackerman, B. P. A processing resource account of age differences in recall. *Canadian Journal of Psychology*, 1982, *36*(2), 325–344.

Shiffrin, R. M., & Schneider, W. Controlled and automatic human information processing: II. Perceptual learning, automatic attending, and a general theory. *Psychological Review*, 1977, *84*, 127–190.

9

A Process Theory of Remembering: Its Application to Korsakoff Amnesia and a Critique of Context and Episodic–Semantic Theories

Constantine X. Poulos and D. Adrian Wilkinson

The conscious remembering of an individual experience is a distinct and separate kind of memory. We take this as given. This phenomenological distinction has been made frequently, and in modern times dates back at least to Ribot (1882). Since then, this kind of memory has been variously referred to as "imaginative" (Bergson, 1896/1911), "familiar-to-me" (Claparède, 1911/1951), "historical" (Krauss, 1930), "temporal" (Nielsen, 1958), "remembrances" (Reiff & Scheerer, 1959), "episodic" (Tulving, 1972), and "autobiographical" (Jacoby & Dallas, 1981). Except when discussing specific theories, we somewhat arbitrarily call this "event" or "aware" memory.

For Korsakoff amnesia, we accept the idea that its central feature involves the singular selective impairment of event memory. This idea was clearly articulated by Claparède (1911/1951), and the notion is also contained in the work of Katzaroff (1911), MacCurdy (1928), Krauss (1930), Koffka (1935), Nielsen (1958), Kinsbourne and Wood (1975), Huppert and Piercy (1976), Rozin (1976), and Weiskrantz and Warrington (1979).

There is now a broad base of data indicating that amnesics normally acquire and retain a wide range of information, exemplified by classical conditioning (Weiskrantz & Warrington, 1979), perceptual–motor skills (Butters, Lewis, Cermak, & Goodglass, 1973), cognitive skills such as reading reversed writing (Cohen & Squire, 1980), and learning a mathematical rule (Wood, Ebert, & Kinsbourne, 1982) (see Moscovitch, 1982, for a fuller list). A remarkable feature of all these findings is that the amnesics consistently show no aware memory of the events of the practice sessions. Hence, there is now a considerable body of evidence indicating a circumscribed deficit in Korsakoff amnesia, consistent with Claparède's (1911/1951) observation.

As suggested by this historical perspective, we feel that the task for current theories is not so much to recognize the phenomenological distinctiveness of event memory as it is to provide a process account of its distinctiveness. For Korsakoff amnesia, this entails providing a process description not only of what Korsakoffs can remember, but also of what they cannot.

In the first section of this chapter, we examine context theory (Huppert & Piercy, 1976) and episodic–semantic theory (Tulving, 1972), which has been applied to amnesia (Kinsbourne & Wood, 1975). In our analysis, we propose that both theories converge in suggesting a process description of event memory on the basis of whether "contextual"

Constantine X. Poulos and D. Adrian Wilkinson. Addiction Research Foundation, Toronto, Ontario, Canada.

information is stored, and that this involves tautological definitions or empirical paradoxes. In the second section, we propose and develop a process description of event memory in terms of how information is processed. In the final section, we apply this process account to findings in Korsakoff amnesia.

Context and Episodic–Semantic Theories

Context Theory

Huppert and Piercy, in an important series of studies (1976, 1977, 1978), proposed that Korsakoff amnesics are selectively deficient in remembering information about context. In one study (1976), amnesic and control subjects studied two groups of complex pictures a day apart. On a subsequent recognition test, amnesics could discriminate previously studied pictures from new ones, but could not identify on which day a recognized picture had been seen previously. Huppert and Piercy suggested a distinction "between memory for an item of information (e.g., a picture, a word, or a unique event) and memory for the context in which that item of information occurred" (1976, p. 18). They pointed out that a similar distinction between memory for item and context had been made in the Norman and Rumelhart (1970) model of normal memory, in which attributes of an item have *attached* to them information about the item's contextual occurrence. Huppert and Piercy proposed that in the amnesic syndrome, there is a "dissociation between memory for items and memory for context; memory for items or attributes of items may be relatively intact while memory for context is grossly impaired" (1976, p. 18).

The distinction made by Huppert and Piercy is appealing, yet perplexing. The general notion may be cast in terms of the kernel or central feature of an event's being encased in a shell that constitutes all the particular trappings of the individual event. In amnesics, the kernel or target item is remembered normally, whereas the shell or context of its occurrence is lost. This dissociation between memory for an item and for its context implies a process distinction, and the basis provided for this distinction rests upon whether contextual information is remembered.

It is critical to note that there are two distinct definitions of the proposition: "Amnesics are deficient in remembering context." On the one hand, "context" can refer to all the circumstances attendant on the individual event; this can be called "context-as-event." However, *in the absence of additional specification*, to assert that "Amnesics are deficient in remembering context" in this sense is simply a restatement of the phenomenology. In a noncircular sense, the deficit can be taken to mean that amnesics fail to encode and/or remember information about situational, task, or temporal stimuli; this can be called "context-as-stimulus." We suggest that these separate meanings of "context" have been used inconsistently in the literature.

Some studies have examined the effects of context-as-stimulus on the performance of amnesics (see Hirst, 1982). For example, Winocur and Kinsbourne (1978) manipulated situational cues and thereby reduced negative transfer in amnesics, though the performance of control subjects was unaffected. This has been interpreted as evidence for context theory, under the assumption that amnesics are deficient in encoding situational stimuli, and therefore are differentially helped when such manipulations are particularly salient (see Hirst, 1982; Stern, 1981). However, since the amnesics benefited from the context shift and the normals did not, the results could as validly be interpreted as indicating that amnesics are more sensitive to context than normals.

Regardless of the interpretation of these studies, the extensive findings that amnesics can acquire and retain a variety of skills normally are clear evidence that they encode and retain information about context-as-stimulus. For example, one aspect of context-as-stimulus involves apparatus or task cues, which are an integral aspect of perceptual–motor skills. (For a similar point, see Moscovitch, 1982, p. 365.) That amnesics learn and retain information about apparatus and task stimuli is clearly indicated by their normal acquisition and retention of pursuit-rotor performance (e.g., Brooks & Baddeley, 1976). Similarly, they are normal in retaining information about the conditional stimulus in Pavlovian conditioning (Weiskrantz & Warrington, 1979). Information regarding the temporal relationship between stimuli is an integral aspect of pursuit-rotor learning; also, the latency of conditional eye-blink response is known to directly reflect the temporal interval between conditioned stimulus and unconditioned stimulus (see Gormezano & Moore, 1969). In addition, for cognitive skills involved in reading transformed text, Kolers (1975) has demonstrated that such skills are remarkably sensitive to stimulus configurations of the text. As previously indicated, amnesics are normal in acquiring such cognitive skills (Cohen & Squire, 1980). It may be noted that in Pavlovian conditioning, the environmental context can serve as the conditioned stimulus (e.g., Siegel, 1976). Since Pavlovian conditioning processes are intact in amnesics, then they should show normal context-specific conditioning. Thus there is a substantial body of evidence that amnesics can encode and retain a variety of stimulus information normally.

In short, if one takes "context" to mean "context-as-event," then context theory reduces to the phenomenological assertion that amnesics are deficient in the conscious recollection of individual events. If "context" is used to mean "context-as-stimulus," the theory is unable to handle the ability of amnesics to learn skills normally.

Episodic–Semantic Theory

Tulving's 1972 article rekindled interest in the idea that memory for an individual event reflects a distinct process. He contrasted "episodic" with "semantic" memory. The notion of episodic memory is straightforward and corresponds closely to Bergson's (1896/1911). That is, it stores individual, autobiographical events, described in terms of perceptible dimensions and temporal–spatial relations. Semantic memory constitutes the organized knowledge a person possesses about words and verbal symbols, their meaning and referents, and rules for the manipulation of these symbols. Semantic memory can be distinguished in that it *does not register perceptible properties of inputs*, but only their cognitive referents. Thus, perceptible attributes of stimulus events are important only for permitting identification of semantic referents of events: "These properties themselves are not recorded in semantic memory" (Tulving, 1972, p. 388).

Some striking conceptual similarities to context theory (Huppert & Piercy, 1976) are best illustrated by Tulving's analysis of an event in which a person hears a short story. For Tulving, all the information about the episode of hearing the story, including the exact words of the story, would be registered in episodic memory. In contrast, only the meaning of the story, or the idea units, are registered in semantic memory. This notion is very similar to Huppert's and Piercy's, in the sense that episodic memory is memory for the "shell" of the individual trappings encasing some central "kernel" of information, which is stored in a different way. (See Kolers, 1979, for a similar analysis of memory theories of reading skills.)

Memory for perceptible inputs is the only basis provided to distinguish episodic memory. As such, the term "perceptible inputs" plays a role equivalent to that of "context" in the theory of Huppert and Piercy. Moreover, we propose that a similar blurring between two separate usages occurs. That is, "perceptible inputs" can mean either a unique event or stimulus information. When "perceptible input" denotes "event," then the proposition that "Perceptible inputs are stored in episodic memory" reduces to a tautology.

If "perceptible input" is used to mean "stimulus information," then the proposition that "Perceptible inputs are stored in episodic memory" fails to differentiate episodic memory from other memory systems. That is, Tulving, Schacter, and Stark (1982) explicitly exclude "cognitive skills (e.g., Cohen & Squire, 1980; Kolers, 1975) and other forms of procedural knowledge" (p. 336) from both episodic and semantic memory. As is well established (e.g., Kolers, 1975), cognitive skills involve the retention of perceptible inputs defined as stimulus information. Thus the basis of a unique process description of episodic memory is lost, since perceptible inputs as stimulus information can be stored both in memory for cognitive skills and in memory for episodes.

Following Tulving's distinction, Kinsbourne and Wood (1975, 1982) have proposed that amnesics are impaired in episodic but not in semantic memory. They describe episodic memory as "context-bound" and semantic memory as "context-free." In contrast to Tulving, they consign cognitive and perceptual–motor skills to semantic memory, and suggest that the findings that amnesics are normal in retaining such "context-free" learning indicate they are selectively impaired in episodic memory. In their discussions, the authors clearly use "memory for context" to mean memory for individual autobiographical events.

In this analysis, we have proposed that both context theory and episodic–semantic theory provide definitions of event memory that are either tautological or empirically contradicted.

A Theory of Processes for Two Kinds of Memory

A Dichotomy and Process Distinction

A GENERAL DICHOTOMY

The dichotomy that we propose is clearly indicated in the writings of Bergson (1896/1911; see Reiff & Scheerer, 1959, p. 25). We begin by assuming that the conscious remembering of an individual experience involves processes that are totally distinct and separate from all other forms of retention of past experience. We propose that such remembering can be viewed as involving a perceptual image of past experience, and we refer to this form of memory as "imaginal memory."

We propose a general process-based dichotomy between imaginal memory and "associative memory" and we assume that everything stored in associative memory ultimately rests on learning or associative acquisition processes. Within associative memory, we subsume such phenomena as conditioning, perceptual learning, perceptual–motor skills, cognitive skills, and "semantic skills." (Perceptual learning and skill learning are frequently described as involving "emergent" organizational features—e.g., procedural rules. We return to this issue in a later discussion of semantic skills.)

Initially, we focus our discussion on separating imaginal memory from learning at a general level. There are a number of areas of learning in which it is clearly unnecessary to invoke such a notion as "imaginal memory" for a process explanation of changes that occur on the basis of past experience. Pavlovian conditioning is a case of "simple" learning in which such changes can be explained without recourse to a process involving event or aware memory (e.g., Pavlov, 1927; Rescorla & Wagner, 1972). The idea that perceptual learning can be understood without aware memory has been familiar since Helmholtz's concept of "unconscious inference," and continues through to Gibson's major work (1979). Similarly, perceptual–motor skill is another area in which learning need not depend on aware memory as a process for acquisition or retention (e.g., Howard, 1968). Finally, Kolers (1973, 1975, 1979) has argued that complex cognitive skills such as reading can be explained without recourse to such a notion as "aware memory." In each of these areas, the retention of previously acquired information can be explained by processes that do not involve the conscious remembering of the individual events of acquisition. (While both imaginal-memory processes and learning processes can co-occur in a given situation, we show later that they are nonetheless distinct and they can be conceptually and experimentally separated.)

PROCESS DISTINCTION

We propose that imaginal memory has *nothing* to do with the formation of associative bonds. However, learning fundamentally involves new associative connections.[1] (By way of contrast, it may be noted that Tulving, 1972, suggested that the formation of associations is unimportant for semantic memory, but may play a role in episodic memory.)

Before contrasting imaginal and associative memory, it is useful to restrict some terms differentially. For associative memory, we say that information is "entered" or "learned" and "elicited." The laying down of information into imaginal memory we term "recording." We use "remembering" to indicate reading out from the "image" or "memory."

A Process Analysis of the Two Memory Systems

IMAGINAL MEMORY

Information is processed in qualitatively different ways in imaginal and associative memory. Specifically, we propose that remembering can be analyzed as involving a perceptual-like act. In contrast, we propose that the elicitation and access of information

---

1. A bundle of associatively bound elements can occur as a unit in imaginal memory; in various situations, it could be a letter, a word, or a well-practiced action. However, the occurrence of such an associative bundle as a unit in imaginal memory is utterly distinct from the processes involved in the formation of new associations.

from associative memory do not comprise the attributes of a perceptual-like act. Of interest here is that certain kinds of information are *only* available through perceptual judgments. Thus, consideration of the kinds of information that can only derive from perceptual judgments can provide a means for distinguishing imaginal memory from associative memory. We suggest that this will provide a means for analyzing event memory not just as a phenomenological given, but as a testable theoretical construct.

Experientially based relational information depends exclusively upon perceptual judgments. Consider an observer who is perceiving a particular spatial array. This observer can make the perceptual judgment that "A is to the left of G." With equal validity, he or she can say, "G is to the right of A." For a temporal array, the observer can make the judgment that "M preceded K," or, equally, "K followed M." These are samples of geometrical and temporal relations. There are two essential points about relational propositions inherent in these examples: First, such relational propositions do not exist in an array in the *absence* of an observer; in addition, the observer may select any point in the array as a point of reference. These are exclusive and inherent properties of perceptual judgments.

We pursue the instigating metaphor that remembering involves a perceptual-like act. Therefore we suggest that inherent and exclusive properties of perceptual acts are also properties of remembering. Specifically, we propose that remembering involves a perceptual-like act in that it *conceptually* involves an array (an image or memory) that is distinct from the observer (the rememberer). The rememberer can make *perceptual judgments* about these past experiences. Hence *relational information about a past experience is only available through imaginal memory*. Later, we identify other types of experientially based perceptual information that are also exclusive properties of imaginal memory.[2]

ASSOCIATIVE MEMORY

To say that someone has learned an associative connection between A and B involves two parts: first, that representations of A and B are stored as elements; and second, that some connection or associative bond between them is formed. By "association" is typically meant that A is conditionally tied, or in terms of process connected, to B. Such *single* associations do not involve reciprocity, such that given B, then A. The processes concerning the connection of elements fall in the general province of learning. Of primary interest here are the questions of how information stored in the elements is accessed and what kind of information is available to the agent. We assume that accessing the information stored in an association does not have the properties of a perceptual-like act. Hence the nature of information thus accessed must be qualitatively different from information obtained through imaginal memory. In this regard, we present two "magical experiments" that serve to contrast processes of imaginal and associative memory. These illustrations provide a means of specifying the kinds of information available from each memory system, and indicate operational procedures for separating them.

___

2. There is other relational information that is not experientially based, such as "The French Revolution preceded the Russian Revolution" and "Toronto is east of Moose Jaw." However, this type of relational information clearly does not depend upon a perceptual judgment, but is generated or derived. In this chapter, we restrict our use of "relational information" to mean information about particular experienced events (i.e., experientially based).

MAGICAL EXPERIMENTS

In our first magical experiment, two male subjects come to the laboratory. One is divested of the ability to form any new imaginal memories; in addition, he is also rendered a "superb" learner. The other is stripped of the ability of store any new information in associative memory, but is granted "superb" imaginal-memory abilities. Thus, our Learner can only process new information into associative memory, and our Rememberer can only process new information into imaginal memory. Each is given a single serial presentation of a long list of unrelated words. Subsequently, both are tested for retention. Given the first word of the list, both can recall the rest in perfect order. In this sense, both the Learner and the Rememberer are identical in storing all the words of the array in their temporal sequence. And hence, on this basis, there is no means of discerning that different processes are involved.

Next, our subjects are given a "probe" word from the list and are asked which word came before it and which word came after it. As indicated, the Rememberer can give the "after" word with ease, and for the "before" word, he "looks" at his temporal memory and says "Oh, yes, that was 'onyx.'" For this person, the question is no more taxing than "What did you eat before the entrée?" Time does not move backward in imaginal memory; however, given an arbitrary reference point, our Rememberer can, with equal facility, make judgments about what immediately preceded it or followed it. In short, information about temporal relations is available through remembering.

Our Learner can specify the word that followed the probe word with facility. However, he would only be able to answer the "before" question by accessing information forward through the serial associative path. The Learner cannot use the probe as an arbitrary reference to access the preceding item. All that can be said of the Learner is that all the elements of the array have been stored in sequence. However, since relational information about temporal order is not available to our Learner, whatever "elicitation" involves, it is not a perceptual-like judgment on stored temporal information.

It is important to note, however, that the target words of the previous experiment are accessible through both an elicited association (for the Learner) and through a memory (for the Rememberer). As previously indicated, a set of associatively bound elements such as a word can occur as a unit in learning and in memory. The fact that words are accessible either through learning or through imaginal memory may operate to obscure the qualitative differences between these processes. (We suggest that there is a clear basis for distinguishing between the two, and we return to this issue later.) However, for the next "experiment" we use nonverbal stimuli for which there are no ready names, and this, we think, will reveal the startling qualitative differences between the two processes.

In this magical experiment, we focus upon the nature of the information that is stored in an element in associative memory. For simplicity, we use a conditioning paradigm to assess the nature of this retained information for our Learner. Imagine that our two subjects are presented with a brief exposure to a complex nonrepresentational abstract painting, and that this is immediately followed by a painful shock. Subsequently, the Rememberer will *recognize* having seen the picture before. (He will remember being shocked, but will exhibit no conditioned fear reaction to the painting.) Furthermore, if any segments of the painting are rearranged, the Rememberer can readily specify exactly which geometrical relations of the painting have been changed. In short, *an exact representation of the configuration of the painting* has been recorded into imaginal memory, and relational information is available through the perceptual-like act of remembering this representation.

Consider now our Learner. When the painting is presented again, the Learner will exhibit a clear conditioned fear reaction to it. By this index, he also *recognizes* the painting. Furthermore, if any segments of the painting are rearranged, the conditioned fear reaction will be reduced in proportion to the number of segments that are moved. Hence, by this measure, *an exact representation of the configuration of the painting* has also been stored in associative memory. Despite this (and this point is crucial), when asked to, the Learner *cannot* directly specify the nature of the changes. His behavior can *only* register that changes have been made in the painting.

We have previously indicated that experientially based information about geometrical relations is an exclusive property of a perceptual act. Furthermore, we have indicated that a perceptual act entails *both* a perceiver and something perceived. We have proposed that accessing information that is associatively stored does *not* have these dual properties. Since it does not, then geometrical relational information about a previous experience is not available from associative memory.

Consider again our Rememberer. When presented with the modified form of the painting, in which some segments have been rearranged, he remembers the image of the original painting. Hence specific differences between this image and the test painting are readily discerned. We have proposed that this remembering functionally constitutes a perceiver and something perceived, and this accounts for the availability to the Rememberer of experientially based information about geometrical relations of the original painting. Consider again our Learner when he is presented with the modified form of the painting. As indicated, his conditioned fear reaction is reduced by the modification. Thus the Learner has stored an exact representation of the original painting. However, *since there are no means by which the Learner can elicit a "copy" of the original painting, all he can do is react to the stimulus configuration at hand.*

Our selection of geometrical information in this experiment has been somewhat arbitrary. We could have altered the colors of the original painting, and this would have reduced the magnitude of the Learner's conditioned fear reaction, relative to that elicited by re-presentation of the original. That is, the Learner's behavior would reflect the fact that this now color-modified painting is different from the stored representation of the original. Yet, if asked to, the Learner could not directly specify which colors had been changed. The reason for this inability is exactly the same as the reasons for his inability to specify geometrical changes. That is, experientially based information about the color of an object or stimulus is an exclusive property of a perceptual act. Stimuli do *not* have the experiential attribute of color in the absence of a perceiver. Since access to associatively stored information does not have the dual properties of a perceiver and something perceived, then experientially based information about the color of the previously presented painting is not available. Again, since there are no means by which the Learner can access a "copy" of the original painting, all he can do is react to the stimulus configuration that is presented.

This line of reasoning has an extraordinary implication. The principle is a general one and applies to all experientially based perceptual attributes of stimuli: color, brightness, loudness, resonance, warmth, and so on. Each of these experiential attributes of stimuli does not exist in the absence of a perceiver. Hence experientially based information of any perceptual attribute of a stimulus is unavailable from a representation of the stimulus that is stored in associative memory. *While an exact representation of a stimulus can be stored in associative memory, it is as if it were stored without color, without form, without any perceptual quality. It is simply "stimulus."*

WORDS AND DENOTATIVE INFORMATION

The names of perceptual qualities are learned. However, such denotative learning does not depend on the remembering of perceptual events. The names of perceptual qualities can also be used to derive information that is distinct from experientially based perceptual information. Take this example: Our Learner is given a serial presentation of photographs of a canary, an emerald, and a strawberry. He can readily learn this series by using the names of objects. If asked to specify the color of the object portrayed after "canary," the Learner can give the appropriate answer with facility. He can generate this by the denotative meaning of "emerald," but this is clearly distinct from the perceptual information, which is experientially based. A clear example is that a person who has always been blind can know that "emeralds are green" and that "canaries are yellow."

As previously indicated, this ability of words to be accessible in either memory system can obscure the differences between the two memory processes. We return to the issue of the denotative and "evocative" meaning of words.

IMAGINAL MEMORY OF COGNITIVE EVENTS: MNEMONICS

We suggest that cognitive events as well as "external" events are recorded in imaginal memory, and that the use of mnemonic devices involves the remembering of particular kinds of cognitive events.

Consider being introduced to a man named Paul whose name you don't want to forget. He has a beard like your friend Peter's, and for you "Peter" is already associated with "Paul." This serial association during introduction to Paul constitutes the mnemonic device (cognitive event). This "associative event" is recorded, and, when you again see Paul, *remembering* the associative event reveals Paul's name. Note that the process described does not involve the formation of a new association, although what is recorded is based on an existing association. However, associative learning proceeds concurrently: Over repeated meetings with Paul, his name and face are directly learned, and the mnemonic is discarded and may in fact be forgotten. In the present view, his name need no longer be remembered because it is now learned. Subjects studying lists of arbitrary paired associates frequently report using such mnemonic ploys (i.e., natural language mediators; see Underwood & Schulz, 1960).

The use of visual imagery to "connect" arbitrary events is also reported by subjects and can dramatically improve performance (e.g., Paivio & Smythe, 1971). The same analysis applies, except that recording of a visual image is involved, rather than the recording of semantic associations.

SEMANTIC MEMORY, SEMANTIC SKILLS, AND OTHER SKILLS

Given the dichotomy that we have suggested between associative and imaginal memory, it is useful to consider, within this framework, the kind of information that

Tulving (1972) has identified as "semantic memory." As previously indicated, "semantic memory" refers to the organized knowledge a person possesses about words and symbols, about their meaning and referents, and about rules for the manipulation of these symbols.

We suggest that there are two separate and distinct questions involved in an analysis of such semantic information. The first concerns the acquisition process by which basic information is entered; the second question concerns the structure or organization of semantic information.

These two issues (acquisition vs. structure), we feel, are conflated in Tulving's description of semantic memory. Tulving suggests that associations do not figure prominently in the study of semantic memory, since "contiguity of input does not seem to be an important determinant of the structure of the mental thesaurus" (1972, p. 397).[3] We suggest that associative processes *ultimately underlie* the acquisition of *denotative* information, which is represented in semantic "knowledge." For example, learning the names of things rests on associative learning. That such learning is almost by definition largely trans-situational does not negate the involvement of associative processes.

Consider now the issue of structure. To assume that associative acquisition processes underlie semantic information *does not entail* that these processes, in and of themselves, are adequate to explain the structure of semantic knowledge. It is logically possible that there are additional higher-order processes that automatically come into play when multiple associative connections involve common elements. Such higher-order processes could determine the structure or "rules" of semantic knowledge. A parallel analysis can apply to cognitive skills and perceptual–motor skills. That is, acquisition is governed by associative factors, but higher-order processes may be involved in accounting for the structure or rules of the acquired skills. Thus, in these terms, one can view semantic knowledge as semantic skills (see Kolers, 1975, 1976, 1979). It is interesting to note that Tulving (1972) assumes that semantic memory is relatively impervious to interference and loss. These attributes also apply to cognitive skills and perceptual–motor skills (see Kolers, 1975, 1979).

Whether it is necessary to invoke additional higher-order processes to explain the structure of semantic knowledge is, however, not relevant to this discussion. The essential point here is that the acquisition of *denotative* information, which is represented in semantic knowledge, is based on an associative process. As such, it is totally distinct from imaginal memory.

INDIVIDUAL AND SECOND-ORDER IMAGINAL MEMORIES

Two broad classes of information are often distinguished in what we term associative memory. One is information representing an individual associative connection. The other involves "concepts" that can result from some "pooling" of information based on multiple

3. As previously indicated, no "perceptible inputs" are stored in semantic memory, and this serves as a basis for differentiating it from episodic memory. However, as indicated, he permits the possibility that associations may play an explanatory role in episodic memory. Whatever the acquisition process for semantic memory may be, it is also presumably distinct from that involved in a *third* type of memory system, referred to as "cognitive and other procedural skills" (Tulving *et al.*, 1982). As indicated, Kolers (1975, 1976) has shown that cognitive skills (e.g., reading) are sensitively dependent on variations of stimulus features. Therefore semantic memory apparently involves an acquisition process separate from episodic memory and separate from cognitive and procedural skills. (Also see Jacoby & Witherspoon, 1982.)

associations involving common elements. Our concern here is only the dual classification—individual versus, call it, "second-order" information.

The intriguing issue arises of whether there are two classes of information in imaginal memory. Clearly the acquisition of an imaginal memory, as described, entails the recording of a single individual experience. However, the possibility remains that there are second-order memories that involve pooling of a number of individual imaginal memories. We wish to raise this issue. There is no reason to assume that such second-order memories cannot occur in imaginal memory, and there is phenomenological and experimental evidence suggesting that they do.

Take, for example, the case of remembering one's bedroom from childhood. Such remembering clearly involves the use of imaginal memory. However, the room may not be remembered as a series of single perceptual experiences. It is as though a perceptual composite of the room has been developed from multiple single experiences. Furthermore, consider the instruction to imagine a cat that is "brilliant red." It is clear that many people would report a vivid visual image. That an appropriate visual image is evoked has clear implications. First, one could not imagine "brilliant redness" without the previous acquisition of an imaginal memory of something "brilliant red." However, the visual image is clearly not based on the memory of any single experience. Hence the perceptual experience of a brilliant red cat may be evoked by the words but be mediated by the imaginal memory system.

Two general points are involved in the present discussion. The first is that "imaginative" processes may involve the imaginal memory system. (For an interesting example of how such imaginative processes can be experimentally investigated, see a recent study by Watkins & Schiano, 1982.) Secondly, as indicated in the second example given above, words such as "brilliant red" can mediate this imaginative process. Thus words can be used to activate the imaginal memory system. This evocative property of words is distinct from the denotative use of words in that perceptual information is not derived, but involves a conscious perceptual-like experience. By providing operational specifications for the phenomenological notion of "aware" or "event" memory, the present formulation provides a basis for conceptually analyzing such issues as how the evocative property of words is related to the imaginal memory system.

OVERVIEW

We have provided a process explanation (and an operational definition) of how the conscious remembering of individual events represents a unique memory system. A general dichotomy between imaginal and associative memory has been proposed. The formation of associative bonds is excluded from imaginal memory. Remembering conceptually involves a perceptual-like act, but accessing information from associative memory does not. We have proposed that experientially based information on the perceptual attributes of a previous experience is an exclusive and defining feature of aware or imaginal memory. Cognitive events can also be recorded into imaginal memory, and this assumption serves as a basis for analyzing the use of mnemonic devices. Finally, it is indicated that the imaginal memory system may underlie the evocative property of words and imaginative processes.

We have suggested a theory of processes—that is, a process description for two memory systems. Within this framework, we have specified the attributes of information particular to each system. It is clear that we have not suggested any particular theory of imaginal memory (or, for that matter any theory of learning), in the sense that we have not specified what independent variables determine entry, storage, and accessibility in either system. This aspect of the systems is not at issue here. Rather, we have proposed a general organizing schema for two conceptually distinct systems of memory.

In the next section, we apply this process description to Korsakoff amnesia, and attempt to integrate salient features of that body of literature within this framework.

Korsakoff Amnesia

We believe that the distinction between imaginal and associative memory can provide a process description of Korsakoff amnesia. We suggest that amnesics have a profound impairment of imaginal memory for new information, whereas their associative processes are essentially normal, like those of the Learner in our magical experiments. A specific deficit of imaginal memory could involve impairment of recording, or memory, or of remembering (encoding, consolidation, or retrieval). For the purposes of the present discussion, we do not try to identify which aspect or aspects of the system are affected. Rather, we attempt to indicate how salient features of Korsakoff amnesia can be analyzed and integrated within this two-process formulation.

Normal Learning

Our proposal that amnesics have normal learning abilities entails that they are normal in entering information into stimulus or response elements of associative bonds, in the formation of such bonds, and in the retention of all this associative information. Hence conditioning and skill learning provide particularly clear views of associative abilities.

The findings that amnesics are normal in conditioning and in acquiring an impressive variety of skills (see Moscovitch, 1982) follow directly and deductively from the present formulation. It is worth noting that, in this view, it is assumed that *all stimuli* are processed, stored, and retained in associative memory in a normal manner. Thus, in marked contrast to the interpretations of the context and episodic–semantic theories, we exclude the implication that amnesics are selectively deficient in encoding and or storing any particular type of stimulus information *per se* (e.g., situational, task, or temporal). Rather, application of the present process theory to amnesia specifies that all stimulus information is entered and stored normally; however, this is true only for associatively processed information.

As indicated, in all the studies (cited by Moscovitch, 1982) showing normal learning by amnesics, the amnesics expressed, either spontaneously or in response to detailed questions (Weiskrantz & Warrington, 1979), no "aware memory" or "conscious remembering" of the individual events of acquisition sessions. In the present formulation, of course, such "aware memory" or "conscious remembering" of individual events is directly tied to the integrity of imaginal memory. Because of the profound impairment of imaginal-memory processes that we suggest is the case for amnesics, the person is unable to "autobiographically explain" his or her newly acquired ability.

Failure to "Learn"

In light of the present process distinction, many of the experiments used to assess memory in amnesics have confounded learning and imaginal memory. We suggest that analysis within the present framework can bring coherence to these findings.

Probably the most consistently demonstrated failure of amnesics to acquire new information in formal tests is their inability to "learn" lists of arbitrarily paired words (i.e., unrelated paired associates). As indicated, normal subjects typically report that they use mnemonics (natural language mediators, semantic associates, visual imagery) in initial performance on this task (Cutting, 1978; Paivio & Smythe, 1971; Underwood & Schulz, 1960). As we have discussed, using mnemonic devices depends on imaginal memory for a cognitive event (the specific mnemonic formed during study). Thus amnesics, with virtually no imaginal memory, would be forced to rely on learning the lists by rote association, which constitutes a much more difficult task and could explain their usually disastrous performance. In fact, Korsakoff amnesics frequently make *no* correct responses over a number of trials (see Cutting, 1978; Hirst, 1982; Rozin, 1976). The marked deficit of amnesics apparently does not reside in an inability to form mnemonics during study. This is most clearly shown by studies where appropriate mnemonics for relating the pairs (either semantic associates or visual imagery) are directly supplied to subjects. While normal subjects' performance is further enhanced, there is evidence that amnesics obtain no benefit and remain profoundly deficient (see Baddeley, 1982; Cutting, 1978). It should be noted that experimental manipulations (e.g., very brief study and test intervals) that constrain the use of mnemonic devices will make the task more difficult. Increasing the difficulty of a memory task usually disproportionately reduces the performance of amnesics. However, according to the present formulation, constraining the use of mnemonic devices will disproportionately *aid* the relative performance of amnesics, since both normals and amnesics will rely principally on rote associative learning.

Priming and Learning

In contrast to their performance on unrelated paired associates, amnesics have been found to be unimpaired in their ability to recall strongly associated pairs, such as "man–woman" (see Cutting, 1978; Hirst, 1982). However, such performance may simply depend upon the phenomenon of "priming." Early studies of priming showed that the single presentation or emission of a word will dramatically elevate the probability of elicitation of that word by an associate (see Underwood & Schulz, 1960). Thus, priming, by itself, could mediate errorless performance for strongly associated word pairs.

Some recent investigations of "priming" are of particular interest here because of findings that in normal subjects there can be a dissociation between measures of "aware memory" and the priming effects of even a single prior presentation of an item. In studies that have demonstrated such a dissociation effect in normals, the effects of priming have been indexed by such measures as perceptual identification (e.g., Jacoby & Dallas, 1981), word-fragment completion (Tulving *et al.*, 1982), and biased elicitation of a lower-frequency homonym (Jacoby & Witherspoon, 1982). Thus, while it is not clear whether priming involves attentional or learning factors, these studies in normals clearly indicate that it is independent of imaginal memory. In this regard, it is germane to note that Jacoby and Witherspoon (1982) found that Korsakoff amnesics were normal in priming.

Jacoby (1982) has emphasized an important aspect of associative phenomena in tests of recognition memory. On the basis of his own and others' work (Mandler, 1979), he argues that there are two bases for recognition judgments. The first of these is based upon aware memory for the events of the previous presentation of the items; the second is based upon and involves assessment of "trace strength," which is reflected in the subject's perceptual fluency in processing the item. This dichotomy in recognition is similar to the account suggested by Huppert and Piercy (1976), who argued that recognition could depend either upon a judgment of "list membership," or of familiarity determined by "trace strength." Thus Jacoby converges with Huppert and Piercy in suggesting that recognition may involve two distinct processes. One of these processes involves aware memory, while the other is either attentional or associatively based. Of particular interest here is that Huppert and Piercy and Jacoby have suggested that since amnesics are impaired in "aware" memory, they rely only on effects like priming. Furthermore, these investigators have indicated how singular reliance on this effect of prior presentation can account for the well-documented susceptibility of amnesics to interference and intrusion errors. Hence, we follow these authors' suggestions and conclude that susceptibility to interference is a secondary and not a causal feature of the symptoms of Korsakoff amnesia.

Findings that cued recall can elevate the performance of amnesics (e.g., McDowall, 1979; Warrington & Weiskrantz, 1970) can also be interpreted as being mediated by the effects of priming. For example, McDowall (1979) found that providing amnesics with the category name facilitated recall of category members that had been previously presented, and hence primed (i.e., members of the target list). Category members have preexperimental associations with the category name; thus they could be evoked by the category name, since they were primed by virtue of their previous presentation. Hence, elevated performance produced by cued recall clearly does not imply that imaginal memory is involved. In this regard, an observation on amnesics by Weiskrantz and Warrington (1975) is to the point: "When patients correctly identify an item in a cued-recall task, they often are uncertain they have seen the item before; i.e., the patients do not appear to know that they are remembering" (p. 423). Thus, in cued-recall tasks, as in newly acquired skills, amnesics have no autobiographical explanation for their successful performance.

Concluding Remarks

Earlier in this chapter, we suggest that a task for current theorizing is not so much to recognize as to explain how the conscious remembering of an individual event represents a unique process. We believe that we have provided such an explanation, based on the assumption that remembering involves a perceptual-like act and is totally distinct from the formation of associative bonds. The proposal that imaginal memory is virtually destroyed in Korsakoff amnesia, while associative abilities continue unabated, integrates findings in amnesia and provides a systematic basis for separating the two kinds of knowing originally identified in Claparède's (1911/1951) clinical insight. In particular, we believe that this formulation identifies the analytic tools that may be used to delineate the specific aspects of imaginal memory that are defective in amnesia.

Finally, we suggest that the present formulation provides a conceptual framework for examining experimentally the memory system that Bergson (1896/1911) called "the memory which imagines."

ACKNOWLEDGMENTS

We thank Louise Goldhar for her assistance with typing the manuscript, and her witty editorial comments. Thanks are also due to Joanne Cordingley for help with the references.

REFERENCES

Baddeley, A. Amnesia: A minimal model and an interpretation. In L. S. Cermak (Ed.), *Human memory and amnesia*. Hillsdale, N.J.: Erlbaum, 1982.

Bergson, H. [*Matter and memory*] (M. Paul & W. Palmer, trans.). New York: Macmillan, 1911. (Originally published, 1896.)

Brooks, D. N., & Baddeley, A. D. What can amnesic patients learn? *Neuropsychologia*, 1976, *14*, 111–122.

Butters, N., Lewis, R., Cermak, L. S., & Goodglass, H. Material specific deficits in alcoholic Korsakoff patients. *Neuropsychologia*, 1973, *11*, 291–299.

Claparede, E. Recognition et moiité. *Archives de Psychologie*, 1911, *11*, 79–90. (Reprinted as Recognition and "me-ness." In D. Rapaport [Ed.], *Organization and pathology of thought*. New York: Columbia University Press, 1951.)

Cohen, N., & Squire, L. Preserved learning and retention of pattern analyzing skills in amnesia: Dissociation of knowing how and knowing that. *Science*, 1980, *210*, 207–210.

Cutting, J. A. A cognitive approach to Korsakoff's syndrome. *Cortex*, 1978, *14*, 485–495.

Gibson, J. J. *Ecological approach to visual perception*. Boston: Houghton Mifflin, 1979.

Gormezano, I., & Moore, J. W. Classical conditioning. In M. H. Marx (Ed.), *Learning: Processes*. London: Collier-Macmillan, 1969.

Hirst, W. The amnesic syndrome: Descriptions and explanations. *Psychological Bulletin*, 1982, *91*, 435–460.

Howard, I. P. Displacing the optical array. In S. J. Freedman (Ed.), *The neuropsychology of spatially oriented behavior*. Homewood, Ill.: Dorsey Press, 1968.

Huppert, F. A., & Piercy, M. Recognition memory in amnesia patients: Effect of temporal context and familiarity of material. *Cortex*, 1976, *12*, 3–20.

Huppert, F. A., & Piercy, M. Recognition memory in amnesic patients: A defect of acquisition? *Neuropsychologia*, 1977, *15*, 643–652.

Huppert, F. A., & Piercy, M. The role of trace strength in recency and frequency judgements by amnesic and control subjects. *Quarterly Journal of Experimental Psychology*, 1978, *30* 347–354.

Jacoby, L. L. Knowing and remembering: Some parallels in the behavior of Korsakoff patients and normals. In L. S. Cermak (Ed.), *Human memory and amnesia*. Hillsdale, N.J.: Erlbaum, 1982.

Jacoby, L. L., & Dallas, M. On the relationship between autobiographical memory and perceptual learning. *Journal of Experimental Psychology: General*, 1981, *110*, 306–340.

Jacoby, L. L., & Witherspoon, D. Remembering without awareness. *Canadian Journal of Psychology*, 1982, *36*, 300–324.

Katzaroff, D. Contribution à l'étude de la recognition. *Archives de Psychologie*, 1911, *11*, 2–78.

Kinsbourne, M., & Wood, F. Short-term memory processes and the amnesic syndrome. In D. Deutsch & J. A. Deutsch (Eds.), *Short-term memory*. New York: Academic Press, 1975.

Kinsbourne, M., & Wood, F. Theoretical considerations regarding the episodic–semantic memory distinction. In L. S. Cermak (Ed.), *Human memory and amnesia*. Hillsdale, N.J.: Erlbaum, 1982.

Koffka, K. *Principles of gestalt psychology*. New York: Harcourt, Brace, 1935.

Kolers, P. A. Remembering operations. *Memory and Cognition*, 1973, *1*, 347–355.

Kolers, P. A. Specificity of operation in sentence recognition. *Cognitive Psychology*, 1975, *7*, 289–306.

Kolers, P. A. A pattern analyzing basis of recognition. In L. S. Cermak & F. I. M. Craik (Eds.), *Levels of processing in human memory*. Hillsdale, N.J.: Erlbaum, 1979.

Krauss, S. Untersuchungen über Aufbau und Störung der menschlichen Handlung. *Archive für die gesamte Psychologie,* 1930, *77*, 649–692.

MacCurdy, J. T. *Common principles in psychology and physiology*. Cambridge, Mass.: Harvard University Press, 1928.

McDowall, J. Effects of encoding instructions and retrieval cueing on recall in Korsakoff patients. *Memory and Cognition*, 1979, *7*, 232–239.

Mandler, G. Organization and repetition. In L. Nilsson (Ed.), *Perspectives on memory research*. Hillsdale, N.J. Erlbaum, 1979.

Moscovitch, M. Multiple dissociations of function in amnesia. In L. S. Cermak (Ed.), *Human memory and amnesia*.

Nielsen, J. M. *Memory and amnesia*. Los Angeles: San Lucas Press, 1958.

Norman, D. A., & Rumelhart, D. E. A system for perception and memory. In D. A. Norman (Ed.), *Models of human memory*. New York: Academic Press, 1970.

Paivio, A., & Smythe, P. C. Word imagery, frequency and meaningfulness in short-term memory. *Psychonomic Science*, 1971, *22*, 333–335.

Pavlov, I. P. [*Conditioned reflexes*] (G. V. Anrep, trans.). London: Oxford University Press, 1927.

Reiff, R., & Scheerer, M. *Memory and hypnotic age regression*. New York International Universities Press, 1959.

Rescorla, R. A., & Wagner, A. R. A theory of Pavlovian conditioning: Variations in the effectiveness of reinforcement and nonreinforcement. In A. Black & W. F. Prokasy (Eds.), *Classical conditioning* (Vol. 2, *Current research and theory*). New York: Appleton-Century-Crofts, 1972.

Ribot, T. A. *Diseases of memory*. New York: Appleton, 1882.

Rozin, P. The psychobiological approach to human memory. In M. R. Rosenzweig & E. L. Bennett (Eds.), *Neural mechanisms of learning and memory*. Cambridge, Mass.: MIT Press, 1976.

Siegel, S. Morphine analgesic tolerance: Its situation specificity supports a Pavlovian conditioning model. *Science*, 1976, *193*, 323–325.

Stern, L. D. A review of theories of human amnesia. *Memory and Cognition*, 1981, *9*, 247–262.

Tulving, E. Episodic and semantic memory. In E. Tulving & W. Donaldson (Eds.), *Organization of memory*. New York: Academic Press, 1972.

Tulving, E., Schacter, D. L., & Stark, H. A. Priming effects in word-fragment completion are independent of recognition memory. *Journal of Experimental Psychology: Learning, Memory, and Cognition*, 1982, *8*, 336–342.

Underwood, B. J., & Schulz, R. W. *Meaningfulness and verbal learning*. Chicago: J. B. Lippincott, 1960.

Warrington, E. K., & Weiskrantz, L. Amnesic syndrome: Consolidation or retrieval? *Nature*, 1970, *228*, 628–630.

Watkins, M. J., & Schiano, D. J. Chromatic imaging: An effect of mental colouring on recognition memory. *Canadian Journal of Psychology*, 1982, *36*, 291–299.

Weiskrantz, L., & Warrington, E. K. The problem of the amnesic syndrome in man and animals. In R. L. Isaacson & K. H. Pribram (Eds.), *The hippocampus* (Vol. 2). New York: Plenum, 1975.

Weiskrantz, L., & Warrington, E. K. Conditioning in amnesic patients. *Neuropsychologia*, 1979, *17*, 187–194.

Winocur, G., & Kinsbourne, M. Contextual cueing as an aid to Korsakoff amnesics. *Neuropsychologia*, 1978, *16*, 671–682.

Wood, F., Ebert, V., & Kinsbourne, M. The episodic–semantic memory distinction in memory and amnesia: Clinical and experimental observations. In L. S. Cermak (Ed.), *Human memory and amnesia*. Hillsdale, N.J.: Erlbaum, 1982.

Preserved Learning Capacity in Amnesia: Evidence for Multiple Memory Systems

Neal J. Cohen

Introduction

The amnesic syndrome is a severe and pervasive disorder of learning and memory that affects both verbal and nonverbal material, irrespective of the modality of stimulus presentation. For example, we know from extensive study of the noted amnesic patient H. M. (e.g., Corkin, Sullivan, Twitchell, & Grove, 1981; Milner, Corkin, & Teuber, 1968; Scoville & Milner, 1957) that the memory impairment can extend to words, digits, paragraphs, faces, names, maze routes, spatial layouts, geometric shapes, nonsense patterns, nonsense syllables, clicks, tunes, tones, public and personal events, and more. H. M. does not know his age, the date, the place where he lives, or the recent history of his mother and father. Nonetheless, it has been shown that H. M. and other patients can, in some circumstances, demonstrate very impressive memory performance. Indeed, amnesic patients can sometimes acquire information at a normal rate and can maintain normal performance across considerable delay intervals. These findings have raised fundamental questions about the nature of the amnesic syndrome, about differences among kinds of memory, and about the way in which memory is organized in the brain. This chapter considers the examples of good memory performance in amnesia, focusing predominantly on controlled experimental findings, and provides a framework for understanding these findings. It is argued that such examples reflect a preserved learning capacity in amnesia, mediated by a memory system that operates independently of the one compromised in amnesia.

The first major claim of this chapter is that the examples of preserved learning in amnesia can be categorized in terms of the following two classes of phenomena: (1) intact ability (i.e., *normal* vis-à-vis control subjects) to acquire and retain a variety of motor, perceptual, and cognitive skills, despite poor memory for the learning episodes and despite impaired memory-test performance for the facts that are normally accumulated in using the skills; and (2) normal facilitation or other alterations of the ability to perform certain processing tests based upon prior exposure to or priming of the to-be-tested stimulus materials (i.e., "repetition-priming effects"), despite impaired recall or recognition memory for these materials. Each class of findings is discussed in turn.

In considering the data, emphasis is placed on comparisons between amnesic patients and control subjects, focusing in particular on evidence for spared (i.e., normal)

Neal J. Cohen. Department of Psychology and Clinical Research Center, Massachusetts Institute of Technology, Cambridge, Massachusetts.

performance by amnesic patients.[1] Ideas about spared learning and retention in amnesia have too often in the past been influenced by anecdotal reports and informal observations, which can seldom be interpreted unambiguously. One often-cited anecdotal account that illustrates this point comes from Claparède (1911). Upon shaking hands with a patient with Korsakoff syndrome, Claparède pricked her finger with a pin hidden in his hand. Subsequently, whenever he again attempted to shake the patient's hand, she promptly withdrew it. When he questioned her about this behavior, she replied, "Isn't it allowed to withdraw one's hand?" and "Perhaps there is a pin hidden in your hand," and finally, "Sometimes pins are hidden in hands" (p. 84). Thus, the patient learned the appropriate response based on previous experience, but she never seemed to attribute her behavior to personal memory of some previously experienced event. One might be tempted to conclude that the acquired avoidance response provides evidence for some spared learning capacity in amnesia. However, though this amnesic patient did show a long-lasting avoidance response, one cannot be sure that the patient's avoidance behavior would last as long as would the avoidance behavior of a normal control subject. Nor can one be sure that the patient's avoidance behavior would be reserved for the perpetrator as specifically as would likely be a control subject's behavior. Barbizet (1970) reported that the response to being pricked with a pin can be quite *short-lived* for an amnesic patient:

> If the examiner pricks his hand with a needle while shaking hands with him, he withdraws it with a cry; twenty seconds later, he will offer his hand again without distrust, and the same performance may be repeated several times. Only after 15 days of conditioning does he begin to show a certain reticence over offering his hand to the examiner several times in close succession, but he will always offer it at the first meeting of the day with complete confidence. (p. 38)

Such considerations give us pause in accepting anecdotal reports as evidence for preserved learning by amnesic patients. The reason for caution is that there appear to be differences among aspects of memory in their effective strength or lifetime in normal human memory: The aspects of memory tapped by some measures are lost or become unavailable earlier during the time after learning than do the aspects of memory tapped by other measures. Given any two aspects of memory that differ with regard to lifetime, one can choose the measures and the delay interval to produce performance that reveals the presence of one in the absence of the other. Relating this argument to the example discussed above, it is reasonable to suppose that for all people, amnesic patients and normal control subjects alike, memory for the perpetrator of the pin-prick episode and for the episode itself could fade before memory for the fact that shaking hands may occasionally have untoward consequences. Indeed, much of our general knowledge about the world has just this character. We can see nothing in this account, then, that warrants a special claim of dissociation among kinds or aspects of memory in amnesia. Only when an aspect of memory performance in amnesic patients is normal with respect to that of control subjects can we confidently entertain the hypothesis of a dissociation in memory.

---

1. A detailed discussion of the need for explicit criteria to establish whether different memory systems are dissociable can be found elsewhere (Cohen & Schacter, 1984). In order to increase the confidence of claims for dissociation, performance based on the operation of a system presumed to be dissociated from that of a damaged system must be intact rather than relatively preserved.

Evidence of Preserved Learning in Amnesia

Acquisition of Skills

PERCEPTUAL–MOTOR SKILLS

The earliest and most clearly documented demonstration of potentially preserved learning in the amnesic syndrome comes from studies of perceptual–motor skills. Milner (1962) and Corkin (1965, 1968) showed that the patient H. M. could exhibit considerable learning and retention of such skills, despite his profound global amnesia. For example, H. M. steadily learned a mirror-tracing task across 3 days of testing, reducing his error score and the time required for completion (Milner, 1962). This occurred without any indication in his verbal reports of his accumulating experience with the task. In addition, despite H. M.'s inability to learn the correct sequence of turns through a 10-choice tactual maze over 80 trials, he nevertheless gradually reduced the time required to complete each trial (Corkin, 1965). H. M. also demonstrated dramatic learning on two tracking tasks: rotary pursuit and bimanual tracking. In each case, H. M. increased his time on target across 7 days of testing. When retested 1 week later on the rotary-pursuit task (bimanual tracking was not retested), H. M.'s performance was at the level of performance attained at the end of training 1 week earlier (Corkin, 1968). It should be noted, however, that H. M.'s rotary-pursuit performance differed from that of the control subjects in two important respects. First, despite H. M.'s obvious learning and retention of the task, his time-on-target performance across sessions was nonetheless inferior to that of the control subjects. Second, the pattern of contact scores (i.e., the change across trials in the number of times the subject falls off and gets back onto target) exhibited by H. M. in acquiring the skill was different from that exhibited by control subjects. That is, the control subjects lowered their contact scores with increasing practice, indicating that they learned how to maintain contact longer with the target and fall off target less often. By contrast, H.M. had higher contact scores with increasing practice. This result suggested that he did not improve his ability to maintain contact with the target, but instead learned to get back on target more rapidly after an error. Such differences between H. M.'s performance and that of the controls seem to argue against a straightforward sparing of capacity for perceptual–motor skill learning, and it has played an important role in some accounts of preserved learning (e.g., Wickelgren, 1979). Yet, further investigations of rotary pursuit indicate that *normal* learning and retention of this perceptual–motor skill can occur in a variety of different amnesic groups and that H. M.'s discrepant performance is related to poor motor capacities rather than poor motor-skill learning capacities. These findings, to be described next, suggest that the learning of perceptual–motor skills in amnesia does indeed reflect a preserved capacity.

Learning and retention of rotary pursuit has been reported in amnesic patients with Korsakoff syndrome (Brooks & Baddeley, 1976; Cermak, Lewis, Butters, & Goodglass, 1973; Cohen, 1981), postencephalitic patients (Brooks & Baddeley, 1976), patients receiving bilateral ECT (Cohen, 1981), and the diencephalic patient N. A. (Cohen, 1981). Most importantly, the time-on-target performance of amnesic patients, in almost all of these cases, was equivalent to that of normal control subjects. But what of H. M.'s failure to exhibit performance comparable to that of the control subjects? Corkin (1968) attributed it not to his memory deficit, but rather to his chronic slowness: He was inferior to the controls in reaction time and in rate of spontaneous activity (serial ordering of digits). This deficit in rate of activity would be penalized heavily in such tasks as rotary pursuit, where the rate of movement is controlled by the apparatus. The view that H. M.'s failure to attain the same level of rotary-pursuit performance as control subjects can be attributed to his chronic slowness receives support from subsequent tests of his skill learning in *untimed* tasks, for which he demonstrated normal learning and retention. This is described below. With regard to the differences between H. M. and his controls in contact scores, it should be noted that these differences were observed when their performance (measured by time on target) also differed. That is, the comparison of contact scores is complicated by the fact that H. M. and the control subjects were not matched for level of performance. In the only other study that reported both time-on-target performance and contact scores (Cohen, 1981), it was found that amnesic patients whose time-on-target performance was equivalent to that of control subjects demonstrated a completely normal pattern of contact scores. Particularly illuminating was the finding that the pattern of contact scores was related closely to the level of time-on-target performance: By comparing various patient and control groups at different levels of difficulty of the task (i.e., requiring tracking at different speeds), it was possible to show a change in the pattern of contact scores from a pattern like that shown by H. M. to that shown by his controls as the level of time-on-target performance increased. Thus, the differences in contact scores could be accounted for solely by differences in level of performance.

Other claims of perceptual–motor learning in amnesic patients come from a study by Brooks and Baddeley (1976), who found a normal reduction across trials in the time needed to complete both the adult version of the Porteus visual maze and a 12-piece jigsaw puzzle. For each of these tasks, amnesic patients exhibited the familiar pattern of excellent retention when retested 1 week after initial learning, despite an inability to remember their previous experience with the tasks. Taken together, the studies of perceptual–motor skill learning suggest a preserved learning capacity in amnesia.

PERCEPTUAL SKILLS

Recent investigations indicate that the capacity for preserved skill learning in amnesia extends beyond perceptual–motor tasks. A particularly clear example comes from a study of mirror reading in amnesia (Cohen & Squire, 1980), based on similar tasks studied with normal subjects (Kolers, 1975, 1976, 1979). Subjects saw triads of 8- to 10-letter low-frequency words presented by mirror reflection in a tachistoscope. Subjects read five blocks of 10 word triads on each of 3 consecutive days and also on a fourth day approximately 13 weeks later. For each block of 10 word triads, half were common to all blocks (repeated) and half were unique (nonrepeated). By analyzing separately the time required to read each nonrepeated and repeated word triad, it was possible to evaluate the ability to acquire the operations or procedures necessary for mirror reading, as well as the ability to benefit from frequent repetition of specific words. The results are shown in Figure 10-1. Results for the nonrepeated word triads indicate that the amnesic patients learned the mirror-reading skill at a rate equivalent to that of matched control subjects, and they retained the skill normally over an interval of 3 months. Results for the repeated word triads indicate the facilitative effect on reading speed of previous experience with

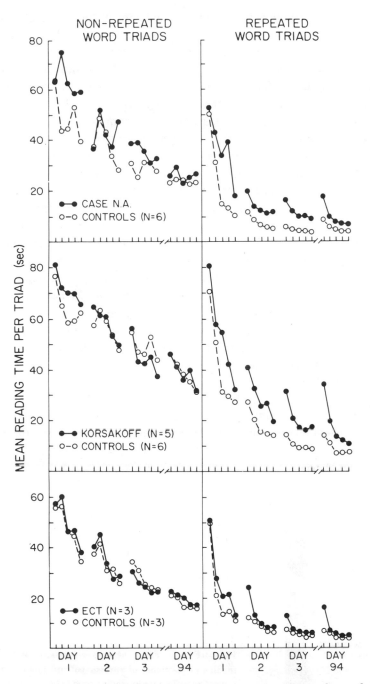

FIGURE 10-1. Acquisition and retention of mirror-reading skill in amnesic patients and normal control subjects. Performance on the nonrepeated (unique) items, which reflects the ability to acquire the rules or procedures necessary for reading mirror-reversed text, was equivalent for the two groups; however, performance on the repeated items, which depends in addition on memory for the specific words presented, was impaired in amnesic patients. (From N. J. Cohen, *Neuropsychological evidence for a distinction between procedural and declarative knowledge in human memory and amnesia.* Unpublished doctoral dissertation, University of California at San Diego, 1981. Reprinted by permission.)

particular word triads for both amnesic patients and control subjects. Note, however, that this facilitative effect on reading speed of repeating specific words was smaller for the patients than for the controls, particularly on the first block of each new testing day. This can be seen more clearly in Figure 10-2, which provides a measure of the forgetting between testing days (mean difference in reading time between the last block of 10 triads on each testing day and the first block on the following testing day). For performance on the nonrepeated word triads, which depends solely on learning the operations or procedures required for mirror reading, there was no forgetting between testing days by either the amnesic patients or the normal control subjects. However, for performance on the repeated word triads, which depends in addition on memory for the specific word triads that were repeated from block to block, there was marked forgetting by the amnesic patients. This dissociation between the intact ability of amnesic patients to acquire the mirror-reading skill and their inability to benefit as much as normal subjects from the repetition of specific items was reflected also in verbal reports. Whereas none of the amnesic patients reported upon questioning that word triads had been repeated during the task, all of the control subjects reported spontaneously that some word triads were repeated frequently. Amnesic patients who were asked to explain why they read some word triads so rapidly claimed invariably that those triads were "easier" than were the others.

Another indication that amnesia is associated with a deficit in specific-item memory, despite completely intact acquisition and retention of the mirror-reading skill, came from a recognition-memory test administered after the third day of testing. The amnesic patients exhibited markedly impaired recognition memory for both the repeated and the non-repeated words that had been read during the course of the experiment. For example, whereas all of the control subjects correctly recognized all 15 repeated words, none of the amnesic patients could identify all of the repeated words. To summarize the results of this experiment, then, amnesic patients learned and retained normally the pattern-analyzing operations or encoding procedures required for mirror reading, but demonstrated poor

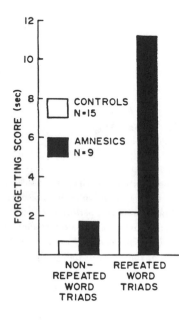

FIGURE 10-2. Effect of between-session forgetting on mirror-reading performance of amnesic patients and normal control subjects. The difference in reading time between the last block of each session and the first block of the subsequent one is equally small in both amnesics and controls for the nonrepeated items, but is disproportionately large in the amnesics for the repeated items. (From N. J. Cohen & L. R. Squire, Preserved learning and retention of pattern analyzing skill in amnesia: Dissociation of knowing how and knowing that. *Science*, 1980, *210*, 207–210. Copyright 1980 by the American Association for the Advancement of Science. Reprinted by permission.)

memory for the specific-item information that would normally result from applying these operations or procedures, and had little or no recollection of the learning experience itself. Moscovitch (1982b) has obtained similar results in a study of mirror reading of lines of text.

COGNITIVE SKILLS

The discrepancy between normal acquisition of skills and impaired memory-test performance for specific-item information can be seen in the cognitive domain as well. Clear support comes from a study of the ability of amnesic patients, including H. M., to learn the cognitive skills required for optimal solution to the Tower of Hanoi puzzle (Cohen & Corkin, 1981). The Tower of Hanoi puzzle is a complex problem-solving task involving at least 31 steps; it has been studied extensively in normal subjects (e.g., Anzai & Simon, 1979; Karat, 1982; Simon, 1975), providing a wealth of information about the strategies used by subjects to solve the puzzle during the course of training. The puzzle consists of five wooden blocks and three pegs, as shown in Figure 10-3. At the outset, all five blocks are arranged on the leftmost peg with the blocks in size order, the smallest block on the top and the largest one on the bottom. Subjects are asked to move the blocks from the leftmost "Start" peg to the rightmost "Finish" peg. They can only move one block at a time, and can never place a larger block on top of a smaller one. To solve the puzzle, subjects must shuttle the blocks back and forth using all three pegs. The optimal solution (i.e., the solution accomplished in the fewest moves possible) requires 31 moves. There is only one sequence of moves that will lead to a 31-move solution. Subjects are asked to solve the puzzle four times on each of 4 consecutive days, with the aim of reaching this optimal solution.

Results with 12 amnesic patients, including H. M., indicated a normal rate of learning for this task across the 4 days of testing (see Table 10-1). Normal acquisition of the cognitive skills required to solve the puzzle occurred despite little or no recollection of having worked at the task previously and despite poor insight into what was being learned. This point was illustrated in a second experiment, in which the puzzle was prepared beforehand to portray various intermediate stages of completion. Some of these configurations, but not others, portrayed stages of completion that subjects would have passed through in solving the puzzle in an optimal way (i.e., that were "on the optimal-solution path"). The patients were markedly impaired in their ability to distinguish configurations

FIGURE 10-3. Schematic for the Tower of Hanoi puzzle. (From N. J. Cohen, *Neuropsychological evidence for a distinction between procedural and declarative knowledge in human memory and amnesia.* Unpublished doctoral dissertation, University of California at San Diego, 1981. Reprinted by permission.)

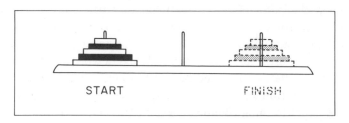

TABLE 10-1. Number of Moves to Solution

Group	Session number			
	1	2	3	4
Amnesics ($n = 12$)	46.6	41.6	37.7	33.4
	(33–100)	(31–63)	(31–55)	(31–51)
Controls ($n = 8$)	48.4	41.6	39.3	34.1
	(31–88)	(31–69)	(31–69)	(31–45)

Note. Minimum number of moves = 31.

that were on the optimal-solution path and that they would have encountered previously from configurations that were not on the optimal-solution path and that might never have been encountered previously. Nonetheless, they were as good as control subjects at completing the puzzle from all stages of completion that were presented to them. In a final experiment, patients were asked to solve the puzzle with the middle peg, and not the rightmost peg, serving as the goal. Successful performance on this transfer task required a different sequence of movements from the one practiced during training on the initial task, though the problem had the same deep structure and could be solved using the same rules. Patients had no trouble solving this transfer task when tested following the fourth day of training in the initial task. These and other findings indicated that the patients had learned the deep structure of the problem, acquiring the cognitive skills necessary to solve the puzzle in the optimal way, despite their profound memory impairments. In addition, long-term relation of the skill was demonstrated in a 1-year follow-up study with the patient H. M., who showed very impressive savings (see Table 10-2).

Repetition-Priming Effects

A second class of examples of preserved learning capacity in amnesia comes from studies of repetition-priming effects. A growing literature documents that the ability of both amnesic patients and normal control subjects to perform a variety of processing tasks (e.g., naming, spelling, categorization) can be facilitated or otherwise altered by prior exposure to (i.e., priming of) the to-be-tested stimulus materials, even when the materials cannot be recalled or recognized.

The facilitation of test performance in amnesia due to repetition priming is perhaps best illustrated by studies involving the identification of fragmented verbal or nonverbal material. The ability of amnesic patients to identify fragmented drawings or words presented in varying degrees of completion was markedly facilitated when retested with the same material; however, the patients could not remember being previously exposed to the material and were impaired in standard tests of recall or recognition (Milner *et al.*, 1968; Warrington & Weiskrantz, 1968, 1970). This facilitation of performance can be seen as reflecting priming of the previously presented drawings or words, rather than a more general learning of how to complete fragmented materials, as indicated by the reported absence of facilitation for presentation of a set of fragmented materials different from what was presented during initial training (Baddeley, 1982; Weiskrantz, 1978).

Similar findings have been obtained in a somewhat different paradigm, in which prior presentation of a list of words was found to bias the completion of three-letter word stems in favor of those words presented previously, rather than other words sharing the same initial letters (e.g., Graf, Squire, & Mandler, 1984; Warrington & Weiskrantz, 1970, 1974). The word-completion performance of amnesic patients was biased to the same extent as was the performance of normal control subjects, despite the patients' markedly impaired recall or recognition of the target words.

It is important to note that in other studies using a superficially identical method, the performance of amnesic patients was again consistently biased toward producing words that had been presented previously, but not to the same extent as the performance of control subjects (Mayes, Meudell, & Neary, 1978; Squire, Wetzel, & Slater, 1978; Wetzel & Squire, 1982). This discrepancy in results can be explained by the nature of the test instructions; its exposition here should help to clarify the nature of the intact priming effects in amnesia (see Graf *et al.*, 1984). In the reports finding the performance of amnesic patients to be poorer than normal, the patients were asked explicitly to recall the previously presented words using the word fragments as cues. Performance with this method of *cued recall* would appear to depend upon explicit, intentional retrieval of episodic memory, which is compromised in amnesia. By contrast, in the reports finding normal performance by amnesic patients, the patients were asked simply to "identify" the word fragments (Weiskrantz, 1982) or were told to "complete each [fragment] to form the first word that came to mind" (Graf *et al.*, 1984), an instruction that seems to direct the subject away from an intentional retrieval of memory for the presented words (Baddeley, 1982; Graf *et al.*, 1984; Jacoby, Chapter 15, this volume). Performance with this method would appear to depend upon some more incidental or automatic process (Baddeley, 1982; Jacoby, Chapter 15, this volume) whereby performance is automatically influenced by the level of activation produced by prior stimulus presentation (Mandler, 1980). Other accounts have called this process "perceptual fluency" (Jacoby & Dallas, 1981; Jacoby & Witherspoon, 1982) or the "hot-tubes effect" (Rozin, 1976). Such a process is here claimed to be intact in amnesia, as is described below.

TABLE 10-2. Patient H. M.: Number of Moves to Solution

	Session number			
	1	2	3	4
Mean	46.3	41.8	37.3	40.0
Range	39–53	34–46	31–42	35–51
	5	6	7	8
Mean	34.5	35.5	33.0	32.0
Range	31–39	35–37	31–35	31–35
	9[a]	10[a]	11[a]	12[a]
Mean	37.5	33.3	32.5	32.0
Range	31–47	31–37	31–35	31–35

Note. Minimum number of moves = 31.
[a]One year later.

Consistent with this account are a number of other findings of repetition-priming effects in performance-based tasks that direct the subject away from intentional memory retrieval. In one study (Jacoby & Witherspoon, 1982), five patients with Korsakoff syndrome were asked orienting questions designed to prime the lower-frequency meanings of selected homonyms (e.g., "Name a musical instrument that employs a reed"). Later, the patients were asked to spell a set of words that included the homonyms (i.e., "reed–read") in addition to nonhomonyms. For the homonyms, the patients tended to respond with the spelling that corresponded to the low-frequency meaning biased by the orienting questions. Indeed, this priming effect was as large for the amnesic patients as it was for normal control subjects, despite the patients' impairment with respect to the controls in recognizing which words they had heard in the orienting questions.

Another study (Moscovitch, 1982a, 1982b) found repetition-priming effects in a lexical-decision task. Subjects were asked to judge whether individually presented words or nonword letter strings were legitimate English words. Decisions were speeded upon re-presentation of the same items, even when the patients could not remember that those items had occurred previously.

Further evidence for repetition-priming effects in amnesic patients despite impaired recall and recognition of the primed material derives from our work on mirror reading (Cohen & Squire, 1980). As already discussed, the performance of the amnesic patients documented in Figure 10-1 illustrates both a normal improvement across trials in reading speed for the nonrepeated items, and a significant but nonetheless subnormal facilitation of performance for repeated items. In our original description of these data, we stressed the dissociation between normal performance on the nonrepeated items and impaired performance on the repeated items. However, what is of interest in the present context is the fact that all amnesic patients showed some amount of facilitation in reading repeated items whose previous occurrence they could not recognize. We would submit that the facilitation for repeated items is the normal repetition-priming effect. Reading words already presented on previous occasions invokes the operation of precisely the same encoding processes on each occasion, leading to an increase in their efficacy or level of activation. This is how Kolers (1979) interpreted the ability of college students to read more quickly pages of geometrically inverted text that had been presented 1 year earlier and had long since been forgotten. But what of the fact that the facilitation of performance for repeated words demonstrated by the amnesic patients failed to match that demonstrated by the control subjects? Based upon the reports of the subjects, it seems most reasonable to conclude that this reflects the amnesic patients' deficit in recall and recognition memory. Upon reading the first word in each repeated triad, the control subjects could recognize it as a repeated item and showed facilitation by recalling the other two members of the triad without having to actually read them. The amnesic patients, on the other hand, could not generate the triad by such a use of memory; they simply read each word in repeated triad more rapidly than they had previously.

Finally, evidence for repetition-priming effects can be inferred from informal observations that amnesic patients can achieve perception in depth of random-dot stereograms more rapidly as a function of previous experience with the stimulus materials and can demonstrate retention of the McCullough color aftereffect (Weiskrantz, 1978), and from the report that amnesic patients can improve their performance in detecting anomalous features of repeatedly presented line drawings from the McGill Picture Anomalies Test (Baddeley, 1982; Warrington & Weiskrantz, 1973).

What is so striking about all of these examples is that prior exposure to stimuli can influence the performance of amnesic patients in a normal manner, even though the patients cannot recall or recognize those same stimuli. Yet, in normal control subjects, too, the facilitative effects of prior experience on subsequent performance with the same materials can be independent of recognition memory (Jacoby & Dallas, 1981; Jacoby & Witherspoon, 1982; Scarborough, Gerard, & Cortese, 1979; Tulving, Schacter, & Stark, 1982). In these studies, prior exposure to a word list facilitated later perceptual identification of the same words when presented very briefly (Jacoby & Dallas, 1981) and facilitated completion of the same words when presented in fragmented form (Tulving *et al.*, 1982), regardless of whether or not the subjects successfully recognized the previous occurrence of those words.

On the face of it, these parallel findings in amnesic patients and normal control subjects would seem easily explained by assuming that recognition is simply a less sensitive index of memory than a performance-bound measure such as word completion. Nelson (1978) has demonstrated elegantly that performance measures of retention based on savings can reveal evidence for memory in normal control subjects at a time after learning when recognition memory is at chance. Applying this account to amnesia, one need only imagine that the memory of amnesic patients is so weak (due to inadequate encoding or faulty storage) or retrieval so inefficient that only the most sensitive tests assessing particular aspects of memory will provide evidence of memory for prior experience. The key to this account is the notion of a unitary memory system with different aspects of memory that differ with respect to functional lifetime and availability, as measured by particular tests. On this view, different aspects of memory could be dissociated by making memory weak and by carefully choosing one's test, as discussed earlier. Such an argument has been advanced by Meudell and Mayes (1981), who tested normal control subjects long after learning and reproduced dissociation between facilitated performance and impaired recognition that is exhibited by amnesic patients soon after learning. By their view, the dissociation between facilitation of performance and impaired recognition memory is related to the differential sensitivity of the two measures to different aspects of memory; it will be observed whenever memory is sufficiently weak, whether in amnesic patients tested soon after learning or in control subjects tested long after learning.

This interpretation of preserved learning capacity in amnesic patients is refuted by the evidence. First, we have already discussed studies demonstrating the independence of recognition memory and priming effects in normal subjects, even when recognition-memory performance is very good. Indeed, the finding of independence means that priming effects are uncorrelated with the level of recognition-memory performance. Accordingly, the results in amnesic patients cannot be explained by supposing that priming simply measures the same underlying memory in a more sensitive way than recognition-memory techniques. Second, the evidence argues against the claim that patterns of amnesic performance simply mimic the patterns of performance that appear in normal subjects during the course of forgetting, when their memory is sufficiently weak. Priming effects for words are as large in amnesic patients as in normal subjects with good memory performance, and they can disappear at an entirely normal rate in amnesics during the time after stimulus presentation. These findings mean that priming effects are normal in amnesic patients, not that priming effects reflect an aspect of memory that is less susceptible to weakening of memory.

All of these examples of priming effects share in common with the instances of skill acquisition already discussed an observable influence of previous experience on subsequent behavior, in the absence of memory for the previous experience itself and despite poor insight about the information that must have been acquired. Priming effects and skill acquisition nonetheless seem to differ in the specificity with which the beneficial effects of experience are expressed: Priming effects are restricted to the enhancement of performance for re-presentation of the identical stimulus materials, and skill learning is generalizable to all material handled by the same operations or procedures. This difference notwithstanding, the facilitation of performance despite impaired memory, characterized by both skill acquisition and repetition-priming effects, suggests a fundamental dissociation between the kind of information processing that underlies the facilitation and the kind of information processing that supports standard memory effects. A proposed account of this difference will be developed in the next section as part of a more general characterization of preserved learning capacity in amnesia. The central claim of the proposal is that the dissociation in amnesia between the tasks on which performance is preserved and tasks on which performance is impaired reflects the operation of two fundamentally separate kinds of knowledge systems; these knowledge systems are in turn mediated by different memory systems, which are afforded independent neurological status.

Characterization of Preserved Learning in Amnesia

The sheer number and variety of the examples of good, and often intact, learning or memory performance by amnesic patients have led to some pessimism about being able to find a dimension or category to embrace all of them (Weiskrantz, 1978; Weiskrantz & Warrington, 1979). However, it is the claim of this chapter that the examples of preserved learning can be understood in terms of intact skill acquisition and intact repetition-priming effects, and that this classification scheme permits the development of a formulation that borrows from cognitive science and neuroscience to account for the phenomenon of preserved learning capacity in amnesia. This formulation is explicated below, taking into consideration a number of other current views (Baddeley, 1982; Kinsbourne & Wood, 1975; Moscovitch, 1982a; Olton, Becker, & Handelmann, 1979; Warrington & Weiskrantz, 1982; Weiskrantz, 1982).

The present formulation draws from the psychological and philosophical literatures a number of proposals of dissociation among different memory systems. For example, Ryle (1949) was impressed by the apparent difference between the knowledge required to perform motor skills and the knowledge of words or facts about the world: "knowing how" as opposed to "knowing that." He argued that access to these two kinds of knowledge was fundamentally different, in that the expression of "knowing that" required the conscious direction of attention to the act of remembering, whereas the expression of "knowing how" was mediated through the performance of a skilled action in a manner that did not involve active attention or conscious recall.

A rather similar view was expressed by Bruner (1969), who distinguished between "memory with record" and "memory without record." As he defined it, "memory with record" refers to the facts we acquire and events we experience in daily life, which are stored away for later use: the words, names, faces, routes, and so forth that are the substance of most memory tests. By contrast, "memory without record" reflects the way in which "encounters are converted into some process that changes that nature of an organism, changes his skills, or changes the rules by which he operates, but are virtually inaccessible in memory as specific encounters" (p. 254). Thus, the processing rules or operating procedures are themselves modified. Skills such as playing golf or tennis improve, despite poor access to the "specific instances that led to the perfection of the [skill]" (p. 254). Memory without record does not require a concomitant memory with record of specific instances.

The notion that memory without record is fundamentally different from memory with record was originally intended to account for the way in which the learning of perceptual–motor skills is distinct from other types of learning. In recent years, experimental evidence has been obtained that would tend to broaden the domain of such a formulation to perceptual skills as well (e.g., Kolers, 1975, 1976, 1979). Examining the ability of normal subjects to read geometrically inverted or otherwise transformed text, Kolers distinguished the acquisition of pattern-analyzing operations or encoding procedures "that are directed at the surface lexical features of the text" (Kolers, 1979, p. 374) from specific memory for the results or outcomes of these operations—"the semantic or other grammatical content of text that is the subject of most contemporary studies" (Kolers, 1979, p. 374). He found that subjects dramatically improved their reading of transformed text with experience, independently of the ability to remember the content of the text. It was suggested that skilled reading, like other perceptual processes, involves the application of analytic operations or procedures that analyze the information at the level of visual patterns to produce a resultant semantic outcome. These operations and procedures can be modified by experience to enhance pattern-analyzing performance; the outcomes are stored independently.

Another somewhat similar distinction has been drawn from the literature on artificial intelligence (AI) (Anderson, 1981, 1982; Winograd, 1975; Winston, 1977), involving "procedural" versus "declarative" knowledge. The distinction between procedural and declarative knowledge is a statement of the contrast between, on the one hand, information that is represented implicitly in the cognitive processes, operations, or procedures that specify its use and that can be accessed only by "running off" particular routines; and, on the other hand, information that is represented explicitly as a set of facts or data structures in a declarative data base and that can be accessed directly on demand. For an example of the difference between these two kinds of representations, consider the ways in which one could program a device to supply answers to multiplication problems. In a declarative system of representation, answers could be generated by consulting a prestored data base of multiplication tables and locating the appropriate entries; adults undoubtedly use this method for accomplishing multiplication of two single-digit numbers. In a procedural system of representation, answers could be generated by actually implementing the multiplication operations, namely by iteratively adding x to itself n times; this is what children must do before they learn the multiplication tables. Thus, in a declarative system, there is explicit access to the data base from which the answers will be selected; whereas in a procedural system, answers are derived through the application of particular algorithms.

The present formulation borrows from the proposals described above in claiming a fundamental distinction between two kinds of knowledge or memory systems; further, it argues that this distinction is honored by the nervous system, as reflected by the differential susceptibility of the two systems to amnesia. Nonetheless, it should be clear that this formulation differs from the proposals described above in various ways. For purposes of explication, however, the terms "procedural" and "declarative" knowledge are used here to label the two knowledge or memory systems, even while acknowledging the differences between the procedural–declarative distinction as originally proposed in the AI literature and the one presently being proposed.[2] By the present account, the acquisition of skills and the phenomenon of priming, both of which can occur in the absence of memory for the stimulus materials presented previously or for the previous learning experience itself, represent a particular class of knowledge dependent upon the integrity of a particular memory system. This kind of knowledge, which is here called "procedural" knowledge, is acquired and expressed by virtue of a memory system that does not permit explicit access to the contents of the knowledge base and does not support the ability to reflect in verbal reports the patient's accumulating experience with the tasks. This implicitly represented procedural knowledge is tied to and expressible only through activation of the particular processing structures or procedures engaged by the learning tasks; it is acquired and retained by virtue of the plasticity inherent in these processing structures or procedures. Thus, experience serves to influence the organization of processes that *guide* performance without access to the knowledge that *underlies* the performance.

By contrast, a different kind of knowledge, which is here called "declarative" knowledge, seems to be represented in a system quite compatible with the traditional memory metaphor of experimental psychology, in which information is said to be first processed or encoded, then stored in some explicitly accessible form for later use, and then ultimately retrieved upon demand. This system acquires and maintains a representation of the specific outcomes of the operations performed by the processing structures or procedures activated by the learning tasks. Thus, whereas representation of procedural knowledge is seen to involve the reorganization or other modification of existing processing structures or procedures, representation of declarative knowledge is claimed to involve the creation of new data structures to represent explicitly the outcomes of engaging these processes or procedures. The content of the declarative-knowledge system constitutes the subject of most experimental investigations of memory and is markedly impaired in amnesic patients, following damage to medial temporal or diencephalic brain structures.

In order to understand the way in which the proposed distinction between memory systems is realized by the nervous system, it is useful to begin with a view of the brain as being comprised of a set of distinct processing and action systems.[3] By virtue of differences among the distinct processing and action systems in their connections, they handle dif-

2. The terms "procedural" and "declarative" are used here partly because I have used them previously, and partly because the dictionary definitions of these terms are very close to the spirit of the present formulation. The use of these terms is *not* meant to imply that the psychological level of description of the AI-inspired distinction is framed appropriately to capture the nature of the difference between the two knowledge or memory systems proposed here. Indeed, I can see no way to "represent" the proposed distinction within the representational framework embodied by the procedural–declarative distinction as it was originally proposed.

3. The notion of distinct processing and action systems is meant to extend across all levels of analysis. It incorporates the facts that the visual system can be seen to process information separately from the auditory system; that within the visual system, area 17 can be seen to process information separately from area 18; and that within area 17, a given column or minicolumn can be seen a functional system, processing information separately from neighboring columns or minicolumns. This is not to deny that the different functional systems cooperate at all levels to produce cognition and action; it merely emphasizes that the enormous anatomical specificity of the nervous system supports multiple levels of information processing and memory storage.

ferent types of information; and due to differences among systems in their architectures, they handle information in different ways. In performing a task, processing structures or procedures within the appropriate processing and action systems are engaged, which permits the plasticities inherent in these systems to produce relatively temporary activations and longer-term modifications of the elements. That is, the operation of processes or procedures within any of these systems is accompanied by direct on-line changes that tune and otherwise increase the efficacy of the relevant processes and procedures. It is such changes that provide the basis for repetition-priming effects (through relatively temporary activations) and that underlie the acquisition of skills (through longer-term modifications). However, because of the differences among systems in the information being processed and in the nature of the processing, the possibilities of communication among systems would seem to be very limited. The format or code of the (procedural) knowledge represented by modification of particular processes and procedures is seen to be so closely tied to the nature of the processes and operations used by any given system that it would be functionally inaccessible to other systems.

As a means of supporting communication among the different systems, a (declarative) code that is fundamentally different from that used by the processing and action systems is seen to be available for storage of the outcomes resulting from the operation of processes or procedures from *all* systems. This common code represents explicitly new data structures derived from the operation of any available process or procedure. The storage of processing outcomes or results in the form of a declarative code permits the ability to compare and contrast information from different processes or processing systems; and it enables the ability to make inferences from and generalizations across facts derived from multiple processing sources. Such a common declarative code thereby provides the basis for access to facts acquired during the course of experience and for conscious recollection of the learning experiences themselves. The declarative system is seen to depend upon the medial temporal and diencephalic brain structures damaged in amnesia. It follows from these considerations that the interruption of such a system would produce a selective impairment of learning and memory: It would spare the ability to benefit from previous experience in the form of skill acquisition and repetition-priming effects, while impairing access to knowledge ordinarily acquired during the learning experience, as well as memory for the learning experience itself. The dissociation between the ability of amnesic patients to benefit from experience and their inability to reflect the experience in their verbal reports has been noted repeatedly in the discussion of the data given above; its importance for understanding the phenomenon of preserved learning has been stressed by a number of other authors (Baddeley, 1982; Jacoby & Witherspoon, 1982; Moscovitch, 1982a; Weiskrantz, 1978). Such a dissociation between good performance and poor verbal reports in amnesia follows naturally from the present formulation of amnesia as a deficit selective to the explicitly represented knowledge that is characteristic of the declarative system, which leaves unimpaired implicitly represented knowledge characteristic of the procedural system. Hence, a virtue of the present formulation is that it does not have to postulate a specific deficit in amnesia in "monitoring" (Weiskrantz, 1978), "evaluative memory" (Baddeley, 1982), or "attribution" (Jacoby, Chapter 15, this volume) processes.

The relationship of these ideas to brain mechanisms of learning and memory can be appreciated by looking at forms of learning that have been analyzed with some success in neurophysiological terms. In the *Aplysia*, for example, habituation of the gill-withdrawal response involves synaptic changes in the same system responsible for the normal response (Kandel, 1976). Here, the mechanisms involved in executing the gill-withdrawal response are themselves modified by experience. Habituation does not seem to require an explicit representation of having experienced a particular pattern of stimulation in a specific place at a specific time. The tuning of visual cortical cells in cats through selective early experience illustrates the same point. Restricting a cat's early experience to horizontal contours modifies the properties of individual cells in the visual cortex, resulting in special sensitivity to horizontally oriented lines (Blakemore, 1974). But there is no sense in which such changes depend upon the declarative knowledge of having undergone a particular experience, or even of the fact that the world is composed primarily of horizontally oriented lines. Rather, the tuning of the visual system by restricted early experience appears to reflect the gradual modification of neuronal structures that are themselves involved in the course of analyzing information and expressing behavior. This kind of modification of neuronal elements seems to provide a clear example of procedural knowledge. It occurs gradually with practice, changing the rules by which an organism operates, without requiring a declarative representation of the specific instances that comprise the learning experience, or of the specific outcomes that result from it. Storage of the specific instances or outcomes, in this view, would require additional brain mechanisms, which are proposed to be damaged in amnesia.

There have been other formulations of amnesia that have also relied on the proposal of dissociations among memory systems. For example, it has been argued (Kinsbourne & Wood, 1975; Schacter & Tulving, 1982, 1983; Wood, Ebert, & Kinsbourne, 1982) that the pattern of deficits and sparing seen in the amnesic syndrome supports Tulving's (1972) proposed distinction between "episodic" and "semantic" memory. As originally proposed, "episodic" memory refers to autobiographical memory for specific temporally dated and spatially located events (e.g., a memory of watching the space shuttle *Columbia* touch down at Edwards Air Force Base), whereas "semantic" memory is context-free knowledge of language, concepts, facts, and rules (e.g., the fact that the space shuttle is a reusable space vehicle built and operated by the United States). The fact that amnesic patients have, on the one hand, preserved general intelligence as well as intact language, perceptual, and social skills, yet, on the other hand, have profoundly impaired memory for day-to-day events and may be confused as to time and place, has been offered in support of the idea that amnesia reflects a selective impairment in episodic memory. What this use of the episodic–semantic distinction to explain amnesia has not adequately appreciated is that the examples offered above confound a comparison between semantic and episodic memory with a comparison between premorbid and post-morbid memory. That is, information that would support performance on intelligence tests and that would mediate language, perceptual, and social skills is acquired rather early in life, during the remote premorbid period (i.e., long before the onset of amnesia). By contrast, memory for day-to-day events and appreciation of current context obviously depends upon recent postmorbid memory. Thus, in this example, the "semantic" information is exclusively permorbid information and the "episodic" information is exclusively postmorbid information. The point is that to evaluate fairly the distinction between semantic and episodic memory in amnesia, one must compare either new learning (postmorbid memory) of both semantic and episodic information, or remote (premorbid) memory for both semantic and episodic information.

Recent work using this strategy indicates clearly that the deficit in new l
the deficit in remote memory both encompass episodic and semantic inforn
example, in the domain of new learning, many studies of the patient H. M. hav
profound impairment not only in many laboratory tests of episodic memory,
tests of such semantic information as memory for public figures (Marslen-Wilson &
Teuber, 1975) and memory for the meanings of new vocabulary words (Gabrieli, Cohen, &
Corkin, 1983). In the vocabulary study, H. M. showed a profound impairment in learning
the meanings of eight words (e.g., "anchorite," "quotidian," "welkin," etc.) over 10 days of
testing in a performance-based paradigm that required the words to be matched to the
appropriate definitions, synonyms, or sentence frames. He showed virtually no savings on
this task, despite at least 15 trials for each word on each of the 10 testing days. In the
domain of remote memory, too, the deficit seems to cover semantic and episodic information alike. Case N. A., patients with Korsakoff syndrome, and patients receiving bilateral
ECT have all demonstrated parallel remote-memory impairments for public (largely
semantic) and personal (episodic) events (Zola-Morgan, Cohen, & Squire, 1983).

Another argument for relating the episodic–semantic distinction to amnesia has
been that the examples of preserved learning in amnesia described earlier might all be
considered to reflect the operation of an intact semantic memory. Yet, it seems apparent
that semantic memory as originally described belongs to the category of declarative
knowledge, while preserved learning of motor, perceptual, and cognitive skills reflects the
operation of a separate procedural system. Schacter and Tulving (1983) have also argued
that the episodic–semantic distinction deals only with information that can be represented
propositionally (i.e., declarative knowledge), and that the acquisition and modification of
procedural knowledge may operate according to fundamentally different rules. It is possible
to accommodate the phenomena within a episodic–semantic framework if one redefines
the terms, so that episodic memory represents the class of context-bound autobiographical
information, and semantic memory represents, *by exclusion*, all other information. In this
case, all the examples of preserved learning in amnesia would indeed reflect the operation
of an intact semantic memory. The question such a move raises, however, is whether there
are any principled reasons for postulating a dissociation in just that form. Stated in
another way, although a dissociation between autobiographical and nonautobiographical
memory is intuitively sensible, the critical question is whether such a dissociation is of a
natural kind. One could just as easily split the memory system into memories for all
animate things versus all inanimate things, or memories for all things with sharp boundaries versus all things with fuzzy boundaries, and so on. The point is that both halves of the
proposed dichotomy must be biologically sensible in order to have given rise to functionally separate systems with differential susceptibility to amnesia. At any rate, regardless
of the usefulness of the episodic–semantic distinction in understanding normal human
memory, there is as yet no compelling evidence for the view that these are two functionally
distinct domains of memory with differential susceptibility to amnesia.

Another proposed distinction among memory systems is the distinction between
"reference" memory and "working" memory (Olton *et al.*, 1979), which was developed
from studies with experimental animals. "Reference" memory is a system claimed to be
involved in learning those aspects of a task that are constant from trial to trial; hence, it
requires no updating or modification across trials. "Working" memory is a contextually

sensitive system for shorter-term storage of the aspects of a task that change from trial to trial, and that must be remembered in order to achieve success on a given trial. According to the reference–working formulation, reference memory is spared in experimental animals with lesions of the hippocampal system, whereas working memory is selectively affected.

However, as has been argued elsewhere (Squire & Cohen, 1979), work with amnesic patients provides difficulty for this account by indicating that the constant features of a task are not automatically protected. That is, constant repetition of declarative information is not sufficient to ensure learning (Cohen, 1981; Corsi, 1972; Drachman & Arbit, 1966). Thus, H. M. was unable to recall a string of digits that was one digit in excess of his immediate memory span, despite 25 consecutive repetitions of the same string (Drachman & Arbit, 1966); he was also unable to exhibit savings in the test of new vocabulary learning, despite 10 days of testing with the materials held constant (Gabrieli et al., 1983). The intact acquisition of skill by amnesic patients is not based upon simple repetition. The preserved learning of procedural knowledge is postulated to occur because of the *nature* of the information, not because of the constancy of the information. Hence, the facts of human amnesia provide no support for the proposed distinction between reference memory and working memory.

Elaborated above are a number of arguments against the viability of the semantic–episodic or the reference–working memory distinctions for understanding the human amnesic syndrome. Nonetheless, these formulations have served an important purpose by arguing for a view of memory as composed of functionally separate systems with different susceptibilities to the effects of brain injury. Such a view of course provides the foundation for the account of dissociation among memory systems offered in this chapter.

Conclusion

Memory, or at least the long-term memory store, has typically been viewed as a unitary system. In an appeal to parsimony, apparent variability in the characteristics of different "aspects" of memory has been attributed to differences in the nature of the encoding received by distinct informational types or by differences in the retrieval operations necessary to gain access to them. On this view, a given learning experience influences a single representational system and can be expressed in performance in somewhat different forms, depending upon the nature and sensitivity of the test employed; or the learning experience establishes a number of different representations, depending upon the attributes to which distinct encoding operations are attuned. But the multiple representations produced by the different encodings are inextricably related and are fundamentally of the same kind. By contrast, it has been the contention of this chapter that the evidence of preserved skill acquisition in memory-impaired amnesic patients, together with the evidence of repetition-priming effects that operate independently of recognition memory in amnesic patients and normal control subjects alike, provide a compelling case for proposing a fundamental dissociation among memory systems. The particular formulation proposed here distinguishes between procedural and declarative knowledge, arguing that these different forms of knowledge are mediated by neuroanatomically distinct memory systems. The present formulation builds upon and has a number of similarities to other distinctions proposed earlier in the philosophical, psychological, and neuropsychological literatures; however, it differs from them in important ways.

It is worth noting that the proposal of multiple memory systems in no way denies the importance of different types of encoding and retrieval operations invoked by distinct classes of information; indeed, the relationship of representation to process is such that the ability of different memory systems to give rise to separate representational classes that differ with regard to their informational content and accessibility demands that there be differences among these memory systems in encoding and retrieval processes. However, the present formulation *does deny* that a unitary memory (i.e., representational) system can maintain its claims of parsimony at the expense of postulating additional distinct processes. That is, it cannot be claimed that a multiple-memory-system view is less parsimonious than a unitary-memory-system view if the unitary system must invoke extra processes not required by the multiple memory systems. The available evidence is therefore taken to be sufficiently compelling to abandon the model of a unitary memory system. Further work will ascertain whether the proposed distinction between procedural and declarative knowledge, or some other proposed distinction, leads to the most useful characterization of memory systems.

ACKNOWLEDGMENTS

My research described in this chapter has been supported by U.S. Public Health Service Grants MH08280 and RR00088. I wish to thank Larry Squire and Suzanne Corkin, with whom various aspects of this work have been conducted. The ideas expressed in this chapter benefit from many conversations with numerous colleagues both at the University of California at San Diego and the Massachusetts Institute of Technology, who are here thanked collectively; however, the ideas have been particularly influenced—though by no means are they necessarily completely shared—by Larry Squire, Lynn Nadel, and Dan Schacter.

REFERENCES

Anderson, J. R. *Cognitive skills and their acquisition.* Hillsdale, N.J.: Erlbaum, 1981.

Anderson, J. R. Acquisition of cognitive skill. *Psychological Review*, 1982, *89*, 369–406.

Anzai, Y., & Simon, H. A. The theory of learning by doing. *Psychological Review*, 1979, *86*, 124–140.

Baddeley, A. Amnesia: A minimal model and an interpretation. In L. S. Cermak (Ed.), *Human memory and amnesia.* Hillsdale, N.J.: Erlbaum, 1982.

Barbizet, J. *Human memory and its pathology.* San Francisco: W. H. Freeman, 1970.

Blakemore, C. Developmental factors in the formation of feature extracting neurons. In F. O. Schmitt & F. G. Worden (Eds.), *The neurosciences: Third study program.* Cambridge, Mass.: MIT Press, 1974.

Brooks, D. N., & Baddeley, A. What can amnesic patients learn? *Neuropsychologia*, 1976, *14*, 111–122.

Bruner, J. S. Modalities of memory. In G. A. Talland & N. C. Waugh (Eds.), *The pathology of memory.* New York: Academic Press, 1969.

Cermak, L. S., Lewis, R., Butters, N., & Goodglass, H. Role of verbal mediation in performance of motor tasks by Korsakoff patients. *Perceptual and Motor Skills*, 1973, *37*, 259–262.

Claparède, E. Recognition et moiité. *Archives de Psychologie* (Genève), 1911, *11*, 79–90.

Cohen, N. J. *Neuropsychological evidence for a distinction between procedural and declarative knowledge in human memory and amnesia.* Unpublished doctoral dissertation, University of California at San Diego, 1981.

Cohen, N. J. & Corkin, S. The amnesic patient. H. M.: Learning and retention of cognitive skill. *Society for Neuroscience Abstracts*, 1981, *7*, 517–518.

Cohen, N. J., & Schacter, D. L. *Are memory systems dissociable?* Unpublished manuscript, 1984.

Cohen, N. J., & Squire, L. R. Preserved learning and retention of pattern analyzing skill in amnesia: Dissociation of knowing how and knowing that. *Science*, 1980, *210*, 207–210.

Corkin, S. Tactually-guided maze learning in man: Effects of unilateral cortical excisions and bilateral hippocampal lesions. *Neuropsychologia*, 1965, *3*, 339–351.

Corkin, S. Acquisition of motor skill after bilateral medial temporal lobe excision. *Neuropsychologia*, 1968, *6*, 255–265.

Corkin, S., Sullivan, E. V., Twitchell, T. E., & Grove, E. The amnesic patient H. M.: Clinical observations and test performance 28 years after operation. *Society for Neuroscience Abstracts*, 1981, *7*, 235.

Corsi, P. M. *Human memory and the medial temporal region of the brain*. Unpublished doctoral dissertation, McGill University, 1972.

Drachman, D. A., & Arbit, J. Memory and the hippocampal complex. *Archives of Neurology*, 1966, *15*, 52–61.

Gabrieli, J. D. E., Cohen, N. J., & Corkin, S. The acquisition of lexical and semantic knowledge in amnesia. *Society for Neuroscience Abstracts*, 1983, *9*, 238.

Graf, P., Squire, L. R., & Mandler, G. The information that amnesic patients do not forget. *Journal of Experimental Psychology: Learning, Memory, and Cognition*, 1984, *10*, 164–178.

Jacoby, L. L., & Dallas, M. On the relationship between autobiographical memory and perceptual learning. *Journal of Experimental Psychology*, 1981, *110*, 306–340.

Jacoby, L. L., & Witherspoon, D. Remembering without awareness. *Canadian Journal of Psychology*, 1982, *36*, 300–324.

Kandel, E. R. *Cellular basis of behavior*. San Francisco: W. H. Freeman, 1976.

Karat, J. A model of problem solving with incomplete constraint knowledge. *Cognitive Psychology*, 1982, *14*, 538–559.

Kinsbourne, M., & Wood, F. Short-term memory processes and the amnesic syndrome. In D. Deutsch & J. A. Deutsch (Eds.), *Short-term memory*. New York: Academic Press, 1975.

Kolers, P. A. Specificity of operations in sentence recognition. *Cognitive Psychology*, 1975, *1*, 289–306.

Kolers, P. A. Pattern-analyzing memory. *Science*, 1976, *191*, 1280–1281.

Kolers, P. A. A pattern-analyzing basis of recognition. In L. S. Cermak & F. I. M. Craik (Eds.), *Levels of processing in human memory*. Hillsdale, N.J.: Erlbaum, 1979.

Mandler, G. Recognizing: The judgment of previous occurrence. *Psychological Review*, 1980, *87*, 252–271.

Marslen-Wilson, W. D., & Teuber, H.-L. Memory for remote events in anterograde amnesia: Recognition of public figures from news photographs. *Neuropsychologia*, 1975, *13*, 353–364.

Mayes, A. R., Meudell, P. R., & Neary, D. Must amnesia be caused by either encoding or retrieval disorders? In M. M. Brunenberg, P. E. Morris, & R. N. Sykes (Eds.), *Practical aspects of memory*. London: Academic Press, 1978.

Meudell, P., & Mayes, A. The Claparède phenomenon: A further example in amnesics, a demonstration of a similar effect in normal people with attenuated memory, and a reinterpretation. *Current Psychological Research*, 1981, *1*, 75–88.

Milner, B. Les troubles de la mémoire accompagnant des lésions hippocampiques bilatérales. In P. Passouant (Ed.), *Physiologie de l'hippocampe*. Paris: Centre National de la Recherche Scientifique, 1962.

Milner, B., Corkin, S., & Tueber, H.-L. Further analysis of the hippocampal amnesic syndrome: 14-year follow-up study of H. M. *Neuropsychologia*, 1968, *6*, 215–244.

Moscovitch, M. Multiple dissociations of function in the amnesic syndrome. In L. S. Cermak (Ed.), *Human memory and amnesia*. Hillsdale, N.J.: Erlbaum, 1982. (a)

Moscovitch, M. A neuropsychological approach to perception and memory in normal and pathological aging. In F. I. M. Craik & S. Trehub (Eds.), *Aging and cognitive processes*. New York: Plenum Press, 1982. (b)

Nelson, T. O. Detecting small amounts of information in memory: Savings for nonrecognized items. *Journal of Experimental Psychology: Human Learning and Memory*, 1978, *4*, 453–468.

Olton, D. S., Becker, J. T., & Handelmann, G. E. Hippocampus, space, and memory. *Behavioral and Brain Sciences*, 1979, *2*, 313–365.

Rozin, P. The psychobiological approach to human memory. In M. R. Rosenzweig & E. L. Bennett (Eds.), *Neural mechanisms of learning and memory*. Cambridge, Mass.: MIT Press, 1976.

Ryle, G. *The concept of mind*. San Francisco: Hutchinson, 1949.

Scarborough, D. L., Gerard, D., & Cortese, C. Assessing lexical memory: The transfer of word repetition effects across task and modality. *Memory and Cognition*, 1979, *7*, 3–12.

Schacter, D. L., & Tulving, E. Amnesia and memory research. In L. S. Cermak (Ed.), *Human memory and amnesia*. Hillsdale, N.J.: Erlbaum, 1982.

Schacter, D. L., & Tulving, E. Memory, amnesia, and the episodic/semantic distinction. In R. L. Isaacson & N. E. Spear (Eds.), *Expression of knowledge*. New York: Plenum Press, 1983.

Scoville, W. B., & Milner, B. Loss of recent memory after bilateral hippocampal lesions. *Journal of Neurology, Neurosurgery and Psychiatry*, 1957, *20*, 11–21.

Simon, H. A. The functional equivalence of problem solving skills. *Cognitive Psychology*, 1975, *7*, 268–288.

Squire, L. R., & Cohen, N. J. Hippocampal lesions: Reconciling the findings in rodents and man. *Behavioral and Brain Sciences*, 1979, *2*, 345–346.

Squire, L. R., Wetzel, C. D., & Slater, P. C. Anterograde amnesia following ECT: An analysis of the beneficial effect of partial information. *Neuropsychologia*, 1978, *16*, 339–347.

Tulving, E. Episodic and semantic memory. In E. Tulving & W. Donaldson (Eds.), *Organization of memory*. New York: Academic Press, 1972.

Tulving, E., Schacter, D. L., & Stark, H. A. Priming effects in word-fragment completion are independent of recognition memory. *Journal of Experimental Psychology: Learning, Memory, and Cognition*, 1982, *8*, 336–342.

Warrington, E. K., & Weiskrantz, L. A new method of testing long-term retention with special reference to amnesic patients. *Nature*, 1968, *217*, 972–974.

Warrington, E. K., & Weiskrantz, L. The amnesic syndrome: Consolidation or retrieval? *Nature*, 1970, *228*, 628–630.

Warrington, E. K., & Weiskrantz, L. An analysis of short-term and long-term memory deficits in man. In J. A. Deutsch (Ed.), *The physiological basis of memory*. New York: Academic Press, 1973.

Warrington, E. K., & Weiskrantz, L. The effect of prior learning on subsequent retention in amnesic patients. *Neuropsychologia*, 1974, *12*, 419–428.

Warrington, E. K., & Weiskrantz, L. Amnesia: A disconnection syndrome? *Neuropsychologia*, 1982, *20*, 233–248.

Weiskrantz, L. A comparison of hippocampal pathology in man and other animals. In K. Elliot & J. Whelan (Eds.), *Functions of the septo-hippocampal system* (CIBA Foundation Symposium No. 58). Amsterdam: Elsevier, 1978.

Weiskrantz, L. Comparative aspects of studies of amnesia. In D. E. Broadbent & L. Weiskrantz (Eds.), *The neuropsychology of cognition*. London: Royal Society of London, 1982.

Weiskrantz, L., & Warrington, E. K. Conditioning in amnesic patients. *Neuropsychologia*, 1979, *17*, 187–194.

Wetzel, C. D., & Squire, L. R. Cued recall in anterograde amnesia. *Brain and Language*, 1982, *15*, 70–81.

Wickelgren, W. A. Chunking and consolidation: A theoretical synthesis of semantic networks, configuring in conditioning, S-R versus cognitive learning, normal forgetting, the amnesic syndrome, and the hippocampal arousal syndrome. *Psychological Review*, 1979, *86*, 44–60.

Winograd, T. Frame representations and the declarative-procedural controversy. In D. G. Bobrow & A. M. Collins (Eds.), *Representation and understanding: Studies in cognitive science*. New York: Academic Press, 1975.

Winston, P. H. *Artificial intelligence*. Reading, Mass.: Addison-Wesley, 1977.

Wood, F., Ebert, V., & Kinsbourne, M. The semantic-episodic memory distinction in memory and amnesia. In L. Cermak (Ed.), *Human memory and amnesia*. Hillsdale, N.J.: Erlbaum, 1982.

Zola-Morgan, S., Cohen, N. J., & Squire, L. R. Recall of remote-episodic memory in amnesia. *Neuropsychologia*, 1983, *21*, 487–500.

11

The Sufficient Conditions for Demonstrating Preserved Memory in Amnesia: A Task Analysis

Morris Moscovitch

"Duplexity" Theories of Memory

Amnesia is not a unitary syndrome. One type of amnesia may differ from another with respect to etiology, locus of brain damage, and associated deficits on a variety of cognitive and memory tasks (Lhermitte & Signoret, 1972; Huppert & Piercy, 1978, 1979; Squire, 1981; Talland, 1965; Moscovitch, 1982a). Although it is not easy to decide which behavioral deficits are obligatory features of all amnesias and which are unique to a particular syndrome, it is possible to specify some characteristics that are common to all amnesic patients. These are best described in terms of the following four types of dissociation: (1) memory from intelligence; (2) secondary, or long-term, memory from primary, or short-term, memory; (3) memory for postmorbid events (anterograde) from that for premorbid ones (retrograde); and (4) awareness from memory. These dissociations are not absolute but relative, in that the initial function in each of these dissociations is the one that is most severely affected, although the second function may also be somewhat impaired (see Moscovitch, 1982a, for an extended discussion).

Of these dissociations, the last one seems to be a contradiction in terms, in that it implies some preserved ability on the part of amnesics to acquire new memories. Indeed, it has long been known that profound amnesia does not preclude the possibility of learning some things well, even though the patient denies any familiarity with the learning situation and seems to lack any awareness of having learned something new (Claparède, 1911; Corkin, 1968; Milner, Corkin, & Teuber, 1968; Talland, 1965; Weiskrantz, 1978). This dissociation between conscious awareness and memory may be translated to a dissociation between two different types of memory systems or modes of remembering, only one of which is preserved in amnesia. Recently, concern with this dissociation between different memory systems has assumed a central position in discussions of amnesia, and it forms the focus of this chapter.

Although it is not always easy to trace the development of this concern, it is fair to say that investigation of memory in nonclinical populations and in nonhuman mammals has had a major influence. Some theorists of normal memory have felt it necessary to postulate at least two types of memory systems or forms of remembering to make sense of the literature. One of the most influential of these has been Tulving's (1972) distinction between "semantic" and "episodic" memory. Originally, the distinction was meant to be purely conceptual but

Morris Moscovitch. Psychology Department, Centre for Studies in Human Development and Unit for Memory Disorders, Erindale College, University of Toronto, Mississauga, Ontario, Canada.

has since evolved into a description of two types of memory systems, one of which is believed to be impaired and the other preserved in amnesia (Diamond & Rozin, 1974, as cited in Rozin, 1976; Kinsbourne & Wood, 1975; Schacter & Tulving, 1982).

Many neuropsychologists interested in animal memory have felt a similar need to postulate the existence of different memory systems if they are to resolve the discrepancy between the effects of hippocampal damage in humans and those in other species. Although some investigators have proposed that deficits in a single stage of the information-processing sequence of a system could account for the observed phenomena (Weiskrantz, 1978), most have chosen the former strategy. For them, the hippocampus mediates one type of memory, and extrahippocampal structures mediate another (Gaffan, 1976; O'Keefe & Nadel, 1978; Olton, Becker, & Handelmann, 1979; Hirsh, 1974; Hirsh & Krajden, 1982; Winocur, 1982; to cite just a few).

At the moment there are at least a dozen candidates in the human and animal literature for what I have called "duplexity" theories of memory (Moscovitch, 1982a). As one might expect, each has its own special features and, depending on the theory, differs from its competitors in either subtle or obvious ways. The theoretical and empirical overlap among these various theories, however, is very great. Each can account for the vast majority of the data, and each fails to capture in its theoretical net a small, but different, proportion of the phenomena reported in the literature. It would be difficult to describe accurately what the similarities and differences are among the various theories in the space assigned to me by the editors of this volume. Even given unlimited space, I would not find the task simple, because many (though not all) of the theories, are still evolving and are sufficiently vague with regard to many of the distinctions one might wish to draw—for example, the distinctions among procedural (Cohen & Squire, 1980), performance (Jacoby & Witherspoon, 1982), and semantic (Rozin, 1976; Schacter & Tulving, 1982) memory or among conscious recollection (Baddeley, 1982), reflection (Johnson, 1983), episodic memory (Schacter & Tulving, 1982), working memory (Olton et al., 1979), and memory with awareness (Jacoby & Witherspoon, 1982). Moreover, the distinctions that separate one theory or hypothesis from another seem quite small in comparison to the basic truth they all capture about amnesia.

A New Proposal

Rather than deal with these models in detail, I would like to propose my own scheme for designating which aspects of amnesic memory are preserved and which are impaired. My formulation differs from the other proposals in two ways. First, whereas all the other proposals focus on distinguishing between different kinds of memory systems or between processes within a particular kind of memory system, I would like to focus instead on task demands or task variables. In this sense, my formulation is neutral with respect to process and mechanism. It is, in fact, more like an operational definition of the types of memory tasks at which amnesics might succeed or fail. Although theoretically neutral, this proposal has the potential for directing research toward delineating the processes or discovering the mechanisms that underlie performance on these different types of tasks. Second, my proposal indicates only the sufficient conditions for demonstrating preserved and impaired memory functions in amnesics, and makes no attempt to suggest the necessary conditions as well.

Amnesics will show savings on tasks that satisfy the following three conditions: (1) The tasks are so highly structured that the goal of the task and the means to achieve it are apparent; (2) the means to achieve the goal are available to the subject (i.e., the response and strategies used to arrive at the goal are already in the subject's repertoire); and (3) success in achieving the goal can be had without reference to a particular postmorbid event or episode. Performance on tasks that satisfy these conditions is guided both by the circumstances and conditions at hand and by the prior strategies and associations that the subject brings to the task. The subject is not asked to remember a prior occasion, but merely to perform the task. The subject is asked to act or choose in the present, not to recollect a previous event or to reflect on past performance. Put another way, successful performance on tasks that satisfy these conditions is limited by the task structure and can be modified by past experience, but it does not depend on conjuring up (i.e., remembering) a previous experience or its outcome. In short, amnesics who cannot "remember," in the ordinary sense of calling to mind a previous event, can nonetheless benefit from past experience on tasks that are highly structured.

I illustrate and support this statement with evidence collected in my laboratory and by other investigators. I will begin with a simple example of a lexical-decision task in which some words and nonwords are repeated at lags of 0, 7, or 29 items. The subject's task is merely to indicate whether a string of letters is a word or not. Reaction time to do so is measured. Scarborough and his colleagues (Scarborough, Cortese, & Scarborough, 1977; Scarborough, Gerard, & Cortese, 1979) showed that performance on the second presentation of an item improves in comparison to performance on the first presentation, as measured by latencies to reach the correct decision. The reaction-time advantage for the repeated item is known as the "repetition-priming effect" and does not decrease substantially with lag between the first and second presentations, even when the two may be separated by as much as 48 hours. The repetition-priming effect, therefore, reflects the consequences of past experience but does not make any demands on the subject to remember a prior event. This is a task that satisfies the conditions for preserved memory in amnesics, because the goals of the task as well as the means to achieve that goal are available to the subject, but success does not require reference to a previous episode. As such, the repetition-priming effect should be as great in amnesic patients as in controls. Our experiment confirmed this prediction (see Figure 11-1). When the materials of the task were kept the same, but the task requirements were changed so that a subject had to decide whether an item appeared for the first or second time on the list, the performance of both the normal and the amnesic subjects changed markedly. For the normal subjects, recognition performance as measured both by latency and accuracy deteriorated with lag. Predictably, amnesic subjects could not perform much above chance levels (see Figure 11-1). Successful performance could not be achieved by simply operating on the materials at hand, but required specific reference to a prior event.

Using somewhat different procedures and materials, but the same rationale, Diamond and Rozin (1974, as cited in Rozin, 1976) and Jacoby and Witherspoon (1982) were able to show preserved priming in amnesic patients. Indeed, many of the demonstrations of the effectiveness retrieval cues in amnesia (Warrington & Weiskrantz, 1970, 1973; Winocur & Weiskrantz, 1976) may simply be examples of a type of repetition-priming effect. In Diamond and Rozin's study, amnesic patients and normal controls studied a list of words and pseudowords created by combining the first and second syllables of two real words. At retention, both groups were presented with the first three letters of the items and asked to guess the word. Studying only real words, but not pseudowords, improved the amnesics'

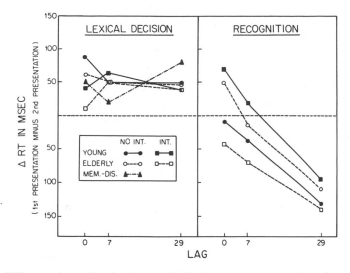

FIGURE 11-1. Differences in reaction time between the first and second presentation of a word in lexical-decision and recognition tasks. The second word was presented at lags of 0, 7, and 29 items. INT refers to interference produced by an interpolated math task between each trial.

performance, whereas studying both helped normal people. The benefits that the study items conferred on performance over new items lasted less than an hour. Diamond and Rozin concluded that successful amnesic performance depended on activating or priming previously stored information (real words). When the correct responses were not present in the subject's repertoire and could not be derived from available materials, the amnesics performed poorly.

In a very important extension of this experiment, Graf, Squire, and Mandler (1984) showed that task instructions were critical. If at retention the amnesic was asked to complete a word, given its initial letters, then performance was normal in that many more study items than new items were completed. If, however, the instructions specified that the subject use these letters as cues for retrieving the study items, amnesic patients' performance did not improve whereas that of normal subjects improved significantly.

These repetition-priming effects are relatively short-lived. Similar effects, however, can be obtained that last for weeks or even months. Identifying Gollin figures (Milner *et al.*, 1968; Warrington & Weiskrantz, 1970) and reading geometrically transformed script (Cohen & Squire, 1980; Moscovitch, 1982b) both improve with practice, and the improvement can be maintained for weeks, even without any exposure to the task during the interval. Moreover, the improvement may be item-specific as well as general to the entire task. The results of our modification of Cohen and Squire's (1980) study on reading transformed script illustrate these points.

Subjects were required to read sentences in normal or transformed script as quickly as possible without making mistakes. The transformation rotated each letter around its vertical axis. On the first day, subjects read 14 sentences in each of the two scripts; 2 hours later they read seven new and seven old sentences of each type and were required to judge after each sentence whether they had read it before. Four to 14 days later, they read 28 sentences of each type, seven of which were new and the rest old, and judged whether they had read the sentences before.

As Figure 11-2 (panel A) shows, recognition accuracy gets worse as we proceed from the young adults to the four memory-disordered subjects, three of whom were early Alzheimer patients with normal IQs who still lived at home. The memory-disordered patients performed at chance levels, with only one of them having even a sense of familiarity with the task, whereas the older adults from the community, with whom they were matched for age and education, performed significantly above chance even at a 2-week delay. In contrast, reading performances measured by speed (see Figure 11-2, panel B) improved as much in the amnesic patients as in the community old. Significantly, the reduction is not uniform across all sets, but is greatest for those that were seen before. This is as true of amnesics as it is of other subjects. Performance on this task as measured by reading speed satisfies the conditions set forth as sufficient to show preserved memory in amnesics, whereas the recognition test does not.

It is not clear why the effects on this task should be so much longer-lasting than the priming effects on lexical-decision tasks, although a number of possibilities come to mind. First, subjects had more practice in the reading of transformed script. The task also took more effort to complete and may have called on the subjects' problem-solving abilities to master, or at least to execute, a new skill. Whatever the process, it is clear that other tasks show similar long-term savings. Among them are solving jigsaw puzzles and anagrams (Baddeley, 1982), playing a new tune on the piano (Gardner, 1974), learning a pursuit-rotor task (Corkin, 1968) and a mirror-drawing task (Milner *et al.*, 1968), and even acquiring a

FIGURE 11-2. Results of modified study on reading transformed script, in terms of recognition accuracy (panel A; numbers indicate the percentage of correct recognition of previously seen sentences and rejection of new sentences) and speed in seconds (panel B). Sets A, B, C, and D each consist of seven sentences.

READING TRANSFORMED SCRIPT
YES–NO RECOGNITION ACCURACY (PERCENT)

(A)

		YOUNG				COMMUNITY OLD				INSTITUTIONALIZED OLD					MEMORY DISORDERED			
		A	B	C	D	A	B	C	D	A	B	C	D		A	B	C	D
	INITIAL	✔	✔			✔	✔			✔	✔			→	✔	✔		
	1-2 HR DELAY	98.0		99.0		93.9		93.9		67.1		81.3		→	42.9		67.6	
	2 WK DELAY	96.9	78.6	78.6	82.6	81.6	54.1	60.2	80.6	35.7	24.1	30.0	82.9	4-14 DAY DELAY	71.4	60.7	46.4	53.5

READING TRANSFORMED SCRIPT
SPEED IN SEC

(B)

		YOUNG				COMMUNITY OLD				INSTITUTIONALIZED OLD					MEMORY DISORDERED			
		A	B	C	D	A	B	C	D	A	B	C	D		A	B	C	D
	INITIAL	18.5	19.6	–	–	34.8	36.9	–	–	42.2	44.7	–	–	→	41.8	44.3	–	–
	2 HR DELAY	9.1	–	15.7	–	23.0	–	33.0	–	35.5	–	44.3	–	→	26.1	–	36.8	–
	2 WK DELAY	7.7	9.7	11.3	12.5	19.2	22.9	26.2	26.5	32.1	36.1	38.2	37.4	4-14 DAY DELAY	19.5	26.3	29.5	34.5

classical conditioning response (Weiskrantz & Warrington, 1979) (see Baddeley, 1982, for a list of other such tasks). In addition, on many of these tasks amnesics give evidence of learning a specific item, and not simply acquiring a general skill or set of multipurpose procedures.

Perhaps the most surprising achievement of amnesic patients is their ability to learn and apply a mathematical rule (Kinsbourne & Wood, 1975) and to solve the Tower of Hanoi puzzle (see Cohen, Chapter 10, this volume), and to show savings on these tasks for months. Unlike the other tasks, these ones do not seem to be as tied to perceptual–motor skills or activation of previously stored information. The Tower of Hanoi, in particular, requires a high order of problem-solving ability.[1] Yet these tasks, too, share the same formal properties that permit them to satisfy the conditions I have proposed for tasks on which amnesics will show savings. Even the Tower of Hanoi is structured so that the goal is clear, the strategies necessary for achieving a solution are available to the subject, and success can be achieved without reference to a prior event.

Comparison with Other Hypotheses

At this point, the reader may ask what the advantage is in knowing the sufficient conditions for demonstrating preserved memory in amnesics. Would not one of the many other hypotheses that have already been proposed do just as well? I think not. First, by being neutral with regard to process or mechanism, one can state what characterizes those tasks on which amnesics show preserved memory without making any commitment to a theoretical framework about the nature of memory in general. Given the deficiencies of many of the available theories, it would seem a decided advantage to maintain a neutral stance at this point and to explore the terrain unfettered by attachments to a particular doctrine. Second, although the conditions that I have proposed resemble many of the available hypotheses, I think that the present proposal fares better than most of these in accounting for the evidence in the human literature. A number of examples illustrate this point.

Many theories assume that amnesic patients have deficits in establishing new associations or in using context to encode or retrieve the appropriate item from memory (Diamond & Rozin, 1974, as cited in Rozin, 1976; Hirsh, 1974; Schacter & Tulving, 1982; Warrington & Weiskrantz, 1973; Wickelgren, 1979; Winocur, 1982a). The experiments cited by Baddeley (1982), as well as our own studies on the reading of inverted script, indicate that improvement in performance is item-specific; this suggests that amnesics can form new, contextually specific associations and not merely acquire a general skill. As a further test of this idea, we had amnesic patients, as well as normal control subjects, study pairs of words that were very weakly associated, as well as sentences that were in the form of noun–verb–noun–noun (e.g., "The boy gave the ticket to the professor"). Later, all the subjects were asked to read separate lists of words and sentences. Each list contained either

1. "The Tower of Hanoi puzzle involves three vertical pegs and a number of doughnut-like disks of graduated sizes that fit on the pegs. At the outset all the disks are arranged pyramidally on one of the pegs, with the largest disk on the bottom. The task is to move all the disks to one of the empty pegs under the constraints that (a) only one disk may be moved at a time, and (b) a disk may never be placed on top of another smaller than itself" (Simon, 1975, p. 269).

old associates or old sentences; new associates or new sentences; or re-paired associates or re-paired sentences. The re-paired associates consisted of old items in which the response member of one pair was joined with the stimulus member of another pair; the re-paired sentences consisted of old nouns and verbs that were reassembled to form new sentences in such a way that no nouns and verbs that appeared together in an old sentence could appear together in a new one.

It was found that all subjects, including amnesics, read the lists consisting of old items significantly faster than lists of either new or re-paired items. There was no difference between the latter two for any of the groups (see Figure 11-3). On a recognition test, the young and normal control subjects could distinguish the old items from the new and re-paired ones, whereas the amnesics performed at chance levels on the sentences and only slightly above chance levels on the paired associates if they were presented twice.

These results indicate that amnesic patients do form associations among new items, but that they can demonstrate this only if the task satisfies the conditions for showing preserved memory in amnesics. What is significant is that for amnesics, as for controls, evidence of facilitated performance was found only for the previously associated items, not for the re-paired items; this indicates that what is stored is the unit, not the individual items. Put another way, the effect is specific and sensitive to the encoding context, even in amnesics, but it can be shown only under the appropriate test conditions.

It might be assumed that the conditions I have proposed simply provide the means for constraining retrieval cues at recognition or recall. This would reduce my proposal to a version of the retrieval-deficit hypothesis of amnesia (Kinsbourne & Wood, 1975; Warrington & Weiskrantz, 1973). This is not the case at all. Given identical cues, amnesics fail to demonstrate the effects of prior experience (savings or storage) if they are asked to decide whether the items were presented previously (i.e., to make reference to a previous event or episode), but not if they are simply required to operate on the information at hand. The various studies our group has reported, as well as those reported by Cohen and Squire (1980), Baddeley (1982), and especially by Graf *et al.* (1984), make this point very clearly.

Theories that emphasize intact semantic memory (Diamond & Rozin, 1974, as cited in Rozin, 1976; Kinsbourne & Wood, 1975; Schacter & Tulving, 1982) in amnesia have

FIGURE 11-3. Reading rate (in seconds) to old, old' (re-paired), and new paired associates and sentences. There were eight memory-disorder (MEM.-DIS.) subjects who read the paired associates, only seven of whom also read the sentences.

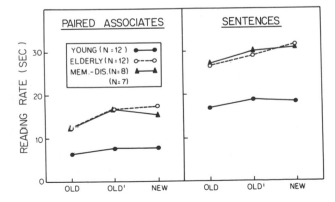

difficulty accounting for the fact that amnesic patients show anterograde amnesia for famous personalities, for world events (Albert, Butters, & Levin, 1979; Squire & Cohen, 1982), and even for words that have become current or that have changed in frequency after the amnesia was established (Cohen, 1983; Moscovitch & Ladowski, 1984). According to the conditions that I have specified, this is not surprising, since the demands of the task in cases where figures or events need to be identified are such that the subject does not enter the task with strategies or responses that enable him or her to arrive at a solution to the questions posed. Not being premorbidly familiar with the items, he or she cannot perform accurately, given the way the task is structured. This still leaves open the possibility that if the tasks were designed to satisfy the conditions set forth, amnesics might demonstrate some knowledge of postmorbid events and personalities.

The conditions I have proposed as sufficient to demonstrate preserved memory in amnesics resemble Cohen and Squire's (1980) and Jacoby and Witherspoon's (1982) hypothesis on the dissociation in amnesia between "procedural" and "declarative" memory and between "objective performance" on tests of savings and "subjective awareness" on tests of deliberate remembering, respectively. Indeed, my earlier ideas about the dissociation of different kinds of memory were influenced by their work and that of Kolers (1976) and by discussions on amnesia at the Lake Morey conference (see Cermak, 1982). I cannot, at the moment, point to any critical differences between my current proposal and that of Jacoby and Witherspoon, except that the two hypotheses emphasize different details. I am more concerned with task variables that distinguish one way of testing memory from another, whereas they concentrate on the cognitive processes that underlie performance on the different tests. This is not the case for Cohen and Squire, whose hypothesis, I believe, differs from mine on some substantive points. My hypothesis is neutral with regard to the type of memory or memory process that is spared in amnesia, defining only the conditions under which preserved memory may be demonstrated. Cohen and Squire, on the other hand, assume that there are two different memory systems, procedural and declarative, and that only the former is spared. Nor is it the case that my conditions regarding task variables are equivalent to the defining characteristics of procedural memory. For Cohen and Squire, procedural memory consists of the procedures or operations used to achieve a goal. No mention is made in their hypothesis of the fact that the subject has the means or strategies available for reaching that goal. This does not imply that the subject necessarily knows the solution beforehand, but that he or she should have the strategies available for arriving at a solution or goal. In addition, they do not mention that if the solution requires reference to a previous postmorbid event, the amnesic should fail at the task. Reference to a particular event need not be part of declarative memory, but could consist of calling to mind particular procedures carried out at a particular time and place.

Let me illustrate the differences with two variations of the Tower of Hanoi puzzle. Imagine an amnesic patient learning to solve the puzzle, except that some arbitrary elements are introduced that have nothing to do with reaching the specified goal, yet are made part of the general procedure. For example, the subject must turn each disk upside down before transferring it to another peg. Would the subject spontaneously perform this action the second time he or she attempts to solve the puzzle? According to my hypothesis, the subject should not, since this procedure is not part of the goal toward which he or she is striving; however, according to Cohen and Squire, this should be as much a part of procedural memory as the procedures used to arrive at a solution. Another rule that might be introduced is that in successive attempts at the puzzle, the principal peg on which the disks are finally arranged alternate from trial to trial. Again, according to my hypothesis, the amnesic patient should fail, since this solution requires reference to a previous event. Cohen and Squire, however, might predict that the subject should succeed, since this rule is properly part of procedural memory.

The reader familiar with psychological controversies can probably anticipate the outcome of this debate. As each side proposes a "definitive" experiment, the other side counters with an alternative experiment or modifies its hypothesis slightly so as to remain consistent with current findings. One very quickly reaches the point of diminishing returns in this scientific debate. But until that point is reached (for investigators in the midst of the controversy, it sometimes never is), much can be learned about the nature of the system under investigation. Amnesia research is now only at the threshold of initiating this type of debate.

One Memory System or Two?

Because the conditions I have set forth apply to task variables, they have nothing to say about this question. Earlier (Moscovitch, 1982a, 1982b), I argued in favor of one type of duplexity theory of amnesia, procedural versus conscious recollection or reflection. The hypothesis I have advanced in the present chapter would be just as valid for theories advocating the existence of a single long-term memory system. According to this view, some memories appear to be retained, whereas others do not, because of the question or tasks we put to the subject. Under one set of conditions, the memory becomes manifest, whereas under another set it remains hidden. It is not as if there are two memories of the same event or separate memories of different aspects of the same event—one for the procedures and one for the outcomes—but, rather, a single memory that reveals itself to different queries. In amnesics, responses are impaired to some queries, but not to others.

It might seem, given this analysis, that it makes no practical difference whether one argues for a unitary or a duplexity theory of memory. Let me cite at least one instance in which this is not the case. I argued (Moscovitch, 1982a), as did others (Milner, 1966; Rozin, 1976; Squire & Cohen, 1982), that some amnesias arise from failure to consolidate postmorbid events. This applies only to memories mediated by the system that is impaired. I was forced to argue, as would any duplexity theorist, that memories of the same event are normal in the memory system that is spared. A unitary-system view, however, could not tolerate an interpretation of amnesia as a consolidation failure, since such memories would never become manifest under any condition.

Summary

I have proposed three conditions that a task must satisfy if amnesics are to demonstrate preserved memory in performing it. By focusing on the task, rather than on underlying processes or mechanisms, I hope to distinguish more clearly the nature of the demands placed on the organism in those situations in which memory is preserved in amnesics from those in which it is impaired. This type of knowledge is critical for the development of a theory of normal and pathological memory.

It is clear from the foregoing that specifying these conditions does not provide a full account of amnesia or explain the various phenomena associated with it. It even remains to be determined whether these conditions apply equally well to all types of amnesic patients and to nonhuman species with damage to memory-related structures. It is hoped that this information will make it easier to elucidate the psychological processes and neurological mechanisms underlying the mnemonic abilities of at least some mammalian species.

ACKNOWLEDGMENTS

This work was supported by a Medical Research Council of Canada Grant and an Ontario Mental Health Foundation Grant to Gordon Winocur and Morris Moscovitch. The research reported in this chapter was conducted in collaboration with Gordon Winocur, Jill Moscovitch, and Don Crapper-McLachlan. I thank them, and also Neal Cohen, Fergus Craik, Larry Jacoby, Gordon Logan, Paul Rozin, Dan Schacter, Larry Squire, and Endel Tulving for their comments and suggestions during the many discussions we have had on amnesia. Many thanks to Nina Minde for help in collecting the data, to Peter Bucenieks for help in analyzing it, and to Maureen Patchett for typing the manuscript.

REFERENCES

Albert, M. S., Butters, N., & Levin, J. Temporal gradients in the retrograde amnesia of patients with alcoholic Korsakoff's disease. *Archives of Neurology*, 1979, *36*, 211–216.

Baddeley, A. D. Amnesia: A minimal model and an interpretation. In L. S. Cermak (Ed.), *Human memory and amnesia*. Hillsdale, N.J.: Erlbaum, 1982.

Cermak, L. S. (Ed.). *Human memory and amnesia*. Hillsdale, N.J.: Erlbaum, 1982.

Claparède, E. Recognition et moiité. *Archives de Psychologie* (Genève), 1911, *11*, 79–90.

Cohen, N. J. Personal communication, 1983.

Cohen, N. J., & Squire, L. R. Preserved learning and retention of pattern-analyzing skill in amnesia: Dissociation of knowing how and knowing that. *Science*, 1980, *210*, 207–210.

Corkin, S. Acquisition of motor skill after bilateral medial temporal-lobe excision. *Neuropsychologia*, 1968, *3*, 255–265.

Gaffan, D. Recognition memory in animals. In J. Brown (Ed.), *Recall and recognition*. New York: Wiley, 1976.

Gardner, H. *The shattered mind*. New York: Random House, 1974

Graf, P., Squire, L. R., & Mandler, G. The information that amnesic patients do not forget. *Journal of Experimental Psychology: Learning, Memory, and Cognition*. 1984, *10*, 164–178.

Hirsh, R. The hippocampus and contextual retrieval from memory: A theory. *Behavioral Biology*, 1974, *12*, 421–444.

Hirsh, R., & Krajden, J. The hippocampus and the expression of knowledge. In R. L. Isaacson & N. E. Spear (Eds.), *The expression of knowledge*. New York: Plenum Press, 1982.

Huppert, F. A., & Piercy, M. Dissociation between learning and remembering in organic amnesia. *Nature*, 1978, *275*, 317–318.

Huppert, F. A., & Piercy, M. Normal and abnormal forgetting in amnesia: Effect of locus of lesion. *Cortex*, 1979, *15*, 385–390.

Jacoby, L., & Witherspoon, D. Remembering without awareness. *Canadian Journal of Psychology*, 1982, *36*, 300–324.

Johnson, M. A multiple entry modular memory system. In G. H. Bower (Ed.), *The psychology of learning and motivation* (Vol. 17). New York: Academic Press, 1983.

Kinsbourne, M., & Wood, F. Short-term memory processes and the amnesic syndrome. In D. Deutsch & A. J. Deutsch (Eds.), *Short-term memory*. New York: Academic Press, 1975.

Kolers, P. Reading a year later. *Journal of Experimental Psychology: Human Learning and Memory*, 1976, *2*, 554–565.

Lhermitte, F., & Signoret, J.-L. Analyse neuropsychologique et différenciation des syndromes amnésiques. *Revue Neurologique*, 1972, *126*, 161–178.

Milner, B. Amnesia following operation on the temporal lobes. In C. W. M. Whitty & O. L. Zangwill (Eds.), *Amnesia*. London: Butterworths, 1966.

Milner, B., Corkin, S., & Teuber, H.-L. Further analysis of the hippocampal amnesic syndrome. *Neuropsychologia*, 1968, *6*, 215–234.

Moscovitch, M. Multiple dissociations of function in amnesia. In L. S. Cermak (Ed.), *Human memory and amnesia*. Hillsdale, N.J.: Erlbaum, 1982. (a)

Moscovitch, M. A neuropsychological approach to perception and memory in normal and pathological aging. In F. I. M. Craik & S. Trehub (Eds.), *Memory and cognitive processes in aging*. New York: Plenum Press, 1982. (b)

Moscovitch, M., & Ladowski, R. *Recall, recognition, and lexical decisions in young and old people for words that changed in frequency between 1944 and 1967*. Manuscript in preparation, 1984.

O'Keefe, J., & Nadel, L. *The hippocampus as a cognitive map*. London: Oxford University Press, 1978.

Olton, D. S., Becker, J. T., & Handelmann, G. E. Hippocampus, space and memory. *Behavioral and Brain Sciences*, 1979, *2*, 313–366.

Rozin, P. The psychobiological approach to human memory. In R. M. Rosenzweig & E. L. Bennett (Eds.), *Neural mechanisms of learning and memory*. Cambridge, Mass.: MIT Press, 1976.

Scarborough, D. L., Cortese, C., & Scarborough, H. Frequency and repetition effects in lexical memory. *Journal of Experimental Psychology: Human Perception and Performance*, 1977, *3*, 1–17.

Scarborough, D. L., Gerard, D., & Cortese, C. Accessing lexical memory: The transfer of word repetition effects across task and modality. *Memory and Cognition*, 1979, *7*, 3–12.

Schacter, D. L., & Tulving, E. Memory, amnesia, and the episodic/semantic distinction. In R. L. Isaacson & N. E. Spear (Eds.), *The expression of knowledge*. New York: Plenum Press, 1982.

Simon, H. A. The functional equivalence of problem solving skills. *Cognitive Psychology*, 1975, *7*, 268–288.

Squire, L. R. Two forms of human amnesia: An analysis of forgetting. *Journal of Neuroscience*, 1981, *1*, 635–640.

Squire, L. and Cohen, N. Remote memory, retrograde amnesia, and the neuropsychology of memory. In L. S. Cermak (Ed.), *Human memory and amnesia*. Hillsdale, N.J.: Erlbaum, 1982.

Talland, G. A. *Deranged memory*. New York: Academic Press, 1965.

Tulving, E. Episodic and semantic memory. In E. Tulving & W. Donaldson (Eds.), *Organization of memory*. New York; Academic Press, 1972.

Warrington, E. K., & Weiskrantz, L. Amnesic syndrome: Consolidation or retrieval? *Nature*, 1970, *228*, 628–630.

Warrington, E. K., & Weiskrantz, L. An analysis of short-term and long-term memory defects in man. In J. A. Deutsch (Ed.), *The physiological basis of memory*. New York: Academic Press, 1973.

Weiskrantz, L. A comparison of hippocampal pathology in man and other animals. In K. Elliot & J. Whelan (Eds.), *Function of the septo-hippocampal system* (CIBA Foundation Symposium No. 58). Amsterdam: Elsevier, 1978.

Weiskrantz, L., & Warrington, E. K. Conditioning in amnesic patients. *Neuropsychologia*, 1979, *17*, 187–194.

Wickelgren, W. A. Chunking and consolidation: A theoretical synthesis of semantic networks, configuring in conditioning S-R versus cognitive learning, normal forgetting, the amnesic syndrome, and the hippocampal arousal system. *Psychological Review*, 1979, *86*, 44–60.

Winocur, G. The amnesic syndrome: A deficit in cue utilization. In L. S. Cermak (Ed.), *Human memory and amnesia*. Hillsdale, N.J.: Erlbaum, 1982. (a)

Winocur, G. Radial-arm-maze behavior by rats with dorsal hippocampal lesions: Effects of cuing. *Journal of Comparative and Physiological Psychology*, 1982, *96*, 155–169. (b)

Winocur, G., & Weiskrantz, L. An investigation of paired-associate learning in amnesic patients. *Neuropsychologia*, 1976, *14*, 97–110.

12

Amnesia Is as Amnesia Does: Toward Another Definition of the Anterograde Amnesias

Steven Mattis and Richard Kovner

We would like to briefly present the results of some of our ongoing research; then, integrating it with a theoretical model and other selected research, we follow the implications of this integration toward a more accurate understanding of the anterograde amnesias.

Recently, we have been engaged in efforts to significantly enhance free recall in patients with severe anterograde amnesias due to bilateral central nervous system (CNS) impairment. Toward this goal, we reported the effect on recall of a technique called "Ridiculously Imaged Stories" (RIS) (Kovner, Mattis, & Goldmeier, 1983). In this experiment, five patients with generalized anterograde amnesias of differing pathophysiologies (two were alcoholic Korsakoff, one had suffered severe head trauma, one had suffered an episode of hypotension/hypoxia, and the last had experienced a bleed of a dominant medial temporal lobe arteriovenous malformation [AVM] with subsequent hydrocephalus that was shunted) were studied.

These subjects were presented with two 20-word lists that were matched for category type, frequency of usage, concreteness, and imagery (Battig & Montague, 1969; Paivio, Yuille, & Madigan, 1968). One list was presented in a standard list-learning paradigm, utilizing selective-reminding cues (Buschke, 1973). The words on the other list were connected by a storyline composed of RIS of highly novel (i.e., arousing) content. For example, the first five words on the RIS list were "headlight," "ink," "refrigerator," "girl," and "lemon." The target items were linked by the following story:

> R. K. was jogging down the highway at night with a *headlight* in the middle of his forehead. It began to rain, but instead of raining water it rained *ink*, blackening out R. K.'s eyeglasses and causing him to stumble along in the middle of the road. Rolling down the highway toward him was a big white *refrigerator* on wheels being driven by a *girl* with *lemons* instead of breasts.

The amnesic subjects and a matched group of normal controls were seen once weekly for learning sessions that lasted for 1½ hours, including a 20-minute free-time break between conditions. The RIS or the selective-reminding control procedure was alternately presented as the first condition in each week's session. At the beginning of a condition each week, a free-recall trial and a recognition-memory probe were administered to assess memory performance at the 1-week intervals.

Steven Mattis. Department of Psychiatry, New York Hospital–Cornell Medical Center, Westchester Division, White Plains, New York.

Richard Kovner. Department of Neurology, Montefiore Medical Center and Albert Einstein College of Medicine, Bronx, New York.

In the first session (Week 1) and in all subsequent sessions (Weeks 2–8), after the 1-week interval recall and recognition measures had been obtained in the RIS condition, the entire story was read to the subject, with the target items' being clearly emphasized as the words to be recalled. A free-recall trial immediately followed (Trial 1). Trials 2, 3, and 4 proceeded without initial presentation of the story. On these trials, subjects were asked to recount the story including target items, and partial cuing was instituted as needed to elicit the target words. Cuing was initiated with context cues (retelling part of the story minus target items—e.g., "The refrigerator on wheels was being driven by a . . ."). If this failed to elicit a target word, a category cue was given (e.g., "kitchen appliance"). If this also failed, the target item was given. On the fifth trial, free recall without any cuing was requested. Immediately following the final free-recall trial, a recognition-memory probe was introduced. This consisted of 40 items (20 target and 20 distractor), with the subject being asked to respond "yes" or "no" as to whether or not each item was on the list being learned.

In the selective-reminding condition, five learning trials were also administered during each session. On Trial 1, all 20 words were read to the subject at the rate of one per 2 seconds. The subject was required to repeat each word to insure correct registration. Selective reminding was then instituted for four trials. In this procedure (Buschke, 1973), the subject is provided with the target items he or she did not produce after his or her recall has been exhausted on each trial. Thus, the level of cuing provided in the selective-reminding condition corresponds to the most concrete level of cuing in the RIS condition (i.e., providing the target word if context and categorical cuing have failed to elicit it). The fifth trial, as in the RIS condition, consisted of free recall followed by a 40-item recognition-memory probe.

By the eighth week of training (i.e., the eighth session), the amnesic group demonstrated free recall of 14 of the 20 words on the target list in the RIS condition after a 1-week interval. This contrasted with free recall of fewer than two target words in the selective-reminding condition. It should be noted again that the stimulus characteristics of the two lists, the frequency of target-word repetitions, and the amount of cuing in both conditions were virtually identical.

Review of the literature and data from the control condition in this study indicate that none of the relevant parameters by themselves could have produced the magnitude of free recall after a 1-week interval demonstrated by our amnesic subjects. Neither repetition *per se* (as seen in this study), the storyline by itself (as exemplified by the typically poor performance of amnesic patients on the Memory Passages subtest of the Wechsler Memory Scale), nor visual imagery techniques without concomitant use of a story (Baddeley & Warrington, 1973; Cermak, 1975; Cutting, 1978) are effective in producing robust recall in patients with generalized amnesias and bilateral CNS impairment.

There is some suggestion (Butters, 1982; Davidoff, Butters, Gerstman, & Mattis, 1979) that highly arousing (i.e., emotionally charged) material may be an independently effective factor in improving paragraph memory in Korsakoff subjects, but nowhere to the degree demonstrated by our amnesic subjects. In order to investigate the saliency of novelty as an independent factor in our technique, in addition to exploring the limitations of our technique in terms of the amount of material that can be learned, two of our five amnesic subjects were studied further. The results to date (Kovner, Mattis, & Pass, 1983) show that our two amnesic subjects were able to learn lists of 80 and 60 words, respectively, in the RIS condition; their free recall of the lists and the associated stories was 100% accurate after intervals ranging from 1 to 7 weeks. Surprisingly, the novel aspects of the storyline did not contribute to the magnitude of free recall. Another storyline, "Logically Imaged Stories" (LIS), was constructed in which the target items were logically (i.e., rather neutrally) linked together. For example, the first five words on the LIS list were "golf," "shoes," "building," "sandwich," and "grass." The LIS story started as follows:

> Mr. Jones was out playing *golf* and was wearing his new *shoes*. While playing, he noticed that one of the cleats was broken, and he returned to the main *building* to get it repaired. Afterward, Mr. Jones bought a *sandwich* at the snack bar and walked out onto the *grass*.

In the LIS condition, the same two amnesic subjects were able to learn an additional 80 and 60 words, respectively, at the same rate as in the RIS condition, with 100% accuracy after intervals of 1 week or more. At present, each subject is capable of recalling all RIS and LIS words (i.e., 160 and 120 words, respectively) in sequence with 100% accuracy after a minimum delay of 1 week. These findings contrast sharply with the observation that at any given session there is an equal probability that our subject will be disoriented as to date and may display other clinically obvious signs of anterograde amnesia.

In the RIS and LIS procedures, new material to be learned was introduced in consecutive blocks of 20 words. We were therefore able to compare the rate of acquisition and efficacy of 1-week free recall of each 20-word list to those before and after. Therefore, any savings effects or disruptive effects of prior word-list exposure on acquisition and recall could be noted. No such effects were in fact observed. Each subject had a steady rate of learning for such 20-word lists, which did not vary as a function of serial-list order or condition (RIS or LIS). Once learned, the material was remarkably invulnerable to distortion, forgetting, and intrusion.

While we are continuing to investigate the parameters contributing to robust free recall in amnesic patients, the results to date indicate that some severely amnesic patients can freely recall virtually unlimited amounts of unrelated items embedded in new stories after intervals of 1 week or more, utilizing the RIS and LIS techniques. Although the learning rates of amnesic subjects using these procedures is significantly slower than normal, the fact remains that in order for them to accomplish this feat they have had to demonstrate the ability to encode, store, retrieve, and organize large amounts of information within a new context. These findings not only seriously challenge current models of anterograde amnesias, which rely heavily on the postulation of unitary deficits in encoding, retrieval, or episodic (contextual) memory as prime causal factors, but also require rethinking as to the definition of an anterograde amnesia.

Most impressive was the fact that our patients made no spontaneous attempts to use our mnemonic techniques to promote recall of everyday events, and showed no savings (i.e., the use of similar strategies) when concurrent control lists of 20 words were introduced. At no time did the subjects attempt to develop their own stories when they were engaged in the selective-reminding procedure or informal list-learning tasks. However, we did not interpret this to mean that the crucial difference between normal and amnesic populations is the failure of amnesic patients to apply conscious strategies during learning.

The inability of our amnesic subjects to initiate such mnemonic strategies spontaneously contrasted sharply with (1) their ability to benefit from the technique when it was externally structured by the examiners, and (2) their ability to invent and effectively use such imaged stories when specifically requested to do so at informal sessions. It appeared to us, clinically, that the patients were able to "chunk," sequence, store, and reorganize stored material, and to retrieve this material, only when the parallel initiating, attentional, and monitoring mechanisms (which normally are automatically self-activated) were stimulated and maintained by the external conditions (i.e., by the RIS and LIS procedures). Indeed, the simplicity of our learning technique, combined with the seeming ease of the amnesic subjects' recall once the stories were learned, suggested that a primary deficit of automatically actuated processing might be involved. As a result, we began to shift our focus away from seeking general defects in encoding, storage, and retrieval functions as possible causes of amnesia, and toward consideration of those processes that influence spontaneous initiation of the necessary cognitive operations.

In the literature on memory and amnesia, there is seemingly only one clearly formulated model of memory—a mathematical model developed by Grossberg (1978, 1982), which explicates the critical role of attentional–inertial processes in learning and memory. Central to his model is the constant, complementary interaction of attentional and orienting subsystems. These two subsystems drive parallel gating mechanisms at given points in neuronal space and time during encoding, storage, and retrieval if expectancies are met (match), or for memory reset by the orienting system if expectancies are not met (mismatch). Grossberg also emphasizes that many of the processing steps necessary for adaptive learning and memory are not accessible to consciousness. He states explicitly,

> The many processing steps such as adaptive filtering, short-term memory mismatch, disinhibition of orienting arousal, short-term memory reset, and so forth, all involve perfectly good neural potentials, signals, and transmitters. However, they are not accessible to consciousness. The conscious experience is, I suggest, the resonant or attentive moment, which seems to be immediate because it is a global event that energizes the system as a whole. (1982, p. 543)

His model would appear to predict, explicitly and implicitly, the patterns of memory disorders and competencies that are consonant with our data.

In addition, Hasher and Zacks (1979) have behaviorally delineated "automatic" and "effortful" processes in normal learning and memory. Speculations as to the effects of disorders in such "automatic" processes on memory are consonant with Grossberg's model, and may serve as at least a first-order approximation of the pattern of deficits manifested by our patients. The automatic, "genetically prepared" processes postulated by Hasher and Zacks are (1) activation of word meaning, (2) discrimination of event frequency, (3) appreciation of the temporal order of events, and (4) discrimination of the spatial location of cues. These processes appear to be of equal efficacy, whether or not they are instructionally embedded in learning tasks (focused vs. incidental learning). These functions, as reported by the authors, also do not seem to show maturational trends once they have reached asymptotic levels early in life.

Lhermitte and Signoret (1972) first observed differences in mnemonic deficit patterns in alcoholic Korsakoff subjects and post-herpes encephalitics that could reflect deficits in the automatic processes postulated above. Post-herpes subjects displayed massive anterograde amnesia on a task requiring spatial location of pictures, but showed better performance on tasks requiring knowledge of temporal order. Korsakoff subjects, by contrast, were able to store information about spatial location, but failed sequential tests. In retrospect, this was perhaps the first indication that a given group of amnesic patients may have a specific defect in one kind of "automatic" process in the presence of another's being relatively intact.

We (Mattis, Kovner, & Goldmeier, 1978) also showed contrasting performance deficits in Korsakoff and post-herpes encephalitis patients in a verbal-recall and recognition-memory paradigm. The post-herpes subjects offered no evidence of any retention on either measure, for a variety of different list organizations. In our contrast of the amnesic disorders of Korsakoff and post-herpes patients in this study, we made the observation concerning activation of word meaning that normal controls and Korsakoff patients had equal recognition memory for truly novel verbal stimuli (i.e., nonsense and Persian words). We can speculate that to the extent that activation of word meaning is unnecessary, normal controls have no advantage. While the commonly observed anomia in post-herpes patients might account in part for poor performance on verbal tasks, the severity of anomia in no way accounts for the complete absence on either recall or recognition tasks of any evidence of encoding, and certainly would not account for the severe defects in nonverbal memory observed by Lhermitte and Signoret (1972). Grossberg (1982) postulates a central role for the hippocampi as the final common pathways of the drive representations, which to a large extent determine cue saliency and selectivity. Failure to gate appropriately may result in equipotentiality or equal saliency of all concurrent cues, so that none are selected to enter short-term or long-term memory. The propensity for bilateral destruction of medial temporal areas in herpes encephalitis makes it likely that these patients would suffer more extensive hippocampal damage than would usually be found in alcoholic Korsakoff syndrome. Thus, a hypothesized difference in the way "automatic" processes may have been affected by the differing lesion distributions in both syndromes may largely account for the observed differences in mnemonic deficits.

In a later study (Kovner, Mattis, Gartner, & Goldmeier, 1981) we contrasted performance of alcoholic Korsakoff and severe posttraumatic amnesic subjects on an instrument we developed, called the Semantic Information Test. This test taps basic semantic knowledge about common, concrete nouns. It was noted that the Korsakoff patients made a disproportionate number of incorrect responses to such absurdly easy questions as these:

A dog can learn to read and write: True or False?
A donkey lays eggs: True or False?

It would seem that at least some of the literature suggesting a lack of deep semantic encoding by alcoholic Korsakoff subjects (Cermak & Reale, 1978) could be interpreted as rather suggesting a deficit in the "automatic" activation of word meaning. This might, in turn, lead to the blurring of cue saliency, with defective transfer to short and long-term memory. Interestingly, the two amnesic subjects reported on in the combined RIS-LIS study (with amnesia due to hypoxia, and left medial temporal lobe AVM and hydrocephalus, respectively) did not differ from normal subjects on the Semantic Information Test. This finding suggests that a deficit in activation of word meaning is not invariably associated with anterograde amnesia. Intuitively, it would seem that a deficit in appreciation of event frequency would be rather universal in amnesic patients, because it may depend on the interactions among the other three postulated "automatic" functions. This has not yet been examined systematically in amnesic patients of different etiologies.

Huppert and Piercy (1976) reported results with alcoholic Korsakoff patients that suggest that the deficit in discriminating temporal order is more salient than their deficit in discriminating event frequency. The experimenters examined recognition memory for pictures and words of different frequency of usage at intervals of 10 minutes, 1 week, and 7 weeks. The Korsakoff subjects displayed relatively good retention of pictures and low frequency of usage words at all intervals. The subjects were also assessed on their ability to discriminate (1) whether or not pictures had been seen 10 minutes or 24 hours previously, or (2) whether the picture presented had been seen before or not. The Korsakoff subjects were severely impaired on the first type of recognition memory and were much less impaired on the second type. This was viewed as a defect in contextual memory, but could also be seen as a deficit in the ability to discriminate temporal order, and in some circumstances frequency. In our work with alcoholic Korsakoff patients (Mattis *et al.*, 1978), we observed that extensive repetition of a 20-word target list using the selective-reminding procedure (Buschke, 1973) did not aid recognition memory. In fact, if recognition-memory probes were introduced after the 4th, 8th, and 12th recall trials of learning on a categorized word list, then by the third probe recognition memory was substantially poorer than on the first probe. One could view this as suggestive of a negative three-way interaction effect among appreciation of temporal order, frequency, and activation of word meaning.

The dense anterograde amnesia of the alcoholic Korsakoff patients, observed on the third recognition-memory probe of the categorized word list, was at times equal in severity to the dense anterograde amnesia demonstrated by the post-herpes encephalitis patients. Which group, or even which specific patients, had the more severe amnesia? The research to date suggests that this question cannot be answered by obtaining a memory score on any given task. In the case described above, we submit that the Korsakoff and the post-herpes patients obtained the same score for different reasons. Thus, by the third probe, the hypothesized interactional effect of deficits in automatic processes would have severely restricted the Korsakoff patients' appreciation of prior events. Their level of defective performance was not as pronounced on the first probe, or even for differently constructed word lists. In contrast, the post-herpes encephalitis patients' postulated generalized failure to gate efficiently resulted in observed failure to appreciate prior events under a wide range of stimulus and task conditions. Thus, differences in mnemonic processes among patient groups or specific patients can only be intelligently discussed within the constraints of given task requirements and cannot be generalized to other situations. In addition, each amnesic subgroup possesses a typical profile of performance abilities under differing task conditions.

To recapitulate, our attempt to develop behavioral techniques that would augment recall in severely amnesic patients has resulted in procedures that promote free recall of large amounts of information in such patients. While we continue to investigate those parameters and combination of parameters that will enable more rapid and extensive acquisition of material, the magnitude of free recall demonstrated by our patients seriously challenges the theoretical framework within which most investigators have been working. Our patients have demonstrated the ability to encode, store, chunk, reorganize in new contexts, and retrieve information reliably. These findings have led us to focus on models of memory that emphasize unconscious, automatic processes. The mathematical model expounded by Grossberg (1982) is, to our knowledge, the only one consonant with our findings and our suggested reinterpretation of the findings of others.

At this point in our understanding of the anterograde amnesias, we would submit (1) that deficits in "automatic" processes play a causal role in the anterograde amnesias; (2) that different distributions of lesions are etiologically related to deficits in different automatic processes; and (3) that, therefore, there are differing resultant patterns of memory disorders as a function of different pathogenic events. We would hope that research toward delineation of the neuroanatomical and neurophysiological substrates of differing deficits in automatic processes will eventually result in an array of specific techniques, both behavioral and pharmacological, that will successfully alleviate the anterograde amnesias.

REFERENCES

Baddeley, A. D., & Warrington, E. K. Memory coding and amnesia. *Neuropsychologia*, 1973, *11*, 159–165.

Battig, W. F., & Montague, W. W. Category norms for verbal items in fifty-six categories. *Journal of Experimental Psychology Monographs*, 1969, *80*, 1–46.

Buschke, H. Selective reminding for analysis of memory and learning. *Journal of Verbal Learning and Verbal Behavior*, 1973, *12*, 543–550.

Butters, N. Personal communication, 1982.

Cermak, L. S. Imagery as an aid to retrieval for Korsakoff patients. *Cortex*, 1975, *11*, 163–169.

Cermak, L. S., & Reale, L. Depth of processing and retention of words by alcoholic Korsakoff patients. *Journal of Experimental Psychology: Human Learning and Memory*, 1978, *4*, 165–174.

Cutting, J. A cognitive approach to Korsakoff's syndrome. *Cortex*, 1978, *14*, 485–495.

Davidoff, D. A., Butters, N., Gerstman, L. J., & Mattis, S. *Motivational aspects of alcoholic Korsakoff's syndrome.* Paper presented at the 7th annual meeting of the International Neuropsychological Society, New York City, 1979.

Grossberg, S. A theory of human memory: Self-organization and performance of sensory–motor codes, maps and plans. *Progress in Theoretical Biology*, 1978, *5*, 233–374.

Grossberg, S. Processing of expected and unexpected events during conditioning and attention: A psychophysiological theory. *Psychological Review*, 1982, *89*, 529–572.

Hasher, L., & Zacks, R. T. Automatic and effortful processes in memory. *Journal of Experimental Psychology: General*, 1979, *108*, 356–388.

Huppert, F. A., & Piercy, M. Recognition memory in amnesic patients: Effect of temporal context and familiarity of material. *Cortex*, 1976, *4*, 3–20.

Kovner, R., Mattis, S. S., Gartner, J., & Goldmeier, E. A verbal semantic deficit in the alcoholic Korsakoff syndrome. *Cortex*, 1981, *17*, 419–426.

Kovner, R., Mattis, S., & Goldmeier, E. A technique for promoting robust free recall in chronic organic amnesia. *Journal of Clinical Neuropsychology*, 1983, *5*(1), 65–71.

Kovner, R., Mattis, S., & Pass, R. *Some amnesic patients can freely recall large amounts of information in new contexts.* Paper presented at the 11th annual meeting of the International Neuropsychological Society, Mexico City, February 1983.

Lhermitte, F., & Signoret, J. L. Analyse neuropsychologique et différenciation des syndromes amnésiques. *Revue Neurologique*, 1972, *126*, 161–178.

Mattis, S., Kovner, R., & Goldmeier, E. Different patterns of mnemonic deficits in two organic amnestic syndromes. *Brain and Language*, 1978, *6*, 179–191.

Paivio, A., Yuille, J. C., & Madigan, S. Concreteness, imagery, and meaningfulness values for 925 nouns. *Journal of Experimental Psychology Monograph*, 1968, *76*(1, Pt. 2).

Memory Localization in the Brain

13

Gordon Winocur

Introduction

Neuropsychological investigations of the amnesic syndrome have focused increasingly in recent years on the neurological substrate underlying memory disorders. Numerous cortical and subcortical centers have been implicated in the mediation of memory, but two brain regions—the medial temporal lobe and the diencephalon—have come in for special attention. The diencephalon and, in particular, the thalamus, have been associated with memory processes since the classic study of Victor, Adams, and Collins (1971), in which pathological analysis was performed on the brains of severely amnesic patients with Korsakoff syndrome. Diencephalic and limbic structures were variously affected in this population, but disease was found most consistently in the area of the dorsomedial thalamus. Subsequent investigations involving patients with more restricted thalamic damage have generally confirmed the importance of this structure for memory processes.

An association between the medial temporal lobe and memory has been widely accepted since the work of Milner and her colleagues (Milner, 1962). In an early study, Scoville and Milner (1957) examined at autopsy the brains of several amnesic patients who had undergone temporal lobectomy. A correlation was reported between the severity of memory loss and extent of damage to the hippocampus; no other affected structure yielded this type of relationship. This finding was extended in studies of the patient H. M., who, following bilateral hippocampectomy, displayed a profound amnesia that was virtually unaccompanied by intellectual impairment or other signs of cognitive change.

Considerable progress has been made in describing the features of memory disorders associated with primary damage in different brain areas. Indeed, we now have hypotheses concerning the respective dysfunctions underlying the various organically based amnesias. This chapter is concerned mainly with diencephalic and medial temporal lobe amnesia, and particularly with the notion that these regions can be functionally dissociated with respect to memory-related operations. New experiments are reported in which existing concepts, based mainly on research with brain-damaged humans, are evaluated in studies using analogous procedures with animals subjected to surgically controlled brain lesions.

Gordon Winocur. Department of Psychology, Trent University, Peterborough, Ontario, Canada.

Diencephalic and Medial Temporal Lobe Amnesia

Human Studies

Investigations by Huppert and Piercy (1979) and by Squire (1981) have consistently pointed to two dissociable forms of amnesia following damage to diencephalic or medial temporal lobe areas. In one study, Huppert and Piercy (1979) presented 120 pictures to groups of Korsakoff amnesics, normal controls, and H. M., and then assessed recognition memory 10 minutes, 24 hours, and 7 days later. At each test, a different sample of 40 target items was interspersed with 40 new distractors. The initial presentation time for each picture was varied between the groups so that, at 10 minutes, performance levels were equivalent. At longer intervals, H. M.'s recognition memory declined, although there was no difference between the Korsakoff and control groups. The results appear to reflect a faster forgetting rate in amnesia that is related to medial temporal lobe damage. In contrast, the rate of forgetting in Korsakoff amnesics, presumed to have primary diencephalic damage, was normal. Confirmatory results, based on similar tests, were reported by Squire (1981) for Korsakoff patients; N. A., an amnesic patient with unilateral thalamic damage; and a group of ECT patients (this group was included because of indirect evidence linking ECT-induced memory loss to medial temporal lobe dysfunction).

The idea of anatomically dissociable forms of amnesia has also been evaluated in experiments involving memory over shorter intervals, but here the evidence is less straight-forward. A frequently used test of short-term memory, the Brown–Peterson test, involves presentation of stimuli (consonant trigrams, words) for a fixed, brief period, followed by a variable filled interval (e.g., 0–60 seconds), after which the subject must recall the stimuli. Medial temporal lobe patients with extensive hippocampal damage are generally impaired on this task, although their actual rate of forgetting appears normal (Milner, 1974).

Patients with diencephalic lesions are also impaired on the Brown–Peterson test, but the results are not entirely consistent. N. A. displayed rapid forgetting (Squire & Slater, 1978), but there is disagreement over the performance of Korsakoff patients, who, because of their presumed thalamic damage, would be expected to show similar loss. Butters and his colleagues (Cermak, Butters, & Goodglass, 1971; Samuels, Butters, Goodglass, & Brody, 1971) reported abnormally fast forgetting in Korsakoff patients, whereas Warrington (Baddeley & Warrington, 1970; Warrington, 1982) has consistently found no differences between Korsakoff patients and control subjects. A critical factor underlying this discrepancy may relate to procedural differences in administering the test. In the Butters *et al.* experiments, subjects were allowed only 2 seconds to study the stimuli, whereas Warrington presented the stimuli for 3 or 4 seconds. Assuming that the studies were comparable in other respects, variable presentation times could account for the observed performance differences, especially if, as has been suggested, diencephalic amnesia can be related to a fundamental deficit at the time of original learning.

This issue was examined recently in a patient, B. Y., who became amnesic after an apparent cardiovascular accident involving the paramedian artery, which supplies blood to the dorsomedial thalamus (Winocur, Oxbury, Roberts, Agnetti, & Davis, in press). CT scans revealed small, bilateral lesions restricted to the region to the dorsomedial nucleus. The Brown–Peterson test was administered to this patient, with stimuli presented for 2 seconds or 4 seconds. The data (see Figure 13-1) show clearly that B. Y. was severely impaired in the 2-second condition, in line with the Butters *et al.* findings, but normal at the delay intervals of 0–9 seconds, in line with Warrington's reports.

These results are consistent with Huppert and Piercy's (1979) and Squire's (1981) general conclusion that the chief difference between diencephalic and medial temporal lobe amnesia can be traced to deficits at different stages of information processing. Their respective positions vary somewhat, but the essential argument is that diencephalic amnesia results from a fundamental deficit very early in the learning process, perhaps at the stage in which information is actually encoded. Patients with medial temporal lobe damage appear better at registering and holding material; this suggests that encoding mechanisms may be more functional. Memory loss in these patients begins to emerge clearly at longer intervals—a pattern that implicates the consolidation or storage of acquired information.

FIGURE 13-1. **Precent recall scores by B. Y. and control group on the Brown–Peterson test. (From G. Winocur, S. Oxbury, R. Roberts, V. Agnetti, & C. Davis, Amnesia in a patient with bilateral lesions to the thalamus.** *Neuropsychologia*, **in press. Copyright by Pergamon Press, Ltd. Reprinted by permission.)**

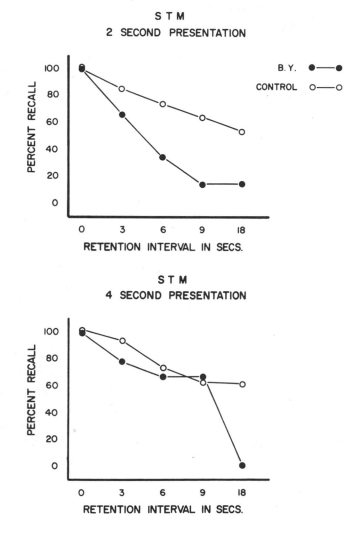

Investigations with brain-damaged humans have been valuable, not only in describing similarities and differences among various types of amnesia, but in providing a basis for integrating the traditional approaches of experimental psychology and neuropsychology. However, their usefulness in characterizing the normal function of a damaged region is limited in part by the degree of inference necessarily involved in describing the locus and extent of damage. Advances in CT technology have greatly aided this effort, but the margin of error remains substantial. In this respect, animal experiments in which brain lesions are produced under controlled conditions, and that use analogous testing procedures, can serve as a valuable complement to human studies.

Animal Studies

Animal investigations, involving different species and a range of tasks, have assessed memory performance in relation to selective brain damage. There is little doubt that the hippocampus, on its own (Jarrard, 1980; Olton, Becker, & Handelmann, 1979; Winocur, 1980) or in combination with other medial temporal lobe structures (e.g., amygdala; see Mishkin, 1978), is critically involved in memory processes. It is also clear that lesions to the thalamus of aminals, particularly in the dorsomedial region, adversely affects memory (Aggleton & Mishkin, 1983; Thompson, 1963).

There has been little attempt to generate, on the basis of these findings, animal models for the types of amnesia described in the preceding section. Nevertheless, at least one line of research illustrates the potential value of such an approach. In a series of studies, Kesner and his associates (Kesner & Wilburn, 1974) electrically stimulated different parts of the brains of rats within seconds of their having received aversive foot shock, contingent upon having displayed learned operant behavior. Retesting for memory of the shock followed at variable intervals, ranging between 64 seconds and 24 hours. Memory loss was consistently reported in hippocampally stimulated animals at long, but *not* at short, intervals. Stimulation of other brain regions (e.g., amygdala, caudate nucleus) yielded different patterns of memory loss.

These results are broadly consistent with the human data suggesting that disruption of hippocampal function causes memory loss that becomes apparent at relatively long intervals following original learning. There appear to be no corresponding animal studies specifically addressing the idea that diencephalic amnesia represents a deficit at an earlier stage of processing. Recently, a systematic investigation was undertaken in my laboratory, in which the effects of hippocampal and thalamic lesions were directly compared on tests of memory; these tests were designed to be analogous to the human tests that provide the strongest evidence for a dissociation between diencephalic and medial temporal lobe amnesia. In both cases, the critical variable interacting with locus of lesion was the length of interval over which information must be remembered.

MEMORY OVER SHORT INTERVALS

This test, based on a procedure first described by Means, Walker, and Isaacson (1970), was designed to parallel the Brown–Peterson test of short-term memory. Groups of rats with hippocampal, dorsomedial thalamic, and sham lesions were initially trained to press a lever for food according to a schedule of continuous reinforcement. When responding had stabilized, the experimental condition was introduced, which consisted essentially of a single-lever alternation problem. Each session consisted of 24 go or no-go trials, in which the lever was present for 20 seconds. On go trials, each lever press produced a food pellet; on no-go trials, pressing the level produced no reinforcement. Between trials, the lever was retracted for 2.5, 5, 10, 20, 40, or 80 seconds. Each interval occurred four times in a session, according to a random schedule, which varied every day. One session per day was administered over 12 consecutive days, with a go trial beginning each session.

Efficient performance on each trial demanded that the animal accurately recall events of the previous trial. For example, an immediately preceding go trial, in which responses were rewarded, was the signal that the next trial, following the return of the lever, would be a no-go trial and that responses should be withheld; the opposite was true if the preceding trial was a no-go trial. Two measures of performance were taken: latency to first response, and the number of responses in the go and no-go trials. If animals learned the task and remembered across the intervals, they would display shorter latencies and more responses in the go than in the no-go trials. Thus, efficiency would be reflected in low go/no-go latency ratios and high go/no-go response ratios. These ratios were computed for the various groups at each delay interval on Days 1 and 12, and are presented in Figures 13-2 and 13-3.

FIGURE 13-2. Latency ratios for hippocampal, thalamic, and operated control groups on the go/no-go task.

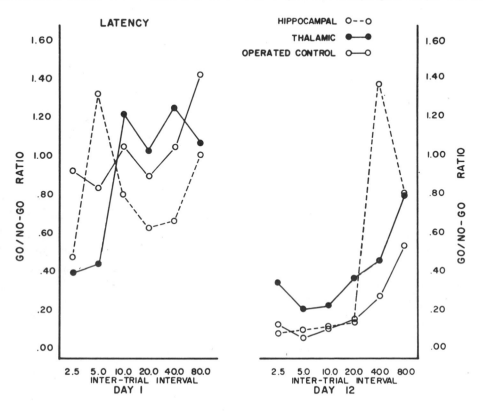

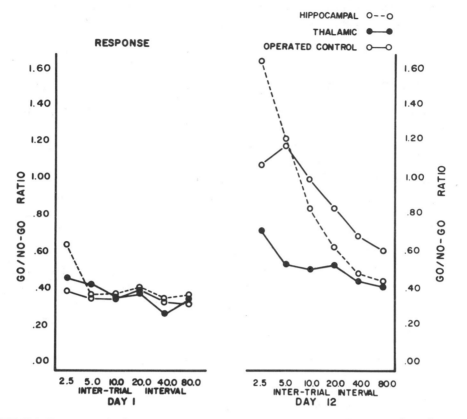

FIGURE 13-3. Response ratios for hippocampal, thalamic, and operated control groups on the go/no-go task.

The results for the two measures were essentially the same. As expected, all groups were equally inefficient on the first day of the experimental condition. The only significant Day 1 effect was that of interval, as all groups showed a performance decline as a function of increased intervals. There was general improvement by Day 12, but on both measures, the thalamic group was significantly worse than the control group at all intervals. The hippocampal group performed as well or better than the other groups at short intervals, but deteriorated at longer intervals. On the response measure, the decline was apparent by the 20-second interval, where the hippocampal group no longer differed significantly from the thalamic group. The decline occurred later, but more dramatically, on the latency measure, where performance of hippocampal animals dropped sharply at the 40-second delay.

Because they showed substantial savings over training, it is clear that all groups learned the basic alternation strategy inherent to the task. Indeed, on Day 12, the hippocampal group performed at least as well as the control group at the shorter intervals. The hippocampal animals' problem clearly was not with the task itself, but in recalling episodic events at relatively long intervals. The thalamic group showed the smallest overall improvement on Day 12, relative to Day 1; this indicates that they probably learned less about the task than the other groups. This—along with the fact that on Day 12, the thalamic group was significantly impaired at even the 2.5-second delay, where the intertrial interval was minimal—confirms the fundamental importance of the thalamus to the learning process.

MEMORY AT LONG INTERVALS

A second series of experiments, involving an avoidance-conditioning procedure, tested recall over extended delay periods. Groups of hippocampal, thalamic, and operated control rats were deprived of water and allowed individual access to a drinking spout for 30 minutes on each of 4 consecutive days. On the fifth day, half the animals received an electric shock when they made contact with the spout; the other half received no shock. Both subgroups were returned to their home cages immediately upon making contact with the spout. A single retest took place 1 hour, 7 days, or 21 days later. The measure of recall of the aversive experience was the animal's latency to drink at test; failure to recall the shock would result in relatively short latencies.

As can be seen in Figure 13-4, when no shock was administered, the three groups showed little change in latency to drink over the various delay periods. In the shock condition, there were no differences between groups following 1-hour and 7-day delays. After 21 days, the hippocampal group was slightly but significantly faster than the control group, indicating some memory loss for the shock. Latency differences between the thalamic group and the other groups were not statistically significant.

The behavior of the hippocampal groups suggests some impairment at relatively long intervals, and, as such, is consistent with results of the previous study. There was no clear evidence of memory deficit in the thalamic group. The data further emphasize that memory loss in cases of thalamic damage relates to performance at original learning. The shock-avoidance study involved a task that all animals were equally able to learn and perform with a high degree of proficiency. Animals with thalamic lesions, initially having learned the task as well as controls, were able to hold and recall the information for long periods of time.

With respect to the importance of original learning in thalamic amnesia, other evidence shows that damage to the structure can contribute to memory loss even when a high level of performance is eventually achieved, if difficulty is encountered at learning. A recent study illustrates this point. Groups of rats with hippocampal, thalamic, or control lesions were administered a visual pattern-discrimination task and retested 5 days later, with or without an intervening task-related experience. The interpolated experience (intended to be a source of interference) consisted of an unsolvable problem, involving stimuli very similar to the original discriminanda.

As can be seen in Table 13-1, there was no difference between the hippocampal and control groups in the number of trials required to reach the original learning criterion. The hippocampal and control groups showed excellent recall in the low-interference condition, but the hippocampal group was severely impaired in relearning the discrimination in the high-interference condition. The thalamic groups, despite reaching criterion, were impaired at original learning and required more trials than controls to relearn the task. The thalamic animals were also affected by the interpolated experience, but to a lesser degree than animals with hippocampal damage. Thus, it would appear that apparently good learning by thalamic animals can mask difficulties during the learning process itself. Over

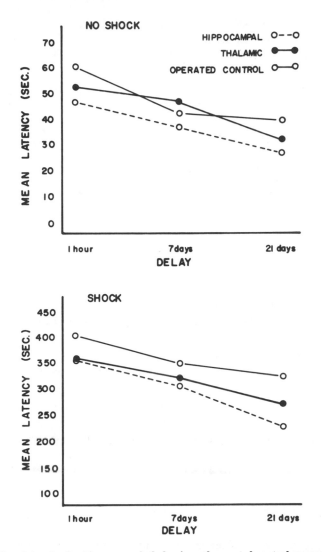

FIGURE 13-4. Mean latencies for hippocampal, thalamic, and operated control groups in the shock-avoidance task.

time, an impoverished representation of the task is likely to be vulnerable to decay, leading, conceivably, to relatively poor recall of important aspects of the task.

These findings also focus on an important aspect of hippocampal amnesia—that is, the role of interference. Animals and humans with hippocampal damage appear disproportionately vulnerable to the disruptive effects of interference. A recently completed study in the shock-avoidance series confirms this general finding and, in addition, shows how interference interacts with the effects of hippocampal lesions to produce memory loss. Using the avoidance paradigm described above, animals were tested at 1-hour and 7-day intervals following shock or no-shock treatments. As a potentially interfering experience, animals in the 7-day groups also received water-approach training in a very similar apparatus between training and testing on the task.

TABLE 13-1. Mean Trials to Criterion by All Groups on the Original Learning (OL) and Relearning (RL) of Discrimination Task in Low- and High-Interference Conditions

	OL	RL
Low interference		
Thalamic	78.8	16.3
Hippocampal	56.0	3.3
Operated control	46.7	5.0
High interference		
Thalamic	81.4	27.1
Hippocampal	43.3	30.0
Operated control	46.0	6.0

Note. Some of these data were reported in Winocur (1979).

Figure 13-5 shows that all groups behaved similarly when tested in the no-shock/interference condition. Following shock, the hippocampal group displayed significantly shorter latencies at the 7-day test than either the thalamic group or the control group, which, in turn, did not differ from each other. The mean response latency for the hippocampal group in the shock/interference condition was approximately 170 seconds; in the shock/no-interference test (see Figure 13-5), the hippocampal group's average latency was over 300 seconds. Taken together, the shock-avoidance and visual-discrimination studies are consistent in showing that the memory of animals with hippocampal damage for previous events is affected not only by the amount of time that has elapsed, but by interference factors that render specific events less salient.

Summary and Conclusions

In this chapter, I have reviewed evidence from animal and human studies, which identify important differences in the characteristics of amnesia associated with different types of brain damage. Animal-based data are consistent with the results of human studies in showing that medial temporal lobe and diencephalic damage produce memory disturbances that can be traced to difficulties at different stages of information processing. Thalamic damage adversely affects original learning in many situations; when this is the case, subsequent memory loss can be demonstrated following very short intervals. In contrast, memory loss following hippocampal damage does not appear as reliably at short intervals, but is typically manifested as elapsed time increases. The evidence indicates that acquired information decays more rapidly during extended delays in hippocampally damaged animals than in animals with thalamic or control lesions. Moreover, interference, in the form of competing response tendencies, appears to interact with the effect of hippocampal lesions in contributing to memory loss. Interference appears to be less of a factor in the case of thalamic amnesia.

It has been proposed (Huppert & Piercy, 1979; Squire, 1981) that memory disturbance following thalamic damage reflects a primary dysfunction at the early stages of

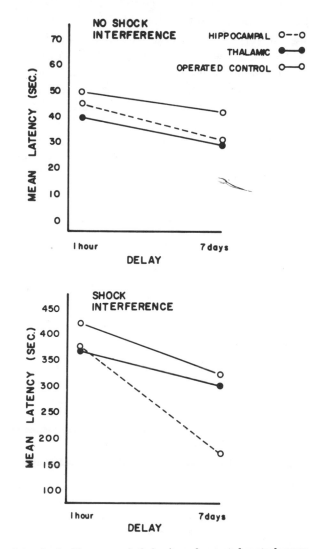

FIGURE 13-5. Mean latencies for hippocampal, thalamic, and operated control groups in the shock-avoidance/
interference task.

processing, when information is registered and encoded. This type of deficiency would
adversely affect the amount and quality of new learning, and, consequently, later memory.
Evidence showing that animals with thalamic lesions display normal forgetting curves and
memory loss that is related to difficulties at original learning is consistent with this general
interpretation.

Recently, Squire, Cohen, and Nadel (1982) have formulated a new position with
respect to medial temporal lobe involvement in memory processes. They propose that this
region contributes to the process whereby important informational elements and their
relationships are identified and stored. Storage of information is thought to be spatially
distributed throughout the brain, involving the neocortex in particular. The medial temporal lobe is crucial in specifying those coherent elements to be incorporated into the

existing body of knowledge, as part of the consolidation process. Damage to the region would block the permanent formation of organized representations, resulting in a loss of memory for recent experiences and, presumably, an impairment of new learning that depends on the elaboration of stored information. Squire *et al.* (1982) do not specifically address the question of interference, but the idea that competing associations would further strain the processing ability of subjects with medial temporal lobe damage is compatible with the model.

Thus the evidence from new animal studies reported in this chapter is generally consistent with currently favored notions concerning the dissociable features of diencephalic and medial temporal lobe amnesia. A particularly encouraging feature of these results is the degree of support they lend to continuing efforts to devise animal models of the different amnesias considered to be a part of the amnesic syndrome.

ACKNOWLEDGMENT

Research reported in this chapter was supported by grants from the Ontario Mental Health Foundation, the Natural Sciences and Engineering Research Council, the Medical Research Council of Canada, and the Scientific Affairs Division of NATO.

REFERENCES

Aggleton, J. P., & Mishkin, M. Visual recognition impairment following medial thalamic lesions in monkeys. *Neuropsychologia*, 1983, *21*, 189–197.

Baddeley, A. D., & Warrington, E. K. Amnesia and the distinction between long- and short-term memory. *Journal of Verbal Learning and Verbal Behavior*, 1970, *9*, 176–189.

Cermak, L. S., Butters, N., & Goodglass, H. The extent of memory loss in Korsakoff patients. *Neuropsychologia*, 1971, *9*, 307–315.

Huppert, F. A., & Piercy, M. Normal and abnormal forgetting in organic amnesia: Effects of locus of lesions. *Cortex*, 1979, *15*, 385–390.

Jarrard, L. E. Selective hippocampal lesions and behavior. *Physiological Psychology*, 1980, *8*, 198–206.

Kesner, R. P., & Wilburn, M. W. A review of electrical stimulation of the brain in context of learning and retention. *Behavioral Biology*, 1974, *10*, 259–293.

Means, L. W., Walker, D. W., & Isaacson, R. L. Facilitated single-alternation go, no-go acquisition following hippocampectomy in the rats. *Journal of Comparative and Physiological Psychology*, 1970, *72*, 278–285.

Milner, B. Les troubles de la mémoire accompagnant des lésions hippocampiques bilatérales. In P. Passouant (Ed.), *Physiologie de l'hippocampe*. Paris: Centre National de la Recherche Scientifique, 1962.

Milner, B. Hemispheric specialization: Scope and limits. In F. O. Schmitt & F. G. Warden (Eds.), *The neurosciences: Third research program*. Cambridge, Mass.: MIT Press, 1974.

Mishkin, M. Memory in monkeys severely impaired by combined but not by separate removal of amygdala and hippocampus. *Nature*, 1978, *273*, 297–298.

Olton, D. S., Becker, J. T., & Handelmann, G. E. Hippocampus, space, and memory. *Behavioral and Brain Sciences*, 1979, *2*, 313–365.

Samuels, I., Butters, N., Goodglass, H., & Brody, B. A comparison of subcortical and cortical damage on short-term visual and auditory memory. *Neuropsychologia*, 1971, *9*, 293–306.

Scoville, W. B., & Milner, B. Loss of recent memory after bilateral hippocampal lesions. *Journal of Neurology, Neurosurgery and Psychiatry*, 1957, *20*, 11–21.

Squire, L. R. Two forms of human amnesia: An analysis of forgetting. *Journal of Neuroscience*, 1981, *1*, 635–640.

Squire, L. R., & Slater, P. C. Anterograde and retrograde memory impairment in chronic amnesia. *Neuropsychologia*, 1978, *16*, 313–322.

Squire, L. R., Cohen, N. J., & Nadel, L. The medial temporal region and memory consolidation: A new hypothesis. In H. Weingartner & E. Parker (Ed.), *Memory consolidation*. Hillsdale, N.J.: Erlbaum, 1982.

Thompson, R. Thalamic structures critical for retention of an avoidance conditioned response in rats. *Journal of Comparative and Physiological Psychology*, 1963, *56*, 261–267.

Victor, M., Adams, R. D., & Collins, G. H. *The Wernicke–Korsakoff syndrome*. Philadelphia: F. A. Davis, 1971.

Warrington, E. K. The double dissociation of short- and long-term memory deficits. In L. S. Cermak (Ed.), *Human memory and amnesia*. Hillsdale, N.J.: Erlbaum, 1982.

Winocur, G. Effect of interference on discrimination learning and recall by rats with hippocampal lesions. *Physiology and Behavior*, 1979, *22*, 339–345.

Winocur, G. The hippocampus and cue-utilization. *Physiological Psychology*, 1980, *8*, 280–288.

Winocur, G., Oxbury, S. Roberts, R., Agnetti, V., & Davis, C. Amnesia in a patient with bilateral lesions to the thalamus. *Neuropsychologia*, in press.

Problems and Prospects for Research on Amnesia

14

Andrew R. Mayes and Peter R. Meudell

Introduction

One major aim of research into organic amnesia is to illuminate the operation of vital neural mechanisms mediating those kinds of memory that are most apparent in humans. To fulfill this aim, researchers have tried to analyze what pattern of memory breakdown is associated with the brain damage that causes amnesia. Researchers may then develop testable theories of information processing and storage from the isolated pattern of memory breakdown and knowledge of the anatomical links of the lesioned brain structures. The current status, problems, and prospects of this program constitute the focus of this chapter.

Organic amnesia in humans conventionally involves a deficit in new learning and memory, accompanied by some memory loss for pretraumatic events; these deficits may be associated with apparently normal intelligence and short-term memory. The amnesic syndrome is believed to be caused by lesions of limbic–diencephalic structures, such as the hippocampus, fornix, mammillary bodies, dorsomedial nucleus of the thalamus, and other thalamic nuclei. Although the syndrome involves a global disturbance in acquiring information about facts and events, relatively normal acquisition of conditioning and a range of perceptual–motor skills has been claimed (see Meudell & Mayes, 1982; Parkin, 1982).

Many theories of the disorder have comprised descriptions of the memory loss in terms of the traditional trichotomy: registration, storage, or retrieval. The apparent normality of cognition in some amnesics led to the proposal that they were suffering from a failure of consolidation (see Milner, 1971). Despite evidence of good cognitive function in some amnesics, other theorists have argued that they suffer from deficits in registration. Thus, Butters and Cermak (1975) claim that amnesics have a problem in effortful encoding, such that they do not spontaneously encode information in terms of meaningful features. In contrast, Hirst (1982) has claimed that the primary failure is in encoding features that are normally automatically processed, which causes a seondary problem in encoding, involving effortful processing. Finally, Weiskrantz and Warrington (1975) have argued that amnesia is a selective disorder of retrieval, caused by an unexplained but excessive degree of interference from other material already in memory.

Recent theorists have been more wary about isolating the affected stage of memory or have denied the appropriateness of characterizing amnesia as a deficit in a specific stage of

Andrew R. Mayes and Peter R. Meudell. Department of Psychology, University of Manchester, Manchester, England, United Kingdom.

memory. Thus, the disorder has been popularly construed as a deficit in the *use* of contextual information, which may secondarily cause problems in registration and retrieval (see Winocur, Kinsbourne, & Moscovitch, 1981). This hypothesis tries to explain the good learning of skills and conditioning tasks as a result of their independence from the use of contextual information. Warrington and Weiskrantz (1982) have suggested that such spared learning may occur when frontal cortex processing systems have been disconnected from limbic memory structures. The two proposals may be complementary, as some evidence supports the view that integrity of the frontal cortex is essential for the normal use of contextual information, which is relevant to recency judgments (see Milner, 1971).

Although Warrington and Weiskrantz (1982) give no indication of the nature of the processes that the limbic memory structures are unable to execute on the disconnected frontally processed information, other theories implicitly do give such an indication. This indication is that the damaged structures normally mediate the functions disturbed in amnesia. They may, for example, be implicated in consolidating certain kinds of memory or in the automatic registration of information. These ascriptions may be too crude, as they take no account of the nature of the inputs to and outputs from the damaged structures in interpreting the lesion-induced deficit.

To assess the data base of the theories described above, one needs to consider several problems inherent in amnesia research. First, there are the interpretive difficulties arising from comparisons of poor and good memory. Second, there is the problem of separating the cognitive deficits that are essentially connected with amnesia from others that are caused by lesions incidental to the memory failure. Third, there is the issue of whether amnesia is a unitary or multiple disorder of memory. Fourth, there is the current uncertainty about the locus of the critical lesion or lesions in amnesia. Lastly, there is the extreme difficulty of ascertaining whether a breakdown is one of registration, storage, or retrieval.

The Pattern of Amnesic Performance and Comparisons of Good and Poor Memory

Memory is not uniformly poor in amnesics. In addition to their capacity to learn and retain a wide range of perceptual–motor and cognitive skills (see Meudell & Mayes, 1982; Parkin, 1982), amnesics have been reported to show good, or even normal, learning of highly associated word pairs (Winocur & Weiskrantz, 1976) and good recall of words that are cued by their initial letters (see Warrington & Weiskrantz, 1974). An amnesic's ability to show these kinds of residual memory is not, however, accompanied by normal feelings of familiarity or recognition for the remembered material. At least in the case of cued recall, this familiarity loss seems to be caused by a genuine deficit in metamemory, rather than a shift to a more cautious criterion for acknowledging memory (Mayes & Meudell, 1981a). Amnesics have also been reported to be abnormally sensitive to proactive interference (Morris, Welch, & Britton, in press; Warrington & Weiskrantz, 1974, 1978; Winocur & Weiskrantz, 1976) and to context-dependent forgetting (Winocur & Kinsbourne, 1978). Disproportionate difficulty in making recency judgments, another problem in using contextual cues, has been described in some amnesics (e.g., see Hirst, 1982); relatedly, some amnesics have been shown to confuse frequency and recency judgments (Huppert & Piercy, 1978). Finally, some amnesics have shown abnormalities in processing semantic information, as evinced by the form of their recognition errors and their failure to show release following a semantic shift in the Wickens's paradigm (see Butters & Cermak, 1975).

These properties of anterograde amnesia have been used to underpin the theories discussed in the introduction. It is assumed that the pattern of memory performance reflects the cause of amnesia. The pattern observed is one dependent on comparisons of good and poor memory. Such comparisons have often been vitiated by floor or ceiling effects, but even when these are not obviously present, scaling effects and other unknown processes may operate so that the poor memory seems qualitatively different from the strong. If poor memories of whatever provenance show the same qualitative differences from strong memory, then the identified pattern may be a general result of testing poor memory, rather than one indicative of the causes of amnesia. For example, although amnesics show a pattern of good cued recall and poor recognition when tested immediately after learning, normal subjects show the same pattern when tested after a long delay (Mayes & Meudell, 1981b; Mortenson, 1980; Squire, Wetzel, & Slater, 1978; Woods & Piercy, 1974). Instead of showing that amnesic retrieval benefits differentially by having possible responses drastically constrained, good cued recall therefore may be a universal feature of poor memory.

Like immediately tested amnesic memory, equivalently poor normal memory, tested after a delay, shows good retention of highly (but not weakly) associated word pairs and sensitivity to contextual shifts (Mayes, Meudell, & Som, 1981). It may also show a dissociation between performance of a perceptual skill and recognition of the items involved (Meudell & Mayes, 1981a). The advantage of semantic over phonemic and graphemic cuing also seems to disappear when poor memory is tested in normal as well as amnesic subjects (Wetzel & Squire, 1982). Finally, errors in eight-choice as compared to two-choice forced recognition are disproportionately increased in immediately tested amnesic memory, but the same pattern is shown by normal subjects tested after a delay, and the effect disappears if a d' rather than "number correct" analysis is performed (Meudell & Mayes, 1981b).

Normal memory can be attenuated to the level of immediately tested amnesic memory either by delaying testing or by reducing learning exposure. Most studies have manipulated only delay, although both manipulations should be effective if the performance pattern is a general feature of poor memory. Excessive interference has been shown in amnesics, using the A-B, A-C paradigm with easily learned items. The ratio of the temporal interval between lists, and between lists and testing, is an important determinant of the degree of interference. This ratio should therefore be preserved if normal subjects are tested after long delays. If this is done, we have tentative evidence that the degree of interference is increased. If, however, memory is attenuated by reducing exposure of the information to be learned, there is no indication that interference is increased (Mayes & Meudell, 1983b). Even so, when list A-C is harder to learn, reducing exposure in normal subjects reproduces the amnesic pattern of results. The effect is caused by differentially poor learning of a harder list, rather than higher levels of interference. This artifact may confound some of the published literature, especially as we have been unable so far to demonstrate excessive interference in our amnesics. In our view, the status of interference in amnesia remains unresolved.

Reduced exposure has the same effect on the pattern of cued recall and recognition as does delayed testing, and, furthermore, the two manipulations appear to influence familiarity judgments in similar ways (Meudell & Mayes, 1984). Analysis showed that both delay and reduced exposure led normal subjects to lose confidence in the accuracy of their memories of cued words: Loss of familiarity may therefore, be a universal feature of poor memory. This conclusion may have some generality since Kunst-Wilson and Zajonc (1980) have also shown that reduced exposure can abolish recognition but leave other aspects of memory intact, and we have earlier noted a delay-induced dissociation between recognition and "skill" memory in a perceptual task (Meudell & Mayes, 1981a). It may be therefore that poor encoding and/or storage of certain features causes loss of familiarity in amnesics and normal subjects following brief exposures.

Effects found in all kinds of poor memory cannot, without further investigation, throw light on the causes of amnesia. Effects that occur only for some kinds of poor memory may do so, and can usefully be examined in normal subjects. Some effects are, however, not seen at all in normal attenuated memory. One of these is the amnesic's confusion of recency with frequency information (Huppert & Piercy, 1978). We have not found the amnesic pattern of confusion in normal subjects, whether their memories were attenuated by delay or reduced exposure (Meudell, Mayes, & Ostergarde, in preparation, 1983). Unlike interference, the confusional phenomenon is not subject to subtle artifacts and so, it may be argued, should illuminate the causes of amnesia. The phenomenon, however, may be incidental to the core amnesic syndrome and may not be a result of limbic system lesions, as is now discussed.

The Frontal Cortex and the Problem of Impairments Incidental to Amnesia

Recent evidence from CT scans shows that at least 80% of amnesics with an alcoholic etiology have frontal cortex atrophy (Butters, as quoted in Moscovitch, 1982). Very severe amnesia is, however, seen without frontal atrophy (e.g., see Mair, Warrington, & Weiskrantz, 1979). Frontal symptoms, incidental to limbic system amnesia, may then be confused with genuine and core amnesic symptoms. Such symptoms can be identified because they should occur in some frontally lesioned patients with only mild memory problems, and not in amnesics with minimal disturbances of the frontal cortex. Similar criteria are applicable to incidental impairments caused by other cortical or brain stem lesions.

Milner (1971) reported that frontal patients show deficits in recency judgments when compared with temporal lobe patients who show recognition problems. Squire (1982) has shown a deficit in recency judgments in alcoholic amnesics, even when their overall level of recognition is matched to controls. Under similar conditions, the patient N. A. and ECT patients do not show this deficit (Squire, Nadel, & Slater, 1981). N. A. is believed to have a selective thalamic lesion, and ECT patients may not be frontally impaired, whereas alcoholic amnesics are known to suffer frontal atrophy. Furthermore, Squire found that alcoholic amnesics' deficits in recency judgments correlated with their performance on "frontal" tests, such as the Wisconsin Card Sort task. So far, confusion of frequency and recency information has only been seen in alcoholic amnesics (Huppert & Piercy, 1978; Meudell *et al.*, 1983), who show frontal atrophy. It is therefore plausible to argue that the severe problems with recency judgments arise from frontal lesions, because the frontal cortex mediates automatic encoding and retrieval, which are necessary for such judgments. Without this system, recency and frequency judgments must be based on how "strong" memories feel.

The hypothesis needs substantiation, as some issues are still unresolved. For example, Hirst (1982) reported that other amnesics show the deficit in recency judgment even when their recognition is matched with that of controls. It is unknown whether these amnesics have frontal atrophy. Also, it is possible that N. A. and ECT patients have mild problems with recency judgment, as Squire *et al.*'s (1981) matching procedure made their task harder for controls. Subjects had to distinguish sentences in two lists, spaced 3 minutes apart, but whereas amnesics began their judgments 10 seconds after List 2, controls began up to 90 minutes later. The ratio of list spacing to the list-testing delay should have been constant to preserve discriminability.

The frontal lobes are also involved in effortful organizational processes, which are important in the registration and retrieval of complex, meaningful information. It is therefore possible that failures in the use of semantic information are incidental consequences of frontal atrophy rather than of limbic lesions. This view is supported by Moscovitch's (1982) observation that frontal patients fail to show release from proactive interference in Wickens's paradigm after a semantic shift, and by Squire's (1982) observation that the deficit of alcoholic amnesics on this task correlates with their performance on "frontal" tests. It is further supported by the observation that even when alcoholic amnesics fail to show release on the shift trial, they seem aware that there has been a shift, but are unable to use this knowledge to aid their memory—a problem that is typical for some frontally lesioned patients (Winocur *et al.*, 1981). Finally, the position receives support from findings of normal release in N. A. and ECT patients (Squire, 1982), an encephalitic patient (Cermak, 1976), and another amnesic without an alcoholic etiology (see Moscovitch, 1982). Some uncertainty remains, however, as Warrington (1982) has reported failure to show release from proactive interference in amnesics who may not have appreciable frontal atrophy.

Is Amnesia a Unitary or a Multiple Disorder?

If the hypotheses discussed above are true, then some frontal lesions may cause amnesic symptoms quite distinct from those produced by limbic system lesions. The preceding two sections indicate that only a few of the effects constituting the amnesic pattern of memory performance may be unique to amnesia. A theory of the deficit must explain all such symptoms if it arises from damage to a single system. If, however, there are several dissociable disorders, this argument no longer applies. It is known, of course, that unilateral temporal lesions cause material-specific amnesias for verbal and visual–spatial information (see Milner, 1971), but it is more relevant to determine whether bilateral lesions of different limbic structures cause distinct amnesias.

Two tentative dissociations have been made. First, it has been shown that amnesics with putative lesions of the diencephalon, such as alcoholic amnesias and N. A., learn slowly but forget at a normal rate; whereas amnesics who putatively have suffered impairments of the medial temporal lobes, such as patient H. M. and ECT patients, not only learn slowly but also forget abnormally fast (Huppert & Piercy, 1979; Squire, 1981). Temporal lobe and diencephalic amnesias may then be associated with different disturbances of the forgetting function.

Second, there is some evidence that retrograde amnesia and anterograde amnesia may be dissociable. Goldberg, Antin, Bilder, Gerstman, Hughes, and Mattis (1981) have described a patient with a very severe retrograde amnesia but with no clear signs even of a residual anterograde amnesia. The case is somewhat peculiar because of the extremely severe retrograde amnesia and the possibility that the critical lesion was located in nonspecific systems of the midbrain. Similar cases with less severe retrograde amnesia have, however, been reported as results of vascular accidents, tuberculous meningitis, and closed head injury (see Wood, Ebert, & Kinsbourne, 1982). Documentation of anterograde amnesia without retrograde amnesia is less sure, although Winocur, Oxbury, Roberts, Agnetti, and Davis (in press) have recently described a man with bilateral thalamic lesions whose anterograde amnesia was accompanied by a retrograde amnesia, which was not clinically detectable. There is also evidence that patients recovered from transient global amnesia, or the effects of a sodium amytal injection on the hemisphere contralateral to where there is preexisting temporal lobe pathology, show permanent amnesia for the period of dysfunction but may recover memory for the pretraumatic or preinjection period (Fredericks, 1979; Milner, 1966).

Retrograde amnesia itself may take several forms. The amnesia may be steeply graded, with memories for events more than a few years prior to trauma being spared (as seems to occur with H. M., N. A., and ECT patients); or it may extend back over decades, with only modest sparing of the oldest memories as occurs in alcoholic and postencephalitic amnesics (see Cohen & Squire, 1981, for a discussion). Goldberg et al.'s (1981) case may represent a still more severe form of retrograde amnesia. On the other hand, limbic lesions may only cause one kind of retrograde amnesia, which is steeply graded. The extensive retrograde amnesia of alcoholic amnesics may arise from a combination of this disorder with a milder but more uniform depression of retrieval deficiency, caused by incidental frontal lesions. Albert, Butters, and Brandt (1981) have, in fact, shown that Huntington choreics who have frontal atrophy display a uniform retrograde amnesia for all memories, regardless of how old these are.

There is one further group of amnesics relevant to theories of amnesia—namely, patients with specific amnesias. Di Renzi (1982) has described amnesias specific to colors, faces, and topography, which arise from neocortical lesions. He claimed that the patients' ability to process these materials was otherwise seemingly normal. It is therefore interesting that Ross (1980) has described a case of selective amnesia for visual material in a man with bilateral occipito-temporal lesions. Ross argued that the sighted parts of this patient's visual fields enabled him to process visual stimuli effectively normally, and that his amnesia was caused by the disconnection of his neocortical visual processing systems from the limbic memory structures of the temporal lobe. If this disconnectionist argument is right, then other specific amnesias would be predicted. Ross's suggestion would also make untenable Warrington and Weiskrantz's view that limbic system amnesia is caused solely by a disconnection of limbic and frontal cortex structures. Specific cortical–limbic disconnections should produce specific components of the amnesic syndrome (in terms of the kinds of memory affected), but only bilateral limbic lesions should cause the whole syndrome.

The Critical Lesion(s) in Amnesia

Attempts to fractionate the amnesic syndrome not only try to see which memory symptoms are inseparable, but also try to determine what lesions cause the separable syndromes. Recent polemics have made clear, however, that even the identification of the critical lesion(s) in the undifferentiated amnesic syndrome is not a matter of universal agreement. Disagreement exists because of the rarity of postmortem analyses of properly characterized amnesics, the relative imprecision of current *in vivo* techniques for locating lesions, and the frequency of adventitious damage. Several views command varying degrees of support. First, a unitary memory deficit is caused by lesions of the hippocampus or serially connected structures, such as the fornix or mammillary bodies (Warrington & Weiskrantz, 1982). Second, permanent and severe amnesia only arises when there is combined damage to a hippocampal–mammillary body–anterior thalamic system and to an amygdala–dorsomedial thalamic nucleus system (Mishkin, 1982). Third, amnesia arises from damage to the temporal stem or to its subcortical projections, such as the dorsomedial nucleus of the thalamus (Horel, 1978). Fourth, hippocampal and diencephalic lesions cause separable amnesic syndromes (Huppert & Piercy, 1979). This last position can be extended as amnesic subvarieties are discovered. For example, posterior hippocampal lesions may be associated with retrograde amnesia, whereas anterior ones may be associated with anterograde amnesia (Penfield & Mathieson, 1974).

There is no clear winner among these contenders, but we would tentatively support the last position. Most evidence comes from studies of animal models, and some of it is hard to assess. For example, Swanson and Cowan (1979) have shown that, in the rat, the subiculum rather than the hippocampus proper projects to the mammillary bodies. This evidence might question the salience for amnesia of hippocampal lesions, lesions of the mammillary bodies, or merely their mutual dependence. More relevantly, Squire and Zola-Morgan (1982) have argued that combined hippocampal–amygdala lesions cause a memory disturbance in monkeys like that of human amnesia, whereas temporal stem lesions do not. Their data are equivocal on the question of whether the combined lesion disturbs memory more severely than a hippocampal lesion.

The use of animal models presupposes that one can identify those tasks (such as delayed nonmatching to sample) on which human amnesics will be impaired, and those tasks (such as visual discrimination) on which human amnesics will be normal. There are two problems with this presupposition. First, as earlier sections of this chapter should make clear, areas of normality and deficit in the memory of human amnesics have not yet been fully mapped. Second, attempts to test human amnesics on tasks for which limbically lesioned monkeys show impairments have produced results that are hard to interpret (Oscar-Berman & Zola-Morgan, 1980a, 1980b). Performance of such tasks may well be achieved via different mediating mechanisms in monkeys and humans. Nevertheless, animal models offer the main hope of locating the structures critical in human amnesia.

Is Amnesia a Disturbance of Registration, Storage, or Retrieval?

If the critical lesion(s) underlying amnesia are known, and the broad pattern of cognitive memory performance in amnesics is also known, then one has two sources of information to help identify the affected memory processes. Knowledge of lesion locus is useful to the extent that the nature of the damaged structure's inputs and outputs are known, along with evidence of its detailed physiological functioning. This kind of knowledge is available for the hippocampus, so if its disruption were critical in amnesia, possible ideas about the nature of the memory loss would be drastically constrained. Knowledge of the pattern of performance in amnesics also suggests which stages of memory are affected—but only weakly. Combination of both informational sources may be vital for locating the affected stage of memory or demonstrating the irrelevance of such an analysis.

Registration, storage, and retrieval are closely interdependent processes, so it is very hard to discover whether one is selectively impaired (see Watkins, 1978). For example, even assuming normal registration, abnormal forgetting may be caused by degradation of storage or abnormal retrieval of what is normally stored. In each case, remembering might be similarly affected by cuing, contextual shifts, and interference. Although a retrieval deficit, unlike one of storage, might be expected to affect pre- and posttraumatic memories equally, the evidence for this is unclear. First, it may be that retrograde and anterograde amnesia are dissociable disorders; second, most evidence suggests that retrograde amnesia usually affects recent, not distant, memories. No current theory of retrieval or the consolidation of storage can plausibly explain retrograde amnesia, which is confined to a period of a few years before trauma.

Two complementary approaches may help isolate the memory stages affected in amnesia. First, researchers should try to discover whether registration and retrieval are normal in amnesics. If they are, then a storage deficit must be involved, as Moscovitch (1982) believes. If they are not, and the deficits cannot be separated from the core symptoms, then the underlying deficit must be one of registration or retrieval. Normal registration of all mnemonically relevant informational features is hard to prove. The range of such features must be known (at present, this is not the case), and then knowledge of different features must be probed in a way the subject cannot predict, at about the time of learning so as to minimize memory load. In our sense, processing a feature is the same as encoding it (with due respect to Hirst, 1982), although this encoding may not result in proper storage. So if a feature is encoded, the encoder should be able to answer questions about it or to demonstrate his or her knowledge at the time, but not necessarily later.

Normal retrieval in the face of poor memory is even harder to ascertain. It is not established by showing normal recall of remote events, as some retrieval processes may be functions of age of memory. The second approach to isolating the memory stage affected in amnesia may be helpful here. This approach tries to identify the physiological and biochemical correlates of learning, storage, and retrieval in normal and amnesic memory. If physiological measures that correlate with memory in control subjects are abnormal in amnesics, then one may be able to identify the memory stage affected. One will at least learn at what stage processing deficiencies become noticeable after information is perceived.

Prospects

It might be argued that the difficulty in identifying amnesia as a defect of registration, storage, or retrieval shows the attempt to be misconceived. The functions of the damaged limbic structures simply may not be describable in these terms. Be that as it may, in our view current knowledge is insufficient for strongly claiming amnesia (or the amnesias) as a defect of one of the stages of memory. A critical review of the literature indicates that the acquisition and retention of cognitive and perceptual–motor skills and conditioning may be relatively well preserved in amnesia. It is unproved whether preserved kinds of learning are heterogeneous or whether they possess critical common features. Conversely, it is clear that semantic memory (in the sense of the term as commonly defined as information contained in our mental dictionaries and encyclopedias) is impaired in amnesics, as well as episodic memory. Semantic memory is deficient in the pretraumatic period, as shown by questionnaires about public events (see Cohen & Squire, 1981), and difficulty in acquiring new semantic information is an aspect of anterograde amnesia.

These generalizations leave open the question of what failures cause the memory deficit that does occur. No one has yet shown that brain lesions may impair one or more kinds of learning relatively spared in limbic amnesia, while sparing the complex kinds of memory affected in amnesia. Until this is shown, it remains possible that these tasks merely require less of a *general* resource provided by the limbic structures. For example, many current theorists argue that spared learning is context-free, or is little influenced by interference or does not depend on feelings of familiarity. Normal mediation of context, familiarity, and interference-prone information is held to depend on intact limbic structures. We have already indicated that careful analysis casts doubt on the strength of this claim. If it is correct, however, one should predict that residual learning in amnesics should be abnormally disturbed when the importance of context, interference, or familiarity is artificially increased. If this does not happen, one can merely say that spared kinds of learning are normal because they depend little on limbic system structures.

Our review shows that no obvious registration or retrieval deficits underlie the impairments in episodic and semantic memory that are caused by limbic system lesions. They have not, however, been conclusively excluded. Future progress will depend on achieving a rapprochement of human and animal research. Development of suitable animal models will help elucidate the anatomy of global amnesia and determine whether the syndrome can be fractionated. This anatomical knowledge will constrain future information- and storage-processing theories of amnesia. Animals may also be used to model more precisely the biochemical disturbances that underlie human amnesia. This is of particular interest, in view of evidence showing the importance of cholinergic abnormalities in amnesia (see Mayes & Meudell, 1983a, for a discussion).

A full rapprochement between human amnesia and animal models of it has not yet been reached. One example of conflict, discussed by Mayes and Meudell (1983a), concerns the popular theory that amnesia is caused by a deficit in the use of contextual information. At present, the human data seem to indicate that deficits of this kind do not occur in limbic system amnesia, whereas the animal data seem to show that hippocampal lesions can affect the use of contextual information (Winocur & Olds, 1978). Success in resolving apparent conflicts of this kind is essential if we are to locate the causes of amnesia and identify the memory functions of the limbic system.

REFERENCES

Albert, M. S., Butters, N., & Brandt, J. Patterns of remote memory in amnesic and demented patients. *Archives of Neurology*, 1981, *38*, 495–500.
Butters, N., & Cermak, L. Some analyses of the amnesic syndromes in brain-damaged patients. In R. Isaacson & K. Pribram (Eds.), *The hippocampus* (Vol. 2). New York: Plenum, 1975.

Cermak, L. S. The encoding capacity of a patient with amnesia due to encephalitis. *Neuropsychologia*, 1976, *14*, 311–326.

Cohen, N. J., & Squire, L. R. Retrograde amnesia and remote memory impairment. *Neuropsychologia*, 1981, *19*, 337–356.

Di Renzi, E. Memory disorders following focal neocortical damage. *Philosophical Transactions of the Royal Society, London*, 1982, *B298*, 73–83.

Fredericks, J. A. M. Transient global amnesia. *International Neuropsychology Society Bulletin*, June 1979, p. 18.

Goldberg, E., Antin, S. P., Bilder, R. M., Jr., Gerstman, L. J., Hughes, J. E. O., & Mattis, S. Retrograde amnesia: Possible role of mesencephalic reticular activation system on long-term memory. *Science*, 1981, *213*, 1392–1394.

Hirst, W. The amnesic syndrome: Descriptions and explanations. *Psychological Bulletin*, 1982, *91*, 435–460.

Horel, J. A. The neuranatomy of amnesia: A critique of the hippocampal memory hypothesis. *Brain*, 1978, *101*, 403–445.

Huppert, F. A., & Piercy, M. The role of trace strength in recency and frequency judgments by amnesic and control subjects. *Quarterly Journal of Experimental Psychology*, 1978, *30*, 346–354.

Huppert, F. A., & Piercy, M. Normal and abnormal forgetting in amnesia: Effect of locus of lesion. *Cortex*, 1979, *15*, 385–390.

Kunst-Wilson, W. R., & Zajonc, R. B. Affective discrimination of stimuli that cannot be recognized. *Science*, 1980, *207*, 557–558.

Mair, W. G. P., Warrington, E. K., & Weiskrantz, L. Memory disorders in Korsakoff's psychosis: A neuropathological and neuropsychological investigation of two cases. *Brain*, 1979, *102*, 749–783.

Mayes, A. R., & Meudell, P. R. How similar is immediate memory in amnesic patients to delayed memory in normal subjects?: A replication, extension and reassessment of the amnesic cueing effect. *Neuropsychologia*, 1981, *19*, 647–654. (a)

Mayes, A. R., & Meudell, P. How similar is the effect of cueing in amnesics and in normal subjects following forgetting? *Cortex*, 1981, *17*, 113–124. (b)

Mayes, A. R., & Meudell, P. R. Amnesia in man and other animals. In A. R. Mayes (Ed.), *Memory in humans and animals*. Wokingham, England: Van Nostrand Reinhold, 1983. (a)

Mayes, A. R., & Meudell, P. R. *Effects of delay and reduced exposure on interference in normal people*. Unpublished manuscript, 1983. (b)

Mayes, A. R., Meudell, P. R., & Som, S. Further similarities between amnesia and normal attenuated memory: Effects with paired associate learning and contextual shifts. *Neuropsychologia*, 1981, *19*, 655–664.

Meudell, P. R., & Mayes, A. R. The Claparède phenomenon: A further example in amnesics, a demonstration of a similar effect in normal people with attenuated memory and a reinterpretation. *Current Psychological Research*, 1981, *1*, 75–88. (a)

Meudell, P. R., & Mayes, A. R. A similarity between weak normal memory and amnesia with two and eight choice word recognition: A signal dectection analysis. *Cortex*, 1981, *17*, 19–30. (b)

Meudell, P. R., & Mayes, A. R. *Normal and abnormal forgetting:* Some comments on the human amnesic syndrome. In A. Ellis (Ed.), *Normality and pathology in cognitive functions*. London: Academic Press, 1982.

Meudell, P. R., & Mayes, A. R. Patterns of confidence loss in cued recall responses of normal people with attenuated memory: Their relevance to a similar amnesic phenomenon. *Neuropsychologia*, 1984, *22*, 41–54.

Meudell, P. R., Mayes, A. R., & Ostergarde, A. *Recovery and frequency judgments in normal people with poor memory*. Manuscript in preparation, 1983.

Milner, B. Amnesia following operation on the temporal lobes. In C. W. M. Whitty & O. L. Zangwill (Eds.), *Amnesia*. London: Butterworths, 1966.

Milner, B. Interhemispheric differences in the localisation of psychological processes in man. *British Medical Bulletin*, 1971, *27*, 272–277.

Mishkin, M. A memory system in the monkey. *Philosophical Transactions of the Royal Society, London*, 1982, *B298*, 85–95.

Morris, R. G., Welch, J. L., & Britton, P. G. The effects of interference on paired associate learning in presenile dementia *Neuropsychologia*, in press.

Mortenson, E. L. The effects of partial information in amnesic and normal subjects. *Scandinavian Journal of Psychology*, 1980, *21*, 75–82.

Moscovitch, M. Multiple dissociations of function in amnesia. In L. S. Cermak (Ed.), *Human memory and amnesia*. Hillsdale, N.J.: Erlbaum, 1982.

Oscar-Berman, M., & Zola-Morgan, S. M. Comparative neuropsychology and Korsakoff's syndrome: I. Spatial and visual reversal learning. *Neuropsychologia,* 1980, *18,* 499–512. (a)

Oscar-Berman, M., & Zola-Morgan, S. Comparative neuropsychology and Korsakoff's syndrome: II. Two choice visual discrimination learning. *Neuropsychologia,* 1980, *18,* 513–528. (b)

Parkin, A. J. Residual learning capability in organic amnesia. *Cortex,* 1982, *18,* 417–420.

Penfield, W., & Mathieson, G. Memory: Autopsy findings and comments on the role of the hippocampus in experimental recall. *Archives of Neurology,* 1974, *31,* 145–154.

Ross, E. D. Sensory-specific and fractional disorders of recent memory in man: I. Isolated loss of visual recent memory. *Archives of Neurology,* 1980, *37,* 193–200.

Squire, L. R. Two forms of human amnesia: An analysis of forgetting. *Journal of neuroscience,* 1981, *1,* 635–640.

Squire, L. R. Comparisons among forms of amnesia: Some deficits are unique to Korsakoff syndrome. *Journal of Experimental Psychology: Learning, Memory, and Cognition,* 1982, *8,* 560–571.

Squire, L. R., Nadel, L., & Slater, P. C. Anterograde amnesia and memory for temporal order. *Neuropsychologia,* 1981, *19,* 141–146.

Squire, L. R., Wetzel, C. D., & Slater, P. C. Anterograde amnesia following ECT: An analysis of the beneficial effects of partial information. *Neuropsychologia,* 1978, *16,* 339–348.

Squire, L. R., & Zola-Morgan, S. The neurology of memory: The case for correspondence between the findings of man and non-human primate. In J. A. Deutsch (Ed.), *The physiological basis of memory* (2nd ed.). New York: Academic Press, 1982.

Swanson, L. W., & Cowan, W. M. The connections of the septal region in the rat. *Journal of Comparative Neurology,* 1979, *186,* 621–656.

Warrington, E. K. The double dissociation of short- and long-term memory deficits. In L. S. Cermak (Ed.), *Human memory and amnesia.* Hillsdale, N.J.: Erlbaum, 1982.

Warrington, E. K., & Weiskrantz, L. The effect of prior learning on subsequent retention in amnesic patients. *Neuropsychologia,* 1974, *12,* 419–428.

Warrington, E. K., & Weiskrantz, L. Further analysis of the prior learning effect in amnesic patients. *Neuropsychologia,* 1978, *16,* 169–177.

Warrington, E. K., & Weiskrantz, L. Amnesia: A disconnection syndrome? *Neuropsychologia,* 1982, *20,* 233–248.

Watkins, M. J. Theoretical issues. In M. M. Gruneberg & P. Morris (Eds.), *Aspects of memory.* London: Methuen, 1978.

Weiskrantz, L., & Warrington, E. K. The problem of the amnesic syndrome in man and animals. In R. L. Isaacson & K. H. Pribram (Eds.), *The hippocampus* (Vol. 2). New York: Plenum, 1975.

Wetzel, C. D., & Squire, L. R. Cued recall in anterograde amnesia. *Brain and Language,* 1982, *15,* 70–81.

Winocur, G., & Kinsbourne, M. Contextual cuing as an aid to Korsakoff amnesia. *Neuropsychologia,* 1978, *16,* 671–682.

Winocur, G., Kinsbourne, M., & Moscovitch, M. The effects of cuing on release from proactive interference in Korsakoff amnesic patients. *Journal of Experimental Psychology: Human Learning and Memory,* 1981, *1,* 56–65.

Winocur, G., & Olds, J. Effects of context manipulation on memory and reversal learning in rates with hippocampal lesions. *Journal of Comparative and Physiological Psychology,* 1978, *92,* 312–321.

Winocur, G., Oxbury, S., Roberts, R., Agnetti, V., & Davis, C. Amnesia in a patient with bilateral lesions to the thalamus. *Neuropsychologia,* in press.

Winocur, G., & Weiskrantz, L. An investigation of paired associate learning in amnesic patients. *Neuropsychologia,* 1976, *14,* 97–110.

Wood, F., Ebert, V., & Kinsbourne, M. The episodic–semantic memory distinction in memory and amnesia: Clinical and experimental observations. In L. C. Cermak (Ed.), *Human memory and amnesia.* Hillsdale, N.J.: Erlbaum, 1982.

Woods, R. T., & Piercy, M. A similarity between amnesic memory and normal forgetting. *Neuropsychologia,* 1974, *12,* 437–445.

15

Incidental versus Intentional Retrieval: Remembering and Awareness as Separate Issues

Larry L. Jacoby

The definition of "amnesia" as "a loss of memory" is misleading in its simplicity. Everyone is subject to memory loss to some extent. Normal memory performance is inconsistent across tasks (e.g., Underwood, Boruch, & Malmi, 1978) and occasions of testing (e.g., Battig, 1979). Thus, memory performance typically lacks the monolithic quality that is implied by the definition of amnesia. Very little attention has been given to the potential significance of variability in memory performance across occasions of testing. However, researchers have focused on the independence of performance on different types of memory tests. According to several reports (e.g., Corkin, 1968; Milner, Corkin, & Teuber, 1968), amnesics preserve a nearly normal ability to employ memory for recent events to aid their interpretation of an ambiguous event (e.g., identification of a fragmented version of a previously presented picture) or as a source of savings revealed in their objective performance (improvement from practice of a pursuit-rotor task). These effects occur, although amnesics deny any sense of subjective familiarity when asked about the experience that gave rise to the effect on performance. That is, effects of recent prior experience on performance can be independent of memory, as assessed by standard tests of recognition memory or recall. This phenomenon has far-reaching implications for the understanding of memory in normals and amnesics. Many of the data described in this chapter were gained from normal subjects rather than amnesics. Using data gained from normals to help our understanding of amnesia seems justified, since many effects found with amnesics, including effects of prior experience in the absence of recognition memory, can also be found with normals.

Some sort of simplifying scheme is obviously needed to help make sense of the various results that are obtained in investigations of memory. One popular scheme has been to distinguish among "encoding" (putting things into memory), "storage" (maintenance in memory), and "retrieval" (recovery of information from memory), and then to specify the locus of deficits in terms of these three stages. It has been debated whether amnesia results from a deficit in encoding (e.g., Cermak, 1979) or a deficit in retrieval (e.g., Warrington & Weiskrantz, 1973). Further, it has been postulated that some amnesics suffer from an abnormally fast rate of forgetting, due to a deficit in storage (Huppert & Piercy, 1979; Squire, 1982). The independence of performance on some tests of memory has been explained by postulating separate memory stores or qualitative differences in memory. The

Larry L. Jacoby. Department of Psychology, McMaster University, Hamilton, Ontario, Canada.

memory that is preserved by amnesics and expressed in performance is attributed to memory for procedures (Cohen & Squire, 1980) or semantic memory (Kinsbourne & Wood, 1975), while the amnesic's poor performance on tests of recognition memory or recall is attributed to a loss of declarative memory (Cohen & Squire, 1980) or episodic memory (Kinsbourne & Wood, 1975).

In contrast to the scheme outlined above, I prefer to emphasize similarities in processing that cut across the memory stores and stages that others have postulated. Similarities in processing are potentially ignored by attempts to specify a deficit in memory as being limited to encoding, storage, or retrieval. In fact, forms of processing that are important for encoding may be equally important for retrieval, making it more fruitful to focus on deficits in processing in general rather than to consider encoding and retrieval problems separately. Thus, this chapter attempts to interpret the memory performance of normals and amnesics within a common processing framework. Both storage and retrieval are seen as sometimes requiring more active elaborative processing than amnesics will spontaneously carry out. The preserved memory in amnesia is treated as being due to effects on retrieval that can be explained in the same way as are effects of incidental versus intentional learning. Finally, effects of prior experience on objective performance and on awareness of remembering are treated as being separable. Rather than being viewed as inherent characteristics of memory, awareness of remembering or feelings of subjective familiarity are seen as relying on the application of a heuristic and as resulting from an attribution process.

Encoding, Storage, and Retrieval

It has been claimed that Korsakoff patients' amnesia results from encoding deficits; namely, in contrast to normals, amnesics reveal less flexibility in their processing of material, and less elaborative processing or processing of meaning (e.g., Cermak, 1979). Further, it has been suggested that it may be possible to repair the patients' memory performance by controlling encoding processes through the use of incidental-learning procedures. Experiments designed along these lines have shown that, as is true for normals, employing incidental-learning tasks that require Korsakoff patients to process the meaning of the material to be remembered, rather than more superficial characteristics, does enhance memory performance. Disappointingly, the control of processing through incidental-learning procedures does not substantially reduce the memory disadvantage of amnesics as compared to normals (Baddeley, 1982; Cermak & Reale, 1978).

Incidental-learning procedures may still leave remaining differences in encoding between normals and amnesics. Normals may do more creative or elaborative processing when answering a question; this additional processing is not strictly required by the task, but may serve to enhance memory performance. Differences in encoding processes of this sort are difficult to detect when easy questions requiring a "yes" or "no" answer are employed in the incidental-learning phase of an experiment. Patients might be as likely as normals to answer the questions correctly, but might still engage in less undetected processing than normals do. The use of more complex questions and additional measures such as reaction times might be useful for detecting existing differences. One could then further equate encoding processes, thereby potentially reducing differences in memory performance between Korsakoff patients and normals.

The ineffectiveness of incidental-learning procedures as a therapeutic device seems more likely to stem from differences in retrieval than from undetected differences in encoding processes. Central to the rationale underlying the use of incidental-learning procedures is the claim that Korsakoff patients are less likely to engage in elaborative processing on their own initiative than are normals, so they must be forced to do so. If patients are unlikely to engage in elaborative processing during encoding, there seems to be no reason to think that they would do so at the time of retrieval. In line with the encoding-specificity hypothesis (e.g., Tulving & Thompson, 1973), gaining maximal benefits from elaborative processing during encoding may require that subjects engage in the same form of processing at the time of test. A failure to engage heavily in elaborative retrieval processing on their own initiative would explain why Korsakoff patients still show a memory deficit even when incidental-learning procedures are employed to increase their elaborative processing during encoding. Just as incidental-learning procedures have been used to manipulate encoding processes, it may be possible to devise "incidental-testing" procedures to control retrieval processes, and thereby to eliminate the difference in memory performance between Korsakoff patients and normals. Following incidental learning, the memory disadvantage of Korsakoff patients may be removed if memory is tested by comparing the effects of the prior training on the objective performance of some subsequent task. In this vein, there have been many reports of nearly "normal" memory revealed by Korsakoff patients on incidental tests (as opposed to standard recall and recognition-memory tests) of this form (e.g., Cohen & Squire, 1980).

Effects on rate of forgetting also may be due to processes similar to those involved in encoding and retrieval. Differences in rate of forgetting have been used to postulate two types of amnesia, with only one of the two types suffering from a deficit in storage. Diencephalic amnesia, of which the Korsakoff syndrome is an example, is characterized by a normal rate of forgetting, whereas bitemporal amnesia (of which the case of the famous patient H. M. is an example) is said to reveal a deficit in storage, being characterized by rapid forgetting (Squire, 1982). To compare forgetting rates, additional exposures of material to be remembered have typically been used to equate the memory performance of amnesics with that of their controls on an initial test (equating degree of learning). The difficulty is that equal performance on an initial test does not imply that the different groups achieved that performance by the same means. Qualitative differences in encoding and retrieval processing may be responsible for the apparent differential rate of forgetting. The finding of fast forgetting is very important for specifying different types of amnesia, regardless of whether fast forgetting is due to qualitative or quantitative differences in memory. What is being advocated here is comparing performance across a variety of retention tests to reveal any qualitative differences in encoding and retrieval processes. It would be particularly interesting to compare the forgetting rate of diencephalic amnesics and bitemporal amnesics, using tests that rely on memory for prior experience being revealed as a source of savings, or other such incidental tests of retrieval.

Preserved Memory in Amnesia

By definition, amnesics are impaired in their ability to reflect on memory for prior episodes or to recognize items as being familiar. However, according to several reports, amnesics preserve a nearly normal ability to employ memory gained from recent experience to facilitate their objective task performance. The most common examples of preserved learning and memory lie in the domain of perceptual–motor skills (Squire, 1982).

The examination of situations that reveal normal savings is important for specifying the aspects of memory that are spared by amnesia. If only perceptual–motor tasks revealed preserved learning and memory, it would seem reasonable to argue that the perceptual–motor system is separate from the rest of memory and is spared by amnesia. However, amnesics also reveal effects of recent prior experience in their performance of verbal tasks. We (Jacoby & Witherspoon, 1982) found that Korsakoff patients' interpretation of the meaning of a homophone (e.g., "read–reed") is influenced by memory for its recent prior presentation. Homophones were presented auditorily in the context of questions that biased interpretation toward the less frequent meaning of the homophone (e.g., "Name a musical instrument that employs a reed"). Subjects were later asked to spell several words; no mention was made that some of the words were homophones that had been presented in the earlier phase of the experiment. Surprisingly, Korsakoff patients showed a slightly greater tendency than did normals to spell homophones in line with the bias produced by the earlier questions (e.g., "reed"). This effect of memory on the interpretation of homophones appeared, although a later test revealed that Korsakoff patients were much less likely than normals to recognize the homophones as having been previously presented. Further analyses revealed that effects on spelling were independent of recognition memory for both normals and amnesics. Normals, like amnesics, show effects of prior experience on performance of perceptual tasks that are independent of recognition memory. For example, we (Jacoby & Dallas, 1981) reported that the prior presentation of a word enhances it subsequent tachistoscopic identification, and that this effect on perception is independent of recognition memory. Data such as those coming from the spelling experiment described above can be used as evidence that the separability of effects on objective performance and recognition memory is general, rather than being restricted to perceptual–motor tasks.

A difference in the sensitivity of the two types of memory tests could underlie the effects of prior experience on objective performance in the absence of recognition memory. In this vein, Meudell and Mayes (1981) argue that evidence of learning without recognition memory is not unique to amnesics, but, rather, is characteristic of weak memory in general. To support their argument, they show that the relationship between normals' ability to detect hidden objects in cartoons and their recognition memory for the cartoons after 17 months is similar to that of amnesics after a delay of 7 weeks. Similarly, Nelson (1978) employed normals and found that a savings measure of retention revealed evidence of memory even when subjects failed a test of recognition memory. Nelson interpreted these results as evidence that the two types of tests differ in their sensitivity. Recognition-memory tests were described as having a higher threshold than do savings measures of memory.

Unfortunately for this differential-sensitivity explanation, weak memory produced by a long delay between study and test is not required to find effects on perceptual tasks in the absence of recognition memory for normals. Savings in perceptual tasks are statistically independent of recognition memory, so that having passed the "high-threshold" test of recognition memory does not coincide with a larger effect of prior experience on "low-threshold" savings measures of retention (Jacoby & Witherspoon, 1982; Tulving, Schacter, & Stark, 1982). Further, some study manipulations have an opposite effect on recognition memory and on performance of a subsequent perceptual task (Jacoby, 1983b). Results of this form are clearly incompatible with the claim that the types of tests differ only in their sensitivity to memory for recent prior experience.

Separate Memory Stores?

Given the independence of recognition memory and memory as revealed by savings, it is tempting to conclude that different memory systems underlie performance on the two types of tests. Common to several accounts is the postulation of two memory systems that differ in terms of the level of abstraction of information that they represent. For example, recognition memory may rely on "episodic" memory, a system that preserves information about individual events, while effects on savings measures of memory rely on "semantic" memory, a system that represents more general, abstract information (Kinsbourne & Wood, 1975). Effects on performance in the absence of recognition memory might be described as being due to the "activation" of an abstract semantic-memory representation that does not preserve information about particular episodes of the sort required to support recognition memory. Tulving *et al.* (1982) have suggested that episodic memory underlies recognition memory, while a rather poorly specified "perceptual" memory that is separate from both episodic and semantic memory is responsible for the independent effect of recent prior experience on their perceptual task (word-fragment completion). Cohen and Squire (1980) postulate two memory systems by distinguishing between "procedural" and "declarative" knowledge, a distinction that is apparently seen as being unrelated to the distinction between semantic and episodic memory. "Procedural" knowledge refers to knowledge for rules or procedures, while "declarative" knowledge refers to information that is based on specific items or data.

If savings in objective performance rely on a more abstract memory representation than does recognition memory, effects on savings should be less specific to the details of the prior presentation of an item than is recognition memory. That is, if the activation of an abstract representation underlies savings, details that are specific to a particular presentation of an item should not be preserved to influence the amount of observed savings. Although effects on perceptual identification can be independent of recognition memory, performance on both types of tests can apparently rely on memory for particular prior episodes. The effect of a prior presentation of a word on its subsequent perceptual identification is subject to the same encoding variables (Jacoby, 1983b) and retrieval variables (Jacoby, 1983a) that have been well documented in studies of recognition memory and recall for particular events. There is no evidence that savings in objective performance necessarily rely on a more abstract representation of prior experience than does recognition memory (Jacoby & Witherspoon, 1982).

The failure to find a difference in specificity of effects also weighs on the distinction between procedural and declarative knowledge employed by Cohen and Squire (1980). Cohen and Squire found that amnesics acquired the skill of reading inverted text as readily as did normals, but had poorer memory for the specific words that had been read. They concluded that procedural learning was unimpaired, although there was a deficit in declarative learning. Cohen and Squire apparently view the reading of inverted text as a general skill or procedure that is invariant across the particular texts to which it is applied—a view that may be unjustified. Kolers and his colleagues (e.g., Kolers, 1979), in their investigations employing normals, have shown that the effects of training are specific to the particular orientation of the text, the words read, the type font, the order of approximation to English, and the spacing of letters. The skill of reading inverted text does not seem to be abstract in the sense of being divorced from the specific material that has been the object of prior practice. Rather than being general, procedures may be so specific to the items to which they are applied that procedural knowledge cannot be treated as being independent of declarative knowledge. Even if a distinction between procedural knowledge and declarative knowledge is justified, it may be more useful to focus on their interaction, rather than treating them as independent systems. Recent work on skill learning has been aimed at determining how declarative knowledge can be used to modify procedural knowledge (Hayes-Roth, Klahr, & Mostow, 1981; Neves & Anderson, 1981). For example, instructions can be seen as a form of declarative information that influences the development of a skill, procedural knowledge. By this view, a loss of the ability to remember declarative information would not invariably leave procedural knowledge unaffected. These considerations undermine the utility of the procedural–declarative knowledge distinction in explaining amnesics' memory performance.

Incidental versus Intentional Retrieval

Rather than postulating separate memory stores, I prefer to employ a distinction between "incidental" and "intentional" retrieval that parallels the distinction between "incidental" and "intentional" learning. Evidently, the only factor common to tasks revealing effects of prior experience that are independent of recognition memory is that in all cases the subject's memory is tested using procedures that do not require intentional retrieval (Baddeley, 1982; Jacoby, 1982). Rather than restriction to a particular type of task (e.g., perceptual–motor tasks), then, it is the incidental nature of retrieval that seems important for preserved learning and memory. Differences between incidental and intentional learning have been described in terms of differences in processing, and a similar approach seems appropriate for describing differences between incidental and intentional retrieval.

It has been suggested that intention is important for learning only to the extent that it is translated into processing or representational activities; incidental learning can be made identical to intentional learning by requiring the incidental learner to engage in the same activities as does the intentional learner (Postman, 1964). If incidental-learning procedures had been successful in removing the memory deficit of amnesics, the effect would have been described as due to a difference in processing rather than a difference in memory stores. That is, separate memory stores would not be identified with incidental and intentional learning. Similarly, the effectiveness of incidental retrieval is perhaps better attributed to an influence on processing, rather than being attributed to a separate memory system that is preserved in amnesia. The independence of incidental retrieval (e.g., effects on perceptual identification) and intentional retrieval (e.g., recognition memory) can also be understood in terms of differences in the type of information processed. Incidental-learning procedures can be devised to produce a parallel independence of effects. If subjects in one condition are required to deal with the meaning of a presented word while those in a second condition deal with its physical appearance, for example, some manipulations would have differential effects on performance in the two conditions. The result would be independence that comes from qualitative differences in encoding. Similarly, the independence of incidental and intentional retrieval can be attributed to qualitative differences in the types of information that are employed during retrieval.

Others have identified types of tasks with independent memory systems. By concentrating on the type of information used by a task, in contrast, highly variable relations among tasks are predicted. Recognition memory can apparently rely either on memory for perceptual characteristics (familiarity) or on memory gained by processing meaning (e.g., see Jacoby & Dallas, 1981; Mandler, 1980). Recognition memory can be made to reflect prior conceptually driven processing (meaning), while effects on perceptual identification are made to reflect prior data-driven processing (memory for perceptual characteristics), so independence of performance on the two types of test can be produced (Jacoby, 1983b). However, the independence of recognition memory and effects on perceptual identification can be removed by altering procedures so as to insure that both types of test use memory gained from prior data-driven processing (Jacoby & Witherspoon, 1982). For normals, savings in performance of a perceptual task and recognition memory can be made dependent on or independent of each other by manipulating factors that influence the type of information that they employ. Consequently, it seems unwise to identify the tasks with independent memory systems.

Differences in processing along with the distinction between incidental and intentional retrieval are useful for interpreting the results of an experiment reported by Graf, Squire, and Mandler (1984). They presented amnesics and controls with a list of words for study in a first phase of an experiment. Words from the first phase were then intermixed with new words to be presented as word fragments, which were to be completed by subjects without instructions that some fragments had been derived from previously presented words. With the use of this incidental-retrieval procedure, amnesics and controls produced equal memory performance. By contrast, in a second experiment, amnesics and their controls were presented with word fragments that were to be used as explicit cues for retrieval of previously studied words (intentional retrieval). The use of intentional-retrieval procedures resulted in poorer memory performance for amnesics than for their controls. Comparisons across the experiments revealed that intentional retrieval produced higher performance than did incidental retrieval for control subjects, but produced the same level of performance as did incidental retrieval for amnesics. Graf et al. (1984) attribute this differential effectiveness of instructions to declarative memory's being intact in control subjects and impaired in amnesics.

As an alternative to their account, differences in processing can be emphasized. It is likely that normal subjects respond to instructions to remember by elaborating retrieval cues in terms of the prior study context. In this vein, Smith, Glenberg, and Bjork (1978) have reported that, for normals, the deleterious effects of a change in environmental context between study and test can be removed by instructing subjects at the time of testing to imagine that they are in the study context. As is true for encoding, it is unlikely that amnesics will engage in this elaborative retrieval processing of their own accord. Similarly, retrieval has been described as an active process that involves reconstruction through setting up plausible retrieval cues (e.g., Lindsay & Norman, 1972). To remember the name of one's third-grade teacher, for example, one begins by remembering where one lived in the third grade, what the school looked like, and so on. Baddeley (1982) suggests that amnesics are less likely to actively generate their own cues for retrieval than are normals.

The account of preserved learning in amnesia in terms of processing differences between incidental and intentional retrieval ignores differences in awareness of remembering. It is striking that a patient can reveal normal memory for a prior experience in his or her objective performance while simultaneously denying any subjective familiarity for that prior experience. The problem of awareness might be treated as being sufficiently serious to justify postulating a separate memory store that is unique in that it allows awareness of remembering. However, a reasonable alternative is to treat subjective familiarity or awareness as arising from additional processing, rather than as an inherent characteristic of a particular memory system. As discussed in the next section, awareness of remembering may rely on the use of heuristics similar to those that have been described as being important in the attribution literature (e.g., Nisbett & Ross, 1980).

The Fluency Heuristic and Awareness of Remembering

Recognition memory seems to require awareness of remembering, although awareness is not required to show savings gained from prior experience in objective performance. Awareness has been treated as being an inherent characteristic of the episodic-memory system, the system responsible for recognition memory (e.g., Tulving *et al.*, 1982). However, that approach gives rise to a problem that is similar to a problem associated with the claim that depth perception is innate. If one decides that depth perception is innate, there is a tendency to think that depth perception is then understood and to forget that it is still necessary to specify the cues that are used to infer depth. Similarly, saying that awareness is an inherent characteristic of episodic memory does not specify the cues on which awareness is based. I prefer to treat awareness of remembering as being an attribution (cf. Nisbett & Ross, 1980), and to regard relative fluency as being one cue that is used for that attribution (Jacoby & Dallas, 1981).

Rather than being directly accessed as an attribute of memory, awareness of remembering may be viewed as involving an attribution process that is similar to the process involved in using the availability heuristic to estimate probabilities (Kahneman & Tversky, 1973). When using the availability heuristic, a person infers that a class of events is a probable one if an instance of that class is highly available (i.e., it can be readily brought to mind). In the awareness of remembering, fluency in performing a task, like availability, is a basis for application of a heuristic. Subjective familiarity or awareness of remembering a particular event resembles probability in being a dimension that is judged by application of a heuristic. Others have treated familiarity as primitive and as serving as a basis for recognition memory (e.g., Mandler, 1980). In contrast, I treat effects of prior experience on performance as primary, and view feelings of subjective familiarity as being due to performance effects' being attributed to prior study. The judgment of familiarity follows effects on performance and requires additional processing. Amnesics may fail to use judgments of relative fluency to monitor their performance. As a result, effects of prior experience on objective performance are not accompanied by feelings of subjective familiarity. The amnesic, then, is seen as being less likely to actively generate plausible retrieval cues at the time of testing, and as also being less likely to monitor his or her own performance to make the attribution of subjective familiarity.

Earlier discussions have centered on judgments of relative perceptual fluency as a heuristic for recognition memory (Jacoby & Dallas, 1981). However, use of the fluency heuristic need not be restricted to judgments of perceptual fluency. One could as well judge fluency of semantic processing as a heuristic for deciding whether or not an item had been encountered during study. In this regard, retrieval of study context has been said to provide an alternative to judging relative perceptual fluency as a basis for recognition memory (Jacoby & Dallas, 1981). For retrieval of study context, however, a subject still has the problem of deciding whether he or she has actually retrieved the study context or has only invented it. The fluency of constructing study context is likely to provide a basis for making the decision. Although there are other cues that one can use to aid in the judgment of whether or not he or she is remembering (e.g., Baddeley, 1982), the fluency heuristic seems to be useful over a wide range of situations.

Several advantages can be gained by treating familiarity as an attribution rather than as an inherent characteristic of memory. First, feelings of familiarity do not invariably arise when we encounter previously experienced people, events, or objects. We do not experience a feeling of familiarity when we encounter a colleague at work, but would experience such a feeling and would be aware of recognizing the colleague if we encountered him or her in an unexpected location. The feeling of familiarity seems to rely on a discrepancy reaction of some sort or on a direct question about recognition that calls for an attribution to be made. Indeed, it would be incredibly disruptive if a subjective feeling of familiarity intruded every time we encountered a previously experienced person, location, object, or event.

Treating familiarity as an attribution also has the advantage of allowing for variability in the relation between effects in performance and a subject's attributions. Effects on performance due to factors other than recent prior experience will sometimes give rise to feelings of subjective familiarity. The higher probability of a false recognition of a high-frequency than a low-frequency word can be seen as due to subjects' mistakenly attributing the performance effects of frequency in the language to prior study. An effect of recent prior experience on performance also will not always be attributed to the correct source. In a study of duration judgments, subjects incorrectly attributed their superior perceptual identification of old words to those words' being presented for a longer duration than were new words (Jacoby & Witherspoon, 1982). As a similar but more commonplace example, when beginning to learn a foreign language, one has the impression that the language is being spoken at an incredibly rapid rate by native speakers and that this rate interferes with comprehension. As a function of experience, the rate at which the language is spoken seems to slow. In this example, effects of prior experience on fluency of comprehension are incorrectly attributed to a difference in speaking rate. In general, effects of prior experience on performance are probably often incorrectly attributed to physical characteristics of the stimuli, rather than their giving rise to feelings of subjective familiarity.

Effects of prior experience on performance may also sometimes be incorrectly attributed to affective factors. Zajonc (1980) has found affective judgments to be influenced by previous presentations of items, although subjects were unable to recognize the items as having been previously presented. He concluded that there is an affective system that is separate from the cognitive system, which is responsible for recognition memory. Zajonc's results can be reinterpreted as being due to effects of prior experience on relative perceptual fluency, which subjects attributed to differences in affect. Effects on perceptual identification, like judgments of affect, can be independent of recognition memory. For both types of measure, the independence of recognition memory may be better described in terms of differences in the information that is processed than in terms of separate memory systems. The stimuli employed by Zajonc were typically meaningless and originally affectively neutral, so subjects may have had no alternative to using judgments of relative perceptual fluency as a heuristic for making judgments about affect.

Concluding Comments

Accounts of amnesia have typically attempted to identify memory deficits as specific to encoding, storage, or retrieval. In actuality, the types of processing required for encoding seem to be very similar to those required for retrieval; elaborative processing is important for both retrieval and encoding. In line with the encoding-specificity principle (Tulving & Thompson, 1973) or memory for operations (Kolers, 1979), the effect of prior study is seen as being restricted by the similarity of encoding and retrieval processing. Effects on encoding and effects on retrieval cannot fruitfully be treated as being separate.

I have treated the distinction between incidental and intentional retrieval as similar to the distinction made earlier between incidental and intentional learning. According to this view, preserved learning and memory are not restricted to any particular set of tasks, such as perceptual–motor tasks, but rather are due to the use of incidental-retrieval procedures to structure the retrieval environment for the amnesic. As has earlier been argued for encoding (e.g., Cermak, 1979), the amnesic will not spontaneously engage in more active, elaborative retrieval processing. Revealing effects of prior study requires that processing at the time of retrieval be similar to that at encoding. Controlling encoding through incidental-learning procedures in combination with intentional-retrieval procedures does not insure this similarity in processing, so is an ineffective means of repairing memory performance.

The amnesic is seen as being incapable of structuring his or her own encoding or retrieval processing without the support that is provided by incidental-encoding and incidental-retrieval procedures. Recent work on metamemory has been aimed at determining how a learner develops the ability to structure his or her learning activities (e.g., Brown, 1975). Corresponding work aimed at retrieval is needed. If one wants to argue that there are separate memory systems, a prerequisite for specifying such systems is gaining control over encoding and retrieval processes to show that differences truly stem from separate memory systems. Incidental-encoding and incidental-retrieval procedures are likely to be useful in this regard.

Awareness of remembering and effects of prior experience on objective performance are separate issues. Rather than being an inherent characteristic of a particular memory system, awareness of remembering is seen as being an attribution that results from the application of a heuristic. By this view, effects of a particular prior experience on performance are not necessarily accompanied by awareness; awareness corresponds to attributing effects on performance to prior experience as a source of those effects. Attributions vary in their veridicality. Effects on performance that arise from prior experience will sometimes be incorrectly attributed to other sources even by normals.

Effects on performance in the absence of recognition memory probably result from the amnesic's not monitoring his or her own performance, as well as from a failure to engage in more active retrieval processing. This failure to monitor performance should be particularly important in the development of certain skills. Most experiments on amnesia have followed a short study period with a single test of memory, so that only a small cross-section of memory performance is observed. A promising direction for future research is to compare the development of various skills, searching for cumulative effects of patients' failure to engage in more active processing and their failure to monitor their own performance.

ACKNOWLEDGMENT

I wish to express my appreciation to Donna Gelfand for her comments on an earlier draft of this chapter.

REFERENCES

Baddeley, A. D. Domains of recollection. *Psychological Review*, 1982, *89*, 708–729.

Battig, W. F. The flexibility of human memory. In L. S. Cermak & F. I. M. Craik (Eds.), *Levels of processing in human memory*. Hillsdale, N.J.: Erlbaum, 1979.

Brown, A. L. The development of memory: Knowing, knowing about knowing, and knowing how to know. In H. W. Reese (Ed.), *Advances in child development and behavior* (Vol. 10). New York: Academic Press, 1975.

Cermak, L. S. Amnesic patients' level of processing. In L. S. Cermak & F. I. M. Craik (Eds.), *Levels of processing in human memory*. Hillsdale, N.J.: Erlbaum, 1979.

Cermak, L. S., & Reale, L. Depth of processing and retention of words by alcoholic Korsakoff patients. *Journal of Experimental Psychology: Human Learning and Memory*, 1978, *5*, 164–175.

Cohen, N. J., & Squire, L. R. Preserved learning and retention of pattern-analyzing skill in amnesia: Dissociation of knowing how and knowing that. *Science*, 1980, *210*, 207–210.

Corkin, S. Acquisition of motor skill after bilateral medial temporal-lobe excision. *Neuropsychologia*, 1968, *6*, 255–266.

Graf, P., Squire, L. R., & Mandler, G. The information that amnesic patients do not forget. *Journal of Experimental Psychology: Learning, Memory, and Cognition*, 1984, *10*, 164–178.

Hayes-Roth, F., Klahr, P., & Mostow, D. J. Advice taking and knowledge refinement: An iterative view of skill acquisition. In J. R. Anderson (Ed.), *Cognitive skills and their acquisition*. Hillsdale, N.J.: Erlbaum, 1981.

Hupert, F. A., & Piercy, M. Normal and abnormal forgetting in organic amnesia: Effect of locus of lesion. *Cortex*, 1979, *15*, 385–390.

Jacoby, L. L. Knowing and remembering: Some parallels in the behavior of Korsakoff patients and normals. In L. S. Cermak (Ed.), *Human memory and amnesia*. Hillsdale, N.J.: Erlbaum, 1982.

Jacoby, L. L. Perceptual enhancement: Persistent effects of an experience. *Journal of Experimental Psychology: Learning, Memory, and Cognition*, 1983, *9*, 21–38. (a)

Jacoby, L. L. Remembering the data: Analyzing interactive processes in reading. *Journal of Verbal Learning and Verbal Behavior*, 1983, *22*, 485–508. (b)

Jacoby, L. L., & Dallas, M. On the relationship between autobiographical memory and perceptual learning. *Journal of Experimental Psychology: General*, 1981, *3*, 306–340.

Jacoby, L. L., & Witherspoon, D. Remembering without awareness. *Canadian Journal of Psychology*, 1982, *36*(2), 300–324.

Kahneman, D., & Tversky, A. On the psychology of prediction. *Psychological Review*, 1973, *80*, 237–251.

Kinsbourne, M., & Wood, F. Short-term memory processes and the amnesic syndrome. In D. Deutsch & A. J. Deutsch (Eds.), *Short-term memory*. New York: Academic Press, 1975.

Kolers, P. A. A pattern-analyzing basis of recognition. In L. S. Cermak & F. I. M. Craik (Eds.), *Levels of processing in human memory*. Hillsdale, N.J.: Erlbaum, 1979.

Lindsay, P. H., & Norman, D. A. *Human information processing*. New York: Academic Press, 1972.

Mandler, G. Recognizing: The judgment of previous occurrence. *Psychological Review*, 1980, *87*, 252–271.

Meudell, P., & Mayes, A. The Claparède phenomenon: A further example in amnesics, a demonstration of a similar effect in normal people with attenuated memory, and a reinterpretation. *Current Psychological Research*, 1981, *1*, 75–88.

Milner, B., Corkin, S., & Teuber, H. L. Further analysis of the hippocampal amnesia syndrome. *Neuropsychologia*, 1968, *6*, 215–234.

Nelson, T. O. Detecting small amounts of information in memory: Savings for nonrecognized items. *Journal of Experimental Psychology: Human Learning and Memory*, 1978, *4*, 453–468.

Neves, D. M., & Anderson, J. R. Knowledge compilation: Mechanisms for the automatization of cognitive skills. In J. R. Anderson (Ed.), *Cognitive skills and their acquisition*. Hillsdale, N.J.: Erlbaum, 1981.

Nisbett, R. E., & Ross, L. *Human inference: Strategies and shortcomings of social judgment*. Englewood Cliffs, N.J.: Prentice-Hall, 1980.

Postman, L. Short-term memory and incidental learning. In A. W. Melton (Ed.), *Categories of human learning*. New York: Academic Press, 1964.

Smith, S. M., Glenberg, A. M., & Bjork, R. A. Environmental context and human memory. *Memory and Cognition*, 1978, *6*, 342–353.

Squire, L. R. The neuropsychology of human memory. *Annual Review of Neuroscience*, 1982, *5*, 241–273.

Tulving, E., Schacter, D. L., & Stark, H. A. Priming effects in word-fragment completion are independent of recognition memory. *Journal of Experimental Psychology: Learning, Memory, and Cognition*, 1982, *8*, 336–342.

Tulving, E., & Thompson, D. M. Encoding specificity and retrieval processes in episodic memory. *Psychological Review*, 1973, *80*, 352–373.

Underwood, B. J., Boruch, R. F., & Malmi, R. A. Compositions of episodic memory. *Journal of Experimental Psychology: General*, 1978, *107*, 393–419.

Warrington, E. K., & Weiskrantz, L. An analysis of short-term and long-term memory defects in man. In J. A. Deutsch (Ed.), *The physiological basis of memory*. New York: Academic Press, 1973.

Zajonc, R. B. Feeling and thinking: Preferences need no inferences. *American Psychologist*, 1980, *35*, 151–175.

Chromomnemonics and Amnesia

16

J. A. Deutsch

Amnesia has popularly been regarded as a state in which there is a global memory loss. In retrograde amnesia, there is a loss of memory preceding the trauma or disease that precipitated the memory loss. In anterograde amnesia, there is an apparent inability to lay down memories as a result of damage to the central nervous system. The present chapter addresses primarily the disorder present in anterograde amnesia.

The patient suffering from anterograde amnesia seems not to recognize people he or she has just met a few minutes ago, or to recall events that have just occurred. This might be taken to indicate a complete inability to form fresh memories. On the other hand, access to memories before the initiating damage is spared, though some retrograde amnesia is generally also present. In other words, the patient can remember things about his or her past as well as a normal person can (Cohen & Squire, 1981; Squire & Cohen, 1979), though there is an inability to remember events just prior to the trauma. Such a retrograde amnesia may extend to events anywhere from seconds to perhaps years of time just prior to the central nervous system (CNS) damage and appears to be a dissociable deficit from anterograde amnesia (Cohen & Squire,1981), at least in certain classes of patients.

However, in spite of the seeming failure of the ability to form or utilize new memories, it appears that certain types of function survive unscathed. For instance, amnesics can learn mirror-tracing tasks (Milner, 1962); pursuit-rotor tasks at a normal rate (Brooks & Baddeley, 1976; Cermak, Lewis, Butters, & Goodglass, 1973; Cohen, 1981); mirror reading, again at a normal rate (Cohen & Squire, 1980); a numerical rule (Wood, Ebert, & Kinsbourne, 1982); and the solutions to certain complex puzzles, again at a normal rate (Cohen, 1981; Cohen & Corkin, 1981). The memory for such learning can also be excellent—for instance, in conditioned eye blink (Weiskrantz & Warrington, 1979) and mirror reading (Cohen, 1981; Cohen & Squire, 1980). It is to be noted that the learning curves of amnesic patients and normals are in many cases superimposable. There is no evidence that amnesic patients learn more slowly initially and then catch up. They also show "priming" effects of the same size as normal subjects (Graf, Squire, & Mandler, 1984; Jacoby & Witherspoon, 1982). For instance, their word-completion behavior or choice of spelling in a subsequent test is influenced by words that were previously presented, to the same extent and over the same time range as in normals. A similar dissociation in mnemonic ability has been described (Mishkin, Spiegler, Saunders, & Malamut, 1982) in monkeys rendered amnesic by combined lesions to the hippocampus and amygdala. Such monkeys can learn a visual-discrimination task at the normal rate,

J. A. Deutsch. Department of Psychology, University of California at San Diego, La Jolla, California.

even when the individual trials are spaced 24 hours apart. However, these monkeys find great difficulty in using the memory of similar visual material after longer than 10 seconds in a matching-to-sample recognition task, where the object just shown must be avoided in order that the reward should be obtained, whereas normal monkeys perform almost flawlessly even after 2 minutes.

There is therefore some dispute about the nature of the deficit in anterograde amnesia. Some have held that there is a specific deficit in the memory of events, as opposed to a memory for habits, or that it is declarative memory that is absent while procedural memory survives. However, in view of the nature of the tasks that the amnesic has recently been shown capable of learning, this has become an increasingly difficult thesis to sustain. Another view explains the amnesic deficit as a loss in the ability to order events or to time-tag them. (For a review of evidence supporting this view, see Hirst & Volpe, 1982.) Such a view has gained recent strong support from the demonstration that amnesics, while they remember certain news items as well as normals, are very much impaired in being able to place them in time. Similarly, while they can recognize items that have been presented to them in succession, their ability to remember when the items occurred is grossly impaired (Hirst & Volpe, 1982). This view of amnesics' disability presents us with a paradox. While the amnesic can learn new habits as well as normal controls, he or she cannot remember the time of events in the past.

Now, it is possible to believe that normal ability to perform such temporal placement is due to a reconstruction of the past by remembering the content of memory. While it might be possible to construct a system that could reconstruct the past from the content of memory, it would seem implausible that this is what we actually do all the time. It may be assumed that in general we place an event in some portion of the past because its memory carries some kind of time marker. However, we can, under special or favorable circumstances, reconstruct when an event occurred from contextual cues. The presence of this alternative method of dating an event makes it difficult to obtain completely unambiguous evidence for the view that anterograde amnesia is due to a loss of time-tagging or time-marking. A patient suffering from such a loss of time-tagging can fall back on reconstructing the past from contextual markers, especially under experimental conditions that favor such a strategy. Squire (1982) has recently argued that a lack of temporal information is a characteristic of Korsakoff patients and not of other amnesics, and that it is not the basic deficit in amnesia. The inability to remember time, it is argued, is due to damage to other neural systems in Korsakoff patients besides those that are damaged in amnesia. However, if it is correct, as is probable, that Korsakoff patients suffer from more widespread damage than other amnesics, we could argue that, to the contrary, such additional damage works to reveal the basic deficit in amnesia more clearly in their case. If there are two mechanisms available to us for reconstructing the time of past events—time-tagging and context—the destruction of one of these mechanisms would lead only to mild impairment of the capacity to reconstruct the time of past events, especially under favorable conditions. It might need damage to both mechanisms for the deficit to reveal itself. It should be noted in this context that Squire (1982) asked his subjects to report which group of previously read sentences a given sentence came from. The associative richness of sentences, read in close succession, would clearly favor the utilization of contextual cues by patients with such capacity still intact, and so would mask their deficit in time-tagging. Put more generally, the deficit in time-tagging might not have emerged in the Squire study, since another mechanism might have been used by subjects.

If a deficit in time-tagging is a basic deficit in amnesia, how would time-tagging be implemented by the nervous system? One possible system would be to attach a time-of-arrival tag to each incoming complex of stimuli and to store such a tag along with each such incoming stimulus complex. Somehow, such a system does not appear very plausible. Another scheme would be to have each memory trace, after it is laid down, change along a continuum of strength with the passage of time. In such a way, the amount of strength of any memory trace would give information about its age. But there are various problems with such a hypothesis. The first is that the dynamic range between zero and maximum trace strength is probably quite narrow and noise quite high, in comparison with the number of different ages the system should ideally represent; thus such a system would give only a rather coarse indication of when something had happened. The second problem is that the strength of a trace, according to many theories, is the strength of a connection between two elements, and this variable of strength would also represent not only time, but the firmness of the associative bond. This would render trace strength an ambiguous indicator of time. A third problem is that what indications we have of the change of such traces with time reveal that the change is not monotonic with time. The trace apparently undergoes a process of growth followed by shrinkage. This would render the dating of any memory ambiguous, as there will always be two points on the curve that are equal in height (except at the maximum).

Does this mean that the idea of time-tagging through variations in trace strength must be discarded? The idea that memories are somehow represented in variations in the strength of synaptic connection is plausible, as in the notion that the strength of a memory or a habit is represented by the strength of a synaptic connection that codes for the memory. But this is only apparently so, as can be seen by the way an analogous problem has been solved by the eye. The eye is able to locate a particular wavelength of light correctly on the spectral continuum, almost independently of the intensity of such a light. This is analogous to the problem that must be solved in memory where a memory can be assigned to a particular time, independently of the strength of such a memory. The inputs to the mechanism in the eye that can extract such information are simple variations in strength of signal, depending on where on an inverted-U curve of sensitivity the wavelength lies and on how intense the energy at that wavelength is. However, to extract such information, the eye uses inputs from three inverted-U curves that partially overlap and have different maxima. Each wavelength will thus assume a value on each of the inverted-U curves. These values are then fed into two different mechanisms. One mechanism sums the values, thus giving information about overall intensity but losing information about the position on the spectrum. The second mechanism computes the ratio of the values on the inverted-U curves, thus giving information about the position on the spectrum of the monochromatic light but discarding information about its intensity.

Such a system can be used in the case of memory. Instead of assuming that a memory trace is represented by a single process that first increases in strength and then decreases, we may assume that each memory trace is represented by a number of processes, simultaneously initiated, but increasing and decreasing in strength at different rates. This would produce the signals that would then be fed into the two kinds of mechanism that are used by the eye. One of these mechanisms would sum the intensities produced by the two processes that increase and decrease with time at different rates. The output of this first mechanism would signal the strength of memory or habit, while losing all information about when the memory was laid down. The second mechanism would extract the ratio between the strength of the signals that had been simultaneously initiated. This second mechanism would thus measure the age of the memory, while losing information about its strength. The number of inverted-U processes initiated by each event to be remembered could be quite numerous. A huge continuum of time must be covered in memory, and an increase in the accuracy in such a system of time-tagging can be achieved by increasing the number of processes initiated as a memory is laid down. Some of these processes may be only very brief, running their up-and-down course within seconds. At the other end of the scale, such processes may be measured in years.

Is there any evidence that such processes with different time constants occur in memory? If rats are taught a habit, they can be retested while under the influence of a drug at different times after initial learning. The drug is injected at the same time before each retest. We thus test the influence of a drug on habits of different age. In such a series of experiments (Deutsch, 1971), cholinergic agents were used. For habits more than 3 days old, it was found that there was an increasing block of memory by anticholinesterases. Such a memory block was almost complete at 2 to 3 weeks, and then declined in habits older than that. There is then evidence of an increase in vulnerability to an anticholinesterase, followed by a decline in such vulnerability after about 14 to 21 days. However, if we look at habits less than 3 days old, there is evidence for a separate maximum, as the curves obtained have a minimum of sensitivity at about 3 days to anticholinesterases. The extra peak for habits less than 3 days old is not very pronounced when we use anticholinesterases, though. Anticholinesterases facilitate weak habits (and synaptic connections) and block strong ones. If before 3 days one of the underlying processes is strong and the other weak, their sum may not be very different after anticholinesterase treatment. On the other hand, a much larger effect should be visible after anticholinergic treatment where there is a subtractive effect on all synaptic transmission that is cholinergically mediated. Consequently, we would expect a large decrement where both curves intersect. As a result, the presence of two such processes is much more dramatically revealed by the use of an anticholinergic. The fact that the effect is much less clearly seen with anticholinesterases shows that the two processes with different time constants sum, and occur in parallel, as is demanded by the theory. (The effect described above must not be taken to mean that the rat has only two such parallel processes available. The times that were sampled preclude observation of other curves at shorter intervals.) If two systems analogous to the ones found in the visual pathway exist in extracting information about the past, then the somewhat paradoxical facts concerning anterograde amnesia can be readily accounted for. The preservation of only the system that sums the strength of the synaptic connections representing a memory, as they wax and wane at different rates, would enable that amnesic to utilize past learning of skills and habits that yields information about their strength but not about when they were laid down. The impairment of the system that compares the strengths of the synaptic connections representing a memory, as they wax and wane at different rates, would leave the amnesic unable to use his or her memory store to determine when in the past its contents occurred and whether they occurred in the past at all.

This "comparator," or "opponent," process is normally set up or connected at the time that memory registration occurs. In the state of anterograde amnesia, such a connection no longer occurs. As mentioned above, the anterograde amnesic does still remember about events that occurred some time before he or she became amnesic, and this means that the mechanisms for comparing strengths of memory trace already connected are preserved. After the precipitating trauma, some trophic influence proceeding from some brain structures may be absent, so that connections are not formed between the synapses modified by learning to form the comparator or opponent mechanism. For instance, it might need a particular balance of transmitter or neuromodulator influence to increase the probability of connection of inhibitory inputs in the comparator mechanism.

I have stated above that the impairment of the system that compares the strengths of the synaptic connections representing a memory would leave the amnesic unable to use his or her memory store to determine when in the past its contents occurred and whether they occurred in the past at all. The rationale for this statement is as follows: When the nervous system detects that something has occurred before, or, in other words, recognizes it, it must compare incoming signals with some stored representation of them. Now, on the theory that has been suggested above, such stored representations consist of alterations of synaptic strength, which then have their output either through the system that sums these strengths or through the opponent system that compares them. It will be recalled that it is this second system that enables such representations to be dated. A part of the signal enabling recognition to occur must then originate either from the output of the summator mechanism or from the output of the comparator (opponent) mechanism. It seems much more probable that the signal used in recognition is derived from the comparator mechanism. One argument for this is that the amnesic patient is grossly deficient in his or her ability to recognize; though this can be regarded as being a circular argument in some sense, it nevertheless constrains interpretation within the context of the theory as already stated. A second argument that could be made is that recognition carries with it some sense of the recency of what is being recognized, and it is not implausible to assume that a perception of when something happened is intrinsic to the feeling of its recognition. Stated in less subjective terms, it is postulated that when incoming signals are matched against their possibly already existing synaptic representations, the output of such synaptic alterations is interrogated via the comparator system. (As stated above, a comparator is formed for each incoming event. As a result, events before injury can be recognized.) An important consequence of this is that if such a comparator system is not formed, recognition of prior occurrence cannot take place, even though synaptic representations forming the memory store exist and have outputs via the summator system.

Let us see how a system with such a deficit would behave under various circumstances. One obvious, trivial consequence is that it could not identify a particular sensory input as having occurred before. There would therefore be a behavioral deficit in tasks where such a capacity to match incoming information with information in store is necessary for success. One such task is recall. When asked to recall, as can easily be seen when recall is difficult, we generate a sequence of alternatives until we come up with one that we recognize. Without this capacity to recognize (or match what we have produced with some part of the contents of the memory store), we would lack the signal of success (recognition) that ordinarily terminates the search. We assume here that the process of generating alternatives is nonrandom, and in fact is driven at least in part by the memory store through the summator system. However, without the success signal derived from the comparator system, the organism may very well produce the correct answer but be unaware of it. (Such production is normally subvocal or prevocal, and it is not normally vocalized unless the success signal arrives.)

Let us contrast the situation described above, where the success signal is derived from a match with the contents of the memory store, to one where the success signal is derived from some other source. Suppose that the patient is not asked to recall a name, but instead to solve a puzzle or to complete a word, as in priming experiments. The success signal, as soon as the right output has been generated, does not depend on the match between such an output and its representation in the memory store; it depends on the capacity to perceive that the puzzle has been solved. In fact, it is a characteristic of all the tasks that have been called "procedural" (mirror tracing and reading, pursuit rotor, various puzzles) that the patient can perceive that he or she has done them right without comparing his or her output to a target stored in memory. It is also a characteristic of the so-called priming tasks. On the other hand, all those that have been called "declarative" have the property that the patient cannot know that he or she has done them right without comparing his or her output to a target stored in memory, and it is this comparison that the patient cannot perform.

We are thus in a position to test between the present hypothesis and the one that is based on the procedural–declarative distinction. According to the present hypothesis, the ability to learn does not depend on whether the subject matter is declarative or procedural. It depends only on the success signal that terminates the search. When the success signal is derived from comparing the present signal with some stored representation of it in memory, the amnesic patient will fail. For instance, if asked to learn a word association or to put a name to a face, the only way that the patient can know he or she is right is to refer to his or her memory of it. On the other hand, if asked to learn a skill or the solution to a puzzle, the patient can know he or she is right by referring to a rule, without recognizing that he or she has seen the solution before.

Now let us look at the definition of "procedural" memory (Squire, 1982): "The critical feature that is procedural here is that there can develop in memory a representation based on experience that changes the way an organism responds to the environment, without affording access to the specific instances that led to this change" (p. 260). According to such a definition, the amnesic patient should be able to learn procedures that are arbitrary, in the sense that the patient cannot know that he or she is right by referring to a rule. The two contrasting theoretical viewpoints could be tested by training amnesic patients on two versions of the same task, both of which would involve the identical set of moves. However, in one case the moves would be presented as the solution of a problem, and in the other as a set of arbitrary moves. In both cases the procedure and the subject matter would be the same, and so both should be learnable, according to procedural-declarative theory of amnesia. On the other hand, according to the theory presently being put forward, improvement from trial to trial should be much better when the moves are placed in the context of a solution to a problem, while progress should be negligible when the same procedure is presented as a set of arbitrary moves whose correctness can only be established by reference to memory.

Now let us examine the definition of "declarative" memory (Squire, 1982): "Thus the ability to develop and store declarative memory (all the bits of specific-item information that are the subject of conventional memory experiments like faces, words and shapes) depends on the integrity of the particular bitemporal and diencephalic brain structures affected in amnesia" (p. 260). According to this definition, the amnesic should not be able to learn tasks consisting of faces, words, and shapes. However, according to the present theory, there should be no difficulty if the task has indications built into it that the right output has been made, and if these indications do not depend on the memory of the task. It is true that most experiments on faces, shapes, and words have arbitrarily paired these items in such a way that a knowledge of successful response is based on access to the memory of previous trials. However, it would be possible to devise learning tasks using such material that could yield learning in amnesics by incorporating a rule in the task. The fulfilling of such a rule could then signal success to the amnesic within the task. For instance, it should be possible to teach the amnesic an association between a word and its anagram, once the rule has been made explicit. But this learning should not be possible without such a rule. For instance, the amnesic should learn to say "veteran" in response to the nonsense word "tavener," but only when told that he or she is learning an anagram. Similarly, he or she should be able to learn paired associates by a modification of the normal procedure. Instead of being asked to recall a word in response to another, the subject should be asked to say any word that occurs to him or her and should be told that he or she is right when the correct word is produced. There should be a decrease in the latency of the production of the correct word. The reason for this is as follows: If asked to recall, the subject is incapable of selecting the correct word to vocalize, because even if the word is internally produced, it will not be recognized as being correct and so no vocal output will occur. On the other hand, if the patient is asked to vocalize words as they occur to him or her, the probability of such production will increase as the synaptic strength mediating the words in memory increases. Such an increase in synaptic strength will reflect itself in output from the summator system and thus will produce an increase in the probability of the correct word. However, the output from the comparator system, which gives the signal that recall has occurred, will remain absent, making it impossible for the patient to complete the normal act of recall.

The theory put forward is designed to explain why the amnesic cannot learn word associations or new facts, recognize new faces or places, and order events in time, while at the same time he is able to acquire various motor, perceptual, and cognitive skills normally and shows normal evidence of memory in priming tasks. The theory supposes that memory is laid down for each incoming event as a set of parallel synaptic changes, each of which varies with time at a different rate. Such information is then utilized via two different circuits analogous to those found in the visual system. One of these sums the concurrent synaptic changes (the summator system), and the other compares them (the comparator system). Generation of material from memory proceeds via the summator system, while recognition of incoming information or the material generated by the summator system occurs via the comparator system. The sole defect in anterograde amnesia is an inability to form new comparators after the trauma. The amnesic is therefore incapable of recognizing the recurrence of incoming events and recognizing that the output of the summator system matches stored information. He or she therefore cannot perform memory tasks that depend on such recognition, but performs normally on memory tasks where the success signal depends on some other kind of match, such as the correct solution of a problem at the time.

In this chapter, processing mechanisms known to be used in the visual system in handling brightness and color have been postulated to operate in the mnemonic system. Such a postulation increases the power and plausibility of any theoretical memory or learning system that relies on strength of connection as one of its basic assumptions to explain behavioral change based on experience. No longer do such theories have to rely exclusively on contextual cues to explain discrimination between the ages of memories. The postulation of processing mechanisms already discovered in the visual system also illuminates the rather paradoxical dissociations of mnemonic function in anterograde amnesia. It seems likely that processing mechanisms that are found to operate in one part of the nervous system are used in another context in other parts of the nervous system. The visual system is at present best understood in its relation between function and underlying mechanisms. And so the eye is our best window to the mind.

ACKNOWLEDGMENTS

My thanks are due to Drs. R. M. Boynton, P. Graf, and L. R. Squire for valuable discussions, and to Professor O. L. Zangwill, who many years ago was my teacher.

REFERENCES

Brooks, D. N., & Baddeley, A. What can amnesic patients learn? *Neuropsychologia*, 1976, *14*, 111–112.

Cermak, L. S., Lewis, R., Butters, N., & Goodglass, H. Role of verbal mediation in performance of motor tasks by Korsakoff patients. *Perceptual and Motor Skills*, 1973, *37*, 259–262.

Cohen, N. *Neuropsychological evidence for a distinction between procedural and declarative knowledge in human memory and amnesia.* Unpublished doctoral dissertation, University of California at San Diego, 1981.

Cohen, N., & Corkin, S. The amnesic patient, H. M.: Learning and retention of a cognitive skill. *Society for Neuroscience Abstracts*, 1981, *7*, 235.

Cohen, N., & Squire, L. R. Preserved learning and retention of pattern analyzing skill in amnesia: Dissociation of knowing how and knowing that. *Science*, 1980, *210*, 207–209.

Cohen, N., & Squire, L. R. Retrograde amnesia and remote memory impairment. *Neuropsychologia*, 1981, *19*, 337–356.

Deutsch, J. A. the cholinergic synapse and the site of memory. *Science*, 1971, *174*, 788–794.

Graf, P., Squire, L. R., & Mandler, G. The information that amnesic patients do not forget. *Journal of Experimental Psychology: Learning, Memory, and Cognition*, 1984, *10*, 164–178.

Hirst, W., & Volpe, B. T. Temporal order judgments with amnesia. *Brain and Cognition*, 1982, *1*, 294–306.

Jacoby, L. L., & Witherspoon, D. Remembering without awareness. *Canadian Journal of Psychology*, 1982, *36*, 300–324.

Milner, B. Les troubles de la mémoire accompagnant des lésions hippocampiques bilatérales. In P. Passouant (Ed.), *Physiologie de l'hippocampe*. Paris: Centre National de la Recherche Scientifique, 1962.

Mishkin, M., Spiegler, B. J., Saunders, R. C., & Malamut, B. L. An animal model of global amnesia. In S. Corkin (Ed.), *Alzheimer's disease: A report of progress*. New York: Raven Press, 1982.

Squire, L. R. Two forms of human amnesia: An analysis of forgetting. *Journal of Neuroscience*, 1981, *1*, 635–640.

Squire, L. R. The neuropsychology of human memory. *Annual Review of Neuroscience*, 1982, *5*, 241–273.

Squire, L. R., & Cohen, N. J. Memory and amnesia: Resistance to disruption develops for years after learning. *Behavioral and Neural Biology*, 1979, *25*, 115–125.

Weiskrantz, L., & Warrington, E. K. Conditioning in amnesic patients. *Neuropsychologia*, 1979, *17*, 187–194.

Wood, F., Ebert, V., & Kinsbourne, M. The episodic–semantic memory distinction in memory and amnesia: Clinical and experimental observations. In L. Cermak (Ed.), *Human memory and amnesia*. Hillsdale, N.J.: Erlbaum, 1982.

Human Hippocampal and Amygdala Recording and Stimulation: Evidence for a Neural Model of Recent Memory

17

Eric Halgren

Introduction

Complementary Experimental Techniques

Neuropsychological experiments correlating the location of a lesion with its psychological effects have demonstrated a crucial role of the medial temporal lobe (MTL) in human recent memory. Stimulation and recording experiments seldom contribute to more precise definition of amnesia, but rather provide complementary information for modeling its neural basis. For example, the amnesia that sometimes results from MTL electrical stimulation is too brief to permit detailed characterization. However, this very brevity may be used to locate in time the contribution of the MTL to memory processes (input, delay, or retrieval). In other circumstances, MTL stimulation may result in overt subjective experiences of recollection or familiarity. These experiences could represent the hyperactivation of processes that are removed by lesions, and thus provide convergent insights into the nature of these processes.

Similarly, MTL recording experiments are only indirectly related to the results of lesion studies. A change in MTL neural activity during a cognitive task does not imply that the MTL is necessary for its performance—only that the task is adequate to involve the MTL reliably. It is likely that this involvement often is peripheral to the neural activity on the pathway from stimulus to response. For example, the task may be to classify names on the basis of gender. One would expect that MTL lesions would not affect this classification, but would produce an inability to recall these names after the task was over (i.e., would abolish incidental learning). Even so, we cannot conclude that the changes in MTL activity which are noted during the name-classification task are related to memory formation; these changes may rather represent peripheral effects, with the critical activity going undetected due to the crudity of our methods.

Eric Halgren. Veterans Administration Southwest Regional Epilepsy Center, Los Angeles, California; Department of Psychiatry and Biobehavioral Sciences, and Brain Research Institute, University of California at Los Angeles School of Medicine, Los Angeles, California.

Need for a Model

The neurobiology of the limbic system and the phenomenology of amnesia have been so intensively studied that it is easy to forget that there is no generally accepted model, however crude, of the neural mechanisms of human recent memory. Our level of ignorance is comparable to knowing that the heart is essential for circulation of the blood without understanding the role of muscular contractions in expelling the blood. Such a neural model is not only necessary for integrating lesion, stimulation, recording, and positron emission tomographic (PET) (Mazziotta, Phelps, & Halgren, 1983) studies with one another; it is also essential for more effective clinical research. Without a neural model, physical treatments that will produce predictable effects on memory cannot be devised, and clinical neuropsychological investigation must remain largely correlational.

The model must include the many elements, neural and mental, that interact in producing memory. Yet this results in a model with so many degrees of freedom that no experiment could observe enough variables with enough precision to provide direct confirmation. This complexity also allows the model to be adjusted post hoc to account for experimental results that are inconsistent with details of the model. There are, nonetheless, critical junctures in the model where further experimental results could force the design of a fundamentally different model. Therefore, rather than review in detail my group's experimental findings, I concentrate in this chapter on identifying the fundamental test points in the choice of a neural model, and on considering how current and future research could contribute to these choices (see Halgren, 1981, 1982, and Halgren, Wilson, Squires, Engel, Walter, & Crandall, 1983, for recent reviews of stimulation and recording studies of the human amygdala and hippocampus). Before presenting these test points, I first discuss in greater detail the clinical context, and then the neural model, in order to make clear the goals of the experimental studies, which are then described.

Complex Partial Seizures

Complex partial seizures (CPS; formerly known as "psychomotor" or "temporal lobe" seizures) may begin with a wide variety of auras, proceed to loss of contact (often with a motionless stare), and then go on to repetitive stereotyped movements (such as chewing). At about the same time that the electrographic seizure discharge ends, these "automatic" movements become more variable and complex, and partially responsive to environmental contingencies (Delgado-Escueta, Enrile-Bascal, & Treiman, 1982). Approximately 2 million Americans are epileptic; perhaps 800,000 of these have CPS, and of these, about 200,000 to 400,000 continue to have seizures under anticonvulsant treatment (Hauser & Kurland, 1975). In selected cases, surgical removal of the epileptogenic focus provides the best hope for seizure relief (Foerster & Penfield, 1930). In a review of the world literature, Jensen (1975) concluded that surgical therapy eliminated seizures altogether in 50–75% of all patients with CPS. More refined diagnostic criteria may raise this proportion to over 90% (Delgado-Escueta & Walsh, 1983; Engel, Crandall, & Rausch, 1981).

Clinical Neuropsychological Evaluation

Clinical neuropsychological evaluation can help eliminate as surgical candidates those patients with inadequate intelligence or interpersonal skills to allow them to benefit from seizure cure, or with multiple deficits possibly indicating diffuse brain damage and/or multifocal epilepsy. For patients who satisfy these criteria, the critical questions remain: (1) Where does the seizure start? and (2) What would be the neuropsychological effects of surgical removal of the focus? Depth recordings have found that CPS most often originate in the MTL, and when the MTL is removed surgically, it is commonly found to be sclerotic (Brown, 1973). MTL sclerosis is often completely or predominately unilateral, according to postmortem studies of patients with CPS (Margerison & Corsellis, 1966). Presumably, this sclerosis underlies the specific verbal and nonverbal memory deficits reported by Milner (1975) and L. B. Taylor (1968) in patients with CPS, probably originating in the dominant or nondominant temporal lobe, respectively. These material-specific memory deficits can be useful, together with other information, in lateralizing an MTL seizure focus. However, if the surgeon is to remove that MTL secure in the knowledge that no global amnesia will result, more reliable methods are necessary to assure that the contralateral MTL can support memory (Penfield & Milner, 1958). The best known of these methods is Wada's intracarotid sodium amytal test, as modified by Milner (Milner, Branch, & Rasmussen, 1962). Following a successful injection, one hemisphere is anesthetized for about 3 minutes. If the contralateral hemisphere, nonanesthetized, has a damaged MTL, then during these 3 minutes the patient will be transiently amnesic. By imitating temporarily the physical effects of contemplated surgery, the test can help the surgeon predict the neuropsychological effects of surgery, and surgery can be canceled if necessary.

It is possible to produce a temporary disruption more precisely localized to the MTL by electrically stimulating these sites with implanted electrodes. This advantage over the Wada test is not sufficient clinical justification for implanting electrodes into the MTL. That risk should only be taken if by all other criteria the patient is likely to benefit from surgical therapy, and if depth recordings are necessary to localize the focus. Once the electrodes are implanted, they must remain in place for a few weeks in order to capture 8 to 10 spontaneous seizures on videotape, as well as synchronized depth–surface EEGs. No additional risk is imposed by recordings of MTL field and action potentials during cognitive tasks administered while awaiting the unpredictable occurrence of a spontaneous seizure. While these studies are in their infancy, they have the potential of providing still more localized and subtle information on the functional status of different MTL synaptic systems (Squires, Halgren, Wilson, & Crandall, 1981). In addition, these studies could lead to improved methods of predicting depth activity from surface recordings, and thus could decrease the number of patients who need depth electrodes.

In sum, the surgical treatment of CPS requires accurate localization of MTL damage as well as of the seizure focus. In order to increase the precision and reliability of this localization, neuropsychological testing paradigms are accompanied by temporary unilateral MTL disruption (the modified Wada test, or electrical stimulation), or by direct recordings of MTL neural activity. Furthermore, since the patients have general intelligence and personality function within the normal range, since they are recorded or stimulated in a fairly normal waking state outside the operating room, and since one may limit recordings to areas and times relatively free of epileptogenic pathology, it is possible to draw inferences regarding normal MTL function from these studies.

A Neural Model for Human Recent Memory

Overview (Assumptions)

The model (see Figure 17-1; for further details and discussion, see Halgren, 1976, and Halgren *et al.*, 1983) assumes that the MTL's function is to contribute to the reexperience of events that have occurred in the "recent" past, or to a subjective experience of familiarity when parts of these prior events recur. The direct neural substrate for the initial experience and the reexperience of events occurs in the (mainly posterior) association cortex (AC). During the initial experience, a trace is laid down in the MTL. This is a gross trace, which does not include every element and relation that made up the original event, but which includes many of the novel juxtapositions of familiar objects or thoughts that made the event unique. This gross trace contributes to recall, in interaction with other cognitive skills that operate on experience in general: Relevant knowledge and questions are organized into "frames" (Minsky, 1975). For example, in remembering what we had for breakfast this morning, the information provided by the specific trace is aided by our knowledge that we usually have eggs (induction), and that breakfast always involves food (deduction). As time passes, either an event is forgotten, or its lessons are extracted and it is absorbed into a frame by losing its specifics, or it becomes a paradigmatic experience forming its own frame (thus forming remote episodic memory). Corresponding to these processes, the MTL trace fades, and the AC incorporates the experience. This happens gradually over the course of hours to years (depending on the event), defining the time course of that memory's susceptibility to disruption and thus the time course of recent memory.

Anatomy and Physiology

It is well known that efferents from frontal, parietal–occipital, and temporal ACs all converge upon the entorhinal cortex and adjacent regions of the parahippocampal gyrus (Jones & Powell, 1970; Seltzer & Pandya, 1976; Van Hoesen & Pandya, 1975; Van Hoesen, Pandya & Butters, 1975). These projections are both direct and through limbic neocortex (cingulate cortex, posterior parahippocampal gyrus, and orbito-frontal cortex). The limbic neocortex projects to the subiculum (Van Hoesen, Rosene, & Mesulam, 1979). The entorhinal cortex is the major source of afferents to the hippocampus, whose main outflow is to subicular cortex. The subicular cortex projects directly to the limbic neocortex (Rosene & Van Hoesen, 1977), which in turn projects back to AC. Of greatest importance, Van Hoesen (1980) has recently shown that the posterior parahippocampal gyrus projects to every region of AC. Potentially, therefore, these fibers could form multiple positive feedback loops between AC and hippocampal formation, with links in limbic neocortex and subiculum. The synapses in the hippocampal segment of this loop are excitatory and highly plastic. A single tetanic activation of several hippocampal synapses leads to long-

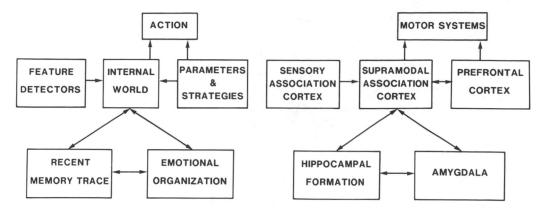

FIGURE 17-1. Division of the brain into different functional regions for the purposes of the model proposed here.

lasting increases in their efficacy—long-term enhancement (LTE; see Bliss & Gardner-Medwin, 1973; McNaughton, 1983). Reciprocal connections between AC and the amygdala along similar routes could also be traced (Price, 1981). These synapses also may show long-lasting changes if repeatedly activated (Goddard, McIntyre, & Leech, 1969).

Our model assumes that the projections from AC onto MTL neurons are (1) cognitive, (2) randomly convergent–divergent, and (3) reciprocal. First, we assume that successive levels of AC contain neurons that respond to progressively more complex features of the environment (Konorski, 1967). At the highest level, these features can no longer be thought of as passively reflecting patterns of sensory inputs. Rather, the highest features are better thought of as endogenous expectations and inferences: They are the elements that compose our cognitive frames. The AC neurons that project to the MTL are assumed to correspond to these cognitive elements. Within a cognitive frame (in the AC), these elements are associated and related in lawful ways corresponding to the underlying structure of our cognitive world. However, we assume that these relations are largely lost in the AC projection to the MTL, where each AC neuron projects to many MTL neurons. This divergence results in the convergence upon individual MTL neurons of excitation from (cortically) unrelated elements in a more or less random fashion. Finally, we assume that if a particular AC neuron excites a particular MTL neuron, then excitation of that MTL neuron will reciprocally excite that same AC neuron.

The Model in Action (see Figure 17-2)

We have now assumed almost everything we need. An event occurs, and its experience is based directly upon the activity of AC neurons. Those AC neurons that code for disparate cognitive elements of this experience convergently excite certain MTL neurons, resulting in tetanic activation and LTE. Later presentation of a cue for recall (e.g., "What did you have for breakfast this morning?") will reactivate the AC substrates for the associated cognitive elements. These activated elements will project to various MTL neurons. However, only those neurons that are hypersensitive due to their prior LTE will

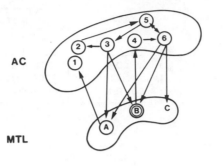

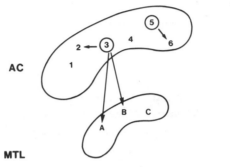

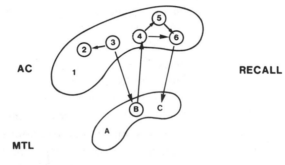

FIGURE 17-2. Neural mechanisms proposed to underlie recent memory. *Input*: At the initial experience of an event, five association cortex (AC) neurons are activated (labeled 2 through 6). These AC neurons excite MTL neurons A, B, and C, but only the synapses from 3 and 6 onto B are enhanced (A did not reach LTE threshold because it does not participate in an active AC ⟷ MTL positive feedback loop; C did not reach LTE threshold because it received too little input from excited AC neurons). *Cue*: Aspects 3 and 5 of the previous event are presented as recall cues. *Recall*: Because the synapse from 3 to B is enhanced, excitation of 3 excites B, which excites 4. Other aspects of the original experience (2, 4, 5, 6) are excited as a result of the interactions within the AC. Together, these processes lead to reconstruction of the AC neural activity pattern present at the original experience.

be activated. These activated neurons will project back to further elements of the original experience. Even partial activation of elements not in the original cue will provide material for inferential processes not requiring the trace. For example, the cues "you," "breakfast," and "this morning" may activate through the MTL the element "eggs," which in turn activates through (nonmemory) inferential processes "bacon" and "orange juice." The (probably preconscious) suggestions of these inferential processes can be probed against the trace. Those that occurred in the original experience will lead to further convergent activation of sensitized MTL elements. In this manner, the cue in a successful recall will lead to a cyclic MTL ⟷ AC interaction, eventually resulting in convergent activation of most of the elements of the original experience.

The MTL may thus be looked upon as a reservoir of random connections, some of which get strengthened as a result of experience, forming temporary positive feedback loops between arbitrary combinations of specific AC neurons. Given that these feedback loops are multisynaptic, and that the AC → MTL connections are so widely divergent, one could not suppose that these reciprocal connections are specified genetically. A dynamic method is possible, however, wherein the only MTL neurons to obtain sustained tetanic activation sufficient to produce LTE are those that participate in a completed reciprocal positive feedback loop (AC → MTL → AC . . .). In other words, as a consequence of divergence and convergence, there are multiple potential passages for excitation from the AC through successive levels of the MTL. Some of these passages may lead to excitation of at least some of the same AC neurons that originated that passage's excitation. Other potential passages may not be reciprocal in this manner. If both types of passages were initially activated at a low level, positive feedback from the AC may be decisive for increasing excitation above the threshold for LTE in the reciprocal passages only.

In addition to these random, but labeled, excitatory passages through the MTL, there are extensive unlabeled lateral and temporal inhibitory interactions between MTL neurons that help focus the excitatory passages. These inhibitory interactions are very strong and well defined in the hippocampus (HC; Knowles & Schwartzkroin, 1981). In addition to its distant projections, a given HC pyramidal cell recurrently excites local interneurons, which inhibit that pyramidal cell's neighbors. Consequently, excitation will tend to become focused in the pyramidal cell that is activated most strongly, relative to its neighbors, and the net proportion of HC pyramidal cells active at any one moment would tend to remain constant across varying levels of excitatory input. Experimental evidence indicates that on an inactive background in the slice preparation, an HC pyramidal cell may be driven by fewer than 5% of its afferents (Andersen, Silfvenius, Sundberg, & Sveen, 1980). Consequently, without lateral inhibition, the divergent excitatory projections in the HC trisynaptic pathway would easily lead to diffuse hyperexcitation. With lateral inhibition, the large number of potential excitatory passages (inherent in a divergent low-threshold system) may compete among each other to produce the passage best representing, as well as reciprocally connected to, the AC neurons activated in the event.

Since the reactivation of the MTL elements during recall should again lead to LTE, the model predicts that the trace will be strengthened by repeated recall. However, what is to prevent repeatedly recalled memories from coming to dominate the MTL? These are precisely those memories that the experimental evidence indicates would be transferred to the AC. Modifying a suggestion of Wickelgren (1979), I would further hypothesize that there is a competition between MTL and AC neurons for synaptic space on other MTL and AC neurons. If a particular constellation of cognitive elements repeatedly recurs, then the corresponding set of AC neurons will fire together and become tightly linked (cf. Hebb, 1949). The MTL neurons that previously projected to them would now be forced to seek synaptic space on AC neurons, which are less tightly "bound" to each other. Thus, consolidation of the neocortical trace automatically frees MTL neurons to engage in other traces. If in addition, AC neurons only project to the MTL if they are unable to secure adequate synaptic space on other AC neurons, then when an AC neuron became tightly bound, it would no longer project to the MTL. Because unbound AC neurons would then be both the source and destination of MTL connections, this further assumption would tighten the AC ⟷ MTL feedback loop.

The neural events that occur when recognition of a recently presented item is probed are the same as those that follow the presentation of a cue for recall of an item, except that in recognition the item and the cue are identical. In recognition, the cues actually consist of the item whose recognition is probed plus the context in which it putatively occurred. It is easy to understand how the presentation of these very rich cues could lead to the recall of further elements of the original event. The contribution of general cognitive inferential processes to this recall may be overwhelmed by the MTL feedback to the overdetermined cues. This feedback, in turn, is hypothesized to provide by mass action the subjective feeling of familiarity that is the actual basis of most of our recognition decisions. Other recognition decisions may not involve the MTL, but rather may be based on facilitated (neocortical) perceptual processing, or on the affective response to such facilitation (Jacoby & Dallas, 1981; Zajonc, 1980).

Test Points Critical for Choosing a Model (see Table 17-1)

A Neoassociationist Model

Memory models (Anderson & Bower, 1973; Boring, 1950; Hilgard, 1956) may be broadly divided into (1) associationist models, which divide experience (British empiricists) or behavior (American learning theorists) into simple elements that are combined on the basis of temporal contiguity (and perhaps reinforcement) into complex ideas or activities; and (2) rationalist models, which emphasize molar (whole-organism) aspects of experience (Gestalt psychologists) or of behavior (e.g., Tolman, 1932/1949). Generally speaking, associationist models are inadequate to account for the phenomena of memory, whereas rationalist models are too poorly defined to suggest neural realizations. The model described here belongs to the group of models termed "neoassociationist" by Anderson and Bowers (1973) because they include both rationalist and associationist capacities in separate, but interacting, parts of the mind. The rationalist part of our model is in AC: The AC contains (undefined) information-processing mechanisms that transcend connectionism in being partially innate (e.g., spatial and linguistic analysis), and in their creativity (of novel outputs and strategies). The associationist part of our model lies in the MTL: It devises no strategy, and processes all information alike, associating elements on the basis of temporal contiguity.

The neural memory model of O'Keefe and Nadel (1978) is also neoassociationist. Like our model, it divides the brain into two interacting parts, neocortex and HC, with

TABLE 17-1. Choice Points for Neural Models of Memory

Choice made	Alternatives	Consequences for model	Evidence
Neoassociationist model	Associationist model (Pavlov) Rationalist model (Kohler)	Divide brain into 2 parts subserving (1) strategic cognition, and (2) plastic associations	Associationist models do not explain memory Rationalist models are too vague
Medial temporal lobe (MTL) is plastic part	MTL is cognitive map (O'Keefe and Nadel)	MTL provides a reservoir of random potential connections for association cortex (AC)	General cognition needs stability, many neurons (AC > MTL) MTL lesions affect memory, not cognition AC lesions affect cognition, not memory
MTL interaction is with awareness	MTL interacts with sensory input (Mishkin) or movement (Olds, Thompson)	Sensory input cannot enter recent memory directly Retrieval from recent memory has no direct influence on behavior	MTL stimulation evokes vivid memories, *déjà vu* Amnesics show behavioral memory without awareness
MTL contains a memory trace	MTL contribution is to encoding, consolidation, retrieval, connection, or vertical-node priming	Properties of long-term enhancement (LTE) imply properties of recent memory	Simultaneous input and output deficit in transient global amnesia or MTL stimulation Event-related potentials in MTL after cognitive closure
MTL output is information-specific	MTL output affects information-processing mode (Wickelgren)	Need numerous reciprocal MTL $\longleftrightarrow$ AC connections	Specificity of hippocampal (HC) place cells in rats HC neuroanatomy

fundamentally different properties. Both models place great emphasis on the ability of complex, idiosyncratic combinations of high-level polysensory attributes (passed from the neocortex) to fire each HC pyramidal cell. Indeed, O'Keefe discovered that most rat HC pyramidal cells will fire in a particular place, regardless of the modality through which that location is sensed (O'Keefe, 1979). However, in O'Keefe and Nadel's (1978) model, it is the HC that is rationalist, whereas the neocortex is associationist! Thus, in their model, place cells acquire their correlates by virtue of innate HC mechanisms for cognitive mapping of the environment. In our model, place correlates arise as an emergent property from (1) the extraction of relevant (i.e., polymodal and/or extrapersonal-space-invariant) attributes by (innate?) AC mechanisms before projection to HC; (2) temporal contiguity, in that different aspects of the environment defining a particular location are experienced simultaneously; and (3) lateral and recurrent inhibition, which tend to encourage the formation of firing-correlates with aspects of the environment that distinguish one place from another. The mechanism proposed here could account for aspects of HC place cells that seem incongruous for a spatial cognitive map: Some place cells have multiple places within a given environment; most place cells have a place correlate in each environment in which they are placed, but these places bear no apparent relationship to one another (Kubie & Ranck, 1983); and, most significantly, adjacent HC neurons have place correlates that are not adjacent, and actually appear entirely unrelated. Furthermore, our proposed mechanism for the formation of HC firing-correlates is more general, and thus is directly applicable to humans, in whom memory deficits following MTL lesions are by no means restricted to orientation within extrapersonal space.

O'Keefe and Nadel's model explicitly predicts that individual HC place cells will respond to attributes of the same place, even if they are not temporally contiguous. It appears that this prediction is true, although unambiguous experimental demonstration is lacking. Our model also proposes how elements that are not strictly temporally contiguous could still come to activate the same neuron. Suppose sets of elements A + B activated the cell at one time, and B + C activated the same cell shortly thereafter. Then presentation of A (as a cue) may activate A + C, a novel combination.

This proposed mechanism could, in humans, form the basis for the behavioral phenomenon known as "proactive interference": When two events have recently occurred in similar contexts and with some overlap in cognitive elements, then the cues from one event are likely to activate elements belonging to the other event (Baddeley, 1976). The cognitive integration and stability that accompany transfer of the trace from the MTL to the neocortex would further account for the resistance to interference that accrues over time.

Other well-established properties of human memory also fit well with the model's assumed separation of the brain into a stable AC, containing general cognitive processes, and a plastic MTL, containing recent-memory traces. For example, many studies (e.g., Bartlett, 1932; Neisser, 1967) have shown that recall is often not a passive reception of an image from the past, but an active reconstruction of an event, using apparently all available cognitive processes in interaction with the specific trace. Separation of the trace from general cognition also permits the trace to directly represent the novel relations between cognitive elements occurring during an event, rather than the elements themselves. Consider the typical situation where the subject is asked to remember a list of words. Clearly, the subject does not store the words themselves; he or she already knows them, and thus only needs to store that they occurred in this list. That is, "storing a word" is actually storing a method for using a cue to access the complicated group of relationships that constitutes a word.

One way of providing such access would be to tag each word with a marker that is strengthened by repetition and weakened by time. However, this so-called "strength theory" cannot account for the ability of subjects to recall words differentially from contexts distinguished on dimensions other than strength (Anderson & Bower, 1972). These experiments imply that, instead of tagging individual items with familiarity, memory traces are formed by strengthening the ties between already familiar elements (strengthened "horizontal associations"). However, further experiments indicate that the interaction of multiple cues in promoting retrieval is too strong to be explained by associations between pairs of existing elements (Ross & Bower, 1981). Rather, it is necessary to postulate that multiple elements of the event are united in a novel element termed a "vertical node" (Wickelgren, 1979) or "schema" (Anderson & Bower, 1973). These postulates find direct correspondences in the neural model proposed here. Novel "vertical nodes" are formed within the MTL as a result of convergent input from AC neurons representing multiple well-learned and cognitively integrated elements. When a subject is recalling a word list, the vertical nodes representing the context are presented as the retrieval cue.

This emphasis on the role of context in retrieval may seem to be at odds with an associationist approach. Actually, the description of memory as based on the association of particular cognitive attributes through individual MTL neurons is largely a matter of convenience. In fact, the firing-correlates of neither MTL neurons nor their afferents need to be recognizably cognitive for the model to work—all that is needed is that the loop through the MTL be reciprocal and plastic. All feedback loops are probed in parallel, and they interact in crucial ways in both AC and MTL limbs. Thus, rather than focusing on specific feedback lines, one could view the model as proposing two interacting sets of neurons, each of which forms an overall pattern of activity influencing the other. Within the time scale of recent memory, the AC is fixed, forming patterns on the basis of multiple information sources, and the MTL is plastic, forming a temporary imprint of the current AC pattern and influencing that AC pattern toward one of its previous modes.

MTL Interaction Is with Awareness

In learning theory, memory functions to connect stimulus to response. Neither stimulus nor response is directly involved in the model proposed here. Recent memory is conceived as one of many influences on the current model of the world (experience) that is constructed in the AC. Sensory stimuli may influence this experience, and thus may help define the content of memories. However, we can also remember thoughts, hallucinations, and dreams formed with minimal or no sensory input. This semi-independence from sensory input helps distinguish our model from that proposed by Mishkin (1982). Similarly, the influence of memory retrieval on the cognitive map has no direct consequences for behavior: Remembering my mother's telephone number doesn't mean I'll call her (alas!).

Experimental studies of memory require a specified sensory input and motor output in order to be controlled and reproducible. Nonetheless, these studies indicate that the presence of an item in awareness may be necessary for it to enter certain categories of memory (Jacoby & Witherspoon, 1982). It has long been recognized that amnesics may show specific behavioral plasticity in the absence of any subjective recognition or recall (Cohen, Chapter 10, this volume; Corkin, 1968; Warrington & Weiskrantz, 1982). It now appears that those categories of memory for which awareness is necessary may be those that are specifically impaired in amnesia.

A close relationship between the subjective phenomena of recent memory and the MTL is further implied by studies of the subjective experiences evoked by MTL stimulation. These phenomena—intense feelings that the current situation has previously been experienced (déjà vu), and vivid images from memory intruding into awareness—can be evoked by low-level electrical stimulation of the amygdala, HC, or parahippocampal gyrus (see Halgren, 1981, 1982; Halgren, Walter, Cherlow, & Crandall, 1978; and Halgren et al., 1983, for reviews). Although our studies were carried out with epileptics undergoing diagnostic procedures prior to surgical treatment, it appears that evoked déjà vu and memory image are not bizarre products of epileptogenic pathology, because (1) these phenomena are evoked with about equal frequency from the side of spontaneous seizure onset as from the contralateral MTL, and simultaneous electrographic monitoring indicates that the latter responses were not due to gross spread of excitation over the commissures; (2) those patients who experienced evoked memory images seldom experienced similar phenomena as auras (evoked déjà vu, however, often does resemble the spontaneous aura); and (3) other authors have reported that déjà vu and memory images may be evoked from the temporal regions of nonepileptic patients (e.g., Ishibashi, Hori, Endo, & Sato, 1964). In general, the mechanism of gross spread of excitation by any means, epileptic or not, can be ruled out by the failure of direct stimulation of limbic and brain stem structures that receive MTL projections to evoke these same mental phenomena (Halgren, 1981, 1982; Halgren et al., 1983). Penfield had earlier found that lateral temporal neocortex stimulation can also evoke memory images and déjà vu (Mullan & Penfield, 1959; Penfield & Perot, 1963). However, Gloor, Olivier, Quesney, Andermann, and Horowitz (1982) found that when both the lateral temporal lobe and the MTL were stimulated with the same parameters in the same subjects, experiential phenomena were only evoked by direct MTL stimulation, or by lateral stimulations that resulted in after-discharge spreading to medial sites.

Although hyperactivation of the MTL thus appears critical for evoking déjà vu or memory images, other characteristics of these stimulation-evoked experiences are para-doxical unless one assumes that the actual content of the experience is defined by the structure that receives the hyperactivated MTL efferents, rather than by the MTL itself. First, despite the MTL's central role, most MTL stimulations do not evoke any mental phenomenon, even if they are powerful enough to evoke afterdischarges. Conversely, while removal of both MTLs will impair the experiences of familiarity and recall, at least for recent events, removal of the stimulated MTL alone generally does not. Thus, while activation of MTL neurons may lead to memory experiences, other data indicate that this activation is neither sufficient (otherwise, all such activations would evoke experiences) nor necessary (otherwise, removal of activated neurons would prevent that experience in other circumstances).

A second line of evidence suggesting that the neurons directly underlying experiences evoked by MTL stimulation are outside the MTL is the great diversity of these experiences, as well as the nature of the factors that select among them. In addition to déjà vu and memory images, MTL stimulation may evoke dream-like images; emotions (especially fear); unformed visceral–sensory, auditory, visual, somaesthetic, or olfactory hallucinations; or other mental phenomena. Which of these categories of experience is evoked is not related to whether the stimulating electrode is in the amygdala, HC, or parahippocampal gyrus, or in the dominant or nondominant hemisphere, but rather to who is being stimulated and in particular to the individual's personality, and to the inter-personal situation at the time of stimulation. These factors could conceivably modulate the direct MTL neural reaction to stimulation. However, such modulation is unlikely to be strong, and, in any case, has not been observed in direct monitoring of MTL activity during electrical stimulations that evoked these various phenomena. On the other hand, personality and interpersonal relations are very likely to alter the context in which a distal structure interprets MTL outflow. Thus, the variety of mental phenomena could represent differing interpretations of a more or less constant MTL hyperoutflow by a distal struc-ture.

A third observation inconsistent with the possibility of MTL neurons' directly underlying the experiences evoked by their stimulation is that these experiences often occur while MTL neurons are engaged in afterdischarges. How could such neurons engage in the coherent, refined information processing that must underlie experiences as complex as memory images? (This argument was first advanced by Hughlings Jackson over 100 years ago; see J. Taylor, 1958.)

According to the model proposed above, the association neocortex is that "distal structure" where the neurons directly define experiences of *déjà vu* or memory images in response to hyperactivation of their afferents from the MTL. Stimulation-induced MTL hyperoutflow could imitate the simultaneous convergent activation of many MTL nodes, which the model proposes to result in the subjective experience of familiarity. Similarly, the model suggests how MTL hyperactivation would lead to memory images. Those AC neurons that directly underlie experience are hypothesized to receive projections from feature detectors in the sensory AC as well as from the MTL. Hyperactivation of the MTL synapses would thus be expected to overpower the sensory inputs to the AC neurons, resulting in a shift in the content of experience from the external environment to endogenous sources. If so, then other endogenous influences besides memory traces should sometimes define the content of experiences evoked by MTL stimulation. Indeed, some of these experiences are too bizarre to be memories, and some can be interpreted as reflecting the patient's psychodynamic concerns in a manner similar to the images of dreams. The characteristics of experiential phenomena evoked by MTL stimulation are thus consistent with our model's hypothesis that, in the normal brain, the subjective experiences of recognition and recall are formed in the AC under MTL influence.

MTL Contains a Memory Trace

A critical feature of the proposed model is that MTL contains a memory trace. Other models assert that the specific deficit responsible for amnesia lies in encoding (Butters & Cermak, 1980), consolidation (Penfield & Milner, 1958), retrieval (Warrington & Weiskrantz, 1973), or connection (of conscious to unconscious memory; see Warrington & Weiskrantz, 1982). Studies of chronic amnesia are of limited value in definitely distinguishing among these possibilities (Piercy, 1977; Squire, 1982). However, MTL electrical stimulation sometimes produces a transient amnesic state with important implications for this question (Halgren *et al.*, 1983). It was found that single pulses of weak electrical current, applied either during the initial presentation of an item or during its subsequent test presentation, produced a pronounced impairment of recognition memory. This is consistent with the finding that during transient global amnesia due to probable vascular impairment of the MTL, the patient is unable to remember events that occurred prior to the onset of amnesia; after the patient returns to normal, he or she is unable to recall what happened during the amnesic period (Fisher & Adams, 1964; Whitty, 1977). These observations imply that MTL amnesia consists of both an inability to form new memory traces and an inability to retrieve recently formed traces. This conclusion is again consistent with our model: New vertical nodes could not be formed in a dysfunctional MTL, and unresponsive MTL neurons could not contribute to retrieval by an intact neocortex. The disruptive effect of single MTL stimulus pulses further implies that the MTL contributes something essential to memory formation within the first second after an item is presented. This is also consistent with the proposal of our model that vertical nodes are formed in the MTL as a result of tetanic activation at the conclusion of feature detection.

MTL activity during memory formation can be more precisely tracked by electrophysiological recordings. The strongest and most regular changes in MTL neural activity during behavior have been termed "endogenous limbic potentials" (ELPs) because they have similar latencies and task correlates to the endogenous components of the scalp-evoked response: N_2-P_3-slow wave (Halgren, Squires, Wilson, Rohrbaugh, Babb, & Crandall, 1980; Halgren *et al.*, 1983; McCarthy, Wood, Allison, Goff, Williamson, & Spencer, 1982; Squires *et al.*, 1981.)

ELPs have large amplitude, phase-reverse within the MTL, and are accompanied by changes in unit activity. Therefore, they are locally generated. Whether they volume-conduct to the scalp to produce some or all of the scalp endogenous potentials is unclear at this time (Halgren, Squires, Wilson, & Crandall, 1982; Wood, McCarthy, Allison, Goff, Williamson, & Spencer, 1982). If so, then specific inferences of limbic dysfunction could be drawn from the abnormal scalp potentials recorded in alcoholism, aging, dementia, and other disorders (Squires *et al.*, 1981). However, even if ELPs do *not* propagate to the scalp, they are correlated with the endogenous scalp potentials across a number of tasks, and thus it is reasonable to suppose that the psychological task correlates that have been worked out for these potentials at the scalp also hold for the limbic potentials. Briefly, these studies (see reviews by Donchin, 1981; Pritchard, 1981) have found that endogenous potentials occur following any attended task-relevant stimulus that conveys information. They are larger when the stimulus indicates a shift within the context of the task. Reaction-time evidence indicates that these potentials begin at about the same time that stimulus apprehension is completed (Desmedt, 1981). In any case, their latency increases with increasing difficulty of stimulus classification (Kutas & Donchin, 1979).

Since these potentials begin after stimulus classification, appear unrelated to the motor response, and can be absent in the presence of good stimulus classification, it is unlikely that they are due to neural processes that underlie performance of these tasks. Rather, all of these characteristics are appropriate for a potential that reflects some aspect of the vertical-node formation event, as outlined in the model proposed above. Node formation only occurs for attended stimuli, cannot begin until the stimulus has been evaluated, and is larger if the stimulus signals a context shift because more nodes are formed.

The specific proposal that the physical basis of the HC recent-memory traces is the same as that of LTE needs to be further tested in animals. The correlations shown by Barnes (1979) are important, but confirmation will require observing the behavioral effects of specific blockers of LTE (Lynch, Halpain, & Baudry, 1983). LTE appears to decay over time and to build up with repeated tetani, with parameters appropriate for the synaptic plasticity that underlies recent memory. Other forms of synaptic plasticity have been identified in the neocortex that might underlie immediate memory (McNaughton, 1983). However, further work is needed to show that LTE occurs under physiological conditions, and that it is characteristic of the HC but not the neocortex.

MTL Output Is Information-Specific

Field potentials can only be generated by the more or less synchronous activity of large numbers of neurons. Therefore, they cannot represent the specific information-processing activities of neurons, but rather the envelopes of background activation that parse that processing. A fundamental choice to be made in designing a neurocognitive model of memory is whether the MTL indeed contributes any specific information to guide retrieval. Most models assume not, supposing that the HC is activated *en masse* at the appropriate time to exert a general control function. For example, in Wickelgren's (1979) model, the HC activates all neocortical unbound nodes willy-nilly, permitting them to compete on more equal footing with the older and more established bound nodes. In such a model it is difficult to understand why individual rat HC pyramidal cells have such individual and specific firing-correlates (O'Keefe, 1979). So far, only a few instances of human HC formation neurons have been found with comparably specific firing-correlates (Halgren, Babb, & Crandall, 1978). Further studies in animals are also needed to determine whether there are enough MTL $\longleftrightarrow$ AC interconnections to carry specific memories, and whether these interconnections are excitatory. It is known that some AC areas both send axons to and receive axons from the same MTL regions (Van Hoesen, 1980). But it is unknown whether single neocortical columns both receive and send MTL axons, and if so, whether such columns have unusual behavioral correlates suggesting that they may embody unbound nodes.

Summary

Patients with uncontrolled seizures may receive electrodes in their HC formation and amygdala (MTL) in order to localize their seizure focus. These electrodes are sometimes stimulated in order to predict the effects of removal of the seizure focus. The electrodes also may be recorded from during cognitive tasks. Interpretation of the results of these studies requires a neurocognitive model for recent memory. The model described here supposes that temporary memory traces are formed when convergent AC efferents induce LTE in the MTL. These traces later provide AC with specific information that aids retrieval. Electrical stimulation of the MTL evokes subjective memory experiences in a manner consistent with this model. The need predicted by the model for MTL function during both trace formation and retrieval is supported by the disruptive effects of MTL stimulation on memory. Endogenous MTL potentials have task correlates and a time course that the model suggests would be expected of neurons involved in formation of the trace. Many aspects of the model remain highly speculative. In particular, a critical question for future study is that of specificity of MTL outflow.

ACKNOWLEDGMENTS

I thank J. Stapleton, M. Smith, J. Winson, G. Heit, and L. Meredith for enlightening discussions; the National Institute of Neurological and Communicative Disorders and Stroke (NS 02332 and NS18741) and the Veterans Administration for research support; P. Crandall, A. V. Delgado-Escueta, J. Engel, Jr., and D. Treiman for providing the clinical context for scientific studies; and N. Squires, C. Wilson, and T. Babb, who collaborated in the research described in this chapter. The views expressed are my own and do not necessarily reflect those of my colleagues or sponsors.

REFERENCES

Andersen, P., Silfvenius, H., Sundberg, S. H., & Sveen, O. A comparison of distal and proximal dendritic synapses on CA1 pyramids in hippocampal slices *in vitro*. *Journal of Physiology* (London), 1980, *307*, 273–299.

Anderson, J. R., & Bower, G. H. Recognition and retrieval processes in free recall. *Psychological Review*, 1972, *79*, 97–123.

Anderson, J. R., & Bower, G. H. *Human associative memory*. Washington, D.C.: Winston, 1973.

Baddeley, A. D. *The psychology of memory*. New York: Basic Books, 1976.

Bartlett, F. C. *Remembering*. Cambridge, England: Cambridge University Press, 1932.

Barnes, C. A. Memory deficits associated with senescence: A neurophysiological and behavioral study in the rat. *Journal of Comparative and Physiological Psychology*, 1979, *93*, 74–104.

Bliss, T. V. P., & Gardner-Medwin, A. R. Long-lasting potentiation of synaptic transmission in the dentate area of the unanaesthetized rabbit following stimulation of the perforant path. *Journal of Physiology*, 1973, *232*, 357–374.

Boring, E. G. *History of experimental psychology*. New York: Appleton-Century-Crofts, 1950.

Brown, W. J. Structural substrates of seizure foci in the human temporal lobe. In M. A. B. Brazier (Ed.), *Epilepsy: Its phenomena in man*. New York: Academic Press, 1973.

Butters, N., & Cermak, L. S. *Alcoholic Korsakoff's syndrome: An information-processing approach to amnesia*. New York: Academic Press, 1980.

Corkin, S. Acquisition of motor skill after bilateral temporal lobe excisions. *Neuropsychologia*, 1968, *6*, 225–265.

Delgado-Escueta, A. V., Enrile-Bascal, F., & Treiman, D. M. Complex partial seizures on closed circuit television and EEG: A study of 691 attacks in 79 patients. *Annals of Neurology*, 1982, *11*, 292–300.

Delgado-Escueta, A. V., & Walsh, G. O. The selection process for surgery of complex partial seizures: Surface EEG and depth electrography. In A. A. Ward, Jr., J. K. Penry, & D. Purpura (Eds.), *Epilepsy*. New York: Raven Press, 1983.

Desmedt, J. E. Scalp-recorded cerebral event-related potentials in man as a point of entry into the analysis of cognitive processing. In F. O. Schmitt, F. G. Worden, G. Adelman, & S. D. Dennis (Eds.), *The organization of the cerebral cortex*. Cambridge, Mass.: MIT Press, 1981.

Donchin, E. Surprise! . . . Surprise? *Psychophysiology*, 1981, *18*, 493–513.

Engel, J. Jr., Crandall, P. H., & Rausch, R. Surgical treatment of the partial epilepsies. In R. N. Rosenberg, R. G. Grossman, S. Schochet, E. R. Heinz, & W. D. Willis (Eds)., *The clinical neurosciences*. New York: Churchill Livingstone, 1981.

Fisher, C. M., & Adams, R. D. Transient global amnesia. *Acta Neurologica Scandinavica*, 1964, *40*(Suppl. 9).

Foerster, O., & Penfield, W. The structural basis of traumatic epilepsy and results of radical operation. *Brain*, 1930, *53*, 99–120.

Gloor, P., Olivier, A., Quesney, L. F., Andermann, F., & Horowitz, S. The role of the limbic system in experiential phenomena of temporal lobe epilepsy. *Annals of Neurology*, 1982, *12*, 129–144.

Goddard, G. V., McIntyre, D. C., & Leech, C. K. A permanent change in brain function resulting from daily electrical stimulation. *Experimental Neurology*, 1969, *25*, 295–330.

Halgren, E. *Activity of human hippocampal formation and amygdala neurons during olfaction, memory, movement, and other behaviors*. Unpublished doctoral dissertation, University of California at Los Angeles, 1976.

Halgren, E. The amygdala contribution to emotion and memory: Current studies in humans. In Y. Ben-Ari (Ed.), *The amygdaloid complex*. Amsterdam: Elsevier/North-Holland, 1981.

Halgren, E. Mental phenomena induced by stimulation in the limbic system. *Human Neurobiology*, 1982, *1*, 251–260.

Halgren, E., Babb, T. L., & Crandall, P. H. Activity of human hippocampal formation and amygdala neurons during memory testing. *Electroencephalography and Clinical Neurophysiology*, 1978, *45*, 585–601.

Halgren, E., Squires, N. K., Wilson, C. L., Rohrbaugh, J. W., Babb, T. L., & Crandall, P. H. Endogenous potentials generated in the human hippocampal formation by infrequent events. *Science*, 1980, *210*, 803–805.

Halgren, E., Squires, N. K., Wilson, C. L., & Crandall, P. H. Brain generators of evoked potentials: The late (endogenous) components. *Bulletin of the Los Angeles Neurological Society*, 1982, *47*, 108–123.

Halgren, E., Walter, R. D., Cherlow, D. G., & Crandall, P. H. Mental phenomena evoked by electrical stimulation of the human hippocampal formation and amygdala. *Brain*, 1978, *101*, 83–117.

Halgren, E., Wilson, C. L., Squires, N. K., Engel, J. Jr., Walter, R. D., & Crandall, P. H. Dynamics of the hippocampal contribution to memory: Stimulation and recording studies in humans. In W. Seifert (Ed.), *Neurobiology of the hippocampus*. New York: Academic Press, 1983.

Hauser, W. A. and Kurland, L. T. Epidemiology of epilepsy in Rochester, Minnesota, 1935–1967. *Epilepsia*, 1975, *16*, 1–66.

Hebb, D. O. *The organization of behavior: A neuropsychological theory*. New York: Wiley, 1949.

Hilgard, E. R. *Theories of learning* (2nd ed.). New York: Appleton-Century-Crofts, 1956.

Ishibashi, R., Hori, H., Endo, K., & Sato, T. Hallucinations produced by electrical stimulation of the temporal lobes in schizophrenic patients. *Tohoku Journal of Medicine*, 1964, *82*, 124–139.

Jacoby, L. L., & Dallas, M. On the relationship between autobiographical memory and perceptual learning. *Journal of Experimental Psychology: General*, 1981, *110*, 206–340.

Jacoby, L. L., & Witherspoon, D. Remembering without awareness. *Canadian Journal of Psychology*, 1982, *36*, 300–324.

Jensen, I. Proceedings of the Scandinavian Neurosurgical Society: Pathology and prognostic factors in temporal lobe epilepsy. Followup after temporal lobe resection. *Acta Neurochirurgica (Wien)*, 1975, *31*, 261–262.

Jones, E. G., & Powell, T. P. S. An anatomical study of converging sensory pathways within the cerebral cortex of the monkey. *Brain*, 1970, *93*, 793–820.

Knowles, W. D., & Schwartzkroin, P. A. Local circuit synaptic interactions in hippocampal brain slices. *Journal of Neuroscience*, 1981, *3*, 876–886.

Konorski, J., *Integrative activity of the brain*. Chicago: University of Chicago Press, 1967.

Kubie, J. L., & Ranck, J. B., Jr. Sensory–behavioral correlates in individual hippocampus neurons in three situations: Space and context. In W. Seifert (Ed.), *Neurobiology of the hippocampus*. New York: Academic Press, 1983.

Kutas, M., & Donchin, E. Variations in the latency of P300 as a function of variations in semantic categorizations. In D. Otto (Ed.), *Multidisciplinary perspectives in event-related brain potential research* (EPA 600/9-77-043). Washington, D.C.: U.S. Government Printing Office, 1979.

Lynch, G., Halpain, S., & Baudry, M. Structural and biochemical effects of high frequency stimulation in the hippocampus. In W. Seifert (Ed.), *Neurobiology of the hippocampus*. New York: Academic Press, 1983.

Margerison, J. H., & Corsellis, J. A. N. Epilepsy and the temporal lobes: A clinical, electroencephalographic and neuropathological study of the brain in epilepsy, with particular reference to the temporal lobes. *Brain*, 1966, *89*, 499–530.

Mazziotta, J. C., Phelps, M. E., & Halgren, E. Local cerebral glucose metabolic response to audiovisual stimulation and deprivation: Studies in human subjects with positron CT. *Human Neurobiology*, 1983, *2*, 11–23.

McCarthy, G., Wood, C. C., Allison, T., Goff, W. R., Williamson, P. D., & Spencer, D. D. Intracranial recordings of event-related potentials in humans engaged in cognitive tasks. *Society for Neuroscience Abstracts*, 1982, *8*, 976.

McNaughton, B. L. Activity dependent modulation of hippocampal synaptic efficacy: some implications for memory processes. In W. Seifert (Ed.), *Neurogiology of the hippocampus*. New York: Academic Press, 1983.

Milner, B. Psychological aspects of focal epilepsy and its neurosurgical management. In D. P. Purpura, J. K. Penry, & R. D. Walter (Eds.), *Advances in neurology*. New York: Raven Press, 1975.

Milner, B., Branch, C., & Rasmussen, T. Study of short-term memory after intracarotid injection of sodium amytal. *Transactions of the American Neurological Association*, 1962, *87*, 224–226.

Minsky, M. A framework for representing knowledge. In P. E. Winston (Ed.), *The psychology of computer vision*. New York: McGraw-Hill, 1975.

Mishkin, M. A memory system in the monkey. *Philosphical Transactions of the Royal Society of London*, 1982, *298*, 83–95.

Mullan, S., & Penfield, W. Illusions of comparative interpretation and emotion. *Archives of Neurology and Psychiatry*, 1959, *81*, 269–284.

Neisser, U. *Cognitive psychology*. New York: Appleton-Century-Crofts, 1967.

O'Keefe, J. A review of the hippocampal place cells. *Progress in Neurobiology*, 1979, *13*, 419–439.

O'Keefe, J., & Nadel, L. *The hippocampus as a cognitive map*. Oxford: Clarendon Press, 1978.

Penfield, W., & Milner, B. Memory deficit produced by bilateral lesion in the hippocampal zone. *Archives of Neurology and Psychiatry*, 1958, *79*, 475–497.

Penfield, W. P., & Perot, P. The brain's record of auditory and visual experience: A final summary and discussion. *Brain*, 1963, *86*, 595–696.

Piercy, M. F. Experimental studies of the organic amnesic syndrome. In C. W. M. Whitty & O. L. Zangwill (Eds.), *Amnesia* (2nd ed.). London: Butterworths, 1977.

Price, J. L. The efferent projections of the amygdaloid complex in the rat, cat and monkey. In Y. Ben-Ari (Ed.), *The amygdaloid complex*. Amsterdam: Elsevier/North-Holland, 1981.

Pritchard, W. S. Psychophysiology of P300. *Psychological Bulletin*, 1981, *89*, 506–540.

Rosene, D. L., & Van Hoesen, G. W. Hippocampal efferents reach widespread areas of cerebral cortex and amygdala in the rhesus monkey. *Science*, 1977, *198*, 315–317.

Ross, B. H., & Bower, G. H. Comparisons of models of associative recall. *Memory and Cognition*, 1981, *6*, 1–16.

Seltzer, B., & Pandya, D. N. Some cortical projection to the parahippocampal area in the thesus monkey. *Experimental Neurology*, 1976, *50*, 146–160.

Squire, L. R. The neuropsychology of human memory. *Annual Review of Neuroscience*, 1982, *5*, 241–273.

Squires, N. K., Halgren, E., Wilson, C., & Crandall, P. H. Human endogenous limbic potentials: Cross-modality and depth/surface comparisons in epileptic subjects. In A. W. K. Galliard & W. Ritter (Eds.), *Tutorials in ERP research: Endogenous components*. Amsterdam: North-Holland, 1981.

Taylor, J. (Ed.). *Selected writings of John Hughlings Jackson* (Vol. 1, *On epilepsy and epileptiform convulsions*). New York: Basic Books, 1958.

Taylor, L. B. Localization of cerebral lesions by psychological testing. *Clinical Neurosurgery*, 1968, *16*, 269–287.

Tolman, E. C. *Purposive behavior in animals and men*. Berkeley: University of California Press, 1949. (Originally published, 1932.)

Van Hoesen, G. W. The cortico-cortical projections of the posterior parahippocampal area in the rhesus monkey. *Anatomical Record*, 1980, *196*, 195.

Van Hoesen, G. W., & Pandya, D. N. Some connections of the entorhinal and perirhinal (area 35) cortices of the rhesus monkey: I. Temporal lobe afferents. *Brain Research*, 1975, *95*, 1–24.

Van Hoesen, G. W., Pandya, D. N., & Butters, N. Some connections of the entorhinal (area 28) and perirhinal (area 35) cortices of the rhesus monkey: II. Frontal lobe afferents. *Brain Research*, 1975, *95*, 25–38.

Van Hoesen, G. W., Rosene, D. L., & Mesulam, M. M. Subicular input from temporal cortex in the rhesus monkey. *Science*, 1979, *205*, 608–610.

Warrington, E. K., & Weiskrantz, L. An analysis of short-term and long-term memory defects in man. In J. A. Deutsch (Ed.), *the physiological basis of memory*. New York: Academic Press, 1973.

Warrington, E. K., & Weiskrantz, L. Amnesia: A disconnection syndrome. *Neuropsychologia*, 1982, *20*, 233–248.

Whitty, C. Transient global amnesia. In C. Whitty & O. Zangwill (Eds.), *Amnesia: Clinical, psychological, and medicolegal aspects*. London: Butterworths, 1977.

Wickelgren, W. A. Chunking and consolidation: A theoretical synthesis of semantic networks: Configuring in conditioning, S-R versus cognitive learning, normal forgetting, the amnesic syndrome, and the hippocampal arousal system. *Psychological Review*, 1979, *86*, 44–60.

Wood, C. C., McCarthy, G., Allison, T., Goff, W. R. Williamson, P. D., & Spencer, D. D. Endogenous event-related potentials following temporal lobe excisions in humans. *Society for Neuroscience Abstracts*, 1982, *8*, 976.

Zajonc, R. B. Feeling and thinking: Preferences need no inferences. *American Psychologist*, 1980, *35*, 151–175.

18

Papez Circuit Revisited: Two Systems Instead of One?

Elkhonon Goldberg

The proliferation of interest in studying memory is encouraging, yet it has led to a considerable fragmentation of the field. Animal studies are separate from human studies; clinical studies are separate from normal studies. Some researchers are interested in information processing without much regard for the machinery involved; others are concerned with making macroscopic brain–behavioral statements without much interest in finer points of information processing. Moreover, there are neuroanatomists and neurochemists who inquire into the machinery without always making explicit attempts at establishing behavioral connections. Finally, we are haunted by the classical nomenclature of "faculties," whereas in fact "memory" certainly does not sit in a separate compartment, unconnected to other "faculties."

Such fragmentation is inevitable, due to the sheer scope and the eclectic nature of the field. Yet we have to admit that it is unfortunate, as long as we believe in the continuity of the evolution of species, in the fact that pathology is altered normality, and in the fact that our psychic manifestations are somehow related to the brain, but also believe that the operations of an information-processing system cannot always be completely deduced from its engineering design.

It is clear that one can approach the same reality with various different questions in mind. Yet awareness of the developments in the adjacent fields of inquiry can help one to move in one's own field, both by offering heuristic clues and by imposing constraints and pointing out impossibilities and inconsistencies that could not be discerned from a relatively limited data base.

Although my interests lie primarily with brain–behavior relations and normal cognition, I find such eclectic awareness helpful. While the research of each of us is restricted to one or another empirical domain, all of us have certain working models of a generalized, eclectic nature, which we hesitate to make public because of their looseness. They are helpful, however, in that they provide a greater context for our specific inquiry, and hence guide it. Since my essential interests in normal cognition have more recently been influenced by neuroanatomical findings, I have decided to take a liberty not usually permitted by the format of professional journals.

This has resulted in a speculative chapter about the interaction of memory and selective arousal, which draws heavily on neuroanatomical and animal experimental findings, leads essentially to formulations about normal cognition, offers implicitly a

Elkhonon Goldberg. Division of Neuropsychology, Department of Psychiatry, Albert Einstein College of Medicine and Montefiore Medical Center, Bronx, New York.

program of future studies that can be best conducted on animals, is written by a clinical neuropsychologist, and further confuses the issue by fragmenting memory into three components (two systems and an interface) instead of one.

The concept of the cortical–thalamic–limbic loops as a critical part of the mechanisms of consolidation and retrieval has become classic (Hebb, 1949; Verzeano, 1977; Vinogradova, 1975). One of the early formulations attempting to identify the components of this functional system was offered by Papez (1937). He proposed a circuit in which the following structures are sequentially arranged: hippocampi–fornix–mammillary bodies–anterior thalamic nucleus–cingulate gyrus. Although Papez's explicit interest lay with emotions, similar loops have been proposed as the substrate of memory.

A close relationship between the limbic structures and ventral subdivisions of mesencephalic tegmentum has been appreciated for some time, and the term "limbic midbrain area" has been introduced to denote this relationship (Nauta, 1958). Recently, an increasing body of evidence has implicated the role of reticulo-limbic interaction in long-term memory. This evidence arises both from animal studies (Flicker, McCarley, & Hobson, 1981; Oades, 1981; Thompson, 1974) and from clinical observations (Goldberg, Antin, Bilder, Gerstman, Hughes, & Mattis, 1981). Both kinds of evidence lead to the conclusion that memory deficits unaccompanied by a generalized impairment of arousal can be caused by lesions in the ventral tegmental area of the mesencephalon. The ventral tegmental area consists largely of reticular nuclei, which project into a number of limbic structures (Carpenter, 1976; Cooper, Bloom, & Roth, 1978; Moore & Bloom, 1979; Nauta & Domesick, 1981; Lewis & Shute, 1967; Shute & Lewis, 1967). It appears, therefore, that the classical concept of the thalamic–limbic–cortical circuit as a substrate of consolidation and retrieval has to be amended to include the mesencephalic reticular component, or, more precisely, the ventral portion of the mesencephalic reticular formation.

The analysis of the anatomy of the reticulo-limbic connections can be revealing in attempting further to define the possible reticular–limbic–thalamic–cortical circuitries. This is the subject of this chapter.

Whereas the classic Papez model postulates a *sequential* arrangement between the two limbic structures most often implicated in memory—hippocampi and mammillary bodies—the analysis of ascending reticular pathways reveals the possibility of a *parallel* access to these two structures via the ascending activating system. Three distinct reticular pathways emerge from the ventral mesencephalic tegmentum: (1) from the ventral tegmental nucleus via the mammillary peduncle into the lateral mammillary bodies; (2) from the ventral tegmental nucleus via a component of the medial forebrain bundle, which projects via the diagonal band nucleus, medial septum, and septo-hippocampal pathway into hippocampi; and (3) from the ventral tegmental area, substantia nigra pars compacta, and nucleus reticularis tegmenti pontis, projecting via a component of the medial forebrain bundle into the fronto-orbital brain, hypothalamus, and amygdala (Lindvall, Bjorklund, Moore, & Stenevi, 1974; MacLean, 1958).

The presence of the first and second projections described above indicates that the ventral tegmental reticular nucleus has *parallel* access to the mammillary bodies and hippocampi, and that it is neuroanatomically possible for one of the two limbic structures to be activated via the reticular formation without the other one being activated at the same time (see Figure 18-1).

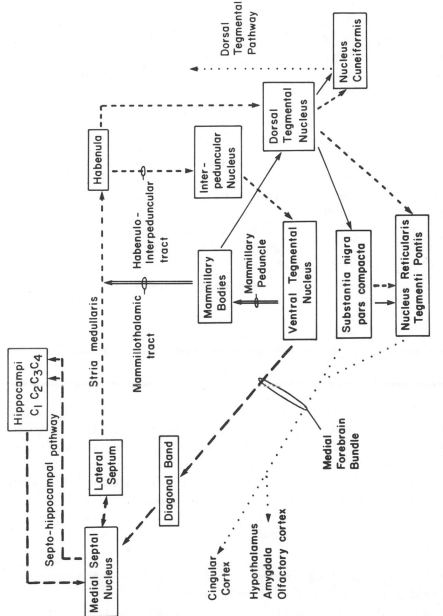

FIGURE 18-1. Ponto-mesencephalic interactions with the two memory circuits: ascending activating influences on the hippocampal system (long broken line); descending inhibitory influences from the hippocampal system (short broken line); ascending activating influences on the mammillary system (double solid line); descending inhibitory influences from the mammillary system (single solid line); ascending pathways unrelated to the two "memory" systems (dotted line).

This duality of the connectedness of the limbic structures with the midbrain reticular formation is further upheld when the descending pathways are considered (see Figure 18-1). Projections descending from the medial mammillary bodies via the mammillo-tegmental tract reach the ventral and dorsal tegmental nuclei, and from the latter, further projections emerge to reach a wide range of other reticular nuclei in the mesencephalon and pons (substantia nigra pars compacta, nucleus reticularis tegmenti pontis, and nucleus cuneiformis). Descending projections from hippocampi travel via the lateral septum and stria medullaris into the habenula, from which further descending pathways reach the ventral tegmental nucleus (via the interpeduncular nucleus) and the dorsal tegmental nucleus, whose further projections have just been described. Nauta and Domesick (1981) refer to these pathways as "the route composed of stria medullaris and fasciculus retroflexus" and "the mammillo-tegmental tract" (p. 166).

Thus the descending limbic reticular projections also appear to be arranged in a parallel fashion so that it is neuroanatomically possible for each of the two structures (mammillary bodies and hippocampi) alone to exert a descending influence upon the whole ensemble of mesencephalic and pontine reticular nuclei, which in their turn are the sources of ascending reticular projections.

It can be therefore concluded that two neuroanatomically distinct loops—hippocampo-reticular and mammillo-reticular—are possible. These two loops have different limbic components—mammillary bodies versus hippocampi—but a shared midbrain component. In other words, both limbic structures are connected with the same population of reticular nuclei.

Such apparent duality of the reticulo-limbic connections leads to the question of whether there are also, functionally, two (rather than one) cortical–thalamic–limbic–mesencephalic loops, which interact with each other (Table 18-1).

The two proposed systems are schematically represented in Figure 18-2 and can be tentatively described as follows:

1. *The mammillary system* comprises the hypothalamus, which is bidirectionally interconnected with the mammillary bodies, which are bidirectionally interconnected with the anterior thalamic nucleus (via the mammillo-thalamic tract), which is bidirectionally interconnected with the cingular cortex.
2. *The hippocampal system* comprises the amygdala, which is bidirectionally interconnected with hippocampi, which are bidirectionally interconnected with vast areas of neocortex (via enthorinal cortex), which is bidirectionally interconnected with the dorsomedial thalamic nucleus, which is bidirectionally interconnected with the amygdala.

In addition, the ventral tegmental nucleus of the mesencephalon should be considered as a reticular component of each of the two systems.

In the two systems, respectively, the mammillary bodies and the hippocampi appear to be the focal points of interface between their mesencephalic reticular, limbic, and thalamo-cortical components.

Aside from the differences listed above in terms of "dry" neuroanatomy, these two parallel circuits can be distinguished in terms of the prevalent neurotransmitter systems involved; that is, the relative role of catecholamines compared to the cholinergic component is greater in the mammillary than in the hippocampal system (Shute & Lewis, 1966). It

TABLE 18-1. Hierarchic Pairwise Comparison of the Components of Two Memory Circuits

Level	Mammillary system	Hippocampal system
Mesencephalic	Ventral tegmental nucleus area	Ventral tegmental nucleus area
Posterior limbic	Mammillary bodies	Hippocampi
Anterior limbic	Hypothalamus	Amygdala
Thalamic	Anterior thalamic nucleus	Dorsomedial thalamic nucleus
Cortical	Cingular cortex	Neocortex

is interesting in this respect that the possibility of two arousal systems' being associated with different neurotransmitter systems (catecholaminergic and cholinergic) was discussed by Routtenberg (1968).

The examination of the two systems reveals that they are internally cohesive and different from each other in several respects. Table 18-1 provides a pairwise hierarchic comparison of the systems. The examination of their respective limbic components reveals that the mammillary system includes the structure that controls behaviors that are significant with respect to the specimen's internal homeostasis (hypothalamus), whereas the hippocampal system includes the structure that can be tentatively described as controlling behaviors significant at a higher level, in the context of the specimen's behavior vis-à-vis the external world and the other specimens of the group, and therefore controlling also the collective homeostasis of the group (amygdala). A similar comparison of the thalamic and cortical components of the two systems reveals that the hippocampal system includes structures involved in the integration of a broad spectrum of perceptual input from the external world, going beyond what is immediately related to the basic homeostatic needs

FIGURE 18-2. Two circuits of reverberation related to memory: the mammillary system (thin solid line); the hippocampal system (broken line). Interface between the two systems is indicated by a thick solid line.

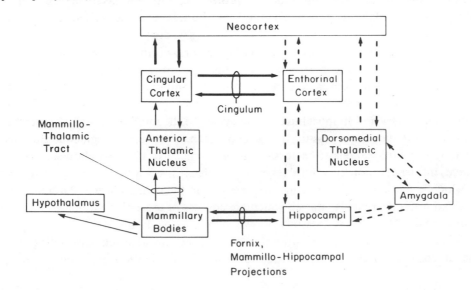

(dorsomedial thalamic nucleus and neocortex); whereas the mammillary system includes structures that are less involved in the integration of biologically "impartial" information and are more immediately involved in subserving basic biological needs (anterior thalamic nucleus and cingulate gyrus).

The components of the mammillary system are phylogenetically older than their counterparts in the hippocampal system. In terms of their respective positions in the cephalic hierarchy, the first system spans from diencephalic to mesocortical levels; the second one is more exclusively telencephalic and embraces neocortex. It is noteworthy that Mishkin, Spiegler, Saunders, and Malamut (1982) proposed the existence of a memory system that is "more primitive than the limbic memory mechanism" and operates independently of it. The mammillary system proposed here appears to fit this description.

Thus there emerges a picture of two possible systems of reverberation: one (mammillary) with a relatively stronger catecholaminergic component, phylogenetically older, and including structures controlling immediately homeostatically significant processes in the specimen; the other one (hippocampal) with a relatively stronger cholinergic component, phylogenetically younger, and including structures that are implicated in processing a wide range of information about the external world and that control behaviors related to the interaction with other specimens in a group.

Whereas the set of mesencephalic reticular nuclei that give rise to ascending projections *into* the two described systems appears to be limited to the ventral tegmental area, the set of reticular nuclei affected by the descending projections arising *from* the two described systems is much more vast, and both systems have access to the same set of mesencephalic and pontine reticular nuclei. This makes it neuroanatomically possible for the activity taking place in either of the two systems to modulate a wide spectrum of arousal phenomena in vast areas of the central nervous system (CNS) far beyond the two delineated circuits (see Figure 18-1).

The reticular nuclei that receive descending projections arising in the mammillary bodies and hippocampi include, in addition to the ventral tegmental nucleus, substantia nigra pars compacta and the nucleus reticularis tegmenti pontis, which are the sources of the ventrally distributed ascending reticular projections into the basal forebrain, hypothalamus, and amygdala via the medial forebrain bundle; and the nucleus cuneiformis, which projects rostrally.

One type of interaction made possible by the organization of pathways described above is enhancement of the reverberation in one (or both) of the described reticular–limbic–thalamic–cortical loops, simultaneous with the inhibition of the activating reticular influence upon other structures. It is noteworthy, in this respect, that the pattern of the descending mammillary and hippocampal pathways upon the midbrain reticular system appears to be hierarchic: The access to the nuclei other than the ventral tegmental nucleus is mediated by an additional relay (the dorsal tegmental nucleus). This may allow separate (independent) influences upon the ventral tegmental nucleus (possibly by way of a positive feedback), which is the source of ascending influences upon the mammillary and hippocampal circuits; and upon the reticular nuclei, which are sources of ascending influences upon the structures outside these loops (possibly by way of a negative feedback).

In effect, a dual system is proposed that allows an area-selective activation of regions of cortex and thalamus in order to foster the facilitation of specific neuronal circuits in the case of consolidation, and the "marking" of particular areas where previously facilitated neuronal circuits reside in the case of retrieval. It is further proposed that the participation of hippocampi and mammillary bodies is needed to sustain such activation and to ensure its spatial selectivity with respect to particular cortical and thalamic areas. In effect, then, the mammillary bodies and hippocampi are viewed as functional extensions of the ventral subdivision of ascending reticular formation, which ensures the considerable degree of spatial specificity of action that the reticular formation proper does not provide.

The idea of several arousal systems is not new (Flicker *et al.*, 1981; Routtenberg, 1968), nor is the idea of several memory circuits (Isaacson, 1972; Thompson, Baumeister, & Rich, 1962). Here I am offering a speculation about two integrated arousal–memory systems. It should be understood that the specific neuroanatomical components of the two proposed systems are tentative and are offered here only to indicate *possible* features of their organization. Mishkin (1982) recently proposed a two-circuit memory model in which amygdala and hippocampus are assigned to different circuits rather than the same circuit.

It is always difficult and potentially spurious to assign anthropomorphic behavioral labels to describe the functions of various brain structures and circuits. For this reason, the following formulations have to be considered as tentative. The presumed cognitive distinction between the two circuits is along the lines of processing that which is mandatory, that is, immediately valuable from the point of view of survival in homeostatic terms (the mammillary system), versus that which is significant in terms of the specimen's interaction with the external world (the hippocampal system). By definition, the latter type of processing embraces a broader spectrum of general orienting information, which is auxiliary and has only remote survival value, than does the former one. Another way to conceptualize this dichotomy in functional terms would be to say that the mammillary system is relatively more involved in immediate pragmatic appraisal ("What does it mean for my immediate biological integrity?"), while being less capable of fine exploratory discriminations; whereas significance judgment provided by the hippocampal system is more indirect and is mediated to a greater degree by fine stimulus exploration in terms of the external world, and is therefore more removed from immediate pragmatic judgment. In this sense, if one imagines a continuum on which various memories are aligned from "neutral" on the left to "affective" on the right, then the contributions of the hippocampal system will be relatively stronger toward the left-hand part of this spectrum and those of the mammillary system toward the right-hand part. It is further possible that motor and proprioceptive discriminations are closer to the domain of the mammillary system, whereas those related to distant exteroceptors are closer to the domain of the hippocampal system. Bernstein (1966) suggested that motor and related proprioceptive functions are phylogenetically older and more immediately "pragmatic" than are the functions of distant exteroceptive integration.

It is clear that any attempt to subdivide knowledge into that which is immediately significant for survival and that which is relatively indifferent with respect to survival is artificial. The two concepts are useful only for defining the extreme points of a continuum along which various real-life learning and recall situations are aligned. This implies that the two proposed "memory systems" are unlikely to work separately; in most cases a joint involvement of the two is expected, but with varied "weights," or degrees of contribution to the mnestic process. One would expect the mammillary system to be relatively more critical in a learning situation that involves direct and effective reward, and the hippocampal system to be relatively more critical in an indifferent situation (e.g., in a word-learning task that carries no significance to the subject).

Such interactive coexistence of the mammillary and hippocampal systems implies the presence of an appropriate neuroanatomical substrate for this interaction. Fornix (hippocampo-mammillary projections) and mammillo-hippocampal projections constitute a loop that can make such an interaction structurally possible. I therefore consider these tracts as the interface between the two systems.

It is obvious that, with phylogenetic progression, the relative weight of the more neutral, auxiliary type of information processing increases from negligible to predominant. The bulk of the knowledge possessed by an average human being has very little immediate reward value, and the pragmatic value of such information, while discernible in the final analysis, is very indirect. This is what we refer to as "accessory information." It is probable that the culturally encouraged impetus for accumulating such information is of a general anticipatory nature; knowledge is obtained "just in case" it may turn out to be of immediate use, and this is the biological justification for it. While in actuality the bulk of such information may never prove to be of real critical need to an individual, the availability of such a redundant information bank enabling broad orientation provides a great survival advantage. Subdivision of labor, which is unique to humans, may provide another justification for learning information that carries no immediate biological value.

It is reasonable to assume that throughout the phylogenetic progression, the role of the mammillary system in memory remains unchanged, and the role of the hippocampal system becomes increasingly prominent. The same can be probably suggested with respect to ontogeny, but in a less linear fashion: Here the distinction is between infancy and early childhood versus the rest of life.

The proposed model of two interacting circuits may help resolve a major controversy existing in memory research: the "human–animal" controversy. Whereas in humans damage to the hippocampi usually leads to memory deficit (Scoville & Milner, 1957), animal experiments have failed to reveal a comparable uniformity of the effect (Isaacson, 1972; Horel, 1978). As long as the assumption of a monolithic, single "memory system" is honored, such discrepancy is disturbing. Indeed, this discrepancy has led to questioning the traditional notion of the role of hippocampi in memory (Horel, 1978).

At the same time, a relatively more limited role of the hippocampal system in subhuman species can be expected on the basis of the foregoing analysis. Furthermore, a prediction (yet to be tested) can be made that the overall role of this system in memory will be inversely correlated with the phylogenetic position of a species.

Experimental paradigms used in clinical studies of brain-damaged populations are different from those employed in animal studies; the latter almost invariably include reinforcement, whereas the former usually do not. Even when human studies attempt to do so, it is not clear that the reinforcement is effective. Although these methodological differences would fail to explain the "human–animal" controversy in the presence of a single "memory system" (Horel, 1978), they are perfectly capable of doing so in the presence of two distinct "memory systems" of the type described above. To verify further the role of the hippocampal system in the memory of subhuman species, a paradigm will have to be designed that is not based on reinforcement, yet is within the species' ethological repertoire. A possible solution to the problem can be obtained by using the habituation of the orienting reflex. The "two-circuit" model would predict impaired performance on such a paradigm following hippocampal lesions in animals.

Compared to the abundant literature on cognitive deficits following hippocampal lesions, the literature on the mammillary bodies is less extensive. This may be due to the fact that cases of isolated damage to the mammillary bodies are rare in humans and that a "clean" access to the mammillary bodies is complicated in animal lesion studies. The hypothesis discussed above would predict considerable memory deficit following the destruction of the mammillary system in animals (with the possible exception of the studies where the orienting-reflex habituation paradigm is used). In humans, we would expect the memory deficits following isolated mammillary lesions to be less significant and to be limited to emotionally colored information and to learning under effective reward conditions.

Since the fornix is, according to this model, an auxiliary component serving as the interface between the two main systems, the lesions of the fornix would be expected to have the least direct impact on memory. This prediction appears to be supported by the existing observations (Hirst, 1982).

The "two-memory-system" model may prove to be capable of accommodating another set of observations central to the field of human memory. It has been reported on numerous occasions that profound retrograde amnesia is less likely to affect early-life memories than it is to affect later-life memories. Providing that it is true that early-life memories are limited to affectively significant material, whereas later-life memories include both affectively significant and affectively indifferent, accessory information, then it is predictable that the deficit of chronologically later memories would be better detected by commonly used tests (which are by and large sensitive to general rather than personally significant information). Furthermore, later-life memories may indeed be more impaired, since damage to either of the two systems, rather than to the mammillary system alone, will affect them.

If it is true that isolated damage to hippocampi is more likely to occur than isolated damage to the mammillary bodies, then the two-memory-system model helps explain also the classical neurological finding known since Claparède, namely, that in amnesias affectively indifferent knowledge suffers more than affectively colored knowledge. Furthermore, it is also known that specific memories of a particular situation can be lost while the knowledge of its affective significance remains intact. In Claparède's classical albeit somewhat crude experiment, an experimenter shook hands with amnesic patients. There was a needle between the experimenter's fingers. Later the patients could not remember ever having seen the experimenter before, yet avoided shaking hands with him, rationalizing it in all kinds of irrelevant ways (e.g., "My hands are dirty") (Luria, 1969).

Nevertheless, one would expect, on the basis of the foregoing hypothesis, that the paradoxical pattern of an amnesia for early-life and/or affectively colored events with a relatively more intact memory for later-life and/or affectively insignificant events can be caused by isolated damage to the mammillary system.

In effect, then, a systematic test of the proposed model requires a matrix of experiments or observations, such that lesions in the mammillary and hippocampal systems would each be combined with both learning and retention of both biologically significant and accessory information both in humans and in animals. Our current knowledge enables us to fill reliably only a few of the emerging 16 cells. We should hope that the developments in the field of memory research will enable us to fill those remaining in the near future.

Because of the need to introduce the proposed model in clear terms, the foregoing discussion has emphasized the separate functional descriptions of its component circuits. The possible outcomes of their interactions have not been addressed in comparable detail.

In the context of the proposed model, such interactions should be expected to be significant, and this may obscure the differential roles of the two circuits. The likelihood of the joint participation of both circuits in most memory processes probably implies that if the assessment of memory uses very sensitive indices, deficits will be found following lesions in either system. On the other hand, relatively crude measures may fail to reveal a deficit following damage to one of the circuits alone, since either circuit can provide some partial basis for learning and/or retrieval in most situations. Finally, it is possible that some degree of plasticity exists across the two circuits, such that an intact circuit is capable of serving the function of the damaged one; this would ultimately mean that, as the findings of Victor, Adams, and Collins (1971) tend to indicate, both circuits have to be damaged in order to produce massive amnesia.

ACKNOWLEDGMENTS

Appreciation is due to Robert M. Bilder for his assistance with neuroanatomical reviews, and to Richard Kovner for his valuable discussion of the manuscript.

REFERENCES

Bernstein, N. A. [*Outlines of the physiology of movements and the physiology of activity*.] Moscow: Meditsina, 1966 (in Russian).

Carpenter, M. B. *Human neuroanatomy*. Baltimore: Williams & Wilkins, 1976.

Cooper, J. R., Bloom, F. E., & Roth, R. H. *The biochemical basis of neuropharmacology*. New York: Oxford University Press, 1978.

Flicker, C., McCarley, R. W., & Hobson, J. A. Aminergic neurons: State control and plasticity in three model systems. *Cellular and Molecular Neurobiology*, 1981, *2*, 123–166.

Goldberg, E., Antin, S. P., Bilder, R. M. Gerstman, L. J., Hughes, J. E. O., & Mattis, S. Retrograde amnesia: Possible role of mesencephalic reticular activation in long-term memory. *Science*, 1981, *213*, 1392–1394.

Hebb, D. O. *The organization of behavior*. New York: Wiley, 1949.

Hirst, W. The amnestic syndrome: Descriptions and explanations. *Psychological Bulletin*, 1982, *3*, 435–460.

Horel, W. K. The neuroanatomy of amnesia. *Brain*, 1978, *101*, 403–450.

Isaacson, R. L. Hippocampal destruction in man and other animals. *Neuropsychologia*, 1972, *10*, 47–64.

Lewis, P. R., & Shute, C. C. D. The cholinergic limbic system: Projections to hippocampal formation, medial cortex, nuclei of the ascending cholinergic reticular system, and the subfornical organ and supra-optic crest. *Brain*, 1967, *90*, 521–540.

Lindval, O., Bjorklund, A., Moore, R. Y., & Stenevi, U. Mesencephalic dopamine neurons projecting to neocortex. *Brain Research*, 1974, *81*, 325–331.

Luria, A. R. Lectures in cognitive psychology taught at University of Moscow, 1969.

MacLean, P. D. Contrasting functions of limbic and neocortical systems of the brain and their relevance to psychophysiological aspects of medicine. *American Journal of Medicine*, 1958, *25*, 611–626.

Mishkin, M. A memory system in the monkey. *Philosophical Transactions of the Royal Society of London*, 1982, *B298*, 85–95.

Mishkin, M., Spiegler, B. J., Saunders, R. C., & Malamut, B. L. An animal model of global amnesia. In S. Corkin, K.L. Davis, J. H. Growden, E. Usdin, & R. J. Wurtman (Eds.), *Alzheimer's disease: A review of progress.* New York: Raven Press, 1982.

Moore, R. Y., & Bloom, F. E. Central catecholamine neuron system: Anatomy and physiology of the norepinephrine and epinephrine systems. *Annual Review of Neuroscience,* 1979, *2,* 113–168.

Nauta, W. J. H. Hippocampal projections and related neural pathways to the midbrain in the cat. *Brain,* 1958, *81,* 319–340.

Nauta, W. J. H., & Domesick, V. B. Ramifications of the limbic system. In S. Matthysse (Ed.), *Psychiatry and the biology of the human brain: A symposium dedicated to Seymour S. Kety.* New York: Elsevier/ North-Holland, 1981.

Oades, R. D. Types of memory or attention?: Impairments after lesions of the hippocampus and limbic ventral tegmentum. *Brain Research Bulletin,* 1981, *7,* 221–226.

Papez, J. W. A proposed mechanism of emotion. *Archives of Neurology and Psychiatry,* 1937, *38,* 725–743.

Routtenberg, A. The two-arousal hypothesis: Reticular formation and limbic system. *Psychological Review,* 1968, *1,* 51–80.

Scoville, W. B., & Milner, B. Loss of recent memory after bilateral hippocampal lesions. *Journal of Neurology, Neurosurgery and Psychiatry,* 1957, *20,* 11–21.

Shute, C. C. D., & Lewis, P. R. Cholinergic and monoaminergic systems of the brain. *Nature,* 1966, *210,* 710–711.

Shute, C. C. D., & Lewis, P. R. The ascending cholinergic reticular system: Neocortical, olfactory and subcortical projections. *Brain,* 1967, *90,* 497–520.

Thompson, R. Localization of the "maze memory system" in the white rat. *Physiological Psychology,* 1974, *2,* 1–17.

Thompson, R., Baumeister, A. A., & Rich, I. Subcortical mechanisms in a successive brightness discrimination habit in the rat. *Journal of Comparative and Physiological Psychology,* 1962, *55,* 487–491.

Verzeano, M. The activity of neuronal networks in memory consolidation. In R. R. Drucker-Colin & J. L. McGaugh (Eds.), *Neurobiology of sleep and memory.* New York: Academic Press, 1977.

Victor, M., Adams, R. D., & Collins, G. H. *The Wernicke–Korsakoff syndrome.* Philadelphia: F. A. Davis, 1971.

Vinogradova, O. S. Functional organization of the limbic system in the process of registration of information: Facts and hypotheses. In R. L. Isaacson & K. H. Pribram (Eds.), *The hippocampus* (Vol. 2, *Neurophysiology and behavior*). New York: Plenum Press, 1975.

19

Comparative Neuropsychology and Alcoholic Korsakoff Disease

Marlene Oscar-Berman

An underlying assumption of the comparative neuropsychological approach is a simple one: Across primates, there are important commonalities in the structure of the central nervous system and its control of behavior.

Introduction

In the past decade, experimental study of human memory dysfunction has blossomed. In contrast to earlier views of organic amnesia as a unitary disorder with a common link of abnormal acquisition, amnesias now are dissociated according to etiology, complexity of symptomatology, and/or locus of cerebral pathology. This unfolding of the diversity of human cognition and its representations in the central nervous system continues. Through the constant interplay between work in the laboratory and work in the clinic, we have emphasized the presence of behavioral deficits in neurological disorders that heretofore have been minimized or ignored (Oscar-Berman, 1978, 1980).

The neurological population we have examined most thoroughly at the Boston University School of Medicine and the Boston Veterans Administration Medical Center consists of patients with alcoholic Korsakoff disease, and their most serious prevailing symptom is anterograde amnesia. Because relatively little is known about how human behavior is altered by brain damage that results from long-term alcohol abuse, we have tried to explore the full extent of neuropsychological deficits and intact skills in these patients and in alcoholics who have not developed Korsakoff disease. To accomplish our goals, we have used sensitive experimental paradigms that measure aspects of perceptual processing, attention, motivation, and disinhibition; we have observed specific abnormalities in all of these functions in Korsakoffs (Oscar-Berman, 1980). If present at all, deficits observed in non-Korsakoff alcoholics were qualitatively similar to those seen in Korsakoffs, but not so severe. Undoubtedly, the various abnormalities we have demonstrated have contributed to the serious memory impairments characteristic of alcoholic Korsakoff syndrome, and can be linked to the underlying pathology in multiple brain sites that is coincident with alcohol abuse.

Marlene Oscar-Berman. Department of Biobehavioral Sciences, Division of Psychiatry, and Aphasia Research Center, Department of Neurology, Boston University School of Medicine, Boston, Massachusetts; Aphasia Research Center, Boston Veterans Administration Medical Center, Boston, Massachusetts.

Neuroradiological and neuropathological evidence from alcoholic patients (with and without amnesia) has implicated bifrontal, bitemporal, and diencephalic brain damage (Victor, Adams, & Collins, 1971; Wilkinson & Carlen, 1981). Most often the damage is diffuse, uncircumscribed, and unselective, prohibiting disclosure of the specific structures that are responsible for specific functional anomalies. Many attempts to solve this problem have relied upon animal models, whereby selective damage to suspected brain structures is deliberately inflicted, and behavioral changes are noted postoperatively (Horel, 1978; Mahut, Zola-Morgan, & Moss, 1982). The reverse process is not common: Rarely do investigators apply to human neurological groups methodology with a history of proven reliability and validity for uncovering and describing the deficits of brain-damaged animals. In situations where this approach has been tried (Ghent, Mishkin, & Teuber, 1962; Weiskrantz, 1971, 1978), results are often negative or uninterpretable because, we think, the neurological groups used have been too heterogeneous with respect to etiology, to symptomatology, and/or to locus of cerebral pathology. Moreover, it is likely that animals with circumscribed lesions have not shown impairments comparable to those observed in human neurological cases, more because of lack of comparability in lesion site and size and in the behavioral paradigms used than because of species differences *per se*. We recognize that variables controlling human performance may involve linguistic mediators and may be more complex than for nonhuman primates, thereby contaminating the results of direct comparisons among species. Nonetheless, the comparative neuropsychological approach already has been fruitful both in demonstrating behavioral abnormalities compatible with known areas of damage (Oscar-Berman & Zola-Morgan, 1980a, 1980b), and in pointing the way heuristically toward uncovering the basic mechanisms behind the observed abnormalities (Öberg & Divac, 1982; Oscar-Berman, 1980; Witt & Goldman-Rakic, 1983). Furthermore, the differences we have observed among different groups of human participants (e.g., alcoholic or brain-damaged control patients) have been important for understanding the full extent of neuropsychological deficits consequent to years of alcohol abuse, and to other disease processes as well (Oscar-Berman & Gade, 1979; Oscar-Berman & Zola-Morgan, 1980a, 1980b).

In short, our most recent probings into neurological disorders in the clinic are based largely upon what we have learned from laboratory investigations employing similar paradigms for human and nonhuman primate participants alike. By analogy to scientific explorations of the frontal lobes, and their multifarious functional and structural models, I wish to describe our continuing efforts to use the comparative neuropsychological approach to understand the neural substrates of human cognition.

Prefrontal Cortex

Telencephalic structures account for about 75% of the weight of the entire human central nervous system, and prefrontal cortex constitutes roughly one-third of human neocortical tissue (Fuster, 1980), nearly twice that found in the chimpanzee telencephalon. Because of the greater size of the human frontal lobes relative to the size in other primates, frontal functions historically were presumed to be unique to humans (Halstead, 1947; Rylander, 1939). With regard to spoken symbolic language functions, this presumption remains valid. However, behavioral homology cannot be separated from neuroanatomical homology

(Bitterman, 1975), and comparative neuroanatomists have demonstrated that nonhuman primates have cortical areas that may correspond to human language areas (Geschwind, 1974; Öberg & Oscar-Berman, 1976).

At present there is no single theory that is adequate to account for other cognitive functions that may be subserved by the frontal lobes, particularly by prefrontal cortex. In nonhuman primates, prefrontal cortex has been inextricably connected to whatever functions are needed for normal performance on delayed-alternation (DA) and delayed-response (DR) tasks (Jacobsen & Nissen, 1937; Warren & Akert, 1964). Such functions have been thought to include short-term memory, spatial memory or appreciation of spatial cues, response inhibition, distractibility, and disinhibition; we do not know how, or whether, these hypothesized functions are related.

Human prefrontal cortex has been postulated to be important in other vaguely defined functions, such as judgment, impulse control, and abstract thinking (Luria, 1966; Warren & Akert, 1964). Such complex alterations in behavior after frontal lobe damage in humans have been more difficult to measure than in experimental monkeys, for two important reasons. First, there is little agreement on precise operational definitions of vague terms such as those just noted; this presents barriers to experimental analysis in the laboratory, where behavioral criteria need to be precisely established. Secondly, although gradients of specialization of prefrontal cortex in dorsal to ventral and anterior to posterior dimensions have been observed in monkeys (Konorski, Teuber, & Zernicki, 1972; Warren & Akert, 1964) and people (Bear, 1983; Valenstein, 1980), subdivision of human prefrontal cortex is complicated by demonstrated lateralized differences in the two hemispheres (Bear, 1983; Geschwind, 1974; Moscovitch, 1979). Nonetheless, patients with alcoholic Korsakoff disease have been observed to exhibit behaviors that are not unlike those demonstrated in monkeys and people with bilateral prefrontal symptomatology.

Thus, Talland (1965) and others have noted poor performance by Korsakoffs in divided-attention tasks (Glosser, Butters, & Samuels, 1976); Korsakoffs also do poorly on DA and DR tasks (Oscar-Berman, Zola-Morgan, Öberg, & Bonner, 1982), exhibit abnormal perseveration of inappropriate responses (Oscar-Berman, 1973; Oscar-Berman et al., 1982), show reduced orienting and habituation responses (Oscar-Berman & Gade, 1979), demonstrate deficits in shifting attention (Oscar-Berman & Samuels, 1977), exhibit increased susceptibility to interference (Moscovitch, 1979; Oscar-Berman & Zola-Morgan, 1980b; Squire, 1982), and have difficulty changing sets (Oscar-Berman, 1973; Rozin, 1976). All of these findings are compatible with clinical signs of frontal lobe pathology (Lhermitte & Signoret, 1976; Luria, 1966), and with anatomical evidence of cortical atrophy (including frontal tissue) in alcoholics (Lishman, 1981; Wilkinson & Carlen, 1981).

It should be emphasized that prior to the early 1970s, the role of frontal lobe structures in Korsakoff syndrome was minimized or ignored. In our own laboratory, emphasis on these and other cognitive deficits in alcoholic Korsakoff patients came principally from results of studies employing the comparative neuropsychological approach. We used Levine's (1966) method for assessing strategy formation and its possible disruption in brain-damaged groups; Levine's method was itself derived from his earlier procedure for measuring strategy formation in normal monkeys (Levine, 1959). We observed that Korsakoffs perseverated (Oscar-Berman, 1973; Oscar-Berman, Sahakian, & Wikmark, 1976) in ways that were very similar to those of monkeys with prefrontal lesions

(Brush, Mishkin, & Rosvold, 1961; Oscar & Wilson, 1966; Wilson & Oscar, 1966). Our subsequent measures of arousal and selective attention, although exploratory at the time, were similar to those used to measure the same functions in nonhuman primates (Pribram & McGuinness, 1975; Wilson, 1978) and in retarded individuals (Zeaman & House, 1963), and our findings of hypoarousal and restricted attention again suggested frontal lobe pathology in alcoholic Korsakoff disease. To what extent all or some of these deficits contribute to—or are independent of—the Korsakoff amnesia awaits future dissociation from impairments in patients with (1) known damage to prefrontal cortex, and (2) similar memory problems in the absence of these other deficits (Cermak, 1976; Freedman & Oscar-Berman, 1984).

The Temporal Lobes

From the latter part of the 19th century until now, brain topography for visually based functions has become more precisely defined (Wilson, 1978). Prior to the 1930s, it was generally believed that cortex of the occipital lobes was the only cortical representation for visual functions (Klüver, 1941). Although there have been numerous confirmations of loss of pattern vision after removal of striate cortex, complete "blindness" following such lesions is not the case (Pasik & Pasik, 1971). In the 1930s, however, the role of the temporal lobes was emphasized when visual agnosia was described as a salient feature of the Klüver–Bucy syndrome in monkeys (Klüver & Bucy, 1939). Other features of the Klüver–Bucy syndrome include perseverative hypermetamorphosis concomitant with the visual agnosia; oral examination and reexamination of objects; hypersexuality; and hyporeactivity to being provoked.

Beginning in the 1950s, functions of the temporal lobes in monkeys were further fractionated. Some abnormal perseverative traits seen in the Klüver–Bucy syndrome (including those related to impaired memory) have been attributed to damage of hippocampal regions (Correll & Scoville, 1965; Mahut et al., 1982), and some of the other functional abnormalities (e.g., hypersexuality and hyporeactivity) have been related to damage in different limbic system structures, such as the amygdala (Pilleri, 1966). Aspects of the visual agnosia, the hypermetamorphosis, and the perseveration of these functions observed in the Klüver–Bucy syndrome were attributed to loss of neocortical tissue. Through isolation of inferotemporal cortex from the amygdala and hippocampus, the direct role of this cortex in visually guided learning was clearly established and separable from the visual functions of striate cortex (Mishkin, 1972; Wilson & Mishkin, 1959). By the late 1960s, inferotemporal cortex was further functionally subdivided into an anterior sector (TE in Bonin & Bailey's [1947] terminology) dealing with visual association, learning–memory behaviors, and a posterior sector (areas OB, OA, and TEO) needed for normal attention to and discrimination among features of visual stimuli (Cowey & Gross, 1970; Mishkin, 1972, 1982; Wilson, 1978).

Whereas bitemporal lobectomies produce the most complete constellation of the Klüver–Bucy syndrome in monkeys, it is unusual to see *all* of the classic Klüver–Bucy signs in a single human individual, unless there also is extensive dementia (as seen in Pick disease). Rather, different combinations of the traits appear together, depending primarily upon locus of damage, which in turn depends upon etiology. Traits resembling visual agnosia and perseverative repetition are well-recognized traits in alcoholic Korsakoff patients, a group whose memory impairments typically have been linked to damage in some part of the Papez circuit (Papez, 1937) or related structures. Because results of nonhuman primate research historically had been able to dissociate visually based learning–memory deficits from those related to visual attention and feature discrimination, we explored the possibility that alcoholic Korsakoff disease affects some aspects of visual behavior while leaving other aspects relatively intact (Oscar-Berman & Zola-Morgan, 1980b). This research project was especially relevant at the time of its inception, because Horel (1978) had proposed that at least one aspect of human amnesia might be related to damaged visual association cortex or its projections into the temporal stem adjacent to the hippocampus. Furthermore, Mishkin (Jones & Mishkin, 1972; Mishkin, 1982) had suggested that human amnesics suffer from an inability to form functional links among sensory association areas (for appreciation of stimulus qualities), the limbic system (for appreciation of reward value), and more recently (Mishkin, 1982), the thalamus (as the last loop in the feedback circuit to visual neocortex).

The two experimental procedures that we chose to use already had been used by other investigators to separate deficits of selective visual perception from those of visual association learning in monkeys with temporal lobe lesions (Cowey & Gross, 1970; Dean, 1976; Iwai & Mishkin, 1969). One task involved the learning of two-choice visual discriminations, each (in succession) to some predetermined criterion; these are called "individual-pair" (IP) discriminations. The other, somewhat more complex task, called "concurrent-pair" (CP) discriminations, also involved the learning of pairs of visual stimuli; but a number of different pairs were presented in random order within each session, such that several discriminations were learned simultaneously.

Monkeys with lesions of the posterior sector of inferotemporal cortex (that which receives projections from the cortical representation of the fovea in striate cortex) failed on acquisition of IP tasks, reflecting their deficits in discriminating or in detecting differences among stimuli. By contrast, monkeys with lesions of anterior inferotemporal cortex were impaired on CP problems, the ones that rely more on intact visual association-learning skills than on perceptual-discrimination ability *per se*. The behavior of Korsakoff patients on these same tasks resembled that of animals with anterior inferotemporal cortical damage; that is, they were able to perform normally on most IP problems, but were seriously impaired on all CP problems. We therefore attributed this pattern of results, in part, to a weakened ability by Korsakoffs to associate stimulus attributes with reinforcement contingencies, and we considered the possible involvement of temporal neocortical tissue (including Horel's postulated temporal stem) and its connections with the amygdala and the thalamus (Mishkin, 1982). This same sentiment was echoed in the results of other experiments within the framework of comparative neuropsychology. For example, we found the pattern of performance of Korsakoffs on visual and on spatial reversal tasks to be almost identical with that of monkeys with damage to temporal pole cortex plus amygdala (an impairment that also was attributed to difficulty in forming new stimulus–reinforcement associations subsequent to unlearning a related old response; see Jones & Mishkin, 1972, and Oscar-Berman & Zola-Morgan, 1980a). The same interpretation can be applied to the deficits we observed when Korsakoffs were tested on differential reinforcement of low rates of response (DRL) and on probability-learning tasks used often in animal laboratories.

In addition, an apparent cleavage between the effects of human and nonhuman hippocampal damage was narrowed when we tested Korsakoffs on DRL schedules and observed that the Korsakoffs (with known damage to structures that connect directly with the hippocampus) performed like animals with hippocampal damage. In probability-learning settings (where one response alternative is reinforced differentially, and usually independently from another), Korsakoffs again behaved like hippocampally damaged animals: They overresponded and did not evidence normal sensitivity to changing reinforcement contingencies (Öberg & Oscar-Berman, 1976; Oscar-Berman, Heyman, Bonner, & Ryder, 1980; Oscar-Berman et al., 1976, 1982). Although the hippocampus has been enlarged during evolution and probably has established "new" connections, its appearance in monkeys and people is similar; anatomical and behavioral homologies are likely. However, it is still not certain that the hippocampus is the *critical* structure that controls behaviors in tasks such as those just discussed. Damage to overlying white matter and surrounding neocortex usually accompanies hippocampal damage, and frequently there are *multiple* sites of pathology (in monkeys and in humans) (Horel, 1978; Weiskrantz, 1978).

There are abundant reciprocal connections between prefrontal cortex and inferotemporal cortex with each other and with other sensory cortical areas (in the occipital and parietal lobes), giving the frontal and temporal lobes polysensory control (Fuster, 1980). Also providing a network of reciprocal interactions with prefrontal and temporal cortex is the limbic system, which, in turn, has influence upon basal ganglia structures, the septum, the hypothalamus, and the mesencephalon (Nauta & Domesick, 1981). It is not unlikely that, as we look further into the types of deficits that are exhibited by alcoholic Korsakoff patients, we will find evidence of damage to those related brain regions, and that the impairments will be dissociated from those of neurological patients whose principal sites of damage are elsewhere in the nervous system (Freedman & Oscar-Berman, 1984; Oscar-Berman, 1980; Oscar-Berman & Zola-Morgan, 1980a, 1980b).

A Lesson for Future Research

The discussion to this point has outlined the comparative neuropsychological approach to understanding how behavior is affected by brain damage associated with alcoholic Korsakoff disease. The most striking outcome was the implication of frontal lobe involvement and damage to temporal lobe structures that were previously not considered to be relevant to the symptoms of Korsakoff disease.

In summary, we know that brain damage in Korsakoffs is widespread and diffuse. Their most obvious symptom is anterograde amnesia, but they have many, many other impairments as well. It is important to understand all of the neuropsychological deficits concomitant with alcohol abuse. Only then can we help to maximize the intact abilities of those who are impaired. Only then will we be able to understand fully the subtle functions that go awry when parts of the brain are damaged, and only then will we know how the brain functions to control human behavior. Since the goals of animal physiological and comparative psychology and human neuropsychology are the same in this regard, there should be some common ground in methodology as well; and that, we think, is comparative neuropsychology.

Epilogue

In describing the apparent discrepancy between human and animal data on memory and its disorders, the Panel on Neurological Aspects of Behavior (National Advisory Neurological and Communicative Disorders and Stroke Council, 1979) noted a question that is as yet unsettled: Do the brain structures responsible for organic amnesias in humans reflect a new order of organization, or are the differences between human and nonhuman primates purely a matter of degree?

The question is still unanswered, but we feel that the comparative neuropsychological approach—one that can employ comparable measures of behavior in different species—points us in the direction of homologous behaviors and homologous neuroanatomical structures.

ACKNOWLEDGMENTS

The writing of this chapter was supported in part by the Medical Research Service of the Veterans Administration and from the following U.S. Department of Health and Human Services grants: NIAAA AA05211 and RSDA AA00061, and NINCDS NS07615 and NS06209.

REFERENCES

Bear, D. Hemispheric specialization and the neurology of emotion. *Archives of Neurology*, 1983, *40*, 195–202.
Bitterman, M. E. The comparative analysis of learning. *Science*, 1975, *188*, 699–709.
Bonin, G. V., & Bailey, P. *The neocortex of Macaca mulatta.* Urbana: University of Illinois Press, 1947.
Brush, E. S., Mishkin, M., & Rosvold, H. E. Effects of object preferences and aversions on discrimination learning in monkeys with frontal lesions. *Journal of Comparative and Physiological Psychology*, 1961, *54*, 319–325.
Cermak, L. S. The encoding capacity of a patient with amnesia due to encephalitis. *Neuropsychologia*, 1976, *14*, 311–326.
Correll, R. E., & Scoville, W. B. Performance on delayed match following lesions of medial temporal lobe structures. *Journal of Comparative and Physiological Psychology*, 1965, *60*, 360–367.
Cowey, A., & Gross, C. G. Effects of foveal prestriate and inferotemporal lesions on visual discrimination by rhesus monkeys. *Experimental Brain Research*, 1970, *11*, 128–144.
Dean, P. Effects of inferotemporal lesions on the behavior of monkeys. *Psychological Bulletin*, 1976, *83*, 41–71.
Freedman, M., & Oscar-Berman, M. *Perseveration and amnesia in neurological disease.* Manuscript submitted for publication, 1984.
Fuster, J. M. *The prefrontal cortex.* New York: Raven Press, 1980.
Geschwind, N. *Selected papers on language and the brain.* Boston: Reidel, 1974.
Ghent, L., Mishkin, M., & Teuber, H. -L. Short-term memory after frontal-lobe injury in man. *Journal of Comparative and Physiological Psychology*, 1962, *55*, 705–709.
Glosser, G., Butters, N., & Samuels, I. Failures in information processing in patients with Korsakoff's syndrome. *Neuropsychologia*, 1976, *14*, 327–334.

Halstead, W. C. *Brain and intelligence: A quantitative study of the frontal lobes.* Chicago: University of Chicago Press, 1947.

Horel, J. A. The neuroanatomy of amnesia: A critique of the hippocampal memory hypothesis. *Brain,* 1978, *101,* 403–445.

Iwai, E., & Mishkin, M. Further evidence on the locus of the visual area in the temporal lobe of the monkey. *Experimental Neurology,* 1969, *25,* 585–594.

Jacobsen, C. F., & Nissen, H. W. Studies of cerebral function in primates: IV. The effects of frontal lobe lesions on the delayed alternation habit in monkeys. *Journal of Comparative and Physiological Psychology,* 1937, *23,* 101–112.

Jones, B. P., & Mishkin, M. Limbic lesions and the problem of stimulus–reinforcement associations. *Experimental Neurology,* 1972, *36,* 363–377.

Klüver, H. Visual functions after removal of the occipital lobes. *Journal of Psychology,* 1941, *11,* 23–45.

Klüver, H., & Bucy, P. C. Preliminary analysis of functions of the temporal lobes in monkeys. *Archives of Neurology and Psychiatry,* 1939, *42,* 979–1000.

Konorski, J., Teuber, H. -L., & Zernicki, B. (Eds.). The frontal granular cortex and behavior. *Acta Neurobiologiae Experimentalis,* 1972, *32*(Whole No. 2).

Levine, M. A model of hypothesis behavior in discrimination learning set. *Psychological Review,* 1959, *66,* 353–366.

Levine, M. Hypothesis behavior by humans during discrimination learning. *Journal of Experimental Psychology,* 1966, *71,* 331–338.

Lhermitte, F., & Signoret, J. -L. The amnesic syndrome and the hippocampal–mammillary system. In M. R. Rosenzweig & E. L. Bennett (Eds.), *Neural mechanisms of learning and memory.* Cambridge, Mass.: MIT Press, 1976.

Lishman, W. A. Cerebral disorder in alcoholism: syndromes of impairment. *Brain,* 1981, *104,* 1–20.

Luria, A. R. *Higher cortical functions in man.* New York: Basic Books, 1966.

Mahut, H., Zola-Morgan, S. M., & Moss, M. Hippocampal resections impair associative learning and recognition memory in the monkey. *Journal of Neuroscience,* 1982, *2,* 1214–1229.

Mishkin, M. Cortical visual areas and their interaction. In A. G. Karczman & J. C. Eccles (Eds.), *The brain and human behavior.* New York: Springer-Verlag, 1972.

Mishkin, M. A memory system in the monkey. *Philosophical Transactions of the Royal Society,* 1982, *B298,* 85–95.

Moscovitch, M. Information processing and the cerebral hemispheres. In M. S. Gazzaniga (Ed.), *Handbook of behavioral neurobiology* (Vol. 2, *Neuropsychology*). New York: Plenum Press, 1979.

National Advisory Neurological and Communicative Disorders and Stroke Council. *Report of the Panel on Neurological Aspects of Behavior* (DHEW Publication No. (NIH) 79-1917). Washington, D.C.: U.S. Government Printing Office, 1979.

Nauta, W. J. H., & Domesick, V. B. Neural associations of the limbic system. In A. L. Beckman (Ed.), *The neural basis of behavior.* Jamaica, N.Y.: Spectrum, 1981.

Öberg, R. G. E., & Divac, I. Neurology and neuropsychology of basal ganglia. *International Neuropsychology Society Program,* 1982, *10,* 43. (Abstract)

Öberg, R. G. E., & Oscar-Berman, M. *Comparative aspects of human neuropsychology.* Paper presented at the meeting of the European Brain and Behavior Society, London, March 1976.

Oscar, M., & Wilson, M. Tactual and visual discrimination learning in monkeys with frontal lesions. *Journal of Comparative and Physiological Psychology,* 1966, *62,* 108–114.

Oscar-Berman, M. Hypothesis testing and focusing behavior during concept formation by amnesic Korsakoff patients. *Neuropsychologia,* 1973, *11,* 191–198.

Oscar-Berman, M. Commentary. In E. Callaway, P. Tueting, & S. H. Koslow (Eds.), *Event related brain potentials in man.* New York: Academic Press, 1978.

Oscar-Berman, M. Neuropsychological consequences of long-term chronic alcoholism. *American Scientist,* 1980, *68,* 410–419.

Oscar-Berman, M., & Gade, A. Electrodermal measures of arousal in humans with cortical or subcortical brain damage. In H. D. Kimmel, E. H. van Olst, & J. F. Orlebeke (Eds.), *The orienting reflex in humans.* Hillsdale, N.J.: Erlbaum, 1979.

Oscar-Berman, M., Heyman, G. M., Bonner, R. T., & Ryder, J. Human neuropsychology: Some differences between Korsakoff and normal operant performance. *Psychology Research,* 1980, *41,* 235–247.

Oscar-Berman, M., Sahakian, B. J., & Wikmark, G. Spatial probability learning by alcoholic Korsakoff patients. *Journal of Experimental Psychology: Human Learning and Memory*, 1976, *2*, 215–222.

Oscar-Berman, M., & Samuels, I. Stimulus preference and memory factors in Korsakoff's syndrome. *Neuropsychologia*, 1977, *15*, 99–106.

Oscar-Berman, M., & Zola-Morgan, S. M. Comparative neuropsychology and Korsakoff's syndrome: I. Spatial and visual reversal learning. *Neuropsychologia*, 1980, *18*, 499–512. (a)

Oscar-Berman, M., & Zola-Morgan, S. M. Comparative neuropsychology and Korsakoff's syndrome: II. Two-choice visual discrimination learning. *Neuropsychologia*, 1980, *18*, 513–526. (b)

Oscar-Berman, M., Zola-Morgan, S. M., Öberg, R. G. E. & Bonner, R. T. Comparative neuropsychology and Korsakoff's syndrome: III. Delayed response, delayed alternation and DRL performance. *Neuropsychologia*, 1982, *20*, 187–202.

Papez, J. W. A proposed mechanism of emotion. *Archives of Neurology and Psychiatry*, 1937, *38*, 725–743.

Pasik, T., & Pasik, P. The visual world of monkeys deprived of striate cortex: Effective stimulus parameters and the importance of the accessory optic system. *Vision Research*, 1971, *3*, 419–435.

Pilleri, G. The Klüver–Bucy syndrome in man. *Psychiatry and Neurology* (Basel), 1966, *152*, 65–103.

Pribram, K. H., & McGuinness, D. Arousal, activation, and effort in the control of attention. *Psychological Review*, 1975, *82*, 116–149.

Rozin, P. The psychobiological approach to human memory. In M. R. Rosenzweig & E. L. Bennett (Eds.), *Neural mechanisms of learning and memory*. Cambridge, Mass.: MIT Press, 1976.

Rylander, G. *Personality changes after operations on the frontal lobes*. London: Oxford University Press, 1939.

Squire, L. R. Comparisons between forms of amnesia: Some deficits are unique to Korsakoff's syndrome. *Journal of Experimental Psychology: Learning, Memory and Cognition*, 1982, *8*, 560–571.

Talland, G. A. *Deranged memory*. New York: Academic Press, 1965.

Valenstein, E. S. (Ed.). *The psychosurgery debate: Scientific, legal, and ethical Perspectives*. San Francisco: W. H. Freeman, 1980.

Victor, M., Adams, R. D., & Collins, G. H. *The Wernicke-Korsakoff syndrome*. Philadelphia: F. A. Davis, 1971.

Warren, J. M., & Akert, K. (Eds.). *The frontal granular cortex and behavior*. New York: McGraw-Hill, 1964.

Weiskrantz, L. Comparison of amnesic states in monkey and man. In L. E. Jarrard (Ed.), *Cognitive processes of nonhuman primates*. New York: Academic Press, 1971.

Weiskrantz, L. A comparison of hippocampal pathology in man and other animals. In K. Elliot & J. Whelan (Eds.), *Functions of the septo-hippocampal system* (CIBA Foundation Symposium No. 58). New York: Elsevier/Excerpta Medica/North-Holland, 1978.

Wilkinson, D. A., & Carlen, P. L. Chronic organic brain syndromes associated with alcoholism: Neuropsychological and other aspects. In Y. Israel, F. Glaser, H. Kalant, R. Popham, W. Schmidt, & R. Smart (Eds.), *Research advances in alcohol and drug problems* (Vol. 6). New York: Plenum Press, 1981.

Wilson, M. Visual system: Pulvinar–extrastriate cortex. In R. B. Masterson (Ed.), *Handbook of behavioral neurobiology* (Vol. 1, *Sensory integration*). New York: Plenum Press, 1978.

Wilson, W. A., & Mishkin, M. Comparison of the effects of inferotemporal and lateral occipital lesions on visually guided behavior in monkeys. *Journal of Comparative and Physiological Psychology*, 1959, *52*, 10–17.

Wilson, W. A., & Oscar, M. Probability learning in monkeys with lateral frontal lesions. *Journal of Comparative and Physiological Psychology*, 1966, *62*, 462–464.

Witt, E. D., & Goldman-Rakic, P. S. Intermittent thiamine deficiency in the rhesus monkey: II. Evidence for memory loss. *Annals of Neurology*, 1983, 13, 396–401.

Zeaman, D., & House, B. T. The role of attention in retardate discrimination learning. In N. R. Ellis (Ed.), *Handbook of mental deficiency*. New York: McGraw-Hill, 1963.

Psychobiological Determinants of Memory Failures 20

Herbert Weingartner

A Point of View

Learning and memory processes are psychobiologically complex and differentiated behaviors. These cognitive processes are, however, amenable to experimental analysis in a manner that allows us to begin to construct verifiable psychobiologically defined theories and models. To accomplish this synthesis of behavioral and biological cognitive research requires critical evaluation and definition of the discriminable psychological dimensions of learning and memory—processes that must be as detailed as our characterization of the biology of cognitive processes. If we are to develop viable models of brain–behavior relationships, then it does not serve us well to carefully map neuroanatomical structures and neurochemical events onto crudely described cognitive behaviors. Cognitive research requires integration, synthesis, and convergence of the psychology and biology of learning and memory. This requires an appreciation of the characteristics of information processing, learning, and memory in unimpaired subjects, in impaired patients, and in lower animals as subjects. These different types of findings and the theories generated from this research must then be integrated with our knowledge of the structures and neurochemical events that mediate cognitive processes.

This chapter first addresses the separate contexts that have characterized the study of learning and memory. Using cognitive research and theory, as well as what is known about the pathology and biology of learning and memory, a framework is outlined for the analysis of learning and memory. This framework is utilized to characterize some common forms of learning–memory failures in humans. Some of the neuropharmacological studies of learning and memory are also briefly reviewed, to further amplify the contrasting ways in which cognitive processes can be altered. Such a synthesis of the psychobiology of cognitive–learning–memory phenomena and theory is clinically useful, not only because it suggests new, more effective diagnostic tools and treatment strategies, but also because it serves as a working framework for more effective strategies for the study of learning and memory.

The Differentiated Structure of Cognitive Processes:
A Brief Historical Overview

A number of long but separate histories of research have been directed at defining the determinants of learning and memory and related cognitive processes. The study of

Herbert Weingartner. Laboratory of Psychology and Psychopathology, National Institute of Mental Health, Bethesda, Maryland.

learning and memory in unimpaired subjects emerged from a tradition of behaviorism and then developed a separate identity. Some three decades ago, computer metaphors began to dominate thinking about memory and learning, so that information processing was viewed in terms of serially ordered as well as parallel discrete systems. These included versions of sensory integration, attention, short-term memory, and long-term memory (Atkinson & Shiffrin, 1968; Waugh & Norman, 1965). More recently, learning and memory were reconsidered in terms of elaborateness of encoding as a way of defining how well something has been learned (Craik & Lockhart, 1972; Craik & Tulving, 1975; Tulving & Watkins, 1975). The study of disturbances in cognition, evident in clinical phenomena, utilized some of the research about cognition from models and methods describing the unimpaired subjects. In general, however, this research proceeded on a separate course (Warrington, 1982). Similarly, cognitive psychologists interested in describing learning and memory in unimpaired subjects made little use of clinical research. Separate, parallel research efforts were accomplished with the aim of describing the structure (behavior) of lower animal learning and memory. Still other research was directed at defining some of the biological determinants of learning and memory (Gold & McGaugh, 1975; McGaugh & Herz, 1972). The major point to be made is that these areas of study were developed separately; this meant that the study of the biology, psychology, and psychopathology of learning and memory each developed its own metaphors, theories, models, and methods of study. For example, a concept such as memory consolidation was used to develop both theory and method in animal learning–memory research, but was either ignored or rejected by investigators of cognitive processes in unimpaired human subjects. This fragmentation of research has weakened and unduly limited the development of powerful theories, methods, and, most of all, the types of questions that might be asked about learning and memory. The framework for the analysis of learning and memory outlined below is necessarily broad and general, but I hope that it may provide a scheme for bringing together these different territories of inquiry about cognition.

Cognition may fail or be altered in a number of different ways. These changes can occur through alteration in some of the following types of cognitive processes outlined and defined below: (1) episodic memory (or its component processes, such as attention); (2) access and use of semantic or knowledge memory (which includes procedural learning); (3) effortful cognitive capacity demanding operations and processes; (4) automatic cognitive operations; (5) reward–reinforcement-related learning–memory operations (including consolidation processes); and (6) retrieval processes. These cognitive systems and processes are viewed as having an integrity of their own, but are also seen as interdependent with overlapping psychological and biological processes and determinants.

Most cognitive research has been concerned with determinants of learning and memory that involve episodic memory (Tulving, 1972). "Episodic" memory refers to processes and central nervous system representation of recently acquired experiences, including information about when events occurred, what preceded and followed these events, and the context of the acquisition of those experiences. Some of the components of episodic memory that have been of interest include sequentially dependent ordered processes, such as sensory integration; attention; working memory; and postprocessing encoding and mediational operations that alter information in working memory. Memory consolidation and maintenance operations and retrieval processes have also been of recent interest. The elaborateness of encoding operations and mediational processes, as well as the determinants of memory and learning, have also been studied extensively, particularly in the last 10 years. Effective encoding of information has been characterized in terms of a number of its aspects, including the nature of stimuli to be remembered; the kind of cognitive operations used to process information, and the effort that is expended in accomplishing these operations.

There has been a recent growing interest in the types of cognitive processes that subjects use in thinking about events. Language behavior, procedural learning, problem solving, decision processes, and mediational processes, which clearly are involved in the evaluation and synthesis of information or experience, are some of the operations that have begun to be studied extensively. These types of cognitive processes all involve in some crucial way "old" learning, or "semantic" or "knowledge" memory. These processes also play a role in episodic memory. The way in which knowledge is stored, its representation, and its role in relation to episodic memory are just a few of the issues that are currently under active investigation. Semantic memory includes information about rules and procedures, logic, meaning, and relation of information acquired throughout a lifetime. Unlike episodic memory, the representation of semantic memory in the central nervous system is not linked to a specific sequence, time, or context. However, retrieval or access to that knowledge base is necessary for us to appreciate the meaning and significance of ongoing events. Another parallel example of the distinction between semantic memory and episodic memory is illustrated by differences in the cognitive operations required in learning and remembering (performing) procedures (the logic and operations required to accomplish many skill tasks), and those required in declarative memory (or memory for where, when, and how learning has taken place) (N. J. Cohen & Squire, 1980). That is, procedural learning is viewed as being based primarily on access to semantic memory, while declarative memory reflects episodic memory.

The amount of effort, or directed cognitive activity requiring cognitive capacity for processing information, is another important determinant that affects both episodic- and semantic-memory processes. Some cognitive processes require sustained effort or active participation on the part of the subject. Other cognitive operations can be accomplished almost automatically or passively and require little cognitive capacity (Hasher & Zacks, 1979; Lewis, 1979). For example, learning and remembering the details of some experience require active effortful cognitive operations and limit the effectiveness of other operations that are performed at the same time. On the other hand, superficial processing conditions, such as forms of shadowing information, monitoring how often an event took place, or remembering some of the surrounding incidental information (e.g., what someone was wearing while presenting information) can be accomplished almost "automatically" without effort and require little of our cognitive capacity. The determinants of memory and learning for effortful and for automatic information processing appear to be different and to involve different psychobiological mechanisms (R. Cohen, Cohen, Weingartner, & Pickar, 1983; Zacks, Hasher, & Sanft, 1982).

The role of the reinforcement–reward system defined by self-stimulation studies of the brain is also important in the establishment of memories and in the performance of learned behaviors. Recent studies of areas of the brain that induce behaviors by altering the self-stimulation rate have been useful in defining some of the chemistry and neuroanatomy of that reward system. These same areas of the brain and neurochemical systems that are involved in stimulation–reward overlap those involved in memory and learning (Kornetsky

& Esposito, 1981). The relationship of the brain systems involved in self-stimulation and reward to the ones involved in learning and memory can be seen as a kind of biological confirmation of Thorndike's law of effect, which was stated some 50 years ago, and its offspring, behaviorism. Specific components of learning–memory processes appear to be altered differentially by conditions that affect the reward system of the brain. This system may have a particular role in affecting the strength of learned behaviors.

Retrieval processes represent a set of operations that includes the generation of strategies involved in searching for previously acquired episodic information and knowledge behaviors. It also involves cognitive behaviors that can be used to evaluate retrieved events. The context in which retrieval is attempted can act to bias the types of search strategies used to search for previously acquired behaviors (Tulving & Thompson, 1973).

Forms of Cognitive Failure

Cognitive dysfunctions are associated with a wide variety of neuropsychiatric–psychiatric–psychological syndromes. Although learning–memory failures are often the obvious and common behavioral expression of these cognitive impairments, the ways in which memory fails may be syndrome-specific. Some of the features and determinants of different types of memory failure are outlined and described below, in terms of the framework for considering information-processing changes that is presented above. The examples of cognitive learning–memory failures chosen are those that might illustrate some specific changes in access to semantic memory, automatic versus effortful processing, reinforcement–reward-related memory phenomena, and retrieval processes.

Progressive Dementias (Failures in Semantic or Knowledge Memory)

The progressive dementias (PDs) represent a variety of syndromes, of which Alzheimer disease is perhaps the most common (Constantinidis, 1978). In PDs, we see progressive and dramatic deterioration in learning, memory, and other forms of cognitive behavior. In the early stages of the disorder, these cognitive changes can superficially resemble those evident in depression or those associated with aging (Craik, 1977; Weingartner & Silberman, 1982). However, more careful evaluation of these changes in learning and memory, even during the early stages of PD, demonstrates that the mechanisms of such information processing impairments are quite different from those associated with cognitive impairments in other disorders.

The PD patient generally fails to establish a "permanent" record of ongoing events in episodic memory (i.e., has failures in recent memory). This is just as evident in processing inherently easily encodable related events (Weingartner, Kaye, Smallberg, Ebert, Gillin, & Sitaram, 1981) as it is evident in learning unrelated, difficult-to-encode events. Unlike the situation in depression, processes that can be accomplished almost automatically are as likely to be disrupted in PD as those that require sustained effort. The PD patient is unable to encode information effectively and therefore fails to learn and remember. This encoding impairment, unlike that seen in patients with Korsakoff disease, is directly related to an impairment in finding and using information that is part of previously acquired knowledge

(Weingartner, Kaye, Ebert, Gillin, Petersen, & Smallberg, 1981; Weingartner, Kaye, Smallberg, Ebert, Gillin, & Sitaram, 1981). PD patients' inability to find or use prior knowledge is reflected in such cognitive behaviors as problems in word finding and naming, difficulties in appreciating the meaning of ongoing events, and problems in logical conceptual thinking (de Ajuriaguerra & Tissot, 1975). The extent to which episodic memory is impaired in these patients is directly related to impairment in accessing knowledge memory (Weingartner, Kaye, Ebert, Gillin, Petersen, & Smallberg, 1981; Weingartner, Kaye, Smallberg, Ebert, Gillin, & Sitaram, 1981). Proposed treatments in the early stages of PDs of an Alzheimer type might logically be directed at facilitating those cognitive processes that would improve access to knowledge memory.

Korsakoff Disease (Impaired Recent Memory with Relatively Preserved Remote Memory and Access to Previously Acquired Knowledge)

A large body of systematic research has been completed that would define the structure of the neuropathology and related cognitive changes in amnesic disorders (Milner, 1970; Victor, Adams, & Collins, 1971). Korsakoff disease (KD) is one of the most common of these amnesic syndromes. There have also been some attempts to model types of amnesias in lower animals (Mishkin, 1978). Despite all these efforts, there remains much uncertainty about the psychobiology of this form of cognitive failure.

There is universal agreement that recent memory is impaired in KD patients, but there are many theories about why memory fails in these patients. Explanations have included consolidation failure; retrieval failure, in terms that can include or exclude output interference; and incomplete encoding of information at the time of acquisition (see Butters & Cermak, 1980, for a review). Defective encoding has been the most frequently used current explanation for why KD patients fail to remember recent events. This currently popular formulation of the KD learning–memory failure parallels the current heuristic emphasis in cognitive psychology, which is away from stage models of information processing and toward a single-trace elaborateness-of-processing explanation of how we learn and remember.

Unlike PD patients, KD patients fail to learn and remember, despite the fact that they are generally capable of accessing and using previously acquired knowledge (Weingartner, Grafman, Boutelle, Kaye, & Martin, 1983). This may account for their success in learning and later performing procedures while failing to recall the context in which that procedural learning took place (N. J. Cohen & Squire, 1980; Corkin, 1968; Milner, Corkin, & Teuber, 1968). Although some structures of previously acquired knowledge (remote memory) are somewhat inaccessible in KD, most aspects of semantic memory are remarkably intact when compared to the readily apparent failures in episodic memory. That is, comparably episodic-memory-impaired PD patients suffer far more in terms of semantic-memory functions (Weingartner et al., 1983). In addition, although conceptual thinking and language processing are somewhat impaired in KD patients, the extent of these cognitive dysfunctions is also not sufficient to account for the severity of recent memory failure. To the naive observer, it is puzzling that the KD patient, who seems reasonably cognitive intact, remembers so very little of ongoing experience.

KD patients also appear amotivational and apathetic. It appears almost as if little of their ongoing cognitive behavior is susceptible to effective and differentiated reinforcement. This lack of drive has frequently been observed, but has not been related in a systematic manner to the nature of the KD memory impairment; it may reflect the effects of limbic system lesions and related neurochemical disturbances. Perhaps the KD memory impairment is a reflection of lesions that disrupt the functional relationship of reward and reinforcement and memory.

Depression (Failure of Effortful Cognitive Operations)

Depressed patients often complain of difficulties in concentration, attention, learning, and memory; much of their subjective experience is confirmed by clinical examinations and laboratory tests of these cognitive functions. The scope and picture of depression-related cognitive impairment may superficially resemble those evident in PD patients. However, the determinants and structure of the cognitive impairment in depressed patients are different and distinguishable from the superficially similar impairments evident in early-stage PD patients.

Depressed patients fail to learn and remember information that requires sustained effort (R. Cohen, Cohen, Weingartner, Smallberg, & Murphy, 1982; Reus, Silberman, Post, & Weingartner, 1979) or the use of elaborate rather than superficial cognitive operations. Cognitive impairments tend not to be evident when the patients are processing and later remembering information that is organized for them and therefore requires little cognitive effort in transforming and then encoding. Similarly, in asking subjects to remember previously processed events, retrieval conditions that require little effort, such as recognition memory, are less likely to indicate impaired memory than those that require more extensive and complex operations. There is also some laboratory data that would suggest that these disruptions in effortful cognitive processes are mediated by changes in catecholamine activity, since drugs that stimulate this system primarily affect effortful processes (Reus et al., 1979). Cognitive operations that can be accomplished relatively automatically are left unimpaired. In addition, while conceptual, procedural, and logical operations are disrupted to some extent in very depressed patients, access to previous knowledge is usually complete and effective if sufficient time is available to the patients. Drugs that disrupt catecholamine activities produce a cognitive picture similar to the one that appears in depression. This pattern of depression-related cognitive impairments should be quite distinct from that seen in PD patients. However, one complicated issue that contributes to the problem of discriminating cognitive failure in depression and in PD is that early-stage PD patients also often present with a depressed picture, which represents a response to their progressive decrease in cognitive effectiveness.

Brain-State-Dependent Learning and Memory
(Context-Dependent Encoding and Retrieval of Information)

A good deal of processed information that is stored in memory is often not freely memorable. When we ask subjects to freely remember previously experienced events without cues or prompts, they may fail to recall or access these events, even though they are available in memory. Such memory failures can be misinterpreted as failures of learning, consolidation, or recent memory. In some instances, such cognitive dysfunctions occur because information has been stored or acquired in one contextual state, such as a mood-specific condition or a drug-altered state, and retrieval is attempted in a very different state. This context-dependent memory failure has been labeled "dissociative" or "state-dependent" learning. It has been most frequently documented in studies of animal learning, but many demonstrations of the phenomena in humans now exist (Overton, 1974; Weingartner, 1978). We know that ethanol, marijuana, and cholinergic drugs, as well as mood states, bias how information is encoded and what types of retrieval strategies subjects generate in searching their memory (Weingartner, 1978). This type of memory failure is really a retrieval failure, since reinstituting context or providing subjects with an appropriate retrieval scheme allows them to recover previously stored experiences.

Neuropharmacological Treatments That Alter Learning and Memory

The cognitive effects of cholinergic, noradrenergic, and dopaminergic drugs, as well as neuropeptides, have been tested extensively (Dunn, 1980; Squire & Davis, 1981). Drugs that affect the serotonin and gamma-aminobutyric acid (GABA) systems have not been relatively well explored in humans, and few of the existing studies have been accomplished in unimpaired subjects. Consequently, there are few data about the specific ways in which learning and memory changes are related to different types of drug treatment. Instead, research efforts have focused on how drugs might reverse cognitive dysfunctions in patients suffering from a variety of disorders. However, useful evaluation and appreciation of these clinical research findings must rest on knowledge about both the biological response of a given drug treatment and the determinants and structure of the target cognitive dysfunction.

Based on an evaluation of the neuropharmacological cognitive studies in humans, it is possible at least to sketch the structure of the psychobiological cognitive response to drug stimuli with relatively specific effects in the central nervous system. In unimpaired subjects, cholinergic antagonists appear to mimic the type of learning–memory failure associated with dementing illness of an Alzheimer type (Caine, Weingartner, Ludlow, & Cudahy, 1981; Drachman & Leavitt, 1974). Cholinergic agonists reverse some of the cognitive disruptions produced by cholinergic antagonists (Sitaram, Weingartner, & Gillin, 1978). Cholinergic agonists, by themselves, appear to affect many aspects of learning and memory, including a consolidation phase of memory processes (Davis, Mohs, Tinklenberg, 1978; Weingartner, Sitaram, & Gillin, 1979).

Drugs that increase catecholamine activity appear to facilitate relatively specific aspects of learning and memory, while drugs that block catecholamine activity disrupt similar kinds of learning–memory processes. The pattern of these cognitive changes is similar to that seen in depression (Reus et al., 1979; Weingartner, Rapoport, Buchsbaum, Bunney, Ebert, Mikkelsen, & Caine, 1980). For example, catecholamine antagonists such as α-methylparatyrosine impair learning and memory while also depressing mood, motivation, and drive. Unlike the situation with cholinergic antagonists, it is the strength and retrieval potential of acquired information that is disrupted by such catecholamine antagonists, although some learning (albeit weak) does take place. The inverse of this pattern of cognitive change is produced by catecholamine agonists such as amphetamine

(Weingartner *et al.*, 1980). Here too, it is the strength of the memory trace and of sustained cognitive effort that seems to be affected most by such drug treatments.

Drugs that alter neuropeptide activity, such as naloxone, can affect "automatic" cognitive processes, while other peptides such as adrenocorticotrophic hormone (ACTH) or its fragments can selectively affect attention (R. Cohen *et al.*, 1983), or, in the case of vasopressin, access to semantic memory and encoding operations (Weingartner, Gold, Ballenger, Smallberg, Post, & Goodwin, 1981; Weingartner, Kaye, Ebert, Gillin, Petersen, & Smallberg, 1981). This class of agents tends to alter cognition more as a drug that would ordinarily affect catecholamine activity would, rather than as a cholinergic drug would. This may be explained by the central nervous system response to neuropeptide treatments.

Much work remains to be completed if we are to obtain a clear picture of how drugs alter learning, memory, and related cognitive processes. However, despite incomplete knowledge, we have many examples of specificity in the cognitive changes produced by different types of drug treatments. The form of these drug-related memory and learning changes parallels the patterns of cognitive dysfunction seen in psychiatric and neurological syndromes.

Summary

Different types of cognitive processes are mediated by different psychobiological mechanisms. This is suggested by studies of specific disruptions of brain systems, such as those produced by learning–memory failures associated with central nervous system lesions, and cognitive changes produced by drugs that alter different neurochemical systems. Studies in impaired and unimpaired subjects, as well as data from studies of memory processes in lower animals, point to the likelihood that cognitive processes, including memory, learning, and information processing, can fail in different ways. Some of the specific types of cognitive operations in which alterations can result in learning–memory changes are attention; short-term versus long-term memory; elaborative and effortful cognitive processes, in contrast to automatic processing operations; acquisition versus retrieval of information in memory; the encoding and transformation of attended events; access and use of well-learned knowledge in semantic memory; and reward-related versus reward-independent learning and memory. Drugs that disrupt different neurochemical systems can mimic neuropathologically specific forms of memory impairments. Similarly, specific neurochemical agonists can reverse or attenuate different forms of cognitive impairments.

REFERENCES

Atkinson, R. C., & Shiffrin, R. M. Human memory: A proposed system and its control processes. In K. W. Spence & J. T. Spence (Eds.), *The psychology of learning and motivation: Advances in theory and research* (Vol. 2). New York: Academic Press, 1968.

Butters, N., & Cermak, L. S. *Alcoholic Korsakoff's syndrome.* New York: Academic Press, 1980.

Cain, E. D., Weingartner, H., Ludlow, C. L., & Cudahy, E. A. Qualitative analysis of scopolamine-induced amnesia. *Psychopharmacology*, 1981, *74*, 74–80.

Cohen, N. J., & Squire, L. R. Preserved learning and retention of pattern-analyzing skill in amnesia: Dissociation of knowing how and knowing that. *Science*, 1980, *210*, 207–210.

Cohen, R., Cohen, M., Weingartner, H., & Pickar, D. High dose naloxone affects task performance in normal subjects. *Psychiatry Research*, 1983, *8*, 127–136.

Cohen, R., Cohen, M., Weingartner, H., Smallberg, S., & Murphy, D. L. Effort in cognitive processes in depression. *Archives of General Psychiatry*, 1982, *39*, 593–597.

Constantinidis, J. Is Alzheimer's disease a major form of senile dementia?: Clinical, anatomical, and genetic data. In R. Katzman, R. D. Terry, & K. L. Bick (Eds.), *Alzheimer's disease.* New York; Raven Press, 1978.

Corkin, S. Acquisition of motor skill after bilateral medial temporal-lobe excision. *Neuropsychologia*, 1968, *6*, 255–266.

Craik, F. I. M. Age differences in human memory. In J. E. Birren & K. W. Schaie (Eds.), *Handbook of the psychology of aging.* New York: Van Nostrand Reinhold, 1977.

Craik, F. I. M., & Lockhart, R. S. Levels of processing: A framework for memory research. *Journal of Verbal Learning and Verbal Behavior*, 1972, *11*, 671–684.

Craik, F. I. M., & Tulving, E. Depth of processing and the retention of words in episodic memory. *Journal of Experimental Psychology: General*, 1975, *1*, 268–294.

Davis, K. L., Mohs, R. C., & Tinklenberg, J. Physostigmine: Improvement of long-term memory processes in normal humans. *Science*, 1978, *201*, 272–274.

de Ajuriaguerra, J., & Tissot, R. Some aspects of language in various forms of senile dementia (Comparisons with language in childhood). In E. H. Lenneberg & E. Lenneberg (Eds.), *Foundation of language development.* New York: Academic Press, 1975.

Drachman, D. A., & Leavitt, J. Human memory and the cholinergic system. *Archives of Neurology*, 1974, *30*, 113–121.

Dunn, A. J. Neurochemistry of learning and memory: An evaluation of recent data. *Annual Review of Psychology*, 1980, *18*, 343–390.

Gold, P. E., & McGaugh, J. L. A single-trace, two-process view of memory storage processes. In D. Deutsch & J. A. Deutsch (Eds.), *Short-term memory.* New York: Academic Press, 1975.

Hasher, L., & Zacks, R. T. Automatic and effortful processes in memory. *Journal of Experimental Psychology: General*, 1979, *108*(3), 356–388.

Kornetsky, C., & Esposito, R. U. Reward and detection thresholds for brain stimulation: Dissociative effects of cocaine. *Brain Research*, 1981, *209*, 496–500.

Lewis, D. J. Psychobiology of active and inactive memory. *Psychological Bulletin*, 1979, *88*, 1054–1083.

McGaugh, J. C., & Herz, M. J. *Memory consolidation.* San Francisco: Albion, 1972.

Milber, B. Memory and the medial temporal regions of the brain. In K. H. Pribram & D. E. Broadbent (Eds.), *Biology of memory.* New York: Academic Press, 1970.

Milner, B., Corkin, S., & Teuber, H. L. Further analysis of the hippocampal amnesic syndrome: 14-year follow-up study of human memory. *Neuropsychologica*, 1968, *6*, 215–234.

Mishkin, M. Memory in monkeys severely impaired by combined but not by separate removal of amygdala and hippocampus. *Nature*, 1978, *273*, 297–298.

Overton, D. A. Experimental methods for the study of state-dependent learning. *Federation Proceedings*, 1974, *33*, 1800–1813.

Reus, V. I., Silberman, E., Post, R. M., & Weingartner, H. D-Amphetamine: Effects on memory in a depressed population. *Biological Psychiatry*, 1979, *14*, 345–356.

Sitaram, N., Weingartner, H., & Gillin, J. C. Human serial learning: Enhancement with arecholine and choline and impairment with scopolamine. *Science*, 1978, *201*, 274–276.

Squire, L. R., & Davis, H. P. The pharmacology of memory: A neurobiological perspective. *Annual Review of Pharmacology and Toxicology*, 1981, *21*, 323–356.

Tulving, E. Episodic and semantic memory. In E. Tulving & W. Donaldson (Eds.), *Organization and memory.* London: Academic Press, 1972.

Tulving, E., & Thompson, D. M. Encoding specificity and retrieval processes in episodic memory. *Psychological Review*, 1973, *80*, 352–373.

Tulving, E., & Watkins, M. J. Structure of memory traces. *Psychological Bulletin*, 1975, *82*, 261–275.

Victor, M., Adams, R. D., & Collins, G. H. *The Wernicke-Korsakoff syndrome.* Oxford, Blackwell, 1971.

Warrington, E. K. The double dissociation of short- and long-term memory deficits. In L. S. Cermak (Ed.), *Human memory and amnesia.* Hillsdale, N.J.: Erlbaum, 1982.

Waugh, N. C., & Norman, D. A. Primary memory. *Psychological Review*, 1965, *72*, 89–104.

Weingartner, H. Human state-dependent learning. In B. T. Ho, D. W. Richards, & D. C. Chute (Eds.), *Drug discrimination and state-dependent learning.* New York: Academic Press, 1978.

Weingartner, H., Gold, P. W., Ballenger, J. C., Smallberg, S. A., Post, R. M., & Goodwin, P. K. Effects of vasopressin on memory. *Science*, 1981, *211*, 601–603.

Weingartner, H., Grafman, J., Boutelle, W., Kaye, W., & Martin, P. Forms of cognitive failure. *Science*, 1983, *221*, 380–382.

Weingartner, H., Kaye, W., Ebert, M., Gillin, J. C., Petersen, R. C., & Smallberg, S. A. Effects of vasopressin on cognitive impairments in dementia. *Life Sciences*, 1981, *29*, 2721–2726.

Weingartner, H., Kaye, W., Smallberg, S. A., Ebert, H., Gillin, J. C., & Sitaram, N. Memory failures in progressive idiopathic dementia. *Journal of Abnormal Psychology*, 1981, *49*(3), 187–196.

Weingartner, H., Kaye, W., Smallberg, S. A., Cohen, R., Ebert, M. H., Gillin, J. C., & Gold, P. Determinants of memory failures in dementia. In S. Corkin, K. Davis, J. Growden, & K. Wiertman (Eds.), *Alzheimer's disease: A Review of progress.* (Vol. 19). New York: Raven Press, 1982.

Weingartner, H., Rapoport, J. L., Buchsbaum, M. S., Bunney, W. E., Ebert, M. H., Mikkelsen, E. J., & Caine, E. D. Cognitive processes in normal and hyperactive children and their response to amphetamine treatment. *Journal of Abnormal Psychology*, 1980, *89*(1), 25–37.

Weingartner, H., & Silberman, E., Models of cognitive impairment. *Psychopharmacology Bulletin*, 1982, *2*, 27–42.

Weingartner, H., Sitaram, N., & Gillin, J. C. The role of the cholinergic nervous system in memory consolidation. *Bulletin of the Psychonomic Society*, 1979, *13*, 9–11.

Zacks, R. T., Hasher, L., & Snaft, H. Automatic encoding of event frequency: Further findings. *Journal of Experimental Psychology*, 1982, *8*(2), 106–116.

21

Assessments of Drug Effects on Human Memory Functions

Jared R. Tinklenberg and Joy L. Taylor

Introduction

During the last few years, we and our collaborators have studied the effects of a wide range of psychoactive drugs on human memory functions. These drugs have included the traditional central nervous system stimulants (amphetamine and methylphenidate), the hypnotics (secobarbital, triazolam, and flurazepam), and anxiolytic (diazepam), an antihistamine (diphenhydramine), and the oral opiate-like drug methadone. We have also investigated some of the cognitive effects of alcohol and cannabis. Recently, we have focused on drugs that in nonhuman studies have improved performance on certain behavioral tasks and thus may have potential for enhancing human memory performance. These drugs include cholinergic agonists, adrenocorticotrophic hormone (ACTH)-like and vasopressin-like peptides, dihydroergotoxine mesylate, and naftidrofuryl.

We have attempted to design our studies so that memory changes induced by these pharmacological interventions could be interpreted in terms of existing models of human information processing (Atkinson & Shiffrin, 1968; Sternberg, 1966, 1969). We had initially hoped that by making systematic pharmacological interventions, drug effects on specific memory functions, such as encoding or consolidation, could be precisely identified. Our findings so far indicate that obtaining such specificity is difficult. Instead, one theme that has emerged from investigating this range of drugs with varying pharmacological characteristics is that their behavioral effects have not been confined to specific memory functions—much less to memory itself. Effects on clerical speed, tracking accuracy, and reaction time (RT) have been observed as well. Perhaps most importantly, the effects of a given drug on nonmemory and memory tasks are usually in the same direction. If a drug impairs verbal recall, for example, it generally impairs RT as well, and vice versa. These results lead us to conclude that many psychoactive agents produce pervasive rather than specific behavioral effects.

Some initial trials of psychoactive drugs have produced results that were at first interpreted as specific drug effects on discrete memory functions. For example, the first studies of ACTH-like peptides suggested that they might enhance "short-term" memory (de Wied & Bohus, 1966). But subsequent studies of these peptides in both humans and nonhumans using different paradigms and experimental manipulations indicated their

Jared R. Tinklenberg and Joy L. Taylor. Laboratory of Clinical Psychopharmacology and Psychophysiology, Veterans Administration Medical Center, Palo Alto, California; Department of Psychiatry and Behavioral Sciences, Stanford University School of Medicine, Stanford, California.

behavioral effects are more pervasive. ACTH-like peptides have been shown to facilitate performance on a range of tasks, including some that do not have a memory component (Tinklenberg & Thornton, 1983). Effects on generalized, nonspecific processes such as attention have become more likely explanations for the behavioral activity of ACTH-like peptides (Kastin, Olson, Sandman, & Coy, 1981; Pigache & Rigter, 1981). For these reasons, we are now hesitant to ascribe specific memory effects to a drug unless the experiment explicitly measures possible drug effects on attention, arousal, and other memory-modulating processes as well.

This theme has led us increasingly to shift away from research strategies that approach drug effects in terms of discrete cognitive functions to a more general, nonspecific perspective. Our current strategy is to attempt to identify one or more factors that could account for such pervasive effects on performance. These factors include attention, arousal, motivation, and affect. To implement this approach, we have found dual tasks to be useful, especially in combination with simultaneous measurements of electrophysiological variables. The dual tasks are used to evaluate attentional "capacity," and the concurrent measures of electrophysiology are used to assess changes in arousal. The next two sections outline our use of dual-task and electrophysiological techniques. Since dual tasks have not been extensively used in studies of drugs and memory function, they are presented here in some detail.

Use of Dual-Task Methodology to Assess Attentional Capacity

In this section, we describe how dual tasks are used to measure attentional capacity indirectly—in particular, how this technique may be applied to the study of drug effects. Some results from two experiments that used this technique to look at the effects of acute doses of benzodiazepines are presented. But first, we describe what we mean by the term "attentional capacity" and what assumptions underlie this model of attention.

Attention as a Limited, Allocatable Resource

Attention involves a "focusing of consciousness." However, as Kahneman (1973) pointed out, the act of focusing entails more than just selecting an object or activity to attend to. We can focus attention in varying degrees of intensity. Moreover, we can divide our attention between activities; however, there is a definite limit on our capacity to do this. When the two activities are easy and undemanding, they can be carried out together with little sense of mental strain. For example, we can plan our day while driving to work. When the difficulty of one or both tasks is increased, limits on simultaneous task performance emerge. Parallel parking, for example, is sufficiently demanding that conversation may be temporarily interrupted. In this case, it seems that attentional resources are diverted away from talking to steering in order to park the car successfully.

These properties of attention led Kahneman (1973) to characterize attention as a limited but allocatable reserve of mental processing capacity necessary for carrying out mental work. The allocation of attention is in some instances voluntary (e.g., as in reading this chapter) and in others involuntary (e.g., as in responding to the call of one's name). In the present discussion, we focus entirely upon conditions involving the voluntary allocation of attention.

A Sketch of the Dual-Task Methodology

The dual-task method is designed to measure attentional capacity indirectly. Essentially, the technique entails having the subject perform two activities simultaneously. In addition, the subject performs each task individually to provide a baseline for the dual-task condition. The decrement in performance observed when the two tasks are done together, relative to the performance observed when they are done separately, provides a measure of the extent to which the available attentional capacity is exceeded. The underlying rationale is presented by Kahneman (1973) and by Norman and Bobrow (1975). Basically, they assume that attentional demands are additive. As long as the joint attentional demands of the two tasks do not exceed attentional capacity, the two tasks can be executed together with no decrement in performance. Simultaneous task performance falters at the point where the combined attentional demands of the two tasks exceed the available capacity. Hence, larger dual-task decrements reflect greater attentional "overloads."

For the dual-task methodology to be a valid measure of attentional capacity, the choice of task pairs is important. Obviously, the two tasks must not be so difficult or incompatible with each other that they cannot be done simultaneously. Conversely, the tasks should be sufficiently attention-demanding that they interfere with each other to a measurable extent. In Kahneman's terminology, sufficient "capacity interference" should be present. It is capacity interference that is of interest; thus, "structural interference" between the two tasks (e.g., attempting to look in two different places at the same time) should be minimized. Consequently, the two tasks chosen should be unlike each other, particularly in terms of perceptual and motor requirements. The attentional literature provides more detailed guidelines for selecting a pair of dual tasks (e.g., see Kerr, 1973; Navon & Gopher, 1979; Norman & Bobrow, 1975).

A study of Lansman (1978) provides an example of the dual-task methodology. A verbal short-term memory task was paired with a simple RT task. The memory task, adapted from Atkinson and Shiffrin's (1968) work, required the subject to keep track of a continually changing set of letter–digit pairs. The RT task involved pressing a key in response to a tone. During the time that subjects were studying the paired associates, the tone was presented at quasi-random intervals. The subjects were never required to recall the paired associates and respond to the tone at the same time.

In the dual-task condition, both recall accuracy and RT were worse, relative to the single-task conditions, in which subjects only rehearsed the paired associates or only listened for the tone. For instance, in the single-task/RT-only conditon, subjects' RTs averaged near 300 msec. When they attempted to rehearse two letter–digit pairs and listen for the tone, their RTs were slowed by over 100 msec. Attempting to rehearse four letter–digit pairs slowed responding to the tone by an additional 40 msec. This result—a slowing in the RT task that is dependent upon the difficulty of the memory task—is most significant. It indicates that the decrement in dual-task performance is not simply a matter of having to coordinate two activities, but that it is also a function of the difficulty or attentional demands of the tasks.

Application of the Dual-Task Methodology to Human Psychopharmacology

The dual-task method can be used to provide a means of measuring a drug's effect on available attentional capacity. This is a most important endeavor, since attentional capacity is considered to underlie nearly every aspect of performance. In memory tasks, for example, the effectiveness of encoding new information has been considered dependent upon attentional resources (Rabinowitz, Craik, & Ackerman, 1982).

We want to emphasize, however, that the measure of "attentional capacity" obtained using these techniques will reflect the capacity available for performing laboratory tasks, rather than the individual's full attentional capacity. The full attentional capacity of an individual probably cannot be measured. Hence, a drug effect on "attentional capacity" does not imply that total attentional capacity is altered. It is conceivable that a drug could alter the amount of attentional resources allocated to the experimental tasks without altering a person's full attentional capacity. A change in motivation could do this. Presently, we have no appropriate means of objectively quantifying changes in motivation. Thus, the dual-task measure of attentional capacity should be interpreted as a measure of available attentional capacity rather than full attentional capacity.

Regardless of whether a drug is affecting full or available attentional capacity, the dual-task technique should be more sensitive than single-task methods. Indeed, in some situations, the single-task condition may not show a reliable drug effect at all. This is because performing a single task may not sufficiently tax attention. Suppose, for example, that under the placebo condition, performing a task at a given level of proficiency requires 75% of an individual's capacity. If, under the drug, capacity is reduced such that achieving the same level of performance now requires 90% of available capacity, the drugged individual will still be able to match the placebo condition. Intuitively, we might describe this as being able to compensate for the effect of the drug by expending more mental effort. Performing two tasks at the same time, which presumably exceeds capacity, would be necessary to detect a reliable and observable effect of the drug.

The dual-task technique has been used primarily in basic research on attention and information-processing demands (e.g., see reviews by Kahneman, 1973; Kerr, 1973; Navon & Gopher, 1979) and in applied research on human factors (e.g., Brown, Simmons, & Tickner, 1967). In the field of human psychopharmacology, it has been used to our knowledge only by Truijens, Trumbo, and Wagenaar (1976) and by us (Hunt & Tinklenberg, 1984; Taylor, 1982).

We now describe two experiments using the dual-task technique to study the effects of acute doses of benzodiazepine. (More complete details are given in Taylor, 1982.) In both experiments, young men received diazepam, flurazepam, or placebo in a double-blind crossover design.

In the first experiment, there were four drug conditions: flurazepam 30 mg at night and placebo the next morning; diazepam 5 mg at night and 5 mg the next morning; diazepam 10 + 10 mg; and placebo both night and morning. Subjects were tested twice in the morning, beginning 1 hour after the morning capsule was taken.

The dual tasks were a verbal short-term memory paired-associates task and a simple RT task adapted from the work of Lansman (1978) and Lansman and Hunt (1982). In the memory task, subjects had to keep track of seven letter–digit pairs. The letter–digit pairs changed continually throughout a 5-minute sequence of trials, such that each time the subject recalled the digit paired with a letter, a new digit was then assigned to the letter. Subjects had 3 seconds to study each new pairing; during some of the study intervals, a tone was sounded. Subjects were instructed to press a key in response to the tone as quickly as possible, but without severely disrupting their concentration on the memory task. If subjects failed to respond to the tone within 1.5 seconds, a "response failure" was recorded.

There were two task conditions: a single-task condition, in which the only task was listening for the tone, and the dual-task condition. The typical dual-task pattern was observed. When the subjects just listened for the tone, RTs averaged about 240 msec. When subjects were given the dual task of studying the paired associates and responding to the tone, RTs to the tone were nearly doubled. Of primary interest was the effect of the drug in the dual-task condition as compared to the single-task condition. In the single task condition, only the higher dose of diazepam (10 + 10 mg) produced a reliable slowing of approximately 40 msec ($p < .05$). Flurazepam and the lower dose of diazepam did not reliably slow RT. Greater slowing was seen for all three active drug conditions in the dual-task condition during the first test session. At this time, flurazepam slowed RTs by 70 msec ($p < .10$), and both doses of diazepam prolonged RTs between 90 and 100 msec ($p < .05$). At the second test session, 2 hours later, the dual-task condition did not show any greater slowing than the single-task condition.

A second interesting effect concerned the number of times subjects failed to respond to the tone within 1.5 seconds. All three active drug conditions increased the frequency of response failures, particularly in the dual-task condition. For example, diazepam 10 + 10 mg increased the number of response failures in the dual-task condition in 12 of 16 subjects (two made more response failures under placebo, and two showed no change; $p < .01$ by the sign test). In the single-task condition, six subjects had more failures ($p < .10$ by the sign test; one made more response failures under placebo, and nine showed no change). The frequency of response failures while under the benzodiazepines was relatively low (about 5% of the trials); however, this rate was twice that of the placebo condition.

Finally, there was no significant effect of any active drug on the accuracy of recalling the paired associates. Accuracy was lowest in the diazepam 10 + 10 mg condition (68% correct) and highest in the placebo condition (72%), but these differences were not statistically reliable ($p > .25$).

To summarize, the benzodiazepines produced a larger dual-task decrement, particularly in the number of response failures in the RT task. This pattern of drug effects is consistent with the notion that the benzodiazepines reduce available attentional capacity. How is it that the greater dual-task decrement emerged in the RT task, more so than in the memory task? One explanation of these results is that RT was particularly vulnerable to the effects of the drugs, because it held lower priority than the memory task. Recall that subjects were instructed not to allow responding to the tone to interfere with their concentration on the paired associates. Using the economic analogy of resource allocation, the lower-priority task would be expected to suffer more if there were a "cutback" in processing resources. Resources to the higher-priority task would remain fairly constant.

Other explanations have nothing to do with task priority. We could hypothesize that the effect was specific to one of the tasks. For example, the drug may have impaired the proficiency or rate of rehearsing the paired associates. Consequently a greater proportion of attentional resources was necessary for maintaining memory accuracy, and fewer resources were available for the RT task.

To explore the nature of dual-task decrements fully, we really need to examine dual-task performance under a wider range of conditions. One means of doing this is to ask the subject to make tradeoffs between the two tasks. In one block of trials, we might instruct subjects to give higher priority to the memory task, and then, in a later block of trials, to give higher priority to the RT task. Varying the priorities in both directions has two advantages. First, it provides a measure of a subject's ability to shift priorities from one task to the other while under the influence of a drug. Second, it permits a much stronger interpretation of the form of the dual-task decrement. If a drug produces a larger dual-task decrement, and the decrement emerges in whichever task has the lower priority, this finding would support the notions that (1) there is a reduction in available capacity and (2) the effect is not task-specific.

In the second experiment (Taylor, 1982), we studied the effects of diazepam (10 + 10 mg) on dual-task performance, in which the priorities of the tasks were varied relative to each other. In addition to the two dual-task conditions, there were two baseline conditions in which each task was performed alone. In this experiment, the two tasks were a spatial short-term memory task and a choice RT task designed by Lansman and Farr (1981). For the memory task, seven plus signs appeared in a random order. The pluses were presented sequentially within a 3×4 grid, but no two pluses ever appeared in the same location. Subjects were given 3 seconds to memorize the pattern. After a 1.5-second delay, subjects were prompted to mimic the sequence by pressing keys on a telephone touch pad. For the RT task, tones were presented to the left and right ears, and it was the subject's task to press one of two keys corresponding to the ear in which the tone was presented. In the dual-task conditions, the tone was always presented during the 3-second study interval. Responses to the two tasks were always at different times and with different hands to minimize structural interference.

Subjects were instructed as to which task should receive the higher priority in each of the two dual-task conditions. However, subjects were explicitly advised that they should not completely ignore the lower-priority task. A nominal payoff system was used to induce subjects to follow the priority instructions. Points were awarded for high levels of performance on both tasks, but the total number of points that could be earned was far greater for the higher-priority task.

Subjects received either diazepam (10 + 10 mg) or placebo in a double-blind crossover design. As in the first experiment, there were two administrations of diazepam: the first at bedtime and the second at 8 A.M. the following day. This particular set of tasks began 2 hours after the administration of the second capsule and lasted 1 hour. Two other tests not described here preceded and followed the dual tasks.

As described earlier, it was predicted that diazepam would produce a larger dual-task decrement and that the decrement would appear primarily in the lower-priority task. There were interesting trends suggesting this pattern of drug effects; however, the differences were not statistically reliable. We first describe the effects of diazepam on the spatial-pattern task in the three task conditions: (1) pattern only; (2) dual-task, with pattern having high priority; and (3) dual-task, with pattern having low priority. Diazepam impaired the recall of the pattern in both dual-task conditions and in the single-task condition as well ($p < .025$). Table 21-1 provides the breakdowns for each task condition. As the table indicates, there was a trend for the diazepam–placebo difference to be larger in the low-priority condition than in the single- and high-priority conditions (.08 vs. .05); however, the interaction between drug and priority condition was not significant. Finally, as the table shows, all subjects, regardless of drug condition, were quite adept at prioritizing the two tasks in accordance with the point system. Memory accuracy under both drug and placebo was highest in the single-task and dual-task/high-priority conditions and lowest in the dual-task/low-priority condition. These results indicate that diazepam did not markedly affect the ability to trade off resources among tasks.

The pattern of drug effects was similar for the RT task. These results are shown in Figure 21-1. Recall accuracy for the pattern (see Table 21-1) is plotted alongside the RT to show the tradeoff in task priorities between the pattern task and the RT task. In every task condition, diazepam slowed RTs to a marginally significant degree ($p < .10$). Again, the slowing of RT tended to be greatest when the RT task was given lower priority. The diazepam–placebo difference was 10 msec in the single-task condition and 13 msec in the high-priority condition. This difference is in contrast to a 60-msec elevation when the tone had a lower priority. Despite these trends, there was little statistical indication of an interaction between drug and task priority ($p > .20$).

The results of the memory and RT tasks, considered together, do not indicate reduced available capacity under diazepam. We consider these trends to be quite interesting. The present experiment involved only 12 subjects. A larger-scale study would probably provide the statistical power necessary to detect reliably larger dual-task decrements.

So far, we have been discussing attentional capacity without regard to its inter-relationships with arousal. In the theoretical literature concerning the model of attentional resources, capacity is generally treated as a fixed, unchanging quantity for the sake of simplicity. However, attentional capacity most likely fluctuates from moment to moment. These fluctuations interact with arousal in a complex fashion (e.g., see Pribram & McGuinness, 1975, in press). Attentional capacity and arousal appear to vary together in the lower and midrange levels of arousal. When arousal is high, allocation of capacity becomes both more uneven and less precise (Kahneman, 1973), and "cue utilization"

TABLE 21-1. Mean Proportion Correct for Recall of Pattern

Drug condition	Single-task condition	Dual-task condition		Mean
		High priority	Low priority	
Diazepam 10 + 10	.69	.65	.52	.62
Placebo	.74	.71	.60	.68

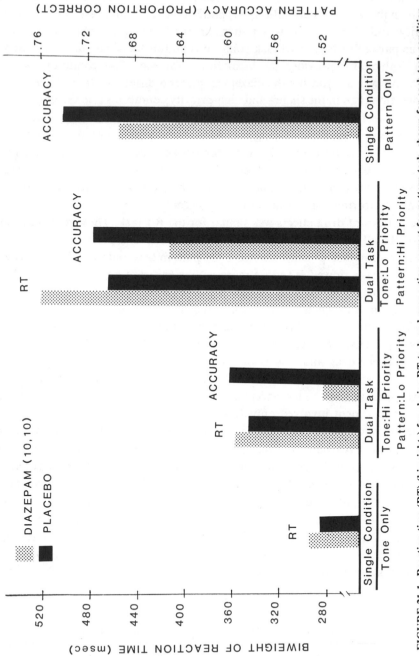

FIGURE 21-1. Reaction time (RT) (biweights) for choice RT task and proportion correct for pattern task, shown for each task condition.

narrows (Easterbrook, 1959). Dual-task performance requires sensitivity to a wider range of cues than does single-task performance. Therefore, if a subject is too highly aroused, his or her dual-task performance may be impaired, especially if a narrow focus of attention is undesirable (Easterbrook, 1959).

Because of these complexities, we find concomitant electrophysiological measures of arousal especially useful to interpret drug effects on task performance. The next section gives an example of these measures. Since electrophysiological measures have been extensively used in drug studies, we do not present technical details, which are available elsewhere (e.g., Tinklenberg, Roth, Pfefferbaum, & Kopell, 1983). What we wish to emphasize is the simultaneous application of these electrophysiological techniques with dual tasks.

Concurrent Electrophysiological Measurements

To help differentiate possible drug effects on specific aspects of memory from effects on nonspecific memory-modulating processes, we find it useful to employ physiological monitoring techniques concurrently with behavioral measures. Of the many possible physiological parameters that might reflect drug effects on the memory-modulating processes often termed "arousal," we have particularly focused on electrophysiological measures of brain activity. The spontaneous electroencephalogram (EEG) and event-related potentials (ERPs) provide useful information when used in conjunction with dual-task performance measures such as those outlined in the previous section. When the EEG is recorded during the task performance and analyzed by fast Fourier transformation, quantitative information is obtained about its power and frequency distribution. These frequency-spectral analyses given general neurophysiological information about the state of the central nervous system during the task performance and provide indices that probably reflect the central level of arousal or activation of the individual at each instant during the task. The capacity for virtually continuous and instantaneous electrophysiological monitoring offers advantages over biochemical measures that may reflect certain memory-modulating processes (e.g., plasma norepinephrine levels, in which continuous measures are difficult or impossible and cannot be time-locked to behavioral performance at a given instant). Since these EEG measures are independent of language, some of the difficulties associated with traditional subjective reports on arousal or activation are circumvented. In addition, EEG changes, as such, are not perceived by the subjects. Subjects cannot monitor "how well" they are doing. Hence, it is difficult to bias EEG results volitionally in a desired direction, and some subjects are less likely to show catastrophic "test anxiety." Additional advantages of electrophysiological measures in drug studies are presented elsewhere (Tinklenberg et al., 1983).

Although our laboratory has emphasized measurement of brain physiology, in certain studies we also monitor other physiological parameters, such as heart rate, temperature, and skin conductance. These peripheral indices may not reflect levels of central nervous system arousal as directly as EEG measures, but in some instances may alert the investigator to nonspecific influences on overall behavioral performance. Since arousal and other memory-modulating processes are probably not unitary phenomena, we argue that any one or two of these peripheral measures used separately may miss important information about drug effects on these processes. Thus, we prefer to employ multiple physiological measures of these peripheral variables. With the advent of microcomputer technology, multiple physiological measures can be made efficiently and economically.

In some instances, simultaneous measures of multiple physiological variables is essential, since monitoring the effects of a drug on a single peripheral parameter will be misleading. The complex reflexes involved in cardiovascular changes provide a salient example. Drug-associated changes in heart rate cannot be easily interpreted unless changes in blood pressure, pulse volume, peripheral resistance, posture, and activity are simultaneously measured. Simple inferences that an increased heart rate reflects greater arousal and a decreased rate less arousal can be erroneous. Obrist (1981) provides a more detailed discussion of this important issue.

Conclusion

In summary, we are impressed by the pervasive behavioral effects of most psychoactive drugs on human memory performance. Although these effects are sometimes interpreted as changes in specific memory functions, we argue that these results can usually be explained more accurately in terms of drug-induced alterations in nonspecific modulating processes, such as attention or arousal. From this perspective, we have been adopting the strategy of explicitly testing for changes in these processes when we make pharmacological interventions in human memory performance. Dual-task methodologies, especially when used with concurrent electrophysiological monitoring, appear to be useful for this explicit testing.

ACKNOWLEDGMENTS

Preparation of this chapter was supported by the Medical Research Service of the Veterans Administration, NIMH Grants MH36609 and MH16744-03, and Palo Alto Veterans Administration–Stanford Clinical Research Grant MH30854.

REFERENCES

Atkinson, R. C., & Shiffrin, R. M. Human memory: A proposed system and its control processes. In K. W. Spence & J. T. Spence (Eds.), *The psychology of learning and motivation: Advances in research and theory* (Vol. 2). New York: Academic Press, 1968.

Brown, I. D., Simmons, D. C., & Tickner, A. H. Measurement of control skills, vigilance, and performance on a subsidiary task during 12 hours of car driving. *Ergonomics*, 1967, *10*, 665–673.

de Wied, D., & Bohus, B. Long term and short term effects on retention of a conditioned avoidance response in rats by treatment with long acting pitressin and alpha-MSH. *Nature*, 1966, *212*, 1481–1486.

Easterbrook, J. A. The effect of emotion on cue utilization and the organization of behavior. *Psychological Review*, 1959, *66*, 183–201.

Hunt, E. B., & Tinklenberg, J. R. *A methodology for studying the effects of drugs on human cognition: An ACTH 4-9 analog (Organon 2766) versus methylphenadate.* Manuscript submitted for publication, 1984.

Kahneman, D. *Attention and effort*. Englewood Cliffs, N.J.: Prentice-Hall, 1973.

Kastin, A. J., Olson, R. D., Sandman, C. A., & Coy, D. H. Multiple independent actions of neuropeptides on behavior. In J. L. Martinez, Jr., R. A. Jensen, R. B. Messing, H. Rigter, & J. L. McGaugh (Eds.), *Endogenous peptides and learning and memory processes*. New York: Academic Press, 1981.

Kerr, B. Processing demands during mental operations. *Memory and Cognition*, 1973, *1*, 401–412.

Lansman, M. *An attentional approach to individual differences in immediate memory*. University of Washington Technical Report, June 1978.

Lansman, M., & Farr, S. *The effect of priority on probe RT*. Paper presented at the meeting of the Psychonomic Society, Philadelphia, November 1981.

Lansman, M., & Hunt, E. Individual differences in secondary task performance. *Memory and Cognition*, 1982, *10*, 10–24.

Navon, D., & Gopher, D. On the economy of the human-processing system. *Psychological Review*, 1979, *86*, 214–255.

Norman, D. A., & Bobrow, D. B. On data-limited and resource-limited processes. *Cognitive Psychology*, 1975, *7*, 44–64.

Obrist, P. A. *Cardiovascular psychophysiology*. New York: Plenum Press, 1981.

Pigache, R. M., & Rigter, H. Effects of peptides related to ACTH on mood and vigilance in man. In T. B. van Wimersma Greidanus (Ed.), *Frontiers of hormone research* (Vol. 8). Basel: Karger, 1981.

Pribram, K. H., & McGuinness, D. Arousal, activation and effort in the control of attention. *Psychological Review*, 1975, *82*(2), 116–149.

Pribram, K. H., & McGuinness, D. Basal forebrain mechanisms in the control of attention. In D. E. Sheer (Ed.), *Houston Symposium on Attention*. New York: Academic Press, in press.

Rabinowitz, J. C., Craik, F. I. M., & Ackerman, B. P. A processing resource account of age differences in recall. *Canadian Journal of Psychology*, 1982, 36, 325–344.

Sternberg, S. High-speed scanning in human memory. *Science*, 1966, *153*, 652–654.

Sternberg, S. The discovery of processing stages: Extensions of Donder's method. In W. G. Koster (Ed.), *Attention and performance II*. Amsterdam: North-Holland, 1969.

Taylor, J. *The effects of benzodiazepines on cognition and performance*. Unpublished doctoral dissertation, University of Washington, 1982.

Tinklenberg, J. R., Roth, W. T., Pfefferbaum, A., & Kopell, B. S. Electrophysiological techniques for geriatric psychopharmacology. In T. J. Crook & S. Ferris (Eds.), *Assessments in geriatric psychopharmacology*. New York: Raven Press, 1983.

Tinklenberg, J. R., & Thornton, J. Neuropeptides in geriatric psychopharmacology. *Psychopharmacology Bulletin*, 1983, *19*, 198–211.

Truijens, C. L., Trumbo, D. A., & Wagenaar, W. A. Amphetamine and barbiturate effects on tasks performed singly and in combination. *Acta Psychologica*, 1976, *40*, 233–244.

Some Behavioral Consequences of Neurochemical Deficits in Korsakoff Psychosis

William J. McEntee and Robert G. Mair

A major achievement of modern neuroanatomy has been the discovery of chemically defined neuronal pathways in the brain that are important for a variety of behavioral functions. Impairments of these neurochemical systems, which presumably synthesize and release specific neurotransmitters, have been implicated in a number of neuropsychiatric diseases, including Parkinson disease, schizophrenia, affective disorders, hyperkinesis (attentional-deficit disorder), and Alzheimer disease, to name a few. To the clinician, a neurochemical approach to the study of neurobehavioral disorders can be a two-edged sword. On the one hand, it can be of heuristic value for understanding the etiology of a neuropsychiatric illness that may not have a clearly localized pathological substrate; the discovery of a neurochemical deficit can also suggest a potential pharmacological treatment for an otherwise untreatable condition. On the other hand, neurochemical measures are influenced by a number of state-dependent variables, and a neurochemical abnormality can be much more difficult to demonstrate clearly than a localized anatomical lesion. This chapter reviews experiments implicating impairments of brain norepinephrine (NE)-containing neuronal systems in Korsakoff psychosis and presents hypotheses we have developed concerning the cognitive consequences of diminished brain NE activity in humans. The discussion illustrates three logical approaches to the neurochemistry of human amnesia. First, we consider evidence that NE activity is diminished in patients with Korsakoff psychosis, and that the degree of this impairment correlates with the severity of the amnesic symptoms of the illness. Second, evidence is reviewed showing that the amnesic symptoms of this disease are improved by treatment with drugs that enhance brain NE activity. Third, behavioral deficits in patients with Korsakoff psychosis are compared to those produced in experimental animals by NE-depleting lesions.

Structure and Function of Central NE Pathways

Cell bodies of NE-containing neurons are located in the brain stem and have axonal projections that ascend and to a lesser extent descend by means of an extensive branching

William J. McEntee and Robert G. Mair. Neurology Service, Veterans Administration Medical Center, Providence, Rhode Island; Division of Neurology, Section of Psychiatry and Human Behavior, Brown University, Providence, Rhode Island.

process that provides terminals throughout the central nervous system (CNS), with very little topographical arrangement (Moore & Bloom, 1979). The locus ceruleus, located in the rostral pons in the lateral extent of the floor of the fourth ventricle, contains the largest collection of NE cell bodies, whose axons ascend in the so-called "dorsal bundle" to form a dense network of NE-releasing terminals throughout the neocortex, with a large input as well to the thalamus, hippocampus, and basal forebrain. Other clusters of NE-containing cell bodies, which compromise the so-called "lateral tegmental group," are located in a number of smaller nuclei scattered through the medulla and pons, which innervate the hypothalamus and other structures in the brain stem, diencephalon, and basal forebrain. The density of NE innervation of cerebral cortex has been estimated at 330,000 terminals per cubic millimeter of rat cerebral cortex, distributed in such a manner that all cortical neurons are within 30 microns of an NE terminal (Descarries, Watkins, & Lapierre, 1977). It has also been demonstrated (Descarries et al., 1977) that the majority of such terminals do not end at classical synapses; this has led to the presumption that most cortical NE is released at nonsynaptic sites in a diffuse fashion and affects a large number of target cells. Thus it seems that the brain noradrenergic system, at least in part, serves a regulatory role for the cerebral cortex.

The physiological properties of NE-containing neurons in the locus ceruleus suggest that the supposed regulatory influence exerted by these neurons on the cerebral cortex may be related to the control of cortical activation. Neurons in the locus ceruleus of cats (Chu & Bloom, 1974), rats (Aston-Jones & Bloom, 1981a; Foote, Aston-Jones, & Bloom, 1980), and squirrel monkeys (Foote et al., 1980) exhibit increased activity, which presumably results in release of increased amounts of NE throughout cerebral cortex, just prior to and throughout the waking phase of the sleep–waking cycle. Similarly, short bursts of locus ceruleus activity have been reported to coincide with phasic changes in EEG activity (Aston-Jones & Bloom, 1981a, 1981b; Chu & Bloom, 1974; Foote et al., 1980). Locus ceruleus neurons have also been shown to be sensitive to external stimulation, being driven at short latencies (15–50 msec) by brief auditory, visual, or somatosensory stimuli, with many being responsive to more than one sensory modality (Aston-Jones & Bloom, 1981b). NE also appears to play a role in facilitating the signal-to-noise properties of postsynaptic neurons, in that iontophoretic application of NE in various brain regions tends to diminish the spontaneous activity of postsynaptic neurons without reducing sensitivity to normal synaptic inputs (Bloom, 1974; Woodward, Moises, Waterhouse, Hoffer, & Freedman, 1979). Intracellular recordings of Purkinje cells in the cerebellum have demonstrated that iontophoretic NE also produces hyperpolarization of neuronal membranes like that of an inhibitory neurotransmitter, but differs in that membrane resistance is increased rather than decreased (Siggins, Oliver, Hoffer, & Bloom, 1971; Woodward et al., 1979). Such an increase in membrane resistance could thus facilitate neurotransmission by enhancing presynaptic release and/or postsynaptic actions of neurotransmitters in a manner opposite to that described by Dudel and Kuffler (1961) for pre- and postsynaptic inhibition at the crayfish neuromuscular junction (which is associated with hyperpolarization coupled to a decrease in membrane resistance). If the Purkinje cell is a reasonable model for the actions of NE on other neurons, then an increase in locus ceruleus activity during periods of behavioral arousal or following sensory stimulation could facilitate neural transmission throughout cortex.

NE Activity in Korsakoff Psychosis

Neurochemical Studies

The bulk of work in mapping the pathways of brain monamine systems has been performed in experimental animals, as there has been difficulty in adapting the techniques for this work to postmortem human brain tissue. Nonetheless, if one extrapolates the animal findings to humans, it appears that the ascending axonal processes of NE-containing neurons are heavily concentrated in periventricular and periaqueductal regions of the brain stem and diencephalon (Lindvall & Bjorklund, 1974); these findings seem to coincide with locations of the pathological lesions found postmortem in patients with Korsakoff psychosis (Malamud & Skillicorn, 1956; Victor, Adams, & Collins, 1971), suggesting that these neurons may be vulnerable to the pathological processes of this disease. Further support for this proposed anatomical coincidence is provided by Young and Kuhar (1980), who, by use of autoradiographic localization methods, have demonstrated high concentrations of alpha adrenoceptors in a number of regions of rat brain; these also seem to correspond to the pathological topography described in postmortem studies of Korsakoff disease (Victor et al., 1971).

If NE-containing neurons are damaged by the lesions associated with Korsakoff psychosis, then less of this monoamine should be present in the brain, and its concentration and that of its metabolites should be decreased in cerebrospinal fluid (CSF) of patients with this illness. CSF samples from humans are generally obtained from the lumbar subarachnoid space. The concentrations of a putative neurotransmitter or its metabolites found in the lumbar CSF depend on a chain of events that includes the activity of enzymes that synthesize or degrade the transmitter, as well as the active and passive transport processes by which molecules move from brain to CSF, from cerebral to lumbar CSF, and from lumbar CSF to the peripheral circulation. In humans, most brain NE is metabolized to 3-methoxy-4-hydroxyphenyl glycol (MHPG), while most brain dopamine (DA) is converted to homovanillic acid (HVA) and most serotonin (5-HT) to 5-hydroxyindoleacetic acid (5-HIAA). These metabolites are subsequently discharged into CSF or blood and eventually are excreted into the urine. The exact proportion of monoamine metabolites in blood and urine that derive from brain metabolism is not known, but it is generally accepted that neurochemical metabolites found in CSF are from the CNS and more accurately reflect the activity of central neurochemical systems than measurements made from other body fluids. We have measured the concentrations of the monoamine metabolites MHPG, HVA, and 5-HIAA in samples of lumbar CSF obtained from 21 patients with Korsaoff psychosis (McEntee, Mair, & Langlais, 1982). The CSF concentrations of each of these metabolites was significantly lower than in samples obtained from age-matched control subjects who were free of neurological or psychiatric disease at the time of their spinal tap. Of the three metabolites, MHPG was reduced most consistently (in all cases) and most extensively (by an average of 45%) when compared to mean control values. Studies of MHPG in lumbar CSF have suggested that as much as 50% of its concentration results from NE catabolism in the spinal canal (Post, Goodwin, Gordon, & Watkin, 1973). Thus, an average reduction of 45% in lumbar CSF MHPG may reflect a substantial deficit in brain NE activity. Although CSF levels of HVA and 5-HIAA were also significantly reduced in the Korsakoff patient population that was studied, they were reduced less consistently and less extensively than that of MHPG.

The relationship between NE and Korsakoff psychosis is underscored by evidence that the concentration of MHPG in lumbar CSF correlates with a general measure of the severity of the disease (i.e., the difference in scores between the full-scale IQ of the Wechsler Adult Intelligence Scale [WAIS] and the memory quotient [MQ] of the Wechsler Memory Scale [WMS]; see McEntee & Mair, 1978), as well as with performance on specific tasks that are sensitive to the amnesic symptoms of this disease—namely, the Memory Passages and Associative Learning subtests of the WMS, recognition memory for odors and for human faces, and a test measuring retrograde amnesia with a multiple-choice format (Mair, McEntee, & Zatorre, 1982). No significant correlation was demonstrated between the CSF concentrations of HVA and 5-HIAA and performance on tasks measuring amnesia. Two observations support the argument that central NE activity is functionally linked to the occurrence of Korsakoff amnesia, and that the correlations between MHPG and memory function are not merely coincidences related to the overall severity of the disease process. First, there was no correlation between the concentration of MHPG and performance on several other tasks that are not direct measures of amnesia, but that are impaired in Korsakoff psychosis (Mair *et al.*, 1982). Second, there is a double dissociation between performance on one of these tasks (the Digit Symbol subtest of the WAIS), the measures of amnesia mentioned above, and the concentrations of CSF HVA (a measure of central DA activity) and MHPG in lumbar CSF (Mair *et al.*, 1982). Performance on the Digit Symbol subtest is generally thought to be sensitive to impairments of visual–perceptual capability and new learning as well as of psychomotor speed—capabilities that have been related to central DA activity in patients with Parkinson disease (Hansch, Syndulko, Cohen, Goldberg, Potvin, & Tourtellotte, 1982). In the 21 Korsakoff patients we have studied, there is a strong correlation between CSF HVA and performance on the Digit Symbol subtest ($r = .71$, $p < .001$). In contrast, very weak correlations were found between MHPG and performance on the Digit Symbol subtest and between HVA and measures of memory impairment (Mair *et al.*, 1982).

Pharmacological Studies

Assuming that damage to brain NE-containing neurons is a causative factor of the amnesic impairments associated with Korsakoff psychosis, then treatment with specific pharmacological agents that enhance central NE activity might improve some of these symptoms. We (McEntee & Mair, 1980) studied the effects of three such drugs on the performance of patients with Korsakoff psychosis on a battery of neuropsychological tests. The drugs were clonidine, a direct alpha$_2$ NE receptor agonist that, unlike most other specific alpha NE receptor agonists, crosses the blood–brain barrier; D-amphetamine, an NE and DA agonist that affects release and reuptake mechanisms and thus requires the presence of presynaptic terminals for its action; and methysergide, a 5-HT blocker, included because of evidence that NE and 5-HT can have opposing effects on some learning tasks. The neuropsychological battery consisted of tests measuring a variety of cognitive functions that are impaired in Korsakoff patients.

The results of the drug study showed that clonidine treatment was associated with improved performance on several tasks measuring anterograde amnesia, but that none of the medications were associated with improved performance on tests measuring retrograde amnesia or on recognition memory of human faces. Likewise, drug treatment resulted in no improvement on the Witkin Children's Embedded Figures test, presumed to measure visual–perceptual ability; the Digit Symbol subtest of the WAIS; or the Carey Faces Test (Carey & Diamond, 1977). Figures 22-1 and 22-2 illustrate changes in performance on those neuropsychometric tests that were affected by clonidine treatment. Figure 22-1 shows results for subtests of the WMS. Clonidine improved performance significantly for two of the subtests on which the MQ is based, Memory Passages and Visual Reproduction. The Memory Passages subtest measures the ability to recall items from an information-laden paragraph, and the Visual Reproduction subtest measures the ability to reproduce a

FIGURE 22-1. The performance of eight persons with Korsakoff psychosis on the subtests of the Wechsler Memory Scale (WMS), prior to any treatment and during each of the drug treatments reported; see text for details. (From W. J. McEntee & R. G. Mair, Memory enhancement in Korsakoff's psychosis by clonidine: Further evidence of a noradrenergic deficit. *Annals of Neurology*, 1980, 7, 466–470. Reprinted by permission of the authors and publisher.)

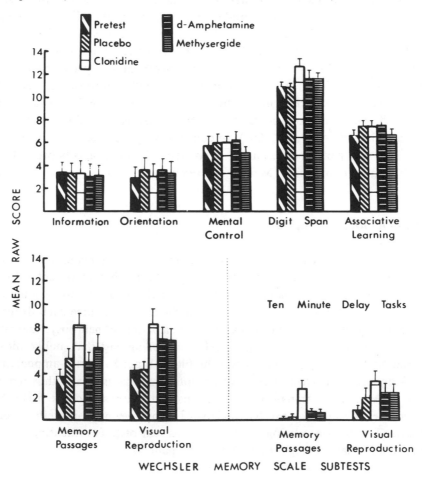

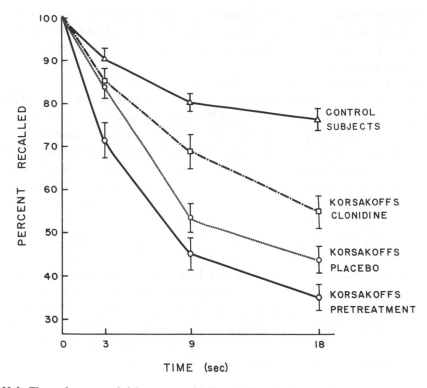

FIGURE 22-2. The performance of eight persons with Korsakoff psychosis and eight age-matched nonalcoholic control subjects on the consonant trigrams test. The performance of the Korsakoff patient is shown prior to the drug treatments administered (McEntee & Mair, 1980) and during the clonidine and placebo treatments. The mean performance by Korsakoff patients during D-amphetamine and methysergide treatments was intermediate between their performance during the clonidine and placebo trials. (This figure is replotted from data reported by Mair, Capra, McEntee, & Engen, 1980, and McEntee & Mair, 1980.)

simple drawing from memory. Both of these tasks measure the recall of information immediately after it has been presented. Modified versions of these two tests were included in the study, in which recall was measured a second time after a delay of 10 minutes. Performance on each of the 10-minute-delay tasks was improved following treatment with clonidine. Taken together, these results suggest that clonidine improves the recall of recently presented information, and that some of this improvement persists for at least 10 minutes. In regard to other WMS subtests measuring the recall of recently presented information, clonidine improved the average performance on the Digit Span task, although this improvement did not reach significance, while performance on the Associative Learning subtest was not affected by any of the treatments. This last result may be explained by the makeup of the test, which is divided into a difficult part that Korsakoff patients failed to learn under any circumstances, and an easy part that they had little trouble learning during the placebo trials.

The only other test for which results improved significantly followed clonidine treatment was the consonant trigrams test, a measure of short-term memory decay based on the Peterson and Peterson (1959) technique. Figure 22-2 presents the results of this task for non-brain-damaged control subjects and Korsakoff patients prior to drug treatment, during clonidine treatment, and during placebo administration. Treatment with clonidine improved recall after the 9- and 18-second delays, although the performance of the Korsakoff patients treated with clonidine was not as good as that of the non-brain-damaged control subjects.

There are some striking parallels between the types of tasks that correlate with CSF MHPG and improve following treatment with clonidine. With the exception of the test for retrograde amnesia (which correlates with CSF MHPG but was not affected by clonidine treatment), these tasks involve the recall of recently presented information. Thus, the results of the neurochemical and neuropharmacological experiments taken together support a hypothesis that diminished brain NE activity at least contributes to the anterograde amnesia that characterizes Korsakoff's psychosis. Such consistency between different experimental approaches is encouraging, although the data do not speak directly to the issue of how diminished NE activity might produce amnesia.

Recent neuropsychological experiments have identified a number of mechanisms that might contribute to the amnesic symptoms of Korsakoff's psychosis. The last section of this chapter reviews some of these ideas in light of animal experiments delineating the behavioral consequences of central NE lesions. Within the constraints of this chapter, this section does not present a comprehensive review of either of these literatures. Our purpose is to consider whether diminished central NE activity is a sufficient cause of Korsakoff amnesia and to speculate on the relationship between this neurochemical deficit and the cognitive impairments associated with Korsakoff psychosis.

NE and Cognition: Some Comparisons and Hypotheses

On the basis of morphological and physiological properties, central NE systems have been described as a neuromodulatory mechanism, organized to facilitate cortical activity during periods of behavioral arousal (Aston-Jones & Bloom, 1981a, 1981b). Psychologists have related central NE systems to a number of aspects of learning, including reinforcement, attention, retention, and fear. Earlier theories tended to view NE activity as being requisite for learning and memory to occur. More recent experiments have demonstrated that animals with near-complete depletion of cortical NE are unimpaired in their ability to learn certain types of tasks, including lever pressing for continuous reinforcement (Mason & Iversen, 1977), T-maze acquisition accuracy (Amaral & Foss, 1975), complex motor manipulation (Mason & Iversen, 1978a), go/no-go alternation (Tremmel, Morris, & Gebhart, 1977), and step-down passive avoidance (Mason & Fibiger, 1978). The ability of lesioned animals to learn these tasks across daily sessions is inconsistent with NE-containing neurons' mediating processes such as reinforcement or memory storage, which are necessary for any learning to occur. NE-depleted animals also exhibit a general tendency to continue responding during extinction trials, when reinforcements are withheld. Mason and Iversen (1979) have argued that an impairment of selective attention, resulting in the formation of less specific stimulus–response associations, is the most parsimonious explanation for this resistance to extinction. Mason and his colleagues have supported this hypothesis by demonstrating a number of other behavioral deficits that are consistent with an impairment of selective attention. For instance, animals with NE-depleting lesions are impaired in their ability to learn and subsequently to reverse a successive-discrimination problem

(Mason & Iversen, 1978b). More directly, they have demonstrated that central NE-depleting lesions impede the development of latent inhibition (Mason & Lin, 1980). In a latent-inhibition task, a stimulus is first presented without reinforcement and thus becomes associated with nonreinforcement. This nonreinforced preexposure tends to impair the ability of intact animals to learn a subsequent discrimination based on that stimulus, presumably because they have learned to ignore the stimulus during their initial exposure to it. The ability of lesioned animals to learn a task mediated by a previously nonreinforced stimulus might therefore be viewed as failure of the selective attentional processes that are necessary for the animals to learn to ignore an irrelevant stimulus.

It is probably premature to conclude that a specific function of NE-containing neurons is to control selective attention. Recently, Ridley, Haystead, Baker, and Crow (1981) demonstrated that the alpha NE blocker acetoperone interferes with the ability of marmosets to learn and then to reverse a visual discrimination problem in a Wisconsin General Testing Apparatus (WGTA). Ridley *et al.* (1981) contend that acetoperone impaired learning by interfering with the animals' abilities to form associations. They also noted that the deficit they observed was similar to that described by Oscar-Berman and Zola-Morgan (1980a, 1980b) among patients with Korsakoff psychosis given a similar task in a modified version of the WGTA. A number of other investigators have argued that the release of NE facilitates the consolidation and retrieval of information from memory stores. For instance, Quartermain and coworkers have demonstrated that pharmacologically induced amnesias can be reversed by injections of clonidine immediately after training trials are completed and immediately before recall testing, but not at intervening times (Freedman, Backman, & Quartermain, 1979; Quartermain, Freedman, Botwinick, & Gutwein, 1977). The use of posttraining injections rules out the possibility that this amelioration of amnesia is the result of improved learning, and the failure of treatments at intervening time intervals (several hours after training or before testing) is inconsistent with clonidine's simply delaying the rate of memory trace decay. A cautionary point should be made, however, that the antiamnesia effects of NE agonists may be task-dependent. In this regard, it has been shown that posttraining injections of NE and DA facilitate the retrieval of different learned behaviors (Quartermain & Altman, 1982; Qartermain, Judge, & Freedman, 1982). Similarly, there is evidence that the facilitatory effects of posttraining injections of NE agonists depend on several conditioning parameters that are known to affect habit strength (Gold & van Buskirk, 1978; Hall, 1977; Quartermain & Botwinick, 1975a, 1975b).

There appear to be a number of analogies between behavioral alterations observed in experimental animals with cortical NE-depleting lesions and neuropsychological deficits demonstrated in patients with Korsakoff psychosis. First, there is evidence that Korsakoff patients and NE-depleted animals can learn certain simple behaviors. This might be explained, in part, by the hypothesis of Cohen and Squire (1980) that in human amnesics that the ability to learn rule-based information or strategies ("knowing how") is spared, but that the acquisition of data-based knowledge ("knowing that") is deficient. Most tasks used in animal learning experiments, and indeed all the tasks that NE-depleted animals have been shown to learn, involve the acquisition of relatively simple response strategies and do not require learning or manipulation of significant amounts of stimulus information. It can thus be argued that animals with NE-depleting lesions are similar to amnesic humans in having a relatively well-preserved ability to "learn how." In contrast, patients with

Korsakoff psychosis and animals with experimentally diminished brain NE activity are dramatically impaired in their abilities to perform more complex tasks, such as reversal of a previously learned association or a discrimination-learning problem (Kinsbourne & Winocur, 1980; Mason & Iversen, 1978b; Oscar-Berman & Zola-Morgan, 1980a, 1980b; Ridley *et al.*, 1981).

Second, although neither of these conditions impair the ability to remember all previously learned information, each has been associated with retrieval deficits that depend on the type of information learned and (at least arguably) on the strength with which the memory trace is established. Patients with Korsakoff psychosis are unimpaired in their remote memory for overlearned verbal information, such as that represented in the Information, Comprehension, and Vocabulary subtests of the WAIS (McEntee *et al.*, 1982; Talland, 1965). When remote memory is tested with information from the past about public events and well-known people, patients with Korsakoff psychosis exhibits a retrograde amnesia that is more severe for information learned in the decade or two prior to the onset of their amnesia (Albert, Butters, & Levin, 1979). Albert, Butters, and Brandt (1980) have argued that the temporal gradient of this retrograde amnesia is caused by a combination of defective encoding of information during the period of alcohol abuse that typically precedes the illness and a general impairment of retrieval mechanisms that interferes with the recall of these poorly formed memory traces.

Third, there is evidence that attention is impaired in patients with Korsakoff psychosis and in animals with NE-depleting lesions. A number of investigators have described a variety of perceptual deficits in patients with Korsakoff psychosis that are consistent with impaired attention. These include increased time required to recognize tachistoscopically presented visual stimuli and longer critical interstimulus intervals in visual backward-masking tasks (Oscar-Berman, Goodglass, & Cherlow, 1973); increased time to decide whether two verbal stimuli are phonetically equivalent (Cermak, Butters, & Moreines, 1974); impaired ability to discriminate differences in odor quality, but no impairment in absolute olfactory sensitivity or odor memory (Mair, Capra, McEntee, & Engen, 1980); diminished capacity to perform dichotic-listening tasks (Glosser, Butters, & Samuels, 1976; Parkinson, 1979); inability to recognize pictures of unfamiliar human faces when the faces are obscured by superficial irrelevant stimuli (hats, wigs, clothes, and facial expression) (Dricker, Butters, Berman, Samuels, & Carey, 1978); and an impaired ability to perform embedded-figures tasks, in which one must find a simple geometric shape hidden in a more complex figure (Glosser, Butters, & Kaplan, 1977; Talland, 1965). More directly, Oscar-Berman and Gade (1979) have reported that patients with Korsakoff psychosis exhibit smaller orienting responses that habituate less rapidly than those of control subjects when they are stimulated with a series of 100-dB auditory stimuli. Baker (1978), in our laboratory, observed a similar result in the orientation response for 12 patients with Korsakoff psychosis, and also demonstrated an increase in the amplitude of the response and improvement in the rate of habituation following treatment with clonidine for two of these patients, who were included in our earlier drug study (McEntee & Mair, 1980). Although pharmacological data are available from only two subjects, this result suggests that primary attention is dependent on the level of central NE activity. There is agreement among most investigators that the capacity for selective or divided attention is modulated by the orientation response (Siddle & Spinks, 1979), although the precise relationships between these processes are unclear. The implication of diminished orientation responses in patients with Korsakoff psychosis thus provides a mechanism that might contribute to or possibly account for other attentional or information-processing deficits associated with this disease.

In his classic monograph on Korsakoff psychosis, Talland (1965) argued that the impairments of perception associated with Korsakoff syndrome, as well as the anterograde and retrograde amnesia, can be ascribed to a general impairment of activation. According to this hypothesis, a premature termination of an activating function limits the abilities to compare and integrate successive stimulus items and thus to perform normally on tests of perception, as well as the capacity to register and consolidate memory traces.

> If function is not sufficiently sustained, perception will not lead to registration since, in order to achieve that, the neural events initiated in perception must extend further in time or in another dimension. . . . The argument here advanced is that registration is not sustained long enough or does not extend sufficiently to embed the process in all the appropriate systems of information storage and, either as a consequence or concomitant effect, to provide for its endurance. (Talland, 1965, pp. 306, 309)

According to Talland's model, the failure to sustain activation also results in a failure to sustain memory-scanning operations required to locate and retrieve information from long-term memory stores. While parts of Talland's model may require modification to account for the results of more recent neuropsychological experiments and for more modern psychological concepts, we agree with his argument that many of the psychological impairments associated with Korsakoff psychosis may be attributed to a generalized impairment of cognitive activation. It is our hypothesis that this impairment of cognitive activation is related to diminished central NE activity.

REFERENCES

Albert, M. S., Butters, N., & Brandt, J. Memory for remote events in alcoholics. *Journal of Studies on Alcoholism*, 1980, *41*, 1071–1081.

Albert, M. S., Butters, N., & Levin, J. Temporal gradients in the retrograde amnesia of patients with alcoholic Korsakoff's disease. *Archives of Neurology*, 1979, *36*, 211–216.

Amaral, D. G., & Foss, J. A. Locus coeruleus lesions and learning. *Science*, 1975, *188*, 377–378.

Aston-Jones, G., & Bloom, F. E. Activity oif norepinephrine-containing locus coeruleus neurons in behaving rats anticipates fluctuations in the sleep–waking cycle. *Journal of Neuroscience*, 1981, *1*, 876–886. (a)

Aston-Jones, G., & Bloom, F. E. Norepinephrine-containing locus coeruleus neurons in behaving rats exhibit pronounced responses to non-noxious environmental stimuli. *Journal of Neuroscience*, 1981, *1*, 887–900. (b)

Baker, E. Unpublished data, 1978.

Bloom, F. E. To spritz or not to spritz: The doubtful valve of aimless iontophoresis. *Life Sciences*, 1974, *14*, 1819–1834.

Carey, S., & Diamond, R. From piecemeal to configurational representation of faces. *Science*, 1977, *195*, 312–314.

Cermak, L. S., Butters, N., & Moreines, J. Some analyses of the verbal encoding deficit of alcoholic Korsakoff patients. *Brain and Language*, 1974, *2*, 141–150.

Chu, N., & Bloom, F. E. Activity patterns of catecholamine-containing pontine neurons in the dorso-lateral tegmentum of unrestrained cats. *Journal of Neurobiology*, 1974, *5*, 527–544.

Cohen, N. J., & Squire, L. R. Preserved learning and retention of a pattern-analyzing skill in amnesia. *Science*, 1980, *210*, 207–210.

Descarries, L., Watkins, K. C., & Lapierre, Y. Noradrenergic axon terminals in the cerebral cortex of the rat: III. Topometric ultrastructural analysis. *Brain Research*, 1977, *133*, 197–222.

Dricker, J., Butters, N., Berman, G., Samuels, I., & Carey, S. The recognition and encoding of faces by alcoholic Korsakoff patients and right hemisphere patients. *Neuropsychologia*, 1978, *16*, 683–695.

Dudel, J., & Kuffler, S. Presynaptic inhibition at the crayfish neuromuscular junction. *Journal of Physiology*, 1961, *155*, 543–562.

Foote, S. L., Aston-Jones, G., & Bloom, F. S. Impulse activity of locus coeruleus neurons in awake rats and monkeys is a function of sensory stimulation and arousal. *Proceedings of the National Academy of Sciences USA*, 1980, *77*, 3033–3037.

Freedman, L. S., Backman, M. F., & Quartermain, D. Clonidine reverses the amnesia induced by dopamine-beta-hydroxylase inhibition. *Pharmacology, Biochemistry and Behavior*, 1979, *11*, 259–263.

Glosser, G., Butters, N., and Kaplan, E. Visuoperceptual processes in brain damaged patients on the digit-symbol substitution task. *International Journal of Neuroscience*, 1977, *7*, 59–66.

Glosser, G., Butters, N., & Samuels, I. Failures in information processing in patients with Korsakoff's syndrome. *Neuropsychologia*, 1976, *14*, 327–334.

Gold, P. E., & van Buskirk, R. P. Post-training brain norepinephrine concentrations: Correlation with retention performance of avoidance training and with peripheral epinephrine modulation of memory processing. *Behavioral Biology*, 1978, *23*, 509–520.

Hall, M. E. Enhancement of learning by cycloheximide and DDC: A function of response strength. *Behavioral Biology*, 1977, *21*, 41–51.

Hansch, E. C., Syndulko, K., Cohen, S. N., Goldberg, F. I., Potvin, A. R., & Tourtellotte, W. W. Cognition in Parkinson disease: An event-related potential perspective. *Annals of Neurology*, 1982, *11*, 599–607.

Kinsbourne, M., & Winocur, G. Response competition and interference effects in paired-associate learning by Korsakoff amnesics. *Neuropsychologia*, 1980, *18*, 541–548.

Lindvall, O., & Bjorklund, A. The organization of the ascending catecholamine neuron systems in the rat brain as revealed by the glxoxylic acid fluorescence method. *Acta Physiologica Scandinavia*, 1974 (Suppl. 414), 1–48.

Mair, R. G., Capra, C., McEntee, W. J., & Engen, T. Odor discrimination and memory in Korsakoff's psychosis. *Journal of Experimental Psychology: Human Perception and Performance*, 1980, *6*, 445–458.

Mair, R. G., McEntee, W. J., & Zatorre, R. J. Brain NE and DA activity: Correlation with specific behavioral deficits in Korsakoff's psychosis. *Neurology*, 1982, *32*, A66–A67.

Malamud, N., & Skillicorn, S. A. Relationship between the Wernicke and Korsakoff syndrome: A clinico-pathologic study of seventy cases. *Archives of Neurology and Psychiatry*, 1956, *76*, 585–596.

Mason, S. T., & Fibiger, H. C. 6 OHDA lesion of the dorsal nonadrenergic bundle alters the extinction of passive avoidance. *Brain Research*, 1978, *152*, 209–214.

Mason, S. T., & Iversen, S. D. Behavioral basis of the dorsal bundle extinction effect. *Pharmacology, Biochemistry and Behavior*, 1977, *7*, 373–379.

Mason, S. T., & Iversen, S. D. Central and peripheral noradrenaline and resistance to extinction. *Physiology and Behavior*, 1978, *20*, 681–686. (a)

Mason, S. T., & Iverson, D. S. Reward, attention, and the dorsal noradrenergic bundle. *Brain Research*, 1978, *150*, 135–145. (b)

Mason, S. T., & Iversen, S. D. Theories of the dorsal bundle extinction effect. *Brain Research Reviews*, 1979, *1*, 107–137.

Mason, S. T., & Lin, D. Dorsal noradrenergic bundle and selective attention in the rat. *Journal of Comparative and Physiological Psychology*, 1980, *94*, 819–832.

McEntee, W. J., & Mair, R. G. Memory impairment in Korsakoff's psychosis: A correlation with brain noradrenergic activity. *Science*, 1978, *202*, 905–907.

McEntee, W. J., & Mair, R. G. Memory enhancement in Korsakoff's psychosis by clonidine: Further evidence of a noradrenergic deficit. *Annals of Neurology*, 1980, *7*, 466–470.

McEntee, W. J., Mair, R. G., & Langlais, P. J. MHPG is always while HVA and 5-HIAA are often diminished in the CSF of patients with Korsakoff's psychosis. *Neurology*, 1982, *32*, A229.

Moore, R. Y., & Bloom, F. E. Central catecholamine neuron systems: Anatomy and physiology of the norepinephrine and epinephrine systems. In W. M. Cowan (Ed.), *Annual review of neuroscience* (Vol. 2). Palo Alto, Calif.: Annual Reviews, 1979.

Oscar-Berman, M., & Gade, A. Electrodermal measures of arousal in humans with cortical or subcortical brain damage. In K. D. Kimmel, E. H. Van Olst, & J. F. Orelebeke (Eds.), *The orienting reflex in humans*. New York: Wiley, 1979.

Oscar-Berman, M., Goodglass, H., & Cherlow, D. G. Perceptual laterality and iconic recognition of visual materials by Korsakoff patients and normal adults. *Journal of Comparative and Physiological Psychology*, 1973, *82*, 316–321.

Oscar-Berman, M., & Zola-Morgan, S. M. Comparative neuropsychology of Korsakoff's syndrome: I. Spatial and visual reeversal learning. *Neuropsychologia*, 1980, *18*, 499–512. (a)

Oscar-Berman, M., & Zola-Morgan, S. M. Comparative neuropsychology of Korsakoff's syndrome: II. Two choice visual discrimination learning. *Neuropsychologia*, 1980, *18*, 513–525. (b)

Parkinson, S. R. The amnesic Korsakoff's syndrome: A study of selective and divided attention. *Neuropsychologia*, 1979, *17*, 67–75.

Peterson, L. R., & Peterson, M. J. Short-term retention of individual verbal items. *Journal of Experimental Psychology*, 1959, *58*, 193–198.

Post, R. M., Goodwin, F. K., Gordon, E. K., & Watkin, D. M. Amine metabolites in human cerebrospinal fluid: Effects of cord transection and spinal fluid block. *Science*, 1973, *179*, 897–899.

Quartermain, D., & Altman, H. J. Facilitation of retrieval by D-amphetamine following ansiomycin induced amnesia. *Physiological Psychology*, 1982, *10*, 283–292.

Quartermain, D., & Botwinick, C. Y. Effect of age of habit on susceptibility to cycloheximide-induced amnesia in mice. *Journal of Comparative and Physiological Psychology*, 1975, *89*, 803–809. (a)

Quartermain, D., & Botwinick, C. Y. Role of the biogenic amines in the reversal of cycloheximide-induced amnesia. *Journal of Comparative and Physiological Psychology*, 1975, *88*, 386–401. (b)

Quartermain, D., Freedman, L. S., Botwinick, C. Y., & Gutwein, B. M. Reversal of cycloheximide-induced amnesia by adrenergic receptor stimulation. *Pharmacology, Biochemistry and Behavior*, 1977, *7*, 259–267.

Quartermain, D., Judge, N. E., & Freedman, E. The role of lisuride and other dopamine agonists in memory retrieval processes. In D. B. Calne, P. Horowski, R. J. MacDonald, & W. Wuttke (Eds.), *Lisuride and other dopamine agonists*. New York: Raven Press, 1982.

Ridley, R. M., Haystead, T. A. J., Baker, H. F., & Crow, T. J. A new approach to the role of noradrenaline in learning: Problem solving in the marmoset after alpha-noradrenergic receptor blockade. *Pharmacology, Biochemistry and Behavior*, 1981, *14*, 849–855.

Siddle, D. A. T., & Spinks, J. A. Orienting response and information processing: Some theoretical and empirical problems. In K. D. Kimmel, E. H. Van Olst, & J. F. Orlebeke (Eds.), *The orienting reflex in humans*. New York: Wiley, 1979.

Siggins, G. R., Oliver, A. P., Hoffer, B. J., & Bloom, F. E. Cyclic adenosine monophosphate and norepinephrine: Effects on transmembrane properties of cerebellar Purkinje cells. *Science*, 1971, *171*, 192–194.

Talland, G. A. *Deranged memory*. New York: Academic Press, 1965.

Tremmel, F., Morris, M. D., & Gebhart, G. F. The affect of forebrain norepinephrine depletion on two measures of response suppression. *Brain Research*, 1977, *126*, 185–188.

Victor, M., Adams, R. D., & Collins, G. H. *The Wernicke-Korsakoff syndrome*. Philadelphia: F. A. Davis, 1971.

Woodward, D. J., Moises, H. C., Waterhouse, B. D., Hoffer, B. J., & Freedman, R. Modulatory actions of norepinephrine in the central nervous system. *Federation Proceedings*, 1979, *38*, 2109–2116.

Young, W. S., & Kuhar, M. J. Noradrenergic alpha-1 and alpha-2 receptors: Light microscopic autoradiographic localization. *Proceedings of the National Academy of Sciences USA*, 1980, *77*, 1696–1700.

23

The Assessment of Memory Disorders in Patients with Alzheimer Disease

Marilyn Albert and Mark Moss

Most neuropsychological studies of memory disorders in humans have been carried out in amnesic patients: patients with alcoholic Korsakoff syndrome, postencephalitic patients, and patients with surgical, embolic, or traumatic brain lesions. While many types of amnesic patients have some degree of personality change and subtle cognitive deficits in other areas besides memory, they are relatively ideal subjects for the study of memory, for two primary reasons. First, there is no question that the memory deficits of these individuals are not their only striking cognitive defects. Second, the nature of their memory disorder is relatively stable over time.

Patients with progressive dementias possess neither of these characteristics. Thus, an examination of their memory deficits is methodologically more complex than a similar examination in amnesic patients. An investigation of dementia patients must take into account the stage of each patient's illness, the limitations imposed by other prominent cognitive defects, the possible heterogeneity of the patient population, and the interactions of age and disease on the patients' memory deficits. Nowhere are these difficulties better exemplified than in the study of patients with presenile and senile dementia of the Alzheimer type. The confusion in the literature regarding the cognitive profile of Alzheimer patients is a reflection of the problems presented by this complexity.

This chapter, therefore, discusses these methodological and conceptual issues in detail. It is our hope that a better appreciation of them will enable researchers in the field to carry out investigations that are more easily comparable to one another and to design experimental procedures that may more accurately assess the memory disorders of Alzheimer patients.

The Stage of Disease

If one wishes to examine the factors that contribute to the memory impairment of Alzheimer patients, it would seem imperative to equate patients for severity of illness. It cannot, for example, be assumed *a priori* that both storage and retrieval mechanisms are disrupted early in the course of disease, and that the absolute severity of impairment reflects only a quantitative and not a qualitative change. It may just as easily be the case

Marilyn Albert. Departments of Psychiatry and Neurology, Massachusetts General Hospital, Division on Aging, Harvard Medical School, Boston, Massachusetts.

Mark Moss. Department of Anatomy, Boston University School of Medicine, Boston, Massachusetts; Department of Psychiatry, Massachusetts General Hospital, Harvard Medical School, Boston, Massachusetts.

that difficulties in retrieval are primarily responsible for the early symptoms of memory dysfunction, and that the increasing severity of impairment reflects the impact of failures in additional aspects of the memory process.

It is, however, not adequate to determine the severity of illness by establishing the number of years that have elapsed since the patient was diagnosed, or even since the family first started noticing the symptoms of disease. Alzheimer disease is, by definition, a progressive disorder with an insidious onset. Rarely can the patient or family describe with any degree of accuracy when the symptoms of disease began. In addition, there are not salient neurological changes that can be used to mark the onset of disease, as in other dementing disorders. For example, the presence of choreic movements or the appearance of focal neurological signs can reasonably be used to determine the onset of Huntington disease or multi-infarct dementia, respectively. The diagnosis of Alzheimer disease is, on the other hand, generally dependent upon a variety of job-related and/or family-related issues that bear only an indirect relationship to the actual onset of disease. In addition, patients with Alzheimer disease vary widely in the rate at which their illness progresses. Some individuals show considerable decline over the course of 1 or 2 years, while others demonstrate only marginal increases in impairment over the same interval.

Under these circumstances, the only meaningful way to equate patients for severity of illness is to assess their behavior objectively. Tests of cognitive performance or activities of daily living (ADL) can be used for this purpose.

However, experience indicates that when such test instruments are used to rate severity of impairment in mildly to moderately impaired patients, they must examine a broad range of cognitive and/or functional activities in order to be accurate. For example, patients who fit the clinical criteria for the diagnosis of Alzheimer disease (e.g., gradually increasing severity of memory impairment evident to family, friends, and professional associates; impaired performance on a variety of standardized memory tests; and a drop of at least one standard deviation on the Wechsler Adult Intelligence Scale [WAIS]) may still make no errors on the Mental Status Questionnaire (Kahn, Goldfarb, Pollack, & Peck, 1966; Reisberg, Ferris, DeLeon, & Crook, 1982) and show no impairment on ADL scales that include only self-maintenance activities (Vitaliano, Breen, Albert, Russo, & Prinz, 1984).

The Dementia Rating Scale (Coblentz, Mattis, Zingesser, Kasoff, Wisniewski, & Katzman, 1973; Mattis, 1976) is a test we have used for this purpose and recommend highly. It is an excellent tool for evaluating mildly or moderately advanced Alzheimer patients. It assesses a wide variety of cognitive functions (i.e., attention, initiation and perseveration, conceptualization, construction, and memory) on a level of difficulty appropriate to the patients. Scores correlate well with the WAIS, and test–retest reliability is extremely high. The major shortcoming of the test is that it does not include an assessment of language. This is easily remedied by the addition of tasks such as confrontation naming and reading.

The Impact of Other Cognitive Defects

In designing experiments to assess memory dysfunction in patients with Alzheimer disease, it is also necessary to keep in mind that although memory loss comprises the most common and dramatic symptom of disease, other areas of dysfunction exist, even early in the course of the illness. It is important, therefore, to be aware of the possibility that such cognitive defects may confound or significantly interact with mnemonic test variables.

For example, mildly to moderately impaired Alzheimer patients usually display difficulty with confrontation naming. That is, they have difficulty producing the name of common objects when presented with line drawings, photographic representations, or actual three-dimensional examples of these objects. In the early stages of disease, patients generally can recognize the object, can accurately describe its function, or can make some association with it (i.e., can produce circumlocutory responses), but cannot provide the correct name. It is easy to see that testing of verbal memory can be confounded with naming deficits of this nature if only verbatim responses are considered to be accurate. Such difficulties might also exaggerate measures of the verbal-encoding deficits of patients with Alzheimer disease. It may be possible statistically to partial out the effect of a naming dysfunction in order to evaluate memory performance *per se* on a verbal-memory task. However, any discussion of performance on a verbal-memory task must, at the very least, acknowledge the possible impact of naming deficits on behavior.

Similarly, in assessing memory, one must be aware of the degree to which Alzheimer patients are perseverative, circumstantial, and stimulus-bound early in the course of the disease. These tendencies can alter a patient's responses in such a way that tasks designed to assess memory may not produce responses that are an accurate reflection of the patient's true ability. For example, in a continuous-recognition paradigm, in which the subject is asked to say whether or not he or she has previously seen the stimulus item, an Alzheimer patient is likely to perseverate in either a negative or a positive response mode, regardless of his or her actual memory for the target item. A forced-choice task, which requires the subject to choose between stimulus pairs (i.e., the target item and a distractor), would be more likely to reveal the subject's actual ability to retain information.

A dramatic example of the way in which such perseverative tendencies can mislead one's conclusion about the underlying nature of a patient's deficits can be seen in the performance of Alzheimer patients on visual–spatial tasks. Figure 23-1 shows the performance of two Alzheimer patients when presented with a page of figures to copy. The top part of each half of the figure shows part of the page as seen by one patient, while the bottom part of each half of the figure shows the performance of the patient. The patients' errors do not appear to result from a misperception of the stimuli; instead, the errors seem to result from a perseveration of the previous figure or of the previous type of response. If the nature of the error were overlooked and only the test score noted, one might conclude that these subjects had visual–spatial deficits.

Similarly, when asked to draw a clock and set the hands at "ten after eleven," many mildly to moderately impaired Alzheimer patients may perseverate their own responses (see Figure 23-2, a and c) or be drawn to the concrete content of the instructions, the words "ten" and "eleven" (Figure 23-2, b and d). However, when these patients are asked to copy a clock, it is clear that their performance is entirely correct.

Furthermore, the instructions and responses required by many memory tasks are often complex. This complexity alone may prevent an Alzheimer patient, who already has difficulty inhibiting irrelevant responses and focusing on the relevant dimensions of the task, from accurately revealing his or her memory ability. It may therefore be necessary for those wishing to assess memory function in Alzheimer patients to develop new tasks with the cognitive profile of such patients clearly in mind.

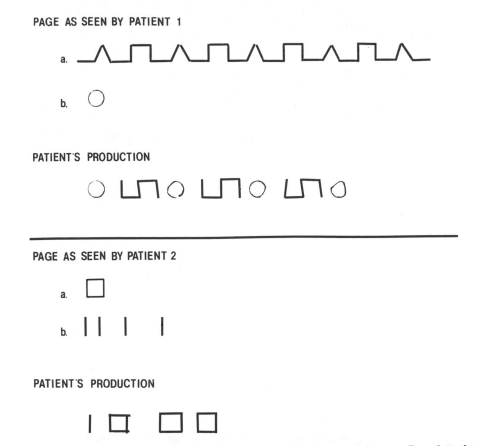

FIGURE 23-1. The performance of two patients with Alzheimer disease when asked to copy figure b on the page after having already copied figure a.

Two such tasks have been developed in our laboratory. One is a delayed non-matching-to-sample task, and the other is a delayed recognition-memory task. Both paradigms are based on memory tests developed for use in primates, and one of their major advantages is that direct comparisons can be made between the performance of neurological patients and monkeys with selective cortical and subcortical lesions. However, these tasks have other important advantages as well:

1. The task instructions are easily understood.
2. The response required is a simple one.
3. Both tasks have a game-like quality that makes them appealing and non-threatening.
4. The subjects are not openly confronted with their failures (e.g., by being drilled on words they have missed) and thus do not become discouraged or uncooperative.
5. Numerous alternate forms of the tasks can easily be designed to be administered on repeated occasions.
6. The tasks permit detailed tracking and quantification of memory ability.

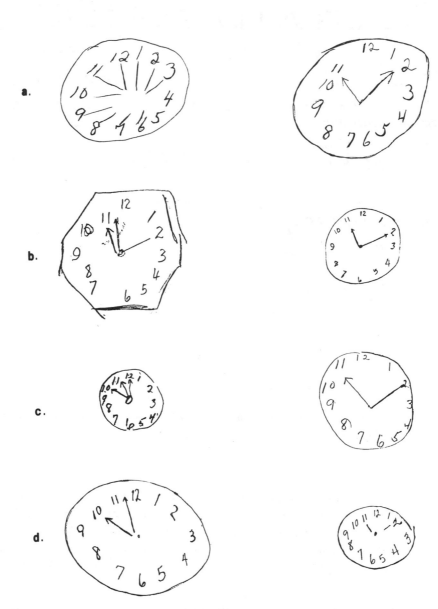

FIGURE 23-2. The drawings of four patients with Alzheimer disease. The left-hand column shows the perform-ance of each patient when asked to draw a clock and set the hands at "ten after eleven." The right-hand column is each patient's copy, performed at a later time and on a separate piece of paper.

In the delayed non-matching-to-sample task, the subject is presented with a three-dimensional "junk" object (e.g., a spoon, ball, pen, etc.). After a delay of 10, 30, 70, or 130 seconds, the subject is asked to point to the object he or she has *not* previously seen. It has recently been shown that monkeys with hippocampal ablations (alone or in combination with removal of the amygdala) show increasing difficulty as the delay interval extends beyond 10 seconds (Mahut, Zola-Morgan, & Moss, 1982; Mishkin, 1978). Patients with

Alzheimer disease demonstrate an almost identical pattern of memory decay (see Figure 23-3).

The delayed recognition-memory task measures the subject's memory span by requiring him or her to identify a new stimulus among an increasing set of previously presented familiar stimuli. It is a modification of a test designed to assess spatial-recognition capacity, with and without visual cues, in monkeys with selective hippocampal lesions (Rehbein, in preparation). For human and monkey subjects alike, stimuli are placed on circular discs. The discs are placed one at a time on a board (see Figure 23-4), in a series of increasing length. Each new disc is added after the prescribed delay interval (during which the subject cannot see the board). The subject's task is merely to point to the new disc that was just added during the delay.

A variety of modalities can be used with patients (e.g., words, colors, patterns, or spatial arrangement) so that material-specific recognition memory can be assessed. When words, colors, or patterns are used, the discs are moved randomly during the delay intervals so that the position of the disc does not provide an additional cue. When the stimulus parameter being tested is the spatial arrangement of the discs, there is, of course, no alteration in the position of the discs during the delay interval.

Primate data directly comparable to human data are not yet available, though it is already clear that monkeys with damage to the hippocampal formation are severely impaired on a spatial form of this task (Rehbein, in preparation). However, we have tested two patient groups with dementing disorders of differing etiologies (patients with Alzheimer disease and patients with Huntington disease) on this delayed recognition-memory task. The preliminary data indicate that both the Huntington patients and the Alzheimer

FIGURE 23-3. The performance of healthy human subjects, normal monkeys, patients with Alzheimer disease, and monkeys with hippocampal lesions on the delayed non-matching-to-sample task. (Monkey data from Mahut, Zola-Morgan, & Moss, 1982.)

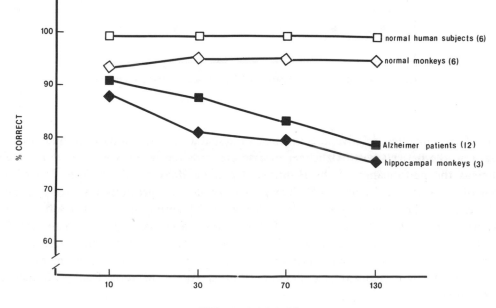

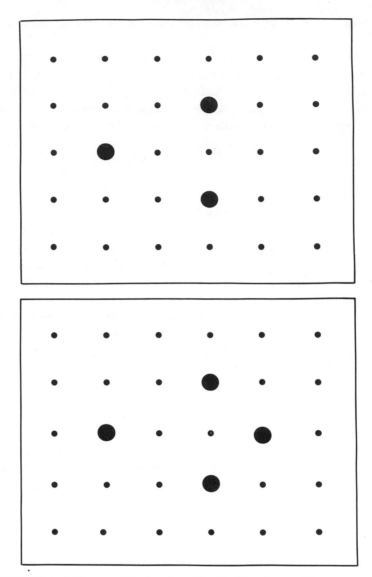

FIGURE 23-4. A diagram of the board used for the delayed recognition-memory task.

patients are impaired, relative to controls, on the spatial, color, and pattern conditions. In addition, the patients with Alzheimer disease are impaired when word stimuli are used, whereas the performance of the Huntington patients does not differ from that of the control subjects (see Figure 23-5). This is consistent with previous findings regarding differences in the cognitive profiles of Alzheimer and Huntington patients (Butters, Sax, Montgomery, & Tarlow, 1978; Rosen & Mohs, 1982) and may help to explain why the memory performance of patients with Huntington disease is improved by the addition of meaningful, contextual verbal information, whereas the test scores of Alzheimer patients remain relatively unchanged by such cuing (Butters, Albert, Miliotis, Phillips, Sterste, & Sax, 1983).

The Heterogeneity of the Patient Population

Investigators involved in Alzheimer disease research are becoming increasingly aware of the fact that the population of patients who meet the DSM-III criteria for progressive degenerative dementia of unknown origin is cognitively heterogeneous and may include identifiable subtypes of patients.

Our experience indicates that, early in the course of disease, the vast majority of Alzheimer patients have a striking impairment in memory function (which is particularly evident with delays) and difficulty with abstraction, set shifting, and maintenance. They often, but not invariably, have naming deficits as well.

Other investigators, as well as ourselves, have described at least two additional types of patients. The first type shows early symptoms of a dramatic language impairment, which has many of the manifestations of an aphasic disorder. This language dysfunction appears in the absence of focal lesions and becomes progressively worse over time. Memory deficits and difficulties with abstraction are evident as the disease progresses, but are far less striking than the language disorder.

The other subgroup of patients reported by various clinicians consists of individuals with dramatic visual–spatial deficits early in the course of disease. These patients will often say that they do not see properly, and may be initially referred for diagnosis by an ophthalmologist. Such individuals have other cognitive deficits (e.g., memory problems), but, again, these are less striking than their visual–spatial impairments.

Thus, even if one limits the investigation of memory disorders to patients in the same stage of disease, as suggested earlier (e.g., mildly to moderately impaired patients),

FIGURE 23-5. The performance of healthy human subjects, patients with Alzheimer disease, and patients with Huntington disease on the delayed recognition-memory span task.

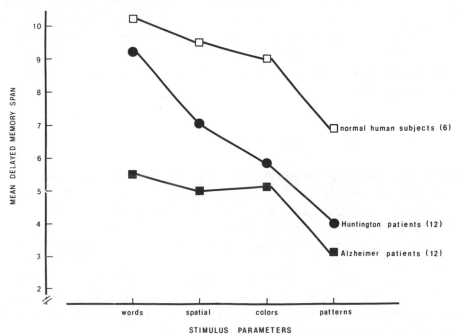

there may be individuals within the group who are quite atypical of the whole, by virtue of the variations in presentation described above. Such heterogeneity may confound one's ability to examine, in a uniform manner, the factors that contribute to the memory impairment of these patients.

In addition to variations in cognitive profiles with groups of Alzheimer patients, there is a great deal of variability in the psychiatric profiles of the patients as well. Depressive symptomatology is quite common early in the course of disease. Family members will typically report an overall diminished level of spontaneity and social involvement from the patient. Other Alzheimer patients first come to the attention of physicians because of inappropriate or aggressive behavior. This is often particularly striking because it is entirely out of character for a patient. By treating these symptoms with appropriate medication or short-term therapy, the functional level of Alzheimer patients can often be greatly improved. While it may not be feasible to select patients according to variations in psychiatric status, these dimensions should at least be quantified and controlled statistically, due to their potential impact on test behavior.

The subtypes we have described may result from differing combinations of neuropathological or neurochemical loss. For example, it is now widely accepted that a depletion of the cholinergic enzyme choline acetyltransferase (CAT) is the most dramatic and consistent chemical marker of Alzheimer disease (Terry & Davies, 1980). Furthermore, much of this loss in the cortex may derive from the degeneration of cells in the nucleus basalis of Meynert and the substantia innominata (Whitehouse, Price, Struble, Clark, & DeLong, 1981), which projects to widespread areas of the cortex and limbic system (Mesulam, VanHoesen, & Rosene, 1977) and contains CAT-positive cells (Levey, Musfon, Mesulam, & Wainer, 1982). However, a moderate to severe loss of cells in the locus ceruleus has also been reported in Alzheimer patients (Mann & Yates, 1981). While there does not appear to be a relationship between the catecholamine enzyme associated with the locus ceruleus (dopamine-β-hydroxylase) and the number of neuritic plaques in the brains of Alzheimer patients (Perry, Tomlinson, Blessed, Perry, Cross, & Crow, 1981), it seems likely that one subgroup of Alzheimer patients is made up of patients with both a cholinergic and a catecholaminergic deficit. It will probably require the careful behavioral description of patients whose neurochemical deficiencies can be measured during life to evaluate this hypothesis.

The Interaction of Age and Disease

There is at least one additional potential source for the heterogeneity one observes in the behavior of Alzheimer patients—that is, the age of the subjects. This is ironic, since the neuropathological similarity between presenile and senile patients (i.e., the presence of neuritic plaques and neurofibrillary tangles) has only recently been recognized (Katzman, 1976). Nevertheless, the term "Alzheimer disease" is now almost universally applied to individuals under and over the age of 65.

This practice has had a salutory effect on efforts to mobilize interest in and support for research and treatment in the area. However, it has often caused investigators to overlook the possibility that important differences may exist between presenile and senile patients of the Alzheimer type.

Investigations in our laboratory indicate that the differences in CT and EEG measures between Alzheimer patients and their controls vary with the age of the population. Measurements that can consistently discriminate patients under 65 from their controls are not useful among older patients (Albert, Naeser, Levine, & Garvey, in press-a), and vice versa (Albert, Naeser, Levine, & Garvey, in press-b; Duffy, Albert, & McAnulty, in press). Similarly, recent epidemiological data indicate that Alzheimer disease has a bimodal distribution in the population, with the younger patients appearing to have a much stronger genetic component (Mortimer & Schuman, 1981).

While these data do not necessarily imply that presenile and senile dementia of the Alzheimer type are two different diseases, they do at least suggest that important age–disease interactions exist that should not be overlooked. Thus, one cannot assume that the factors that contribute to the memory disorders of younger and older Alzheimer patients are identical without first comparing the groups for possible differences.

To date, we have only found such age–disease interactions in the naming behavior of patients with Alzheimer disease. When presenile and senile patients are equated for overall level of severity (using the Dementia Rating Scale), there remains a large and significant difference between the naming scores of younger and older patients (see Figure 23-6). Further investigations will be needed in order to determine whether the memory performance of Alzheimer patients is differentially affected by age as well.

FIGURE 23-6. A comparison between patients with Alzheimer disease (aged 45–64 and 65–85) and healthy age-equivalent controls on a confrontation-naming task. There is a significant difference between the older and younger controls ($p < .001$), a significant difference between the older and younger Alzheimer patients ($p < .001$), and a significant age $\times$ disease interaction. The Alzheimer patients were equated for level of severity on an activities of daily living (ADL) scale and the Dementia Rating Scale.

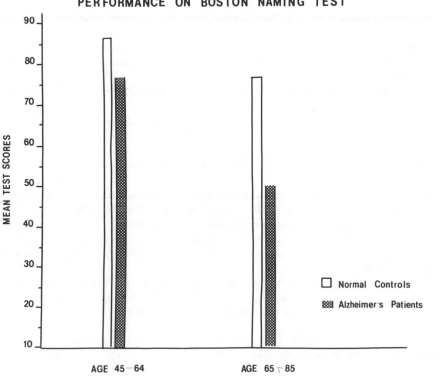

ACKNOWLEDGMENT

The preparation of this chapter was supported by Grant PO1-AG-02269 from the National Institute on Aging to Beth Israel Hospital and the Harvard Medical School.

REFERENCES

Albert, M. S., Naeser, M. A., Levine, H. L., & Garvey, J. Ventricular size in patients with presenile dementia of the Alzheimer type. *Archives of Neurology*, in press. (a)

Albert, M. S., Naeser, M. A., Levine, H. L., & Garvey, J. Mean CT density numbers in patients with senile dementia of the Alzheimer's type. *Archives of Neurology*, in press. (b)

Butters, N., Albert, M. S., Miliotis, P., Phillips, J., Sterste, A., & Sax, D. S. The effect of verbal mediators on the pictorial memory of brain-damaged patients. *Neuropsychologia*, 1983, *21*, 307–323.

Butters, N., Sax, D. S., Montgomery, K., & Tarlow, S. Comparison of the neuropsychological deficits associated with early and advanced Huntington's disease. *Archives of Neurology*, 1978, *35*, 585–589.

Coblentz, J. M., Mattis, S., Zingesser, L. H., Kasoff, S. S., Wisniewski, H. M., & Katzman, R. Presenile dementia: Clinical aspects and evaluation of cerebrospinal fluid dynamics. *Archives of Neurology*, 1973, *29*, 299–308.

Duffy, F. H., Albert, M. S., & McAnulty, G. Brain electrical activity in patients with presenile and senile dementia of the Alzheimer's type. *Annals of Neurology*, in press.

Kahn, R. L., Goldfarb, A. I., Pollack, M., & Peck, A. Brief objective measures for the determination of mental status in the aged. *American Journal of Psychiatry*, 1966, *118*, 326–328.

Katzman, R. The prevalence and malignancy of Alzheimer's disease. *Archives of Neurology*, 1976, *22*, 217–218.

Levey, A., Mufson, E. J., Mesulam, M. M., & Wainer, B. H. Co-localization of choline acetyltransferase and acetylcholinesterase in the mammalian forebrain. *Society for Neuroscience Abstracts*, 1982, *8*, 134.

Mahut, H., Zola-Morgan, S., & Moss, M. Hippocampal resections impair associative learning and recognition memory in the monkey. *Journal of Neuroscience*, 1982, *2*, 1214–1229.

Mann, D. M. A., & Yates, P. O. Dementia and cerebral noradrenergic innervation. *British Medical Journal*, 1981, *282*, 474–475.

Mattis, S. Dementia Rating Scale. In R. Bellack & B. Karasu (Eds.), *Geriatric psychiatry*. New York: Grune & Stratton, 1976.

Mesulam, M. M., VanHoesen, G. W., & Rosene, D. L. Substantia innominata, septal area and nuclei of the diagonal band in the rhesus monkey: Organization of efferents and their acetylcholinesterase histo-chemistry. *Society for Neuroscience Abstracts*, 1977, *3*, 202.

Mishkin, M. Memory in monkeys severely impaired by combined but not by separate removal of amygdala and hippocampus. *Nature*, 1978, *273*, 297–298.

Mortimer, J. A., & Schuman, L. M. (Eds.). *The epidemiology of dementia*. New York: Oxford University Press, 1981.

Perry, E. K., Tomlinson, B. E., Blessed, G., Perry, R. H., Cross, A. J., & Crow, T. J. Neuropathological and biochemical observations on the noradrenergic system in Alzheimer's disease. *Journal of Neurological Science*, 1981, *51*, 279–287.

Reisberg, B., Ferris, S. H., DeLeon, M. J., & Crook, T. The global deterioration scale for assessment of primary degenerative dementia. *American Journal of Psychiatry*, 1982, *139*, 1136–1139.

Rehbein, L. Doctoral dissertation, Northeastern University, in preparation.

Rosen, W., & Mohs, R. Evolution of cognitive decline in dementia. In S. Corkin, K. L. Davis, J. H. Growdon, E. Usdin, & R. J. Wurtman (Eds.), *Alzheimer's disease: A report of progress in research*. New York: Raven Press, 1982.

Terry, R. D., & Davies, P. Dementia of the Alzheimer's type. *Annual Review of Neuroscience*, 1980, *3*, 77–95.

Vitaliano, P. P., Breen, A. R., Albert, M. S., Russo, J., & Prinz, P. N. Memory, attention, and functional status in community residing Alzheimer type dementia patients and optimally healthy aged. *Journal of Gerontology*, 1984, *39*, 58–64.

Whitehouse, P. J., Price, D. L., Struble, R. G., Clark, J. T., & DeLong, M. R. Alzheimer's disease: Evidence for selective loss in the nucleus basalis. *Annals of Neurology*, 1981, *10*, 122–126.

24

Observations on Amnesia after Nonmissile Head Injury

Harvey S. Levin, Andrew Papanicolaou, and Howard M. Eisenberg

Head injury is the most common etiology of memory disorder, but it has attracted less investigative interest than alcoholic Korsakoff syndrome or rare cases of mesial temporal lobe surgery. Perhaps this apparent neglect of posttraumatic amnesia (PTA) reflects a reluctance to study memory problems that are frequently complicated by disturbed consciousness and attentional deficits. In this chapter, we assess the relationship between impaired consciousness and the gross amnesic defects characteristic of the early stages of recovery after head injury. We also discuss recent findings concerning the presence of a temporal gradient in retrograde amnesia (RA) produced by head injury. Lastly, we present preliminary evidence for a noninvasive, physiological measure of subacute amnesia after head-injured patients emerge from coma.

Subacute Amnesia in Relation to Impaired Consciousness and Attention

PTA (anterograde amnesia) is one of the most distinctive features of closed head injury (CHI), occurring even after mild head trauma that produces brief or no loss of consciousness (Russell, 1932; Yarnell & Lynch, 1970). RA for events before a head injury is relatively brief in relation to the duration of anterograde amnesia, typically spanning an interval measured in minutes or seconds in mild or moderate head injuries (Russell, 1935; Russell & Nathan, 1946). Consistent with clinical observations of amnesic periods in patients with relatively undisturbed consciousness after mild head injury, Ommaya and Gennarelli (1974) postulated that the structural irregularity and variation in tissue densities of the limbic and fronto-temporal cortices contribute to the vulnerability of these structures to injury, with resulting memory impairment, while the neural substrate for alertness (e.g., mesencephalic brain stem) is less vulnerable.

In contrast to amnesic disorders with an insidious onset (e.g., Korsakoff syndrome), moderate and severe head injury is typically followed immediately by a period of anterograde amnesia concomitant with a variable degree of disturbance in level of consciousness. Lethargy, agitation, incoherent talkativeness, inappropriate behavior, hallucinations, euphoria, and fluctuations in autonomic functioning frequently accompany anterograde amnesia during the early stages of emergence from coma following CHI (Moore & Ruesch, 1944; Russell, 1932). In view of these marked behavioral aberrations, Moore and Ruesch

Harvey S. Levin, Andrew Papanicolaou, and Howard M. Eisenberg. Division of Neurosurgery, The University of Texas Medical Branch, Galveston, Texas.

referred to this phase of recovery as "posttraumatic psychosis" rather than PTA. This constellation of features raises the question of whether PTA is but one of numerous manifestations of globally impaired consciousness, or the most prominent cognitive deficit during this stage of recovery. PTA also differs from alcoholic Korsakoff syndrome because computed tomographic (CT) scanning and surgical findings permit antemortem clinico-pathological correlation after head injury. Furthermore, advances in the clinical grading of coma provide a quantitative index of the severity of brain injury (Teasdale & Jennett, 1974).

Following publication of Russell's clinical data on estimates of PTA, Moore and Ruesch (1944) employed quantitative cognitive and psychomotor tasks to study impaired attention and other aspects of disturbed consciousness after CHI. While Russell and his colleagues focused on the amnesia characteristic of the early stage of recovery from head injury, they also acknowledged the presence of other early sequelae compatible with disturbed consciousness. Although recent research has emphasized the disruption of memory (cf. Schacter & Crovitz, 1977), there has been also a resurgence of interest in the contribution of attentional deficit to apparent memory disorder (Geschwind, 1982). The phenomenon of "islands" of intact memory—that is, preserved recall of isolated incidents during an otherwise amnesic period—may reflect the waxing and waning of attention.

Definition and Measurement of PTA

Ritchie Russell reported the first systematic studies of early recovery from head injury in his 1932 paper. He initially characterized this interval as the duration of disturbed consciousness (i.e., the "loss of full consciousness"). Accordingly, there was no differentiation of anterograde amnesia from coma or impaired consciousness (see Figure 24-1). In fact, Russell and Nathan (1946) defined the duration of PTA as the interval of "impaired consciousness." In 1961 Russell and Smith revised the earlier formulation by emphasizing impaired memory. They defined PTA as the duration of disturbance (of consciousness) during which "current events have not been stored." This definition has gained wide acceptance as an index of severity of CHI (cf. Jennett & Teasdale, 1981). Other investigators, however, have preferred to measure the duration of anterograde amnesia apart from the period of impaired consciousness as defined by the Glasgow Coma Scale (Teasdale & Jennett, 1974).

Procedures to measure PTA resemble traditional techniques of the mental status examination and are typically constrained by the necessity for brief bedside testing. Russell and his colleagues studied head-injured patients who had been transferred to the Military Hospital for Head Injuries in Oxford. To develop a uniform index of severity of brain insult for a large series of patients who were initially treated in diverse field hospitals under wartime conditions, Russell employed a retrospective interview that yielded an estimate of the interval of impaired consciousness (i.e., the period of both coma and anterograde amnesia; see Figure 24-1). Although this strategy yields prognostically useful information, particularly when other indices of acute neurological impairment are not available (Russell & Smith, 1961), it assumes that patients can distinguish between "real memory" and repeated briefing by their families during the early stages of recovery. Moreover, retrospective estimates of the duration of PTA are frequently discrepant from estimates given by the

EARLY STAGES OF RECOVERY FROM CLOSED HEAD INJURY

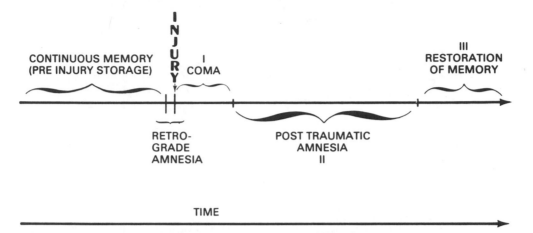

FIGURE 24-1. Sequence of acute alterations in memory after CHI. The periods of coma (I) and PTA (II) have been traditionally combined to yield a total interval of impaired consciousness that extends until continuous memory for ongoing events (III) is restored. (From H. S. Levin, A. L. Benton, & R. G. Grossman, *Neurobehavioral consequences of closed head injury*. New York: Oxford University Press, 1982. Reprinted by permission.)

patient during the early stage of recovery (Gronwall & Wrightson, 1980). Consequently, investigators have recently developed techniques to evaluate PTA directly, beginning when the patient emerges from coma (i.e., exhibits eye opening and obeys commands) (Fortuny, Briggs, Newcombe, Ratliff, & Thomas, 1980; Levin, O'Donnell, & Grossman, 1979). Although patients in this stage of recovery from CHI usually utter comprehensible speech, intubation may require modification of standard procedures, such as substituting a multiple-choice recognition format for verbal recall.

The Galveston Orientation and Amnesia Test (GOAT) was derived from a brief questionnaire of temporal orientation (Benton, Van Allen, & Fogel, 1964) and was expanded to include items testing orientation to person, place, and circumstances, in addition to a detailed description of the first postinjury memory and the last event before the injury. Although these latter items are frequently difficult to verify, they provide traditional measures of PTA and RA. Based on the distribution of scores in young adults who recovered from mild CHI (intact eye opening, preserved ability to obey commands, and comprehensible speech on admission, with no neurological deficit or CT evidence of hematoma or contusion), various levels of performance were defined and applied to a prospective series of head injuries of varying severity.

Daily administration of the GOAT yields a recovery curve depicting the restoration of orientation and resolution of gross amnesia, as illustrated in Figure 24-2. We operationally defined duration of PTA as the interval during which the GOAT score is below a borderline level of performance recorded in the standardization group (≤ 75). We found a strong relationship between the severity of initial neurological impairment (Glasgow Coma Scale score) and the duration of PTA as defined by the GOAT. The duration of PTA, as measured by the GOAT, was also related to overall recovery at least 6 months postinjury.

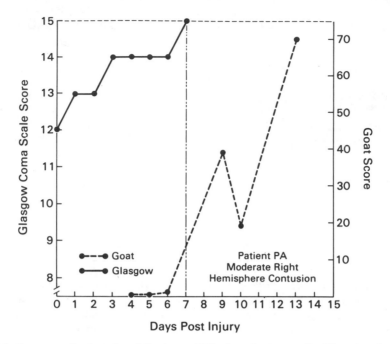

FIGURE 24-2. Recovery of orientation following a CHI of moderate severity. There is a 1-week delay in restoration of full orientation and resolution of gross amnesia after ratings of the patient's level of consciousness reach the ceiling of the Glasgow Coma Scale.

A similar technique to measure PTA directly was subsequently developed by Fortuny *et al.* (1980), who supplemented questions of orientation with a brief picture-recall test and asked the patient to recall the examiner's name. The investigators defined the termination of PTA as the point when the patient had 3 consecutive days of correct recall. The authors found that this brief test yielded estimates of PTA that agreed closely with the results of clinical examination by neurosurgeons.

Consistent with the results of direct measurement of PTA, Russell (1971) recommended that the "return of orientation" be used to signal the end of PTA. Gronwall and Wrightson (1980) serially interviewed a consecutive series of patients with mild head injury, beginning in the emergency room (an average interval of less than 2 hours postinjury). The authors determined that PTA ended when a patient exhibited "return of continuous memory" (i.e., was able to recall ongoing events related to his or her treatment and the circumstances of injury). Although Gronwall and Wrightson found a significant overall relationship between recovery of orientation and return of continuous memory, there were a sufficient number of dissociations (e.g., impaired recall of ongoing events despite normal orientation) to lead the authors to dispute the functional equivalence of disorientation and PTA. Whether this dissociation occurs after more severe CHI awaits further study. Clinical experience, however, suggests that marked disorientation and impaired memory are closely related during the early stages of recovery following coma.

Duration of PTA in Relation to the Duration of Coma

Direct measurement of PTA offers the opportunity to elucidate the early postcomatose stages of memory deficit following head injury. We have employed this technique to inquire about the relationship between the duration of coma and the period of PTA. Apart from the theoretical aspect of this relationship (see Figure 24-3), it would be clinically useful to predict the duration of gross confusion and marked behavioral disturbance after patients emerge from coma. Jennett and Teasdale (1981) estimated from an international data bank that the duration of PTA is about four times the length of the interval until speech returns after CHI, but details of measuring PTA were not given.

The pilot phase of the Coma Data Bank Network, which was developed by the National Institute of Neurological and Communicative Disorders and Stroke (NINCDS), has provided an opportunity to study consecutive admissions at six university hospitals for severe CHI (i.e., Glasgow Coma Scale score $\leq$ 8, consistent with no eye opening, inability to obey commands, and failure to utter comprehensible words). The GOAT was administered serially to survivors while they were hospitalized, yielding a direct measure of PTA (number of days postcoma until the GOAT score reached a normal level of $\geq$ 75) in 50 cases.

FIGURE 24-3. Duration of coma plotted against the duration of PTA in 50 head-injured patients whose findings were entered into the pilot phase of the NINCDS Coma Data Bank Network.

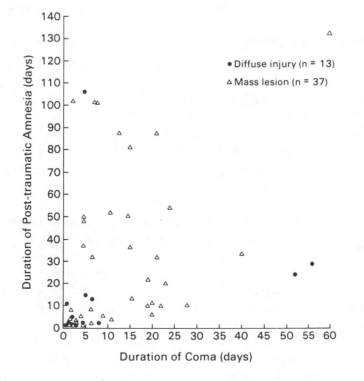

Plotting the duration of PTA against the duration of coma (coma was considered to end when the eyes opened to some stimulus and the patient obeyed commands and uttered comprehensible speech) yielded a relationship (see Figure 24-3) characterized by excessive variability to permit linear predication, despite statistical significance (Kendall rank-order correlation coefficient of .30, $p < .003$). Figure 24-3 shows several cases of markedly prolonged PTA despite relatively brief periods of coma. There was no feature common to these atypical cases or to patients whose PTA resolved rapidly after an interval of coma. From these preliminary findings, we surmise that there are other important determinants of PTA duration, apart from duration of coma.

RA and Ribot's Law of Regression

Ribot (1882) reviewed the published case studies of his era, which included detailed descriptions of amnesia for events before and after head injury. From these cases and reports of other etiologies of amnesia, Ribot proposed the law of regression, which holds that the susceptibility of a memory to disruption is inversely proportional to its age. He considered those memories to be unstable that were the "most recent recollections," because they had been "rarely repeated" and were therefore without "permanent associations."

Consistent with this view, Russell and Nathan (1946) found that the retrograde effects of amnesia rarely exceeded 30 minutes, except in patients with more severe CHI as reflected by a duration of PTA exceeding 1 day. Furthermore, Russell (1935) described a CHI patient who initially exhibited an RA that extended 9 years into the past while he was in PTA. During the following 10 weeks, he gradually recollected events in the remote past, beginning with the earliest memories, until his recall for past events was restored to within a few minutes of the accident. Russell and Nathan (1946) confirmed the shrinkage of RA in a series of CHI patients in whom the chronological sequence of recovery of remote memory typically paralleled the resolution of PTA. Benson and Geschwind (1967) reported an impressive case of shrinking RA in a head-injured patient whose retrograde loss was reduced from 2 years to 24 hours during the first 3 months after injury.

Since case reports of head-injured patients based on recall of autobiographical events and orientation have supported Ribot's law, we predicted that administration of a test of remote memory to patients in PTA would yield a temporal gradient (i.e., relative sparing of the oldest memories). To test this prediction, we employed a measure of recognition memory for names of former television programs broadcast for a single year (Squire & Slater, 1975), which has a comparable level of difficulty across time periods. We revised the test by including more recent shows and deleting programs too old for use with young head-injured patients. The television questionnaire was administered orally to 18 CHI patients (median age = 19 years, range = 16–39) who were in various stages of PTA, as reflected by their GOAT scores (median = 45, range = 10–79). All patients were enrolled in an inpatient rehabilitation program at the Plaza Del Oro Hospital, Houston, after sustaining a moderate to severe CHI (median Glasgow Coma Scale score on admission to trauma unit = 6, range = 4–10). To mitigate the effects of attentional deficit, we administered only 10 of the 30 items in each session. We also gave a self-administered, multiple-choice form of the test to 117 undergraduate students (mean age = 20 years, $SD = 7.7$)

who had resided in Texas (mean $=$ 19.9 years, $SD=$ 3.1) and owned a television during the time period encompassed by the test.

Figure 24-4 shows the percentage of correct recognition of the names of the television programs plotted against the time period during which they were broadcast. It is seen that the head-injured patients consistently recognized fewer programs than the control group, irrespective of the time period. There is no consistent trend for a temporal gradient in the remote memory of the CHI patients, as their performance parallels the pattern of the control group. We are extending our investigation of traumatic RA after head injury to include detailed autobiographical information that is verified by the family and a test of recognition of faces of persons who rose to prominence during specific time periods.

Our preliminary findings are apparently at variance with previous studies showing a temporal gradient in remote memory of patients with alcoholic Korsakoff syndrome or medial temporal lobe damage (Albert, Butters, & Levin, 1979; Squire & Cohen, 1982). This disparity can be at least partially explained by the insidious onset of anterograde-memory deficit, which disrupts storage of new information in patients with Korsakoff syndrome, while access to previously acquired knowledge may be relatively preserved. In contrast, we presume that young victims of CHI with no antecedent neuropsychiatric disorder had normal long-term memory consolidation during the preinjury time periods covered by the television questionnaire. Consequently, we infer that the RA of the head-injured patients is primarily attributable to retrieval failure. Since Squire and his coworkers have shown that recall procedures can produce a temporal gradient when no sparing of remote memory is seen on recognition, our interpretation awaits confirmation by recall procedures.

FIGURE 24-4. Percentage of correct recognition of the titles of former television programs, plotted as a function of the time period during which they were broadcast.

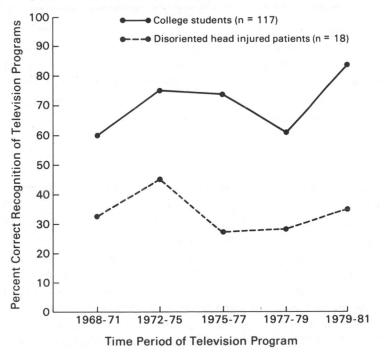

Evoked-Potential Correlates of PTA

Clinicians and investigators typically describe patients during the early stages of recovery from CHI as being "in" or "out" of PTA—expressions that denote a distinctive neurological condition. Although the cognitive and behavioral disturbances characteristic of PTA are more complex than the responses used to rate the depth of coma, this early stage of recovery can be distinguished from the behavioral characteristics of head-injured patients who have achieved full orientation and are no longer confused or grossly amnesic. As previously suggested (Levin, Benton, & Grossman, 1982), PTA may constitute a specific neurophysiological state in which learning does not transfer to the post-PTA stage of recovery (Overton, 1978). We are unaware, however, of any study showing a physiological correlate of PTA.

We postulated that aberrations in the P300, a late positive-going component of the auditory evoked potential (AEP) that purportedly reflects cognitive processing of a rare unpredictable stimulus (Pritchard, 1981), would parallel the resolution of PTA during the early stage of recovery from head injury. The appearance of this late AEP component after presentation of the rare tone is generally attributed to its greater salience, which engages focal attention and, presumably, more elaborate processing than the frequently occurring predictable stimulus. The precise nature of this processing, however, is unclear (see Pritchard, 1981, for an informative review).

Therefore, we proposed that the appearance of the P300 requires at least that the patient recognize the salience of the rare stimulus as opposed to the frequent one. However, recognition can only occur if there is registration in memory of both the physical parameters and the temporal features of both stimuli, as well as appreciation of their differences. As such, it would be expected that severely impaired attention and memory during PTA precludes the possibility of recognition and differential processing of the rare stimulus and would be reflected by the absence of the P300. The failure to retain information about the frequent tone and to appreciate the distinctiveness of the rare tone would result in identical AEP waveforms to both stimuli. We predicted that oriented CHI patients, who have emerged from PTA and therefore exhibit less severe deficits of attention and memory, would be capable of differentially processing the rare stimulus. A P300 should therefore appear in these head-injured patients, albeit delayed, due to their inefficient speed of cognitive processing (see Squires, Goodin, & Starr, 1979) in comparison with normal subjects.

We have compared AEPs recorded from a train of frequent 500-Hz tones to AEPs recorded from rare 1000-Hz tones that appear at random intervals (probability of .2). These stimuli are delivered binaurally through headphones at the same intensity level (65-dB sound pressure level). All recordings are made from the vertex (C_z) with linked-ear reference. A Nicolet Med-80 system is used for data collection and reduction. Up to this point we have obtained data from five normal adult volunteers, five comatose patients (GOAT score = 0), five disoriented or marginally oriented patients (GOAT score = 60–75), and two fully oriented CHI patients (GOAT score $\geq$ 80). All CHI patients were young adults studied during their initial hospitalization on our service. Both the patients and the normal subjects were asked to listen to the tones, but no response was requested.

Representative waveforms to the two tones from one subject in each group are shown in Figure 24-5A. Figure 24-5B represents mean latencies (and *SD*'s) of the major

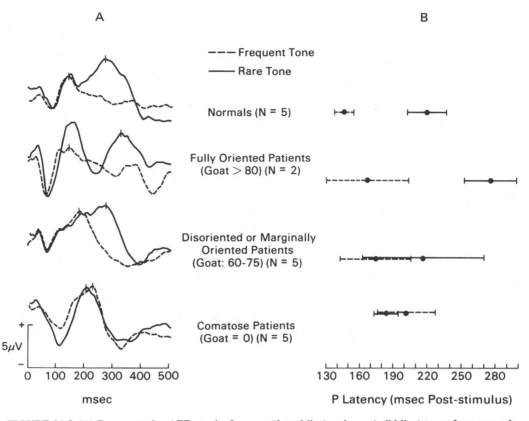

FIGURE 24-5. (A) Representative AEPs to the frequent (dotted-line) and rare (solid-line) tones from one subject in each group. The major positive peaks are marked by vertical lines. (B) The means and standard deviations of the peak latencies of the rare- and frequent-tone AEPs for each group of subjects.

positive peak for the frequent and rare tones. It is seen that the latency of the prominent (P2) peak in the AEP to the frequent tone increases with the severity of disturbance of consciousness. Secondly, the latency of the P300 response to the rare tone increases from the results obtained in normals to those obtained in the fully oriented CHI patients, but then it regresses towards and closely approximates the mean latency of the P2 to the frequent-tone AEP in the disoriented and in the comatose groups.

These data suggest that (1) the AEP response to the rare tone consists of two positive peaks (P2 and P300), the first most likely representing preattentive and the second attentive processing of the salient stimulus. In normal subjects the latter process is represented by the P300, and so it is with the fully awake, oriented CHI patients. During PTA (GOAT score = 60–75), however, when CHI patients fail to consistently recognize the difference between the two tones and to appreciate the saliency of the rare one, the latency differences of the rare- and frequent-tone peaks tend to overlap. In fact, the two prominent positive peaks to the rare tone cannot be distinguished clearly in the waveforms (see Figure 24-5A) of head-injured patients while they are in PTA. Finally, in comatose patients (GOAT score = 0), who are consistently unable to process the two stimuli differentially, the rare-tone AEP response seems to represent the same preattentive processing to this stimulus as to the frequent tones (i.e., no differential response).

We are cognizant that these interpretations are conjectural, based as they are on small groups of patients. However, we believe that the procedures we are using afford the possibility of establishing a direct physiological measure of recovering memory and attention during PTA.

Directions for Future Research

We anticipate application of information-processing paradigms and nonverbal measures to elucidate further the PTA and RA that characterize the early stages of recovery from nonmissile head injury. As we have shown, impaired consciousness is related to PTA duration, but other factors are also contributory. Concurrent assessment of various types of attention (e.g., selective vs. vigilant) could determine the contribution of nonretentive defects to PTA. In this connection, the P300 or other physiological measures may prove to be useful.

We also anticipate that amnesia resulting from brain injury will be studied more intensively to elucidate the neuropsychology of memory. Technological advances in activation and imaging procedures could permit visualization of regional changes in cerebral metabolism that parallel the resolution of traumatic amnesia. In contrast to most etiologies of memory disorder, the onset of traumatic amnesia can be precisely determined; preinjury neurological functioning is typically normal; and the new generation of CT scanners can frequently disclose the localization of focal injuries.

ACKNOWLEDGMENTS

Research reported in this chapter was supported by Grant NS 07377-12, Center for the Study of Nervous System Injury; Grants 80-233 and 82-47, the Moody Foundation; Contract NS 9-2308, Coma Data Bank Network; and Contract NS 9-2314, Comprehensive CNS Trauma Center. Portions of the data reported here were contributed to the National Institute of Neurological and Communicative Disorders and Stroke (NINCDS) Coma Data Bank Network by Donald P. Becker, MD, Medical College of Virginia; Howard M. Eisenberg, MD, The University of Texas Medical Branch; Robert G. Grossman, MD, Baylor College of Medicine; John A. Jane, MD, University of Virginia; Lawrence F. Marshall, MD, University of California, San Diego; and Kamran Tabaddor, MD, Albert Einstein College of Medicine. Selma Kunitz and her staff of the NINCDS Office of Biometry and Field Studies contributed ongoing support, and their assistance is gratefully acknowledged. We are grateful to Patricia Smith and Lori Bertolino for assistance in data analysis, and to Sarah De Los Santos for manuscript preparation.

REFERENCES

Albert, M. S., Butters, N., & Levin, J. Temporal gradients in the retrograde amnesia of patients with alcoholic Korsakoff's disease. *Archives of Neurology*, 1979, *36*, 211–216.
Benson, D. F., & Geschwind, N. Shrinking retrograde amnesia. *Journal of Neurology, Neurosurgery and Psychiatry*, 1967, *30*, 539–544.
Benton, A. L., Van Allen, M. W., & Fogel, M. L. Temporal orientation in cerebral disease. *Journal of Nervous and Mental Disease*, 1964, *139*, 110–119.
Fortuny, L. A. I., Briggs, M., Newcombe, F., Ratcliff, G., & Thomas, C. Measuring the duration of post traumatic amnesia. *Journal of Neurology, Neurosurgery and Psychiatry*, 1980, *43*, 377–379.
Geschwind, N. Disorders of attention: A frontier in neuropsychology. *Philosophical Transactions of the Royal Society of London: Biological Sciences*, 1982, *298*, 173–185.

Gronwall, D., & Wrightson, P., Duration of post-traumatic amnesia after mild head injury. *Journal of Clinical Neuropsychology*, 1980, *2*, 51–60.

Jennett, B., & Teasdale, G. *Management of head injuries*. Philadelphia: F. A. Davis, 1981.

Levin, H. S., Benton, A. L., & Grossman, R. G. *Neurobehavioral consequences of closed head injury*. New York: Oxford University Press, 1982.

Levin, H. S., O'Donnell, V. M., & Grossman, R. G. The Galveston Orientation and Amnesia Test: A practical scale to assess cognition after head injury. *Journal of Nervous and Mental Disease*, 1979, *167*, 675–684.

Moore, B. E., & Ruesch, J. Prolonged disturbances of consciousness following head injury. *New England Journal of Medicine*, 1944, *230*, 445–452.

Ommaya, A. K., & Gennarelli, T. A. Cerebral concussion and traumatic unconsciousness: Correlation of experimental and clinical observations on blunt head injuries. *Brain*, 1974, *97*, 633–654.

Overton, D. A. Major theories of state dependent learning. In B. T. Ho, D. W. Richards III, & D. L. Chute (Eds.), *Drug discrimination and state dependent learning*. New York: Academic Press, 1978.

Pritchard, W. S. Psychophysiology of P300. *Psychological Bulletin*, 1981, *89*, 506–540.

Ribot, T. *Diseases of memory: An essay in the positive psychology*. New York: Appleton, 1882.

Russell, W. R. Cerebral involvement in head injury. *Brain*, 1932, *55*, 549–603.

Russell, W. R. Amnesia following head injuries. *Lancet*, 1935, *ii*, 762–763.

Russell, W. R. *The traumatic amnesias*. New York: Oxford University Press, 1971.

Russell, W. R., & Nathan, P. W. Traumatic amnesia. *Brain*, 1946, *69*, 183–187.

Russell, W. R., & Smith, A. Post-traumatic amnesia in closed head injury. *Archives of Neurology*, 1961, *5*, 4–17.

Schacter, D. L., & Crovitz, H. F. Memory function after closed head injury: A review of the quantitative research. *Cortex*, 1977, *13*, 150–176.

Squire, L. R., & Cohen, N. J. Remote memory, retrograde amnesia, and the neuropsychology of memory. In L. S. Cermak (Ed.), *Human memory and amnesia*. Hillsdale, N.J.: Erlbaum, 1982.

Squire, L. R., & Slater, P. C. Forgetting in very long-term memory as assessed by an improved questionnaire technique. *Journal of Experimental Psychology: Human Learning and Memory*, 1975, *1*, 50–54.

Squires, K., Goodin, D., & Starr, A. Event related potentials in development, aging, and dementia. In D. Lehmann & E. Callaway (Eds.), *Human evoked potentials: Applications and problems*. New York: Plenum Press, 1979.

Teasdale, G., & Jeannett, B. Assessment of coma and impaired consciousness: A practical scale. *Lancet*, 1974, *ii*, 81–84.

Yarnell, P. R., & Lynch, S. Progressive retrograde amnesia in concussed football players: Observation shortly postimpact. *Neurology*, 1970, *20*, 416.

25

The Study of Human Memory with Neuro-Imaging Techniques

Terry L. Jernigan

The development of three-dimensional neuro-imaging techniques, which allow *in vivo* visualization of the brain, represents a major advance in neuroscience. Transmission computed tomography (TCT), which uses estimates of X-ray attenuation and tomographic reconstruction to provide images of cerebral structure, is now widely used in clinical research. Positron emission tomography (PET), a method by which the distribution of a labeled (emitting) substance of biological significance is visualized, has only recently been used for research, but the field is growing rapidly. Tomographic nuclear magnetic resonance (NMR) images, based on various aspects of an atom's behavior in the presence of specific magnetic fields, have so far been obtained in only a few clinical studies. The relative strengths and weaknesses of these methods have been the subjects of numerous discussions in the medical and biophysical literatures and are complex topics. Technical descriptions and comparisons of the methods are not attempted here. Rather, the focus of this chapter is on the relevance of these techniques in the study of human memory, and on conceptual issues considered to be critical to the success of neuro-imaging studies of cognition. Some of the issues discussed are by no means uniquely relevant to neuro-imaging research; however, it is hoped that describing the forms that such old problems take in this new area of research may prove a valuable exercise.

In most TCT and PET studies relevant to human memory, groups of people with cognitive deficits are examined, sometimes in comparison to normal controls. Such groups are typically composed of demented patients, in whom memory is particularly impaired, or of alcoholic or elderly subjects, in whom less dramatic memory changes are often reported. The aim of such studies is usually not to elucidate the cerebral bases of memory, but to investigate or describe the cerebral correlates of the diseases and thereby to gain understanding of their pathophysiology. The cognitive or neuropsychological assessments are usually of secondary importance to the investigator and are not collected with the goal of testing hypotheses about memory dysfunction *per se*. Rarely, a case study appears in which amnesia is thought to be the result of a discrete lesion (Squire & Moore, 1979), or a striking memory change is seen after cerebral infarction (Ross, 1980a, 1980b; Ladurner, Skvarc, & Sager, 1982). These studies are exceptions in that they specifically address the localization of mnemonic functions.

Since the goal of most neuro-imaging studies of elderly, alcoholic, or demented subjects is not the localization of cognitive impairment, perhaps it is not surprising that

Terry L. Jernigan. Psychology Service, Veterans Administration Medical Center, Palo Alto, California.

almost no new information on this topic has been gleaned from them. Nevertheless, investigators often attempt to draw inferences about the structural substrates of the memory impairments observed in their patient populations. Most often these inferences are drawn on the basis of the correlation of scores on memory tests with measures of atrophy on TCT, or with uptake of fluorodeoxyglucose (FDG) as measured by PET. Admittedly, these observations of correlation greatly strengthen the case for pursuing the study of human memory with brain scans. They do not, of course, establish the structural correlates of the deficits. Before the results of these correlations are summarized, a number of conceptual problems in this research area are discussed.

Conceptual Issues

Many errors of interpretation are probably related to a tendency to conceptualize neuro-images as "pictures of brain density" or "maps of brain function." In fact, of course, the data that give rise to these images are transformations of some particular aspect of brain structure or function. Such transformations, however, are exceedingly complex. To be sure, they are strongly related to certain characteristics of the brain (e.g., tissue density), but they are actually multifactorial *estimates* of these characteristics. Students of psychological-measurement theory are well aware of the interpretive difficulties that arise as a result of uncertainties about the relative proportions of reliable and error variance in their measurements (and, within the reliable variance, the specific factor variances). Rarely, however, does one encounter a discussion of the potential influence of these variables on the results of neuro-imaging studies, even when the methods of quantifying the image data are very crude. It would seem a safer course to approach neuro-images more as one would approach intelligence—by initially exploring the relationships between different techniques for measuring images, with the goals of discovering the sources of artifacts, estimating the reliabilities, and identifying different components of the variance. Having adopted this approach, one is sobered by the difficulties of establishing relationships between poorly understood brain measures and poorly understood cognitive measures. Seen in this light, however, the negative results of naive studies are more plausible and therefore less discouraging.

It behooves the investigator in this area to keep in mind, in addition to the difficulties described above, that the correlations he or she observes are viewed, as it were, through the "lens" of the particular disorder that afflicts the patients examined. For example, in our studies of alcoholics (Jernigan, Zatz, Ahumada, Pfefferbaum, Tinklenberg, & Moses, 1982), much more cortical sulcal widening was present than is observed in normals, but only slightly more ventricular fluid volume. In these subjects a neuro-psychological test, Trailmaking—Form B, correlated highly with sulcal widening measures but not at all with ventricular measures. In a group of elderly subjects, however, with substantially more ventricular enlargement, the same measure correlated significantly with both ventricular and sulcal measures; in fact, with regression analyses, it could be shown that the sulcal measure did not significantly improve the prediction of this deficit over the ventricular measure alone. Numerous issues arise in the interpretation of such a result, but the point here is that the constraints on one's observations imposed by the cerebral disorder itself must be considered. Inferences about brain–behavior relationships must be consistent not only with the pattern of findings within a particular patient group, but with the constellation of patterns occurring over a variety of groups in which different cerebral pathologies are present.

As in many research areas, low measurement validity and the practice of giving the same label to measures of different things account for most of the discrepancies in the neuro-imaging literature. After these, however, probably the greatest source of discrepancy is the use of data-analytic methods that capitalize on chance variability. By this, I refer to instances in which investigators collect lots of measurements, test the "significance" of many relationships, and present the "significant" results as representing the underlying neurobehavioral structure. The standard injunction issued by the experimentally trained psychologist in response to this problem is "Adopt a model!" The rationale here is that studies guided by specific models, involving specific hypotheses, produce only those measures representing factors in the model. Although the utility of a working model in research is beyond question, I would advocate a middle-of-the-road position on this issue. Robert Crowder makes a cogent argument that even the most appealing models adopted from the domain of cognitive psychology have enjoyed little real success when tested with clinical data (Crowder, 1982). In his closing remarks, when describing a theoretically problematic syndrome in an aphasic, he makes the following statements:

> The symptom was not, in all probability, discovered by putting the aphasic through the standard information-processing experiments of the time. Instead, I suspect, it was naturalistic observation informed by theoretical sophistication (and a bit of luck) that did the trick. Theoretical sophistication comes from frontline immersion in basic research and the research literature but it does not require that the theories be put to test with factorial experiments including Korsakoff and controls as one factor. Perhaps somewhat more of this observational approach with amnesics might assist us in getting an idea of the phenomenon with which we are dealing. (pp. 40–41)

The approach that Crowder is suggesting may be different from the one that I describe, and is certainly different from the representative clinical studies of patients with memory impairments reviewed below. My position is that it is appropriate in many cases to aim clinical studies at the descriptive level of analysis. This is not to endorse those clinical studies in which no *a priori* hypotheses are made; this practice is never justified. Nor do I suggest that clinical investigators make inferential statements based on descriptive results. In my opinion, the best studies test hypotheses, but include extensive post hoc analyses conducted in the service of generating new hypotheses consistent with the data. Needless to say, this generative process is aided immeasurably by theoretical sophistication. It is well to recognize that neuro-imaging studies produce kinds of data that have not previously been available, and that those data that were available were not adequate to support plausible models of those phenomena we investigate with imaging techniques.

Reported Correlations of Structure and Function

The following summary of findings should not be interpreted to imply that correlations between memory measures and measures of brain atrophy are invariably obtained. The majority of those reports that are published and that mention such data do note correlations, but this may be a highly biased sample of the relevant studies. This section reviews findings in alcoholics, normal elderly subjects, and demented subjects, respectively. With the exception of a few PET reports, all of the studies reviewed used TCT.

In a very large sample of people, 20 to 65 years of age, in which 29% of the subjects reported drinking "too much" and 10% were classified as "excessive drinkers," a measure of word learning was correlated with linear measures of the ventricular spaces and with subjective ratings of cortical atrophy (Bergman, Borg, Hindmarsh, Idestrom, & Mutzell, 1980). Similar recent-memory tests from the Wechsler Memory Scale (WMS) were correlated with widths of ventricular and sulcal fluid spaces in a group of chronic alcoholics and in a smaller group of Korsakoff amnesics (Wilkinson & Carlen, 1980).

In elderly subjects, a clinical evaluation of "memory and information" was correlated with maximum ventricular areas, but not with an undescribed measure of cortical atrophy (Roberts & Caird, 1976). In another study, however, a clinical "memory and orientation" assessment correlated with ratings of cortical atrophy but not with measures of ventricular enlargement (Jacoby, Levy, & Dawson, 1980). The Visual Reproduction score from the WMS correlated weakly with measures of sulcal and ventricular width in another study of 60- to 100-year-old people (Earnest, Heaton, Wilkinson, & Manke, 1979). When an otherwise unselected group of elderly people with diffuse cerebral atrophy were studied, correlations were obtained between a measure of delayed recall of words and frontal ventricular width. In the same study, the score on the Squire Television Test of remote memory correlated with sylvian fissure width, which is thought to reflect anterior temporal atrophy (Wu, Schenkenberg, Wing, & Osborn, 1981).

In patients with known or suspected dementia, measures of global atrophy, ventricular enlargement, and sulcal widening correlated with clinical and standardized measures of immediate, recent, and remote memory (de Leon, Ferris, George, Reisberg, Kricheff, & Gershon, 1980; Gutzmann & Avdaloff, 1980; Kaszniak, Garron, & Fox, 1979; Kaszniak, Garron, Fox, Bergen, & Huckman, 1979). In one study, measures of digit span and recent memory for prose, designs, and verbal associates were correlated with a measure of reduced discriminability of white and gray matter on the cortical vertex (George, de Leon, Ferris, & Kricheff, 1981).

It should be emphasized that in all of these reports correlation coefficients were small—about .30 to .40 in most cases, occasionally .40 to .60 in demented samples. In an early study of seven demented patients using PET, the results suggested that this new technique would allow predictions of much greater magnitude (Ferris, de Leon, Wolf, Farkas, Christman, Reisberg, Fowler, MacGregor, Goldman, George, & Rampal, 1980). Correlations between regional estimates of FDG uptake and subtests of the Guild Memory Test (recall of prose, designs, and paired associates) ranged from .73 to .92. Unfortunately, no attempt was made to examine regional differences in these relationships. In a later report, when 11 patients had been studied, the results were essentially the same (Farkas, Ferris, Wolf, de Leon, Christman, Reisberg, Alavi, Fowler, George, & Reivich, 1982). In the latest study of which I am aware, of 10 patients with presumptive Alzheimer disease, the initial results revealed high correlations (above .70) between ratios of right frontal to left frontal FDG concentrations and cognitive measures (Friedland, Budinger, Ganz, Yano, Mathis, Koss, Ober, Huesman, & Derenzo, 1983).

In summary, ample evidence exists to suggest that changes observable on neuro-images are associated with disordered memory in several patient groups. Unfortunately, almost no attempts have been made to establish what, if any, independent effects on memory may be attributed to changes in different cerebral structures. It is suggestive that measures of the sylvian fissures, third ventricle, and frontal horns have repeatedly been correlated with tests of recent and remote memory, but the analyses used in the studies are not adequate to implicate the adjacent regions. The following is an outline of some initial attempts that my colleagues and I have made to address this problem with TCT. Most of the results I mention are not yet published because of their tentative nature, though some of the results have been presented at meetings.

An Approach to Neurobehavioral Research

In an initial study of normal elderly schoolteachers, the cognitive correlates of cerebral atrophy were examined (Jernigan, Zatz, Feinberg, & Fein, 1980). Our hypotheses were that performance on tests of immediate, recent, and remote memory would decline with increasing cerebral atrophy. A test of immediate memory (digit span) was correlated with visual ratings as well as automated volume measures of ventricular enlargement, and remote-memory scores (Albert, Butters, & Levin, 1979) were correlated with measures of cortical atrophy, both in perisylvian and vertex areas, and with third ventricular width. The recent-memory scores (verbal paired associates) were not significantly correlated with any measure of atrophy. In post hoc analyses, we discovered that in the subset of subjects who performed poorly on the paired-associates test, the scores were correlated with widening of the third ventricle and other measures of atrophy in the region of the thalamus and sylvian fissure.

Recently we completed a second study of 50 elderly volunteers. The subjects were 49 to 82 years of age. No correlation was observed between digit span performance and any of three measures of atrophy. We can only speculate that this discrepancy may have been due to sampling error, or to differences in the composition of the two samples. The results with the paired-associate scores were similar to those in the earlier study: Only in low-scoring subjects were the significant relationships with measures of perisylvian cortical atrophy. The remote-memory score was again correlated with measures of vertex cortical atrophy and perisylvian cortical atrophy.

Unfortunately, none of these results allow us to conclude that any particular area of the brain is implicated in the memory impairments of our subjects. Let us take remote memory as an example. We assume that performance on this test reflects ability to recall information that has been previously encoded. Since the score has been correlated with measures of atrophy in two independent samples of elderly people, we will assume that this is a reliable finding, and not a product of spurious association. We have collected several measures of atrophy: one of vertex sulcal widening (VSUL), which we hope reflects primarily atrophy of the cortical convexity; one of enlargement of the sylvian and inter-hemispheric fissures (FTSUL), which we hope reflects primarily frontal and anterior temporal cortical atrophy; and one of ventricular enlargement (VEN), which we hope reflects primarily atrophy of central gray matter and subcortical white matter. The remote-memory score (recall) shows correlation with the sulcal measures, but not with the ventricular measure (see Table 25-1). The two cortical measures are correlated with recall to approximately the same degree. When the three atrophy measures are entered into a regression to predict recall, no variable has a significant regression coefficient (see Table

TABLE 25-1. Measures of Association between Cognitive and CT Variables

Measure	VEN	FTSUL	VSUL
Correlation coefficients			
Recall	.05	−.35*	−.39**
Trails B	.41**	.24	.27
t statistics for regression coefficients			
Recall	1.52	−1.62	−1.71
Trails B	2.72**	−.35	1.52

*$p < .05$.

**$p < .01$.

25-1). The regression coefficients in this case relate to the *unique* contributions of the variables to the prediction. In this case, the regression coefficient for VEN is low because it is not predictive of recall, but those for the sulcal measures are low because they do not have high unique predictability (i.e., either one will do as well). The question in which we are most interested involves the degree to which some measures have significantly greater unique relationship to deficits than do other measures. The differences between the regression coefficients tell us something about this. In order to test the hypothesis that the measures differ in this respect, we must test the significance of the differences we observe between the regression coefficients. A convenient method for doing this is as follows: For the two CT measures of interest, we compute both their sum and their difference. Then instead of the two measures, we enter these two new combinations of them, with the additional CT measure, into the regression to predict the recall measure. If the difference measure has a significant regression coefficient, then the two CT measures have significantly different unique relation to the recall measure. Table 25-2 contains the results of these analyses for the recall measure. Both VSUL and FTSUL are significantly more strongly related to recall than is VEN, but no significant difference is found between the two sulcal measures.

These results provide evidence that sulcal widening is more disruptive of recall than is ventricular enlargement in this population. Unfortunately, however, one could argue that the lack of association with ventricular enlargement was simply due to a lack of sensitivity in the ventricular measure, relative to the cortical measures. For example, if we had rated the ventricles blindfolded, the same result would have occurred, even if ventricular enlargement was strongly related to recall. Such an argument would be difficult to make, however, if we could establish a double dissociation—that is, if some other measure showed the opposite pattern of correlations with these atrophy measures.

To illustrate the methods we use to attempt to establish such a dissociation, I include the results of these analyses for another measure we have repeatedly found to be correlated with atrophy, Trailmaking—Form B (Trails B). Examination of Tables 25-1 and 25-2 reveals the following pattern of results: In this case, the simple correlation for VEN is significant, but not those for the sulcal measures. A similar pattern is observed for the regression coefficients, since the ventricular measure is uniquely predictive of Trails B in

TABLE 25-2. t Statistics for Differences between Pairs of Regression Coefficients

Measure	VEN/FTSUL	VEN/VSUL	FTSUL/VSUL
Recall	2.04**	2.37**	.06
Trails B	1.70*	.78	1.03

*$p < .10$.
**$p < .05$.

this set of predictors. The difference between the regression coefficients, however, only approaches significance in the case of VEN/FTSUL. Therefore, in this case, we are not able to state definitely that a specific relationship exists between the sulcal measures and recall. If the regression coefficient for VEN had been significantly different from those for the sulcal measures, we could argue that since the ventricular measure is sufficiently sensitive to show a unique relation to Trails B, the unique relationship of the sulcal measures to recall must not be due to variations in measurement sensitivity. Although our criteria have not been met, we are encouraged to see this pattern in our results. Perhaps if we had compared the pattern observed with recall to that with a measure more factorially pure than Trails B, the desired outcome would have occurred.

Clearly, a variety of additional issues must be resolved before we can conclude that the loss of cortical tissue is responsible for the impairment of remote memory in old age. The analyses described above are summarized here to illustrate an approach to the use of neuro-images for establishing which changes in which structures disrupt mnemonic function. We hope to begin soon to use this approach to study PET results in aged and demented subjects. With this technique, a great increase in sensitivity to cerebral function is anticipated. This gain is likely to yield high dividends if we proceed cautiously and thoughtfully. Early studies will, of necessity, be exploratory. It is most important that our explorations be guided by multidimensional models of the phenomena we observe, and that we acknowledge that with complex models most results may be explained in a multitude of ways.

ACKNOWLEDGMENT

I am grateful to Al Ahumada, Jr., and Leslie M. Zatz for many helpful discussions during the preparation of this chapter. This work was supported by the Medical Research Service, Veterans Administration Medical Center, Palo Alto, California.

REFERENCES

Albert, M. S., Butters, N., & Levin, J. Temporal gradients in the retrograde amnesia of patients with alcoholic Korsakoff's disease. *Archives of Neurology*, 1979, *36*, 211–216.

Bergman, H., Borg, S., Hindmarsh, T., Idestrom, C. M., & Mutzell, S. Computed tomography of the brain, clinical examination and neurological assessment of a random sample of men from the general population. *Acta Psychiatrica Scandinavica*, 1980, *62*, 47–56.

Crowder, R. G. General forgetting theory and the locus of amnesia. In L. S. Cermak (Ed.), *Human memory and amnesia*. Hillsdale, N.J.: Erlbaum, 1982.

de Leon, M. J., Ferris, S. H., George, A. E., Reisberg, B., Kricheff, I. I., & Gershon, S. Computed tomography evaluations of brain–behavior relationships in senile dementia of the Alzheimer's type. *Neurobiology of Aging*, 1980, *1*, 69–79.

Earnest, M. P., Heaton, R. K., Wilkinson, W. E., & Manke, W. F. Cortical atrophy, ventricular enlargement and intellectual impairment in the aged. *Neurology*, 1979, *29*, 1138–1143.

Farkas, T., Ferris, S. H., Wolf, A. P., de Leon, M. J., Christman, D. R., Reisberg, B., Alavi, A., Fowler, J. S., George, A. E., & Reivich, M. F-2-deoxy-2-fluoro-D-glucose as a tracer in the positron emission tomographic study of senile dementia. *American Journal of Psychiatry*, 1982, *139*, 352–353.

Ferris, S. H., de Leon, M. J., Wolf, A. P., Farkas, T., Christman, D. R., Reisberg, B., Fowler, J. S., MacGregor, R., Goldman, A., George, A. E., & Rampal, S. Positron emission tomography in the study of aging and senile dementia. *Neurobiology of Aging*, 1980, *1*, 127–131.

Friedland, R. P., Budinger, T. F., Ganz, E., Yano, Y., Mathis, C. A., Koss, B., Ober, B. A., Huesman, R. H., & Derenzo, S. E. Regional cerebral metabolic alterations in dementia of the Alzheimer type: Positron emission tomography with 18-fluorodeoxyglucose. *Journal of Computer Assisted Tomography*, 1983, *7*, 590–598.

George, A. E., de Leon, M. J., Ferris, S. H., & Kricheff, I. I. Parenchymal CT correlates of senile dementia (Alzheimer disease): Loss of gray–white matter discriminability. *American Journal of Neuroadiology*, 1981, *2*, 205–213.

Gutzmann, H., & Avdaloff, W. Mental impairment (dementia) and cerebral atrophy in geriatric patients. *Mechanisms of Ageing and Development*, 1980, *14*, 459–468.

Jacoby, R. J., Levy, R., & Dawson, J. M. Computed tomography in the elderly: I. Normal population. *British Journal of Psychiatry*, 1980, *136*, 249–255.

Jernigan, T. L., Zatz, L. H., Ahumada, A. J., Pfefferbaum, A., Tinklenberg, J. R., & Moses J. A. CT measures of cerebrospinal fluid volume in alcoholics and normal volunteers. *Psychiatry Research*, 1982, *7*, 9–17.

Jernigan, T. L., Zatz, L. M., Feinberg, I., & Fein, G. Measurement of cerebral atrophy in the aged by computed tomography. In L. W. Poon (Ed.), *Aging in the 1980's: Psychological issues*. Washington, D.C.: American Psychological Association, 1980.

Kaszniak, A. W., Garron, D. C., & Fox, J. Differential effects of age and cerebral atrophy upon span of immediate recall and paired-associate learning in older patients suspected of dementia. *Cortex*, 1979, *15*, 285–295.

Kaszniak, A. W., Garron, D. C., Fox, J. H., Bergen, D., & Huckman, M. Cerebral atrophy, EEG slowing, age, education, and cognitive functioning in suspected dementia. *Neurology*, 1979, *29*, 1273–1279.

Ladurner, G., Skvarc, A., & Sager, W. D. Computer tomography in transient global amnesia. *European Neurology*, 1982, *21*, 34–40.

Roberts, M. A., & Caird, F. I. Computerized tomography and intellectual impairment in the elderly. *Journal of Neurology, Neurosurgery and Psychiatry*, 1976, *39*, 986–989.

Ross, E. D. Sensory-specific and fractional disorders of recent memory in man: I. Isolated loss of visual recent memory. *Archives of Neurology*, 1980, *37*, 193–200. (a)

Ross, E. D. Sensory-specific and fractional disorders of recent memory in man.: II. Unilateral loss of tactile recent memory. *Archives of Neurology*, 1980, *37*, 267–272. (b)

Squire, L. R., & Moore, R. Y. Dorsal thalamic lesion in a noted case of chronic memory dysfunction. *Annals of Neurology*, 1979, *6*, 503–506.

Wilkinson, D. A., & Carlen, P. L. Relationship of neuropsychological test performance to brain morphology in amnesic and non-amnesic chronic alcoholics. *Acta Psychiatrica Scandinavica*, 1980, *62*, 89–101.

Wu, S., Schenkenberg, T., Wing, S. D., & Osborn, A. J. Cognitive correlates of diffuse cerebral atrophy determined by computed tomography. *Neurology*, 1981, *31*, 1180–1184.

Studies of Memory in Nonhuman Primates

Although a great deal can be learned about the neuropsychology of memory by studying humans, in the end one must also turn to experimental animals, in which brain–behavior relationships can be studied rigorously with a variety of techniques. With this approach, questions about which brain regions are involved in memory, which have not yet been answered with certainty in human studies, can be addressed directly.

This section consists of seven chapters describing how the neuropsychology of memory has been investigated in the monkey. Three different approaches are represented. The first attempts to characterize the properties of single cortical and subcortical neurons and then to make inferences about the normal organization of memory and about the roles of separate brain regions. What makes this approach fruitful is that neurons can be found that are sensitive to both fixed and acquired properties of stimuli, including their physical features, their reward value, and whether or not they need to be remembered. The second approach derives from the study of human amnesia and the finding that damage to particular brain regions can produce strikingly selective deficits in learning and memory. The goal with monkeys is to establish animal models of human amnesia and thereby to identify with certainty which brain areas must be damaged to produce the syndrome as well as to study in detail the contributions of these brain areas to normal memory functions. The third approach, in a sense, builds on the success of the second and asks broader questions about the overall organization of memory in the brain: Where is memory stored? How do the two cortical hemispheres interact in memory storage? What are the separate contributions of frontal cortex, inferotemporal cortex, and the other sensory, motor, and association areas? One of the major themes to emerge from work with monkeys is the close correspondence between the findings for monkeys and the findings for humans.

26

Neurophysiological Investigations of Different Types of Memory in the Primate

Edmund T. Rolls

Introduction

In this chapter, investigations of the neural basis of different types of memory in the primate, using recordings of the activity of single neurons during the performance of different types of memory task by monkeys, are described. The aims of this approach are to define the extent to which the neural processing involved in different types of memory may be dissociable and separately localized; to determine the type of computation being performed in relation to memory in different parts of the central nervous system and to trace the processing through the system from input to output; and, by increasing understanding of normal memory processing, to clarify our understanding of disorders of memory. The types of memory processing considered here include the formation of learned associations between stimuli and reward or punishment, the disconnection of such stimulus–reinforcement associations, recognition memory, sensory–motor habit formation, and short-term habituation to patterned visual stimuli.

The Formation of Stimulus–Reinforcement Associations

The Lateral Hypothalamus and Substantia Innominata

During investigations of the neurophysiological control of feeding, my colleagues and I (Rolls, Burton, & Mora 1976) found neurons in the lateral hypothalamus and substantia innominata of the hungry monkey that responded to the sight of food but not of nonfood objects. Because these neurons responded to a wide range of visual stimuli that signified food for the hungry monkey, it appeared possible that the responses of these neurons became associated with the sight of food during learning. To test this, the activity of these neurons was recorded while the monkeys learned and performed a visual discrimination in which one visual stimulus—for example, a circle—indicated that a monkey could make a lick response to obtain food, and a different stimulus—for example, a square—indicated that the monkey must not make a lick response, or it would obtain aversive hypertonic saline. It was found that in this task the responses of these neurons became associated with the visual stimulus that signified food; that the responses of these neurons preceded and predicted the feeding responses of the monkey; and that the responses of the

Edmund T. Rolls. Department of Experimental Psychology, University of Oxford, Oxford, England, United Kingdom.

neurons were not due just to mouth movements made by the monkey (Mora, Rolls, & Burton, 1976; Rolls, Sanghera, & Roper-Hall, 1979; Rolls *et al.*, 1976). Moreover, if a particular visual stimulus was no longer associated with reward, as in extinction, then the neuron ceased to respond to that stimulus, and if the association of the stimuli with reinforcement was reversed in the visual discrimination, then the responses of the neurons also reversed, remaining associated with whichever visual stimulus was associated with reward (Mora *et al.*, 1976; Rolls, Sanghera, & Roper-Hall, 1979).

These experiments thus provided evidence that there were neurons in the lateral hypothalamus and substantia innominata with responses that occurred to visual stimuli associated with reinforcement. Visual information could reach these basal forebrain neurons through the inferior temporal visual cortex and amygdala. This is indicated by anatomical evidence for connections from the inferior temporal cortex to the amygdala (Herzog & Van Hoesen, 1976; Turner, Mishkin, & Knapp, 1980) and from the amygdala to the basal forebrain (Nauta, 1961) (see Figure 26-1). It is also indicated by the evidence that lesions of the anterior part of the temporal lobe (or of the amygdala or the temporal lobe neocortex) lead to the Klüver–Bucy syndrome, in which monkeys respond to nonfood objects as if they were food, and have deficits in learning tasks in which visual stimuli must be associated with reinforcement (Akert, Gruesen, Woolsey, & Meyer, 1961; Jones & Mishkin, 1972; Klüver & Bucy, 1939; Spiegler & Mishkin, 1981). To determine where along this pathway the responses of neurons might become associated with reinforcing visual stimuli, recordings were made of the activity of neurons in the inferior temporal visual cortex and amygdala while rhesus monkeys performed visual discriminations. Recordings were also made while they were shown visual stimuli associated with positive reinforcement such as food; stimuli associated with negative reinforcement, such as aversive hypertonic saline; and neutral visual stimuli (Rolls, Judge, & Sanghera, 1977; Sanghera, Rolls, & Roper-Hall, 1979).

FIGURE 26-1. Some of the pathways described in the text are shown on this lateral view of the rhesus monkey brain. (Abbreviations: amyg, amygdala; central s, central sulcus; Hyp, hypothalamus–substantia innominata–basal forebrain; Lat f, lateral (or Sylvian) fissure; m, mammillary body; Sup Temp s, superior temporal sulcus; 7 = posterior parietal cortex, area 7.)

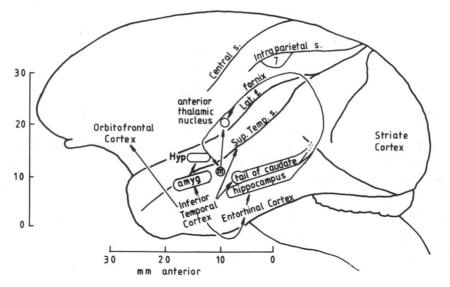

Inferior Temporal Visual Cortex

It was found that during visual discriminations inferior temporal neurons often had sustained visual responses with latencies of 100–140 msec to the discriminanda, but that these responses did not depend on whether the visual stimuli were associated with reward or punishment (in that the neuronal responses did not alter during reversals, when the previously rewarded stimulus was made to signify aversive saline and the previously punished stimulus was made to signify reward) (Rolls *et al.*, 1977). The conclusion, that the responses of at least the majority of inferior temporal neurons during visual discriminations do not code for whether a visual stimulus is associated with reward or punishment, is also consistent with the findings of Ridley, Hester, and Ettlinger (1977), Jarvis and Mishkin (1977), Gross, Bender, and Gerstein (1979), and Sato, Kawamura, and Iwai (1980). Further, it was found that inferior temporal neurons did not respond only to food-related visual stimuli, or only to aversive stimuli, and were not dependent on hunger; rather, in many cases their responses depended on physical aspects of the stimuli, such as shape, size, orientation, color, or texture (Rolls *et al.*, 1977).

Amygdala

In recordings made from 1754 amygdaloid neurons, it was found that 113 (6.4%), of which many were in a dorsolateral region of the amygdala known to receive inputs directly from the inferior temporal visual cortex (Herzog & Van Hoesen, 1976), had visual responses that in most cases were sustained while the monkey looked at effective visual stimuli (Sanghera *et al.*, 1979). The latency of the responses was 100–140 msec or more. The majority (85%) of these visual neurons responded more strongly to some stimuli than to others, but physical factors (such as orientation, color, and texture) that accounted for the responses could not usually be identified. It was found that 22 (19.5%) of these visual neurons responded primarily to foods and to objects associated with food, but for none of these neurons did the responses occur uniquely to food-related stimuli, in that they all responded to one or more aversive or neutral stimuli. Further, although some neurons responded in a visual discrimination to the visual stimulus that indicated food reward, but not to the visual stimulus associated with aversive saline, only minor modifications of the neuronal responses were obtained when the association of the stimuli with reinforcement was reversed in the reversal of the visual discrimination. A comparable population of neurons with responses that were apparently partly but not uniquely related to aversive visual stimuli was also found (Sanghera *et al.*, 1979). These findings thus suggest that the amygdala could be involved in an early stage of the processing by which visual stimuli are associated with reinforcement, but that neuronal responses here do not code uniquely for whether a visual stimulus is associated with reinforcement (see Rolls, 1981b).

Thus the responses during stimulus–reinforcement association learning, as well as the effective stimuli and the response latencies, of neurons recorded in the anatomical sequence inferior temporal cortex–amygdala–hypothalamus, suggest that visual processing along this pathway becomes increasingly dependent on previous reinforcement. There is little relation to reinforcement in the inferior temporal visual cortex; some effect of reinforcement becomes evident in the amygdala; and full elaboration of neuronal responses in relation to reinforcement becomes evident in the basal forebrain.

The Disconnection of Associations between Visual Stimuli and Reinforcement

Lesions

The disconnection of associations between visual stimuli and reinforcement may involve separate mechanisms from those involved in their formation. The orbito-frontal cortex is implicated by lesion evidence in these disconnection processes. Lesions of the orbito-frontal cortex impair (1) reversals of visual discriminations, in that the monkeys make responses to the previously reinforced stimulus or object; (2) extinction, in that responses continue to be made to the previously reinforced stimulus; (3) go/no-go tasks, in that responses are made to the stimulus that is not associated with reward; and (4) passive avoidance, in that responses are made when they are punished (Butter, 1969; Iversen & Mishkin, 1970; Jones & Mishkin, 1972; Tanaka, 1973; see also Fuster, 1980, and Rosenkilde, 1979). In contrast, the formation of associations between visual stimuli and reinforcement is much less affected by these lesions than by temporal lobe lesions, as tested during visual-discrimination learning; and the reversal of a spatial-response task, in which responses must be prevented to a position rather than to an object previously associated with reinforcement, is less impaired by orbito-frontal than by hippocampal lesions (Jones & Mishkin, 1972).

Neuronal Activity in the Orbito-Frontal Cortex

To investigate the possible functions of the orbito-frontal cortex in the disconnection of stimulus–reinforcement associations, recordings were made of the activity of 494 orbito-frontal neurons during the performance of a go/no-go task, reversals of a visual-discrimination task, extinction, and passive avoidance (Thorpe, Rolls, & Maddison, 1983; see also Rolls, 1981a). First, neurons were found that responded in relation to the preparatory auditory or visual signal used before each trial (15.1%), or nondiscriminatively during the period in which the discriminative visual stimuli were shown (37.8%). These neurons are not considered further here. Second, 8.6% of neurons had responses that occurred discriminatively during the period in which the visual stimuli were shown. The majority of these neurons responded to whichever visual stimulus was associated with reward, in that the stimulus to which they responded changed during reversal. However, six of these neurons required a combination of a particular visual stimulus in the discrimination *and* reward in order to respond. Further, none of this second group of neurons responded to all the reward-related stimuli (including different foods) that were shown, so that in general this group of neurons coded for a combination of one or some visual stimuli *and* reward. Thus information that particular visual stimuli had previously been associated with reinforcement was represented in the responses of orbito-frontal neurons. Third, 9.7% of neurons had responses that occurred after the lick response was made to obtain reward in the task. Some of these responded independently of whether a reward of fruit juice was obtained, or whether aversive hypertonic saline was obtained on trials on which the monkey licked in error or was given saline in the first trials of a reversal. Through these neurons, information that a lick had been made was represented in the orbito-frontal cortex. Other neurons in this third group responded only when fruit juice was obtained, and thus through these neurons information that reward had been given on that trial was represented in the orbito-frontal cortex. Other neurons in this group responded when saline was obtained when a response was made in error; or when saline was obtained on the first few trials of a reversal (but not in either case when saline was simply placed in the mouth); or when reward was not given in extinction; or when food was taken away instead of being given to the monkey. However, these neurons did not respond in all these situations in which reinforcement was omitted or punishment was given. Thus, through these neurons, task-selective information that reward had been omitted or punishment given was represented in the responses of these orbito-frontal neurons.

These three groups of orbito-frontal neurons could together provide for computation of whether the reinforcement previously associated with a particular stimulus was still being obtained, and for generation of a signal if a match was not obtained. This signal could be partly reflected in the responses of the last subset of neurons with task-selective responses to nonreward or to unexpected punishment. This signal could be used to alter the monkey's behavior—leading, for example, to reversal to one particular stimulus but not to other stimuli; to extinction to one stimulus but not to others; and so on. It could also lead to the altered responses of the orbito-frontal differential neurons found as a result of the learning occurring during the reversal of the visual discrimination, so that their responses indicate appropriately whether a particular stimulus is now associated with reinforcement.

Thus the orbito-frontal cortex contains neurons that appear to be involved in altering behavioral responses when these are no longer associated with reward or become associated with punishment. In the context of the disconnection of stimulus–reinforcement associations, it appears that without these neurons the primate is unable to correct its behavior when disconnection becomes appropriate. The orbito-frontal neurons could be involved in the actual breaking of the association, or in the alteration of behavior when other neurons signal that the connection is no longer appropriate. The observation that humans with damage to the frontal lobe may know that a particular strategy is inappropriate and may be able to verbalize the correct solution, and yet may be unable to correct their inappropriate responses (Teuber, 1964), suggests that the ability to unlearn the association is intact, but that with damage to the frontal lobe this particular type of unlearning cannot influence behavioral response mechanisms. On the other hand, as shown here, the orbito-frontal cortex contains neurons with responses that could provide the information necessary for, and the basis for, the unlearning. In relation to how associations between stimuli and reinforcement are broken and the way in which this influences behavioral responses, it is clearly of importance to investigate further with lesion and recording techniques the orbito-frontal neurons described here, which are implicated in at least one of these processes by the evidence presented.

Neuronal Responses Related to Recognition Memory

Another output pathway from the inferior temporal cortex projects to the entorhinal cortex, which in turn has connections to the hippocampus (Van Hoesen & Pandya, 1975a, 1975b) (see Figure 26-1). On anatomical evidence, there is thus a potentially important sequence for visual information, as follows: inferior temporal cortex–entorhinal cortex–

hippocampus–fornix–mammillary bodies–anterior thalamus. There is evidence relating damage to different parts of this sequence to anterograde amnesia in humans, evident as a major deficit in learning to recognize new stimuli (Mair, Warrington, & Weiskrantz, 1979; Milner, 1972; Scoville & Milner, 1957). Recently, the evidence relating hippocampal damage to the amnesia has been questioned, and instead it has been suggested that damage to cortical association fibers in the temporal stem (Horel, 1978) or combined damage to the hippocampus and amygdala (Mishkin, 1978) is important in producing the amnesia. To determine in which of the postulated neural systems neuronal activity is related to visual recognition, and to investigate how neuronal processing in the identified system is related to visual recognition memory, recordings are now being made in the monkey from the different systems implicated in amnesia.

The recordings are being made from single neurons while the monkeys are performing a visual-recognition task of the type impaired in anterograde amnesia in humans. Each visual stimulus is shown twice per day—once as novel; and on a second trial, after 0–17 other intervening items in the recognition task, as familiar, when the monkey can lick to obtain fruit juice if it recognizes the stimulus correctly. It is an important feature of this task that it is not a test of a relatively short-term form of memory capacity, in which the monkey has to remember which of two often repeated stimuli it saw most recently (as in a delayed matching-to-sample task). Rather, it is a test of a relatively long-term recognition capacity (the pairs of stimuli can be separated by 15 minutes), which is not disrupted by even 17 intervening judgments for different stimuli. Indeed, measurements can be made of the number of intervening items over which a neuron can respond differently to novel and familiar stimuli, thus allowing quantitative comparisons of the "memory span" of neurons in different brain regions (see Rolls, Perrett, Caan, & Wilson, 1982).

In recordings made during the performance of this task, a population of neurons was found at the anterior border of the thalamus that responded to the stimuli only when they were familiar. The activity of these neurons was not related to lick responses. Further, in the different (visual-discrimination) task, a number of these neurons were found to respond both to the familiar reward-associated stimulus to which the monkey always licked, and to the familiar aversive stimulus to which it did not lick. This shows that in a reward association task these neurons respond on the basis of familiarity, providing evidence for a dissociation of recognition and stimulus–reinforcement association memories.

Analysis of the responses of these neurons in the serial visual-recognition task showed that the responses to familiar stimuli were time-locked to the onset and duration of the visual stimulation (brief exposures producing brief responses). The response latencies were in the range 100–200 msec. A 100-msec exposure of the stimulus was sufficient for the stimulus to be encoded, and a 100-msec exposure was also sufficient for a recognition-related response. The magnitude of the neuronal response on trials with familiar stimuli decreased as the number of trials between the first (novel) and second (familiar) presentation of the same stimulus increased. The rate of this decay or "forgetting" varied from cell to cell and was best described by an exponential function. Repeated exposure tended to slow the rate of forgetting, and two or three repeated presentations prolonged some cell "memories" for more than 100 intervening trials. The neurons showed some ability to respond to stimuli as familiar, despite changes in viewing conditions and transformations such as 90-degree rotation.

These neurons are in an anterior midline thalamic region, in or close to which there is often damage in humans with memory disorder of the Korsakoff type (Mair *et al.*, 1979; Victor, Adams, & Collins, 1977). This region is close to and probably connected with the thalamic region in which lesions produce memory impairment in monkeys (Aggleton & Mishkin, 1981). Also, this region is closely connected with temporal lobe regions that have been implicated in amnesia (see Rolls *et al.*, 1982).

This type of experiment thus indicates that neuronal activity related to recognition can be found in one of the systems implicated in amnesia. It suggests fascinating possibilities for tracing the processing related to recognition memory through the system, as well as for quantifying to what extent neuronal activity in different regions is related to the formation of memories that can persist over long time intervals that include interfering stimuli. This type of experiment also allows parameters affecting such memory mechanisms to be investigated, and has in addition provided evidence on the separate nature of stimulus–reinforcement association memory and recognition memory (see Rolls *et al.*, 1982). Preliminary experiments using this technique are providing indications that neuronal activity in the prefrontal convexity cortex is related more to short-term types of memory task involving recency judgments (e.g., delayed matching-to-sample tasks; see also Fuster, 1980) than to longer-term recognition-task performance, so that these prefrontal neurons may play a role in recency rather than in longer-term recognition memory.

Neuronal Activity Related to Memory in Other Brain Regions

In the tail of the caudate nucleus, which (in common with many of the other systems described in this chapter) receives inputs from the inferior temporal visual cortex (see Figure 26-1 and Rolls, 1981a), neurons have been found that respond to visual stimuli (Caan, Perrett, & Rolls, 1984; see also Rolls, 1981a). These neurons show rapid pattern-specific habituation to repeated visual stimuli, and are usually dishabituated by one intervening stimulus. On the basis of this and lesion evidence, it has been suggested that these striatal neurons are part of a system for behavioral orientation to new patterned visual stimuli, and for subsequent behavioral habituation to such stimuli (Caan *et al.*, 1984). It is because these neurons respond to patterned visual stimuli, and are likely to receive their visual inputs from the inferior temporal visual cortex, that it is suggested that they are involved in habituation to pattern-specific but not to simpler visual stimuli (Caan *et al.*, 1984). Insofar as the responses of these neurons are of this type, their activity is related to a particular type of "short-term" memory.

In the head of the caudate nucleus, neurons are found that respond with relatively short latencies (e.g., 130 msec) on reward trials in a visual-discrimination task (Rolls, Thorpe, & Maddison, 1983). However, these neurons typically do not respond when the reward-related visual stimulus is simply shown to the monkey outside the visual-discrimination task; nor do they respond to a range of other visual stimuli associated with rewards, such as a variety of foods. Thus their responses do not appear to be visual responses to stimuli associated with reinforcement. It is important that on these criteria the responses of these neurons are different from those of the hypothalamic neurons described above, which do respond in these situations and are therefore described as having responses to visual stimuli associated with food reinforcement. The neurons in the head of the caudate nucleus also do not respond when the monkey makes the lick movement when it is not performing the visual-discrimination task, so that the responses of these neurons do not appear to be unconditionally movement-related. Rather, these neurons appear to respond only when particular responses are being initiated to particular stimuli (see Rolls *et al.*, 1983), and it is thus suggested that they are part of a system for rapid "stimulus–motor-response" performance, in which a relatively inflexible habit system may be set up as a result of extensive previous experience.

Conclusions

The points made in this chapter indicate how the neurophysiological approach is contributing toward our understanding of the neural processing related to different types of memory. In addition, a number of general points can be made. First, the neurophysiological investigations described provide evidence that there are different types of memory, with dissociations being found among the types of memory in relation to which individual neurons respond. On this basis, it is possible to distinguish between the formation of stimulus–reinforcement associations (amygdala); the disconnection of stimulus–reinforcement associations (orbito-frontal cortex); recognition memory (midline thalamus); relatively short-term pattern-specific memory useful for orientation to new or changing patterned visual stimuli (tail of the caudate nucleus); and recency memory (prefrontal cortex–inferior temporal visual cortex). Second, at least partial dissociations are found among the types of memory to which neuronal activity is related in different brain regions. Some of the dissociations found in the work described here are indicated in the preceding sections (although, particularly in the case of the thalamus, the neuronal responses in the regions indicated could reflect the result of the computation rather than the computation itself). This type of finding provides evidence for at least partial localization of different types of memory function. Third, it is possible to some extent at present, and is likely to become more feasible, to trace processing from one area to the next and to determine how each area contributes to the processing. This amounts to determining the transfer function of each stage. Of course, before this can be done, the type of neuronal activity at each stage of processing must be determined, and this is part of the point of the present work. Fourth, by analyzing neuronal activity at each stage of the processing, one gains insight into the actual computation being performed at each stage. It is interesting to consider how this relates to the "function" of an area, as determined by the effects of damage. Thus for example on the basis of the effects of damage to the orbito-frontal cortex, one can infer that its "function" is in the disconnection of stimulus–reinforcement associations or the correction of behavioral responses, yet only a small proportion of neurons respond at the time when the behavior has to be corrected (e.g., in extinction; see above). Instead, many orbito-frontal neurons fire in relation to the events required to compute that reward is no longer associated with a particular stimulus. Thus some neurons respond selectively to visual stimuli, some to particular visual *when* they are associated with reward, and others in relation to the delivery of reward or punishment itself. Information of all these types is essential for the computation that a particular visual stimulus that was formerly associated with reward is no longer associated with reward. Thus, the recordings of neuronal activity during the performance of a task can provide evidence on the nature of the computation being performed in a particular area, and on how this computation is related to different types of memory.

ACKNOWLEDGMENTS

I have worked on some of the experiments described here with M. J. Burton, W. Caan, S. Judge, F. Mora, D. I. Perrett, M. K. Sanghera, S. J. Thorpe, and F. A. W. Wilson; their collaboration is sincerely acknowledged. I also thank Dr. C. Leonard for reading a draft of this chapter. This research was supported by the Medical Research Council and the Wellcome Trust.

REFERENCES

Aggleton, J., & Mishkin, M. Recognition impairment after medial thalamic lesions in monkeys. *Society for Neuroscience Abstracts*, 1981, *8*, 236.

Akert, K., Gruesen, R. A., Woolsey, C. N., & Meyer, D. R. Klüver–Bucy syndrome in monkeys with neocortical ablations of temporal lobe. *Brain*, 1961, *84*, 480–498.

Butter, C. M. Perseveration in extinction and in discrimination reversal tasks following selective prefrontal ablations in *Macaca mulatta*. *Physiology and Behavior*, 1969, *4*, 163–171.

Caan, W., Perrett, D. I., & Rolls, E. T. Responses of striatal neurons in the behaving monkey: 2. Visual processing in the caudal neostriatum. *Brain Research*, 1984, *290*, 53–65.

Fuster, J. M. *The prefrontal cortex*. New York: Raven Press, 1980.

Gross, C. G., Bender, D. B., & Gerstein, G. L. Activity of inferior temporal neurons in behaving monkeys. *Neuropsychologia*, 1979, *17*, 215–229.

Herzog, A. G., & Van Hoesen, G. W. Temporal neocortical afferent connections to the amygdala in the rhesus monkey. *Brain Research*, 1976, *115*, 57–69.

Horel, J. A. The neuroanatomy of amnesia: A critique of the hippocampal memory hypothesis. *Brain*, 1978, *101*, 403–445.

Iversen, S. D., & Mishkin, M. Perseverative interference in monkey following selective lesions of the inferior prefrontal convexity. *Experimental Brain Research*, 1970, *11*, 376–386.

Jarvis, C. D., & Mishkin, M. Responses of cells in the inferior temporal cortex of monkeys during visual discrimination reversals. *Society for Neuroscience Abstracts*, 1977, *3*, 1794.

Jones, B., & Mishkin, M. Limbic lesions and the problem of stimulus–reinforcement associations. *Experimental Neurology*, 1972, *36*, 362–377.

Klüver, H., & Bucy, P. C. Preliminary analysis of functions of the temporal lobes in monkeys. *Archives of Neurosurgery and Psychiatry*, 1939, *42*, 979–1000.

Mair, W. G. P., Warrington, E. K., & Weiskrantz, L. Memory disorder in Korsakoff's psychosis: A neuropathological and neuropsychological investigation of two cases. *Brain*, 1979, *102*, 749–783.

Milner, B. Disorders of learning and memory after temporal lobe lesions in man. *Clinical Neurosurgery*, 1972, *19*, 421–446.

Mishkin, M. Memory severely impaired by combined but not separate removal of amygdala and hippocampus. *Nature*, 1978, *273*, 297–298.

Mora, F., Rolls, E. T., & Burton, M. J. Modulation during learning of the responses of neurons in the hypothalamus to the sight of food. *Experimental Neurology*, 1976, *53*, 508–519.

Nauta, W. J. H. Fiber degeneration following lesions of the amygdaloid complex in the monkey. *Journal of Anatomy*, 1961, *95*, 515–531.

Ridley, R. M., Hester, N. S., & Ettlinger, G. Stimulus- and response-dependent units from the occipital and temporal lobes of the unanaesthetized monkey performing learnt visual tasks. *Experimental Brain Research*, 1977, *27*, 539–552.

Rolls, E. T. Processing beyond the inferior temporal visual cortex related to feeding, memory, and striatal function. In Y. Katsuki, R. Norgren, & M. Sato, (Eds.), *Brain mechanisms of sensation*. New York: Wiley, 1981. (a)

Rolls, E. T. Responses of amygdaloid neurons in the primate. In Y. Ben-Ari (Ed.), *The amygdaloid complex.* Amsterdam: Elsevier, 1981. (b)

Rolls, E. T., Burton, M. J., & Mora, F. Hypothalamic neuronal responses associated with the sight of food. *Brain Research*, 1976, *111*, 53–66.

Rolls, E. T., Judge, S. J., & Sanghera, M. K. Activity of neurons in the inferotemporal cortex of the alert monkey. *Brain Research*, 1977, *130*, 229–238.

Rolls, E. T., Perrett, D. I., Caan, A. W., & Wilson, F. A. W. Neuronal responses related to visual recognition. *Brain*, 1982, *105*, 611–646.

Rolls, E. T., Sanghera, M. K., & Roper-Hall, A. The latency of activation of neurons in the lateral hypothalamus and substantia innominata during feeding in the monkey. *Brain Research*, 1979, *164*, 121–135.

Rolls, E. T., Thorpe, S. J., & Maddison, S. P. Responses of striatal neurons in the behaving monkey: 1. Head of the caudate nucleus. *Behavioural Brain Research*, 1983, *7*, 179–210.

Rosenkilde, C. E. Functional heterogeneity of the prefrontal cortex in the monkey: A review. *Behavioral and Neural Biology*, 1979, *25*, 301–345.

Sanghera, M. K., Rolls, E. T., & Roper-Hall, A. Visual responses of neurons in the dorsolateral amygdala of the alert monkey. *Experimental Neurology*, 1979, *63*, 610–626.

Sato, T., Kawamura, T., & Iwai, E. Responsiveness of inferotemporal single units to visual pattern stimuli in monkeys performing discrimination. *Experimental Brain Research*, 1980, *38*, 313–319.

Scoville, W. B., & Milner, B. Loss of recent memory after bilateral hippocampal lesions. *Journal of Neurology, Neurosurgery and Psychiatry*, 1957, *20*, 11–21.

Spiegler, B. J., & Mishkin, M. Evidence for the sequential participation of inferior temporal cortex and amygdala in the acquisition of stimulus–reward associations. *Behavioural Brain Research*, 1981, *3*, 303–317.

Tanaka, D. Effects of selective prefrontal decortication on escape behavior in the monkey. *Brain Research*, 1973, *53*, 161–173.

Teuber, H.-L. The riddle of frontal lobe function in man. In J. M. Warren & K. Akert (Eds.), *The frontal granular cortex and behavior.* New York: McGraw-Hill, 1964.

Thorpe, S. J., Rolls, E. T., & Maddison, S. Neuronal activity in the orbito-frontal cortex of the behaving monkey. *Experimental Brain Research*, 1983, *49*, 93–115.

Turner, B. H., Mishkin, M., & Knapp, M. Organization of the amygdalopetal modality-specific cortical association areas in the monkey. *Journal of Comparative Neurology*, 1980, *191*, 515–543.

Van Hoesen, G. W., & Pandya, D. N. Some connections of the entorhinal (area 28) and perirhinal (area 35) cortices in the monkey: I. Temporal lobe afferents. *Brain Research*, 1975, *95*, 1–24. (a)

Van Hoesen, G. W., & Pandya, D. N. Some connections of the entorhinal (area 28) and perirhinal (area 35) cortices in the monkey: III. Efferent connections. *Brain Research*, 1975, *95*, 39–59. (b)

Victor, M., Adams, R. D., & Collins, G. H. *The Wernicke–Korsakoff syndrome.* Oxford: Blackwell, 1977.

The Cortical Substrate of Memory

27

Joaquin M. Fuster

When he was "in search of the engram," Lashley (1950) had to come to terms with the puzzling fact that very large portions of the cerebral cortex can be extirpated in animals without detriment to their performance of conditioned discriminations and complex habits. He concluded that it is not possible to demonstrate the localization of a memory trace anywhere in the cortex: The so-called "associative areas" are not storehouses for specific memories. His principle of "mass action" derived largely from finding that the behavioral deficit resulting from a given cortical ablation was mostly dependent on the quantity of tissue removed, and very little dependent on its location within a general area.

One reason for Lashley's conclusions and controversial principle is to be found in his having used the rat for many of his experiments; the cerebral cortex of this animal is poorly differentiated. Furthermore, it seems that he did not consider enough the possibility that some of his ablated animals were able to perform their behaviors with the aid of a variety of cues (visual, spatial, proprioceptive, etc.). Removal of the central representation of one type of cue left the animal still capable of using that of another. In other words, Lashley's conclusions did not properly take into account that the deposition of memory is essentially an associative phenomenon, and so is recall. Thus, in the absence of one associative avenue, a conditioned response can be effected through another.

In the primate, one can also observe functional sparing after extensive cortical ablation, a degree of equipotentiality, and a semblance of "mass action" in several cortical areas. This is hardly surprising, in view of the richness of associative connectivity that exists in the monkey's cortex. However, it is in fact the primate data that oblige us to accept the specialization of certain parts of associative cortex in certain forms of memory, and, at the very least, to adopt a moderate position somewhere between the localizationist and holistic extremes in all that concerns the cortical representation of the engram.

It is now apparent that, in the primate brain, the memory of a sensory event is principally represented in a large cortical district near the primary sensory area for events of the same modality. Let us consider vision, for example. Because in the monkey the lesions of the inferior temporal cortex (area TE of Von Bonin and Bailey) result in difficulties in acquisition and retention of visual discriminations, and not of discriminations of other modalities (Gross, 1973), it is reasonable to suppose that the inferotemporal area is the cortical district essential for visual memory, or at least is involved in some crucial aspect of the representation of visual objects. In any event, the involvement of inferotemporal cortex in visual phenomena is understandable in the light of well-known anatomical and physiological data. On the one hand, the inferotemporal cortex is known to

Joaquin M. Fuster. Department of Psychiatry and Brain Research Institute, School of Medicine, University of California at Los Angeles, Los Angeles, California.

receive most of its input, through the circumstriate belt, from the striate area (Jones, 1974). On the other hand, inferotemporal neurons are known to denote a variety of visual features, such as form, contrast, and color, though their receptive fields are considerably larger than those of neurons in the striate cortex (Gross, Rocha-Miranda, & Bender, 1972).

The study of inferotemporal cells in the behaving monkey has contributed two pieces of evidence that not only give further credence to the role of the inferotemporal cortex in visual memory, but also provide some hints of organization and mechanism. These hints are as follows: (1) The reaction of inferotemporal cells to visual stimuli is dependent not only on the physical features of the stimuli, but on their behavioral relevance and on the attention of the animal (Fuster & Jervey, 1981; Gross, Bender, & Gerstein, 1979; Mikami & Kubota, 1980); (2) some inferotemporal cells undergo stimulus-dependent discharge during the retention of visual stimuli in a short-term memory task (Fuster & Jervey, 1981, 1982). Both of these are discussed later.

Our findings in the inferotemporal cortex (Fuster, Bauer, & Jervey, 1981; Fuster & Jervey, 1981, 1982) are consistent with, and to some extent support, the following general views on the role of the cerebral cortex in the formation, retention, and recall of memory. Of course, some of the notions expressed below are still quite tentative.

Practically all regions of the cortex participate in the formation of memory. This statement sounds less gratuitous if we consider the known commitment of large expanses of cortex to the analysis of the many kinds of sensory information that the organism can obviously remember or associate with learned responses. However, it would appear that the participation and purview of primary sensory areas in memory is quite different from those of parasensory or associative areas, such as the inferotemporal area. Indeed, there is reason to believe that after certain critical events in early ontogeny, primary areas are relatively set in their organization. Their cell assemblies are organized according to preprogrammed patterns of internal and external connectivity, and, as a result, their analytical function is stably determined. It appears that the participation of primary areas in the formation of memory is largely dependent on, if not limited to, their role as the sensory analyzers of what is to have access to memory. The memory they retain and recall is, by and large, the "memory of the species."

Associative areas, on the other hand, have fewer prior commitments than primary areas. At all ages, their plasticity is much greater, and their participation in the retention and recall of memory is probably to a large extent determined by the history of the organism. Yet their role in individual memory does not exempt associative areas from sensory analysis. Quite the contrary; at those levels of cortical organization the two are inextricably related to one another. For example, the inferotemporal cortex clearly participates in the analysis of sensory features, though we do not yet know according to what parameters. Nor do we know the nature of the transformations of sensory data between the primary cortical analyzer (i.e., the striate cortex) and the inferotemporal cortex. However, it is also clear that the inferotemporal cortex, in addition to being capable of analyzing, can somehow retain visual information.

Indeed, when we reach cortical areas engaged in sensory perception, we have to accept the very real possibility that the same nerve cells may be involved in both sensory analysis and memory in these areas, for it is practically impossible to conceive of perceptual analysis that is not firmly anchored in memory. For this and other reasons, there is no need to postulate separate cell populations for perception and memory. Memory may simply be a latent function of the very same cells that analyze sensory information in the context of past experience, such analysis being the essence of perception. There is no need to postulate a tangible store of the engram, other than a network of cells and fibers with connections previously potentiated by virtue of synaptic changes. Memory would simply be the latent possibility (indeed, probability) that a population of cells capable of representing a stimulus constellation will be reactivated when one or a few of the elements of the constellation appear before the organism. The recall of the others, of the complete constellation, is essentially an associative phenomenon. Association, in turn, is most probably the consequence of a condition that no reasonable learning theory can do without: the repetitive temporal coincidence or contiguity of stimuli. This coincidence or contiguity facilitates certain connections and synaptic processes within the cell population, in such a manner that when one of the stimuli is again encountered, the whole population will be reactivated. The population will resonate, so to speak, and the stimulus with its associated "following" will be thus recognized and categorized (Hayek, 1952).

Recognition and categorization, however, may be realized by many different (i.e., nonisomorphic) cell groups' forming a repertoire that occupies a vast cortical region (several regions, if cross-modality association is involved). Each cell group may recognize a signal only more or less well, and thus, because of the large margin of flexibility and indeterminacy, such a system of cell groups may be called "degenerate." This is the essence of the distributed and group-selective theory of neural memory that Edelman (1978) proposed on the basis of analogies with immune systems. The principal merit of that theory is that it allows for recognition and recall even in the presence of large variations of the input signal. Only a system capable of doing that can achieve "stimulus constancy," an absolutely necessary capability of any neural system of perception and memory.

At present there is no practical method for studying the formation of the functional associations within and between the cell groups of associative cortex that we presume to be at the foundation of perception and memory. Such study should be done by monitoring cellular activity in several domains simultaneously and analyzing changes in reactivity as a function of repeated cooccurrence of stimuli with each other and with behavioral responses of the animal. Without that, we have no adequate electrophysiological control of permanent memory formation, retention, or recall at the cellular level.

What is now possible is to verify the participation of isolated cells in the encoding of diverse stimuli and then, by behavioral manipulations, to force the animal to retain temporarily, and later to recognize, each of the stimuli. It is reasonable to expect that this will allow us to assess the participation of the cells under study in the retention and recall of sensory information. The behavioral manipulation best suited to do that is to train and test the experimental animal in the performance of a delayed matching-to-sample (DMS) task. A typical visual DMS task requires, at the start of each trial, the recognition of a visual stimulus, one attribute of which (e.g., color) must be retained and, after a short period, recognized again, for a particular behavioral response (see Figure 27-1). Thus, in such a task, the information being retained for the short term is like a "memory within a memory"—a piece of information whose behavioral relevance is restricted to the trial and conveniently bracketed in time.

The importance of attention and relevance in stimulus recognition by nerve cells is suitably revealed by changing the context of a stimulus whose physical characteristics remain constant—that is, by studying unit reactions both in a context in which the stimulus

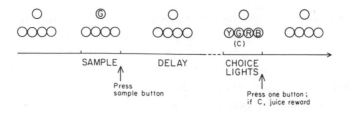

FIGURE 27-1. Event sequence in a trial of a delayed matching-to-sample (DMS) task. The experimental animal, a monkey, is facing a panel with five stimulus–response buttons. A trial begins with presentation, on the top button, of a colored light (in this case green, indicated by G), which serves as the sample for the trial. The animal presses the button, thus acknowledging perception of the color light and turning it off. After a period of delay of a few seconds or minutes, four colored lights, one of them the sample, appear in the lower buttons (Y, yellow; G, green; R, red; B, blue). Choice of the sample color is then rewarded with fruit juice. The color of the sample and its position in the lower buttons are changed randomly from trial to trial. Note that the animal is thoroughly familiar with the four colors in the context of the task and, in order to perform the latter correctly, must perceive (i.e., recognize) the color for each trial and retain it in its absence for the duration of the delay.

is relevant and in a context in which it is not. Consider, for example, the reactions of inferotemporal cells to compound visual stimuli serving as sample stimuli in DMS (see Figure 27-2). The stimuli consist of symbols on colored backgrounds. Depending on the symbol, the animal must either pay attention to the background color or ignore that color. Some cells, in that situation, will react differently to different colors only if color discrimination is relevant and necessary for subsequent behavior.

In monkeys performing the DMS task, we made the interesting observation of inferotemporal cells that, while the animal has to retain a color, show sustained changes of discharge of magnitude often related to the color being retained. It is important to note that the discharge of such cells is usually altered only during presentation and retention of stimuli, and returns to the normal spontaneous rate as soon as the stimuli have been behaviorally utilized and their memorization is no longer necessary. It is also important that cells with sustained and color-dependent discharge during retention need not show alterations of discharge during presentation of the stimuli for retention or for comparative match (see Figure 27-3).

In summary, our single-unit experiments demonstrate, in the first place, that the reactions of some inferotemporal cells to a stimulus are not only determined by the physical characteristics of the stimulus, but by its behavioral relevance, which in turn may be determined by the context in which it appears. The fact that a cell reacts differentially to different stimuli of equal relevance (e.g., the color samples in DMS) simply reflects the participation of the cell in encoding the attribute (e.g., color) that distinguishes the stimuli. However, the difference in reaction may be only one of degree, suggesting that, in addition, the cell participates in the encoding of other attributes that are common to all the test stimuli of a task (e.g., position, shape, brightness, etc.). Thus, the cell may participate in several populations, each encoding a separate attribute. By virtue of prior associations, the cell may recognize more than one attribute of a given stimulus, or all of them together. Indeed, it does not seem that any of the groups of cells constituting the functional "modules" of the inferotemporal cortex encode one and only one stimulus attribute or feature.

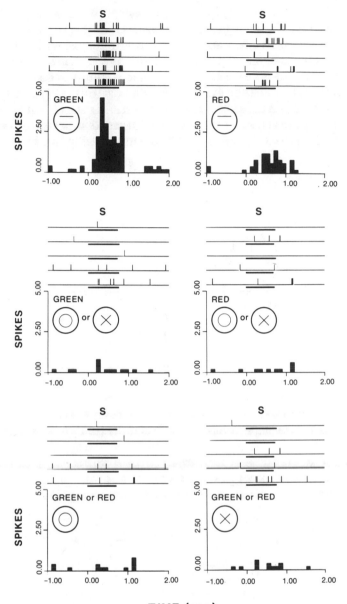

TIME (sec)

FIGURE 27-2. Reactions of an inferotemporal cell to the sample (S, sample period) in DMS trials with combinations of symbol and color. Every graph shows sample-period discharge in five trials (average-frequency histogram at the bottom). Color was relevant when the sample contained the symbol = , but irrelevant when it contained either of the other two symbols; in the first instance, the animal had to retain the color and ignore the symbol, and in the second the animal had to retain the symbol and ignore the color. The cell reacts preferentially to green if color is relevant.

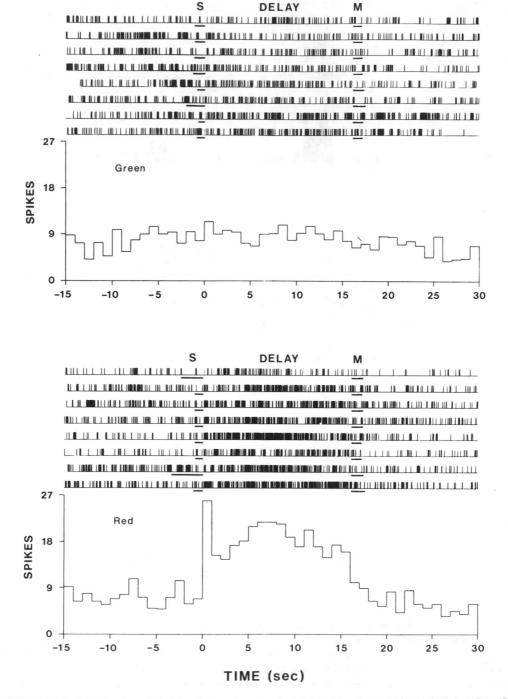

FIGURE 27-3. Activity of a cell in inferotemporal cortex during 16 trials of a DMS task with two colors (S, sample; M, match). In this display, the records of trials with the same sample color have been grouped together. The two average-frequency histograms are time-locked with the termination of the sample and the beginning of the choice lights. The cell is activated during the 16-second delay of red-sample trials. That activation ends with the end of trial.

The sustained (in some cases, differential) discharge of some inferotemporal cells during the delay of a DMS task, while the stimulus is no longer present, probably reflects their participation in the retention of the stimulus as demanded by the task. That retention is a form of short-term memory. Therefore, it is tempting to infer that the DMS trial is an abbreviated process of memory formation, and that what those cortical cells do during the retention period is a microcosm, or at least a stage, of what they normally do in the formation of memory for the long term. All we would need, to add plausibility to the inference, would be to postulate a mechanism that converts sustained discharge into a permanent structural change, such as it might occur at the synaptic level, whereby the cell—and the population to which it belongs—would be reactivated on every reappearance of the stimulus. In such a mechanism, it is not difficult to include speculatively the role of the hippocampus, which receives all manner of sensory inputs (notably from inferotemporal cortex, through the entorhinal area) and which is thought to be important for memory consolidation.

Because some inferotemporal cells show differential discharge only during the delay or retention period, it seems possible that the retention function, in addition to being carried out by cells that participate in perception and recognition, is carried out also by certain cells that do not. Such cells may be specialized in the retention process and cooperate with the others in that process.

At all events, the inferotemporal cortex is not the only associative cortical area implicated in visual short-term memory. At least one other is implicated as well: the prefrontal cortex. Anatomically, the two areas are known to be interconnected (Jones & Powell, 1970; Pandya, Dye, & Butters, 1971). Furthermore, we know that the prefrontal cortex, as well as the inferotemporal cortex, is important for performance of the DMS task (Bauer & Fuster, 1976). Single-unit and behavior data from recent cortical cooling experiments are giving us indications of a functional relationship between the two cortical domains.

The role of the prefrontal cortex in short-term memory is most likely supramodal and related to the temporal organization of behavior that short-term memory tasks, such as DMS, require (Fuster, 1980). Thus the inferotemporal cortex probably supports a visual-memory task primarily because it is visual, and the prefrontal cortex because it requires temporal organization of stimuli and motor responses (Fuster, 1981). However, the role of the prefrontal cortex in cooperation with the inferotemporal cortex, in the case of visual memory, is probably not essentially different from the role of the prefrontal cortex in cooperation with other associative areas in other modalities of memory. Furthermore, it is possible that the prefrontal role is needed for the short-term memory performance of any modality only inasmuch as it requires the temporal integration of sensory information with motor acts. Prefrontal cells would contribute the associations with movement to a widely distributed cortical system, while cells in posterior associative cortex would contribute the sensory associations. Thus we return to the idea of a wide system of associative memory to which many areas contribute by reason of their specialization in the various sensory and motor modalities. Large parts of that system are activated by a behaviorally relevant stimulus and contribute to its perception, memory, and recall.

In conclusion, memory resides less in neurons than in relationships between neurons. A given memory resides in a contingent of neurons only as much and as firmly as they are interconnected. Thus the memory is as widely distributed over the cortex as the cells in the network for that memory are. A given cell or group of cells may be part of many such networks or distributed systems of associations, and therefore of many memories.

REFERENCES

Bauer, R. H., & Fuster, J. M. Delayed-matching and delayed-response deficit from cooling dorsolateral prefrontal cortex in monkeys. *Journal of Comparative and Physiological Psychology*, 1976, *90*, 293–302.

Edelman, G. M. Group selection and phasic reentrant signaling: A theory of higher brain function. In G. M. Edelman & V. B. Mountcastle (Eds.), *The mindful brain*. Cambridge, Mass.: MIT Press, 1978.

Fuster, J. M. *The prefrontal cortex*. New York: Raven Press, 1980.

Fuster, J. M. Prefrontal cortex in motor control. In V. B. Brooks (Ed.), *Handbook of physiology: Nervous system* (Vol. 2, *Motor control*). Baltimore: Williams & Wilkins, 1981.

Fuster, J. M., Bauer, R. H., & Jervey, J. P. Effects of cooling inferotemporal cortex on performance of visual memory tasks. *Experimental Neurology*, 1981, *71*, 398–409.

Fuster, J. M., & Jervey, J. P. Inferotemporal neurons distinguish and retain behaviorally relevant features of visual stimuli. *Science*, 1981, *212*, 952–955.

Fuster, J. M., & Jervey, J. P. Neuronal firing in the inferotemporal cortex of the monkey in a visual memory task. *Journal of Neuroscience*, 1982, *2*, 361–375.

Gross, C. G. Inferotemporal cortex and vision. In E. Stellar & J. M. Sprague (Eds.), *Progress in physiological psychology* (Vol. 5). New York: Academic Press, 1973.

Gross, C. G., Bender, D. B., & Gerstein, G. L. Activity of inferior temporal neurons in behaving monkeys. *Neuropsychologia*, 1979, *17*, 215–229.

Gross, C. G., Rocha-Miranda, C. E., & Bender, D. B. Visual properties of neurons in inferotemporal cortex of the macaque. *Journal of Neurophysiology*, 1972, *35*, 96–111.

Hayek, F. A. *The sensory order*. Chicago: University of Chicago Press, 1952.

Jones, E. G. The anatomy of extrageniculate visual mechanisms. In F. O. Schmitt & F. G. Worden (Eds.), *The neurosciences*. Cambridge, Mass.: MIT Press, 1974.

Jones, E. G., & Powell, T. P. S. An anatomical study of converging sensory pathways within the cerebral cortex of the monkey. *Brain*, 1970, *93*, 793–820.

Lashley, K. S. In search of the engram. *Symposium of the Society for Experimental Biology*, 1950, *4*, 454–482.

Mikami, A., & Kubota, K. Inferotemporal neuron activities and color discrimination with delay. *Brain Research*, 1980, *182*, 65–78.

Pandya, D. N., Dye, P., & Butters, N. Efferent cortico-cortical projections of the prefrontal cortex in the rhesus monkey. *Brain Research*, 1971, *31*, 35–46.

28

Memories and Habits: Some Implications for the Analysis of Learning and Retention

Mortimer Mishkin and Herbert L. Petri

Spared Learning and Retention in Amnesia

Bilateral damage to either the medial part of the temporal lobe or the medial diencephalon, whether from disease, accidental injury, or surgical intervention, can result in a severe and global anterograde amnesia (for reviews, see Butters, 1979, and Squire, 1982). Patients who demonstrate these profound memory deficits can, nevertheless, still learn and retain certain types of tasks. The amnesic patient H. M., for example, was able to learn and retain the responses associated with mirror tracing over a period of a few days, even though he had no recollection of having performed the task before (Milner, 1962). He later demonstrated the same phenomenon on both a pursuit-rotor task (Corkin, 1968) and a visual maze (Milner, Corkin, & Teuber, 1968). Other amnesic patients have been able to learn and retain similar behaviors (Brooks & Baddeley, 1976; Cermak, Lewis, Butters, & Goodglass, 1973; Gardner, 1975; Starr & Phillips, 1970). Initially, these examples of spared retention in amnesic cases were assumed to be limited to the learning of motor skills. Now, however, there is considerable evidence that a wide variety of other behaviors, not related in any obvious way to learning of motor skills, can also be learned and retained (Cohen & Squire, 1980; Gaffan, 1972; Sidman, Stoddard, & Mohr, 1968; Warrington & Weiskrantz, 1968, 1974; Weiskrantz & Warrington, 1970, 1979; Winocur & Weiskrantz, 1976).

Recent research on animals parallels the studies of human amnesia by indicating that either medial temporal damage (Mishkin, Spiegler, Saunders, & Malamut, 1982) or medial diencephalic damage (Aggleton & Mishkin, 1983) produces a severe and global anterograde amnesia in monkeys. Yet, despite their profound memory deficits, monkeys with medial temporal lesions can learn a difficult visual pattern discrimination presented with repeated trials, and they do so at about the normal rate (Mishkin, 1954; Zola-Morgan, Squire, & Mishkin, 1982). Furthermore, they can learn repeated-trial object discriminations at a nearly normal rate even though the successive trials are presented 1 to 2 minutes apart (Orbach, Milner, & Rasmussen, 1960), an interval that causes them to fail completely on one-trial tests of object recognition and object–reward associative recall (Mishkin *et al.*, 1982). Indeed, in a recent experiment (Malamut, Saunders, & Mishkin, in press), it was found that amnesic monkeys could learn an object-discrimination task as quickly as unoperated animals even when the intertrial interval was 24 hours. These results in amnesic

Mortimer Mishkin. Laboratory of Neuropsychology, National Institute of Mental Health, Bethesda, Maryland.
Herbert L. Petri. Department of Psychology, Towson State University, Baltimore, Maryland.

monkeys thus present the same paradox of normal learning and retention in spite of rapid forgetting that is exhibited by amnesic patients.

What are we to make of the fact that both patients and experimental animals can be amnesic in some situations and yet not in others? The conclusion to which most investigators have come is that there are at least two different forms of retention, only one of which is affected in amnesia (Cohen & Squire, 1980; Cormier, 1981; Cutting, 1978; Gaffan, 1974; Graf, Mandler, & Haden, 1982; Hirsh, 1974; Hirst, 1982; Huppert & Piercy, 1976; Kinsbourne & Wood, 1975; O'Keefe & Nadel, 1978; Olton, Becker, & Handelmann, 1979; Stern, 1981; Warrington & Weiskrantz, 1982; Wickelgren, 1979). Starting from this same premise, Mishkin, Malamut, and Bachevalier (1984) have proposed that there are two separate retention systems in the brain, which store the effects of experience in fundamentally different ways. The model is most similar conceptually to the one initially advanced by Hirsh in 1974 (see also Hirsh, 1980; Hirsh & Krajden, 1982), though it differs from his in its specification of the underlying neural mechanisms.

A Neural Model

The model proposes that experiences are stored in both a memory system and a habit system (Mishkin *et al.*, 1984). The memory system utilizes circuits within the limbo-diencephalic regions of the brain, together with closely associated neocortical regions, particularly those located in the anterior temporo-insular and prefrontal areas. Cortical activation of the limbo-diencephalic circuit is assumed to result in the storage of the neural representation of a stimulus configuration within the higher-order sensory cortical area that triggered the circuit. This neural representation may become associated, in turn, with the neural representations of other stimulus configurations in either the same or different modalities, or with the neural representations of affective states, environmental places, or behavioral acts. The neural representations of these states, places, and acts are assumed to be stored in the other parts of the memory system to which the higher-order sensory cortical areas project and with which the stored stimulus representations become linked. The memory system is presumed to store these experiences, both the individual items and their associations, in as little as one trial. The content of the store is information or knowledge, and the process for which the system is responsible is cognition. In the terminology of other investigators, the memory system is responsible for episodic memory (Kinsbourne & Wood, 1975), vertical associative memory (Wickelgren, 1979), declarative knowledge (Cohen & Squire, 1980), and elaborative processing (Graf *et al.*, 1982).

The system just described is the one that is impaired in amnesia. The second system, or habit system, which is presumed to mediate the learning ability that remains despite amnesia, is also presumed to store experiences, but in an entirely different manner from the first. This second system is likely to involve connections of the cortex with the striatum (Mishkin *et al.*, 1984) and associated structures within the extrapyramidal system (Thompson, 1982) and cerebellum (McCormick, Lavond, Clark, Kettner, Rising, & Thompson, 1981; Swanson, Teyler, & Thompson, 1982; Yeo, Hardiman, Glickstein, & Russell, 1982). It is hypothesized that activity within this cortico-striatal system stores the changed probability that a specific stimulus or a specific environment will evoke a specific response, purely as a result of the reinforcement contingencies operating in the situation.

Unlike the memory system, the habit system is assumed to require more than a single trial for the result to be reflected in mastery of a task; each successful trial strengthens the habit incrementally. Habits, by definition, are associations, but these can be distinguished from associative memories in that habits are exclusively noncognitive stimulus–response bonds. Again, in the terminology of others, the habit system is responsible for semantic memory (Kinsbourne & Wood, 1975), horizontal associative memory (Wickelgren, 1979), procedural knowledge (Cohen & Squire, 1980), and integrative processing (Graf *et al.*, 1982).

Some Implications for Learning Theory

The dual-systems model of retention suggests a possible resolution of one of the most fundamental controversies in psychology—namely, the controversy regarding what is learned (cf. Hirsh, 1974). One group of psychologists has argued that responses are learned, while a second group has argued that what is acquired is factual knowledge. This controversy can be traced back to the differing philosophical approaches of empiricism and rationalism, out of which the behaviorist and cognitivist schools developed. As argued by Bower and Hilgard (1981), however, it is logically possible that higher organisms can "acquire both . . . procedural (habitual skills) and factual knowledge" (p. 5).

The dual-systems model of retention likewise suggests that we do not have to choose between behaviorist and cognitivist explanations of learning. Rather, the data from amnesic patients imply—and the neural model proposes—that both types of learning occur, with each neural circuit storing different products of experience. Research outcomes over the last several decades that have seemed to support either the behaviorist or the cognitivist view may have resulted from differential involvement of the habit and memory systems. That is, a particular experimental paradigm may naturally favor retention by one or the other neural mechanism. Indeed, Spence (1940), a forceful proponent of behaviorism, pointed out the dissimilarity between the tasks he used and those used by Krechevsky (1938), an equally forceful proponent of cognitivism. But while the nature of a particular task may accentuate retention by one neural system relative to the other, such instances may be the exceptions. *Most instances of learning could well involve both the memory and the habit systems, because each of the ingredients that make up a learning experience may enter into the learning process in both ways.* While all the implications of this notion remain to be worked out, in the rest of this chapter we briefly outline some of them.

Stimulus Elements versus Configurations

The stimulus–response (S-R) approach to learning, begun by theorists such as Thorndike (1898) and further elaborated by behaviorists such as Watson (1914), Spence (1936), and Hull (1943), assumed that an association is made between all the individual stimulus elements in a situation and the specific response that is reinforced in the presence of these stimuli. The S-R approach thus emphasized that each of the specific components of a complex stimulus (e.g., size, shape, hue) gain the power to evoke the conditioned response.

Consequently, the final behavior of the organism depends on the algebraic summation of the excitatory strengths of all the sampled stimulus elements.

In contrast to these S-R behaviorist views, cognitivists have typically treated stimuli as configurations that take on meaning. For example, Tolman (1932) argued that stimuli serve as signs that point toward or predict the presence of a goal. Similarly, the Gestalt school of psychology (e.g., Koffka, 1928) emphasized that organisms solve problems by understanding the meaning of a holistic event. Thus, for Tolman and the Gestaltists, stimuli were viewed as configurations to which meaning becomes attached, and which thereby provide information to the organism about its environment. Stimulus configurations were also central to the cognitivist Lashley, who proposed that only stimuli for which an animal is "set to react" will gain associative strength, and that these stimuli are "generally those which combine readily according to Gestalt laws of perception" (Lashley, 1942, p. 260).

The disagreements between the behaviorist and cognitivist schools of thought about what constitutes the stimulus in a learning experiment were never resolved, and although the controversy has diminished in recent years, it still surfaces in subdued form in various arenas. For example, Sutherland and Mackintosh (1971) argue in cognitivist style that the blocking effect of an initial conditioned stimulus (CS) on a second CS presented later (i.e., the Kamin effect) is due to competition for attention; if the first CS predicts events perfectly, then the second CS provides no new information and is ignored (Mackintosh, 1978). Rescorla and Wagner (Rescorla & Wagner, 1972; Wagner & Rescorla, 1972), on the other hand, argue in behaviorist style that during training the initial CS can continue to gain associative strength to the point where the second stimulus cannot be associated, but only because little room for additional associative strength remains. McArthur (1982) has provided an excellent review of a parallel conflict between the Gibsonian explanations of perception, which emphasize detection of the physical invariances in the stimulation impinging on the sensory apparatus, and constructivist explanations, which emphasize the necessity of memory, knowledge, and expectation for unambiguous perception. Thus, in perception as well as in learning, behaviorists and cognitivists continue to debate.

But perhaps a choice between the two positions is unnecessary. The dual-systems model suggests that stimuli can enter into learning in both ways—that is, both as elements and as configurations. We suggest that in the habit system each of the components of a stimulus complex becomes connected by reinforcement to a specific response, as the behaviorists have argued, whereas in the memory system (specifically within the sensory portion of that system located in the anterior temporo-insular region), the neural representations of stimuli are stored as configurations to which significance can subsequently become attached, as the cognitivists have proposed. Thus, the model suggests that stimulus elements and configurations can enter into the stored product of experience in separate systems simultaneously. But while a stimulus element is a necessary component of a habit, a stimulus configuration, as we point out below, is not a necessary component of an associative memory.

Responses versus Acts

The S-R behaviorist approach emphasized that learning is reducible to the formation of conditioned reflexes (Watson, 1930) or to the acquisition of simple movements (Guthrie,

1935) or habits (Hull, 1943). Given the necessary drive and reinforcement, response acquisition was regarded as essentially automatic, requiring neither awareness of the stimulus that evokes it nor of the outcome to which it leads. By contrast, the cognitive approach, again typified by Tolman's views, regarded learned behavior not simply as muscle contractions or glandular secretions, but as acts (Tolman, 1932). The choice of the term "act" was meant to imply that the behavior is purposive or intentional, and is therefore directed toward some goal expected on the basis of past experience. In a view similar to Tolman's, the Gestalt approach argued that although S-R can take place it is atypical and occurs only "when meaning or natural organization was absent" (Hilgard & Bower, 1975, p. 271).

A closely related debate concerned the way in which behavior to be learned is generated and selected. S-R approaches have stressed the gradual emergence of a habit through the selective reinforcement of one among many competing responses (Hull, 1943) or the shaping of a final response through the reinforcement of successive approximations (Ferster & Skinner, 1957). In all such models, some response is initially evoked by the stimulus or generated by an internal state, and this response is gradually modified by experience. Cognitive theorists, on the other hand, have argued that behavior is most often volitional and is far more flexible than S-R theorists propose, in that it can be quickly altered to fit the animal's purpose. This flexibility was often characterized as hypothesis testing, insightful problem solving, or the intentional selection of responses (Krechevsky, 1938).

In an attempt to account for the appearance of purposiveness in learned behavior, the behaviorists introduced intervening variables, such as feedback from fractional anticipatory goal responses (Hull, 1930, 1931) and fractional frustration responses (Amsel, 1958). A particularly striking use of intervening variables to deal with learned behavior that appears to represent the essence of cognition is Skinner's (1945, 1957) proposal that language consists of socially reinforced verbal responses to inferred private stimuli. Although these positions were parsimonious in their attempt to comprehend all learning within a single framework, the price was increased complexity of the framework combined with a loss of behaviorist purity.

Relinquishment of a single framework may allow a return to purer versions of both contending views. Thus, the dual-systems model proposes that automatic responses and intentional acts can be learned concurrently, but each according to its own rules. As indicated earlier, the habit system stores the changing probability that a given stimulus or situation will elicit a specific response; the response, consequently, is an obligatory component of a habit. An act, by contrast, is not an obligatory component of a memory, and indeed is just one of many possible components. For although associative memories may be formed between stimuli and acts, they may also be formed between one stimulus and another, between a stimulus and an emotion, between an emotion and an act, or even between one act and another. When an act does enter into an associative memory, it must do so, according to the model, on the basis of an acquired connection with the stored neural representation of that act. Just as the neural representations of stimulus configurations (but not of stimulus elements) are presumed to be stored in the higher-order sensory cortical areas, the neural representations of acts (but not of responses) are presumed to be stored in the higher-order sensory–motor cortical areas (e.g., lateral prefrontal, premotor, superior parietal).

Needs versus Motives

Hull (1943, 1951, 1952), a primary advocate of the S-R approach, initially emphasized the role of physiological needs or tissue deficits in the generation of drive (and drive stimuli), which in turn had to be reduced in order for learning to occur. Shortly after Hull developed these ideas, a number of studies on curiosity, manipulation, and exploration suggested that other motives, not obviously related to physiological needs, also generated learning. For example, Harlow and his colleagues found that monkeys would learn to take apart mechanical puzzles for no externally administered reward (Harlow, 1950; Harlow, Harlow, & Myer, 1950) and would also acquire a new response simply for the reward of exposure to sensory stimuli (Butler, 1953; Butler & Alexander, 1955; Butler & Harlow, 1954). Similarly, Hebb (1966) noted that play behavior and the learning it affords ordinarily occur when physiological needs are inactive, and that in primates, such play is often almost "entirely mental, with a minimum of muscular activity" (Hebb, 1966, p. 239). The recognition that there are motives that have no apparent basis in tissue deficits or other physiological needs was one major factor that eventually led to the demise of the drive-reduction theory of learning (Bolles, 1967).

But perhaps burial of the drive-reduction theory was premature. In the dual-systems model of retention, there is room for learning both through reduction of bodily needs and through the fulfillment of cognitive motives. The most important distinction between the two processes, however, is not the one between lower-order needs and higher-order motives, but the difference between ways in which needs and motives enter into learning. Thus, when tissue deficits and their concomitant internal stimuli or milieus lead to the acquisition of habitual responses that reduce those deficits, the drive and its reduction are necessary conditions of learning, but not components of the learned connections. In the memory system, conversely, satisfaction of cognitive motives—which can range all the way from the cognitive correlates of bodily needs through affective states to intellectual curiosity—is not a necessary condition for learning, as has been amply demonstrated by the literature on incidental learning (Hasher & Zacks, 1979; Mechanic, 1962); but when motives do participate in memory formation, then, according to the model, they become integral components of the association, inasmuch as motives (like all other components in memory) are stored neural representations. The locus of the store in this case is presumably the amygdalo-hypothalamic system and the cortex closely related to it (e.g., orbito-frontal and anterior cingulate regions).

Reinforcements versus Incentives

As with the other ingredients of the learning experience, the final ingredient we wish to discuss is likewise treated in very different ways by the two opposing schools of learning theory. Beginning with Thorndike's (1898) declaration of the law of effect, behaviorists have viewed the response outcome as the key to learning. Thus, either the presentation of a positive reinforcer or the withdrawal of a negative reinforcer will strengthen a habit or increase response probability. The power of reinforcement to control the acquisition of responses has been demonstrated most forcefully by the Skinnerian school (Ferster & Skinner, 1957).

For cognitive theorists such as Tolman (1932), on the other hand, reinforcement was not a necessary condition for learning, as demonstrated by studies on latent learning (e.g., Blodgett, 1929). According to the cognitivists, "reinforcers" serve not to increase response probability, but to confirm or disconfirm an expectancy. The expectancy, in turn, provides the incentive for future acts. In short, behavior is purposive or goal-directed in conformity with past learning. On the other hand, it is clear that substantial informational learning can occur in the absence of any behavior, or, indeed, of any purpose (i.e., through disinterested observation alone).

We suggest, again, that learning may involve both response strengthening and expectancy development, but that these two different storage processes are controlled by separate neural systems. The dual-systems model proposes that the response outcome can serve as the reinforcer that strengthens S-R associations within the habit system, but that the same anticipated outcome can also serve as an incentive within the memory system. In the latter case, the incentive is presumed to be stored as a neural representation, which then becomes another component of associative memory. Exactly as in the distinction between a need and a motive, the distinction between a reinforcer and an incentive is that a reinforcer is a necessary condition for, but not a component in, a learned association, whereas an incentive may be a component of a learned association but is not a necessary one.

There is one way in which an incentive may differ from the other components of the memory system that have already been discussed, and that is that an incentive could itself be a learned association. This association may take the form of either a stimulus–affect (e.g., food, money) or an act–affect (e.g., exploration, sport) linkage, in which case the stored neural representation of an incentive would actually be an associative memory that could nevertheless operate as a single, albeit complex, component.

One important by-product of the dual-systems model of retention is the likelihood that the loss of learning, like the learning itself, follows different principles in the two systems: Habits are probably not forgotten but are extinguished as a result of nonreinforcement; conversely, memories are clearly not extinguished through nonreinforcement, but are instead forgotten. That is, within the memory system, neural representations presumably become unavailable either through decay, if they have not been consolidated, or through the processes of proactive and retroactive interference, if they have been.

Concluding Comment

This chapter has presented the view that the ingredients of a learning experience—sensory, motor, motivational, satisfactional—can enter into the learning process in two ways: as memories stored in a cortico-limbic system and as habits stored in a cortico-striatal system. A potential strength of this dual-systems model is that it may suggest solutions to problems regarding learning that have proven to be particularly recalcitrant to theoretical analysis (reversal learning, avoidance learning, partial-reinforcement extinction effect, etc.). The source of this potential explanatory power is that although the habit and memory systems may ordinarily be synergistic, they may also operate independently and may sometimes even conflict. Awareness of these many possibilities, and their combinations, may encourage renewed attempts to solve some of the difficult puzzles that continue to trouble the analysis of learning and retention.

ACKNOWLEDGMENT

Herbert L. Petri is a recipient of Faculty Research and Faculty Development Grants from Towson State University, Baltimore, Maryland.

REFERENCES

Aggleton, J. P., & Mishkin, M. Visual recognition impairment following medial thalmic lesions in monkeys. *Neuropsychologia*, 1983, *21*, 189–197.

Amsel, A. The role of frustrative nonreward in noncontinuous reward situations. *Psychological Bulletin*, 1958, *55*, 102–119.

Blodgett, H. C. The effect of the introduction of reward upon the maze performance of rats. *University of California Publications in Psychology*, 1929, *4*, 113–134.

Bolles, R. C. *Theory of motivation*. New York: Harper & Row, 1967.

Bower, G. H., & Hilgard, E. R. *Theories of learning* (5th ed.). Englewood Cliffs, N.J.: Prentice-Hall, 1981.

Brooks, D. N., & Baddeley, A. What can amnesic patients learn? *Neuropsychologia*, 1976, *14*, 111–122.

Butler, R. A. Discrimination learning by rhesus monkeys to visual-exploration motivation. *Journal of Comparative and Physiological Psychology*, 1953, *46*, 95–98.

Butler, R. A., & Alexander, H. M. Daily patterns of visual exploratory behavior in the monkey. *Journal of Comparative and Physiological Psychology*, 1955, *48*, 247–249.

Butler, R. A., & Harlow, H. F. Persistence of visual exploration in monkeys. *Journal of Comparative and Physiological Psychology*, 1954, *47*, 258–263.

Butters, N. Amnesic disorders. In K. Heilman, & E. Valenstein (Eds.), *Clinical neuropsychology*. New York: Oxford University Press, 1979.

Cermak, L. S., Lewis, R., Butters, N., & Goodglass, H. Role of verbal mediation in performance of motor tasks by Korsakoff patients. *Perceptual and Motor Skills*, 1973, *37*, 259–262.

Cohen, N. J., & Squire, L. R. Preserved learning and retention of pattern-analyzing skill in amnesia: Dissociation of knowing how and knowing that. *Science*, 1980, *210*, 207–210.

Corkin, S. Acquisition of motor skill after bilateral medial temporal-lobe excision. *Neuropsychologia*, 1968, *6*, 255–265.

Cormier, S. M. A match–mismatch theory of limbic system function. *Physiological Psychology*, 1981, *19*, 3–36.

Cutting, J. A cognitive approach to Korsakoff's syndrome. *Cortex*, 1978, *14*, 485–495.

Ferster, C. B., & Skinner, B. F. *Schedules of reinforcement*. New York: Appleton-Century-Crofts, 1957.

Gaffan, D. Loss of recognition memory in rats with lesion of the fornix. *Neuropsychologia*, 1972, *10*, 327–341.

Gaffan, D. Recognition impaired and association intact in the memory of monkeys after transection of the fornix. *Journal of Comparative and Physiological Psychology*, 1974, *86*, 1100–1109.

Gardner, H. *The shattered mind*. New York: Knopf, 1975.

Graf, P., Mandler, G., & Haden, P. E. Simulating amnesic symptoms in normal subjects. *Science*, 1982, *218*, 1243–1244.

Guthrie, E. R. *The psychology of learning*. New York: Harper & Row, 1935.

Harlow, H. F. Learning and satiation of response in intrinsically motivated complex puzzle performance by monkeys. *Journal of Comparative and Physiological Psychology*, 1950, *43*, 289–294.

Harlow, H. F., Harlow, M. K., & Meyer, D. R. Learning motivated by a manipulation drive. *Journal of Experimental Psychology*, 1950, *40*, 228–265.

Hasher, L., & Zacks, R. T. Automatic and effortful processes in memory. *Journal of Experimental Psychology: General*, 1979, *108*, 356–388.

Hebb, D. O. *A textbook of psychology*. Philadelphia: W. B. Saunders, 1966.

Hilgard, E. R., & Bower, G. H. *Theories of learning* (4th ed.). Englewood Cliffs, N.J.: Prentice-Hall, 1975.

Hirsh, R. The hippocampus and contextual retrieval of information from memory: A theory. *Behavioral Biology*, 1974, *12*, 421–444.

Hirsh, R. The hippocampus, conditional operations, and cognition. *Physiological Psychology*, 1980, *8*, 175–182.

Hirsh, R., & Krajden, J. The hippocampus and the expression of knowledge. In R. L. Isaacson & N. E. Spear (Eds.), *The expression of knowledge*. New York: Plenum, 1982.

Hirst, W. The amnesic syndrome: Descriptions and explanations. *Psychological Bulletin*, 1982, *91*, 435–460.

Hull, C. L. Knowledge and purpose as habit mechanisms. *Psychological Review*, 1930, *37*, 511–525.

Hull, C. L. Goal attraction and directing ideas conceived as habit phenomena. *Psychological Review*, 1931, *38*, 487–506.

Hull, C. L. *Principles of behavior: An introduction to behavior theory*. New York: Appleton-Century-Crofts, 1943.

Hull, C. L. *Essentials of behavior*. New Haven: Yale University Press, 1951.

Hull, C. L. *A behavior system: An introduction to behavior theory concerning the individual organism*. New Haven: Yale University Press, 1952.

Huppert, F. A., & Piercy, M. Recognition memory in amnesic patients: Effect of temporal context and familiarity of material. *Cortex*, 1976, *12*, 3–20.

Kinsbourne, M., & Wood, F. Short-term memory processes and the amnesic syndrome. In D. Deutsch & J. A. Deutsch (Eds.), *Short-term memory*. New York: Academic Press, 1975.

Koffka, K. [*The growth of the mind: An introduction to child psychology*] (2nd ed.) (R. M. Ogden, trans.). New York: Harcourt, Brace, 1928.

Krechevsky, I. A study of the continuity of the problem-solving process. *Psychological Review*, 1938, *45*, 107–133.

Lashley, K. S. An examination of the "continuity theory" as applied to discriminative learning. *Journal of General Psychology*, 1942, *26*, 241–265.

Mackintosh, N. J. Cognitive or associative theories of conditioning: Implications of an analysis of blocking. In S. H. Hulse, H. Fowler, & W. K. Honig (Eds.), *Cognitive processes in animal behavior*. Hillsdale, N.J.: Erlbaum, 1978.

Malamut, B. L., Saunders, R. C., & Mishkin, M. Monkeys with combined amygdalo-hippocampal lesions succeed in object discrimination learning despite 24-hour intertrial intervals. *Behavioral Neuroscience*, in press.

McArthur, D. J. Computer vision and perceptual psychology. *Psychological Bulletin*, 1982, *92*, 283–309.

McCormick, D. A., Lavond, D. G., Clark, G. A., Kettner, R. E., Rising, C. E., & Thompson, R. F. The engram found? Role of the cerebellum in classical conditioning of nictitating membrane and eyelid responses. *Bulletin of the Psychonomic Society*, 1981, *18*, 103–105.

Mechanic, A. Effects of orienting task, practice, and incentive on simultaneous incidental and intentional learning. *Journal of Experimental Psychology*, 1962, *64*, 383–399.

Milner, B. Les troubles de la mémoire accompagnant des lésions hippocampiques bilatérales. In P. Passouant (Ed.), *Physiologie de l'hippocampe*. Paris: Centre National de la Recherche Scientifique, 1962. (English translation in P. M. Milner & S. Glickman [Eds.], *Cognitive processes and the brain*. New York: Van Nostrand, 1965.)

Milner, B., Corkin, S., & Teuber, H.-L. Further analysis of the hippocampal amnesic syndrome: 14-year follow-up study of H.M. *Neuropsychologia*, 1968, *6*, 215–234.

Mishkin, M. Visual discrimination performance following partial ablations of the temporal lobe: II. Ventral surface versus hippocampus. *Journal of Comparative and Physiological Psychology*, 1954, *47*, 187–193.

Mishkin, M., Malamut, B., & Bachevalier, J. Memories and habits: Two neural systems. In G. Lynch, J. L. McGaugh, & N. M. Weinberger (Eds.), *Neurobiology of learning and memory*. New York: Guilford Press, 1984.

Mishkin, M., Spiegler, B. J., Saunders, R. C., & Malamut, B. L. An animal model of global amnesia. In S. Corkin, K. L. Davis, J. H. Growden, E. Usdin, & R. J. Wurtman (Eds.), *Alzheimer's disease: A report of progress in research*. New York: Raven Press, 1982.

O'Keefe, J., & Nadel, L. *The hippocampus as a cognitive map*. London: Oxford University Press, 1978.

Olton, D. S., Becker, J. T., & Handelmann, G. E. Hippocampus, space, and memory. *Brain and Behavioral Sciences*, 1979, *2*, 313–365.

Orbach, J., Milner, B., & Rasmussen, T. Learning and retention in monkeys after amygdala–hippocampus resection. *Archives of Neurology*, 1960, *3*, 230–251.

Rescorla, R. A., & Wagner, A. R. A theory of Pavlovian conditioning: Variations in the effectiveness of reinforcement and nonreinforcement. In A. H. Black & W. F. Prokasy (Eds.), *Classical conditioning II: Current research and theory*. New York: Appleton-Century-Crofts, 1972.

Sidman, M., Stoddard, L. T., & Mohr, J. P. Some additional quantitative observations of immediate memory in a patient with bilateral hippocampal lesions. *Neuropsychologia*, 1968, *6*, 245–254.

Skinner, B. F. The operational analysis of psychological terms. *Psychological Review*, 1945, *52*, 270–277.

Skinner, B. F. *Verbal behavior*. New York: Appleton-Century-Crofts, 1957.

Spence, K. W. The nature of discrimination learning in animals. *Psychological Review*, 1936, *43*, 427–449.

Spence, K. W. Continuous versus noncontinuous interpretations of discrimination learning. *Psychological Review*, 1940, *47*, 271–288.

Starr, A., & Phillips, L. Verbal learning and motor memory in the amnesic syndrome. *Neuropsychologia*, 1970, *8*, 75–81.

Stern, L. D. A review of theories of human amnesia. *Memory and Cognition*, 1981, *9*, 247–262.

Squire, L. R. The neuropsychology of human memory. *Annual Review of Neuroscience*, 1982, *5*, 241–273.

Sutherland, N. S., & Mackintosh, M. J. *Mechanisms of animal discrimination learning*. New York: Academic Press, 1971.

Swanson, L. W., Teyler, T. J., & Thompson, R. F. Hippocampal long-term potentiation: Mechanisms and implications for memory. *Neurosciences Research Program Bulletin*, 1982, *20*(5), 613–769.

Thompson, R. Brain lesions impairing visual and spatial reversal learning in rats: Components of the "general learning system" of the rodent brain. *Physiological Psychology*, 1982, *10*, 186–198.

Thorndike, E. L. Animal intelligence: An experimental study of the associative processes in animals. *Psychological Review Monograph*, 1898, *2*(8).

Tolman, E. C. *Purposive behavior in animals and men*. New York: Century, 1932.

Wagner, A. R., & Rescorla, R. A. Inhibition in Pavlovian conditioning: Application of a theory. In R. A. Boakes & M. S. Holliday (Eds.), *Inhibition and learning*. London: Academic Press, 1972.

Warrington, E. K., & Weiskrantz, L. New method of testing long-term retention with special reference to amnesic patients. *Nature*, 1968, *217*, 972–974.

Warrington, E. K., & Weiskrantz, L. The effect of prior learning on subsequent retention in amnesic patients. *Neuropsychologia*, 1974, *12*, 419–428.

Warrington, E. K., & Weiskrantz, L. Amnesia: A disconnection syndrome? *Neuropsychologia*, 1982, *20*, 233–248.

Watson, J. B. *Behavior: An introduction to comparative psychology*. New York: Holt, 1914.

Watson, J. B. *Behaviorism*. New York: Norton, 1930.

Weiskrantz, L. R., & Warrington, E. K. Verbal learning and retention by amnesic patients using partial information. *Psychonomic Science*, 1970, *20*, 210–211.

Weiskrantz, L. R., & Warrington, E. K. Conditioning in amnesic patients. *Neuropsychologia*, 1979, *17*, 187–194.

Wickelgren, W. A. Chunking and consolidation: A theoretical synthesis of semantic networks, configuring in conditioning, S-R versus cognitive learning, normal forgetting, the amnesic syndrome, and the hippocampal arousal system. *Psychological Review*, 1979, *86*, 44–60.

Winocur, G., & Weiskrantz, L. An investigation of paired associate learning in amnesic patients. *Neuropsychologia*, 1976, *14*, 97–110.

Yeo, C. H., Hardiman, M. J., Glickstein, M., & Russell, I. S. Lesions of cerebellar nuclei abolish the classically conditioned nictitating membrane response. *Society for Neuroscience Abstracts*, 1982, *8*, 22.

Zola-Morgan, S., Squire, L. R., & Mishkin, M. The neuroanatomy of amnesia: Amygdala–hippocampus versus temporal stem. *Science*, 1982, *218*, 1337–1339.

Consolidation of Memory: The Hippocampus Revisited

29

Helen Mahut and Mark Moss

Early Studies of Memory Consolidation

When Hebb (1949) provided a model of neural cortical representations of external events that organisms acquire (i.e., cell assemblies), these representations were also conceived of as the substrate of active two-stage memory processes. In agreement with the original theory proposed by Müller and Pilzecker (1900), Hebb's two-stage model, elaborated in more sophisticated physiological terms by P. M. Milner (1957, 1960), permits the following postulates: (1) Traces of events persist initially as a form of activity within cortical assembly elements, due to temporary increases in synaptic efficiency (short-term memory); and (2) though initial traces may involve multiple, partially overlapping cell assemblies, only traces of frequently rehearsed events, or those of events with special motivational significance to the organism, are gradually consolidated through permanent structural changes within some assemblies and become the substrate of long-term memory. The identification of the brain mechanisms that mediate memory processes and a precise specification of their properties continue to be focal concerns of neuropsychology.

Early studies in Hebb's laboratory established that memory could be disrupted by electrical stimulation of the thalamic intralaminar–midline system known to project to, and affect normal function of, wide cortical areas (Hanbery, Ajmone-Marsan, & Dilworth, 1954). Retardation was found in the learning of the visual–spatial Hebb–Williams maze in rats (Mahut, 1962) and of a visual object-discrimination task in cats (Mahut, 1964). Of particular interest was the finding in the latter study that stimulation did not impair the retention of a task acquired 2 months earlier without stimulation, and that no deleterious effects were obtained when stimulation after each choice was delayed by 20 sec. In later studies, the anatomy and temporal characteristics of memory traces became of primary interest. Because the intralaminar–midline thalamic system has reciprocal connections with the caudate nucleus, and because the hippocampus had been implicated by clinical studies in amnesia (Penfield & Milner, 1958; Scoville & Milner, 1957), electrodes were implanted, in different groups of rats, in the caudate nucleus, in the intralaminar–midline nuclei (Herkenham, 1974; Mahut, 1965), and in the dorsal and ventral hippocampus (Gary-Bobo & Mahut, 1968). The animals were taught a visual-discrimination task in a T-maze. Low-intensity current (10 μA) was delivered, for different groups of rats, either before, during,

Helen Mahut. Department of Psychology, Northeastern University, Boston, Massachusetts.

Mark Moss. Department of Anatomy, Boston University School of Medicine, Boston, Massachusetts; Department of Psychiatry, Massachusetts General Hospital, Harvard Medical School, Boston, Massachusetts.

or after each choice. While no impairment was found when stimulation was delivered before the choice in any of the four groups, all groups of rats were significantly impaired when stimulation was given after each choice, and only the caudate group was significantly impaired when stimulation was given during the choice.

There were two surprising aspects of these studies. One was the very short time required for the initial strengthening of memory traces: While rats were impaired when stimulated *immediately* after each choice, they were unimpaired when stimulation was delayed by as little as 2 sec. The effectiveness of this specific delay was undoubtedly a special case due to the locus of stimulation, to the nature of the task, or to both of these factors. Nonetheless, it should be noted that Hebb (1961) demonstrated improvement in the learning of a recurrent string of nine digits embedded in a series of changing strings that had to be attended to and repeated by normal subjects. It does appear, therefore, that whatever initial consolidation changes must occur in the nervous system, they must begin to occur within a very brief time.

The second aspect concerned the role of the hippocampus at different stages of learning. Since electrical stimulation of the hippocampus results readily in seizures and arrest of ongoing behavior, the current intensity was lowered to 4–6 μA; and, to detect possible abnormalities not reflected in behavior, hippocampal activity was monitored throughout all learning sessions. For the most part, reduced intensity precluded overt seizures, but, as stimulation continued over days, several types of EEG abnormalities began to appear in the record. Much to our surprise, however, rats were able to attain the learning criterion in the presence of abnormal discharges, followed by a typically flat postseizure record (see Figure 29-1). A conclusive interpretation of these results was complicated not only by the possible spread of current, and that of abnormal discharges, to adjacent structures, but also by a motivational factor: Many of the 68 rats with electrode tips in the hippocampus pressed a bar in a Skinner box to obtain stimulation at higher intensities than those used in the learning experiments, in spite of occasional seizures.[1] There was a suggestion, however, that normal activity in the thalamus–caudate–hippocampus circuits must provide the cortex with the necessary facilitation of initial consolidation processes, but that its role may diminish as memory traces become strengthened.

These results were obtained on the background of a prevailing pessimistic belief that there was a real discontinuity between human and nonhuman species in the role played by the hippocampus in memory functions (Drachman & Ommaya, 1964; Iversen & Weiskrantz, 1964; Milner, 1970; Orbach, Milner, & Rasmussen, 1960). Yet the results were oddly compatible with clinical findings. Anterograde amnesia had been uncovered in patients after bilateral ablations of the uncinate–amygdaloid region, hippocampus, and hippocampal gyrus (Scoville & Milner, 1957). A similarly profound memory loss was found in one patient after a unilateral temporal lobectomy with a preexisting, long-standing damage to the opposite temporal lobe. In a second patient, amnesia developed when excision of uncus and hippocampal zone was added to a partial unilateral temporal lobectomy, with a preexisting lesion in the corresponding area of the contralateral temporal lobe. No com-

1. The highest and most sustained rates of bar pressing, without accompanying seizures, were obtained from the subiculum, but this anatomical finding could not be appreciated at the time. Because the results obtained with the use of stimulation techniques could not be unambiguously interpreted in terms of learning deficits, and because we began to uncover retention deficits in monkeys after damage to the hippocampus, projects with rats were abandoned.

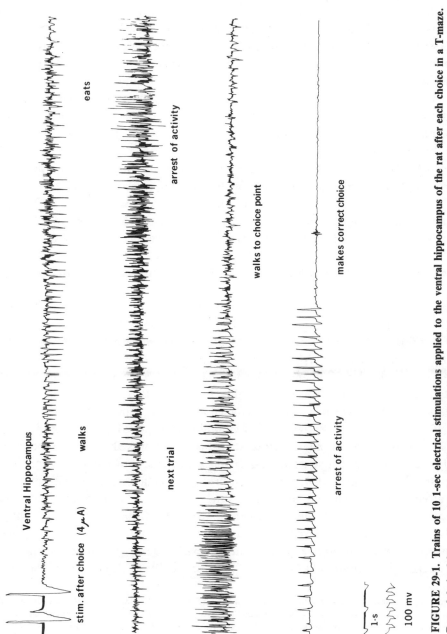

FIGURE 29-1. Trains of 10 1-sec electrical stimulations applied to the ventral hippocampus of the rat after each choice in a T-maze. Record derived from the same electrode placement, Session 10, Trial 4. First day of learning criterion (at least 18 correct in 20 consecutive trials).

parable loss was found after ablations that were limited to the uncinate–amygdaloid region (Scoville & Milner, 1957), and the severity of the deficit appeared to be correlated with the extent of hippocampal tissue removed (Penfield & Milner, 1958). In all cases, short-term memory, as measured by the digit span, was intact, but the patients were unable to retain verbal or nonverbal material for more than a few minutes, particularly if their attention was distracted. Remote memories were relatively intact, but retrograde amnesia covered preoperative periods from 3 months to approximately 3 years. In reviewing these cases, Milner (1962) concluded that the findings pointed to the hippocampus as the critical structure in memory though, in the absence of cases with selective excisions of the hippocampus, the possible role of additional damage to the amygdala had to remain an open question.[2] In line with the notion that memory is an active, two-stage process, she proposed the following: (1) While removal of the hippocampus does not affect long-established associations, it makes it most difficult to establish lasting new memory traces; (2) given the length of retrograde amnesia, consolidation of memory must be a continued, long process; and (3) permanent changes must occur in structures beyond the hippocampus, and, while new associations not yet independent of hippocampal activity are lost, consolidated cortical long-term traces become eventually autonomous.

The critical role of the hippocampus was reemphasized when, in one of the amnesic patients with unilateral left temporal lobectomy, autopsy revealed an extensive atrophy of the right hippocampus (Milner, Corkin, & Teuber, 1968). Also, the severity of the memory deficit for visual or verbal material was found to be correlated with the amount of hippocampal tissue included in the right or left lobectomies, respectively (Corsi, 1969; Milner & Teuber, 1968). Extensive follow-up examinations of one of Dr. Scoville's patients (H. M.), with permanent anterograde amnesia after bitemporal lobectomy, firmly established that short-term memory, as measured by digit span (Drachman & Arbit, 1966; Milner, 1966) and related tests (Wickelgren, 1968), is within normal range, while the salient deficit remains in the establishment of new associations with longer delays, in more than one modality. This distinction was underlined by the finding that, on delayed matching-to-sample tasks, H. M.'s performance fell to chance levels after 1 min with auditory stimuli (Prisko, 1963) and after 30 sec with visual stimuli (Prisko, 1963; Sidman, Stoddard, & Mohr, 1968). It is not surprising, therefore, that this patient was also found to be severely impaired on tasks of cumulative learning over repeated trials, showing little progress from one block of stimuli to the next with continuous recognition tasks (Milner & Teuber, 1968) or when attempting to learn a visual (Milner, 1962, 1968) or tactual (Corkin, 1965) simple maze. However, in spite of his global amnesia, patient H. M. performed competently on tests of motor skill and on some cognitive tasks (Milner, 1968).

In order to obtain precise verification of surgical damage in brains without pre-existing neurological abnormalities, several early studies were explicitly designed to re-

2. Two early reports described a severe memory loss on the background of mental confusion and deterioration. In the first case (Grünthal, 1947), there was acute onset of hypoglycemia in an old patient, followed shortly by death. Autopsy revealed hardly any pathology in the neocortex and none in the hippocampal gyrus. However, pronounced atrophy and cell loss were found in the dentate gyrus and Ammon's horn. In the second case, with long survival (Glees & Griffith, 1952), autopsy revealed that the hippocampus, hippocampal and fusiform gyri, and a large portion of the fornix fibers had been destroyed bilaterally by a vascular accident. Interestingly, no pathological changes were noted in the amygdala or mammillary bodies. It is regrettable that in the only two known cases of selective damage to the hippocampal system, no psychological testing was possible, and it is surprising that no premorbid history was provided.

produce in monkeys impairments resembling those found in the clinic. In most cases, removals included the amygdala, as well as the hippocampus and hippocampal gyrus; retrograde as well as anterograde learning capacities were assessed, with special emphasis on those tasks in which a delay was interposed between the presentation of the stimuli and the animals' response. Mild but significant impairments were found in postoperative retention and relearning of visual and tactual discriminations (Orbach *et al.*, 1960) and of matching-to-sample tasks without delays (Correll & Scoville, 1965; Drachman & Ommaya, 1964). Postoperative acquisition of a visual pattern discrimination under conditions of massed trials was impaired (Orbach *et al.*, 1960), as was the concurrent learning of several pairs of visual patterns, with a given pair presented after intervals of either several seconds or 5 min (Correll & Scoville, 1965, 1970).

The belief that there are real phylogenetic differences in the role of medial temporal lobe structures in memory was based on the finding that both retrograde and anterograde amnesia appeared to be less global than that found in patients. It also stemmed from the fact that those monkeys that were able to relearn a matching-to-sample task without delays were not unduly disturbed by the further introduction of delays of up to 12 sec. Finally, it was felt that, rather than an abnormally rapid decay of memory traces, interpair interference may have been responsible for the impairment on the concurrent discrimination task. It is easy to see, in retrospect, that the disappointment felt by the authors was unfounded. The study by Drachman and Ommaya (1964) and that of Correll and Scoville (1965) did demonstrate retrograde deficits in visual associative learning, and the delays used were well within the short-term span. When, later, different tests of recognition memory became available, deficits in associative and recognition memory were found with delays of 30 sec and longer.

The Hippocampus Revisited

Earlier studies used tasks that required both pre- and postoperative prolonged training; furthermore, the ablations combined damage to two major structures, the amygdala and hippocampus, each structure subserving presumably distinct functions. In fact, in some cases, damage to both structures had been shown to produce more severe, but also different, effects than selective damage to either structure alone (Correll & Scoville, 1965; Mahut, 1971). Yet, interactive effects were not the rule: With the exception of one task (object-discrimination reversal), monkeys with combined removals were impaired on tasks on which monkeys with selective hippocampal removals were impaired, and were not impaired on tasks on which monkeys with hippocampal removals were not impaired (Mahut, 1971). It was thought necessary, therefore, to dissect the mnemonic functions of medial temporal lobe structures by using two approaches. In one, we varied the site of lesion and tested the effects of ablations in both visual and tactual modalities. In the other, we varied the age at which damage to the hippocampal system was inflicted.

Since anterograde, rather than retrograde, amnesic defects in patients were most severe, of main interest was the reexamination of anterograde effects of amygdalo-hippo-campal ablations on long-term retention of simple object discriminations that could be learned in one short session, without overlearning. At the same time, we focused our attention on the effects of selective hippocampal removals. However, in the course of this early work, mnemonic disturbances were attributed to damage of a brain structure related to the hippocampus: Deficits in visual retention and associative learning have been found to follow anterior inferotemporal cortical ablations (Iversen & Weiskrantz, 1964; Iwai & Mishkin, 1968), and growing anatomical evidence revealed close connections between the anterior inferotemporal cortex and hippocampus through the entorhinal area (Moss, 1974; Van Hoesen & Pandya, 1975; Van Hoesen, Pandya, & Butters, 1972). Therefore, a direct comparison among the effects on memory of inferotemporal, entorhinal, and hippocampal ablations became of direct interest.

Deficits associated with bitemporal lobectomies in patients were found to be nonspecific as to modality, and projections from several cortical association areas to the entorhinal cortex and thence to the hippocampus were described in monkeys (Van Hoesen et al., 1972). The latter could constitute one possible anatomical basis for supramodal effects. One of our concerns, therefore, was to determine whether resections of the hippocampus would result in deficits that were independent of sensory modality.

As a new test of memory became available, more closely resembling tests used in the clinic than did standard laboratory tasks (Gaffan, 1974; Mishkin & Delacour, 1975), assessment of visual recognition memory after hippocampal ablations became possible.

Results obtained in all these projects have been reported previously and are only briefly described here; however, some emphasis is placed on the nature of the tasks that were used.

1. With a task that required either retention or reversal of an object discrimination on alternate days, monkeys with amygdalo-hippocampal, hippocampal, or entorhinal, but not those with inferotemporal cortical, ablations were impaired on retention days, but not on reversal days. Hippocampal removals were also followed by a similar impairment when the task was given in the tactual modality (Mahut, Moss, & Zola-Morgan, 1981).

2. Hippocampal and entorhinal ablations resulted in an impairment in retention of simple object discriminations after intervals of 1 and 24 hr and, surprisingly, in a milder impairment after 48-hr intervals. Monkeys with inferotemporal cortical ablations were impaired only at the shortest of the three intervals (Mahut et al., 1981).

3. As expected, monkeys with inferotemporal cortical ablations were impaired on the concurrent object-discrimination task, but so were those with hippocampal or entorhinal ablations. This task involved the presentation of eight pairs of objects in an intermingled fashion in each session, until the animals learned to discriminate every pair. In the tactual mode, however, hippocampal, but not inferotemporal, ablations were followed by a deficit (Moss, Mahut, & Zola-Morgan, 1981). Conceivably, therefore, monkeys with neocortical ablations were impaired because of a primary defect in recognizing the physical attributes of several pairs of objects presented concurrently in the *visual modality*, whereas the impairment of monkeys with hippocampal ablations may have been due primarily to a deficit in retention of object–reward associations that was *independent of modality*. A more detailed, day-by-day, analysis of the performance of monkeys with hippocampal removals suggested that they were abnormally susceptible to proactive and retroactive interpair interference in both visual and tactual modes, a characteristic associated earlier with combined amygdalo-hippocampal removals (Correll & Scoville, 1970). It is important to note, however, that interpair interference was found to be less pronounced in those monkeys that had undergone prior extensive training with several different object-discrimination tasks.

4. Impairment after hippocampal removals was also found on a task of visual recognition. In this task, monkeys were trained with the use of a trial-unique non-matching-to-sample procedure (Mishkin, 1978; Mishkin & Delacour, 1975) to indicate whether they could discern, after a *single* previous presentation, a familiar (i.e., previously presented) from a novel (i.e., not previously presented) test object. In one version of the task, delays between familiarization with the sample object and its re-presentation with a novel one were increased in steps from 10 to 30, 70, and 130 sec. In another version, several sample objects were presented serially, and each list was followed by nonmatching trials of each list member with a novel object. Though monkeys with hippocampal ablations were significantly impaired with delays, particularly with 130-sec delays, the impairment was more marked with lists, and it approximated that shown by one monkey with a combined amygdalo-hippocampal ablation. Analysis of the pattern of errors made on individual items with all list lengths revealed an intact primacy effect, but, once again, an abnormal sensitivity to interference among items, in particular to proactive interference (Mahut, Zola-Morgan, & Moss, 1982). It should be noted that this impairment was still present as late as 5 years after surgery.[3]

Sensitivity to Massed Practice

Detailed analyses of performance on the concurrent object-discrimination task and on the list version of the recognition-memory task revealed an abnormal sensitivity to interference—a symptom that may parallel the vulnerability to distraction of patients with bitemporal lobectomies. Perhaps the unexpected and paradoxical finding of a greater impairment of operated monkeys in object-discrimination retention after 1-hr than after 48-hr intervals (described in the previous section) was due to a related enhanced sensitivity to massed, as opposed to distributed, practice? To see whether this notion was correct, we took the following four steps: First we reexamined the performance of all the monkeys that had been tested in our laboratory on the successive-retentions task with 1-, 24-, and 48-hr intervals, in all previous projects (Mahut *et al.*, 1981; Mahut & Zola, 1976, 1977; Moss, 1979; Zola, 1973). The final list included operated control monkeys (our surgical failures with unilateral fornix sections or unilateral removals of the entorhinal area), normal monkeys, and those with either inferotemporal cortical, entorhinal, or hippocampal ablations, as well as those with bilateral sections of the fornix (see Table 29-1).

While no significant differences among groups were found in initial acquisition, significant differences were found among groups with 1-hr (Kruskal–Wallis one-way analysis of variance: $H = 18.6, p < .001$), 24-hr ($H = 21.3, p < .001$), and 48-hr ($H = 16.1$,

---

3. The impairment on the recognition-memory task, particularly severe with the list version, is at variance with the absence of impairment or mild impairment after hippocampal removals as reported by Mishkin (1978). Yet, in both studies, the same testing procedure was used with comparable delays and the same list lengths. Furthermore, the ablations sustained by four of the six monkeys in our hippocampal group seem to correspond to the ablations in two of Mishkin's three monkeys with selective ablations of the hippocampus. The discrepancy between the two sets of results is puzzling, particularly since monkeys in our study were considerably more sophisticated experimentally than were those tested by Mishkin. The difference could be due, perhaps, to the fact that, while our study assessed anterograde effects of hippocampal damage, the results reported by Mishkin reflect the absence of retrograde effects.

TABLE 29-1. Performance of Normal Monkeys, Operated Controls, and Four Experimental Groups on the Successive-Retentions Task at Three Different Time Intervals

		Initial learning Group mean		Five retentions Group mean	
	n	Trials per pair of objects	Errors	Trials	Errors
1 hr					
Normal	12	38.1	16.0	43.8	18.7
AIT	4	45.8	20.3	152.8	76.0_b
Entorhinal	3	41.0	19.3	89.3	38.3_b
Fornix	5	34.8	15.2	163.8	76.6_a
Hippocampal	5	43.0	22.0	170.0	78.0_a
24 hr					
Normal	16	40.8	18.3	49.7	20.0
Oper. C.	7	38.4	16.9	44.1	18.0
AIT	4	46.0	25.0	62.0	26.8
Entorhinal	3	50.7	24.7	96.0	40.7_b
Fornix	13	35.3	15.3	125.4	50.9_a
Hippocampal	8	36.2	20.1	128.1	53.7_a
H-7-Am		41.5	16.0	88	39
48 hr					
Normal	9	38.6	17.9	40.7	17.7
Oper. C.	3	35.7	18.3	23.3	11.0
AIT	4	45.8	20.3	20.8	8.5
Entorhinal	3	46.3	23.3	64.7	25.7
Fornix	8	44.4	18.6	109.9	43.8_b
Hippocampal	6	47.2	19.3	88.2	39.2_b
H-7-Am		31.5	24.0	115	45

Note. Abbreviations: AIT, anterior inferotemporal cortical ablation; Oper. C., operated control group; H-7-Am, bilateral amygdalohippocampal ablation. Subscripts a and b denote significantly more errors than those made by monkeys in the normal control groups (a: $p < .002$, two-tailed; b: $p < .02$, two-tailed).

$p < .01$) intervals. Significant differences were found between individual groups of experimental monkeys and those in both the normal and operated control groups, but, for the sake of clarity, only differences between experimental and normal groups are indicated in Table 29-1.

As a second step, the performance of monkeys in all groups was examined as a function of successive retentions. The data obtained in this step, and those obtained in the next step, were analysed by the use of two-way analyses of variance; when appropriate, these analyses were followed by *a posteriori* between-group comparisons using the Newman–Keuls paired-comparisons test (Kirk, 1968). To simplify the illustration of the results, only data obtained by normal monkeys and by those in the hippocampal, inferotemporal, and entorhinal groups are shown in Figure 29-2. Significant group, retention, and group $\times$ retention interactions were found with all three intervals (F ratios were significant at levels of confidence from $p < .01$ to $p < .00001$). Significant differences in performance between monkeys in each of the experimental groups and those in the normal group (p's $< .05$) are indicated by solid black symbols in Figure 29-2. This view of the results confirmed that normal monkeys retained only imperfectly the discriminations

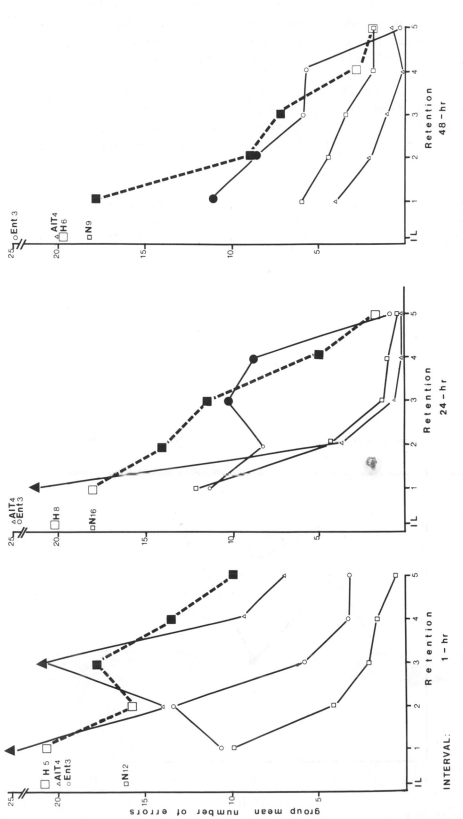

FIGURE 29-2. Mean group accuracy of performance attained by four groups of monkeys on the successive-retentions task with three different intervals. Solid symbols indicate significant differences in performance, as compared to normal control group. Abbreviations: IL, errors on initial learning; N, normal; Ent, entorhinal; AIT, anterior inferotemporal cortical; H, hippocampal.

practiced in previous sessions and that several sessions were needed to attain close to errorless performance. The salient aspect of performance of monkeys with hippocampal ablations was that the number of errors decreased more rapidly as the intersession intervals became longer.

As a third step, we examined the extent to which the effects of repeated practice were reflected in performance on the first, and on a few subsequent, trials *within* a session. Errors made on Retention 5 with 24-hr intervals, and those made on Retentions 4 and 5 with 48-hr intervals, were not included in the statistical analyses, because the performance

FIGURE 29-3. Mean group accuracy attained by monkeys in the normal and in two experimental groups at the beginning of each testing session on all five retentions, at 1-hr intervals. Solid symbols indicate significant differences in performance, as compared to normal control group (Newman-Keuls test, *p*'s < .05). Abbreviations: N, normal; AIT, anterior inferotemporal cortical; H, hippocampal.

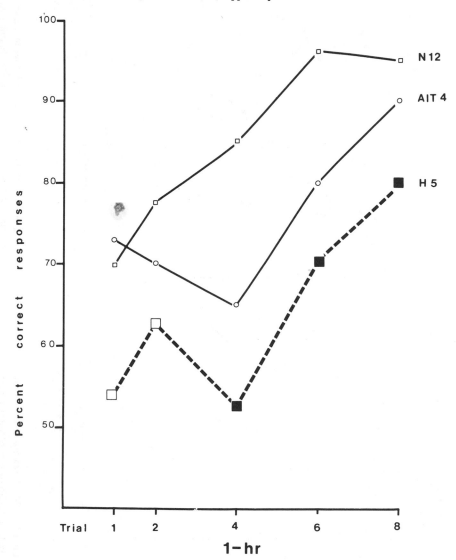

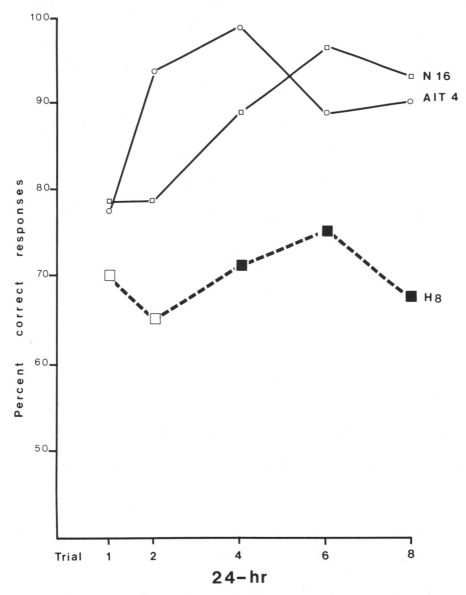

FIGURE 29-4. Mean group accuracy attained by monkeys in the normal and in two experimental groups at the beginning of each testing session on all five retentions, at 24-hr intervals. Solid symbols indicate significant differences in performance, as compared to normal control group (Newman-Keuls test, p's < .05). Abbreviations: N, normal; AIT, anterior inferotemporal cortical; H, hippocampal.

of monkeys with hippocampal ablations on those retentions was no longer significantly impaired. Significant group and trial effects were found with all three intervals, but a significant group × trial interaction was found only with 48-hr intervals. Significant differences in performance among monkeys in the normal, hippocampal, and inferotemporal groups are indicated by solid black symbols in Figures 29-3, 29-4, and 29-5.

Though we were not surprised to see that monkeys with hippocampal ablations were not significantly less accurate on Trial 1 than were normal monkeys, we were not

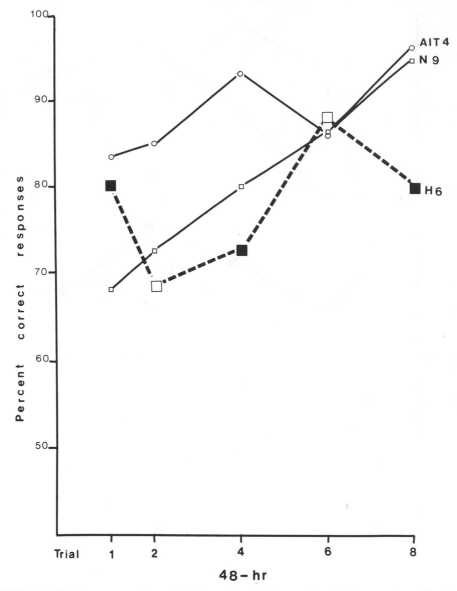

FIGURE 29-5. Mean group accuracy attained by monkeys in the normal and in two experimental groups at the beginning of each testing session on all five retentions, at 48-hr intervals. Solid symbols indicate significant differences in performance, as compared to normal control group (Newman-Keuls test, *p*'s < .05). Abbreviations: N, normal; AIT, anterior inferotemporal cortical; H, hippocampal.

prepared to find that they were significantly *more* accurate with the longest (48-hr) intervals. It should be noted, however, that regardless of their efficient performance on the first trials, monkeys with hippocampal ablations made more errors than did normal monkeys on subsequent trials.

The fourth step was undertaken in an attempt to find other instances of unimpaired, or paradoxically facilitated, retention on the first trial of training sessions separated by long (24-hr) delays. To this end, we examined the data obtained on a visual pattern-

TABLE 29-2. Visual Pattern-Discrimination Task

Group	Errors	% correct in last 100 trials
Normal (n = 15)	Range: 48–224 $\bar{X}$ = 128.3	90–95
Hippocampal		
H-1	99	90
H-2	123	92
H-3	138	90
H-4	142	90
H-5	258	90
H-6	353	91
H-7	364	90
H-8 (AIT)	311	76
H-9 (AIT)	355	73
H-10 (AIT)	305	69
H-11 (AIT)	379	50
H-12 (AIT)	413	50
H-13	403	48
H-Am-1	123	90
H-Am-2	157	90
H-Am-3	173	90

Note. Abbreviations: AIT, additional, inadvertent damage to inferotemporal neocortex; H-Am, combined amygdalo-hippocampal ablation.

discrimination task by 15 normal and 16 hippocampectomized monkeys. Of the latter, 9 were significantly impaired; 13 of this group had sustained radical bilateral removals, while in the remaining 3, combined amygdalo-hippocampal ablations included only the most anterior portion of the hippocampus. Only 5 of the 16 monkeys sustained varying degrees of inadvertent damage to the inferotemporal neocortex, and in one (H-13), there was gliosis of the inferotemporal cortex (see Table 29-2).

The errors made on Trial 1 were plotted for four approximately equal consecutive blocks of trials, to take into account possible changes in performance with continued training.[4] The results, illustrated in Table 29-3, seem to be in accord with the findings obtained on the successive-retentions task with three different intersession intervals.

It appears, therefore, that when monkeys were required to remember after either 1-hr, 24-hr, or 48-hr intervals which of two equally familiar objects was associated with reward, normal monkeys showed incomplete retention for past events at the beginning of each session, but a capacity for rapid relearning within a few seconds. After hippocampal damage, while retention of past events equaled that of normal monkeys on the first trial, it was the capacity to relearn within a session that was impaired. These findings are compatible with the notion that operated monkeys perform best under conditions of distributed practice; together with the sensitivity to proactive and retroactive interference, they define at least two characteristics of those brain systems that mediate learning in the absence of hippocampus. It should be noted that similar properties have been ascribed by O'Keefe and Nadel (1978) to their conceptual "taxon" system, which mediates learning in organisms deprived of the "locale" system through damage to the hippocampus.

4. This method of analysis was suggested by Dr. Zola-Morgan.

TABLE 29-3. Visual Pattern-Discrimination Task: Mean Percentages of Correct Responses Made by Normal and Operated Monkeys on Trial 1 in All Daily Sessions, Divided into Four Blocks

			Block		
Group	*n*	I	II	III	IV
Normal	15	54	60	64	56
Hippocampal					
H1–H4	4	42	50	31	80
H5–H7	3	79	26	86	28
H8–H12	5	71	72	75	68
H13	1	33	67	33	85
H-Am	3	64	61	50	81

Note. Abbreviation: H-Am, combined amygdalo-hippocampal ablation. Underlined numbers represent percentages of responses that were significantly greater than chance.

Effects of Hippocampal Damage as a Function of Age

Monkeys with hippocampal ablations sustained in infancy, at 2 months of age, were impaired postoperatively (at 3 to 5 months of age) on the object-discrimination retention task with 24- and 48-hr intervals between successive retention tests. They were also impaired on a spatial (left–right) discrimination-reversal task. Impairments on both types of tasks equaled in severity those found in age-control juvenile monkeys operated upon at 2 years of age. Two years later, on the second retest with the same tasks, the impairments became attenuated or were no longer present.[5] At 5 to 6 years of age, the same operated monkeys performed with normal ease on a previously unencountered task, in which discriminations between members of eight pairs of objects had to be learned concurrently and were not impaired as a group on the spatial (left–right) delayed-alternation task, though both tasks were sensitive to hippocampal damage in older monkeys. At the same time, however, they were significantly impaired on the trial-unique delayed non-matching-to-sample recognition-memory task (Rehbein, Zola-Morgan, Mahut, & Moss, 1980). On this task, both the severity of the impairment and a greater difficulty experienced with lists than with delays paralleled the performance of monkeys operated upon as juveniles (Mahut *et al.*, 1982). In view of the unexpected dissociation of performance between the two classes of tasks, we decided to reassess visual and spatial learning capacities with the use of three other trial-unique recognition-memory or associative-memory tasks. One was an object–reward association task in which monkeys had to remember which of two equally familiar objects had been associated with food reward 10 to 130 sec earlier (Gaffan, 1974). The second was a spatial-recognition task in which they had to discern, on every trial, an unfamiliar location of one of two identical plaques on an 18-well food tray (Rehbein, 1984). Operated monkeys were impaired with 70- and 130-sec delays on the first task, and with all delays on the second. The third task assessed recognition with increasing

---

5. This project was carried out in close collaboration with Dr. Zola-Morgan.

memory loads (Rehbein, 1984; Rehbein & Mahut, 1983). After the first recognition trial, and on all subsequent trials, previously presented objects continued to be re-presented, but a novel object was added on each successive trial. Intervals between presentations of the samples and their re-presentations with a novel item were 5 sec. Two series of different objects were used in each daily session, and testing with each series was terminated for a given monkey as soon as it failed to displace the most recently presented novel item. Intervals between series were 15 sec. The same procedure was used in the location-recognition version of the task, except that, instead of objects, identical discs covered food wells located in different positions on the tray. After 32 training sessions, the memory "span" attained for objects ranged between 5 and 12 for individual normal monkeys, with a group mean of 8 objects; for location, it ranged from 4 to 9, with a group mean of 5.1 locations. In contrast, the "span" attained by operated monkeys was significantly shorter: It ranged from 1 to 5 items, with group means of 3.5 and 2.6 for the object and location tests, respectively (Newman–Keuls test, p's $< .01$).

Summary and Interpretation

The main goal of our work has been to clarify the role of the hippocampus in memory. In our early work, we found that ablation of this structure in the monkey resulted in anterograde deficits in concurrent object-discrimination learning and in retention of object discriminations after 1-hr and 24-hr intervals. Even partial deafferentation of the hippocampus through ablation of the entorhinal area was sufficient to produce equivalent deficits. Also, some of the deficits were found to be independent of sensory modality. Later, when new tests (Gaffan, 1974) became available, which resembled closely those used in the clinic, it was possible to demonstrate visual recognition-memory deficits with delays as short as 30 to 130 sec, and with lists of as few as five serially presented items. Detailed analyses of performance revealed an abnormal sensitivity of operated monkeys to interitem interference as well as to massed practice. Parallel studies of the effects of hippocampal damage in infancy revealed the presence of deficits in recognition memory for object quality, or location, as well as in object–reward associative memory, as late as 5 to 6 years following surgery.

Yet not all functions are affected by hippocampal damage in the monkey. Operated animals perform with normal ease on tasks such as left–right, spatial delayed response (Mahut, 1971; Orbach et al., 1960), go/no-go (nonspatial) delayed alternation (Mahut, 1971), and object-discrimination reversal (Jones & Mishkin, 1972; Mahut, 1971), and not all operated animals are impaired in learning two-choice visual-discrimination tasks (cf. Table 29-2). In addition, as described in the present report, retention of past events, even after 48-hr delays, is unimpaired on the first trial of each daily session of 20 trials. In the special case of hippocampal damage sustained in infancy, followed by practice with two-choice discrimination tasks, long-term effects included a deficit in recognition memory but an absence of deficit on two previously unencountered learning tasks with repeated trials and 24-hr intervals between sessions. These instances of spared capacity to learn are in line with normal rates of learning of a perceptual task (mirror drawing) shown by patient H. M. (Milner, 1962), as well as with his ability to learn certain puzzles (Cohen & Corkin, 1981). Similarly, performance of a mirror-reading task has been shown to improve over days in amnesic patients with neuropathological, or traumatic, damage of medial thalamic structures (Cohen & Squire, 1980). Therefore, a neural system must exist that can mediate learning in the absence of memory systems, and its nature is best understood in the light of a challenging hypothesis advanced by Hirsh (1974, 1980) and by Hirsh and Krajden (1982). By extending the views of O'Keefe and Nadel (1978), Hirsh considers the hippocampus as a cognitive, Tolmanian, system, which mediates knowledge about relations among all stimuli instead of the more narrow knowledge about space alone. Rather than ensuring consolidation of memory, the hippocampus is seen as a system that mediates the selective processes determining which limited subset of memories, out of many potentially relevant memories stored in the cortex, will guide behavior at any given time. However, the brain is also assumed to contain an associative-learning system that operates, literally, in the Hullian sense of an incremental buildup of stimulus–response associations through reinforcement. On this view "a strong association . . . involving a given stimulus must exist only when the representation of that stimulus is incorporated into no more than one association" (Hirsh & Krajden, 1982, p. 215). Hence, previous learning interferes with subsequent learning, as we find to be the case after hippocampal damage in monkeys. In agreement with O'Keefe and Nadel (1978), Hirsh suggests that the hippocampus mediates cognitive aspects of memory but not its associative aspects (Hirsh & Krajden, 1982).

Given the existence of two distinct systems, their interactions must be complex, for "on some occasions the two systems compete; on others, they cooperate. Each has capacities that the other does not. There are certain features of knowledge that cannot be attained without using the capacities of both" (Hirsh & Krajden, 1982, p. 214). It seems to us that the first necessary step would be to identify the neural system that is capable of mediating stimulus–response learning; for several reasons, the striatum might prove to be a promising target. By virtue of its afferent and efferent pathways, it can be viewed as a functional interface between cortical and motor systems, on the one hand, and between cortical and reinforcement systems, on the other. In addition to the sensory–motor areas, several other cortical areas are known to project to the caudate–putamen complex in the dorsal striatum (Van Hoesen, Yeterian, & Lavizzo-Mourey, 1981; Yeterian & Van Hoesen, 1978; for review, see Graybiel & Ragsdale, 1979). In turn, the dorsal striatum gives origin to two distinct pathways. One projects to the pallidum and provides a link with subthalamic and midbrain modulating motor systems. The other projects to substantia nigra, and it is this reciprocal striato-nigral pathway that links the dorsal and ventral (nucleus accumbens) sectors of the striatum with both limbic structures (amygdala, hippocampus) and dopamine-containing cells in the midbrain (Kelley & Domesick, 1982; Kelley, Domesick, & Nauta, 1982; for review, see Graybiel & Ragsdale, 1979). So far, supporting behavioral evidence is scant, though one important relevant finding may be that, in rats, both aversive and appetitive classical conditioning can be facilitated retroactively by noncontingent, selective activation of nigro-striatal fibers (Coulombe & White, 1980; Major & White, 1978). More direct support comes from the demonstration that brightness-discrimination learning is impaired by lesions of the caudate nucleus in cats (Olmstead, Villablanca, Marcus, & Avery, 1976) and that, in the monkey, lesions of the tail of the caudate nucleus, which receives projections from the inferotemporal neocortex (Whitlock & Nauta, 1956; Yeterian, 1978, as cited by Graybiel & Ragsdale, 1979), impair postoperative retention of a visual pattern-discrimination task (Divac, Rosvold, & Szwarcbart, 1967). Clearly a reexamination of striatal functions with more diverse and appropriate behavioral tests is needed. It remains to be seen whether the new evidence will justify the undertaking of the more formidable task of specifying the different levels of interaction that might obtain between the striatal learning system and the hippocampal, or thalamic, memory systems.

ACKNOWLEDGMENTS

We thank Dr. Nelson Butters for informative discussions of some controversial, and less controversial, aspects of human amnesia; Dr. Steve Harkins for his unstinted help with statistical analyses; and Lucio Rehbein for sharing with us the data obtained in his projects. Dr. W. J. H. Nauta was kind enough to assess the reports of Grünthal (1947) and Glees and Griffith (1952). Helen Mahut also acknowledges rewarding and helpful discussions with Richard Hirsh.

REFERENCES

Cohen, N., & Corkin, S. The amnesic patient, H. M.: Learning and retention of a cognitive skill. *Society for Neuroscience Abstracts*, 1981, *7*, 235.

Cohen, N., & Squire, L. Preserved learning and retention of pattern-analyzing skill in amnesia: Dissociation of knowing how and knowing that. *Science*, 1980, *210*, 207–210.

Corkin, S. Tactually-guided maze-learning in man: Effects of unilateral cortical excisions and bilateral hippocampal lesions. *Neuropsychologia*, 1965, *3*, 339–351.

Corsi, P. *Verbal memory impairment after unilateral hippocampal excisions.* Paper presented at the 40th Annual Meeting of the Eastern Psychological Association, Philadelphia, 1969.

Correll, R. E., & Scoville, W. B. Performance of delayed match following lesions of medial temporal lobe structures. *Journal of Comparative and Physiological Psychology*, 1965, *60*, 360–367.

Correll, R. E., & Scoville, W. B. Relationship of ITI to acquisition of serial visual discriminations following temporal rhinencephalic resection in monkey. *Journal of Comparative and Physiological Psychology*, 1970, *70*, 464–469.

Coulombe, D., & White, N. The effect of post-training lateral hypothalamic self-stimulation on aversive and appetitive classical conditioning. *Physiology and Behavior*, 1980, *25*, 267–272.

Divac, I., Rosvold, H. E., & Szwarcbart, M. Behavioral effects of selective ablations of the caudate nucleus. *Journal of Comparative and Physiological Psychology*, 1967, *63*, 184–190.

Drachman, D. A., & Arbit, J. Memory and the hippocampal complex. *Archives of Neurology*, 1966, *15*, 52–61.

Drachman, D. A., & Ommaya, A. K. Memory and the hippocampal complex. *Archives of Neurology*, 1964, *10*, 411–425.

Gaffan, D. Recognition impaired and association intact in the memory of monkeys after transection of the fornix. *Journal of Comparative and Physiological Psychology*, 1974, *86*, 1100–1109.

Gary-Bobo, E., & Mahut, H. Unpublished data, 1968.

Glees, P., & Griffith, H. B. Bilateral destruction of the hippocampus (cornu ammonis) in a case of dementia. *Monatschrift für Psychiatrie und Neurologie*, 1952, *123*, 193–204.

Graybiel, A. M., & Ragsdale, C. W. Fiber connections of the basal ganglia. In M. Cuenod, G. W. Kreutzberg, & F. E. Bloom (Eds.), *Development and chemical specificity of neurons: Progress in brain research.* Amsterdam: Elsevier, 1979.

Grünthal, E. von. Über das klinische Bild nach umschriebenem beiderseitigem Ausfall des Ammonshornrinde. *Monatschrift für Psychiatrie und Neurologie*, 1947, *113*, 1016.

Hanbery, J., Ajmone-Marsan, C., & Dilworth, M. Pathways of non-specific thalamo-cortical projection systems. *Electroencephalography and Clinical Neurophysiology*, 1954, *6*, 103–118.

Hebb, D. O. *The organization of behavior.* New York: Wiley, 1949.

Hebb, D. O. Distinctive features of learning in the higher animal. In J. F. Delafresnay (Ed.), *Brain mechanisms and learning.* Oxford: Blackwell, 1961.

Herkenham, M. *The relationship of the nonspecific thalamus to mechanisms of attention and memory in the rat.* Unpublished doctoral dissertation, Northeastern University, 1974.

Hirsh, R. The hippocampus and contextual retrieval of information from memory: A theory. *Behavioral Biology,* 1974, *12,* 421–444.

Hirsh, R. The hippocampus, conditional operations, and cognition. *Physiological Psychology,* 1980, *8,* 175–182.

Hirsh, R., & Krajden, J. The hippocampus and the expression of knowledge. In R. L. Isaacson & N. E. Spear (Eds.), *The expression of knowledge.* New York: Plenum Press, 1982.

Iversen, S. D., & Weiskrantz, L. Temporal lobe lesions and memory in the monkey. *Nature,* 1964, *201,* 740–742.

Iwai, E., & Mishkin, M. *Two visual foci in the temporal lobe of monkeys.* Paper presented at the Japan–U.S. Joint Seminar on Neurophysiological Basis of Learning and Behavior, Kyoto, Japan, 1968.

Jones, B., & Mishkin, M. Limbic lesions and the problem of stimulus–reinforcement associations. *Experimental Neurology,* 1972, *36,* 362–377.

Kelley, A. E., & Domesick, V. B. The distribution of the projection from the hippocampal formation to the nucleus accumbens in the rat: An anterograde- and retrograde-horseradish peroxidase study. *Neuroscience,* 1982, *7,* 2321–2335.

Kelley, A. E., Domesick, V. B., & Nauta, W. J. H. The amygdalostriatal projection in the rat. An anatomical study by anterograde and retrograde tracing methods. *Neuroscience,* 1982, *7,* 615–630.

Kirk, R. E. *Experimental design: Procedures for the behavioral sciences.* Belmont, Calif.: Brooks-Cole, 1968.

Mahut, H. Effects of subcortical electrical stimulation on learning in the rat. *Journal of Comparative and Physiological Psychology,* 1962, *55,* 472–477.

Mahut, H. Effects of subcortical electrical stimulation on discrimination learning in cats. *Journal of Comparative and Physiological Psychology,* 1964, *58,* 390–395.

Mahut, H. Unpublished data, 1965.

Mahut, H. Spatial and object reversal learning in monkeys with partial temporal lobe ablations. *Neuropsychologia,* 1971, *9,* 409–424.

Mahut, H., Moss, M., & Zola-Morgan, S. Retention deficits after combined amygdalo-hippocampal and selective hippocampal resections in the monkey. *Neuropsychologia,* 1981, *19,* 201–225.

Mahut, H., & Zola, S. Effects of early hippocampal damage in monkeys. *Society for Neuroscience Abstracts,* 1976, *2,* 829.

Mahut, H., & Zola, S. Ontogenetic time-table for the development of three functions in infant macaques and the effect of early hippocampal damage upon them. *Society for Neuroscience Abstracts,* 1977, *3,* 428.

Mahut, H., Zola-Morgan, S., & Moss, M. Hippocampal resections impair associative learning and recognition memory in the monkey. *Journal of Neuroscience,* 1982, *2,* 1214–1229.

Major, R., & White, N. Memory facilitation by self-stimulation reinforcement mediated by the nigro-neostriatal bundle. *Physiology and Behavior,* 1978, *20,* 723–733.

Milner, B. Les troubles de la mémoire accompagnant des lésions hippocampiques bilatérales. In P. Passouant (Ed.), *Physiologie de l'hippocampe.* Paris: Centre National de la Recherche Scientifique, 1962.

Milner, B. Amnesia following operation on the temporal lobes. In C. W. M. Whitty & O. L. Zangwill (Eds.), *Amnesia.* London: Butterworths, 1966.

Milner, B. Visual recognition and recall after right temporal-lobe excision in man. *Neuropsychologia,* 1968, *6,* 191–209.

Milner, B., Corkin, S., & Teuber, H.-L. Further analysis of the hippocampal amnesic syndrome: 14-year follow-up study of H. M. *Neuropsychologia,* 1968, *6,* 215–234.

Milner, B., & Teuber, H.-L. Alteration of perception and memory in man: Reflections on methods. In L. Weiskrantz (Ed.), *Analysis of behavioral change.* New York: Harper & Row, 1968.

Milner, P. M. The cell assembly: Mark II. *Psychological Review,* 1957, *64,* 242–252.

Milner, P. M. Learning in neural systems. In M. C. Yovits & S. Cameron (Eds.), *Self-organizing systems.* New York: Pergamon Press, 1960.

Milner, P. M. *Physiological psychology.* New York: Holt, Rinehart & Winston, 1970.

Mishkin, M. Memory in monkeys severely impaired by combined, but not by separate removal of amygdala and hippocampus. *Nature,* 1978, *273,* 297–298.

Mishkin, M., & Delacour, J. An analysis of short-term visual memory in the monkey. *Journal of Experimental Psychology: Animal Behavior Processes,* 1975, *1,* 326–334.

Moss, M. *Differential projections of two sectors of the inferotemporal cortex in the rhesus monkey.* Paper presented at the Fourth Annual Meeting of the Society for Neuroscience, St. Louis, 1974.

Moss, M. *The role of the hippocampal system in concurrent discrimination of monkeys.* Unpublished doctoral dissertation, Northeastern University, 1979.

Moss, M., Mahut, H., & Zola-Morgan, S. Concurrent discrimination learning of monkeys after hippocampal, entorhinal or fornix lesions. *Journal of Neuroscience,* 1981, *1*, 227–240.

Müller, E. E., & Pilzecker, A. Experimentelle beiträge zur lehre von Gedachtniss. *Zeitschrift für Psychologie und Physiologie der Sinnersorgans: Erganzungsband,* 1900, *1*.

O'Keefe, J., & Nadel, L. *The hippocampus as a cognitive map.* Oxford: Clarendon Press, 1978.

Olmstead, C. E., Villablanca, J. R., Marcus, R. J., & Avery, D. L. Effects of caudate nuclei or frontal cortical ablations in cats: IV. Bar pressing, maze learning, and performance. *Experimental Neurology,* 1976, *53*, 670–693.

Orbach, J., Milner, B., & Rasmussen, T. Learning and retention in monkeys after amygdala–hippocampus resection. *Archives of Neurology,* 1960, *3*, 230–251.

Penfield, W., & Milner, B. Memory deficit produced by bilateral lesions in the hippocampal zone. *Archives of Neurology and Psychiatry,* 1958, *79*, 475–497.

Prisko, L. H. *Short-term memory in focal cerebral damage.* Unpublished doctoral dissertation, McGill University, 1963.

Rehbein, L. *Long-term deleterious effects on visual and spatial memory functions after damage to the hippocampal system in infancy.* Doctoral dissertation in preparation, Northeastern University, 1984.

Rehbein, L., & Mahut, H. Long-term deficits in associative and spatial recognition memory after early hippocampal damage in monkeys. *Society for Neuroscience Abstracts,* 1983, *9*, 639.

Rehbein, L., Zola-Morgan, S., Mahut, H., & Moss, M. Failure of sparing, or recovery, of recognition memory after early hippocampal resections in the rhesus macaque. *Society for Neuroscience Abstracts,* 1980, *6*, 88.

Scoville, W. B., & Milner, B. Loss of recent memory after bilateral hippocampal lesions. *Journal of Neurology, Neurosurgery and Psychiatry,* 1957, *20*, 11–21.

Sidman, M., Stoddard, L. T., & Mohr, J. P. Some additional quantitative observations of immediate memory in a patient with bilateral hippocampal lesions. *Neuropsychologia,* 1968, *6*, 245–254.

Van Hoesen, G. W., & Pandya, D. N. Some connections of the entorhinal (area 28) and perirhinal (area 35) cortices of the rhesus monkey: I. Temporal lobe afferents. *Brain Research,* 1975, *95*, 1–24.

Van Hoesen, G. W., Pandya, D. N., & Butters, N. Cortical afferents to the entorhinal cortex of the rhesus monkey. *Science,* 1972, *175*, 1471–1473.

Van Hoesen, G. W., Yeterian, E. H., & Lavizzo-Mourey, R. Widespread cortico-striate projections from temporal cortex of the rhesus monkey. *Journal of Comparative Neurology,* 1981, *199*, 205–219.

Whitlock, D. G., & Nauta, W. J. H. Subcortical projections from the temporal neocortex in *Macaca mulatta. Journal of Comparative Neurology,* 1956, *106*, 183–212.

Wickelgren, W. A. Sparing of short-term memory in an amnesic patient: Implications for strength theory of memory. *Neuropsychologia,* 1968, *6*, 235–244.

Yeterian, E. H., & Van Hoesen, G. W. Cortico-striate projections in the rhesus monkey. The organization of certain cortico-caudate connections. *Brain Research,* 1978, *139*, 43–63.

Zola, S. *Effects of fornix transection on reversal learning in the monkey.* Unpublished doctoral dissertation, Northeastern University, 1973.

30

Toward an Animal Model of Human Amnesia: Some Critical Issues

Stuart Zola-Morgan

Background

The objective of the neuropsychological analysis of memory is to understand its organization and neurological foundations. Here I describe two approaches that we and others have taken to achieve a neuropsychological analysis. The first has been to study the nature of memory deficits in amnesic patients of varying etiologies, and many of the notions discussed here stem from findings and ideas developed from these investigations. The second approach has been directed toward the development of an animal model of human amnesia by studying monkeys with lesions of specific brain regions where damage is thought to cause amnesia in humans. These studies have taken their lead from our research on the nature of human amnesia and have addressed a number of neuropsychological issues that must be resolved in order to achieve a satisfactory animal model.

Although there had been occasional earlier attempts to develop animal models of memory (Jacobsen & Elder, 1936) it is only since the 1950s, when the findings from the famous temporal lobe amnesic patient H. M. were reported (Scoville & Milner, 1957), that investigators have made an intensive effort to reproduce the amnesic syndrome in animals. Unfortunately, the outcome of such investigations has been somewhat disappointing, because damage in animals to the brain areas often implicated in the human cases has not always seemed to produce effects that matched the human amnesic syndrome in important ways. An extensive and controversial literature has accumulated for a number of species and a number of brain areas (for reviews of this literature, see Douglas, 1967; Isaacson, 1972; Squire & Zola-Morgan, 1983; Weiskrantz, 1978). These difficulties notwithstanding, the search has continued, because the achievement of an animal model would give us a tremendous advantage toward understanding the underlying mechanisms of memory. Animal models of human amnesia could identify with certainty which brain regions must be damaged to produce amnesia, and they could lead to more detailed neurobiological studies of learning and memory.

In this chapter, I discuss some of the issues pertinent to achieving an animal model of amnesia. Research on the neuropsychology of human amnesia has provided a number of criteria that must be satisfied before we can consider the goal of an animal model of human amnesia to have been attained. As may be seen, our ability to identify with certainty the critical brain areas involved in amnesia and our understanding of what tasks are appro-

Stuart Zola-Morgan. Veterans Administration Medical Center, San Diego, California; Department of Psychiatry, University of California at San Diego School of Medicine, La Jolla, California.

priate for studying amnesia have been two long-standing areas of uncertainty. I believe we are now very close to resolving these issues.

Issues

What Are the Brain Structures Whose Damage Is Responsible for Amnesia?

In considering the neuropathology of human amnesia, it has often been supposed that all amnesias are alike and that amnesia results from damage to one of a group of anatomically related structures (e.g., the hippocampal formation of the medial temporal lobe and the mammillary bodies in the diencephalon, which are connected by the fornix). However, recent neuropsychological data from both humans and monkeys have suggested that this functional link is not so obligatory as once thought, and that diencephalic and medial temporal amnesia may be distinct entities. The distinction between diencephalic and temporal lobe amnesia was first suggested by Lhermitte and Signoret (1972), and has recently been supported by a comparison of forgetting rates between groups of amnesic patients (Huppert & Piercy, 1978, 1979; Squire, 1981). Using a method designed to equate the retention of performance shortly after learning, these investigators have shown that patients with diencephalic amnesia (patients with Korsakoff syndrome and the well-studied amnesic case N. A.) exhibited a normal rate of forgetting, while the temporal lobe case H. M. and patients receiving electroconvulsive therapy (ECT) were found to exhibit abnormally rapid forgetting. (The data for H. M., however, were somewhat ambiguous.) We have recently applied this method to study forgetting rates in monkeys with selective lesions of the diencephalon (dorsomedial nucleus of the thalamus) and of the temporal lobe area (conjoint lesions of the hippocampus and amygdala). While the results of this preliminary study paralleled those just described for humans (rapid forgetting by monkeys with medial temporal lobe damage, but not by those with diencephalic damage), other studies using these same groups of monkeys suggested that those with medial temporal lobe damage were more severely amnesic than those with diencephalic damage (Zola-Morgan & Squire, 1982). Thus, it would be important to repeat these studies with operated groups whose amnesia is precisely equivalent. Additional evidence that diencephalic and temporal lobe amnesias are different entities comes from analyses suggesting that the retrograde amnesia associated with each area of damage is different in extent (see Squire & Cohen, 1984, for review). Finally, damage to the fornix, a major pathway that connects the hippocampal system to the diencephalon, does not seem to have significant effects on memory in either humans (see Squire & Moore, 1979, for review) or monkeys (see Zola-Morgan, Dabrowska, Moss, & Mahut, 1983, for review). Thus, there does not appear to be any strong evidence for functionally linking the diencephalon and the temporal lobe, and in my discussion I assume that the amnesia resulting from damage to each of these areas are distinct entities, at least to some extent.

DIENCEPHALIC AMNESIA

Although damage to the mammillary bodies is invariably associated with Korsakoff syndrome, the best studied of the diencephalic amnesias (see Barbizet, 1970; Mair, Warrington, & Weiskrantz, 1979), there is uncertainty as to whether mammillary body damage is responsible for amnesia. Some have favored the view that damage to the dorsomedial thalamic nucleus correlates best with amnesia (Victor, Adams, & Collins, 1971), and a crucial role for this region is also supported by the finding that the well-studied amnesic case N. A. has a lesion there (Squire & Moore, 1979).

The available evidence leads to no easy conclusion at this time about the relative importance of the mammillary bodies and the dorsomedial nucleus. Indeed, it may be incorrect to suppose that one structure or the other is the critical one. Other neuro-pathological data suggest that amnesia can occur when lesions are present in the mammillary bodies but not in the dorsomedial nucleus (Brion & Mikol, 1978), or when lesions are present in the dorsomedial nucleus but not the mammillary bodies (Mills & Swanson, 1978). Perhaps combined damage to both structures would cause more severe amnesia than when either structure is damaged alone, but quantitative data are not yet available to permit a test of this idea.

The time is clearly ripe for some of these ideas to be tested in a rigorous way in animals, but to date only a few studies of diencephalic amnesia have been accomplished (see Markowitsch, 1982, and Squire & Zola-Morgan, 1983, for reviews). An important consideration here is the appropriateness of the behavioral tests. Clearly, the tests used to evaluate the effects of brain lesions in monkeys must be ones that can be characterized as sensitive to amnesia in humans. With this criterion in mind, I know of no studies that have investigated the effects of mammillary body damage in monkeys. Indeed, their location in the brain makes circumscribed and selective lesions of these structures difficult to achieve. Their proximity to life-sustaining brain stem areas and to the blood supply of the Circle of Willis probably explains why over the past 30 years so few studies have been published concerning the behavioral effects of their damage. Recently, Dr. Nelson Butters and his colleagues at the Veterans Administration Medical Center in Boston developed a technique for the surgical removal of the mammillary bodies in monkeys and presented evidence for impaired delayed-alternation performance (Holmes, Jacobsen, Stein, & Butters, 1982). Dr. Butters has been kind enough to allow me to observe the surgical approach used by his colleagues, and studies of the effects of damage to the mammillary bodies using tasks sensitive to amnesia are now under way in our own laboratory and in his.

Damage to the dorsomedial nucleus of the thalamus in monkeys has been investigated in three recent studies, all of which reported impairments on the same amnesia-sensitive task, the trial-unique delayed non-matching-to-sample task (described in a later section). The lesions in one study were large and involved much of the medial aspects of both the anterior and medial thalamic nuclei (Aggleton & Mishkin, 1983a). In the two other studies, the lesions were smaller and limited either to the anterior (Aggleton & Mishkin, 1983b) or posterior (Zola-Morgan & Squire, 1982) portion of the dorsomedial nucleus. Both lesions significantly impaired performance. The deficit associated with lesions to the anterior dorsomedial nucleus was relatively mild, and the deficit associated with lesions to the posterior extent of the nucleus was severe. Interestingly, the impairment seen in the monkeys with posterior dorsomedial nucleus lesions was about as severe as that seen in the monkeys that had sustained combined damage to anterior and medial thalamic nuclei (Aggleton & Mishkin, 1983a).

The study by Zola-Morgan and Squire (1982) also demonstrated that when a multiple-exposure condition was used, analogous to that of the Huppert and Piercy (1978, 1979) and Squire (1981) studies on human amnesia, monkeys with lesions of the medial temporal lobe (hippocampus and amygdala combined) exhibited abnormally rapid forgetting, while the monkeys with dorsomedial lesions exhibited normal forgetting rates. It is possible that with larger, more complete lesions of the dorsomedial nucleus, this dissociation between the effects of diencephalic and temporal lobe damage would not occur, but it is also possible that the posterior portion of the nucleus may be an especially critical region whose damage is sufficient to produce these behavioral effects. In support of the latter notion are the findings from another recent study in monkeys that deficits on delayed response and delayed alternation correlated significantly with the extent of damage to the posterior portion of the dorsomedial nucleus (Isseroff, Rosvold, Galkin, & Goldman-Rakic, 1982).

TEMPORAL LOBE AMNESIA

Although the traditional view has been that damage to the hippocampal formation is the critical event responsible for temporal lobe amnesia (e.g., case H. M., cases of encephalitis), a review of the animal literature from the last 30 years does not lead immediately to any easy generalization about the effects on memory of hippocampal damage (see Squire & Zola-Morgan, 1983, for review). Two recently formulated hypotheses have raised the possibility of the involvement of other brain regions. Mishkin (1978, 1982) has suggested that to produce the severe impairment in memory resembling that seen in human amnesia, it is necessary to remove both the hippocampus and the amygdala. This hypothesis is, of course, consistent with the fact that the removal in patient H. M. involved both of these structures (Scoville & Milner, 1957). Horel (1978) has argued that hippocampal damage does not produce amnesia at all. He has presented a compelling case that, instead, amnesia results from damage to an area called the "temporal stem" (TS) or "albal stalk," a bundle of white-matter fibers containing the afferents and efferents by which the temporal cortex makes connections with more medial and more anterior parts of the brain. The TS lies adjacent to the hippocampus and the amygdala, and Horel has argued that the surgical approach used for H. M.'s temporal lobe removals very likely damaged this region.

Using a task known to be sensitive to human amnesia, the delayed non-matching-to-sample task, we have evaluated these two current hypotheses about which brain regions must be damaged to produce the disorder (see Figure 30-1). Monkeys with bilateral transections of the white matter of the TS were unimpaired, but monkeys with conjoint lesions of the hippocampus and amygdala (HA) exhibited a severe memory deficit (Zola-Morgan, Squire, & Mishkin, 1982). These results provide a clear basis for rejecting the hypothesis that TS damage causes amnesia.

While monkeys with HA lesions were markedly impaired on the non-matching-to-sample task, it is not yet entirely clear whether hippocampal lesions themselves cause the greater part of this impairment or whether amygdala damage contributes to it in a crucial way. One would think that 30 years of research could by now have answered the question of whether damage to the hippocampus alone is sufficient to cause an amnesia of the severity seen in humans. In fact, we are only now close to a resolution of that issue, as I describe next.

Whereas the effects of HA damage just described do suggest an impairment like that present in human amnesia, the hypothesis that a severe amnesia can be produced only by conjoint HA lesions, and not by lesions limited to the hippocampus, demands more than

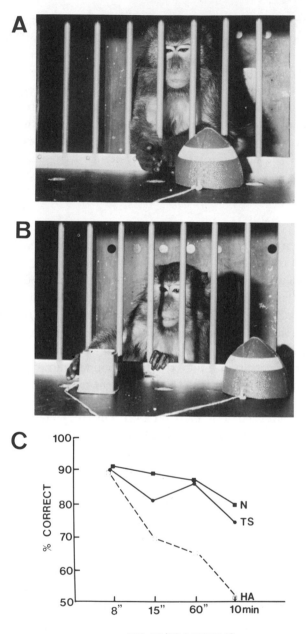

FIGURE 30-1. The trial-unique delayed non-matching-to-sample task. (A) The sample: The monkey first displaces a single object covering the middle well of a three-well food tray and obtains a reward. (B) The choice: Approximately 8 seconds later, the monkey sees two objects, the original one and a novel one. The monkey must displace the novel object to obtain a reward. New pairs of objects are used on every trial, and once the monkey learns the basic 8-second task, the interval between the sample and choice parts of the trial can be increased from seconds to minutes and even to hours. This task is sensitive to medial temporal lobe and to diencephalic damage in monkeys. (C) Normal monkeys (N), monkeys with temporal stem (TS) lesions, and monkeys with conjoint lesions of the hippocampus and the amygdala (HA) were tested on progressively longer delays, presented in sequence from 8 seconds to 10 minutes. The HA group was severely impaired. The TS group was normal.

the observation that conjoint lesions can cause impairment on certain tasks. It is also critical that the deficit following combined lesions is more severe than the deficit following selective hippocampal lesions.

The performance of operated groups with lesions limited to the hippocampus has been compared directly to that of groups with HA lesions on many kinds of tasks, but there have only been two direct comparisons involving tasks that are believed to be sensitive to human amnesia. Using the delayed non-matching-to-sample task, Mishkin (1978) reported that monkeys with separate hippocampal or amygdala damage were only mildly impaired, while those with combined removals of both structures exhibited a severe impairment. In the second study that has afforded the needed comparison, monkeys with hippocampal lesions and those with combined HA removals demonstrated equally impaired performance on a retention test of simple object discriminations (Mahut, Moss, & Zola-Morgan, 1981). Unfortunately, the comparisons in these studies are complicated by the fact that in the first study, histological reconstructions of the combined lesions were not available, and that in the second, the monkeys with the combined lesions had less complete hippocampal damage than the monkeys with lesions restricted to the hippocampus.

In summary, these two studies together provide some limited support for the idea that combined HA lesions cause greater impairment than hippocampal lesions alone; however, because of uncertainty about histology, the case is not yet a strong one. In addition on some tasks that seem suitable for assessing memory, such as the delayed retention of object discriminations and the learning of concurrent discriminations, the impairment can be quite severe following hippocampal lesions alone (Mahut et al., 1981; Moss, Mahut, & Zola-Morgan, 1981). There is also evidence (Mahut, Zola-Morgan, & Moss, 1982) that on the non-matching-to-sample task, monkeys with hippocampal lesions alone can be more severely impaired than those reported by Mishkin (1978).

To determine whether a hippocampal lesion or a conjoint HA lesion best produces amnesia, the two operated groups must be compared directly on several tasks sensitive to amnesia. One precaution that must be taken in all such comparisons is that there must be equivalence between the extent of the hippocampal damage in the monkeys with the restricted lesions and in the monkeys with the combined lesions. Recently, we reviewed the literature on the effects of medial temporal damage in monkeys (Squire & Zola-Morgan, 1983). When all studies were considered together, there was a decided tendency for the anterior third of the hippocampus to be spared in monkeys with lesions of the hippocampus alone and for it to be included in monkeys with the combined lesions. This difference could give the impression of there being greater amnesia in the group with combined lesions even if the hippocampus itself were the critical structure. It should be noted that in the one study cited earlier (Mahut et al., 1981), this nonequivalence of lesions happened to occur in the opposite direction.

The possibility that the anterior hippocampus might sometimes be spared is obviously relevant to interpreting the studies in monkeys and is especially relevant to making inferences about the human surgical cases. Case H. M., for example, developed profound amnesia following a removal that included the anterior two-thirds of the hippocampus. Studies with monkeys derived from this paradigmatic case and designed to test the importance of the hippocampus in memory function would be of uncertain validity if the lesions spared the anterior third of the hippocampus.

Recent anatomical findings indicate that a lesion that spared the anterior third of the hippocampus would not entirely deafferent and deefferent this structure. While most if not all of the subcortical connections that travel via the fornix (DeVito, 1980; Poletti & Creswell, 1977; Swanson & Cowan, 1979; Valenstein & Nauta, 1959) would be disrupted, much of the reciprocal projections of entorhinal cortex, medial frontal cortex, and the amygdala via the subiculum (Rosene & Van Hoesen, 1977) would be left intact.

In summary, the notion that combined HA damage produces more severe deficits than hippocampal damage on certain tasks suitable for the study of amnesia has some evidence to support it. Yet direct comparisons are still needed across several tasks in which histological reconstruction can verify the equivalence of the hippocampal removals in each group. Recent studies of the delayed non-matching-to-sample task suggest that the combined HA lesion produces a more severe deficit than hippocampal lesions alone, even when the hippocampal lesion can be shown histologically to be complete (Zola-Morgan & Squire, 1984b; Murray & Mishkin, 1984). Questions that remain concern the severity of the deficit associated with separate hippocampal lesions, and whether the more severe deficit associated with HA lesions is due to amygdala damage *per se* or to damage to periamygdaloid tissue including neocortex (Zola-Morgan & Squire, 1984b).

Thus, considerable headway has been made toward identifying candidate structures in the diencephalon and in the temporal lobe that must be damaged to produce amnesia. As I indicate next, a number of suitable tasks for testing memory in the monkey have emerged in the last few years, so that it should be possible to identify precisely those brain regions that must be damaged to produce human amnesia.

What Are the Tasks Appropriate for Studying Amnesia?

It seems fair to say that it has been uncertainty about which tasks are appropriate to detect amnesia, more than any other factor, that has thwarted attempts to establish an animal model of human amnesia. In the case of the behavioral tasks used to study memory in the monkey, it is now clear that they vary in how relevant they are to the human amnesic syndrome. This is a crucial new point in our understanding of what it is that we must be able to demonstrate in an animal model; it stems directly from recent investigations, which have shown that the amnesic syndrome in humans applies to a narrower domain of learning and memory than was once thought.

The traditional view of the amnesic syndrome has been that, despite their impairments, these patients can under some circumstances exhibit good learning and retention across long intervals. The best known examples of this observation come from the learning of perceptual–motor skills. Case H. M., for example, exhibited progressive learning of mirror tracing, pursuit rotor, and bimanual tracking across several days of testing (Corkin, 1968; Milner, 1962), despite reporting on each day that he had no memory of having performed the task before. During the last 10 years, investigators have compiled a considerable list of tasks that are less clearly perceptual–motor, but that can elicit signs of retention in patients who by other indications are profoundly amnesic (Cohen, 1981; Weiskrantz, 1978; Wood, Ebert, & Kinsbourne, 1982). A particularly good example is the demonstration that amnesic patients improved their skill at learning to read mirror-reversed words over a 3-day period and then retained the skill at a normal level 3 months later (Cohen & Squire, 1980; Cohen, 1981). Yet many of the patients did not remember having worked at the task before, and all were amnesic for the particular words that they read. Similar findings have recently been demonstrated using a complex cognitive problem-solving task, the Tower of Hanoi problem (Cohen & Corkin, 1981).

Both diencephalic and medial temporal lobe patients seem to be capable of acquiring the skills or processes needed for mirror reading, but they cannot acquire facts about the world, the outcomes, or the results of having used these skills (i.e., the fact that they have been tested or the ability to recognize as familiar the words that they have read). These findings have suggested a distinction, developed in more detail elsewhere (Cohen, 1981; Cohen & Squire, 1980; Squire & Cohen, 1984), between skills that are spared in amnesia and information based on specific facts, or outcomes of engaging in skills, that are impaired in amnesia.

This distinction can be usefully applied to the study of monkeys with lesions in those areas of the brain thought responsible for amnesia. Specifically, when the tasks used to assess memory in monkeys are scrutinized with this distinction in mind, it is clear that some of them should be sensitive to amnesia, whereas others would be expected to reveal either a mild memory impairment or none at all. This framework thus allows a test of its own validity, in that we can begin to make *a priori* predictions about a task's sensitivity to amnesia, based on our evaluation of the task requirements (see Squire & Zola-Morgan, 1983, for the application to several tasks of the proposed distinction between memory systems). In addition, in our own parallel program of human and animal neuropsychological research, we can validate tasks that have been developed for monkeys by administering them, essentially unchanged, to our amnesic patient populations. Several tasks, such as concurrent learning (Correll & Scoville, 1965a; Moss *et al.*, 1981; Oscar-Berman & Zola-Morgan, 1980; Zola-Morgan & Squire, in press) and the delayed retention of object discrimination (Mahut *et al.*, 1981; Zola-Morgan & Squire, in press), have been shown to be sensitive to amnesia in humans and to diencephalic and temporal lobe damage in monkeys. The best studied of these amnesia-sensitive tasks is the delayed non-matching-to-sample task (Mishkin & Delacour, 1975), which requires the monkey to recognize which of two objects it has previously seen (see Figure 30-1). This task reveals a clear impairment even with delays as short as 15–30 seconds in monkeys with medial temporal lesions (Mahut *et al.*, 1982; Mishkin, 1978; Zola-Morgan *et al.*, 1982; Zola-Morgan & Squire, in press) and in those with damage to the dorsomedial nucleus (Aggleton & Mishkin, 1983a,b; Zola-Morgan & Squire, 1982).

In contrast to these tasks, which are amnesia-sensitive, other tasks can be identified for use with monkeys that appear to depend substantially on skills or procedures. These tasks presumably would not be sensitive to diencephalic or medial temporal lobe damage in either humans or monkeys. Visual pattern-discrimination learning in the monkey, which is acquired gradually across days, seems to be an example of such a task (see Squire & Zola-Morgan, 1983, and Zola-Morgan & Squire, 1984a, for discussion). Monkeys with conjoint HA lesions are typically only mildly, if at all, impaired on such tasks (see Squire & Zola-Morgan, 1983, for a review of this literature); and monkeys with lesions of other brain regions that have been implicated in human amnesia (e.g., medial thalamus) also perform pattern-discrimination tasks successfully, despite failing at other tasks that are sensitive to human amnesia (Aggleton & Mishkin, 1983a; Isseroff *et al.*, 1982; Zola-Morgan & Squire, 1982).

In an attempt to parallel the finding from human amnesia of preserved motor skills, we have developed a set of motor-skill tasks for use with monkeys (Zola-Morgan & Squire,

1983, 1984a). One of these requires the monkey to learn to manipulate a food object (a fragile breadstick) around a series of barriers without dropping or breaking it. A second task requires the monkey to learn to retrieve a candy (a Life Saver) threaded onto a thin metal tube that has a right-angle bend (Davis, McDowell, Deter, & Steele, 1956). In order to obtain the Life Saver reward, the monkey must move it around the bend to the end of the tube (see Figure 30-2). Monkeys with conjoint HA lesions developed this skill over a period of several days at the same rate as normal control monkeys, and their retention of this skill after a 1-month interval was identical to that of the normal control monkeys (see Figure 30-2).

With tasks like those described in this section, and with the framework developed from investigations of human amnesia, considerable headway has been made in constructing a test battery by which a profile of amnesia in the monkey can be developed. The

FIGURE 30-2. (A) The Life Saver motor-skill task. In order to obtain the Life Saver, the monkey must learn to thread it around a bend to the end of the tube. Performance on this task by monkeys does not seem to be affected by medial temporal lesions. (B) Acquisition of the Life Saver motor-skill task by monkeys with conjoint HA lesions was as good as that of normal control monkeys. After a 1-month interval, the operated and normal control groups demonstrated equal levels of retention of the skill.

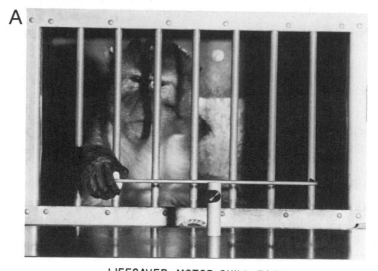

A

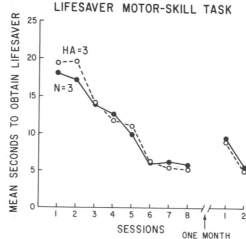

B

LIFESAVER MOTOR-SKILL TASK

brain regions in monkeys whose damage is responsible for the memory defects should be identifiable with this approach. In the remaining sections of this chapter, I discuss some additional characteristics of human amnesia that should direct our attempts toward the achievement of an animal model.

Retrograde versus Anterograde Amnesia

In humans, both anterograde and retrograde amnesia vary, depending on the form of amnesia studied, and their particular characteristics can be used to develop a taxonomy of memory disorders (Squire, 1981; Squire & Cohen, 1984). The distinction between retrograde and anterograde amnesia is an important one. For example, the fact that H. M. can recall events that occurred prior to his surgery better than events that occurred after his surgery (Marslen-Wilson & Teuber, 1975; Scoville & Milner, 1957) shows that (1) the brain regions damaged In H. M. are involved in the formation of memory rather than its retrieval; and (2) memory is not permanently stored in these structures. Moreover, the fact that H. M. has difficulty recalling events from 1 to 3 years prior to his surgery (Scoville & Milner, 1957) has suggested that these regions are involved in maintaining memory for a considerable time after learning (Squire & Cohen, 1982; Squire, Cohen, & Nadel, in press). In addition, patients who undergo ECT for the relief of chronic depression demonstrate a temporally limited retrograde amnesia, covering the period of a few years prior to treatment without affecting the period prior to that time (Squire & Cohen, 1982). Thus, findings from research on human amnesia suggest that the susceptibility of memory to disruption can decrease for as long as a few years after learning.

Unfortunately, these ideas and the distinction between retrograde and anterograde amnesia have frequently been overlooked by investigators attempting to replicate in animals the memory impairments seen in patients. Although some investigators (Orbach, Milner, & Rasmussen, 1960) have compared in monkeys the postoperative acquisition of a task (anterograde amnesia) with the postoperative retention of preoperative learning (retrograde amnesia), the time interval between preoperative learning and the surgery has probably been too brief to demonstrate a discontinuity between these two temporal domains of memory. It is, of course, difficult to know how to extrapolate from the human findings an appropriate learning–surgery interval for monkeys in order to demonstrate a temporally limited retrograde amnesia, but experiments including intervals of 6 months or longer would be of considerable interest.

Experimental strategies such as this would permit a comparison of premorbid and postmorbid memory, as well as a comparison of the nature of diencephalic and temporal lobe involvement in memory functions. Studies of human amnesia have emphasized that the discontinuity between these two temporal domains of memory is important in understanding the functional organization of memory, as well as the function of those brain structures that produce memory impairment when damaged.

The Effects of Distraction

When patient H. M. was able to rehearse and was not distracted, he maintained perfect performance on consonant trigrams up to delays of 40 seconds (Sidman, Stoddard, & Mohr, 1968) and was able to retain a three-digit number perfectly for at least 15 minutes

(Milner, 1959). Although intertrial mental activity (e.g., rehearsal) has traditionally been discussed primarily in the context of human performance and specifically in the context of verbal tasks, the concept may be useful in understanding the representational capacity of nonhuman animals (Wagner, Rudy, & Whitlow, 1973).

It is difficult to judge the demands of the non-matching-to-sample task used with monkeys, which involves easily discriminable objects and no distraction between sample and match. Studies in our laboratory have shown that the impaired performance on the non-matching-to-sample task of monkeys with conjoint HA lesions deteriorates even further when they are required to perform an irrelevant distracting task during the delay (Zola-Morgan & Squire, in press). Perhaps monkeys with hippocampal lesions, who have been reported to show relatively mild deficits on this task, would under conditions of distraction exhibit deficits comparable to those elicited by the conjoint removals.

Modality-General Defects

The McGill temporal lobe studies (Kimura, 1963; Milner, 1966, 1968) have led to the conclusion that memory processes are in some respects not modality-specific. Impairments in memory observed in the visual modality are typically found also in the auditory or tactile mode (Milner, 1966, 1968). These results imply that damage in monkeys to those brain structures responsible for amnesia should produce modality-general defects.

This notion has not yet been systematically explored, but monkeys with medial temporal lesions have demonstrated impairments that appear to be modality-general, just as in the human cases. Thus, monkeys with hippocampal lesions were impaired on concurrent-learning tasks in both the visual and tactual modalities (Moss, et al., 1981), and monkeys with conjoint HA lesions were impaired on both tactual and visual versions of the delayed non-matching-to-sample task (Mishkin, 1978; Murray & Mishkin, 1983; Zola-Morgan et al., 1982). Both the hippocampus and the amygdala receive input from more than one sensory modality (Jones & Powell, 1970; Turner, Mishkin, & Knapp, 1980; Van Hoesen, Pandya, & Butters, 1972; Whitlock & Nauta, 1956), and it is important to administer tests of memory in more than one modality to determine whether these inputs in the monkey have functional significance, as they appear to in humans.

For studies of the effects of medial temporal damage, at least, there is another reason for administering tasks in a modality, in addition to the visual one. The surgical approach used for making lesions of the medial temporal area may inadvertently result in damage to area TE, visual association cortex (Gross, 1975; Von Bonin & Bailey, 1947). When such damage occurs, impairments on visual-memory tasks are more difficult to interpret. Testing in a modality that would not be affected by damage to brain areas involved in visual information processing could serve as a behavioral control for the neocortical damage.

At this time, no information is available in monkeys regarding the possible modality-general nature of the effects of diencephalic damage.

Prospects

The development of an experimental model for the study of a clinical disease entity in humans has always been one of the goals of neuroscience research. Attempts to establish an animal model of human amnesia in the monkey began more than a quarter of a century ago, and we are only now beginning to bring the monkey data and the human data into good correspondence. I believe that we have demonstrated that neuropsychological investigations of amnesia in monkeys and humans can be mutually facilitatory. The promising developments in work with monkeys is in part a result of recent developments from human neuropsychological research. These developments, in turn, will allow us to develop a profile of amnesia in the monkey and to begin to identify with certainty the brain structures whose damage is responsible for the defects of memory in both humans and monkeys. The promise of an animal model of human amnesia is an exciting one, and I believe that achievement of the model is close at hand.

ACKNOWLEDGMENTS

This work was supported by the Veterans Administration and by NIH/NIMCDS Grant No. NS19063. I thank Larry Squire for his encouragement and for his comments on various sections of this chapter, and I thank Nicholas for waiting to be born until this chapter was completed.

REFERENCES

Aggleton, J. P., & Mishkin, M. Visual recognition impairment following medial thalamic lesions in monkeys. *Neuropsychologia*, 1983, *21*, 189–197. (a)

Aggleton, J. P., & Mishkin, M. Memory impairment following restricted medial thalamic lesions in monkeys. *Experimental Brain Research*, 1983, *52*, 199–209. (b)

Barbizet, J. *Human memory and its pathology.* San Francisco: W. H. Freeman, 1970.

Brion, S., & Mikol, J. Atteinte du noyau latéral dorsal du thalamus et syndrome de Korsakoff alcoolique. *Journal of Neurosciences*, 1978, *38*, 249–261.

Cohen, N. J. *Neuropsychological evidence for a distinction between procedural and declarative knowledge in human memory and amnesia.* Unpublished doctoral dissertation, University of California at San Diego, 1981.

Cohen, N. J., & Corkin, S. Learning and retention of a cognitive skill. *Society for Neuroscience Abstracts*, 1981, *7*, 235.

Cohen, N. J., & Squire, L. R. Preserved learning and retention of pattern-analyzing skill in amnesia: Dissociation of knowing how and knowing that. *Science*, 1980, *210*, 207–210.

Corkin, S. Acquisition of motor skill after bilateral medial temporal-lobe excision. *Neuropsychologia*, 1968, *6*, 225–265.

Correll, R. E., & Scoville, W. B. Effects of medial temporal lesions on visual discrimination performance. *Journal of Comparative and Physiological Psychology*, 1965, *60*, 175–181. (a)

Correll, R. E., & Scoville, W. B. Performance on delayed match following lesions of medial temporal lobe structures. *Journal of Comparative and Physiological Psychology*, 1965, *60*, 360–367. (b)

Davis, R. T., McDowell, A. A., Deter, C. W., & Steele, J. P. Performance of rhesus monkeys on selected laboratory tasks presented before and after a large single dose of whole body X-radiation. *Journal of Comparative and Physiological Psychology*, 1956, *49*, 20–26.

DeVito, J. L. Subcortical projections to the hippocampal formation in squirrel monkey (*Saimiri sciureus*). *Brain Research Bulletin*, 1980, *3*, 285–289.

Douglas, R. J. The hippocampus and behavior. *Psychological Bulletin*, 1967, *67*, 416–442.

Gross, C. G. Inferotemporal cortex and vision. In E. Stellar & J. M. Sprague (Eds.), *Progress in physiological psychology* (Vol. 5). New York: Academic Press, 1975.

Holmes, E. J., Jacobson, S., Stein, B. M., & Butters, N. Spatial memory and long term retention following mammillary body lesions in monkeys. *Society for Neuroscience Abstracts*, 1982, *8*, 23.

Horel, J. A. The neuroanatomy of amnesia: A critique of the hippocampal memory hypothesis. *Brain*, 1978, *101*, 403–445.

Huppert, F. A., & Piercy, M. Dissociation between learning and remembering in organic amnesia. *Nature*, 1978, *275*, 317–318.

Huppert, F. A., & Piercy, M. Normal and abnormal forgetting in organic amnesia: Effects of locus of lesion. *Cortex*, 1979, *15*, 385–390.

Isaacson, R. L. Hippocampal destruction in man and other animals. *Neuropsychologia*, 1972, *10*, 47–64.

Isseroff, A., Rosvold, H. E., Galkin, T. W., & Goldman-Rakic, P. S. Spatial memory impairments following damage to the mediodorsal nucleus of the thalamus in rhesus monkeys. *Brain Research*, 1982, *232*, 97–113.

Jacobsen, C. F., & Elder, J. H. The effect of temporal lobe lesions on delayed response in monkeys. *Comparative Psychology Monography*, 1936, *13*, 61–66.

Jones, E. G., & Powell, T. P. S. An anatomical study of converging sensory pathways within the cerebral cortex of the monkey. *Brain*, 1970, *93*, 793–820.

Kimura, D. Right temporal-lobe damage. *Archives of Neurology*, 1963, *8*, 264–271.

Lhermitte, F., & Signoret, J.-L. Analyse neuropsychologique et différenciation des syndromes amnésiques. *Revue Neurologique*, 1972, *126*, 161–178.

Mahut, H., Moss, M., & Zola-Morgan, S. Retention deficits after combined amygdala–hippocampal and selective hippocampal resections in the monkey. *Neuropsychologia*, 1981, *19*, 201–225.

Mahut, M., Zola-Morgan, S., & Moss, M. Hippocampal resections impair associative learning and recognition memory in the monkey. *Journal of Neuroscience*, 1982, *9*, 1214–1229.

Mair, W. G. P., Warrington, E. K., & Weiskrantz, L. Memory disorder in Korsakoff's psychosis: A neuropathological and neuropsychological investigation of two cases. *Brain*, 1979, *102*, 749–783.

Markowitsch, H. J. Thalamic mediodorsal nucleus and memory: A critical evaluation of studies in animals and man. *Neuroscience and Biobehavioral Reviews*, 1982, *6*, 351–380.

Marslen-Wilson, W. D., & Teuber, H.-L. Memory for remote events in anterograde amnesia: Recognition of public figures from newsphotographs. *Neuropsychologia*, 1975, *13*, 353–364.

Mills, R. P., & Swanson, P. D. Vertical oculomotor apraxia and memory loss. *Annals of Neurology*, 1978, *4*, 149–153.

Milner, B. Memory defect in bilateral lesion. *Psychiatric Research Reports*, 1959, *11*, 43–52.

Milner, B. Les troubles de la mémoire accompagnant des lésions hippocampiques bilatérales. In P. Passouant (Ed.), *Physiologie de l'hippocampe*. Paris: Centre National de la Recherche Scientifique, 1962.

Milner, B. Amnesia following operation on the temporal lobes. In C. W. M. Whitty & O. L. Zangwill (Eds.), *Amnesia*. London: Butterworths, 1966.

Milner, B. Disorders of memory after brain lesions in man. Preface: Material-specific and generalized memory loss. *Neuropsychologia*, 1968, *6*, 175–179.

Mishkin, M. Memory in monkeys severely impaired by combined but not by separate removal of amygdala and hippocampus. *Nature*, 1978, *273*, 297–298.

Mishkin, M. A memory system in the monkey. *Philosophical Transactions of the Royal Society*, 1982, *298*, 85–95.

Mishkin, M., & Delacour, J. An analysis of short-term visual memory in the monkey. *Journal of Experimental Psychology: Animal Behavior Processes*, 1975, *1*, 326–334.

Moss, M., Mahut, H., & Zola-Morgan, S. Concurrent discrimination learning of monkeys after hippocampal, entorhinal, or fornix lesions. *Journal of Neuroscience*, 1981, *1*, 227–240.

Murray, E., & Mishkin, M. Severe tactual memory deficits in monkeys after combined removal of the amygdala and hippocampus. *Brain Research*, 1983, *270*, 340–344.

Murray, E., & Mishkin, M. Personal communication, 1984.

Orbach, J., Milner, B., & Rasmussen, T. Learning and retention in monkeys after amygdala–hippocampus resection. *Archives of Neurology*, 1960, *3*, 230–251.

Oscar-Berman, M., & Zola-Morgan, S. M. Comparative neuropsychology and Korsakoff's syndrome: II. Two choice visual discrimination learning. *Neuropsychologia*, 1980, *18*, 513–525.

Poletti, C. E., & Creswell, G. Fornix system efferent projections in the squirrel monkey: An experimental degeneration study. *Journal of Comparative Neurology*, 1977, *175*, 101–128.

Rosene, D. L., & Van Hoesen, G. Hippocampal efferents reach widespread areas of cerebral cortex and amygdala in the Rhesus monkey. *Science*, 1977, *198*, 315–317.

Scoville, W. B., & Milner, B. Loss of recent memory after bilateral hippocampal lesions. *Journal of Neurology, Neurosurgery and Psychiatry*, 1957, *20*, 11–21.

Sidman, M., Stoddard, L. T., & Mohr, J. P. Some additional observations of immediate memory in a patient with bilateral hippocampal lesions. *Neuropsychologia*, 1968, *6*, 245–254.

Squire, L. R. Two forms of human amnesia: An analysis of forgetting. *Journal of Neuroscience*, 1981, *1*, 635–640.

Squire, L. R., & Cohen, N. J. Remote memory, retrograde amnesia, and the neuropsychology of memory. In L. Cermak (Ed.), *Human memory and amnesia*. Hillsdale, N.J.: Erlbaum, 1982.

Squire, L. R., & Cohen, N. J. Human memory and amnesia. In G. Lynch, J. L. McGaugh, & N. M. Weinberger (Eds.), *Neurobiology of learning and memory*. New York: Guilford Press, 1984.

Squire, L. R., Cohen, N. J., & Nadel, L. The medial temporal region and memory consolidation: A new hypothesis. In H. Weingartner & E. Parker (Eds.). *Memory consolidation*. Hillsdale, N.J.: Erlbaum, in press.

Squire, L. R., & Moore, R. Y. Dorsal thalamic lesion in a noted case of chronic memory dysfunction. *Annals of Neurology*, 1979, *6*, 503–506.

Squire, L. R., & Zola-Morgan, S. The neurology of memory: The case for correspondence between the findings for human and nonhuman primate. In J. A. Deutsch (Ed.), *The physiological basis of memory* (2nd ed.). New York: Academic Press, 1983.

Swanson, L. W., & Cowan, W. M. The connections of the septal region in the rat. *Journal of Comparative Neurology*, 1979, *186*, 621–656.

Turner, B. H., Mishkin, M., & Knapp, M. Organization of the amygdalopetal modality-specific cortical association areas in the monkey. *Journal of Comparative Neurology*, 1980, *191*, 515–543.

Valenstein, E. S., & Nauta, W. J. H. A comparison of the distribution of the fornix system in the rat, guinea pig, cat, and monkey. *Journal of Comparative Neurology*, 1959, *3*, 337–363.

Van Hoesen, G. W., Pandya, D. N., & Butters, N. Cortical afferents to the entorhinal cortex of the rhesus monkey, *Science*, 1972, *175*, 1471–1473.

Victor, M., Adams, R. D., & Collins, G. H. *The Wernicke-Korsakoff syndrome*. Philadelphia: F. A. Davis, 1971.

Van Bonin, G., & Bailey, P. *The neocortex of Macaca mulatta*. Urbana: University of Illinois Press, 1947.

Wagner, A. R., Ruby, J. W., & Whitlow, J. W. Rehearsal in animal conditioning. *Journal of Experimental Psychology*, 1973, *97*, 407–426. (Monograph)

Weiskrantz, L. A comparison of hippocampal pathology in man and other animals. In K. Elliot & J. Whelan (Eds.), *Functions of the septo-hippocampal system*. (CIBA Foundation Symposium No. 58). Amsterdam: Elsevier, 1978.

Whitlock, D. G., & Nauta, W. J. H. Subcortical projections from the temporal cortex in *Macaca mulatta*. *Journal of Comparative and Physiological Psychology*, 1956, *56*, 183–212.

Wood, F., Ebert, V., & Kinsbourne, M. The episodic semantic memory distinction in amnesia: Clinical and experimental observations. In L. Cermak (Ed.), *Human memory and amnesia*. Hillsdale, N.J.: Erlbaum, 1982.

Zola-Morgan, S., Dabrowska, J., Moss, M., & Mahut, H. Enhanced perceptual novelty in the monkey after fornix sections but not after hippocampal ablations. *Neuropsychologia*, 1983, *21*, 433–454.

Zola-Morgan, S., & Squire, L. R. Two forms of amnesia in monkeys: Rapid forgetting after medial temporal lesions but not diencephalic lesions. *Society for Neuroscience Abstracts*, 1982, *8*, 24.

Zola-Morgan, S., & Squire, L. R. Intact perceptuo-motor skill learning in monkeys with medial temporal lobe lesions. *Society for Neuroscience Abstracts*, 1983, *9*, 27.

Zola-Morgan, S., & Squire, L. R. Preserved learning in monkeys with medial temporal lesions: Sparing of motor and cognitive skills. *Journal of Neuroscience*, 1984, *4*, 1072–1085. (a)

Zola-Morgan, S., & Squire, L. R. Performance of monkeys with separate and combined lesions of the hippocampus and amygdala on delayed nonmatching to sample. *Society for Neuroscience Abstracts*, 1984, *10*. (b)

Zola-Morgan, S., & Squire, L. R. Medial temporal lesions in monkeys impair memory on a variety of tasks sensitive to human amnesia. *Behavioral Neuroscience*, in press.

Zola-Morgan, S., Squire, L. R., & Mishkin, M. The neuroanatomy of amnesia: Amygdala-hippocampus versus temporal stem. *Science*, 1982, *218*, 1337–1339.

Some Thoughts and Some Experiments on Memory 31

Robert W. Doty

Some Thoughts on Memory

Perhaps the most astonishing aspect of human memory is its seeming unsaturability. The detail, the variety are limitless—from erudition to erotica, trivia to profundity, Palestrina to Resphigi, Hannibal's elephants amok at Zama, thane of Cawdor, the odontoceti, lupens at Popocatepetl. There are well-documented examples of the qualitative magnitude and remarkable permanence of this mnemonic store (e.g., Hunter, 1977; Luria, 1968; Standing, 1973), but a usefully quantitative statement as to the full or attainable capacity seems impossible to deduce. And is it really unsaturable, or after a certain stage must memories be erased or overlaid to make way for the new? If it is not saturable, what is the status of the vacant repository—say, at 20 years of age—destined to accumulate and retain many decades of events, 21×10^6 waking seconds per year? Schüz (1978) calculates that during the first 26 days of its life, when it is presumably learning most of its behavioral repertoire, a rat grows 500,000 dendritic spines per second (!); but then this complement must serve for the remainder of its life. If dendritic spines provide a substrate for memory, it must be in some subtle aspect of their operative role rather than their mere number; or else the proportion of "mnemonic space" devoted to later as compared to early life must be orders of magnitude smaller than it seems.

In number and complexity, however, it would appear that the cortical machinery is adequate to the vastness of the mnemonic task attributable to it—a billion synapses and several kilometers of axon collaterals (Braitenburg, 1978) for each of its roughly 500,000 cubic millimeters in man (Blinkov & Glezer, 1968). The permutations and combinations of spatial–temporal patterns among the billions of neuronal elements are clearly sufficient to approach the practical infinity of the mnemonic capacity. But if a memory is a partial repetition of some past pattern (e.g., Marczynski, Wei, Burns, Choi, Chen, & Marczynski, 1982), by what process can this pattern again be unfolded and replayed, almost at will? And to what template is it compared (for, uncannily, one can judge also the veracity of the recall)?

Inscrutable, these questions are part of the larger mystery—how the few million millisecond pulses of retinal ganglion cells each instant produce the steady, vivid, and gapless scene continually perceived. If this integrative magic is presently incomprehensible, so too must be its pallid reproduction on the screen of memory. What puzzles most, of course, is the experiential unity forged from the spatially and temporally dispersed, multimillioned, semireliable digital events in those bizarrely crafted elements, the neurons (e.g., Doty, 1975). Is this any more remarkable than that a lamp is composed of atoms? Yes, for while the unity

Robert W. Doty. Center for Brain Research, University of Rochester Medical Center, Rochester, New York.

"lamp" transcends in quality its countless elemental constituents, and is temporally nonstationary in its photon emission, its processes are neither self-ordering nor self-renewing; nor, it seems safe to infer, does its action within itself yield anything remotely like unified experience. Somehow in brains the ceaseless ionic jostle of the mean-free-path in the micellar medium does not degrade the form; the neuron and the memory are independent of which particular atoms constitute them, so long as the arrangement is stochastically stable.

Form, presumably, is paramount; but this tells nothing still of the experienced integration, an enormous eigenfunction within brain space and neuronal time. One's ignorance here is so profound that it is tempting to assume that some yet unrealized physical principle may ultimately be needed to provide the solution. Quantum mechanics certainly offers ample evidence that brain-dependent mentality is incompatible with the comprehension of physical processes at the photon level. The challenge to understanding is not just the familiar enigma of the quantized wave, but a seeming resolution of the Einstein–Podolsky–Rosen paradox (Einstein, Podolsky, & Rosen, 1935) in such a way as to alter conceptualizations of physical reality far more basically than did the Michelson–Morley elimination of the hypothesized "ether." Discussing a logical situation arising from applying Heisenberg's "uncertainty principle" to two identical systems, Einstein *et al.* (1935) state:

> We see therefore that, as a consequence of two different measurements performed upon the first system, the second system may be left in states with two different wave functions. On the other hand, since at the time of measurement the two systems no longer interact, no real change can take place in the second system in consequence of anything that may be done to the first system. This is, of course, merely a statement of what is meant by the absence of an interaction between the two systems. Thus, it is possible to assign two different wave functions to the same reality (the second system after the interaction with the first). (p. 799)

As Einstein *et al.* frame it, the choice is between quantum mechanics providing an incomplete picture of reality, or more than one reality existing concurrently.

Einstein presumed that the answer to such an experiment would be in favor of a single physical reality; but a series of experiments, now culminating in those of Aspect, Grangier, and Roger (1982), seems decisive in proving this expectation wrong (see d'Espagnat, 1979, for extensive discussion; see also Davies, 1980, Robinson, 1982, and Rohrlich, 1983, for a different point of view). In other words, multiple realities exist and are conjured up by human action. Memory or consciousness in such a world may possibly be more than a molecular arrangement; although, if so, it is presently impossible to perceive in even the most tenuous way in what manner this quantum-mechanical riddle could apply. The caveat is simply offered here that the nature of physical reality still eludes human grasp, shadows on the wall of Plato's cave; and that consciousness, so schooled by memory, may likewise remain inexplicable so long as this is so.

However, while assuaging the embarrassment of one's ignorance, such resort to possibly nescient principles should not deter the search for more conventional explanations. A good place to begin is with the unexpected mnemonic feats of insects. With brains having probably fewer than a million neurons (Strausfeld, 1976), although often at a density 10 or more times greater than in mammalian neocortex, many species (e.g., ants, bumblebees, honeybees, wasps, hover flies) are able to recognize landmarks in an often very extensive territory (see Wehner, 1981, for a thorough and perceptive review). By this means they return with high accuracy to a feeding, nesting, or hovering site, or they systematically patrol a chosen area. To do this requires a highly sophisticated matching of current to past visual input, with interpretations of sequence, direction, distance, and parallactic compensation. Some of the ranges, and therefore the areas with which acquaintance is demanded, are truly enormous—several hundred meters or even a few kilometers in radius—as established by the return of the insects after displacement over these distances. In some cases, recognition has been demonstrable after an unpracticed lapse of several days.

It is perhaps malicious to remark how all this superb spatial orientation is achieved without benefit of a hippocampus. More instructive is the fact that a "start recording" signal seems to be required to open the mnemonic register to input. This is evidenced by the "orientation flight" that the insect customarily makes prior to leaving the point to which it will return, and by the compatibility of Cartwright and Collett's (1982) "snapshot" hypothesis with their data and computer modeling. Clearly, a "start" signal is an essential part of the process, together with preservation of the order of encountered images, and the ability to sequence them in reverse order during the return journey. From such considerations, it can be seen that the "dating" of memories, so characteristic of human recollection, is an intrinsic requirement at the primitive level for a mnemonic trace to be useful. If the hippocampus does indeed have something to do with memory, particularly with recognizing spatial orientation, as so vividly illustrated by O'Keefe and Nadel (1978) and Olton (1978), then it is tempting to hypothesize that the transition to theta rhythm that invariably accompanies self-generated motion through space (e.g., Vanderwolf, Kramis, & Robinson, 1978) serves as the "start recording" signal. In other words, as the animal starts to move about in its environment, invariably producing an onset of theta rhythm, this opens a mnemonic register for the sequence of stimuli to be encountered.

An almost paradigmatic example of the failure of such a "start recording" signal has been produced by transection of the fornix (Shapiro, Hulse, & Olton, 1982). Following deletion of this pathway, probably required for the relevant theta activity, a rat can still perform a well-learned sequence (i.e., can follow a set of rules); but in the absence of the "start recording" signal, it fails to register the sequence of sensorial events as it does so, and hence remains unaware of where it has been despite the accuracy of its rule following (see Olton, Chapter 33, this volume).

If the hippocampal theta rhythm actually is the manifestation of a "start recording" mechanism, then the remarkable consistency of this rhythm during the "paradoxical" stage of sleep (e.g., Vanderwolf et al., 1978), when the movement is restrained by active inhibition at segmental levels, might illuminate the otherwise mysterious relation between this stage of sleep and the learning of motor performances, as observed by Bloch, Hennevin, and Leconte (1979). Yet if so, it would seem that the dreams of rats must somehow have considerably more coherence than those of men.

One of the more instructive features of the paradigm developed by Shapiro et al. (1982) is the clear distinction it provides between memory for rules and memory for events, a distinction also obvious in most human amnesias (Squire, 1982). This, then, is one of the other major problems in endeavors to understand mnemonic phenomena—that there are many different forms of memory, and that it is usually not evident exactly which form is under investigation, or to what degree the different forms of memory share common mechanisms. I have addressed these problems to some degree previously (Doty, 1979) in pointing out two distinctly different means by which neurons may retain the consequences of their past: the "ionic" versus the "macromolecular" mechanisms.

Some alteration of its ionic milieu is an inevitable concomitant of voltage fluctuation in any neuron; depending upon many factors, such as type of neuron, concentration and type of ionic species, and so on, the alteration will endure for various periods of time, in some cases perhaps for several days. Such ionic changes will also produce various metabolic responses. Ionic changes take on a new significance and complexity with the discovery that neurons commonly possess more than one voltage-dependent ionic process (e.g., Jahnsen & Llinas, 1982). Ultimately, however, the ionic fluctuation *per se* is impermanent, and thus differs decisively from a "macromolecular" mnemonic mechanism, in which an essentially permanent change, probably akin to that occurring in immunocytochemistry, is effected in the neuron. The hypothesized macromolecular process also offers an explanation for the frequently overlooked "temporal paradox," required at the synaptic level for associative learning or conditioning, in which an antecedent stimulus undergoes an alteration in its significance contingent upon occurrence of a subsequent, different stimulus. The "macromolecular" scheme (Doty, 1979) also subsumes, of course, the development of what is coming to be known as a "Hebb synapse" (Hebb, 1949), in which effectiveness is hypothesized to be augmented consequent to concurrent synaptic events.

In what follows (and, indeed, in essentially all experiments on memory), the distinction between "ionic" versus "macromolecular" bases cannot be discerned, save that all neural activity has ionic consequences, and that most memories are permanent and hence are inferred to have a macromolecular component.

Interhemispheric Mnemonic Transfer

A challenging feature of the relation posited between neocortex and memory is the bi-hemispheric arrangement of the cortex, its mirror-image duplication. Nubio Negrão and I (Doty & Negrão, 1973; Doty, Negrão, & Yamaga, 1973) have proposed that this hemispheric duplication does not produce a duplication of memory traces, because the corpus callosum (CC) (1) prevents the formation of bilateral traces and (2) allows each hemisphere access to traces stored in the other. By thus precluding redundant, bilateral engrams, the CC effectively doubles the mnemonic capacity of the brain and makes hemispheric specialization possible.

This proposal for a mnemonic function of the CC arose with the observation that macaques, trained to respond to electrical excitation of striate cortex, generalized their responses to such excitation only within the originally "trained" hemisphere after the CC had been cut. This has not proven to be the case for macaques with split optic chiasm trained to normal visual inputs (Butler, 1968; Downer, 1962; Hamilton, 1977; Myers, 1962; Noble, 1968; Sullivan & Hamilton, 1973). This contradiction seems likely to be attributable either to the fact that the stimulus originated at the cortex in the Doty–Negrão experiments, or that for our experiments both hemispheres were otherwise receiving normal visual input, whereas in the monkeys with chiasm transected, not only was about half the system deafferented, but the nonresponding eye-hemisphere was unoccupied by any direct visual input (i.e., the eye was covered).

There are several other important contentions or contradictions in this area. First, Risse and Gazzaniga (1978) were unable to find evidence for "readout" of an engram in one hemisphere by the other. In eight patients undergoing carotid angiography, they also anesthetized the left hemisphere briefly with amobarbital while placing an object in the left hand. When recovered, the patients were unable to name the object, although six of the patients could, with the left hand, identify the object, thus showing that the right hemisphere was in possession of the information. Retrieval of the information, however, probably would involve an extremely complex process—the translation of right-hemispheric kinesthetic engrams into left-hemispheric verbal code—which, despite the protestations of Risse and Gazzaniga as to the simplicity of this task, two patients could not perform after anesthetization even for objects presented prior to the anesthesia. A much more convincing case for lack of accessibility would have been failure to identify the objects blindly with the right hand.

Another set of problems involves the anterior commissure (AC). In our experiments with electrical excitation of striate cortex, Negrão and I found that it presented a striking contrast to the CC, for if only the AC were intact during training, the monkeys were unequivocally responsive bilaterally after its transection. In other words, the AC, unlike the CC in these experiments, produced a bilateral engram; and we thus predicted that in cases with agenesis of the CC, language functions would be found bilaterally. This appears to be true (Gott & Saul, 1978; Lortie, Lassonde, & Ptito, 1981; Sauerwein, Lassonde, & Geoffroy, 1981), although the data are still very fragmentary (Chiarello, 1980).

Finally, while all are agreed that the AC can transfer mnemonic visual information in macaques or chimpanzees (Black & Myers, 1964; Butler, 1979; Doty & Negrão, 1973; Downer, 1962; Gazzaniga, 1966; Sullivan & Hamilton, 1973), there is still debate over the facility with which this occurs. The experiments described below suggest, however, that the AC has a remarkable capability for the interhemispheric transfer of detailed visual information. This is probably also true in man (Chiarello, 1980; Risse, LeDoux, Springer, Wilson, & Gazzaniga, 1978), although there is also a strong denial (McKeever, Sullivan, Ferguson, & Rayport, 1981).

The present experiments are being performed on macaques with optic chiasm transected transphenoidally, using the approach developed by Downer (1962). In addition, either the CC is cut, leaving the AC as the only forebrain commissure; or the AC and most of the CC is transected, leaving only about 5 mm of the splenium intact. All the monkeys are still alive, but since all transections are performed under direct, microscopically aided vision, there is little reason to believe that the surgery was not as intended.

Each monkey wears a lightweight mask (see Figure 31-1) equipped with rotary solenoid shutters to restrict vision to one or the other eye-hemisphere in whatever manner desired. The monkey faces an array of three small vertically stacked rear-projection screens (see Figure 31-2) on which high-quality photographic images can be displayed. Its task is to identify ("match") from a pair of images on upper and lower screens the one ("sample") previously seen on the center screen (see Figure 31-2). It is rewarded with water or juice for touching the center screen with the "sample" and the correct screen for the "match." Errors are punished with a puff of air to the face, a loud horn, and a delay of 45 sec to the next trial. Typical times are 3 sec for intertrial interval, 3 sec to respond to "sample," and 10 sec between extinction of "sample" and presentation of choice for "match." Most latencies for the "match" are about 1 sec or less, although a 5-sec time is allowed.

It bears emphasis that a different pair of images is used for each of the 50–60 daily trials, and in such circumstances, as shown elsewhere (Overman & Doty, 1980), an essentially permanent memory is formed of the "sample"; one monkey tested after a 4-day interval had 76% correct responses for 25 trials, and six others at 2 days had responses ranging from 76% to 86% correct.

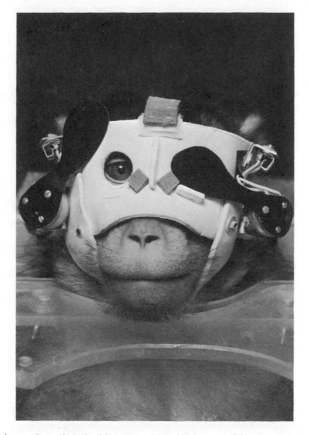

FIGURE 31-1. Monkey in mask equipped with rotary solenoid shutters. Visual pathway has been surgically restricted so that view of the world through one eye passes only to the corresponding half of the brain. When the one shutter closes and the other opens, the experimenter can observe whether the monkey recognizes with the "new" eye and brain what the other eye and brain have perceived, and can thereby with this technique analyze how visual memories are transferred from one half of the brain to the other.

The advantage of such a delayed matching-to-sample procedure for assaying inter-hemispheric mnemonic transfer or hemispheric specialization is immediately obvious. Rather than training an animal for days or weeks to make a discrimination using one hemisphere and then repeating the process with the other, as has been the procedure for the great majority of experiments on "split-brain" monkeys for the past 20 years, the capabilities of each hemisphere can here be assessed almost on a trial-by-trial basis.

The initial quest has been to identify categories of visual stimuli that differentiate the capabilities of the splenium versus the AC, or of one hemisphere versus the other. To date, no such categories have been found (Doty, Gallant, & Lewine, 1982). For colored images of complex objects (e.g., packages, tools, electronic components, flowers, toys) with a 10-sec delay between "sample" and "match," accuracy is 95% or better for intra-hemispheric comparison or for interhemispheric comparison in either direction. The only interesting moment in these trials came when the monkey with the CC fully transected and the AC intact viewed for the first time, 1 month after callosotomy, the colored images with one eye and was required to identify them 2 sec later with the other. For the first two trials it appeared totally baffled when called upon to choose between the two images presented to

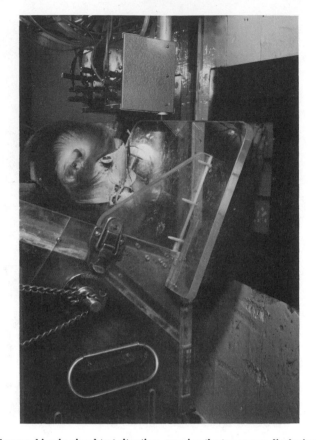

FIGURE 31-2. Monkey working in visual test situation, pressing the top screen displaying three yellow squares, which appeared previously on the center screen in a different geometrical arrangement. It thus correctly chooses the number of objects, three, rather than the larger number displayed on the bottom screen. In an actual run, the solenoids to the shutters would be connected so as to require use of different eyes for initial versus subsequent viewing.

the "nonviewing" eye to make the match, and it failed to make any choice in the 5 sec allowed. With the third trial, it responded correctly; it failed to respond on the fourth trial; and then it resumed its usual essentially errorless performance. For the 50-trial session, the monkey made only one error of commission, and it failed to respond a total of 10 times, 5 times with each eye. On the next day there was no hesitation or failure to respond, and only one error in going from left to right and two from right to left, for a total score of 94% correct. Thus this animal showed only a brief period of confusion and hesitation when forced for the first time to rely on the AC for interhemispheric communication; this is remarkable only because in the same situation the animal with only 4–5 mm of the splenium intact showed not the slightest hesitation and was 92% correct in its first session.

Presentation of the same images as black-and-white rather than colored slides reduces the accuracy of response to about 85% correct, and pure, featureless color is surprisingly difficult. Even when the monotony of the task is relieved by interspersing the pure colors among trials using complex colored objects, the general average is only 75% correct. For the monkey with only the AC intact, the interhemispheric mnemonic comparison is also at this level for alphanumeric material, or for judging "number" of objects (as in Figure 31-2)—both, however, with only a 2-sec interval. The latter problem required significant retraining of the animals, first simply on the concept of "few" versus "many," and then on one or two objects versus three to five. Since the monkeys had previously learned to select the "match" from a pair of radically different objects, the task of choosing on the basis of number alone was exceptionally difficult; the objects, although different for each trial, were here the same for both "sample" and "match" and were distinguished only by their number. The animal with only splenium intact never got beyond the 75% level for "few" versus "many" at 2 sec.

The animal with the splenium intact was also very poor (60% correct) at matching colored projections of human faces, whereas the one with only AC intact could make 90% correct interhemispheric comparisons (for a 2-sec interval); this performance was comparable to that of an intact monkey, which attained 87% correct. The choices for the "match" always paired males with males, Caucasians with Caucasians, bearded with bearded, and so forth, and eyeglasses were absent in all cases. It is of considerable interest that the monkey achieving the 90% correct identification responded aggressively, by vigorously and repeatedly striking the screen, when first presented with several of the male (but not the female) faces.

The intention had been to use Japanese Kanji, ranging from two to six strokes, as a class of stimuli testing geometrical analysis. Despite more than 3000 trials, use of different-colored backgrounds, intervals of .5–4 sec, etc., the monkeys still lingered at the chance 50–55% level. There thus appears to be an unexpected difference here in the capacity of macaque and human visual systems; human observers, wholly illiterate in Japanese, had not the slightest difficulty performing the task perfectly with a 10-sec delay. Obviously, it would be of interest to test children or illiterate peoples in this regard, in an effort to discern the origin of this striking macaque–human difference—the more so, since most of the animals perform reasonably well even with interhemispheric mnemonic transfer of alphanumeric material.

In sum, the AC and splenium appear equal in their ability to provide identification of complex colored or black-and-white images, or pure colors, when viewed with one hemisphere after having been observed 10 sec previously by the other. The AC can also serve in this capacity for number of objects, human faces, or alphanumeric material, and the poor performance in this regard of the monkey forced to use only the splenium is probably attributable to general behavior rather than specific deficiency. There certainly has been no evidence of any lack of efficiency of the AC system for making such interhemispheric mnemonic comparisons; nor has there been any evidence of hemispheric specialization for identifying or transferring the various types of visual images employed.

ACKNOWLEDGMENTS

It is a pleasure to thank John A. Gallant for his dedicated and skillful assistance in training the monkeys and constructing the apparatus. I am also grateful to Jeffrey D. Lewine for many fruitful discussions, and to Louise R. Levy, Mary G. Capozzi, and Nancy G. Dintruff for secretarial assistance. The research was supported by Grant No. BNS82-08583 from the National Science Foundation.

REFERENCES

Aspect, A., Grangier, P., & Roger, G. Experimental realization of Einstein–Podolsky–Rosen–Bohm *Gedanken-experiment:* A new violation of Bell's inequalities. *Physical Review Letters,* 1982, *49,* 91–94.

Black, P., & Myers, R. E. Visual function of the forebrain commissures in the chimpanzee. *Science,* 1964, *146,* 799–800.

Blinkov, S. M., & Glezer, I. I. [*The human brain in figures and tables*] (B. Haigh, trans.). New York: Plenum Press, 1968.

Bloch, V., Hennevin, E., & Leconte, P. Relationship between paradoxical sleep and memory processes. In M. A. B. Braizer (Ed.), *Brain mechanisms in memory and learning: From the single neuron to man* (IBRO Monograph Series, Vol. 4). New York: Raven Press, 1979.

Braitenberg, V. Cortical architectonics: General and areal. In M. A. B. Brazier & H. Petsche (Eds.), *Architectonics of the cerebral cortex* (IBRO Monograph Series, Vol. 3). New York: Raven Press, 1978.

Butler, C. R. A memory-record for visual discrimination habits produced in both cerebral hemispheres of monkey when only one hemisphere has received direct visual information. *Brain Research,* 1968, *20,* 152–167.

Butler, C. R. Interhemispheric transfer of visual information via the corpus callosum and anterior commissure in the monkey. In I. S. Russell, M. W. van Hof, & G. Berlucchi (Eds.), *Structure and function of the cerebral commissures.* London: Macmillan, 1979.

Cartwright, B. A., & Collett, T. S. How honeybees use landmarks to guide their return to a food source. *Nature,* 1982, *295,* 560–564.

Chiarello, C. A house divided? Cognitive functioning with callosal agenesis. *Brain and Language,* 1980, *11,* 128–158.

Davis, P. *Other worlds.* New York: Simon & Schuster, 1980.

d'Espagnat, B. The quantum theory and reality. *Scientific American,* 1979, *241*(5), 158–181.

Doty, R. W. Consciousness from neurons. *Acta Neurobiologiae Experimentalis (Warsaw),* 1975, *35,* 791–804.

Doty, R. W. Neurons and memory: Some clues. In M. A. B. Braizer (Ed.), *Brain mechanisms in memory and learning: From the single neuron to man* (IBRO Monograph Series, Vol. 4). New York: Raven Press, 1979.

Doty, R. W., Gallant, J. A., & Lewine, J. D. Interhemispheric mnemonic transfer in *Macaca nemestrina. Society for Neuroscience Abstracts,* 1982, *8,* 628.

Doty, R. W., & Negrão, N. Forebrain commissures and vision. In R. Jung (Ed.), *Handbook of sensory physiology* (Vol. 7/3B). Berlin: Springer-Verlag, 1973.

Doty, R. W., Negrão, N., & Yamaga, K. The unilateral engram. *Acta Neurobiologiae Experimentalis (Warsaw),* 1973, *33,* 711–718.

Downer, J. L. deC. Interhemispheric integration in the visual system. In V. B. Mountcastle (Ed.), *Interhemispheric relations and cerebral dominance.* Baltimore: Johns Hopkins University Press, 1962.

Einstein, A., Podolsky, B., & Rosen, N. Can quantum-mechanical description of physical reality be considered complete? *Physical Review,* 1935, *47,* 777–780.

Gazzaniga, M. S. Interhemispheric communication of visual learning. *Neuropsychologia,* 1966, *4,* 183–189.

Gott, P. S., & Saul, R. E. Agenesis of the corpus callosum: Limits of functional compensation. *Neurology,* 1978, *28,* 1271–1279.

Hamilton, C. R. Investigations of perceptual and mnemonic lateralization in monkeys. In S. Harnad, R. W. Doty, L. Goldstein, J. Jaynes, & G. Krauthamer (Eds.), *Lateralization in the nervous system.* New York: Academic Press, 1977.

Hebb, D. O. *The organization of behavior.* New York: Wiley, 1949.

Hunter, I. M. L. An exceptional memory. *British Journal of Psychology,* 1977, *68,* 155–164.

Jahnsen, H., & Llinas, R. Electrophysiological properties of guinea pig thalamic neurons studied *in vitro. Society for Neuroscience Abstracts,* 1982, *8,* 413.

Lortie, J., Lassonde, M., & Ptito, M. Dichotic listening in callosal agenesis. *Society for Neuroscience Abstracts,* 1981, *7,* 381.

Luria, A. R. [*The mind of a mnemonist: A little book about a vast memory*] (L. Solataroff, trans.). New York: Basic Books, 1968.

Marczynski, T. J., Wei, J. Y., Burns, L. L., Choi, S. Y., Chen, E., & Marczynski, G. T. Visual attention and neuronal firing patterns in the feline pulvinar nucleus of thalamus. *Brain Research Bulletin,* 1982, *8,* 565–580.

McKeever, W. F., Sullivan, K. F., Ferguson, S. M., & Rayport, M. Typical cerebral hemisphere disconnection deficits following corpus callosum section despite sparing of the anterior commissure. *Neuropsychologia,* 1981, *19,* 745–755.

Myers, R. E. Discussion, In V. B. Mountcastle (Ed.), *Interhemispheric relations and cerebral dominance.* Baltimore: Johns Hopkins University Press, 1962.

Noble, J. Paradoxical interocular transfer of mirror-image discriminations in the optic chiasm sectioned monkey. *Brain Research,* 1968, *10,* 127–151.

O'Keefe, J., & Nadel. L. *The hippocampus as a cognitive map.* Oxford: Clarendon Press, 1978.

Olton, D. S. The function of septo-hippocampal connections in spatially organized behavior. In K. Elliot & J. Whelan (Eds.), *Function of the septo-hippocampal system* (CIBA Foundation Symposium No. 58). Amsterdam: Elsevier, 1978.

Overman, W. H., Jr., & Doty, R. W. Prolonged visual memory in macaques and man. *Neuroscience,* 1980, *5,* 1825–1831.

Risse, G. L., & Gazzaniga, M. S. Well-kept secrets of the right hemisphere: A carotid amytal study of restricted memory transfer. *Neurology,* 1978, *28,* 950–953.

Risse, G. L., LeDoux, J., Springer, S. P., Wilson, D. H., & Gazzaniga, M. S. The anterior commissure in man: Functional variation in a multisensory system. *Neuropsychologia,* 1978, *16,* 23–31.

Robinson, A. L. Quantum mechanics passes another test. *Science,* 1982, *217,* 435–436.

Rohrlich, F. Facing quantum mechanical reality. *Science,* 1983, *221,* 1251–1255.

Sauerwein, H., Lassonde, M., & Geoffroy, G. A tachistoscopic study of intra- and interhemispheric processing of visual information in callosal agenesis. *Society for Neuroscience Abstracts,* 1981, *7,* 382.

Schüz, A. Some facts and hypotheses concerning dendritic spines and learning. In M. A. B. Brazier & H. Petsche (Eds.), *Architectonics of the cerebral cortex* (IBRO Monograph Series, Vol. 3). New York: Raven Press, 1978.

Shapiro, M. L., Hulse, S. H., & Olton, D. S. Hippocampal function and the memory for serial patterns. *Society for Neuroscience Abstracts,* 1982, *8,* 311.

Squire, L. R. The neuropsychology of human memory. *Annual Review of Neuroscience,* 1982, *5,* 241–243.

Standing, L. Learning 10,000 pictures. *Quarterly Journal of Experimental Psychology,* 1973, *25,* 207–222.

Strausfeld, N. J. *Atlas of an insect brain.* Berlin: Springer-Verlag, 1976.

Sullivan, M. V., & Hamilton, C. R. Memory establishment via the anterior commissure of monkeys. *Physiology and Behavior,* 1973, *11,* 873–879.

Vanderwolf, C. H., Kramis, R., & Robinson, T. E. Hippocampal electrical activity during waking behaviour and sleep: Analyses using centrally acting drugs. In K. Elliot & J. Whelan (Eds.), *Function of the septo-hippocampal system* (CIBA Foundation Symposium No. 58). Amsterdam: Elsevier, 1978.

Wehner, R. Spatial vision in anthropods. In H. Autrum (Ed.), *Handbook of sensory physiology* (Vol. 7/6C). Berlin: Springer-Verlag, 1981.

32

The Organization of Memory in
Nonhuman Primate Model Systems

Karl H. Pribram

Introduction

The Problems

It is scarcely more than three decades since Lashley, continuing the theme of his 1929 *Brain Mechanisms and Intelligence* in his 1950 article "In Search of the Engram," declared his failure to locate the memory trace. By contrast, today the evidence from carefully performed clinical neuropsychological studies (which continue a 19th-century tradition) provides a plethora of localizable disturbances of memory processes. However, interpretation of the data from these studies often remains difficult, because lesions in humans do not carve the brain according to functionally operating anatomical systems. Nor do these studies completely contradict Lashley: Deficits are not limited to specific memory traces (e.g., recognition of one's grandmother), but involve classes of memory processes. We are thus faced with the problem of reconciling the nature of engram storage with the nature of memory processing.

Further, the attempt to characterize and classify processes has served up series of dichotomies that vary from investigator to investigator. What is the relationship between "procedural" and "referential" processes? Between "episodic" and "working" memory? And between all of these and others, such as "semantic" processing? There is thus at present no agreement as to the relationship among dichotomous formulations—only a monumental Tower of Babel to confuse those not directly involved in the research.

Some of these problems can be addressed by studying nonhuman primate models. There is a relevant body of such evidence, which is currently ignored in studies made on human neuropsychological patients. In this chapter I review this evidence, which suggests that the various aspects of memory can be arranged hierarchically, according to the brain systems that have been identified as being involved. The specifics of the hierarchy proposed will most likely be subject to changes as new evidence accrues. However, I maintain that the complexities of memory will not be understood until the relationship among them, and their relationships to brain systems, become clarified.

At least seven different memory mechanisms can be identified. At base, these involve perceptual and motor skills on the one hand, and the episodic processing of novel (registration) on a familiar (extinction) events on the other. Skills are enhanced by search

Karl H. Pribram. Neuropsychology Laboratories, Departments of Psychology and of Psychiatry and the Behavioral Sciences, Stanford University, Stanford, California.

and sampling procedures to form referential processes. Episodic processes become sensitive to the spatial–temporal structure that describes the context within which the episodes occur and allows transfer of training in one context to another. In turn, referential and contextual processes interact to produce declarative language.

Each of the nodes of the hierarchy has a forebrain system identified with it (see Figure 32-1). Thus perceptual skills involve the extrinsically connected primary sensory systems; motor skills involve the extrinsically connected motor systems. Processing novelty involves systems converging on the amygdala; processing the familiar involves those converging on the hippocampus. Search and sampling are disturbed by resections of the intrinsic cortex of the parietal–temporal–preoccipital convexity, which lies between the extrinsic projection areas; probabilistic programming is disturbed by resections of the far frontal intrinsic cortex. ("Extrinsic" denotes relatively direct connections with the periphery; "intrinsic" indicates that such connections are indirect.) The methods and data from which these conclusions stem are described below.

The Multiple-Dissociation Technique

The experimental analysis of subhuman primate psychosurgical preparations has uncovered a host of memory disturbances. The initial technique by which these brain–behavior relationships were established is called the method of "multiple dissociation" (Pribram, 1954), akin to what Teuber named the method of "double dissociation" of signs of brain trauma in humans. The *multiple*-dissociation technique depends on classifying the behavioral deficit produced by cortical ablations into "yes" and "no" instances on the basis of some arbitrarily chosen criterion; then plotting on a brain map the total extent of tissue associated with each of the categories "ablated: deficit" and "ablated: no deficit"; and finally finding the intercept of those two areas (essentially subtracting the "nos" from the

FIGURE 32-1. Diagram of the relationships among types of learning and memory processes. Note that the functions of the neural systems described in this chapter make up the endpoints of each of the branches of the tree. The term "contextual" is used in relation to such terms as "working memory" (based on the alternation paradigm), "declarative" (based on computer-programming paradigms), or "pragmatic" (based on linguistic paradigms) because it is more general in meaning. The term "referential" is used, where in linguistics and cognitive psychology the term "semantic" would apply.

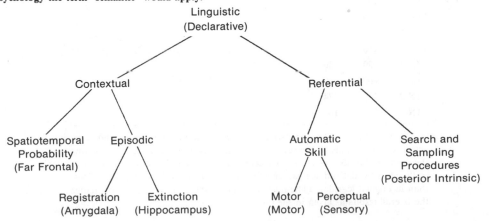

"yeses-plus-nos"). This procedure is repeated for each type of behavior. The resulting map of localization of disturbances is then validated by making lesions restricted to the site determined by the intersect method and showing that the maximal behavioral deficit is obtained by the restricted lesion. (See Table 32-1 and Figure 32-2.)

Once the neurobehavioral correlation has been established by the multiple-dissociation technique, two additional experimental steps are undertaken. First, holding the lesion constant, a series of variations is made of the task on which performance was found defective. These experimental manipulations determine the limits over which the brain-behavior disturbance correlations hold, and thus allow reasonable constructions of models of the psychological processes impaired by the various surgical procedures.

Second, neuroanatomical and electrophysiological techniques are engaged to work out the relationships between the brain areas under examination and the rest of the

TABLE 32-1. Simultaneous Visual-Choice Reaction

Operates without deficit			Operates with deficit			Nonoperated controls		
	Pre	Post		Pre	Post		Pre	Post
OP 1	200	0	PTO 1	120	272	C 1	790	80
OP 2	220	0	PTO 2	325	F	C 2	230	20
OP 3	380	0	PTO 3	180	F	C 3	750	20
LT 1	390	190	PTO 4	120	450	C 4	440	0
LT 2	300	150	T 1	940	F			
H 1	210	220	T 2	330	F			
HA	350	240	VTH 1	320	F			
FT 1	580	50	VTH 2	370	F			
FT 3	50	0	VTH 3	280	F			
FT 4	205	0	VTH 4	440	F			
FT 5	300	200	VT 1	240	F			
FT 6	250	100	VT 2	200	F			
DL 1	160	140	VT 3	200	890			
DL 2	540	150	VT 4	410	F			
DL 3	300	240	VT 5	210	F			
DL 4	120	100						
MV 1	110	0						
MV 2	150	10						
MV 3	290	130						
MV 4	230	10						
MV 5	280	120						
CIN 1	120	80						
CIN 2	400	60						
CIN 3	115	74						
CIN 4	240	140						

Note. Pre- and postoperative scores on a simultaneous visual-choice reaction of the animals whose brains are diagrammed in Figure 32-2, indicating the number of trials taken to reach a criterion of 90% correct on 100 consecutive trials. Deficit is defined as a larger number of trials taken in the "retention" test than in original learning. (The misplacement of the score H 1 does not change the overall results as given in the text.)

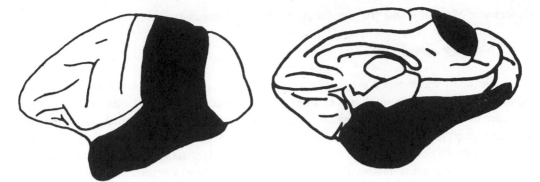

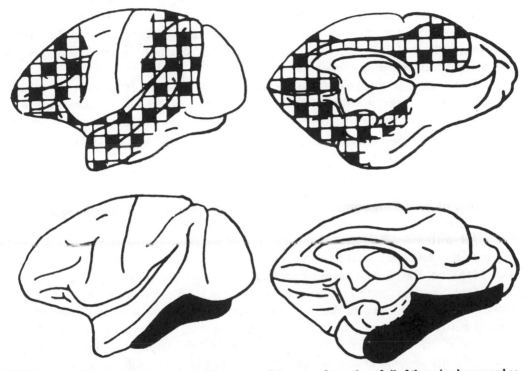

FIGURE 32-2. The upper diagram represents the sum of the areas of resection of all of the animals grouped as showing deficit. The middle diagram represents the sum of the areas of resection of all of the animals grouped as showing no deficit. The lower diagram represents the intercept of the area shown in the black in the upper diagram and that *not* checkerboarded in the middle diagram. This intercept represents the area invariably implicated in visual-choice behavior in these experiments.

nervous system. These experimental procedures allow the construction of reasonable models of the functions of the areas and of the mechanisms of impairment.

Two major classes of memory processes have been delineated by the first of these operations: "referential" and "contextual." The following sections of this chapter take up these processes, while the final sections deal with modeling the neural mechanisms that underlie the processes.

Reference Memory and the Posterior Cortical Convexity

Sensory Specificity

Between the sensory projection areas of the primate cerebral mantle lies a vast expanse of parietal–temporal–preoccipital cortex. Clinical observation has assigned disturbance of many gnostic and language functions to lesions of this expanse. Experimental psychosurgical analysis in subhuman primates, of course, is limited to nonverbal behavior; within this limitation, however, a set of sensory-specific agnosias (losses in the competence to choose among cues) has been produced. Distinct regions of primate cortex have been shown to be involved in each of the modality-specific memory functions: anterotemporal in gustation (Bagshaw & Pribram, 1953), inferotemporal in vision (Mishkin & Pribram, 1954), midtemporal in audition (Dewson, Pribram, & Lynch, 1969; Weiskrantz & Mishkin, 1958), and occipito-parietal in somesthesis (Pribram & Barry, 1956; M. Wilson, 1975). In each instance, choice reactions learned prior to surgical interference are lost to the subject postoperatively, and great difficulty (using a "savings" criterion) in reacquisition is experienced, if task solution is possible at all.

The behavioral analysis of these sensory-specific memory deficits has shown that they involve a restriction in sampling of alternatives—a true information-processing deficit, a deficit in reference memory. Perhaps the easiest way to communicate this is to review the observations, thinking, and experiments that have led to the present view of the function of the inferotemporal cortex in vision.

Search and Sampling

All sorts of differences in the physical dimensions of the stimulus (e.g., size) influence the deficiency in choice that occurs after inferotemporal lesions (Mishkin & Hall, 1955), but the disability is more complex—as illustrated in the following story:

One day, when testing my lesioned monkeys at the Yerkes Laboratories at Orange Park, Florida, I sat down to rest from the chore of carrying a monkey a considerable distance between home cage and laboratory. The monkeys, including this one, were failing miserably at the visual-discrimination tasks being administered. It was a hot, muggy, typical Florida summer afternoon, and the air was swarming with gnats. My monkey reached out and caught a gnat. Without thinking, I also reached for a gnat, and missed. The monkey reached out again, caught a gnat, and put it in its mouth. I reached out—and missed again! Finally the paradox of the situation forced itself on me. I took the beast back to the testing room; it was still deficient in making visual choices, but when no choice was involved, its visually guided behavior appeared to be intact. On the basis of this observation, the hypothesis was developed that *choice* was the crucial variable responsible for the deficient discrimination following inferotemporal lesions. As long as a monkey does not have to make a choice, its visual performance should remain intact.

To test this hypothesis, monkeys were trained in a Ganzfeld made of a translucent light fixture large enough so the animal could be physically inserted into it (Ettlinger, 1957). The animal could press a lever throughout the procedure but was rewarded only during the period when illumination was markedly increased for several seconds at a time.

Soon response frequency became maximal during this "bright" period. Under such conditions, no differences in performance were obtained between inferotemporally lesioned and control animals. The result tended to support the view that if an inferotemporally lesioned monkey did not have to make a choice, it would show no deficit in behavior, since in another experiment (Mishkin & Pribram, 1954) where choice was involved, the monkeys failed to distinguish between differences in brightness.

In another instance (Pribram & Mishkin, 1955), we trained the monkeys on a very simple object-discrimination test, using an ashtray and a tobacco tin. These animals had been trained for 2 or 3 years prior to surgery and were sophisticated problem solvers. This, plus ease of task, produced only a minimal deficit in the simultaneous-choice task. When given the same cues successively, the monkeys showed a deficit when compared with their controls, despite their ability to differentiate the cues in the simultaneous situation.

This result gave further support to the idea that the problem for the operated monkeys was not so much in "seeing," but in being able to *refer* in a useful or meaningful way to what they had seen previously. Not only the stimulus conditions, but an entire range of response determinants appeared to be involved in specifying the deficit. To test this more quantitatively, I next asked whether the deficit would vary as a function of the *number* of alternatives in the situation (Pribram, 1959). It was expected that an informational measure of the deficit could be obtained, but something very different appeared when I plotted the number of errors against the number of alternatives (see Figure 32-3).

If one plots repetitive errors made before the subject finds a peanut—that is, the number of times a monkey searches the same cue—versus the number of alternatives in the situation, one finds that there is a hump in the curve, a stage where control subjects make

FIGURE 32-3. Graph of the average number of repetitive errors made in the multiple-object experiment during those search trials in each situation when the additional—that is, the novel—cue was first added.

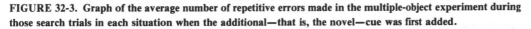

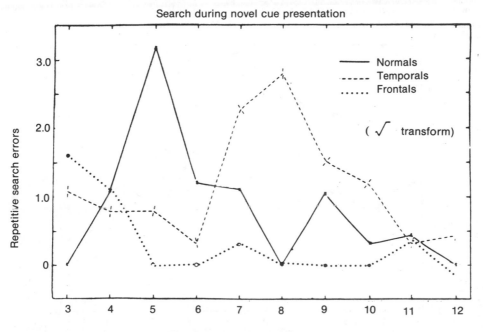

many repetitive errors. The monkeys do learn the appropriate strategy, however, and go on to complete the task with facility. What intrigued me was that during this stage the monkeys with inferotemporal lesions were doing better than the controls! This seemed a paradox. As the test continued, the controls no longer made so many errors, whereas the lesioned subjects began to accumulate errors at a greater rate than shown earlier by the controls.

When a stimulus-sampling model was applied to the analysis of the data, a difference in sampling was found (see Figure 32-4). The monkeys with inferotemporal lesions showed a lowered sampling ratio; they sampled fewer cues during the first half of the experiment. Their defect can be characterized as a restriction on the number of alternatives searched and sampled. Their sampling competence, their competence to process information, had become impaired. The limited sampling restricted the ability to construct an extensive semantic-memory store and to reference that memory during retrieval.

Automatic (Skilled) versus Controlled (Procedural) Processing

There is evidence that, for some tasks at least, memory processes need only the primary projection, input–output systems of the brain. Shiffrin and Schneider (Schneider & Shiffrin, 1977; Shiffrin & Schneider, 1977) and Treisman (1977) have developed tasks that differentiate between automatic and controlled processing. They differ in that tasks that can be automatically processed involve overlearned skills, in which a choice can

FIGURE 32-4. Graph of the average proportion of objects (cues) that were sampled (except novel cue) by each of the groups in each of the situations. To sample, a monkey had to move an object until the content or lack of content of the food well was clearly visible to the experimenter. As was predicted, during the first half of the experiment the curve representing the sampling ratio of the posteriorly lesioned group differed significantly from the others at the .024 level (according to the nonparametric Mann–Whitney U test).

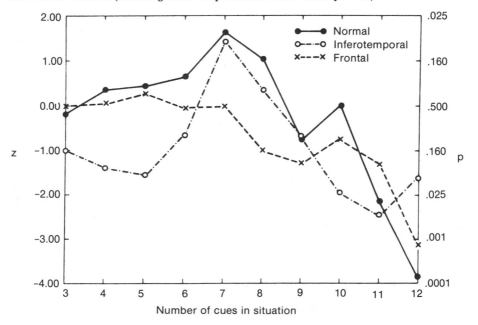

proceed without serial search (as indicated by short reaction times that are relatively independent of sample size). Thus the number of alternatives from which a cue is chosen has no effect on reaction time, since all are processed in parallel fashion. Controlled processing involves an earlier stage of skill and requires a serial search, with reaction time dependent on the number of alternatives.

To determine what brain systems were involved in these two types of reference-memory tasks, we used a modification of Treisman's displays and measured the event-related electrical activity recorded from the striate and peristriate cortex, the infero-temporal lobe, the far frontal cortex, and the percentral cortex. The subject had to select a green square from a set of colored squares and diamonds, each of equal contour and luminance when compared to the rewarded cue.

The following display combinations were used in the experiment described here: (1) a simple disjunctive display, in which the green square had to be identified in a background of eight red diamonds; (2) a more complicated disjunctive display, in which the green square had to be identified in a background of red diamonds, white circles, and blue triangles that were not held identical; (3) the conjunctive display, in which the green square had to be identified in a background of green diamonds, red diamonds, and red squares. The results showed that changes in brain electrical responses recorded from the primary sensory areas reflected the number of distinct features in the display. Conversely, changes in potentials recorded from the posterior intrinsic association cortex—and, initially, when the task was novel in the far frontal intrinsic association cortex—reflected the difficulty of the task as determined by the number of alternatives and the conjunctive–disjunctive dimension of the displays.

Other experiments have allowed us to make a dissociation between the brain electrical activity evoked in the primary sensory projection cortex and the posterior intrinsic association cortex of the temporal lobe (Nuwer & Pribram, 1979; Rothblat & Pribram, 1972). These earlier studies, as well as the current ones, showed that the brain electrical activity evoked in the primary sensory receiving areas was largely determined by the features in the stimulus display, irrespective of whether they were being reinforced; whereas the electrical potential changes evoked in the temporal cortex were primarily related to the cognitive operations involved (i.e., the choices based on categorizing and pigeonholing) (Broadbent, 1974). Clear and consistent involvement of the frontal cortex was found only on occasions when the task was novel or when the reinforcing contingencies were shifted between runs. This relationship to novelty is consonant with the results described below.

Episodic Memory and the Limbic Forebrain

Contextual Memory

The second major division of the cerebral mantle to which memory functions have been assigned by clinical observation lies on the medial and basal surface of the brain and extends forward to include the poles of the frontal and temporal lobes. This fronto-limbic portion of the hemisphere is cytoarchitecturally diverse. The expectation that different parts might be shown to subserve radically different functions was therefore even greater than that entertained for the apparently uniform posterior cortex. To some extent, this expectation was not fulfilled: Lesions of the fronto-limbic region, irrespective of location (dorsolateral frontal, caudate, cingulate–medial frontal, orbito-frontal, temporal polar–amygdala, and hippocampal) disrupted "delayed-alternation" behavior. The alternation task demands that the subject alternate responses between two cues (for example, between two places or between two subjects) on successive trials. On any trial, the correct response is dependent on the outcome of the previous response. This suggests that the critical variable characterizing the task is its temporal organization. In turn, this leads to the supposition that the disruption of alternation behavior produced by fronto-limbic lesions results from an impairment of the process by which the brain achieves its temporal organization. This supposition was only in part confirmed by further analysis: It became necessary to impose severe restrictions on what is meant by "temporal organization," and important aspects of spatial organization were also severely impaired. For instance, *skills* are not affected by fronto-limbic lesions, nor are discriminations of melodies. Retrieval of long-held memories also is little affected; rather, a large range of short-term memory processes is involved. These clearly include tasks that demand matching from memory the spatial location of cues (as in the delayed-response problem) (Anderson, Hunt, Vander Stoep, & Pribram, 1976), as well as their temporal order of appearance (as in the alternation task; Pribram, Plotkin, Anderson, & Leong, 1977). A similar deficit is produced when, in discrimination tasks, shifts in which cue is rewarded are made over successive trials (Mishkin & Delacour, 1975). The deficit appears whenever the organism must fit the present event into a "context" of prior occurrences, and there are no cues that address this context in the situation at hand at the moment of response.

The Registration of Events as Episodes

As noted, different parts of the fronto-limbic complex would, on the basis of their anatomical structure, be expected to function somewhat differently within the category of contextual memory processes. Indeed, different forms of contextual amnesia are produced by different lesions. In order to be experienced as memorable, events must be fitted to context. A series of experiments on the orienting reaction to novelty and its registration has pointed to the amygdala as an important locus in the "context-fitting" mechanism. The experiments were inspired by the results from Sokolov's laboratory (Sokolov, 1960).

Sokolov presented human subjects with a tone beep of a certain intensity and frequency, repeated at irregular intervals. Galvanic skin response (GSR), heart rate, finger and forehead plethysmograms, and electroencephalogram (EEG) were recorded. Initially, these records showed the perturbations that were classified as the orienting response. After several repetitions of the tone, these perturbations diminished and finally vanished. They habituated. Originally, it had been thought that habituation reflected a *lowered* sensitivity of the central nervous system to inputs. But when Sokolov *decreased* the intensity of the tone beep, leaving the other parameters unchanged, a full-blown orienting response was reestablished. Sokolov reasoned that the central nervous system could not be desensitized, but that it was less responsive to sameness: When any difference occurred in the stimulus, the central nervous system became *more* sensitive. He tested this idea by rehabituating his subjects and then occasionally omitting the tone beep, or reducing its duration without changing any other parameter. As predicted, his subjects now oriented to the unexpected silence.

The orienting reaction and habituation are thus sensitive measures of the process by which context is organized. We therefore initiated a series of experiments to analyze in detail the neural mechanisms involved in orientating and its habituation. This proved more difficult than we imagined. The dependent variables—behavior, GSR, plethysmogram, and EEG—are prone to dissociate (Koepke & Pribram, 1971). Forehead plethysmography turned out to be especially tricky, and we eventually settled on behavior, GSR, heart and respiratory responses, and EEG as most reliable.

The results of the first of these experiments (Schwartzbaum, Wilson, & Morrissette, 1961) indicated that, under certain conditions, removal of the amygdaloid complex can enhance the persistence of locomotor activity in monkeys who would normally decrement their responses. The lesion thus produces a disturbance in the habituation of motor activity (see Figure 32-5).

The results of the experiments on the habituation of the GSR component of the orienting reaction (Bagshaw, Kimble & Pribram, 1965) also indicate clearly that amygdalectomy has an effect (see Figure 32-6). The lesion profoundly reduces GSR amplitude in situations where the GSR is a robust indicator of the orienting reaction. Concomitantly, deceleration of heartbeat, change in respiratory rhythm, and some aspects of EEG indices of orienting also are found to be absent (Bagshaw & Benzies, 1968). As habituation of motor activity (Schwartzbaum et al., 1961) and also habituation of earflicks (Bateson, 1969) had been severely retarded by these same lesions, we concluded that the autonomic indicators of orienting are in some way crucial to subsequent behavioral habituation. We identified the process indicated by the autonomic components of the orienting reaction as "registering" the novel event.

However, the registration mechanism is not limited to novelty. Extending the analysis to a classical conditioning situation (Bagshaw & Coppock, 1968; Pribram, Reitz,

FIGURE 32-5. Postoperative activity scores of normal and amygdalectomized monkeys for successive blocks of three sessions under conditions of constant illumination and more intense, varied illumination.

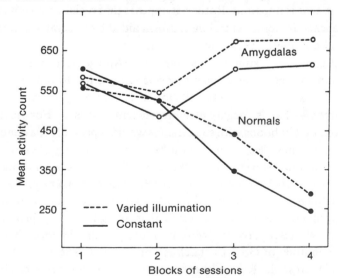

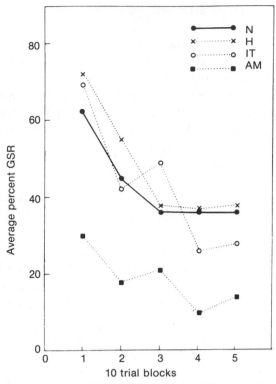

FIGURE 32-6. Curves of percentages of GSR response to the first 50 presentations of the original stimulus for the normal group (N) and three experimental groups (H, IT, AM) (i.e., monkeys with hippocampal, inferotemporal, and amygdala resections).

McNeil, & Spevack, 1979) and using the GSR as a measure of conditioning, we found that normal monkeys not only condition well but produce earlier and more frequently anticipatory GSRs as time goes by. Amygdalectomized subjects fail to make such anticipatory responses. As classical conditioning of a striped muscle proceeds normally, it is not the conditioning *per se* that is impaired. Rather, it appears that registration entails some active process akin to rehearsal—some central mechanism aided by visceral–autonomic processes that maintains and distributes excitation over time.

Behavioral experiments support this suggestion. Amygdalectomized monkeys placed in operant situations or the two-cue task described above fail to take proper account of reinforced events (Schwartzbaum, 1960a, 1960b). This deficiency is dramatically displayed whenever punishment—that is, negative reinforcement—is used. For instance, an early observation showed that baboons with such lesions would repeatedly (day and day and week after week) put lighted matches in their mouths, despite showing obvious signs of being burned (Fulton, Pribram, Stevenson, & Wall, 1949). These observations were further quantified in tasks measuring avoidance of shock (Pribram & Weiskrantz, 1957). The results of these two experiments were confirmed in other laboratories and with other species so often that the hypothesis needed to be tested that amygdalectomy produces an altered sensitivity to pain. We (Bagshaw & Pribram, 1968) put this hypothesis to the test and showed that the amplitude of GSR to shock is not elevated as it would be were there an elevation of the pain threshold. Rather, the threshold is, if anything, reduced by the ablation.

This experimental result suggests that amygdalectomy produces its effects by way of a "loss of fear," defined as a disturbance in "registering" the noxious event by placing it in context. In other words, the animal does not remember the noxious event, so that its recurrence is experienced as novel and not fear-producing.

Processing the Familiar

Context is not composed solely of the registration of reinforcing and deterrent events. Just as important are the errors, the nonreinforced aspects of a situation, especially if on previous occasions they have been reinforced. It is resection of the primate hippocampal formation (Douglas & Pribram, 1966) that produces relative insensitivity to errors, to frustrative nonreward (Gray, 1975), and more generally to the familiar, nonreinforced aspects of the environment (the $S^{\triangle}$ of operant conditioning, the negative instances of mathematical psychology). In their first experience with a discrimination-learning situation, subjects with hippocampal resections show a peculiar retardation, provided there are many nonrewarded alternatives in that situation. For example, in an experiment using a computer-controlled automated testing apparatus (DADTA) (Drake & Pribram, 1976; Pribram, 1969), the subject faced 16 panels; discriminable cues were displayed on only two of these panels, and only one cue was rewarded. The cues were displayed in various locations in a random fashion from trial to trial.

Hippocampectomized monkeys were found to press the unlit and unrewarded panels for thousands of trials, long after their unoperated controls ceased responding to these "irrelevant" items. It is as if in the normal subject, a "ground" is established by enhancing "inattention" (extinction) to all the negative instances of those patterns that do not provide a relevant "figure." This "inattention" is an active, evaluating process, as indicated by the behavior shown during shaping in a discrimination-reversal task, when the demand is to respond to the previously nonreinforced cue: Unsophisticated subjects often begin by pressing on various parts of their cage and the testing apparatus before they hit upon a chance response to the nonrewarded cue.

These and many similar results indicate that the hippocampal formation is part of an evaluative mechanism that helps to establish the "ground," the familiar aspects of context.

Working Memory and the Frontal Cortex

The Spatial–Temporal Structure of Context

In some respects, the far frontal resection produces memory disturbances characteristic of both hippocampectomy and amygdalectomy, though not so severe. Whereas medial temporal lobe ablations impair context formation by way of habituation of novel and familiar events, far frontal lesions wreak havoc on yet another contextual dimension—that of organizing the spatial and temporal structure of the context (Anderson et al., 1976; Pribram et al., 1977). This effect is best demonstrated by an experiment that changed the parameters of the classical alternation task. Instead of interposing equal intervals between trials (go right, go left every 5 sec) in the usual way, couplets of right–left were formed by extending the intertrial interval to 15 sec before each right trial (right, 5 sec; left, 15 sec; right, 5 sec; left, 15 sec; . . .). When this was done, the performance of the far frontally lesioned monkeys improved immediately and was indistinguishable from that of the controls (Pribram *et al.*, 1977; Pribram & Tubbs, 1967). This result suggests that for the subject with a bilateral far frontal ablation, the alternation task is experienced similarly to reading this page without any spaces between the words. The spaces, like the holes in doughnuts, provide the contextual structure, the parceling or parsing of events by which the outside world can be coded and deciphered.

Context as a Function of Reinforcing Contingencies

Classically, disturbance of "working" short-term memory has been ascribed to lesions of the frontal pole. Anterior and medial resections of the far frontal cortex were the first to be shown to produce impairment on delayed-response and delayed-alternation problems. In other tests of context formation and fitting, frontal lesions also take their toll. Here, also, impairment of conditioned avoidance behavior, of classical conditioning, and of the orienting GSR is found. Furthermore, as shown in Figure 32-7, error sensitivity is reduced in operant conditioning. After several years of training on mixed and multiple schedules, the animals were extinguished over 4 hours. The frontally lesioned animals failed to extinguish in the 4-hour period, whereas the control monkeys did (Pribram, 1961).

FIGURE 32-7. Graph of performance of three groups of monkeys under conditions of extinction in a mixed-schedule operant conditioning situation. Note the slower extinction of the frontally lesioned monkeys.

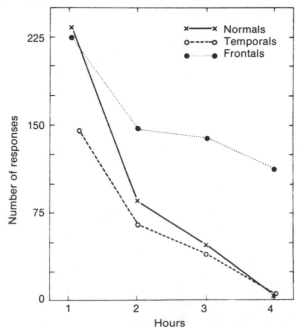

This failure in extinction accounts in part for poor performance in the alternation already described: The frontally lesioned animals again make many more repetitive errors. Even though they do not find a peanut, they go right back and keep looking (Pribram, 1959).

This result was confirmed and amplified in a study by W. A. Wilson (1962) and another by us (Pribram et al., 1977), in which we asked whether errors followed alternation or nonreinforcement. We devised a situation in which both lids over two food wells opened simultaneously, but the monkey could obtain the peanut only if it had opened the baited well. Thus the monkey was given "complete" information on every trial, and the usual correction technique could be circumvented. There were four procedural variations: correction-contingent, correction-noncontingent, noncorrection-contingent, and noncorrection-noncontingent. The contingency referred to whether the position of the peanut was altered on the basis of the monkey's responses (correct or incorrect) or whether its position was changed independently of the monkey's behavior. We then analyzed the relationship between each error and the trial that preceded that error. Table 32-2 shows that for the normal monkeys, the condition of reinforcement and nonreinforcement of the previous trial made a difference; for the frontally lesioned monkeys, this was not the case. Change in location, however, affected both normal and frontal subjects about equally. In this situation, as well as in an automated computer-controlled version of the alternatives problem (Drake & Pribram, 1976; Pribram, 1969), frontal subjects were simply uninfluenced by rewarding or nonrewarding consequences of their behavior.

In a multiple-choice task (Pribram, 1959) (see Figure 32-8), the procedure calls for a strategy of returning to the same object for five consecutive times—that is, to criterion—and then a shift to a novel item. The frontally lesioned animals are markedly deficient in doing this. Again, the conditions of reinforcement are relatively ineffective in shaping behavior in animals with frontal lesions, and the monkeys' behavior becomes nearly

TABLE 32-2. Percentage of Alternation as a Function of Response and Outcome of Preceding Trial

Subject	Preceding trial			
	A-R	A-NR	NA-R	NA-NR
Normal				
394	53	56	40	45
396	54	53	36	49
398	49	69	27	48
384	61	83	33	72
Total	55	68	34	52
Frontal				
381	49	51	41	43
437	42	46	27	26
361	49	48	38	35
433	43	39	31	32
Total	46	46	33	33

Note. Comparison of the performance of frontally ablated and normal monkeys on alternations made subsequent to reinforced (R) and nonreinforced (NR) and an alternated (A) and nonalternated (NA) response.

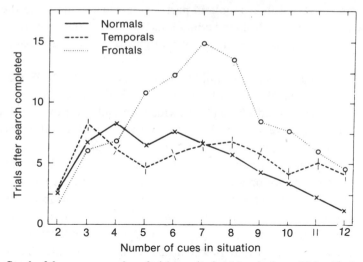

FIGURE 32-8. Graph of the average number of trials to criterion taken in the multiple-object experiment by each group in each of the situations after search was completed—that is, after the first correct response. Note the difference between the curves for the controls and for the frontally operated group, a difference that is significant at the .05 level by an analysis of variance ($F = 8.19$ for 2 and 6 df) according to McNemar's procedure performed on normalized (by square-root transformation) raw scores.

random when compared to that of normal subjects (Pribram, Ahumada, Hartog, & Roos, 1964). Behavior of the frontally lesioned monkeys thus appears to be minimally controlled by expected outcomes.

The Memory Store

Distributed Memory

As noted in the introduction, the experiments of Lashley demonstrated that specific memory traces remain intact after extensive resection—up to 85%—of the primary visual cortex. These results make it imperative to assume that input becomes widely distributed. Several mechanisms have been proposed to account for such distribution (see reviews by Eich, 1982; Murdock, 1979, 1982; Pribram, 1982), and how such distributed systems are organized (Cooper, 1973; Edelman, 1974; Pribram, 1966, 1982). Here I want to present direct evidence that indeed distribution does occur.

We trained monkeys to discriminate between a circle and a set of vertical stripes by pressing the right or left half of a plastic panel upon which the cues were briefly projected (for .01 msec). Transient electrical responses were meanwhile recorded from fine electrode wires, and these electrical responses (from single neurons or small neuronal aggregates) were related by computer analysis to the stimulus, response, and reinforcement contingencies of the experiments (Bridgeman, 1982; Pribram, Spinelli, & Kamback, 1967). Thus we could distinguish from the record whether the monkey had looked at a circle or at the stripes, whether it had obtained a reward or made an error, and whether it was about to press the right or the left leaf of the panel. Interestingly enough, not all of these brain patterns were recorded from all of the electrode locations: From some, input-related patterns were obtained best; from others, the reinforcement-related patterns were best derived; and still others gave us best the patterns that were response-related. This was despite the fact that *all placements were within the primary visual system*, which is characterized anatomically by being homotopic with the retina. It appears therefore not only that optic events are distributed widely over the system, but that response- and reinforcement-related events reliably reach the input systems. Such results surely shake further one's confidence in the ordinary view that input events must be transmitted to the "association" area for associative memory to be effected.

Semantic Competence

As noted above, the diminution in reference memory that follows lesions of the posterior convexity is specific to the sensory mode served by the cortex that has been injured (Gordon, 1983; Warrington, Logue, & Pratt, 1971; Warrington & Rabin, 1971; Warrington & Weiskrantz, 1973) and is therefore often interpreted as a change in channel capacity. Elsewhere (Pribram & McGuinness, 1975) I have reviewed the evidence that the competence of neural channels that process sensory input is involved, not channel capacity. Further, the lesion sites that result in these changes involve the intrinsic (or associational) systems related to specific primary extrinsic sensory systems, and not the sensory systems *per se*. The question therefore arises as to how competence is altered by lesions of the intrinsic systems of the brain.

One reasonable answer to this question can be framed in terms of coding and retrieval. Changes in competence following lesions to intrinsic cortical systems are changes in the mechanisms that address the long-term distributed store. This leads to the dilemma that strategies of retrieval must also be represented and stored in the brain, or they would not be disturbed by the lesion. It might be argued that such strategies are innate. Be that as it may, the changes in competence following lesions appear to become manifest in behaviors such as language, which is clearly learned. Whatever the innate competence for the behavior, it has been considerably modified by experience. What, then, are the characteristics of such modifiable competences?

One possible answer to this question is that the intrinsic systems of the forebrain operate corticofugally to preprocess sensory input on its route through the projection systems. In this way, the sensory input becomes coded and recoded on the basis of experience.

There are several advantages to this formulation. First, it helps considerably in systematizing data. Second, it answers a persistent unanswered question originally formulated by Von Monakov (1914): Can disturbances in memory (such as the agnosias) be completely dissociated from disturbances in sensory functions? Van Monakov asked these questions specifically: (1) Can agnosia occur in the absence of involvement of the primary projection systems? (2) Does agnosia occur in the absence of primary sensory difficulties? Von Monakov's answer to the second question was an unequivocal "no," an opinion shared by Bay (1964) on the basis of more recent and carefully controlled studies. Von Monakov, after reviewing the anatomical data, also gave a tentative "no" to the first question, although he was neither completely convinced nor convincing on this point. The preprocessing formulation and the data presented below indicate that the correct answer is more complex.

The Mechanisms of Re-Membering the Dismembered Store

Recovery Functions

The experimental findings detailed here allow one to specify a possible mechanism to account for the lesion-produced memory deficits: The posterior intrinsic cortex, by way of efferent tracts leading to the basal ganglia and brain stem (most likely to the colliculi or surrounding reticular formation; see Pribram 1958, 1960a, 1977), can be suggested to partition the events that occur in the associated projection cortex and to classify and categorize these events according to one or another schema. This suggestion was tested in experiments (Spinelli & Pribram, 1966, 1967), in which the intrinsic cortex was electrically stimulated and records were made of recovery functions and receptive field properties of cells within the projection systems.

Records were made in awake monkeys. Paired flashes were presented, and recordings made from electrodes implanted in the occipital cortex. The respones to 50 such paired flashes were accumulated on a computer for average transients. The flash–flash interval was varied from 25 to 200 msec. All records were made from striate (visual) cortex.

FIGURE 32-9. A plot of the recovery functions obtained in five monkeys before and during chronic cortical stimulation. Note the relative amplitude of the second response as a function of interflash interval.

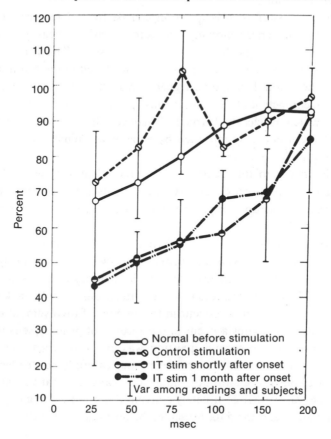

The top traces were recorded prior to the onset of stimulation, and the lower ones after stimulation of the inferotemporal region had begun. Note that with cortical stimulation, the recovery function was depressed—that is, recovery was delayed. Figure 32-9 shows the average of such effects in five subjects. Chronic stimulation of the inferotemporal cortex produced a marked increase in the processing time taken by cells in the visual system.

A parallel experiment was conducted in the auditory system (Dewson, 1968). In this study, made with cats, removals of the auditory homologue of the inferotemporal cortex were performed. This homologue is the insular–temporal region of the cat. Dewson (1964) had shown that its removal impairs complex auditory discrimination (speech sounds), leaving simple auditory discrimination (pitch and loudness) intact. Removal, in addition, alters paired-click recovery cycles recorded as far peripherally as the cochlear nucleus. Bilateral ablation shortens the recovery cycle markedly. Of course, control ablations of the primary auditory projection cortex and elsewhere have no such effect. Thus we have evidence that chronic stimulation of the "association" cortex selectively prolongs, while ablation selectively shortens, the recovery time of cells in the related primary sensory projection system.

Receptive Fields

These results have been extended in both the auditory and visual modes. Alterations of visual receptive fields recorded from units at the optic nerve, geniculate, and cortical levels of the visual projection systems were produced by electrical stimulation of the inferotemporal cortex. The anatomy of the corticofugal pathways of these controls over sensory input also is under study. In the auditory system, the fibers lead to the inferior colliculus, and from there (in part via the superior olive) to the cochlear nucleus (Dewson, Nobel, & Pribram, 1966). In our studies of the visual pathways, the fibers from the inferotemporal cortex lead via the putamen (Reitz & Pribram, 1969) to the pretectal–collicular region as the site of interaction between the corticofugal control mechanism and the visual input system.

Contextual memory mechanisms have also become subject to neurophysiological analysis. Again, as in the case of the sensory-specific memory processes, corticofugal efferent control mechanisms have been demonstrated. Results obtained in my laboratory show that in many instances these controls are the reciprocals of those involved in the sensory-mode-specific processes (Lassonde, Ptito, & Pribram, 1981; Spinelli & Pribram, 1967). Others (Skinner & Lindsley, 1973) have shown that the most likely pathways of operation of the fronto-limbic mechanisms involve the brain stem reticular formation. Here, however, as in the case of the sensory-specific memory processes, control can be exerted as far peripherally as the primary sensory neuron (Spinelli & Pribram, 1967; Spinelli, Pribram, & Weingarten, 1965).

Channel Redundancy

In general terms, the operation of efferents from sensory-specific posterior systems tend to reduce, and those from the fronto-limbic systems tend to enhance, redundancy in the input channels (i.e., the primary projection systems). This presumably is accomplished by inhibition and disinhibition of the ongoing interneuronal regulatory processes within the afferent channels—both those by which neurons regulate the activities of their neighbors, and those that decrease a neuron's own activity.

Redundancy control must work something like a multiplexing circuit. In neurophysiological terms, when the recovery time of neurons in the sensory projection system is increased by posterior "association" cortex stimulation, fewer cells are available at any given moment to receive the concurrent input. Each of a successive series of inputs thus will find a different set of cells in the system available to excitation. There is a good deal of evidence that, in the visual system at least, there is plenty of reserve capacity—redundancy—so that information transmission is not, under ordinary circumstances, hampered by such "narrowing" of the channel (Attneave, 1954). Ordinarily a particular input excites a great number of fibers in the channel, ensuring replication of transmitted information. Just as lateral inhibition in the retina has the effect of reducing redundancy (Barlow, 1961), so the operation of the sensory-specific posterior "association" cortex increases the density of information within the input channel.

Conversely, the functions of the fronto-limbic mechanism enhance redundancy, making more cells available at any given moment to concurrent input. This diminishes the density of information processed at any moment and enhances temporal resolution.

The Brain Model of the Memory Mechanism

The Model

The evidence presented here makes it not unlikely that one function of the posterior intrinsic and fronto-limbic formations of the forebrain is to code events occurring within the input systems. As noted, the distribution of information (dismembering) implies an encoding process that can reduplicate events. Regrouping the distributed events (remembering) also implies some sort of coding operation—one similar to that used in decoding binary switch settings into an octal format and that into assembly and still higher-order programming language. An impaired coding process would be expected to produce grave memory disturbances. Lesion-produced amnesias—reference and contextual—therefore reflect primary malfunctions of coding mechanism, and not the destruction of localized engrams.

Concretely, the intrinsic cortex is thus conceived to program, or to structure, an input channel. This is tantamount to saying that the input in the projection systems is coded by the operation of the intrinsic cortex. In its fundamental aspects, computer programming is a coding operation: The change from direct machine operation through assembler to one of the more manipulable computer languages involves a progression from the setting of binary switches to conceptualizing combinations of such switch settings in "octal" code; then assembling the numerical octals into alphabetized words and phrases; and finally parceling and parsing phrases into sentences, routines, and subroutines. In essence, these progressive coding operations minimize interference among the configurations of occurrence and recurrence of the events.

Implications

The model has several important implications. First, the nonrecovered cells, the ones that are still occupied by excitation initiated by prior inputs, will act as a context or short-term memory buffer against which the current input is matched. A match–mismatch operation of this sort is demanded by models of the process of recognition and selective attention spelled out on other occasions by Craik (1943), Sokolov (1960), Bruner (1957), MacKay (1956), and myself (Pribram, 1960a, 1963a, 1963b). These "occupied" cells thus form the matrix of "uncertainty" that shapes the pattern of potential information—that is, the "unexpectancy" that determines the selection of input signals that might or might not occur. The normal functions of the posterior cortex are assumed to increase the complexity of this context, while those of the fronto-limbic systems would simplify and thus allow readier registration and parceling.

Second, in a system of fixed size, reduction of redundancy increases the degree of correlation possible with the set of external inputs to the system, while enhancement of redundancy has the opposite effect. The number of alternatives or the complexity of the item to which an organism can attend is thereby controlled (Garner, 1962). This internal alteration in the functional structure of the classic sensory projection system thus allows attention to vary as a function of the spatial and temporal resolution that excitations can achieve, with the result that events of greater or lesser complexity can be attended to. The sharper the spatial resolution, the greater the "uncertainty," and thus the more likely that any set of inputs will be sampled for information. Conversely, the greater the temporal resolution, the more likely that attention is focused, and that events become grouped, memorable, and certain. In the extreme, the sharpening of the appetite for information becomes what the clinical neurologist calls "stimulus-binding." Its opposite is agnosia, the inability to identify events because they fail to fit the oversimplified context of the moment.

Third, this corticofugal model of the functions of the so-called association systems relieves us of the problem of higher- and higher-order infinite regress—an association-area "homunculus" who synthesizes and abstracts from inputs, only to pass on these abstractions to a still higher "homunculus," perhaps the one who makes decisions, and so on. Former ways of looking at the input–output relationships of the brain invariably have come up against this problem (implicit or explicit) of "homunculi" inside "homunculi."

According to the model presented here, there is no need for this type of infinite regress. The important functions of perception, decision, and so on are going on within the primary sensory and motor projection systems. Other brain regions, such as the posterior intrinsic sensory-specific systems and the fronto-limbic systems, exert their effects by altering the functional organization of the primary systems. Thus these intrinsic systems are not "association" but "associated" systems; they simply alter the configuration of input–output relationships processed by the projection systems. In computer language, the intrinsic systems function by supplying *subroutines* in a hierarchy of programs—subroutines contained within, and not superimposed from above on, the more fundamental processes. In this fashion, the infinite higher-order abstractive regress is avoided. One could argue that in its place a downward regress of subroutines is substituted. I would answer that this type of regress, through progressive differentiation, is the more understandable and manipulable of the two.

A final advantage of the model is that the signal itself is not altered; the invariant properties of a signal are unaffected (unless channel capacity is overreached). It is only the organization of the channel itself—the matrix within which the signal is transmitted—that is altered. Thus the same signal carries more or less information, depending on the "width" of the channel. Further, the signal carries different meanings, depending on the particular structure or organization of the redundancy of the channel.

Summary

Experimentally produced local forebrain damage does demonstrably impair memory functions. However, the impairment apparently is not so much a removal of localized engrams as an interference with the mechanisms that ordinarily code neural events so as to allow facile storage and retrieval. Thus, the evidence shows that anatomically the memory trace is distributed within a neural system by means of an en-coding process, while as a function of de-coding, the distributed, dismembered engram is reassembled—that is, re-membered. Thus, what and whether something is remembered is in large part dependent on how it is, and that it is adequately coded.

Two major classes of memory mechanisms have been identified: "reference" and "contextual." Each of these classes is subdivided into others. Reference memory is composed of sets of sensory-specific skilled, automatic processes, on the one hand, and another set of sensory-specific search and sampling procedures on the other. Contextual memory is composed of a mechanism that registers episodes, another that processes the familiar, and a third that works to organize the spatial–temporal structure of context. How these memory mechanisms interact to produce declarative linguistic processes remains to be investigated.

REFERENCES

Anderson, R. M., Hunt, S. C., Vander Stoep, A., & Pribram, K. H. Object permanancy and delayed response as spatial context in monkeys with frontal lesions. *Neuropsychologia*, 1976, *14*, 481–490.

Attneave, F. Some informational aspects of visual perception. *Psychological Review*, 1954, *61*, 183–193.

Bagshaw, M. H., & Benzies, S. Multiple measures of the orienting reaction to a simple non-reinforced stimulus after amygdalectomy. *Experimental Neurology*, 1968, *20*, 175–187.

Bagshaw, M. H., & Coppock, H. W. GSR conditioning deficit in amygdalectomized monkeys. *Experimental Neurology*, 1968, *20*, 188–196.

Bagshaw, M. H., Kimble, D. P., & Pribram, K. H. The GSR of monkeys during orienting and habituation and after ablation of the amygdala, hippocampus and inferotemporal cortex. *Neuropsychologia*, 1965, *3*, 111–119.

Bagshaw, M. H., & Pribram, K. H. Cortical organization in gustation (*Macaca mulatta*). *Journal of Neurophysiology*, 1953, *16*, 499–508.

Bagshaw, M. H., & Pribram, J. D. The effect of amygdalectomy on shock threshold of the monkey. *Experimental Neurology*, 1968, *20*, 197–202.

Barlow, H. B. Possible principles underlying the transformations of sensory messages. In W. Rosenblith (Ed.), *Sensory communication*. Cambridge, Mass.: MIT Press, 1961.

Bateson, P. P. G. Ear movements of normal and amygdalectomized monkeys. Personal communication, 1969.

Bay, E. Principles of classification and their influence on our concepts of aphasia. In A. V. S. de Reuck & M. O'Connor (Eds.), *Disorders of language* (CIBA Foundation Symposium). Boston: Little, Brown, 1964.

Bridgeman, B. Multiplexing in single cells of the alert monkey's visual cortex during brightness discrimination. *Neuropsychologia*, 1982, *20*(1), 33–42.

Broadbent, D. E. Division of function and integration. In F. O. Schmitt & F. G. Worden (Eds.), *The neurosciences: Third study program*. Cambridge, Mass.: MIT Press, 1974.

Bruner, J. S. On perceptual readiness. *Psychological Review*, 1957, *64*, 123–152.

Cooper, L. N. A possible organization of animal memory and learning. In F. Lindquist & S. Lindquist (Eds.), *Proceedings of the Nobel Symposium on Collective Properties of Physical Systems*. New York: Academic Press, 1973.

Craik, K. J. W. *The nature of explanation*. Cambridge, England: Cambridge University Press, 1943.

Dewson, J. H., III. Speech sound discrimination by cats. *Science*, 1964, *3619*, 555–556.

Dewson, J. H., III. Efferent olivo cochlear bundle: Some relationships to stimulus discrimination in noise. *Journal of Neurophysiology*, 1968, *31*, 122–130.

Dewson, J. H., III, Nobel, K. W., & Pribram, K. H. Corticofugal influence at cochlear nucleus of the cat: Some effects of ablation of insular–temporal cortex. *Brain Research*, 1966, *2*, 151–159.

Dewson, J. H., III, Pribram, K. H., & Lynch, J. C. Ablations of temporal cortex in the monkey and their effects upon speech sound discriminations. *Experimental Neurology*, 1969, *24*, 579–591.

Douglas, R. J., & Pribram, K. H. Learning and limbic lesions. *Neuropsychologia*, 1966, *4*, 197–220.

Drake, K. U., & Pribram, K. H. DADTA IV: A computer based video display and recording system for behavioral testing. In P. B. Brown (Ed.), *Computer technology in neuroscience*. New York: Wiley, 1976.

Edelman, G. M. Specificity and mechanism at the lymphoid cell surface. In F. O. Schmitt & F. G. Worden (Eds.), *The neurosciences: Third study program*. Cambridge, Mass.: MIT Press, 1974.

Eich, J. M. A composite holographic associative recall model. *Psychological Review*, 1982, *89*(6), 627–661.

Ettlinger, G. Visual discrimination following successive unilateral temporal excisions in monkeys. *Journal of Physiology (London)*, 1957, *140*, 38–39.

Fulton, J. F., Pribram, K. H., Stevenson, J. A. F., & Wall, P. D. Interrelations between orbital gyrus, insula, temporal tip and anterior cingulate. *Transactions of the American Neurological Association*, 1949, 175–179.

Garner, W. R. *Uncertainty and structure as psychological concepts*. New York: Wiley, 1962.

Gordon, W. P. Memory disorders in aphasia: I. Auditory immediate recall. *Neuropsychologia*, 1983, *21*, 325–339.

Gray, J. A. *Elements of a two-process theory of learning*. London: Academic Press, 1975.

Koepke, J. E., & Pribram, K. H. Effect of milk on the maintenance of sucking in kittens from birth to six months. *Journal of Comparative and Physiological Psychology*, 1971, *75*, 363–377.

Lashley, K. S. *Brain mechanisms and intelligence*. Chicago: University of Chicago Press, 1929.

Lashley, K. S. In search of the engram. *Symposium of the Society for Experimental Biology*, 1950, *4*, 454–482.

Lassonde, M. C., Ptito, M., & Pribram, K. H. Intracerebral influences on the microstructure of visual cortex. *Experimental Brain Research*, 1981, *43*, 131–144.

MacKay, D. M. The epistemological problem for automata. In *Automata studies*. Princeton, N.J.: Princeton University Press, 1956.

Mishkin, M., & Delacour, J. An analysis of short-term visual memory in the monkey. *Journal of Experimental Psychology: Animal Behavior Processes*, 1975, *1*(4), 326–334.

Mishkin, M., & Hall, M. Discrimination along a size continuum following ablation of the inferior temporal convexity in monkeys. *Journal of Comparative and Physiological Psychology*, 1955, *48*, 97–101.

Mishkin, M., & Pribram, K. H. Visual discrimination performance following partial ablations of the temporal lobe: I. Ventral versus lateral. *Journal of Comparative and Physiological Psychology*, 1954, *47*, 14–20.

Murdock, B. B. Convolution and correlation in perception and memory. In L. G. Nilsson (Ed.), *Perspectives on memory research*. Hillsdale, N.J.: Erlbaum, 1979.

Murdock, B. B. A theory for the storage and retrieval of item and associative information. *Psychological Review*, 1982, *89*(6), 609–626.

Nuwer, M. R., & Pribram, K. H. Role of the inferotemporal cortex in visual selective attention. *Electroencephalography and Clinical Neurophysiology*, 1979, *46*, 389–400.

Pribram, K. H. Toward a science of neuropsychology: Method and data. In R. A. Patton (Ed.), *Current trends in psychology and the behavioral sciences*. Pittsburgh: University of Pittsburgh Press, 1954.

Pribram, K. H. Neocortical function in behavior. In H. F. Harlow (Ed.), *Neocortical function in behavior.* Madison: University of Wisconsin Press, 1958.

Pribram, K. H. On the neurology of thinking. *Behavior Science*, 1959, *4*, 265–287.

Pribram, K. H. The intrinsic systems of the forebrain. In J. Field & H. W. Magoun (Eds.), *Handbook of physiology* (Vol. 2, *Neurophysiology*). Washington, D.C.: American Physiological Society, 1960. (a)

Pribram, K. H. A review of theory in physiological psychology. *Annual Review of Psychology*, 1960, *11*, 1–40. (b)

Pribram, K. H. A further experimental analysis of the behavioral deicit that follows injury to the primate frontal cortex. *Experimental Neurology*, 1961, *3*, 432–466.

Pribram, K. H. The new neurology: Memory, novelty, thought and choice. In G. H. Glaser (Ed.), *The EEG and behavior.* New York: Basic Books, 1963. (a)

Pribram, K. H. Reinforcement revisited: A structural view. In M. Jones (Ed.), *Nebraska Symposium on Motivation* (Vol. 11). Lincoln: University of Nebraska Press, 1963. (b)

Pribram, K. H. Some dimensions of remembering: steps toward a neuropsychological model of memory. In J. Gaito (Ed.), *Macromolecules and behavior.* New York: Academic Press, 1966.

Pribram, K. H. DADTA III: An on-line computerized system for the experimental analysis of behavior. *Perceptual and Motor Skills*, 1969, *29*, 599–608.

Pribram, K. H. New dimensions in the functions of the basal ganglia. In C. Shagass, S. Gershon, & A. J. Friedhoff (Eds.), *Psychopathology and brain dysfunction.* New York: Raven Press, 1977.

Pribram, K. H. *Languages of the brain: Experimental paradoxes and principles in neuropsychology.* New York: Brandon House, 1982.

Pribram, K. H., Ahumada, A., Hartog, J., & Roos, L. A progress report on the neurological processes distributed by frontal lesions in primates. In J. M. Warren & K. Akert (Eds.), *The frontal granular cortex and behavior.* New York: McGraw-Hill, 1964.

Pribram, K. H., & Barry, J. Further behavioral analysis of the parieto-temporo-preoccipital cortex. *Journal of Neurophysiology*, 1956, *19*, 99–106.

Pribram, K. H., & McGuinness, D. Arousal, activation and effort in the control of attention. *Psychological Review*, 1975, *82*(2), 116–149.

Pribram, K. H., & Mishkin, M. Simultaneous and successive visual discrimination by monkeys with inferotemporal lesions. *Journal of Comparative and Physiological Psychology*, 1955, *48*, 198–202.

Pribram, K. H., Plotkin, H. C., Anderson, R. M., & Leong, D. Information sources in the delayed alternation task for normal and "frontal" monkeys. *Neuropsychologia*, 1977, *15*, 329–340.

Pribram, K. H., Reitz, S., McNeil, M., & Spevack, A. A. The effect of amygdalectomy on orienting and classical conditioning in monkeys. *Pavlovian Journal*, 1979, *14*(4), 203–217.

Pribram, K. H., Spinelli, D. N., & Kamback, M. C. Electrocortical correlates of stimulus response and reinforcement. *Science*, 1967, *157*, 94–96.

Pribram, K. H., & Tubbs, W. E. Short-term memory, parsing and the primate frontal cortex. *Science*, 1967, *156*, 1765.

Pribram, K. H., & Weiskrantz, L. A comparison of the effects of medial and lateral cerebral resections on conditioned avoidance behavior in monkeys. *Journal of Comparative and Physiological Psychology*, 1957, *50*, 74–80.

Reitz, S. L., & Pribram, K. H. Some subcortical connections of the inferotemporal gyrus of monkeys. *Experimental Neurology*, 1969, *25*, 632–645.

Rothblat, L., & Pribram, K. H. Selective attention: Input filter or response selection? *Brain Research*, 1972, *39*, 427–436.

Schneider, W., & Shiffrin, R. M. Controlled and automatic human information processing: I. Detection, search and attention. *Psychological Review*, 1977, *84*, 1–66.

Schwartzbaum, J. S. Changes in reinforcing properties of stimuli following ablation of the amygdaloid complex in monkeys. *Journal of Comparative and Physiological Psychology*, 1960, *53*, 388–395. (a)

Schwartzbaum, J. S. Response to changes in reinforcing conditions of barpressing after ablation of the amygdaloid complex in monkeys. *Psychological Report*, 1960, *6*, 215–221. (b)

Schwartzbaum, J. S., Wilson, W. A., Jr., & Morrissette, J. R. The effects of amygdalectomy on locomotor activity in monkeys. *Journal of Comparative and Physiological Psychology*, 1961, *54*, 334–336.

Shiffrin, R. M., & Schneider, W. Controlled and automatic human information processing: II. Perceptual learning, automatic attending, and a general theory. *Psychological Review*, 1977, *84*, 127–190.

Skinner, J. E., & Lindsley, D. B. The nonspecific mediothalamic–frontocortical system: Its influence on electrocortical activity and behavior. In K. H. Pribram & A. R. Luria (Eds.), *Psychophysiology of the frontal lobes*. New York: Academic Press, 1973.

Sokolov, E. N. Neuronal models and the orienting reflex. In M. A. Brazier (Ed.), *The central nervous system and behavior*. New York: Josiah Macy, Jr., Foundation, 1960.

Spinelli, D. N., & Pribram, K. H. Changes in visual recovery functions produced by temporal lobe stimulation in monkeys. *Electroencephalography and Clinical Neurophysiology*, 1966, *20*, 44–49.

Spinelli, D. N., & Pribram, K. H. Changes in visual recovery function and unit activity produced by frontal cortex stimulation. *Electroencephalography and Clinical Neurophysiology*, 1967, *22*, 143–149.

Spinelli, D. N., Pribram, K. H., & Weingarten, M. A. Centrifugal optic nerve responses evoked by auditory and somatic stimulation. *Experimental Neurology*, 1965, *12*, 303–319.

Treisman, A. Focused attention in the perception and retrieval of multidimensional stimuli. *Perception and Psychophysics*, 1977, *22*(1), 1–11.

Von Monakov, C. *Die Lokalisation im Grosshien und der Abbau der Function Durch Korticale*. Wiesbaden: Bergmann, 1914.

Warrington, E. K., Logue, V., & Pratt, R. T. C. The anatomical localisation of selective impairment of auditory verbal short-term memory. *Neuropsychologia*, 1971, *9*, 377–387.

Warrington, E. K., & Rabin, P. Visual span of apprehension in patients with unilateral cerebral lesions. *Quarterly Journal of Experimental Psychology*, 1971, *23*, 423–431.

Warrington, E. K., & Weiskrantz, L. An analysis of short-term and long-term memory defects in man. In J. A. Deutsch (Ed.), *The physiological basis of memory*. New York: Academic Press, 1973.

Weiskrantz, L., & Mishkin, M. Effects of temporal and frontal cortical lesions on auditory discrimination in monkeys. *Brain*, 1958, *81*, 406–414.

Wilson, M. Effects of circumscribed cortical lesions upon somesthetic and visual discrimination in the monkey. *Journal of Comparative and Physiological Psychology*, 1975, *50*, 630–635.

Wilson, W. A., Jr. Alternation in normal and frontal monkeys as a function of response and outcome of the previous trial. *Journal of Comparative and Physiological Psychology*, 1962, *55*, 701–704.

Studies of Memory in Nonprimates: Physiology, Pharmacology, and Behavior

When one turns from human subjects, clinical patients, and monkeys to other experimental animals, one finds the biology of memory being investigated with a broad spectrum of strategies and techniques. These can be pursued relatively inexpensively in smaller laboratory animals such as rats, rabbits, and cats, and a strong tradition of anatomy and physiology involving these species is available. At its best, a program of work in this tradition can lead to cumulative knowledge about the organization of learning and memory. Several experimental systems are already available for both vertebrates and invertebrates. Indeed, the number of systems and paradigms already available seems sufficient to test the generality of newly discovered processes and mechanisms, but not too small to risk missing major mechanisms used by organisms to accomplish learning and memory.

The 22 chapters in this section represent the major approaches currently being taken. They also illustrate the wide range of questions under study, from questions about animal models of the same clinical syndromes discussed in earlier chapters, to questions about cellular mechanisms of learning in vertebrates and invertebrates. Four major experimental techniques can be identified: lesions and behavioral analysis; recording of cellular activity in behaving animals; electrical stimulation of identified neural pathways; and pharmacological manipulation of specific transmitter systems or metabolic pathways. These techniques are being applied, separately or in combination, to several well-established experimental systems. For example, favorable model systems for studying associative learning at the cellular level, especially simple forms of classical conditioning, have been developed in both vertebrates and invertebrates. In addition, the study of aversively and appetitively motivated learning has been standardized by the widespread use of passive-avoidance tasks and the eight-arm radial maze. Both tasks can be used to study one-trial learning, and acquired information persists for hours, days, or weeks, depending on the experimental conditions. Finally, the widely studied phenomenon of long-term potentiation, an instance of long-lasting plasticity in an identified neural pathway, offers a model system for studying memory in vertebrates at the synaptic level and for asking questions about the possible behavioral–functional significance of synaptic events.

In all of this work, two different themes or goals can be discerned. One goal is to identify the locus in the brain of information storage and to characterize the cellular events that occur in information-containing pathways. A second goal is to identify the brain systems that modulate or influence the development or maintenance of information storage and to understand the particular role of these brain systems. Information will be needed from each of these ventures, if a broad understanding is to be achieved about how the brain accomplishes memory. Although occasionally a chauvinistic voice is heard, favoring one approach or one experimental question over another, we still know too little about memory to ignore any possible lead.

Animal Models of Human Amnesias

33

David S. Olton

Introduction

Animal models provide a valuable means of investigating the neural mechanisms under-lying normal memory and the types of pathology responsible for the different syndromes of amnesia.[1] Although experiments with people can include very sophisticated psychological analyses, they are substantially limited by ethical considerations in terms of their neural analyses. And although *in vitro* or invertebrate preparations are appropriate for some types of applications (Kandel, 1976, p. 39), they are simply incapable of providing the information required here. Thus, the precision of control and the accuracy of measurement necessary to conduct basic neurological analyses can be obtained only with animal models.

When writing for contributions to this volume, the editors requested chapters that were "conceptually oriented and . . . a discussion of the assumptions and perspectives peculiar to each contributor's areas." With these requests in mind, I have written a chapter that discusses the general nature of research with animal models of human amnesias without referring to any particular model. Many of the points made here are already familiar to those working in the field, and are implicitly incorporated into research protocols. But they rarely get stated explicitly. I hope that this discussion helps make the principles underlying this approach clear, and provides a general framework which can be used to compare the different models currently available and to develop new ones (Minckler, Bauer, & Ringenberg, 1972).

Validity

A model is valid to the extent that it measures what it claims to measure. In the present context, the issue is whether or not the experimental procedures for the animals elicit the intended cognitive processes and neural mechanisms. Thus, all the components of the comparative approach are relevant. Some of the points that are particularly helpful in developing and evaluating an animal model are summarized below.

---

1. This statement is not meant to imply that ethical considerations do not apply to experiments with animals. Clearly they do. But as long as one does not wish to give animals all the rights that are given to people, there is the possibility of better experimental procedures with animals. The issue, then, resolves around the decision of whether the pain and discomfort produced by the experiment are justified by the increment in knowledge obtained.

David S. Olton. Department of Psychology, Johns Hopkins University, Baltimore, Maryland.

Conceputal Validity

Memories are composed of associations, and many characteristics of these associations have been described in detail. To the extent that an animal model is valid, the description of the cognitive processes involved in the animals' memory should be consistent with already established conceptual frameworks (see the discussions in Hulse, Fowler, & Honig, 1978; Premack, 1983; Roitblat, 1982; Roitblat, Bever, & Terrace, 1983). Furthermore, the model should be able to identify and describe the ways in which these processes influence memory and performance.

For example, virtually all memory systems are subject to interference; the ability to remember any given item decreases as the number of items to be remembered increases. The shape of the function relating the amount of interference produced by each additional item varies markedly, depending on the type of information to be remembered, but the presence of a positive function is ubiquitous. The interference is common to all memory systems, and its presence in an animal model strengthens the validity of that model.

As illustrated in this volume, many different types of memory systems have been proposed. Relating one system to another can often be difficult, and expecting an animal model to fit into every conceptual framework is unrealistic. Nonetheless, any model ought to be able to deal with a set of core issues considered by most every memory system (Teuber, 1955, p. 288).

Behavioral Validity

Performance in virtually every task requires some type of memory. Thus, every task is a "memory" task. Likewise, virtually every other psychological process is also required: sensation, motor movement, motivation, and so on. Consequently, no task is a pure measure of just memory.

Still, steps can be taken to enhance the relative importance of the memory component and to suppress the relative importance of other components (see Di Renzi, 1982, pp. 4–6, 173; Lezak, 1976, pp. 119–120). Providing very salient and familiar stimuli to be remembered, being certain that the animal is well trained in the general experimental procedure, minimizing the response requirements—these and many other steps can help to emphasize the memory aspects of the task. In essence, the goal is to develop a task that is both sensitive to and selective for the desired cognitive process: sensitive, so that even minor changes in the process of interest produce substantial behavioral changes; selective, so that even substantial changes in other processes produce at most only minor behavioral changes in this task.

If memory is a major factor influencing performance, then variables (such as interference) that affect memory also ought to affect the components of that performance (such as choice accuracy) that depend on this memory. In a complementary fashion, variables that affect other psychological processes ought to have relatively little effect on these components, and should affect other ones instead. Manipulations can also be made in order to identify the discriminative stimuli guiding the animals' choice behavior and to be certain that some alternative, simplified strategy has not been adopted. In this way, the validity of the behavioral task as a measure of memory can be assessed.

Neurological Validity

The same input–output relations can be attained by a variety of different mechanisms. Even if a model does have a well-developed conceptual basis and an appropriate behavioral task, it still may not involve the desired neurological system. Consequently, some comparison of the effects of similar lesions in people and in animals must be made. The outcomes of this comparison, however, must be interpreted with care. Brain damage in people is rarely discrete, and the description of that damage is usually very limited. Thus, the likelihood that the lesion in the animal is identical to that in the human is very small, and a detailed matching of the amnesic syndromes is unlikely.

The outcome of this experimental test is somewhat asymmetrical. A close approximation of the syndrome in animals to that in people provides strong support for the validity of the model. Discrepancies between the syndromes could be due to a variety of factors, however, one of which is the complicated pattern or unknown extent of the brain damage in the people. Consequently, a general similarity of the two syndromes may be taken as providing this type of validity.

Ethological Validity

Animals have evolved in natural habitats, not laboratories, and this historical perspective should influence the ways in which we decide to test animals. Certainly when developing a model, and also when evaluating one, taking the animal's point of view in the experiment can be very helpful.

Ultimately, the animal is the one who must perform the task, and the experimenter must communicate the desired set of instructions to the animal as clearly as possible. We are often justified in using technology to make our experiments more efficient in terms of the amount of experimenter time required to conduct them. But the benefits of saving experimenter time can be offset by the costs incurred in making the task overly complex for the animal. Adopting the animal's perspective can often point out these false savings, and can help suggest ways of making the task more efficient for the animal as well as for the experimenter.

In their natural habitats, animals face a variety of different problems, the solution of which is aided by a good memory (Kamil & Sargent, 1981; Krebs, 1978). The ability to solve these problems effectively can have a substantial influence on a species' fitness, so that adaptation and natural selection have had an enduring opportunity to change the cognitive processes involved in remembering. For example, many animals have a constant series of decisions to make when searching for food: where to go, when to go there, what to eat after arriving, how long to stay, where to go next, and so forth. Thus, if one wants to ask questions about an animal's memory, understanding the general types of problems posed by the environment can assist in designing tasks and evaluating the extent to which any given task elicits natural memory processes.

Another consequence of considering ethological variables is the ability to ask specific questions about specific animals. Studies of foraging patterns indicate that predators often have search strategies that are particularly well adapted to the distribution of prey in their environment. Thus, in contrast to the general problems common to many animals that are discussed above, these variations are specific to certain combinations of predators and prey. For example, some predators deplete their food source in a single visit, and the source then takes some time to replenish its food. For these predators, the optimal strategy is to shift from one source to another, and not to return to a previously visited source until it has had sufficient time to replenish its food (Cole, Hainsworth, Kamil, Mercier, & Wolf, 1982; Kamil, 1977). Other types of predators have other response-reinforcement contingencies, and are likely to find additional prey if they remain in a previously visited site in which they have found food. These personal and evolutionary histories can have a substantial impact on an animal's preferred search strategy, and the extent to which the animal's preference matches the demands of the task chosen by the experimenter can in turn have a substantial influence on performance.

Interpretation

Brain Lesions

Amnesias are often caused by brain damage, and animal models of human amnesias commonly use lesions in order to trace the brain mechanisms involved in normal memory and to describe the pathological changes producing amnesic syndromes. The use of brain lesions, however, might be doomed to failure for a variety of different reasons. Some are general: The brain might be so complicated with dynamic interactions that this approach will not be a useful way of examining its functional organization (Gregory, 1961). Others are more specific. If a system has only a single input and a single output, and no spontaneous activity, then a lesion anywhere along it will have the same result (no output for a given input) even though the system might have many different functional stages, each producing a different transformation of the signal (Webster, 1973; Weiskrantz, 1974). In such a case, lesions by themselves will not elucidate the function of the system (although lesions in conjunction with stimulation and recording will).

But, equally strong arguments can be made for assuming that the lesion method will work. Technicians commonly use both the techniques and the logic lesion analysis to diagnose faulty equipment and to identify the system that has failed. The neurological examinations given in the clinic are an indication of the extent to which appropriate analyses can locate the site of pathology (Bannister, 1978), and much of physiological psychology is based on the results obtained with lesions.

Even though *a priori* feelings about the usefulness of brain lesions vary, the issue can be addressed empirically. If the lesion analysis is not appropriate, then the results obtained from it should be uninterpretable by themselves and should be inconsistent when compared with conclusions drawn from the other two methods of examining the relationships between structure and function (stimulation and recording). Fortunately, neither of these predictions is true. The results of lesion experiments are internally consistent, using the same logic that applies in other fault-finding situations, and the view of the brain drawn from lesion analyses is generally consistent with that obtained from other techniques.[2]

2. This statement is not meant to imply that lesion experiments are the standard against which all other techniques are meant to be judged. There is no outside standard of truth in the search for structure–function relations (or at least if there is, it has not been revealed to me). Consequently, the question of validity is really one

Such an optimistic viewpoint is by no means intended to minimize the difficulties involved in examining structure–function relationships with brain lesions (or with any other technique). At a very fundamental level, we really do not know how to define "structure," "function," or "relationship" (Orbach, 1982; Young, 1970). And the brain is clearly a very active system (Finger & Stein, 1982; Rowland, 1966; Schoenfeld & Hamilton, 1977; Teuber, 1974); progressive changes may continue for years after a lesion. Nonetheless, we have made progress with well-designed lesion experiments, and there is no reason to believe that we must stop here.

Dissociations

We are often told that the finding of "no effect" between groups is not of interest. Editors tell us that the lack of an effect can occur for so many reasons that such experiments are not worth publishing. Statisticians tell us that all the analyses are designed to detect differences and cannot be used to measure similarities.

In spite of these warnings, the lack of effect, when combined with the presence of an effect, is not only interesting, but absolutely critical in order to move from the observational level of analysis to the conceptual level of analysis (Platt, 1964; Teuber, 1955, pp. 277–278, 283–288; Tulving, 1979, p. 31). Consider the experimental finding that after a lesion in structure A, behavior X is impaired. Although the observation is obviously correct as it stands, interpretation is virtually impossible because the impairment could have occurred for many different reasons: lack of sensory input, no memory for the appropriate associations, decreased motivation, failure of motor output, and so on. Only when unimpaired behaviors are found can some decision be made among these various interpretations. If, for example, psychophysical tests show that perceptual processes are intact, then the impairment in behavior X is not likely to be due to lack of sensory input. If tests of motor abilities show that these are fundamentally intact, then the impairment in behavior X is not likely to be due to inappropriate motor output. This process of gradually eliminating inappropriate explanations is critical if an experimenter is to arrive at the correct interpretation, and it can be accomplished only by identifying functions that are not impaired and contrasting those with functions that are impaired.

Dissociations appear in two dimensions. Behavioral dissociations are of this form: Following a lesion in structure A, behavior X is impaired, but not behaviors Y or Z. These dissociations are useful in describing the extent to which a given neural system is selectively involved in a particular function. The functions involved in the unimpaired behavioral tasks are identified and subtracted from the list of possible explanations for the impairment in behavior X; the remaining explanations are treated in the same way. The greater the number of dissociations, the greater the specificity of structure A for function X.

Neurological dissociations are of this form: Following a lesion in structure A but not in structures B or C, behavior X is impaired. These dissociations indicate the extent to

of converging operations. Each of the three techniques (stimulation, lesion, recording) available to study structure–function relationships has its own set of advantages and disadvantages, and no one of them has any more right to be considered as the best standard than the others. Where conclusions from all three are similar, we can be more confident that they are correct than we can be when the conclusions disagree.

which a given behavior involves a particular structure. The structures in which lesions do not impair the behavior are identified and subtracted from the list of all possible structures; the remaining structures are considered as candidates for a functional system, subject to the same types of tests with respect to other behaviors.

Placement of Lesions

Following a lesion, the brain often demonstrates a great deal of plasticity, and changes in the areas that remain intact may continue for an extended period of time. If these changes are accompanied by a behavioral recovery of function, additional experiments are necessary to determine the neural mechanisms involved in this recovery (Finger & Stein, 1982). A correlation between neural plasticity and behavioral recovery cannot be used to imply causality.

These additional experiments are particularly important if incomplete lesions are made. In such a case, recovery might be mediated by other structures (in which case the damaged structure might not be necessary for that function), or might be mediated by recovery in the same structure (in which case the damaged structure might be necessary for that function). Distinguishing between these alternative interpretations is important, but can only be done with other experiments which are rarely carried out. Thus, experiments with incomplete lesions cannot provide critical information about structure–function relationships (Handelmann, Olton, & Evans, in press).

Unless the goal is to examine specifically the mechanisms of recovery of function, complete lesions are desirable. Note that "complete" does not mean "large." If the structure in question has only 100 cells, then a complete lesion destroys only 100 cells. If recovery of function is found after complete lesions, then one can confidently conclude that the structure in question is not necessary for the recovered function.

Conclusions

The use of brain lesions to investigate the functional organization of neural systems involved in memory and the pathological changes producing amnesia is a complicated endeavor. Nonetheless, certain steps can be taken to make it relatively more useful. With the enhanced emphasis on cognitive processes in animals (Premack, 1983; Roitblat, 1982), psychology is providing us with the conceptual framework and experimental procedures to examine memory processes in animals in great detail. The challenge for neuropsychology is to take these developments and use them to understand the functional organization of the brain.

The explicit statement of some of the criteria to be used for developing and evaluating animal models of amnesia should help to meet this challenge in two ways. First, it should provide a framework for experimenters to judge the relative merits of different models. Second, it should stimulate some further discussion, so that an even better framework can be attained.

ACKNOWLEDGMENTS

Preparation of this chapter was supported in part by Research Grant MH24213 from the National Institute of Mental Health to David S. Olton. I appreciate comments and suggestions on the manuscript from N. Cohen, D. Hepler, M. Mishkin, M. Shapiro, E. Tulving, G. Wenk, and G. Winocur, and I thank O. Rossman for typing.

REFERENCES

Bannister, R. *Brain's clinical neurology*. New York: Oxford University Press, 1978.

Cole, S., Hainsworth, F. R., Kamil, A. C., Mercier, T., & Wolf, L. L. Spatial learning as an adaptation in hummingbirds. *Science*, 1982, *217*, 655–657.

Di Renzi, E. *Disorders of space exploration and cognition*. New York: Wiley, 1982.

Finger, S., & Stein, D. G. (Eds.). *Brain damage and recovery*. New York: Academic Press, 1982.

Gregory, R. L. The brain as an engineering problem. In W. H. Thorpe & O. L. Zangwill (Eds.), *Current problems in animal behavior*. Cambridge, England: Cambridge University Press, 1961.

Handelmann, G. E., Olton, D. S., & Evans, M. J. The hippocampal system mediates recovery of behavioral function after loss of the CA3 pyramidal cells. *Brain Research*, in press.

Hulse, S. H., Fowler, H., & Honig, W. K. *Cognitive processes in animal behavior*. Hillsdale, N.J.: Erlbaum, 1978.

Kamil, A. C. Systematic foraging by a nectar-feeding bird, the amakihi (*Loxops virens*). *Journal of Comparative and Physiological Psychology*, 1977, *92*, 388–396.

Kamil, A. C., & Sargent, T. D. *Foraging behavior: Ecological, ethological, and psychological approaches*. New York: Garland STPM Press, 1981.

Kandel, E. R. *Cellular basis of behavior*. San Francisco: W. H. Freeman, 1976.

Krebs, J. R. Optimal foraging: Decision rules for predators. In J. R. Krebs & N. B. Davies (Eds.), *Behavioural ecology*. Oxford: Blackwell Scientific Publications, 1978.

Lezak, M. D. *Neuropsychological assessment*. New York: Oxford University Press, 1976.

Minckler, T. A., Bauer, T. E., & Ringenberg, L. M. Modeling as a tool in neuroscience. In J. Minkler (Ed), *Introduction to neuroscience*. St. Louis: C. V. Mosby, 1972.

Orbach, J. (Ed.). *Neuropsychology after Lashley*. Hillsdale, N.J.: Erlbaum, 1982.

Platt, J. R. Strong inference. *Science*, 1964, *146*, 347–353.

Premack, D. The codes of man and beasts. *Behavioral and Brain Sciences*, 1983, *6*, 125–167.

Roitblat, H. L. The meaning of representation in animal memory. *Behavioral and Brain Sciences*, 1982, *5*, 353–372.

Roitblat, H. L., Bever, T. G., & Terrace, H. S. *Animal cognition*. Hillsdale, N.J.: Erlbaum, 1983.

Rowland, V. Sterotaxic techniques and the production of lesions. In L. Martini & W. F. Ganong (Eds.), *Neuroendocrinology* (Vol. 1). New York: Academic Press, 1966.

Schoenfeld, T. A., & Hamilton, L. W. Secondary brain changes following lesions: A new paradigm for lesion experimentation. *Physiology and Behavior*, 1977, *18*, 951–967.

Teuber, H. L. Physiological psychology. *Annual Review of Psychology*, 1955, *6*, 267–296.

Teuber, H. L. Recovery of function after lesions of the central nervous system: History and prospects. *Neurosciences Research Program Bulletin*, 1974, *12*, 132–145.

Tulving, E. Memory research: What kind of progress? In L.-G. Nilsson (Ed.), *Perspectives on memory research*. Hillsdale, N.J.: Erlbaum, 1979.

Webster, W. G. Assumptions, conceptualizations, and the search for the functions of the brain. *Physiological Psychology*, 1973, *1*, 346–350.

Weiskrantz, L. Brain research and parallel processing. *Physiological Psychology*, 1974, *2*, 53–54.

Young, R. M. *Mind, brain, and adaptation in the nineteenth century: Cerebral localization and its biological context from Gall to Ferrier*. Oxford: Clarendon Press, 1970.

Memory: Time Binding in Organisms

Garth J. Thomas

An almost universally postulated concept that has wide intuitive appeal in the study of memory supposes that dynamic (time-changing) events are recoded into relatively timeless, nondynamic events at a neural level (trace or engram). Organisms have an almost continuous "blooming, buzzing confusion" of sensory input to brain. Crucial aspects of these sensory processes are converted into relatively timeless (unchanging) codes to be used to control subsequent behavior. We can do no better than postulate Semon's engram (Schacter, 1982). At the present time in neuroscience, the structural change that comprises the engram in unknown at the cellular level of the nervous system. We can, however, infer some hypothetical properties of the trace from behavior.

Thus, a primary (and banal) notion of this chapter is that the engram must be considered as a hypothetical construct. It is inferred from current choice behavior, the correctness of which depends on the organism's past commerce with the cue stimuli that are critical in guiding those discriminative responses. However, such a simple formulation does not exhaust the phenomenon of memory behavior. There is a long and honorable tradition of dividing memory into at least two types. The earliest instance is, perhaps, William James' division of memory into "primary" and "secondary" (James, 1890). There are many later instances: "habit memory" versus "pure memory" (Bergson, 1910); "knowing how" versus "knowing that" (Ryle, 1949); "memory without record" versus "memory with record" (Bruner, 1969); "episodic memory" versus "semantic memory" (Tulving, 1972); "reference memory" versus "working memory" (Honig, 1978); and, of course, the distinction of much current preoccupation: "short-term memory" versus "long-term memory." An interesting neuroscience point has been made by Squire (1982): Some aspects of these distinctions (and there are many more) are "honored by the nervous system."

The present chapter proposes another distinction between types of memory: "dispositional memory" versus "representational memory." The distinction really is quite old. It is close to the old distinction of "symbolic memory" versus "nonsymbolic memory" that grew out of Hunter's work (1913, 1920) with delayed response and delayed alternation in the early years of this century. Also, it is very similar to Honig's recent distinction between "reference memory" and "working memory" (1978).

Dispositional memory is most generally characterized by a memory-indicating discrimination that is made with regard to crucial sensory events present at the organism's sensorium at the time of choice. The concept says nothing about the distinction between classical and instrumental conditioning. In both kinds of conditioning, past experiences with the conditioned stimulus (CS) and unconditioned stimulus (UCS) have allowed the

Garth J. Thomas. Center for Brain Research, University of Rochester Medical Center, Rochester, New York.

organism to extract from its continuous flow of sensory inputs a "correlation" between a cue stimulus and is contingent consequences, stimulus–stimulus (S-S) or stimulus–response (S-R).

Such "learnings" are usually slow, require many repetitions (trials), and are built up gradually through cumulative memories of past contingent relationships. One supposes (speculatively) that such memory capabilities are very old in evolution—probably as old as a synaptic nervous system that permits "optional" transmission (Sherrington's term). Even lowly invertebrates with some degree of plasticity in their behavior can habituate, (i.e., eliminate responses to nonnoxious stimuli) when they are repeated frequently: For example, the sea cucumber can "learn and remember" *not* to withdraw its siphon in response to a light touch!

The term "dispositional" designates this type of memory, because the discriminative responses that indicate *memory* are all experience-dependent changes in dispositions to respond to sensory events that are represented in sensory input at the time of choice. A differential reaction to S+ and S− depends on the remembered disposition. Also, the present chapter offers no new suggestions regarding this type of memory. The current psychology of learning is primarily concerned with and seems to say all that we presently know about the phenomenon.

Representational memory, on the other hand, requires not only that the organism remember an experience-dependent disposition, but also that its nervous system contain a "representation" of a critical cue to guide a memory-indicating discrimination; and it must make a choice (respond discriminatively) to that brain representation when there is no crucial and current environmental event induced in the organism's sensorium at the time of choice that can serve as a cue. The "cue" is in the head of the organism, not in sensory-induced representations of environmental events. It is speculated that this type of memory capability can be found only in warm-blooded vertebrates (mammals and birds), so it appears rather late in the evolution of brain. Furthermore, within mammals, the capacity is most developed in humans. It underlies, in lower mammals, what Tolman referred to as the ability to develop an "expectancy." Also, all tasks or problems that are conventionally presented to organisms to study memory confound both dispositional and representational memory. There are a few behavioral tasks that represent relatively "pure" instances of representational memory. Some are delayed response, delayed alternation, matching-to-sample, and possibly trace conditioning—to name only a few that come quickly to mind (regarding trace conditioning, see Solomon, Vander Schaft, Nobre, Weisz, & Thompson, 1983).

None of the ideas expressed above are particularly novel. More novel points are made below that serve largely to "operationalize" the ideas expressed above (and others).

Significantly successful delayed alternation in a two-alternative situation is commonly supposed to depend on a representational memory of the previous trial to guide the choice on the subsequent trial. There are ambiguities regarding interpretation. Perhaps the animals are learning and remembering (as dispositional memory) a response schedule (go right, go left, etc.). Consequently, the preference is for what is called a paired-run procedure, which is currently in use with rats in a T-maze. The paired-run procedure consists of an adaptation of the widely used test in memory research of "matching (or non-matching)-to-sample." It differs from the conventional matching-to-sample task in that a complex, brain-built cue of *place*—a perception constructed by brain from multiple sensory cues

over a period of time while the organism is locomoting—usually controls the discrimination, rather than a specific sensory stimulus (a form, a wavelength, an object, etc.). And the
discriminative response consists of locomoting to a "place" rather than pushing a panel,
pecking a key, or displacing an object. Such modifications bring the test task into
congruence with species-specific dispositions and capabilities of the small-brained rat.

Basically, a trial consists of two runs in a T-maze. On the first run of a trial, the
guillotine door to only one of the two goal boxes (GBs) is opened, and which GB door is
opened is determined by a balanced, irregular schedule. The rat has no choice to make; it
simply must run to the only GB available in order to get food reward. On the second run of
a trial, the doors to both GBs are opened, and it must make a choice. It can be faced with
either one of two problems: If the rat is in a "shift" group, entering the GB opposite the one
available on the previous one-door run will yield reinforcement (nonmatch). If the rat is in
a "stay" group, the correct response that yields reward is to go to the same GB entered on
the previous trial (match). Actually, the shift (nonmatch) task is much easier and is
mastered quickly, presumably because of the species-specific disposition of rats (and
probably other animals that locomote to forage) to alternate. However, with about twice
the number of trials as required for the shift (nonmatch) task, rats can master the stay
(match) task. Both are, nonetheless, representational-memory tasks. The adequacy of the
memory for the first run (one door) is indicated by the accuracy of choice on the two-door
run. When the rats are given 12 trials per session (24 runs), and if they are correct 10, 11, or
12 times, they are discriminating significantly ($p < .02$, expanded binomial).

Figure 34-1, by schematic diagrams, indicates procedural matters and some hypothetical constructs about trace strength. Consider the top row (A). The vertical "blips"
indicate runs; two pairs of runs are shown (two trials). The blip to the far left and the third
blip indicate "information runs." The door to one arm of the T-maze (or the other,

FIGURE 34-1. A schematic diagram to illustrate procedural events (A), the hypothetical strength of the memory
traces, and the place in time of the hypothetical reset (B). Abbreviations: I, information run; C, choice run; T_A and
T_B, any two trials; IRI, interrun interval; ITI, intertrial interval; PI, place for events yielding proactive interference (between a choice run and its succeeding information run); RI, place for events yielding retroactive
interference (between an information run and its succeeding choice run); R, reset.

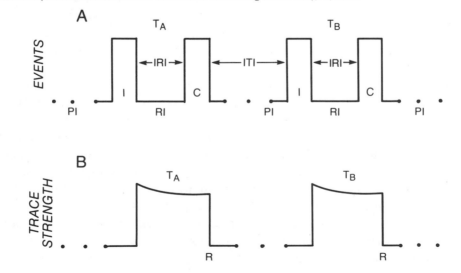

depending on a balanced, irregular schedule) is opened. The rat runs down the stem of the T-maze and into the only available GB, where it is fed when the experimenter pushes in a food dish *after* the GB is entered. After a few seconds of eating, the rat is removed, and the interrun interval (IRI) begins. (The IRI can be an independent variable.) After the IRI, the rat is placed back into the start box (SB) and given its "choice run." This time the doors to both GBs are opened, and the rat is again rewarded, but only if it makes a correct choice. Correctness depends on whether the rat is working on a shift or stay problem. Sometime during (or immediately after—the B part of the diagram shows "immediately after"), a hypothetical reset mechanism erases the traces from both runs. Thus, the rat faces the next pair of runs in the session with a "clean slate" as regards traces from previous runs. Stimulus events that happen after the previous reset and before the next information run have the potential for interfering with traces of the information run in question and would be an instance of proactive interference. Stimulus events that occur during the IRI (i.e., after an information run but before the succeeding choice run) would commonly be said to have a potential for retroactive interference on traces of the preceding information run. However, that terminology presumes that the interfering effect is on the storage (or registration) of traces of the information run. If the IRI interference events affect retrieval, perhaps it, too, should be called proactive interference.

The procedures and theory described in this chapter have little to say regarding what constitutes an interfering event. Presumably, as seems to be the case in most memory experiments, similarity between the interpolated events and the event to be remembered would constitute the main factor. *A priori*, one would think that novel stimuli that evoke exploratory or investigatory responses would have high interfering value for rats because they also would involve place cues.

The reset mechanism does have the survival utility of protecting the organism against effects of proactive interference when it is faced with a sequence of very similar discriminations. The only evidence that there must be a reset mechanism is the fact that a plot of errors against successive trials produces a horizontal (or a nonsignificantly downward sloping) line, rather than an upward sloping line, which would obtain if there were a tendency to make more errors the farther into a session the organism goes.

The second row of the diagram (B) of Figure 34-1 indicates the state of relevant hypothetical traces. With the occurrence of the information run, a memory trace of the alley entered is set up in the animal's brain. During the IRI, a slight decay is indicated by a small decrease in trace strength. There is no evidence for that decay. It is presumed to occur because all nonrandom structures are supposed to decay toward random (according to the second law of thermodynamics) as a function of time. However, at the end of the IRI, there is still considerable trace left. After the hypothetical reset, the trace strength plunges to zero. When the rat is confronted with the next information run of the succeeding trial, there are no potentially interfering traces left from previous runs. (The "clear" button of its "calculator" has been pushed.)

Why the new designation of two types of memory? First of all, "dispositional" and "representational" seem to be more descriptive than other terms of what is interpreted as going on when organisms remember. Also, very similar previous typologies entail extra presumptions that restrict generality. For example, Honig's (1978) distinction between reference and working memory is very similar to the distinction between dispositional and representational memory. It is presumed, especially by Olton, Becker, and Handelmann

(1979), that the working memories last until the "end of the trial," where the reset takes place. It seems to me that the division of the continuous flow of stimulation–behavior into trials is an artifact of the behaviorist's laboratory. Such an important hypothetical mechanism for memory as "reset" that frees the behavior of higher vertebrates from the "tyranny of stimulation" would not have evolved if the traces lasted until the end of the trial. Then the only selective pressures to evolve the necessary brain circuits mediating representational memory would be from procedures in behaviorists' laboratories.

A similar problem arises with the distinction between long-term and short-term memory. At the empirical level, such a distinction depends on viewing the traces as time-dependent. Admittedly, at a theoretical (interpretational) level, the distinction is made in terms of the hypothetical information processing involved, not time *per se*. However, until the information processing can be empirically specified, the difference between long-term and short-term memories seems to be a matter of duration, and there is considerable variation from species to species and situation to situation.

This latter point clearly raises the problem of just how long representational memories last. (Dispositional memories last a long time, even a lifetime!). Presumably, representational memories do not last very long because they are especially vulnerable to retroactive interference. But how long they last is not strictly time-dependent. Their fate is to be destroyed by retroactive interference, and how much retroactive interference there is depends on circumstances that is, salience and similarity to the information in the information run, that impinge as stimuli on the organism's sensorium during the IRI.

A most relevant problem concerns the nature of the hypothetical reset mechanism. From research to date, there is little known about it, other than it must exist. *A priori*, two possibilities come to mind:

1. The mechanism could be cue-controlled and learned. The information processing by the brain, in a sense, says, "Remember after one-door runs; forget after 2-door runs.

2. Reset also could result from autochthonous changes in trace processing: The trace lasts until it is *used* (minus the presumed decay). Even though not *used*, the critical trace system would not last long because of its vulnerability to retroactive interference from similar *usages*. In a living organism, the brain is always "busy." There is continuous sensory input—some types of which are more interfering than others (presumably). However, there is the possibility that the reset mechanism is triggered by the trace system's being used; that is, whenever a discriminative response uses the trace system to guide a choice, that use destroys the trace system. The trace system, thus, is good for only one usage—and we call that fact a "reset."

All of this semantic "wheel spinning" is speculative, however. Clever and original research will have to be done to yield precise and operationally convincing characterizations. The following brief account summarizes some relevant research with rats.

The earliest study from our laboratory at the University of Rochester Medical Center (Thomas, 1978) on the memory problem used contingently rewarded delayed alternation by rats in a T-maze and found that posterodorsal septal lesions affected memory. Transection of the postcommissural fornix had no effect. Also, the posterodorsal septal lesions (precommissural fornix?) enhanced the susceptibility of rats to interference effects of intertrial delays and intertrial rotation. A subsequent study (Thomas, 1979) found that both spontaneous alternation (reinforced for running but not for alternating) and contingently reinforced alternation were seriously impaired by posterodorsal septal lesions, but the spontaneous alternation did not recover with continued training, as the contingently rewarded alternation did.

The recovery phenomenon was puzzling. We (Thomas & Brito, 1980) showed that normal (intact) rats would gradually recover alternation efficiency (contingently reinforced) when the intertrial interval (ITI) was lengthened from 0 to 90 sec. However, rats with posterodorsal septal lesions, although they could recover with 0-sec delay between trials, continued at chance levels of performance with a 90-sec ITI, which suggested that the recovery phenomenon depended in part on the extent of demands placed upon the representational-memory circuits. The study also found that the representational-memory system involved more than just the septo-hippocampal system. Lesions to medial frontal cortex (area 32) also produced a "loss with recovery" of the representational-memory task.

Further studies pursued the "anatomical problem." We found (Brito, Thomas, Davis, & Gingold, 1982) that lesions of mediodorsal thalamus also resulted in "loss with recovery," as did lesions in prelimbic cortex and posterodorsal septum. In a different T-maze, we (Thomas, Brito, & Stein, 1980) observed the "loss with recovery" after small lesions in the medial septal nucleus. However, the recovery was not as robust as that observed previously.

More recent studies using the paired-run procedure described above have found that it, like contingently rewarded alternation, is sensitive to medial septal lesions (Thomas & Spafford, 1984). We (Stanton, Thomas, & Brito, 1984) found the same thing (loss with recovery) in paired-run tests of both shift and stay tasks, although the recovery was not robust and the animals did not achieve preoperative levels of performance. We (Stanton et al., 1984) also obtained a gradual falling off in memory with IRIs of up to 210 sec in normal animals.

Also, lesions in additional anatomical structures were found by Yu and Wong (1982) to result in a loss with recovery of a paired-run representational-memory task. They found that olfactory bulbectomy dropped paired-run accuracy temporarily to chance levels, which is puzzling until one considers the projection to the olfactory bulbs from the homologue of the nucleus basalis of Meynert (nucleus basalis magnocellularis in rats). Small bilateral lesions in nucleus basalis magnocellularis had no deleterious effect after an IRI of only 10 sec, but there was a marked impairment with more difficult tasks, that is, after IRIs of 90 and 180 sec (Ordy, Thomas, & Blosser, 1983). Organisms with more highly evolved brains can handle more complicated representational-memory tasks, and probably it takes more brain to handle such complicated problems. For example, Spiegler and Mishkin (1981) found that after amygdaloid lesions monkeys were impaired in remembering (choosing) one from a number of stimulus objects that had been held in representational memory. With rats, amygdaloid lesions had no effect on representational memory for a single place (arm) in a T-maze (Ordy et al., 1983). Likewise, findings (Thomas & Gash, 1982) indicate that bilateral lesions that transected the mammillo-thalamic tracts resulted in the usual "loss with recovery."

Throughout these experiments, controls have consisted of just surgical controls (no brain damage) or various cortical lesions (dorsolateral frontal cortex, anterior cingulate cortex, or posterior visual cortex). None of these lesions had any effect on representational memory. Suggestive results are also indicated by misplaced lesions. Thus, a lesion in the anterior part of the medial septum had no effect. Neither did a lesion that was too posterior and was located mostly in paraventricular nucleus of the thalamus.

As these various structures do not form a preferentially and anatomically inter-connected system, one can only conclude that a good bit of brain is critically involved in the hypothetical circuitry that mediates representational-memory capabilities. Perhaps there are parallel circuits, and partial destruction of any one of them temporarily impairs representational memory. The rats do not forget what to do in the maze; they simply suffer impairment of the ability to guide a choice discrimination by their memory of the previous run, be it with contingently reinforced alternation or the paired-run procedure. Of course, the obvious conclusion is that the brain "honors" (to use Squire's word) the distinction between dispositional and representational memory.

We have also investigated other aspects of representational memory (Brito & Thomas, 1981). We found that posterodorsal septal lesions not only impaired retention of a contingently reinforced alternation task, but the lesions also slowed (but did not prevent) postoperative original learning. In addition, we showed that both learning and retention of single alternation in a runway (patterning) was impaired by posterodorsal lesions. How-ever, subsequent research (see Brito, Thomas, & Stanton, 1982) suggests that performances of "patterning" may not represent an unequivocal instance of representational memory. With the use of a plus-shaped elevated maze, we (Thomas, Brito, Stein, & Berko, 1982) found that, regardless of the location of the SB, performance was impaired by small medial septal lesions when correct alternation depended on a memory from the previous run, but performance was not impaired by the medial septal lesions when correct responding could be done on the basis of dispositional memory.

It has been known for a long time that the primary anterior input to the hippo-campus from the medial septal nucleus is predominately (if not entirely) cholinergic (e.g., see Dudar, 1975). The lesion studies in which the septo-hippocampal system was disrupted (medial septal lesions and postero-dorsal septal lesions) produced a significant and dramatic (if only temporary) impairment in representational memory. Therefore, it would be ex-pected that anticholinergic drugs would also impair performance on tasks that depend critically on representational memory. Such, indeed, seems to be the case.

Bilateral intracerebral injections of scopolamine into the hippocampus impaired contingently rewarded alternation but had a minor (at the highest dose) or no effect (at lower doses) on dispositional memory, measured as retention of a visual discrimination by the same rats in the same maze (Davis, Brito, Stopp, & Stanton, 1982). Likewise, in another laboratory and with a different experimenter (Ordy, Thomas, & Dunlap, 1982), bilateral intracerebral injections in hippocampus of scopolamine also impaired representa-tional memory with three different IRIs (0, 45, and 90 sec). In addition, there was a marked slowing of choice time, but a minor or nonsignificant effect on start and run times in the T-maze. It was observed that the rats acted during choice as if they were looking for a distinctive cue in the environment, but it was not there. It was in their brains and had been weakened or obliterated by the scopolamine. Their choice times were longer than normal because they tended to spend time in "vicarious trial and error," as Tolman called it.

Finally, atropine sulfate given intraperitoneally impaired representational memory in a dose-dependent manner in rats given the paired-run test. Methyl atropine at the highest dose (20 mg/kg) had no effect (Kasckow, Thomas, & Herndon, in press). The drug studies mentioned above are not yet definitive because some preliminary observations and experiments (unpublished) have found a marked tolerance (in terms of percentage correct choices) that appears after repeated intraperitoneal injections of both scopolamine and atropine.

It is disappointing to find little in the previous work on memory that impinges crucially on the ideas expressed in this chapter. There are two main reasons. First, as was said earlier, every learning–memory task that is used in memory research with lower animals involves both dispositional and representational memory. Therefore, any manipulations such as lesions or drugs can have consequences on memory performance, but usually they show up only as statistically significant effects with groups (the "sociology of rats"). The paired-run procedure separates the two types of memory and yields a (relatively) pure instance of representational memory as the chief dependent variable. This fact results in substantial depression of performance-indicating memory by those independent variables that impair representational memory. The effect shows up in every animal. This "pure case" isolation of representational memory is accomplished by two strategies:

1. A problem (adopted from matching-to-sample) must be selected in which, at the time of choice, there is no environmental event antecedent to the organism's sense organs that can act as a cue to guide a discrimination; correct discriminations can be made only if the organism's brain furnishes a cue representation of the information run (i.e., a *memory*).

2. In order to get a pure case of representational memory, all other sources of variance must be eliminated (or minimized). This is accomplished by extensive adaptation to habituate all disturbing neophobic and investigatory responses and by extensive pre-training of all dispositional learnings that are involved. The one-door trials and the pretesting training on the paired-run procedure before the introduction of a memory-affecting independent variable are necessary if one is to observe robust effects. Before the independent variables are introduced (drugs and lesions, so far), variance must be reduced by driving the animals against the ceiling of 100% accuracy to minimize effects of dispositional memory. The task requires that on each information run, a trial-specific learning must take place. On each succeeding choice run, the effectiveness of that learning is tested by the accuracy of the following choice. Choice accuracy is very sensitive to any faltering of the representational system. Of course, accuracy of performance would falter if any of the independent variables also affected the relevant dispositional-memory system. So far, no such independent variables have been found. It would be interesting to discover an independent variable whose manipulation would impair performance on a dispositional-memory task without disturbing basic discrimination ability or a representational-memory performance. (This presumes nothing so trite as loss of the ability to "remember" a visual discrimination after the severing of optic nerves!)

The second problem with relating the present notions to much of previous work on memory derives from concerns with generality. Much theory about memory seems to derive from empirical observations of the performance of humans. Memory in humans must be terribly species-specific as regards behavioral characteristics. *Homo sapiens* is the only organism with a high degree of linguistic facility. The human ability to make two types of responses—to discriminate at a nonlinguistic level (as in "lower" animals), and also to make use of a "second signal system" (Pavlov's term) that mediates linguistic discriminative responses (and the fact that these systems can interact in ways that are largely unknown but that probably change culturally over time)—makes it possible that effective rehearsal can take place. That capacity completely negates the possibility of discovering how a culture-free nervous system forms and uses memory traces and their time course. Consider, for instance, a human doing the paired-run procedure. During the information run, the person could say, "It's the left alley." During the IRI the person could frequently say to himself or herself, "It's the left one." Rehearsal (saying "It's the left one") could result in a tremendous lengthening of the apparent effective age of the memory. Nonlinguistic organisms can presumably, "rehearse" only by maintaining a fixed posture during the IRI (i.e., "pointing" toward the alley they went to on the information run). Observation and experimentation shows that they do not maintain a fixed orientation. They often whirl around and rush about during the IRI; they are handled by the experimenter during the IRI, which would also tend to break up any fixed orientation.

As an example of the difficulties of studying neural mechanisms of memory in the exceedingly complex human brain, consider the primary paradigm experiment on short-term memory by Peterson and Peterson (1959). By having their subjects busy their linguistic capacities with successive subtraction of threes to eliminate any effects of rehearsal, Peterson and Peterson found that the accuracy of the discrimination indicating memory (recalling the item to be remembered after one exposure) dropped off rapidly and approached zero after the passage of 18 sec. However, the rapidly falling performance curve does not define the time-binding capacity of the memory system. It reflects the deterioration of memory that results from retroactive inference by unknown stimulation. Brain clearly can "hold" representational memories longer than that. Some of Mac-Corquodale's (1947) rats in McCord's (1939) four-direction jumping-stand task for delayed response could discriminate at better than chance levels after 4 min and some sec of delay. In our study (Stanton *et al.*, 1984), the group median was close to chance (50%) accuracy with IRI delays of 210 sec, but some animals could do significantly better than chance (10 or more correct in 12 trials, expanded binomial) at that delay. In that case, the source of retroactive interference came from time spent during IRIs in the animal's home cage. One still does not know what would happen to the trace with zero retroactive interference, because even while restrained in its home cage, the rat's brain was active. In any event, the trace for a single experience lasted longer than 18 sec. The 18-sec length does not describe an intrinsic property of short-term memory traces. Instead, it indicates the declining success of discrimination guided by a hypothetical trace under conditions of no rehearsal and unknown retroactive interference effects.

Another difficulty with studying humans, besides the added complexity of the problem posed by their linguistic capabilities (and the obvious proscription of intrusive research with them), stems from their highly developed representational-memory capacity and the presumed complex interactions that are possible with dispositional memories. It is difficult to envision behavioral tests that could be applied to humans in which relatively pure instances of representational versus dispositional memories could be investigated. Perhaps there would be some possibility of applying the notions. One might suppose that a person suffering from an "amnesic syndrome" of short-term memory (Lhermitte & Signoret, 1976) might be able to discriminate eggs from sausage when they were set before him or her (a dispositional-memory task), but that the person would display marked impairment in differentially responding to a question as to which one he or she had for breakfast (a representational-memory task).

All this is not to say that memory research on humans has no point. Clearly, the memory capabilities of humans, although perhaps species-unique, presumably depend on basic neural mechanisms common to "higher" vertebrates. The argument simply is that it would be especially difficult, if not impossible, to elucidate basic neural mechanisms of memory with humans. The unique possession of linguistic capacity and the possibility of cultural (learned) modification of the interactions between linguistic and nonlinguistic discrimination poses the most difficult obstacle to elucidating the basic mechanisms of brain for time binding. Obviously, the characteristics of memory in humans, and their modification by drugs, disease, age, and brain injury, need further and continuous investigation. But the most general formulation will derive from study of evolutionarily simpler, culture-free, and nonlinguistic brains.

ACKNOWLEDGMENTS

I am indebted to Dr. Mark E. Stanton for many useful discussions concerning the memory problem, and to Charlotte Askins, Mary Capozzi, and Nancy Dintruff for assistance in preparing the manuscript.

REFERENCES

Bergson, H. L. [*Matter and memory*] (N. M. Paul & W. S. Palmer, trans.). London: Allen, 1910.

Brito, G. N. O., & Thomas, G. J. T-maze alternation, response patterning, and septo-hippocampal circuitry in rats. *Behavioural Brain Research*, 1981, *3*, 319–340.

Brito, G. N. O., Thomas, G. J., Davis, B. J., & Gingold, S. I. Prelimbic cortex, mediodorsal thalamus, septum and delayed alternation in rats. *Experimental Brain Research*, 1982, *46*, 52–58.

Brito, G. N. O., Thomas, G. J., & Stanton, M. E. Septo-hippocampal disconnections and go–no go discrimination in rats. *Behavorial and Neural Biology*, 1982, *34*, 427–432.

Bruner, J. S. Modalities of memory. In G. A. Talland & N. C. Waugh (Eds.), *The pathology of memory*. New York: Academic Press, 1969.

Davis, B. J., Brito, G. N. O., Stopp, L. C., & Stanton, M. E. Memory and the septo-hippocampal cholinergic system in the rat. *Society for Neuroscience Abstracts*, 1982, *8*, 322.

Dudar, J. D. Effects of septal nuclei stimulation on release of acetylcholine in rabbit hippocampus. *Brain Research*, 1975, *83*, 123–133.

Honig, W. K. Studies of working memory in the pigeon. In S. H. Hulse, H. Fowler, & W. K. Honig (Eds.), *Cognitive processes in animal behavior*. Hillsdale, N.J.: Erlbaum, 1978.

Hunter, W. S. The delayed reaction in animals and children. *Behavior Monographs*. 1913, *2*, 1–86.

Hunter, W. S. The temporal maze and kinesthetic sensory processes in the white rat. *Psychobiology*, 1920, *2*, 1–17.

James, W. *The principles of psychology* (Vol. 1). New York: Henry Holt, 1890.

Kasckow, J. W., Thomas, G. J., & Herndon, R. M. Performance factors in regard to impaired memory and tolerance induced by atropine sulfate. *Physiological Psychology*, in press.

Lhermitte, F., & Signoret, J.-L. The amnesic syndromes and the hippocampal–mammillary system. In M. R. Rosenzweig & E. L. Bennett (Eds.), *Neural mechanisms of learning and memory*. Cambridge, Mass.: MIT Press, 1976.

MacCorquodale, K. An analysis of certain cues in the delayed response. *Journal of Comparative and Physiological Psychology*, 1947, *40*, 239–253.

McCord, F. The delayed reaction and memory in rats. *Journal of Comparative Psychology*, 1939, *27*, 1–37.

Olton, D. S., Becker, J. T., & Handelmann, G. E. Hippocampus, space, and memory. *Behavioral and Brain Sciences*, 1979, *2*, 313–365.

Ordy, J. M., Thomas, G., & Dunlap, W. Cholinergic drug effects on recent memory in aged rats. *Society for Neuroscience Abstracts*, 1982, *8*, 442.

Ordy, J. M., Thomas, G., Dunlap, W., & Blosser, J. Comparison of memory in rats after lesions in medial septal area, nuc. basalis magnocellularis, and amygdala. *Society for Neuroscience Abstracts*, 1983, *9*, 639.

Peterson, L. R., & Peterson, M. J. Short-term memory of individual verbal items. *Journal of Experimental Psychology*, 1959, *58*, 193–198.

Ryle, G. *The concept of mind*. London: Hutchinson, 1949.

Schacter, D. L. *Stranger behind the engram: Theories of memory and the psychology of science*. Hillsdale, N.J.: Erlbaum, 1982.

Solomon, P. R., Vander Schaaft, E. C., Nobre, A. C., Weisz, D. J., & Thompson, R. F. Hippocampus and trace conditioning of the rabbit's nictitating membrane response. *Society for Neuroscience Abstracts*, 1983, *9*, 645.

Spiegler, B. J., & Mishkin, M. Evidence for the sequential participation of inferior temporal cortex and amygdala in the acquisition of stimulus–reward associations. *Behavioural Brain Research*, 1981, *3*, 303–317.

Squire, L. R. The neuropsychology of human memory. *Annual Review of Neuroscience*, 1982, *5*, 241–273.

Stanton, M. E., Thomas, G. J., & Brito, G. N. O. Posterodorsal septal lesions impair performance on both shift and stay working memory tasks. *Behavioral Neuroscience*, 1984, *98*, 405–415.

Thomas, G. J. Delayed alternation in rats after pre- or postcommissural fornicotomy. *Journal of Comparative and Physiological Psychology*, 1978, *92*, 1128–1136.

Thomas, G. J. Comparison of effects of small lesions in posterodorsal septum on spontaneous and rerun correction (contingently reinforced) alternation in rats. *Journal of Comparative and Physiological Psychology*, 1979, *93*, 685–694.

Thomas, G. J., & Brito, G. N. O. Recovery of delayed alternation in rats after lesions in medial frontal cortex and septum. *Journal of Comparative and Physiological Psychology*, 1980, *94*, 808–818.

Thomas, G. J., Brito, G. N. O., & Stein, D. P. Medial septal nucleus and delayed alternation in rats. *Physiological Psychology*, 1980, *8*, 467–472.

Thomas, G. J., Brito, G. N. O., Stein, D. P., & Berko, J. K. Memory and septo-hippocampal connections in rats. *Journal of Comparative and Physiological Psychology*, 1982, *96*, 339–347.

Thomas, G. J., & Gash, D. M. *Hypothalamic lesions and representational memory in rats*. Unpublished research, Center for Brain Research, University of Rochester Medical Center, 1982.

Thomas, G. J., & Spafford, P. S. Deficits for representational memory induced by septal and cortical lesions (singly and combined) in rats. *Behavioral Neuroscience*, 1984, *98*, 394–404.

Tulving, E. Episodic and semantic memory. In E. Tulving & W. D. Donaldson (Eds.), *Organization of memory*. New York: Academic Press, 1972.

Yu, S., & Wong, C. *Comparative effects of medial septal lesions and olfactory bulbectomy on representational memory and olfactory discrimination*. Unpublished manuscript, Center for Brain Research, University of Rochester Medical Center, 1982.

35

Posterior Parietal Association Cortex and Hippocampus: Equivalency of Mnemonic Function in Animals and Humans

Raymond P. Kesner and Bruce V. DiMattia

In recent years there has been a renewed interest in a neural system analysis of the structural organization of memory in humans and animals. This interest has been kindled by the improved methods of detecting brain damage in humans through a variety of scanning techniques, as well as by improved behavioral methodology for studying multiple components of the cognitive system in both animals and humans. Since brain damage leading to memory pathology in humans tends to be extensive and extremely variable, it is of critical importance to develop animal models that mimic functionally similar mnemonic deficits following more localized brain damage. The paucity in the number of existing models derives from the hesitation of some scientists to accept the assumption of both mental (i.e., mnemonic function) and neural evolutionary continuity and from the lack of suitable testing methods to access cognitive function in animals.

In this chapter, we propose a correspondence between animals and humans in terms of brain–memory function. More specifically, we attempt to demonstrate that damage to either the hippocampus or the posterior parietal association cortex (PPC) results in functionally different sets of mnemonic deficits and residual capacities in both animals and humans. We also propose a theoretical framework aimed at integrating a neural system analysis of brain function with the structural organization of memory.

Hippocampus: Humans

In humans it has been assumed that the hippocampus is critically involved in some aspect of memory, because bilateral medial temporal lobe damage that includes the hippocampus produces a profound amnesia for new information. Patients with such damage appear to forget quite readily events that occur in their daily lives. As an example, they are usually unable to tell what they have done throughout the day, including food they have eaten or people they have met. In contrast, they are able to communicate normally at least about events that have occurred prior to their brain damage or are occurring at present. Further, their verbal skills are intact, and they can carry out mental arithmetic. Thus, one cardinal feature of the amnesic syndrome in these patients appears to be an impairment of processes associated with long-term memory (LTM) for specific events, with normal operation of

Raymond P. Kesner and Bruce V. DiMattia. Department of Psychology, University of Utah, Salt Lake City, Utah.

processes associated with short-term memory (STM). One elegant study (Baddeley & Warrington, 1970) serves to illustrate this main point. It is well known that immediate free recall of a list of words results in a serial-position curve with better memory performance for the first items (primacy effect) and the last items (recency effect), compared to items located in the middle of the list. It has been proposed by some theorists that the primacy effect reflects information storage in LTM, while the recency effect reflects information processing in STM (Atkinson & Shiffrin, 1968). However, it should be noted that there are other interpretations for the serial-position effect. For example, it has been suggested that the recency effect reflects automatic availability of information requiring little attention, whereas the primacy effect reflects the utilization of controlled or effortful attention-directing activity (Hasher & Zacks, 1979; Kinsbourne & Wood, 1982; Shiffrin & Schneider, 1977). Baddeley and Warrington (1970) presented 10 unrelated words to amnesic and control patients, followed by an immediate test of free recall. Compared to controls, amnesic patients had an impaired primacy effect, but no impairment of the recency effect. A similar pattern of results was obtained in patient H. M. and patients with large left hippocampus removal (Milner, 1978).

This pattern of results suggests that amnesic patients can remember the (specious) present by maintaining distinctive information within STM with the use of automatic processes that do not require active attention. In contrast, these patients do not effectively utilize controlled or effortful attention processes (e.g., rehearsal or other mnemonic strategies) that are usually employed in the encoding and storage of new distinctive information within LTM. This inability to use appropriate processes of active attention might limit the distinctiveness of new events and might result in accelerated forgetting. Indeed, it has been shown that patient H. M. and patients receiving electroconvulsive shock therapy, which presumably alters hippocampus function, show more rapid forgetting when performance on an STM test has been equated for possible problems with level of initial learning (Huppert & Piercy, 1977, 1979; Squire, 1981).

It should be noted that the theoretical framework mentioned above suggests a role for memory function within the hippocampus based on some process component of memory, without specifying the exact nature of the memory to be processed. Given a renewed interest in the structural organization of memory, it is not surprising that in recent years there has been an emphasis on a second cardinal feature of amnesic patients— namely, that they can learn reasonably well and can retain a variety of rules of specific perceptual–motor skills (tracking, mirror tracing, eyelid conditioning) and pattern-analyzing skills (mirror reading, rule-based verbal paired-associate learning, rules of card games), while not remembering any of their previous performances of the task, the specific contingencies of the task, or the time and place at which they learned the task. This dissociation can be thought of as reflecting a distinction between episodic and semantic memory (Kinsbourne & Wood, 1975; Tulving, 1972), working and reference memory (Olton, Becker, & Handelmann, 1980), or between procedural or rule-based memory ("knowing how") and declarative or data-based memory ("knowing that") (Cohen & Squire, 1980). There are many recent examples of this dissociation. To mention a few, Weiskrantz and Warrington (1979) demonstrated that amnesic patients could acquire and retain classical eyelid conditioning, but that they could neither remember performing the task nor describe the apparatus or the procedure. Cohen and Squire (1980) demonstrated that amnesic patients could acquire and retain a mirror-reading skill, but that between sessions they could not remember repeated words that made up the reading task. In summary, this feature of the amnesic syndrome emphasizes the nature of hippocampus involvement in the structural organization of memory by suggesting that the hippocampus actively encodes distinctive temporal–spatial aspects of events (context), which reflect declarative knowledge, rather than encoding rules, which would reflect procedural knowledge.

Based on this constellation of deficits and residual capacities, it can be argued that the hippocampus represents a specific neural substrate for declarative or episodic knowledge concerning distinctive events that occur within a specific context. It is possible that the context is influenced by both external stimuli and internal states. Based on previous experiments in our laboratory, it appears that the hippocampus subserves declarative knowledge of primarily the external context, independently from coding of internal contextual states (Kesner & Hardy, 1983). The processing of internal states might be mediated by other neural regions (e.g., amygdala).

The processing of external contextual information as a subset of declarative knowledge can involve both automatic and controlled attention processes. It would appear that hippocampus-damaged patients can utilize external contextual information only in situations in which automatic attention processes are sufficient for efficient performance. Thus, as a working hypothesis, one can characterize the hippocampus-damaged patient as having deficits in memory tasks that require effortful or controlled attention in the processing of declarative knowledge concerning the external context.

Hippocampus: Animals

For many years, attempts to develop an animal model of the human amnesic syndrome with presumed hippocampus damage have been unsuccessful. A number of suggestions have been made to resolve this discrepancy. The first and simplest idea is that the function of the hippocampus is different in animals and humans. A second possibility is that the amnesic syndrome produced by medial temporal lobe lesions in humans is not due to hippocampus damage, but to damage of other structures. For example, Horel (1978) suggested that damage to the temporal stem containing input and output pathways of temporal cortex and amygdala is necessary for memory impairment. This idea was based on an extensive review of the literature and on the experimental observation that cuts of the temporal stem in monkeys abolished a preoperatively learned visual pattern discrimination. Mishkin (1978), on the other hand, suggested that the amnesic syndrome is due not only to hippocampus damage, but to a combination of hippocampus plus amygdala damage. He demonstrated in monkeys that in a delayed matching-to-sample task neither amygdala nor hippocampus lesions alone produced a deficit, but a severe performance deficit was observed with combined lesions.

A third possibility is that the hippocampus is critically involved in some aspect of LTM, but that the tasks used to test memory in animals are not equivalent to those used to test human memory. For example, Iversen (1976) has argued that the major effect of hippocampus lesions leading to LTM deficits is excessive interference. Since most animal tests tend to be simple and very repetitive, there often is little interference, and deficits might not be expected.

Based on the assumption that in the past inadequate tests of memory function have been employed, we would like to demonstrate that more complex tests of mnemonic function might indeed reveal that the same cardinal features described above for amnesic patients apply to hippocampus-damaged rats. Previously, it was demonstrated that sub-seizure levels of electrical stimulation of the dorsal hippocampus during or after a training trial can result in a disruption of retention at a long-term retention test (minutes to hours) without altering performance on a short-term retention test (seconds to minutes) in one-trial passive-avoidance, one-trial appetitive-learning, and eight-choice spatial matching-to-sample tasks (Berman & Kesner, 1976; Bierley, Kesner, & Novak, 1983; Kesner & Conner, 1974). It is assumed that electrical stimulation serves as a temporary disruptive agent of normal dorsal hippocampus function. One could argue, however, that electrical stimulation of the hippocampus does not represent a comparable condition to that seen with brain damage in amnesic patients. Thus, we present the results of two studies aimed at demonstrating that hippocampus-damaged rats have dysfunctions and residual capacities similar to those observed in amnesic patients with presumed hippocampus damage.

In the first study, rats were first trained to perform in an Olton eight-arm radial maze (see Olton & Samuelson, 1976). Following acquisition, animals received during the study phase of the trial (one per day) a piece of Froot Loop cereal as reinforcement in one of the eight arms of the maze. The arm containing the food was varied randomly from day to day. Ten seconds after finding the food, the animal was returned to its home cage for either a 1-min or a 2-hr delay period. Following the delay period, the animal was returned to the maze and given a retention test (test phase). Correct performance during the test phase required the animal to return to the previously reinforced arm (i.e., the animal had to use a "win-stay" rule) in order to receive an additional piece of Froot Loop cereal. An error was defined as an entry into an arm not containing the reinforcement. After extensive training, rats could remember the correct arm (made few errors) after a 1-min or a 2-hr delay period.

Animals then received dorsal hippocampus lesions and were retested for 16 trials at each delay period. The order of presentation of each delay period was randomly determined. The mean number of errors per trial based on the last 8 trials per delay prior to the lesion and 16 trials per delay after the lesion is shown in Figure 35-1. One can clearly observe that the lesioned animals made few errors at 1-min delay, but significantly more errors at 2-hr delay. These results are consistent with previous findings using electrical brain stimulation of the hippocampus in the same task (Bierley et al., 1983). They also support the idea that hippocampus-lesioned animals can apply the "win–stay" rule for relatively short delay periods resulting in normal STM performance, but cannot apply the rule at long delay periods (perhaps because of inability to use active attention processes), resulting in a deficient LTM performance. Note also that one can interpret these data as representing an example of accelerated forgetting and are thus consistent with the Huppert and Piercy data (1977, 1979).

In a second study (Kesner & Novak, 1982), rats were trained on an eight-arm radial maze for Froot Loop reinforcement. After extensive training, each animal was allowed on each trial (one per day) to visit all eight arms in an order that was randomly selected for that trial. The sequencing of the eight arms was accomplished by sequential opening of Plexiglas doors (one at a time) located at the entrance of each arm. This constituted the study phase. Immediately (within 20 sec) after the animal had received reinforcement from

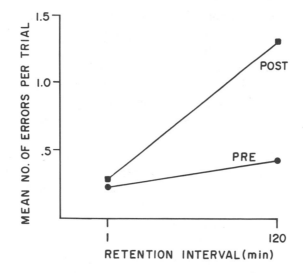

FIGURE 35-1. Mean number of errors per trial at short (1-min) and long (120-min) retention delays before (pre) and after (post) dorsal hippocampus lesions.

the last of the eight arms (i.e., completed the study phase), the test phase began. Only one test was given for each trial and consisted of opening two doors simultaneously. On a random basis, either the first and second, fourth and fifth, or seventh and eighth doors that occurred in the sequence were selected for the test. The rule to be learned, leading to an additional reinforcement, was to choose the arm that occurred earlier in the sequence. All rats displayed a serial-position curve—that is, prominent retention (a performance better than chance [50%]) for the recency and primacy components of the list, but no retention (chance performance) for the middle portion of the list. The same animals were then given additional trials, with a 10-min delay between study and test phases. This procedure resulted in a disruption of the recency portion of the serial-position curve without markedly altering the primacy component. It is important to note that this is the first demonstration of a prominant serial-position curve in rats. Some animals then received a dorsal hippo-campus lesion, while other animals served as sham-operated controls. Since the sham operation had no deleterious effect on the serial-position curve, the other animals were subsequently subjected to dorsal hippocampus lesions. At the immediate test, the lesioned animals displayed excellent retention only for the recency component of the list, but no retention (chance performance) for the primacy component. All animals were then given additional tests, with a 10-min delay between study and test phases. Under those conditions, hippocampus-lesioned animals performed at chance levels for all items of the list, indicating that they had no memory for order information. The results of this experiment are remarkably similar to the performance of amnesic patients, including H. M., on memory for a list of items (Baddeley & Warrington, 1970; Milner, 1978), in that hippocampus damage disrupted the primacy but not the recency component of the serial-position curve. Furthermore, with an additional delay between presentation and retention test, the hippocampus-lesioned animals demonstrated no retention—a finding that is similar to what has been described clinically with amnesic patients.

More recently, we have been able to show that rats can also display a serial-position curve for memory of items (places on a maze), given that a "win–stay" rule is required (DiMattia & Kesner, in press). Preliminary data suggest that hippocampus-lesioned animals show memory for the later items (recency component), but poor memory for the early items (primacy component) in the list. Thus, in hippocampus-damaged rats it has been possible to reproduce one cardinal feature of the amnesic syndrome—namely, a disruption of processes associated with LTM for specific external contextual events without altering processes associated with STM.

An additional important observation in this study is that lesioned rats could remember the previously learned rule (choose the arm that occurred earlier in the sequence), given that the retention test employed a choice between the last items of the sequence. This suggests that hippocampus damage does not interfere with the ability to remember the rule and that the deficit in remembering the early items of a particular sequence might have been due to the inability to direct attention to the specific and unique details characteristic of appropriate encoding of the early items. Thus, the studies mentioned above provide some indirect support for the second cardinal feature of the amnesic syndrome—namely, that specific rules can be learned and remembered, while the time and place at which the initial information was experienced are forgotten.

Posterior Parietal Association Cortex: Humans

Damage to the PPC in humans results in a number of intellectual and behavioral deficits. Among these are disorders of attention, affect, personality, sensation, motor control, spatial perception, spatial memory, and certain specific intellectual capacities, such as the ability to write or to perform mathematical operations. The particular constellation of symptoms observed in a subject is somewhat dependent upon whether the damage is to the dominant or the nondominant hemisphere. For example, clinical investigations have shown that the dominant PPC plays a role in language processes and that the nondominant PPC plays a role in spatial processes (Ruff & Volpe, 1981; Saffran & Marin, 1975; Warrington & Shalice, 1969). It is for this reason that we concentrate our discussion on the nondominant hemisphere in humans when making comparisons to bilateral damage of the PPC in animals, although it is to be recognized that a certain degree of functional overlap exists between the two human lobes. For example, although the symptom of topographical amnesia might occur primarily after damage to the nondominant hemisphere, a certain percentage of subjects with damage to the dominant hemisphere also manifest the disturbance (McFie & Zangwill, 1960). Furthermore, a bilateral lesion in humans often results in an even greater deficit than what might be expected from a unilateral lesion.

With respect to mnemonic information processing, humans with PPC damage have deficits for information concerning spatial aspects of their environment. These deficits include such symptoms as an inability to draw maps or diagrams of familiar spatial locations and a general loss of "topographic sense," which may involve the loss of long-term geographic knowledge, as well as an inability to form a "cognitive map" of new environments. Memory for spatial events thus appears to be impaired (Benton, 1969; Di Renzi, Faglioni, & Villa, 1977).

In addition, there is a profound inattention (sensory neglect) to all sensory stimuli impinging upon a patient with PPC damage from the side contralateral to the lesion. For example, such a patient might fail to dress on the side of his or her body contralateral to the side of the lesion, and in the extreme case, might deny the existence of his or her hand on that side. Further, when asked to draw on a sheet of paper, such a patient might concentrate his or her drawing on the contralateral side of the paper.

It is interesting to note that although PPC patients exhibit a deficit in attention to spatial stimuli, the deficit appears to be dependent upon the level of difficulty of the particular task at hand. For instance, Di Renzi *et al.* (1977) described a patient, M. A., who was able to perform on a test of spatial memory span with the same level of accuracy as normal individuals. This test required the patient to point to cubes previously tapped by the examiner. However, M. A. was unable to solve a more difficult spatial task, the visual stylus maze (Milner, 1965), and exhibited topographical disorientation, despite the fact that there was no global amnesia and performance on other cognitive and verbal tests was normal.

Another example of the apparent dependency of the occurrence of a spatial attention deficit on the level of difficulty of the task might possibly be found in the phenomenon referred to as "extinction." A patient recovering from total contralateral neglect is at first able to detect a stimulus only when presented to the ipsilateral side, but is eventually able to respond to a stimulus object when it is presented in either spatial hemifield. However, if the task is made slightly more difficult by means of the simultaneous presentation of two similar stimuli, one to each side of the patient, the patient is able to notice only the stimulus on the side ipsilateral to the lesion.

A final example, somewhat related to the previous one, is found in the fact that PPC patients sometimes manifest what has been described as a "piecemeal" approach to spatial problems (Paterson & Zangwill, 1944), such as drawing or block constructions. Here, the patient is apparently only able to attend to one object at a time or to one isolated segment of a problem, which leads to an inability to integrate elementary spatial relations into a composite whole. For example, the patient might be able to describe isolated parts of a painting, but is unable to describe the general theme of the work. Warrington and her colleagues (Warrington & Taylor, 1973) have described a similar phenomenon. Patients with right PPC lesions, although capable of recognizing objects shown in familiar views, are badly impaired when it comes to recognizing objects in unfamiliar views. The implication is that the processing of rudimentary spatial relations occurs automatically, while higher-level integration of spatial relations within the immediate external environment requires more effortful processing involving the PPC.

Thus, based on this constellation of deficits and residual capacities, it can be argued that the PPC represents a specific neural substrate for procedural or semantic knowledge concerning space. Furthermore, it is possible that the application of rules utilizing information about spatial events within a "cognitive map" might operate independently of temporal-coding processes. Rules associated with procedural knowledge concerning time might be mediated by other cortical regions (e.g., frontal cortex). The application of mnemonic rules requires attention, which might vary in degree along a continuum from automatic to controlled or effortful processing (Hasher & Zacks, 1979; Shiffrin & Schneider, 1977). It would appear that PPC patients can utilize spatial rules only when relatively automatic attention is required. Thus, as a working hypothesis, one can characterize the PPC patient as having deficits in memory tasks requiring effortful or controlled attention in applying procedural knowledge concerning space.

Posterior Parietal Association Cortex: Animals

Monkeys with PPC lesions appear to manifest a constellation of deficits that is quite similar to the one typically observed in humans with right PPC damage. The symptom of contralateral neglect, for instance, although somewhat less profound than in humans, is nevertheless present in the monkey. Further, monkeys, as with humans, exhibit deficits on spatial problems; they are deficient in their ability to find their way back to their home cage from the center of a room and in their ability to solve maze tasks.

In agreement with the human data, we now offer support for the postulation that the degree of difficulty of a task is an important determinant of the manifestation of a spatial deficit in animals. First, monkeys with PPC lesions are able to solve easy bent-wire "route-finding" tasks (Petrides & Iversen, 1979), but, relative to normal control animals, they are unable to solve a similar but more difficult version of the task. Second, monkeys with PPC lesions perform significantly worse on a landmark-reversal task (Pohl, 1973) than on a place-reversal task. As anticipated, the landmark-reversal task is considerably more difficult for animals to learn than the place-reversal task, suggesting that the former task might require relatively more controlled or effortful processing than the latter. Third, the phenomenon of extinction that is seen in human PPC patients is likewise seen in monkeys, albeit to a somewhat less profound degree.

Findings from behavioral–electrophysiological experiments with monkeys lend additional support to the idea that PPC is perhaps critically involved in the mediation of effortful attention in applying procedural knowledge concerning space. Neurons have been identified that are only active when the monkey is effortfully attending to an object in its visual field. The object not only must be in a specific sector of the visual field in order to trigger increased firing rates, but also must be within arm's reach and must have some motivational significance for the animal (Mountcastle, Lynch, Georgopoulos, Sakata, & Acuna, 1975). Additionally, cells may require that the object be moving in a specific direction, often with the additional requirement that the movement be within a specific area of immediate extrapersonal space. In other words, these nerve cells will show a change in response level only if the animal is paying attention to a number of critical inputs that are present, suggesting high-level, multifarious integration of stimulus information that is predominantly spatial in nature.

Hence, it appears that there are important correspondences between humans and monkeys in terms of attention deficits and poor performance on learning tasks that require learning of spatial rules.

Ablations of PPC in the rat have been consistently associated with learning deficits on mazes and maze-like tasks, a finding that compares well with the evidence from humans and monkeys. However, with rats, very few tasks have been employed that have specifically tested for spatial-memory deficits, and little systematic analysis of attention requirements of the tasks has been carried out.

We have recently demonstrated that we can vary the degree of required attention that an animal must employ in order to solve a maze task. Rats were given lists of spatial events (arms) in an Olton eight-arm radial maze. During the study phase of a trial, animals were allowed to enter five arms, one at a time. Both the order and the subset of five of eight arms were varied from trial to trial. They were then given a test of their memory for the arms visited during the study phase by means of a forced-choice testing procedure (see Roberts & Smythe, 1979), in which the animals were presented with one previously visited arm and one novel arm. The animal had to choose between these two test arms in order to obtain additional reinforcement. One group of rats was required to return to the previously visited arm (win–stay), and a second group was required to choose the novel arm (win–shift). It is assumed that these two conditions have differential attention requirements, because (1) the win–shift procedure is considerably easier for the animal to learn than the win–stay procedure; and (2) with the win–stay procedure rats have shown a serial-position curve that includes significant primacy and recency effects, whereas with the win–shift procedure only recency effects have been seen (DiMattia & Kesner, in press).

We now present a study that was designed to test whether there might be a greater correspondence between animals and humans by investigating the effects of PPC lesions in the rat on memory for a list of items in the task mentioned above. Rats trained as described above in the win–stay or win–shift procedure were given aspiration lesions of the PPC. They were then given postlesion testing. The percentage of correct responses as a function of serial position, strategy required, and pre- versus postoperative tests is shown in Figures 35-2 and 35-3. In the win–stay condition, rats' ability to perform was deleteriously affected by bilateral removal of PPC (see Figure 35-2); that is, there was a disruption of memory performance for every position on the list. However, comparable lesions of PPC did not produce any impairment of postoperative performance in the win–shift condition (see Figure 35-3), which presumably requires less attention. It should be noted that sham-operated animals did not show a deficit in the win–stay condition.

In the task requiring the win–stay strategy, the results could be interpreted as reflecting a deficit in controlled attention processing and an inability to utilize the appropriate spatial rules. No differential disruptive effects on primacy and recency compo-

FIGURE 35-2. Percentages of correct responses as a function of serial position for win–stay animals before (pre) and after (post) PPC lesions.

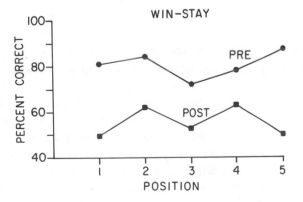

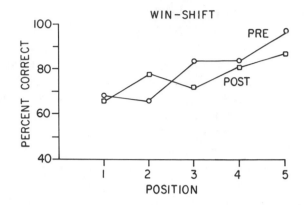

FIGURE 35-3. Percentages of correct responses as a function of serial position for win–shift animals before (pre) and after (post) PPC lesions.

nents of the list were expected, because the PPC does not process rules concerning temporal aspects of the environment. Furthermore, one can eliminate the possibility that PPC lesions produced adverse effects on motor performance or motivational systems, because PPC-damaged animals showed no memory deficits in the win–shift condition, which is identical in every respect to the win–stay condition except for the specific rule that must be employed during the test phase of a trial. In the task requiring the win–shift strategy, the results could reflect residual capacity of PPC-damaged animals, allowing for the application of relatively automatic attention processes to spatial rules. However, one cannot rule out the possibility that for successful performance in the win–shift condition, a different nonspatial rule (e.g., a response rule) might be of greater importance.

Thus, this study provides some support for an equivalency of mnemonic function (utilization of controlled attention processes applied to the operation of spatial rules) of the PPC in both rats and humans.

Attribute Model of Memory

Given that there is a correspondence in rats and humans in mnemonic function of the hippocampus and the PPC, it should also be possible to apply a common theoretical framework. We have previously proposed an attribute theory of memory organization (Kesner, 1980). The theory is based on the assumption that LTM consists of a set or bundle of traces, each representing some attribute or feature of a learning experience. This assumption is not novel; rather, it has become generally accepted as a model of memory representation by many theoreticians studying human information processing (Bower, 1967; Tulving, 1972; Underwood, 1969) and more recently in the study of animal memory (Spear, 1976). This multidimensional scaling of the memory trace contrasts with the assumption that the structure of memory consists of a monolithic or dual trace.

Within this multidimensional framework of memory, there are at least four possible explanations of how memories are stored. First, it is possible that attributes are organized in a hierarchical fashion, based upon importance. Thus, the most important attributes may be stored at one level of the hierarchy and may determine the storage of less important attributes at different levels. Second, it is possible that attributes are organized independently, all attributes being of equal importance. The third possibility suggests that attributes can be stored independently, but that specific attributes can be stored at differential rates. The fourth possibility suggests that attributes are organized in a heterarchical network employing both sequential and independent systems. As an example of the last possibility, one could envision that the coding of spatial–temporal attributes of an event might be processed simultaneously as a subset of contextual attributes and as a subset of procedural and declarative knowledge. In addition, contextual attributes might be processed as subsets of procedural and declarative knowledge.

A second assumption of the theory is that different neural "units" subserve different attributes. The neuroanatomical "unit" of analysis (e.g., synapse, synaptic conglomerate, synaptic assembly, neuron, neural assembly, junctional thicket, simple circuit, neural region, system, or complex system; see Welker, 1976) cannot be specified at the present time. We arbitrarily use neural regions, such as the hippocampus and the PPC, as the initial neural units of analysis; however, with more refined techniques, specific subregions within each of the larger units might emerge as the more critical units of analysis. The stronger version of the assumption would propose that each specific neural region stores (contains the mnemonic representation of) a specific attribute or set of attributes. The weaker version of the assumption would propose that each specific neural region processes only information represented by a specific attribute or set of attributes. The organization of these attributes will largely be determined by the anatomical and functional nature of the interconnections of the critical neural regions subserving the important attributes.

A third assumption is that critical neural regions will be in an active state when in the presence of a corresponding set of attributes associated with the processing of mnemonic information. The duration and degree (e.g., number of local circuits) of activation is greatly influenced by attention processes (automatic and controlled). Thus, automatic attention processes would result in short duration and less extensive activation of critical neural circuits providing for accessibility to (1) information at short time delays (STM) in the case of temporal attributes, (2) information of the immediate spatial environment in the case of spatial attributes, and (3) information concerning the short-term aspects of the external context in the case of spatial–temporal attributes.

In contrast, controlled attention processes would increase the duration and the number of activated critical neural circuits and thus would increase the probability that (1) in the case of temporal attributes, information might be accessible at longer time delays (LTM); (2) in the case of spatial attributes, information might have access to multiple relationships between and among spatial components of the immediate environment; and (3) in the case of spatial–temporal attributes, information might be accessible to long-term aspects of the external context. Furthermore, it should be noted that implicit in this formulation is the assumption that temporal attributes employ largely duration of activation, whereas spatial attributes employ largely extent of activation of critical neural circuits as a means of coding information.

Within the context of the attribute theory of memory, we have proposed that the hippocampus encodes, stores, and retrieves information concerning the utilization of declarative knowledge of the external context, consisting of both temporal and spatial attributes. Furthermore, prolonged and extensive activation of the hippocampus occurs whenever the task requires controlled attention coupled with the presence of a distinctive external context.

In contrast, the PPC encodes, stores, and retrieves information concerning the utilization of procedural knowledge (rules) of spatial attributes of the external environment. These spatial attributes would be employed in remembering the location and movements of objects, relative to body position and the immediate surrounding space. Furthermore, extensive but not necessarily prolonged activation of the PPC occurs whenever the learning situation requires effortful or controlled attention, coupled with the need to apply spatial rules.

The attribute model of memory can easily account for the hippocampus and PPC syndromes in animals and humans. Given that the hippocampus is limited to the controlled and effortful processing of temporal and spatial attributes encompassing a subset of the external context, deficits would be expected only when distinctive events that have occurred in specific places must be remembered at some later time (in the order of minutes, hours, days). No deficits (residual memory capacity) would be expected when distinctive spatial events have to be remembered immediately, in which case automatic attention processing might suffice and/or involve the operation of rules. In the case of PPC, its function appears to be limited to the processing of rules associated with spatial attributes requiring effortful attention. Thus, deficits would be expected only when spatial rules need to be utilized in situations requiring a great deal of attention. No deficits (residual memory capacity) would be expected when spatial rules need to be utilized in situations requiring relatively automatic attention processes or when temporal rules need to be used.

The attribute theory as applied to brain–memory function in humans and animals has many similarities to the idea that there are two types of memory—namely, episodic or declarative memory versus semantic or procedural memory—but it is more explicit in identifying the specific attributes and critical neuronal substrates that are involved in these two types of memory. Furthermore, this version of the attribute theory incorporates the process of attention to provide for extent and duration of neuronal activation of critical circuits mediating corresponding attributes. Also, the multidimensional nature of the attribute theory implies that many other neural regions are involved in the coding of different attributes (e.g., amygdala in coding of internal context, frontal cortex in coding of temporal rules) that contribute to the structural organization of memory.

In summary, we hope that we have established a correspondence in brain–memory function between animals and humans on both an empirical and a conceptual level.

REFERENCES

Atkinson, R. C., & Shiffrin, R. M. Human memory: A proposed system and its control process. In K. W. Spence & J. T. Spence (Eds.), *Advances in the psychology of learning and motivation: Research and theory* (Vol. 2). New York: Academic Press, 1968.

Baddeley, A. D., & Warrington, E. K. Amnesia and the distinction between long- and short-term memory. *Journal of Verbal Learning and Verbal Behavior*, 1970, *9*, 176–189.

Benton, A. L. Disorders of spatial orientation. In P. J. Vinken & G. W. Bruyn (Eds.), *Handbook of clinical neurology* (Vol. 3). Amsterdam: North-Holland, 1969.

Berman, R. F., & Kesner, R. P. Posttrial hippocampal, amygdaloid and lateral hypothalamic electrical stimulation: Effects upon memory of an appetitive experience. *Journal of Comparative and Physiological Psychology*, 1976, *90*, 260–267.

Bierley, R. A., Kesner, R. P., & Novak, K. J. Episodic long-term memory in the rat: Effects of hippocampal stimulation. *Journal of Comparative and Physiological Psychology*, 1983, *97*, 42–48.

Bower, G. A multicomponent theory of the memory trace. In K. W. Spence & J. T. Spence (Eds.), *The psychology of learning and motivation* (Vol. 1). New York: Academic Press, 1967.

Cohen, N. J., & Squire, L. R. Preserved learning and retention of pattern-analyzing skill in amnesia: Dissociation of knowing how and knowing that. *Science*, 1980, *210*, 207–210.

DiMattia, B. V., & Kesner, R. P. Serial position curve in rats: Automatic versus controlled information processing. *Journal of Experimental Psychology: Animal Behavior Processes*, in press.

Di Renzi, E., Faglioni, P., & Villa, P. Topographical amnesia. *Journal of Neurology, Neurosurgery and Psychiatry*, 1977, *40*, 498–505.

Hasher, L., & Zacks, R. T. Automatic and effortful processes in memory. *Journal of Experimental Psychology: General*, 1979, *108*, 356–388.

Horel, J. The neuroanatomy of amnesia: A critique of the hippocampal memory hypothesis. *Brain*, 1978, *101*, 403–445.

Huppert, F. A., & Piercy, M. Recognition memory in amnesic patients: A deficit of acquisition? *Neuropsychologia*, 1977, *15*, 643–652.

Huppert, F. A., & Piercy, M. Normal and abnormal forgetting in organic amnesia: Effect of locus of lesion. *Cortex*, 1979, *15*, 385–390.

Iversen, S. D. Do hippocampal lesions produce amnesia in animals? *International Review of Neurobiology*, 1976, *19*, 1–49.

Kesner, R. P. An attribute analysis of memory: The role of the hippocampus. *Physiological Psychology*, 1980, *8*, 189–197.

Kesner, R. P., & Conner, H. S. Effects of electrical stimulation of limbic system and midbrain retricular formation upon short- and long-term memory. *Physiology and Behavior*, 1974, *12*, 5–12.

Kesner, R. P., & Hardy, J. D. Long-term memory for contextual attributes: Dissociation of amygdala and hippocampus. *Behavioural Brain Research*, 1983, *8*, 139–149.

Kesner, R. P., & Novak, J. Serial position curve in rats: Role of the dorsal hippocampus. *Science*, 1982, *218*, 173–174.

Kinsbourne, M., & Wood, F. Short-term memory processes and the amnesic syndrome. In D. Deutsch & J. A. Deutsch (Eds.), *Short-term memory*. New York: Academic Press, 1975.

Kinsbourne, M., & Wood, F. Theoretical considerations regarding the episodic–semantic memory distinction. In L. S. Cermak (Ed.), *Human memory and amnesia*. Hillsdale, N.J.: Erlbaum, 1982.

McFie, J., & Zangwill, O. L. Visual-constructive disabilities associated with lesions of the left cerebral hemisphere. *Brain*, 1960, *83*, 243–260.

Milner, B. Visual-guided maze learning in man: Effects of bilateral hippocampal, bilateral frontal, and unilateral cerebral lesions. *Neuropsychologia*, 1965, *3*, 317–338.

Milner, B. Clues to the cerebral organization of memory. In P. A. Buser & A. Rougeul-Buser (Eds.), *Cerebral correlates of conscious experience*. Amsterdam: Elsevier, 1978.

Mishkin, M. Memory in monkeys severely impaired by combined but not by separate removal of amygdala and hippocampus. *Nature*, 1978, *273*, 297–298.

Mountcastle, V. B., Lynch, J. C., Georgopoulos, A., Sakata, H., & Acuna, C. Posterior parietal association cortex of the monkey: Command functions for operations within extrapersonal space. *Journal of Neurophysiology*, 1975, *38*, 871–908.

Olton, D. S., Becker, J. T., & Handelmann, G. E. Hippocampal function: Working memory or cognitive mapping? *Physiological Psychology*, 1980, *8*, 239–246.

Olton, D. S., & Samuelson, R. J. Remembrance of places passed: Spatial memory in rats. *Journal of Experimental Psychology: Animal Behavior Processes*, 1976, *2*, 97–116.

Paterson, A., & Zangwill, O. L. Recovery of spatial orientation in the post-traumatic confusion state. *Brain*, 1944, *67*, 54–58.

Petrides, M., & Iversen, S. D. Restricted posterior parietal lesions in the rhesus monkey and performance on visuospatial tasks. *Brain Research*, 1979, *161*, 63–77.

Pohl, W. Dissociation of spatial discrimination deficits following frontal and parietal lesions in monkeys. *Journal of Comparative and Physiological Psychology*, 1973, *82*, 227–239.

Roberts, W. A., & Smythe, W. E. Memory for lists of spatial events in the rat. *Learning and Motivation*, 1979, *10*, 313–336.

Ruff, R. L., & Volpe, B. T. Environmental reduplication associated with right frontal and parietal lobe injury. *Journal of Neurology, Neurosurgery, and Psychiatry*, 1981, *44*, 382–386.

Saffran, E. M., & Marin, O. S. M. Immediate memory for word lists and sentences in a patient with deficient auditory short-term memory. *Brain and Language*, 1975, *2*, 420–433.

Shiffrin, R. M., & Schneider, W. Controlled and automatic human information processing: II. Perceptual learning, automatic attending, and a general theory. *Psychological Review*, 1977, *3*, 1–17.

Spear, N. E. Retrieval of memories: A psychobiological approach. In W. K. Estes (Ed.), *Handbook of learning and cognitive processes* (Vol. 4, *Attention and memory*). Hillsdale, N.J.: Erlbaum, 1976.

Squire, L. R. Two forms of human amnesia: An analysis of forgetting. *Journal of Neuroscience*, 1981, *1*, 635–640.

Tulving, E. Episodic and semantic memory. In E. Tulving & W. Donaldson (Eds.), *Organization of memory*. New York: Academic Press, 1972.

Underwood, B. J. Attributes of memory. *Psychological Review*, 1969, *76*, 559–573.

Warrington, E. K., & Shallice, T. The selective impairment of auditory verbal short-term memory. *Brain*, 1969, *92*, 885–896.

Warrington, E. K., & Taylor, A. M. The contribution of the right parietal lobe to object recognition. *Cortex*, 1973, *9*, 152–164.

Weiskrantz, L., & Warrington, E. K. Conditioning in amnesic patients. *Neuropsychology*, 1979, *17*, 187–194.

Welker, W. I. Brain evolution in mammals: A review of concepts, problems and methods. In R. B. Masteron, M. E. Bitterman, B. Campbell, & N. Hotton (Eds.), *Evolution of brain and behavior in vertebrates*. Hillsdale, N.J.: Erlbaum, 1976.

36

On Recoveries from Impairments of Remembering

Donald R. Meyer and Patricia Morgan Meyer

We begin this account of the kind of work we do, how it got started, and what has come of it by examining two kinds of want ads. The first ad is as follows:

> HELP WANTED: Male. A traveling salesman for hot new lines of merchandise. Unlimited opportunities for real live wire. Contact X, who will be at the hotel for the convention.

The second ad is as follows:

> HELP WANTED: Couple. To care for animals and children. Steady work with no heavy lifting. Reasonable wages and chance to buy the place when present owner retires. Contact Y, whose address is RFD 1.

Essentially, we opted for the second kind of job, and have spent our entire professional careers at Ohio State University. Its inhabitants describe it as The Big Farm. As yet, we do not have a clear title to it, but we do have a piece of the action, and have lived very comfortably because the "children"—our students—have helped us with the livestock. Moreover, although we hate to pack things, we have visited many of our colleagues, and only very rarely have we found that the grass in their pastures was greener than our own.

Our having stayed put has enabled us to carry out a long-term program of studies of recoveries of function after injuries to the brain. The program has now been in progress for 25 years. It has served a double purpose of providing us with data and of giving our students hands-on experience with neuropsychological research. Early on, we standardized our principal behavioral and neurosurgical procedures, and we kept them simple so that incoming students could learn them within a month or so. Then, when the students had passed muster in the eyes of a Big Sister or Brother—that is, a senior graduate student who was thoroughly familiar with the methods—their initial assignments were to replicate a just-completed study in the program. Hence we were invariably the first to know when there was something the matter with a finding, and also when a finding could be relied upon as being quantitatively correct.

We continue to use the same procedures, but from study to study we employ them in different combinations. We consider the creative part of what we do as making decisions as to what kinds of combinations are likeliest to bear fruit. That part of neuropsychology is hard, and it simply is not something that a graduate student can learn within a few weeks

Donald R. Meyer and Patricia Morgan Meyer. Department of Psychology, Ohio State University, Columbus, Ohio.

or months. Nor does it come naturally to people who are masters of other subfields of neuroscience, for they often have had no exposure whatsoever to the science of animal behavior.

We propose to illustrate the workings of the program by describing the steps that we have followed in arriving at a proof of the existence of a function that the cortex performs as a whole. We consider it to be the first rigorous proof of such a concept. It is based upon deductions from impairments of performance of a black–white discrimination problem, a task in which the subject is usually trained to exist from a choice compartment by passing through a white door. The measures are mean trials to reach a criterion of 9 correct choices in 10 trials, which normal Long–Evans rats will meet in 25 trials if trained with our contemporary methods.

The scores we discuss have been obtained from studies of approximately 2000 subjects. Most of the scores are accurate to within one or two trials. Not in any instance is a score's standard error larger than approximately 10% of the mean. Hence we dispense with statistical tests of differences, and we accept null hypotheses when different groups of subjects have the same scores. Also, we mention that some of the comparisons made here are between subjects that were studied in the 1960s and others that were studied in the 1980s. We can make such comparisons because the program was designed to include procedures for detection of long-term changes in our methods and our subjects. We have picked up some drifts from time to time, but none that would affect the conclusions we draw in this review.

We have studied the effects upon performance of the problem of a very large variety of one-stage and two-stage injuries to the neocortex. However, the ones that are of interest to us here were ablations either of a quadrant of the cortex or else of several quadrants of the cortex. An injury to a posterior quadrant is termed a PQ. An injury to an anterior quadrant is termed an AQ. AQ + PQ injuries, if on the same side, are termed UH for unilateral hemidecortications. If they are on different sides, such injuries are termed CQ, or cross-quadrant hemidecortications. A combination of PQ + PQ is BP, bilateral posterior, and a combination of AQ + AQ is BA, bilateral anterior. A combination of AQ + AQ + PQ + PQ is CD, for such an injury completely decorticates the subject.

We are mainly concerned with four kinds of training procedures. N means that the subject was not given training at some stage in study. L designates the subject's first training on the problem. R_1 means that the subject was tested for retention through retraining on the problem, and R_2 means that the subject was given an additional test of retention.

In most of the studies, the injuries were serially inflicted. We illustrate our designations of groups by considering a rat that would be described as an $L-PQ_1-R_1-UH_2-R_2$ preparation. In such a study, the rat would be trained on the problem (L) while it was normal; it would then be subjected to a first-stage injury to a posterior quadrant of the cortex (PQ_1); it would then be given interoperative retraining (R_1); it would then be subjected to a second-stage contralateral AQ + PQ ablation (UH_2), and it would then be retested for performance of the problem after having sustained two injuries that destroyed three-quarters of its neocortex.

One could think at first glance that no simple sense could possibly be made of the results of such a complex procedure. However, we are firm believers in the maxim that you cannot really tell whether a strategy will work unless and until you have tried it. When we first studied serial preparations, we were also dubious about them. However, we have found that it often does not matter how a serial preparation has been treated, and that at the same time there are certain kinds of treatments that yield extremely powerful effects. Hence we next describe some don'ts and dos, and then we show why the dos make a difference and the don'ts don't.

The black–white problem is a "visual" discrimination problem. Much of the posterior cortex of the rat consists of "visual" areas. An $L-BP-R_1$ preparation requires about 25 mean trials to relearn the problem, and an $L-BA-R_1$ preparation requires about 17 trials. Hence, since the scores are accurate to within one or two trials, we conclude that the cost of a BP injury is greater than and differs from the cost of a BA injury by 8 mean trials.

We term the difference a measure of the posterior-specific deficit. We tentatively regard it as related to the fact that BP subjects are permanently and absolutely form-blind. Thus we have found that although they can learn differential-flux and differential-contour problems, they are wholly unable to learn a task in which the only cues are differences between the spatial orientations of contours. In passing, we note that BP subjects can master many "visual-form" problems, but that is only so because the problems are inadequate as tests of visual-form perception.

Importantly, although a BP subject has a greater impairment than a BA, a PQ ablation has the same effect as an AQ. That is, regardless of whether the procedure is $L-AQ-R_1$ or $L-PQ-R_1$, the animals will relearn the task (R_1) in approximately 8–9 trials. That number is very interesting. Thus 8–9 trials is half of the cost of a one-stage BA ablation, and hence $AQ + AQ = 2(AQ) = BA$! Hence not only are the consequences of anterior injuries concordant with a law of mass action, but they also are expressible as linear sums of the effects of partial anterior injuries.

Although that relationship is evidently invalid for $PQ + PQ$, or BP, we have found it to be an excellent predictor of the consequences of other two-quadrant injuries. Thus $L-UH-R_1$ subjects and $L-CQ-R_1$ preparations relearn the problem at rates that are approximately the same. In passing, we note that one of the results was off the mark by 4 mean trials, which may perhaps be all right but leaves us with a wish to examine the facts a little closer.

Next we examine some re-relearning scores of animals prepared with two-stage injuries to the cortex. The simplest paradigms are $L-AQ_1-R_1-AQ_2-R_2$ and $L-PQ_1-R_1-PQ_2-R_2$. We now become concerned with the R_2 scores while remembering that the R_1 scores for the groups were the same. We have found from such studies that serial anteriors have almost no R_2 impairment; thus they will re-relearn in 3 trials or so following their second-stage ablations. In contrast, serial posterior preparations require about 8 mean trials, which is not very different from the R_1 cost of a first-stage PQ ablation.

The foregoing findings prompted us to think that there might be a function that is shared by all quadrants of the cortex, regardless of the fact that different quadrants of the cortex also have different subfunctions. Thus we were impressed by our observation that two-quadrant subjects, except for BPs, require about twice as many R_1 trials as subjects with one-quadrant injuries. We were also impressed by the fact that the cost of a BP injury was 8 trials more than the cost of a BA injury, and that 8 trials was also the difference between the cost of a BP injury and the sum of the costs of individual PQ injuries. But we then began to wonder whether we were sane, for we knew that it was not very likely that linear equations would accurately describe the effects of combinations of injuries that had each destroyed many millions of cells.

However, since we had not invented the scores, we decided to see how far we could get with the following set of assumptions. The first was that the cost of a first-stage injury to a quadrant was 8.5 trials. The second was that injuries to more than one quadrant have linearly additive effects, provided that the injuries do not bilaterally destroy the posterior cortex. The third was that the latter kinds of injuries have an added cost of 8 trials, for subjects thus prepared will also exhibit the posterior-specific deficit. The fourth was that interoperative retraining will correct the quadrant impairments, and will also induce a protection of remembering from the consequences of any further injury, provided that the injury does not complete the destruction of the posterior cortex. The fifth was that under the last-mentioned circumstance, retraining will not protect a subject from the 8-trial cost of an injury that destroys or completes the destruction of both posterior quadrants of the cortex, but will nonetheless protect it from any other costs of subsequent injuries to the cortex.

We found that those assumptions were consistent with every R_1 and R_2 finding we had thus far encountered. For example, we had found that CD subjects relearn the problem in an estimated 38 trials, and that $(4 \times 8.5) + 8$ adds up to 42 trials. BP subjects relearn the problem in approximately 25 trials, and $(2 \times 8.5) + 8$ adds up to 25 trials. Other kinds of two-quadrant preparations require about 17 trials, but they do not have the posterior deficit, and hence they relearn the problem in (2×8.5) trials.

However, although our theory was consistent with scores we already knew about, we were very well aware that we would need to validate it by testing its predictions of scores that we did not know about. Therefore, we conducted a study in which we examined the performances of serial preparations with one- or two-quadrant first-stage injuries and second-stage injuries that completed the destruction of three quadrants of the neocortex. The paradigms were $L-AQ_1-R_1-BP_2-R_2$, $L-PQ_1-R_1-CQ_2-R_2$, $L-CQ_1-R_1-AQ_2-R_2$, $L-UH_1-R_1-PQ_2-R_2$, and $L-UH_1-R_1-AQ_2-R_2$.

We predicted that the first two groups would relearn the problem (R_1) in 8.5 trials; we observed that their combined score for R_1 tests was 8.1 ± 1.4 trials. We also predicted that the last three groups would require about 17 R_1 trials, because their first-stage injuries destroyed two quadrants; we observed that their combined score for R_1 tests was 15.5 ± 1.1 trials. We also predicted that the R_2 impairments of subjects whose second-stage injuries destroyed or completed the destruction of the posterior cortex would be about 8 mean trials; we observed that the R_2 mean for those groups was $8.9 \pm .68$ trials. We also predicted that the R_2 impairments of the other two groups would be small, because such subjects were left with one intact posterior quadrant; we observed that the R_2 mean for those groups was $3.6 \pm .70$ trials.

Since, in our opinion, those outcomes show that there is in fact a function that the cortex performs as a whole, we next discuss the question of the nature of the holistic function. When asked for their opinions, most of our colleagues have guessed that the impairments are due either to injuries to the activating system or else to a system that stores the engrams or structural traces of memories. The first idea has been hard to put to rest, because there is in fact a distributed set of projections to the cortex that arises in the core of the brain. The second idea has also been tenacious, but not because experiments support it; instead, it has persisted because it is plausible and almost impossible to disprove.

We have closely studied both of those ideas. First we consider the activation theory, or "level-of-arousal" theory. A rat that has just sustained an injury to its cortex is not particularly peppy, but after a few days it is almost as lively as an unoperated animal. Hence, if the holistic effects of such ablations are due to changes in arousal, one would think that the R_1 postoperative impairment of an L–BP–R_1 preparation would gradually lessen as a function of time for recovery. However, such a subject will relearn the problem in approximately 25 trials, and it does not matter whether the R_1 test is conducted on the 12th day following the surgery or 4 weeks following the surgery.

The activation theory of the holistic function is also inconsistent with a finding for serial preparations. It has long been established that serially inflicted injuries to the core of the brain stem have lesser effects upon arousal than one-stage injuries. Hence one would think that if our outcomes were due to changes in level of arousal, an L–PQ_1–N–PQ_2–R_1 preparation would relearn the problem at a somewhat faster rate than a one-stage L–BP–R_1 preparation. But that is not so; the groups relearn the problem at the same rate.

Having thus dispensed with the activation theory, we now give our reasons for doubting the theory that the holistic function has something to do with memory storage. The first telling evidence against such a concept was provided by LeVere and Morlock. They observed that even though a BP subject takes about as many trials to relearn the problem as to learn it, preoperative training on the black–white task will markedly retard the rate at which the subject will learn a reversal of the problem. We have looked at their results by training normal rats to choose the black instead of the white door, and by then training them to choose the white door following a BP operation. We found that the subjects required 50 trials to learn the reversed discrimination—in other words, more trials would be required for a CD subject to relearn the problem. Hence, although a BP subject is unable to remember a black–white problem that it learned prior to surgery, such a subject still has a memory for the problem, and the memory is substantially intact.

Then what is the nature of the holistic function of the cortex? The answer is neither memory storage nor arousal, but retrieval of memories from storage. Our most recent support for that conclusion has come from studies of second-stage effects. As we have observed, interoperative retraining will correct the holistic impairment, regardless of what kinds of first-stage and second-stage injuries are sustained by the subjects. The traditional view of such recoveries has been that interoperative retraining on the problem develops a substitutive habit, or else protects ultimate performance of the problem by giving the subjects overtraining. But now we can say, and with considerable assurance, that interoperative retraining corrects the impairment by developing a system that permits the subjects to utilize memories that were formed before their injuries were sustained.

Our proof of that contention is as follows: An L–PQ_1–R_1–PQ_2–R_2 preparation re-relearns the problem (R_2) in about 8 trials. In contrast, a preoperatively overtrained subject that is not given interoperative training—that is, an L–R_1–PQ_1–N–PQ_2–R_2 preparation—requires 25 trials to re-relearn the problem (R_2). Also interoperative training on the problem conveys no protection of ultimate performance if given to a subject that was not trained prior to surgery, for an N–PQ_1–L–PQ_2–R_1 preparation also takes approximately 25 trials to relearn the problem (R_1). Hence interoperative retraining corrects impairments of the holistic function by developing a new mechanism for retrieval of preoperatively established memories.

Now we close our presentation of data with a very brief account of some effects we have observed in subjects with perinatal injuries. First, we note that we discovered long ago that adult $N-BA_1-L-BP_2-R_1$ preparations relearn the problem at exactly the same rate as $L-BP-R_1$ subjects. Also, we discovered long ago that the converse was true, for $N-BP_1-L-BA_2-R_1$ subjects relearn the problem at exactly the same rate as $L-BA-R_1$ subjects. In passing, we note that the two observations are supportive of our last generalization, for neither type of subject had a memory to remember at the time that it was given interoperative training on the problem.

However, if the first operations are performed when the animals are 7 days old, and training on the problem and the second operation are delayed until the subjects are adults, one catches a different kind of fish. Under such conditions, regardless of whether the early operation is a BA_1 or a BP_1, the subjects have enormous impairments of remembering following the second-stage ablations. Thus, instead of taking only 17 or 25 mean trials to relearn the problem, the animals require about as many trials as one-stage CD preparations.

We take this to mean that after very early injuries to the cortex, the surviving components of the holistic system have much greater roles in the process of remembering that they would have if the injuries had been inflicted when the brain was reasonably mature. We know almost nothing about the nature of the alterations, but our findings from electrophysiological studies appear to have excluded the possibility that the outcomes are due to reorganizations of the visual mechanisms of the brain. Also, we have asked whether early BP subjects are capable of learning a form-discrimination problem if tested in adulthood. We have found that they are not, and that has strengthened our belief that the posterior deficit can be distinguished from impairments of the holistic function.

We think that our experiments with perinatal subjects, in which we have found a symmetrical effect of BA and BP ablations, offer further strong support for our conclusion that the cortex is equipotentially involved in the process of remembering of memories. The other supports are that first-stage effects are governed by law of mass action if we discount posterior-specific impairments; that posterior-specific impairments can be dissociated from impairments whose severities are independent of the loci of the injuries to the cortex; and that interoperative retraining will effect a protection of remembering that is independent of the loci and extents of first-stage and second-stage injuries. We can see no problems with the argument, but we invite the comments of our colleagues.

Now we comply with our editors' requests for our perceptions of shores dimly seen. Where should we go, and what would be some routes that we ourselves do not propose to follow? The first question has a simple answer; we shall do what our subjects tell us to. There have been some occasions when we misunderstood their messages. On most of those occasions, the messages were garbled by our own erroneous beliefs that their deficits would sooner or later be explained as mainly being due to the effects of the injuries upon the brain's visual mechanisms. We think that our having had that attitude to start with has cost us both about 10 years, but the time was not completely wasted, because we have managed to accomplish a fair amount of work in the field of visual physiology.

From time to time, our colleagues have asked us what theories we were testing in our investigations. Our answer has been that we were keeping many theories in mind, but were mainly in the business of answering questions that were posed by our prior investigations. Thus, for example, we did not set out to show that the cortex has an equipotential function and that the function is remembering; instead, those conclusions eventually emerged as the simplest explanation of a very large variety of findings. They are relevant, of course, to the theories of Gall, of Flourens, of Pavlov, and of Lashley, and also to the theories of von Monakow, Franz, and Walter Hunter. And these are just a few of our heroes; there are others too numerous to mention.

When we first began our work, we were interested in two general questions: Where are memories stored within the brain, and what are the bases of recoveries from injuries to the brain? At that time the cortex was widely believed to be the brain's major memory bank, and recoveries of functions were generally regarded as *prima facie* evidence of sloppy neurosurgical techniques. The celebrated studies were those reporting impairments that did not go away, and if the effects could be viewed as mnemonic impairments, that was how they were viewed.

We approached those questions by using nearly every behavioral procedure we had heard of. We thought that we would surely find a basis for believing that at least some memories can be eradicated by at least some injuries to the cortex. In the process we examined the classical proofs, of which the most durable was Lashley's, who thought that the black–white engram is stored in the visual neocortex, provided that the cortex is intact. But as we have shown in this review, the proof he offered was defective. There was nothing the matter with his facts, but he drew the wrong conclusion because he believed that an impairment of remembering, if profound and enduring, implies that a subject no longer has a memory to remember. And although we have shown in a variety of ways that such a presumption is pernicious, it has misled and still is continuing to mislead a remarkable number of scientists with interests in the central neural substrates of memories.

During that endeavor, we were struck by the fact that there were very few proofs to be considered. We thought that was odd, because the question of whether the cortex has a role in memory storage had been studied for a century. Then, about a dozen years ago, it finally began to dawn upon us that one cannot destroy memories by destroying the cortex, because it does not store memory traces. We have recently reviewed our explorations of that hypothesis. We do not describe them here, because the work has involved some very close analyses of neuropsychological procedures, and many neuroscientists appear to have found them as difficult to follow as it is for us to follow a neurochemist's metabolic pathways. But our bottom line was simple: There is no proof whatever that memories are stored by cortex, although injuries to it will produce severe disorders of attending, of perceiving, of thinking through, and of storing or retrieving information.

Since our own investigations had led us to conclude that memories are hard to destroy, we looked at the question of whether they could be destroyed with methods we had not employed ourselves. The commonest of those were procedures in which the animals were given a task that they could learn in one trial, and were then subjected to treatments which were aimed at blocking the formation of long- term or structural memory traces. A few years ago, we observed that such procedures had yielded impairments of remembering, but that no one had shown that the impairments were due to effects upon developments of memories. We argued that the neuropsychological results were consistent with the notion that long-term traces are formed very rapidly indeed, and hence were inconsistent with the notion that the traces are formed via syntheses of protein or peptide molecules. Approximately 7 years have now elapsed since we first presented that conclusion, and we know of no subsequent empirical result that would give us any reason to doubt it.

However, very recently, R. F. Thompson and his colleagues have observed that cerebellar injuries that spare unconditioned responses will suppress remembering of conditioned responses and will block their formation after surgery. If those findings mean what they seem to, we believe that the study is destined to become a neuropsychological classic. Insofar as we are presently aware, it presents the only evidence we have that the engram or trace of a memory can be destroyed by a survivable injury to the brain of a mammal. Hence we believe that the lead should be pursued, and we wish that we had the time to do that; but we still have not run out of problems that can best be explored with our own paradigms.

First on our list is the problem of how large a first-stage injury has to be in order for retraining to induce a protection of ultimate remembering from the otherwise unfortunate effects of further injuries to the cortex. We have shown that an injury to any of the quadrants of the cortex is sufficient for the purpose, even though the injuries have relatively modest effects upon performance of the problem. The question we are presently examining is whether a first-stage injury that is far too small to bring about an R_1 impairment will nonetheless enable a subject with a huge second-stage injury to re-relearn the problem very promptly. We now have a limited amount of pilot data suggesting that very tiny injuries—that is, ablations of perhaps 2 or 3 cubic millimeters of the cortex—will yield that result, regardless of where the injury to the cortex is inflicted.

We believe that such protections provide an explanation of Hughlings Jackson's law of momentum, which Jackson deduced from his observation that a slowly growing lesion may become enormous before the victim of the process is compelled to seek the advice of a physician. Thus we suggest that after the process has begun, memories that the victim continues to employ will continue to be accessible. When the lesion is still in its very early stages, those memories will be easy to recall, but as it advances, new recollections will be harder and harder for the victim. In passing, we note that such an explanation does not account for Ribot's law, but that we have dealt with that problem in our other recent synopsis of our studies.

There are evidently many kinds of questions that our studies of recoveries have posed but have not addressed. From time to time, our colleagues in other neurosciences have asked us why we have not addressed these questions, and have argued that we ought to do so, despite their being questions that are not in our fields of expertise. When we have pointed that out, they have urged us to get ourselves retreaded as neuro-something-elses, and have strongly intimated that they think that the era of neuropsychology is over. However, we are not about to do that, because we have found that our own piece of pie is tough enough. We believe that our colleagues are good at what *they* do, and we believe that we are good at what *we* do. At least, we have a lot of practice. Hence we are pleased to offer them procedures that will yield more interesting measures of behavior than the counters of activity wheels, and we are also pleased to offer them our knowledge of what the measures mean. They are welcome to try them for themselves, but we have other questions to attend to besides the questions that they might wish to raise.

ACKNOWLEDGMENT

This chapter was prepared with support from the Donald Jansen Fund of Ohio State University.

SUGGESTED READINGS

Beattie, M. S., Gray, T. S., Rosenfeld, J. A., Meyer, P. M., & Meyer, D. R. Residual capacity for avoidance learning in decorticate rats: Enhancement of performance and demonstration of latent learning with D-amphetamine treatments. *Physiological Psychology*, 1978, *6*, 279–287.

Cloud, M. D., Meyer, D. R., & Meyer, P. M. Inductions of recoveries from injuries to the cortex: Dissociation of equipotential and regionally specific mechanisms. *Physiological Psychology*, 1982, *10*, 66–73.

LeVere, T. E., & Morlock, G. W. The nature of visual recovery following posterior decortication in the hooded rat. *Journal of Comparative and Physiological Psychology*, 1973, *83*, 62–67.

Hata, M. G., Diaz, C. L., Gibson, C. F., Jacobs, C. E., Meyer, P. M., & Meyer, D. R. Perinatal injuries to extra-visual cortex enhance the significance of visual cortex for performance of a visual habit. *Physiological Psychology*, 1980, *8*, 9–14.

McCormick, D. A., Lavond, D. G., Clark, G. A., Kettner, R. E., Rising, C. E., & Thompson, R. F. The engram found?: Role of the cerebellum in classical conditioning of nictitating membrane and eyelid responses. *Bulletin of the Psychonomic Society*, 1981, *18*, 103–105.

Meyer, D. R. Access to engrams. *American Psychologist*, 1972, *27*, 124–133.

Meyer, D. R., & Beattie, M. S. Some properties of substrates of memory. In L. H. Miller, C. A. Sandman, & A. J. Kastin (Eds.), *Neuropeptide influences on brain and behavior*. New York: Raven Press, 1977.

Meyer, P. M. Recovery of function following lesions of the subcortex and neocortex. In D. G. Stein, J. J. Rosen, & N. Butters (Eds.), *Plasticity and recovery of function in the central nervous system*. New York: Academic Press, 1974.

Meyer, D. R., & Meyer, P. M. Dynamics and bases of recoveries of functions after injuries to the cerebral cortex. *Physiological Psychology*, 1977, *5*, 133–165.

Meyer, P. M., & Meyer, D. R. Memory, remembering, and amnesia. In R. L. Isaacson & N. E. Spear (Eds.), *The expression of knowledge*. New York: Plenum Press, 1982.

Nonspecific Neural Mechanisms Involved in Learning and Memory in the Rat

37

Robert Thompson

Introduction

Are there discrete regions of the mammalian brain that are essential for the normal performance of a broad spectrum of laboratory tasks, or are the brain mechanisms underlying the performance of one kind of learned activity totally separable from those underlying the performance of another kind of learned activity? This issue has largely been ignored by experimental neuropsychologists, despite the fact that its resolution may provide important clues to the understanding of the neurobiological basis of learning and memory.

On the one hand, it can be argued that since neither learning nor memory is unitary phenomenon—there may be stimulus–response learning, cognitive-map learning, semantic learning, reference memory, working memory, episodic memory, and the like (see Oakley, 1981)—the neural substratum for one class of learned responses may have nothing in common with that for another class of learned responses.

On the other hand, it can be argued that the performance of most learned responses (particularly those acquired by subjects in a free-moving, unrestrained situation) requires the engagement of those brain systems subserving such activities as arousal, selective attention, and motor control. Since each of these activities may represent a unitary process, it would follow that nonspecific neural mechanisms would indeed be involved in learning and memory.

Despite its weaknesses and limitations, the lesion method would appear to constitute the simplest and most straightforward way to determine the possible existence of nonspecific neural mechanisms subserving learning and memory. Two different experiments suggest themselves. In one (a memory experiment), normal laboratory animals would be trained on a variety of tasks and then subjected to bilateral lesions of different cortical or subcortical regions. Following an appropriate recovery period, the animals would be tested for retention of each of the tasks learned preoperatively. Those lesion placements producing retention losses on all of the tasks investigated could conceivably define those sites within the brain that have nonspecific functions in the performance of learned responses. In the second (a learning experiment), different groups of laboratory animals would first be subjected to bilateral cortical or subcortical lesions and subsequently would be trained on a variety of tasks. Those lesion placements producing acquisition deficits on all of the tasks

Robert Thompson. Fairview State Hospital, Costa Mesa, California; Department of Physical Medicine and Rehabilitation, University of California at Irvine Medical Center, Orange, California.

investigated could similarly be viewed as defining those sites within the brain that have nonspecific functions in the performance of learned responses.

Although all learning studies may be viewed as memory studies, to the extent that learning requires storage of information, the possibility exists that the pattern of results generated by the learning experiment suggested above will not be exactly the same as that generated by the corresponding memory experiment. Lashley (1929), for example, showed that occipital damage in rats impairs retention, but not acquisition, of a light–dark discrimination problem. In contrast, Brady, Schreiner, Geller, and Kling (1954) reported that amygdaloid damage in cats impairs acquisition, but not retention, of an active-avoidance problem. The clinical literature also suggests that certain brain lesions may be associated with serious anterograde amnesia with little retrograde amnesia (see Squire, 1982, for a review of this literature), while other brain lesions may be associated with the converse pattern of amnesic effects (Goldberg, Antin, Bilder, Hughes, & Mattis, 1981).

On the strength of the foregoing observations, it is proposed that those nonspecific mechanisms (if they do indeed exist) involved in learning will not precisely coincide with those involved in memory. For convenience, any nonspecific mechanisms underlying learning are termed the "general learning system" (GLS), and any underlying memory is termed the "general memory system" (GMS).

For a number of years, I have been using the lesion method for the purpose of identifying the GMS of the rat brain. The results of this effort are briefly described here, followed by a description of some recent data bearing upon the identification of the GLS of the rat brain. The balance of this chapter is devoted to a discussion and an interpretation of these findings.

The General Memory System

The first hint that a GMS exists within the rat brain came from a series of studies comparing the effects of different cortical and subcortical lesions on retention of two habits: a visual discrimination and an inclined-plane (vestibular–proprioceptive–kinesthetic) discrimination in albino rats (see Thompson, 1982b, for a review of these studies). Both habits were established under the motive of escape–avoidance of foot shock. In the case of the visual habit, the animals were tested on a white–black and/or a horizontal–vertical discrimination problem in a Thompson–Bryant box. The inclined plane problem involves testing blinded animals in a single-unit T-maze that could be titled 11° from the horizontal axis; the task was to choose the upward sloping alley and to avoid the adjacent downward sloping alley.

Figure 37-1 summarizes some of the results of these experiments (see also Thompson, Arabie, & Sisk, 1976). Three functionally separate groups of brain structures were identified. One group was concerned only with retention of the visual discrimination; the second was concerned only with retention of the inclined-plane discrimination; and the third *was concerned with retention of both habits.*

That this third group may indeed constitute the major part of the GMS of the rat brain is suggested by the results of lesion studies on other types of laboratory tasks. Thus, normal rats trained on a maze with three blind alleys (Thompson, 1974, 1978a) or a series of latch-box problems (Spiliotis & Thompson, 1973; Thompson, Gates, & Gross, 1979)

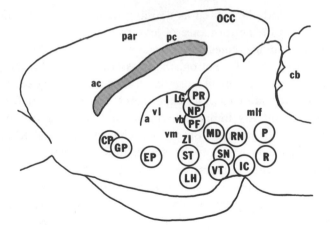

FIGURE 37-1. Schematic drawing of a parasagittal section of the rat brain, showing the relative positions of lesion placements producing retention deficits on the inclined-plane discrimination only (lowercase letters), visual discrimination only (capital letters), and both discriminations (encircled capital letters). Abbreviations: a (A), anterior thalamus; ac (AC), anterior cingulate cortex; amy, amygdaloid complex; cb, cerebellum; cbc, cerebellar cortex; CG, mesencephalic central gray; CP, intermediate caudo-putamen; DH, dorsal hippocampus; DM, mediodorsal thalamus; e, eye; EP, entopeduncular nucleus; FR, frontolateral cortex; GP, globus pallidus; IC, interpeduncular–central tegmental area; l (L), lateral thalamic complex; LG, lateral geniculate bodies; LH, posterolateral hypothalamus; MB, mammillary bodies; MD, mesodiencephalic reticular formation; MFB, rostral medial forebrain bundle; mlf, medial longitudinal fasciculus; mrf, dorsomedial mesencephalic reticular formation; NA, nucleus accumbens; NP (np), nucleus posterior thalami; OCC, occipital cortex; OLF, olfactory bulb; P, pontine reticular formation; par (PAR), parietal cortex; pc (PC), posterior cingulate cortex; PF, parafascicular nucleus; PO, preoptic–supraoptic hypothalamus; PR (pr), pretectum; R, median raphe; RCP, rostral caudo-putamen; RN, red nucleus; S, septal area; sc, superior colliculus; SN, substantia nigra; ST, subthalamic nucleus; vb, ventrobasal thalamus; VH, ventral hippocampus; VHY, ventromedial hypothalamus; vl (VL), ventrolateral thalamus; vm (VM), ventromedial thalamus; VT, ventral tegmental area; ZI (zi), zona incerta.

were found to exhibit serious retention losses following lesions to any one of the structures included within this third group. Retention deficits in active- and/or passive-avoidance responses were also associated with selective lesions to this third group (Thompson, 1978b).

    In summary, the latest findings from my laboratory suggest that the GMS of the rat brain is composed of portions of the basal ganglia (intermediate caudo-putamen, globus pallidus, entopeduncular nucleus, subthalamus, substantia nigra, and red nucleus), limbic midbrain area (ventral tegmental area, interpeduncular–central tegmental area, and median raphe), and brain stem reticular formation (particularly the ventral zone, including its rostral extension into the posterolateral hypothalamus, parafascicular nucleus, nucleus posterior thalami, and pretectum).

The General Learning System

Since the components of the GMS were largely exposed by examining retention of both a visual discrimination and a vestibular–proprioceptive-kinesthetic discrimination in brain-damaged rats, it seems reasonable to assume that the components of the GLS could likewise be exposed by studying *acquisition* of similar discriminations in brain-damaged rats. This enterprise was initiated by determining which lesion placements in rats would produce significant deficits in original learning and reversal learning of a position habit formed in a single-unit T-maze adapted for the motive of escape–avoidance of foot shock. (These two spatial discriminations are most likely mediated by the processing of vestibular–proprioceptive–kinesthetic signals; see Douglas, Clark, Erway, Hubbard, & Wright, 1979, and Thompson, Hale, & Bernard, 1980.) Of the 38 different cortical and subcortical sites canvassed with bilateral lesions, 29 were found to be associated with acquisition deficits on both the original and the reversal learning. Subsequently, it was determined whether selective lesions to these 29 brain sites would also produce significant deficits in original and reversal learning of a white–black discrimination habit formed in a Thompson–Bryant box. Any one of the foregoing sites found to be critical for acquisition of these two visual problems would qualify as a component of the GLS of the rat brain.

Figure 37-2 summarizes some of the results of this investigation (see also Thompson, 1982a, 1982c). Of the 29 brain regions sampled with lesions, 12 were found to be implicated in acquisition of the white–black discrimination habit and its reversal. These regions consisted of the occipital cortex, globus pallidus, ventrolateral thalamus, lateral thalamic complex, parafascicular nucleus, posterolateral hypothalamus, substantia nigra, red nucleus, mesencephalic central gray, interpeduncular–central tegmental area, median raphe, and pontine reticular formation.

In light of earlier findings (Thompson, 1978a) supplemented by other observations recently made in my laboratory, it seems reasonable to include all of the foregoing structures, except the occipital cortex, within the GLS of the rat brain. The occipital cortex is excluded from the GLS on the grounds that bilateral damage to this region fails to impair acquisition of other types of nonvisual discriminations (Finger & Frommer, 1968; Thompson, 1982a).

FIGURE 37-2. Schematic drawing of a parasagittal section of the rat brain, showing the relative positions of lesion placements producing no deficits in learning of spatial discrimination (lowercase letters), visual discrimination (capital letters), and both spatial and visual discrimination (encircled capital letters). (See Figure 37-1 for abbreviations.)

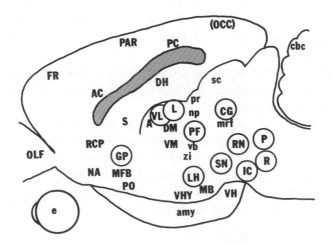

In summary, it would appear that the GLS of the rat brain is composed of most of those structures found to be included within the GMS (see Table 37-1). The intermediate caudo-putamen, entopeduncular nucleus, subthalamus, ventral tegmental area, and mesodiencephalic reticular formation, which are constituents of the GMS, have yet to be examined in relation to their inclusion within the GLS.

Differences between the Two Nonspecific Systems

As noted in Table 37-1, a few major differences are present between the composition of the GLS and that of the GMS. The former contains the ventrolateral thalamus, the lateral thalamic complex, and the mesencephalic central gray, while the latter contains the nucleus posterior thalami and the pretectum. Although these differences are of considerable interest, it would be premature to speculate at this time about their functional significance. It must be emphasized that independent groups of animals were used to investigate the composition of the GLS and GMS. Such an experimental design allows for the possibility that variations in lesion topography and/or lesion magnitude could be responsible for the observed disparities. A within-subjects design, in which the same brain-damaged animals would be assessed for both acquisition and retention performance, is needed to establish whether a given brain structure belongs to one or both nonspecific systems.

Some Limitations and Weaknesses

Employing the lesion method to localize nonspecific neural mechanisms underlying learning and memory is not without its weaknesses and limitations (see also Thompson, 1982a, 1982c). It is well established, for example, that the appearance of a learning or retention deficit in brain-damaged animals may be contingent not only upon lesion topography, but upon lesion magnitude, whether or not the lesions are produced in one or two stages, the length of the recovery period, the age and previous experience of the subject, the nature and difficulty of the task, and the like (Finger, 1978; Stein, Rosen, & Butters, 1974). Of equal concern is the difficulty in determining whether a learning or retention deficit exhibited by brain-damaged animals arises from destruction of cells at the site of the lesion, interruption of fiber pathways coursing through the lesioned area, or secondary brain changes initiated by the lesion (Schoenfeld & Hamilton, 1977). And with respect to the "global" deficits observed in the current series of experiments, it remains unclear whether one sector of a given component of the GLS or GMS is implicated in visual tasks and another sector in spatial tasks, or whether the entire component contributes equally to the performance of both visual and spatial tasks.

The foregoing is but an abbreviated list of weaknesses inherent in the lesion method. How, then, is it possible to interpret lesion data of the kind presented in this chapter in relation to the existence and composition of nonspecific mechanisms subserving learning and memory? In the case of the GLS, it will be recalled that 38 different cortical and subcortical regions were canvassed with lesions. Of these, only 11 (excluding the occipital cortex) were associated with learning losses on both visual and spatial discriminations. It

TABLE 37-1. The Composition of the GLS and GMS

Brain region	GLS	GMS
Intermediate caudo-putamen	?	X
Globus pallidus	X	X
Entopeduncular nucleus	?	X
Ventrolateral thalamus	X	
Lateral thalamic complex	X	
Parafascicular nucleus	X	X
Nucleus posterior thalami		X
Pretectum		X
Posterolateral hypothalamus	X	X
Subthalamic nucleus	?	X
Substantia nigra	X	X
Ventral tegmental area	?	X
Red nucleus	X	X
Interpeduncular–central tegmental area	X	X
Median raphe	X	X
Mesencephalic central gray	X	
Mesodiencephalic reticular formation	?	X
Pontine reticular formation	X	X

Note. A given component is indicated by the letter "X" within a cell.

may be inferred, therefore, that these 11 brain regions, which are included with the GLS, are potentially more involved in the overall learning process than the remaining 27 brain regions that have been excluded from the GLS. A similar inference can be made in connection with the GMS.

Neocortex, Hippocampus, and Diencephalon

The cerebral cortex, hippocampus, mediodorsal thalamic nucleus, and mammillary bodies are the regions of the mammalian brain most frequently mentioned in connection with learning and memory. Yet, not one of these regions qualified as a component of either the GLS or GMS of the rat brain. This, of course, does not imply that neocortical, hippo-campal, or medial diencephalic regions of the rat brain are devoid of any role in learning and memory. Rather, it means that these regions may be critical for the performance of certain classes of learned activities, but are not critical for the performance of other classes of learned activities. In other words, these telencephalic and diencephalic structures have *specific* functions in learning and memory that are to be contrasted with the seemingly nonspecific functions in learning and memory served by the respective components of the GLS and GMS.

Are these data on the rat in conflict with the clinical literature? From one point of view, they may not be. For example, there appear to be no reports in the clinical literature that a single cortical lesion will produce nonspecific learning and/or memory defects (Russell, 1981). Furthermore, although patients with hippocampal or medial diencephalic lesions may exhibit an amnesic syndrome, certain domains of learning and memory may be spared. Thus, amnesic patients have been reported to learn a simple spatial discrimination (Oscar-Berman & Zola-Morgan, 1980), simple visual discriminations (Gaffan, 1972; Oscar-Berman & Zola-Morgan, 1980), and perceptual (or perceptual–motor) skills (Brooks & Baddeley, 1976; Cohen, & Squire, 1978, 1980) about as rapidly as controls. From another point of view, however, a conflict may indeed exist. This relates to the paucity of evidence in the clinical literature that lesions in the region of the pallidum, parafascicular nucleus, posterolateral hypothalamus, substantia nigra, red nucleus, or pontine reticular formation (some of the components of the rat's GLS and GMS) are associated with nonspecific learning and memory disorders (however, see Albert, 1978, on "subcortical dementia").

An Interpretation

The data on the provisional identification of the GLS and GMS of the rat brain can be approached from two contrasting theoretical perspectives. The first would be molecular in nature, treating each component or set of components as contributing in some specific way to the performance of a variety of learned behaviors, with little regard for the manner in which these separate contributions are functionally united. Thus, the nigro-striatal complex may function in arousal–activation processes; the interpeduncular–central tegmental area and median raphe may play a role in behavioral inhibition; the parafascicular nucleus may be concerned with escape–avoidance responses to noxious stimuli; the pontine reticular formation and red nucleus may contribute to motor control; and so forth. The second perspective, being a holistic one, would treat the GLS and GMS as functional entities, serving some bewilderingly complex role in the overall learning and memory process. That this latter perspective may have some merit in the present context is indicated by the remarkable degree of morphological interconnectivity existing among the various components of the GLS (Thompson, 1982c) and GMS (Thompson, 1982b).

It seems plausible to suppose that any nonspecific mechanisms involved in learning and memory not only should lie at the interface between the sensory and motor systems of the brain, but should have the potential to exert their influences on both of these domains. These influences would conceivably play a role in such psychological processes as arousal, selective attention, motivation, and motor readiness. A theoretical construct that encompasses all of the foregoing psychological processes is an "anticipatory set" or "expectancy." Anticipatory sets, long recognized to be an important factor in learning and memory, have been conceived by Sperry (1955) to intermediate between sensory and motor events and to exert an organizing effect on the brain—through the mobilization of facilitory and inhibitory processes—on both the sensory and motor sides. Sperry has argued cogently "that in the brain of the conditioned animal a well-organized facilitory set appears prior to the incidence of the conditioned stimulus"; he concludes, "It is this special pattern of central facilitation—absent before training and developed through training—that is directly responsible for channelling the sensory impulses into the proper motor response" (Sperry, 1955, p. 43). I propose, although the proposal is speculative and undoubtedly simplistic, that the core structures concerned with the development (learning) and expression (memory) of anticipatory sets comprise the respective constituents of the GLS and GMS.[1]

This hypothesis has the potential to bridge the gap between lesion data, on the one hand, which tend to implicate relatively localized neural assemblies in learning and memory, and neurophysiological data, on the other, which suggest the participation of most brain regions in learning and memory. Consider, for example, the findings of E. Roy John and his associates (John, 1967, 1972; John & Schwartz, 1978) on the synchronous endogenous components recorded from widespread neural regions during the performance of conditioned responses. It is not inconceivable that these widespread neural changes associated with learning and memory arise from the activation of the GLS-GMS, which generates the complex synchronization observed in many different parts of the brain. Of equal importance is the possibility that the emergence of these endogenous processes is in some way related to the arousal of an anticipatory set. John and Schwartz (1978) have already alluded to such a possibility: "The most parsimonious explanation of endogenous processes in ERPs is that they reflect the subjective evaluation of incoming information in the context of expectations derived from previous experience" (p. 25).

Conclusions

The results of this series of experiments lead to the conclusion that nonspecific mechanisms underlying learning and memory do indeed exist within the rat brain, and that they inhabit an extensive anatomical region embracing elements of the basal ganglia, thalamus, hypothalamus, limbic midbrain area, and brain stem reticular formation. The component parts of this anatomical ensemble are not remarkably different from those proposed by John to make up the "representational systems" responsible for the appearance of endogenous processes associated with learning and memory. The extent to which the functional significance of these nonspecific mechanisms is related to the mediation of anticipatory sets as conceived by Sperry is a matter of future study.

REFERENCES

Albert, M. L. Subcortical dementia. In R. Katzman, R. D. Terry, & K. L. Bick (Eds.), *Alzheimer's disease: Senile dementia and related disorders.* New York: Raven Press, 1978.
Brady, J. V., Schreiner, L., Geller, I., & Kling, A. Subcortical mechanisms in emotional behavior: The effect of rhinencephalic injury upon the acquisition and retention of a conditioned avoidance response in cats. *Journal of Comparative and Physiological Psychology*, 1954, *47*, 179–186.

1. Two comments must be made in connection with this hypothesis. First of all, it supersedes the one that I developed earlier in a discussion concerning the functional organization of the rat brain (Thompson, 1982b). (In the earlier report, the GMS—or "integrating block"—was conceived to participate mainly in motor control.) The second comment relates to the contribution of *specific mechanisms* in the establishment of anticipatory sets. It should be apparent that the GLS, for example, is presumed to have the distinguishing feature of participating in the formation of a wide variety of anticipatory sets. However, acquisition of anticipatory sets would also depend upon the engagement of specific mechanisms. In the case of a "visual" anticipatory set, the specific mechanism would include the classical visual pathways, while a "vestibular-proprioceptive-kinesthetic" anticipatory set, in contrast, would include a different ensemble of structures, such as the parietal cortex, cingulate cortex, and cerebellum (see Thompson, 1982b).

Brooks, D. N., & Baddeley, A. D. What can amnesic patients learn? *Neuropsychologia*, 1976, *14*, 111–122.

Cohen, N. J., & Squire, L. R. Impaired motor memory and intact motor skills acquisition in anterograde amnesia. *Society for Neuroscience Abstracts*, 1978, *4*, 256.

Cohen, N. J., & Squire, L. R. Preserved learning and retention of pattern-analyzing skill in amnesia: Dissociation of knowing how and knowing that. *Science*, 1980, *210*, 207–210.

Douglas, R. J., Clark, G. M., Erway, L. C., Hubbard, D. G., & Wright, C. G. Effects of genetic vestibular defects on behavior related to spatial orientation and emotionality. *Journal of Comparative and Physiological Psychology*, 1979, *93*, 467–480.

Finger, S. (Ed.). *Recovery from brain damage: Research and theory.* New York: Plenum Press, 1978.

Finger, S., & Frommer, G. P. Effects of cortical lesions on tactile discrimination graded in difficulty. *Life Sciences*, 1968, *7*, 897–904.

Gaffan, D. Loss of recognition memory in rats with lesions of the fornix. *Neuropsychologia*, 1972, *10*, 327–341.

Goldberg, E., Antin, S. P., Bilder, R. M., Hughes, J. E. O., & Mattis, S. Retrograde amnesia: Possible role of mesencephalic reticular activation in long-term memory. *Science*, 1981, *213*, 1392–1394.

John, E. R. *Mechanisms of memory.* New York: Academic Press, 1967.

John, E. R. Switchboard versus statistical theories of learning and memory. *Science*, 1972, *177*, 850–864.

John, E. R., & Schwartz, E. L. The neurophysiology of information processing and cognition. *Annual Review of Psychology*, 1978, *29*, 1–29.

Lashley, K. S. *Brain mechanisms and intelligence.* Chicago: University of Chicago Press, 1929.

Oakley, D. A. Brain mechanisms of mammalian memory. *British Medical Bulletin*, 1981, *37*, 175–180.

Oscar-Berman, M., & Zola-Morgan, S. M. Comparative neuropsychology and Korsakoff's syndrome: I. Spatial and visual reversal learning. *Neuropsychologia*, 1980, *18*, 499–512.

Russell, E. W. The pathology and clinical examination of memory. In S. B. Filskov & T. J. Boll (Eds.), *Handbook of clinical neuropsychology.* New York: Wiley, 1981.

Schoenfeld, T. A., & Hamilton, L. W. Secondary brain changes following lesions: A new paradigm for lesion experimentation. *Physiology and Behavior*, 1977, *18*, 951–967.

Sperry, R. W. On the neural basis of the conditioned response. *British Journal of Animal Behavior*, 1955, *3*, 41–44.

Spiliotis, P. H., & Thompson, R. The "manipulative response memory system" in the white rat. *Physiological Psychology*, 1973, *1*, 101–114.

Squire, L. R. The neuropsychology of human memory. *Annual Review of Neuroscience*, 1982, *5*, 241–273.

Stein, D. G., Rosen, J. J., & Butters, N. (Eds.). *Plasticity and recovery of function in the central nervous system.* New York: Academic Press, 1974.

Thompson, R. Localization of the "maze memory system" in the white rat. *Physiological Psychology*, 1974, *2*, 1–17.

Thompson, R. *A behavioral atlas of the rat brain.* New York: Oxford University Press, 1978. (a)

Thompson, R. Localization of a "passive avoidance memory system" in the white rat. *Physiological Psychology*, 1978, *6*, 263–274. (b)

Thompson, R. Brain lesions impairing visual and spatial reversal learning in rats: Components of the "general learning system" of the rodent brain. *Physiological Psychology*, 1982, *10*, 186–198. (a)

Thompson, R. Functional organization of the rat brain. In J. Orbach (Ed.), *Neuropsychology after Lashley.* Hillsdale, N.J.: Erlbaum, 1982. (b)

Thompson, R. Impaired visual and spatial reversal learning in brain-damaged rats: Additional components of the "general learning system" of the rodent brain. *Physiological Psychology*, 1982, *10*, 293–305. (c)

Thompson, R., Arabie, G. J., & Sisk, G. B. Localization of the "incline plane discrimination memory system" in the white rat. *Physiological Psychology*, 1976, *4*, 311–325.

Thompson, R., Gates, C. E., & Gross, S. A. Thalamic regions critical for retention of skilled movements in the rat. *Physiological Psychology*, 1979, *7*, 7–21.

Thompson, R., Hale, D. B., & Bernard, B. B. Brain mechanisms concerned with left–right differentiation in the white rat. *Physiological Psychology*, 1980, *8*, 309–319.

38

Hippocampal Neuronal Firing, Context, and Learning

John L. Kubie and James B. Ranck, Jr.

For many years there has been general agreement that context is important in learning. Starting about 15 years ago, serious consideration of the issue increased with studies of context in classical conditioning, in human neuropsychology (especially in studies of aging and amnesia), in cognitive psychology, and in the interpretation of hippocampal lesions in animals. The diversity of interest has led to many different uses of the word "context." Few of these uses are precisely specified, and some of the uses do not even overlap each other. For instance, among the clearer definitions of "context" are these: background stimuli (as opposed to foreground stimuli), time and place, tonic stimuli, stimuli that are not attended to by the animal, and phasic stimuli other than the target stimulus (where the target stimulus is defined by the experimenter).

Experimental Observations

Our interest in context stems from the data we have collected on the patterns of firing of hippocampal neurons. Over the past several years we have been recording from single complex-spike cells[1] in Ammon's horn and comparing the firing of a single neuron across several very different situations—usually an operant chamber, a radial maze, and a large home pen, with the same distal cues in all three situations (Kubie & Ranck, 1983). We expected to find consistencies of firing across situations, and were surprised to find very few. What we found was that, for virtually every neuron, two aspects of unit firing were profoundly situation-specific: the spatial firing of the unit and the background firing of the unit. Since O'Keefe and Dostrovsky's (1971) first description, many studies have confirmed that for the rat and rabbit most complex-spike cells in Ammon's horn fire spatially. That is, when a rat is awake, a spatial unit will fire faster than about 2 spikes per second if and only if the animal is in a particular part of its environment. We also found that most cells fired spatially, but we found that the spatial fields (or place fields) were situation-specific: Knowledge of a spatial field in one situation did not help us predict the unit's spatial field in another situation. A cell was capable of having spatial fields in one, two, or all three

---

1. There are two kinds of neurons that can be recorded in Ammon's horn: complex-spike cells and theta cells (Fox & Ranck, 1981). Complex-spike cells are more than 90% of the neurons and are presumably pyramidal cells. Theta cells are interneurons.

John L. Kubie and James B. Ranck, Jr. Department of Physiology, Downstate Medical Center, Brooklyn, New York.

situations. If a rat was returned to a situation hours later, the spatial field of the neuron was the same. The spatial field of neurons was always tested to see whether it was defined by local or distal cues by rotating the apparatus 90 degrees in the recording room. In all cases, spatial fields in the radial-arm maze were defined by distal cues, and spatial fields in the operant chamber and the home pen were defined by local cues. Thus, not only does a single neuron have different spatial fields in different situations, but a place is defined by different types of cues in different situations. A second and more surprising aspect of unit firing that was situation-specific was background firing rate (defined either as firing outside the spatial field or as firing of less than 2 per second). In extreme cases, a cell could be totally off for 10 minutes in one environment, and then could go to a healthy overall firing rate in the next environment, both inside and outside its spatial field. There was no tendency for any particular environment to elicit fast background firing any more than any other environment. This slow background firing was also stable if the rat returned to the same situation hours later. These data made us consider the possibility that situation-specific firing actually represented context-specific firing, and that the hippocampus is part of the neural system that processes (or produces) context.

Objects and Contexts

We were troubled by the use of the word "context"—it seemed correct yet undefined. In trying to link what we knew about the nervous system to a useful definition of "context," we have found it useful to compare two ways in which the mammalian forebrain uses sensory information: to perceive contexts and to identify objects. We have made the simple hypothesis that these two processes are accomplished by different neural systems, which use different processing methods and whose output is used for different purposes. The hippocampus is presumably part of the context-identifying system. What we are going to do for much of this chapter is describe characteristics of the context-identifying system, and, to a lesser degree, the object-identifying system. The goal is to derive a definition of contexts (and objects) that fits both neurobiology and our intuitive notions of what these words should mean.

First, we discuss object detection. It is our hypothesis that sensory processing in the telencephalon is divided into two channels: one for perceiving contexts and the other for identifying objects. Below the telencephalon, these two types of information processing are not differentiated. Common nouns, such as "spoon," "television set," "horse," "chair," "rock," "leaf," and "telephone booth," are all object labels. For a particular object to be identified as a member of an object class, it must pass some test with respect to its stimulus features. For instance, for the visual image of a chair to be identified, the relations of its edges and contours must pass the chair test. Once this set of features has passed the chair test, it no longer is a set of features, but a singular chair. What is useful is that the features do not have to be analyzed over and over again once the object has been recognized. Although it is not totally clear to us how the identification process occurs, objects appear to have three characteristic features: they have continuous contours; they are solid; and they have a size such that the entire contour can be conveniently viewed. Recent neuro-anatomical and physiological work suggests that the visual system has a subsystem devoted to object detection.

Contextual Processing

Knowledge of context appears to be derived from at least two types of sensory information: (1) tonic information from the environment, and (2) information concerning the spatial relationships of objects in the environment.

Tonic Inputs

Tonic input has, at times, been considered the defining feature of context (Wenzel & Zeigler, 1977). For a rat, one might consider several types of tonic information—for instance, constant background sounds or light level. But we are particularly intrigued by the idea that odors permeating an environment may be particularly important tonic cues that help to define a context. We know of no studies of animal behavior that address this possibility directly. On anatomical and physiological grounds, it makes some sense that odors might frequently play this type of role. The olfactory bulbs have substantial projections to the gateway to the hippocampal complex, the entorhinal cortex (Scalia & Winans, 1976). Stimulation of the olfactory bulb produces excitatory postsynaptic potentials (EPSPs) in the hippocampus (Yokota, Reeves, & MacLean, 1970). Even in humans, for whom odors presumably play a less important role than for the rat, odors may play significant roles in context and memory. For people, odor cues are frequently hard to name, but they can frequently evoke images of scenes or events and can help us recall some of our earliest memories. Regardless of which sense modalities contribute the greatest tonic input to the hippocampus, one can well imagine that environment-specific tonic inputs to the hippocampus could well affect the rates or patterns of background activity seen across the neurons of the hippocampus.

Spatial Inputs

Space and context are intertwined[2] (Nadel & Wilner, 1980). Context is not just a list or stimuli, or a list of replaceable stimuli (e.g., Restle, 1957), or a list of complex stimuli; context must involve relationships between and among stimuli, and many of these relationships are spatial. We have found it convenient to divide stimuli into two categories when considering their spatial relationships: stimuli that are used to identify objects, and stimuli that are used as "frames of reference."

Frame-of-reference stimuli are stimuli from gross environmental features that are not objects. Horizons, walls, shorelines, streets, and mountains generate stimuli that are used as part of a frame of reference. (There are stimuli that do not fit into either the object or the frame-to-reference category—e.g., a cloud, rain.) While it seems unlikely that context can exist without a perceived frame of reference, it seems very likely that contexts

2. There are many ways in which the brain processes contextual information. We are not talking about the ways in which the parietal lobe and the superior colliculus process space; the types they process are often called "personal space." We are talking about a mode of spatial processing that deals with spatial relations between and among stimuli, some of which are immediately acting on sensory receptors, but not all of which need be acting on sensory receptors simultaneously. This mode seems to involve the hippocampus.

could be perceived without objects. We are currently studying rats placed within chambers that have clear frame-of-reference cues but no clear object cues—namely, a large rectangular box with one white wall, and a large cylinder with a wide, white vertical stripe on the wall. The spatial and background firing of the hippocampal complex-spike cells in these environments is perfectly normal.

Object detection and discrimination are probably not integral parts of the context system. We imagine that object detection goes on independently of context. But once an object is detected, we imagine that it can contribute to the development of a context or a spatial map. We imagine that during the process of object detection and discrimination, an object is attended to. After the object has been identified, keeping track of its location is complex. The object may move in and out of sensory fields and is usually not the focus of attention. Yet, to a large degree, the object remains identified. Moreover, the object becomes a feature of the context. As a human or a rat enters a familiar environment, we imagine that familiar objects are not repeatedly identified, yet they are kept track of. When an object becomes part of a spatial map or context, some information about the distances and angles between the object and other map stimuli (objects and frame-of-reference cues) must be retained. One simple model that would explain the spatial firing of hippocampal neurons is that the firing of hippocampal neurons is tuned to the perceptual angle(s) between or among environmental features. This model could and should be tested. If something of this nature turns out to be the case, it would indicate that information about the perceived angles between and among stimuli from the environment is a basic part of spatial and contextual processing.

Features of Context

A context cannot be studied with only knowledge of the environment an animal inhabits, because context is a way in which an animal actively interprets its environment. Context is the result of how a particular animal processes information. It is a special kind of perception. To study context, therefore, we must know about both the animal and its environment. Since we think that the hippocampus is involved in processing contextual information, we can study context by studying the firing of hippocampal neurons in behaving animals. Contextual processing can also be studied in purely behavioral experiments. Some stimuli, such as a horizon, are likely to be involved in contextual processing, but stimuli are not inherently contextual or noncontextual. Most stimuli are used simultaneously in contextual processing and other processing (e.g., object discrimination and reflexes).

We imagine that an animal perceives a context at any given time, and we imagine that it perceives only one context. This context may be familiar or novel, and it may be stable or changing, but there is one and only one. A context will remain the same in the face of some variation of its parts. The slow, situation-specific firing in Ammon's horn changes abruptly when a rat is placed in a different one of the three situations we have studied. We imagine that this change in firing correlates with the rat's perception of a new context. There are only casual observations on the development of place fields or slow firing of hippocampal neurons when a rat is placed in a novel environment. When the rat is first placed in the environment, there is a slow, apparently nonspecific firing of complex-spike cells; this firing gradually speeds up or slows down to a steady level in a few minutes. Place fields may be seen in 1 to 5 minutes. We imagine that changes in the firing patterns of complex-spike cells correspond to changes in the perceived context as the rat becomes familiar with the environment. From these observations, it seems that a context can change slowly or abruptly in particular cases. Whether context changes slowly or abruptly in a particular case is an important issue, which can be partially addressed by studying the firing of complex-spike cells in changing situations.

Attention is similar to context in that approximately one and only one thing can be attended to at a time. We imagine, however, that attention and context are controlled by entirely different neural and behavioral systems. Different things can be attended to in the same context, and the same thing can be attended to in different contexts.

Contextual stimuli are not necessarily the objects of attention. Only a small portion of the sensory information coming into an animal is attended to, and a much larger portion may contribute to context. The fact that a stimulus is attended to does not mean that it cannot contribute to context. Rather, attention, or lack of it, is independent of and irrelevant to context. The place field of a single neuron in Ammon's horn is largely independent of the behavior of the animal. For instance, the location of the place field and the firing rate while in the place field are approximately the same, whether a rat runs through an apparatus on its own or is carried through in the hand of the experimenter. We imagine that the rat is attending to very different things in the two cases.

In the visual system of primates, attention usually involves foveation and hence a more detailed sensory processing. Much of the visual contribution to context is probably extrafoveal and does not receive detailed processing. Similarly, contextual stimuli from other sensory systems may not receive analysis as detailed as the analysis required by stimuli that are attended to. Almost all behavioral work, even on context, has studied stimuli that are intense or that are probably the objects of attention. But this is probably a minor part of contextual processing. We personally find it hard to think about sensory events that are not attended to—not only because of a shortage of data, but also because of the difficulty in using our own personal experience as a guide. Things that we do not attend to, we are not aware of. We consider it possible that there are certain classes of external stimuli that we never attend to and that we may never be aware of, these stimuli may contribute to context; some of these may be olfactory.

Context and Learning

In talking about memory and context, it is useful to separate out three kinds of memory: memory for discrete events, procedural memory, and spatial memory. There are other kinds of memory that do not fall into these categories. First, our conclusions are as follows: Memory for discrete events is heavily dependent on context (and hence on the hippocampus); and certain kinds of spatial memory are also heavily dependent on context (and hence on the hippocampus).

Memory for discrete events is the same as "episodic memory," as defined by Tulving (1972) and Kinsbourne and Wood (1982). It also includes "working memory" as defined by

Honig (1978) and Olton, Becker, and Handelmann (1979), but is a larger category. Memory for discrete events involves both a memory for a single event and the ability to distinguish one event from another. Therefore, one-trial learning is not necessarily a memory for a discrete event. We imagine that contextual information is used to store and retrieve a memory of a discrete event—ideas previously developed by Hirsh (1974) and Kinsbourne and Wood (1982). Context can be thought of as the basis of the filing system. Some deficits seen after hippocampal lesions in animals are well explained by a loss of memory for discrete events—for instance, the loss of ability to perform on a schedule of differential reinforcement of low rate of response (DRL). Olton *et al.* (1979) have argued that working-memory deficits are the principal deficits seen after hippocampal lesions in animals. Human amnesics have a major deficit in memory for discrete events (Kinsbourne & Wood, 1982).

"Procedural memory" is the terminology of Squire and Zola-Morgan (1983); they also call it "skill learning." They describe procedural learning as based on procedures or rules rather than specific facts or data. It is "knowing how" as opposed to "knowing that." Procedural learning includes motor learning, simple delayed classical conditioning, and even some cognitive skills. Procedural memory does not use contextual information. Indeed, it is important for many skills to be used in many contexts (Kinsbourne & Wood, 1982). Contextual cues may be explicitly ignored. Squire (1982) has reviewed those kinds of memory that are unaffected in human amnesics and has shown that they all fit the category of procedural memory. There has been no thorough review of the effects of hippocampal lesions in animals on procedural memory. It seems that much of the learning that is spared after hippocampal lesions (most operant learning and discrimination learning) would be classified as procedural. We know of no clear procedural-learning task that is affected by hippocampal lesions.

The hippocampus and the contextual system are also probably involved in certain kinds of spatial memory. We have described above the experimental results on the relation of context and the spatial firing of complex-spike cells in the hippocampus, and we have given our reasoning on the relationship between space and context. O'Keefe and Nadel (1978) have argued that many of the deficits seen after hippocampal lesions in animals can be explained by a loss of spatial ability, including spatial memory. There is much to what they say.

There are memories that are not easily classified as episodic or procedural or spatial. For instance, there are memories of the facts of American history, there are memories of individuals we have met, and there are memories of the features of familiar objects. The fact that these memories are difficult to classify indicates that we are very far from a totally useful memory taxonomy. There is, however, one further idea we would like to present. We have speculated above that two telecephalic sensory processing systems may exist—a context system and an object system. Perhaps context categories are used for filing episodic memories and spatial memories, while object categories are used for filing other types of memory.[3]

---

3. *Note added in proof.* Since the preparation of this chapter, Mishkin, Ungerleiter, and Macko (1983) have published a summary of anatomical, electrophysiological, and behavioral work in the monkey concerning cortical processing of visual information. This paper describes two cortical information-processing pathways: an object-identifying pathway through the inferior temporal cortex, and a spatial-analysis pathway through the inferior parietal cortex. The finding of an anatomical substrate for these two systems is a necessary step in demonstrating the dichotomy we discuss between the processing of objects and spatial contexts.

ACKNOWLEDGMENT

This work was supported by National Institutes of Health Grant NS 14497.

REFERENCES

Fox, S. E., & Ranck, J. B., Jr. Electrophysiological characteristics of hippocampal complex-spike cells and theta cells. *Experimental Brain Research*, 1981, *41*, 399–410.

Hirsh, R. The hippocampus and contextual retrieval of information from memory: A theory. *Behavioral Biology*, 1974, *12*, 421–444.

Honig, W. K. Studies of working memory in the pigeon. In S. H. Hulse, H. Fowler, & W. K. Honig (Eds.), *Cognitive processes in animal behavior*. Hillsdale, N.J.: Erlbaum, 1978.

Kinsbourne, M., & Wood, F. Theoretical considerations regarding the episodic–semantic memory distinction. In L. S. Cermak (Ed.), *Human memory and amnesia*. Hillsdale, N.J.: Erlbaum, 1982.

Kubie, J. L., & Ranck, J. B., Jr. Sensory–behavioral correlates in individual hippocampal neurons in three situations: Space and context. In W. Seifert (Ed.), *Neurobiology of the hippocampus*. New York: Academic Press, 1983.

Mishkin, M., Ungerleiter, L. G., & Macko, K. A. Object vision and spatial vision: Two cortical pathways. *Trends in Neuroscience*, 1983, *6*, 414–417.

O'Keefe, J., & Dostrovsky, J. The hippocampus as a spatial map. Preliminary evidence from unit activity in the freely-moving rat. *Brain Research*, 1971, *34*, 171–175.

O'Keefe, J., & Nadel, L. *The Hippocampus as a cognitive map*. London: Oxford University Press, 1978.

Olton, D. S., Becker, J. T., & Handlemann, G. E. Hippocampus, space, and memory. *Behavioral and Brain Sciences*, 1979, *2*, 313–365.

Nadel, L., & Wilner, J. Context and conditioning: A place for space. *Physiological Psychology* , 1980, *8*, 218–228.

Restle, F. Discrimination of cues in mazes: A resolution of the place-versus-response question. *Psychological Review*, 1957, *64*, 217–228.

Scalia, F., & Winans, S. S. New perspectives on the morphology of the olfactory system: Olfactory and vomeronasal pathways in mammals. In R. L. Doty (Ed.), *Mammalian olfaction, reproductive processes, and behavior*. New York: Academic Press, 1976.

Squire, L. R. The neuropsychology of human memory. *Annual Review of Neuroscience*, 1982, *5*, 241–273.

Squire, L. R., & Zola-Morgan, S. The neurology of memory: The case for correspondence between the findings for man and non-human primates. In J. A. Deutsch (Ed.), *The physiological basis of memory* (2nd ed.). New York: Academic Press, 1983.

Tulving, E. Episodic and semantic memory. In E. Tulving & W. D. Donaldson (Eds.), *Organization of memory*. New York: Academic Press, 1972.

Wenzel, B. M., & Zeigler, H. P. (Eds.). Tonic functions of sensory systems. *Annals of the New York Academy of Sciences*, 1977, *290*, 1–435.

Yokota, T., Reeves, A. G., & MacLean, P. D. Differential effects of septal and olfactory valleys on intracellular responses of hippocampal neurons in awake, sitting monkeys. *Journal of Neurophysiology*, 1970, *33*, 96–107.

Neuronal Substrates of Basic Associative Learning **39**

Richard F. Thompson, Gregory A. Clark, Nelson H. Donegan,
David G. Lavond, John Madden IV, Laura A. Mamounas,
Michael D. Mauk, and David A. McCormick

The nature of the memory trace has proved to be among the most baffling questions in science. In order to analyze mechanisms of information storage and retrieval, it is first necessary to identify and localize the brain systems, structures, and regions that are critically involved. With a very few exceptions, such information has not yet been obtained. This problem of localization has been perhaps the greatest barrier to progress in the field (Hebb, 1949; Lashley, 1929; Thompson, Berger, & Madden, 1983).

In recent years the "model system" approach to analysis of the neuronal substrates of learning and memory has been valuable and productive. The basic notion is to utilize a preparation showing a clear form of associative learning in which neuronal analysis is possible. When a suitable preparation has been developed, the first issue that must be addressed is that of identifying the neuronal structures and systems that are involved in a given form of learning. Most typically, this has been approached using lesions, electrophysiological recording, and anatomical methods. A critical aspect is circuit analysis—tracing the neuronal pathways and systems from the conditioned stimulus (CS) channel to the motor neurons. As the essential structures and pathways are defined, it becomes possible to localize and analyze cellular mechanisms underlying learning and memory (Cohen, 1980; Ito, 1982; Kandel & Spencer, 1968; Thompson, Berger, Cegavske, Patterson, Roemer, Teyler, & Young, 1976; Thompson, Berger, & Madden, 1983; Thompson, McCormick, Lavond, Clark, Kettner, & Mauk, 1983; Thompson & Spencer, 1966; Tsukahara, 1981; Woody, Yarowsky, Owens, Black-Cleworth, & Crow, 1974). One of the many advantages of utilizing a few well-defined model systems for analysis of brain substrates of learning and memory is that knowledge is cumulative and can be generalized across laboratories.

We have adopted a particularly clear-cut and robust form of associative learning in the intact mammal as a model system: classical conditioning of the rabbit nictitating membrane (NM) and eyelid response to an acoustic CS, using a corneal airpuff, as unconditioned stimulus (UCS). This simple form of learning, first developed for behavioral analysis by Gormezano, is very well characterized behaviorally (Gormezano, 1972), has

Richard F. Thompson, Nelson H. Donegan, David G. Lavond, Laura A. Mamounas, and Michael D. Mauk. Department of Psychology, Stanford University, Stanford, California.

Gregory A. Clark. Center for Neurobiology and Behavior, Columbia University, New York, New York.

John Madden IV. Departments of Physiology and of Psychiatry and the Behavioral Sciences, Stanford University Medical School, Stanford, California.

David A. McCormick. Department of Neurology, Stanford University Medical School, Stanford, California.

proved extremely valuable for analysis of theoretical issues in learning by Wagner and associates (Donegan & Wagner, in press; Wagner, 1969, 1971, 1981), and is particularly well suited for neurobiological analysis (Disterhoft, Kwan, & Low, 1977; Thompson *et al.*, 1976). A number of laboratories are now using this preparation for the study of neuronal substrates of learning and memory (e.g., see Thompson, McCormick, Lavond, *et al.*, 1983). Eyelid conditioning exhibits the same basic laws of learning in a wide range of mammalian species, including humans, and is prototypical of classical conditioning of striated muscle responses.

We have developed evidence elsewhere arguing against the possibility that the essential neuronal plasticity forming the memory trace develops in the CS channel (here, the primary auditory system). In brief, using a signal detection paradigm where the animal gives conditioned responses (CRs) on only half the trials to a constant-intensity threshold-level acoustic CS, the evoked neuronal activity in primary auditory-relay nuclei is present and identical in both detection and nondetection trials (Kettner & Thompson, 1982). The memory-trace system(s) must be differentially active or activated on trials when learned responses are emitted or not emitted. Other evidence argues against localization of the trace to reflex pathways and alpha or startle-response pathways: In particular, the minimum latency of the well-learned response is about 80 msec, much too long for these short latency pathways. Still other evidence argues against localization of the trace to motor neurons (see Thompson, McCormick, Lavond, *et al.*, 1983). Here we focus on putative sites of neuronal plasticity that may serve to code learning and memory for "simple" CRs. Classical conditioning of the rabbit NM–eyelid response may be viewed as but one instance of the general class of specific, adaptive CRs learned with an aversive UCS.

Even in this relatively simple associative-learning situation, it appears that several "memory-trace" systems may develop in the brain. In his treatment of classical conditioning, Konorski (1967) distinguished between two classes of CRs: diffuse, preparatory CRs and precise, consummatory CRs. A similar distinction has been made by Weinberger (1982) in his survey of aversive conditioning between "nonspecific" and "specific" CRs. Nonspecific responses are usually autonomic, but also include generalized body movements, are learned rapidly, and prepare the organism to do something. Such responses are often viewed as manifestations of a "conditioned emotional state" or "acquired drive" (e.g., conditioned fear) (Brown & Jacobs, 1949; Frey & Ross, 1968; Konorsky, 1967; Miller, 1948; Mowrer, 1947; Rescorla & Solomon, 1967). They presumably reflect the basic association between the neutral CS and the "emotogenic" properties of the UCS. Conditioning of specific responses (e.g., eyelid closure or leg flexion) involves learning precise, adaptive CRs that deal specifically with the UCS and require more extensive training. Prokasy (1972) has suggested a similar dichotomy based on occurrence of learned responses. In his terms, the first phase, lasting until the occurrence of the first CR, consists in detection of the CS-UCS contingency and initial selection of the appropriate adaptive response, and the second phase concerns the increase in relative frequency of the specific, adaptive learned response.

A third type of memory-trace system involves higher brain structures such as the hippocampus and might be called complex, cognitive, or "declarative" (e.g., see Squire, 1982). In the "simple" standard-delay, classically conditioned NM–eyelid response in the rabbit, at least these three trace systems appear to develop, as we describe in detail below. It appears that the "nonspecific response" memory trace may be necessary for development of the "specific adaptive response" memory trace, which in turn may be necessary for development of at least a part of the "cognitive" memory trace (see Thompson, Barchas, Clark, Donegan, Kettner, Lavond, Madden, Mauk, & McCormick, in press; Thompson, Berger, & Madden, 1983; Thompson, McCormick, Lavond, *et al.*, 1983).

Initial Localization of the Memory Trace for the Discrete, Adaptive Learned Response: The Cerebellum

Animals can learn the standard NM–eyelid CR following ablation of all brain tissue above the level of the thalamus (Enser, 1974; Norman, Buchwald, & Villablanca, 1977). Several inferences are possible from this result, perhaps the most parsimonious being that a "primary memory-trace" circuit exists below the level of the thalamus for the standard CR. This is not to say that higher brain structures do not normally play important roles and develop substantial learning-induced neuronal plasticity. Indeed, the hippocampus does so (see below).

Over the past 4 years, we have been in the process of completing an extensive and detailed mapping of the midbrain–brain stem, recording neuronal-unit activity in already trained animals (McCormick, Lavond, & Thompson, 1983; Thompson *et al.*, in press). Learning-related increases in unit activity are prominent in certain regions of the cerebellum (both in cortex and deep nuclei), in certain regions of the pontine nuclei, and in the red nucleus. Such unit activity is also seen in certain regions of the reticular formation, and of course in the cranial motor nuclei engaged in generation of the behavioral response— portions of the third, fifth, sixth, accessory sixth, and seventh nuclei. The results to date of the mapping studies point to substantial engagement of the cerebellar system in the generation of the CR.

Current studies in which we have recorded neuronal-unit activity from the deep cerebellar nuclei (dentate and interpositus nuclei) over the course of training have in some locations revealed a striking pattern of learning-related growth in activity (McCormick, Clark, Lavond, & Thompson, 1982). In the example shown in Figure 39-1, the animal did not learn on Day 1 of training. Unit activity showed evoked responses to tone and airpuff onsets but no response in association with the reflex NM response, in marked contrast to unit recordings from the cranial motor nuclei. On Day 2 the animal began showing CRs, and the unit activity in the medial dentate nucleus developed a "model" of the CR. On Day 3, the learned behavioral response and the cerebellar model of the learned response were well developed, but there was still no clear model of the reflex behavioral response. The cerebellar-unit model of the learned response precedes the behavioral response signifi- cantly in time. Another example is shown in Figure 39-2. This animal was given unpaired training before acquisition began. Average histograms revealed that the unit activity showed only minimal responses to the tone and airpuff during the unpaired day of training. However, during acquisition, as the animal learned, the unit activity developed a model of the CR. Again, there is no clear model of the unconditioned response (UCR). *A neuronal model of the learned behavioral response appears to develop* de novo *in the cerebellum.*

In current work, we have found that lesions ipsilateral to the trained eye in several locations in the neocerebellum—large ablations of the lateral portion of the hemisphere, localized electrolytic lesions of the dentate–interpositus nuclei and surrounding fibers, and discrete lesions of the superior cerebellar peduncle (see Figure 39-3)—permanently abolish

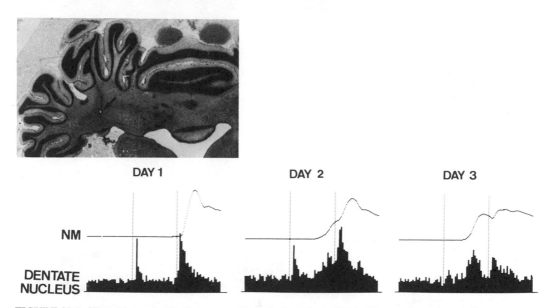

FIGURE 39-1. Histograms of unit cluster recordings obtained from the medial dentate nucleus during classical conditioning of NM–eyelid response. The recording site is indicated by the arrow. Each histogram bar is 9 msec in width, and each histogram is summed over an entire day of training. The first vertical line represents the onset of the tone, and the second vertical line represents the onset of the airpuff. The trace above each histogram is the averaged movement of the animal's NM for an entire day, with "up" being the extension of the NM across the cornea. The total duration of each histogram and trace is 750 msec. The pattern of increased discharges of cerebellar neurons appears to develop a neuronal "model" of the amplitude–time course of the learned behavioral response. (From D. A. McCormick, G. A. Clark, D. G. Lavond, & R. F. Thompson, Initial localization of the memory trace for a basic form of learning. *Proceedings of the National Academy of Sciences*, 1982, 79(8), 2731–2742. Reprinted by permission.)

the CR but have no effect on the UCR and do not prevent subsequent learning by the contralateral eye (see Figure 39-4) (Clark, McCormick, Lavond, Baxter, Gray, & Thompson, 1982; McCormick, Clark, Lavond, & Thompson, 1982; McCormick, Guyer, & Thompson, 1982; McCormick, Lavond, Clark, Kettner, Rising, & Thompson, 1981). The result with electrolytic lesions has recently been replicated exactly by Yeo, Hardiman, Glickstein, and Russell (1982), using light as well as tone CSs and a periorbital shock rather than the corneal airpuff as the UCS. If training is given after unilateral cerebellar lesion, the ipsilateral eye cannot learn, but the contralateral eye learns normally (Lincoln, McCormick, & Thompson, 1982). Lesions in several locations in the ipsilateral pontine brain stem produce a similar selective abolition of the CR (Desmond & Moore, 1982; Lavond, McCormick, Clark, Holmes, & Thompson, 1981). Although some uncertainty still exists, the learning-effective lesion sites in the pontine brain stem appear to track the course of at least a part of the superior cerebellar peduncle.

Taken together, these results indicate that the cerebellum is an obligatory part of the learned-response circuit for NM–eyelid conditioning. Since decerebrate animals can learn the response, this would seem to localize an essential component of the memory trace to the ipsilateral cerebellum and/or its major afferent–efferent systems. The fact that a neuronal-unit "model" of the learned behavioral response develops in the cerebellar deep nuclei and may precede the behavioral response by as much as 50 msec or more would

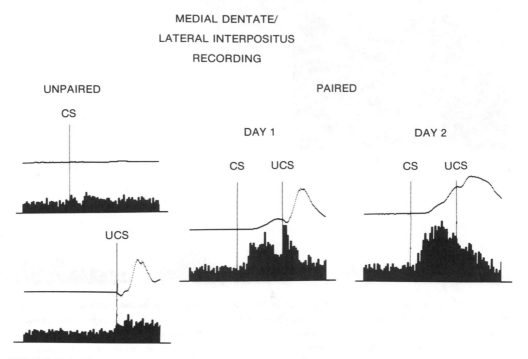

MEDIAL DENTATE/
LATERAL INTERPOSITUS
RECORDING

UNPAIRED   PAIRED

CS   DAY 1   DAY 2

UCS   CS   UCS   CS   UCS

FIGURE 39-2. Histograms of unit recordings obtained from a chronic electrode implanted on the border of the dentate–interpositus nuclei in one animal. The animal was first given random, unpaired presentations of the tone and airpuff (104 trials of each stimulus) and then trained with 2 days of paired training (117 trials each day). Each histogram is an average over the entire day of training indicated. The upper trace represents movement of the NM, with "up" being closure. The first vertical line represents the onset of the CS, while the second line represents the onset of the UCS. Each histogram bar is 9 msec in duration. Notice that these neurons develop a model of the CR, but not the UCR, during learning. (McCormick & Thompson, unpublished observations.)

FIGURE 39-3. Reconstructions of cerebellar lesions effective in abolishing the ipsilateral conditioned NM–eyelid response. A is a typical unilateral aspiration of the lateral cerebellum and dentate–interpositus nuclei. B represents a unilateral electrolytic lesion of the dentate–interpositus nuclei (DIX) in which the overlying cortex is spared. C is a localized unilateral lesion of the superior cerebellar peduncle (SPX). All reconstructions are through the broadest extent of each lesion. Abbreviations: ANS, ansiform lobe; CN, cochlear nucleus; D, dentate nucleus; F, fastigial nucleus; ANT, anterior lobe; FL, flocculus; I, interpositus nucleus; IC, inferior colliculus; IO, inferior olive; IP, inferior cerebellar peduncle; PF, paraflocculus; SC, superior colliculus; SP; superior cerebellar peduncle; VM, vermal lobes; VII, seventh nucleus. (Unpublished observations.)

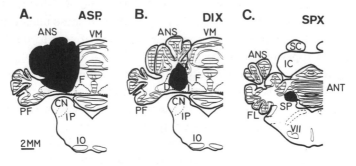

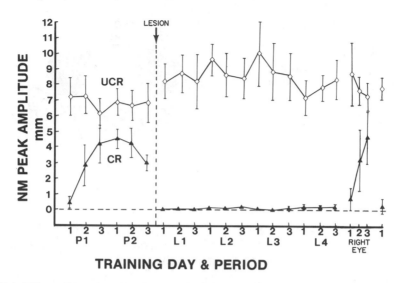

TRAINING DAY & PERIOD

FIGURE 39-4. Effects of ablation of left lateral cerebellum on the learned NM–eyelid response (six animals). Solid triangles indicate the amplitude of the CR; open diamonds indicate the amplitude of the UCR. All training was to left eye (ipsilateral to lesion), except where labeled "right eye." The cerebellar lesion completely and permanently abolished the CR of the ipsilateral eye, but had no effect on the UCR. P_1 and P_2 indicate initial learning on the 2 days prior to the lesion. L_1–L_4 are 4 days of postoperative training to the left eye. The right eye was then trained and learned rapidly. The left eye was again trained and showed no learning. Numbers on abscissa indicate 40-trial periods, except for "right eye," which are 24-trial periods. (From D. A. McCormick, G. A. Clark, D. G. Lavond, & R. F. Thompson, Initial localization of the memory trace for a basic form of learning. *Proceedings of the National Academy of Sciences*, 1982, 79 (8), 2731–2742. Reprinted by permission.)

seem to localize the process to cerebellum or its afferents, for which the cerebellum is a manditory relay. This time period is consistent with the minimum onset latency for CRs in well-trained animals (about 80 msec) and is very close to the minimum CS-UCS interval that can support learning.

The possibility that unilateral cerebellar lesions produce a modulatory disruption of a memory trace localized elsewhere in the brain seems unlikely. If so, it must be efferent from the cerebellum, since discrete lesions of the superior cerebellar peduncle abolish the learned behavioral response. Yet the neuronal model of the learned response is present within the ipsilateral cerebellum. In current studies, we have trained animals with both eyes and have made bilateral ablations of the lateral cerebellum. The lesions permanently abolish the conditioned NM–eyelid response on both sides. (The smallest effective bilateral lesions do not produce any persisting signs of motor dysfunction.) Such animals have been repeatedly retrained for as long as 3 months postoperatively and show no relearning at all of the CR with either eye (Thompson *et al.*, in press) (see Figure 39-5).

In a related project, we have found that the lateral ipsilateral cerebellum is also essential for classical conditioning of the flexion reflex in the hind limb (Thompson *et al.*, in press). Rabbits are initially trained with a shock UCS to the left hind paw, using the same conditions otherwise as in NM–eyelid training (i.e., tone CS), and electromyogram (EMG) activity is recorded from flexor muscles of both hind limbs. Both hind limbs develop an equivalent learned flexor response, consistent with the rabbit's normal model of locomotion. Ablation of the left lateral cerebellum permanently abolishes this conditioned

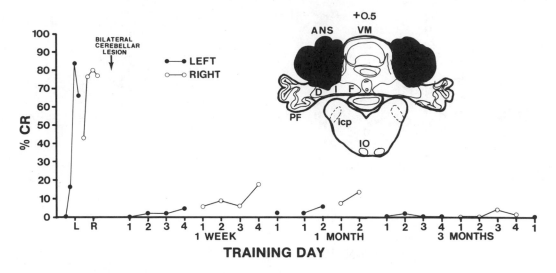

FIGURE 39-5. Effects of bilateral neocerebellar lesion on the conditioned NM–eyelid response of one animal. Before lesion, the animal's left NM–eyelid was trained (L), with subsequent training of the right NM–eyelid (R). Each data point is an average of 30 trials. A bilateral cerebellar aspiration was performed, and the animal was allowed to recover 1 full week. The animal was then given 4 full days of training (120 trials each day) to the left and then the right NM–eyelid, followed by 1 additional day of training on the left. At 1 month postlesion, the animal was again trained 2 days on each side. At 3 months postlesion, the animal again received 4 days of training per side, followed by 1 final day on the left. Each data point after (L) and (R) represents 1 full day of training. Histology revealed that the ansiform and paramedian lobes and the dorsal aspect of the dentate–interpositus nuclei were removed bilaterally. Note that although the animal learned the response initially in fewer than 90 trials, subsequent training of 1440 trials on the left side and 1200 trials on the right over a period of 3 months failed to reinstate this learned response. (Lavond, McCormick, & Thompson, unpublished observations.)

response in both hind limbs (see Figure 39-6). Training (i.e., paw-shock UCS) is then given to the right hind limb, and both hind limbs relearn. When training is then shifted back to the left hind limb, the learned response in both hind limbs rapidly extinguishes. These results demonstrate that the left cerebellar lesion does not simply prevent the animal from making the learned response in the left hind limb; they support the view that the memory trace for the learning of hind limb flexion, like the NM–eyelid learned response, is established unilaterally in the cerebellum. There is an earlier Soviet report indicating that complete removal of the cerebellum in dogs well trained in leg-flexion conditioning permanently abolished the discrete leg-flexion response (Karamian, Fanaralijian, & Kosareva, 1969).

From these results, we infer that the cerebellum is essential for the learning of all discrete, adaptive motor responses, at least for classical conditioning with an aversive UCS. In terms of localization of the putative memory trace, our evidence at present is most consistent with localization to the dentate–interpositus nuclei. Composite diagrams are shown in Figure 39-7, indicating regions that are ineffective in abolishing the learned NM–eyelid response, a minimum effective lesion, and recording sites where a neuronal model of the learned response develops in the cerebellar deep nuclei. Note that the neuronal model and the effective lesion site are virtually identical, involving the most

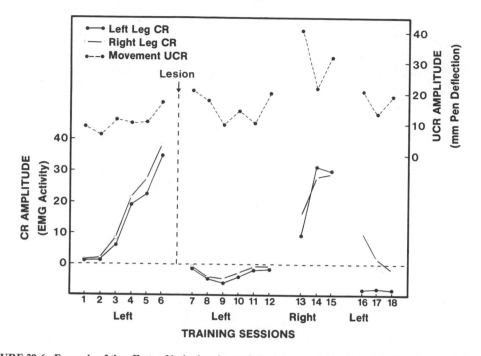

FIGURE 39-6. Example of the effects of lesioning the cerebellar deep nuclei ipsilateral to the side of training on leg-flexion CRs and UCRs in the rabbit. In each session 30 training trials were presented, wherein a 350-msec auditory CS overlapped and terminated with a 100-msec paw-shock UCS. During Sessions 1–12 and 16–18, the shock UCS was delivered to the left paw (ipsilateral to the side of the lesion), and during Sessions 13–15 the shock UCS was shifted to the right paw. (The bilateral leg-flexion UCRs to the paw-shock UCS were measured by means of a stabilimeter device.) (Donegan & Thompson, unpublished observations.)

medial portion of the dentate nucleus and the most lateral portion of the interpositus nucleus. Large cortical cerebellar lesions are ineffective in abolishing the learned response: The small critical region of the dentate–interpositus must be damaged (see also Figure 39-3). We do not yet know whether the cerebellar cortex plays an important role in initial learning; it does not appear to be essential for the memory of the learned response.

Finally, in current work we have found that microinjection of as little as 2 nmol of bicuculline methiodide directly into this same region—the medial dentate–lateral interpositus nuclear area—causes a selective and reversible abolition of both the behavioral CR and the neuronal model of the CR (recorded with a microelectrode .75mm ventral to the tip of the microinfusion cannula) (see Figure 39-8). This selective bicuculline abolition of the learned response occurs, regardless of how well trained or overtrained the animal is. The fact that high concentrations of gamma-aminobutyric acid (GABA) have been localized to these nuclear regions (Okada, Nitsch-Hassler, Kim, Bak, & Hassler, 1971), coupled with the observations by Chan-Palay (1977, 1978) demonstrating autoradiographic localization of GABA receptors in this region, provides a basis for tentatively postulating that bicuculline produces its selective abolition of the CR in a traditional way—through blockage of inhibitory GABAminergic transmission. Note that there is no increase in spontaneous unit activity following bicuculline infusion in the recordings shown in Figure 39-8; thus the abolition of the CR seems not to be due to abnormally increased cellular activity. Instead,

A. NONEFFECTIVE

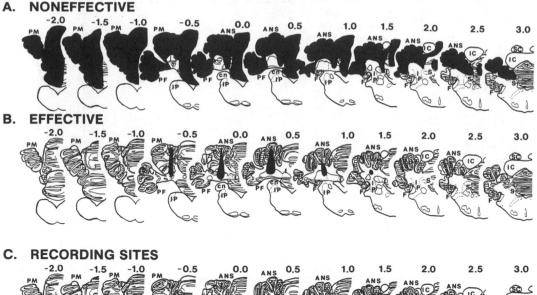

B. EFFECTIVE

C. RECORDING SITES

FIGURE 39-7. Summary of lesion and recording studies. A is a composite of the cerebellar tissue removed (in four animals) without permanent abolition of a previously learned NM–eyelid response. B is a representative stereotaxic lesion of one animal, which permanently abolished the learned response. C indicates seven recording sites (stars) that reveal models of the CR. The "3" at level 0.5 indicates that there are three stars at this level. The recordings from Figures 39-1 and 39-2 are two of these three stars. Note that the effective and noneffective lesions are closely complementary, and that the recording sites that reveal models of the CR exist in the same region as the effective lesion. This region is within the medial dentate–lateral interpositus nuclei. (McCormick & Thompson, unpublished observations.)

it seems more likely to be blocking inhibitory synaptic transmission that is in some way essential for the generation of the CR. One calls to mind Eugene Roberts's notion of GABAminergic processes' playing a key role in learning (Roberts, 1976, 1980). This result also demonstrates that abolition of the CR by lesions in this region cannot be due to nonspecific persisting effects of the lesion. The bicuculline abolition of the CR dissipates over time—with CRs returning to baseline levels by the end of the test session (see Figure 39-8).

It seems a very reasonable possibility that the memory trace for learning of classical (and instrumental?) discrete, adaptive motor responses occurs in the cerebellum. Perhaps the most prominent feature of such learned responses is their precise timing. At least in aversive learning, the CR is under very strong control by the CS-UCS interval in terms of onset latency and temporal morphology, and is always timed to be at maximum at or shortly before the time when the onset of the UCS occurs. The cerebellum is very well designed to provide such precise timing (Eccles, Ito, & Szentagothai, 1967). Indeed, the

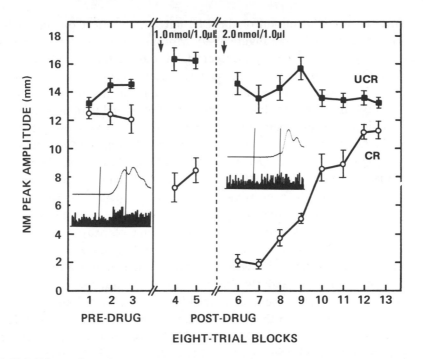

FIGURE 39-8. Effects of localized microinjection of bicuculline methiodide into the medial dentate–lateral interpositus region on the well-learned NM–eyelid response. Closed squares and open circles represent the peak amplitude of the UCR and CR, respectively. Each training block consists of eight averaged trials, with a variable 30-sec intertrial interval. Left panel: Mean NM response amplitude during three blocks of predrug baseline conditioning. Center panel: Mean NM response amplitude for two blocks following microinjection of 1 nmol bicuculline methiodide into dentate–interpositus. Right panel: Mean NM response amplitude for eight blocks following microinjection of 2 nmol of bicuculline methiodide. Note inserts within left and right panels: The upper trace in each histogram represents the averaged NM response; the lower trace depicts the corresponding dentate–interpositus multiple-unit peristimulus histogram. The bin width is 9 msec. The first vertical line in each histogram indicates tone onset; the second vertical line indicates airpuff onset. The predrug histogram is an average of Blocks 2 and 3; the postdrug histogram is an average of Blocks 6 and 7. (Mauk, Madden, Barchas, & Thompson, unpublished observations.)

cerebellum has been suggested by several authors as a possible locus for the coding of learned motor responses (Eccles *et al.*, 1967; Ito, 1970, 1982; Marr, 1969) as has the red nucleus (Tsukahara, 1981) and the inferior olive (Llinas, Walton, Hillman, & Sotelo, 1975).

Opiate Actions on the Learned Response: Conditioned Fear?

Opiate and endogenous opioid actions have been implicated in aversive learning in a large number of studies (Martinez, Rigter, Jensen, Messing, Vasquez, & McGaugh, 1981). As we have noted earlier, behavioral analyses of aversive learning suggest that it may occur as two processes or phases, the first involving "conditioned fear," and the second concerned with learned performance of discrete, adaptive motor responses.

Systemic intravenous (i.v.) administration of morphine (5.0 mg/kg) to animals that have just learned the NM–eyelid response to criterion causes an immediate and naloxone-reversible (i.v. .1 mg/kg) abolition of the CR, but has no effect on the UCR (Mauk, Warren, & Thompson, 1982) (see Figure 39-9). Morphine has no effect on neuronal-unit activity evoked by the tone CS in the central nucleus of the inferior colliculus. The abolition of the CR occurs on the trial immediately after injection, prior to presentation of the next UCS. It would seem that morphine is acting directly on some aspect of the associative process. In a series of studies using both central and peripheral administration of highly specific opiate analogues (e.g., morphiceptin), it was shown that the opiate abolition of the CR is entirely a central action and can be obtained by activation of mu receptors (see Figures 39-10 and 39-11) (Mauk, Madden, Barchas, & Thompson, 1982). The most immediate and profound effects are obtained with administration to the rostral region of the fourth ventricle, suggesting involvement of opiate-receptor-rich systems in this region. Application of the same kind and amount of opiate in the fourth ventricle also selectively abolishes the classically conditioned slowing of heart rate in response to periorbital shock in the rabbit (Lavond, Mauk, Madden, Barchas, & Thompson, 1982).

    We have suggested that this selective fourth-ventricle opiate abolition of both the learned NM–eyelid response and the learned heart rate response might be due to a common action on some part of the "conditioned fear" system in the brain stem (Thompson *et al.*, in press). Consistent with this interpretation is the fact that overtraining protects against the effects of opiates on the NM–eyelid CR (Mauk, Castellano, Rideout, Madden, Barchas, & Thompson, 1983) (see Figure 39-12). It is as though the presumed cerebellar system develops some degree of "functional autonomy" when the specific adaptive response

FIGURE 39-9. The effect of i.v. administration of morphine on NM CRs and UCRs. Rabbits were trained to a criterion of eight CRs in nine consecutive trials and were given two additional blocks of trials (baseline conditioning) before injection of morphine (5 mg/kg). Scores for the CR and UCR were determined by the peak amplitude of the NM extension during CS and UCS periods, respectively. Dotted lines indicate preinjection response baselines. (From M. D. Mauk, J. T. Warren, & R. F. Thompson, Selective, naloxone-reversible morphine depression of learned behavioral and hippocampal responses. *Science*, 1982, *216*, 434–435. Copyright 1982 by the American Association for the Advancement of Science. Reprinted by permission.)

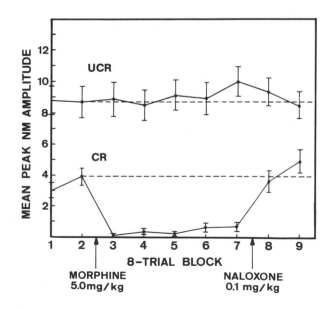

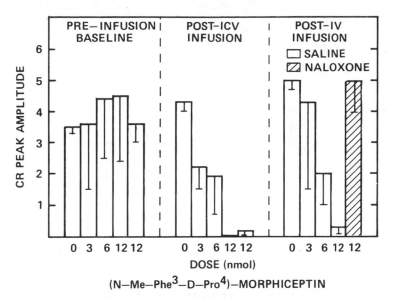

FIGURE 39-10. The effect of intracerebroventricular (ICV) infusion (fourth ventricle) of the potent and highly selective *mu* receptor agonist [N-Me-Phe³-D-Pro⁴]morphiceptin on NM CRs. Animals were trained to criterion baseline conditioning (left panel). ICV infusion of [N-Me-Phe³-D-Pro⁴]morphiceptin produced a dose-dependent abolition of CRs (center panel). This effect was reversed in animals given i.v. injections of naloxone 2.5 mg/kg (right panel). (From M. D. Mauk, J. Madden IV, J. D. Barchas, & R. F. Thompson, Opiates and classical conditioning: Selective abolition of conditioned responses by activation of opiate receptors within the central nervous system. *Proceedings of the National Academy of Sciences*, 1982, 79, 7598–7602. Reprinted by permission.)

FIGURE 39-11. Systemic administration of [N-Me-Phe³-D-Pro⁴]morphiceptin has no effect on CRs, supporting a central site of action. Each animal was given serial systemic doses of [N-Me-Phe³-D-Pro⁴]morphiceptin in doses ranging from .1 to 10 times those effective via central administration (i.e., 1.2 to 120 nmol; see Figure 39-10).

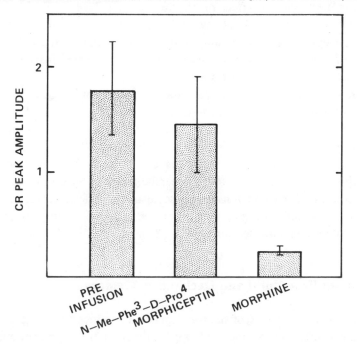

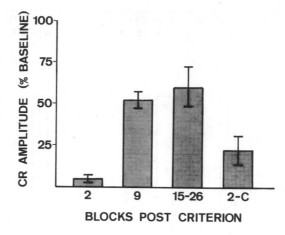

FIGURE 39-12. The effect of additional baseline conditioning blocks (overtraining) on morphine abolition of CRs. CR amplitudes following a 5 mg/kg injection of morphine are presented in terms of preinjection baseline. Each group received different amounts of overtraining before injection: 2 blocks ($n = 13$), 9 blocks, ($n = 4$), 15–20 blocks ($n = 7$). The final group (2-C) was a control for consolidation effects ($n = 6$). (From M. D. Mauk, T. G. Castellano, J. A. Rideout, J. Madden, IV, J. D. Barchas, & R. F. Thompson, Overtraining reduces opiate abolition of classically conditioned responses. *Physiology and Behavior*, 1983, *30*, 493–495. Reprinted by permission.)

is well learned; conditioned fear is no longer so critical. There are, of course, other essential neuronal substrates for the learned heart rate response, including portions of the amygdala and the hypothalamus (Cohen, 1980; Kapp, Gallagher, Applegate, & Frysinger, 1982; Smith, Astley, DeVit, Stein, & Walsh, 1980). Interestingly, administration of opiates to the central nucleus of the amygdala abolishes the conditioned heart rate slowing in the rabbit (Kapp *et al.*, 1982) but has no effect on the just-learned NM–eyelid response (Mauk, Madden, Barchas, & Thompson, 1982). We only suggest that there may be localized (and possibly common) opiate actions on some part of the conditioned fear circuitry in the vicinity of the fourth ventricle that is necessary for both responses—learned heart rate and the initial learning of the NM–eyelid response.

In current work, we have found that bilateral lesions of the deep cerebellar nuclei (dentate–interpositus region) that completely prevent learning of the NM–eyelid response with either eye do not prevent learning of the conditioned heart rate slowing (Lavond, Lincoln, McCormick, & Thompson, in press). In short, the "fear" system appears to be essential for learning of the discrete, adaptive response, with its memory trace presumably established in the cerebellar system, but the cerebellar trace system is not essential for learning of nonspecific "fear" responses. These results and speculations are consistent with the large literature implicating opioids in learned fear and anxiety, as well as with the behavioral literature on aversive learning.

The Hippocampus: Procedural and Declarative Memory

One of the more striking aspects of neuronal plasticity induced by simple conditioning procedures is the marked engagement of unit activity in the hippocampus (Swanson, Teyler, & Thompson, 1982). In a series of studies, Berger, Thompson, and associates

(Berger, Laham, & Thompson, 1980; Berger & Thompson, 1978a, 1978b, 1978c, 1982; Berry & Thompson, 1978; Hoehler & Thompson, 1980; Thompson, Berger, Berry, Hoehler, Kettner, & Weisz, 1980) found that the majority of identified pyramidal neurons sampled in the CA3-CA1 region of the dorsal hippocampus developed a very clear neuronal "model" of the learned behavioral NM–eyelid response in the rabbit (see Figure 39-13). Over a wide range of conditions that impair or alter acquisition, maintenance, or extinction of the learned NM–eyelid response, the learning-induced increase in hippocampal-unit activity precedes and accurately predicts subsequent behavioral learning performance (Berger et al., 1980; Berger & Thompson, 1978b; Thompson et al., 1980; Thompson, Berger, & Madden, 1983). The hippocampal response has all the properties one would wish of a direct measure of the inferred process of learning in the brain. Yet, as noted above, animals can learn simple CRs without a hippocampus.

This is not the place to review the vast literature on effects of hippocampal lesions on learning and more generally on behavior (e.g., see O'Keefe & Nadel, 1978; Olton, Becker, & Handelmann, 1979). However, it is to be emphasized that the hippocampus does become essential even in simple conditioning paradigms when greater demands are placed on the memory system, as in latent inhibition, discrimination reversal, and trace conditioning (Berger & Orr, 1983; Orr & Berger, 1981; Solomon & Moore, 1975; Thompson, McCormick, Lavond, et al., 1983; Weisz, Solomon, & Thompson, 1980; see also Berger, Chapter 40, this volume). Where it has been studied in such paradigms, unit activity in the hippocampus becomes markedly engaged (Thompson, Berger, & Madden, 1983).

A number of authorities in the field of human learning and memory have distinguished two "kinds" of memory, which Squire (Squire, 1982) has recently termed "procedural" and "declarative." Damage to diencephalic or hippocampal–temporal structures in humans results in marked deficits in the formation of declarative memory, but not of procedural memory. Squire and associates have proposed that declarative memory may be a new development in evolution that corresponds with the elaboration of the hippocampus and other higher brain systems.

Simple classical conditioning paradigms would seem to be instances of procedural memory. However, when the tasks are made more complex, it is possible that "declarative" memory becomes involved and that the hippocampus then plays a more critical role. In the context of Squire's theory, it might be suggested that declarative memory has developed from the more ancient procedural memory system, the latter involving the cerebellum. If so, then one might expect the hippocampal system to become engaged in all learning paradigms, even though it is essential only in situations that require some aspect of "declarative" memory. A further expectation would be that the cerebellar system may itself play a role in the engagement of the hippocampal system, at least in procedural learning.

In current work, we have obtained precisely this result (Clark et al., 1982). In well-trained animals exhibiting the hippocampal neuronal response model of the behavioral response (both CR and UCR components—see Figures 39-13 and 39-14), ipsilateral electrolytic lesions of the medial dentate–lateral interpositus region that abolish the learned behavioral response also abolish the neuronal model in the CS period in the hippocampus (see Figure 39-14). When the animal is then trained on the other eye, which learns, the learning-predictive neuronal response in the CS period in the hippocampus returns. When training is then shifted back to the eye ipsilateral to the cerebellar lesion, which still cannot relearn, the hippocampal response in the CS period gradually extinguishes as the previous CR in the contralateral eye extinguishes.

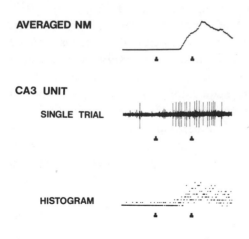

FIGURE 39-13. Examples of the discharge pattern of an identified hippocampal pyramidal neuron responding during trial periods in a rabbit well trained in the conditioned NM–eyelid response. Upper trace: NM response averaged over the number of trials (see Figure 39-1). Center trace: Single-trial example of the discharge pattern of the pyramidal neuron. Lower trace: Histogram (3-msec time bins) of the cell discharge over the same number of trials as for the NM response shown above. First cursor represents tone CS onset; second cursor represents airpuff UCS onset. Total trace duration was 750 msec. Note that the pattern of increased frequency of cell discharge closely models the amplitude–time course of the behavioral NM response. (Berger & Thompson, unpublished observations.)

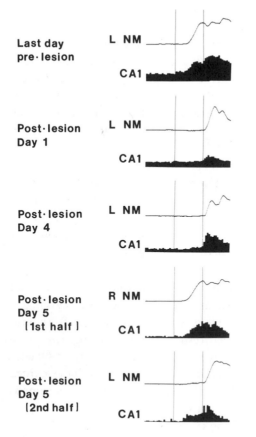

FIGURE 39-14. NM and hippocampal-unit (CA1) responses before and after lesions of the dentate–interpositus nuclei and surrounding fibers. Top trace: NM response. Bottom trace: Peristimulus histogram of hippocampal multiple-unit discharges (15-msec time bins). First vertical line represents tone onset; second vertical line represents airpuff onset. Total trace length was 750 msec. Prelesion, postlesion Day 1–4 represents averages from the entire 117-trial training session; on postlesion Day 5, training was switched to the right (nonlesioned side) eye, then returned to the left side. Lesion of the dentate–interpositus nuclei was found to abolish both the learned NM–eyelid and hippocampal-unit responses. However, training on the right (nonlesioned) side reinstated this hippocampal response as well as the right NM–eyelid response. Subsequent training on the left again failed to produce CRs on the left, although the hippocampal response remained. (Clark, McCormick, Lavond, & Thompson, unpublished observations.)

The marked involvement of the hippocampus in simple learning paradigms and its essential role under some conditions suggests that the more complex "cognitive" or "declarative" aspects of learning and memory can also be studied using the model system approach with conditioned responses.

ACKNOWLEDGMENTS

The work reported here was supported in part by research grants from the National Science Foundation (BNS 81-17115), the National Institutes of Health (NS23368), the National Institute of Mental Health (MH26530), and the McKnight Foundation. Grants to single authors included National Institute of Mental Health Grant No. MH23861 (John Madden IV), Predoctoral Fellowships from the National Institute of Mental Health Nos 1F31 MH08513-01 (Gregory A. Clark) and 5F31 MH08673-02 (David A. McCormick); Neuroscience Training Grant No. 1T32 MH17047-01 (Laura A. Mamounas); and Postdoctoral Fellowship from the National Institute of Mental Health Nos. 1F32 MH08576-01 (Nelson H. Donegan) and 2F32 MH08233-03 (David G. Lavond).

We would like to extend our gratitude to Jack Barchas for his support and guidance in our collaborative efforts.

REFERENCES

Berger, T. W., Laham, R. I., & Thompson, R. F. Hippocampal unit–behavior correlations during classical conditioning. *Brain Research*, 1980, *193*, 229–248.

Berger, T. W., & Orr, W. B. Hippocampectomy selectively disrupts discrimination reversal in conditioning of the rabbit nictitating membrane response. *Behavioural Brain Research*, 1983, *8*, 49–68.

Berger, T. W., & Thompson, R. F. Identification of pyramidal cells as the critical elements in hippocampal neuronal plasticity during learning. *Proceedings of the National Academy of Sciences*, 1978, *75*, 1572–1576. (a)

Berger, T. W., & Thompson, R. F. Neuronal plasticity in the limbic system during classical conditioning of the rabbit nictitating membrane response: I. The hippocampus. *Brain Research*, 1978, *145*, 323–346. (b)

Berger, T. W., & Thompson, R. F. Neuronal plasticity in the limbic system during classical conditioning of the rabbit nictitating membrane response: II. Septum and mammillary bodies. *Brain Research*, 1978, *156*, 293–314. (c)

Berger, T. W., & Thompson, R. F. Hippocampal cellular plasticity during extinction of classically conditioned nictitating membrane behavior. *Behavioural Brain Research*, 1982, *4*, 63–76.

Berry, S. D., & Thompson, R. F. Prediction of learning rate from the hippocampal EEG. *Science*, 1978, *200*, 1298–1300.

Brown, J. S., & Jacobs, A. The role of fear in the motivation and acquisition of responses. *Journal of Experimental Psychology*, 1949, *39*, 747–759.

Chan-Palay, V. *Cerebellar dentate nucleus, organization, cytology and transmitters*. Berlin: Springer-Verlag, 1977.

Chan-Palay, V. Autoradiographic localization of γ-aminobutyric acid receptors in the rat central nervous system by using [^{3}H]muscimol. *Proceedings of the National Academy of Sciences* 1978, *75*(2), 1024–1028.

Clark, G. A., McCormick, D. A., Lavond, D. G., Baxter, K. Gray, W. J., & Thompson, R. F. Effects of electrolytic lesions of cerebellar nuclei on conditioned behavioral and hippocampal neuronal responses. *Society for Neuroscience Abstracts*, 1982, *8*, 22.

Cohen, D. H. The functional neuroanatomy of a conditioned response. In R. F. Thompson, L. H. Hicks, & B. V. Shryrkov (Eds.), *Neural mechanisms of goal-directed behavior and learning*. New York: Academic Press, 1980.

Desmond, J. E., & Moore, J. W. A brain stem region essential for classically conditioned but not unconditioned nictitating membrane response. *Physiology and Behavior*, 1982, *28*, 1029–1033.

Disterhoft, J. F., Kwan, H. H., & Low. W. D. Nictitating membrane conditioning to tone in the immobilized albino rabbit. *Brain Research*, 1977, *137*, 127–144.

Donegan, N. H., & Wagner, A. R. Conditioned diminution and facilitation of the UCR: A sometimes-apparent-process interpretation. In I. Gormezano, W. F. Prokasy, & R. F. Thompson (Eds.), *Classical conditioning III: Behavioral, neurophysiological and neurochemical studies in the rabbit*. Hillsdale, N.J.: Erlbaum, in press.

Eccles, J. C., Ito, M., & Szentagothai, J. *The cerebellum as a neuronal machine*. New York: Springer-Verlag, 1967.

Enser, D. Personal communication, 1974.

Frey, P. W., & Ross, L. E. Classical conditioning of the rabbit eyelid response as a function of interstimulus interval. *Journal of Comparative and Physiological Psychology*, 1968, *65*, 246–250.

Gormezano, I. Investigations of defense and reward conditioning in the rabbit. In A. H. Black & W. F. Prokasy (Eds.), *Classical conditioning II: Current research and theory*. New York: Appleton-Century-Crofts, 1972.

Hebb, D. O. *The organization of behavior*. New York: Wiley, 1949.

Hoehler, F. K., & Thompson, R. F. Effect of the interstimulus (CS-UCS) interval on hippocampal unit activity during classical conditioning of the nictitating membrane response of the rabbit (*Oryctrolagus cuniculus*). *Journal of Comparative and Physiological Psychology*, 1980, *94*, 201–215.

Ito, M. Neurophysiological aspects of the cerebellar motor control system. *International Journal of Neurology*, 1970, *7*, 162–176.

Ito, M. Cerebellar control of the vestibulo-ocular reflex: Around the flocculus hypothesis. *Annual Review of Neuroscience*, 1982, *5*, 275–296.

Kandel, E. R., & Spencer, W. A. Cellular neurophysiological approaches in the study of learning. *Physiological Review*, 1968, *48*, 65–134.

Kapp, B. S., Gallagher, M., Applegate, C. D., & Frysinger, R. C. The amygdala central nucleus: contributions to conditioned cardiovascular responding during aversive pavlovian conditioning in the rabbit. In C. D. Woody (Ed.), *Conditioning: Representation of involved neural functions*. New York: Plenum Press, 1982.

Karamian, A. I., Fanaralijian, V. V., & Kosareva, A. A. The functional and morphological evolution of the cerebellum and its role in behavior. In R. Llinas (Ed.), *Neurobiology of Cerebellar Evolution and Development: First International Symposium*. Chicago: American Medical Association, 1969.

Kettner, R. E., & Thompson, R. F. Auditory signal detection and decision processes in the nervous system. *Journal of Comparative and Physiological Psychology*, 1982, *96*, 328–331.

Konorski, J. *Integrative activity of the brain*. Chicago: University of Chicago Press, 1967.

Lashley, K. S. *Brain mechanism and intelligence*. Chicago: University of Chicago Press, 1929.

Lavond, D. G., Lincoln, J. S., McCormick, D. A., & Thompson, R. F. Effect of lesions of the lateral cerebellar nuclei on conditioning of heart-rate and nictitating membrane/eyelid responses in the rabbit. *Brain Research*, in press.

Lavond, D. G., Mauk, M. D., Madden, J., IV, Barchas, J. D., & Thompson, R. F. Central opiate effect on heart-rate conditioning. *Society for Neuroscience Abstracts*, 1982, *8*, 319.

Lavond, D. G., McCormick, D. A., Clark, G. A., Holmes, D. T., & Thompson, R. F. Effects of ipsilateral rostral pontine reticular lesions on retention of classically conditioned nictitating membrane and eyelid responses. *Physiological Psychology*, 1981, *9*, 335–339.

Lincoln J. S., McCormick, D. A., & Thompson, R. F. Ipsilateral cerebellar lesions prevent learning of the classically conditioned nictitating membrane/eyelid response. *Brain Research*, 1982, *242*, 190–193.

Llinas, R., Walton, K., Hillman, E. D., & Sotelo, C. Inferior olive: Its role in motor learning. *Science*, 1975, *190*, 1230–1231.

Marr, D. A theory of cerebellar cortex. *Journal of Physiology*, 1969, *202*, 437–470.

Martinez, J. L., Rigter, H., Jensen, R. A., Messing, R. B., Vasquez, B. J., & McGaugh, J. L. Endophin and enkephalin effects on avoidance conditioning: The other side of the pituitary–adrenal axis. In J. L. Martinez, R. A. Jansen, R. B. Messing, H., Rigter, & J. L. McGaugh (Eds.), *Endogenous peptides and learning and memory processes*. New York: Academic Press, 1981.

Mauk, M. D., Castellano, T. G., Rideout, J. A., Madden, J., IV, Barchas, J. D., & Thompson, R. F. Overtraining reduces opiate abolition of classically conditioned responses. *Physiology and Behavior*, 1983, *30*, 493–495.

Mauk, M. D., Madden, J., IV, Barchas, J. D., & Thompson, R. F. Opiates and classical conditioning: Selective abolition of conditioned responses by activation of opiate receptors within the central nervous system. *Proceedings of the National Academy of Sciences*, 1982, *79*, 7598–7602.

Mauk, M. D., Warren, J. T., & Thompson R. F. Selective, naloxone-reversible morphine depression of learned behavioral and hippocampal responses. *Science*, 1982, *216*, 434–435.

McCormick, D. A., Clark, G. A., Lavond, D. G., & Thompson, R. F. Initial localization of the memory trace for a basic form of learning. *Proceedings of the National Academy of Sciences*, 1982, *79*(8), 2731–2742.

McCormick, D. A., Guyer, P. E., & Thompson, R. F. Superior cerebellar peduncle selectively abolish the ipsilateral classically conditioned nictitating membrane/eyelid response of the rabbit. *Brain Research*, 1982, *244*, 347–350.

McCormick, D. A., Lavond, D. G., Clark, G. A., Kettner, R. E., Rising, C. E., & Thompson, R. F. The engram found?: Role of the cerebellum in classical conditioning of nictitating membrane and eyelid responses. *Bulletin of the Psychonomic Society*, 1981, *18*(3), 103–105.

McCormick, D. A., Lavond, D. G., & Thompson, R. F. Neuronal responses of the rabbit brainstem during performance of the classically conditioned nictitating membrane (NM) eyelid response. *Brain Research*, 1983, *271*, 73–88.

Miller, N. E. Studies of fear as an acquirable drive: I. Fear as motivation and fear-reduction as reinforcement in learning of new responses. *Journal of Experimental Psychology*, 1948, *38*, 89–101.

Mowrer, O. H. On the dual nature of learning: A reinterpretation of "conditioning" and "problem-solving." *Harvard Educational Review*, 1947, *17*, 102–148.

Norman, R. J., Buchwald, J. S., & Villablanca, J. R. Classical conditioning with auditory discrimination of the eyeblink in decerebrate cats. *Science*, 1977, *196*, 551–553.

Okada, Y., Nitsch-Hassler, C., Kim, J. S., Bak, I. J., & Hassler, R., Role of gamma-aminobutyric acid (GABA) in the extrapyramidal motor system: I. Regional distribution of GABA in rabbit, rat guinea pig and baboon CNS. *Experimental Brain Research*, 1971, *13*, 514–518.

O'Keefe, J., & Nadel, L. *The hippocampus as a cognitive map*. New York: Oxford University Press, 1978.

Olton, D. S., Becker, J. T., & Handelmann, G. E. Hippocampus, space, and memory. *Behavioral and Brain Sciences*, 1979, *2*, 313–365.

Orr, W. B., & Berger, T. W. Hippocampal lesions disrupt discrimination reversal learning of the rabbit nictitating membrane response. *Society for Neuroscience Abstracts*, 1981, *7*, 648.

Prokasy, W. F. Developments with the two-phase-model applied to human eyelid conditioning. In A. H. Black & W. R. Prokasy (Eds.), *Classical conditioning II: Current research and theory*. New York: Appleton-Century-Crofts, 1972.

Rescorla, R. A., & Solomon, R. L. Two process learning theory: Relationships between Pavlovian conditioning and instrumental learning. *Psychological Review*, 1967, *74*, 151–182.

Roberts, E. Desinhibition as an organizing principle in the nervous system: The role of the GABA system. In E. Roberts, T. N. Chase, & D. B. Tower (Eds.), *GABA in nervous system function*. New York: Raven Press, 1976.

Roberts, E. Epilepsy and antiepileptic drugs: A speculative synthesis. In G. H. Glaser, J. K. Penny, & D. M. Woodbury (Eds.), *Antiepileptic drugs: Mechanisms of action*. New York: Raven Press, 1980.

Smith, O. A., Astley, C. A., DeVit, J. L., Stein, J. M., & Walsh, K. E. Functional analysis of hypoothalamic control of the cardiovascular responses accompanying emotional behavior. *Federation Proceedings*, 1980, *39*(8), 2487–2494.

Solomon, P. R., & Moore, J. W. Latent inhibition and stimulus generalization for the classically conditioned nictitating membrane response in rabbits (*Cryctolagus cuniculus*) following dorsal hippocampal ablation. *Journal of Comparative and Physiological Psychology*, 1975, *89*, 1192–1203.

Squire, L. The neurophysiology of human memory. *Annual Review of Neuroscience*, 1982, *5*, 241–273.

Swanson, L. W., Teyler, T. J., & Thompson, R. F. (Eds.). Hippocampal LTP: Mechanisms and functional implications. *Neurosciences Research Program Bulletin*, 1982, *20*(5).

Thompson, R. F., Barchas, J. D., Clark, G. A., Donegan, N., Kettner, R. E., Lavond, D. G., Madden, J., Mauk, M. D., & McCormick, D. A. Neuronal substrates of associative learning in the mammalian brain. In D. L. Alkon & J. Farley (Eds.), *Primary neural substrates of learning and behavioral change*. Princeton, N.J.: Princeton Unversity Press, in press.

Thompson, R. F., Berger, T. W., Berry, S. D., Hoehler, F. K., Kettner, R. E., & Weisz, D. J. Hippocampal substrate of classical conditioning. *Physiological Psychology*, 1980, *8*(2), 262–279.

Thompson, R. F., Berger, T. W., Cegavske, C. F., Patterson, M. M., Roemer, R. A., Teyler, T. J., & Young, R. A. A search for the engram. *American Psychologist*, 1976, *31*, 209–227.

Thompson, R. F., Berger, T. W., and Madden J., IV. Cellular processes of learning and memory in the mammalian CNS. *Annual Review of Neuroscience*, 1983, *6*, 447–491.

Thompson, R. F., McCormick, D. A., Lavond, D. G., Clark, G. A., Kettner, R. E., & Mauk, M. D. The engram found?: Initial localization of the memory trace for a basic form of associative learning. In J. M. Sprague & A. N. Epstein (Eds.), *Progress in psychobiology and physiological psychology*. New York: Academic Press, 1983.

Thompson, R. F., & Spencer, W. A. Habituation: A model phenomenon for the study of neuronal substrates of behavior. *Psychological Review*, 1966, *173*, 16–43.

Tsukahara, N. Synaptic plasticity in the mammalian central nervous system. *Annual Review of Neuroscience*, 1981, *4*, 351–379.

Wagner, A. R. Stimulus selection and "modified continuity theory." In G. H. Bower & J. T. Spence (Eds.), *Psychology of learning and motivation* (Vol. 3). New York: Academic Press, 1969.

Wagner, A. R. Elementary associations. In H. H. Kendler & J. T. Spence (Eds.), *Essays in neobehaviorism: A memorial volume to Kenneth M. Spence*. New York: Appleton-Century-Crofts, 1971.

Wanger, A. R. SPO: A model of automatic memory processing in animal behavior. In N. E. Spear & R. R. Miller (Eds.), *Information processing in animals: Memory mechanisms*. Hillsdale, N.J.: Erlbaum, 1981.

Weinberger, N. M. Effects of conditioned arousal on the auditory system. In A. L. Beckman, (Ed.), *The neural basis of behavior*. Jamaica, N.Y.: Spectrum, 1982.

Weisz, D. J., Solomon, P. R., & Thompson, R. F. The hippocampus appears necessary for trace conditioning. *Bulletin of the Psychonomic Society*, 1980, *193*, 244. (Abstract)

Woody, C. D., Yarowsky, P., Owens, J., Black-Cleworth, P., & Crow, T. Effect of lesions of coronal motor areas on acquisition of conditioned eye blink in the cat. *Journal of Neurophysiology*, 1974, *37*, 385–394.

Yeo, C. H., Hardiman, M. J., Glickstein, M., & Russell, I. S. Lesions of cerebellar nuclei abolish the classically conditioned nictitating membrane response. *Society for Neuroscience Abstracts*, 1982, *8*, 22.

Neural Representation of Associative Learning in the Hippocampus

40

Theodore W. Berger

Over the past several years, we have been investigating the role of the hippocampus and other limbic system structures during associative learning in subprimate mammals. We have been using classical conditioning of the nictitating membrane (NM) response as a model system for this analysis, because the NM preparation has a number of features that make it ideal for a cellular analysis of learning-induced neural plasticity. The rationale for use of this particular behavioral preparation (see Thompson, Berger, Cegavske, Patterson, Roemer, Teyler, & Young, 1976), as well as the rationale for the model systems approach to a neurobiological analysis of learning, has been outlined previously and is not reviewed here (see D. H. Cohen, 1974; Kandel, 1976; Woody, 1974). However, some of the basic tenets and objectives of the model systems approach will be discussed below in the context of our recent work on the hippocampal system and its role in associative learning.

Very briefly, the behavior we are measuring is extension of the rabbit NM over the corneal surface in response to an airpuff as unconditioned stimulus (UCS) (see Gormezano 1972). The full behavioral reflex is actually eyelid closure as well as NM extension, and involves all the ocular motor nuclei (Berthier & Moore, 1980; McCormick, Lavond, & Thompson, 1982). The motoneurons that are essential specifically for the membrane response, however, are located in the abducens and accessory abducens nucleus of the pons (Disterhoft & Shipley, 1980; Gray, MacMaster, Harvey, & Gormezano, 1981). The NM response is measured separately from eyelid closure by using clips to hold the eyelids open during training. NM extension is readily conditioned in the cat as well as the rabbit (Patterson, Berger, & Thompson, 1979; Patterson, Olah, & Clement, 1977), using a variety of sensory modalities as conditioned stimuli (CSs), though we have used primarily auditory cues.

Characteristics of Hippocampal Pyramidal Cell Activity during Classical Conditioning of the NM Response

In several past reports, we have shown that classical conditioning of the rabbit NM response is associated with substantial changes in the activity of hippocampal pyramidal neurons (Berger, Alger, & Thompson, 1976; Berger & Thompson, 1978a, 1978b, 1982). In our initial studies we used a simple conditioning procedure—a delay paradigm—in which

Theodore W. Berger. Departments of Psychology and Psychiatry, University of Pittsburgh, Pittsburgh, Pennsylvania.

the CS (tone) precedes the UCS (100-msec duration corneal airpuff) by 250 msec and terminates with offset of the UCS. Chronic recording techniques were used to record multiple or single-unit extracellular activity in or near the pyramidal cell layers of the hippocampus. In one series of studies, a bipolar stimulation electrode was chronically implanted in the fornix for electrophysiological identification of recorded pyramidal neurons (Berger & Thompson, 1978a; Berger, Rinaldi, Weisz, & Thompson, 1983).

Results showed that the activity of hippocampal pyramidal neurons is markedly altered by conditioning and that the conditioning-induced response of pyramidal cells has several interesting characteristics. First, pyramidal cell activity becomes altered during the very early phases of conditioning. With the parameters we used for training, behavioral conditioned responses (CRs) are typically exhibited after approximately 100 trials. In contrast, pyramidal cell activity changes within the first 10 trials. Second, within conditioning trials, pyramidal cells increase frequency of firing over pretrial, background rates (see Figure 40-1). This heightened frequency of firing increases gradually with conditioning, so that at asymptotic levels increases in frequency of several hundred percent above baseline rates are not uncommon. Spontaneous firing rates do not appear to be altered. Third, the increased frequency of pyramidal cell discharges is not evenly distributed throughout the trial period. Instead, a positive correlation exists between the probability of cell firing and amplitude of the NM CR (see Figure 40-1). As a result of this relationship, the pattern of pyramidal cell activity within trials correlates strongly with amplitude–time properties of the learned behavioral response (Berger, Laham, & Thompson, 1980). Thus, there are two major features of the neural plasticity shown by hippocampal pyramidal cells during conditioning: (1) an increase in overall frequency across trials, and (2) a specific pattern of discharge within trials (at the heightened frequency) that reflects parameters of the learned behavior.

Finally, the hippocampal discharge that develops with training also shifts temporally in the later phases of conditioning to have a shorter latency from CS onset. Early in the conditioning process, when animals exhibit only unconditioned responses (UCRs) to CS-UCS pairings, the frequency of hippocampal cell firing increases, and the pattern of hippocampal discharges parallels the amplitude–time course of the behavioral response.

FIGURE 40-1. Extracellularly recorded responses of two (A and B) single hippocampal pyramidal neurons during classical conditioning of the rabbit NM response. For this and all subsequent similar figures, upper traces represent the averaged NM response for total number of trials during which the cell was recorded; lower traces are peristimulus time histograms showing total number of action potentials recorded. Left arrow indicates tone onset; right arrow indicates airpuff onset. Total trace length equals 750 msec.

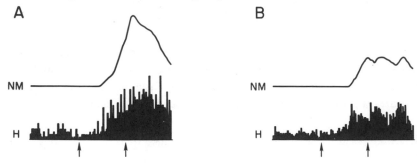

But during this early phase of conditioning, increased hippocampal cellular activity occurs in the post-UCS onset period in association with the behavioral UCR. Later in training, as onset of the NM response moves forward in time into the CS-UCS interval and becomes defined as a CR, onset of hippocampal cell firing also shifts into the CS-UCS interval in parallel with the behavior.

Hippocampal cellular plasticity during NM conditioning is specifically related to associative learning. The critical feature of classical conditioning is the temporal contiguity between the CS and the UCS. If the CS precedes the UCS by a very short temporal interval (e.g., 50 msec) or by very long intervals (e.g., greater than 4 sec), no behavioral conditioning is observed (Gormezano, 1972). Behavioral conditioning only occurs within a limited range of CS-UCS temporal contiguity. Hippocampal cellular plasticity develops only within the same range of optimal contiguity that results in behavioral learning. When the CS and UCS are separated temporally by 30 sec (i.e., when an explicitly unpaired paradigm is used for training), no changes in hippocampal activity are seen (see Figure 40-2) (Berger & Thompson, 1978b). If the CS precedes the UCS by only 50 msec, no behavioral learning occurs, and no increases in hippocampal activity are detectable. Within the interstimulus range of 150–1000 msec, behavioral conditioning readily occurs, and hippocampal cellular plasticity also is robust (Hoehler & Thompson, 1980).

Definition of Learning-Related Neural Plasticity

It is significant that changes in hippocampal cellular activity initially occur within the UCS period. Many electrophysiological analyses of learning-related neural activity make the *a priori* assumption that "conditioned" unit activity is activity that changes within the CS-UCS interval in a classical conditioning paradigm, or activity that changes after stimulus (S[D]) onset but before behavioral movement in an instrumental learning paradigm. The results described above are clearly an example of "conditioned" unit activity, because increased levels of hippocampal firing occur only during learning or during performance of the learned behavior. Changes in hippocampal activity also occur before behavioral learning develops when across-trial comparisons are made. Yet the increased hippo-

FIGURE 40-2. Extracellularly recorded responses of two (A and B) single hippocampal pyramidal neurons during presentations of airpuff alone. Arrow indicates airpuff onset. Data were collected during explicitly unpaired presentations of tones and airpuffs (intertrial interval: average 30 sec). No evoked responses to tone presentation were ever seen under these conditions, so the latter data are not shown. Total trace length equals 750 msec.

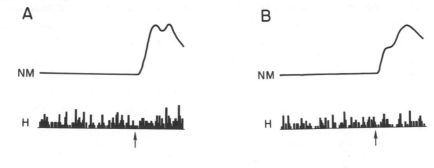

campal firing appears first in the post-UCS onset period with the behavioral UCR, and not during the CS-UCS interval. Importantly, Gormezano (1972) has shown that the first NM CRs exhibited by an animal during the course of training occur not in the CS-UCS interval, but in the post-UCS-onset period (as shown by the occurrence of NM responses on CS-alone "test" trials). Thus, at least in the NM paradigm, conditioned behavior first occurs with a latency that exceeds the CS-UCS interval, so it is reasonable to find learning-induced neural plasticity first occurring with a similar latency. Experimental paradigms that do not allow examination of UCS-related unit activity (e.g., use of a shock UCS) may be ignoring learning-related neural plasticity that develops early in the course of conditioning.

The fact that learning-induced neural plasticity need not occur only during the CS-UCS interval has important implications of interpreting unit–behavior relationships during learning. For example, correlations between the across-trial time courses of changes in unit activity and changes in behavior are often used to conclude whether a brain structure is "essential" or necessary for behavioral learning. In our NM paradigm, changes in hippocampal activity first occur within the UCS period and gradually move forward in time into the CS-UCS interval. If a comparison is made between the time course of unit changes in the UCS period and the time course of learned behavior ("learned behavior" is defined as NM movement in the CS-UCS interval), hippocampal neural plasticity is seen as preceding behavioral learning by a considerable degree. On the other hand, if a comparison is made between unit changes in the CS-UCS interval and the development of learned behavior, the time courses are approximately parallel.

Frequency versus Pattern Codes of Learning-Related Unit Activity

One of the particularly striking features of the hippocampal neural response that develops during NM conditioning is the pattern of cell discharge within trial periods. As seen in Figure 40-1, the summed across-trial activity of a single pyramidal neuron can display a surprisingly good correlation with the amplitude–time course of the NM CR. This observation illustrates that while frequency of firing is the measure of cellular changes most often used, learning-related information can be transmitted through other parameters of cell activity as well (such as temporal pattern, number, latency, etc.; see Perkel & Bullock, 1968). If only a frequency measure is used, cellular activity from many different brain structures may appear similar, because differences in pattern of response are ignored. Likewise, changes in discharge pattern may occur with training in the absence of changes in overall frequency, so that activity of some cells may be judged to be unrelated to learning when in fact changes in their pattern of firing would indicate an intimate involvement (see Gabriel & Saltwick, 1980). In our investigation of physiologically distinguished classes of hippocampal neurons, we found several cell types that increased overall frequency within conditioning trials. Examination of their pattern of firing, however, revealed that some cells were responding with a close relationship to the learned behavior (see Figure 40-3A), some to the CS (see Figure 40-3B), and others with a close relationship to a rhythmic, slow-wave potential (theta rhythm) known to be generated by the hippocampus (see Figure 40-3C).

The distinction being made here is relevant to more than just a cataloguing of differences in cell types. Differences between frequency and pattern of discharge may

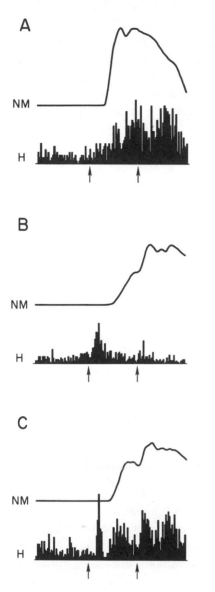

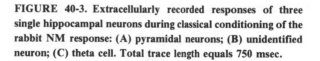

FIGURE 40-3. Extracellularly recorded responses of three single hippocampal neurons during classical conditioning of the rabbit NM response: (A) pyramidal neurons; (B) unidentified neuron; (C) theta cell. Total trace length equals 750 msec.

provide important clues as to the functional role of a given cell or brain structure during learning. For example, across-trial changes in the frequency of hippocampal pyramidal cell firing occur both during tone–airpuff conditioning of the NM response (Berger *et al.*, 1976) and during tone–shock conditioning of leg flexion (Thompson, Berger, Berry, & Hoehler, 1980). While increases in discharge frequency are common to both learning paradigms, the within-trial pattern of cell firing is different under the two conditions. During NM conditioning, the pattern of hippocampal activity parallels features of the NM response, whereas during leg-shock conditioning the pattern of hippocampal activity parallels features of muscular flexion (as measured by electromyogram [EMG]). Thus, changes in frequency indicate whether or not hippocampal neurons become activated, while the pattern of cell firing indicates the specific information being transmitted. Perhaps the most instructive analogy is that frequency measures of pyramidal cell activity are similar to the "enabling" function of solid-state memory. When the memory chip is "enabled," it is functional within the larger circuit, in the same sense that increased firing frequency of a cell population will increase the relative effect of that population on its postsynaptic target. Pattern measures, on the other hand, are similar to the contents of the memory chip. The chip may be enabled under all learning conditions, but its content may vary, depending on the particular behavior to be learned.

Distributed Memory Systems

Frequency and pattern do not exhaust the number of different codes that are known to be used by central nervous system (CNS) neurons (see Perkel & Bullock, 1968). Sometimes even the use of both frequency and pattern criteria will fail to distinguish between learning-related cell responses that are obviously different. For example, neurons may exhibit identical responses as measured by frequency and pattern, but may differ in terms of latency from CS onset. Again drawing on our observations of hippocampal pyramidal neurons, we found that important differences could be distinguished among pyramidal cells that respond during conditioning with both a heightened frequency and a pattern of discharge that parallels the NM response. Some pyramidal neurons exhibit a response that correlates with all components of the conditioned NM behavior (i.e., components of the NM response that occur in the CS-UCS interval, as well as components that occur in the UCS interval). Other pyramidal cells, however, exhibit a response that correlates only with NM movement in the CS-UCS interval or only with movement in the UCS interval (see Figure 40-4). These differences can be quantified by comparing latency to onset of the NM response and latency to onset of the hippocampal-unit response. In other words, for some pyramidal cells the latency to conditioned increase in frequency precedes NM onset; for others the latency is coincident with NM onset; and for still others the latency follows NM onset. For all cells, however, frequency of firing increases with training, and the pattern of firing correlates positively with the NM amplitude–time course (verified statistically).

Again, this observation has implications that go beyond a descriptive accounting of the activities of different cells in one learning paradigm. Our earlier studies using multiple-unit recordings revealed that the activity of groups of hippocampal neurons collectively displayed an excellent "model" of the NM CR (Berger, Laham, & Thompson, 1980). That is, the correlation between a poststimulus time histogram of multiple-unit hippocampal activity (from the pyramidal cell region) recorded over trials and the averaged NM response for those same trials develops gradually over the course of training and reaches substantial values (exceeding .80 and sometimes .90). The multiple-unit results showed that, in almost all recordings, all components of the NM response are reflected in the cumulated hippocampal unit histogram. Results of the single-unit analysis referred to above, however, reveal that the composite response seen in multiple-unit recordings does not reflect the summation of homogeneous pyramidal cell activity, but instead is a synthesis of heterogeneous responses of several subgroups of pyramidal neurons. On any given trial, one subpopulation of pyramidal cells contributes a discharge correlated with the earliest component of the NM response, while other subpopulations discharge in correlation with later components. The principle that emerges from such a result is that

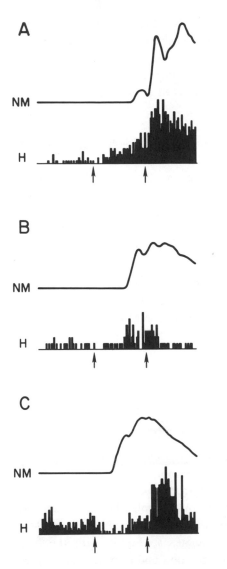

FIGURE 40-4. Responses of three different pyramidal neurons during NM classical conditioning. Note that summed activity of cell shown in A parallels all phases of the NM response. Activities of cells shown in B and C parallel only early and late phases, respectively, of the NM response. Total trace length equals 750 msec.

subpopulations of neurons can exhibit what might be termed a "cooperativity" in the production of a learning-related neural response. In other words, the unit CR exhibited by a total population of hippocampal pyramidal neurons is "distributed" among several subpopulations.

The fact that some pyramidal neurons exhibit a complete model of the NM response also suggests that there may be hierarchy of cell types within the hippocampus. This is consistent with both anatomical and physiological data indicating that synaptic interactions exist between pyramidal cells (MacVicar & Dudek, 1981; Swanson, Wyss, & Cowan, 1978). A hierarchical arrangement would have the functional advantage that certain components of a memory trace may be altered or operated upon without changing other components. For example, if an animal is trained at one CS-UCS interval and then switched to another, NM behavior in the CS-UCS interval is significantly altered, whereas the UCR to the UCS is not. A distributed memory system like the one described above would allow activity of cells correlating with the NM CR in the CS-USC interval to be altered independently of cells correlating with later, unconditioned components of the NM response. A hierarchical system would further provide final-stage neural elements to synthesize the new hippocampal "model" of the animal's learned behavior.

Transmission of Learning-Related Neural Activity through Multisynaptic Systems

One of the basic tenets of the model systems approach to a neurobiological analysis of learning is an emphasis on the use of response systems in which the behavior is discrete, stereotyped, and completed within a relatively short time period. The advantage is that, under such conditions, neural activity related to associative learning can be easily identified by electrophysiological techniques. Changes in the frequency of cell firing are most easily detected over a relatively small time sample, and specific patterns of cell activity are most easily identified if the pattern is relatively invariant. The assumption is that if the animal's behavior is discrete and highly stereotyped, so is the cellular activity underlying that behavior. From the preceding discussion, it should be clear that the NM preparation shares the characteristics outlined above, and that those characteristics have aided in the identification of specific and different patterns of neural activity—not only in the hippocampus, but in other areas of the brain as well (e.g., medial septum—see Berger & Thompson, 1977; auditory nuclei—see Kettner & Thompson, 1982; cerebellum—see R. F. Thompson, Clark, Donegan, Lavond, Madden, Mamounas, Mauk, & McCormick, Chapter 39, this volume; abducens nucleus—see Cegavske, Patterson, & Thompson, 1979).

One of the advantages to investigating learning-dependent signals like the hippocampal response is the feasibility of examining its transmission over multisynaptic pathways. In mammalian systems, learning-dependent neural responses may develop or be present in structures that are many synapses removed from motoneurons mediating the behavioral response. The hippocampus is just such an example. The motoneurons responsible for NM movement lie in the abducens and accessory abducens nucleus of the pons. The fact that hippocampal activity correlates so highly with the NM response suggests that hippocampal output may converge upon abducens motoneuronal activity via some multisynaptic circuit. Verifying this hypothesis, however, requires (1) anatomically identifying multisynaptic pathways that are potentially used to transmit information to motoneurons, and (2) electrophysiologically recording the activity of principal neurons composing the pathway(s) to determine whether a given circuit is actually utilized during conditioning. Given the divergent nature of most mammalian efferent systems, the second task of recording along identified nodes of multisynaptic pathways can be a formidable undertaking. If the learning-related response is a subtle change in cell firing or a complex sequence of variations in firing that occur over a substantial time course, documenting transmission of the signal over successive projection sites would be even more difficult. That task is greatly facilitated, however, when the learning-dependent neural event to be "tracked" along a circuit is a discrete, well-defined signal with a high signal-to-noise ratio. The feasibility of tracking the hippocampal unit response to an efferent target site was demonstrated in a study we completed several years ago (Berger & Thompson, 1977). Multiple-unit activity was recorded simultaneously from electrodes chronically implanted in the hippocampus and its subcortical target, the lateral septum, during NM conditioning. Results showed that highly similar response patterns were recorded from both structures, and the similarity of the two learning-dependent signals was easily discernible and could be verified statistically (see Figure 40-5).

Multiple Mammalian Memory Systems

Our interest in tracking the hippocampal-unit response along efferent pathways is part of an overall strategy to determine the behavioral significance of hippocampal activity during classical conditioning. If the hippocampal-unit response can be recorded at successive points in a multisynaptic circuit to the level of the motoneuron, then a causal relationship between hippocampal activity and learned NM behavior is supported. Another parallel approach we are using, however, is examining the effects of hippocampal lesions on NM conditioning. If lesions of the hippocampus prevent or retard NM conditioning, it would provide further evidence for a causal relationship between hippocampal activity and learned NM behavior.

It is clear from both neuropsychological work (e.g., N. J. Cohen & Squire, 1980; Milner, 1970; Sidman, Stoddard, & Mohr, 1968) and animal research (e.g., Olton, Becker, & Handelmann, 1979; O'Keefe & Nadel, 1978; Squire & Zola-Morgan, 1982), however, that the hippocampal system is not necessary for all types of learning, and that multiple memory systems exist in the mammalian brain (see also Squire, 1981). Several distinctions or dimensions along which to define these different memory systems have been proposed— for example, declarative versus procedural memory (Cohen & Squire, 1980), working versus reference memory (Honig, 1978), taxon versus locale systems (O'Keefe & Nadel, 1978), contextual retrieval versus performance line (Hirsh, 1974), and memory versus habit systems (see Mishkin & Petri, Chapter 28, this volume). An element common to all of these conceptions is not only that multiple memory systems exist, but that they are interconnected and functionally interact in fundamental ways. If the hippocampus is essential only for certain types of classical conditioning tasks, then other brain structures and the memory systems they mediate must be responsible for learning that does not require the hippo-campus. The lesion studies we are conducting should distinguish the subset of learning conditions that require the hippocampal system, while tracking hippocampal-unit activity

FIGURE 40-5. Multiple-unit recording of cells in pyramidal region of hippocampus at early (A) and late (B) phases of conditioning, and simultaneous recording of cells in lateral septum (lower histograms) at same phases of conditioning. Total trace length equals 750 msec.

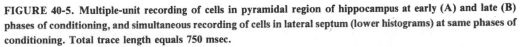
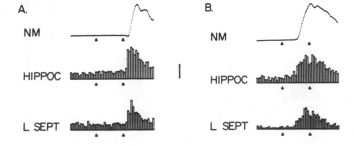

along its efferent pathways should identify points of interface between the hippocampus and neural systems that mediate other learning. We believe we have localized such an interface (see next section), though further work still remains in order for us to substantiate our belief.

First, however, it is clear that the hippocampus is not necessary for learning in the simple delay task that was used in the studies described above (Schmaltz & Theios, 1972; Solomon & Moore, 1975). On the other hand, we have recently shown that hippocampal damage does interfere with two-tone discrimination reversal learning of the rabbit NM response (Berger & Orr, 1982). More specifically, we compared the behavior of animals with hippocampal–subicular lesions to that of normal animals and of animals with lesions of just the neocortex overlying hippocampus. Results showed that there were no significant differences between operated control animals and animals given hippocampal or neocortical lesions in the development of initial differential CRs (see Figure 40-6). In contrast, hippocampal lesions severely affected reversal learning. In all hippocampal lesion cases, failure at reversal learning resulted from continued responding to the new CS− (the initial CS+) rather than low levels of responding to the new CS+ (the initial CS−) (see Figure 40-7). Animals in all groups, including hippocampal lesions, readily increased CR rates to the new CS+ in the reversal phase of training.

A number of laboratories have reported that bilateral hippocampectomy sometimes results in increased resistance to extinction when animals are tested in a variety of different tasks. The possibility existed, then, that the effects of hippocampectomy on reversal learning could be accounted for in terms of increased resistance to extinction to the previous CS+. To test this hypothesis, we prepared two additional groups of animals: operated controls and animals with hippocampal lesions. All animals were conditioned

FIGURE 40-6. Effect of bilateral hippocampal ablation on initial discrimination and reversal learning of the rabbit NM response. Solid bars represent results for operated controls; crossed bars represent results for animals with a neocortical lesion; open bars represent results for animals with a hippocampal lesion. Error bars show *SEM*'s.

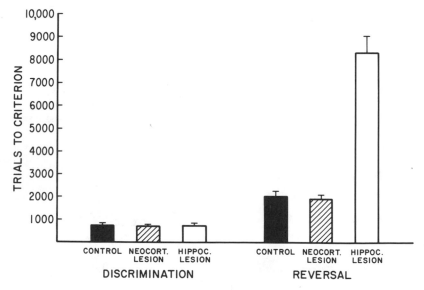

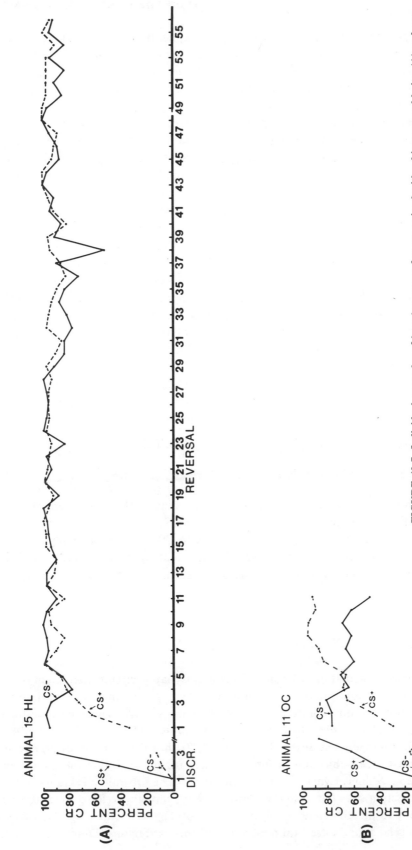

FIGURE 40-7. Individual examples of learning curves for one animal with a hippocampal lesion (A) and one operated control animal (B). Note that animal with a hippocampal lesion fails to learn the reverse discrimination because of continued responding at high and equal rates to both the CS+ and the CS−.

453

using a delay paradigm and extinguished using an explicitly unpaired paradigm. Results showed that hippocampectomy had no effect on the rate of acquisition of NM CRs, and, more importantly, no effect on rates of extinction (Berger & Orr, 1983). Thus, the effect of hippocampectomy on reversal learning cannot be explained as a lesion-induced increased resistance to extinction.

The mnemonic function lost after hippocampectomy that is necessary for successful discrimination reversal is still an unresolved issue, and proper treatment of the issue goes beyond the scope of this chapter (but see Berger & Orr, 1983). It is important, however, to emphasize the manner in which animals with hippocampal lesions fail at reversal learning: by responding at high and equal rates to the CS+ and the CS−. An animal's ability to exhibit learned behavior (extension of the NM) upon presentation of a CS is unaffected by hippocampal damage. This residual ability may be analogous to what has been termed "procedural memory" (Squire, 1982) or "habit system" (Mishkin & Petri, Chapter 28, this volume). Procedural or rule-based memories are known to be unaffected by hippocampal damage in humans (N. J. Cohen & Squire, 1980). In contrast, an animal's ability to distinguish among multiple CSs so as to respond appropriately to the CS+ and the CS− is affected by hippocampal damage. This ability may be analogous to what has been termed "declarative" or "recognition" memory. Declarative or data-based memories are known to be affected by hippocampal damage in humans (N. J. Cohen & Squire, 1980). Whether or not these analogies are appropriate obviously require further investigation. For the rabbit NM preparation, however, two different brain systems have been found to mediate two different mnemonic functions. As just reviewed, the hippocampus is essential for the mnemonic function needed for discrimination reversal. Thompson and associates (see R. F. Thompson *et al.*, Chapter 39, this volume), on the other hand, have recently identified the cerebellar system as essential for what may be termed "procedural memory," or an animal's ability to respond to any CS. Lesions of the deep cerebellar nuclei or the superior cerebellar peduncle completely abolish the NM CR even in a simple delay paradigm (McCormick, Clark, Lavond, & Thompson, 1982). Together, these data suggest that the cerebellar system mediates an animal's ability to develop a CR to any CS, while the hippocampal system mediates an animal's ability to respond differentially to CSs under more complex learning conditions. The hippocampal system, then, through multisynaptic efferent projections, may modulate the cerebellar system during such learning situations as discrimination reversal.

Anatomical Interconnections between Multiple Memory Systems

We are in the process of anatomically identifying multisynaptic circuits that might transmit information from the hippocampus to other brain systems (including the cerebellum), and ultimately to motoneurons controlling the NM response. We began by investigating hippocampal cortical and subcortical targets in the rabbit, and we corroborated observations first made by others (Swanson & Cowan, 1977) that the majority of hippocampal efferents project to the subiculum, a limbic cortical region adjoining the hippocampus (Berger, Swanson, Milner, Lynch, & Thompson, 1980). The subiculum is known to have a number of projection sites (Swanson & Cowan, 1977), though we have concentrated on subicular output to the cingulate gyrus, because in other species the cingulate gyrus has been shown to send axons to several nonlimbic subcortical regions (Domesick, 1969).

From experiments that are still in progress, we have found that the same regions of the subiculum that receive efferents from hippocampus give rise to a prominent projection to the retrosplenial component of the posterior cingulate gyrus (Semple-Rowland, Bassett, & Berger, 1981). Subicular efferents terminate solely within retrosplenial cortex and do not extend into the granular, cingulate cortex (as defined by Rose & Woolsey, 1948). The primary sites of subicular terminations are layers I and IV of retrosplenial, though predominently IV. The cells of origin for this system lie within the subiculum only and not in other subregions of the subicular complex (e.g., presubiculum or parasubiculum). A topographical organization exists to this system such that anterior regions of dorsal subiculum project to more antero-medial portions of retrosplenial, while ventral subicular cells project to more postero-lateral retrosplenial zones.

The significance of the hippocampal–subicular–retrosplenial system is that we have also recently shown that the primary efferent targets of the retrosplenial cortex are the ventral pontine nuclei (Bassett & Berger, 1981). More specifically, cells of layer V of retrosplenial send efferents predominately to the ventral, the lateral, and the paramedian gray of the ventral pons. These pontine nuclei are known to be major afferents to the cerebellar cortex in rabbit (Brodal & Jansen, 1946), and thus may serve as the final link in a relatively short multisynaptic circuit capable of transmitting information from the hippocampus to the cerebellum. If our future electrophysiological experiments verify that the hippocampal pyramidal cell response that develops during NM conditioning is in fact transmitted along this pathway, we will have identified an interface between the two types of memory systems referred to earlier (e.g., declarative and procedural).

Hippocampal-Unit Activity during Discrimination Reversal Learning of the NM Response

Since hippocampal functioning is required for discrimination reversal learning, it becomes of interest to know (1) whether hippocampal pyramidal neurons respond differentially to the CS+ and the CS− in a manner consistent with the animal's behavior, and (2) whether the activity of hippocampal pyramidal cells is uniquely different during reversal learning versus initial discrimination learning. We are currently examining the activity of two types of hippocampal neurons during discrimination and reversal learning: pyramidal cells and what have been termed theta cells. Pyramidal neurons are identified by (1) collision techniques with the use of bipolar stimulating electrodes implanted in the fornix, a major hippocampal efferent pathway, and/or (2) spontaneous firing characteristics. Theta cells are identified by spontaneous firing characteristics described by others (Ranck, 1973) and ourselves (Berger & Weisz, in press). Results to date have shown that pyramidal neurons gradually develop a differentially enhanced response to the CS+ over the course of initial discrimination conditioning. During CS+ trials there is a strong correlation between the probability of cell firing and the amplitude of the NM CR (see Figure 40-8). On CS− trials during which the animal displays a NM CR, hippocampal pyramidal cells also exhibit heightened unit responding; when the animal does not show a CR on CS− trials, pyramidal neurons also do not show an enhanced response. During reversal conditioning, the differential response of pyramidal cells also reverses, though not enough units have yet been examined during reversal to give a more complete description. Theta cells have been recorded only during discrimination conditioning to date. In contrast to pyramidal cells,

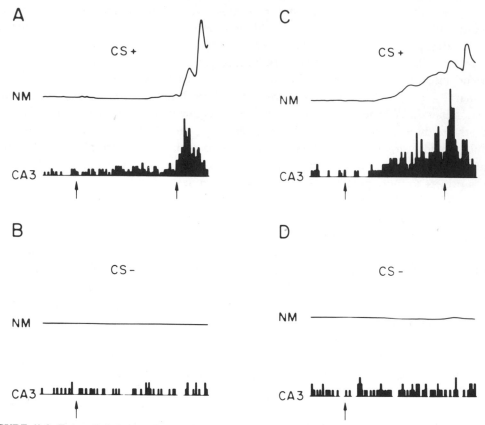

FIGURE 40-8. Extracellularly recorded responses of two single pyramidal neurons during two-tone discrimination conditioning of rabbit NM extension. A and B show an example of one cell recorded at an early phase of discrimination training. C and D show an example of a different cell recorded at the point of asymptotic discrimination learning. Left arrow indicates tone onset; right arrow indicates airpuff onset. Total trace length equals 1250 msec.

theta cells do not show a differential response to the CS+ and the CS−, or else show only very slight differences (see Figure 40-9). Irrespective of whether or not the animal exhibits a behavioral CR, theta cells respond with a train of bursts at the theta frequency (6–8 Hz) triggered by onset of the CS (+ or −). At this point in our analysis, then, we know that hippocampal pyramidal cells do exhibit differential responses to the CS+ and CS− during discrimination and reversal conditioning, and that differential hippocampal responding parallels differential behavioral NM responding. No major differences are apparent between pyramidal cell activity during learning of the initial discrimination and learning of the reverse discrimination, though further work is necessary to resolve this issue conclusively.

Linear versus Nonlinear Characteristics of Synaptic Transmission

What we are proposing for the immediate future, then, is to record from single neurons at each point in the subicular–retrosplenial–pontine system during discrimination reversal learning to determine whether projection cells at each site exhibit the learning-induced pattern of activity shown by hippocampal pyramidal neurons. In combination with extracellular single-unit recording, we will use chronically implanted stimulation electrodes to verify that the neurons we are recording are functionally part of the circuit we have described anatomically. For example, units recorded from subiculum will be those that are either synaptically activated by stimulating hippocampus or antidromically activated by stimulation of retrosplenial cortex. If our current working hypothesis is correct, both types of cells should exhibit an increased frequency of firing and a pattern of discharge matching that of hippocampal pyramidal neurons.

A potential difficulty with this approach lies in the assumption that the characteristics of synaptic transmission at each point in the described pathway will be linear. We have stressed that tracking the hippocampal-unit response along a series of synapses is facilitated by the unit response being discrete, paralleling parameters of the behavioral CR, and having a high signal-to-noise ratio. To the extent that input–output characteristics of, for example, hippocampal–subicular synapses are linear, the first two characteristics should be preserved and thus should be identifiable in subicular unit responding. Maintaining the same signal-to-noise ratio would depend on the relative spontaneous rates of the pre- and postsynaptic elements. Decreases in the signal-to-noise ratio of the hippocampal response would be problematic, but only in the limit (i.e., when the signal-to-noise

FIGURE 40-9. Extracellularly recorded responses of a theta cell during CS+ (A) and CS− (B) trials of a two-tone discrimination paradigm. C shows summed unit response and averaged NM response for all CS− trials on which animal exhibited a CR. D shows results for all CS− trials on which the animal did not exhibit a CR.

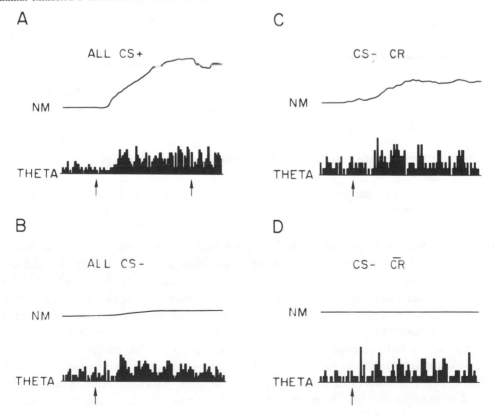

ratio approaches 1.0). A much greater obstacle to transsynaptic identification of learning-related unit responses is the potential for nonlinearities in synaptic transmission. It is possible that synaptic relations between two cells (or brain structures) are predominantly nonlinear, so that transformations of discharge patterns would result. An example would be if the hippocampal-unit response was differentiated due to rapid and potent recurrent inhibition of the postsynaptic cell. If the differentiation transformation was major, equating the pre- and postsynaptic response would be difficult. If nonlinearities are suspected, the solution is to determine the input–output characteristics of a given synapse, and techniques are available for making such evaluations (Marmarelis & Marmarelis, 1978). If non-linearities in transmission are found, the nature of those nonlinearities can be characterized, and predictions can be made as to the manner in which the hippocampal-unit response would be altered by propagation through that synapse. Comparing the predicted result with the empirical result will allow conclusions as to whether or not a learning-related signal is transmitting along a given pathway.

Nonlinear transformations of a synaptically transmitted signal also have implications for interpreting unit–behavior relationships. We have interpreted the hippocampal-unit response as a "model" of the topography of the NM CR, because of the high correlation that exists between the unit pattern and all parameters of the behavioral pattern (Berger, Laham, & Thompson, 1980). Whether the same correlation holds after transmission through several synapses remains to be determined. The manner in which the correlation may be altered is obviously significant. For example, if a series of synapses successively differentiates the hippocampal-unit response, onset of hippocampal firing would be the most important component of the unit response, and thus its potential role in initiation of NM CR would be more likely. In contrast, if a series of synapses successively integrates the hippocampal-unit response, cellular firing at distal sites, which is initiated by hippocampal pyramidal cell activity, would extend into the intertrial interval. In other words, in the latter case, hippocampal output may engage or mediate consolidation processes that must occur in each of the posttrial periods for successful learning (McGaugh & Herz, 1972).

Within-Trial versus Between-Trial Learning-Related Cellular Activity

The second possibility mentioned above raises an important point regarding most electro-physiological analyses of associative learning: Namely, unit activity is usually sampled within the conditioning trial and not between conditioning trials (i.e., during the intertrial interval). This bias has been strengthened in recent years with the widespread use of model behavioral systems, like the rabbit NM response, that are characterized by discrete behavioral responses. As mentioned above, memory-consolidation processes essential for learning have been shown to have a critical temporal variable extending into the posttrial period (McGaugh & Herz, 1972). Most present electrophysiological analyses of learning (including our own) do not sample those consolidation processes to the extent that they are reflected in unit activity during the intertrial interval (for a notable exception, see Weisz, Clark, & Thompson, 1984), or for that matter, between-session unit activity (see Disterhoft & Segal, 1978). The importance of the within-trial–between-trial distinction is that within-trial unit discharges like the hippocampal response probably reflect the end result or product of consolidation processes, rather than the consolidation processes themselves. To the extent that we wish to study the processes electrophysiologically, unit activity during intertrial intervals or between sessions would have to be monitored.

The choice to record unit activity only within conditioning trials is obviously, in part, a practical one. If cellular responses were monitored throughout the entire session of a multisession learning paradigm, the deluge of data might be impossible to organize, store, and analyze. A second and perhaps more important issue, however, is the method one would use for analysis. The most commonly used methods of evaluating learning-related unit responses are those that rely on discrete time intervals (e.g., poststimulus time histograms). Unit activity in the intertrial interval might be analyzed by simply segregating that time into discrete epochs. But while changes in the activity of different epochs of the intertrial interval might be detected, reducing the data into a concise, descriptive measure is the primary difficulty. However, epochs of electroencephalographic recordings are often summarized by autocorrelation and power spectrum analyses. Similar techniques might be used or developed for point processes such as action potentials (e.g., interspike interval distributions).

ACKNOWLEDGMENTS

The research described in this chapter was supported by grants from the McKnight Foundation, the National Science Foundation (BNS 80-21395), and the National Institute of Mental Health (RCDA, MH00343).

REFERENCES

Bassett, J. L., & Berger, T. W. Non-thalamic efferent projections of the posterior cingulate gyrus in the rabbit. *Society for Neuroscience Abstracts*, 1981, *1*, 885.

Berger, T. W., Alger, B., & Thompson, R. F. Neuronal substrate of classical conditioning in the hippocampus. *Science*, 1976, *192*, 483–485.

Berger, T. W., Laham, R. I., & Thompson, R. F. Hippocampal unit–behavior correlations during classical conditioning. *Brain Research*, 1980, *193*, 229–248.

Berger, T. W., & Orr, W. B. Role of the hippocampus in reversal learning of the rabbit nictitating membrane response. In C. D. Woody (Ed.), *Conditioning: Representation of involved neural functions*. New York: Plenum Press, 1982.

Berger, T. W., & Orr, W. B. Hippocampectomy selectively disrupts discrimination reversal conditioning of the rabbit nictitating membrane response. *Behavioural Brain Research*, 1983, *8*, 49–68.

Berger, T. W., Rinaldi, P., Weisz, D., & Thompson, R. F. Single unit analysis of hippocampal cellular activity during classical conditioning of rabbit nictitating membrane response. *Journal of Neurophysiology*, 1983, *50*, 1197–1219.

Berger, T. W., Swanson, G. W., Milner, T. A., Lynch, G. S., & Thompson, R. F. Reciprocal anatomical connections between hippocampus and subiculum: Evidence for subicular innervation of regio superior. *Brain Research*, 1980, *183*, 265–276.

Berger, T. W., & Thompson, R. F. Limbic system interrelations: Functional division among hippocampal–septal connections. *Science*, 1977, *197*, 587–589.

Berger, T. W., & Thompson, R. F. Identification of pyramidal cells as the critical elements in hippocampal neuronal plasticity during learning. *Proceedings of the National Academy of Sciences*, 1978, *75*, 1572–1576. (a)

Berger, T. W., & Thompson, R. F. Neuronal plasticity in the limbic system during classical conditioning of the rabbit nictitating membrane response: I. The hippocampus. *Brain Research*, 1978, *145*, 323–346. (b)

Berger, T. W., & Thompson, R. F. Hippocampal cellular plasticity during extinction of classically conditioning nictitating membrane behavior. *Behavioural Brain Research*, 1982, *4*, 63–76.

Berger, T. W., & Weisz, D. J. Single unit analysis of hippocampal pryamidal and granule cells and their role in classical conditioning of the rabbit nictitating membrane response. In I. Gormezano, W. F. Prokasy, & R. F. Thompson (Eds.), *Classical conditioning III: Behavioral, neurophysiological and neurochemical studies in the rabbit*. Hillsdale, N.J.: Erlbaum, in press.

Berthier, N. E., & Moore, J. W. Role of extraocular muscles in the rabbit (*Oryctolagus cuniculus*) nictitating membrane response. *Physiology and Behavior*, 1980, *24*, 931–937.

Brodal, A., & Jansen, J. The ponto-cerebellar projection in the rabbit and cat. *Journal of Comparative Neurology*, 1946, *84*, 31–118.

Cegavske, C. F., Patterson, M. M., & Thompson, R. F. Neuronal unit activity in the abducens nucleus during classical conditioning of the nictitating membrane response in the rabbit. *Journal of Comparative and Physiological Psychology*, 1979, *93*, 595–609.

Cohen, D. H. The neural pathways and informational flow mediating a conditioned autonomic response. In L. DiCara (Ed.), *Limbic and autonomic nervous systems research*. New York: Plenum Press, 1974.

Cohen, N. J., & Squire, L. R. Preserved learning and retention of pattern analyzing skill in amnesia: Dissociation of knowing how and knowing that. *Science*, 1980, *210*, 207–209.

Disterhoft, J. F., & Segal, M. Neuron activity in rat hippocampus and motor cortex during discrimination reversal. *Brain Research Bulletin*, 1978, *3*, 583–588.

Disterhoft, J. R., & Shipley, M. T. Accessory abducens nucleus innervation of rabbit retractor bulbi motoneurons localized with HRP retrograde transport. *Society for Neuroscience Abstracts*, 1980, *6*, 478.

Domesick, V. B. Projections from the cingulate cortex in the rat. *Brain Research*, 1969, *12*, 196–320.

Gabriel, M., & Saltwick, S. E. Rhythmic theta-like unit activity of the hippocampal formation during acquisition and performance of avoidance behavior in rabbits. *Physiology and Behavior*, 1980, *24*, 303–312.

Gormezano, I. Classical conditioning: Investigations of defense and reward conditioning in the rabbit. In A. H. Black & W. R. Prokasy (Eds.), *Classical conditioning II*. New York: Appleton-Century-Crofts, 1972.

Gray, T. S., MacMaster, S. E., Harvey, J. A., & Gormezano, I. Localization of retractor bulbi motoneurons in the rabbit. *Brain Research*, 1981, *226*, 93–106.

Hirsh, R. The hippocampus and contextual retrieval of information from memory: A theory. *Behavioral Biology*, 1974, *12*, 421–444.

Hoehler, F. K., & Thompson, R. F. Effect of the interstimulus (CS-UCS) interval on hippocampal unit activity during classical conditioning of the nictitating membrane response of the rabbit (*Oryctolagus cuniculus*). *Journal of Comparative and Physiological Psychology*, 1980, *94*, 201–215.

Honig, W. K. Studies of working memory in the pigeon. In S. H. Hulse, H. Fowler, & W. K. Honig (Eds.), *Cognitive processes in animal behavior*. Hillsdale, N.J.: Erlbaum, 1978.

Kandel, E. R. *Cellular basis of behavior*. San Francisco: W. H. Freeman, 1976.

Kettner, R. E., & Thompson, R. F. Auditory signal detection and decision processes in the nervous system. *Journal of Comparative and Physiological Psychology*, 1982, *96*, 328–331.

MacVicar, B. A., & Dudek, F. E. Electronic coupling between pyramidal cells: A direct demonstration in rat hippocampal slices. *Science*, 1981, *213*, 782–785.

Marmarelis, P. Z., & Marmarelis, V. Z. *Analysis of physiological systems*. New York: Plenum, 1978.

McCormick, D. A., Clark, G. A., Lavond, D. G., & Thompson, R. F. Initial localization of the memory trace for a basic form of learning. *Proceedings of the National Academy of Sciences*, 1982, *79*, 2731–2742.

McCormick, D. A., Lavond, D. G., & Thompson, R. F. Concomittent classical conditioning of the rabbit nictitating membrane and eyelid responses: Correlations and implications. *Physiology and Behavior*, 1982, *28*, 769–775.

McGaugh, J. L., & Herz, M. J. *Memory consolidation*. San Francisco: Albion, 1972.

Milner, B. Memory and the medial temporal regions of the brain. In K. H. Pribram & D. E. Broadbert (Eds.), *Biology and memory*. New York: Academic Press, 1970.

O'Keefe, J., & Nadel, L. *The hippocampus as a cognitive map*. London: Oxford University Press, 1978.

Olton, D. S., Becker, J. T., & Handelmann, G. E. Hippocampus, space, and memory. *Behavioral and Brain Sciences*, 1979, *2*, 313–365.

Patterson, M. M., Berger, T. W., & Thompson, R. F. Hippocampal neuronal plasticity recorded from cat during classical conditioning. *Brain Research*, 1979, *163*, 339–343.

Patterson, M. M., Olah, J., & Clement, J. Classical nictitating membrane conditioning in the awake, normal, restrained cat. *Science*, 1977, *196*, 1124–1126.

Perkel, D. H., & Bullock, T. *Neurosciences Research Program Bulletin*, 1968, *6*.

Ranck, J. B., Jr. Studies on single neurons in dorsal hippocampal formation and septum in unrestrained rats: I. Behavioral correlates and firing repertoires. *Experimental Neurology*, 1973, *41*, 461–555.

Rose, J. E., & Woolsey, C. N. Structure and relations of limbic cortex and anterior thalamic nuclei in rabbit and cat. *Journal of Comparative Neurology*, 1948, *89*, 279–347.

Schmaltz, L. W., & Theios, J. Acquisition and extinction of a classically conditioned response in hippocampectomized rabbits (*Oryctolagus cuniculus*). *Journal of Comparative and Physiological Psychology*, 1972, *79*, 328–333.

Semple-Rowland, S. L., Bassett, J. L., & Berger, T. W. Subicular projections to retrosplenial cortex in the rabbit. *Society for Neuroscience Abstracts*, 1981, *7*, 886.

Sidman, M., Stoddard, L. T., & Mohr, J. P. Some additional quantitative observations of immediate memory in a patient with bilateral hippocampal lesions. *Neuropsychologia*, 1968, *6*, 245–254.

Solomon, P. R., & Moore, J. W. Latent inhibition and stimulus generalization of the classically conditioned nictitating membrane response in rabbits (*Oryctolagus cuniculus*) following dorsal hippocampal ablation. *Journal of Comparative and Physiological Psychology*, 1975, *89*, 1192–1203.

Squire, L. R. Two forms of human amnesia: An analysis of forgetting. *Journal of Neuroscience*, 1981, *1*, 635–640.

Squire, L. R. The neuropsychology of human memory. *Annual Review of Neuroscience*, 1982, *5*, 241–273.

Squire, L. R., & Zola-Morgan, S. The neurology of memory: The case for correspondence between the findings for man and non-human primate. In J. A. Deutsch (Ed.), *The physiological basis of memory* (2nd ed.). New York: Academic Press, 1982.

Swanson, L. W., & Cowan, W. M. An autoradiographic study of the organization of the efferent connections of the hippocampal formation in the rat. *Journal of Comparative Neurology*, 1977, *172*, 49–84.

Swanson, L. W., Wyss, J. M., & Cowan, W. M. An autoradiographic study of the organization of intrahippocampal association pathways in the rat. *Journal of Comparative Neurology*, 1978, *181*, 681–716.

Thompson, R. F., Berger, T. W., Berry, S. D., & Hoehler, F. K. The search for the engram: II. In D. McFadden (Ed.), *Neural Mechanisms in Behavior: A Texas symposium*. New York: Springer-Verlag, 1980.

Thompson, R. F., Berger, T. W., Cegavske, C. R., Patterson, M. M., Roemer, R. A., Teyler, T. J., & Young, R. A. The search for the engram. *American Psychologist*, 1976, *31*, 209–227.

Weisz, D. J., Clark, G. A., & Thompson, R. F. *Increased excitability in dentate gyrus during NM conditioning in rabbit*. Manuscript in preparation, 1984.

Woody, C. D. Aspects of the electrophysiology of cortical processes related to the development and performance of learned motor responses. *The Physiologist*, 1974, *17*, 49–69.

41

Forebrain–Brain Stem Interaction: Conditioning and the Hippocampus

John W. Moore and Paul R. Solomon

Introduction

In order to understand how the hippocampus modulates classical conditioning, one needs a clear idea of the neural systems that underlie each component of the entire constellation of behaviors modified by pairing a given unconditioned stimulus (UCS) with a given conditioned stimulus (CS). One of the advantages of the nictitating membrane (NM) response is that the conditioned response (CR) produced by using a relatively focused UCS, such as airpuff to the eye or mild electrostimulation to the orbital region, appears to be confined to reflexes involving the relatively small number of skeletal muscles associated with the protection of the eyes (Berthier & Moore, 1980b; McCormick, Lavond, & Thompson, 1982). This preparation has already provided many insights into the role of the hippocampus in learning (Moore & Solomon, 1980). Recent discoveries concerning the location in the brain of the basic events necessary for the formation and expression of the NM CR set the stage for studies designed to clarify precisely how these regions, the cerebellum and pontine brain stem, and the hippocampus interact.

Our research in the hippocampus and learning has been based on the assumption that classical conditioning, and such phenomena as stimulus generalization and discrimination, are best understood in terms of information processing and related mathematical models. Within the conceptualization, one typically assumes that each successive stage of information processing might be assigned to distinct functional systems of the brain. We have assigned to the hippocampus the task of tuning out irrelevant events (Moore & Stickney, 1980, 1982; Solomon, 1977; Solomon & Moore, 1975). This view is consistent with the more general notion that the hippocampus is involved in coding the temporal relationships in the classical conditioning situation, especially when the CS and the UCS are temporally remote (Moore, 1979b; Solomon, 1979, 1980).

There is a clear alternative to the idea that anatomically distributed systems perform the specialized tasks associated with information processing in conditioning and learning. Rather than thinking of the brain as an assembly line for the transformation of raw sensory energy into behavior, it is possible that many of the component processes occur at the level of single neurons, each of which is capable of adjusting synaptic inputs in such a way as to yield not only conditioning, but the derivative phenomena of latent inhibition, blocking, conditioned inhibition, and so forth, as well (see Barto & Sutton, 1982; Sutton & Barto,

John W. Moore. Department of Psychology, University of Massachusetts, Amherst, Massachusetts.
Paul R. Solomon. Department of Psychology, Williams College, Williamstown, Massachusetts.

1981). It is even possible that the brain is analogous to a society of individuals (neurons) that has evolved in a symbiotic relationship with other organ systems to promote collective survival and replication. A good case for viewing neurons as goal-seeking individuals has been presented by Klopf (1982).

The idea that individual neurons may behave according to the same principles of learning and adaptation as whole organisms may seem fanciful to one approaching these problems from the perspective of psychology, with its emphasis of the self-concept, but not so unreasonable from the perspective of other disciplines, particularly in view of Sperry's (e.g., 1982) findings with split-brain preparations.

Hippocampus and the NM CR

The first indication that neuronal activity in the hippocampus is correlated with the NM CR came from a study by Berger, Alger, and Thompson (1976). These authors reported that both single-unit and multiple-unit activity in the pyramidal cell layer of hippocampus increased during the first few pairings of the CS and UCS. This increased neuronal activity preceded the behavioral response by as much as 35–40 msec and formed a temporal model of the NM response (Berger, Clark, & Thompson, 1980). Initially, the hippocampal response preceded the unconditioned response (UCR), but as CRs begin to occur, the neuronal response moved forward in the interstimulus interval, paralleling the CR and preceding it by 35–40 msec (see also Patterson, Berger, & Thompson, 1979).

Although these results suggest that the hippocampus is involved in acquisition of the CR, this characterization of the role of hippocampus in conditioning is difficult to support, since bilateral hippocampal ablations do not affect acquisition of the CR (e.g., Solomon & Moore, 1975). Moreover, careful analysis of the latency and topography of the CRs does not reveal any difference between animals with hippocampal ablations and controls. The paradox between the electrophysiological data and the results of lesion studies gave rise to two important questions regarding the role of the hippocampus in conditioning of the NM response: (1) Precisely what role, if any, is the hippocampus playing in acquisition of the CR? (2) Are there paradigms within the context of the NM CR for which the hippocampus is essential?

Conditioning Tasks for Which the Hippocampus Appears Critical

Although hippocampal lesions do not disrupt acquisition of the NM CR in a simple delay paradigm, we and others have shown that these lesions are disruptive in more complex conditioning tasks involving the NM response (see Solomon, 1979, for a review). One such task is latent inhibition, in which nonreinforced preexposure to a stimulus prior to conditioning retards conditioning to that stimulus when it is subsequently paired with the UCS in normal rabbits, but not in rabbits with hippocampal lesions. We (Solomon & Moore, 1975) reported that, whereas 450 tone preexposures resulted in a decrement in conditioning in normal rabbits and rabbits with neocortical ablations, animals with dorsal hippocampal ablations conditioned as fast as non-preexposed controls. This finding has now been replicated in the rat (McFarland, Kostas, & Drew, 1978).

A second task in which hippocampal lesions produce disruption is blocking. In blocking, experience with one stimulus (CS_A) that has been paired with the UCS blocks conditioning to a second stimulus (CS_B) when the two are subsequently presented together and repeated paired with the original UCS (Kamin, 1968; Marchant & Moore, 1973). Animals with hippocampal lesions do not show the blocking effect and thus show CRs to CS_B presented alone (Solomon, 1977). Similar results have been reported for rats in the conditioned emotional response (CER) paradigm (Rickert, Bennett, Lane, & French, 1978).

Successive acquisition and extinction sessions typically produce increasingly rapid reacquisition and extinction of the NM CR in normal rabbits (Smith & Gormezano, 1965), but rabbits with hippocampal ablations do not show more rapid extinction with repeated sessions (Schmaltz & Theios, 1972). Recently, Orr and Berger (1981) have reported that rabbits with dorsal hippocampal ablations can acquire but cannot reverse a two-tone discrimination (see also Berger, 1982). This is consistent with work on hippocampal lesions and reversal discrimination in other preparations (see Hirsch, 1974, for a review).

These studies suggest that the hippocampus is essential for certain types of conditioning tasks. Furthermore, these findings might all be encompassed within the tuning-out hypothesis. It has also been suggested that the hippocampus is involved in the association of temporally remote events (Moore, 1979b, p. 231; Solomon, 1980; see also Rawlins, Feldon, & Gray, 1982). A direct way to evaluate this hypothesis is to examine the role of the hippocampus in a task in which the CS ad UCS are temporally separated. Trace conditioning is one such task. Unlike delay conditioning, in which the CS and UCS usually overlap, in trace conditioning the CS goes on and off prior to the UCS. For conditioning to occur in this paradigm, some neuronal representation (i.e., trace) of the CS must persist to mediate the association with the UCS and for conditioning to occur. One such study of trace conditioning involves a 250-msec tone (80 dB), followed by a 500-msec period in which no stimuli were present (the trace interval), followed by a 100-msec airpuff UCS (Weisz, Solomon, & Thompson, 1980). Animals were run for 118 trials per day, using a variable-interval 60-sec intertrial interval. Using these parameters, normal animals acquired the response (eight CRs in any block of nine trials) within 4 days. These animals appeared to acquire the response much in the way normal animals acquire the response in a delay paradigm. Hippocampal rabbits, by contrast, did not acquire what has been referred to as an adaptive CR. They occasionally emitted short latency responses at the tone onset (600–700 msec prior to airpuff onset), which lasted for about 100 msec. These responses were often present early in training and, unlike normal CRs, were invariant in terms of latency and topography. When switched to a delay-conditioning paradigm, hippocampal animals readily acquired a normal-appearing CR.

In an ongoing study, one of us (Solomon) has been investigating multiple-unit neuronal responses in area CA1 of the hippocampus. The paradigm is the same as that used in the lesion study. Data (frequency of cell firings) were collected separately for the 750 msec immediately preceding the CS onset (the baseline period), for the combined CS and trace periods (750 msec), and for the 750-msec post-UCS onset period. The preliminary results of this study indicate that multiple-unit activity in the hippocampus increases early in conditioning (sometimes in the first block of CS-UCS pairings) and well before the emergence of the CR. At this stage, the cells appear to begin bursting during the CS and continue to do so after the termination of the CS and throughout the 500-msec trace period. As in the case of delay conditioning, the cells also increase their firing rate during the UCS presentation. Later in conditioning, as CRs begin to emerge, the unit activity precedes the behavioral CR and models it as in delay conditioning. The bursting seen earlier in conditioning during the CS and the trace period is no longer present. Recording of neuronal activity during trace conditioning appears to provide a useful method for examining which structures and systems are involved in maintaining a neural representation of stimuli during the conditioning process.

It is noteworthy that amnesic patients appear to have no difficulty acquiring an eyeblink CR in a delay-conditioning paradigm (Weiskrantz & Warrington, 1979). It will be interesting to see whether amnesic patients are impaired in trace conditioning, latent inhibition, blocking, and the like.

The Role of the Hippocampus in Delay Conditioning

Although removal of much of the hippocampal formation does not disrupt simple delay conditioning, there are a number of other manipulations that both alter hippocampal neuronal activity and disrupt conditioning. These studies provide a clue to the role of the hippocampus in delay conditioning in the intact animal. Berry and Thompson (1979) reported that small medial septal lesions both blocked hippocampal theta and retarded acquisition of the NM CR. Similarly, Solomon and Gottfried (1981) found that microinjections of scopolamine directly into the medial septum—another manipulation that blocks hippocampal theta (Stumpf, Petsche, & Gogolak, 1962)—also retarded CR acquisition. In each instance, the appearance of the first CRs was greatly retarded, but once CRs begin to occur, conditioning proceeded at a normal rate and reached asymptotic levels.

The results of these studies are consistent with a study by Berry and Thompson (1978) correlating hippocampal theta with acquisition of the NM response. In this study, the authors were able to predict the rate of acquisition of the NM CR by examining hippocampal EEG immediately prior to conditioning. Rabbits that displayed relatively high levels of activity in the theta range (2–8 Hz) conditioned significantly faster than animals that had a preponderance of activity in a higher frequency range (8–22 Hz).

Because systemic administration of scopolamine in the rabbit both alters hippocampal neuronal activity by blocking hippocampal theta and retards acquisition of the NM CR (Harvey & Gormezano, 1981; Moore, Goodell, & Solomon, 1976), this manipulation provides a useful tool for examining the relationship between altered neuronal activity in hippocampus and retarded acquisition of the NM CR. Specifically, if the retardation of conditioning following systemic administration of scopolamine is due to altered neuronal activity in hippocampus, there should be no retardation of conditioning in scopolamine-treated rabbits with hippocampal ablation. Solomon, Solomon, Schaaf, and Perry (1983) report just such an effect. In this study, animals with hippocampal ablations, animals with neocortical ablations, or unoperated controls were given either scopolamine or saline injections. The animals were then conditioned to a light CS and eye-shock UCS in a delay-conditioning paradigm. The data from this study are consistent with the results of earlier studies in indicating that (1) dorsal hippocampal ablation does not affect acquisition of the NM CR, and (2) systemic administration of scopolamine retards acquisition of the CR in normal animals and those with neocortical ablations. The most interesting finding of the study, however, is that scopolamine, which alters hippocampal neuronal activity and retards conditioning in normal rabbits, did not affect conditioning in rabbits with hippocampal ablations. These results suggest that certain patterns of neuronal activity in hippocampus are more detrimental to conditioning than is ablating the structure.

The notion that a malfunctioning structure may be more detrimental to conditioning than none at all has been suggested before in regard to hippocampus (Berry & Thompson, 1979; Isaacson, 1974; Solomon, 1980). This concept may be useful in explaining paradoxical data from a variety of sources. For example, although Berry and Thompson (1979) demonstrated that small medial septal lesions disrupt acquisition of the NM CR, an earlier study (Lockhart & Moore, 1975) found that large septal lesions (encompassing the medial and lateral septum) had no effect on simple acquisition. It is possible to account for these data by hypothesizing that lesions of the medial septum, a primary afferent to hippocampus, disrupt conditioning by producing altered neuronal activity in hippocampus, which then has its effects on conditioning by modulating other essential structures and systems in the brain. When the lesion is extended to the lateral septum (a primary hippocampal efferent), however, the altered neuronal activity might not effect these essential systems. In this regard, lateral septal lesions function much in the same way as hippocampal lesions in the Solomon *et al.* (1983) study. Of course, these hypotheses are testable by examining the effects of altering hippocampal neuronal activity with manipulations such as scopolamine in animals with lateral septal lesions. We should point out, however, that recently discovered anatomical pathways in the rabbit from hippocampus via the subiculum to cingulate cortex and to pons (e.g., Bassett & Berger, 1981) provide an alternate pathway for the flow of information from the hippocampus. The contribution of this pathway will also have to be evaluated.

In sum, there is now good reason to believe that even though the hippocampus is not essential for acquisition of the NM CR in the simple delay paradigm, it can play a modulatory role. Given this information, it now seems important to seek answers to two questions:

1. With what neuronal system or systems in the brain is the hippocampus interacting to disrupt conditioning?
2. What is the mechanism of this disruption?

Although the answer to the second question will require substantially more research, there are already some good indications as to the answer to the first.

A Neuronal Model

Moore (1979a) incorporated evidence on the role of the hippocampus in NM conditioning into a neuronal model. Recent developments outlined above provide an opportunity to update the model. Its key features are here summarized.

1. Pairing an UCS with an CS produces learning because of the contiguous converging action of these two afferent pathways onto neurons of the pontine reticular formation. These Hebbian-type learning neurons are afferent to motoneurons responsible for the NM response as observed at the periphery. Furthermore, these learning neurons and their synaptic inputs form a neural circuit parallel to that subserving the UCR.

2. The output of the learning neurons is characterized as having both fast- and slow-conducting components. The fast-conducting component allows action potentials to be propagated rapidly toward the forebrain. Assuming that the temporal density of action potentials from learning neurons mimics the topography of the CR, the fast-conducting component provides the forebrain (including the hippocampus) with an *efference copy* of the CR to be executed. Such ascending information would be useful for integrating the CR into other behavioral systems and for higher-level information processing, such as what might be necessary for tuning out irrelevant events or for processes of declarative, as opposed to procedural, memory (see Cohen & Squire, 1980). The slow output, arising from axon collaterals, is responsible for driving motor neurons. The difference in conduction velocity for the two output components in the model has been attributed to differences in fiber diameter, mylineation, branch points, and number of intervening synapses in each pathway. Postulation of two output branches with different speeds accounts for the finding noted above—that CR-modeling activity recorded from the hippocampus tends to precede the behavioral CR.

3. The motoneurons responsible for the NM response are assumed to lie within the abducens nucleus on the side of the brain stem ipsilateral to the UCS.

4. The active form of learned inhibition associated with conditioned inhibition training originates at the level of the midbrain and projects caudally to inhibit the learning neurons via inhibitory (hyperpolarizing) synapses. Evidence implicating the midbrain in conditioned inhibition came from Mis (1977). Subsequent studies have shed little further light on the neural substrates of conditioned inhibition (Berthier & Moore, 1980a; Blazis & Moore, 1982; Moore, Yeo, Oakley, & Steele-Russell, 1980).

5. The septo-hippocampal complex performs the task of preventing afferent information arising from stimuli that do not predict the UCS from reaching the learning neuron. Axoaxonic synaptic configurations and presynaptic inhibition are the suggested mechanism for this tuning-out function. This descending influence is very likely not monosynaptic, and the number of synaptic relays to learning neurons remains conjectural. In any event, this aspect of the model remains true to the tuning-out hypothesis by preventing irrelevant stimuli from acquiring control over behavior.

We discuss each point in turn. There is now good evidence from combined lesion and electrophysiological studies that the pontine brain stem contains premotor neurons that are essential for learning and the performance of the NM CR (Desmond, Berthier, & Moore, 1981; Desmond & Moore, 1982; Lavond, McCormick, Clark, Holmes, & Thompson, 1981; Moore, Desmond, & Berthier, 1982). Furthermore, the critical neurons appear to lie in a strip immediately dorsal to and extending rostrally from the motor trigeminal nucleus (Desmond & Moore, 1983). This is the supratrigeminal region described by Mizuno (1970). In addition, the interpositus region of the ipsilateral cerebellum appears to be essential for the NM CR (McCormick, Clark, Lavond, & Thompson, 1982; McCormick, Guyer, & Thompson, 1982; McCormick, Lavond, Clark, Kettner, Rising, & Thompson, 1981; Yeo, Hardiman, Glickstein, & Steele-Russell, 1982), and it is entirely possible that the primary locus of the engram for the NM response and other conditioned somatic responses resides within this structure (Thompson, 1982). In this role, neurons of the supratrigeminal reticular formation would be a link in the flow of commands that activates relevant motor neurons (McCormick, Guyer, & Thompson, 1982).

There is now also good evidence to support the idea that the neural circuits responsible for the NM CR are parallel to that of the UCR. Lesions of the brain stem or cerebellum that eliminate the CR appear to have no effect on the UCR, which remains intact. As a cautionary note, however, a systematic physiological study of the UCR, like that no normal rabbits reported by Moore and Desmond (1982), has yet to be undertaken for animals with CR-disrupting lesions. Other evidence that the neural pathways subserving the CR and UCR are parallel comes from studies showing that morphine attenuates CRs but not UCRs (Mauk, Warren, & Thompson, 1982) and that scopolamine (which retards conditioning, as noted above) has no effect on the UCR (Moore *et al.*, 1976).

The most important recent development regarding the second grouping of features of the model concerns the question of whether CR-modeling activity recorded from the hippocampus is indeed the result of rostrally projecting efference copy of the CR. Affirmative evidence comes from a recent study by Clark, McCormick, Lavond, Baxter, Gray, and Thompson (1982), showing that cerebellar lesions that eliminate the NM CR also eliminate the temporal model of the CR recorded from the hippocampus. Evidence concerning the morphology of learning neurons—which are necessary to support the idea of two output systems, a fast-conducting one to the forebrain and a slow-conducting one to the motoneurons—awaits further research on the respective contributions of the cerebellum and pontine reticular formation to the CR.

Concerning the third feature of the model listed above, it has now been well established that the NM response is a passive consequence of eyeball retraction (Berthier & Moore, 1980b; Cegavske, Thompson, Patterson, & Gormezano, 1976). Defensive eyeball retraction is thought to be primarily due to activation of motoneurons of the accessory abducens nucleus (Berthier & Moore, 1983; Disterhoft & Shipley, 1980; Gray, McMaster, Harvey, & Gormezano, 1981; Torigoe, Wenokor, & Cegavske, 1981), although some retractor bulbi motoneurons are also within the abducens nucleus. Other extraocular muscles participate in eyeball retraction (Berthier & Moore, 1980b), and this reflex is highly integrated with the eye blink, which is in turn mediated by the facial nerve (McCormick, Lavond, & Thompson, 1982). The reflex pathway of the UCR is as yet somewhat obscure, but the rostral components of the sensory trigeminal complex, including the principal nucleus, are thought to be the primary sensory component of this reflex (Berthier & Moore, 1983). Thus, the central sensory components of the UCR pathway are quite near to the supratrigeminal region implicated by lesion and electrophysiological studies (Desmond & Moore, 1982, 1983). Finally, horseradish peroxidase studies indicate that neurons in the supratrigeminal region project to the accessory abducens nucleus (Desmond, Rosenfield, & Moore, 1983).

The fourth feature of the model concerns the likely origin of active learned inhibitory influences on premotor neurons responsible for conditioning. Although there has been very little clarification of this point, a variety of indirect indications suggest that "reward" systems of the posterior hypothalamus might underlie conditioned inhibition of the NM response (Berthier & Moore, 1980a). Consistent with this hypothesis are horseradish peroxidase data indicating projections from the posterior lateral hypothalamus (and elsewhere) to the parabrachial nucleus, anatomically very near to the supratrigeminal region implicated in the NM CR (Hamilton, Ellenberger, Liskowsky, & Schneiderman, 1981). A similar pattern of projections from the hypothalamus to regions of the cerebellum implicated in this behavior remains to be demonstrated.

The feature of the model that remains the least documented is listed under the fifth group of features. Direct monosynaptic projections from the hippocampal formation to the supratrigeminal region and deep cerebellar nuclei have not been demonstrated, to our knowledge, and there is no evidence to date bearing on the mode of axonal terminations or synaptic mechanisms underlying the tuning-out interpretation. The problem is compounded by the large number of multisynaptic mediators that could, in principle, convey such instructions to the pontine recticular formation or cerebellum.

Nevertheless, the evidence in support of the idea that the hippocampus is involved in tuning out irrelevant events remains good. For example, the apparent inability of animals with hippocampal lesions to reverse an acquired discrimination, noted above (e.g., Orr & Berger, 1981), might be viewed in terms of inability to learn to ignore the CS that had, prior to reversal, been paired with the reinforcing event. The new information that may be difficult to encompass within the tuning-out hypotheses are the studies cited above that suggest hippocampal involvement in trace conditioning.

The mechanisms by which the hippocampus might bridge the temporal gap between a CS and a UCS in trace conditioning are many. Perhaps the hippocampus is involved in sustaining reverberating activity within sensory systems coding the CS. Clearly, then, the hippocampus might perform more than one task within the information-processing framework in which we have viewed learning. Significant evidence bearing on this point comes from a recent study demonstrating that theta cells and complex-spike cells within the hippocampus are differentially activated during different learning tasks, suggesting two functionally distinct neuronal systems (Christian, West, & Deadwyler, 1982).

Further Research

Experiments such as the Christian et al. (1982) study seem particularly promising for further clarifying the functions of the hippocampal formation in classical conditioning. Their approach and those of Berger (e.g., 1982) and others provide evidence on what the various types of neurons within the septo-hippocampal complex are doing during particular tasks. This strategy needs to be extended into experiments involving compound stimuli (e.g., blocking), latent inhibition, and other paradigms involving higher demands of information processing and memory. Such experiments would seem to be particularly useful if they included concurrent chronic unit recording from brain stem and cerebellar components that are the basic building blocks of the CR.

REFERENCES

Barto, A. G., & Sutton, R. S. Simulation of anticipatory responses in classical conditioning by a neuron-like adaptive element. *Behavioural Brain Research*, 1982, *4*, 221–235.

Bassett, J. L., & Berger, T. W. Non-thalamic efferent projections of the posterior cingulate gyrus in the rabbit. *Society for Neuroscience Abstracts*, 1981, *7*, 885.

Berger, T. W. Hippocampal pyramidal cell activity during two-tone discrimination and reversal conditioning of the rabbit nictitating membrane response. *Society for Neuroscience Abstracts*, 1982, *8*, 146.

Berger, T. W., Alger, B. E., & Thompson, R. F. Neuronal substrates of classical conditioning in the hippocampus. *Science*, 1976, *192*, 483–485.

Berger, T. W., Clark, G. A., & Thompson, R. F. Learning dependent neuronal responses recorded from limbic system brain structures during classical conditioning. *Physiological Psychology*, 1980, *8*, 155–167.

Berry, S. D., & Thompson, R. F. Prediction of learning rate from hippocampal EEG. *Science*, 1978, *200*, 1298–1300.

Berry, S. D., & Thompson, R. F. Medial septal lesions retard classical conditioning of the nictitating membrane response of rabbits. *Science*, 1979, *205*, 2009–2010.

Berthier, N. E., & Moore, J. W. Disrupted conditioned inhibition of the rabbit nictitating membrane response following mesencephalic lesions. *Physiology and Behavior*, 1980, *25*, 667–673. (a)

Berthier, N. E., & Moore, J. W. Role of extraocular muscles in the rabbit (*Oryctolagus cuniculus*) nictitating membrane response. *Physiology and Behavior*, 1980, *24*, 931–937. (b)

Berthier, N. E., & Moore, J. W. The nictitating membrane response: An electrophysiological study of the abducens nerve and nucleus and the accessory abducens nucleus in rabbit. *Brain Research*, 1983, *258*, 201–210.

Blazis, D. E. J., & Moore, J. W. Naloxone does not impair conditioned inhibition of the rabbit's nictitating membrane response. *Bulletin of the Psychonomic Society*, 1982, *20*, 122–123.

Cegavske, C. F., Thompson, R. F., Patterson, M. M., & Gormezano, I. Mechanisms of efferent neuronal control of the reflex nictitating membrane response in the rabbit (*Oryctolagus cuniculus*). *Journal of Comparative and Physiological Psychology*, 1976, *90*, 411–423.

Christian, E. P., West, M. O., & Deadwyler, S. A. Differential functional response correlates of hippocampal cell types in the behaving rat. *Society for Neuroscience Abstracts*, 1982, *8*, 146.

Clark, G. A., McCormick, D. A., Lavond, D. G., Baxter, K., Gray, W. J., & Thompson, R. F. Effects of electrolytic lesions of cerebellar nuclei on conditioned behavioral and hippocampal neuronal responses. *Society for Neuroscience Abstracts*, 1982, *8*, 22.

Cohen, N. J., & Squire, L. R. Perceived learning and retention of pattern analyzing skill in amnesia: Dissociation of knowing how and knowing that. *Science*, 1980, *210*, 207–210.

Desmond, J. E., Berthier, N. E., & Moore, J. W. Brain stem elements essential for the classically conditioned nictitating membrane response of rabbit. *Society for Neuroscience Abstracts*, 1981, *7*, 650.

Desmond, J. E., & Moore, J. W. A brain stem region essential for the classically conditioned but not the unconditioned nictitating membrane response. *Physiology and Behavior*, 1982, *28*, 1029–1033.

Desmond, J. E., & Moore, J. W. A supratrigeminal region implicated in the classically conditioned nictitating membrane response. *Brain Research Bulletin*, 1983, *10*, 765–773.

Desmond, J. E., Rosenfield, M. E., & Moore, J. W. An HRP study of brain stem afferents to the accessory abducens region and dorsolateral pons in rabbit: Implications for the conditioned nictitating membrane response. *Brain Research Bulletin*, 1983, *10*, 747–763.

Disterhoft, J. F., & Shipley, M. T. Accessory abducens innervation of rabbit retractor bulbi motoneurons localized with HRP retrograde transport. *Society for Neuroscience Abstracts*, 1980, *6*, 478.

Gray, T. S., McMaster, S. E., Harvey, J. A., Gormezano, I. Localization of retractor bulbi motoneurons in the rabbit. *Brain Research*, 1981, *226*, 96–106.

Hamilton, R. B., Ellenberger, H., Liskowsky, D., & Schneiderman, N. Parabrachial area as mediator of bradycardia in rabbits. *Journal of the Autonomic Nervous System*, 1981, *4*, 261–281.

Harvey, J. A., & Gormezano, I. Drug effects on classical conditioning of the rabbit nictitating membrane response. *Society for Neuroscience Abstracts*, 1981, *7*, 359.

Hirsch, R. The hippocampus and contextual retrieval of information from memory: A theory. *Behavioral Biology*, 1974, *12*, 421–444.

Isaacson, R. L. *The limbic system*. New York: Plenum, 1974.

Kamin, L. H. "Attention-like" processes in classical conditioning. In M. R. Jones (Ed.), *Miami Symposium on the Prediction of Behavior*. Miami, Fla.: University of Miami Press, 1968.

Klopf, A. H. *The hedonistic neuron*. Washington, D.C.: Hemisphere, 1982.

Lavond, D. G., McCormick, D. A., Clark, G. A., Holmes, D. T., & Thompson, R. F. Effects of ipsilateral rostral pontine reticular lesions on retention of classically conditioned nictitating membranes and eyelid responses. *Physiological Psychology*, 1981, *9*, 335–339.

Lockhart, M., & Moore, J. W. Classical differential and operant conditioning in rabbits (*Oryctolagus cuniculus*) with septal lesions. *Journal of Comparative and Physiological Psychology*, 1975, *88*, 147–154.

Marchant, H. G., & Moore, J. W. Blocking on the rabbit's conditioned nictitating membrane response in Kamin's two-stage paradigm. *Journal of Experimental Psychology*, 1973, *101*, 155–158.

Mauk, M. D., Warren, J. T., & Thompson, R. F. Selective naloxone-reversible morphine depression of learned behavioral and hippocampal responses. *Science*, 1982, *216*, 434–436.

McCormick, D. A., Clark, G. A., Lavond, D. G., & Thompson, R. F. Initial localization of the memory trace for a basic form of learning. *Proceedings of the National Academy of Sciences*, 1982, *79*, 2731–2735.

McCormick, D. A., Guyer, P. E., & Thompson, R. F. Superior cerebellar peduncle lesions selectively abolish the ipsilateral classically conditioned nictitating membrane/eyelid response of the rabbit. *Brain Research*, 1982, *244*, 347–350.

McCormick, D. A., Lavond, D. G., Clark, G. A., Kettner, R. E., Rising, C. E., & Thompson, R. F. The engram found?: Role of cerebellum in classical conditioning of the nictitating membrane and eyelid responses. *Bulletin of the Psychonomic Society*, 1981, *18*, 103–105.

McCormick, D. A., Lavond, D. G., & Thompson, R. F. Concomitant classical conditioning of the rabbit nictitating membrane and eyelid responses: Correlations and implications. *Physiology and Behavior*, 1982, *28*, 769–775.

McFarland, D. J., Kostas, J., & Drew, W. G. Dorsal hippocampal lesions: Effects of preconditioning CS exposure on flavor aversion. *Behavioral Biology*, 1978, *22*, 398–404.

Mis, F. W. A midbrain–brainstem circuit for conditioned inhibition of the nictitating membrane response in the rabbit (*Oryctaolagus cuniculus*). *Journal of Comparative and Physiological Psychology*, 1977, *91*, 975–988.

Mizuno, N. Projection fibers from the main sensory trigeminal nucleus and the supratrigeminal region. *Journal of Comparative Neurology*, 1970, *139*, 457–472.

Moore, J. W. Brain processes and conditioning. In A. Dickinson & R. A. Boakes (Eds.), *Mechanisms of learning and motivation: A memorial volume to Jerzy Konorski*. Hillsdale, N.J. Erlbaum, 1979. (a)

Moore, J. W. Information processing in space–time by the hippocampus. *Physiological Psychology*, 1979, *7*, 224–232. (b)

Moore, J. W., & Desmond, J. E. Latency of the nictitating membrane response to periocular electro-stimulation in unanesthetized rabbits. *Physiology and Behavior*, 1982, *28*, 1041–1046.

Moore, J. W., Desmond, J. E., & Berthier, N. E. The metencephalic basis of the conditioned nictitating membrane response. In C. D. Woody (Ed.), *Conditioning: Representation of involved neural function*. New York: Plenum, 1982.

Moore, J. W., Goodell, N. A., & Solomon, P. R. Central cholinergic blockade by scopolamine and habituation, classical conditioning, and latent inhibition of the rabbit's nictitating membrane response. *Physiological Psychology*, 1976, *4*, 395–399.

Moore, J. W., & Solomon, P. R. (Eds.). Role of the hippocampus in learning and memory. *Physiological Psychology* (special issue), 1980, *8*, 145–296.

Moore, J. W., & Stickney, K. J. Formation of attentional–associative networks in real time: Role of the hippocampus and implications for conditioning. *Physiological Psychology*, 1980, *8*, 207–217.

Moore, J. W., & Stickney, K. J. Goal tracking in attentional–associative networks: Spatial learning and the hippocampus. *Physiological Psychology*, 1982, *10*, 202–208.

Moore, J. W., Yeo, C. H., Oakley, D. A., & Steele-Russell, I. Conditioned inhibition of the nictitating membrane response in decorticate rabbits. *Brain Behavior Research*, 1980, *1*, 397–409.

Orr, W. B., & Berger, T. W. Hippocampal lesions disrupt discrimination reversal learning of the rabbit nictitating membrane response. *Society for Neuroscience Abstracts*, 1981, *7*, 648.

Patterson, M. M., Berger, T. W., & Thompson, R. F. Neural plasticity recorded from cat hippocampus in classical conditioning. *Brain Research*, 1979, *163*, 339–343.

Rawlins, J. N. P., Feldon, J., & Gray, J. A. Behavioral effects of hippocampectomy depend on inter-event intervals. *Society for Neuroscience Abstracts*, 1982, *8*, 22.

Rickert, E. J., Bennett, T. L., Lane, P., & French, J. Hippocampectomy and the attenuation of blocking. *Behavioral Biology*, 1978, *22*, 147–160.

Schmaltz, L. W., & Theios, J. Acquisition and extinction of a classically conditioned response in hippocampectomized rabbits (*Orytolagus cuniculus*). *Journal of Comparative and Physiological Psychology*, 1972, *79*, 328–333.

Smith, M., & Gormezano, I. Effects of alternating classical conditioning and extinction sessions on the conditioned nictitating membrane response of the rabbit. *Psychonomic Science*, 1965, *3*, 91–92.

Solomon, P. R. Role of the hippocampus in blocking and conditioned inhibition of the rabbit's nictitating membrane response. *Journal of Comparative and Physiological Psychology*, 1977, *91*, 407–417.

Solomon, P. R. Temporal versus spatial information processing views of hippocampal function. *Psychological Bulletin*, 1979, *86*, 1272–1279.

Solomon, P. R. A time and a place for everything?: Temporal processing views of hippocampal function with special reference to attention. *Physiological Psychology*, 1980, *8*, 254–261.

Solomon, P. R., & Gottfried, K. E. The septo-hippocampal cholonergic system and classical conditioning of the rabbit's nictitating membrane response. *Journal of Comparative and Physiological Psychology*, 1981, *95*, 322–330.

Solomon, P. R., & Moore, J. W. Latent inhibition and stimulus generalization of the classically conditioned nictitating membrane response in rabbits (*Oryctolagus cuniculus*) following dorsal hippocampal ablation. *Journal of Comparative and Physiological Psychology*, 1975, *89*, 1192–1203.

Solomon, P. R., Solomon, S. D., Schaaf, E. V., & Perry, H. E. Altered activity in the hippocampus is more detrimental to classical conditioning than removing the structure. *Science*, 1983, *220*, 329–331.

Sperry, R. Some effects of disconnecting the cerebral hemispheres *Science*, 1982, *217*, 1223–1226.

Stumpf, C., Petsche, H., & Gogolak, G. The significance of the rabbits septum as a relay station between the midbrain the hippocampus: II. The differential influence of drugs upon both cell firing pattern and the hippocampus theta activity. *Electroencephalography and Clinical Neurophysiology*, 1962, *14*, 212–219.

Sutton, R. S., & Barto, A. G. Toward a modern theory of adaptive networks. *Psychological Review*, 1981, *88*, 135–170.

Thompson, R. F. Personal communication, 1982.

Torigoe, Y., Wenokor, W., & Cegavske, C. F. Neural substrates of the classically conditioned rabbit nictitating membrane preparation: Trigeminal system afferents. *Society for Neuroscience Abstracts*, 1981, *7*, 753.

Weiskrantz, L., & Warrington, E. K. Conditioning in amnesic patients. *Neuropsychologia*, 1979, *17*, 187–194.

Weisz, D. W., Solomon, P. R., & Thompson, R. F. The hippocampus appears necessary for trace conditioning. *Bulletin of the Psychonomic Society*, 1980, *16*, 244. (Abstract)

Yeo, C H., Hardiman, M. J., Glickstein, M., & Steele-Russell, I. Lesions or cerebellar nuclei abolish the classically conditioned nictitating membrane response. *Society for Neuroscience Abstracts*, 1982, *8*, 22.

42

The Amygdala: A Neuroanatomical Systems Approach to Its Contribution to Aversive Conditioning

Bruce S. Kapp, Jeffrey P. Pascoe, and Michael A. Bixler

Introduction

As is apparent from the size and diversity of this volume, numerous approaches to the physiological analysis of memory are in use, each offering a unique contribution to the elucidation of the manner by which the brain stores information. Central to many of these approaches is a delineation of the specific neuroanatomical systems that contribute to memory, with the subsequent goal of defining the exact nature of their contribution. These efforts have provided evidence implicating a function for numerous brain areas in memory, including the hippocampus, cerebellum, thalamus, frontal cortex, and amygdala, to name but a few. Our research over the past several years has been devoted to an investigation of the contribution(s) of the amygdala to learning and to memory processes, particularly of aversive events. Our earlier research (Gallagher & Kapp, 1978; Gallagher, Kapp, Musty, & Driscoll, 1977) demonstrated that pharmacological interventions within the rat amygdala immediately following passive-avoidance conditioning produced retention deficits. This finding was consistent with observations that (1) postconditioning electrical stimulation of the amygdala produces retention deficits (Gold, Macri, & McGaugh, 1973; McDonough & Kesner, 1971), and (2) lesions of the amygdala interfere with the acquisition of a variety of aversively conditioned responses (Blanchard & Blanchard, 1972; Goddard, 1964).

      The exact nature of the contribution(s) of the amygdala to learning and memory for aversive events has remained obscure, although several theories have been suggested. For example, lesions of the amygdala attenuate species-typical emotional (e.g., fear) responses to both unconditioned *and* conditioned threatening stimuli. These observations have led to the proposal that these lesions attenuate the arousal of fear, which accounts for the lesion-induced deficits in the acquisition of conditioned responding during fear-motivated aversive conditioning (Spevack, Campbell, & Drake, 1975). Such an interpretation can be extended to account for the effects of postconditioning amygdaloid manipulations on retention (Kapp & Gallagher, 1979) of aversive conditioning. Hence, an analysis designed to understand the exact contribution of the amygdala to learning and memory, particularly of aversive experiences, must incorporate an analysis of the contributions of the amygdala to fear arousal and the involvement of fear in aversive conditioning.

Bruce S. Kapp, Jeffrey P. Pascoe, and Michael A. Bixler. Department of Psychology, University of Vermont, Burlington, Vermont.

Neuroanatomical data have demonstrated that the amygdala is comprised of a heterogeneous group of nuclei, each with its own unique afferent and efferent connections (Ben-Ari, 1981). Hence, it is not unreasonable to assume that different neuroanatomical systems within the amygdala contribute differentially to various behaviors (Lehman & Winans, 1982), as well as to different aspects of learning and memory processes. Therefore, an important component in an analysis designed to determine the exact nature of the contribution(s) of the amygdala in learning and memory processes is to attempt to define the specific systems of the amygdala that contribute to these processes. Through an initial definition of these systems, important insights may be provided for additional research designed to elucidate the exact nature of the contribution(s) of the amygdala in learning and memory processes. We have recently adopted such a neuroanatomical systems approach.

The Amygdaloid Central Nucleus: Contributions to the Acquisition of Conditioned Cardiovascular Responding in the Rabbit

Several findings prompted us to begin our neural systems analysis of the amygdala by focusing on the amygdaloid central nucleus (see Figure 42-1) and its contribution to the acquisition of conditioned bradycardia in the rabbit during Pavlovian fear conditioning. Among these were two reports demonstrating that lesions confined primarily to the central nucleus resulted in deficits in the acquisition of passive-avoidance responding in rats (Grossman, Grossman, & Walsh, 1975; McIntyre & Stein, 1973). Since such responding

FIGURE 42-1. A coronal section through the rabbit amygdala showing the components of the central nucleus. Abbreviations: Ce$_m$, medial component of the central nucleus; Ce$_l$, lateral component of the central nucleus; Co$_m$, posteromedial cortical nucleus of the amygdala; La, lateral nucleus of the amygdala; Me, medial nucleus of the amygdala; OT, optic tract; P, putamen.

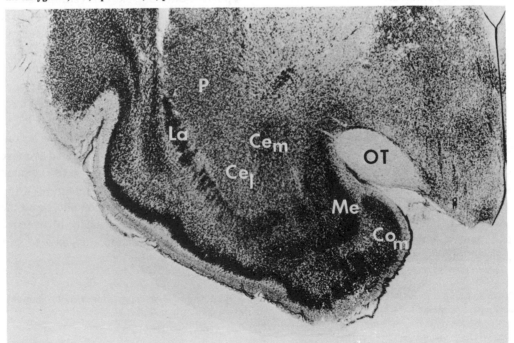

typically involves conditioned species-typical fear responding (e.g., freezing) to apparatus cues, these results were consistent with the interpretation, based on the effects of larger lesions, that lesions of the amygdala interfere with the arousal of fear. Second, stimulation of the central nucleus was consistently reported to elicit somatic and autonomic components of affective behavior, including those described as fear-like (Hilton & Zbrozyna, 1963; Roldan, Alvarez-Pelaez, & Fernandez de Molina, 1974; Ursin & Kaada, 1960), a finding consistent with the data from lesion studies. For these reasons, we chose initially to examine the central nucleus.

Our rationale for initially investigating response acquisition was based on the assumption that a detailed knowledge of the neural systems involved in response acquisition should lend further insights into how these systems may contribute to, or interact with systems responsible for, the storage of information necessary for the subsequent expression of that response under the appropriate environmental contingencies. The conditioned bradycardia response system in the rabbit was chosen because it offered several advantages over response systems typically used to assess acquisition and retention processes in learning and memory research (e.g., active- and passive-avoidance responses). First, the parameters of this rapidly conditioned response, a cardiodeceleration accompanied by a depressor response, have been well defined in the rabbit (Fredericks, Moore, Metcalf, Schwaber, & Schneiderman, 1974; Powell & Kazis, 1976; Schneiderman, VanDercar, Yehle, Manning, Golden, & Schneiderman, 1969). Second, the final pathway for the expression of the response is primarily via the vagus nerves (Fredericks *et al.*, 1974). Third, electrical stimulation of the central nucleus in the cat has been reported to produce a pattern of species-typical affective responses, including significant cardiovascular alterations (Hilton & Zbrozyna, 1963; Stock, Schlör, Heidt, & Buss, 1978). These observations suggested a function for the central nucleus in cardiovascular adjustments to threatening stimuli. Indeed, an anatomical substrate for such a contribution was provided by the demonstration of a direct projection from the central nucleus to dorsal medullary cardiovascular regulatory nuclei in the cat (Hopkins & Holstege, 1978). Finally, bradycardia occurs in response to a predator in the rabbit (von Frisch, 1966) and may represent one of a number of species-typical emotional responses that can come under the influence of associative control via Pavlovian conditioning. As such, this response may be analogous to the species-typical emotional response of freezing in the rat. This latter response is readily conditioned, is typically measured in examining the effects of various agents on retention in learning and memory experiments, and is markedly attenuated by amygdaloid lesions.

Central Nucleus Manipulations: Effects on the Acquisition of Conditioned Bradycardia

Our first experiment sought to determine the effect of lesions of the central nucleus on the acquisition of the conditioned bradycardia response, using a standard Pavlovian aversive conditioning procedure (Kapp, Frysinger, Gallagher, & Haselton, 1979). Both large and small bilateral lesions produced a significant attenuation of the magnitude of the conditioned bradycardia response to a 5-second tone conditioned stimulus (CS). No significant effects were observed on baseline heart rate or on the heart rate orienting response to a novel tone stimulus (see Figure 42-2). It should be noted that it is possible that the effects observed were a function of damage to fibers of passage, rather than to

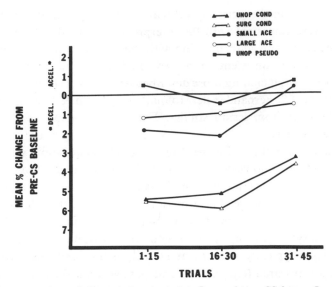

FIGURE 42-2. Mean percentage of change in heart rate to a 5-second tone CS from a 5-second pre-CS baseline for 45 conditioning trials during aversive Pavlovian conditioning in which the CS was paired with a 2.0-mA, 500-msec eyelid shock (UCS). Each group contained eight animals. Data points represent group means for 15 trial blocks. Abbreviations: Small Ace, a group with lesions damaging approximately 50% or less of the central nucleus; Large Ace, a group with lesions damaging more than 50% of the central nucleus; Unop Cond, an unoperated control group; Surg Cond, a surgical control group; Unop Pseudo, an unoperated control group receiving random, unpaired presentations of the CS and UCS.

damage to the central nucleus *per se*. While this alternative explanation is viable, in additional experiments receptor agonists and antagonists injected into the region of the central nucleus also affected the magnitude of the conditioned bradycardia response (Gallagher, Kapp, Frysinger, & Rapp, 1980; Gallagher, Kapp, McNall, & Pascoe, 1981). Hence, it would appear that the observed effects are a function of manipulations of the central nucleus *per se*.

Central Nucleus Projections to Cardioregulatory Nuclei in the Dorsal Medulla of the Rabbit

While these experiments suggested a contribution for the central nucleus in the acquisition of the conditioned bradycardia response, the exact nature of the contribution remained unknown. However, emerging anatomical evidence at the time yielded some important insights. Hopkins and Holstege (1978) had demonstrated a projection in the cat from the region of the central nucleus to autonomic regulatory nuclei of the dorsal medulla—the nucleus of the solitary tract and the vagal dorsal motor nucleus. Since the conditioned bradycardia response in the rabbit is primarily under vagal control, and since cardioinhibitory neurons that could serve as the origin of the final pathway for the expression of the conditioned bradycardia response are located within the vagal dorsal motor nucleus in the rabbit (Schwaber & Schneiderman, 1975), we sought to determine whether such a projection existed in the rabbit.

Our results (see Figure 42-3) demonstrated that the central nucleus projected directly to the vagal dorsal motor nucleus, the nucleus of the solitary tract, and the nucleus ambiguus (Schwaber, Kapp, & Higgins, 1980; Schwaber, Kapp, Higgins, & Rapp, 1982). The projection originated in the medial component of the nucleus and in an uninterrupted continuum extending anteriorly through the substantia innominata and into the lateral component of the bed nucleus of the stria terminalis. The projection encapsulated and terminated within the dorsal motor nucleus of the vagus and terminated within the nucleus of the solitary tract, where it was observed to innervate areas recipient of cardiovascular baroreceptor afferents in the rabbit (Schwaber, Kapp, Higgins, & Rapp, 1980).

Cardiomotor Function for the Central Nucleus in the Expression of Conditioned Bradycardia: An Initial Working Hypothesis

Our anatomical observations endow the central nucleus with the potential to exert a rather direct influence on the autonomic nervous system and on cardioinhibitory neurons that may mediate the expression of the conditioned response. Taken together with the demonstration that manipulations of the central nucleus attenuate the magnitude of the conditioned response, these findings suggested the working hypothesis that the central nucleus functions, at least in part, in the motoric expression of the conditioned bradycardia response (and perhaps other autonomic responses) to the CS. This effect could be mediated by either a direct or an indirect (e.g., via the nucleus of the solitary tract) influence on vagal cardioinhibitory neurons in the vagal dorsal motor nucleus.

If this hypothesis were valid, then it might be predicted that (1) electrical stimulation of the central nucleus would produce autonomic responses, including vagally mediated bradycardia and depressor responses, in the rabbit, and (2) changes in central nucleus neuronal activity would develop to the CS during Pavlovian conditioning at about the time when the conditioned bradycardia response emerges to the CS. These predictions have been confirmed in recent experiments.

First, stimulation of the central nucleus in both anesthetized and awake rabbits produced short-latency, vagally mediated bradycardia and depressor responses accompanied by alterations in respiration (see Figure 42-4), most frequently an increased frequency and decreased depth (Kapp, Gallagher, Underwood, McNall, & Whitehorn, 1982; Applegate, Kapp, Underwood, & McNall, 1983). Both the cardiovascular and respiratory responses were of the same pattern as those observed to the CS during Pavlovian fear conditioning (Powell & Kazis, 1976; Yehle, Dauth, & Schneiderman, 1967), and were maximal upon stimulation of the medial central nucleus, the component from which the projection to the medulla arises. Furthermore, the cardiovascular responses may well be due to stimulation of the cells of origin of the central nucleus descending projection, which may either directly or indirectly activate vagal preganglionic cardioinhibitory neurons in the vagal dorsal motor nucleus. Second, in recent experiments in which multiple-unit activity was recorded from the central nucleus during Pavlovian fear conditioning (Applegate, Frysinger, Kapp, & Gallagher, 1982), a significant increase in short-latency multiple-unit activity developed to the CS over the course of the conditioning procedure in a number of cases (see Figures 42-5 and 42-6). This increased activity emerged at the time when the conditioned bradycardia response emerged to the CS.

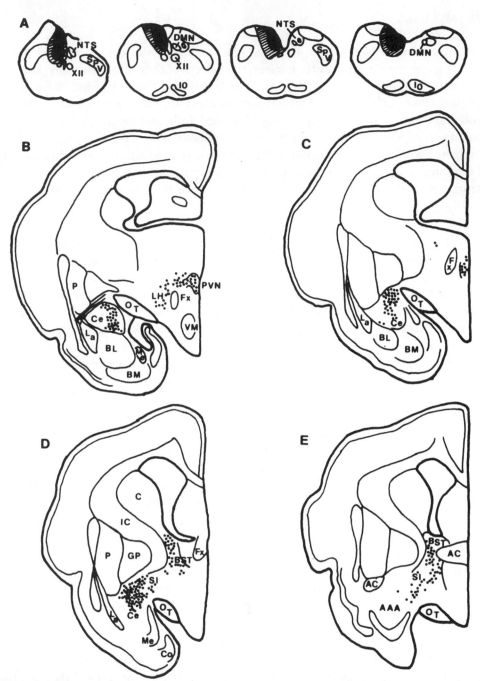

FIGURE 42-3. Labeled neurons in the central nucleus of the amygdala, following four injections of horseradish peroxidase (HRP) at different rostral-caudal levels of the dorsal vagal motor nucleus (DMN)–nucleus tractus solitarius (NTS) complex. Each dot represents one labeled neuron from that section alone. A indicates injection sites; B-E represent caudal to rostral levels, respectively. Abbreviations: AAA, anterior amygdaloid area; AC, anterior commissure; BL, basolateral nucleus of the amygdala; BM, basomedial nucleus of the amygdala; BST, bed nucleus of the stria terminalis; C, caudate nucleus; Ce, central nucleus of the amygdala; Co, cortical nucleus of the amygdala; DMN, dorsal motor nucleus of the vagus nerve; Fx, fornix; GP, globus pallidus; IC, internal capsule; IO, inferior olive; LH, lateral hypothalamus; La, lateral nucleus of the amygdala; Me, medial nucleus of the amygdala; NTS, nucleus of the solitary tract; OT, optic tract; P, putamen; PVN, paraventricular nucleus of the hypothalamus; SI, substantia innominata; SPV, spinal trigeminal complex; VM, ventromedial nucleus of the hypothalamus; XII, hypoglossal nucleus.

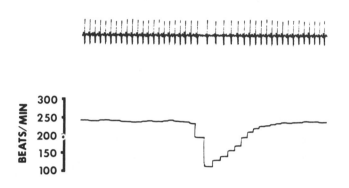

FIGURE 42-4. Heart rate and respiration responses produced by stimulation of the medial central nucleus in the awake, loosely restrained rabbit. The upper trace shows the respiration response, while the lower trace is the cardiotachograph response produced by a 1-second stimulus train (40 μA, 100 Hz, .5-msec pulse duration).

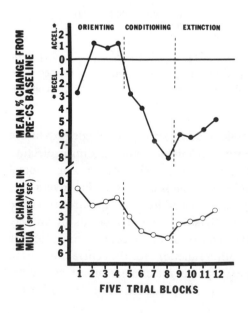

FIGURE 42-5. Mean heart rate change and mean multiple-unit activity (MUA) change from a central nucleus placement in response to a 5-second tone CS for five trial blocks across three phases of an aversive Pavlovian conditioning procedure: a 20-trial orienting phase in which the CS was presented alone, a 20-trial conditioning phase in which the CS and UCS were paired, and a 20-trial extinction phase in which the CS was again presented alone. Note the significant increase in MUA to the CS that emerged during the conditioning phase and that paralleled the development of the conditioned bradycardia response to the CS.

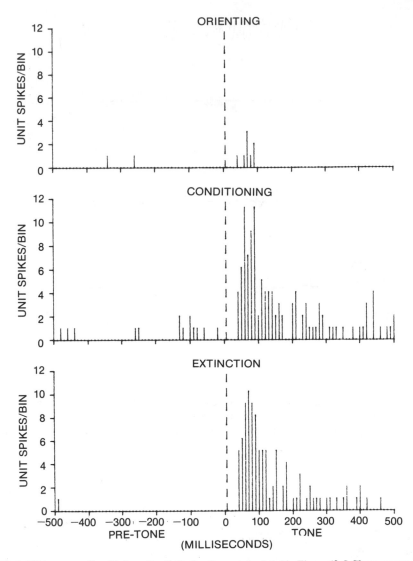

FIGURE 42-6. Histograms of multiple-unit activity for the case depicted in Figure 42-5. Shown are unit spikes/10 msec bin, summed across each of the 20 trials of orienting, conditioning, and extinction, for the 500 msec preceding and the first 500 msec of the CS. Note the low spontaneous pre-CS activity, and the short-latency increases in activity that emerged during the conditioning phase.

In summary, our behavioral, neuroanatomical, and electrophysiological data are consistent with the working hypothesis that the central nucleus and its descending projection may provide an anatomical substrate for the motoric expression of the conditioned bradycardia response, and perhaps other conditioned responses, during Pavlovian fear conditioning. This hypothesis is admittedly speculative, and additional experiments will be necessary to test its validity. Furthermore, we emphasize that our analysis in no way precludes a contribution of other brain areas to the acquisition of the conditioned response (Buchanan & Powell, 1982), nor does it eliminate other functions for the central nucleus in the acquisition of the conditioned response. For example, in the context of our earlier discussion, the deficit in the conditioned bradycardia response produced by manipulations of the central nucleus may reflect, in addition to a deficit in the motoric expression of the conditioned response, a deficit in the arousal of a central fear state that is induced by the noxious unconditioned stimulus (UCS) and that becomes conditioned to the CS. If the conditioned bradycardia response that emerges to the CS represents one of a constellation of responses accompanying the conditioned fear state, then an attenuation in the arousal of fear to the noxious UCS would lead to a weakened association between the CS and fear and would be reflected in an attenuation of the magnitude of the conditioned bradycardia response.

If the central nucleus also functions more generally in the arousal of fear, then it might be expected that manipulations of the central nucleus would interfere not only with autonomic manifestations of the fear state, but also with a variety of other behavioral responses dependent upon the arousal of fear. That this is the case has recently been demonstrated by Werka, Skär, and Ursin (1978). Lesions confined primarily to the central nucleus in rats produced decreased emotionality as reflected in altered open-field behavior, as well as deficits in the acquisition of one-way active avoidance, the acquisition of which is dependent upon fear motivation. The authors interpreted this response profile as consistent with a lesion-induced reduction of fear. These results, together with those demonstrating that lesions of the central nucleus produce deficits in the acquisition of passive avoidance behavior, demonstrate that such lesions alter both conditioned and unconditioned behavioral responses that depend upon the arousal of fear. Hence, the central nucleus may also function in the arousal of fear. Although these hypotheses are attractive in the light of the extant literature, a third hypothesis is viable: Response acquisition deficits observed following lesions of the central nucleus may reflect an interference with a neural system that is directly responsible for the formation and/or the preservation of the association made between the CS and fear.

In summary, while our data suggest a motoric function for the central nucleus in the acquisition of conditioned bradycardia, these data by no means preclude alternative functions for this nucleus. Indeed, in the final analysis, the central nucleus may possess such a multifunctional role in aversive learning and memory processes.

The Central Nucleus of the Amygdala: A Component within a Larger System Involved in Emotional Learning

Our neuroanatomical analysis of the central nucleus projection to autonomic regulatory nuclei of the dorsal medulla offered insights into one of its possible functions—that of a cardiomotor role in the expression of conditioned bradycardia. Hence, additional neuroanatomical analyses of the connections of the central nucleus with other forebrain and brain stem structures should lead to a more complete understanding of its function(s) in aversive conditioning. Recent evidence, including our own, suggests that the central nucleus is a primary component within a larger forebrain system that may be involved in the regulation of the autonomic nervous system. Figure 42-7 presents a schematic summary of some of the major afferent and efferent connections of the central nucleus, based primarily on observations in rats and rabbits. While a detailed description of each of these connections is beyond the scope of our present discussion, we wish to emphasize several aspects of this system.

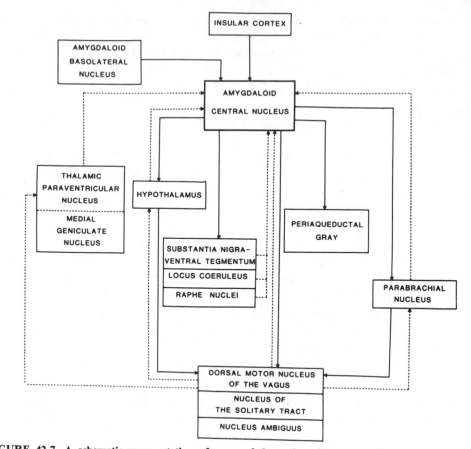

FIGURE 42-7. A schematic representation of some of the major afferent and efferent projections of the amygdaloid central nucleus based on data from rats and rabbits. Dotted lines represent ascending projections, either direct or indirect, to the central nucleus, many of which originate in the nucleus of the solitary tract.

First, many of the areas with which the central nucleus connects have been implicated in autonomic, including cardiovascular, regulation (Evans, 1976; Hamilton, Ellenberger, Liskowsky, Gellman, & Schneiderman, 1980; Kaada, 1951; Stock *et al.*, 1978). Second, much of the influence of the central nucleus is upon the hypothalamus, dorsal medulla, and other brain stem structures, since these areas receive the bulk of its efferent projection system. Third, the central nucleus is recipient of a rather significant projection from the insular cortex (see Figure 42-8). This cortex has been demonstrated in rats to be a recipient of projections from brain stem nuclei (e.g., parabrachial nucleus) involved in processing visceral sensory information (Saper, 1982). Finally, the central nucleus, as well as other components of this system, is a recipient of direct projections from the nucleus tractus solitarius, an area within which visceral sensory afferents synapse (Ricardo & Koh, 1978). Hence, not only does the central nucleus possess the potential to regulate the viscera; its activity and the activity in other areas with which it connects may be modulated by sensory information originating in the viscera. We believe that this latter aspect has important implications for a further understanding of the contributions of the central nucleus and its associated system in aversive conditioning. It is to a discussion of several converging lines of evidence implicating the possible importance of visceral afferent activity in emotion and aversive conditioning that we now turn.

Visceral Sensory–Central Nucleus Interactions:
Potential Contributions to Emotional Arousal and Aversive Conditioning

Several lines of evidence suggest the possibility that various components of the system depicted in Figure 42-7 can be influenced by visceral activity. First, the general visceroceptive region of the nucleus of the solitary tract has been shown to project directly to the central nucleus, as well as to other areas (e.g., the hypothalamus, paraventricular thalamic nucleus, parabrachial nucleus) of this system. Of particular significance is the fact that this

FIGURE 42-8. Dark-field photomicrograph of the distribution of silver grains within the medial central nucleus of the rabbit, following an injection of [³H]proline/[³H]leucine (60 nl) into the insular cortex. Note the well-defined boundaries of the medial central nucleus produced by the label. Exposure time was 8 weeks. OT, optic tract.

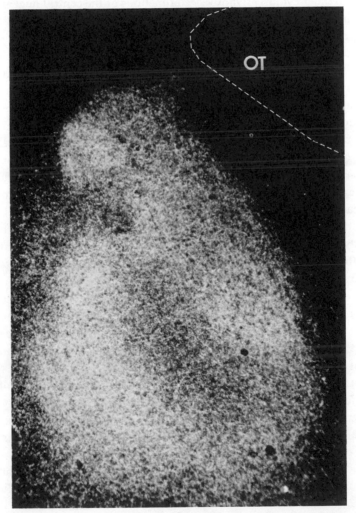

projection arises from the region of the A2 catecholaminergic neurons of the nucleus of the solitary tract (Ricardo & Koh, 1978)—neurons that have been demonstrated to receive a monosynaptic input from visceral afferents of the vagus nerve (Sumal, Blessing, Joh, Reis, & Pickel, 1982). Second, stimulation of the vagus nerve in the awake monkey produces alterations in the firing rates of neurons located within the central nucleus and insular cortex (Radna & MacLean, 1981), a finding consistent with the earlier results of Dell and Olson (1951). Furthermore, that cardiovascular afferent activity can influence components of this system has been shown by the demonstration that stimulation of the cat aortic depressor or carotid sinus nerves produces alterations in the firing frequency of central nucleus neurons (Cechetto & Calaresu, 1981). Similarly, stimulation of the aortic depressor nerve in rabbits has been shown to produce changes in unit activity throughout the parabrachial region (Hamilton *et al.*, 1980), a region projecting directly to the central nucleus. These accumulated data support the notion that the system depicted in Figure 42-7 not only possesses the potential to influence the viscera, but also can be rather directly influenced by visceral autonomic activity.

What is the possible behavioral significance of this visceral influence, particularly with respect to the previously hypothesized functions of the central nucleus (and perhaps of the system in Figure 42-7) in the arousal of fear, the conditioning of fear, and/or the motoric expression of various responses accompanying fear? The answer to this question is far from clear. However, if the system in Figure 42-7 does function in one or more of the processes described above, and if visceral influence is an important component of the system, then it would be predicted that manipulations of visceral activity might produce alterations in, for example, the arousal of emotions (e.g., fear) and fear-motivated conditioning. Indeed, several lines of research suggest that manipulations of the peripheral autonomic nervous system can profoundly influence emotional arousal, as well as the acquisition of aversively conditioned responses. Such manipulations may produce their effects, at least in part, via visceral sensory feedback upon the system depicted in Figure 42-7.

For example, that cardiovascular sensory activity can produce profound influences on emotional behavior has been demonstrated in the studies of Bizzi, Libretti, Mallion, and Zanchetti (1961) and Bartorelli, Bizzi, Libertti, and Zanchetti (1960). Stimulation of carotid body chemoreceptors in acute, prechiasmatic, decerebrate cats produced immediate outbursts of "rage-like" behavior. Decreases in carotid sinus pressure also induced these outbursts, while increases blocked their spontaneous occurrence. Furthermore, these outbursts were dependent upon the integrity of brain mechanisms lying rostral to the pontobulbar region. The authors suggest that these pressoceptive and chemoceptive influences are exerted on higher nervous mechanisms controlling complex patterned responses that may subserve consciousness and emotion. While these authors do not mention outbursts of "fear-like" behavior, the extent to which components of the observed behavioral pattern are similar to those that occur during intense states of fear cannot be excluded. Nevertheless, the results suggest that visceral sensory activity may exert profound influences on the arousal of emotion, perhaps via influences on the system depicted in Figure 42-7. Such evidence is consistent with the notion that this system may function in the arousal of fear.

If visceral sensory feedback contributes to the arousal and/or conditioning of fear, then manipulations of the autonomic nervous system also would be predicted to affect the conditioning of fear, particularly in situations designed to measure fear acquisition directly. Corwin and Slaughter (1979) have provided evidence in support of this prediction using a conditioned emotional response (CER) paradigm, in which conditioned suppression to CS presentation provides a measure of conditioned fear. They demonstrated that electrical stimulation of the cervical vagus nerve in rats coincident with the presentation of the noxious foot-shock UCS during paired CS-UCS acquisition trials significantly attenuated conditioned suppression to the CS during subsequent retention testing. Vagal stimulation immediately preceding foot shock was ineffective. Since conditioned suppression is dependent upon the arousal and conditioning of fear to the CS, the deficits observed may reflect an interference with either or both of these processes. Such an interference could result from a stimulation-induced alteration in visceral feedback upon the system depicted in Figure 42-7—feedback that is normally produced by the noxious UCS and that contributes to these processes.

While vagal stimulation may produce deficits in conditioned suppression by directly altering visceral afferent feedback, vagal stimulation affects the activity of both afferent sensory and efferent motor fibers carried in the nerve. Hence, the observed deficits could also be a function of abnormal changes in visceral motor activity—changes that lead to abnormal afferent feedback. In this respect, it is of interest that blockade of the efferent peripheral parasympathetic system with atropine methyl nitrate has been reported to produce a delay in the emergence of conditioned eye-blink responding in rabbits during Pavlovian aversive conditioning (Albiniak & Powell, 1980). The authors suggest that afferent feedback consequent to parasympathetic activation during conditioning may be an important requirement for optimal acquisition of this aversively conditioned response. Blocking the visceral efferent component presumably results in alterations in visceral sensory feedback. It should be noted, however, that the generality of the effects of parasympathetic efferent blockade on the acquisition of conditioned responding during aversive conditioning is not clear, since DiVietti and Porter (1969) found no effects of pharmacologically induced parasympathetic efferent blockade in rats on acquisition of conditioned suppression in a CER paradigm.

While the evidence presented above suggests that manipulations of the parasympathetic system can produce deficits in fear conditioning and in the acquisition of aversively conditioned responses, the effects of manipulations of the sympathetic system on these processes are equivocal. Perhaps the most widely known study is that of Wynne and Solomon (1955), who investigated the acquisition of avoidance responding in dogs following surgical removal of the sympathetic nervous system. Such removal not only eliminates the visceral–motor component of the system, but also sensory feedback from its activation. The results, although variable, generally demonstrated that this treatment produced deficits in the acquisition of the conditioned avoidance response. Interestingly, the one dog in this study subjected to parasympathetic blockade demonstrated extremely deficient response acquisition, a finding consistent with the results of Corwin and Slaughter (1979) and Albiniak and Powell (1980). While the results of Wynne and Solomon (1955), as well as more recent studies (Joseph & Powell, 1980), suggest that sympathectomy can produce deficits in the acquisition of aversively conditioned responding, a number of studies report that immunosympathectomy produces minimal or no effects on the acquisition of such responding (Van-Toller & Tarpy, 1974). Hence, the influence of the sympathetic nervous system on the acquisition of conditioned responding during fear-motivated avoidance conditioning is far from clear and is deserving of further research.

Finally, consistent with the results suggesting that manipulations of the peripheral autonomic nervous system may affect fear-motivated conditioning are the results showing that agents exerting their effects primarily on the peripheral autonomic nervous system can affect retention of fear-motivated conditioning (Martinez, 1982). For example, peripherally administered epinephrine, which acts primarily on the peripheral nervous system, has been demonstrated to produce a dose-dependent facilitation or deficit in retention of passive-avoidance conditioning when administered immediately following the conditioning session (Gold & van Buskirk, 1975). Since epinephrine is effective only when given shortly following conditioning, the possibility exists that it interacts with, and alters, the response of the peripheral autonomic nervous system to the training foot shock. These abnormal changes could be fed back upon the system in Figure 42-7 to influence the establishment of a central state of fear and/or the conditioning of that state to environmental stimuli. Obviously, the validity of these speculations awaits further research. Nevertheless, these converging lines of evidence point to an anatomical system in need of further investigation, particularly with respect to its contribution to fear motivation, fear conditioning, and memory of aversive experiences.

Conclusions

By incorporating a neuroanatomical systems approach to amygdala functions in learning, important insights have been obtained concerning the contributions of one amygdala system, the central nucleus, to aversive conditioning processes. Indeed, based in part on its anatomical connections with medullary autonomic regulatory nuclei, the central nucleus may function not only in the motoric expression of the conditioned bradycardia response, but also in the arousal of fear. Additional research incorporating neuroanatomical systems analyses to determine the interactions of the central nucleus with other forebrain and brain stem structures should aid in further defining the functions of the central nucleus in these processes, as well as in determining the existence of additional functions (e.g., associative) for this nucleus in aversive conditioning.

REFERENCES

Albiniak, B. A., & Powell, D. A. Peripheral autonomic mechanisms and Pavlovian conditioning in the rabbit (*Oryctolagus cuniculus*). *Journal of Comparative and Physiological Psychology*, 1980, *94*, 1101–1113.
Applegate, C. D., Frysinger, R. C., Kapp, B. S., & Gallagher, M. Multiple unit activity recorded from amygdala central nucleus during Pavlovian heart rate conditioning. *Brain Research*, 1982, *238*, 457–462.
Applegate, C. D., Kapp, B. S., Underwood, M. D., & McNall, C. L. Autonomic and somatomotor effects of amygdala central nucleus stimulation in awake rabbits. *Physiology and Behavior*, 1983, *31*, 353–360.
Bartorelli, C., Bizzi, E., Libretti, A., & Zanchetti, A. Inhibitory control of sino-carotid pressoreceptive afferents on hypothalamic autonomic activity and sham rage behavior. *Archives Italiennes de Biologie*, 1960, *98*, 308–326.
Ben-Ari, Y. (Ed.). *The amygdaloid complex* (INSERM Symposium No. 20). Amsterdam: Elsevier/North-Holland, 1981.

Bizzi, E., Libretti, A., Mallion, A., & Zanchetti, A. Reflex chemoceptive excitation of diencephalic sham rage behavior. *American Journal of Physiology*, 1961, *200*, 923–926.

Blanchard, D. C., & Blanchard, R. J. Innate and conditioned reactions to threat in rats with amygdaloid lesions. *Journal of Comparative and Physiological Psychology*, 1972, *81*, 281–290.

Buchanan, S. L., & Powell, D. A. Cingulate cortex: Its role in Pavlovian conditioning. *Journal of Comparative and Physiological Psychology*, 1982, *96*, 755–774.

Cechetto, D., & Calaresu, F. R. Single units in the amygdala of the cat responding to stimulation of buffer nerves. *Society for Neuroscience Abstracts*, 1981, *7*, 365.

Corwin, J. V., & Slaughter, J. S. Effects of vagal stimulation on the learning of specific and diffuse conditioned suppression. *Behavioral and Neural Biology*, 1979, *25*, 364–370.

Dell, P., & Olson, R. Projections thalamiques, corticales et cérébelleuses des afférences viscérales vagales. *Comptes Rendus des Séances de la Société de Biologie et de Ses Filiales* (*Paris*), 1951, *145*, 1084–1088.

DeVietti, T. L., & Porter, P. B. Modification of the autonomic component of the conditioned emotional response. *Psychological Reports*, 1969, *24*, 951–958.

Evans, M. H. Stimulation of rabbit hypothalamus: Caudal projections to respiratory and cardiovascular centers. *Journal of Physiology* (*London*), 1976, *260*, 205–222.

Fredericks, A., Moore, J. W., Metcalf, F. U., Schwaber, J. S., & Schneiderman, N. Selective autonomic blockade of conditioned and unconditioned heart rate changes in rabbits. *Pharmacology, Biochemistry and Behavior*, 1974, *2*, 493–501.

Gallagher, M., & Kapp, B. S. Manipulation of opiate activity in the amygdala alters memory processes. *Life Sciences*, 1978, *23*, 1973–1978.

Gallagher, M., Kapp, B. S., Frysinger, R. C., & Rapp, P. Beta-adrenergic manipulation in amygdala central n. alters rabbit heart rate conditioning. *Pharmacology, Biochemistry and Behavior*, 1980, *12*, 419–426.

Gallagher, M., Kapp, B. S., McNall, C., and Pascoe, J. P. Opiate effects in the amygdala central nucleus on heart rate conditioning in rabbits. *Pharmacology, Biochemistry and Behavior*, 1981, *14*, 497–505.

Gallagher, M., Kapp, B. S., Musty, R. E., & Driscoll, P. A. Memory formation: Evidence for a specific neurochemical system in the amygdala. *Science*, 1977, *189*, 423–425.

Goddard, G. V. Functions of the amygdala. *Psychological Bulletin*, 1964, *62*, 89–109.

Gold, P. E., Macri, J., & McGaugh, J. L. Retrograde amnesia produced by subseizure amygdala stimulation. *Behavioral Biology*, 1973, *9*, 671–680.

Gold, P. E., & van Buskirk, R. B. Facilitation of time dependent memory processes with post-trial epinephrine injections. *Behavioral Biology*, 1975, *13*, 145–153.

Grossman, S. P., Grossman, L., & Walsh, L. Functional organization of the rat amygdala with respect to avoidance behavior. *Journal of Comparative and Physiological Psychology*, 1975, *88*, 829–850.

Hamilton, R. B., Ellenberger, H. H., Liskowsky, D. R., Gellman, M. D., & Schneiderman, N. Parabrachial nucleus as a mediator of bradycardia in rabbits. *Society for Neuroscience Abtracts*, 1980, *6*, 816.

Hilton, S. M., & Zbrozyna, A. W. Amygdaloid region for defense reactions and its efferent pathway to the brainstem. *Journal of Physiology* (*London*), 1963, *165*, 160–173.

Hopkins, D. A., & Holstege, G. Amygdaloid projections to the mesencephalon, pons and medulla oblongata in the cat. *Experimental Brain Research*, 1978, *82*, 529–547.

Joseph, J., & Powell, D. A. Peripheral 6-hydroxydopamine administration in the rabbit (*Oryctolagus cuniculus*): Effects on Pavlovian conditioning. *Journal of Comparative and Physiological Psychology*, 1980, *94*, 1114–1125.

Kaada, B. R. Somato-motor, autonomic and electrocorticographic responses to electrical stimulation of "rhinencephalic" and other structures in primates, cat and dog. *Acta Physiologica Scandinavica*, 1951, *24*(Suppl. 83), 1–258.

Kapp, B. S., Frysinger, R. C., Gallagher, M., & Haselton, J. Amygdala central nucleus lesions: Effects on heart rate conditioning in the rabbit. *Physiology and Behavior*, 1979, *23*, 1109–1117.

Kapp, B. S., & Gallagher, M. Opiates and memory. *Trends in Neuroscience*, 1979, *2*, 177–180.

Kapp, B. S., Gallagher, M., Underwood, M. D., McNall, C., & Whitehorn, D. Cardiovascular responses elicited by electrical stimulation of the amygdala central nucleus in the rabbit. *Brain Research*, 1982, *234*, 251–262.

Lehman, M. N., & Winans, S. S. Vomeronasal and olfactory pathways to the amygdala controlling male hamster sexual behavior: Autoradiographic and behavioral analyses. *Brain Research*, 1982, *240*, 27–41.

Martinez, J. L. Conditioning: Modification by peripheral mechanisms. In C. D. Woody (Ed.), *Conditioning: Representation of involved neural functions*. New York: Plenum Press, 1982.

McDonough, J. H., & Kesner, R. P. Amnesia produced by brief electrical stimulation of the amygdala or dorsal hippocampus in cats. *Journal of Comparative and Physiological Psychology*, 1971, *77*, 171–178.

McIntyre, M., & Stein, D. Differential effects of one versus two stage amygdaloid lesions on activity, exploratory and avoidance behaviors in the albino rat. *Behavioral Biology*, 1973, *9*, 451–465.

Powell, D. A., & Kazis, E. Blood pressure and heart rate changes accompanying classical eyeblink conditioning in the rabbit (*Oryctolagus cuniculus*). *Psychophysiology*, 1976, *13*, 441–447.

Radna, R. J., & MacLean, P. D. Vagal elicitation of respiratory-type and other unit responses in basal limbic structures of squirrel monkeys. *Brain Research*, 1981, *213*, 45–61.

Ricardo, J. A., & Koh, E. T. Anatomical evidence of direct projections from the nucleus of the solitary tract to the hypothalamus, amygdala, and other forebrain structures in the rat. *Brain Research*, 1978, *153*, 1–26.

Roldan, E., Alvarez-Pelaez, R., & Fernandez de Molina, A. E. Electrographic study of the amygdaloid defense response. *Physiology and Behavior*, 1974, *13*, 779–787.

Saper, C. B. Convergence of autonomic and limbic connections in the insular cortex of the rat. *Journal of Comparative Neurology*, 1982, *210*, 163–173.

Schneiderman, N., VanDercar, D. H., Yehle, A. L., Manning, A. A., Golden, T., & Schneiderman, E. Vagal compensatory adjustment: Relationship to heart-rate classical conditioning in rabbits. *Journal of Comparative and Physiological Psychology*, 1969, *68*, 175–183.

Schwaber, J. S., Kapp, B. S., & Higgins, G. The origin and extent of direct amygdala projections to the region of the dorsal motor nucleus of the vagus and the nucleus of the solitary tract. *Neuroscience Letters*, 1980, *20*, 15–20.

Schwaber, J. S., Kapp, B. S., Higgins, G., & Rapp, P. The origin, extent and terminal distribution of direct amygdala central nucleus projections to the dorsal motor nucleus and nucleus of the solitary tract. *Society for Neuroscience Abstracts*, 1980, *6*, 816.

Schwaber, J. S., Kapp, B. S., Higgins, G. A., & Rapp, P. Amygdaloid and basal forebrain direct connections with the nucleus of the solitary tract and the dorsal motor nucleus. *Journal of Neuroscience*, 1982, *2*, 1424–1438.

Schwaber, J. S., & Schneiderman, N. Aortic nerve activated cardioinhibitory neurons and interneurons. *American Journal of Physiology*, 1975, *299*, 783–790.

Spevack, A. A., Campbell, C. T., & Drake, L. Effects of amygdalectomy on habituation and CER in rats. *Physiology and Behavior*, 1975, *15*, 199–207.

Stock, G., Schlör, K. H., Heidt, H., & Buss, J. Psychomotor behavior and cardiovascular patterns during stimulation of the amygdala. *Pflugers Archives*, 1978, *376*, 177–184.

Sumal, K. K., Blessing, W. W., Joh, T. H., Reis, D. J., & Pickel, V. M. Ultrastructural evidence that vagal afferents terminate on catecholaminergic neurons in the nucleus tractus solitarius. *Society for Neuroscience Abstracts*, 1982, *8*, 429.

Ursin, H., & Kaada, B. R. Functional localization within the amygdaloid complex in the cat. *Electroencephalography and Clinical Neurophysiology*, 1960, *12*, 1–20.

Van-Toller, C., & Tarpy, R. M. Immunosympathectomy and avoidance behavior. *Psychological Bulletin*, 1974, *81*, 132–137.

von Frisch, O. Herzfrequenzänderung bei Drückreaktion junger Nestflüchter. *Zeitschrift für Tierpsychologie*, 1966, *23*, 497–500.

Werka, T., Skär, J., & Ursin, H. Exploration and avoidance in rats with lesions in the amygdala and piriform cortex. *Journal of Comparative and Physiological Psychology*, 1978, *92*, 672–681.

Wynne, L. C., & Solomon, R. L. Traumatic avoidance learning: Acquisition and extinction in dogs deprived of normal peripheral autonomic function. *Genetic Psychology Monographs*, 1955, *52*, 241–284.

Yehle, A., Dauth, G., & Schneiderman, N. Correlates of heart-rate classical conditioning in curarized rabbits. *Journal of Comparative and Physiological Psychology*, 1967, *64*, 98–104.

43

The Neurophysiology of Learning:
A View from the Sensory Side

Norman M. Weinberger

Introduction

The processes of learning and memory are not "content-free." They always involve the learning and remembering of something, or some things. Although there is not yet general agreement about just what is learned and remembered (e.g., stimulus–response connections, relationships among stimuli), the things learned and remembered require adequate stimulation of receptors in sensory systems, adequate transduction of such stimulation, and some degree of processing of the resultant electrophysiological events within sensory systems. One need adopt neither the extreme empiricism of Locke nor the moderate nativism of Kant to accept these statements as starting points for the neuropsychology of learning and memory. One need only reject the extreme nativism of Plato that all learning is merely recall because all knowledge is present at birth.

In approaching learning, my colleagues and I have assumed that the *initial* neural events that occur during learning are particularly worthy of study. Further, we have assumed that such events might well develop within the sensory system of a "stimulus about which something is learned." As this system is the "first place" in which the stimulus is processed, it might also be the site of initial events that are specific to learning. In choosing to study the "sensory side," we were also cognizant of certain tactical advantages: The general functions of sensory systems are better understood than are the functions of many other brain systems; there is a large body of relevant data from the fields of psychophysics and sensory physiology; and input and output paths are well known for most sensory loci. We selected the auditory system for study because of the relative ease with which stimulus parameters can be varied.

The very idea that learning modifies the processing of stimuli by sensory systems presents a paradox. Certainly, sensory systems must correctly analyze the *physical* parameters of stimuli. But, if they also respond to the *psychological* parameters of stimuli (i.e., the *meaning* or *significance* of stimuli), one would expect ambiguity in the response of the system. I return to this issue later, in considering the effects of learning upon the thalamocortical auditory system.

That learning might alter sensory function does not imply that such sensory system changes would necessarily account for other learning-related changes in the central nervous system. But it should be recognized that any learning-induced "functional filtering" by

Norman M. Weinberger. Department of Psychobiology and Center for the Neurobiology of Learning and Memory, University of California at Irvine, Irvine, California.

sensory systems could affect consequent processing elsewhere in the brain. At this point, our view is simply that sensory systems do provide a convenient and advantageous entry point into the complex universe of neural events underlying learning.

What follows is a brief account of problems, attempted solutions, findings, and tentative conclusions involved in our study of learning from the "sensory side," and some implications for the neurophysiology of learning from "all sides." The absence of a review of the pertinent literature is due to limitations of space and format, and not to a lack of acquaintance or appreciation.

Considerations of Behavior

Animals learn continually, and they often learn quickly. In fact, they learn more quickly than is usually acknowledged. The most common measures of animal learning involve recording behaviors that are obvious, easily observed, and usually designated by the experimenter: for example, limb flexion, movement of the nictitating membrane, eye blink, running or not running, walking or not walking, jumping, eating or not eating, drinking or not drinking, and so on. In contrast, less common measures of learning are less obvious, usually require electrophysiological recording, and generally are not designated by the experimeter: for example, changes in heart rate, blood pressure, diameter of the pupil, respiration, skin conductance (GSR), and small, nondirected movements.

Within the skin domain of Pavlovian (classical) conditioning, the obvious behaviors are acquired more slowly than the less obvious behaviors. A résumé of studies of defensive conditioning, encompassing reptiles, birds, and mammals, revealed a bimodal distribution in the rate of acquisition: The obvious behaviors require about 70–900 trials, while the less obvious behaviors require about 5–35 trials (Weinberger, 1982a). Furthermore, when both types of responses are measured simultaneously within the same animal, the same relationship holds (Schneiderman, 1972).

The distinction between behaviors acquired slowly and rapidly is not adequately captured by terms such as "obvious" and "less obvious," although these terms may help explain the experimenter's choice of responses for the study of the neurobiology of learning and memory. Neither is a distinction of somatic versus autonomic responses adequate, for although slowly required responses are all somatic, rapidly acquired responses are both somatic (changes in respiration and "motor restlessness") and autonomic (heart rate, GSR, blood pressure, and pupil movement). This difference in the rates of acquisition is underscored by the finding that the two types of somatic motor behavior are acquired at different rates within the same animal: Nondirected, conditioned motor restlessness develops before limb flexion in the dog undergoing defensive conditioning (Anohkin, 1961).

Elsewhere, I have drawn the distinction on the basis of the degree of *specificity* to the nature of the unconditioned stimulus (UCS) (Weinberger, 1982a). The point requires elaboration here. Slowly acquired (somatic) conditioned responses (CRs) are *all* specific to the UCS. For example, when a limb is shocked, the animal develops a flexion CR, not an eye-blink CR or a nictitating membrane CR. In stark contrast, rapidly acquired CRs are not specific to the nature of the UCS.[1] Several and perhaps all such responses are elicited by all UCSs. We regard these "nonspecific" CRs as indices of a rapidly acquired state of conditioned excitability, while we believe that the specific CRs are "coping" responses that are directed at altering the aversive impact of noxious environmental stimulation. In common parlance, animals quickly learn that the CS predicts the UCS, and they become excited by the previously neutral CS. They learn more slowly what to do, or attempt to do, about the UCS.[2]

Whether the development of specific CRs depends upon the prior acquisition of nonspecific CRs is unknown. In any event, development of nonspecific CRs surely reflects learning-induced changes in the central nervous system, which may be important, if not essential, for the development of specific CRs that are acquired later. In short, the study of the most rapidly developing neural events during learning should have a firm place in the neurobiology of learning, because such events will precede, rather than be correlates of, the obvious, specific somatic behaviors upon which attention has been focused heretofore.

Rapid Associative Learning with Controls for Stimulus Constancy

In the study of the "sensory side," we have been committed to the assumption (or perhaps merely to the hope) that it would be possible, through electrophysiological means, to "trace the fate" of a stimulus within its sensory system as the *meaning* of that stimulus was changed by learning. This immediately raised the problem of how to be certain that changes of evoked activity in the auditory system are due to changes in the meaning of a stimulus, rather than to (inadvertent) changes in the effective pattern and intensity of stimulation at the receptors, as the subjects move during the acquisition of a designated behavior. The strategy of recording sensory system activity during behavioral learning required us to employ extreme tactics that, paradoxically, apparently eliminated behavior.

Our two goals of tracking sensory system activity during behavioral learning and studying initial events in learning could be met by recording within the auditory system during the acquisition of rapidly acquired nonspecific CRs. However, in order to be certain that changes in evoked activity could be directly interpreted as being caused by changes in stimulus meaning, rather than changes in stimulus intensity, it was essential that acoustic stimulation be constant at the tympanic membrane. This required simultaneous elimination of four sources of stimulus inconstancy: (1) position of the head with respect to the sound source (Marsh, Worden, & Hicks, 1962), (2) sound-shadowing by movements of the pinna (Wiener, Pfeiffer, & Backus, 1966), (3) masking noise produced by an animal's own movements (Baust & Berlucchi, 1964; Imig & Weinberger, 1970) and (4) contraction of the middle ear muscles (Galambos & Rupert, 1959; Starr, 1964). These can be completely eliminated simultaneously only by abolishing all movements, which is best accomplished by pharmacological block of neuromuscular transmission. Although this eliminates all somatic behavior, autonomic CRs develop rapidly during classical conditioning, and, as

---

1. Rapid conditioning (fewer than 60 trials) of a specific somatic response has been accomplished by combined electrical stimulation of the motor cortex and hypothalamus as the UCS (Voronin, Gerstein, Kudryashov, & Ioffe, 1975). Hypothalamic stimulation is well known to cause pupillary dilation and other autonomic signs; this is consistent with the view that the central states underlying rapidly acquired nonspecific CRs are necessary for the development of specific CRs.

2. This view clearly implies that specific somatic classical CRs have instrumental components. A detailed discussion of this issue cannot be provided here.

explained above, these nonspecific CRs provide the opportunity to study the *initial* neural changes during learning.

We selected pupillary dilation for the behavioral index of learning, using classical defensive conditioning (UCS = mild electrocutaneous stimulation) in the cat. As there were only fragmentary prior data on pupillary conditioning (Gerall & Obrist, 1962), we first studied this response system under a variety of training conditions to determine whether animals under neuromuscular blockade learn in a normal fashion. This is the case, as the pupillary dilation response exhibits all of the major behavioral phenomena discovered by Pavlov: habituation and dishabituation (Cooper, Ashe, & Weinberger, 1978; Weinberger, Oleson, & Ashe, 1975); acquisition and extinction (Ashe, Cassady, & Weinberger, 1976; Oleson, Westenberg, & Weinberger, 1972); discrimination, both within the auditory modality and between the auditory and somatosensory modalities (Ashe, Cooper, & Weinberger, 1978; Oleson, Vododnick, & Weinberger, 1973; Oleson *et al.*, 1972; Ryugo & Weinberger, 1978); discrimination reversal (Oleson, Ashe, & Weinberger, 1975; Oleson *et al.*, 1972), conditioned inhibition (Weinberger, Oleson, & Haste, 1973); and inhibition of delay (Oleson *et al.*, 1973) (see Figure 43-1). Thus, the cat under neuromuscular blockade is an appropriate preparation for the neurophysiological "tracking" of the CS during learning.

FIGURE 43-1. Learning curves for the pupillary dilation response of the cat. Each point represents the mean (±1 *SE*) for a group of 12 animals. During sensitization ("Sens."), white noise, tone, and shock were presented randomly. During conditioning ("Cond."), white noise (CS+) was always followed by shock. Discrimination training ("Disc.") consisted of the presentation of conditioning trials and presentation of tone alone (CS−) randomly. Note the decrement in response to acoustic stimuli during sensitization, and the rapid acquisition of the pupillary CR during conditioning (during Trials 6-10). Discrimination between the CS+ and CS− develops during the final phase of training. The broken horizontal line is the average dilation to acoustic stimuli during sensitization (control level). (From J. H. Ashe, C. L. Cooper, & N. M. Weinberger, Mesencephalic multiple-unit activity during acquisition of conditioned pupillary dilation. *Brain Research Bulletin*, 1978, 143-154. Reprinted by permission.)

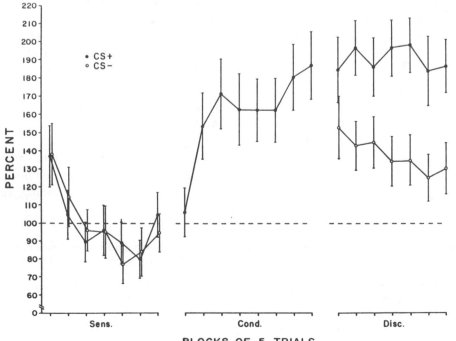

The Effects of Learning on Neuronal Discharges in the Auditory System

During repeated presentation of acoustic stimuli alone, the pupillary dilation response habituates, and so do the multiple-unit responses of neurons in the primary auditory cortex; both behavioral and neural responses habituate at the same rate. In contrast, the first central synaptic station, the cochlear nucleus, continues to respond, without decrement, to each stimulus (Weinberger *et al.*, 1975). During differential conditioning, neuronal discharges in auditory cortex develop differential increased responses to reinforced (CS+) and a nonreinforced (CS−) acoustic stimuli, respectively, during the rapid acquisition of a differential pupillary dilation CR (Oleson *et al.*, 1975). These effects were reversed when the reinforcement contingencies were reversed 1 week later. As in the case of habituation, the pupillary and cortical responses change at approximately the same rates. (The cochlear nucleus displayed similar effects, but its changes developed *after* the appearance of discharge plasticity in the auditory cortex.)[3]

These modifications of evoked activity in the auditory system are central in origin, because the cochlear microphonic (i.e., the auditory receptor potential) is not altered during pupillary conditioning (Ashe *et al.*, 1976).

In order to determine the possible source of learning-induced changes in the response of the auditory cortex, we recorded simultaneously from the two thalamic sources of input to primary auditory cortex, the magnocellular (MGm) and ventral (MGv) medial geniculate nuclei. The MGm developed discharge plasticity during acquisition of the pupillary dilation CR, whereas the MGv exhibited no changes at all (Ryugo & Weinberger, 1976, 1978) (see Figures 43-2 and 43-3). This is particularly noteworthy, because MGm and MGv have different anatomical and physiological properties. The MGm is nonlemniscal, lacking tonotopic organization (Aitkin, 1973; Morest, 1964, 1965), in contrast to the MGv, which is part of the tonotopic, lemniscal auditory system (Aitkin & Webster, 1972; Jones & Rockel, 1971; Morest, 1964).

This *differential plasticity* in the medial geniculate nucleus has been found also in the rabbit during instrumental avoidance conditioning (Gabriel, Miller, & Saltwick, 1976) and in the rat during classical appetitive conditioning (Birt & Olds, 1981). Therefore, the thalamic auditory system contains a lemniscal component, the MGv, which is insensitive to the significance of acoustic stimuli, and a nonlemniscal component, the MGm, which is involved in the acquired significance of sounds. Further, these different roles are correlated with different intrinsic structure, as well as different physiological properties with respect to the analysis of sounds. (See Ryugo & Weinberger, 1978, for additional details.) These findings provide prime evidence that normal anatomical and physiological characteristics of brain structures are directly related to learning; they support the view that some types of neurons (e.g., thalamic relay neurons) are nonplastic, while other types of cells (e.g., thalamic nonspecific units) are plastic with respect to learning.

Although multiple-unit recordings may be adequate for locating signs of discharge plasticity, they are totally inadequate for drawing conclusions about the effects of learning on single cells. A single-unit study of MGm (one neuron per training session) revealed that

3. These findings are inconsistent with the report of Halas, Beardsley, and Sandlie (1970) that the cochlear nucleus changes before the auditory cortex; the major difference between studies is that Halas *et al.* used a much more liberal criterion of change than that used by Oleson *et al.* Also, Halas *et al.* failed to record concurrent behavior in their muscle-relaxed preparations.

FIGURE 43-2. Camera lucida reconstruction of the medial geniculate nucleus from Golgi material. Typical distribution of neuronal types through the middle of the medial geniculate body of the adult cat. Coronal section, Golgi-Cox. Abbreviations: D, dorsal division; M, medial division; VL, ventral division, pars lateralis; VO, ventral division, pars ovoida. (From D. K. Ryugo & N. M. Weinberger, Differential plasticity of morphologically distinct neuron populations in the medial geniculate body of the cat during classical conditioning. *Behavioral Biology,* **1978,** *22,* **275–301. Reprinted by permission.)**

while discharge plasticity developed in the vast majority of neurons, the patterns and direction of change fell into various classes. There were increases and decreases in evoked activity, the latter being masked in previous multiple-unit recordings. Discharge plasticity developed extremely rapidly, within 10 or fewer trials (see Figure 43-4). Increases and decreases in background activity also developed during learning.

　　　Plasticity in the MGm may be either intrinsic or relayed from another source. This issue awaits final resolution. However, ascending auditory synapses within the MGm are plastic, as long-term potentiation (LTP) can be induced in this nucleus by brief, high-

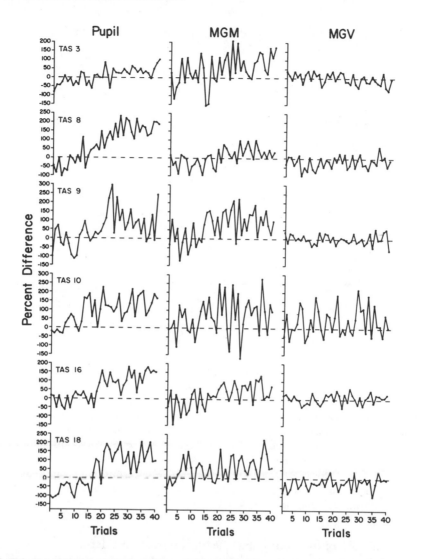

FIGURE 43-3. Trial-by-trial plots of pupillary, MGm, and MGv response changes during conditioning. Each point represents the normalized response to the CS+ during its 1.0-sec presentation, expressed as a percent difference score relative to its mean sensitization value (dashed line). Both pupil and MGm neuronal activity exhibit a systematic growth of responsivity during conditioning. MGv neuronal activity fails to demonstrate such CR enhancement. Data are from animals that developed pupillary conditioning and had placements in MGm and MGv of the same medial geniculate body. Note the modest positive slopes and high degree of variance across trials. These are not merely due to the lack of averaging in these trial-by-trial records, but due to the fact that conditioning has opposite effects on different neurons; multiple-unit recordings are a mixture of data from these neurons. (See Figure 43-4.) (From D. K. Ryugo & N. M. Weinberger, Differential plasticity of morphologically distinct neuron populations in the medial geniculate body of the cat during classical conditioning. *Behavioral Biology*, 1978, *22*, 275–301. Reprinted by permission.)

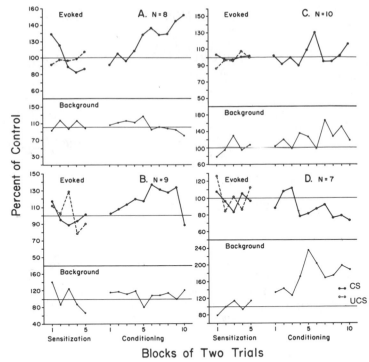

FIGURE 43-4. Learning curves for single neurons in the MGm during pupillary conditioning. Neurons were divided into four groups based on statistical tests of evoked activity: (A) increased and maintained discharges; (B) increased responses, not maintained after 18 trials; (C) no change in evoked firing; (D) decreased response. Note that background activity increases for C (and D), so that all groups developed changes in evoked or background activity, or both. Note the rapid rates of change (e.g., significant alterations by Trials 8–10 during conditioning). Control (100%) is the average activity during the prior sensitization period. The variety of effects on single cells probably accounts for the modest positive slopes of evoked multiple-unit activity (see Figure 43-3). (Reprinted by permission from Figure 9, page 78, in *The Neural Basis of Behavior* by Alexander L. Beckman (Ed.). Copyright 1982 by Spectrum Publications, Inc., Jamaica, New York.)

frequency stimulation of its major input, the brachium of the inferior colliculus (see Figure 43-5) Gerren & Weinberger, 1981, 1983; Weinberger, 1982b). Incidentally, the relevance of LTP to learning is supported by these findings, as LTP develops in a structure that exhibits pronounced plasticity during behavioral learning.

Further investigations of single-unit discharges in primary auditory cortex during conditioning revealed rapid changes in evoked activity of the majority of cells to an acoustic CS during the acquisition of the pupillary CR (Hopkins & Weinberger, 1980). As in the case of the MGm, we found both increased and decreased discharges, and also neurons that exhibited no change (see Figure 43-6). Thus, although the thalamo-cortical auditory system changes its response as a function of stimulus meaning, an increase in significance does not cause merely an increase in neuronal responses, as suggested by the results of multiple-unit studies. As found in the MGm, learning was also accompanied by changes in background, as well as evoked, activity.

Next, we studied so-called secondary auditory cortex (AII) because it receives no input from the MGv but does receive input from the MGm; it is nontonotopic auditory cortex. We found that almost all neurons (21 out of 22) developed plasticity in evoked activity (Diamond & Weinberger, 1982). Background activity either increased or decreased significantly in *all* neurons. This extraordinary degree of plasticity has not been reported for other brain loci. The absence of nonplasticity may reflect the lack of input from the nonplastic MGv. Evoked activity increased for some cells, and decreased for others, as in AI and MGm (see Figure 43-7). This reinforces the idea that the acquisition of significance by a stimulus does not result merely in an increased response of all plastic neurons, and it suggests that some other dimensions of sensory function may be modified by learning, as discussed below.

Recapitulation

Study of the "sensory side" in learning requires the exercise of extreme care, and therefore the use of unusual tactics to insure stimulus constancy at the level of the receptors. In the

FIGURE 43-5. Long-term potentiation (LTP) in the MGm of the anesthetized cat. Monosynaptic responses in the MGm, elicited by periodic stimulation (.2 Hz) of the brachium of the colliculus (BIC), developed increased amplitude (A) and decreased latency (B) following brief, high-frequency stimulation of the BIC (100–300 Hz, 385-msec trains). Each point represents the averaged data from 7 out of 10 experiments that exhibited potentiation of amplitude (A) and 8 out of 10 experiments that exhibited decreases in latency (B). High-frequency stimulation is denoted by the solid rectangle. Vertical bars represent ±1 *SE*. (From R. Gerren & N. M. Weinberger, Long term potentiation in the magnocellular medial geniculate nucleus of the anesthetized cat. *Brain Research*, 1983, *265*, 138–142. Reprinted by permission.)

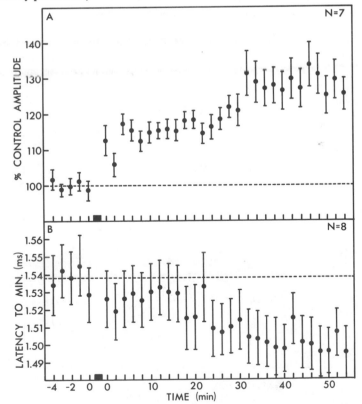

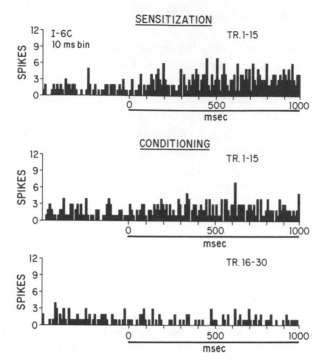

FIGURE 43-6. An example of discharge plasticity for a single neuron in primary auditory cortex (AI) during acquisition of the pupillary dilation conditioned reflex. In this case, evoked discharges decreased during conditioning, whereas background activity was not altered significantly. Note the decrease during the first 15 trials of conditioning, relative to sensitization, and the even greater decrease in response during Trials 16–30. The CS was 1 sec of white noise. The horizontal line under each histogram represents the period of CS presentation. "Background activity" is defined as discharges occurring before CS onset.

FIGURE 43-7. Learning curves for evoked activity of single neurons (recorded one per training session) in auditory cortical field AII during aquisition of the pupillary dilation conditioned reflex. Note the rapid development of changes in evoked discharges during conditioning, within 5 trials for decreases and 10 trials for increases. Values are relative to the evoked activity during the last 5 trials of sensitization. CSs were pure tone or white noise, 1-sec duration.

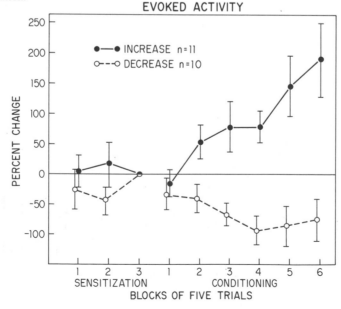

present case, these involved elimination of obvious, somatic behavior by neuromuscular blockade. Yet, autonomic behavior—specifically, dilation of the pupil—is normal under such circumstances. Therefore, it was feasible to study the activity evoked by a cue while that stimulus changed meaning from a novel or neutral sound to that of a positive or negative CS, as indexed independently by concurrent behavioral change.

As the meaning of a sound changes during learning, the response of the auditory system to the *physical* parameters of that stimulus does not change within the *subcortical, lemniscal pathway*.[4] Thus, the auditory cortex receives unmodulated information about the intensity and pattern of air pressure at the tympanic membrane. This conclusion follows from the finding that the discharges of the thalamic lemniscal neurons that project to the primary auditory cortex, the neurons of the MGv, are not altered during learning. In contrast, a nonlemniscal thalamic auditory nucleus, the MGm, develops discharge plasticity simultaneously with changes in a *psychological* parameter, the significance, of sound. Single neurons in this region exhibit such changes within a few trials after a sound is paired with a UCS. This effect is at least as rapid an associational change as any reported previously.

The primary auditory cortex receives information about both the physical and the psychological parameters of sound, as both the nonplastic MGv and the plastic MGm project to this region. These findings may help resolve the paradox described previously: How can a sensory system process both the physical and the psychological parameters of stimuli without a resultant ambiguity in the responses of its neurons? It seems that the two processes are maintained separately through the thalamic level during initial learning. The coalescence of both types of information about sound first occurs in the primary auditory cortex, and thus its responses may be ambiguous, in that the discharges of any single neuron reflect two types of analysis. In this sense, the primary auditory cortex is not the highest level of pure sensory analysis, if that term is employed to indicate the final state of analysis of pressure waves at the tympanic membrane, because its neurons are also influenced by the acquired meaning of sounds. Therefore, it may be more appropriate to regard so-called primary auditory cortex as "auditory-cognitive."

Cortical field AII is remarkable in that virtually all of the neurons sampled to date develop discharge plasticity rapidly during conditioning. Its neurons do not receive direct information about the physical aspects of sound, as they receive no direct projections from the MGv. It does receive input from MGm, as do all cortical auditory fields; thus its plasticity may reflect, in part, the plasticity that develops in this nucleus.

Additional Remarks

Knowledge of the dynamic involvement of sensory systems in learning is still quite primitive. It might have been complete at this time, had studies consistently failed to find that associative processes alter sensory system activity. Such findings would have preserved the dominant notion that the function of sensory systems is limited to analysis of the status of sensory receptors. Although this purely analytic function would undoubtedly involve

---

4. This statement does not account for the changes in the cochlear nucleus that develop after those in the auditory cortex. Changes in the cochlear nucleus might be expected to affect evoked activity in the ventral medial geniculate nucleus, but this apparently does not happen. This problem awaits resolution.

highly complex physiological processes, including the complicity of centrifugal components of sensory systems, one would nonetheless have been able to disregard any more direct role of sensory systems in learning and memory. Indeed, in the case of the auditory system, the weight of evidence supports this view for the *subcortical lemniscal component* of the auditory system.

This outcome suggests that discharge plasticity in the auditory system is not required for tasks that can be mastered by animals lacking auditory cortex. Thus, there may be many situations for which the dynamic role of the auditory system in learning and memory could be disregarded.[5] It is not particularly novel to point out that animals can learn many things in the absence of neocortex. However, it is interesting to realize that in so doing, the subjects are learning without the benefit of a major site of plasticity that is induced by learning—indeed, plasticity that develops very rapidly as well.

Primary auditory cortex is apparently less plastic during learning than is so-called secondary auditory cortex. The extraordinary degree of plasticity of AII is of interest for at least two reasons. First, it provides highly plastic brain tissue for further analysis. Second, it has possible implications for a general understanding of sensory cortex.

In regard to this second reason, the visual, somatosensory, and auditory cortices are each comprised of multiple fields that are more or less modality-specific. An understanding of the relations among fields within a modality has not been realized. Neither have there been adequate tests of ideas about the existence of multiple fields. It is generally assumed that each field has a designated function, and that the fields together manage the cortical affairs of each modality. The dominant notions are that multiple sensory fields indicate either serial or parallel processing, or perhaps a combination of these. That the fields might be differentially plastic with respect to learning and memory apparently has not been considered widely. The findings discusses above indicate that an adequate characterization of sensory cortex may well require assessment with respect to plasticity during learning.

I have emphasized that associative conditioning occurs very rapidly, as indicated by the development of CRs that are not specific to the particular characteristics of the UCS. Further, the electrophysiological changes that develop in the thalamo-cortical auditory system are equally rapid. We do not regard these correlations as having a direct causal relationship, so that ablation of the MGm and auditory cortex would probably not preclude the development of nonspecific CRs. Regardless of this issue, I wish to emphasize that changes on the sensory side are among the most rapidly developing manifestations of physiological plasticity during learning, and that they are well developed long before specific somatic CRs make their appearance. It is possible, but we think unlikely, that such pronounced changes on the sensory side are "side effects" of learning. Yet, until the role of these events is better understood, they are unlikely to be incorporated into dominant conceptions of the neurobiology of learning and memory. Recent findings of associatively induced alterations in photoreceptors (Alkon, Lederhendler, & Shoukimas, 1982) and the olfactory bulb (Freeman, 1980) both emphasize the involvement of the sensory side in learning and memory and increase the urgency of determining the functions of sensory systems in learning and memory.

5. Plasticity in the MGm could still play a role in such situations, if this nucleus is plastic in the absence of auditory cortex.

The "Sensory Side" in the Study of Neural Semiotics

There is a general tendency to regard the simultaneous recording of neuronal and behavioral data during learning as attempts to determine the particular neural circuit underlying a selected learned response. This approach continues to yield important findings, particularly with respect to the reduction of learning events to intracellular and molecular mechanisms. Our research on the "sensory side" has the complementary goal of determining the systems-level processes underlying learning. Questions of function at the systems level can be addressed experimentally, and are of critical importance in understanding the involvement of sensory systems in learning, regardless of the particular synaptic processes that underlie instances of learning-induced neuronal plasticity.

It is well to realize that the electrophysiological changes accompanying learning are merely signs, not necessarily significates. The field of neural semiotics with respect to learning and memory has hardly been initiated. If electrophysiological signs of learning are to lead to testable schemata regarding psychological functions, it will be beneficial and perhaps even necessary to determine the functional significance of such effects. Here, the study of learning from the sensory side offers some tactical advantages, because at least one function of sensory systems is well known—that is, analysis of the physical characteristics of stimuli. Neurons in sensory systems, including sensory cortex, have been studied extensively with respect to their receptive fields and thresholds. It is now possible to determine whether or not alterations in the responses of, for example, neurons in primary auditory cortex are signs of changes in their tuning functions or sensitivity, or not. This type of information would provide a more solid base for further investigation and speculation than is presently available. For example, the acquired significance of stimuli may involve a "retuning" of auditory cortex within the general tonotopic organization of AI, such that the field serves in some capacity as an adaptive filter, a short-term store in which neurons are "recruited" to process particularly significant stimuli. These and other possible functions will remain equally unfounded until data of the appropriate sort are obtained.

ACKNOWLEDGMENTS

Research reported here was supported by research and training grants from the National Institute of Mental Health (MN 11250, 51342, 11095, 22712, 05440, 14599, and 05420); the National Institute of Neurological and Communicative Disorders and Stroke (BNS 76-81924); the National Science Foundation (NS 16108); and the Monsanto Company. I wish to thank Lisa A. Weinberger for typing the manuscript.

REFERENCES

Aitkin, L. M. Medial geniculate body of the cat: Responses to tonal stimuli of neurons in medial division. *Journal of Neurophysiology*, 1973, *36*, 275–283.

Aitkin, L. M., & Webster, W. R. Medial geniculate body of the cat: Organization and responses to tonal stimuli of neurons in ventral division. *Journal of Neurophysiology*, 1972, *35*, 365–380.

Alkon, D. L., Lederhendler, I., & Shoukimas, J. J. Primary changes of membrane currents during associative learning. *Science*, 1982, *215*, 693–695.

Anohkin, P. K. A new conception of the physiological architecture of conditioned reflex. In A. Fessard, R. W. Gerard, & J. Konorski (Eds.), *Brain mechanisms and learning*. Oxford, England: Blackwell Scientific, 1961.

Ashe, J. H., Cassady, J. M., & Weinberger, N. M. The relationship of the cochlear microphonic potential to the acquisition of a classically conditioned pupillary dilation response. *Behavioral Biology*, 1976, *16*, 45–62.

Ashe, J. H., Cooper, C. L., & Weinberger, N. M. Mesencephalic multiple-unit activity during acquisition of conditioned pupillary dilation. *Brain Research Bulletin*, 1978, *3*, 143–154.

Baust, W., & Berlucchi, G. Reflex response to clicks of cat's tensor tympani during sleep and wakefulness and the influence thereon of the auditory cortex. *Archives Italiennes de Biologie*, 1964, *102*, 686–712.

Birt, D., & Olds, M. Associative response changes in lateral midbrain tegmentum and medial geniculate during differential appetitive conditioning. *Journal of Neurophysiology*, 1981, *46*, 1039–1055.

Cooper, C. L., Ashe, J. H., & Weinberger, N. M. Effects of stimulus omission during habituation of the pupillary dilation reflex. *Physiological Psychology*, 1978, *6*, 1–6.

Diamond, D. M., & Weinberger, N. M. Physiological plasticity of single neurons in secondary auditory cortex (AII) during pupillary conditioning in cat. *Society for Neuroscience Abstracts*, 1982, *8*(1), 317.

Freeman, W. J. Evidence for an olfactory search image or representation in the EEG of conditioned cats and rabbits. *Advances in Physiological Science*, 1980, *16*, 421–429.

Gabriel, M., Miller, J. D., & Saltwick, S. E. Multiple unit activity of the rabbit medial geniculate nucleus in conditioning, extinction, and reversal. *Physiological Psychology*, 1976, *4*, 124–134.

Galambos, R., & Rupert, A. Action of middle ear muscles in normal cats. *Journal of the Acoustical Society of America*, 1959, *31*, 349–355.

Gerall, A. A., & Obrist, P. A. Classical conditioning of the pupillary dilation response of normal and curarized cats. *Journal of Comparative and Physiological Psychology*, 1962, *55*, 486–491.

Gerren, R., & Weinberger, N. M. Long lasting facilitation of a monosynaptic response in the magnocellular medial geniculate nucleus of the anesthetized cat. *Society for Neuroscience Abstracts*, 1981, *7*, 752.

Gerren, R., & Weinberger, N. M. Long term potentiation in the magnocellular medial geniculate nucleus of the anesthetized cat. *Brain Research*, 1983, *265*, 138–142.

Halas, E. S., Beardsley, J. V., & Sandlie, M. E. Conditioned neuronal responses at various levels in conditioning paradigms. *Electroencephalography and Clinical Neurophysiology*, 1970, *28*, 468–477.

Hopkins, W., & Weinberger, N. M. Modification of auditory cortex single unit activity during pupillary conditioning. *Society for Neuroscience Abstracts*, 1980, *6*, 424.

Imig, T. J., & Weinberger, N. M. Auditory system multi-unit activity and behavior in the rat. *Psychonomic Science*, 1970, *18*, 164–165.

Jones, E. G., & Rockel, A. J. The synaptic organization in the medial geniculate body of afferent fibers ascending from the inferior colliculus. *Zeitschrift für Zellforschung und Mikroskopische Anatomie*, 1971, *113*, 44–66.

Marsh, J. T., Worden, F. G., & Hicks, L. Some effects of room acoustics on evoked auditory potentials. *Science*, 1962, *137*, 280–282.

Morest, D. K. The neuronal architecture of the medial geniculate body of the cat. *Journal of Anatomy (London)*, 1964, *98*, 611–630.

Morest, D. K. The laminar structure of the medial geniculate body of the cat. *Journal of Anatomy (London)*, 1965, *99*, 143–160.

Oleson, T. D., Ashe, J. H., Weinberger, N. M. Modification of auditory and somatosensory system activity during pupillary conditioning in the paralyzed cat. *Journal of Neurophysiology*, 1975, *38*, 1114–1139.

Oleson, T. D., Vododnick, D. S., & Weinberger, N. M. Pupillary inhibition of delay during Pavlovian conditioning in paralyzed cat. *Behavioral Biology*, 1973, *8*, 337–346.

Oleson, T. D., Westenberg, I. S., & Weinberger, N. M. Characteristics of the pupillary dilation response during Pavlovian conditioning in paralyzed cats. *Behavioral Biology*, 1972, *7*, 829–840.

Ryugo, D. K., & Weinberger, N. M. Differential plasticity or morphologically distinct neuron populations in the medial geniculate body of the cat during classical conditioning. *Society for Neuroscience Abstracts*, 1976, *2*, 435.

Ryugo, D. K., & Weinberger, N. M. Differential plasticity of morphologically distinct neuron populations in the medial geniculate body of the cat during classical conditioning. *Behavioral Biology*, 1978, *22*, 275–301.

Schneiderman, N. Response system divergencies in aversive classical conditioning. In A. H. Black & W. F. Prokasy (Eds.), *Classical conditioning II: Current research and theory*. New York: Appleton-Century-Crofts, 1972.

Starr, A. Influence of motor activity on click-evoked responses in the auditory pathway of waking cats. *Experimental Neurology*, 1964, *10*, 191–204.

Voronin, L. L., Gerstein, G. L., Kudryashov, I. E., & Ioffe, S. V. Elaboration of a conditioned reflex in a single experiment with simultaneous recording of a neural activity. *Brain Research,* 1975, *92*, 385–403.

Weinberger, N. M. Effects of conditioned arousal on the auditory system. In A. L. Beckman (Ed.), *The neural basis of behavior*. Jamaica, N. Y.: Spectrum, 1982. (a)

Weinberger, N. M. Sensory plasticity and learning: The magnocellular medial geniculate nucleus of the auditory system. In C. D. Woody (Ed.), *Conditioning: Representation of involved neural function*. New York: Plenum, 1982. (b)

Weinberger, N. M., Oleson, T. D., & Ashe, J. H. Sensory system neural activity during habituation of the pupillary orienting reflex. *Behavioral Biology*, 1975, *15*, 283–301.

Weinberger, N. M., Oleson, T. D., & Haste, D. Inhibitory control of conditional pupillary dilation response in the paralyzed cat. *Behavioral Biology*, 1973, *9*, 307–316.

Wiener, F. M., Pfeiffer, R. R., & Backus, S. N. On the sound pressure transformation by the head and auditory meatus of the cat. *Acta Oto-Laryngologica*, 1966, *61*, 255–269.

An Essay on Latent Learning

Neil E. Berthier and Charles D. Woody

Presentation of conditioned stimuli (CSs) and unconditioned stimuli (UCSs) separately, before associative training, can lead to either retardation or acceleration of subsequent conditioning. The effects of the stimulus preexposures are latent, awaiting conditioning or some other appropriate circumstance to be manifest. In this chapter we discuss latent neurophysiological effects of stimulus preexposures, as well as their behavioral manifestations. For the sake of simplicity, we separate preexposures into those of stimuli that normally serve as CSs and produce little or no overt motor response, and those of stimuli that normally serve as UCSs and produce a conspicuous motor response resembling the one to be conditioned.

CS Preexposure

Pavlov (1928) noted that a single CS presentation facilitated performance of a subsequent motor response. However, Lubow and Moore (1959) found that presenting animals with repeated (as few as 10) light or rotatory stimuli, before using light and rotation as CSs in classical conditioning of leg flexion, led to retarded acquisition of conditioned motor performance. Others (e.g., Carlton & Vogel, 1967; Lubow & Siebert, 1969; Siegel, 1969a, 1969b) confirmed the observation that multiple CS preexposures could lead to retardation of subsequent conditioning.

Lubow and Moore termed their result "latent inhibition," and suggested that it could reflect conditioning of responses incompatible with elaboration of the subsequent conditioned response (CR), thereby retarding later conditioning. Alternatively, they suggested that the retardation could be due to adaptation of the animal to the CS during preexposure, much like the adaptation postulated by Pavlov to account for inhibitory effects on motor performance of stimulus repetition during extinction.

Rescorla (1971) and Reiss and Wagner (1972) showed that CS preexposures could also lead to a reduction in the ability of the CS to command attention. Rescorla's experiment tested the ability of the preexposed CS to disrupt responses already conditioned to a second CS. The assumption was that a CS to which an animal was insensitive or inattentive would be ineffective in distracting the animal from performance of a CR established to a different CS. Rescorla found that novel CSs disrupted CRs elicited by a second CS, whereas preexposed CS did not. This result led him to conclude that the

Neil E. Berthier and Charles D. Woody. Brain Research Institute, Mental Retardation Research Center, Departments of Anatomy and Psychiatry, University of California at Los Angeles Medical Center, Los Angeles, California.

preexposed CS lost its ability to command attention. Rescorla termed this a reduction in the salience of the stimulus; however, inhibition of transmission of the preexposed CS through a nerve network could also explain the apparent loss of the stimulus's salience. This type of inhibition could be isomorphic with the "latent inhibition" of Lubow and Moore.

UCS Preexposure

In other studies, unpaired UCSs were given before conditioning in which the same UCS was paired associatively with a CS.

Retardation of Subsequent Conditioning

Many of these studies reported retardation of subsequent conditioning by 30 to 500 preexposures to UCSs. UCS preexposures produced retardation of human eyelid conditioning (Hobson, 1968; Taylor, 1956), human finger withdrawal (MacDonald, 1946), conditioned emotional response (CER) conditioning (Baker & Mackintosh, 1979; Baker, Mercier, Gabel, & Baker, 1981; Kremer, 1971; Siegel & Domjan, 1971), taste aversion conditioning (Best & Domjan, 1979; Domjan & Best, 1977), conditioned suppression (Randich, 1981; Randich & LoLordo, 1979), and rabbit eyelid and nictitating membrane conditioning (Mis & Moore, 1973; Siegel & Domjan, 1971).

Taylor (1956) suggested an explanation for this effect. She considered the emotional reactivity of the subject to the UCS to be important in the formation of the CR. In the context of Hullian theory, a noxious UCS would result in an emotional reaction that could increase the drive level of the subject to perform a conditioned avoidance response. The persistence of an increased drive until the next trial would increase conditioned responding (Runquist, Spence, & Stubbs, 1958; Spence, 1958). Repeated UCS presentations prior to conditioning would have the opposite effect: The emotional reactivity of the subject would be decreased through adaptation or habituation to the noxious UCS. The subjects would then show retarded acquisition of the CR because of decreased emotional reactivity (Spence, 1958; Taylor, 1956).

Mis and Moore (1973) suggested another explanation for retardation of conditioning after UCS preexposures, on the basis of the following observation. If a bell was used as a CS and paired with UCS in the first stage of an experiment, and a second CS, such as light, was paired with the bell and the UCS in the second phase, the second stimulus (the light) was found to elicit fewer CRs than if it was not paired with an already conditioned stimulus (Kamin, 1968). In this paradigm, conditioning to the bell was thought to interfere with conditioning to the light. Mis and Moore suggested that the contextual stimuli during UCS preexposures acted as CSs, interfering with conditioning to the CS in the second phase of the experiment in a manner analogous to that shown by Kamin.

A third explanation to be considered is as follows: UCSs themselves have CS-like effects and can be used as CSs to produce CRs. Thus, the same mechanisms that served for latent inhibition following CS presentation could support some forms of inhibition following UCS presentation.

Facilitation of Subsequent Conditioning

Repetitive presentation of UCSs does not always retard subsequent conditioning. Matsumura and Woody (1982) presented a series of 1500 glabella-tap UCSs 1 week before conditioning and found *facilitation* of subsequent eye-blink CRs. The phenomenon was termed "latent facilitation," since the facilitation was manifest by more rapid conditioning subsequent to the UCS preexposures. The facilitation was evident on the third day of conditioning training and was preceded on earlier days by an inhibition of CR performance relative to that of the naive control group. Animals that were given UCSs 4 weeks before conditioning did no show any facilitation of the rate of CR acquisition, and did not reach 80% CR performance levels even on the 10th day of training. The latter may reflect a separate latent inhibition, also arising from the UCS presentations (Matsumura & Woody, 1982). In other experiments, Randich and LoLordo (1979) found that three preexposures of a shock that was subsequently used as UCS in CER conditioning led to facilitation of conditioning 1 day later. If more than three presentations of the UCS were given, subsequent conditioning was inhibited.

Pseudoconditioning: An Unrecognized Form of Latent Facilitation?

Grether (1938) first used the term "pseudoconditioning" in a fear-conditioning experiment. A bell was used as CS and flash powder or a snake blowout as UCS. Initially, presentation of the CS did not elicit fear responses in the subjects. However after the animals were presented with the UCS several times (thereby eliciting unconditioned fear responses), subsequent CS presentations elicited vigorous fear responses. Because the CS and UCS were never paired together, the acquisition of these responses to the CS was termed "pseudoconditioning." Retention of the pseudoconditioned fear response was observed for several days.

Many other investigators have replicated Grether's basic finding: Schlosberg (1934) in tail-movement conditioning of the rat; Harlow (1939a) in movement conditioning of goldfish; Harlow (1939b) and Harlow and Toltzien (1940) in fear conditioning in the cat; Grant and Meyer (1941) and Harris (1941) in conditioned finger withdrawal in humans; Wickens and Wickens (1940) in conditioned leg movement in human neonates; Grant and Dittmer (1940) in galvanic skin response (GSR) conditioning in humans; Wickens and Wickens (1942) in rat fear conditioning; Grant (1943a, 1943b) in human eyelid conditioning; and Sheafor and Gormezano (1972) in rabbit jaw-movement conditioning. In each of these pseudoconditioning studies, except those of Grant (1943a) and Sheafor and Gormezano (1972), a strong aversive UCS was used.

A number of other experiments in which UCSs were presented failed to produce pseudoconditioning. Among these studies were those of Fitzwater and Reisman (1952), Smith and Baker (1960), Champion and Jones (1961), Zerbolio, Reynierse, Weisman, and Denny (1965), and Overmier and Curnow (1969).

The usual definitions stipulate that pseudoconditioned responses are the result of temporally separated sets of CS and UCS pairings (Grant & Dittmer, 1940; Harris, 1943). However, in most pseudoconditioning experiments, only a few CS preexposures have been given. Also with pseudoconditioning, subsequent pairings of CS and UCS are unncessary to elicit the acquired motor response. We suggest that the experiments in which pseudo-conditioning was obtained are analogous to those in which latent facilitation of subsequent conditioning was obtained by preexposure to UCSs. That is, the primary factor for inducing subsequent motor performance is UCS presentation. Experiments in which no pseudoconditioning occurred may have resulted in latent inhibition similar to that seen with repetitive CS or UCS presentations.

Two other interpretations of pseudoconditioning have been suggested. One derives from the observation that sensitization may develop when intense, noxious UCSs are used. This may have occurred in pseudoconditioning of finger withdrawal by Grant and Meyer (1941) and Harris (1941), where several strong electric shocks to the finger caused finger withdrawal to previously neutral stimuli.

The second interpretation depends on generalization of responses from the UCS to the previously neutral CS. Wickens and Wickens (1942) demonstrated this in rats using a light as CS and an electric foot shock as UCS. They reasoned that if stimulus generalization was involved, the degree of pseudoconditioning would be dependent on the degree of commonality between the CS and UCS. In their experiment, rats made more pseudoconditioned responses to the CS if both the CS and UCS had either sudden or gradual onsets. If the CS had a sudden onset and the UCS a gradual onset (or vice versa), rats made relatively few pseudoconditioned responses.

Two other experiments illustrate the role of stimulus generalization in pseudoconditioning. Harlow (1939a) observed pseudoconditioned responses when he maximized the degree of generalization by using a strong electric shock as UCS and a weak electric shock as CS. Also, Grant and Dittmer (1940) produced a gradient of stimulus generalization in human GSR pseudoconditioning. Grant and Dittmer used electric shock of a spot on the back of the subject as UCS. They repeatedly presented the UCS during the first stage of the experiment. During the testing stage, a vibrotactile CS at the same spot on the back elicited pseudoconditioned responses. If the vibrotactile stimulus was moved to any of four other places on the back, the size of the pseudoconditioned response depended on the distance of the CS from the location at which UCS was given.

Either the sensitization or the generalization postulated above could reflect an underlying facilitatory physiological process, such as latent facilitation, by which certain stimuli could more easily evoke specific motor responses. Sensitization, however, would be expected to involve presynaptic rather than postsynaptic mechanisms of neural facilitation (Carew, Castellucci, & Kandel, 1979); generalization would not.

Interpolated UCS Presentations during Conditioning: Inhibition or Facilitation?

In the course of conditioning training, Kimble, Mann, and Dufort (1955) presented subjects with 20 unpaired UCSs after an initial 20 CS-UCS pairings. A control group receiving 20 CS-UCS pairings instead of the unpaired UCSs, but was otherwise treated identically. During subsequent conditioning, subjects of each group performed at the same level; the group receiving CS-UCS pairings was not significantly better at learning the CR than the group receiving UCS presentations alone. This result has been controversial, since attempts to replicate it by others have failed, perhaps for procedural reasons (e.g.,

Champion, 1961; Dufort & Kimble, 1958; Goodrich, Ross, & Wagner, 1957; McAllister & McAllister, 1960). Limitations of space prevent us from reviewing the literature concerning these differences, but in some instances it appears that interpolated UCS presentations may indeed lead to facilitation rather than inhibition of the acquisition of CRs.

Neurophysiological Studies

Effects of UCS-Like Neural Stimulation

Cellular effects of UCS-like neural stimulation have been examined in neurons of the motor cortex of cats. Following electrical stimulation of the pyramidal tract, a satisfactory UCS for conditioning (O'Brien, Wilder, & Stevens, 1977), changes in excitability that lasted for hours were found in pyramidal tract (PT) cells of the motor cortex by Bindman, Lippold, and Milne (1982). The PT cells are layer V pyramidal cells that project to motoneurons or to interneurons that in turn project to motoneurons (Kuypers, 1958; Sakai & Woody, 1980). The increases in excitability in these cells after strong PT stimulation may be related to the excitability increases described below that have been found after conditioning.

Electrophysiological Studies of Neural Mechanisms of Conditioning

In cats conditioned to eye blink, Woody and colleagues found postsynaptic changes in neural excitability in cells to the motor cortex and facial nucleus that projected polysynaptically to the muscles supporting performance of the CR (Brons & Woody, 1980; Jordan, Jordan, Brozek, & Woody, 1976; Matsumura & Woody, 1982; Woody, 1982a; Woody & Black-Cleworth, 1973). Excitability was tested by direct electrical stimulation and was defined as the level of depolarizing current required for repeated spike initiation. The increases in excitability could also be brought about by repetitive, nonassociative presentations of the UCS, and persisted for longer than 4 weeks if the UCS was paired associatively with a CS during training (Brons & Woody, 1980; Matsumura & Woody, 1982). The time course of the neural changes was similar to that of the behavioral effects described earlier. In conditioned animals, the changes facilitated performance of the CR by facilitating transmission along specific motor pathways leading to production of the conditioned movement. Additional findings indicated that these changes supported maintenance of learning savings following extinction, as well as latent facilitation of subsequently learned CRs.

After discriminative eye-blink conditioning, other increases in neural excitability were found to support reception of the CS in preference to the discriminative stimulus (S^D) (Woody, Knispel, Crow, & Black-Cleworth, 1976). These changes were facilitatory of neural transmission and occurred in neurons of the association cortex that were selectively receptive to the CS. (They likely occur in neurons of other regions of the central nervous system as well). These changes depended on associative presentations of the CS and UCS for their induction and reflected a different cellular mechanism from that supporting latent facilitation, since they were disclosed by weak extracellular stimulation but not by intracellular stimulation (Woody et al., 1976).

Other inhibitory changes in neural excitability occurred in neurons of the motor cortex following repetitive presentations of the UCS (Brons, Woody, & Allon, 1982). These changes involved all motor projective groups of cells that were tested, irrespective of their projections. Since these inhibitory changes in neural excitability are nonspecific in terms of their motor representation, they may support the form of latent inhibition that follows CS presentations, as well as the one that follows UCS presentations.

Table 44-1 summarizes some of the neural mechanisms that can be related to simple forms of learned behavior. Further information on the subcellular basis of these mechanisms may be found elsewhere (Woody, 1982b).

Nomenclature of Latent Learning

There are several advantages to describing latent inhibition and facilitation of subsequent motor performance in response to a test stimulus in terms of the underlying physiological mechanisms.

1. The strong correlation between physiology and behavior provides an improved basis for definition. Although the mechanism and the behavior need not always be isomorphic with respect to each other in terms of inhibition or facilitation because of reciprocal neuronal organization (e.g., facilitation produced by inhibition of inhibition), they may usually be expected to be so, at least in the context of the findings described above.

2. Under the proposed nomenclature, behavioral effects previously described separately in terms of latent inhibition, conditioned inhibition, blocking, overshadowing, preconditioning, pseudoconditioning, and so on, would be defined with reference to their

TABLE 44-1. Some Simple Features of Behavior and Relatable Neural Mechanisms

Habituation[a]	Presynaptic inhibition
Sensitization	Presynaptic facilitation
Latent facilitation	Postsynaptic facilitation
Latent inhibition	Inhibition reflected by decreased neural excitability to weak (nA) extracellular current
Conditioning	
Motor specificity	Postsynaptic facilitation (persistent)
Discriminative reception	Facilitation reflected by increased neural excitability to weak (nA) extracellular current
Sensory preconditioning	Facilitation reflected by increased neural excitability to weak (nA) extracellular current

Note. A detailed description of the behavioral and electrophysiological studies on which this table is based has been given elsewhere (Woody, 1982). Some recent studies (see review by Kandel & Schwartz, 1982) that suggest a presynaptic basis of conditioning in invertebrates are inconsistent with earlier studies that have convincingly demonstrated postsynaptic neural changes with associative conditioning in other invertebrates (see Alkon, 1979; Woolacott & Hoyle, 1976). Much of the evidence supporting presynaptic changes depends on obtaining an accurate voltage clamp of the presynaptic terminals, an accomplishment that is methodologically problematic.

[a]Habituation has nine reflex outcomes, but as yet only one established physiological mechanism. Similar considerations apply to the other processes listed herein.

underlying neural mechanisms. This seems reasonable, because the neural mechanisms and their locations within the neural circuitry appear to be the primary determinants of the behavior.

3. Terms such as "pseudoconditioning" are vague in their meaning and are easily misconstrued to imply phenomena of little behavioral or physiologic significance.

4. The latent, nonassociative effects of stimulus repetition merit recognition because they play an inescapable and potentially significant role in "associative" processes such as conditioning.

ACKNOWLEDGMENTS

We thank Dr. Lynn Bindman for helpful comments during preparation of the manuscript. We gratefully acknowledge the support of our research by Grants BNS 78-24146, HD 05958-12, and AFOSR F49620-83-C-0077.

REFERENCES

Alkon, D. L. Voltage-dependent calcium and potassium ion conductances: A contingency mechanism for an associative learning model. *Science*, 1979, *205*, 810–816.

Baker, A. G., & Mackintosh, N. J. Preexposure to CS alone, US alone, or CS and US uncorrelated: Latent inhibition, blocking by context, of learned irrelevance. *Learning and Motivation*, 1979, *10*, 278–294.

Baker, A. G., Mercier, P., Gabel, J., & Baker, P. Contextual conditioning and the US preexposure effect in conditioned fear. *Journal of Experimental Psychology: Animal Behavior Processes*, 1981, *7*, 109–128.

Best, M. R., & Domjan, M. Characteristics of the lithium-mediated proximal US preexposure effect in flavor-aversion conditioning. *Animal Learning and Behavior*, 1979, *4*, 433–440.

Bindman, L. J., Lippold, O. C. J., & Milne, A. R. A post-synaptic mechanism underlying long-lasting changes in the excitability of pyramidal tract neurones in the anaesthetized cat. In C. D. Woody (Ed.), *Conditioning: Representation of involved neural functions*. New York: Plenum, 1982.

Brons, J. F., & Woody, C. D. Long-term changes in excitability of cortical neurons after Pavlovian conditioning and extinction. *Journal of Neurophysiology*, 1980, *44*, 605–615.

Brons, J., Woody, C. D., & Allon, N. Changes in the excitability to weak intensity electrical stimulation of units of the pericruciate cortex in cats. *Journal of Neurophysiology*, 1982, *47*, 377–388.

Carew, T. J., Castellucci, V. F., & Kandel, E. R. Sensitization in *Aplysia:* Restoration of transmission in synapses inactivated by long-term habituation. *Science*, 1979, *205*, 417–419.

Carlton, P. L., & Vogel, J. R. Habituation and conditioning. *Journal of Comparative and Physiological Psychology*, 1967, *63*, 348–351.

Champion, R. A. Supplementary report: Interpolated UCS trials in GSR conditioning. *Journal of Experimental Psychology*, 1961, *62*, 206–207.

Champion, R. A., & Jones, J. E. Forward, backward and pseudo-conditioning of the GSR. *Journal of Experimental Psychology*, 1961, *62*, 58–61.

Domjan, M., & Best, M. R. Paradoxical effects of proximal UCS preexposure: inference with and conditioning of a taste aversion. *Journal of Experimental Psychology: Animal Behavior Processes*, 1977, *3*, 310–321.

Dufort, R. H., & Kimble, G. A. Ready signals and the effect of interpolated UCS presentations in eyelid conditioning. *Journal of Experimental Psychology*, 1958, *56*, 1–7.

Fitzwater, M. E., & Reisman, M. N. Comparisons of forward, simultaneous, backward, and pseudo-conditioning. *Journal of Experimental Psychology*, 1952, *44*, 211–214.

Goodrich, K. P., Ross, L. E., & Wagner, A. R. Performance in eyelid conditioning following interpolated presentations of the US. *Journal of Experimental Psychology*, 1957, *53*, 214–217.

Grant, D. A. The pseudo-conditioned eyelid response. *Journal of Experimental Psychology*, 1943, *32*, 139–149. (a)

Grant, D. A. Sensitization and association in eyelid conditioning. *Journal of Experimental Psychology*, 1943, *32*, 201–212. (b)

Grant, D. A., & Dittmer, D. G. A tactile generalization gradient for a pseudo-conditioned response. *Journal of Experimental Psychology*, 1940, *26*, 404–412.

Grant, D. A., & Meyer, H. I. The formation of generalized response sets during repeated electric shock stimuli. *Journal of General Psychology*, 1941, *24*, 21–38.

Grether, W. F. Pseudo-conditioning without paired stimulation encountered in attempted backward conditioning. *Journal of Comparative Psychology*, 1938, *25*, 91–96.

Harlow, H. F. Forward conditioning, backward conditioning, and pseudo-conditioning in the goldfish. *Journal of Genetic Psychology*, 1939, *55*, 49–58. (a)

Harlow, H. F. Pseudo-conditioned responses in the cat. *Psychological Bulletin*, 1939, *36*, 625. (b)

Harlow, H. F., & Toltzien, F. Formation of pseudo-conditioned responses in the cat. *Journal of General Psychology*, 1940, *23*, 367–375.

Harris, J. D. Forward conditioning, backward conditioning, pseudo-conditioning and adaptation to the CS. *Journal of Experimental Psychology*, 1941, *28*, 491–502.

Harris, J. D. Studies on nonassociative factors inherent in conditioning. *Comparative Psychology Monographs*, 1943, *18*, 1–74.

Hobson, G. N. Effects of UCS adaptation upon conditioning in low and high anxiety men and woman. *Journal of Experimental Psychology*, 1968, *76*, 360–363.

Jordan, S. E., Jordan, J., Brozek, G., & Woody, C. D. Intracellular recordings of antidromically identified facial motoneurons and unidentified brain stem interneurons of awake, blink conditioned cats. *The Physiologist*, 1976, *19*, 245.

Kamin, L. J. Predictability, surprise, attention and conditioning. In B. A. Campbell & R. M. Church (Eds.), *Punishment and aversive behavior*. New York: Appleton-Century-Crofts, 1968.

Kandel, E. R., & Schwartz, J. H. Molecular biology of learning: Modulation of transmitter release. *Science*, 1982, *218*, 433–443.

Kimble, G. A., Mann, L. I., & Dufort, R. H. Classical and instrumental eyelid conditioning. *Journal of Experimental Psychology*, 1955, *49*, 407–417.

Kremer, E. Truly random and traditional control procedures in CER conditioning in the rat. *Journal of Comparative and Physiological Psychology*, 1971, *76*, 441–448.

Kuypers, H. G. J. M. An anatomical analysis of cortico-bulbar connexions to the pons and lower brain stem in the cat. *Journal of Anatomy*, 1958, *92*, 198–218.

Lubow, R. E., & Moore, A. U. Latent inhibition: The effect of non-reinforced pre-exposure to the conditioned stimulus. *Journal of Comparative and Physiological Psychology*, 1959, *52*, 415–519.

Lubow, R. E., & Siebert, C. Latent inhibition in the CER paradigm. *Journal of Experimental Psychology*, 1969, *68*, 136–138.

MacDonald, A. The effect of adaptation to the unconditioned stimulus upon formation of conditioned avoidance responses. *Journal of Experimental Psychology*, 1946, *36*, 1–12.

Matsumura, M., & Woody, C. D. Excitability changes of facial motoneurons of cats related to conditioned and unconditioned facial motor responses. In C. D. Woody (Ed.), *Conditioning: Representation of involved neural functions*. New York: Plenum, 1982.

McAllister, W. R., & McAllister, D. E. The influence of the ready signal and unpaired UCS presentation on eyelid conditioning. *Journal of Experimental Psychology*, 1960, *60*, 30–35.

Mis, F. W., & Moore, J. W. Effect of preacquisition UCS exposure on classical conditioning of the rabbit nictitating membrane response. *Learning and Motivation*, 1973, *4*, 108–114.

O'Brien, J. H., Wilder, M. B., & Stevens, C. D. Conditioning of cortical neurons in cats with antidromic activation as the unconditioned stimulus. *Journal of Comparative and Physiological Psychology*, 1977, *91*, 918–929.

Overmier, J. B., & Curnow, P. F. Classical conditioning, pseudoconditioning and sensitization in "normal" and forebrainless goldfish. *Journal of Experimental Psychology*, 1969, *68*, 193–198.

Pavlov, I. P. *Lectures on conditioned reflexes*. New York: International Publishers, 1928.

Randich, A. The US preexposure phenomenon in the conditioned suppression paradigm: A role for conditioned situational stimuli. *Learning and Motivation*, 1981, *12*, 321–341.

Randich, A., & LoLordo, V. M. Preconditioning exposure to the UCS affects the acquisition of conditioned emotional response. *Learning and Motivation*, 1979, *10*, 245–277.

Reiss, S., & Wagner, A. R. CS habituation produces "latent inhibition" effect but no active "active inhibition." *Learning and Motivation*, 1972, *3*, 237–245.

Rescorla, R. A. Summation and retardation tests of conditioned inhibition. *Journal of Experimental Psychology*, 1971, *75*, 77–81.

Runquist, W., Spence, K. W., & Stubbs, E. W. Differential conditioning and intensity of the UCS. *Journal of Experimental Psychology*, 1958, *55*, 51–53.

Sakai, H., & Woody, C. D. Identification of auditory responsive cells in the coronal–pericruciate cortex of awake cats. *Journal of Neurophysiology*, 1980, *44*, 223–231.

Schlosberg, H. Conditioned responses in the white rat. *Journal of Genetic Psychology*, 1934, *45*, 303–335.

Sheafor, P. J., & Gormezano, I. Conditioning the rabbit's (*Oryctolagus cuniculus*) jaw movement response. *Journal of Comparative and Physiological Psychology*, 1972, *81*, 449–456.

Siegel, S. Effect of CS habituation on eyelid conditioning. *Journal of Comparative and Physiological Psychology*, 1969, *68*, 245–248. (a)

Siegel, S. Generalization of latent inhibition. *Journal of Comparative and Physiological Psychology*, 1969, *69*, 157–159. (b)

Siegel, S., & Domjan, M. Backward conditioning as an inhibitory procedure. *Learning and Motivation*, 1971, *2*, 1–11.

Smith, J. C., & Baker, H. D. Conditioning in the horseshoe crab. *Journal of Experimental Psychology*, 1960, *53*, 279–281.

Spence, K. W. A theory of emotionally based drive (D) and its relation to performance in simple learning situations. *American Psychologist*, 1958, *13*, 131–141.

Taylor, J. A. Level of conditioning and intensity of adaptation stimulus. *Journal of Experimental Psychology*, 1956, *51*, 127–130.

Wickens, D. D., & Wickens, C. A study of conditioning in the neonate. *Journal of Experimental Psychology*, 1940, *26*, 94–102.

Wickens, D. D., & Wickens, C. D. Some factors related to pseudo-conditioning. *Journal of Experimental Psychology*, 1942, *31*, 518–526.

Woody, C. D. Acquisition of conditioned facial reflexes in the cat: Cortical control of different facial movements. *Federation Proceedings*, 1982, *41*, 2160–2168. (a)

Woody, C. D. *Memory, learning, and higher function*. New York: Springer-Verlag, 1982. (b).

Woody, C. D., & Black-Cleworth, P. Differences in excitability of cortical neurons as a function of motor projection in conditioned cats. *Journal of Neurophysiology*, 1973, *36*, 1104–1116.

Woody, C. D., Knispel, J. D., Crow, T. J., & Black-Cleworth, P. Activity and excitability to electrical current of cortical auditory receptive neurons of awake cats as affected by stimulus association. *Journal of Neurophysiology*, 1976, *39*, 1045–1061.

Woolacott, M. H., & Hoyle, G. Membrane resistance changes associated with single, identified neuron learning. *Society for Neuroscience Abstracts*, 1976, *2*, 339.

Zerbolio, D. J., Reynierse, J. H., Weisman, R. G., & Denny, M. R. Pseudoconditioning? *Journal of Comparative and Physiological Psychology*, 1965, *59*, 271–274.

45

Between Model Systems and Memory: The Use of Physiological Plasticity in Hippocampus to Identify Cellular Chemistries Involved in Memory Storage

Gary Lynch and Michel Baudry

Behavioral neurobiology, as its name indicates, requires the synthesis of several types of scientific study. As applied to memory research, the marriage between cell biology and psychology has often been a tempestuous one, possibly because the needs and demands of the partners are not consonant. Nor has it always been the case that the partners have had a clear idea of what they expect from each other. Psychologists are interested in the cellular mechanisms that produce memories, but have difficulties in providing neurochemists with guidelines for recognizing those mechanisms. Neurobiologists have uncovered several promising examples of the plasticity of neuronal circuitries, but usually under conditions that seem only remotely related to those found in behaving animals.

The use of model systems represents one attempt to obviate these problems. A preparation is used that exhibits properties analogous to memory, yet at the same time is amenable to neurobiological investigation. It is perhaps fair to say that models must "give" at one end or the other of the dimension from neuronal chemistry to behavior: The more the preparation has properties that resemble memory, the less accessible it is to biochemistry. Why this should be so is a subject beyond the scope of this review. In the following sections, we first consider the difficulties attendant on defining properties of memory that can be used to evaluate the utility of a model. Second, we briefly summarize work on one preparation and a cellular hypothesis concerning memory that has arisen from it. Finally, means of extending the results of the research on the model to neuropsychological studies are discussed.

Memory Properties as Defining Characteristics of a Useful Model

Expected Isomorphisms

To what extent should we expect the neurophysiological changes that subserve learning to incorporate the behaviorally defined attributes of memory? Memory formation, at a minimum, involves attention, perception, and the association of central representations of external stimuli; it is dependent upon the state of the animal (hormones, arousal, etc.), as well as upon the degree to which the brain is "set" or prepared to connect the

Gary Lynch and Michel Baudry. Center for the Neurobiology of Learning and Memory, University of California, Irvine, California.

elements to be associated. Beyond this, and most critically, a memory can only be detected through the operation of a poorly defined retrieval system that links stored information to cognition and behavior. This retrieval system may have rules of its own and may be physically and functionally distinct from the site and process underlying memory. Each of these stages in storage and recall can be expected to impose some set of constraints on memory as a behavioral phenomenon. If the simplified preparation to be used is intended to model the actual storage step—the production of a lasting trace—then it is likely that it will lack one or more of the features of memory as that phenomenon is described in neuro-psychological terms. The associative property of memory serves as an example. Theorists have commonly insisted that a reasonable neuronal model of how information is stored should exhibit modification only under conditions in which at least two electrical events occur in temporal contiguity. The most famous example of this is the "Hebb synapse" (Hebb, 1949), in which the triggering event is simultaneous activity in pre- and postsynaptic elements (see Figure 45-1a). A second version of the associative idea involves the near-simultaneous arrival of impulses in two elements at a common target (see Figure 45-1b). These ideas assume that the site of association and the site of storage coincide, but there is no necessary reason why this should be so. Figure 45-1c illustrates an alternative possibility. In this, multiple inputs produce an altered discharge in a target, which then modifies the synapses *it* forms; in this case, the site of interaction could be distant from the altered connections.

The presence of multiple stages in memory storage and usage also makes it difficult to develop *a priori* predictions about the effects on models of treatments that influence

FIGURE 45-1. Schematic representation of associative mechanisms of learning. (a) Hebb's synapse: The modified synapse (*) is the result of the simultaneous firing of the afferent input and of the target cell. (b) The modified synapses (*) are the result of the simultaneous firing of two converging afferent inputs to the same target cell. (c) The modified synapse (*) is the result of high-frequency firing of a cell due to simultaneous firing of two converging afferent inputs.

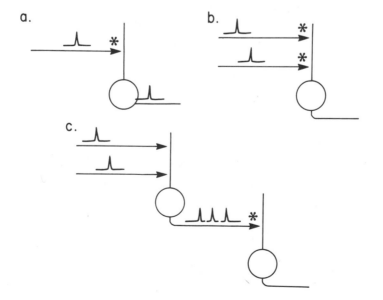

memory formation in intact animals. Electroconvulsive shock and hormone treatments have been shown to produce powerful effects on the memorial system, but it is not at all obvious that these are exerted on the actual storage process.

In a word, it is not clear how much of memory we should expect to find in a model of memory storage. This is a serious problem, because obviously we need some criteria for separating plausible from implausible models. In the following section, we attempt to extract features of memory that should be useful in this regard, and in doing so suggest that the problems described above are compounded by ambiguities in the behavioral descriptions of memory.

Multiple Forms of Memory?

Are we searching for a single cellular event that corresponds to a unique behavioral event? This rather obvious and fundamental question does not have a simple answer. Lesions to the hippocampus and adjacent structures in humans and animals eliminate the ability to form certain types of memory, while leaving other learning skills intact (see O'Keefe & Nadel, 1978, and Squire, 1982, for reviews). The nature of the distinction between what is lost and what is retained is the subject of controversy, but there is agreement that some types of memory storage require these limbic areas, while others do not. Beyond this, different types of training appear to produce qualitatively different types of memory. Some types of information seem to be gained in a very few learning trials, while others require repetitive exposures (practice) to the material to be memorized. Again, what separates the types of memories is the subject of a long debate, but the possibility that qualitatively different phenomena are involved is a real one.

This poses a problem for the development of suitable models for studying memory. If there are multiple memories, then there may be multiple cellular processes used to store memories. Moreover, one must select between initiating conditions that are abrupt or "one-trial" in nature and those that are repetitive and spaced in time. In a sense, the user of a model has to decide upon a behavioral target.

Temporal Parameters

Memory has one defining quality that is of great use in developing a model system: It persists for extraordinarily long periods. This property alone separates memory from a host of other psychological processes, and hence can be used to evaluate the plausibility of the model and of any potential cellular substrates. Having made this point, we must add that little can be said beyond the simple statement that memories are very durable. First, there is the problem of how long it takes for a memory to form. Years of research on "memory consolidation" have yielded conflicting temporal gradients for memory storage. It is clear that memory is susceptible to disruption for periods ranging from minutes to years, according to the experimental situation. Whether this indicates that two forms of storage (and hence two types of cellular processes) are involved or not has yet to be settled. Thus the researcher does not know whether the memory analogue in the model should appear immediately or slowly, or whether multiple processes or a unitary event is desirable.

Similarly, it is unclear how long memories last. Do they decay with time, or are they essentially permanent but in an informational sense degraded by the appearance of similar memories? Is storage accurate and durable, but retrieval inaccurate? These are old issues in psychology, but they pose immediate difficulties for the user of a model.

Physiological Constraints on Model Systems

While the psychological variables needed to define a plausible model of memory are somewhat vague, the physiological constraints are obvious. The nervous system operates with signals that have defined durations and frequencies, and the events used to trigger a memory analogue should correspond to these parameters. Similarly, the manifestation of memory can be expected to be an alteration in the probability or frequency of a physiological signal. However, this does not provide a clear description of the pattern of electrical signals to be used in the model system, a fact that is reflected by the multiple forms of electrical stimulation in studies of this type.

The use of physiological signals presents a severe problem in biochemical studies of model systems. Biochemical assays usually require large amounts of tissue, while standard physiological procedures activate very discrete numbers of elements. Furthermore, there is no way to separate physiologically stimulated from nonstimulated elements in biochemistry; hence, for any lasting effects of electrical activity to manifest themselves in a test tube, it is necessary for a significant fraction of the sample to have participated in that activity.

Thus a model system must reconcile the psychological to the physiological levels of analysis, while at the same time allowing the coordination of physiological and biochemical methodologies. There are some specialized chemical techniques that can be applied to discrete, physiological systems, but the great majority of analytical techniques cannot readily be used in such situations. One faces a choice between letting available chemical methods define hypotheses about physiological events—in this case, those related to memory mechanisms—or modifying the physiological preparation so that it meets the contraints imposed by the selected biochemical techniques.

Hippocampal Long-Term Potentiation

Hippocampal long-term potentiation (LTP) has enjoyed increasing popularity as a model of memory. In the following sections, we consider this phenomenon in the light of the behavioral and physiological constraints discussed above, and then review attempts to use it in biochemical investigations.

LTP was discovered by Bliss and his associates (Bliss & Gardner-Medwin, 1973; Bliss & Lømo, 1973) in the course of physiological studies on the perforant path, the major afferent of the hippocampal formation. This and subsequent work has been reviewed elsewhere (e.g., Lynch & Baudry, 1983). LTP is an increase in the size and amplitude of extracellular and intracellular responses evoked by single-pulse stimulation of fibers following a brief period of high-frequency stimulation. The effect is uniquely stable, and LTP has been followed in chronically implanted rats for weeks or months.

LTP meets certain of the physiological and behavioral constraints that define a plausible model system. It is induced by stimulation parameters that are not greatly different from spike train patterns found in behaving animals. While its duration is uncertain, it clearly lasts for a long time. The time required to develop the effect appears to be less than 5 minutes, but, as discussed above, this cannot be realistically compared with the time needed to form a memory. Interestingly enough, it has been argued that LTP requires the simultaneous activation of a sizable population of axons and hence may be viewed as an associative phenomenon (McNaughton, Douglas, & Goddard, 1978). Finally, both Bliss and Lφmo (1973) and Barnes (1979) report data suggesting that LTP becomes stronger and more enduring if spaced episodes of high-frequency stimulation are used; in a sense, then, it appears to incorporate a "practice" parameter.

While the pattern of stimulation typically used to induce LTP does not grossly deviate from the physiologically meaningful, the synchronous activation of large numbers of adjacent fibers is probably not a "real-world" occurrence. However, potentiation of very small evoked potentials has been observed (Lynch & Baudry, 1983), suggesting that future experiments may yet bring stimulation conditions in line with axonal firing that might well be found in behaving animals.

In all, and while it is still a poorly defined effect, LTP can be taken as a reasonable analogue of the memory process (Swanson, Teyler, & Thompson, 1982). Therefore, it is possible that the cellular events that produce this phenomenon are actually used by the brain to encode memories. The obvious next question is whether hippocampal LTP can be subjected to anatomical and biochemical experiments.

Biochemical Studies of LTP in Slices of Hippocampus

Physiologically viable slices are readily prepared from hippocampus and are capable of generating stable LTP. Slices of laminated structures such as hippocampus possess a number of properties suggesting that they could be used to study biochemical correlates of physiological events (see Lynch & Schubert, 1980, for a review):

1. Slices can be rapidly removed from the recording chamber to the biochemical apparatus.
2. By using multiple stimulating electrodes, it is possible to activate a large population of axons and synapses. This is extremely difficult to accomplish with brain regions *in situ*.
3. Slices of laminated structures can be dissected to prepare relatively homogeneous populations of afferents and target cells.

Taking advantage of these features, we have shown that high-frequency stimulation under conditions that lead to the induction of LTP produces a selective effect on the phosphorylation of the mitochondrial enzyme pyruvate dehydrogenase (Browning, Baudry, & Lynch, 1982; Browning, Dunwiddie, Bennett, Gispen, & Lynch, 1979) and an increase in glutamate receptor binding to synaptic membrane fractions (Baudry, Oliver, Creager, Wieraszko, & Lynch, 1980; Lynch, Halpain, & Baudry, 1982).

There is experimental evidence linking the activity of the enzyme in question (which is controlled by a phosphorylation–dephosphorylation mechanism) to the level of calcium buffering provided by the mitochondria (Browning, Baudry, Bennett, & Lynch, 1981; Browning, Bennett, Kelly, & Lynch, 1981). Hence we proposed that a perturbation of the cytoplasmic calcium levels brought about by an action on mitochondrial calcium uptake is an early step in the sequence leading to LTP.

In support of this, recent experiments have shown that intracellular injections of a calcium chelator block the production of LTP (Lynch, Larson, Kelso, Barrionuevo, & Schottler, 1983). While the issue is still in question, there is reason to believe that the glutamate-binding site in hippocampal membrane is linked to the receptor for the synaptic transmitter (see Baudry & Lynch, 1981, for a review). If this proves to be true, an increase in the number of receptors becomes a likely explanation of LTP.

Does a link exist between the two changes associated with LTP (calcium and glutamate receptors)? Calcium causes a marked and irreversible increase in the numbers of glutamate-binding sites in membranes prepared from hippocampus (Baudry & Lynch, 1979). This action appears to be mediated by the activation of a low-threshold calcium-sensitive proteolytic enzyme (Baudry, Bundman, Smith, & Lynch, 1981; Baudry & Lynch, 1980). These observations can be combined into a reasonable straightforward hypothesis about the origins of LTP, and this is described in Figure 45-2. This idea has been discussed at length elsewhere (Lynch & Baudry, 1983).

At this point, the hypothesis is quite tentative. The linkage between the biochemical (phosphorylation and receptor changes) and physiological (LTP) events induced by high-frequency stimulation is purely correlational. Moreover, the involvement of the proteolytic enzyme in LTP has yet to be tested. With these caveats, it can be said that some of the biochemical correlates of LTP are measurable and may be due to identified cellular processes found in synaptic membranes. The system thus manages to span the gap between

FIGURE 45-2. Hypothesis concerning the cellular mechanisms responsible for long-term changes in synaptic efficiency in hippocampus. (1) High-frequency firing of the presynaptic element results in the calcium influx into the postsynaptic element. (2) Through an as-yet-unidentified mechanism, the α-subunit of pyruvate dehydrogenase (α-PDH) becomes phosphorylated, resulting in a decreased calcium transport in mitochondria. (3) These events produce an increased local concentration of calcium. (4) Calcium activates a low-threshold calcium-dependent neutral protease, calpain I. (5) The proteolytic activity induces the degradation of several proteins associated with the cytoskeletal network such as fodrin or microtubule-associated proteins (MAPs). (6) These changes in membrane-linked proteins unmask glutamate receptors and eventually allow a change in the shape of the dendritic spines. Within minutes the α-PDH is dephosphorylated, low calcium concentration is restored, turning off calpain I activity. (Modified from G. Lynch & M. Baudry, Rapid structural modifications in rat hippocampus—evidence for its occurrence and an hypothesis concerning how it is produced. In A. Morrison & P. Strick [Eds.], *Changing concepts of the nervous system*. New York: Academic Press, 1982. Used by permission.)

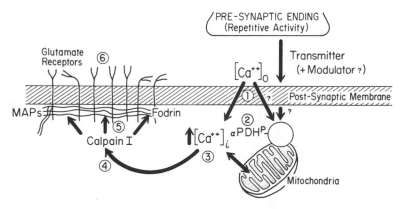

a physiological model (LTP) of a behavior (memory) and chemistry, albeit with some bending of the rules discussed above.

Returning from Model Systems to Behavior

In the preceding sections, we have advanced a cellular explanation for hippocampal LTP, a physiological phenomenon that has some resemblance to memory. It hardly need be stressed that the "proteinase *cum* receptor" hypothesis for LTP has not yet been rigorously tested. But, having advanced to this point, the question of relating what is learned at the slice level to animal behavior becomes pertinent. The *in vitro* experiments provide some suggestions (rather than strong predictions) for neuropsychological research. Frequency of cell discharges may be related not only to information processing, as they are typically viewed, but to the modification of neuronal circuitries as well. Thus the distinctive discharge pattern that induces LTP may be an indication, when observed in chronic recording experiments, of sites that are inscribing some representation of immediately preceding events. The fact that LTP is so readily elicited in some regions and not in others may also be of significance to neuropsychological theories about the brain structures that encode memory. At least by this one physiological measure, brain systems are not equivalently plastic. The biochemical experiments also support this idea, in that the effects of calcium on one class of receptors are much more pronounced in some structures than others (Baudry & Lynch, 1980). These findings could be taken as evidence in support of the idea that the actual storage of information is not a ubiquitous property in brain circuitries. Anatomical maps of the distribution of various types of plasticity may ultimately be available for comparison with those obtained by studying the consequences of lesions on memory.

If research on model systems is to influence the neuropsychology of memory, it is likely that it will do so through the use of defined experimental manipulations. One of the most encouraging features of the hypothesis that has emerged from the slice experiments is the unusual property of the proposed biochemical mechanism. The threshold calcium concentration for activating the proteinase is high enough that it is unlikely that this enzyme participates in "routine" physiological events. Thus it should be possible to use drugs that interfere with it without causing the disruption of normal brain operation. It is obviously necessary to test this point before proceeding with behavioral experiments, but the possibility for a new, clearly defined, and potentially selective pharmacology is a real one. Thus, the value of the model discussed above and others like it will depend upon the degree to which they suggest new candidates for the substratum of memory that can be examined or manipulated in the intact animal (Lynch & Baudry 1984).

REFERENCES

Barnes, C. A. Memory deficits associated with senescence: A neurophysiological and behavioral study in the rat. *Journal of Comparative and Physiological Psychology*, 1979, *93*, 74–104.

Baudry, M., Bundman, M., Smith, E., & Lynch, G. Micromolar levels of calcium stimulate proteolytic activity and glutamate receptor binding in rat brain synaptic membranes. *Science*, 1981, *212*, 937–938.

Baudry, M., & Lynch, G. Regulation of receptor by cations. *Nature*, 1979, *282*, 748–750.

Baudry, M., & Lynch, G. Regulation of hippocampal glutamate receptors: Evidence for the involvement of a calcium-activated protease. *Proceedings of the National Academy of Sciences USA*, 1980, *77*, 2298–2302.

Baudry, M., & Lynch, G. Hippocampal glutamate receptors. *Molecular and Cellular Biochemistry*, 1981, *38*, 5–18.

Baudry, M., Oliver, M., Creager, R., Wieraszko, A., & Lynch, G. Increase in glutamate receptors following repetitive electrical stimulation in hippocampal slices. *Life Sciences*, 1980, *27*, 325–330.

Bliss, T. V. P., & Gardner-Medwin, A. R. Long-lasting potentiation of synaptic transmission in the dentate area of the unanaesthetized rabbit following stimulation of the perforant path. *Journal of Physiology* (*London*), 1973, *232*, 357–374.

Bliss, T. V. P., & Lømo, T. Long-lasting potentiation of synaptic transmission in the dentate area of the anaesthetized rabbit following stimulation of the perforant path. *Journal of Physiology* (*London*), 1973, *232*, 331–356.

Browning, M., Baudry, M., Bennett, W., & Lynch, G. Phosphorylation-mediated changes in pyruvate dehydrogenase activity influence pyruvate-supported calcium accumulation by brain mitochondria. *Journal of Neurochemistry*, 1981, *36*, 1932–1940.

Browning, M., Bennett, W., Kelly, P., & Lynch, G. The 40,000 Mr brain phosphoprotein influenced by high-frequency synaptic stimulation is the alpha subunit of pyruvate dehydrogenase. *Brain Research*, 1981, *218*, 255–266.

Browning, M., Baudry, M., & Lynch, G. Evidence that high-frequency stimulation influences the phosphorylation of pyruvate dehydrogenase and that the activity of this enzyme is linked to mitochrondrial calcium sequestration. In W. H. Gispen & A. Routtenberg (Eds.), *Progress in brain research* (Vol. 56). Amsterdam: Elsevier, 1982.

Browning, M., Dunwiddie, T., Bennett, W., Gispen, W., & Lynch, G. Synaptic phosphoproteins: Specific changes after repetitive stimulation of the hippocampal slice. *Science*, 1979, *203*, 60–62.

Hebb, D. O. *The organization of behavior*. New York: Wiley, 1949.

Lynch, G., & Baudry, M. Origins and manifestations of neuronal plasticity in the hippocampus. In W. Willis (Ed.), *Clinical neurosciences* (Vol. 5). New York, Edinburgh, London, and Melbourne: Churchill Livingstone, 1983.

Lynch, G., & Baudry, M. The biochemistry of memory: A new and specific hypothesis. *Science*, 1984, *224*, 1057–1063.

Lynch, G., Halpain, S., & Baudry, M. Effects of high-frequency synaptic stimulation on glutamate receptor binding studies with a modified *in vitro* hippocampal slice preparation. *Brain Research*, 1982, *244*, 101–111.

Lynch, G., Larson, J., Kelso, S., Barrionuevo, G., & Schottler, F. Intracellular injections of EGTA block the induction of hippocampal long-term potentiation. *Nature*, 1983, *305*, 719–721.

Lynch, G., & Schubert, P. The use of *in vitro* brain slices for multidisciplinary studies of synaptic function. *Annual Review of Neuroscience*, 1980, *3*, 1–22.

McNaughton, B. L., Douglas, R. M., & Goddard, G. V. Synaptic enhancement in fascia dentata: Cooperativity among coactive afferents. *Brain Research*, 1978, *157*, 277–293.

O'Keefe, J., & Nadel, L. *The hippocampus as a cognitive map*. London: Oxford University Press, 1978.

Squire, L. R. The neuropsychology of memory. *Annual Review of Neuroscience*, 1982, *5*, 241–273.

Swanson, L. W., Teyler, T. J., & Thompson, R. F. Hippocampal long-term potentiation: Mechanisms and implications for memory. *Neurosciences Research Program Bulletin*, 1982, *20*, 5.

46

Does Long-Term Potentiation/Synaptic Enhancement Have Anything to Do with Learning or Memory?

Richard Morris and Mark Baker

Introduction

> *Whether or not the intact animal makes use in real life of a property which has been revealed by synchronous, repetitive volleys to a population of fibres the normal rate and pattern along which are unknown, is another matter.—Bliss and Lømo (1973, p. 355)*

The phenomenon of long-term potentiation (LTP) or synaptic enhancement refers to a sustained increase in synpatic efficacy brought about by tetanizing afferent fibers at high frequency. Bliss and Lømo's (1973) original experiments involved preparing anesthetized rabbits with two pairs of stimulating and recording electrodes. A stimulating electrode was placed in the perforant path coming from the entorhinal cortex, and a recording electrode was placed near the granule cells of the dentate gyrus on both sides of the brain. Extracellular field potentials were recorded in response to low-frequency (one per 3 sec) stimuli delivered to either perforant path. Higher-frequency stimuli (15 per sec) were then delivered briefly to one side of the brain only. Bliss and Lomo found that the size of the field potentials recorded in response to subsequent low-frequency stimuli was larger on the side of the brain that had received tetanization than on the control side, and that the increased response was sustained for several hours. They called this phenomenon "long-lasting potentiation." It was soon replicated in the rat in both *in vivo* (Douglas & Goddard, 1975) and *in vitro* (Schwartzkroin & Wester, 1975) preparations, and has since been observed in other species, including mice, cats, and squirrel monkeys. Now called either LTP or enhancement, the phenomenon is widely studied (see Figure 46-1).

Based upon the premise that synaptic changes of some kind must have some role in memory, three features of enhancement have attracted interest: (1) its long time course, pointing to a possible role in either memory consolidation or storage; (2) its occurrence in the hippocampus, a structure widely implicated in memory; and (3) the fact that it can be triggered by brief tetani, perhaps analogous to the way that brief, unique stimulus events can set up traces in memory. These points are discussed in the next section.

The purpose of this chapter, which is more an expression of our ignorance than of current knowledge, is to consider some of the problems involved in going beyond mere

Richard Morris and Mark Baker. Psychological Laboratory, University of St. Andrews, St. Andrews, Fife, Scotland.

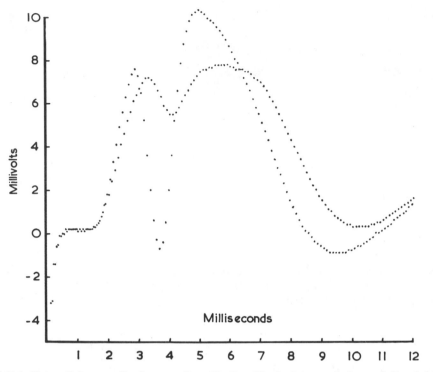

FIGURE 46-1. Extracellular recording from near the cell bodies of the dentate gyrus before and after a brief tetanic stimulus for .25 sec. The evoked potential shows an increased slope between 2 and 3 msec and a greater peak amplitude. The population spike, an extracellular index of the total number and synchrony of firing of the granule cells, also increases. EPSP amplitude and slope typically show greater stability during low-frequency test stimuli, but larger percentage increases in the population spike are often found after tetanization. In studies of the time course of enhancement, subthreshold stimuli that do not evoke a population spike are often used.

speculation to establish the functional significance of synaptic enhancement. Four strategies of investigation are considered. These are (1) a *correlational* strategy, in which correlations are sought between the susceptibility or time course of enhancement in individual animals on the one hand and rates of learning or forgetting on the other; (2) a *prior-enhancement* strategy, in which stimulation sufficient to produce it is given initially and the effects of this stimulation upon behavior are then examined; (3) a *prior-learning* strategy, in which the order of events is reversed and the effects of prior learning upon synaptic efficacy are studied; and finally (4) a *blockage/facilitation* strategy, in which steps are taken to influence enhancement (e.g., pharmacologically) and any subsequent effects upon learning and memory are recorded. With respect to this last approach, models of the underlying biochemical mechanisms will prove invaluable.

This division of experimental approaches into four operationally distinct categories is somewhat arbitrary, but it provides a vehicle with which to make two main points: First, recent studies of hippocampal function point to specific learning and memory paradigms to exploit in studies of enhancement. And second, formal models of how changes in synaptic efficacy might account for aspects of memory deserve careful consideration in the design of experiments.

Synaptic Plasticity and Learning

Throughout this chapter, we use the term "enhancement" in preference to "LTP" to draw attention to the differences between posttetanic potentiation and long-term changes in synaptic efficacy. The reasons for doing so are linked to the probability that distinct pre- and postsynaptic mechanisms are involved, respectively (McNaughton, 1983). Several recent experiments (e.g., Douglas, Goddard, & Riives, 1982; Krug, Brodemann, & Ott, 1982; Lynch, Kelso, Barrionuevo, & Schottler, 1983) point to an exclusively postsynaptic mechanism for the long-lasting effects. In Lynch *et al.*'s (1983) study, chelation of calcium by ethylene-bis(oxyethylenenitrite)tetraacetic acid (EGTA) injected via an intracellular electrode totally blocked enhancement in that cell while leaving surrounding cells unaffected. However, other work (e.g., Dolphin, Errington, & Bliss, 1982; Sastry, 1982; Skrede & Malthe-Sorensson, 1981) indicates that sustained facilitation of transmitter release, or changes in presynaptic excitability, may also be involved in long-term effects. If these phenomena are caused by the same presynaptic mechanisms as those involved in short-term posttetanic potentiation, McNaughton's (1982, 1983) sharp distinction between potentiation and enhancement could prove unsound. However, the controversy over pre- and postsynaptic mechanisms should soon be resolved, and the current confusing terminology should be replaced with terms specifically describing the underlying biochemical subprocesses.

The question of whether changes in synaptic efficacy are pre- or postsynaptic may seem irrelevant to a discussion of the functional significance of synaptic changes. Why does it matter whether the synaptic regulation is achieved by controlling transmitter release or by controlling receptor sensitivity? Both effects (or neither) may be involved in learning, but the different time courses of potentiation and enhancement point to their having different roles within a putative memory mechanism (Goddard, 1980). Moreover, a postsynaptic mechanism allows for cooperativity between different afferent fibers in realizing the conditions for enhancement on either pathway (Levy & Steward, 1979; McNaughton, Douglas, & Goddard, 1978), while in the absence of presynaptic modulation, cooperativity is unlikely to be a property of a presynaptically controlled mechanism. It is, perhaps, not surprising that habituation in invertebrates involves a presynaptic mechanism (Kandel, 1978), since the behavioral phenomenon is little more than a decline in the "gain" along a sensory–motor pathway (it is more complicated in higher vertebrates). More complex forms of learning in mammals, involving the processing of multiple sensory cues in space and time, and the sequencing of appropriate motor output, require the possibility for interactive additive and subtractive effects. The dendrites of the granule and pyramidal cells of the hippocampus, with their branching processes and protruding spines, could provide a substrate for the integration of multimodal and temporally separated inputs. By the same token, postsynaptic mechanisms for up- or down-regulating the numerous inputs to a dendritic tree independent of one another, together with other mechanisms regulating postsynaptic excitability and the conducting properties of dendrites, would be very useful.

Most research on enhancement has been done on the CA1 pyramidal or dentate granule cells of the hippocampus. With its simple layered structure, the hippocampus is well suited both for extracellular field-potential analysis in whole animals and for intracellular studies using the "slice" preparation. According to Bliss (1982), the "simple" anatomy of the hippocampus was as important as, if not more important than, the clinical findings of Scoville and Milner (1957) in his initial decision about where to start looking for mechanisms of synaptic plasticity in the brain. However, recent work has shown that the phenomenon also occurs in neocortex (Kasamatsu, Toyama, Maeda, & Sakaguchi, 1981; Lee, 1983) and in the superior cervical ganglion (Brown & McAfee, 1982). The Brown and McAfee study reported both posttetanic potentiation with a decay time of 3–5 min and LTP with a far longer time course, ranging from 30 to 200 min (the maximum time for which recordings were taken). These results suggested that long-term changes in synaptic efficacy may be a "more general feature of synaptic function" than has hitherto been recognized. However, in some studies, hippocampal enhancement appears to be nondecremental; this implies that, while long-term effects may not be unique to the hippocampus, different time courses may be observed inside and outside this structure. Attention to the time course of synaptic changes recorded *in vivo*, rather than just their presence or absence, will be valuable in functional studies, as will attention to whether a particular type of learning is likely to involve the hippocampus (e.g., on the basis of lesion data).

The third feature of enhancement that has suggested its possible role in learning is that it can be triggered by (relatively) brief tetani. Whereas Bliss and Lømo (1973) used tetani up to 15 sec long, recent studies have followed Douglas in using very short (1/50th sec) trains of high-frequency stimuli (250–400 Hz). Cells in the hippocampus and elsewhere in the brain are known to fire with these parameters, and thus the possibility that conditions of behavioral learning may induce high-frequency activation cannot be dismissed. However, attention must be drawn to the difference between synchronous firing of numerous fibers (in a physiological study) and the asynchronous firing of selected afferent fibers (as might, in principle, occur during learning). Theoretical models of neural networks that can store information (e.g., Marr, 1971) always require separate activation of different cells by distinct events. It is not at all clear whether we can mimic these conditions in behaving animals with any accuracy using presently available physiological techniques. A corollary of this is that the hypothesis under investigation is not, strictly speaking, whether enhancement is involved in learning so much as whether the processes that go to make up the observed phenomenon of enhancement are involved. This subtle but important distinction proves very important when we turn our attention to the effects of prior learning upon changes in synaptic efficacy.

Strategies for Investigating Functional Significance

Correlational Strategy

If enhancement mimics a process that occurs naturally during learning, within-group variations in its magnitude or decay measured in a physiological experiment may be caused by factors that would also influence rates of learning or forgetting in a behavioral study. It follows that correlations might be found between parameters of behavioral performance and synaptic enhancement.

Barnes (1979) trained middle-aged and old rats to perform a difficult place-learning task. Released onto a brightly lit table, rats had to find their way to one of several dark enclosures—a kind of laboratory burrow—hidden beneath the table. The rats learned over 4 days to escape with an average latency of 40 sec, making no more than about four errors per trial at asymptote. They then had to find a different burrow elsewhere and were trained for 2 more days. As at the start of training, the rats again made errors, but they improved to varying degrees with further training. Stimulating and recording electrodes were implanted in the perforant path (PP) and dentate gyrus (DG), respectively. The rats were given low-frequency test stimuli interspersed with four sessions of brief high-frequency tetanization. An increase in the slope of the extracellular excitatory postsynaptic potential (EPSP) occurred after each high-frequency session, but repeated low-frequency test sessions revealed a gradual decline in its magnitude. As with the behavioral data, there was measurable interanimal variability. The interesting result, for present purposes, was a significant negative correlation between the retention of enhancement and the performance of the rats on the place-learning task at asymptote. Moreover, the correlation was significant in both the middle-aged and old groups, and, in keeping with the behavioral data, the old rats showed a poor retention of enhancement over a 24-hr period. Barnes (1979) interpreted these results in terms of decreased "reliability" or "preservation" of memories in the senescent animals.

The Barnes (1979) study, with data recorded from over 59 animals, is one of the new thorough published studies indicating a relationship between synaptic enhancement and learning. However, Barnes (1982) is well aware that it provides relatively weak evidence for identifying a causal relationship. In the light of the studies mentioned above as showing long-term effects outside the hippocampus, it is possible that the decay-time constant is a common parameter of synaptic plasticity in several brain regions. The significant correlation Barnes found may, therefore, be coincidental.

There are, in principle, two ways of getting round this problem using the correlation approach. One would be to examine the time course of synaptic changes in different brain regions in the same animal and to show that the best or only correlations were to be found between the retention of *hippocampal* enhancement and learning. This would be both difficult and tedious. A more profitable approach would be to examine different learning tasks. The question is, what tasks?

The numerous theories and dichotomies concerning the role of the hippocampus in learning and memory present a confusing picture. Unfortunately, the controversy over interpretation of the known facts obscures widespread agreement that certain procedures (such as place-learning tasks) are definitely impaired by hippocampal lesions, while others (such as the initial acquisition of classical conditioning) are not. We use the term "widespread" advisedly, for agreement is not universal: Thompson, Berger, Berry, Hoehler, Kettner, and Weisz (1980) have objected to the "logic of the lesion approach" on the grounds that it has "not been overly helpful in detailed analysis of the roles of brain structures in behavioral movement. Why then, should we expect so much more from the lesion approach with regard to far more complex aspects of behavior such as learning and memory?" (Thompson *et al.*, 1980, p. 274). Whether they would wish to press their argument in the light of more recent results concerning the effects of cerebellar lesions on nictitating membrane conditioning (Thompson, 1982), is unclear.

In any event, recent lesion studies and other experiments following a quite different approach show that quite subtle changes in the efficacy of hippocampal intrinsic circuitry may have profound effects upon "hippocampally sensitive" tasks. For example, Sutherland,

Whishaw, and Kolb (1983) have shown that *unilateral* depletion of dentate granule cells by intrahippocampal administration of colchicine can cause as great an impairment on a spatial water maze as bilateral lesions of the hippocampus. Their results, together with recent behavioral (Schenk & Morris, 1982) and anatomical studies (Van Hoesen, 1982), point to the importance of inputs to the hippocampus from parahippocampal cortical regions relayed via the modifiable excitatory synapses of the dentate molecular layer. Attacking the issue in a quite different way, Schwegler and Lipp (1981) report that genetic differences in the density of the mossy fiber innervation from DG to area CA3 of the hippocampus of mice correlate negatively with two-way active-avoidance learning, a task known to be *improved* by hippocampal lesions. And Barnes, Nadel, and Honig (1980) have reported that senescent rats can learn a simple T-maze very well, but that their strategies of learning are different from those used by young rats. "Probe" trials at the end of training indicated that they tended to use "response" strategies more often and "place" strategies less often. Differential retention of enhancement may not, therefore, correlate with all types of learning. It would be most interesting to know whether the retention of enhancement across a group of animals is correlated only with performance on hippocampally sensitive rather than hippocampally insensitive tasks.

Prior Enhancement

If genetic or aging-induced changes have at least some of their effects upon memory through variation in the relative plasticity of neurons within the hippocampus, could similar effects be brought about directly? Two opposing predictions concerning the effects of prior enhancement upon subsequent learning can be made: (1) The improved "efficacy" of the synapses will allow a better throughput of information to the hippocampus memory system, thereby improving learning; or (2) if the process of learning demands differential strengthening of relevant synapses within a population, then strengthening the whole or a major proportion of the whole population should retard learning and weaken memory.

We are aware of several experiments presently under way, but the only published report (Skelton, Phillips, & Miller, 1981) used a "detection" rather than a "learning" paradigm. Two problems that this and other work should (ideally) deal with are these: (1) Does tetanic stimulation affect all types of learning equally? and (2) How should "nonspecific" effects of stimulation be controlled? The "types of learning" dissociation, outlined in the previous section, should be attempted to ensure that the effects of electrical stimulation are not solely upon sensory or motor processes or upon motivational level. And the "nonspecificity" criterion requires the use of control groups that receive electrical stimulation to other pathways in the brain, or stimulation at low frequencies that do not induce enhancement. The prior-enhancement strategy is more powerful than strictly correlational studies, because it provides a comparison between animals that may differ *only* with respect to synaptic efficacy of particular groups of synapses in the hippocampus.

The "detection" study met part of the second but not the first of these criteria. In a preliminary experiment, rats were trained to work for food reward in response to direct electrical stimulation to the PP rather than in response to an exteroceptive discriminative stimulus (S[D]). Suprathreshold stimulating current was used, such that many granule cells fired. After 400 trials of training, half the rats responded after the PP stimulus rather than just before its presentation, with the probability of granule cell discharge being one factor responsible for rapid discriminative conditioning (Skelton, Phillips, & Miller, 1982). In the main study, subthreshold stimulating current was used for the behavioral training phase, but this was preceded either by 10 short tetani at 200 Hz (enhancement group) or by 10 single pulses (control group). In the subsequent behavioral training, the enhancement group learned to use the PP stimulus and an S^D more quickly than the control group. This, whatever "information" is conveyed by a single synchronous volley to the PP was augmented by prior enhancement.

This study shows that if induced cell discharge is critical in order for an animal to learn to detect intracranial stimulation, then increasing the probability of discharge will improve learning. This is an interesting result, but whether the "detection" paradigm tells us anything new about enhancement is another matter. For it is already established that enhancement will augment population-spike amplitude to a single suprathreshold volley, and the "detection" paradigm is simply a behavioral way of showing this. Moreover, it is known that several procedures other than enhancement can alter neuronal excitability. It would be interesting to know whether simultaneous PP and locus ceruleus stimulation, which augments population-spike amplitude but fails to affect LTP (Abraham & Goddard, 1982), would also augment PP stimulus detectibility in the Skelton *et al.* paradigm. This would provide a basis for arguing that enhancement is one of a variety of ways in which DG cell excitability may be up- or down-regulated to modulate information transfer into the hippocampus. But the fact that enhancement is a homosynaptic change leads us to suspect that there is more to the story than this.

The crucial question raised by Barnes's correlational data is whether variations in the retention of enhancement are causally related to storage and consolidation of information transferred through the hippocampus in the course of learning. In a recent pilot study, one of us (Baker) gave bilateral tetanizing stimulation to the PP in five rats, measuring the enhancement produced using low-frequency test stimuli. Later these and other operated control rats were tested on a spatial-memory task. No differences in the rate of learning by the two groups were observed, nor were any differences in retention seen. However, there were several problems with this pilot study, and we now plan another, using chronically implanted electrodes, multiple tetani over several days, and a shorter interval between the start of training and the end of PP tetanization. For the present, despite the wealth of published data on the effects of stimulation to the hippocampus on memory (e.g., Kesner, 1980), we know of no published evidence showing that prior stimulation at parameters sufficient to cause enhancement will induce any changes in the rate of learning of a hippocampally sensitive task.

Prior Learning

> *. . . any change which can be demonstrated in a population of synapses following relatively brief behavioral manipulations is unlikely to represent a mechanism of memory, unless the storage capacity of the system is extremely low.—McNaughton (1983, p. 245)*

Experiments following the prior-learning strategy involve training an animal in a given task and then, either during or after the learning experience, looking for changes in synaptic effectiveness in selected pathways in the brain.

Before an illustrative study is discussed, this apparently straightforward approach requires careful scrutiny. One serious problem is that if the relevant synaptic changes are thought to be the *site* of memory storage, one is surely searching for a needle in a haystack. We cannot improve upon McNaughton's cautionary note, quoted above. Changes in field EPSPs are most likely to be found if the memory capacity of the system is anything other than trivial.

Formal neural network models of memory (e.g., Gardner-Medwin, 1976; Marr, 1971) lead to exactly the same prediction. In Gardner-Medwin's model of simple and "progressive" recall, "elements of experience" set up activity in a group of cells via their extrinsic input. These cells are interconnected by pathways terminating in Hebb synapses (Hebb, 1949). Learning involves concurrent activity in all the cells activated by an event and in the pathways interconnecting them, resulting in some of the Hebb synapses' becoming effective. Recall involves activating a subset of the cells, which then triggers the entire ensemble via the now effective interconnecting pathways. Within this scheme, it turns out that two parameters are particularly critical for correct performance: (1) the threshold for firing a cell, which is controlled by a tonic inhibitory input acting equally on all cells; and (2) either the number of events that the network has to learn or the proportion of cells active during any one event, with decreases in either parameter improving the accuracy of recall. The model therefore bears out McNaughton's assertion in a mathematically formalized way. It also includes the idea of modulation of neuronal excitability via separate synapses from those used to "store" information (brain stem inputs to the hippocampus and/or inhibitory interneurons?).

Single-unit recording experiments do not yet offer unambiguous support for these deductions, still less for these models of memory. On the one hand, there are experiments showing that complex-spike cells are usually quiescent in freely moving rats until the animal enters a specific and familiar part of the environment (see O'Keefe, 1979, for review). On the other hand, there are studies (e.g., Thompson *et al.*, 1980) indicating that an enormous proportion of the pyramidal cells of the entire hippocampus (up to 80%) are active during nictitating membrane conditioning. The former studies point to a fairly high storage capacity in the hippocampus; the latter do not. One clue to the puzzle this poses is provided in recent data of Kubie and Ranck (1981), who show that a single complex-spike cell may have a place field in each of two separate contexts. This can be accommodated within a model like that of Gardner-Medwin (1976) if it is assumed that an "element of experience" corresponds to a single cell rather than to a single place. This is a reasonable way of applying Gardner-Medwin's model to O'Keefe's data, except that it forces one into assuming that the hippocampus is the site of long-term storage—a view that is probably unwise. An alternative approach would be to assume that the hippocampus functions much more as a temporary- or working-memory sort of device, putting together maps or associations as required, and then transferring this information elsewhere for permanent storage. Marr's (1971) model, which deserves far more careful analysis than space permits here, considers the idea of information transfer between "archicortex" (i.e., hippocampus) and neocortex. In addition, Squire, Cohen, and Nadel (1982) have developed a similar idea in proposing that the hippocampus is involved in "consolidation" for a limited time after initial learning. In their model, long-term storage occurs within "ensembles" of neurons in the neocortex, and the hippocampus is responsible for reorganizing this long-term store, particularly with respect to "declarative" knowledge. The precise role of the mechanisms of plasticity revealed in the phenomenon of enhancement within their scheme is unfortunately left vague. No clear-cut prediction about how field EPSPs might change during or after learning can be derived.

The point we wish to make is that while McNaughton's argument about storage capacity is correct, the inference to be drawn is unclear. Instead of using the argument to doubt the involvement of the hippocampus in memory given certain experimental results, we should perhaps recognize that the storage capacity of the hippocampus may in fact be low. Perhaps an upper limit is seen in exploratory behavior, where small numbers of cells encode information about different parts of an environment; whereas in defensive conditioning, which is being subserved by neural circuits elsewhere in the brain, there is no need to store much information.

A second problem involved in attempting to examine the effects of prior learning upon enhancement arises out of what Ranck has called "Vanderwolf's dilemma." Learning usually involves systematic changes in behavior that are not shown by control animals. In classical conditioning, for example, a conditioned response (CR) develops over the course of training reflecting the animal's ability to predict the arrival of the unconditioned stimulus (UCS) (see Dickinson, 1980, p. 21 ff). Activation of behavior reflecting the underlying learning will involve cell firing, activity along pathways, and transmitter release that in and of itself has *nothing* to do with learning and memory storage or consolidation (e.g., at alpha motoneurons). But how, runs the dilemma, can those neural events specifically associated with learning be dissociated from those merely associated with the behavior generated by the animal's new knowledge? It does not appear to be widely realized that, with respect to conditioning, the truly random control procedure of Rescorla (1967) may fail to do this.

One strategy would be to look at spontaneous behavior of roughly similar form. Vanderwolf and his colleagues, who have done this (e.g., Vanderwolf & Ossenkopp, 1982), report that various dissociable patterns of hippocampal EEG activity show no special relationship to learning. Thompson *et al.* (1980), on the other hand, claim that multiple- and single-unit activity in the hippocampus increase specifically during conditioning and do not occur during spontaneous membrane movements (Thompson, 1982). The dilemma is not, therefore, insuperable, but it certainly implies that choosing an appropriate control group in an experiment may be as difficult as choosing the appropriate experimental group.

Skelton, Scarth, Wilkie, Miller, and Phillips (1982) gave rats 9 days of operant conditioning, followed or preceded by 9 days of noncontingent reinforcement (crossover design). Two hours before each daily session, evoked potentials were recorded from the DG in response to stimulation of the PP. A range of current intensities (20–400 μA) was used to establish input–output curves for each rat on each day. The results showed pronounced changes in granule cell excitability, coupled to the conditioning procedure. The input–output curves were unchanged relative to baseline measurements 2 hr before noncontingent sessions, while prior to days when the rats had to earn reward, population-spike amplitude was increased. Skelton *et al.* tentatively concluded that "similar neuronal events may underlie both LTP and at least one component of the neural basis of learning."

This was a well-designed experiment. The use of noncontingent food in the control group equated reward consumption and any circadian factors involved in motivation over the course of the experiment. The crossover design ensured that any biased assignment to groups on the sensitive population-spike amplitude measure could not give rise to a falsely positive result. But, like the unfortunate kittens of Held and Hein's (1963) gondola experiment, it is essential to know more about what the rats actually did in the experiment. Were the two groups showing comparable patterns of behavior? The trick of doing the electrophysiological session just before the conditioning session may have got round the Vanderwolf dilemma, but it is known that quite subtle differences in behavior can cause marked changes in hippocampal evoked potentials (Winson & Abzug, 1978).

Other studies purporting to show changes in enhancement as a consequence of learning (e.g., Weisz, 1980) are also subject to the objection that they may be caused more by the changes in behavior induced by learning than by learning itself. A recent study by Jaffard and Jeantot (1981), examining the phenomenon of paired-pulse facilitation after different kinds of learning, is relevant here. Twin pulses at an interval of 60 msec were delivered to the commissural fibers on one side of the brains of mice, and recordings were taken from the contralateral hippocampus. The results showed that the magnitude of paired-pulse facilitation was greatly increased 1 hr after rats spent 15 min performing an operant task, relative to the facilitation of rats remaining in their home cages. The effect was apparently absent 5 min and 24 hr after conditioning, showing that prior conditioning may cause time-dependent changes in synaptic efficacy that have nothing to do with enhancement.

Blockade/Facilitation

A fourth strategy entails augmenting or interfering with the processes responsible for causing changes in synaptic efficiency during learning. If such changes occur, then manipulations known to affect enhancement should also affect specific learning subsystems.

Recent work includes both *direct* and *indirect* approaches—that is, attempts to manipulate enhancement by procedures that are tightly linked to formal theories of the process (direct approach), through to procedures that empirically, but for unknown reasons, affect enhancement (indirect approach). An interesting example of the latter is recent work by Jordan and Clark (1983), who have found that rats nutritionally deprived in infancy (via dietary restriction of the dam during pregnancy and lactation) demonstrate impairments in the development and retention of enhancement. These rats are known to show spatial working-memory deficits on a radial maze (Jordan, Cane, & Howells, 1981).

A more direct attack concerns the role of noradrenalin in normal hippocampal function. The diffuse noradrenergic input from the locus ceruleus to the hippocampus is well established from studies using fluorescence microscopy. Biochemical studies have shown that noradrenalin acts via a β-receptor to alter levels of cAMP in cortical nerve cells (Greengard, 1976) and so to modulate protein phosphorylation. It is apparently through this action that noradrenaline (NA) inhibits spontaneous activity in the hippocampus. Recently, Bliss, Goddard, Robertson, and Sutherland (1980) have shown that depletion of forebrain NA following 6-hydroxydopamine (6-OHDA) infusion into the dorsal nor-adrenergic bundle (DNB) causes a sustained impairment in the generation of enhancement. Successive conditioning trains were given to the perforant path at 20-min intervals. A significant difference in enhancement emerged early in conditioning, but no difference in the subsequent decline in enhancement was apparent. This is a puzzling dissociation, from which it is hard to draw any clear-cut prediction about noradrenergic modulation of learning in a "hippocampally sensitive" task. Hagan, Alpert, Morris, and Iversen (1982) failed to find any effects of up to 99% depletion of NA upon place learning, using a water maze known to be very sensitive to the effects of gross hippocampal lesions. Measures of latency, path length, and directionality all showed equally rapid learning in animals with sham lesions and depleted animals. It is surprising, in our view, that massive depletion of a putative neurotransmitter with such an important innervation of the hippocampus should be apparently without effect. However, Abraham and Goddard's (1982) recent report that stimulation in the locus ceruleus modulates granule cell excitability without affecting either the asymptotic amplitude or the subsequent decay of enhancement argues against any major involvement of noradrenalin in the normal processes modulating it.

Another approach, this time involving facilitation of enhancement, is seen in studies of posttrial mesencephalic reticular stimulation (Bloch & Laroche, 1981). They have shown that posttrial stimulation may (1) facilitate the learning of various tasks, and (2) accelerate the conditioning of hippocampal multiple-unit activity. Unfortunately, Bloch and Laroche (1981, Experiment 1) failed to include groups receiving CS alone, UCS alone, or CS-UCS random pairings, so the significance of medial reticular formation (MRF) stimulation in *specifically* accelerating conditioning was not clearly established (assuming that these "control" groups are accepted as adequate). These authors have also shown (3) that MRF stimulation may increase the amplitude of a population spike in the dentate by up to 130% when it precedes the stimulating shock to the perforant path, and (4) that successive trains of MRF stimulation after high-frequency tetanization of the perforant path can increase the duration of enhancement. In the latter case, control rats showed a decay of enhancement back to control values in 2 days, while MRF-stimulated rats showed a decay lasting 4–5 days. However, the MRF stimulation also increased the magnitude of enhancement, and this effect alone could account for the apparent decay-time effects, as in Bliss *et al.*'s (1980) study. Assuming that these results cannot be accounted for solely in terms of changed neuronal excitability (see McNaughton, 1983), the facilitation of enhancement by MRF stimulation points to a possible brain stem mechanism with which particularly significant events can be registered more strongly in memory.

Finally, a pharmacological approach is suggested by a recent theoretical model of the biochemical mechanism of enhancement. Lynch and Baudry (1982) propose that tetanization results in a series of Ca^{++}-triggered processes. Normally, Ca^{++} is actively sequestered by mitochondria, but, through the action of an unknown trigger, the alpha-subunit of pyruvate dehydrogenease (α-PDH) is phosphorylated and the sequestration of Ca^{++} shut down temporarily. Thus, Ca^{++} levels remain elevated, and these trigger the action of a high-molecular-weight protease, probably calpain, to bring about a stabilization of otherwise unstable postsynaptic receptors. The receptor stabilization is "fixed" by a morphological change in the shape of dendritic spines.

Recently, Baudry, Smith, Siman, and Lynch (1982) have shown that thiol-proteinase inhibitors (e.g., leupeptin) may block Ca^{++}-triggered increases in [^{3}H]glutamate receptor binding. The effect is dose-dependent, and total blockade is achieved, *in vitro*, with 80 nM leupeptin. We therefore decided to investigate the effects of leupeptin upon both enhancement (which it should block in a dose-dependent manner) and behavioral learning. Both experiments (in conjunction with Lynch and Baudry) are presently under way. In one pilot behavioral study using intraperitoneal (i.p.) injections of either leupeptin or placebo alone, rats were trained to find a hidden escape platform in a large water maze using procedures described by Morris (1981). No effects of the drug were observed during 16 trials of acquisition, but massed training trials were used; with hindsight, this may not have been ideal for observing what we anticipated would be a subtle effect. Retention tests were then carried out 5, 48, and 240 hr later to test the ability of the rats to search for the escape platform, which had, unknown to them, been removed from the apparatus. We found that the leupeptin group searched in a different way—more often in several places in the pool (in each of three replications, $p < .01$). On a strict ratio measure, the leupeptin group searched relatively *less* often in the correct place. However, we were unable to classify the strategies used by the different rats in any discrete manner, or to distinguish the group differences from those that might have been expected strictly from nonspecific changes in activity level. Accordingly, we are currently attempting alternative approaches to the problem. It is encouraging that the observed trends, although not significant, emerged in retention—bearing out a prediction originally made by Barnes and McNaughton (1980, p. 270) on the basis of their correlational studies.

Conclusion

We have discussed four strategies for investigating the relationship between enhancement and learning. In summary, we are frankly skeptical that the prior-learning strategy will be helpful, although it is ostensibly a direct approach to take. In the absence of appropriate controls for nonspecific behavioral and physiological effects, the prior-enhancement strategy could be misleading, but well-controlled studies offer a potentially useful approach. Correlational work would be more valuable if it were possible to dissociate between those types of learning and memory to which hippocampal enhancement is related and those that involve other neural circuits. Finally, the blockade/facilitation approach is potentially very powerful, provided care is taken to use pharmacological or other agents with relatively specific effects. It is important to stress that an "operational" approach such as we outline must soon be replaced by experiments based upon formal models of the neural mechanisms of learning. Such models should explain the striking dissociation between those types of learning that do and those that do not involve the hippocampus.

ACKNOWLEDGMENTS

This work was financed by travel grants awarded to Richard Morris by the Wellcome Trust and the Guarantors of Brain, and by a Science and Engineering Research Council Studentship award to Mark Baker.

REFERENCES

Abraham, W. C., & Goddard, G. V. Modulation of synaptic transmission and LTP in rat dentate gyrus by stimulation in or near the locus coeruleus. *Society for Neuroscience Abstracts*, 1982, *8*, 131.10
Barnes, C. A. Memory deficits associated with senescence: A neurophysiological and behavioral study in the rat. *Journal of Comparative and Physiological Psychology*, 1979, *93*, 74–104.
Barnes, C. A. Personal communication, 1982.

Barnes, C. A., & McNaughton, B. L. Spatial memory and hippocampal synaptic plasticity in senescent and middle-aged rats. In D. G. Stein (Ed.), *The psychobiology of aging: Problems and perspectives.* Amsterdam: Elsevier, 1980.

Barnes, C. A., Nadel, L., & Honig, W. K. Spatial memory deficit in senescent rats. *Canadian Journal of Psychology*, 1980, *34*, 29–39.

Baudry, M., Smith, E., Siman, R., & Lynch, G. *Calcium regulation of glutamate receptor binding in hippocampal slices.* Paper presented at The Brain in Health and Disease: First World Congress of the International Brain Research Organization, Lausanne, Switzerland, 1982.

Bliss, T. V. P. Personal communication, 1982.

Bliss, T. V. P., & Lømo, T. Long-lasting potentiation of synaptic transmission in the dentate area of the anaesthetised rabbit following stimulation of the perforant path. *Journal of Physiology (London)*, 1973, *232*, 331–356.

Bliss, T. V. P., Goddard, G. V., Robertson, H. A., & Sutherland, R. J. *Noradrenalin depletion reduces long-term potentiation in the rat hippocampus.* Paper presented at the 28th International Congress of Physiological Sciences, Budapest, 1980.

Bloch, V., & Laroche, S. Conditioning of hippocampal cells: Its acceleration and long-term facilitation by post-trial reticular stimulation. *Behavioural Brain Research*, 1981, *3*, 23–42.

Brown, T. H., & McAfee, D. A., Long-term synaptic potentiation in the superior cervical ganglion. *Science*, 1982, *215*, 1411–1413.

Dickinson, A. *Contemporary animal learning theory.* Cambridge, England: Cambridge University Press, 1980.

Dolphin, A. C., Errington, M. L., & Bliss, T. V. P. Long-term potentiation of the perforant path *in vivo* is associated with increased glutamate release. *Nature*, 1982, *297*, 496–498.

Douglas, R. M., & Goddard, G. V. Long-term potentiation of the perforant path-granule cell synapse in the rat hippocampus. *Brain Research*, 1975, *86*, 205–215.

Douglas, R. M., Goddard, G. V., & Riives, M. Inhibitory modulation of long-term potentiation: Evidence for a postsynaptic locus of control. *Brain Research*, 1982, *240*, 259–272.

Gardner-Medwin, A. R. The recall of events through the learning of associations between their parts. *Proceedings of the Royal Society (Series B)*, 1976, *194*, 375–402.

Goddard, G. V. Component properties of the memory machine: Hebb revisited. In P. W. Jusczyk & R. M. Klein (Eds.), *The nature of thought: Essays in honour of D.O. Hebb.* Hillsdale, N.J.: Erlbaum, 1980.

Greengard, P. A possible role for cyclic nucleotides and phosphorylated membrane proteins in the postsynaptic actions of neurotransmitters. *Nature*, 1976, *260*, 101–105.

Hebb, D. O. *The organization of behavior.* New York: Wiley, 1949.

Hagan, J. J., Alpert, J., Morris, R. G. M., & Iversen, S. D. *The effects of catecholamine depletion on spatial learning in the rat.* Manuscript submitted for publication, 1982.

Held, R., & Hein, A. Movement produced stimulation in the development of visually guided behaviour. *Journal of Comparative and Physiological Psychology*, 1963, *56*, 872–876.

Jordan, T. C., Cane, S. E., & Howells, K. F. Deficits in spatial memory performance induced by early undernutrition. *Developmental Psychobiology*, 1981, *14*, 317–325.

Jordan, T. C., & Clark, G. A. Early undernutrition impairs hippocampal long-term potentiation in adult rats. *Behavioral Neuroscience*, 1983, *97*, 100–110.

Jaffard, R., & Jeantot, Y. Post-training changes in excitability of the commissural path-CA1 pyramidal cell synapse in the hippocampus of mice. *Brain Research*, 1981, *220*, 167–172.

Kandel, E. R. *A cell-biological approach to learning: Grass Foundation Lecture.* Society for Neuroscience, 1978.

Kasamatsu, Y., Toyama, K., Maeda, J., & Sakaguchi, H. Long-term potentiation investigated in a slice preparation of striate cortex of young kittens. *Neuroscience Letters*, 1981, *26*, 269–274.

Kesner, R. P. An attribute analysis of memory: The role of the hippocampus. *Physiological Psychology*, 1980, *8*, 189–197.

Krug, M., Brodemann, R., & Ott, T. Blockade of LTP in the dentate gyrus of freely moving rats by the glutamic acid antagonist (GDEE). *Brain Research*, 1982, *249*, 57–62.

Kubie, J. L., & Ranck, J. B., Jr. Sensory-behavioral correlates in individual hippocampal neurons of the rat across four situations. *Society for Neuroscience Abstracts*, 1981, *7*, 119.2

Lee, K. Sustained modification of neuronal activity in the hippocampus and neocortex. In W. Seifert (Ed.), *Neurobiology of the hippocampus.* London: Academic Press, 1983.

Levy, W. B., & Steward, O. Synapses as associative memory elements in the hippocampal formation. *Brain Research*, 1979, *175*, 233–245.

Lynch, G., & Baudry, M. Rapid structural modification in rat hippocampus: Evidence for its occurrence and a hypothesis concerning how it is produced. In R. C. Morrison & A. Strick (Eds.), *Changing concepts of the nervous system*. London: Academic Press, 1982.

Lynch, G., Kelso, S., Barrionuevo, G., & Schottler, F. Intracellular injections of EGTA block the induction of hippocampal long-term potentiation. *Nature*, 1983, *305*, 719–721.

McNaughton, B. L. Long-term synaptic enhancement and short-term potentiation in rat fascia dentata act through different mechanisms. *Journal of Physiology (London)*, 1982, *324*, 249–262.

McNaughton, B. L. Activity dependent modulation of hippocampal synaptic efficacy: Some implications for memory processes. In W. Seifert (Ed.), *Neurobiology of the hippocampus*. London: Academic Press, 1983.

McNaughton, B. L., Douglas, R. M., & Goddard, G. V. Synaptic enhancement in fascia dentata: Cooperativity among coactive elements. *Brain Research*, 1978, *157*, 277–293.

Marr, D. Simple memory: A theory for archicortex. *Philosophical Transactions of the Royal Society of London (Series B)*, 1971, *262*, 23–82.

Morris, R. G. M. Spatial localization does not depend upon the presence of local cues. *Learning and Motivation*, 1981, *12*, 239–260.

O'Keefe, J. A review of the hippocampal place cells. *Progress in Neurobiology*, 1979, *13*, 419–439.

Rescorla, R. A. Pavlovian conditioning and its proper control procedures. *Psychological Review*, 1967, *74*, 71–80.

Sastry, B. R. Presynaptic change associated with long-term potentiation in hippocampus, *Life Sciences*, 1982, *30*, 2003–2008.

Schenk, F., & Morris, R. G. M. *Incomplete recovery of place-navigation deficit by rats with lesions of entorhinal cortex after various training procedures*. Paper presented at the Conference on the Neurobiology of Learning and Memory, Irvine, California, 1982.

Schwartzkroin, P. A., & Wester, K. Long-lasting facilitation of a synaptic potential following tetanisation in the *in vitro* hippocampal slice. *Brain Research*, 1975, *89*, 107–119.

Schwegler, H., & Lipp, H. P. Correlations between two-way avoidance performance and the relative sizes of hippocampal synaptic fields in regio inferior of mice with randomized genotype. *Neuroscience Letters*, 1981, *7*, S237.

Scoville, W. B., & Milner, B. Loss of recent memory after bilateral hippocampal lesions. *Journal of Neurology, Neurosurgery and Psychiatry*, 1957, *20*, 11–21.

Skelton, R. W., Phillips, A. G., & Miller, J. J. Long-term potentiation facilitates the acquisition of perforant path stimulation as a discriminative stimulus. *Society for Neuroscience Abstracts*, 1981, *7*, 245.9.

Skelton, R. C., Phillips, A. G., & Miller, J. J. *Electrical stimulation of the perforant path input into the hippocampus as a discriminative stimulus*. Paper presented at the Second International Symposium on Drugs as Discriminative Stimuli, Beerse, Belgium, 1982.

Skelton, R. C., Scarth, A., Wilkie, D. M., Miller, J. J., & Phillips, A. G. Synaptic activation of dentate granule cells by perforant path stimulation is facilitated by a learning experience. *Society for Neuroscience Abstracts*, 1982, *8*, 215.7.

Skrede, K. K., & Malthe-Sorensson, D. Increased resting and evoked release of transmitter following repetitive electrical tetanisation in hippocampus: A biochemical correlate to long-lasting synaptic potentiation. *Brain Research*, 1981, *208*, 436–441.

Squire, L. R., Cohen, N. J., & Nadel, L. The medial temporal region and memory consolidation: A new hypothesis. In H. Weingartner & E. Parker (Eds.), *Memory consolidation*. Hillsdale, N.J.: Erlbaum, 1982.

Sutherland, R. J., Whishaw, I. Q., & Kolb, B. A behavioral analysis of spatial localization following electrolytic, kainate or colchicine induced damage to the hippocampal formation in the rat. *Behavioural Brain Research*, 1983, *7*, 133–153.

Thompson, R. F. *Neuronal substrates of learning and memory: A dual process theory* Paper presented at the Conference on the Neurobiology of Learning and Memory, Irvine, California, 1982.

Thompson, R. F. Personal communication, 1982.

Thompson, R. F., Berger, T. W., Berry, S. D., Hoehler, F. K., Kettner, R. E., & Weisz, D. J. Hippocampal substrates of classical conditioning. *Physiological Psychology*, 1980, *8*, 262–279.

Van Hoesen, G. W. The para-hippocampal gyrus: New observations regarding its cortical connections in the monkey. *Trends in Neurosciences*, 1982, *5*, 345–350.

Vanderwolf, C H., & Ossenkopp, K. P. Are there patterns of brain slow-wave activity specifically related to learning and memory? In C. Ajmone-Marsan & H. Matthies (Eds.), *Neuronal plasticity and memory formation*. New York: Raven Press, 1982.

Weisz, D. J. Dentate single-unit and field potential activity during NM conditioning in the rabbit. *Society for Neuroscience Abstracts*, 1980, *6*, 787.

Winson, J., & Abzug, C. Neuronal transmission through hippocampal pathways dependent upon behaviour. *Journal of Neurophysiology*, 1978, *41*, 716–732.

The CA3 Pyramidal Cell in the Hippocampus: Site of Intrinsic Expression and Extrinsic Control of Memory Formation

47

Aryeh Routtenberg

Introduction

My colleagues and I have recently discovered that stimulation of an identified cell type in the hippocampus, the granule cell, significantly lowers the probability that a particular item of information will be retrieved (Collier, Miller, Quirk, Travis, & Routtenberg, 1981; Collier, Miller, Travis, & Routtenberg, 1982). This cell system, then, has a powerful impact on information storage.

In this chapter, I would like to discuss briefly what these results might mean. Our findings suggest the following:

1. It is now possible to define the particular role in memory of identified cells in the hippocampal formation.
2. A certain cell type—the CA3 pyramidal cell—may be part of the circuit that stores the molecular change involved in memory formation; that is, it may contain the molecular machinery of the mammalian memory mechanism.
3. Another cell type—the granule cell—may be critical for the control (erasure, resetting, elimination) of memory; that is, it may be a forgetting mechanism.
4. An important distinction should be made between the memory mechanism (an intrinsic process) and the forgetting or modulating mechanism (an extrinsic process).
5. Stimulation that disrupts memory, rather than disrupting the memory process as has been typically thought, may actually enhance or exaggerate the function of the forgetting mechanism.

Intrinsic and Extrinsic Mechanisms of Memory Formation

It is useful to emphasize the fourth point made above—namely, that there exist two components to the process of synaptic plasticity: an intrinsic mechanism, which forms, via biochemical and structural changes in synaptic strength, the circuit underlying the memory; and an extrinsic mechanism, which can enhance or prevent this change in synaptic strength (see Krasne, 1978).

Aryeh Routtenberg. Departments of Psychology and Neurobiology/Physiology, Northwestern University, Evanston, Illinois.

The intrinsic and extrinsic systems in the vertebrate brain are not known. One can, however, list a set of results that would provisionally identify a cell as part of an intrinsic or extrinsic memory system. First, a destructive lesion would prevent memory formation, or, in the case of an extrinsic system only, could enhance memory formation. Second, a nondestructive manipulation, such as electrical stimulation, of this particular cell type would enhance or disrupt memory formation. Third, given that the transmitter of that cell type were known, then blockade of that transmitter should, if the system were intrinsic, prevent memory formation. If the system were extrinsic, blockade should prevent or enhance memory formation.

We have recently obtained a set of results that identifies an extrinsic system within the hippocampus. In our studies of the granule cells of the dentate gyrus (Collier *et al.*, 1981, 1982), nonepileptogenic electrical stimulation of these cells has a powerful yet specific erasure effect on remembering a particular location in the environment. Second, immunocytochemical evidence indicates that opioid peptides are contained within these cells (Fitzpatrick & Johnson, 1981; Gall, Brecha, Karten, & Chang, 1981; Stengaard-Pedersen, Fredens, & Larsson, 1981) and thus constitute a potential transmitter in this system. Based on this information, we have attempted to block the effect of stimulation with a opioid peptide blocking agent, naloxone. We have found, in fact, that naloxone, completely blocks the erasure effect of stimulation. Third, we evaluated the effects of naloxone by itself on memory and found that naloxone had no blocking effect, but had a facilitating effect when given alone.

Since blockage of a known granule cell transmitter does not block memory, this suggests that the mossy fiber system is not intrinsic to the memory-formation process. The fact that its blockade may enhance memory storage suggests that this is an extrinsic system that normally dampens the memory-formation process. Such a conclusion provokes two further suggestions: First, electrical stimulation, rather than disrupting granule cell function, may be enhancing or driving its function, which is to dampen or erase memory. Second, since the mossy fiber system would need to exert its control over an intrinsic system, it is reasonable to suppose that the CA3 pyramidal cell, its primary target, may in fact be an intrinsic system. In the next section, I consider some of the evidence that supports this suggestion.

The CA3 Pyramidal Cell: Memory Storage Site in the Hippocampus

In this section, I consider the CA3 cell in the following terms:

1. Characterization of the anatomy and physiology of its inputs and their interactions.
2. Identification of the transmitters and their mode of action.
3. Description of time-locked alterations in neuronal activity in the CA3 cell with conditioning.
4. Analysis of the type of control each input exerts on the CA3 cell to produce the time-locked alteration in neuronal activity following conditioning.

In the next few sections, I review briefly some of the evidence that bears on these points.

Before doing so, it is valuable to consider certain functional characteristics of this structure. Since the initial description in 1958 by Penfield and Milner of memory impairments following hippocampal damage, considerable evidence has been gathered confirming the critical importance of the hippocampal formation in laying down the memory trace (for recent review, see Olton, 1983; Squire, 1982). Within this wealth of data, certain key points are worth emphasizing.

First, while the memory impairment that is most devastating involves the inability to store new information (anterograde amnesia), there is, as well, a sizable retrograde amnesia that may extend 1 to 3 years prior to the operation. This finding suggests that the hippocampal formation itself stores information for considerable periods of time. The lesion removes items in a long-term memory store from memory storage. We propose that CA3 pyramidal cells represent one site for the cellular changes in hippocampus that underlie this long-term storage. We would predict that biochemical changes in these cells would persist for weeks or years after the occurrence of the event. We have recently observed long-term biochemical alterations on Protein F1 (see what follows) using long-term potentiation (LTP) in chronic animals (Lovinger, Akers, Nelson, Barnes, McNaughton, & Routtenberg, in press).

Second, it has long been recognized that impairments are not observed unless a near-total bilateral removal of hippocampal formation is achieved. In addition, total removal of the hippocampus unilaterally has little effect on the memory formation process. A recent disconnection analysis of hippocampal formation by Olton, Walker, and Wolf (1982) has emphasized this point. The significance of these findings lies in the replicated circuitry of the hippocampus. This apparent redundancy suggests that CA3 pyramidal cells, as part of slightly different circuits, may each store some aspect of the memory, so that sufficient reconstruction is possible even when considerable damage is rendered by partial lesions. (Also, redundancy may contribute to self-knowledge about memory, as in "I know I know that"; see Routtenberg, 1980.) With respect to the complete unilateral removal of the hippocampus and the lack of noticeable effect on memory, one may presume that the hippocampal commissural system is normally capable of carrying all the information that is stored in CA3 cell circuitry of one hippocampus to its contralateral twin.

Third, it has recently been observed that certain types of new memory can be formed in patients with extensive bilateral hippocampal damage. Thus, while such individuals fail to store new data or information (declarative memory), they are able to store new rules (procedural memory) (Cohen & Squire, 1980). The patient is capable of procedural or habit memory or "knowing how," but is not capable of declarative or data memory or "knowing that." In this case, one must conclude that procedural memories can be formed in other brain locations. This is not to exclude that possibility that procedural memories do not interact with declarative memories. We propose, in fact, that such an event can occur at the CA3 pyramidal cell.

To summarize what has been said up to this point, to our knowledge, this is the first attempt both to identify a particular cell in the vertebrate nervous system with the site of memory storage and to propose how inputs to that cell participate in the mechanism for that storage. We define "memory storage" as a process that occurs when a network of neurons related by synaptic transmission demonstrates change. We propose that such a change in synaptic activity leading to memory storage is brought about by a functionally diverse set of inputs to the CA3 pyramidal cell in the hippocampal formation. Based on its known physiological and anatomical properties, each input is classified with respect to its capacity to change (intrinsic) or regulate change (extrinsic). As depicted schematically in Figure 47-1, it is suggested that changes in intrinsic memory circuits are enhanced by extrinsic cholinergic control and dampened by an extrinsic opioid system present within the hippocampal formation. In the next section, I consider these CA3 inputs.

Intrinsic Inputs to the CA3 Cell

Converging lines of evidence suggest that both intrinsic and extrinsic inputs, as defined earlier, synapse on the CA3 pyramidal cells. By virtue of the relation among these inputs memory formation can be expressed. In Figure 47-1, a schematic summary of these inputs is presented.

On purely anatomical grounds, the input from the entorhinal cortex must be considered intrinsic. The entorhinal cortex receives specific information from neocortical inputs (Van Hoesen, Pandya, & Butters, 1975) and transfers such (declarative) information to the CA3 pyramidal cell. We can surmise from the work of Andersen, Blackstad, and Lømo (1966) that this input is capable of frequency potentiation, yet there is no evidence available to indicate how inputs that may be extrinsic to this system would influence this potentiation. Another intrinsic system is likely to be the commissural input, from the contralateral CA3 (Buszaki, 1980; Buszaki & Czech, 1981).

It is interesting to consider the possibility that these intrinsic systems are part of the neural circuitry representing declarative memory. Thus, the data or facts in the environment coded by neocortical systems enter the CA3 pyramid via entorhinal and commissural pathways.

FIGURE 47-1. Simplified hippocampal circuit to illustrate the intrinsic (entorhinal) and extrinsic (granule cell, medial septal area, and locus ceruleus) inputs to the CA3 pyramidal cells.

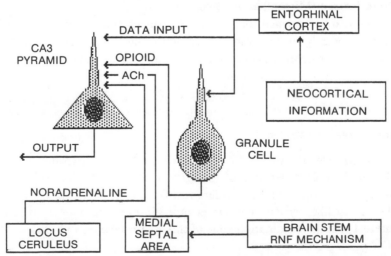

Extrinsic Inputs to the CA3 Cell

SEPTAL CHOLINERGIC INPUT

Considerable evidence from both animals (Deutsch, 1971) and man (Drachman & Leavitt, 1974) indicates that cholinergic transmission in brain is a critical part of the memory-formation process (Squire & Davis, 1981). Cholinergic blockade using the muscarinic receptor blocking agent, scopolamine, produces amnestic effects when administered peripherally or when applied to the hippocampal formation. Moreover, pathology of cholinergic systems is associated with severe memory deficits in presenile dementia of the Alzheimer type.

It has been known for more than a decade that the cells of the medial septal nucleus are the chief source of cholinergic input to the hippocampus (see Mitchell, Rawlins, Steward, & Olton, 1982, for review). Of special interest to the description of input systems on the CA3 pyramids are the following facts: (1) Both light-microscopic (Meibach & Siegel, 1977) and ultrastructural (Rose, Hattori, & Fibiger, 1976) evidence indicates that the major zone of termination of the cholinergic fibers from the medial septal area is the stratum radiatum in the CA3 region; (2) lesions of the medial septal area produce an impairment in spatial memory that is dependent on lesion size (Mitchell *et al.*, 1982; Winson, 1978). Thus, the cholinergic input to the CA3 region appears to be of critical importance in certain types of memory formation. It is perhaps relevant that the CA3 cell receives, relative to other hippocampal targets, the largest monosynaptic input from the medial septal area (Rose *et al.*, 1976).

The assertion that an intact cholinergic system is critical for the memory-formation process raises the possibility that it is an intrinsic one as suggested by Squire and Davis (1981). This seems rather unlikely since, as indexed by hippocampal theta activity (Routtenberg, 1968) or neuronal activity in the septal area (Segal, 1976), the cholinergic system is driven by activation from the brain stem and limbic system (Routtenberg, 1970). Thus, the impact of this input may be extrinsic, directed at specifying the *significance* of the facts or data (and thus potentially containing procedural information), rather than containing the *code* for the data itself. Consistent with the view that the cholinergic system is extrinsic is the fact that medial septal lesions have a minor influence on memories that have already been formed (Mitchell *et al.*, 1982).

It may also be expected that the locus ceruleus system, projecting from the dorsal pons monosynaptically to the stratum radiatum in the CA3 zone (Swanson & Hartman, 1975), can have a similar extrinsic influence on hippocampal pyramidal cell activity. Evidence from Segal (1977a) is consistent with this view.

MOSSY FIBER OPIOID INPUT

I now consider the mossy fiber input to the CA3 cell. Evidence presented earlier indicated that the opioid peptides of the granule cells exert a powerful extrinsic control over memory formation. As noted earlier (e.g., Gall *et al.*, 1981), the granule cells and their axons, the mossy fiber system, contain enkephalin-like immunoreactivity (ELI). It is of special interest that the termination zone of this ELI is coextensive with the terminal zone of the mossy fiber system. It has been suggested, therefore, that mossy fiber terminals contain opioid peptide material.

The site of mossy fiber terminals has been known for more than two decades (Blackstad & Kjaerheim, 1961; Raisman, Cowan, & Powell, 1965). Its location on the suprapyramidal portion of the apical dendrite of CA3 pyramidal cells overlaps with a segment of the cholinergic input to these same cells. There is no specific information on the nature of the interaction between septo-hippocampal terminals and mossy fiber terminals with respect to their influence on CA3 cells.

ACTIVITY OF CA3 CELLS DURING LEARNING AND
THEIR CRITICAL IMPORTANCE FOR LEARNING

A detailed analysis of unit responses in nine different regions of limbic cortex during differential conditioning and its extinction has been provided (Segal, 1973). The postconditioned stimulus time histogram of unit responses in medial septal area, dentate gyrus, CA1, CA3, and entorhinal cortex were compared during each stage of learning. Segal notes,

> In regard to the main experimental question, e.g., does the hippocampus learn? the answer seems to be yes. Data from the pseudoconditioning and extinction sessions seem to substantiate this answer. *Area CA3 of the hippocampus seems to be a focus of change in both the transition from pseudoconditioning to conditioning and from conditioning to extinction.* (1973, p. 850; italics mine)

These data indicate that selective and specific alterations can be observed in the CA3 cell during conditioning. These results do nothing to discourage the selection of the CA3 pyramidal cells as a focus of intrinsic and extrinsic control of plasticity. In the next section, evidence concerning the necessity of the CA3 cell is reviewed.

Kainic Acid Selectively Destroys CA3 Cells and Impairs Memory. There is now excellent evidence that kainic acid, a selective cellular excitatory neurotoxin, preferentially destroys CA3 pyramidal cells (e.g., Nadler, Perry, Gentry, & Cotman, 1980). The reason for this selectivity has not been discovered, though it is clear that other hippocampal cell types, granule cells, and CA1 and CA2 pyramids are not as sensitive to the toxic effects of kainate as are the CA3 pyramids. These results suggest that the CA3 pyramidal cell has special cellular and biochemical properties that are different from other cell types within the hippocampal formation.

The intriguing possibility of studying the effects on memory of a selective lesion of the CA3 cells is clearly suggested by these findings. This would permit the evaluation of the critical or essential nature of these cells for learning and memory. Handelmann and Olton (1981) have shown, in fact, that bilateral CA3-selective kainate lesions produced a permanent inability to learn the radial-arm maze task. In a group of animals trained prior to kainate injections, impairment was present, but some savings was in evidence. In broad terms, CA3 cell damage produces a profound anterograde amnesia and a significant but less profound retrograde loss. These results are reminiscent of the pattern of memory loss observed in human patients with extensive hippocampal destruction.

CHOLINERGIC–OPIATERGIC INTERACTION

I have reviewed evidence, then, that spatial overlap exists between the opioid and cholinergic input onto two dendritic zones of the CA3 cell, the stratum oriens and the stratum lucidum. There is evidence, in fact, that opioids can control the release of acetylcholine from presynaptic terminals. In the hippocampal formation, Segal (1977b) demonstrated that iontophoretically induced excitation by acetylcholine was antagonized by the prior application of morphine. In the cerebral cortex, Jhamandas and Sutak (1980) observed that the release of acetylcholine measured with the Mitchell cup technique was significantly reduced by opioid peptides and synthetic analogues. They also observed that naloxone blocked this opiate control of acetylcholine release.

It is our hypothesis, based on the data just reviewed, that the opioid mossy fiber system controls the effects of acetylcholine at the CA3 cell. Thus, amnesia-producing stimulation of the opioid system (Collier *et al.*, 1981, 1982) may produce a cholinergic blockade—an effective treatment for producing amnesia.

Memory Storage and the CA3 Pyramidal Cell

The diagram presented in Figure 47-1 is intended as a guide to the proposed description of events that occur at the CA3 pyramidal cell during the memory-formation process. For this analysis, I consider three inputs to the CA3 cell: the medial septal input, the granule cell input, and the entorhinal cortex input.

Consider first the data input from the entorhinal cortex. Andersen *et al.* (1966) have indicated that it is difficult to generate an evoked spike in CA3 with such an input, since this input is at the outer dendrites and would not depolarize the cell body sufficiently.

Consider now the septal input. It is possible to enhance or prolong the effect of a commissural input to the CA3 cell by either iontophoretic application of acetylcholine or stimulation of the medial septal area (Krnjevic & Ropert, 1982). It may be presumed that a similar cholinergic-enhancing effect would be observed with the entorhinal cortex input, though no information is currently available on this point. Of special interest is the fact that acetylcholine by itself or medial septal stimulation by itself does not activate the CA3 pyramidal cell system. During memory formation, we propose that input from both the entorhinal system and the cholinergic system are required. The timing of these inputs would be critical. Under any level of moderate activation leading to theta activity, inputs coming from entorhinal cortex would have a greater impact on CA3 cells, increasing the likelihood of cell firing and also prolonging such firing. Under normal physiological conditions, neither input alone would be able to provoke firing; their co-occurrence would increase the probability of generating a spike output from the CA3 cell.

What is the role of the opioid-containing granule cells in this system? Little electrophysiological information exists on opioid effects on CA3 pyramidal cells. Available studies (e.g., Masukawa & Prince, 1982) have not studied opioid effects in the context of stimulation of the granule cells. Recently we have found that iontophoretic naloxone can reduce the electrophysiological effects on CA3 pyramidal cells in response to granule cell stimulation (Routtenberg, Dalkara, & Krnjevic, 1984). To suggest how opioids might function at the CA3 pyramidal cell, the schematic network shown in Figure 47-1 focuses on the fact that the opioid-containing axons of the granule cells terminate at the same CA3 pyramidal cell dendritic location as the cholinergic axons of the medial septal area. Brain stem mechanisms of arousal and reinforcement (discussed in Routtenberg, 1978), which input to the medial septal region, provide a cholinergic, frequency-specific ("theta") input to the CA3 pyramids, increasing excitability. This is accomplished by raising potassium ion conductance (Dodd, Dingledine, & Kelly, 1981; Krnjevic & Ropert, 1982). This increase in excitability enhances reactivity to other inputs, such as those from entorhinal cortex.

We propose that by controlling the release of acetylcholine onto CA3 cells, opioids play a critical gating role, essentially editing the contents of memory, in the process of regulating CA3 cell reactivity. The model in Figure 47-1 predicts that granule cell opioids control memory formation by an anticholinergic action. This fits well with evidence that cholinergic antagonists produce deficits in memory processes that parallel the losses observed with hippocampal lesions.

Of interest here are the results from our laboratory concerning the erasure effects of granule cell stimulation (Collier et al., 1981, 1982). In our view, the erasure effects on memory occur as a result of a blockade of the cholinergic system. This could occur in two ways: presynaptically, by blocking acetylcholine release, or postsynaptically, by changing the membrane properties of the CA3 cell so that cholinergic input is no longer effective. Since granule cell stimulation is effective as an erasing agent 10 minutes after the memory has been stored (Collier & Routtenberg, in press), it suggests that the consequence of cholinergic action may be maintained even after cholinergic transmission has been terminated. Thus, granule cell input may have two actions: first, to control cholinergic release and second, to reverse cholinergic consequences once release has occurred.

What are these consequences and how might they be related to storage processes? With respect to the consequence of cholinergic action, there is evidence from Alkon, Lederhendler, and Shoukimas (1982) and Acosta-Urquidi, Neary, and Alkon (1982) that directly links alterations in conditioning-induced potassium conductance with changes in neural protein phosphorylation. Furthermore, the change in conductance is related to a calcium-dependent protein kinase. While these data are from the invertebrate *Hermissenda*, it is possible that alterations in potassium conductance in CA3 may also be related to changes in phosphoprotein metabolism. It is interesting, for example, that we have recently discovered that the phosphorylation state of a 47,000-molecular-weight phosphoprotein predicts the change in synaptic enhancement or long-term potentiation. This phosphoprotein, interestingly, is regulated by a calcium-dependent protein kinase (Routtenberg, Lovinger, Cain, Akers, & Steward, 1983).

In sum, it is proposed that the consequence of cholinergic input would be to change potassium conductance of the CA3 pyramidal cell through a protein phosphorylation step regulated by a calcium-dependent protein kinase. Since recent advances have been made in our understanding of protein phosphorylation (Gispen & Routtenberg, 1982), this suggestion is appropriately vulnerable to solution.

How might this change in protein phosphorylation lead to a more stable storage? Inputs from entorhinal cortex would be influenced by this alteration in CA3 cell membrane properties, since the cell would fire, or, at the least, depolarization would be enhanced or prolonged. This co-occurrence of presynaptic entorhinal activity and alterations in post-synaptic membrane conductance may be an essential ingredient in bidirectional synaptic communication (Tarrant & Routtenberg, 1977). Such communication leads to a morphological alteration of those particular synapses where increased presynaptic data input and elevated postsynaptic reactivity co-occur. Since posttranslational alterations leading to these morphological stabilizations have a finite half-life, one recognizes in this proposal the need for a continual updating or maintenance mechanism in the storage of memories in the CA3 cell. Such an updating process has been suggested on the basis of neuropsychological data (Squire, Cohen, & Nadel, 1982). It is of interest that the schema proposed here would not require *de novo* protein synthesis (Squire & Davis, 1981), but would be dependent solely on posttranslational modification of existing proteins (Routtenberg, 1982), such as occurs by the protein phosphorylation step.

Summary

In this brief chapter, I have emphasized the following points:

1. Our understanding of the cellular mechanisms in the hippocampus that lead to memory formation is rudimentary. Recent clues from our laboratory concerning a special role in editing or erasing memory for the granule cells in the dentate gyrus point to a strategy in solving this problem.

2. We know little of the particular circuits that store memory (intrinsic system) and those that regulate that storage (extrinsic system). Certain criteria are listed that would enable this specification in mammalian systems. In the hippocampus, and in particular the inputs to the CA3 cell, it is suggested that the granule cell—mossy fiber system and the medial septal–hippocampal pathway are part of the extrinsic system. The entorhinal–dentate or perforant path and the commissural pathway are suggested as components of the intrinsic system.

3. The cellular location for memory storage in the hippocampus has been suggested to be the CA3 pyramids. The storage process is enhanced or deterred by the regulatory influences of the extrinsic fiber pathways that input to the CA3 cell.

4. The molecular mechanism for storage in the CA3 cell may depend on a posttranslational modification of existing proteins. Recent evidence from our laboratory indicates the selective participation of a calcium-dependent phosphoprotein in the synaptic plasticity underlying memory storage.

REFERENCES

Acosta-Urquidi, J., Neary, J. T., & Alkon, D. L. Ca^{2+}-dependent protein kinase regulation of $K^+(V)$-currents: A possible biochemical step in associative learning of *Hermissenda*. *Society for Neuroscience Abstracts*, 1982, *8*, 753.

Andersen, P., Blackstad, T. W., & Lømo, T. Location and identification of excitatory synapses on hippocampal pyramidal cells. *Experimental Brain Research*, 1966, *1*, 236–248.

Alkon, D. L., Lederhendler, I., & Shoukimas, J. J. Primary changes of membrane currents during retention of associative learning. *Science*, 1982, *215*, 693–694.

Blackstad, T. W., & Kjaerheim, A. Special axo dendritic synapses in the hippocampal cortex: Electron and light microscopic studies on the layer of mossy fibers. *Journal of Comparative Neurology*, 1961, *117*, 133–159.

Buzsaki, G. Long-term potentiation of the commissural path–CA1 pyramidal cell synapse in the hippocampus of the freely moving rat. *Neuroscience Letters*, 1980, *19*, 203–296.

Buzsaki, G., & Czech, G. Commissural and perforant path interactions in the rat hippocampus: Field potentials and unitary activity. *Experimental Brain Research*, 1981, *43*, 429–438.

Cohen, N. J., & Squire, L. R. Preserved learning and retention of pattern-analyzing skill in amnesia: Dissociation of knowing how and knowing that. *Science*, 1980, *210*, 207–210.

Collier, T. J., Miller, J. S., Quirk, G., Travis, J., & Routtenberg, A. Remembering rewards in the environment: Endogenous hippocampal opiates modulate reinforcement–memory associations. *Society for Neuroscience Abstracts*, 1981, *7*, 359.

Collier, T. J., Miller, J. S., Travis, J., & Routtenberg, A. Dentate gyrus granule cells and memory: Electrical stimulation disrupts memory for places rewarded. *Behavioral and Neural Biology*, 1982, *34*, 227–239.

Collier, T. J., & Routtenberg, A. Selective impairment of declarative memory following stimulation of dentate gyrus granule cells: A naloxone-sensitive effect. *Brain Research*, in press.

Deutsch, J. A. The cholinergic synapse and the site of memory. *Science*, 1971, *174*, 788–794.

Dodd, J., Dingledine, R., & Kelly, J. S. The excitatory action of acetylcholine on hippocampal neurons of the guinea pig and rat maintained *in vitro*. *Brain Research*, 1981, *207*, 109–127.

Drachman, D. A., & Leavitt, J. L. Human memory and the cholinergic system: A relationship to aging? *Archives of Neurology*, 1974, *27*, 113–121.

Fitzpatrick, D., & Johnson, R. P. Enkephalin-like immunoreactivity in the mossy fiber pathway of the hippocampal formation of the tree shrew (*Tupaia glis*). *Neuroscience*, 1981, *6*, 2485–2494.

Gall, G., Brecha, N., Karten, H. J., & Chang, K.-J. Localization of enkephalin-like immunoreactivity to identified axonal and neuronal populations of the rat hippocampus. *Journal of Comparative Neurology*, 1981, *198*, 335–350.

Gispen, W. H., & Routtenberg, A. (Eds.). *Progress in brain research* (Vol. 56, *Functions of brain phosphoproteins*). Amsterdam: Elsevier/North-Holland, 1982.

Handelmann, G. E., & Olton, D. S. Spatial memory following damage to hippocampal CA3 pyramidal cells with kainic acid: Impairment and recovery with preoperative training. *Brain Research*, 1981, *217*, 41–58.

Jhamandas, K., & Sutak, M. Action of enkephalin analogues and morphine on brain acetylcholine release: Differential reversal by naloxone and an opiate pentapeptide. *British Journal of Pharmacology*, 1980, *71*, 201–210.

Krasne, F. B. Extrinsic control of intrinsic neuronal plasticity: An hypothesis from work on simple systems. *Brain Research*, 1978, *140*, 197–216.

Krnjevic, K., & Ropert, N. Electrophysiological and pharmacological characteristics of facilitation of hippocampal population spikes by stimulation of the medial septum. *Neuroscience*, 1982, *7*, 2165–2183.

Lovinger, D. M., Akers, R. F., Nelson, R. B., Barnes, C. A., McNaughton, B. L., & Routtenberg, A. Protein F1 (47 kD, 4.5 pI) *in vitro* phosphorylation increased by and directly related to three day growth of long term synaptic enhancement. *Society for Neuroscience Abstracts*, in press.

Masukawa, L. M., & Prince, D. A. Enkephalin inhibition of inhibitory input to CA1 and CA3 pryamidal neurons in the hippocampus. *Brain Research*, 1982, *249*, 271–280.

Meibach, R. C., & Siegel, A. Efferent connections of the septal area in the rat: An analysis utilizing retrograde and anterograde transport methods. *Brain Research*, 1977, *119*, 1–20.

Mitchell, S. J., Rawlins, J. N. P., Steward, O., & Olton, D. S. Medial septal area lesions disrupt θ rhythm and cholinergic staining in medial entorhinal cortex and produce impaired radial arm maze behavior in rats. *Journal of Neuroscience*, 1982, *2*, 292–302.

Nadler, J. Y., Perry, B. W., Gentry, C., & Cotman, C. W. Degeneration of hippocampal CA3 pyramidal cells induced by intraventricular kainic acid. *Journal of Comparative Neurology*, 1980, *192*, 333–359.

Olton, D. S. Memory functions and the hippocampus. In W. Seifert (Ed.), *Neurobiology of the hippocampus*. London: Academic Press, 1983.

Olton, D. S., Walker, J. A., & Wolf, W. A. A disconnection analysis of hippocampal function. *Brain Research*, 1982, *233*, 241–253.

Penfield, W., & Milner, B. Memory deficit produced by bilateral lesions in the hippocampal zone. *AMA Archives of Neurology and Psychiatry*, 1958, *79*, 475–497.

Raisman, G., Cowan, W. M., & Powell, T. P. S. The extrinsic afferent, commissural and association fibres of the hippocampus. *Brain*, 1965, *88*, 963–995.

Rose, A. M., Hattori, T., & Fibiger, H. C. Analysis of the septo-hippocampal pathway by light and electron microscopic autoradiography. *Brain Research*, 1976, *108*, 170–174.

Routtenberg, A. The two-arousal hypothesis: Reticular formation and limbic system. *Psychological Review*, 1968, *75*, 51–80.

Routtenberg, A. Hippocampal activity and brainstem reward–aversion loci. *Journal of Comparative and Physiological Psychology*, 1970, *72*, 161–170.

Routtenberg, A. The reward system of the brain. *Scientific American*, 1978, *239*, 122–131.

Routtenberg, A. Redundancy in the nervous system as substrate for consciousness: Relation to the anatomy and chemistry of remembering. In J. M. Davidson & R. J. Davidson (Eds.), *Psychobiology of consciousness*. New York: Plenum Press, 1980.

Routtenberg, A. Memory formation as a posttranslational modification of brain proteins. In C. J. Ajmone-Marsan & H. Matthies (Eds.), *Neuronal plasticity and memory formation*. New York: Raven Press, 1982.

Routtenberg, A., Dalkara, T., & Krnjevic, K. Hippocampal mossy fiber opioid regulation of CA3 pyramidal cell excitability: Iontophoretic study in intact hippocampal formation. *Federation Proceedings*, 1984, *24*.

Routtenberg, A., Lovinger, D., Cain, S., Akers, R., & Steward, O. Effects of long-term potentiation of perforant path synapses in the intact hippocampus on *in vitro* phosphorylation of a 47 kD protein (F-1). *Federation Proceedings*, 1983, *42*, 755.

Segal, M. Flow of conditioned responses in limbic telencephalic system of the rat. *Journal Neurophysiology*, 1973, *36*, 840–854.

Segal, M. Brain stem afferents to the rat medial septum. *Journal of Physiology*, 1976, *261*, 617–631.

Segal, M. The effects of brainstem priming stimulation on interhemispheric hippocampal responses in the awake rat. *Experimental Brain Research*, 1977, *28*, 529–541. (a)

Segal, M. Morphine and enkephalin interactions with putative neurotransmitters in rat hippocampus. *Neuropharmacology*, 1977, *16*, 587–592. (b)

Squire, L. R. The neuropsychology of human memory. *Annual Review of Neuroscience*, 1982, *5*, 241–273.

Squire, L. R., Cohen, N., & Nadel, L. The medial temporal region and memory consolidation: A new hypothesis. In H. Weingarter & E. Parker (Eds.), *Memory consolidation*. Hillsdale, N.J.: Erlbaum, 1982.

Squire, L. R., & Davis, H. P. The pharmacology of memory: A neurobiological perspective. *Annual Review of Pharmacology and Toxicology*, 1981, *21*, 323–356.

Stengaard-Pedersen, K., Fredens, K., & Larsson, L.-I. Enkephalin and zinc in the hippocampal mossy fiber system. *Brain Research*, 1981, *212*, 230–233.

Swanson, L. W., & Hartman, B. K. The central adrenergic system: An immunofluorescence study of the location of cell bodies and their efferent connections in the rat utilizing dopamine-β-hydroxylase as a marker. *Journal of Comparative Neurology*, 1975, *163*, 467–506.

Tarrant, S., & Routtenberg, A. The synaptic spinule in the dendritic spine: Electron microscopic study of the hippocampal dentate gyrus. *Tissue and Cell*, 1977, *9*, 461–473.

Van Hoesen, G. W., Pandya, D. N., & Butters, N. Some connections of the entorhinal (area 28) and perirhinal (area 35) cortices of the rhesus monkey: II. Frontal lobe afferents. *Brain Research*, 1975, *95*, 25–38.

Winson, J. Loss of hippocampal theta rhythm results in spatial memory deficit in the rat. *Science*, 1978, *201*, 160–163.

Strategies in Studying the Cell Biology of Learning and Memory

Steven Rose

Every neuroscientist since the days of Hebb—or even since the days of Ramón y Cajal—has known how memories are encoded in the brain. There is changed connectivity in particular neuronal circuits as a consequence of synaptic remodeling, and this modified connectivity, which underlies altered electrical properties of the circuit, forms the memory trace. Learning consists of making the circuit modification, while recall consists of re-activating the circuit. Everyone knows this; the only trouble lies in proving it—or convincing troublesome psychologists that there is such a unitary phenomenon as memory, convincing systems theorists that memories may be dispersed yet may have a point location, and convincing molecular biologists that connectivity matters more than the primary sequence of ribonucleic acid (RNA) or protein.

The truth of the matter is that despite two decades and more of intensive experimentation, large numbers of published papers, and endless reviews and conferences, we are only a little way toward the goal of answering the question of what precisely *are* the molecular and cellular events that, occurring consequent on a training experience, encode it in such a way that the trained animal's subsequent behavior is adaptively altered—the operationally based definition of learning upon which all experimentation in this area is based. The reasons for this relative lack of progress are, I think, fivefold, and it may be instructive to consider them before passing to an attempt to develop a rational strategy for advance.

First, there is a real problem in defining the psychological phenomenon (phenomena?) of memory in a way that makes it (or them) amenable to neurobiological investigation. While we need not go all the way with Hubbard (1982) in arguing that Proust's madeleine cake will always tell one more about the phenomenology of memory than any amount of training chicks to discriminate colors or rats not to jump off shelves, there is conceptual doubt over the very nature of the phenomenon we are seeking to explain. Yet definitionial rigor in the psychological sciences, as the experience of behaviorism has surely taught us, is achieved only at the expense of either biological or experiential validity.

Second, quite apart from the problem of deciding which biochemical system or cell structure to study, the biochemical or morphological problem is genuinely very difficult. Supposing that an engram is formed by synaptic modulation, any observed changes are likely to be very small against the totality of brain activity at any time. All animals that can learn are likely to be doing so a good proportion of the time, irrespective of the observer.

Steven Rose. Brain Research Group, Department of Biology, The Open University, Milton Keynes, MK76AA, United Kingdom.

Changes induced by an experimenter are therefore superimposed against this "background" brain activity. Pharmacologists and endocrinologists are used to working with changes in measured variables of 50% and upward. Most changes found in studying the neurochemical and neuromorphological sequelae of training are of the order of 8–15% of maximal enzyme activity (or of incorporation rate or whatever), even when defined brain regions or molecular species are studied in an effort to exclude "irrelevant" background. Such changes are scarcely above noise level and demand relatively large sample sizes to drive them to statistical significance—and they do not give one much margin for manipulation.

Third, there has been the problem of defining the questions that are being asked of the system. It has become conventional to distinguish two classes of biochemical approaches, interventive and correlative. In the first type, inhibitors of particular systems (for instance, of protein synthesis) are introduced, and the sequelae for learning and recall are observed; in the second, the animal is trained, and consequent biochemical changes are measured. The problem with both approaches is that interpretations of them may be ambiguous. A drug that speeds or inhibits memory formation may do so by effects on attentional or perceptual processes or motor capacity, and even if it does act on central memory processes, its biochemical mode of action may be unclear—as when it was shown (e.g., Hambley & Rogers, 1979) that the inhibitory effects of cycloheximide on learning capacity in chicks are probably not due so much to inhibition of protein synthesis as to the consequent intracellular accumulation of amino acids, such as glutamate. Equally, a biochemical change that is detected consequent on training might be a sequel of stress or sensory stimulation.

These caveats do not matter if the aim of the experiment is to point to cellular aspects of processes that are merely *necessary* if memory formation is to occur. For instance, many of the studies exploring the pharmacological role of peptide fragments in learning and memory (Martinez, Jensen, Messing, & McGaugh, 1981) probably fall into this category, since these fragments are part of what Agranoff and colleagues once called the "now print" signal for the system (Agranoff, Burrell, Dokas, & Springer, 1976). That is, they are part of mechanisms concerned with attention, stress, rehearsal responses, or whatever, which are aspects of the control process involved in telling the organism, "Hey, that's important, I must remember it." They are thus general to many memories, not specific to a particular one. Such processes are likely to be at least as important, from the point of view of the clinician or human psychologist, as the mysterious engram itself. Nonetheless, the caveats do matter if one is to attempt a reductionist dissection, not of the concomitants of training or even learning, but of what I have called the cell-biological correspondents of the memory trace itself (Rose, 1981b, 1982). By this term I mean those processes, at the level of cell structure and/or chemistry, that are the necessary, sufficient, and specific components of the engram, as opposed to the processes required for reading the engram in or out. If one wants an analogy, the difference is between the recording head of a tape recorder (which can translate all sounds, regardless of their content, onto the tape) and the tape message itself. My concern is with the latter. Clarity in defining the questions being asked at the cellular level and their presumed relationship to psychologically defined phenomena is thus essential.

Fourth, progress has been hindered by a failure to choose the right model in which to explore the cellular correspondents of memory formation. It was perhaps inevitable that early attempts should use adult laboratory rodents trained on the avoidance or appetitive tasks beloved of the experimental psychologist, especially as rodent neurochemistry was already well mapped. However, to seek measurable biochemical change consequent on relatively trivial learning tasks in an already very experienced animal (if any creature who has matured in a laboratory animal house can be so described) is a bit like putting the needle in the hay field rather than limiting it to the haystack, while "strengthening" such learning tasks normally involves stressing the animal in ways that must themselves impose biochemical consequences. There are three ways out of this dilemma:

1. To choose simplified mammalian preparations that show properties that may be regarded as mimicking learning, such as hippocampal potentiation.
2. To work with "simple" nervous systems, such as Kandel's elegant *Aplysia* experiments (Kandel & Schwartz, 1982).
3. To use "natural" learning in young precocial animals.

The last of these approaches has been our strategy, the argument being that (1) young animals are epigenetically predisposed to learn important things about their environment, and these memories are important to them as survival mechanisms; (2) such learning may be "more important" to the very young animal, and hence the cellular changes may be larger or more easily detectable.

The objection to the first and second approaches may be that such simplified preparations either are not really "learning" in the proper sense, or are doing so by mechanisms different from those employed by vertebrates; the objection to the third approach is that early learning is superimposed on a period of rapid biochemical maturation whose effects need to be separated out from those due to training. In addition, the use of a precocial animal whose basic neuroanatomy, neurochemistry, and genetics are less well known than those of the rodent has generated some problems in the prosecution of our own experiments.

Fifth, the characteristic of a mature and progressive field of science is that there is an accepted body of credible observations, replicable among laboratories, on which further work can be built. This has not until recently been the case in the field of the cell biology of memory. Different groups have used very different learning systems, from tissue slices to mice learning "fear of the dark"; they have studied different biochemical systems; and they have rarely attempted to replicate one another's findings. Instead, advertently or inadvertently, a widespread skepticism has been encouraged as to whether any of the published data referred to in the two decades of reviews of the field are to be regarded as "safe." Such anarchy is typical of an immature research field, but after all these years, it is time we grew up.

It is worth asking, not wholly irrelevantly, why it is that theoretical biology is such a sickly child compared with its healthy experimental sibling, while the reverse seems true for physics, where theoreticians flourish (Levy Leblond, 1976). Perhaps it is because experiments in biology are relatively cheap and easy, while in physics they are expensive and difficult. It is so simple for us to do experiments showing that when training occurs neurochemical X is activated, or that injection of drug Y interferes with the process of recall of a learned task, that thinking about the *meaning* of such observations is not encouraged. But I believe that some thought has become essential if we are to develop a rational strategy. The question is this: By what criteria are we to judge whether any cell-biological change we observe is a constituent of the engram? I have recently proposed a set of such criteria that, in my view, any such change must meet. As I have discussed these elsewhere in print (Rose, 1981a, 1981b) as well as at a number of conferences, and have reviewed some of our own experiments with imprinting and passive-avoidance learning in the chick in relation to them, I propose here merely to list the proposed criteria without discussion, and then to proceed to describe a recent experiment of ours that I think clarifies the way they may be used to identify an aspect of engram formation.

My six proposed criteria for any proposed biochemical correspondent of memory formation are as follows:

1. The process or metabolite must show neuroanatomically localized changes in level or rate during memory formation.
2. The time course of the change in biochemistry must match the time course of the specific phase of memory formation of which it is the correspondent.
3. Stress, motor activity, or other necessary but not sufficient predispositions or concomitants of learning must not in themselves and in the absence of memory formation result in the changes of Criterion 1.
4. If the cellular/biochemical changes of Criterion 1 are inhibited during the period over which memory formation should occur, the memory formation should be inhibited, and vice versa.
5. Removal of the anatomical locus (or loci) at which the changes of Criterion 1 occur should interfere with the process of memory formation and/or recall, depending on when, in relation to the training, the region is removed.
6. Neurophysiological recording from the locus (or loci) of the changes of Criteria 1 and 5 should detect altered cellular responses during and/or as a consequence of memory formation.

I suspect that this list is likely to be neither exhaustive nor completely convincing to a neuropsychologist, implying, as it appears to, a unilinear process of trace formation that at best is clearly an oversimplification and at worst may be simply misguided. I offer it nonetheless as a heuristic device, in the hope that someone will improve it; more importantly, I present it because it offers a checklist against which experiments in the field can be judged. In my view, any experiment that attempts to offer a biochemical or cell-biological measure of memory formation must be designed to test that measure against one or more of these criteria, if it is to advance the field and not to be mere stamp collecting.

I have elsewhere (Rose, 1981a) endeavored to show where our own experiments on passive-avoidance learning and imprinting in the day-old chick fit into the schema, and how they may be judged against the criteria. I want here to describe one very recent experiment, explicitly designed to judge the evidence that enhanced synthesis of glyco-proteins (a major class of synaptic membrane recognition molecules) may be part of the process of engram formation in passive-avoidance learning, against Criteria 3 and 4.

When [^{3}H]fucose is injected systemically into an animal, it is steadily incorporated into brain glycoproteins over a period of some hours. Fucose incorporation is a useful marker from the biochemist's point of view, as there is little free intracellular fucose; almost all the added precursor finds its way into the glycoproteins, which are synthesized in the cell body and later incorporated into cell membranes, including synaptic membranes. The fucose incorporation into glycoproteins, which may be a measure of turnover or of synthesis, involves a number of enzymic steps and the enzymes fucokinase and fucosyltrans-ferase. We had already shown that, when day-old chicks are trained on a passive-avoidance learning task, there is an increased incorporation of [^{3}H]fucose into brain glycoproteins, especially the glycoproteins present in a crude synaptic membrane fraction; this increase persists for some hours (up to 24) following training (Burgoyne & Rose, 1980; Sukumar, Rose, & Burgoyne, 1980). There is a corresponding increase in the activity of fucokinase enzyme (Lössner & Rose, 1983), which begins to suggest a plausible biochemical picture of how such enhanced synthesis may be occurring—or, at least, changes the biochemical question into one about how the fucokinase activity might be regulated. It is interesting, for example, that the enzyme is Ca^{2+}-dependent (McCabe, 1983).

In the training procedure, the bird is offered a bright chrome bead, at which it pecks spontaneously. If the bead is coated with an unpleasant-tasting substance (we use the bitter-tasting methylanthranilate), the bird will peck the bead, show a characteristic disgust response, and thereafter avoid pecking at a similar-looking but dry bead. This one-trial passive-avoidance learning task was introduced by Cherkin (1969) and has been used extensively by Gibbs and her colleagues (Gibbs & Ng, 1977). To find that a single peck at a methylanthranilate-coated bead results in a long-lasting increase in fucose incorporation, when compared with that of birds that had pecked a similar but water-coated bead, is exciting. However, it obviously raises this question: Is the increase an aspect of engram formation—of specific synaptic remodeling—or is it (merely) a consequence of the stress of the unpleasant taste or other concomitants of the experience?

The bird cannot learn the avoidance response without experiencing the taste of the methylanthranilate. However, it can experience the taste without remembering, and this fact enables one to dissect the effects of the taste on subsequent biochemistry from the effects of taste plus memory—the key demand of Criteria 3 and 4. Some years ago, Benowitz and Magnus (1973) showed that transcranial subconvulsive electric shock administered im-mediately after the training renders the animals amnesic, so that they will peck the bead on subsequent re-presentation. If the shock is delayed to some minutes after the training, the birds show recall and avoid the bead on subsequent re-presentation. We could thus perform an experiment involving six groups of birds:

1. Controls, unshocked, which had pecked a water-coated bead and which peck on re-presentation later.
2. Controls, immediately shocked, which also peck on re-presentation.
3. Controls, given delayed shock, which also peck on re-presentation.
4. Trained birds, unshocked, which have pecked a methylanthranilate-coated bead, and avoid it on re-presentation.
5. Trained birds, immediately shocked, which *peck* on re-presentation.
6. Trained birds, given delayed shock, which avoid on re-presentation.

Now, in this experimental design, Groups 5 and 6 have had identical experiences: They have pecked methylanthranilate-coated beads and have been shocked. The only difference is in the *time* of shock relative to training, and hence Group 5 is amnesic and Group 6 shows recall. A biochemical change that is consequent on some general aspect of training should appear in Groups 4, 5, and 6. If it is part of the memory-storage process, it should be present in 4 and 6, compared with 1 and 3, but should be absent in 5, which should be identical to 2. Hence it is possible to design an experiment with a predicted outcome as a test of the hypothesis that any particular biochemical process is a correspondent of memory formation.

We used this design with [^{3}H]fucose incorporation into glycoprotein on the biochemical marker (Rose & Harding, in press). To avoid the possibility that the immediate experience of training and electroshock, such as blood flow changes, were responsible for any biochemical effect, the precursor was not administered until after all behavioral measures, including testing (to confirm recall or amnesia), had been carried out. In brief, birds were trained and electroshock was administered either immediately (within 30 sec) or 10 min after training. 30 min after training, birds were tested; 15 min later, they were injected with [^{3}H]fucose; and after a further 3 hr, they were killed and fucose incorporation into macromolecules in several brain regions was determined. The measure thus refers to cellular events taking place not during training itself, but during a subsequent consolidation phase of memory fixation.

The results showed, first, that electroshock itself was without effect on subsequent incorporation of [^{3}H]fucose into glycoprotein. Second, and as anticipated, the effect of training (Group 4) was to increase subsequent fucose incorporation into specific brain regions (the anterior forebrain roof and forebrain base, as defined by Bateson, Horn, & Rose, 1975) by some 26% ($p < .05$). Third, this increase also occurred in the same brain regions of the birds of Group 6—that is, those birds that had been trained and electroshocked but still showed memory for the taste of the bead. Fourth, the increase was abolished in the birds of Group 5, which had been trained, had been electroshocked immediately, and were amnesic. Incorporation in these birds was similar to that in their matching control group, 2.

Hence, passive-avoidance training results in subsequent region-specific increases in brain fucose incorporation into brain glycoproteins (Criterion 1). Inhibition of memory formation prevents the increase from occurring (Criterion 4). Training itself, in the absence of memory formation, is insufficient to produce an increase in incorporation (Criterion 3).

Increased fucose incorporation into glycoprotein thus meets three of the criteria required for it to be considered as part of the process of engram formation in this learning paradigm. Whether this process meets the demands of the second criterion, that of the compatibility of its time course with that of memory formation, remains to be investigated. The methodology of the fucose incorporation cannot provide information as to localization of the changes to specific cells, but we (Kossut & Rose, in press) have been able to use the 2-deoxyglucose method to show that, consequent on passive-avoidance training, there is enhanced cell metabolism in a nucleus of the forebrain base (palaeostriatum augmentatum) and the medial and posterior hyperstriatum ventrale of the forebrain roof (a prerequisite to meeting Criterion 5). Taken together, this combination of methods and experiments is intended to provide an approach to a rational strategy of mapping the biochemical correspondents of memory formation.

However, a further point should be emphasized. Biochemists studying the sequelae of training are often content to show changes that occur *during* the learning process itself—as, for example, where we ourselves have shown brief, transient changes in the maximal binding activity of the muscarinic receptor in passive-avoidance learning (e.g., Rose, Gibbs, & Hambley, 1980)—or in the hours immediately following training, as we have shown in the experiment I describe here. Yet even the longest-term biochemical changes are undetectable after, say, 48 hr posttraining, although of course the memory persists.

How can the persistence of the memory be reconciled with the claim that the transient, brief biochemical event is an aspect of the engram?

There are two possible (though not mutually exclusive) answers to this question. One could be that we are looking at the wrong biochemical process—that, for instance, enhanced glycoprotein synthesis is a step toward something else, perhaps a lasting increase in the amount of some lipid constituents of the synaptic membrane. The second is that the increased metabolic activity we observe is concerned with the active remodeling of membrane—that engram formation involves a change in the shape of the synapses (either the presynaptic bouton or the postsynaptic structure—e.g., the dendritic spine). This morphological remodeling, rather than changed molecular composition or amount of the membrane, would provide the sought-for circuit building. However, once the membrane was remodeled, normal metabolic processes would maintain it in its new form, and a changed rate of some biochemical process would no longer be detectable.

If this were true—and there is already some evidence of morphological sequelae of training in terms of changes in synapse and dendritic shape and size from several laboratories—we should be able to detect changed synaptic structures in those brain regions showing biochemical change, as, for instance, in passive-avoidance learning. In our laboratory we are beginning to embark on this further hunt for the elusive cellular form of the engram (Stewart, Rose, King, Gabbott, & Bourne, 1984). Despite its long gestation, troubled childhood, and difficult adolescence, there is reason to hope that the cell biology of memory may be about to enter its majority at last.

ACKNOWLEDGMENTS

I wish to thank all past and present members of the Brain Research Group for discussions over the years, especially Sue Harding, Margaret Kossut, Norah McCabe, and Mike Stewart; Pat Bateson and Larry Benowitz for many critical and innovative conversations; Jane Bidgood for impeccable typing; and the Science and Engineering Research Council, Medical Research Council, and National Institutes of Health, under whose support much of this work has been carried out.

REFERENCES

Agranoff, B. W., Burrell, H. R., Dokas, L. A., & Springer, A. D. Progess in biochemical approaches to learning and memory. In M. Lipton, A. Di Mascio, & K. Killam (Eds.), *Psychopharmacology*. New York: Raven Press, 1976.

Bateson, P. P. G., Horn, G., & Rose, S. P. R. Imprinting: correlations between behavior and incorporation of ^{14}C-uracil into chick brain. *Brain Research*, 1975, *84*, 207–220.

Benowitz, L., & Magnus, J. G. Memory storage processes following one trial aversive conditioning in the chick. *Behavioral Biology*, 1973, *8*, 367–380.

Burgoyne, R. D., & Rose, S. P. R. Subcellular localization of increased incorporation of ^{3}H-fucose following passive avoidance learning in the chick. *Neuroscience Letters*, 1980, *19*, 343–348.

Cherkin, A. Kinetics of memory consolidation: Role of amnestic treatment parameters. *Proceedings of the National Academy of Sciences USA*, 1969, *63*, 1094–1101.

Gibbs, M., & Ng. K. T. Psychobiology of memory: Towards a model of memory formation. *Biobehavioral Reviews*, 1977, *1*, 113–136.

Hambley, J. W., & Rogers, L. J. Retarded learning induced by amino acids in the neonatal chick. *Neuroscience*, 1979, *4*, 677–684.

Hubbard, R. Discussion. In S. P. R. Rose (Ed.), *Towards a liberatory biology*. London: Allison & Busby, 1982.

Kandel, E. R., & Schwartz, J. H. Molecular biology of learning: Modulation of transmitter release. *Science*, 1982, *218*, 433–442.

Kossut, M., & Rose, S. P. R. Differential 2-deoxyglucose uptake into chick brain structures during passive avoidance training. *Neuroscience*, in press.

Levy Leblond, J. M. Ideology of/in contemporary physics. In H. A. Rose & S. P. R. Rose (Eds.), *The radicalisation of science*. London: Macmillan, 1976.

Lössner, B., & Rose, S. P. R. Passive avoidance training increases fucokinase activity in right forebrain base of day old chicks. *Journal of Neurochemistry*, 1983, *41*, 1357–1363.

Martinez, J. L., Jensen, R. A., Messing, R. B., & McGaugh, J. L. *Endogenous peptides and learning and memory processes*. New York: Academic Press, 1981.

McCabe, N. Unpublished data, 1983.

Rose, S. P. R. Criteria for investigating the biochemistry of memory formation. In R. Rodnight, H. S. Bachelard, & W. L. Stahl (Eds.), *Chemisms of the brain*. Edinburgh: Churchill Livingstone, 1981. (a)

Rose, S. P. R. What should a biochemistry of learning and memory be about? *Neuroscience*, 1981, *6*, 811–821. (b)

Rose, S. P. R. From causations to translations: a dialectical solution to a reductionist enigma. In S. P. R. Rose (Ed.), *Toward a liberatory biology*. London: Allison & Busby, 1982.

Rose, S. P. R., Gibbs, M., & Hambley, J. W. Transient increase in forebrain muscarinic cholinergic receptor binding following passive avoidance training in the young chick. *Neuroscience*, 1980, *5*, 169–172.

Rose, S. P. R., & Harding, S. Training increases ^{3}H-fucose incorporation in chick brain only if followed by memory storage. *Neuroscience*, in press.

Stewart, M. G., Rose, S. P. R., King, J. S., Gabbott, P. L. A., & Bourne, R. Hemispheric asymmetry of synapses in chick medial hyperstratum ventrale following passive avoidance training: A stereological investigation. *Developmental Brain Research*, 1984, *12*, 261–269.

Sukumar, R., Rose, S. P. R., & Burgoyne, R. Increased incorporation of ^{3}H-fucose into chick brain glycoproteins following training on a passive avoidance task. *Journal of Neurochemistry*, 1980, *34*, 1000–1006.

Studying Stages of Memory Formation with Chicks and Rodents

Mark R. Rosenzweig and Edward L. Bennett

The complete story of how organisms acquire, store, retrieve, and use information will certainly be a complicated one, and contributions will be needed from many disciplines and levels of analysis. Within this large field, we have chosen to investigate the basic processes and modulatory influences in the stages of memory formation in nonhuman vertebrates. In this chapter we try to make clear what this program means, including some of the main assumptions that underlie it, and the perspectives and aims of our research. Although we cite some experimental studies with regard to discussion of methods, findings, and unsettled questions, this presentation is not intended to be a review of our research or of the field in which it lies; for such reviews, see papers such as the following: Rosenzweig (1984), Rosenzweig and Bennett (1984), Dunn (1980), Gibbs and Ng (1977), and Squire and Davis (1981).

Assumptions Underlying the Research Program

A basic assumption in this field is the concept of the memory trace—that is, that memory is stored in the nervous system by physical–chemical alterations of neurons and/or neural circuits. Most investigators have also concluded that memory traces can take two or more forms that differ in duration. At a minimum, there are held to be short-term labile traces and long-term stable traces, and the same information can be maintained by either form of trace. It is possible that the short-term and long-term traces are parallel and independent processes, but many investigators suppose that the short-term traces are transformed into or lead to the development of long-term traces, probably through intermediate forms and processes. One often speaks of stages in the development of long-term memory, although there is little agreement as to either the number of putative stages or the processes involved in each stage. There is some evidence that neurochemical processes underlie the early stages, and that these lead eventually to structural (anatomical) changes, which underlie long-term memory.

We also employ the concept, which has been developing since the early 1970s, that formation of memory traces involves both necessary processes (sometimes called "intrinsic") and also modulatory (or "extrinsic") influences that affect the rate or level of the basic processes (Rosenzweig, Bennett, & Flood, 1981). A related but separate concept is that

Mark R. Rosenzweig. Department of Psychology, University of California, Berkeley, California.

Edward L. Bennett. Melvin Calvin Laboratory, Lawrence Berkeley Laboratory, Berkeley, California.

there are intrinsic neural circuits that hold memories and extrinsic circuits that modulate the activity of the intrinsic memory circuits (Krasne, 1976, 1978). Here we are considering neurochemical processes rather than circuits. In the near future, the two kinds of consideration—how (neurochemically) and where (anatomically) memory traces are formed —may be joined as investigators ask what neurochemical processes occur in modulatory circuits. For example, taking indications from recent findings of Thompson and his group (Thompson, Clark, Donegan, Lavond, Lincoln, Madden, Mamounas, Mauk, McCormick, & Thompson, 1984), it may be worthwhile to study neurochemical processes during learning both in deep cerebellar nuclei (which are part of the intrinsic circuit for motor conditioning) and in the hippocampus (which appears to modulate such conditioning).

A further assumption basic to our work is that some aspects of the neuropsychology of memory can be studied only in brains organized according to the vertebrate plan. The importance of studying roles of different brain regions and structures (such as the cerebellum and hippocampus) in learning and memory formation is one of the reasons why we are doing research with vertebrate subjects. Many observations on brain-injured people have suggested specific roles for different brain structures. These indications are being pursued in experimental studies with animals by such techniques as making localized lesions or injecting pharmacological agents into specific structures. Such research cannot be done with invertebrate subjects, although relatively simple invertebrates are proving useful in studying basic cellular events in learning (e.g., Alkon, 1980, 1983; Kandel & Schwartz, 1982). Even a complex invertebrate such as an octopus, which has a large and elaborately structured brain and which learns readily, cannot be used to study the roles of structures in the human brain in learning and memory, because the octopus brain is organized differently from the human brain. On the other hand, all vertebrate brains show the same basic plan of organization, and many findings about functions of a brain structure obtained in one vertebrate species have later been confirmed in others, including human beings. It is also for this reason that there is interest in testing with laboratory vertebrates conclusions reached with invertebrates, to see whether or not they may apply to human beings.

Even if behavioral (cognitive) research demonstrated a sequence of stages of memory that differed in duration and had somewhat different functional characteristics—and this has not yet been accomplished to the satisfaction of many workers in the area—this would not guarantee that there was a separate neurochemical process corresponding to each behaviorally defined stage. Although such correspondence of behavioral stages to neuro-chemical stages is perhaps the simplest hypothesis that could be offered, many investigators expect that the eventual picture will be far more complex. Thus, Kety (1976) has argued strongly for a multiplicity of underlying processes:

> There were forms of memory before organisms developed nervous systems, and after that remarkable leap forward it is likely that every new pathway and neural complexity, every new neurotransmitter, hormone, or metabolic process that played upon the nervous system and subserved a learning process was preserved and incorporated. (p. 321)

Other investigators also see the task of delineating the process involved in formation of memory as extremely complex. For example, Richard Mark (1979) supposes that these processes are about as complex and varied as those involved in carbohydrate metabolism, with numerous parallel pathways and shunts. In this case there may be no single steps that are crucial to the formation of memory, no bottlenecks at which the whole process can be halted. Going even further in this direction of thinking, a recent report that demonstrates strong synergistic effects of cholinergic agents on memory specifically refuses to attribute the effects to action on the acetylcholine (ACh) system:

> It is simplistic to consider that a drug, even if it were known to be highly specific in its mechanism of action on an isolated transmitter system, would necessarily have the same mechanism of action affecting a complex overall process such as memory formation. Thus, the question of what is the mechanism of action of a drug on memory processing is at best a difficult question. (Flood, Smith, & Cherkin, 1983, p. 42)

In spite of such cautionary evaluations concerning the possibility of tracing the neurochemical processes involved in formation of memory, we believe that efforts in this direction are worthwhile. Well-conceived research is almost certain to produce valuable new information and to eliminate some hypotheses as untenable; it may even show that some current hypotheses withstand the challenges of new tests and can encompass a wider range of phenomena than now known. We are encouraged by certain existing evidence to believe that there may, in fact, be at least some obligatory neurochemical processes in the formation of memory. This evidence demonstrates that the formation of long-term memory requires a pulse of protein synthesis (lasting on the order of minutes) somewhere within the posttraining period (lasting on the order of hours). By permitting brief "windows" of partial inhibition to occur at various periods after training (i.e., starting at 105 min, 225 min, or 445 min posttraining), we found that the closer such a pulse of protein synthesis follows training, the more effective it is in establishing long-term memory (Flood, Bennett, Orme, & Rosenzweig, 1975b). Because evidence of the necessity of protein synthesis in the posttraining period is important for our general position, we outline it briefly in the next section and provide references to fuller accounts.

One further assumption should be stated in this section, because it underlies our thinking about the eventual relevance of research in this field for ameliorating both normal and deficient memory processes. This assumption is that each of the stages of memory formation, and each of the necessary processes and modulatory influences involved, shows variation among individual learners and is subject to various sorts of malfunctions. Thus, individual differences in ability to remember, as well as deficiencies in memory, may arise from many causes or combinations of causes. Improving memory in one individual may therefore require quite different means from what will be effective in another. To the extent that the major processes and the most effective modulatory influences can be identified and measured, it should be possible to design rational programs of intervention to improve memory. In many cases, more than one process or modulatory influence within a stage may call for amelioration; in other cases, more than one stage may be functioning below a desirable level. Whenever more than a single aspect (whether within a stage or among stages) requires remediation, synergistic effects may be realized by appropriate combinations of treatments.

The study of synergistic effects of treatments on memory formation may lead to useful therapeutic procedures and may also aid the investigation of stages of memory formation. As Flood *et al.* (1983) have suggested, synergistic effects could be useful therapeutically, since reduced dosages could minimize toxicity and side effects, could help prevent the development of tolerance, and could also reduce the cost of drugs used in treatments. Study of synergistic effects may also aid the investigation of sequential dependence among stages of memory. If there is sequential dependence, then combinations of agents with quite different actions that affect different stages might well produce synergistic effects. If, on the other hand, there are parallel but different memories of different duration, then modulating the strength of one would not affect the others, and synergistic effects would not be expected.

The Necessity of Protein Synthesis for Formation of Long-Term Memory

The editors of this volume have wisely urged contributors to attempt to specify their positions clearly and to distinguish them from other positions with which they might be confused. We wish therefore to stress the temporal constraints of the protein-synthesis hypothesis that we have stated in the preceding section (p. 557). This should help to distinguish our position from both some general and some specific hypotheses. An example of such a general hypothesis is the statement by some investigators that since protein synthesis enters into so many neurochemical processes, it is inconceivable that it would not be involved in memory formation somewhere along the line, and perhaps at several stages. In response to this generalist position, we note that if protein synthesis is blocked in the brain prior to training and continuing for a period of hours thereafter, this does not prevent learning from occurring, nor does it prevent short-term or intermediate-term recall; but it does prevent formation of long-term memory. Furthermore, the inhibition of protein synthesis must be initiated close to the time of training if it is to be amnestic; this requirement helps to distinguish our position from certain specific alternative hypotheses, which we discuss shortly. Meanwhile, however, let us describe briefly some of the main aspects of research on the protein-synthesis hypothesis of formation of long-term memory.

Tests of this hypothesis were initiated by Flexner, Flexner, Stellar, de la Haba, and Roberts (1962), and much current research follows their basic approach. (Some of the history of this topic has been given by Agranoff, 1984, Squire & Davis, 1981, and Rosenzweig & Bennett, 1984.) The research design involves three main components: (1) giving animal subjects brief training that, without further treatment, would yield evidence of retention at a later test (e.g., 1 day, 7 days); (2) administering to some subjects an inhibitor of protein synthesis at various times close to training; and (3) comparing test performance of experimental and control subjects. Both active and passive behavioral tests have been used in order to obviate certain problems with interpretation of results. While the majority of such studies have employed training with aversive consequences, inhibition of protein synthesis has also been demonstrated to prevent long-term memory for positive reinforcements; this is reviewed elsewhere (Rosenzweig & Bennett, 1984).

In the early 1970s, interpretation of results concerning the protein-synthesis hypothesis of memory formation was clouded by serious problems, such as the following: (1) The inhibitors of protein synthesis that were available for research (puromycin and cycloheximide) were rather toxic, and this impeded experiments and complicated interpretation of results; (2) it appeared that inhibition of protein synthesis could prevent memory formation after weak training but not after strong training. The discovery by Bennett, Orme, and Hebert (1972) that anisomycin is an effective amnestic agent in rodents paved the way to resolution of the main challenges to the protein-synthesis hypothesis of memory formation. Anisomycin was found to be of much lower toxicity than other protein-synthesis inhibitors; in mice 25 times the effective amenstic dose was not lethal, whereas cycloheximide had to be used at close to a lethal dose. Since anisomycin has low toxicity and an appropriate dose can be used to produce 80% inhibition in brain for about 2 hr, it can be given repeatedly at 2-hr intervals to vary the duration of cerebral inhibition at the amnestic level. Using this technique in his doctoral research with us and extending inhibition to as long as 14 hours, James Flood found that the stronger the training, the longer the inhibition had to be maintained to prevent formation of memory (Flood, Bennett, Rosenzweig, & Orme, 1975a).

If the inhibition of protein synthesis is to prevent formation of memory, our results with mice show that it must be initiated within a very few minutes after training. Work with chicks indicates that the inhibitor can be administered as long as 20 min after training and still produce amnesia. Once the brief critical period is past (and its exact time course may vary with task and species), we have not found even prolonged subsequent inhibition to prevent formation of memory. We should also note one claim that in addition to this early critical period, there is a second one, 6–8 hr after training, when inhibition of protein synthesis can also prevent formation of long-term memory for an active-avoidance task in the rat (Matthies, 1982). The existence of a second period of susceptibility to protein-synthesis inhibition has not, to our knowledge, yet been corroborated.

Alternative Interpretations

Alternative interpretations of the amnesic effects of inhibition of cerebral protein synthesis have been offered by some investigators. Let us consider here briefly two such hypotheses: (1) Inhibition of protein synthesis blocks formation of memory, not because of its direct effects, but rather because it modifies concentrations of catecholamine neurotransmitters. (2) Protein synthesis inhibition blocks formation of memory because it interferes with paradoxical sleep, and in rodents paradoxical sleep must occur within a few hours of learning if long-term memory is to be formed.

In evaluating the hypothesis that protein-synthesis inhibition blocks memory formation because it modifies concentrations of catecholamine neurotransmitters, we verified that anisomycin does reduce catecholamine concentrations, but found that this reduction amounted to a maximum of 15–20%—far less than the 50–80% claimed in some reports. Then, in a series of experiments, we demonstrated that although single injections of catecholamine inhibitors or protein-synthesis inhibitors can cause amnesia for weak training, stronger training can be overcome only by multiple injections of anisomycin; multiple injections of catecholamine inhibitors are ineffective (Bennett, Rosenzweig, & Flood, 1977). Furthermore, in conditions where three successive injections of anisomycin are required to block memory formation, replacing one of these injections by a catechol-amine inhibitor prevents the occurrence of amnesia, whereas substituting an injection of cycloheximide (a protein-synthesis inhibitor) maintains amnesia. In further experiments, Flood, Smith, and Jarvik (1980) have compared the effect on memory formation of localized administration of the catecholamine inhibitors α-methyl-p-tyrosine methyl ester or diethyldithiocarbamic acid with the effects of the protein-synthesis inhibitors cycloheximide and anisomycin. Although all drugs caused amnesia when administered to the hippocampus, the drugs differed in their effects on memory formation when administered to other brain regions, including the brain stem and amygdala. The experiments cited in this paragraph provide a clear demonstration that the effects of inhibition of protein synthesis on memory cannot be attributed solely to effects on the catecholamine system(s).

When the temporal constraints for blocking formation of long-term memory by inhibiting protein synthesis are compared to the time courses of changes in catecholamine systems caused by inhibition of protein synthesis, this also demonstrates that effects on catecholamine levels are not critically involved in such amnesia. Specifically, experiments show that a few minutes of protein synthesis in the posttraining period are sufficient to guarantee formation of long-term memory, whereas changes in catecholamine levels caused by inhibition of protein synthesis are much slower to develop (on the order of an hour).

Let us turn now to the hypothesis that protein-synthesis inhibition prevents formation of long-term memory because it interferes with the occurrence of paradoxical sleep (PS, also called rapid-eye movement [REM] sleep). Bloch and collaborators reported that the amount of REM sleep increased after learning in the rat, and that preventing REM sleep for a period of 3 hr after shuttle-box training impaired formation of long-term memory (Bloch, 1976; Leconte & Hennevin, 1971). Pearlman and Greenberg (1973), using shuttle-box learning and discrimination learning, confirmed that deprivation of REM sleep for 3 hours after training impaired long-term retention. Fishbein and associates, pursuing this line of research, then found that anisomycin in amnestic doses prevents the occurrence of REM sleep for several hours (Fishbein & Gutwein, 1977); these results were corroborated by Rojas-Ramirex, Aguilar-Jiminez, Posada-Andrews, Bernal-Pedraza, and Drucker-Colin (1977). It is such findings that suggested the hypothesis stated at the start of this paragraph.

This REM–memory hypothesis has gained some currency, but we believe that a more searching review of the research in this area does not support it. In the first place, whereas Bloch and associates and Pearlman and Greenberg reported that occurrence of REM sleep during the first 3 hr after training is critical for formation of long-term memory, Fishbein (who started his work in this topic with Bloch) now states that PS in the 3 hr after training is not essential for memory formation, but that stability and maintenance of memory is dependent on PS's occurring over a protracted time period (Fishbein & Gutwein, 1981; Gutwein, Shiromani, & Fishbein, 1980). Thus the basic observation about posttraining REM sleep and memory formation is still in question. Also, methodological problems about studies investigating REM sleep and memory have been raised by Harris, Overstreet, and Orbach (1982). Even if REM sleep somewhere in the hours following training is definitely found to affect memory formation, it is clear that this effect does not have the precise time requirements that have been found for the amnesic effect of inhibition of protein synthesis. Furthermore, in experiments involving injections of anisomycin, whereas a dose of 40 mg/kg was as effective as one of 120 mg/kg in delaying onset of REM sleep, the larger dose was clearly the more amnestic (Gutwein et al., 1980). Thus, attributing the amnesic effects of protein inhibition to effects on REM sleep does not bear up under critical examination.

More generally, examination of a wide range of drugs shows little or no effect between whether a drug defers REM sleep and whether it is amnestic. For example, excitants such as methamphetamine, moderate doses of kainic acid, and scopolamine in low doses keep animals awake but may improve retention (Flood, 1983).

To the extent that catecholamine transmitters and REM sleep affect the formation of long-term memory, they may participate in modulatory systems rather than being part of necessary processes.

Program of Research

Review of research accomplished so far concerning neurochemical events during hypothesized stages of memory formation has disclosed many suggestive findings and some hypotheses that have stood up to empirical tests, but also has revealed many limitations and gaps in existing knowledge (Rosenzweig & Bennett, 1984). As Dunn has noted, "The most obvious deficit in the literature reviewed is the rarity with which experiments from one laboratory are replicated in another . . . there is also some persisting doubt as to the consistency of effects found within a laboratory" (1980, p. 360). Since this is so, we feel the necessity of attempting to replicate what we see as some of the most important reports in the literature. Only then will we know whether we can build upon and extend them, or whether we must revise some of the empirical structure of findings and the theoretical edifices that have been erected upon them.

The best-integrated investigation of neurochemical processes in the earlier stages of memory formation appears to be that of Marie E. Gibbs and Kim T. Ng, using young chicks as subjects (e.g., Gibbs & Ng, 1977). It seems desirable, therefore, to attempt to replicate some of the most critical of these studies, and if this is successful, to extend them to further tests of hypotheses about basic neurochemical processes and modulatory influences in stages of memory formation. In order to learn what processes may be general among vertebrates, it is also important to see whether one can extend to the chick some important findings that have been made in this field with mice and rats, and to attempt to extend to rodents some of the main findings obtained with chicks. Along with the studies in behavioral pharmacology, appropriate parallel neurochemical studies are required as we have done in past research with the mouse.

A brief statement of the methods, findings, and formulations of Gibbs and Ng is in order here to provide concrete background for our proposals. Gibbs and Ng propose a three-stage sequential model of memory formation—that is, one in which each stage depends directly on the preceding one. The stages are called short-term memory (STM), labile memory (which we prefer to call intermediate-term memory, or ITM), and long-term memory (LTM). The findings come mainly from experiments on one-trial aversive training of chicks, a method that Gibbs adopted from Cherkin (Cherkin, 1969; Cherkin & Lee-Teng, 1965; Lee-Teng & Sherman, 1966). Chicks peck spontaneously at small targets; especially attractive are shiny targets, such as a steel bead. If the target has been dipped in a bitter liquid, one peck suffices to train lasting avoidance behavior. Cherkin and associates continue to use this method to study effects of pharmacological agents on the formation of memory (e.g., Davis, Pico, & Cherkin, 1982), but they are mainly concerned with different questions from those considered here. This training method was somewhat modified by Mark and M. E. Watts (now M. E. Gibbs), and they showed that it was suitable for testing the effects of intracranial injection of drugs on memory formation in chicks (Mark & Watts, 1971; Watts & Mark, 1971a, 1971b). To overcome possible sources of confounding, chicks have been trained in a positively reinforced discrimination task that requires less than 5 min of training (Gibbs & Ng, 1977; Rogers, Drennen, & Mark, 1974), and in multiple-trial aversive training (Gibbs & Bennett, 1976).

STM is hypothesized by Gibbs and Ng to occur as a result of neuronal hyperpolarization, which results from increased potassium conductance across neuronal membranes following stimulation. Evidence for this hypothesis comes from several kinds of observations. One is the finding that intracerebral injections of depolarizing agents, such as glutamate and lithium chloride, disrupt the STM phase of memory formation (Gibbs & Ng, 1979). Since the magnitude of potassium conductance is a function of the concentrations of extracellular and intracellular calcium (Jansen & Nicholls, 1973), Gibbs, Gibbs, and Ng (1979) tested their proposed mechanism of STM by administering calcium chloride in the chick forebrain just prior to passive-avoidance training. Results demonstrated that when calcium chloride was injected 5 min before training, STM lasted four times as long as normally. On the other hand, lanthanum chloride injected intracerebrally prevented calcium flux across neuronal membranes, and this was found to abolish the STM stage of memory formation. The chick data indicate that STM is in its most active phase from 5 to 10 min after one-trial training, and that it then declines rapidly.

During the ITM stage of memory formation, Gibbs and Ng hypothesize, affected neurons are hyperpolarized as in the STM stage, but now the hyperpolarization is produced by activation of the sodium pump. Evidence supporting this hypothesis comes from experiments in which sodium pump inhibitors (ouabain or ethacrynic acid) were injected into chick forebrain shortly before or just after training. Such injections resulted in a decline of memory 10–15 min after passive-avoidance training—that is, at the end of the STM phase. Thus it appeared that these agents did not alter STM formation and function, but abolished the ITM stage. In such experiments LTM did not form either, as was demonstrated by amnesia upon testing 24 hr posttraining. These findings support the sequentially dependent, multistage model of memory formation. It has been found that D-amphetamine and norepinephrine (NE) counteract ouabain-induced amnesia through stimulation of NE release, which in turn acts to increase the activity of the sodium pump (Gibbs, 1976; Gibbs & Ng, 1977). Ouabain-caused amnesia has also been reversed by injection of the sodium pump stimulator diphenylhydantoin (DPH) shortly after training. The fact that DPH did not overcome amnesia induced by potassium chloride suggested that STM does not rely on sodium pump activity (Gibbs & Ng, 1976). ITM is reported to be most active in the chick between 15 and 30 min after training, after which it decays (Gibbs & Ng, 1977).

The LTM phase is reported by Gibbs and Ng (1977) to become optimal in the chick about 60 minutes after training. Formation of LTM in the chick can be disrupted by administration of inhibitors of protein synthesis, such as cycloheximide or anisomycin. When such inhibitors are injected close to the time of training, memory remains strong for about 30 min; then it begins to decline, and by 60 min posttraining it is significantly weaker than that of controls. Thus these observations on the chick accord with findings by us and others that formation of LTM in the mouse requires protein synthesis shortly after training.

Frieder and Allweis, from research on hypoxia-induced amnesia in the rat, have proposed three-phase (Frieder & Allweis, 1978) or four-phase (Frieder & Allweis, 1982a, 1982b) models of memory. In their model, however, the phases are not strictly sequential, but appear to show some parallel processing. Frieder and Allweis (1982b) state that it would be premature to compare their results and model in detail with those of Gibbs and Ng (1977), since neither the species, the learning task, the retention measure, nor the inhibitors were the same in the two laboratories. "However," they conclude, "the fact that multiphase models are necessary to encompass the data in such very different studies strengthens the argument for the existence of several operationally distinguishable neurochemical processes and memory-holding mechanisms in the consolidation of memory" (1982b, p. 1069). We agree, and we also believe that these results show again the desirability of being able to compare chick and rodent results obtained in the same laboratory and under conditions as comparable as possible.

Specific parts of our program, which we would invite other investigators to join, include the following components:

1. Attempt to extend to the mouse and rat the research on STM and ITM that has been done in the chick. As part of this work, investigate more thoroughly than has yet been done the sequential dependence (or lack thereof) among the stages of memory formation.
2. Attempt to increase the effectiveness of treatments by employing combinations of agents, both those that presumably act on a single stage or process (following findings reported by Flood et al., 1983) and combinations that may act on different stages of memory formation.
3. Test the replicability of reports on several stages of memory formation in the chick—STM, ITM, and LTM. The main work reported with the chick by Gibbs and associates has been inhibition of each stage or counteracting inhibition; we will also attempt to enhance each stage.
4. Attempt to reproduce in the chick some of the main findings on protein synthesis and LTM in the mouse—for example, that stronger training requires a longer period of inhibition of protein synthesis to produce amnesia.
5. Employ novel agents to investigate various stages of memory formation. For example, in a preliminary study (Bennett et al., 1972), we found that streptovitacin A appears to inhibit the later stages of protein synthesis in memory formation.
6. Parallel the behavioral studies by investigating the neurochemical actions and the localization–diffusion of the agents employed.

Substantial progress toward defining the basic processes and modulatory influences that act upon successive stages in the formation of memory should, we are confident, provide rational bases for ameliorating both deficient and normal memory processes.

ACKNOWLEDGMENTS

This project has received support from National Institute of Mental Health Grant No. 1 RO1 MH36042-01A1 and from the Office of Energy Research, Office of Health and Environmental Research, U.S. Department of Energy under Contract No. DE-AC03-76SF00098.

Helpful comments on a draft of this chapter were made by Marie Alberti, Susan Benloucif, James F. Flood, Sheri J. Mizumori, Teresa Patterson, and Michael J. Renner.

REFERENCES

Agranoff, B. W., Current biochemical approaches to memory formation. In G. Lynch, J. L. McGaugh, & N. M. Weinberger (Eds.), *Neurobiology of learning and memory*. New York: Guilford, 1984.

Alkon, D. L. Cellular analysis of a gastropod (*Hermissenda crassicornis*) model of associative learning. *Biological Bulletin*, 1980, *159*, 505–560.

Alkon, D. L. Learning in a marine snail. *Scientific American*, 1983, *249* (1), 70–84.

Bennett, E. L., Orme, A., & Hebert, M. Cerebral protein synthesis inhibition and amnesia produced by scopalamine, cycloheximide, streptovitacin A, anisomycin and emetine in rat. *Federation Proceedings*, 1972, *31*, 838.

Bennett, E. L., Rosenzweig, M. R., & Flood, J. F. Protein synthesis and memory studied with anisomycin, In S. Roberts, A. Lajtha, & W. H. Gispen (Eds.), *Mechanisms, regulation and special functions of protein synthesis in the brain*. Amsterdam: Elsevier/North-Holland, 1977.

Bloch, V. Brain activation and memory consolidation. In M. R. Rosenzweig & E. L. Bennett (Eds.), *Neural mechanisms of learning and memory*. Cambridge, Mass.: MIT Press, 1976.

Cherkin, A. Kinetics of memory consolidation: Role of amnesic treatment parameters. *Proceedings of the National Academy of Sciences USA*, 1969, *63*, 1094–1101.

Cherkin, A., & Lee-Teng, E. Interruption by halothane of memory consolidation in chicks. *Federation Proceedings*, 1965, *24*, 328.

Davis, J. L., Pico, R. M., & Cherkin, A. Memory enhancement induced in chicks by L-prolyl-L-leucyl-glycineamide. *Pharmacology Biochemistry and Behavior*, 1982, *17*, 893–896.

Dunn, A. J. Neurochemistry of learning and memory: An evaluation of recent data. *Annual Review of Psychology*, 1980, *31*, 343–390.

Fishbein, W., & Gutwein, B. M. Paradoxical sleep and memory storage processes. *Behavioral Biology*, 1977, *19*, 425–464.

Fishbein, W., & Gutwein, B. M. Paradoxical sleep and a theory of long-term memory. In W. Fishbein (Ed.), *Sleep, dreams, and memory*. Jamaica, N.Y.: Spectrum, 1981.

Flexner, J. B., Flexner, L. B., Stellar, E., de la Haba, G., & Roberts, R. B. Inhibition of protein synthesis in brain and learning and memory following puromycin. *Journal of Neurochemistry*, 1962, *9*, 595–605.

Flood, J. F. Personal communication, 1983.

Flood, J. F., Bennett, E. L., Orme, A. E., & Rosenzweig, M. R. Effects of protein synthesis inhibition on memory for active avoidance training. *Physiology and Behavior*, 1975, *14*, 177–184. (a)

Flood, J. F., Bennett, E. L., Orme, A. E., & Rosenzweig, M. R. Relation of memory formation to controlled amounts of brain protein synthesis. *Physiology and Behavior*, 1975, *15*, 97–102. (b)

Flood, J. F., Smith, G. E., & Cherkin, A. Memory retention: Potentiation of cholinergic drug combinations in mice. *Neurobiology of Aging*, 1983, *4*, 37–43.

Flood, J. F., Smith, G. E., & Jarvik, M. E. A comparison of the effects of localized brain administration of catecholamine and protein synthesis inhibitors on memory processing. *Brain Research*, 1980, *197*, 153–165.

Frieder, B., & Allweis, C. Transient hypoxic-amnesia: Evidence for triphasic memory-consolidating mechanism with parallel processing. *Behavioral Biology*, 1978, *22*, 178–189.

Frieder, B., & Allweis, C. Memory consolidation: Further evidence for the four-phase model from the time courses of diethyldithiocarbamate and ethacrinic acid amnesias. *Physiology and Behavior*, 1982, *29*, 1071–1075. (a)

Frieder, B., & Allweis, C. Prevention of hypoxia-induced transient amnesia by post-hypoxic hyperoxia. *Physiology and Behavior*, 1982, *29*, 1065–1069. (b)

Gibbs, M. E. Effects of amphetamine on short-term, protein independent memory in day-old chicks. *Pharmacology Biochemistry and Behavior*, 1976, *4*, 305–309.

Gibbs, M. E., & Barnett, J. M. Drug effects on successive discrimination learning in young chicks. *Brain Research Bulletin*, 1976, *1*, 295–299.

Gibbs, M. E., Gibbs, C. L., & Ng, K. T. The influence of calcium on short-term memory. *Neuroscience Letters*, 1979, *14*, 355–360.

Gibbs, M. E., & Ng, K. T. Diphenylhydantoin facilitation of labile, protein-independent memory. *Brain Research Bulletin*, 1976, *1*, 203–208.

Gibbs, M. E., & Ng, K. T. Psychobiology of memory: Towards a model of memory formation. *Biobehavioral Reviews*, 1977, *1*, 113–136.

Gibbs, M. E., & Ng, K. T. Neuronal depolarization and the inhibition of short-term memory formation. *Physiology and Behavior*, 1979, *23*, 369–375.

Gutwein, B. M., Shiromani, J., & Fishbein, W. Paradoxical sleep and memory: Long-term disruptive effects of anisomycin. *Pharmacology Biochemistry and Behavior*, 1980, *12*, 377–384.

Harris, P. F., Overstreet, D. H., & Orbach, J. Disruption of passive avoidance memory by REM sleep deprivation: Methodological and pharmacological considerations. *Pharmacology Biochemistry and Behavior*, 1982, *17*, 1119–1122.

Jansen, J. K. S., & Nicholls, J. G. Conductance changes, an electrogenic pump and the hyperpolarization of leech neurons following impulses. *Journal of Physiology (London)*, 1973, *229*, 635–655.

Kandel, E. R., & Schwartz, J. H. Molecular biology of learning: Modulation of transmitter release. *Science*, 1982, *218*, 433–443.

Kety, S. S. Biological concomitants of affective states and their possible roles in memory processes. In M. R. Rosenzweig & E. L. Bennett (Eds.), *Neural mechanisms of learning and memory*. Cambridge, Mass.: MIT Press, 1976.

Krasne, F. B. Invertebrate systems as a means of gaining insight into the nature of learning and memory. In M. R. Rosenzweig & E. L. Bennett (Eds.), *Neural mechanisms of learning and memory*. Cambridge, Mass.: MIT Press, 1976.

Krasne, F. B. Extrinsic control of intrinsic neuronal plasticity: An hypothesis from work on simple systems. *Brain Research*, 1978, *14*, 197–216.

Leconte, P., & Hennevin, E. Augmentation de la durée de "Sommeil Paradoxal" consécutive à un apprentissage chez le rat. *Comptes Rendus Hebdomadaires des Séances de l'Académie des Sciences, Paris*, 1971, *273*, 86–88.

Lee-Teng, E., & Sherman, S. M. Memory consolidation of one-trial learning in chicks. *Proceedings of the National Academy of Sciences USA*, 1966, *56*, 926–931.

Mark, R. F. Concluding comments, In M. A. B. Brazier (Ed.), *Brain mechanisms in memory and learning*. New York: Raven Press, 1979.

Mark, R. F., & Watts, M. E. Drug inhibition of memory formation in chickens: I. Long-term memory. *Proceedings of the Royal Society, London (Biology)*, 1971, *178*, 439–454.

Matthies, H. Plasticity in the nervous system: An approach to memory research. In C. Ajmone-Marsan & H. Matthies (Eds.), *Neuronal plasticity and memory formation*. New York: Raven Press, 1982.

Pearlman, C. A., & Greenberg, R. A. Posttrial REM sleep: A critical period for consolidation of shuttle-box avoidance. *Animal Learning and Behavior*, 1973, *1*, 49–51.

Rogers, J. L., Drennen, H. D., & Mark, R. F. Inhibition of memory formation in the imprinting period: Irreversible action of cycloheximide in young chickens. *Brain Research*, 1974, *79*, 213–233.

Rojas-Ramirez, J. A., Aguilar-Jiminez, E., Posada-Andrews, A., Bernal-Pedraza, J. G., & Drucker-Colin, R. R. The effects of various protein synthesis inhibitors on the sleep–wake cycle of rats. *Psychopharmacology*, 1977, *53*, 147–150.

Rosenzweig, M. R. Experience, memory, and the brain. *American Psychologist*, 1984, *39*(4), 365–376.

Rosenzweig, M. R., & Bennett, E. L. Basic processes and modulatory influences in the stages of memory formation. In G. Lynch, J. L. McGaugh, & N. M. Weinberger (Eds.), *Neurobiology of learning and memory*. New York: Guilford, 1984.

Rosenzweig, M. R., Bennett, E. L., & Flood, J. F. Pharmacological modulation of formation of long-term memory. In G. Adam, I. Meszaros, & E. I. Banyai (Eds.), *Advances in physiological sciences*. (Vol. 17, *Brain and behavior*). London: Pergamon Press, 1981.

Squire, L. R., & Davis, H. P. The pharmacology of memory: A neurobiological perspective. *Annual Review of Pharmacology and Toxicology*, 1981, *21*, 323–356.

Thompson, R. F., Clark, G. A., Donegan, N. H., Lavond, D. G., Lincoln, J. S., Madden, J., IV, Mamounas, L. A., Mauk, M. D., McCormick, D. A., & Thompson, J. K. Neuronal substrates of learning and memory: A "multiple-trace" view. In G. Lynch, J. L. McGaugh, & N. M. Weinberger (Eds.), *Neurobiology of learning and memory*. New York: Guilford, 1984.

Watts, M. E., & Mark, R. F. Drug inhibition of memory formation in chickens: II. Short-term memory. *Proceedings of the Royal Society, London (Biology)*, 1971, *178*, 455–464. (a)

Watts, M. E., & Mark, R. F. Separate actions of ouabain and cycloheximide on memory. *Brain Research*, 1971, *25*, 420–423. (b)

Memory Modulation: Roles of Peripheral Catecholamines

50

Paul E. Gold

Time-Dependent Effects on Memory

Recently, there has been an evolution of the research area termed "memory consolidation" to the more current area of "memory modulation." For many years, it has been clear that, if administered shortly after a training experience, many acute treatments would produce retrograde amnesia. The effectiveness of these treatments in producing amnesia diminishes as time between training and treatment is increased; the time course is called the "retrograde-amnesia gradient." In those experiments that focused attention on theoretical models of short- and long-term memory, the retrograde-amnesia gradient was assumed to reflect the time necessary to from long-term memory.

It is of course obvious that the biological processes that underlie memory storage must take time. If one knew the necessary length of time (is it milliseconds, minutes, hours?), one could exclude many biological processes as the possible mechanism(s) underlying memory storage. Estimates of the time constant, derived from amnesia studies, generally ranged from seconds to a few hours (cf. McGaugh & Dawson, 1972). The arguments regarding which time constant was correct led to a series of studies that both resolved such controversies and, in my view, irrevocably altered the utility and future goals of this research field. Because of the significance of this issue for later—and current—research, it is useful to review the most salient features of these experiments.

Quite frequently, retrograde-amnesia gradients were observed to vary across laboratories. In some cases, the differences could be attributed to such variables as species, training procedures, time of day, or treatment (McGaugh & Herz, 1972). However, the differences across laboratories remained a nagging problem. The resoltion of the issue came from studies in several laboratories beginning in the late 1960s. These findings indicated that the length of a retrograde-amnesia gradient varied directly with the severity of the treatment. For example, Alpern and McGaugh (1968) reported that use of different stimulation parameters of electroconvulsive shock resulted in different amnesia gradients. Cherkin (1969) found that as the concentration and exposure time of chicks receiving the inhalant drug fluorothyl was increased, the retrograde-amnesia gradient could be extended from a few seconds to 24 hr. Similarly, amnesia gradients produced by supraseizure cortical stimulation varied with the intensity of the stimulation train (Gold, Macri, & McGaugh, 1973). A major organizing principle, one that seems intuitive in retrospect,

Paul E. Gold. Department of Psychology, University of Virginia, Charlottesville, Virginia.

emerged: The length of a retrograde-amnesia gradient is determined in large part by the intensity of the treatment.

While it is always useful to gain a general framework that accommodates previously discrepant results, this rule had a very serious implication for the major rationale underlying memory-consolidation studies. Using these procedures, one could no longer expect to determine a time constant for memory consolidation. Because the length of a particular gradient varies with treatment parameters, the gradient evaluates the effectiveness of the treatment in interfering with memory storage, rather than evaluating the temporal properties of processes underlying that storage. The collated results of memory-consolidation experiments can be explained by a variety of models ranging from a single memory trace (Gold & McGaugh, 1975) to multiple traces (McGaugh, 1968; McGaugh & Dawson, 1972). Thus, the results clarify neither the temporal properties of memory-storage processes nor the number of memory-trace systems involved in storage.

Memory Modulation

Still, two major properties of memory storage require explanation. First, a variety of posttraining treatments can alter later retention performance; second, each of these treatments loses this effectiveness as the interval between training and treatment is extended. The question remains regarding the biological significance of transient postexperiential susceptibility to agents that affect memory. It is important to note that, in addition to treatments that impair memory, there are many posttraining manipulations that can enhance later retention performance (McGaugh, 1973). Thus, whatever the biological underpinnings of memory storage may be, the mechanisms retain a transient susceptibility to treatments that can alter these processes, both improving and impairing later performance of learned responses. This realization was a key to considering the possibility that a set of the normal physiological responses to training might be endogenous modulators of memory storage (cf. Gold & McGaugh, 1978). The physiological processes to be considered here need not be a direct component of the memory-storage processes—that is, these events do not require the informational specificity one would hope to find in memory mechanisms—but should modulate memory-storage processes. Thus, it may be possible to study the endogenous neurobiological events that promote or impair memory storage without first identifying the mechanisms underlying that storage. Of course, it may be hoped that examination of the systems modulating memory will provide information about the possible nature of those processes as well.

What are the requirements that would lead to investigation of particular candidates for modulatory systems? First, the modulatory responses should be activated endogenously by the training procedures and correlated with later retention performance. For example, if animals are trained on a foot-shock task, one might consider arousal level, release of stress-related hormones from the pituitary-adrenal axis or from the sympathetic-adrenomedullary system, or release of brain norepinephrine. Results obtained with each of these systems are discussed below, with the exception of arousal level. Because it is so difficult to define appropriate measures of arousal, we have restricted this research to the more specific neuroendocrine systems. Second, it should be possible to manipulate the relevant neuroendocrine systems and show predictable effects on later retention performance. If animals are trained with foot shock as described above, particularly if a relatively mild foot shock is used, posttraining injections of some hormones might enhance later retention performance. Finally, at least some of the traditional treatments that enhance or impair memory (e.g., electrical stimulation of the brain, electroconvulsive shock, antibiotics) might be expected to act through these neuroendocrine memory-modulating systems.

Measurements and Manipulations of Peripheral Epinephrine

In the preceding section, one of the critical questions raised is whether the endogenous systems are activated by training procedures. To assess this possibility, we selected catecholamine systems because of the considerable information relating activation of these systems to stress (e.g., Stone, 1975) and because of the very sensitive assays available. Release of peripheral catecholamines can be studied quite directly by assaying epinephrine and norepinephrine content of plasma obtained through chronic catheters (e.g., in the tail artery; see Chiueh & Kopin, 1978). Rats were trained in a one-trial inhibitory (passive)-avoidance task. The results obtained with plasma epinephrine are shown in Figure 50-1 (McCarty & Gold, 1981). Note that plasma epinephrine content was very sensitive to training procedures. Animals merely placed in the training apparatus for the first time (no foot shock) exhibited a twofold increase in epinephrine levels. A weak foot shock, one that resulted in only modest levels of acquisition, had little effect on plasma epinephrine concentrations. However, the response to a stronger foot shock, which resulted in very good later retention performance, was a dramatic 10-fold increase in plasma epinephrine levels. Similar results were obtained with plasma norepinephrine levels. Thus, peripheral catecholamine levels were very sensitive to these training procedures.

The major question, however, is whether these responses can modulate memory-storage processes. To test this possibility, rats were trained with a weak foot shock and received posttrial subcutaneous injections of epinephrine; retention performance was tested 24 hr later. The aim here was to mimic the endogenous response to a stronger foot shock, and thereby to determine whether the epinephrine response might modulate memory storage. The results of one experiment of this type are shown in Figure 50-2 (Gold & van Buskirk, 1975). Note that the saline-injected control animals exhibited relatively low retention latencies. Those animals that received moderate doses of epinephrine had retention latencies significantly higher than those of the saline-injected controls. A higher dose, in this study, was ineffective. However, under other conditions, high doses can produce amnesia (Gold & van Buskirk, 1976a). Thus, posttraining epinephrine injections can modulate memory in a dose-related manner. Similar inverted-U dose–response relationships have been observed with a variety of treatments, including adrenocorticotrophic hormone (ACTH) (Gold & van Buskirk, 1976a, 1976b), amphetamine (Haycock, van Buskirk, & Gold, 1977; Krivanek & McGaugh, 1969), pentylenetetrazol (Krivanek, 1971), and other drugs (cf. McGaugh, 1973). Furthermore, the optimal memory-enhancing epinephrine doses result in plasma epinephrine levels comparable to those observed immediately after a strong foot shock (McCarty & Gold, 1981). Also, at least one traditional amnesic treatment—supraseizure electrical stimulation of frontal cortex—produces a significant increase in plasma epinephrine above that elicited by high foot-shock training (Gold & McCarty, 1981). These results support strongly the view that the

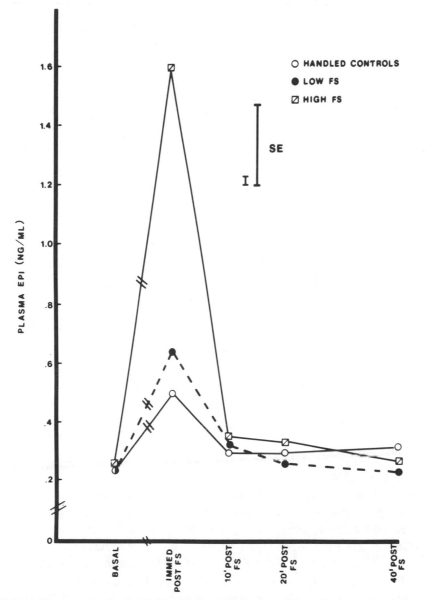

FIGURE 50-1. Plasma levels of epinephrine (ng/ml) under basal conditions (home cage) and immediately, 10, 20, and 40 min after the rats were placed in a test chamber and received a low (.6 mA, .5-sec duration) or high (3.0 mA, 2.0-sec duration) foot shock. Handled controls were placed in the apparatus but received no foot shock. Values are means for six to seven animals per group; the range of standard errors is indicated. (From R. McCarty & P. E. Gold, Plasma catecholamines: Effects of footshock level and hormonal modulators of memory storage. *Hormones and Behavior*, 1981, *15*, 168–182. Reprinted by permission.)

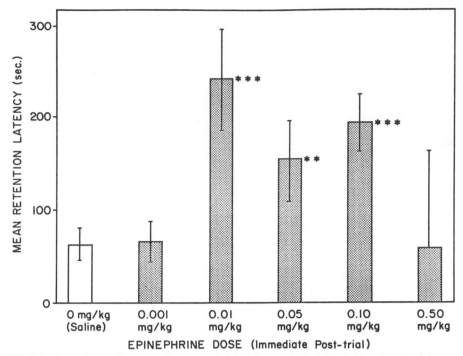

FIGURE 50-2. Retention performance for rats trained with a weak foot shock (.7 mA, .4 sec) in a one-trial inhibitory (passive)-avoidance task. Note that immediate posttraining injections of epinephrine enhanced memory at several intermediate doses. (From P. E. Gold & R. B. van Buskirk, Facilitation of time-dependent memory processes with posttrial epinephrine injection. *Behavioral Biology*, 1975, *13*, 145–153. Reprinted by permission.)

posttraining neuroendocrine state of an organism can modulate the storage of the specific information of the training events.

A further characteristic of hormonal modulation of memory is that the effects on later retention performance are time-dependent. For example, epinephrine injections delayed by 30 min or more after training do not significantly alter later retention performance (Gold & van Buskirk, 1975, 1976a, 1976b). Thus, the results of the epinephrine studies described here exhibit the major characteristics of all memory-consolidation studies. A single hormone can both enhance memory and produce amnesia, and these effects diminish as the time after training is increased. With regard to the earlier discussion about the significance of such temporal gradients, one can now see a simpler and more biological interpretation of retrograde-enhancement gradients. The intent of these studies is to mimic, as closely as possible, specific components of physiological responses to training. One critical variable is the dose administered. In addition, matching endogenous patterns of release also requires that the procedure approximate the temporal characteristics of that release. Thus, because the endogenous hormonal release follows training with a very short latency, injections of the hormones should and do have the largest effects if administered immediately after training. Therefore, manipulations that act on memory through such endogenous systems require that the dose and temporal properties match the magnitude and synchrony of the endogenous events.

There is evidence that peripheral catecholamines may contribute to the amnesias produced by a variety of agents. As noted briefly, frontal cortex stimulation produces retrograde amnesia and also produces increased plasma epinephrine levels. Posttrial injections of amphetamine, a central and peripheral adrenergic agonist, can enhance or impair memory. The effects of this agent may also be mediated by peripheral catecholamines; central injections of amphetamine do not affect memory, while systemic injections of the peripherally acting analogue, 4-hydroxyamphetamine, can modulate memory (Martinez, Jensen, Messing, Vasquez, Soumieru-Mourat, Gedes, Liang, & McGaugh, 1980; Martinez, Vasquez, Rigter, Messing, Jensen, Liang, & McGaugh, 1980). Two inhibitors of adrenergic function, diethyldithiocarbamate and reserpine, produce amnesias that can be reversed by peripheral catecholamine injections (Meligeni, Ledergerber, & McGaugh, 1978; Walsh & Palfai, 1979).

These drugs are all known to act on catecholamine systems, and the evidence suggests that their effects on memory are mediated at least in part through peripheral adrenergic mechanisms. More generally, it may be the case that many classes of amnestic agents act by overstimulation of peripheral catecholamine release. This question was examined by using adrenergic receptor antagonists to attenuate the effects on memory of many amnestic treatments (cf. Gold, McCarty, & Sternberg, 1982). In one study (Gold & Sternberg, 1978), animals received an intraperitoneal (i.p.) injection (2 mg/kg) of phenoxybenzamine 30 min prior to inhibitory-avoidance training. The phenoxybenzamine dose was selected to be below a level that might itself enhance or impair retention performance, but above a dose necessary to impair α-adrenergic receptor function. Shortly after training, animals received one of several amnestic treatments, including supraseizure frontal cortex stimulation, convulsant doses of pentylenetetrazol, subseizure electrical stimulation of the amygdala, diethyldithiocarbamate (a norepinephrine-synthesis inhibitor), and cycloheximide (a protein-synthesis inhibitor). In each case, amnesia was observed in animals pretreated with saline, but amnesia was not seen in those animals pretreated with the adrenergic antagonist. If administered peripherally, each of several α- and β-adrenergic antagonists examined thus far will attenuate amnesia (Sternberg & Gold, 1980, 1981b). Central injections of the antagonists do not attenuate amnesia (Sternberg & Gold, 1981a), supporting a special role for peripheral catecholamines in mediating these amnesias. Thus, these results suggest that many treatments may act on memory through mechanisms that include catecholamine systems.

Although peripheral catecholamine responses to each of these amnesic treatments have not yet been examined (except frontal cortex stimulation, as described above), it is interesting to note that most treatments that produce amnesia are also physiological stressors (e.g., they elicit seizures, they inhibit protein or neurotransmitter synthesis). It is possible, then, that if animals were trained under conditions of relatively low stress, these amnesic agents might actually enhance memory (in a manner analogous to that seen with epinephrine). Posttrial injections of diethyldithiocarbamate or cycloheximide can enhance memory under such training conditions (Hall, 1977; Haycock, van Buskirk, & McGaugh, 1976). Also, in a recent experiment, we (Sternberg, Gold, & McGaugh, 1983) found that seizure-producing frontal cortex stimulation could also enhance or impair later retention performance. The direction of the effects on memory varied with foot-shock level, and both effects could be blocked with peripheral injections of propranolol, a β-adrenergic receptor antagonist.

These results all point toward peripheral adrenergic modulation of memory-storage processing. One area of research that has as yet received little attention is the generality of the role of peripheral catecholamines in memory storage for a variety of training situations.

Most of the results described above have been repeated in active avoidance or an escape visual-discrimination Y-maze task (e.g., Sternberg & Gold, 1980, 1981b). As in the inhibitory-avoidance tasks, these procedures both used foot-shock motivation in training. Recently, we found that epinephrine can also retroactively facilitate memory for water-motivated Y-maze training (Sternberg, Gold, & McGaugh, 1984). It is possible that some neuroendocrine responses (perhaps epinephrine) may modulate memory in many types of situations. Other responses that are more specifically related to particular motivational classes (e.g., cholecystokinin for food tasks; see Novin & Vanderweek, 1979; Smith & Gibbs, 1979) may also be more specific in the range of situations in which the hormones modulate memory.

An understanding of the mechanisms by which peripheral catecholamines act on memory requires additional information about the manner by which the amines can act on the brain. Epinephrine does not readily cross the blood–brain barrier (Axelrod, Weil-Malherbe, & Tomchick, 1959). Nonetheless, several central effects of peripheral epinephrine have been identified. Epinephrine injections produce electrographic arousal (Baust, Niemczyk, & Vieth, 1963), affect brain norepinephrine concentrations (Gold & van Buskirk, 1978), modulate long-term potentiation (Delanoy, Gold, & Tucci, 1983; Delanoy, Merrin, & Gold, 1982), and alter the rate of amygdala kindling (Welsh & Gold, 1983). These latter neurophysiological preparations are discussed in more detail below. Thus, an important unresolved issue is not whether peripheral catecholamines act on brain, but how they do so. One possibility is that epinephrine acts via vascular responses—an action that appears to mediate the electrographic arousal described by Baust et al. (1963). Another possibility is that epinephrine might act on memory via parasympathetic (e.g., vagal) or sympathetic afferents that could monitor epinephrine levels or peripheral actions and relay the information to the central nervous system. It will be useful (and, one hopes, possible in the near future) to identify the organismic processes that mediate the transduction of peripheral catecholamine responses into behaviorally and biologically significant brain consequences.

Modulation of Long-Term Potentiation

Memory modulation, as described here, refers to processes parallel to memory-storage processes that can potentiate or attenuate the storage processes. Optimal use of this information includes studying the way in which neuroendocrine responses interact with the neurobiological storage mechanisms. Although it would be desirable to address this question directly by examining neuroendocrine modulation of long-lasting neuronal change initiated by training, there is little agreement on which functional alterations are most relevant to memory. There is a rapidly growing list of enduring changes in brain structure and function resulting from experience or brain damage (e.g., Juraska, Greenough, Elliott, Mack, & Berkowitz, 1980; Lynch & Baudry, Chapter 45, this volume; Routtenberg, Chapter 47, this volume), and it may be hoped that the documentation and analyses of these plasticities will continue. Possibly, several of these candidate mechanisms will collectively comprise the bases of memory storage. It would not be surprising to learn eventually that there are many classes of brain change, which may be anatomically widespread. With all training procedures, animals learn to make appropriate responses on the basis of associations that include not only the specific stimulus conditions selected by the experimenter (e.g., conditioned stimulus–unconditioned stimulus [CS-UCS] pairings), but also on the basis of a broader context that includes such variables as relevance of the training to evolutionary constraints on learning, stimulus and response generalization, and interoceptive and exteroceptive cues. It may be impossible to train an animal to make a specific association without training it to make simultaneously many other individualized associations. A corollary of this view is that it may not be possible to train an animal with any procedure in order to generate a single neuronal change that represents a specific experimenter-defined association. Nonetheless, it is still a reasonable and desirable goal to learn about those processes initiated by experiences that result in lasting brain change.

Within this conceptual framework, we began to examine neuroendocrine modulation of one example of neuronal plasticity: long-term potentiation (LTP). LTP is characterized by a long-lasting change in a monosynaptic evoked response following high-frequency stimulation of the afferent pathway. Because LTP has rapid onset and long duration, this phenomenon may reflect a form of neuronal alteration engaged in memory-storage processing (Goddard, 1980; Lynch, Browning, & Bennett, 1979). Combined with the anatomical specificity of the functional alterations, these characteristics make the preparation well suited for studying neuroendocrine modulation of a specific neuronal change (Delanoy et al., 1982, 1983). Under physiological control in anesthetized rats, a bipolar stimulating electrode was placed in the angular bundle (perforant path), and a monopolar electrode was placed in the granule cell layer of the dentate gyrus. The high-frequency stimulation parameters were adjusted on the basis of pilot studies, such that the percent change observed in the population-spike amplitude would be a 50–100% increase above prestimulation values. The results of one experiment are shown in Figure 50-3. Amphetamine was selected for the initial studies, because this agent has a relatively broad dose range, which can enhance behaviorally assessed memory (Krivanek, 1971). Note that intermediate amphetamine doses (.01–3.0 mg/kg) significantly enhanced the population-spike amplitude observed for high-frequency stimulation. No significant changes were observed in control amphetamine-treated animals (i.e., animals that did not receive the high-frequency trains). More recently, we found that peripheral epinephrine injections can also enhance LTP in an inverted-U dose–response manner. Also, we have used this preparation to define the receptor class that mediates these adrenergic effects on LTP. Peripheral injections of clonidine, an $alpha_2$ adrenergic agonist, but not methoxamine (an $alpha_1$ agonist) or isoproterenol (a beta agonist), can also enhance LTP.

These results demonstrate that LTP can be regulated by adrenergic agonists. In several respects, the modulation is remarkably similar to that observed in behavioral studies. In each case, drug facilitation of LTP is characterized by an inverted-U dose–response relationship with adrenergic stimulation; optimal LTP-enhancing doses are comparable to optimal doses for memory enhancement. Furthermore, LTP is sensitive to peripheral injections of epinephrine, suggesting that adrenergic modulation includes peripheral actions. In addition, there are two apparent differences between LTP and memory modulation. First, although high doses of adrenergic agonists can produce amnesia, we have not observed similar effects in LTP experiments; high doses neither enhance nor impair LTP. Second, adrenergic modulation of LTP appears to be mediated by $alpha_2$ receptors in particular, but modulation of memory storage can be observed by drugs that act on either alpha or beta receptors. As discussed earlier, if memory storage is likely to involve several neurobiological processes, it may not be surprising that adrenergic modulation includes a broader spectrum of effective drugs for memory storage than for a single example of neuronal change.

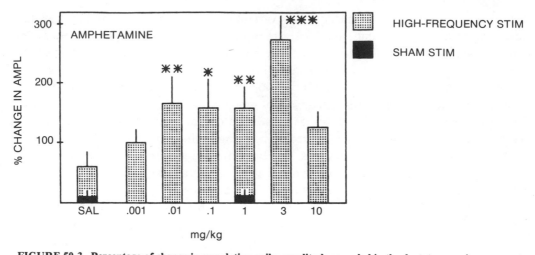

FIGURE 50-3. Percentage of change in population-spike amplitude recorded in the dentate gyrus in response to stimulation of the angular bundle. Anesthetized rats received saline or amphetamine injections 25 min prior to administration of 10 high-frequency stimulation trains. The results illustrated here are based on 10 averaged evoked responses taken 15–20 min after potentiation. Note that saline-treated and amphetamine-treated groups that did not receive the potentiation trains (small black bars) showed little change in population-spike amplitude over this interval. Those animals that received amphetamine injections prior to high-frequency stimulation (.01–3.0 mg/kg, i.p) exhibited enhanced potentiation. (*$p < .05$, **$p < .01$, ***$p < .001$). (From R. L. Delanoy, J. S. Merrin, & P. E. Gold, *Modulation of long-term potentiation (LTP) by adrenergic agonists.* Paper presented at the 12th Annual Meeting of the Society for Neuroscience, Minneapolis, 1982. Used by permission of the authors.)

Enduring Consequences of an Epinephrine Injection

There are several perspectives through which one might interpret memory modulation. In addition to the combined manipulation–correlation studies and the examinations of neuro-biological analogues of memory described here, the hormonal responses have also been considered to be part of a state that may be associated with the immediately preceding experience (Izquierdo, Perry, Dias, Souza, Elisabetsky, Carrasco, Orsingher, & Netto, 1981; Zornetzer, 1978). One interpretation of this view is that the central nervous system may store the information that a punctate neuroendocrine response has occurred. If so, evidence of a residual neurobiological consequence of the endocrine response should be discernible. The results of a recent set of experiments (Welsh & Gold, 1983) suggest that a single epinephrine injection may indeed have a long-lasting effect on brain function.

When administered once daily, electrical stimulation of the amygdala elicits pro-gressive increases in both brain and behavioral seizures (Goddard, 1969; Goddard, Mc-Naughton, Douglas, & Barnes, 1978). This phenomenon, termed "kindling," is often studied as a memory analogue because of the presistence of the neuronal changes. The increases in the seizures elicited by amygdala stimulation are often still evident months after the preceding trial (cf. McNamara, Byrne, Dashieff, & Fitz, 1980; Racine, 1978). Initially, we planned to examine neuroendocrine modulation of this phenomenon in a manner similar to that employed in the LTP studies. Our first results, however, have distracted us from this plan. These results indicate that a single epinephrine injection retards the development of kindling and does so in a proactive manner, lasting at least several days after the injection. The results of one experiment (Welsh & Gold, 1984) are illustrated in Figure 50-4. Animals received unilateral stimulation (250 μA, 60 Hz, .1 msec, 1-sec train) of the amygdala. This stimulation train is sufficient to elicit brief afterdischarges in all animals, but is below a level necessary to observe full behavioral convulsions. Animals that received a single epinephrine injection (2 mg/kg) 30 min or 24 hr prior to the first kindling trial developed longer afterdischarges and full behavioral convulsions at a rate that lagged behind that of the saline-treated animals by several days. Thus, a single epinephrine injection has a long-lasting effect on these measures (afterdischarge duration and behavioral convulsions) of brain function. These findings suggest the possibility that endogenous release of hormones may also be "stored" for a substantial period of time. Perhaps general views on the informational content of training experiences are too narrow and should be expanded to include mechanisms that underlie enduring consequences of relatively abrupt endocrine responses.

Concluding Remarks

This chapter begins with a review of the transition from using retrograde amnesia as a tool for defining psychological attributes of memory storage (short- and long-term memory) to procedurally analogous studies intended to identify biological processes that regulate the neuronal bases of memory formation. From both manipulations and measurements of

FIGURE 50-4. Effects of a single epinephrine injection (2 mg/kg) on later amgydala afterdischarge kindling. Rats received the injection 30 min prior to the first kindling trial (unilateral amygdala stimulation, 250 μA, 60 Hz, .1-msec pulses, 1-sec train). Note the apparent long-lasting retardation of the rate of kindling in those animals that received epinephrine. (From K. Welsh & P. E. Gold, Attenuation of epileptogenesis: Proactive effect of a single epinephrine injection of amygdaloid kindling. *Behavioral and Neural Biology*, 1984. Reprinted by permission.)

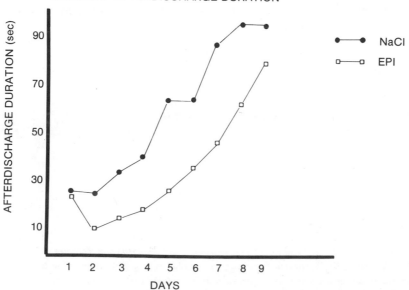

peripheral epinephrine, it is clear that this hormonal factor can modulate memory for several classes of learned responses. Furthermore, there is support for the view that peripheral catecholamine responses may underlie retrograde amnesia and memory enhancement produced by several treatments. In addition, peripheral catecholamines appear to have the capacity to modulate at least one form of neuroplasticity, LTP. By analogy, these results strengthen the notion that LTP may involve mechanisms used in memory storage. Furthermore, the findings suggest that peripheral adrenergic systems may regulate functional changes in the central nervous system. Finally, recent findings provide early indications that transient increases in peripheral catecholamine levels may themselves produce a long-lasting change in brain function (a form of memory storage?).

In this chapter, the primary example of a humoral factor important in memory modulation has been the adrenal medullary hormone, epinephrine. However, one should not conclude that epinephrine, compared to other hormonal or neurotransmitter systems, is necessarily unique in this regard. For example, comparable evidence could in many cases have been presented for brain norepinephrine (cf. Gold & McGaugh, 1978), vasopressin (van Wimersma Griedanus, Bohus, & de Wied, 1981), ACTH (Gold & Delanoy, 1981), opioids, and other endogenous peptides (cf. Martinez, Jensen, Messing, Rigter, & McGaugh, 1981). One should be aware that catecholamines, in particular, are likely to lead research on memory modulation—both because they are released by stressful situations, implying readily available correlative results in avoidance tasks, and because of the vast repertoire of drugs and assays available for this research. On the other side, for example, although support can be generated for the role of glutamate in memory (Baudry & Lynch, 1980), the lack of an appropriate collection of receptor agonists and antagonists or methods to study glutamate release and metabolism will undoubtably retard the development of our understanding of glutamate involvement in memory. Thus, the emphasis here on epinephrine may reflect a selection bias based on current methodological constraints. Because it may be impossible to manipulate a single hormonal system or transmitter system without simultaneously altering a host of other systems, it seems unlikely that we will identify single humoral factors responsible for memory modulation or memory storage. Instead, as comparable techniques became available for other neuromodulatory systems, it will be important to identify the role each plays in memory modulation and storage.

ACKNOWLEDGMENTS

This research was supported by grants from the National Institutes of Mental Health (MH 31141) and Aging (AG D1642) and by a fellowship from the James McKeen Cattell Foundation.

REFERENCES

Alpern, H. P., & McGaugh, J. L. Retrograde amnesia as a function of duration of electroshock stimulation. *Journal of Comparative and Physiological Psychology*, 1968, *65*, 265–269.
Axelrod, J., Weil-Malherbe, H., & Tomchick, R. The physiological disposition of ^{3}H epinephrine and its metabolite metanephrine. *Journal of Pharmacology and Experimental Therapy*, 1959, *127*, 251–256.
Baudry, M., & Lynch, G. Hypothesis regarding the cellular mechanisms responsible for long-term synaptic potentiation in the hippocampus. *Experimental Neurology*, 1980, *68*, 202–204.

Baust, W., Niemczyk, H., & Vieth, K. The action of blood pressure on the ascending reticular activating system with special reference to adrenalin-induced EEG arousal. *Electroencephalography and Clinical Neurophysiology*, 1963, *15*, 63–72.

Cherkin, A. Kinetics of memory consolidation: Role of amnesic treatment parameters. *Proceedings of the National Academy of Sciences USA, 1969, 63*, 1094–1101.

Chiueh, C. C., & Kopin, I. J. Hyperresponsivity of spontaneously hypertensive rats to indirect measurement of blood pressure. *American Journal of Physiology*, 1978, *234*, H690–H695.

Delanoy, R. L., Gold, P. E., & Tucci, D. L. Amphetamine effect on long-term potentiation of dentate granule cells. *Pharmacology, Biochemistry and Behavior*, 1983, *18*, 137–139.

Delanoy, R. L., Merrin, J. S., & Gold, P. E. *Modulation of long-term potentiation (LTP) by adrenergic agonists.* Paper presented at the 12th Annual Meeting of the Society for Neuroscience, Minneapolis, 1982.

Goddard, G. V. Component properties of the memory machine: Hebb revisited. In P. W. Jusczyk & R. M. Klein (Eds.), *The nature of thought: Essays in honor of D. O. Hebb.* Hillsdale, N.J.: Erlbaum, 1980.

Goddard, G. V., McNaughton, B. L., Douglas, R. M., & Barnes, C. A. Synaptic change in the limbic system: Evidence from studies using electrical stimulation with and without seizure activity. In K. E. Livingston & O. Hornykiewicz (Eds.), *Limbic mechanisms.* New York: Plenum Press, 1978.

Gold, P. E., & Delanoy, R. L. ACTH modulation of memory storage processing. In J. Martinez (Ed.), *Endogenous peptides and memory.* New York: Academic Press, 1981.

Gold, P. E., Macri, J., & McGaugh, J. L. Retrograde amnesia gradients: Effects of direct cortical stimulation. *Science*, 1973, *179*, 1343–1345.

Gold, P. E., & McCarty, R. Plasma catecholamines: Changes after footshock and seizure-producing frontal cortex stimulation. *Behavioral and Neural Biology*, 1981, *31*, 247–260.

Gold, P. E., McCarty, R., & Sternberg, D. B. Peripheral catecholamines and memory modulation. In C. Ajmone-Marsan & H. Matthies (Eds.), *Neuronal plasticity and memory formation.* New York: Raven Press, 1982.

Gold, P. E., & McGaugh, J. L. A single-trace, two-process view of memory storage processes. In D. Deutsch & J. A. Deutsch (Eds.), *Short-term memory.* New York: Academic Press, 1975.

Gold, P. E., & McGaugh, J. L. Endogenous modulators of memory storage processes. In L. Carenza, P. Pancherra, & L. Zichella (Eds.), *Clinical psychoneuroendocrinology in reproduction.* New York: Academic Press, 1978.

Gold, P. E., & Sternberg, D. B. Retrograde amnesia produced by serveral treatments: Evidence for a common neurobiological mechanism. *Science*, 1978, *201*, 367–369.

Gold, P. E., & van Buskirk, R. B. Facilitation of time-dependent memory processes with posttrial epinephrine injection. *Behavioral Biology*, 1975, *13*, 145–153.

Gold, P. E., & van Burskirk, R. B. Effect of posttrial hormone injections on memory processes. *Hormones and Behavior*, 1976, *7*, 509–517. (a)

Gold, P. E., & van Buskirk, R. B. Enhancement and impairment of memory processes with posttrial injections of adrenocorticotrophic hormone. *Behavioral Biology*, 1976, *16*, 387–400. (b)

Gold, P. E., & van Buskirk, R. B. Posttraining brain norepinephrine concentrations: Correlation with retention performance of avoidance training and with peripheral epinephrine modulation of memory processing. *Behavioral Biology*, 1978, *23*, 509–520.

Hall, M. E. Enhancement of learning by cycloheximide and DDC: A function of response strength. *Behavioral Biology*, 1977, *21*, 41–51.

Haycock, J. W., van Buskirk, R. B., & Gold, P. E. Effects on retention with posttraining amphetamine injections in mice: Interaction with pretraining experiences. *Psychopharmacologia*, 1977, *54*, 21–24.

Haycock, J. W., van Buskirk, R., & McGaugh, J. L. Facilitation of retention performance in mice by posttraining diethyldithiocarbamate. *Pharmacology, Biochemistry and Behavior*, 1976, *5*, 525–528.

Izquierdo, I., Perry, M. L., Dias, R. D., Souza, D. O., Elisabetsky, E., Carrasco, M. A., Orsingher, O. A., & Netto, C. A. Endogenous opioids, memory modulation, and state dependency. In J. L. Martinez, R. A. Jensen, R. B. Messing, H. Rigter, & J. L. McGaugh (Eds.), *Endogenous peptides and learning and memory processes.* New York: Academic Press, 1981.

Juraska, J., Greenough, W., Elliott, C., Mack, K., & Berkowitz, R. Plasticity in adult rat visual cortex: An examination of several cell populations after differential rearing. *Behavioral and Neural Biology*, 1980, *29*, 157–167.

Krivanek, J. Facilitation of avoidance learning by pentylenetetrazol as a function of task difficulty, deprivation and shock level. *Psychopharmacologia*, 1971, *20*, 213–229.

Krivanek, J. A., & McGaugh, J. L. Facilitating effects of pre- and post-trial amphetamine administration on discrimination learning in mice. *Agents and Actions*, 1969, *1*, 36–42.

Lynch, G., Browning, M., & Bennett, W. F. Biochemical and physiological studies of long-term synaptic plasticity. *Federation Proceedings*, 1979, *38*, 2117–2122.

Martinez, J. L., Jensen, R. A., Messing, R. B., Rigter, H., & McGaugh, J. L. (Eds.). *Endogenous peptides and learning and memory processes*. New York: Academic Press, 1981.

Martinez, J. L., Jensen, R. A., Messing, R. B., Vasquez, B. J., Soumieru-Mourat, B., Gedes, D., Liang, K. C., & McGaugh, J. L. Central and peripheral actions of amphetamine on memory storage. *Brain Research*, 1980, *182*, 157–166.

Martinez, J. L., Vasquez, B. J., Rigter, H., Messing, R. B., Jensen, R. A., Liang, K. C., & McGaugh, J. L. Attentuation of amphetamine-induced enhancement of learning by adrenal demedullation. *Brain Research*, 1980, *195*, 433–443.

McCarty, R., & Gold, P. E. Plasma catecholamines: Effects of footshock level and hormonal modulators of memory storage. *Hormones and Behavior*, 1981, *15*, 168–182.

McGaugh, J. L. A multi-trace view of memory storage. In D. Bovet, F. Bovet-Nitti, & A. Oliverio (Eds.), *Recent advances on learning and retention*. Rome: Roma Accademia Nazionale Dei Lincei, 1968.

McGaugh, J. L. Drug facilitation of learning and memory. *Annual Review of Pharmacology*, 1973, *13*, 229–241.

McGaugh, J. L., & Dawson, R. G. Modification of memory storage processes. In W. K. Honig & P. H. R. James (Eds.), *Animal memory*. New York: Academic Press, 1972.

McGaugh, J. L., & Herz, M. J. *Memory consolidation*. San Francisco: Albion, 1972.

McNamara, J. O., Byrne, M. C., Dashieff, R. M., & Fitz, J. C. The kindling model of epilepsy: A review. *Progress in Neurobiology*, 1980, *15*, 139–159.

Meligeni, J. L., Ledergerber, S., & McGaugh, J. L. Norepinephrine attenuation of diethyldithiocarbamate-induced amnesia. *Brain Research*, 1978, *149*, 155–164.

Novin, D., & Vanderweek, D. A. Visceral involvement in feeding: There is more to regulation than the hypothalamus. In J. M. Sprague & A. N. Epstein (Eds.), *Progress in psychobiology and physiological psychology*. New York: Academic Press, 1979.

Racine, R. J. Kindling: The first decade. *Neurosurgery*, 1978, *3*, 234–252.

Smith, G. P., & Gibbs, J. Postprandial satiety. In J. M. Sprague & A. N. Epstein (Eds.), *Progress in psychobiology and physiological psychology*. New York: Academic Press, 1979.

Sternberg, D. B., & Gold, P. G. Effects of α- and β-adrenergic receptor antagonists on retrograde amnesia produced by frontal cortex stimulation. *Behavioral and Neural Biology*, 1980, *29*, 289–302.

Sternberg, D. B., & Gold, P. E. Intraventricular adrenergic antagonists: Failure to attenuate retrograde amnesia. *Physiology and Behavior*, 1981, *27*, 551–555. (a)

Sternberg, D. B., & Gold, P. E. Retrograde amnesia produced by electrical stimulation of the amygdala: Attenuation with adrenergic antagonists. *Brain Research*, 1981, *211*, 59–65. (b)

Sternberg, D. B., Gold, P. E., & McGaugh, J. L. Memory facilitation and impairment with supraseizure electrical brain stimulation: Attenuation with pretrial propranolol injections. *Behavioral and Neural Biology*, 1983, *38*, 261–268.

Sternberg, D. B., Gold, P. E., & McGaugh, J. L. *Epinephrine enhancement of memory for appetitive training*. Manuscript in preparation, 1984.

Stone, E. A. Stress and catecholamines. In A. J. Friedhoff (Ed.), *Catecholamines and behavior* (Vol. 1). New York: Plenum Press, 1975.

van Wimersma Griedanus, T. B., Bohus, B., & de Wied, D. Vasopressin and oxytocin in learning and memory. In J. L. Martinez, R. A. Jensen, R. B. Messing, H. Rigter, & J. L. McGaugh (Eds.), *Endogenous peptides and learning and memory processes*. New York: Academic Press, 1981.

Walsh, T. J., & Palfai, T. Peripheral catecholamines and memory: Characteristics of syrosingopine-induced amnesia. *Pharmacology, Biochemistry and Behavior*, 1979, *11*, 449–452.

Welsh, K., & Gold, P. E. Attenuation of epileptogenesis: Proactive effect of a single epinephrine injection on amygdaloid kindling. *Behavioral and Neural Biology*, 1984, *40*, 179–185.

Zornetzer, S. F. Neurotransmitter modulation and memory: A new neuropharmacological phrenology. In M. S. Lipton, A. DiMascio, & K. F. Killam (Eds.), *Psychopharmacology: A generation of progress*. New York: Raven Press, 1978.

51

Neurochemical Modulation of Memory: A Case for Opioid Peptides

Michela Gallagher

In the years since Russell and Nathan's (1946) clinical description of retrograde amnesia in humans, a significant area of neurobiological research has focused on this interesting phenomenon. In the earliest investigation using laboratory animals, a potentially useful model of memory processes in humans was provided by the finding that posttraining administration of electroconvulsive shock could impair later retention of a recently learned response (Duncan, 1949). Providing a further parallel to the reports of retrograde amnesia in humans, the effects of posttraining treatments in other animals were found to be time-dependent; the sooner the agent was administered after training, the greater the amnesic effect (McGaugh, 1966). In the many studies conducted in the past few decades, effects on time-dependent memory have been demonstrated for a very large number of treatments (for recent reviews, see Dunn, 1980; Squire & Davis, 1981). However, the continued use of posttraining treatments to study memory has occurred against a background of changing views regarding the significance of the results obtained in these studies.

In the earliest theoretical formulations, the period of susceptibility to amnesic treatments was proposed to reflect the time course for the formation of a long-term memory for the training experience (McGaugh, 1966). Posttraining treatments were viewed as acting on a biological storage process independently of the many functions that operate during training (i.e., sensory processing, arousal, motivation, etc.). A major aim of the research conducted at that time was to identify the neural machinery for long-term memory formation in the brain. Treatments such as electrical stimulation of restricted brain regions and interference with selected biochemical and neurochemical processes were used as amnesic treatments that could potentially reveal the specific sites and mechanisms involved.

More recently, a growing interest has focused on the possibility that biological concomitants of arousal and/or affective states may modulate memory processes (Kety, 1970). Various authors have proposed that modulation of the neural changes underlying memory could arise from visceral/autonomic and neuroendocrine activity in the periphery, as well as from brain systems underlying the central processing of motivational and reinforcing aspects of experiences (Gold & McGaugh, 1975, 1978; Kety, 1970, 1976). Alterations in the activity of such systems could be elicited by training, and, in their persistence for a period of time after training, could contribute at least to the initial stages of the time-dependent process during which memories appear to achieve an increasingly

Michela Gallagher. Department of Psychology, University of North Carolina, Chapel Hill, North Carolina.

invulnerable state. Although memory for the content of an experience could still be viewed as occurring through modifications in selected synaptic connections within the neural circuitry of the brain, the control of these changes might be regulated by neural and hormonal influences arising from widespread activity in both the peripheral and central components of the nervous system. The adaptive advantage of such mechanisms, which would insure preservation of information about significant events, was emphasized originally by Kety (1970); in the past decade, some empirical support for this view has emerged from the work of a number of investigators (see de Wied & Bohus, 1979), and recent reviews in Martinez, Jensen, Messing, Rigter, & McGaugh, 1981).

Within this evolving framework, opioid peptides have recently attracted interest as contributing to some aspect of time-dependent memory. It has been natural to regard this system as providing a link between motivation and memory processes. Opiates are generally recognized to possess powerful mood-altering properties—in particular, decreasing affective responses to aversive stimuli. In addition, a number of reports have indicated that opioid peptide systems may be activated by noxious and/or stressful events, providing an endogenous mechanism that may be capable of attenuating the impact of aversive experiences on an animal (Barta & Yashpal, 1981; Madden, Akil, Patrick, & Barchas, 1977; Rossier, French, Rivier, Ling, Guillemin, & Bloom, 1977; Rossier, Guillemin, & Bloom, 1978). Within this context, the results of numerous studies using aversive training procedures might be consistent with the proposal that the effects of opiate treatments on time-dependent memory are due to the regulation of motivational states by opioid peptide systems.

In general, opiate agonists such as morphine and several opioid peptides have been found to produce retrograde amnesia when administered at low doses shortly after avoidance training (Castellano, 1975; Gallagher & Kapp, 1978; Izquierdo, 1979; Izquierdo & Dias, 1981; Izquierdo, Paiva, & Elisabetsky, 1980; Izquierdo, Sousa, Carrasco, Dias, Perry, Eisinger, Elisabetsky, & Vendite, 1980; Jensen, Martinez, Messing, Spiehler, Vasquez, Soumireu-Mourat, Liang, & McGaugh, 1978; Kovács, Bohus, & de Wied, 1981; Martinez & Rigter, 1980). These effects have been shown to be time-dependent, and in a number of these investigations the effects of agonists were blocked by concurrent posttraining administration of the opiate antagonist naloxone (Castellano, 1975; Gallagher & Kapp, 1978; Izquierdo, 1979; Izquierdo, Sousa, Carrasco, Dias, Perry, Eisinger, Elisabetsky, & Vendite, 1980). Based on these studies, it appears that activation of opiate receptor mechanisms for a period of time after training can impair retention of recent learning. Perhaps more compelling evidence that opioid peptides normally regulate some aspect of memory processes is provided by the consistent finding that posttraining administration of naloxone by itself produces increased retention—an effect that has also been reported to be time-dependent (Gallagher, 1982a, 1982b; Gallagher & Kapp, 1978; Izquierdo, 1979; Messing, Jensen, Martinez, Spiehler, Vasquez, Soumireu-Mourat, Liang, & McGaugh, 1979; Zimmerman, Gorelick, & Colber, 1980). The interpretation that this effect of naloxone is due to its specific opiate antagonist property was strongly supported by the results of a recent study conducted in our laboratory, in which we found that retention of passive-avoidance conditioning in rats could be enhanced by a variety of opiate antagonist agents, including naloxone, naltrexone, diprenorphine, and levallorphan (Gallagher, 1982a, 1982b). In agreement with the characterization of opiate receptors, we also reported that enhancement of retention exhibited stereospecificity for one of these agents. Dextrallorphan, the inactive enantiomer of levallorphan, produced no effect on retention. These results indicate that blocking opiate receptors can enhance retention of avoidance conditioning.

A strikingly consistent pattern of results has emerged from these studies using aversive training procedures: It has been demonstrated that impairment and enhancement of time-dependent memory can be produced by agonist and antagonist treatment, respectively. These effects could be related to a selective shift in motivational processes, with agonists attenuating the posttraining state of some systems normally activated by aversive inputs and antagonists enhancing or prolonging these activities. Although this interpretation addresses the results of studies that have used avoidance training procedures, it fails to account for the results of recent studies indicating that posttraining opiate treatments can also alter retention of nonaversive experiences. The results of studies using nonaversive tasks have shown that retention may be altered in a manner paralleling that observed when aversive training procedures are used (Bostock & Gallagher, 1982; Gallagher, King, & Young, 1983; Izquierdo, 1979; Izquierdo & Graudenz, 1980).

We have recently observed that posttraining administration of an opiate antagonist enhances later performance on a food-rewarded task. Our experiments with rats were based on testing procedures previously developed to examine a form of maze learning. Olton and Samuelson (1976) first reported that rats can be readily trained to visit each arm of an elevated eight-arm radial maze only once during a session, when a food pellet is placed at the end of each arm. Animals normally learn to perform this task accurately by identifying and remembering each arm of the maze, based on information provided by spatial cues in the environment surrounding the test apparatus (O'Keefe & Conway, 1978; Suzuki, Augerinos, & Black, 1980). In other words, the places on the maze are identified by their location in the testing room. This task has been used as a memory-testing procedure by introducing a delay between the fourth and fifth arm choices, and recent studies indicate that rats can remember the initial four arm choices and can accurately choose the remaining four arms at delays up to approximately 6 hours (Beatty & Shavalia, 1980a, 1980b).

In our experiments, rats were initially trained on an eight-arm maze to a criterion performance consisting of no more than two errors on 3 consecutive days, using a 6-hour delay imposed between the fourth and fifth arm choices. Experimental testing occurred following this initial training, when rats were challenged by placing the maze in new spatial environments (new rooms). In the new rooms, posttraining drug or vehicle injections occurred immediately after the initial four arm choices, at the beginning of a 6-hour delay, on each day of testing until criterion performance was achieved. A within-subjects design was used, in which the same animals received experimental and control treatments in different new rooms.

The effects of posttraining opiate antagonist administration on the development of criterion performance in new spatial environments are presented in Table 51-1. In this experiment, two groups of rats received initial training, and then both groups were tested in two novel environments. For each group, an opiate antagonist—either naloxone (2 mg/kg) or diprenorphine (1 mg/kg)—was administered following the first four arm choices in one of the new rooms, and posttraining injections of the saline vehicle were administered when rats were tested in the other room. The order of opiate antagonist and saline treatments was counterbalanced for both groups. Compared to the saline treatment condition, posttraining opiate antagonist administration enhanced maze performance.

TABLE 51-1. Effects of Posttraining Opiate Antagonist Administration on Maze Performance

Treatment condition	Trials to criterion (mean $\pm$ SEM)	Errors to criterion (mean $\pm$ SEM)
Saline treatment		
Naloxone group[a]	5.38 $\pm$ .71	12.0 $\pm$ 2.89
Diprenorphine group[b]	4.90 $\pm$ .70	12.2 $\pm$ 3.03
Opiate antagonist treatment		
Naloxone group[a]	3.25 $\pm$ .63*	4.4 $\pm$ 2.74*
Diprenorphine group[b]	3.60 $\pm$ .49*	5.8 $\pm$ 2.89*

[a] $n = 8$.
[b] $n = 10$.
*$p < .005$ compared to saline treatment.

Compared to their performance in the saline condition, every animal in the naloxone treatment group took fewer trials to reach criterion in the naloxone condition. Diprenorphine also reliably enhanced performance on this task, as reflected in significantly fewer trials to criterion and fewer errors when compared to the performance of the same animals in the saline condition.

In a subsequent experiment, 10 additional rats received initial maze training as described above, followed by testing in four different novel environments. In these environments, animals received either no treatment, posttraining injection of the saline vehicle, naloxone (2 mg/kg) administration immediately after the first four arm choices, or naloxone (2 mg/kg) administration at a 2-hour delay after the first four arm choices. The results of this experiment, which are presented in Table 51-2, indicate that the effect of posttraining naloxone administration on this task appears to be time-dependent. Whereas the naloxone/no-delay treatment significantly enhanced maze performance when compared to both of the control (no treatment, saline vehicle) conditions, the naloxone/2-hour-delay treatment did not significantly alter performance.

The results of these experiments are consistent with the observations of Collier, Miller, Quirk, Travis, and Routtenberg (1981), who used a food-rewarded spatial learning task and reported that naloxone administration prevented retrograde amnesia, which had been produced by electrical stimulation of the hippocampal formation. These studies may indicate that interfering with activation of opiate receptors can also improve time-

TABLE 51-2. Time-Dependent Effects of Posttraining Naloxone Administration on Maze Performance

Treatment condition	Trials to criterion (mean $\pm$ SEM)	Errors to criterion (mean $\pm$ SEM)
No treatment	4.7 $\pm$ .64	11.2 $\pm$ 3.12
Saline	4.8 $\pm$ .75	10.6 $\pm$ 3.29
Naloxone/no delay	3.5 $\pm$ .67*	3.7 $\pm$ 1.27*
Naloxone/2-hour delay	4.0 $\pm$ .89	7.0 $\pm$ 2.93

*$p < .001$ compared to control treatments.

dependent memory when rewarding, rather than aversive, stimuli are used in the training procedure.

Of further interest are the results of studies that have examined the effects of posttraining treatments on retention of nonreinforced presentations of stimuli. Izquierdo and colleagues were the first to report that posttraining opiate treatments altered retention of a nonaversive experience, as reflected in habituation to presentations of an auditory stimulus (Izquierdo, 1979; Izquierdo & Graudenz, 1980; Izquierdo, Paiva, & Elisabetsky, 1980). Administration of morphine or opioid peptides after repeated presentations of a tone was reported to decrease retention of habituation in rats tested 24 hours later. Enhancement of retention was observed when naloxone was administered immediately after the habituation session. The results from these studies are consistent with our recent report that naloxone administration can also enhance retention of nonreinforced exposure to an auditory stimulus, as reflected in subsequent increased latent inhibition of classically conditioned heart rate responding in rabbits (Bostock & Gallagher, 1982).

Although these investigations using nonaversive tasks are as yet few in number, the results are quite consistent. When viewed together with the results of investigations using aversive training procedures, it appears that opiate treatments can produce comparable effects on retention, independent of the specific reinforcement contingencies or even the presence or absence of reinforcement during training. Within the context of the previous discussion, any selective shift in affect or in the value of reinforcement, either less negative or more positive, produced by opiates would not be predicted to produce comparable effects on retention across these different tasks. These collective findings pose an interesting challenge to the view that modulation of memory may occur through the activity of systems primarily linked to the motivational and/or reinforcing aspects of the experiences to be remembered.

However, a more general role for opiate-sensitive mechanisms in memory processes may be related to recent suggestions that opioid peptides regulate some aspect of selective attention. Opiate antagonist administration has been reported to increase measures of selective attention in humans (Arnsten, Segal, Neville, & Hillyard, 1981; Gritz, Shiffman, Jarvik, Schlesinger, & Charuvastra, 1976) and in rats (Arnsten & Segal, 1979; Arnsten, Segal, Loughlin, & Roberts, 1981). In rats, the enhancement observed with naloxone was found to be stereospecific, and low doses of morphine were found to produce an opposite effect. Perhaps it may be reasonable to propose that biological systems that serve to regulate the processing of salient stimuli during initial exposure may also modulate storage of the information provided by those events. This proposal is a more general statement of the view that changes in the activity of biological systems that are brought about during significant experiences (i.e., those with either rewarding or aversive value) may contribute to a state that is conducive to the changes in neural function underlying memory. Memory modulation may also be provided by systems linked to the sampling and processing of environmental events, independent of the reinforcing properties of these events. This suggestion would be particularly consistent with the results of studies examining the effects of opiates, both agonist and antagonist, on memory for nonreinforced exposure to stimuli (i.e., retention of habituation and latent inhibition).

An understanding of the functional significance of opioid peptide influences on memory would be aided by identification of the specific components of opioid peptide systems that are involved. A number of different opioid peptides are found in the periphery as well as in the central nervous system, with different patterns of distribution (e.g., see Sar, Stumpf, Miller, Chang, & Cuatrecasas, 1978; Watson, Khachturian, Coy, Taylor, & Akil, 1982). In light of the heterogeneity of opioid peptides the uniform effects of posttraining opiate treatments on retention across a variety of tasks may not even reflect a common underlying mechanism.

Although little is known about which components of opioid peptide systems are involved in memory, it has been demonstrated that opiate-sensitive mechanisms within the amygdala complex contribute to memory processes, at least when an aversive conditioning procedure is used (Gallagher & Kapp, 1978). We reported that microinjections of opiates, both agonist and antagonist, into the amygdala complex of rats after passive-avoidance training produce effects on retention that are comparable to those produced by systemic drug administration. Opiate agonist administration into the amygdala produced retrograde amnesia, an effect that was shown to be stereospecific and time-dependent. Opiate antagonist administration, by itself, increased retention of passive-avoidance conditioning; this effect was also found to be time-dependent. Some of the results from this study are presented in Figure 51-1. It is important to note that no effects on retention of passive-avoidance conditioning have been observed when posttraining opiate injections are made into some other brain structures containing high concentrations of opioid peptides, including the basal ganglia and periaqueductal gray (Gallagher & Kapp, 1978; Kesner & Calder, 1980). Therefore, not all components of brain opioid peptide systems serve a comparable memory function.

At a time when studies on opiates and memory had almost exclusively involved the use of aversive training procedures, we suggested that opiate-sensitive mechanisms within the amygdala might provide an interface between motivational states and memory processes (Gallagher & Kapp, 1981). This suggestion was originally based on a variety of evidence indicating that a component of the neural circuitry within the amygdala complex is part of a brain system that regulates the arousal of negative affective responses (i.e., fear) to both conditioned and unconditioned aversive or threatening stimuli. Indeed, our proposal that opiate-sensitive sites within the amygdala might be capable of altering the arousal of fear

FIGURE 51-1. Effects of opiate agents administered into the amygdala complex immediately after training on retention of passive avoidance. Median retention latencies and intraquartile ranges are given for groups of rats (n's = 7–10). Control groups consisted of an unoperated group and a vehicle-injected group, which did not differ from each other. Significant decreases and increases in retention were produced by agonist (levorphanol) and antagonist (naloxone) administration, respectively ($p < .02$, Mann–Whitney U test, two-tailed).

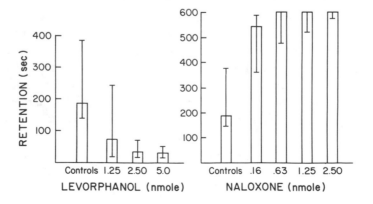

was also found to be consistent with the effects of opiate manipulations in the amygdala on the acquisition of a learned response in rabbits when a Pavlovian fear-conditioning procedure was used (Gallagher, Kapp, McNall, & Pascoe, 1981). Since more recent evidence indicates that the effects of posttraining opiate treatment are not restricted to memories acquired through aversive training, it may now be interesting to examine whether intracranial opiate manipulations within the amygdala complex alter retention when nonaversive tasks are employed. The results of such investigations may further contribute to our understanding of amygdala opioid peptide function and may also serve as one approach to the question of whether a common mechanism underlies the apparently similar effects of opiate treatments on time-dependent memory across a variety of testing procedures.

REFERENCES

Arnsten, A. T., & Segal, D. S. Naloxone alters locomotion and interaction with environmental stimuli. *Life Sciences*, 1979, *25*, 1035–1042.

Arnsten, A. T., Segal, D. S., Loughlin, S. E., & Roberts, D. C. S. Evidence for an interaction of opioid and noradrenergic locus coeruleus systems in the regulation of environmental stimulus directed behavior. *Brain Research*, 1981, *222*, 351–363.

Arnsten, A., Segal, D. S., Neville, H., & Hillyard, S. Naloxone augments electrophysiological measures of selective attention in man. *Society for Neuroscience Abstracts*, 1981, *7*, 659.

Barta, A., & Yashpal, K. Regional redistribution of β-endorphin in the rat brain: The effect of stress. *Progress in Neuro-Psychopharmacology*, 1981, *5*, 595–598.

Beatty, W. W., & Shavalia, D. A. Rat spatial memory: Resistance to interference at long retention intervals. *Animal Learning*, 1980, *8, 550*–552. (a)

Beatty, W. W., & Shavalia, D. A. Spatial memory in rats: Time course of working memory and effect of anesthetics. *Behavioral and Neural Biology*, 1980, *28*, 454–462. (b)

Bostock, E., & Gallagher, M. Naloxone-induced facilitation of latent inhibition in rabbits. *Society for Neuroscience Abstracts*, 1982, *8*, 148.

Castellano, C. Effects of morphine and heroin on discrimination learning and consolidation in mice. *Psychopharmacologia (Berlin)*, 1975, *42*, 235–242.

Collier, T. J., Miller, S., Quirk, G., Travis, J., & Routtenberg, A. Remembering rewards in the environment: Endogenous hippocampal opiates modulate reinforcement memory associations. *Society for Neuroscience Abstracts*, 1981, *7*, 359.

de Wied, D., & Bohus, B. Modulation of memory processes by neuropeptides of hypothalamic–neurohypophyseal origin. In M. A. B. Brazier (Ed.), *Brain mechanisms in memory and learning: From the single neuron to man*. New York: Raven Press, 1979.

Duncan, C. P. The retroactive effect of electroshock on learning. *Journal of Comparative and Physiological Psychology*, 1949, *42*, 32–44.

Dunn, A. J. Neurochemistry of learning and memory: An evaluation of recent data. *Annual Review of Psychology*, 1980, *31*, 343–390.

Gallagher, M. Facilitation of retention for passive avoidance conditioning produced by opiate antagonists. *Society for Neuroscience Abstracts*, 1982, *8*, 148. (a)

Gallagher, M. Naloxone enhancement of memory processes: Effects of other opiate antagonists. *Behavioral and Neural Biology*, 1982, *35*, 375–382. (b)

Gallagher, M., & Kapp, B. S. Manipulation of opiate activity in the amygdala alters memory processes. *Life Sciences*, 1978, *23*, 1973–1978.

Gallagher, M., & Kapp, B. S. Influence of amygdala opiate-sensitive mechanisms, fear-motivated responses, and memory processes for aversive experiences. In J. L. Martinez, Jr., R. A. Jensen, R. B. Messing, H. Rigter, & J. L. McGaugh (Eds.), *Endogenous peptides and learning and memory processes*. New York: Academic Press, 1981.

Gallagher, M., Kapp, B. S., McNall, C. L., & Pascoe, J. P. Opiate effects in the amygdala central nucleus on heart rate conditioning in rabbits. *Pharmacology, Biochemistry and Behavior*, 1981, *14*, 497–505.

Gallagher, M., King, R. A., & Young, N. B. Opiate antagonists improve memory. *Science*, 1983, *221*, 975–976.

Gold, P. E., & McGaugh, J. L. A single-trace, two-process view of memory storage processes. In D. Deutsch & J. A. Deutsch (Eds.), *Short-term memory*. New York: Academic Press, 1975.

Gold, P. E., & McGaugh, J. L. Neurobiology and memory: Modulators, correlates and assumptions. In T. Teyler (Ed.), *Brain and learning*. Stamford, Conn.: Greylock, 1978.

Gritz, E. R., Shiffman, S. M., Jarvik, M. E., Schlesinger, J., & Charuvastra, V. C. Naltrexone: Physiological and psychological effects of single doses. *Clinical Pharmacology and Therapeutics*, 1976, *19*, 773–776.

Izquierdo, I. Effect of naloxone and morphine on various forms of memory in the rat: Possible role of endogenous opiate mechanisms in memory consolidation. *Psychopharmacology*, 1979, *66*, 199–203.

Izquierdo, I., & Dias, R. D. Retrograde amnesia caused by Met-, Leu-, and dis-Tyr-Met-enkephalin in the rat and its reversal by naloxone. *Neuroscience Letters*, 1981, *22*, 189–193.

Izquierdo, I., & Graudenz, M. Memory facilitation by naloxone is due to release of dopaminergic and beta-adrenergic systems from tonic inhibition. *Psychopharmacology*, 1980, *67*, 265–268.

Izquierdo, I., Paiva, A. C. M., & Elisabetsky, E. Posttraining intraperitoneal administration of Leu-enkephalin and beta-endorphin causes retrograde amnesia for two different tasks in rats. *Behavioral and Neural Biology*, 1980, *28*, 246–250.

Izquierdo, I., Sousa, D. O., Carrasco, M. A., Dias, R. R., Perry, M. L., Eisinger, S., Elisabetsky, E., & Vendite, D. A. Beta-endorphin causes retrograde amnesia and is released from the rat brain by various forms of training and stimulation. *Psychopharmacology*, 1980, *70*, 173–177.

Jensen, R. A., Martinez, J. L., Jr., Messing, R. B., Spiehler, V., Vasquez, B. J., Soumireu-Mourat, B., Liang, K. C., & McGaugh, J. L. Morphine and naloxone alter memory in the rat. *Society for Neuroscience Abstracts*, 1978, *4*, 260.

Kesner, R. P., & Calder, L. D. Rewarding periaqueductal gray stimulation disrupts long-term memory for passive avoidance learning. *Behavioral and Neural Biology*, 1980, *30*, 237–249.

Kety, S. The biogenic amines in the central nervous system: Their possible roles in arousal, emotion and learning. In F. O. Schmitt (Ed.), *The neurosciences: Second study program*. Cambridge, Mass.: MIT Press, 1970.

Kety, S. Biological concomitants of affective states and their possible role in memory processes. In M. R. Rosenzweig & E. L. Bennett (Eds.), *Neural mechanisms of learning and memory*. Cambridge, Mass.: MIT Press, 1976.

Kovács, G. L., Bohus, B., & de Wied, D. Retention of passive avoidance behavior in rats following α- and γ-endorphin administration: Effects of post-learning treatments. *Neuroscience Letters*, 1981, *22*, 79–82.

Madden, J., IV, Akil, H., Patrick, R. L., & Barchas, J. D. Stress induced parallel changes in central opioid levels and pain responsiveness in the rat. *Nature*, 1977, *265*, 358–360.

Martinez, J. L., Jr., & Rigter, H. Endorphins alter acquisition and consolidation of an inhibitory avoidance response in rats. *Neuroscience Letters*, 1980, *19*, 197–201.

Martinez, J. L., Jr., Jensen, R. A., Messing, R. B., Rigter, H., & McGaugh, J. L. (Eds.). *Endogenous peptides and learning and memory processes*. New York: Academic Press, 1981.

McGaugh, J. L. Time-dependent processes in memory storage. *Science*, 1966, *153*, 1351–1358.

Messing, R. B., Jensen, R. A., Martinez, J. L., Jr., Spiehler, V. R., Vasquez, B. J., Soumireu-Mourat, B., Liang, K. C., & McGaugh, J. L. Naloxone enhancement of memory. *Behavioral and Neural Biology*, 1979, *27*, 266–275.

O'Keefe, J., & Conway, D. H. Hippocampal place units in the freely moving rat: Why they fire when they fire. *Experimental Brain Research*, 1978, *31*, 573–590.

Olton, D. S., & Samuelson, R. J. Remembrance of places past: Spatial memory in rats. *Journal of Experimental Psychology: Animal Behavior Processes*, 1976, *2*, 97–116.

Rossier, J., French, E. D., Rivier, C., Ling, N., Guillemin, R., & Bloom F. Foot-shock induced stress increases β-endorphin levels in blood but not brain. *Nature*, 1977, *270*, 618–620.

Rossier, J., Guillemin, R., & Bloom, F. Foot-shock induced stress decreases Leu^5-enkephalin immunoreactivity in rat hypothalamus. *European Journal of Pharmacology*, 1978, *48*, 465–466.

Russell, W. R., & Nathan, P. W. Traumatic amnesia. *Brain*, 1946, *69*, 280–300.

Sar, M., Stumpf, W. E., Miller, R. J., Chang, K. J., & Cuatrecasas, P. Immunohistochemical localization of enkephalin in rat brain and spinal cord. *Journal of Comparative Neurology*, 1978, *182*, 17–38.

Squire, L. R., & Davis, H. P. The pharmacology of memory: A neurobiological perspective. *Annual Review of Pharmacology and Toxicology*, 1981, *21*, 323–356.

Suzuki, S., Augerinos, G., & Black, A. H. Stimulus control of spatial behavior on the eight-arm maze in rats. *Learning and Motivation*, 1980, *11*, 1–18.

Watson, S. J., Khachturian, H., Coy, D., Taylor, L., & Akil, H. Dynorphin is located throughout the CNS and is often co-localized with alpha-neo-endorphin. *Life Sciences*, 1982, *31*, 1773–1776.

Zimmerman, E. G., Gorelick, D. A., & Colber, D. L. Facilitation of passive avoidance behavior by post-trial administration of naloxone and ethanol in mice. *Society for Neuroscience Abstracts*, 1980, *6*, 167.

Brain Substrates of Senescent Memory Decline　52

Steven F. Zornetzer

Overview

My intent in this chapter is to discuss memory decline in aging. Since good and extensive reviews of this general area have been written recently (Dean, Scozzafava, Goas, Regan, Beer, & Bartus, 1981; Jensen, Messing, Martinez, Vasquez, Spiehler, & McGaugh, 1981; Kubanis & Zornetzer, 1981), I focus this chapter upon a more narrow consideration of the possible etiological factors underlying senescent memory decline. Specifically, I review and evaluate the so-called "cholinergic hypothesis" of age-related memory decline. I give reasons why I feel this hypothesis is too narrow to account for the data; I consider an alternative, or at least supplemental, hypothesis that I feel is both more robust and testable; finally, I will describe recent work done in my laboratory that reflects upon these issues.

There is an important caveat that needs to be mentioned from the outset. The study of neurobiological and associated behavioral changes occurring with normal aging is often blurred by the study of these same phenomena in age-related pathological conditions. This is best illustrated by the recent proliferation of interest in, and new data pertaining to senile dementia of the Alzheimer type (SDAT). If, as some have suggested (see below), SDAT is nothing more than an acceleration of normal aging processes, the data obtained from normal aging animals (which do not develop SDAT) may indeed be a valid model for studying some aspects of human SDAT. Conversely, clinical-pathological correlates of human SDAT may provide important insights into normal aging. Of course, we should keep in mind that this need not be the case at all, and that the basic assumption may be faulty (e.g., data obtained from normal aged organisms might have little or no relationship to SDAT, and vice versa).

Background and Rationale

A common deficit in both normal aging and SDAT is a decline in memory. The dramatic loss of cholinergic neurons observed in SDAT has led to the hypothesis that degeneration of cholinergic systems may be responsible for the loss of higher-order function in these individuals. Recent data suggest that there is a relation between the severity of the clinical expression of SDAT and transmitter-specific changes in cholinergic neurons located in the basal forebrain (Bowen, Smith, White, Goodhart, Spillane, Flack, & Davison, 1977;

Steven F. Zornetzer. Office of Naval Research, Arlington, Virginia.

Davies & Maloney, 1976; Perry, Perry, Blessed, & Tomlinson, 1977). These changes are believed to occur specifically in magnocellular cholinergic basal forebrain systems located in the medial septum, diagonal band of Broca, and nucleus basalis of Meynert. These data, coupled with the recent hypothesis (Price, Whitehouse, Struble, Clark, Coyle, Delong, & Hedreen, 1982) that degenerating cholinergic neurons and terminals originating in basal forebrain give rise to neuritic plaques, support the growing conventional wisdom that pathogenetic processes primary to the basal forebrain cholinergic system are closely associated with SDAT.

Since SDAT is thought to represent an acceleration of normal aging processes, it has been proposed that cholinergic dysfunction may underlie normal age-related memory deficits (Drachman & Leavitt, 1974; Drachman & Sahakian, 1980). The finding that, in young subjects, blockade of cholinergic systems results in interruption of normal memory processes (Drachman, 1977) has strengthened this hypothesis. Disturbingly, however, interventive strategies designed to stimulate cholinergic systems have not resulted in significant generalized improvement in age-related memory loss (Ferris, Sathananthan, Reisberg, & Gershon, 1979; Mohs, Davis, Tinklenberg, Hollister, 1980; Mohs, Davis, Tinklenberg, Hollister, Yesavage, & Kopell, 1979; Vroulis & Smith, 1981).

The Plot Thickens

Although basal forebrain cholinergic activity has taken "center stage" with respect to its pathogenetic importance in age-related memory loss, it is very unlikely, given our current knowledge of brain complexity, that any single neurotransmitter would selectively and exclusively be involved in disorders of cognitive function and memory (cf. Zornetzer, 1978). Other neurotransmitter systems have been implicated in normal memory processes, particularly catecholamines and opioids (Gallagher & Kapp, 1978; Messing, Jensen, Martinez, Spiehler, Vasquez, Soumireu-Mourat, Liang, & McGaugh, 1979; Stein, Belluzzi, & Wise, 1975; Zornetzer, Abraham, & Appleton, 1978). A growing literature has also described multiple neurochemical (Finch, 1978; Maggi, Schmidt, Ghetti, & Enna, 1979; Ponzio, Brunello, & Algeri, 1978; Simpkins, Mueller, Huang, & Meites, 1977), neuro-anatomical (Brizzee & Ordy, 1979; Landfield, Rose, Sandles, Wohlstadter, & Lynch, 1977; Rogers, Silver, Shoemaker, & Bloom, 1980; Sladek & Sladek, 1979), and behavioral (Barnes, 1979; Bartus, 1979; Bartus, Dean, & Flemming, 1979; Gold & McGaugh, 1975; Kubanis, Gobbel, & Zornetzer, 1981; Zornetzer, Thompson, & Rogers, 1982) changes in aged animals. It is therefore possible that age-related memory deficits may result from concurrent changes in several neurotransmitter systems. This point can be made even more strongly in the case of SDAT, in which there is widespread degeneration and cell loss seen in postmortem tissue (cf. Brody, 1955, 1970, 1976). Rather than review the entire morphological and neurotransmitter literature on age-related brain changes, let us focus upon available data for noncholinergic neuronal systems believed to employ primarily a single neurotransmitter. For purposes of both example and personal interest, the paragraphs below focus on the noradrenergic nucleus locus ceruleus (LC).

Vijayashanker and Brody (1979) were the first to report significant cell loss of LC neurons in senescent human brain. These data were extended by Bondereff, Mountjoy, and Roth (1982), who recently reported that in patients with SDAT, cell loss in LC was significantly greater than occurred with normal aging. Further, two subclasses of SDAT patients could be identified: a group having severe cognitive impairment and 80% cell loss in LC, and a less impaired group with correspondingly less LC cell loss. These data are particularly exciting, for a number of reasons. First, this system, like the basal forebrain cholinergic system, constitutes a neurotransmitter-specific (specific to norepinephrine, or NE) brain region that shows significant cell loss with both normal aging and SDAT. Second, and importantly, the extent of cell loss in LC appears directly correlated with the degree of impaired cognitive function. This second point is interesting, in that it parallels the observations and speculations that the four major pathomnemonic findings in Alzheimer disease (neurofibrillary tangles, senile plaques, granulo-vacuolar degeneration, and Hirano bodies) are similarly related in prevalence to the severity of impaired cognitive function. Accordingly, all of these changes are also found in normal aged brains, but they are quantitatively more frequent in SDAT brain (Appel, 1981). These data from the noradrenergic LC suggest that age-related cognitive decline may be quantitatively related to transmitter-specific dysfunction(s).

Age-related LC cell loss can also be related to melanin and/or lipofuscin accumulation in pigmented cells. Mann and Yates (1974a, 1974b) reported a linear increase in melanin content in cells of the human LC and substantia nigra from birth to age 60. Beyond the age of 60 there is a decline in mean melanin content, which has been attributed to selective degeneration of the most heavily pigmented cells. One interpretation of these data is that melanin, and possibly lipofuscin, accumulation interferes with essential cellular biosynthetic and metabolic systems, ultimately leading to cell death.

Other, more functional data support these morphological findings regarding catecholamine-specific cell loss in normal aging and SDAT. Several investigations have reported reduced activity of catecholamine systems in aged rat brain (Algeri, 1978; Finch, 1973, 1976). Further, a reduced activity with age of tyrosine hydroxylase, the rate-limiting enzyme in the synthesis of catecholamines, has been reported for humans (Cote & Kremzner, 1974; McGeer, Fibiger, McGeer, & Wickson, 1971; McGeer & McGeer, 1973) and rodents (Algeri, 1978). Postmortem studies in humans have reported reduced levels of dopamine (DA) and NE related to age (Adolfsson, Goffries, Roos, & Winblad, 1979; Carlsson & Winblad, 1976).

Clearly, from this brief discussion of the data describing age-related changes in catecholamine systems, there is good reason for us to consider the possibility that these systems, particularly the noradrenergic nucleus LC, may be as important as the age-related changes occurring in basal forebrain cholinergic systems, which have received greater attention. Further, there is considerable additional support for the idea that the LC system plays an essential modulatory role in metabolic (Abraham, Delanoy, Dunn, & Zornetzer, 1979), sensory–motor (Aston-Jones & Bloom, 1981), attentional (Mason, 1981), and higher-order (memory) functions (Zornetzer et al., 1978) in normal aged subjects. These data, coupled with both published and new data from my own laboratory, strongly reinforce the hypothesis that functional decline of the noradrenergic LC system may be directly implicated in normal age-related cognitive decline and the more precipitous functional decline observed in SDAT.

Recent anatomical studies have suggested that there are several brain loci where functional interactions could occur among the LC, nucleus basalis, and other neurotransmitter-defined systems of interest (e.g., the DA cells of the substantia nigra–ventral tegmental area and the widespread opiate-containing systems). Of particular interest in this chapter are the interactions between noradrenergic (NE) neurons of the LC and cholinergic neurons (acetylcholine, or ACh) of the nucleus basalis. Although it is known that LC axons traverse the basal forebrain regions that contain nucleus basalis neurons (Fallon, 1983a; Fallon, Kozrell, & Moore, 1978; Fallon & Moore, 1978), there has not been convincing evidence that LC innervates these neurons. Based on the density of the LC fibers in these regions, such a projection would be sparse at best. Likewise, a projection from nucleus basalis neurons to the LC has not been demonstrated. The presence of moderately dense acetylcholinesterase (AChE)-positive neuropil in, and around, the LC could be the dendrites of AChE-positive cells (cholinoceptive but not cholinergic) or another cholinergic input. A more likely site of noradrenergic–cholinergic interaction is in cerebral cortex, where dense noradrenergic innervation (Morrison, Grzanna, Molliver, & Coyle, 1978) and cholinergic innervation (Jacobowitz & Palkovitz, 1974) overlap, especially in layers I and II. A more isolated, but nonetheless dense, catecholamine innervation of layer II of supragenual cortex arises in the central tegmental area (Lindvall, Bjorklund, Moore, & Stenevi, 1974; Moore & Bloom, 1978). Connections between the two major catecholamine cell groups provide a second level of interaction. These include the innervation of the LC by the ventral tegmental area and a possible reciprocal innervation of the ventral tegmental area by the LC (Jones & Moore, 1977).

Another important consideration to keep in mind is the role of opiate interactions with the catecholamine and cholinergic systems. In this regard, there is some evidence for anatomical projections of opiate-containing neurons to cholinergic neurons of the basal forebrain (Fallon, 1983b) and LC (Herkenham & Pert, 1982). Reciprocal projections of the cell groups to opiate-containing cells are unknown, but based on the widespread localization of opiate cell bodies and terminals, such connections may exist and could be significant in the etiology of SDAT.

As an interim summary, it can be concluded that at least 10 projections could account for interactions among cholinergic, catecholaminergic, and opiate systems as they relate to SDAT. The regions of greatest potential for interaction of cholinergic and catecholaminergic systems are the superficial layers of the cerebral cortex.

The LC and Age-Related Memory Decline

In 1976, studies were begun in young adult rodents that implicated an important role of the nucleus LC in memory processes (Zornetzer et al., 1978; Zornetzer & Gold, 1976). These studies were amplified and further supported by others (see Gold & Zornetzer, 1983, and Zornetzer, 1978, for reviews). One particularly interesting study (Stein et al., 1975) reported that pharmacological inhibition of brain NE synthesis resulted in impaired memory. Administration of NE directly into forebrain ventricular systems, thereby bypassing synthesis inhibition, restored normal memory function.

Interest in relating information regarding the LC and memory function to problems of age-related memory decline were further stimulated with the reports indicating that significant functional and morphological impairment of the LC occurs with both normal aging and SDAT (see above). Studies were begun in my laboratory to investigate directly the possibility that memory decline in aging could be attributed to LC dysfunction.

LC Lesions Produce α-Adrenergic and DA Receptor Supersensitivity

In normal aged brains (both human and nonhuman), significant and selective changes in brain neurotransmitter receptors have been reported. These receptor changes include cholinergic (Freund, 1980; Lippa, Critchett, Bartus, Harrington, & Pelham, 1979; Perry, 1980; Reisine, Yamamura, Bird, Spokes, & Enna, 1978; Strong, Hicks, Hsu, Bartus, & Enna, 1980), β-adrenergic (Greenberg & Weiss, 1978; Maggi *et al.*, 1979; Misra, Shelat, & Smith, 1980; Schocken & Roth, 1977), α-adrenergic (Misra *et al.*, 1980), dopaminergic (Creese, Burt, & Snyder, 1976; Severson & Finch, 1980), GABA-ergic (Govoni, Lodda, Soabo, & Trabucchi, 1977), and glutaminergic (Baudry, Arst, & Lynch, 1981) receptors. Since it has been reported that LC cell bodies are lost with age (Vijayashankar & Brody, 1979), we (Prado de Carvalho & Zornetzer, 1982) designed a study to determine whether LC cell loss, produced experimentally, results in receptor changes in target cell populations normally receiving these LC projections. One rationale for this study was that it represented a first step in a series of studies designed to evaluate some consequences, in forebrain target regions, of LC dysfunction with age.

Briefly, clonidine (CLON), an α-adrenergic pre- and postsynaptic receptor agonist, when combined with apomorphine (APO), a DA receptor agonist, in previously reserpinized rodents, was known to produce marked locomotor stimulation (Anden, Carrodi, Fuxe, Hokfelt, Hokfelt, Rydin, & Svensson, 1979). CLON alone, administered to reserpinized animals, results in little or no locomotor activation. These and other data suggested a role for the cooperativity of both NE and DA in the expression of locomotor activity. Our study investigated the alteration in NE-DA transmitter cooperativity, and by extension, provided us the opportunity to evaluate indirectly α-adrenergic receptor sensitivity through altered CLON dose–response curves.

The results of our experiments indicated that rodents with LC cell body damage were more responsive to both APO and CLON than normal animals. Our interpretation of these data was that subsequent to LC neuron terminal loss, both α-adrenergic (sensitive to CLON stimulation) and DA (sensitive to APO stimulation) receptors became supersensitive.

The implications of these data for the aging brain may be far-reaching. Thus, if in aged brain there is LC cell loss (as has been reported by multiple investigators in human brain), then perhaps there is also a resulting receptor supersensitivity for some classes of receptors (α-receptors, DA receptors, β-receptors, etc.). Additional, as yet undocumented, receptor sensitivity changes in other classes of receptor types may also occur. Such a speculation is particularly relevant of LC-originating NE terminals, which both project to extensive forebrain regions and modulate (enable or disenable) numerous other neurotransmitter actions (cf. Siggins & Bloom, 1981).

Regarding senescent brain and SDAT, of particular interest is whether experimental manipulation of the LC-originating NE system results in functional changes in the basal forebrain cholinergic system. In support of this possibility is the finding that LC terminals share common postsynaptic targets with basal forebrain cholinergic neurons in the diagonal band of Broca, medial septal area, and hippocampal formation (Segal, 1976). Additionally, large regions of cerebral cortex receive NE and ACh terminal field projections from the LC and basal forebrain, respectively. Is it possible that LC-derived NE serves as a chemical modulator of cholinergic function in forebrain and, in turn, modulates memory function as well?

Direct Electrical Activation of LC Cell Bodies Results in Prevention of Age-Related Memory Loss

Aged organisms, ranging from humans to mice, develop memory dysfunction (see Kubanis & Zornetzer, 1981, for an extensive review). During the past 3 years I have begun studying these age-related memory impairments in aged rats and mice (Kubanis et al., 1981; Kubanis, Zornetzer, & Freund, 1982; Zornetzer et al., 1982). One conclusion from the data obtained to date is that, generally, aged rodents do not have severe acquisition or learning deficits. Rather, they have an accelerated loss of recently acquired information (i.e., they forget faster than do young rodents). This accelerated loss of recently acquired information appears quite general to a variety of learning–memory situations (i.e., short-term, intermediate-term, and long-term memory; see Zornetzer et al., 1982).

Considerable interest and effort has been (and is being) devoted to developing effective interventive, usually pharmacological, strategies to ameliorate these age-related memorial and cognitive deficits (Etienne, Gauthier, Johnson, Collier, Mendis, Dastoor, Cole, & Muller, 1978; Hier & Caplan, 1980; Hughes, Williams & Currier, 1976; Loew, 1980; Scott, 1979). In general, two main approaches are being used. The first involves administration of agents that increase the efficacy of the cholinergic system in the brain. Such treatments include precursor loading with lecithin and/or choline (Boyde, Grahan-White, Blockwood, Glen, & McQueen, 1977; Mohs et al., 1980) or administration of anticholinesterases (Drachman & Sahakian, 1980). The second strategy has led to the development of a new class of pharmacological agents, the nootropics, believed to improve cognitive function in the aged. Accordingly, such agents as piracetam, hydergine, vincamine, centrophenoxine, and the like, which have varied actions on brain blood flow and/or metabolism (see Ban, 1978), are being tested. To date, their efficacy in improving cognitive function in the elderly is not convincing.

A careful evaluation of each of these research approaches leads to two observations: (1) There has been an excessively narrow and exclusive focus upon the cholinergic system and memory impairment, and (2) the data reported thus far are collectively neither convincing nor impressive (with occasional notable exceptions; see Bartus & Dean, 1980). Perhaps the latter observation is derived from the former observation?

Manipulation of central catecholamines in aging brain represents an alternative to the two research strategies described briefly above. The NE-containing LC is certainly another candidate transmitter-specific system likely to be involved in cognitive function (see above). The fact that LC neurons and their terminal field receptors show widespread age-related changes makes the LC an ideal system to study. Accordingly, the hypothesis tested in the study reported below was this: "Can experimental manipulation of the LC alter normally expected age-related memory decline?" The results provide exciting new data suggesting that age-related memory failure in senescent rodents can be significantly retarded as a result of direct LC activation. A brief description of these experiments follows.

The initial phase of the experiment simply documented, using the male C57BL/6J mouse, that aged (24-month-old) animals remember more poorly than young (5-month-old) controls. To demonstrate this, I used a single-trial step-down inhibitory-avoidance apparatus (see Kubanis et al., 1981, for details). The results are shown in Figure 52-1.

The second phase of the experiment was designed as a direct test of the hypothesis stated above. Groups of mice, either 5 months or 18 months old at the start of the experiment, were surgically prepared (using stereotaxic procedures) with chronic indwelling electrodes targeted bilaterally for the nucleus LC. This is a well-established procedure in my laboratory (cf. Prado de Carvalho & Zornetzer, 1981).

Following a 10-day postsurgical recovery period, mice began an electrical stimulation regimen consisting of regular stimulation of the LC at 48-hr intervals for a period of 6 months. Thus, at the termination of this prolonged period of intermittent electrical stimulation, mice were either 11 months or 24 months of age. Stimulation parameters were either 100-μA or 50-μA current at 60 Hz using .1-msec biphasic pulses. Each stimulation session lasted 10 minutes, with stimulation actually administered intermittently during this period.

The third phase of the experiment began one week after the last electrical stimulation was administered. All mice were trained in the step-down inhibitory-avoidance task. Mice were then tested 24 hr later for retention of the shock-avoidance response. As the results shown in Figure 52-2 indicate, 24-month-old sham-stimulated mice typically forget (i.e., have a shorter step-down latency) the inhibitory-avoidance response when tested 24 hr after learning. The data from the 24-month-old mice that received chronic and repeated LC electrical stimulation are shown in Figure 52-2.

As these data indicate, mice receiving regular, repeated prior electrical stimulation of the LC showed improved performance, compared to aged controls, when tested 24 hr after learning. In fact, performance of the LC-stimulated aged mice was indistinguishable from that of young controls.

Pharmacological Activation of the LC Results in Prevention of Age-Related Memory Loss

Surgical intervention and electrode implantation in the brain represents a rather extreme procedure for ameliorating age-related memory decline. In an attempt to circumvent this problem, a pharmacological approach seemed more desirable. Accordingly, our first pharmacological approach to LC activation involved the use of piperoxane, an α_2-noradrenergic receptor blocking agent shown to have an excitatory action upon LC neurons (Cedarbaum & Aghajanian, 1976) when administered systemically. Piperoxane is believed to activate LC neurons by directly blocking autoinhibition and collateral inhibition in the nucleus of the LC. These intranuclear inhibitory projections utilize the α_2-receptor. Thus, α_2 blockade results in release from inhibition and greater LC cell firing (Cedarbaum & Aghajanian, 1976). Presumably, elevated LC cell firing would result in correspondingly greater synaptic release of NE at the many terminal fields of the LC in forebrain and other brain regions.

The experimental protocol was designed to parallel the electrical stimulation experiment just described. Mice, 5 months and 18 months of age at the start of the experiment, were divided into independent groups. Animals received either .5 or 1.5 mg/kg piperoxane or saline, administered intraperitoneally (i.p). Injections were given once every 48 hr for 6 months. Injection sites were systematically varied to avoid producing peritoneal irritation or infection.

At the end of the 6-month drug administration period, all mice had a 1-week drug-free period prior to behavioral training and memory testing. At the end of this week, mice were trained and tested on the step-down inhibitory-avoidance task, as described previously.

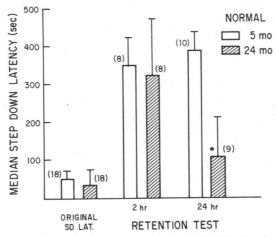

FIGURE 52-1. Median step-down latency (sec) of aged and young C57BL/6J male mice. The figure indicates that original step-down latencies in naive mice did not differ between young and aged groups. When tested 2 hr after training, both young and aged mice had a long step-down latency, suggesting good memory of the inhibitory-avoidance response. Independent groups of mice tested 24 hr after training indicated that aged, but not young, mice now had a significant ($p < .02$) performance deficit, suggesting memory loss.

The results of this experiment are shown in Figure 52-3. Mice aged 24 months that had received repeated administration of piperoxane showed no performance deficit compared to young controls. Aged control mice, which had received saline, performed as expected—that is, these mice had a significant age-related performance deficit when tested 24 hrs after training. It should be noted that prior long-term piperoxane treatment did not appear to alter initial step-down latencies in the mice. This observation would argue against the possibility that the piperoxane effect was due merely to altered activity or anxiety levels. These data are interpreted to suggest that piperoxane, a pharmacological agent capable of increasing LC cell activity, is also capable of significantly reducing age-related memory impairment.

FIGURE 52-2. The effects of prior 6-month intermittent electrical stimulation of the LC upon memory of the inhibitory-avoidance response. All stimulation was ended 1 week prior to training. The data indicate that stimulation at 50-μA current resulted in significant facilitation in performance in aged mice. Young mice, curiously, were not affected by the treatment. The higher current level (150 μA) did not result in significant facilitation of performance.

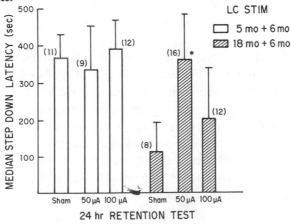

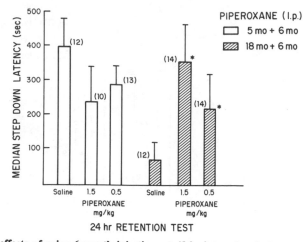

FIGURE 52-3. The effects of prior 6-month injection, at 48-hr intervals, of piperoxane upon memory of the inhibitory-avoidance response. Drug administration was ended 1 week prior to training. The data indicate that both doses of piperoxane (.5 and 1.5 mg/kg, i.p.) resulted in significant improvement in performance of aged, but not young, mice.

Summary and Conclusions

The implications that can be derived from these preliminary results are very important. First, the data suggest that age-related memory loss need not be inevitable. Appropriate interventive strategies can at least delay their onset. The extent to which this delay can be maintained relative to lifespan is not understood at present. Many more careful experiments need to be conducted. Second, activation of LC electrical activity appears to be an important condition leading to the persistence of youthful memory function into senescence. The result of both the electrical stimulation and the piperoxane treatments would suggest that the LC is a common target for the site of action of the two treatments. The question of what is necessary versus sufficient LC activation, vis-à-vis memory function, is not presently understood. The 6-month protocol used in the two experiments described above was based upon the assumption that if LC cell function was normally diminished during aging, the point of onset for such diminished function would probably be during "middle age," which for the C57BL/6J mouse is about 18 months (Finch, 1978). Accordingly, long-term artificial activation of the LC was provided in an attempt to sustain and/or mimic greater LC functional output.

At this juncture it is important to determine (1) the mechanism through which LC activation serves to sustain youthful memory function in aged rodents and (2) the optimal parameters for obtaining improved memory function. Presumably the effect is in some way related to cellular changes occurring, or perhaps not occurring, at distant terminal projection fields receiving LC synaptic endings. One very interesting possibility is that NE-containing LC terminals and/or postsynaptic receptors modulate basal forebrain cholinergic activity directly. Alternatively, LC terminals may interact at common cortical postsynaptic target sites with cholinergic terminals. In either case, loss of normal LC function with aging might result in diminished cholinergic efficacy.

REFERENCES

Abraham, W. C., Delanoy, R. L., Dunn, A. J., & Zornetzer, S. F. Locus coeruleus stimulation decreases deoxyglucose uptake in mouse cerebral cortex. *Brain Research*, 1979, *172*, 387–392.

Adolfsson, R., Gottfries, C.-G., Roos, B. E., & Windblad, B. Postmortem distribution of dopamine and homovanillic acid in human brain, variations related to age and a review of the literature. *Journal of Neural Transmission*, 1979, *45*, 81–105.

Algeri, S. Biochemical changes in central catecholaminergic neurons of the senescent rat. In *Neuro-psychopharmacology: Proceedings of the 10th Congress of the Collegium International Neuropsychopharmacologicum, Quebec, July 1976* (Vol. 2). New York: Pergamon Press, 1978.

Anden, N. E., Carrodi, H., Fuxe, K., Hokfelt, B., Hokfelt, T., Rydin, C., & Svensson, T. Evidence for a central noradrenaline receptor stimulation by clonidine. *Life Sciences*, 1970, *9*, 513–523.

Appel, S. H. Alzheimer's disease. In S. J. Enna, T. Samorajski, & B. Beer (Eds.), *Brain neurotransmitters and receptors in aging and age-related disorders* (Vol. 17). New York: Raven Press, 1981.

Aston-Jones, G., & Bloom, F. E. Norepinephrine-containing locus coeruleus neurons in behaving rats exhibit pronounced responses to non-noxious environmental stimuli. *Journal of Neuroscience*, 1981, *1*, 887–900.

Ban, T. A. Vasodilators, stimulants and anabolic agents in the treatment of geropsychiatric patients. In M. A. Lipton, A. DiMascio, & K. F. Killam (Eds.), *Psychopharmacology: A generation of progress*. New York: Raven Press, 1978.

Barnes, C. A. Memory deficits associated with senescence: A neurophysiological and behavioral study in the rat. *Journal of Comparative and Physiological Psychology*, 1979, *93*, 74–101.

Bartus, R. T. Physostigmine and recent memory: Effects in young and aged non-human primates. *Science*, 1979, *206*, 1087–1089.

Bartus, R. T., & Dean, R. L. Facilitation of aged primate memory via pharmacological manipulation of central cholinergic activity. *Neurobiology of Aging*, 1980, *1*, 145–152.

Bartus, R. T., Dean, R. L., III, & Flemming, D. L. Aging in the rhesus monkey: Effects on visual discrimination learning and reversal learning. *Journal of Gerontology*, 1979, *34*, 209–219.

Baudry, M., Arst, D. S., & Lynch, G. Increased [³H]glutamate receptor binding in aged rats. *Brain Research*, 1981, *223*, 195–198.

Bondareff, W., Mountjoy, C. Q., & Roth, M. Loss of neurons of origin of the adrenergic projection to cerebral cortex (nucleus locus coeruleus) in senile dementia. *Neurology*, 1982, *32*, 164–168.

Bowen, D. M., Smith, C. B., White, P., Goodhart, M. J., Spillane, J. A., Flack, R. H. A., & Davison, A. N. Chemical pathology of the organic dementias. *Brain*, 1977, *100*, 397–426.

Boyde, W. D., Grahan-White, J., Blockwood, G., Glen, I., & McQueen, J. Clinical effects of choline in Alzheimer senile dementia. *Lancet*, 1977, *ii*, 711.

Brizzee, K. R., & Ordy, J. M. Age pigments cell loss and hippocampal function. *Mechanisms of Ageing and Development*, 1979, *9*, 43–162.

Brody, H. Organization of the cerebral cortex: III. A study of aging in the human cerebral cortex. *Journal of Comparative Neurology*, 1955, *102*, 511–556.

Brody, H. Structural changes in the aging nervous system. In H. T. Blumenthal (Ed.)., *Interdisciplinary topics in gerontology* (Vol. 7). Basel: S. Karger, 1970.

Brody, H. An examination of cerebral cortex and brain stem aging. In R. D. Terry & S. Gershon (Eds.), *Aging: Neurobiology of aging*. New York: Raven Press, 1976.

Carlsson, A., & Windblad, B. The influence of age and time interval between death and the autopsy on dopamine and 3-methoxytryramine levels in human basal ganglia. *Journal of Neural Transmission*, 1976, *83*, 271–276.

Cedarbaum, J. M., & Aghajanian, G. K. Noradrenergic neurons of the locus coeruleus: Inhibition by epinephrine and activation by the α-antagonist piperoxane. *Brain Research*, 1976, *112*, 413–419.

Cote, L. J., & Kremzner, L. T. Changes in Neurotransmitter Systems with increasing age in human brain. In *Transactions of the American Society for Neurochemistry, 5th Annual Meeting*, New Orleans, Louisiana, 1974.

Creese, I., Burt, D. R., & Snyder, S. H. Dopamine receptor binding predicts clinical and pharmacological potencies of anti-schizophrenic drugs. *Science*, 1976, *192*, 481–483.

Davies, P., & Maloney, A. Selective loss of central cholinergic neurons in Alzheimer's disease. *Lancet*, 1976, *ii*, 1403.

Dean, R. L., Scozzafava, J., Goas, J. A., Regan, B., Beer, B., & Bartus, R. T. Age-related differences in behavior across the life-span of the C57BL/6J mouse. *Experimental Aging Research*, 1981, *7*, 427–451.

Drachman, D. A. Memory and cognitive function in man: Dose the cholinergic system have a specific role? *Neurology*, 1977, *27*, 783–790.

Drachman, D. A., & Leavitt, J. Human memory and the cholinergic system: A relationship to aging? *Archives of Neurology*, 1974, *30*, 113–121.

Drachman, D. A., & Sahakian, B. J. Memory and cognitive function in the elderly. *Archives of Neurology*, 1980, *37*, 674–675.

Etienne, P., Gauthier, S., Johnson, G., Collier, B., Mendis, T., Dastoor, D., Cole, M., & Muller, H. F. Clinical effects of choline in Alzheimer's disease. *Lancet*, 1978, *i*, 500–509.

Fallon, J. H. The Islands of Calleja complex: II. Connections of medium and large-sized cells. *Brain Research Bulletin*, 1983, *10*, 775–798. (a)

Fallon, J. H. Personal communication, 1983. (b)

Fallon, J. H., Kozrell, D. A., & Moore, R. Y. Catecholamine innervation of the basal forebrain: II. Amygdala, suprahinal cortex and entorhinal cortex. *Journal of Comparative Neurology*, 1978, *180*, 509–532.

Fallon, J. H., & Moore, R. Y. Catecholamine innervation of the basal forebrain: III. Olfactory bulb, anterior olfactory nucleus, olfactory tubercle, and piriform cortex. *Journal of Comparative Neurology*, 1978, *180*, 533–544.

Ferris, S. H., Sathananthan, G., Reisberg, B., & Gershon, S. Long-term choline treatment of memory-impaired elderly patients. *Science*, 1979, *205*, 1039–1040.

Finch, C. Catecholamine metabolism in the brains of aging male mice. *Brain Research*, 1973, *52*, 267–276.

Finch, C. E. The regulation of physiological changes during mammalian aging. *Quarterly Review of Biology*, 1976, *51*, 49–83.

Finch, C. E. Age-related changes in brain catecholamines: A synopsis of findings in C57BL/6J mice and other rodent models. *Advances in Experimental Medicine and Biology*, 1978, *113*, 15–39.

Freund, G. Cholinergic receptor loss in brains of aging mice. *Life Sciences*, 1980, *26*, 371–375.

Gallagher, M., & Kapp, B. S. Manipulation of opiate activity in the amygdala alters memory processes. *Life Sciences*, 1978, *23*, 1973–1978.

Gold, P. E., & McGaugh, J. L. Changes in learning and memory during aging. In I. M. Ordy & K. R. Brizzee (Eds.), *Neurobiology of aging*. New York: Plenum Press, 1975.

Gold, P. E., & Zornetzer, S. F. The mnemon and its juices. Neuromodulation of memory processes. *Behavioral and Neural Biology*, 1983, *38*, 151–189.

Govoni, S., Loddo, P., Spano, P. F., & Trabucchi, M. Dopamine receptor sensitivity in brain and retina of rats during aging. *Brain Research*, 1977, *138*, 565–570.

Greenberg, L. H., & Weiss, B. β-Adrenergic receptors in aged rat brain: Reduced number and capacity of pineal gland to develop supersensitivity. *Science*, 1978, *201*, 61–63.

Herkenham, M., & Pert, C. B. Light microscopic localization of brain opiate receptors: A general autoradiographic method which preserves tissue quality. *Journal of Neuroscience*, 1982, *2*, 1129–1149.

Hier, D. B., & Caplan, L. R. Drugs for senile dementia. *Drugs*, 1980, *20*, 74–80.

Hughes, J. R., Williams, J. G., & Currier, R. D. An ergot alkaloid preparation (hydergine) in the treatment of dementia: Critical review of the clinical literature. *Journal off the American Geriatric Society*, 1976, *24*, 490–497.

Jacobowitz, D. M., & Palkovitz, M. Topagraphic atlas of catecholamine and acetylcholinesterase-containing neurons in the rat brain: I. Forebrain (telencephalon, diencephalon). *Journal of Comparative Neurology*, 1974, *157*, 13–28.

Jensen, R. A., Messing, R. B., Martinez, J. L., Vasquez, B. J., Spiehler, V. R., & McGaugh, J. L. Changes in brain peptide systems and altered learning and memory processes in aged animals. In J. L. Martinez, R. A. Jensen, R. B. Messing, H. Rigter, & J. L. McGaugh (Eds.), *Endogenous peptides and learning and memory processes*. New York: Academic Press, 1981.

Jones, B. E., & Moore, R. Y. Ascending projections of the locus coeruleus in the rat: II. Autoradiographic study. *Brain Research*, 1977, *127*, 23–53.

Kubanis, P., Gobbel, G., & Zornetzer, S. F. Age-related memory deficits in Swiss mice. *Behavioral and Neural Biology*, 1981, *32*, 241–247.

Kubanis, P., & Zornetzer, S. F. Age-related behavioral and neurobiological changes: A review with an emphasis on memory. *Behavioral and Neural Biology*, 1981, *31*, 115–172.

Kubanis, P., Zornetzer, S. F., & Freund, G. Memory and postsynaptic cholinergic receptors in aging mice. *Pharmacology, Biochemistry and Behavior*, 1982, *17*, 313–322.

Landfield, P. W., Rose, G., Sandles, L., Wohlstadter, T., & Lynch, G. Patterns of astroglial hypertrophy and neuronal degeneration in the hippocampus of aged, memory-deficient rats. *Journal of Gerontology*, 1977, *32*, 3–12.

Lindvall, O., Bjorklund, A., Moore, R. Y., & Stenevi, U. Mesencephalic dopamine neurons projecting to neocortex. *Brain Research*, 1974, *81*, 325–331.

Lippa, A. S., Critchett, D. J., Bartus, R. T., Harrington, W., & Pelham, R. W. Electrophysiological and biochemical evidence for age-related alterations in hippocampal cholinergic functioning. *Society for Neuroscience Abstracts*, 1979, *5*, 8.

Loew, D. M. Pharmacological approaches to the treatment of senile dementia. In L. Amaducci, A. N. Davidson, & P. Antuono, *Aging of the brain and dementia* (Vol. 13). New York: Raven Press, 1980.

Maggi, A., Schmidt, M. J., Ghetti, B., & Enna, S. J. Effect of aging of neurotransmitter receptor binding in rat and human brain. *Life Sciences*, 1979, *24*, 367–374.

Mann, D. M. A., & Yates, P. O. Lipoprotein pigments—their relationship to aging in the human nervous system: I. The lipofuscin content of nerve cells. *Brain*, 1974, *97*, 481–488. (a)

Mann, D. M. A., & Yates, P. O. Lipoprotein pigments—their relationship to aging in the human nervous system: II. The melanin content of pigmental nerve cells. *Brain*, 1974, *97*, 489–498. (b)

Mason, S. T. Noradrenaline in the brain: Progress in theories of behavioral function. *Progress in Neurobiology*, 1981, *16*, 263–303.

McGeer, E. G., Fibiger, H. C., McGeer, P. L., & Wickson, V. Aging and brain enzymes. *Experimental Gerontology*, 1971, *6*, 391–396.

McGeer, E. G., & McGeer, P. L. Some characteristics of brain tryosine hydroxylase. In A. J. Mandell (Ed.), *New concepts in neurotransmitter regulation*. New York: Plenum Press, 1973.

Messing, R. B., Jensen, R. A., Martinez, J. L., Spiehler, V. R., Vasquez, B. J., Soumireu-Mourat, B., Liang, K. C., & McGaugh, J. L. Naloxone enhancement of memory. *Behavioral and Neural Biology*, 1979, *27*, 266–275.

Misra, C. H., Shelat, H. S., & Smith, R. C. Effect of age on adrenergic and dopaminergic receptor binding in rat brain. *Life Sciences*, 1980, *27*, 521–526.

Mohs, R. C., Davis, K. L., Tinklenberg, J. R., & Hollister, L. Choline chloride effects on memory in the elderly. *Neurobiology of Aging*, 1980, *1*, 21–25.

Mohs, R. C., Davis, K. L., Tinklenberg, J. R., Hollister, L., Yesavage, J. A., & Kopell, B. S. Choline chloride treatment of memory deficits in the elderly. *American Journal of Psychiatry*, 1979, *136*, 1275–1277.

Moore, R. Y., & Bloom, F. E. Central catecholamine neurone systems: Anatomy and physiology of the dopamine systems. *Annual Review of Neuroscience*, 1978, *1*, 129–169.

Morrison, J., Grzanna, R., Molliver, M., & Coyle, J. The distribution and orientation of noradrenergic fibers in neocortex of the rat: An immunofluorescence study. *Journal of Comparative Neurology*, 1978, *181*, 17–40.

Perry, E. K. The cholinergic system in old age and Alzheimer's disease. *Age and Aging*, 1980, *9*, 1–8.

Perry, E. K., Perry, R., Blessed, G., & Tomlinson, B. Necropsy evidence of central cholinergic deficits in senile dementia. *Lancet*, 1977, *i*, 189.

Prado de Carvalho, L., & Zornetzer, S. F. The involvement of the locus coeruleus in memory. *Behavioral and Neural Biology*, 1981, *31*, 173–186.

Prado de Carvalho, L., & Zornetzer, S. F. Alpha-noradrenergic receptor supersensitivity following discrete electrolytic lesions of the nucleus locus coeruleus: A behavioral demonstration. *Journal of Neural Transmission*, 1982, *53*, 23–31.

Price, D. L., Whitehouse, P. J., Struble, R. G., Clark, A. W., Coyle, J. T., Delong, M. R., & Hedreen, J. C. Basal forebrain cholinergic systems in Alzheimer's disease and related dementias. *Neuroscience Commentaries*, 1982, *1*, 84.

Ponzio, F., Brunello, N., & Algeri, S. Catecholamine synthesis in brain of aging rats. *Journal of Neurochemistry*, 1978, *30*, 1617–1620.

Reisine, T. D., Yamamura, H. I., Bird, E. D., Spokes, E., & Enna, S. J. Pre- and postynsaptic neurochemical alterations in Alzheimer's disease. *Brain Research*, 1978, *149*, 477–481.

Rogers, J., Silver, M. A., Shoemaker, W. J., & Bloom, F. E. Senescent changes in a neurobiological model system: Cerebellar Purkinje cell electrophysiology and correlative anatomy. *Neurobiology of Aging*, 1980, *1*, 3–11.

Schocken, D. D., & Roth, G. S. Reduced β-adrenergic receptor concentrations in aging man. *Nature (London)*, 1977, *267*, 856–858.

Scott, F. L. A review of some current drugs used in the pharmcotherapy of organic brain syndrome. In A. Cherkin, C. E. Finch, N. Kharasch, T. Makinodon, F. L. Scott, & B. S. Strehler (Eds.), *Aging* (Vol. 8, *Physiology and cell biology of aging*). New York: Raven Press, 1979.

Segal, M. Brain stem afferents to the rat medial system. *Journal of Physiology*, 1976, *261*, 617–631.

Severson, J. A., & Finch, C. E. Age changes in human basal ganglion dopamine receptors. *Federation Proceedings*, 1980, *39*, 508.

Siggins, G. R., & Bloom, F. E. Modulation of unit activity by chemically coded neurons. In O. Pompeiano & C. Ajmone-Marsan (Eds.), *Brain mechanisms and perceptual awareness*. New York: Raven Press, 1981.

Simpkins, J. W., Mueller, G. P., Huang, H. H., & Meites, J. Evidence for depressed catecholamine and enhanced serotonin metabolism in aging male rats: Possible relation to gonadotrophin secretion. *Endocrinology*, 1977, *100*, 1672–1678.

Sladek, J. R., & Sladek, C. D. Relative quantitation of monoamine histofluorescence in young and old non-human primates. *Advances in Experimental Medicine and Biology*, 1979, *113*, 231–240.

Stein, L., Belluzzi, J. D., & Wise, C. D. Memory enhancement by central administrations of norepinephine. *Brain Research*, 1975, *84*, 329–335.

Strong, R., Hicks, P., Hsu, L., Bartus, R. T., & Enna, S. J. Age-related alterations in the rodent brain cholinergic system and behavior. *Neurobiology of Aging*, 1980, *1*, 59–63.

Vijayashankar, H., & Brody, H. A quantitative study of the pigmental neurons in the nuclei locus coeruleus and subcoeruleus in man as related to aging. *Journal of Neuropathology and Experimental Neurology*, 1979, *38*, 490–497.

Vroulis, G. A., & Smith, R. C. Cholinergic drugs and memory disorders in Alzheimer's type dementia. In S. J. Enna, T. Samorajski, & B. Beer (Eds.), *Brain neurotransmitters and receptors in aging and age-related disorders* (Vol. 17). New York: Raven Press, 1981.

Zornetzer, S. F. Neurotransmitter modulation and memory: A new pharmacological phrenology? In M. A. Lipton, A. DiMascio, & K. F. Killam (Eds.), *Psychopharmacology: A generation of progress*. New York: Raven Press, 1978.

Zornetzer, S. F., Abraham, W. C., & Appleton, R. Locus coeruleus and labile memory. *Pharmacology, Biochemistry and Behavior*, 1978, *9*, 227–234.

Zornetzer, S. F., & Gold, M. The locus coeruleus: Its possible role in memory consolidation. *Physiology and Behavior*, 1976, *16*, 331–336.

Zornetzer, S. F., Thompson, R., & Rogers, J. Rapid forgetting of aged rats. *Behavioral and Neural Biology*, 1982, *36*, 49–60.

53

Cholinergic Pharmacology, Behavior, and Age-Related Memory Decline

Hasker P. Davis and H. L. Roitblat

Senile dementia presently affects over 2 million Americans, and this number will dramatically increase in the coming decades. A cardinal feature of cognitive disturbances in senile dementia is severe memory impairment. To a lesser extent, many aged individuals are also plagued by memory decline. During the last decade, evidence has accumulated in several different neuroscience fields to suggest that decline of the cholinergic system may have a major role in age-related memory disturbances.

Memory decline in the aged is an active area of research in the field of behavioral pharmacology. In examining the contributions of this field to our understanding of age-related memory deficits, it is useful to keep in mind the different assumptions and methodologies employed in studies directed at memory and those directed at amelioration of a memory deficit. Any drug that improves memory performance is of interest if one is searching for a drug to retard memory decline. This perspective is not, however, sufficient for an understanding of memory and cholinergic dysfunction. Instead, pharmacological contributions to this idea have primarily come from studies directed at understanding how memories are stored in the brain. In studies from this perspective, cholinergic drugs have been used as tools to investigate the cholinergic system's role in memory and to draw inferences from behavioral effects about the structure and processes of memory (Squire & Davis, 1981).

Generally, the strategy of behavioral-pharmacological studies has been to manipulate some aspects of drug administration and then to measure the behavior that follows. The converse strategy, which is the manipulation of behavior, may be equally enlightening, but has generally been neglected in pharmacological studies with aged animals. In contrast, other areas of the neurosciences have been greatly enriched by varying the functional requirements of behavioral tasks. For example, behavioral analyses of memory in neuropathological patients suggest that there may be different kinds of memories (Cohen & Squire, 1980), and that different psychological processes of memory are potentially mediated by different neural structures (Butters & Cermak, 1980; Olton, 1983; Squire, 1982).

In this chapter we outline the studies that have led to the hypothesis that age-associated memory impairment is due, at least in part, to cholinergic dysfunction. Following this, ideas about the potential of cholinergic treatments that have emerged from these studies are critically examined. Finally, we discuss the contribution of behavioral-

Hasker P. Davis. Department of Psychology, St. John's University, Jamaica, New York.

H. L. Roitblat. Department of Psychology, Columbia University, New York, New York.

pharmacological studies to our understanding of memory in old animals, and argue that the future development of this field will depend on a more sophisticated view of the cognitive capacities of animals.

The Cholinergic System as a Memory Site

Much of the foundation for the idea that cholinergic dysfunction has a primary role in age-associated memory deficits is derived from early behavioral-pharmacological studies of the effects of cholinergic agents in young animals. Deutsch and coworkers investigated the behavioral effects of the inhibitors of acetylcholinesterase, physostigmine and diisopropylfluorophosphate, and the anticholinergic drug scopolamine (see Deutsch, 1971; Squire & Davis, 1981). In a series of studies, it was found that when all factors except the training-test interval were held constant, cholinergic drugs either had no effect, facilitated retention, or impaired retention (Deutsch, 1971). For example, diisopropylfluorophosphate impaired retention of a 14-day-old Y-maze escape habit that was well remembered by controls, but the same dose facilitated retention at 28 days after learning, a time when controls exhibited poor retention.

Deutsch (1971) has proposed that these findings can be explained by assuming that memory involves, in part, changes in sensitivity of specific cholinergic synapses with time after initial learning. However, because many drugs that affect other neurotransmitters can facilitate or impair retention, some have questioned whether the role of cholinergic neurons in memory is greater than that of other neurotransmitters (Bartus, Dean, Beer, & Lippa, 1982). For example, manipulation of the neuropeptide vasopressin can profoundly affect retention of newly learned material (Squire & Davis, 1981). Such a finding by itself does not address the way in which memory is affected or provide information about the physiological substrate of memory, because performance changes could be due to alterations in other factors, such as arousal or attention, that might be important in the modulation of memory. The effects of a vasopressin manipulation are consistent with these alternatives, since effects are always in the same direction. In contrast, cholinergic drugs appear to affect memory representation directly. It is difficult to account for cholinergic drugs having different effects on retention levels in terms of nonspecific effects or alteration in such factors as attention or arousal when the only manipulated variable is the age of memory. To determine whether a neurotransmitter directly affects memory representation or simply modulates memory, it will be useful to know whether synaptically active drugs can exert differential effects on retention as a function of the age of memory. To date, such findings have been obtained only with pharmacological agents that affect cholinergic neurons.

Cholinergic Drugs Improve Retention in Old Animals

If cholinergic neurons are part of a system for memory representation, then age-related disturbances in memory may be due in part to cholinergic dysfunction. In addition to the data described above, further support for this idea is provided by neurochemical, neuro-anatomical, and electrophysiological investigations of the cholinergic system (for reviews, see Bartus *et al.*, 1982; Price, Whitehouse, Struble, Clark, Coyle, Delong, & Hedreen, 1982). In brief, the major findings are the following: Choline acetyltransferase activity, acetylcholinesterase activity, the density of muscarinic receptors, acetylcholine synthesis and release, and the number of cholinergic neurons in the nucleus of Meynert all decrease in aged animals and/or in aged humans diagnosed as having Alzheimer disease. Electrophysiological response of neurons to iontophoretically applied acetylcholine is reduced in old rats. Thus, since this system shows marked impairment with age, it is thought that drugs that would enhance the efficacy of cholinergic transmission in remaining neurons might ameliorate memory impairments in old subjects.

While cholinomimetic drugs have been extensively investigated in young animals and have been shown to improve performance in a variety of tasks, relatively few studies have been carried out in older animals. Physostigmine and arecoline, a postsynaptic cholinergic stimulator, are reported to improve short-term memory performance of old monkeys in a delayed matching-to-sample (DMTS) task (Bartus, 1979; Bartus, Dean, & Beer, 1980). Similarly, these same drugs improve retention performance in aged human subjects with Alzheimer disease (for reviews, see Bartus *et al.*, 1982; Squire & Davis, 1981).

Cholinergic Drugs as Treatment for Impaired Memory

Pharmacologically, the therapeutic usefulness of cholinergic drugs is constrained by their unpleasant side effects, rapid metabolism, and by a narrow effective dosage range that shows marked variability in aged subjects (Bartus, 1979). At a psychological level, studies of young and old animals have demonstrated that the effects of cholinergic drugs are determined by the age of the memory and the cognitive characteristics of the subject. For example, rats that are slow maze learners respond to physostigmine differently than fast maze learners (for reviews, see Deutsch, 1971; Squire & Davis, 1981). These same types of variables influence the therapeutic effects of cholinergic drugs on memory in humans, and thereby make them unlikely treatment agents (Mohs & Davis, 1979).

These limitations might be reduced in old subjects if a steady state of improved cholinergic function were established. In this respect, the acetylcholine precursors choline and phosphatidylcholine hold promise as long-term treatments. Dietary loading of choline may enhance acetylcholine synthesis and release, and thereby may have a positive effect on memory. For example, facilitation of memory performance was demonstrated by mice maintained on an enriched choline diet for 4–5 months prior to learning a passive-avoidance habit at 13 months of age (Bartus, Dean, Goas, & Lippa, 1980). In contrast to this positive finding in mice, negative findings have almost universally been reported for memory-impaired humans (Bartus *et al.*, 1982). One possible explanation for these findings is that impaired presynaptic controls for synthesis and release of acetylcholine are no longer responsive to increased precursor levels in demented humans. Accordingly, the positive behavioral effect in mice might have occurred because choline loading was initiated prior to the development of presynaptic disturbances that accompany aging. It is important to note that a basic requirement for long-term precursor treatments is the validity of their assumed enhancement of acetylcholine synthesis and release. This assumption is controversial for short-term precursor loading (Bartus *et al.*, 1982), and no evidence exists for time periods on the order required for long-term treatment.

Despite the disappointing long-term therapeutic results obtained with cholinergic drugs, these studies are consistent with the idea that memory disorders accompanying aging are related to cholinergic dysfunction. Thus, despite their shortcomings as treatments, cholinergic drugs have been usefully employed in behavioral-pharmacological studies to increase our insight into the physiological substrate of memory impairments associated with aging. We have become more aware of the types of drugs and modes of action that might be usefully employed in older subjects. For example, since the integrity of receptors generally remains intact in older subjects, cholinergic drugs that have their effect postsynaptically still seem promising.

We now discuss another function of behavioral-pharmacological studies, which is to provide insight into memory's structure and processes. In this realm, drug studies of memory decline, particularly in aged animals, have fallen short of their goal because of a restricted study and view of the psychological processes of memory that can be drawn from behavioral analyses.

Behavior

Behavioral pharmacologists have concentrated on the use of a few well-chosen techniques to study memory in the aged. Studies have emphasized more or less simple tasks, such as passive avoidance, learned taste aversion, and the single- or multiple-unit T-maze. These tasks have powerful advantages for the study of memory, such as ease of training, the ability to identify the quantity of information learned, and single-trial learning, so that the point at which information is learned can be specified with some precision. Despite their advantages, however, these techniques are based on outmoded theoretical assumptions and an impoverished view of the phenomena of animal memory.

It has been more or less traditional for behavioral pharmacologists to view memory as a linear chain transferring information from a sensory register through one or more short-term stores and then to a long-term or permanent store. Behavioral pharmacologists tend to interpret results within this framework as affecting either short-term or long-term memory. Time, however, is only one of the many operational characteristics of memory. A number of behavioral experiments have found evidence for multiple kinds of memory processes, and some investigators employing cognitive analyses of animal memory have found it useful to view memory in terms of a functional contrast between working and reference memory (Honig, 1978). However, the idea of a functional distinction between working and reference memory is controversial (Morris, 1983), and may be more of an operational distinction that reflects performance on variant and invariant aspects of a task.

In most of the tasks used to study the pharmacology of memory, the main interest is in the retention of the results of a learning episode. Typically, a subject is exposed to a novel stimulus or situation; the subject is then presented with a novel consequence for a given response; and retention of that response is measured at various times. In short, these investigations have concentrated on uncovering the physiological mechanism responsible for the formation and retention of stimulus–response (S-R) or perhaps stimulus–stimulus (S-S) associations, indexed by the subject's response at the next presentation of that stimulus. In contrast, behavioral analyses of animal memory have tended to concentrate on tasks in which a well-trained subject is required to base its performance on stimuli that are no longer present. The memory test emphasizes retention of a particular discriminative stimulus appearing on that trial, indexed by the subject's response at various times after the termination of that stimulus. For example, in DMTS, the correct choice is predicated on the particular sample that started the trial. During the delay, the animal must remember the identity of the familiar sample stimulus. Working memory retains information about those particular events occurring on a trial that are temporally relevant in determining the correct response (e.g., the sample in DMTS). Because these events change from episode to episode (samples alternate randomly from trial to trial in DMTS), the information in working memory is irrelevant to and can interfere with later performance; hence, the optimal strategy is to flush or reset the contents of working memory between trials.

In addition to the information held in working memory, certain rules are needed to specify the relationship between events and responses (e.g., in DMTS, the correct choice following each sample; an identity relationship is not necessary). This information does not change from trial to trial or from day to day and is held in reference memory, along with other aspects of the subject's knowledge base concerning general rules and procedures that apply to all trials. In tasks such as DMTS, both kinds of information are necessary for adequate performance.

Although there are clearly other ways to divide memory functioning, the distinction between working and reference memory has proved useful in understanding the memory performance in a radial-arm maze, in which a number of arms (typically eight) radiate from a central platform like spokes from a wheel (Olton, 1978). Each trial begins with a single piece of food at the end of each arm. The subject typically a rat, is placed in the center of the maze and allowed to enter arms to retrieve the food there. After a small amount of training, rats find approximately 7.5 pieces of food in their first 8 choices; this means that they remember which arms they have visited, and refrain from revisiting an arm already depleted of food (Olton, 1978).

Performance of rats in a radial-arm maze appears to depend on the existence of a cognitive map of the experimental environment, which, because it remains constant from trial to trial, is held in reference memory. This cognitive map appears to be oriented relative to the configuration of extramaze cues in the environment. As the animal visits an arm, it enters that location on a list in working memory or equivalently marks the location on the map (Roitblat, 1982b).

The radial-arm maze is a potentially important piece of equipment in the behavioral-pharmacological laboratory, because working performance has some remarkable features. It is relatively long-lived; rats can reportedly tolerate delays of at least 4–6 hours between the fourth and fifth choices with little decrement in their choice accuracy (Beatty & Shavalia, 1980). While other investigators (Markowska, Burešova, & Bureš, 1983) reported that accurate working performance is restricted to shorter interchoice delays more consistent with the temporal character of territory patroling by rats in their natural habits, effects of pharmacological agents on eight-arm-maze working performance by young and old rodents will be of considerable interest.

Certain interventions are reported to produce a dissociation between working-memory and reference-memory functioning (reviewed by Olton, 1983). If certain arms in a radial-arm maze are never baited, then the animal could avoid visiting those arms on the basis of information stored in reference memory. Accurate performance for the remaining arms, however, would still require working memory in order for the animal to avoid revisiting arms. Following lesions to the fimbria fornix, rats made errors to both kinds of arms, but avoidance of the never-baited arms quickly recovered (Olton & Papas, 1979). This and other studies indicate that the hippocampus is necessary for working-memory functioning.

Experiments that are not designed to assess memory processes may be relatively nonselective for and insensitive to different types of memory processes. While an assumption of a single memory process, one containing only S-R associations at that, may once have been appropriate, the currently available data argue that this is no longer true. Behavioral data clearly show that the representations underlying animal memory are more complex than simple S-R connections (Roitblat, 1982a). Physiological data suggest that the mechanisms instantiating those representations differ as a function of certain kinds of task demands—namely, those appropriate to an operational/functional distinction between working and reference memory (Olton, 1983).

The sorts of tasks outlined above and the kinds of theories to which they lead are significantly different from those utilized previously in the experimental analysis of behavior. Instead, a new cognitive perspective is emerging, one that takes a more sophisticated view of the processes occurring in animals. According to this perspective, a complete theory of memory—or, more generally, a specification of the representational system used by an organism—requires specifications along five dimensions (Roitblat, 1982b). The "domain" of a representation is the limited class of situations in which it is used and to which to applies. A representation can be situation-specific or more general; its domain is a specification of its limits of applicability. The "content" of a representation consists of the particular features that it preserves and the features that can be derived from it. Two representations are informationally equivalent if the same features are preserved by both. The "code" of a representation specifies the mapping relation between features of the representation and features of the experience that is being represented. The coding relationship may be simple and isomorphic or arbitrarily complex. The "medium" of a representation, the aspect most studied by psychopharmacologists, is the physical instantiation of the representational system. The medium itself does not provide information about the experience; it merely supports, the way paper supports ink, the information carrying aspects of the representation. Finally, the "dynamics" of a representation pertain to its changes over time, including the formation, translation (recording), transduction (change in medium), and forgetting of information in the representation.

Conclusion

Studies employing cholinergic drugs provide a key part of the evidence for the idea that cholinergic neurons are involved in age-related memory decline. These studies, however, have not adequately explored how memory changes in old subjects. Instead, investigators of the pharmacology of memory have contented themselves with an oversimplified S-R view of memory that concentrates on memory's temporal characteristics. Based on this view, it is not surprising that doubts have arisen about the relevance of animal behavior to issues in human memory (Norman, 1973; Talland, 1969). Studies of animal cognition provide a new perspective and a variety of new tasks that, if exploited, can allow behavioral pharmacologists to study memory from a broader and more functional perspective.

REFERENCES

Bartus, R. T. Physostigmine and recent memory: Effects in young and aged nonhuman primates. *Science*, 1979, *206*, 1087–1089.

Bartus, R. T., Dean, R. L., & Beer, B. Memory deficits in aged cebus monkeys and facilitation with central cholinomimetics. *Neurobiology of Aging*, 1980, *1*, 145–152.

Bartus, R. T., Dean, R. L., Beer, B., & Lippa, A. S. The cholinergic hypothesis of geriatric memory dysfunction. *Science*, 1982, *217*, 408–417.

Bartus, R. T., Dean, R. L., Goas, J. A., & Lippa, A. S. Age-related changes in passive avoidance retention: Modulation with dietary choline. *Science*, 1980, *209*, 301–303.

Beatty, W. W., & Shavalia, D. A. Rat spatial memory: Resistance to retroactive interference at long retention intervals. *Animal Learning and Behavior*, 1980, *8*, 550–552.

Butters, N., & Cermak, L. S. *Alcoholic Korsakoff's syndrome: An information-processing approach to amnesia.* New York: Academic Press, 1980.

Cohen, N., & Squire, L. R. Preserved learning and retention of pattern analyzing skill in amnesia: Dissociation of knowing how and knowing that. *Science*, 1980, *210*, 207–210.

Deutsch, J. A. The cholinergic synapse and the site of memory. *Science*, 1971, *174*, 788–794.

Honig, W. K. Studies of working memory in the pigeon. In S. H. Hulse, H. Fowler, & W. K. Honig (Eds.), *Cognitive processes in animal behavior*. Hillsdale, N.J.: Erlbaum, 1978.

Markowska, A., Burešova, O., & Bureš, J. An attempt to account for controversial estimates of working memory persistence in the radial maze. *Behavioral and Neural Biology*, 1983, *38*, 97–112.

Mohs, R. C., & Davis, K. L. Cholinomimetic drug effects on memory in young and elderly adults. In A. I. M. Glen & L. J. Whalley (Eds.), *Alzheimer's disease: Early recognition of potentially reversible deficits*. Edinburgh: Churchill Livingstone, 1979.

Morris, R. G. M. An attempt to dissociate spatial-mapping and working-memory theories of hippocampal function. In W. Seifert (Ed.), *Neurobiology of the hippocampus*. London: Academic Press, 1983.

Norman, D. A. What have the animal experiments taught us about human memory? In J. A. Deutsch (Ed.), *The physiological basis of memory*. New York: Academic Press, 1973.

Olton, D. S. Characteristics of spatial memory. In S. H. Hulse, H. Fowler, & W. K. Honig (Eds.), *Cognitive processes in animal behavior*. Hillsdale, N.J.: Erlbaum, 1978.

Olton, D. S. Memory functions and the hippocampus. In W. Seifert (Ed.), *Neurobiology of the hippocampus*. London: Academic Press, 1983.

Olton, D. S., & Papas, B. C. Spatial memory and hippocampal function. *Neuropsychologia*, 1979, *17*, 669–682.

Price, D. L., Whitehouse, P. J., Struble, R. J., Clark, A. W., Coyle, J. T., DeLong, M. R., & Hedreen, J. C. Basal forebrain cholinergic systems in Alzheimer's disease and related dementias. *Neuroscience Commentaries*, 1982, *1*, 84–92.

Roitblat, H. L. Discrete vs. graded processes in pigeon working memory. In M. L. Commons & A. R. Wagner (Eds.), *Harvard Symposium in the Quantitative Analysis of Behavior*. Cambridge, Mass.: Ballinger, 1982. (a)

Roitblat, H. L. The meaning of representation in animal memory. *Behavioral and Brain Sciences*, 1982, *5*, 353–406. (b)

Squire, L. R. The neuropsychology of human memory. *Annual Review of Neuroscience*, 1982, *5*, 241–273.

Squire, L. R., & Davis, H. P. The pharmacology of human memory: A neurobiological perspective. *Annual Review of Pharmacology and Toxicology*, 1981, *21*, 323–356.

Talland, G. A. Interaction between clinical and laboratory research on memory. In G. A. Talland & N. C. Waugh (Eds.), *The pathology of memory*. New York: Academic Press, 1969.

54

Cellular Neurophysiological and Behavioral Studies of Learning in Mollusks

Terry Crow

Introduction

Traditionally, studies of the physiology of learning and memory are multidisciplinary, having been conducted at a variety of levels, from the perspective of a cell biologist to that of a neuropsychologist. A major focus of the experimental strategy of neuropsychologists has been to examine different areas of the vertebrate brain for neural changes associated with learned behavior. An explicit assumption of this approach is that once neural correlates of learning are identified in anatomically well-defined neural structures, then an analysis of the cellular mechanisms of learning and memory will soon follow. However, this particular strategy used in investigating mechanisms of learning has been hindered by the enormous cellular complexity of vertebrate nervous systems. A different approach to research on basic mechanisms of learning and memory has been provided by the analysis of cellular modifications associated with learned behavior in neural systems consisting of a relatively small number of neurons. Toward this end, the study of simple learned behaviors in invertebrate nervous systems, such as those of the gastropod mollusks, has made a considerable contribution toward a possible understanding of basic mechanisms underlying learning and memory.

The purpose of this review is to give a brief summary of this favorable strategy of addressing questions concerning basic mechanisms of learning, and then to discuss from a behavioral and cellular perspective current experimental findings generated from studies of associative learning in mollusks. In order to accomplish this, I use examples from my own laboratory, as well as from other laboratories working in this area, that have resulted in several general principles of invertebrate learning that may be relevant to learning and memory in mammals. Three of the preparations that are discussed here are marine mollusks, *Aplysia, Hermissenda,* and *Pleurobranchaea*; the fourth, *Limax*, is a terrestrial mollusk.

Analysis of Small Nervous Systems

As is the case for any experimental system, cellular and behavioral studies of gastropod mollusks have certain advantages, as well as various limitations. The cellular advantages of using gastropod mollusks for studies of basic mechanisms of learning are numerous. Some of these are as follows:

Terry Crow. Department of Physiology, School of Medicine, University of Pittsburgh, Pittsburgh, Pennsylvania.

1. The nervous systems consist of a relatively small number of neurons, which are usually organized into discrete ganglia with cell bodies located on the surface.
2. The nervous systems, therefore, are easily isolated and visualized.
3. In many examples, the size of the neurons is larger than central neurons in mammals.
4. Some of the neurons are identifiable, enabling investigators to study the same cell or functional cell type from different specimens.
5. In most examples, these nervous systems can be examined under the most favorable cellular neurophysiological conditions, and in some cases cellular techniques that are subject to technical constraints in complex systems (e.g., voltage-clamp techniques) can be successfully applied to these systems (for a review of this research strategy, see Kandel, 1976).

Conditions of Learning

The major weakness of using invertebrates in early studies of learning and memory was behavioral. Initial attempts at demonstrating associative learning in gastropod mollusks were usually negative. However, since nonassociative behavioral modifications had been demonstrated and were amenable to a cellular analysis in mollusks, insects, and crustaceans, there was hope that more complex forms of learning would be found. This early belief became a reality, since more recent work has shown that many of these earlier behavioral limitations can be overcome. Examples of associative learning have now been demonstrated in a number of gastropod mollusks (Carew, Hawkins, & Kandel, 1983; Carew, Walters, & Kandel, 1981; Crow & Alkon, 1978; Crow & Offenbach, 1979, 1983; Davis, Villet, Lee, Rigler, Gillette, & Prince, 1980; Gelperin, 1975; Mpitsos & Collins, 1975; Mpitsos & Davis, 1973; Sahley, Gelperin, & Rudy, 1981; Sahley, Rudy, & Gelperin, 1981; Walters, Carew, & Kandel, 1979, 1981). All of these examples represent some form of aversive conditioning. For these cases, the conditions that produce the learning are well documented, and since most of the operational criteria for associative learning have been met in these mollusks, the results suggest that at the behavioral level of analysis the characteristics of classical conditioning in mollusks may be similar to conditioning in vertebrates. Classical conditioning was investigated in *Aplysia* and *Pleurobranchaea* by pairing the chemosensory stimulus (the conditioned stimulus, or CS) with shock (the unconditioned stimulus, or UCS), which resulted in modification of behavior when the animals were tested in the presence of the CS (Mpitsos & Collins, 1975; Mpitsos & Davis, 1973; Walters *et al.*, 1979, 1981). More recently, the siphon and gill-withdrawal reflex in *Aplysia* was shown to undergo classical conditioning by pairing a tactile CS with tail shock (UCS) (Carew *et al.*, 1981). Somewhat more complex conditioning, such as differential aversive conditioning, has now been demonstrated in both *Pleurobranchaea* (Davis *et al.*, 1980) and *Aplysia* (Carew *et al.*, 1983). One of the most striking examples of the similarity in conditioning between mollusks and vertebrates comes from studies of toxicosis conditioning in the terrestrial mollusk *Limax maximus*. Behavioral investigations of *Limax* using the toxicosis-conditioning paradigm has yielded results that are virtually identical to toxicosis-conditioning studies with rodents (Sahley, Gelperin, & Rudy, 1981; Sahley, Rudy, & Gelperin, 1981). Since in *Limax* higher-order conditioning, blocking, conditioned inhibition, and UCS preexposure effects have been demonstrated, toxicosis conditioning appears to be qualitatively similar for *Limax* and mammals.

The marine mollusk *Hermissenda crassicornis* (see Figure 54-1) has proved to be a successful preparation for behavioral and cellular neurophysiological studies of associative learning. *Hermissenda* exhibits an example of associative learning that resembles aversive conditioning. Conditioning has been studied in *Hermissenda* by pairing illumination (CS) with rotation (presumed aversive UCS), which results in the modification of normally positive phototactic behavior. The choice of the conditioning paradigm used with *Hermissenda* was based upon the anatomical and physiological properties of the two sensory systems that mediate the CS and UCS. Light and rotation were selected as the CS and UCS in order to stimulate these two converging pathways, the visual and gravity-detecting pathways, with natural stimuli. The conditioning procedure involves pairing light with rotation of a modified turntable (see Figure 54-2). The automated conditioning and testing apparatus has been described in detail elsewhere (Tyndale & Crow, 1979) and is only described briefly here. Since *Hermissenda* is positively phototactic, the association of light with a putative aversive stimulus (rotation) would be expected to result in a modification of the normal positive phototaxis in the presence of the CS (light). It is not known that rotation is aversive to *Hermissenda*, although rotation has been previously shown to be an effective UCS in toxicosis-conditioning studies (Braun & McIntosh, 1973). For conditioning and behavioral measurements, the animals were placed in glass tubes filled with seawater, which were inserted into clips on the surface of the turntable (see Figure 54-2). A starting gate consisting of a small foam plug was inserted in a small opening near the outside ends of the tubes during training to insure that all animals were subjected to the

FIGURE 54-1. Photograph of the Pacific nudibranch mollusk *Hermissenda crassicornis*. The nervous system is located posterior to the two rhinophores. (Courtesy of Dr. June Harrigan.)

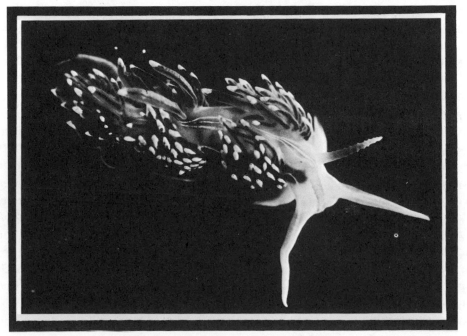

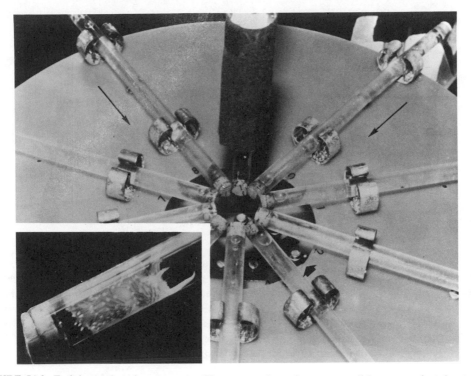

FIGURE 54-2. Training and testing apparatus. The response latencies to enter a light spot projected onto the center of the turntable by an overhead illuminator were recorded automatically when the *Hermissenda* moved toward the light source (direction of arrows) and interrupted the light between illuminator and photocells (arrowhead). *Hermissenda* were subjected to different behavioral treatments consisting of light and rotation while confined to the ends of glass tubes filled with seawater. (From T. Crow & D. L. Alkon, Retention of an associative behavioral change in *Hermissenda. Science*, 1978, *201*, 1239–1241. Copyright 1978 by the American Association for the Advancement of Science. Reprinted by permission.)

same gravitational force during rotation. A pretest–train–retest procedure was used, in which the time taken by individual animals to locomote from one end of the tube into a center-illuminated area at the opposite end of the tube was measured automatically. In subsequent studies, the time taken to initiate locomotion in the presence of light was also measured (Crow & Offenbach, 1979, 1983). Following pretest baseline measurements, the animals received 50 trials of light paired with rotation each day for 3 consecutive days. Both a delayed and a trace conditioning procedure were effective in modifying phototactic behavior. Numerous control groups were run to assess the contribution of nonassociative factors to the modified phototactic behavioral response. Some of these are summarized in the data shown in Figure 54-3. The overall finding of this initial study was that temporally specific light and rotation resulted in a long-term modification of the normally positive phototatic response of *Hermissenda*. This example of associative learning is sensitive to the same order and temporal constraints found in mammalian studies of conditioning. Truly random control procedures result in changes in behavior that are significantly different from paired groups (Crow & Alkon, 1978). The conditioned modification of phototactic behavior is also stimulus-specific, since the behavior of the conditioned animals is only

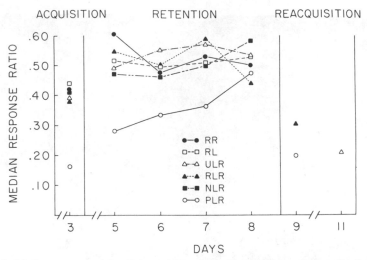

FIGURE 54-3. Median response ratios for acquisition, retention, and reacquisition of a long-term behavioral change in response to a light stimulus in *Hermissenda* (random rotation, random light, unpaired light and rotation, nothing, and paired light and rotation). The response ratio, in the form $A/(A + B)$, compared the latency during the test (B) with the baseline response latency (A). Group data consist of two independent replications for all control groups and three independent replications for the experimental group. (From T. Crow & D. L. Alkon, Retention of an associative behavioral change in *Hermissenda*. *Science*, 1978, *201*, 1239–1241. Copyright 1978 by the American Association for the Advancement of Science. Reprinted by permission.)

changed in the presence of the CS (light) and does not change when the behavior is tested in the absence of the CS (dark) (Crow & Offenbach, 1979, 1983).

These results can be contrasted with the initial attempt at conditioning *Hermissenda*, which was not successful, although nonassociative changes in phototactic behavior resembling sensitization were demonstrated (Alkon, 1974). Since the recent behavioral work has demonstrated temporally specific modifications of phototactic behavior (Crow & Alkon, 1978), a question can be raised concerning the conditions that are sufficient to produce the associative learning. A partial understanding of this issue comes from an examination of the procedures used to study sensitization in *Hermissenda*. In this study, groups of animals were placed in seawater-filled containers and were then trained and tested *en masse* by pairing light with rotation of the container. A modified delayed paradigm was used, in which the light preceded rotation by 45 seconds and then terminated after 25 seconds of rotation, with a 105-second interval between trials. After 3 hours of training, phototactic behavior was modified; however, the effects were nonassociative, since a control group that received explicitly unpaired light and rotation also exhibited the modified phototactic behavior, and this control group was not significantly different from the experimental group. Therefore, the results from the initial study indicate that the behavioral effects were due to nonassociative factors and thus resembled sensitization. The nature of the nonassociative effects produced by conditioning have recently been examined in more detail. These results indicated that the nonassociative contribution to the modification of phototactic behavior depends on the number of conditioning trials and the time between training and testing. As shown in Figures 54-4 and 54-5, when the *Hermissenda* are tested following 5 or 10 conditioning trials, the short-term effects on phototactic

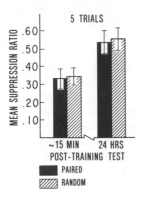

FIGURE 54-4. Time dependence of nonassociative effects of five conditioning trials on phototactic behavior. Both paired ($n = 17$) and random control ($n = 17$) groups showed significant suppression following five conditioning trials when tested 15 minutes after conditioning. However, the nonassociative effect was short-lasting since both groups had returned to baseline measures when tested 24 hours following conditioning ($p < .01$). Thus, five trials produce only short-term nonassociative effects. (From T. Crow, Conditioned modification of locomotion in *Hermissenda crassicornis*: Analysis of time-dependent associative and nonassociative components. *Journal of Neuroscience*, 1983, *3*, 2621–2628. Reprinted by permission.)

behavior are due to nonassociative factors (Crow, 1983a). In contrast to the results from 5 or 10 trials, 50 conditioning trials produce short-term associative effects on behavior when the time between training and testing is extended (Crow, 1983a; see Figure 54-6). However, 3 days of training, consisting of a total of 150 trials, produce long-term changes in phototactic behavior that are dependent on associative factors. The nonassociative component observed after 3 days of training decrements rapidly during the first hour following the termination of behavioral training and is not observed 24 hours following the last conditioning trial (see Figure 54-7).

Where Is the Memory Stored?

Having described the conditions that produce associative learning in molluskan preparations, the question can be raised concerning the locus of the cellular changes that mediate conditioned behavior. Generally, the strategy for this research has been to identify the

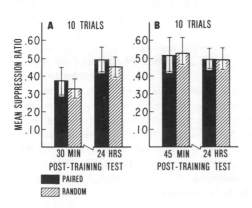

FIGURE 54-5. Time dependence of nonassociative effects produced by 10 conditioning trials. (A) Both paired ($n = 10$) and random control ($n = 10$) groups showed significant behavioral suppression following 10 conditioning trials when tested 30 minutes after conditioning ($p < .05$). However, the changes were short term since tests of the same animals 24 hours after conditioning did not reveal significant suppression. (B) Neither paired ($n = 10$) nor random control ($n = 10$) groups showed significant behavioral suppression following 10 conditioning trials when tested 45 minutes and 24 hours after conditioning. Thus, 10 trials produce only short-term nonassociative effects on phototactic behavior. (From T. Crow, Conditioned modification of locomotion in *Hermissenda crassicornis*: Analysis of time-dependent associative and nonassociative components. *Journal of Neuroscience*, 1983, *3*, 2621–2628. Reprinted by permission.)

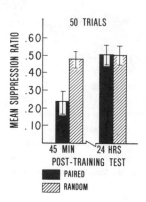

FIGURE 54-6. Transient associative effects produced in a single training session. Fifty conditioning trials result in significant differences in phototactic suppression between paired ($n = 19$) and random control ($n = 10$) groups when tested 45 minutes after training ($p < .01$). However, the associative effects were short term since both groups had returned to baseline levels when tested 24 hours after training. (From T. Crow, Conditioned modification of locomotion in *Hermissenda crassicornis*: Analysis of time-dependent associative and nonassociative components. *Journal of Neuroscience*, 1983, *3*, 2621–2628. Reprinted by permission.)

sensory and motor pathways that mediate the example of conditioning, to examine the cellular and synaptic organization of the pathways (CS and UCS pathways), to identify changes in the pathways that are correlated with the conditioning, and then to identify cellular mechanisms that can account for the learned behavior.

As a start in this analysis, correlates of conditioning have been examined. The studies of neural correlates of conditioning in the mollusks indicate that the neural changes are presynaptic to the motor neurons that mediate the behavioral response. In *Pleurobranchea*, pairing food (squid homogenate) with shock results in an inhibition of the feeding command neurons (paracerebral neurons) in the presence of the CS (food) (Davis & Gillette, 1978). The plasticity in this system is thought to be the result of an enhanced excitability of inhibitory interneurons that synapse on the paracerebral neurons. In both *Aplysia* and *Hermissenda*, neural correlates of conditioning have been found in sensory neurons in the CS pathway (Crow & Alkon, 1980; Hawkins, Abrams, Carew, & Kandel,

FIGURE 54-7. Comparison of posttraining retention (60 minutes) following single-session (50 trials) and multiple-session (150 trials) training. (A) The associative effects produced by single-session training were short term since the paired ($n = 20$) and random control ($n = 20$) groups were not significantly different from each other when tested 60 minutes after one conditioning session (50 trials). However, significant associative effects were detected 60 minutes after multiple-session training (150 trials) ($p < .01$). (B) The associative effects produced by multiple-session training were long term since the paired group was significantly different from random controls when tested 24 hours after training ($p < .01$). Thus, single-session training (50 trials) produces both short-term associative and nonassociative effects, while multiple-session training produces a long-lasting associative effect. (From T. Crow, Conditioned modification of locomotion in *Hermissenda crassicornis*: Analysis of time-dependent associative and nonassociative components. *Journal of Neuroscience*, 1983, *3*, 2621–2628. Reprinted by permission.)

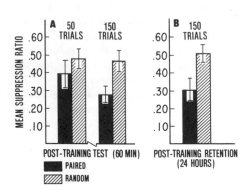

1983; Walters & Byrne, 1983). In these systems, the memory trace appears to be stored in the primary sensory neurons of the CS pathway. Of course, these results do not preclude the existence of multiple sites of memory storage in other parts of the nervous system. However, these findings suggest that the changes in the primary sensory neurons produced by conditioning may be sufficient to explain the modifications of behavior found with these examples of associative learning. In addition, these examples of conditioning suggest that the behavioral modifications may be understood in terms of basic membrane properties of the neurons mediating the response and their synaptic connections, as opposed to the development of an emergent property of an ensemble of neurons. The evidence from all of these cases of neural correlates of conditioning indicate that learning involves changes of preexisting neural connections, rather than the growth or formation of new synaptic connections.

Conditioned Modification of Primary Sensory Neurons in the CS Pathway

In *Hermissenda*, the anatomy of the CS and UCS pathways has been examined in detail (Alkon, 1976). This preparation was introduced to neurobiology by early studies of the visual system (Dennis, 1967). Because of the favorable anatomy of the central nervous system, it is possible to study the cellular organization and synaptic interaction between two sensory systems (CS and UCS pathways) in an isolated nervous system. The circumoesophageal nervous system of *Hermissenda* is shown in the diagram in Figure 54-8. The relative simplicity of the eyes and gravity-detecting statocysts, and the well-defined synaptic interactions between the individual photoreceptors within each eye and statocyst hair cells, make *Hermissenda* a favorable preparation for cellular neurophysiological analysis (Alkon, 1976; Crow, Heldman, Hacopian, Enos, & Alkon, 1979). The eyes and statocysts are easily isolated and visualized, since they are located on the dorsal surface of the nervous system between the paired cerebropleural and pedal ganglia (see Figure 54-8). Each eye contains only five photoreceptors, which can be classified into two types on the basis of anatomical and functional criteria. One of these types (designated as Type B), of which there are three photoreceptors, exhibits long-term plastic capabilities produced by the conditioning procedure.

As a start in the cellular investigation of associative learning in *Hermissenda*, conditioned changes in the CS pathway were investigated by recording intracellularly, from the primary sensory neurons, the photoreceptors in the eyes of conditioned animals. The conditioned changes in the sensory neurons survived the surgical isolation of the nervous system. Following 3 days of behavioral training, Type B photoreceptors from conditioned animals showed a higher spontaneous firing rate, were more depolarized under conditions of dark adaptation, and exhibited an increase in input resistance, relative to Type B photoreceptors in random control groups (Crow & Alkon, 1980). These correlates were subsequently shown to be intrinsic to the photoreceptors and not due to synaptic effects from a presynaptic source following conditioning (see Figure 54-9).

The following experiments were conducted in order to localize the conditioned changes to the primary sensory neurons. Since the occurrence of spike activity and synaptic potentials in the intracellular recordings complicated the conclusions that can be drawn from such experiments, cellular correlates were analyzed further in axotomized prepara-

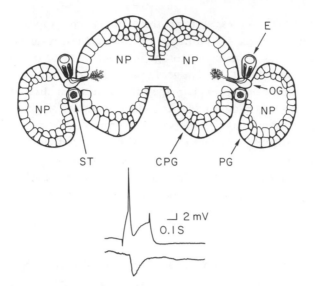

FIGURE 54-8. Diagram of the dorsal surface of the circumoesophageal nervous system of *Hermissenda crassicornis*. Two Type B photoreceptor somata (black areas in each eye), their axons, and their terminal processes have been drawn schematically. Photoreceptors receive synaptic input from other photoreceptors at their terminal endings in the neuropil. Abbreviations: E, eye; OG, optic ganglion; NP, neuropil; ST, statocyst; CPG, cerebropleural ganglia; PG, pedal ganglia. Intracellular recordings from two Type B photoreceptors within the same eye are shown to illustrate the direct inhibitory interactions between Type B photoreceptors. A current pulse delivered to one Type B photoreceptor evokes a spike (top trace), which is followed by an inhibitory postsynaptic potential in the second Type B photoreceptor (bottom trace). This result is invariant from preparation to preparation. The top of the spike in A has been retouched. (From T. Crow, E. Heldman, V. Hacopian, R. Enos, & D. L. Alkon, Ultrastructure of photoreceptors in the eye of *Hermissenda* labeled with intracellular injection of horseradish peroxidase. *Journal of Neurocytology*, 1979, *8*, 181-195. Reprinted by permission.)

tions, in which spike activity and synaptic input were eliminated by cutting the optic nerve. This procedure is effective, since in *Hermissenda* the area of phototransduction is spatially separated from the areas of synaptic input and spike generation. An analysis of the axotomized preparations following conditioning revealed that the photoreceptors from the trained animals were more depolarized and exhibited an increased input resistance, as compared to those of random control groups (Crow & Alkon, 1980; see Figure 54-9). How could such a conditioned change be encoded in a primary sensory neuron? It was hypothesized that conditioning produced a decrease in a steady-state dark-adapted K^+ current in the Type B photoreceptors modulated by light and/or voltage. One prediction of the encoding of memory by a modification of a membrane current would be a change in the photoreceptor's response to the CS (light). Consistent with this hypothesis was the finding of a change in the waveform of light-evoked generator potentials recorded from Type B photoreceptors of conditioned animals (Crow & Alkon, 1980). The results of the neural correlates studies could be explained in part by a decrease of a light- and/or voltage-dependent K^+ current in the Type B photoreceptors (Crow & Alkon, 1980). This hypothesis has been supported by recent findings of a reduction in a rapidly inactivating voltage-dependent K^+ current similar to the A current (I_A) (Alkon, Lederhendler, & Shoukimas, 1982). The change in I_A produced by conditioning may explain the change in the membrane conductance found in dark-adapted Type B photoreceptors; however, it is unclear how this change contributes to the change in the photoresponse of conditioned animals. Indeed, recent evidence from a model that incorporated a 30% reduction in the A current, which simulated the biophysical observations following conditioning, showed little effect upon the generator potential ($<$ 1 mV change in the peak generator potential) (Shoukimas & Alkon, 1983). In addition, recent evidence has shown that conditioning does not significantly alter the transient peak of the light-evoked generator potential in Type B photoreceptors (Crow, 1983c), although the light-adapted photoresponse is significantly

FIGURE 54-9. Cellular changes in cut nerve preparations from experimental and random control animals. (A) Receptor potentials of dark-adapted Type B photoreceptor from an experimental animal (light paired with rotation). Responses evoked by brief light flashes of increasing intensity: 4, $-$log 3.0; 3, $-$log 2.0; 2, $-$log 1.0; 1, $-$log 0.5. Dashed line indicates resting membrane potential, and lower trace indicates duration of light flash. The absence of spikes and synaptic potentials indicates that the photoreceptor soma was successfully isolated from the area of spike initiation and synaptic input. (B) Representative linear current–voltage relationship of dark-adapted isolated (cut nerve) Type B photoreceptors from experimental (paired) and random control groups. (C) Examples of changes in membrane potential of dark-adapted isolated Type B photoreceptors from experimental and random control animals. Electrotonic potentials were evoked by hyperpolarizing square current pulses (bottom traces) through a balanced bridge. Resistance measurements taken with the single electrode–bridge circuit are consistent with data from experiments in which the photoreceptors were impaled simultaneously with two microelectrodes for current injection and voltage recording. (From T. Crow & D. L. Alkon, Associative behavioral modification in *Hermissenda*: Cellular correlates. *Science*, 1980, *209*, 412–414. Copyright 1980 by the American Association for the Advancement of Science. Reprinted by permission.)

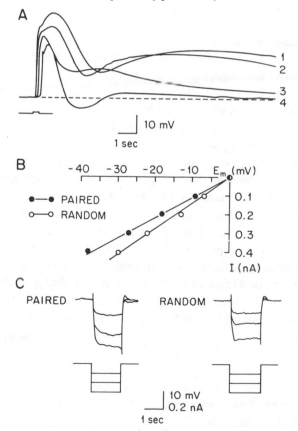

reduced in conditioned animals (Crow, 1983b, 1983c). Since the change in the A current cannot explain the changes in photoresponses following conditioning, it indicates that other cellular changes in the sensory cells make a contribution to the behavioral response to illumination following conditioning. In order to address this, additional experiments have been conducted to further examine cellular correlates of conditioning in the Type B photoreceptors. These studies have focused on changes in photoreceptor adaptation following conditioning.

Conditioned Modification of Sensory Adaptation

The sensitivity of a photoreceptor depends upon its history of illumination. After a cell has been stimulated with light, its sensitivity is reduced; that is, the cell becomes light-adapted. Adaptation is a general feature of sensory receptors, whether they be rapidly adapting mechanoreceptors or more slowly adapting photoreceptors of *Hermissenda*. Since adaptation is a ubiquitous feature of sensory receptors, modification of sensory sensitivity may play a role in the encoding and storage of memory in these systems. In order to test this hypothesis, light-evoked photoreceptor desensitization was used as a cellular probe to study plasticity produced by conditioning (Crow, 1982, 1983b). The amount of desensitization produced by an adapting light flash was examined in Type B photoreceptors from conditioned and random control groups. The adapting light desensitized the photoreceptors from both groups of animals, although the magnitude of the desensitization depended on the prior behavioral history of the animal (conditioned vs. random control) and the intensity of the adapting flash. The photoreceptors from the conditioned *Hermissenda* exhibited significantly more desensitization produced by adapting light, at intensities that were similar to the light intensity of the test CS used in behavioral testing. In addition, recovery of sensitivity was slower following the adapting flash in Type B photoreceptors of conditioned animals. Could this change in visual sensitivity that is produced by conditioning be explained by the previously reported reduction in I_A, the fast voltage-dependent K^+ current? In order to test this, photoreceptor desensitization was examined under experimental conditions in which I_A was blocked with the pharmacological K^+ channel blocker 4-aminopyridine. Blocking I_A with 4-aminopyridine did not produce the significant increase in photoreceptor desensitization that was produced by the conditioning procedure. Therefore, the conditioning effects could not be mimicked by blocking the previously identified rapidly inactivating voltage-dependent K^+ current I_A. The changes in visual sensitivity produced by conditioning could be explained by increases in intracellular Ca^{++} produced by an increase in a voltage-dependent Ca^{++} current, or by release of Ca^{++} from intracellular stores. However, since desensitization occurs when photoreceptors are voltage-clamped at the resting membrane potential, this indicates that in addition to the previously reported voltage-dependent conductance changes, conditioning must alter other cellular processes involved with sensory adaptation. What type of mechanism could account for long-term changes in visual sensitivity? Modification of light- and/or voltage-dependent Ca^{++} conductances or Ca^{++}-dependent K^+ conductances may play a role, since Ca^{++} is involved in photoreceptor adaptation. Modifications in the release of Ca^{++} from intracellular stores or alterations in the reuptake and storage of Ca^{++} could modulate conductances that may contribute to this type of memory encoding. The proposed mechanism(s) may be involved in the expression of the learning.

Discussion and Conclusions

One of the major goals of studies concerned with mechanisms of learning and memory is the identification of the neural locus of the change produced by the learning. This is a necessary prerequisite for later physiological investigations of mechanisms. This goal has now been met in a number of invertebrate preparations. The results of our cellular neurophysiological studies of *Hermissenda* indicate that one locus is in the primary sensory cells of the CS pathway. How general would such a finding be for other gastropod mollusks? Recent evidence consistent with this proposal comes from investigations of cellular analogues of classical conditioning in two different populations of primary mechanoreceptors in *Aplysia* (Hawkins *et al.*, 1983; Walters & Byrne, 1983). The conditioned modifications found in sensory systems are not unique to invertebrate learning. Conditioned alterations in CS-evoked neural activity have been reported both in the auditory and visual systems of vertebrates (for a review, see Weinberger, in 1982).

A question can be raised concerning the logic for building plastic properties into primary sensory neurons: How can these cells store memories of past experiences and also provide an accurate representation of the external environment? In the case of *Hermissenda*, it is not surprising to find plasticity at the level of primary sensory cells, since single photoreceptors perform cellular functions that are carried out by second-order and intrinsic neurons in more complex systems. Phototransduction and spike generation (frequency coding) take place in the same neuron, and in this system lateral inhibition is the result of direct inhibitory synaptic interactions between the primary sensory neurons. In the anatomically more complex sensory systems of vertebrates, many of these functions are performed by intrinsic interneurons of second-order cells. Consequently, one could speculate that it would be more likely to find plasticity in the higher-order neurons of vertebrate sensory systems. Moreover, it has been suggested that not all of the B photoreceptors within each eye are modified by conditioning. Since this simple eye is not an image-forming system, the basic function of light-intensity discrimination can be performed by those photoreceptors that are not modified by the conditioning procedure. Building plasticity into sensory systems allows the flexibility of acquiring sensory learning that can selectively modify a number of different response systems. How the nervous system of *Hermissenda* integrates information on light intensity with the memory of past experiences to generate changes in phototactic behavior is not yet understood.

The behavioral studies of classical conditioning in gastropod mollusks suggests that learning follows the same rules or operations as in vertebrate learning. However, the fact that different species exhibit the same behavioral changes in response to similar conditioning paradigms does not imply that they do so by the same mechanism. Mechanisms of learning found in invertebrates will have to be tested in other species in order to conclude that similar mechanisms of learning are found at all phylogenetic levels. The more similarities that are found in different examples of plasticity, the stronger the basis for the belief that common neural mechanisms may be involved in similar examples of learning across diverse species. This, of course, awaits verification from cellular studies of vertebrates. If this assumption is true, then the invertebrates will have made a contribution toward our understanding of basic mechanisms, due primarily to the technical advantages that they offer for the experimental analysis of associative learning.

ACKNOWLEDGMENTS

The work reported in this chapter and the preparation of the chapter were supported by National Institutes of Health Grant No. HD15793.

REFERENCES

Alkon, D. L. Associative training of *Hermissenda*. *Journal of General Physiology*, 1974, *64*, 70–84.

Alkon, D. L. The economy of photoreceptor function in a primitive nervous system. In J. F. Zettler & R. Weiler (Eds.), *Neural principles in vision*. New York: Springer-Verlag, 1976.

Alkon, D. L., Lederhendler, I., & Shoukimas, J. J. Primary changes of membrane currents during retention of associative learning. *Science*, 1982, *215*, 693–695.

Braun, J. J., & McIntosh, H., Jr. Learned taste aversions induced by rotational stimulation. *Physiological Psychology*, 1973, *1*, 301–304.

Carew, T. J., Hawkins, R. D., & Kandel, E. R. Differential classical conditioning of a defensive withdrawal reflex in *Aplysia californica*. *Science*, 1983, *219*, 397–400.

Carew, T. J., Walters, E. T., & Kandel, E. R. Classical conditioning in a simple withdrawal reflex in *Aplysia californica*. *Journal of Neuroscience*, 1981, *1*, 1426–1437.

Crow, T. Sensory neuronal correlates of associative learning in *Hermissenda*. *Society for Neuroscience Abstracts*, 1982, *8*, 824.

Crow, T. Conditioned modification of locomotion in *Hermissenda crassicornis*: Analysis of time-dependent associative and nonassociative components. *Journal of Neuroscience*, 1983, *3*, 2621–2628. (a)

Crow, T. Conditioned modification of sensory adaptation in *Hermissenda* photoreceptors. *Federation Proceedings*, 1983, *42*, 1346. (b)

Crow, T. Modification of B-photoreceptor adaptation predicts differential light responding following conditioning in *Hermissenda*. *Society for Neuroscience Abstracts*, 1983, *9*, 167. (c)

Crow, T., & Alkon, D. L. Retention of an associative behavioral change in *Hermissenda*. *Science*, 1978, *201*, 1239–1241.

Crow, T., & Alkon, D. L. Associative behavioral modification in *Hermissenda*: Cellular correlates. *Science*, 1980, *209*, 412–414.

Crow, T., Heldman, E., Hacopian, V., Enos, R., & Alkon, D. L. Ultrastructure of photoreceptors in the eye of *Hermissenda* labeled with intracellular injection of hoseradish peroxidase. *Journal of Neurocytology*, 1979, *8*, 181–195.

Crow, T., & Offenbach, N. Response specificity following behavioral training in the nudibranch mollusk *Hermissenda crassicornis*. *Biological Bulletin*, 1979, *157*, 364.

Crow, T., & Offenbach, N. Modification of the initiation of locomotion in *Hermissenda*: Behavioral analysis. *Brain Research*, 1983, *271*, 301–310.

Davis, W. J., & Gillette, R. Neural correlate of behavioral plasticity in command neurons in *Pleurobranchaea*. *Science*, 1978, *199*, 801–804.

Davis, W. J. Villet, J., Lee, D., Rigler, M., Gillette, R., & Prince, E., Selective and differential avoidance learning in the feeding and withdrawal behavior of *Pleurobranchaea californica*. *Journal of Comparative Physiology—A Sensory Neural and Behavioral Physiology*, 1980, *138*, 157–165.

Dennis, M. J. Electrophysiology of the visual system in a nudibranch mollusc. *Journal of Neurophysiology*, 1967, *30*, 1439–1465.

Gelperin, A. Rapid food-aversion learning by a terrestrial mollusk. *Science*, 1975, *189*, 567–570.

Hawkins, R. D., Abrams, T. W., Carew, T. J., & Kandel, E. R. A cellular mechanism of classical conditioning in *Aplysia*: Activity-dependent amplification of presynaptic facilitation. *Science*, 1983, *219*, 400–404.

Kandel, E. R. *Cellular basis of behavior*. San Francisco: W. H. Freeman, 1976.

Mpitsos, G. J., & Collins, S. D. Learning: Rapid aversive conditioning in the gastropod mollusk *Pleurobranchaea*. *Science*, 1975, *188*, 954–957.

Mpitsos, G. J., & Davis, W. J. Learning: Classical and avoidance conditioning in the mollusk *Pleurobranchaea*. *Science*, 1973, *180*, 317–320.

Sahley, C., Gelperin, A., & Rudy, J. W. One-trial associative learning in a terrestrial mollusc. *Proceedings of the National Academy of Sciences USA*, 1981, *78*, 640–642.

Sahley, C., Rudy, J. W., & Gelperin, A. An analysis of associative learning in the terrestrial mollusc *Limax maximus*: I. Higher-order conditioning, blocking, and a transient US-preexposure effect, *Journal of Comparative Physiology—A Sensory Neural and Behavioral Physiology*, 1981, *144*, 1–8.

Shoukimas, J. J., & Alkon, D. L. Effect of voltage-dependent K^+ conductances upon the initial generator response in B-photoreceptor of *H. crassicornis*. *Biophysical Journal*, 1983, *41*, 37a.

Tyndale, C. L., & Crow, T. An IC control unit for generating random and nonrandom events. *IEEE Transactions on Biomedical Engineering*, 1979, *BME-26*, 649–655.

Walters, E. T., & Byrne, J. H. Associative conditioning of single sensory neurons suggests a cellular mechanism for learning. *Science*, 1983, *219*, 405–408.

Walters, E. T., Carew, T. J., & Kandel, E. R. Classical conditioning in *Aplysia californica*. *Proceedings of the National Academy of Sciences USA*, 1979, *76*, 6675–6679.

Walters, E. T., Carew, T. J., & Kandel, E. R. Associative learning in *Aplysia*: Evidence for conditioned fear in an invertebrate. *Science*, 1981, *211*, 504–506.

Weinberger, N. M. Sensory plasticity and learning: The magnocellular medial geniculate nucleus of the auditory system. In C. D. Woody (Ed.), *Conditioning: Representation of involved neural functions*. New York: Plenum, 1982.

Author Index

Abraham, W. C., 527, 531, 532*n.*, 589, 590, 597*n.*, 600*n.*
Abrams, T. W., 614, 620*n.*
Abzug, C., 530, 535*n.*
Ackerman, B. P., 10, 12*n.*, 63, 66*n.*, 216, 223*n.*
Acosta-Urquidi, J., 543, 544*n.*
Acuna, C., 392, 397*n.*
Adams, R. D., 122, 133*n.*, 177, 180*n.*, 192, 193*n.*, 195, 202*n.*, 207, 211*n.*, 226, 235*n.*, 275, 278*n.*, 318, 329*n.*
Adolfsson, R., 590, 597*n.*
Aggleton, J. P., 125, 132*n.*, 275, 277*n.*, 287, 296*n.*, 318, 323, 327*n.*
Aghajanian, G. K., 594, 597*n.*
Agnetti, V., 123, 124*n.*, 133*n.*, 139, 144*n.*
Agranoff, B. W., 548, 553*n.*, 558, 564*n.*
Ahumada, A. J., 259, 265*n.*, 354, 362*n.*
Aitkin, L. M., 493, 501*n.*
Ajmone-Marsan, C., 297, 313*n.*
Akers, R., 538, 543, 545*n.*, 546*n.*
Akert, K., 196, 202*n.*, 270, 277*n.*
Akil, H., 580, 584, 586*n.*, 587*n.*
Alavi, A., 261, 265*n.*
Albert, M. L., 414, 415*n.*
Albert, M. S., 58, 61*n.*, 111, 113*n.*, 139, 142*n.*, 232, 233*n.*, 236–246, 237, 242, 245, 246*n.*, 253, 256*n.*, 262, 264*n.*
Albiniak, B. A., 485, 486*n.*
Alexander, H. M., 292, 294*n.*
Alger, B., 443, 459*n.*, 462, 469*n.*
Algeri, S., 589, 590, 597*n.*, 599*n.*
Alkon, D. L., 500, 501*n.*, 509*n.*, 510*n.*, 543, 544*n.*, 556, 564*n.*, 609, 611, 611*n.*, 612, 612*n.*, 614–616, 616*n.*, 617, 617*n.*
Allison, T., 178, 181*n.*, 182*n.*
Allon, N., 509, 510*n.*
Allport, D. A., 15, 22*n.*
Allweis, C., 562, 564*n.*
Alpern, H. P., 566, 576*n.*
Alpern, M., 48, 53*n.*
Alpert, J., 531, 533*n.*
Altman, H. J., 231, 235*n.*
Alvarez-Pelaez, R., 475, 488*n.*
Amaral, D. G., 230, 233*n.*
Amsel, A., 291, 294*n.*
Anden, N. E., 592, 597*n.*
Andermann, F., 176, 180*n.*
Andersen, P., 171, 179*n.*, 539, 542, 544*n.*
Anderson, J R., 44, 44*n.*, 95, 101*n.*, 150, 156*n.*, 172, 174, 180*n.*
Anderson, R. M., 348, 351, 360*n.*, 362*n.*
Anohkin, P. K., 490, 502*n.*
Antin, S. P., 139, 143*n.*, 184, 192*n.*, 409, 416*n.*
Anzai, Y., 89, 101*n.*
Appel, S. H., 590, 597*n.*

Applegate, C. D., 436, 440*n.*, 477, 486*n.*
Appleton, R., 589, 600*n.*
Aquilar-Jiminez, E., 560, 565*n.*
Arabie, G. J., 409, 416*n.*
Arbit, J., 100, 102*n.*, 300, 313*n.*
Arnsten, A. T., 583, 585*n.*
Arst, D. S., 592, 597*n.*
Ashe, J. H., 492, 492*n.*, 493, 502*n.*, 503*n.*
Aspect, A., 331, 338*n.*
Astley, C. A., 436, 441*n.*
Aston-Jones, G., 225, 233*n.*, 234*n.*, 590, 597*n.*
Atkinson, R. C., 4, 11*n.*, 204, 210*n.*, 213, 215, 222*n.*, 386, 396*n.*
Attneave, F., 358, 360*n.*
Augerinos, G., 581, 587*n.*
Avdaloff, W., 261, 265*n.*
Avery, D. L., 312, 315*n.*
Axelrod, J., 572, 576*n.*

Babb, T. L., 178, 179, 180*n.*
Bachem, A., 46, 53*n.*
Bachevalier, J., 288, 295*n.*
Backman, M. F., 231, 234*n.*
Backus, S. N., 491, 503*n.*
Baddeley, A. D., 4, 11*n.*, 69, 79, 81*n.*, 85, 86, 90–92, 94, 97, 101*n.*, 105, 108, 109, 113*n.*, 116, 121*n.*, 123, 132*n.*, 146, 150, 152, 153, 155*n.*, 157, 164*n.*, 174, 180*n.*, 287, 294*n.*, 386, 389, 396*n.*, 414, 416*n.*
Bagshaw, M. H., 344, 349, 350, 360*n.*
Bahrick, H. P., 58, 61*n.*
Bahrick, P. S., 58, 61*n.*
Bailey, P., 197, 200*n.*, 326, 329*n.*
Bak, I. J., 431, 441*n.*
Baker, A. G., 505, 510*n.*
Baker, E., 56, 61*n.*, 232, 233*n.*
Baker, H. D., 506, 512*n.*
Baker, H. F., 231, 235*n.*
Baker, M., 521–535
Baker, P., 505, 510*n.*
Ballenger, J. C., 210, 212*n.*
Ban, T. A., 593, 597*n.*
Bannister, R., 370, 373*n.*
Barbizet, J., 84, 101*n.*, 317, 327*n.*
Barchas, J. D., 426, 433*n.*, 434, 435*n.*, 436, 436*n.*, 440*n.*, 441*n.*, 580, 586*n.*
Barlow, H. B., 49, 53*n.*, 358, 360*n.*
Barnes, C. A., 178, 180*n.*, 517, 519*n.*, 524–526, 532, 532*n.*, 533*n.*, 538, 545*n.*, 574, 577*n.*, 589, 597*n.*
Barnett, J. M., 562, 564*n.*
Barrionuevo, G., 518, 520*n.*, 523, 534*n.*
Barry, J., 344, 362*n.*
Barta, A., 580, 585*n.*
Bartlett, F. C., 5, 11*n.*, 174, 180*n.*

Subject Index